SCOTT FORESMAN

READING STREET

COMMON CORE 

Program Authors

Peter Afflerbach
Camille Blachowicz
Candy Dawson Boyd
Elena Izquierdo
Connie Juel
Edward Kame'enui
Donald Leu
Jeanne R. Paratore
P. David Pearson
Sam Sebesta
Deborah Simmons
Susan Watts Taffe
Alfred Tatum
Sharon Vaughn
Karen Kring Wixson

Glenview, Illinois

Boston, Massachusetts

Chandler, Arizona

Upper Saddle River, New Jersey

We dedicate Reading Street to Peter Jovanovich.

His wisdom, courage, and passion for education are an inspiration to us all.

The Acknowledgments page appears in the back of the book immediately following the Oral Vocabulary section and constitutes an extension of this copyright page.

ISBN-13: 978-0-328-72532-8
ISBN-10: 0-328-72532-3
1 2 3 4 5 6 7 8 9 10 V003 16 15 14 13 12

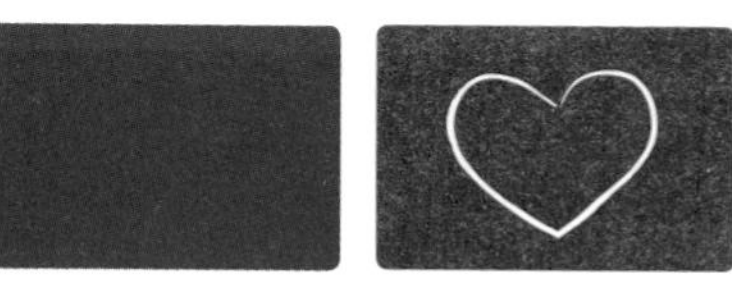

Program Authors

Peter Afflerbach, Ph.D.
Professor; Department of Curriculum and Instruction,
University of Maryland; College Park, Maryland
Areas of Expertise: Common Core State Standards English Language Arts Work Team, Assessment, and Comprehension

Camille L. Z. Blachowicz, Ph.D.
Professor; National College of Education, National-Louis University; Skokie, Illinois
Areas of Expertise: Vocabulary and Comprehension

Candy Dawson Boyd, Ph.D.
Professor, School of Education; Saint Mary's College; Moraga, California
Areas of Expertise: Children's Literature and Professional Development

Elena Izquierdo, Ph.D.
Associate Professor, University of Texas at El Paso
Area of Expertise: English Language Learners

Connie Juel, Ph.D.
Professor of Education; Stanford University; Stanford, California
Areas of Expertise: Phonics, Oral Vocabulary, and Intervention

Edward J. Kame'enui, Ph.D.
Dean-Knight Professor of Education and Director, Institute for the Development of Educational Achievement, and the Center on Teaching and Learning;
College of Education; University of Oregon
Areas of Expertise: Assessment, Intervention, and Progress Monitoring

Donald J. Leu, Ph.D.
John and Maria Neag Endowed Chair in Literacy and Technology Board of Directors, International Reading Association; University of Connecticut; Storrs, Connecticut
Areas of Expertise: Comprehension, Technology, and New Literacies

Jeanne R. Paratore, Ed.D.
Professor of Literacy, Language, and Cultural Studies; Boston University School of Education; Boston, Massachusetts
Areas of Expertise: Intervention and Small Group Instruction

P. David Pearson, Ph.D.
Professor of Language, Literacy and Culture, and Human Development;
Graduate School of Education; University of California; Berkeley, California
Areas of Expertise: Common Core State Standards English Language Arts Work Team, Comprehension

Sam L. Sebesta, Ph.D.
Professor Emeritus; Curriculum and Instruction College of Education,
University of Washington; Seattle, Washington
Areas of Expertise: Children's Literature, Reader Response, and Motivation

Deborah Simmons, Ph.D.
Professor in the Department of Educational Psychology, College of Education and Human Development, Texas A&M University
Areas of Expertise: Literacy Development, Phonics, and Intervention

Susan Watts Taffe, Ph.D.
Associate Professor and Program Coordinator, Literacy and Second Language Studies,
School of Education; University of Cincinnati; Cincinnati, Ohio
Areas of Expertise: Vocabulary, Comprehension, and New Literacies

Alfred Tatum, Ph.D.
Associate Professor and Director, UIC Reading Clinic, University of Illinois at Chicago
Areas of Expertise: Adolescent Literacy, Reader Response, and Motivation

Sharon Vaughn, Ph.D.
H. E. Hartfelder/The Southland Corporation Regents Professor;
University of Texas; Austin, Texas
Areas of Expertise: Literacy Development, Intervention, Professional Development, English Language Learners, Vocabulary, and Small Group Instruction

Karen Kring Wixson, Ph.D.
Dean of Education, University of North Carolina, Greensboro
Areas of Expertise: Common Core State Standards English Language Arts Work Team, Assessment, Small Group Instruction

Consulting Authors

Jeff Anderson, M.Ed.
Author and National Literacy Staff Developer

Jim Cummins, Ph.D.
Professor; Department of Curriculum, Teaching and Learning; University of Toronto

Tahira A. DuPree Chase, Ed.D.
Director of Curriculum and Instruction, Mt. Vernon City School District, New York

Lily Wong Fillmore, Ph.D.
Professor Emerita; Graduate School of Education, University of California, Berkeley

Georgia Earnest Garcia, Ph.D.
Professor; Language and Literacy Division, Department of Curriculum and Instruction, University of Illinois at Urbana-Champaign

George A. Gonzalez, Ph.D.
Professor (Retired); School of Education,
University of Texas-Pan American, Edinburg

Adria Klein, Ph.D.
Professor Emeritus; School of Education, California State University, San Bernadino

Lesley Maxwell, M.S., CCC-SLP
Director of Clinical Education, Clinical Associate Professor; Department of Communication Sciences and Disorders, MGH Institute of Health Professions

Valerie Ooka Pang, Ph.D.
Professor; School of Teacher Education, San Diego State University

Sally M. Reis, Ph.D.
Board of Trustees Distinguished Professor; Department of Educational Psychology, University of Connecticut

Jon Scieszka, M.F.A.
Children's Book Author and Founder of GUYS READ, First National Ambassador for Young People's Literature 2008

Grant Wiggins, Ed.D.
President of Authentic Education, coauthor of *Understanding by Design*

Nurture the love of reading.

Help students learn to read *and* love to read. *Reading Street Common Core* supports reading, writing, and language development. Amazing literature on amazing devices inspires students in a whole new way.

Literature students love

The best literary and informational text

On devices they crave!

Whiteboards, tablets, computers, mobile devices

Build a foundation for reading.

Reading Street Common Core helps students develop foundational skills for reading more complex text. Common Core experts helped design the plan. Classroom results prove it works.

Early Reading Success

Reading Street students outperformed their peers by 15 percentile points, even though they started below the comparison students.

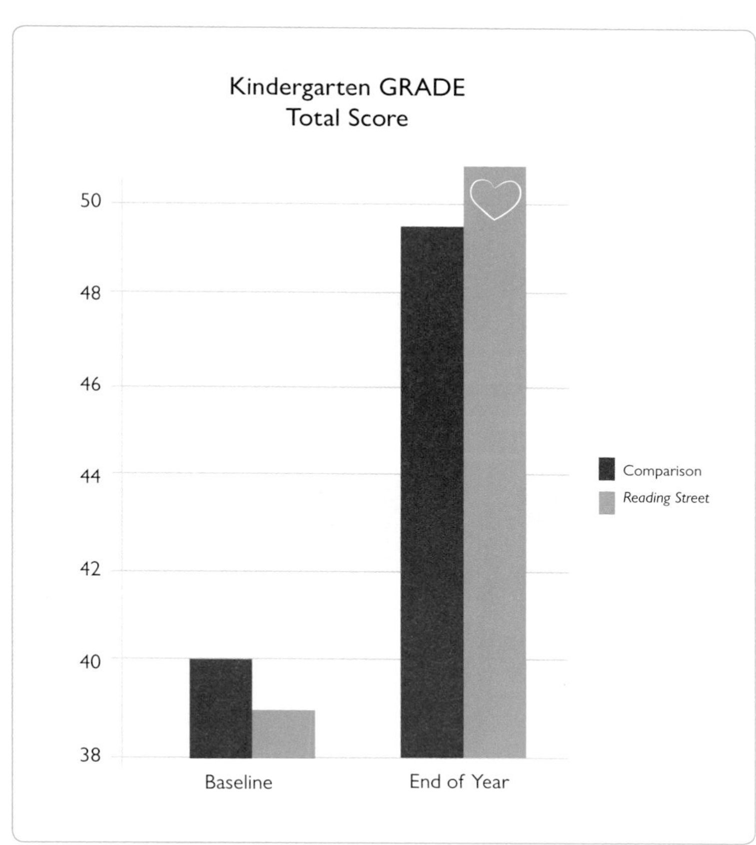

Greater Reading Enjoyment Later

Fourth-grade *Reading Street* students had more positive attitudes toward reading.

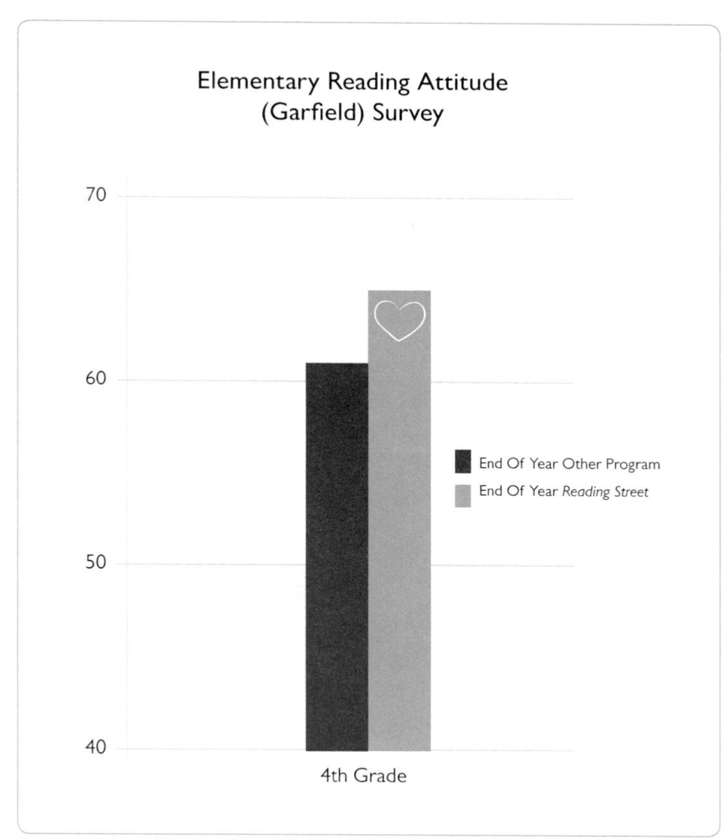

"The texts children read provide them with a foundation not just for what they're going to read, but also for what they're going to write and talk about."

Jeanne R. Paratore, Ed.D.
Program Author

Grow student capacity.

Reading Street Common Core builds students' capacity to read complex texts. Zoom in on elements critical to the Common Core State Standards.

Text-Based Comprehension

Modeling, analysis, and guided practice prepare students for more demanding text.

DAYS 2 & 3

1ST READ

Access Text If students need help, then...

CONNECT TO CONCEPT Look at the pictures on page 147. Look at the chipmunk. This is a chipmunk; describe what it looks like. Encourage children to answer the question in complete sentences. Yes, the chipmunk is light brown with dark brown strips. I think it is eating something. Ask children to describe the ant, raccoon, and bird.

AUTHOR'S PURPOSE What is the author's purpose for writing this selection? How do you know? (The author's purpose is to give information about animals and plants in a forest. These pages tell facts about bugs and leaves.)

Common Core State Standards
Informational Text 8. Identify the reasons an author gives to support points in a text.

Life in the Forest
by Claire Daniel

Genre **Expository text** tells facts about real places. Next you will read about the plants and animals in a forest.

Question of the Week
How are plant and animal communities important to each other?

146 147

Student Edition pp. 146–147

We can find life in the forest.
It is a busy place!

Sun shines on the leaves and helps them grow. Bugs like munching on them. Yum, yum! Bugs can eat lots and lots.

Sun helped these leaves get wide and flat.

148 149

Student Edition pp. 148–149

2ND READ

Close Reading

INFER • TEXT EVIDENCE Look at the pictures on p. 147. How can you tell what kinds of animals and plants you are going to read about? Point to the pictures where you found this information.

SYNTHESIS What if the sun never shined on leaves? How would this change the community? (If the sun never shined, the leaves would never grow. There would be no leaves for the bugs to munch on.)

Science **CONNECT TO SCIENCE** Different parts of a plant help it get what it needs to live. Roots take in water from the soil. Leaves use sunlight and a green pigment called chlorophyll to make food.

ELL
Academic Language Have pairs find other things in their environment that are *wide* and *flat*, like the leaf on p. 148.

146-147 Communities • Unit 2 • Week 5

Life in the Forest 148-149

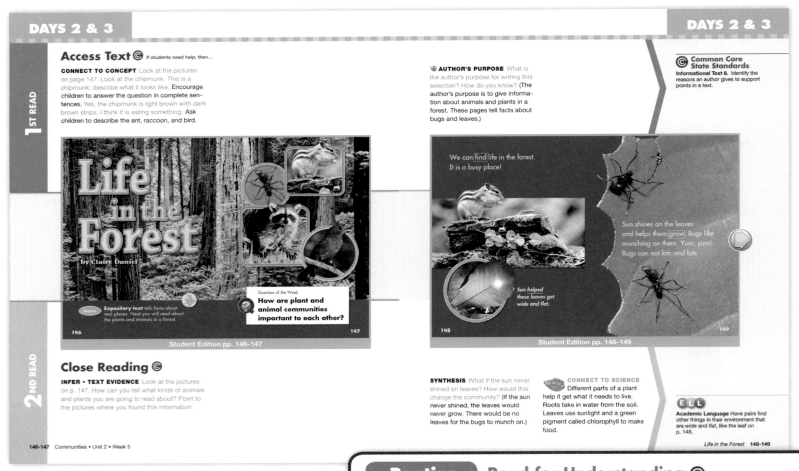

Read for Understanding Routine

Routines provide weekly opportunities to develop deep understanding and build higher-order thinking skills through Close Reading.

Routine **Read for Understanding**

Deepen understanding by reading the selection multiple times.

1. **First Read**—use the **Access Text** notes to help children clarify understanding.
2. **Second Read**—use the **Close Reading** notes to help children draw knowledge from the text.

Content Knowledge

Weekly and unit instruction is built around science and social studies concepts. These concepts connect every piece of literature, vocabulary, and writing, allowing students to develop deep knowledge.

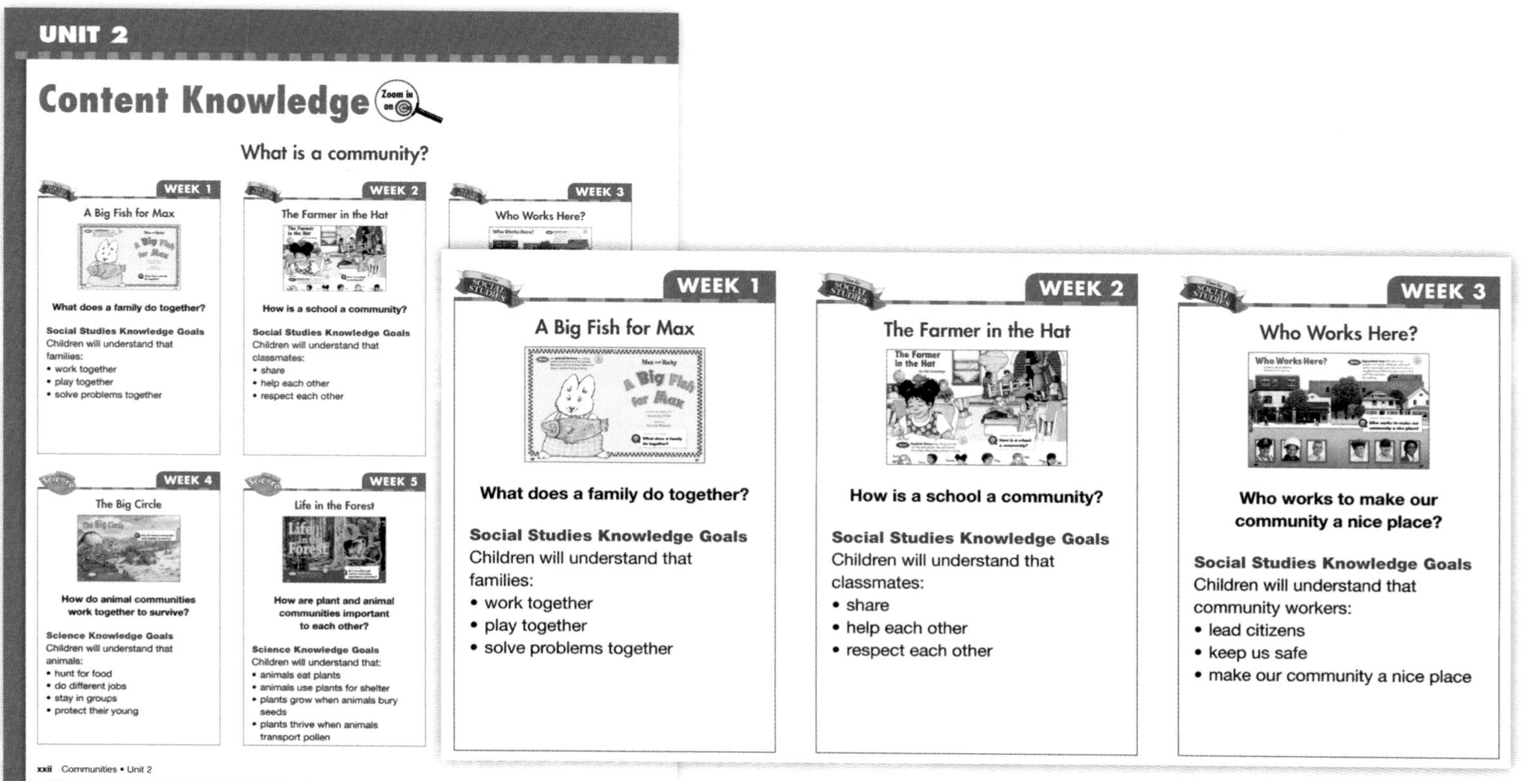

UNIT 2

Content Knowledge

What is a community?

WEEK 1

A Big Fish for Max

What does a family do together?

Social Studies Knowledge Goals
Children will understand that families:
- work together
- play together
- solve problems together

WEEK 2

The Farmer in the Hat

How is a school a community?

Social Studies Knowledge Goals
Children will understand that classmates:
- share
- help each other
- respect each other

WEEK 3

Who Works Here?

Who works to make our community a nice place?

Social Studies Knowledge Goals
Children will understand that community workers:
- lead citizens
- keep us safe
- make our community a nice place

WEEK 4

The Big Circle

How do animal communities work together to survive?

Science Knowledge Goals
Children will understand that animals:
- hunt for food
- do different jobs
- stay in groups
- protect their young

WEEK 5

Life in the Forest

How are plant and animal communities important to each other?

Science Knowledge Goals
Children will understand that:
- animals eat plants
- animals use plants for shelter
- plants grow when animals bury seeds
- plants thrive when animals transport pollen

xxii Communities • Unit 2

Writing

Varied writing tasks help students write to inform or explain.

DAILY

- 10-minute mini-lessons on writing traits and craft allow students to write in response to their reading
- Quick Write routine for writing on demand

WEEKLY

- Different writing product each week
- Writing mini-lessons and organizational models
- Mentor text to exemplify good traits

UNIT

- One- or two-week Writing Workshops
- Writing process lessons

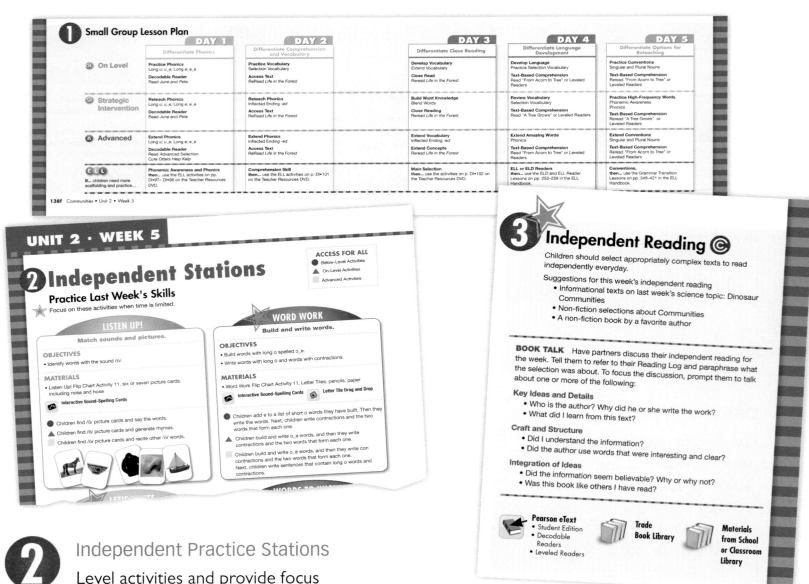

Inspire confidence.

"What do I do in group time?" Follow the simple 3-step plan. *Reading Street Common Core* provides a road map to help you teach with confidence. You'll know exactly where to go and what to do next.

1 Teacher-Led Small Groups

See how to differentiate instruction day by day.

1 Small Group Lesson Plan

	DAY 1 Differentiate Phonics	DAY 2 Differentiate Comprehension and Vocabulary	DAY 3 Differentiate Close Reading	DAY 4 Differentiate Language Development	DAY 5 Differentiate Options for Reteaching
OL On Level	**Practice Phonics** Long *u*; *u_e*; Long *e*; *e_e* **Decodable Reader** Read *June and Pete*	**Practice Vocabulary** Selection Vocabulary **Access Text** ReRead *Life in the Forest*	**Develop Vocabulary** Extend Vocabulary **Close Read** Reread *Life in the Forest*	**Develop Language** Practice Selection Vocabulary **Text-Based Comprehension** Read "From Acorn to Tree" or Leveled Readers	**Practice Conventions** Singular and Plural Nouns **Text-Based Comprehension** Reread "From Acorn to Tree" or Leveled Readers
SI Strategic Intervention	**Reteach Phonics** Long *u*; *u_e*; Long *e*; *e_e* **Decodable Reader** Read *June and Pete*	**Reteach Phonics** Inflected Ending *-ed* **Access Text** ReRead *Life in the Forest*	**Build Word Knowledge** Blend Words **Close Reading** Reread *Life in the Forest*	**Review Vocabulary** Selection Vocabulary **Text-Based Comprehension** Read "A Tree Grows" or Leveled Readers	**Practice High-Frequency Words** Phonemic Awareness Phonics **Text-Based Comprehension** Reread "A Tree Grows" or Leveled Readers
A Advanced	**Extend Phonics** Long *u*; *u_e*; Long *e*; *e_e* **Decodable Reader** Read Advanced Selection *Cute Otters Help Kelp*	**Extend Phonics** Inflected Ending *-ed* **Access Text** ReRead *Life in the Forest*	**Extend Vocabulary** Inflected Ending *-ed* **Extend Concepts** Reread *Life in the Forest*	**Extend Amazing Words** Phonics **Text-Based Comprehension** Read "From Acorn to Tree" or Leveled Readers	**Extend Conventions** Singular and Plural Nouns **Text-Based Comprehension** Reread "From Acorn to Tree" or Leveled Readers
ELL **If...** children need more scaffolding and practice...	**Phonemic Awareness and Phonics then...** use the ELL activities on pp. DI•97– DI•98 on the Teacher Resources DVD.	**Comprehension Skill then...** use the ELL activities on p. DI•101 on the Teacher Resources DVD.	**Main Selection then...** use the activities on p. DI•102 on the Teacher Resources DVD.	**ELL or ELD Readers then...** use the ELD and ELL Reader Lessons on pp. 252–259 in the ELL Handbook.	**Conventions, then...** use the Grammar Transition Lessons on pp. 346–421 in the ELL Handbook.

138f Communities • Unit 2 • Week 5

UNIT 2 • WEEK 5

2 Independent Stations

Practice Last Week's Skills

Focus on these activities when time is limited.

ACCESS FOR ALL
- Below-Level Activities
- On-Level Activities
- Advanced Activities

LISTEN UP!

Match sounds and pictures.

OBJECTIVES
- Identify words with the sound /o/.

MATERIALS
- Listen Up! Flip Chart Activity 11, six or seven picture cards, including nose and hose

Interactive Sound-Spelling Cards

- Children find /ō/ picture cards and say the words.
- Children find /ō/ picture cards and generate rhymes.
- Children find /ō/ picture cards and recite other /ō/ words.

WORD WORK

Build and write words.

OBJECTIVES
- Build words with long o spelled o_e.
- Write words with long o and words with contractions.

MATERIALS
- Word Work Flip Chart Activity 11, Letter Tiles, pencils, paper

Interactive Sound-Spelling Cards Letter Tile Drag and Drop

- Children add e to a list of short o words they have built. Then they write the words. Next, children write contractions and the two words that form each one.
- Children build and write o_e words, and then they write contractions and the two words that form each one.
- Children build and write o_e words, and then they write con contractions and the two words that form each one. Next, children write sentences that contain long o words and contractions.

3 Independent Reading

Children should select appropriately complex texts to read independently everyday.

Suggestions for this week's independent reading
- Informational texts on last week's science topic: Dinosaur Communities
- Non-fiction selections about Communities
- A non-fiction book by a favorite author

BOOK TALK Have partners discuss their independent reading for the week. Tell them to refer to their Reading Log and paraphrase what the selection was about. To focus the discussion, prompt them to talk about one or more of the following:

Key Ideas and Details
- Who is the author? Why did he or she write the work?
- What did I learn from this text?

Craft and Structure
- Did I understand the information?
- Did the author use words that were interesting and clear?

Integration of Ideas
- Did the information seem believable? Why or why not?
- Was this book like others I have read?

Pearson eText
- Student Edition
- Decodable Readers
- Leveled Readers

Trade Book Library

Materials from School or Classroom Library

2 Independent Practice Stations

Level activities and provide focus when time is limited.

3 Independent Reading

Suggest concept-related reading and partner activities.

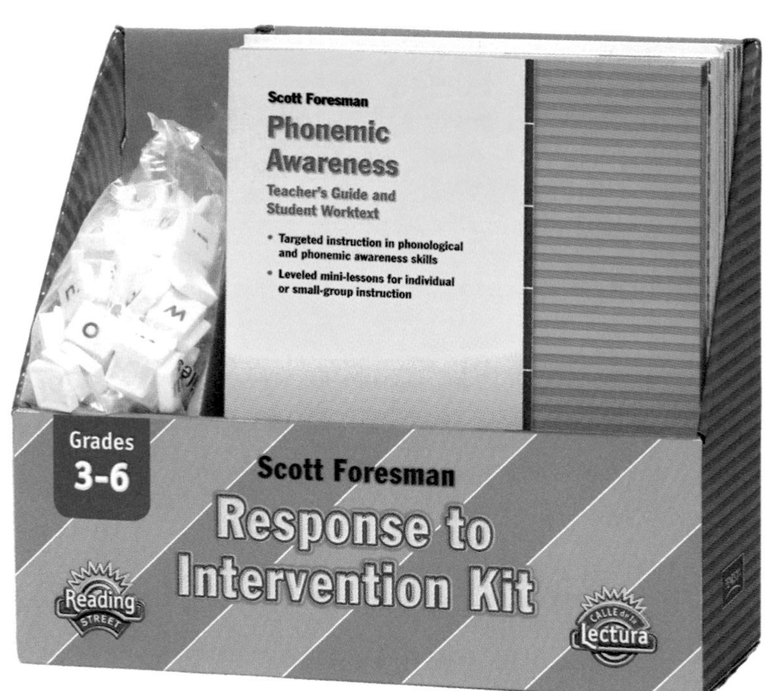

Response to Intervention Kit

Tier 2 RTI Kit provides a targeted focus and leveled mini-lessons for individuals and small groups.

Intensive Intervention

My Sidewalks Intensive Intervention

Conceptually related to *Reading Street, My Sidewalks* provides 30 weeks of instruction for struggling readers.

"What we need to do is to increase the support strategies to help students cope with complex text."

P. David Pearson
Program Author

YOU ARE HERE

UNIT 6 Freedom

UNIT 1 Living and Learning

TABLE OF CONTENTS

UNIT 2
Smart Solutions

UNIT 3
People and Nature

UNIT 4
One of a Kind

UNIT 5
Cultures

eStreet Interactive
www.ReadingStreet.com

Freedom

What does it mean to be free?

The Story of the Statue of Liberty

NARRATIVE NONFICTION

Why do we have symbols that represent freedom?

Paired Selection
A Nation of Immigrants
TEXTBOOK

Happy Birthday Mr. Kang

REALISTIC FICTION

What does it mean to grant freedom?

Paired Selection
Once Upon a Constitution
EXPOSITORY TEXT

Talking Walls: Art for the People

PHOTO ESSAY

Why is freedom of expression important?

Paired Selection
The History of Palindromes
PALINDROMES

Two Bad Ants

ANIMAL FANTASY

Why are rules and laws important to freedom?

Paired Selection
Hiking Safety Tips
ONLINE SOURCES

Atlantis

LEGEND

What is the best way to keep your freedom?

Paired Selection
The Monster in the Maze
DRAMA

Skills Overview

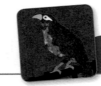

Key
T Tested Skill
◎ Target Skill

		 WEEK 1	 WEEK 2	 WEEK 3
		The Story of the Statue of Liberty Narrative Nonfiction, pp. 374–385 **A Nation of Immigrants** Textbook, pp. 390–391	**Happy Birthday Mr. Kang** Realistic Fiction, pp. 402–419 **Once Upon a Constitution** Expository Text, pp. 424–427	**Talking Walls: Art for the People** Photo Essay, pp. 438–451 **The History of Palindromes** Palindromes, pp. 456–457
Build Content Knowledge ◎	**Integrate Science and Social Studies**	Time for Social Studies: History; Cultures: Symbols; Government History	Time for Social Studies: Community; Responsibility; Cultures	 Freedom of Expression; Immigration; Murals as History
	Weekly Question	*Why do we have symbols that represent freedom?*	*What does it mean to grant freedom?*	*Why is freedom of expression important?*
	Knowledge Goals	Students will understand that symbols • remind us of our history • remind us of our unity • stand for freedom	Students will understand that freedom • can be granted to animals • means pursuing interests • can be granted through laws	Students will understand that freedom of expression • allows us to express ideas or feelings • can spread a message
Get Ready to Read	**Phonics/Word Analysis**	**T** ◎ Vowel Sounds for /ü/ and /u̇/	**T** ◎ Schwa	**T** ◎ Final Syllables
	Literary Terms	Word Choice	Metaphor	Personification
Read and Comprehend	**Comprehension**	**T** ◎ **Skill** Fact and Opinion ◎ **Strategy** Questioning **Review Skill** Author's Purpose	**T** ◎ **Skill** Cause and Effect ◎ **Strategy** Inferring **Review Skill** Theme	**T** ◎ **Skill** Graphic Sources ◎ **Strategy** Important Ideas **Review Skill** Fact and Opinion
	Vocabulary	**T** ◎ Prefix *un-*	**T** ◎ Antonyms	**T** ◎ Unknown Words
	Fluency	Rate	Appropriate Phrasing	Accuracy
Language Arts	**Writing**	Notes Trait: Focus/Ideas	Poetry: Limerick Trait: Organization	Description Trait: Word Choice
	Conventions	**T** Capital Letters	**T** Abbreviations	**T** Combining Sentences
	Spelling	Vowel Sounds in *moon* and *foot*	Schwa	Final Syllables
	Listening and Speaking	Announcement	Express an Opinion	Talk Show

 WEEK 4	 WEEK 5	 WEEK 6
Two Bad Ants Animal Fantasy, pp. 468–485 **Hiking Safety Tips** Online Sources, pp. 490–491	**Atlantis** Legend, pp. 502–519 **The Monster in the Maze** Drama, pp. 524–529	**Optional Review**
 Community; Rules and Laws	 Freedom	 Freedom
Why are rules and laws important to freedom?	*What is the best way to keep your freedom?*	*What does freedom mean?*
Students will understand that rules and laws:keep order • keep us safe • remind us to do the right thing	Students will understand that keeping freedom means • defending it • working together • having necessary laws	Connect the Question of the Week to the Big Question
 Prefixes *im-, in-*	Related Words	
Imagery	Foreshadowing	
T **Skill** Literary Elements: Plot and Theme **Strategy** Story Structure **Review Skill** Cause and Effect	T **Skill** Generalize **Strategy** Inferring **Review Skill** Literary Elements: Plot and Theme	**Review** Unit 6 Target Comprehension Skills and Strategies
T Prefixes and Suffixes *un-, dis-, -ful*	T Homographs	**Review** Unit 6 Target Vocabulary Skills
Rate	Expression	**Review** Unit 6 Fluency Skills
Comic Book Trait: Conventions	Writing for Tests: Historical Fiction Trait: Word Choice	Quick Write for Fluency
T Commas	**T** Quotations and Parentheses	**Review** Unit 6 Conventions
Prefixes, Suffixes, and Endings	Related Words	**Review** Unit 6 Spelling Patterns
Description	Song	

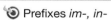

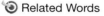

Assessment

5 Steps to Success on Reading Street

RIGHT IN YOUR TEACHER'S EDITION

Step 1

Begin the Year

The Assessment Handbook provides ideas and support to begin the school year and beyond.

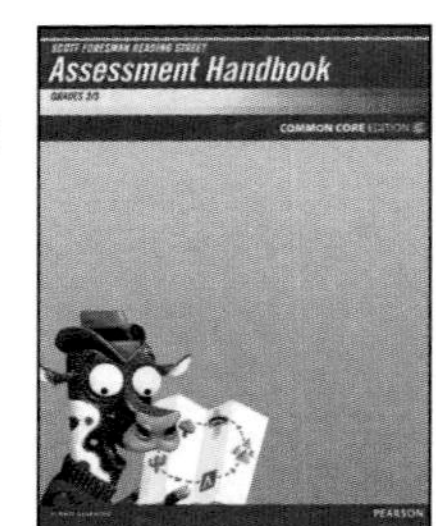

The Baseline Group Test helps identify where students are. Use the Baseline Test results to make initial grouping decisions and to differentiate instruction based on ability levels.

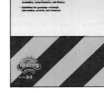

Online Assessment
Save time by using digital assessments. All Reading Street assessments are available on ExamView and in SuccessTracker.

Step 2

Every Day

During the day, use these tools to monitor student progress.

- **Corrective Feedback** provides point of use support.

Corrective feedback	If... students are unable to answer the comprehension questions, then... use the Reteach lesson in *First Stop*.

- **Monitor Progress** boxes each day check retelling, fluency, and oral vocabulary.

Don't Wait Until Friday MONITOR PROGRESS Check Retelling

If... students have difficulty retelling,
then... use the Retelling Cards/Story Sort to scaffold their retellings.

Step 3

Every Week

- **Weekly Assessments** on Day 5 check comprehension and fluency.

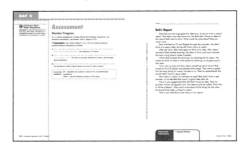

- **Weekly Tests** assess target skills for the week.

- **Fresh Reads** assesses fluency and comprehension as students read a new passage.

- **Reading Street Sleuth** assesses students' ability to find clues in text through close reading.

Step 4

Every Unit

- **Unit Benchmark Tests** assess mastery of unit skills: comprehension, vocabulary, phonics, conventions, and writing.
- **Unit Benchmark Tests** provide professional development and support with performance-based assessment.

- **Performance-Based Assessments** assess students' ability to demonstrate text-based comprehension and application of higher-order thinking skills.

Step 5

End the Year

- **End-of-Year Benchmark Test** measures student mastery of skills covered in all six units with options for performance-based assessment.

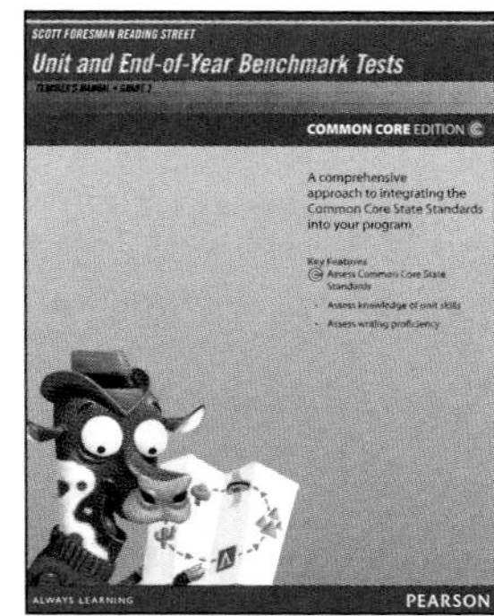

5 Steps to Success on Reading Street

1. Begin the Year
2. Every Day
3. Every Week
4. Every Unit
5. End the Year

Digital Assessment

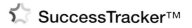

SuccessTracker™

eStreet Interactive
www.ReadingStreet.com

Implementing eStreet Interactive

Power up your classroom and put time back on your side!

eStreet Interactive
www.ReadingStreet.com

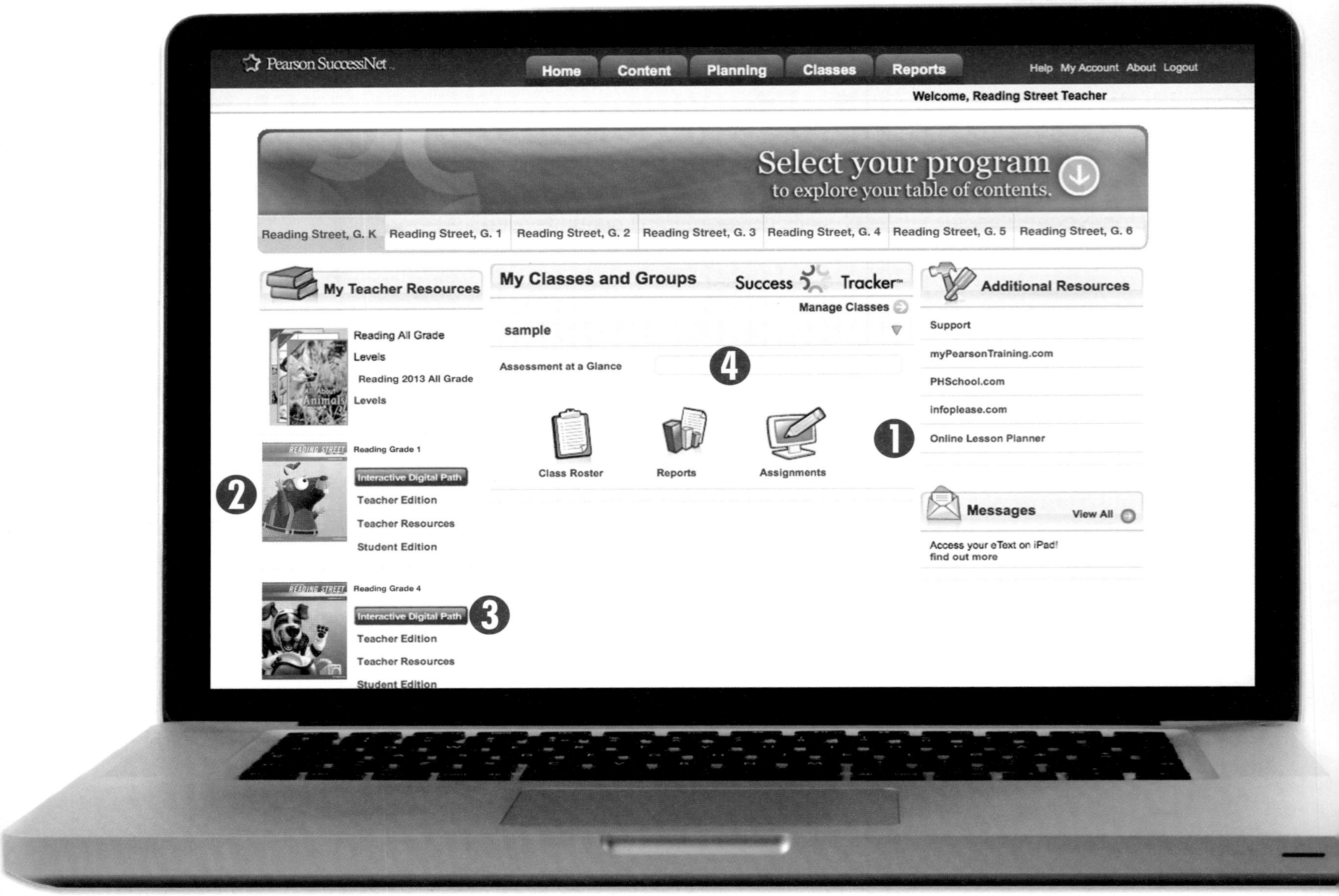

Additional Digital Support

AudioText CD
Background Building Audio CD
Teacher Resources DVD

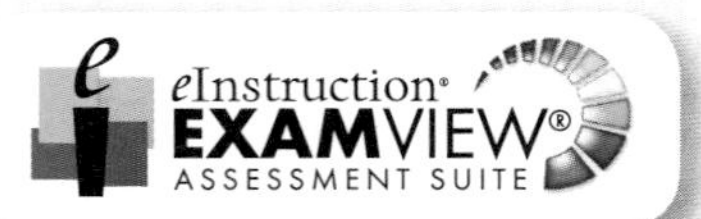

Plan

Customize your daily plan by clicking, dragging, and posting!

- Online Lesson Planner
- Online Teacher's Edition

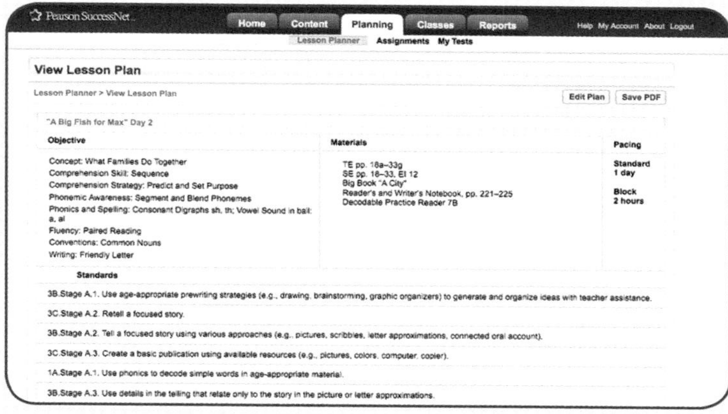

Online Lesson Planner

Teach

Engage through interactive media!

- Concept Talk Videos
- Letter Tile Drag and Drop
- Envision It! Animations
- Grammar Jammer

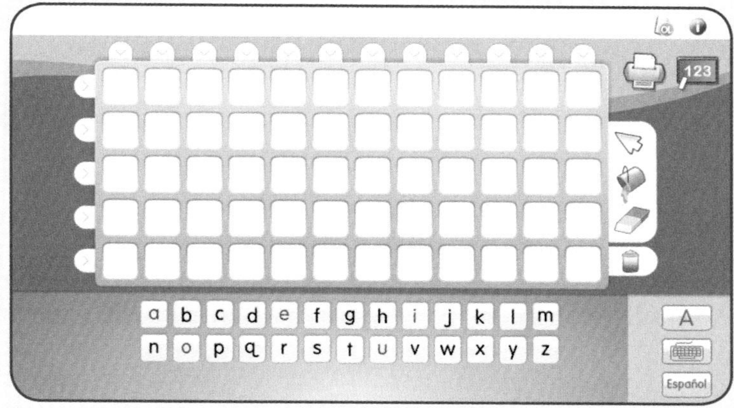

Letter Tile Drag and Drop

Practice

Motivate through personalized practice activities!

- Story Sort
- Pearson eText
- Journal
- Vocabulary Activities
- Leveled Reader Database

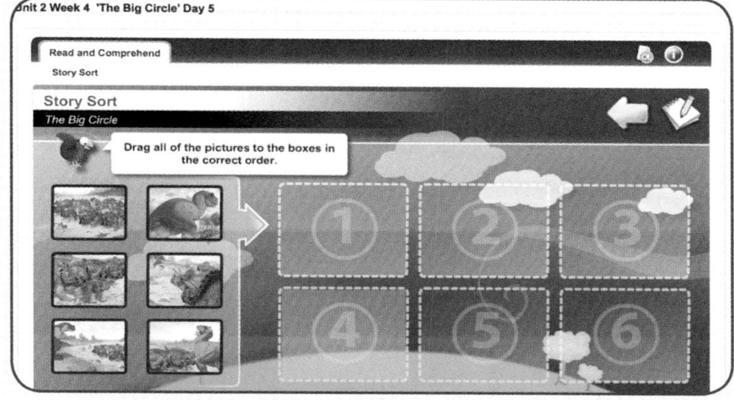

Story Sort

Manage and Assess

Respond to individual needs!

- Monitor student progress
- Assign
- Prescribe
- Remediate

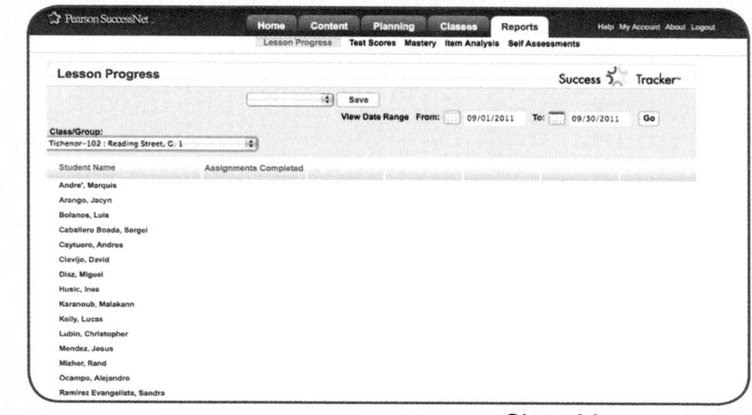

Class Management

Content Knowledge

What does freedom mean?

WEEK 1

The Story of the Statue of Liberty

Why do we have symbols that represent freedom?

Social Studies Knowledge Goals
Students will understand that symbols
- remind us of our history
- remind us of our unity
- stand for freedom

WEEK 2

Happy Birthday Mr. Kang

What does it mean to grant freedom?

Social Studies Knowledge Goals
Students will understand that freedom
- can be granted to animals
- means pursuing interests
- can be granted through laws

WEEK 3

Talking Walls: Art for the People

Why is freedom of expression important?

Social Studies Knowledge Goals
Students will understand that freedom of expression
- allows us to share ideas or feelings
- can spread a message

WEEK 4

Two Bad Ants

Why are rules and laws important to freedom?

Social Studies Knowledge Goals
Students will understand that rules and laws
- keep order
- keep us safe
- remind us to do the right thing

WEEK 5

Atlantis: The Legend of a Lost City

What is the best way to keep your freedom?

Social Studies Knowledge Goals
Students will understand that keeping freedom means
- defending it
- working together
- having necessary laws

Indiana Common Core Edition 

This Week's Target Skills and Strategies

Target Skills and Strategies	Common Core State Standards for English Language Arts	Indiana Academic Standards for English Language Arts
Phonics and Spelling **Skill:** Vowel Sounds in *moon* and *foot*	**CCSS Foundational Skills 3.** Know and apply grade-level phonics and word analysis skills in decoding words. **(Also CCSS Language 2.f.)**	**IN 3.1** Students understand the basic features of words. They select letter patterns and know how to translate them into spoken language using phonics, syllables, word parts, and context. They apply this knowledge to achieve fluent oral and silent reading.
Text-Based Comprehension **Skill:** Fact and Opinion	**CCSS Informational Text 1.** Ask and answer questions to demonstrate understanding of a text, referring explicitly to the text as the basis for the answers.	**IN 3.2.2** Ask questions and support answers by connecting prior knowledge with literal information from the text. **(Also IN 3.2.3)**
Strategy: Questioning	**CCSS Informational Text 1.** Ask and answer questions to demonstrate understanding of a text, referring explicitly to the text as the basis for the answers. **(Also CCSS Informational Text 3.)**	**IN 3.2.2** Ask questions and support answers by connecting prior knowledge with literal information from the text. **(Also IN 3.2.3)**
Vocabulary **Skill:** Prefix *un-* **Strategy:** Word Structure	**CCSS Language 4.b.** Determine the meaning of the new word formed when a known affix is added to a known word (e.g., agreeable/disagreeable, comfortable/uncomfortable, care/careless, heat/preheat).	**IN 3.1.8** Use knowledge of prefixes and suffixes to determine the meaning of words.
Fluency **Skill:** Rate	**CCSS Foundational Skills 4.b.** Read on-level prose and poetry orally with accuracy, appropriate rate, and expression on successive readings.	**IN 3.1.3** Read aloud grade-level-appropriate literary and informational texts fluently and accurately and with appropriate timing, change in voice, and expression.
Listening and Speaking Announcement	**CCSS Speaking/Listening 4.** Report on a topic or text, tell a story, or recount an experience with appropriate facts and relevant, descriptive details, speaking clearly at an understandable pace.	The Indiana Academic Standards for Listening and Speaking are not currently assessed on ISTEP+ assessments. Educators and students should implement the Common Core Standards for Speaking and Listening as soon as possible.
Six-Trait Writing **Trait of the Week:** Focus/Ideas	**CCSS Writing 8.** Recall information from experiences or gather information from print and digital sources; take brief notes on sources and sort evidence into provided categories.	**IN 3.5.8** Write or deliver a research report that has been developed using a systematic research process.
Writing Notes	**CCSS Writing 8.** Recall information from experiences or gather information from print and digital sources; take brief notes on sources and sort evidence into provided categories. **(Also CCSS Writing 2.b.)**	**IN 3.5.8** Write or deliver a research report that has been developed using a systematic research process.
Conventions **Skill:** Capital Letters	**CCSS Language 2.a.** Capitalize important words in titles.	**IN 3.6.7** Capitalize correctly geographical names, holidays, historical periods, and special events.

This Week's Cross-Curricular Standards and Resources

Cross-Curricular Indiana Academic Standards for Science and Social Studies

Science
IN 3.2.6 Describe how the properties of earth materials make them useful to humans in different ways. Describe ways that humans have altered these resources to meet their needs for survival.

Social Studies
IN 3.3.3 Identify the northern, southern, eastern and western hemispheres; cardinal and intermediate directions; and determine the direction and distance from one place to another.

Reading Street Sleuth

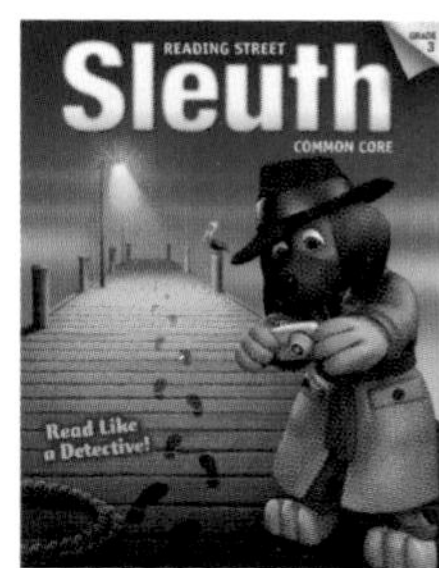

America's National Bird
pp. 68–69

Follow the path to close reading using the Super Sleuth tips:

- Gather Evidence
- Ask Questions
- Make Your Case
- Prove it!

More Reading in Science and Social Studies

Concept Literacy

Below Level

On Level

Advanced

ELL

ELD

ISBN-13: 978-0-328-73392-7 ISBN-10: 0-328-73392-X

Your 90-Minute Reading Block

	Whole Group	Formative Assessment How do I make my small groups flexible?	Small Group OL On Level SI Strategic Intervention A Advanced What are my other students reading and learning every day in Small Groups?
DAY 1	**Content Knowledge** Build Oral Language/Vocabulary **Phonics/Word Analysis** Read **Decodable Reader** **Text-Based Comprehension** **Selection Vocabulary** **Research and Inquiry** Step 1–Identify and Focus Topic **Spelling Pretest** Connect to Phonics/Word Analysis	**Monitor Progress** Check Oral Vocabulary	Differentiate Vocabulary **Build Word Knowledge** OL Practice Amazing Words SI Reteach Amazing Words A Extend Amazing Words OL SI A **Text-Based Comprehension** Read *Reading Street Sleuth,* pp. 68–69 or Leveled Readers A Inquiry Project ELL Access Vocabulary
DAY 2	**Content Knowledge** Build Oral Language/Vocabulary **Phonics/Word Analysis** **Vocabulary Skill** **Text-Based Comprehension** Read Main Selection, using Access Text Notes **Research and Inquiry** Step 2–Navigate/Search **Spelling** Connect to Phonics/Word Analysis	**Monitor Progress** Formative Assessment: Check Word Reading	Differentiate Comprehension **Build Word Knowledge** OL Practice Selection Vocabulary SI Reteach Selection Vocabulary A Extend Selection Vocabulary OL SI A **Access Text** Read *The Story of the Statue of Liberty* A Inquiry Project ELL Access Comprehension Skill
DAY 3	**Content Knowledge** Build Oral Language/Vocabulary **Phonics/Word Analysis** Read **Decodable Passage** **Text-Based Comprehension** Read Main Selection, using Close Reading Notes **Fluency** **Research and Inquiry** Step 3–Analyze Information **Spelling** Connect to Phonics/Word Analysis	**Monitor Progress** Check Retelling	**Differentiate Close Reading** OL SI **Reread to Develop Vocabulary** A **Reread to Extend Vocabulary** OL SI A **Close Reading** Read *The Story of the Statue of Liberty* A Inquiry Project ELL Access Main Selection
DAY 4	**Content Knowledge** Build Oral Language/Vocabulary **Phonics/Word Analysis** Read **Decodable Passage** Read **Content Area Paired Selection with Genre Focus** **Let's Learn It!** Vocabulary/Fluency/Listening and Speaking **Research and Inquiry** Step 4–Synthesize **Spelling** Connect to Phonics/Word Analysis	**Monitor Progress** Check Fluency	Differentiate Vocabulary **Build Word Knowledge** OL Develop Language Using Amazing Words SI Review/Discuss Amazing Words A Extend Amazing Words and Selection Vocabulary OL SI A **Text-Based Comprehension** Read "A Nation of Immigrants" A Inquiry Project ELL Access Amazing Words
DAY 5	**Content Knowledge** Build Oral Language/Vocabulary **Text-Based Comprehension** **Vocabulary Skill** **Phonics/Word Analysis** **Assessment** Fluency, Comprehension **Research and Inquiry** Step 5–Communicate **Spelling Test** Connect to Phonics/Word Analysis	**Monitor Progress** Formative Assessment: Check Oral Vocabulary **Monitor Progress** Fluency; Comprehension	Differentiate Reteaching OL **Practice Capital Letters** SI **Review Capital Letters** A **Extend Capital Letters** OL SI A **Text-Based Comprehension** Reread *Reading Street Sleuth,* pp. 68–69 or Leveled Readers A Inquiry Project ELL Access Conventions and Writing

Daily Independent Options

What do my other students do when I lead Small Groups?

★ **Independent Reading**

Suggestions for this week's independent reading:

- Fiction selections about life in a city
- Fiction selections about life in the country
- An information-rich Web site about cities

Book Talk

Foster critical reading and discussion skills through independent and close reading.

Students should focus on discussing one or more of the following:

- Key Ideas and Details
- Craft and Structure
- Integration of Ideas

Pearson eText
- Student Edition
- Decodable Readers
- Leveled Readers

Trade Book Library

Materials from School or Classroom Library

Independent Stations
Practice Last Week's Skills

★ Focus on these activities when time is limited.

★ **Word Wise**
Word Work
★ **Read for Meaning**
Let's Write!
Words to Know
Get Fluent

Assessment Resources

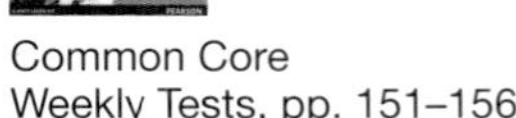

Common Core Weekly Tests, pp. 151–156

Common Core Fresh Reads for Fluency and Comprehension, pp. 151–156

Common Core Unit 6 Benchmark Test

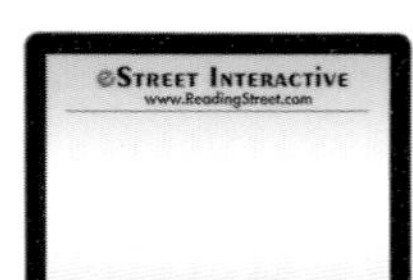

Common Core Success Tracker, ExamView, and Online Lesson Planner

Focus on Common Core State Standards ©

The Story of the Statue of Liberty

by Betsy & Giulio Maestro

Question of the Week
Why do we have symbols that represent freedom?

Genre **Narrative nonfiction** gives information about real people and events in the form of a story. What special event does this selection tell about?

Let's Think About Reading!

374

Main Selection, pp. 374–385

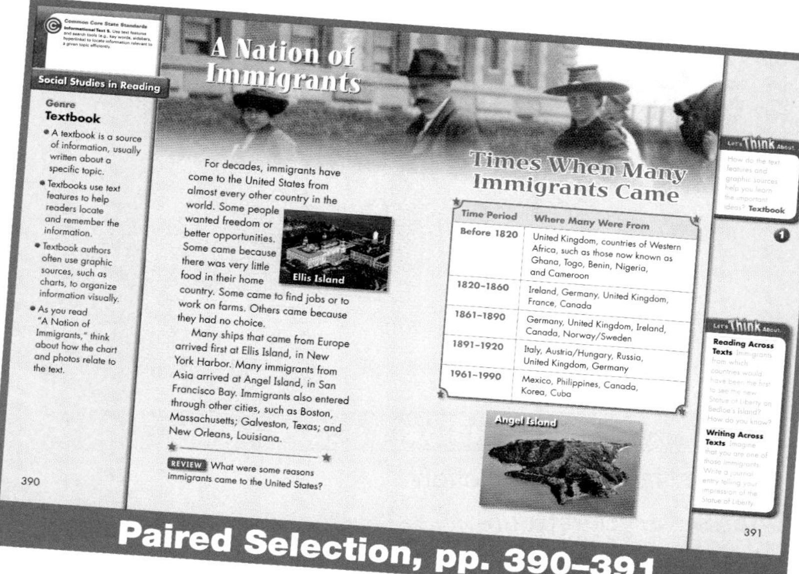
Common Core State Standards
Informational Text 5. Use text features and search tools (e.g., key words, sidebars, hyperlinks) to locate information relevant to a given topic efficiently.

Social Studies in Reading

Genre
Textbook

- A textbook is a source of information, usually written about a specific topic.
- Textbooks use text features to help readers locate and remember the information.
- Textbook authors often use graphic sources, such as charts, to organize information visually.
- As you read "A Nation of Immigrants," think about how the chart and photos relate to the text.

390

A Nation of Immigrants

For decades, immigrants have come to the United States from almost every other country in the world. Some people wanted freedom or better opportunities. Some came because there was very little food in their home country. Some came to find jobs or to work on farms. Others came because they had no choice.

Many ships that came from Europe arrived first at Ellis Island, in New York Harbor. Many immigrants from Asia arrived at Angel Island, in San Francisco Bay. Immigrants also entered through other cities, such as Boston, Massachusetts; Galveston, Texas; and New Orleans, Louisiana.

REVIEW What were some reasons immigrants came to the United States?

Ellis Island

Times When Many Immigrants Came

Time Period	Where Many Were From
Before 1820	United Kingdom, countries of Western Africa, such as those now known as Ghana, Togo, Benin, Nigeria, and Cameroon
1820–1860	Ireland, Germany, United Kingdom, France, Canada
1861–1890	Germany, United Kingdom, Ireland, Canada, Norway/Sweden
1891–1920	Italy, Austria/Hungary, Russia, United Kingdom, Germany
1961–1990	Mexico, Philippines, Canada, Korea, Cuba

Angel Island

Let's Think About...
How do the text features and graphic sources help you learn the important ideas? **Textbook**

1

Let's Think About...
Reading Across Texts Immigrants from which countries would have been the first to see the new Statue of Liberty on Bedloe's Island? How do you know?
Writing Across Texts Imagine that you are one of those immigrants. Write a journal entry telling your impression of the Statue of Liberty.

391

Paired Selection, pp. 390–391

Text-Based Comprehension

Fact and Opinion
CCSS Informational Text 1.

Questioning
CCSS Informational Text 1., CCSS Informational Text 3.

Fluency

Rate
CCSS Foundational Skills 4.b.

Writing and Conventions

Trait: Focus/Ideas
CCSS Writing 8.

Writing Mini-Lesson: Notes
CCSS Writing 2.b., CCSS Writing 8.

Conventions: Capital Letters
CCSS Language 2.a.

Oral Vocabulary

Amazing Words

impressive	competition
tribute	recognizable
enlighten	disgrace
contribution	staggering
dedication	fund

CCSS Language 6.

Selection Vocabulary

Prefix *un-*
CCSS Language 4.b.

Word Structure
CCSS Language 4.b.

crown	symbol	unforgettable
liberty	tablet	unveiled
models	torch	

Phonics and Spelling

Vowel Sounds in *moon* and *foot*
CCSS Foundational Skills 3., CCSS Language 2.f.

few	bookmark
school	balloon
true	suit
goose	chew
fruit	glue
cookie	Tuesday
cushion	bushel
noodle	

Challenge Words

bamboo	barefoot
mildew	renewal
soothe	

Listening and Speaking

Announcement
CCSS Speaking/Listening 4.

Preview Your Week

Why do we have symbols that represent freedom?

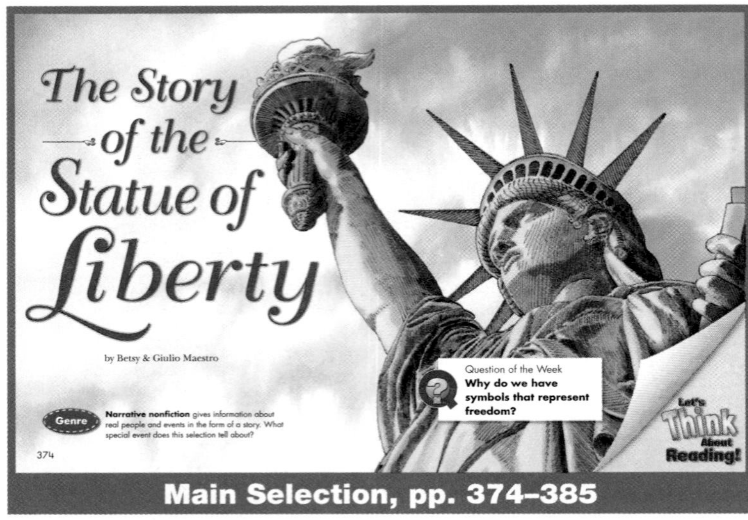

Main Selection, pp. 374–385

Genre: Narrative Nonfiction

Vocabulary: Prefix *un-*

Text-Based Comprehension: Fact and Opinion

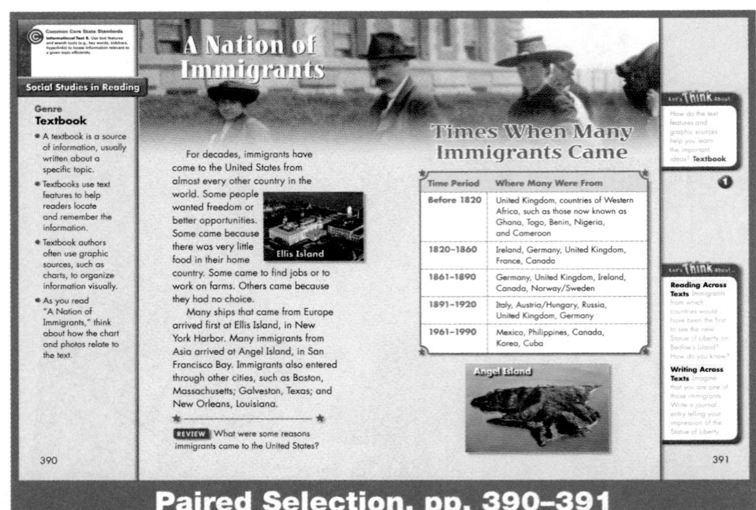

Common Core State Standards
Informational Text 5. Use text features and search tools (e.g., key words, sidebars, hyperlinks) to locate information relevant to a given topic efficiently.

Social Studies in Reading

Genre
Textbook

- A textbook is a source of information, usually written about a specific topic.
- Textbooks use text features to help readers locate and remember the information.
- Textbook authors often use graphic sources, such as charts, to organize information visually.
- As you read "A Nation of Immigrants," think about how the chart and photos relate to the text.

390

A Nation of Immigrants

For decades, immigrants have come to the United States from almost every other country in the world. Some people wanted freedom or better opportunities. Some came because there was very little food in their home country. Some came to find jobs or to work on farms. Others came because they had no choice.

Many ships that came from Europe arrived first at Ellis Island, in New York Harbor. Many immigrants from Asia arrived at Angel Island, in San Francisco Bay. Immigrants also entered through other cities, such as Boston, Massachusetts; Galveston, Texas; and New Orleans, Louisiana.

Ellis Island

REVIEW What were some reasons immigrants came to the United States?

Times When Many Immigrants Came

Time Period	Where Many Were From
Before 1820	United Kingdom, countries of Western Africa, such as those now known as Ghana, Togo, Benin, Nigeria, and Cameroon
1820–1860	Ireland, Germany, United Kingdom, France, Canada
1861–1890	Germany, United Kingdom, Ireland, Canada, Norway/Sweden
1891–1920	Italy, Austria/Hungary, Russia, United Kingdom, Germany
1961–1990	Mexico, Philippines, Canada, Korea, Cuba

Angel Island

Let's Think About...
How do the text features and graphic sources help you learn the important ideas? **Textbook**

1

Let's Think About...
Reading Across Texts Immigrants from which countries would have been the first to see the new Statue of Liberty on Bedloe's Island? How do you know?

Writing Across Texts Imagine that you are one of those immigrants. Write a journal entry telling your impression of the Statue of Liberty.

391

Paired Selection, pp. 390–391

Social Studies in Reading

Genre: Textbook

Build Content Knowledge

KNOWLEDGE GOALS
Students will understand that symbols

- remind us of our history
- remind us of our unity
- stand for freedom

THIS WEEK'S CONCEPT MAP
Develop a concept-related graphic organizer like the one below over the course of this week.

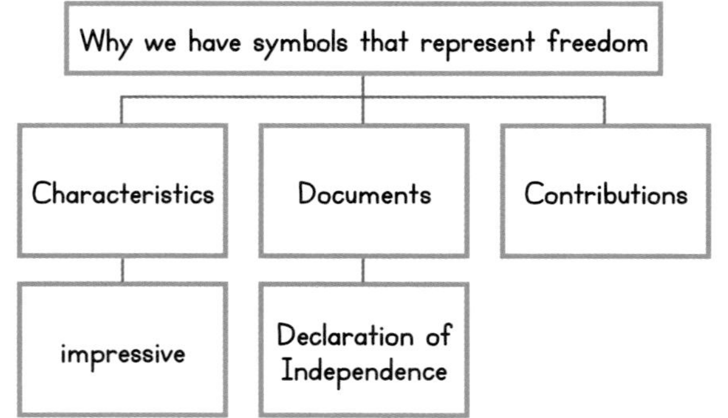

BUILD ORAL VOCABULARY
This week, students will acquire the following academic vocabulary/domain-specific words.

Amazing Words

impressive	dedication	disgrace
tribute	competition	staggering
enlighten	recognizable	fund
contribution		

OPTIONAL CONCEPT-BASED READING Use the Digital Path to access readers offering different levels of text complexity.

Concept Literacy

Below-Level

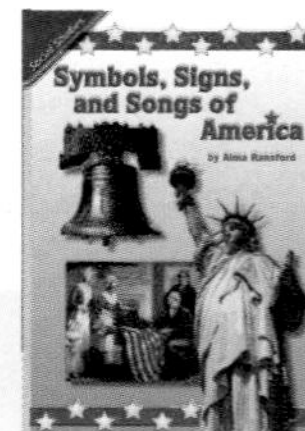

On-Level

Advanced

ELL

ELD

This Week's Digital Resources

eStreet Interactive
www.ReadingStreet.com

Get Ready to Read

Big Question Video This video introduces students to the Big Question and facilitates discussion of the concept for the unit.

Concept Talk Video Use this video on the Digital Path to build interest and introduce the weekly concept of symbols of freedom.

Pearson eText Read the eText of the Student Edition pages on Pearson SuccessNet for comprehension and fluency support.

Envision It! Animations Use this engaging animation on the Digital Path to explain the target comprehension skill, Fact and Opinion.

Read and Comprehend

Journal Use the Word Bank on the Digital Path to have students write sentences using this week's selection vocabulary words.

Background Building Audio CD This audio CD provides essential background information about symbols of freedom to help students read and comprehend the weekly texts.

Pearson eText Read the eText of the main selection, *The Story of the Statue of Liberty,* and the paired selection, "A Nation of Immigrants," with audio support on Pearson SuccessNet.

Vocabulary Activities A variety of interactive vocabulary activities on the Digital Path help students practice selection vocabulary and concept-related words.

Story Sort Use the Story Sort Activity on the Digital Path after reading *The Story of the Statue of Liberty* to involve students in summarizing.

Language Arts

Grammar Jammer Select a stimulating animation on the Digital Path to provide an engaging grammar lesson that will hold students' attention.

Pearson eText Find the Student Edition eText of the Let's Write It! and Let's Learn It! pages with audio support on Pearson SuccessNet.

Additional Resources

Teacher Resources DVD-ROM Use the following resources on the TR DVD or on Pearson SuccessNet throughout the week:

- Amazing Word Cards
- Reader's and Writer's Notebook
- Writing Transparencies
- Daily Fix-It Transparencies
- Scoring Rubrics
- Grammar Transparencies
- ELL Support
- Let's Practice It!
- Graphic Organizers
- Vocabulary Cards

This Week's Skills

Phonics/Word Analysis
Vowel Sounds /ü/ and /u̇/

Comprehension
Skill: Fact and Opinion
Strategy: Questioning

Language
Vocabulary: Prefix *un-*
Conventions: Capital Letters

Fluency
Rate

Writing
Notes

5-Day Planner

DAY 1

Get Ready to Read

Content Knowledge 366j
Oral Vocabulary: *impressive, tribute, enlighten, contribution*
Monitor Progress
Check Oral Vocabulary

Phonics/Word Analysis 368a
Vowel Sounds /ü/ and /u̇/
READ Decodable Reader 26A
Reread for Fluency

Read and Comprehend

Text-Based Comprehension 370a
Fact and Opinion
Questioning

Fluency 370–371
Rate

Selection Vocabulary 371a
crown, liberty, models, symbol, tablet, torch, unforgettable, unveiled

Language Arts

Research and Inquiry 371b
Identify and Focus Topic

Spelling 371c
Vowel Sounds in *moon* and *foot,* Pretest

Conventions 371d
Capital Letters

Handwriting 371d
Cursive Letters *T* and *F*

Writing 371e
Notes

DAY 2

Get Ready to Read

Content Knowledge 372a
Oral Vocabulary: *dedication, competition*

Phonics/Word Analysis 372c
Vowel Sounds /ü/ and /u̇/
Monitor Progress
Check Word Reading

Literary Terms 372d
Word Choice

Read and Comprehend

Vocabulary Skill 372e
Prefix *un-*

Fluency 372–373
Rate

Text-Based Comprehension 374–375
READ *The Story of the Statue of Liberty*—1st Read

Language Arts

Research and Inquiry 381b
Navigate/Search

Conventions 381c
Capital Letters

Spelling 381c
Vowel Sounds in *moon* and *foot*

Writing 381d
Notes

DAY 3

Get Ready to Read

Content Knowledge 382a
Oral Vocabulary: *recognizable, disgrace*

Phonics/Word Analysis 382c
Fluent Word Reading
Vowel Sounds /ü/ and /u̇/
DECODE AND READ
Decodable Practice Passage 26B

Read and Comprehend

Text-Based Comprehension 382e
Fact and Opinion
Questioning
READ *The Story of the Statue of Liberty*—2nd Read
Monitor Progress Check Retelling

Fluency 387b
Rate

Language Arts

Research and Study Skills 387c
Time Line

Research and Inquiry 387d
Analyze Information

Conventions 387e
Capital Letters

Spelling 387e
Vowel Sounds in *moon* and *foot*

Writing 388–389
Notes

DAY 4

Get Ready to Read

Content Knowledge 390a
Oral Vocabulary: *staggering, fund*

Phonics/Word Analysis 390c
Review Suffixes
Fluent Word Reading
DECODE AND READ
Decodable Practice Passage 26C

Read and Comprehend

Genre 390g
Textbook
READ "A Nation of Immigrants" —Paired Selection

Fluency 392–393
Rate
Monitor Progress Check Fluency

Vocabulary Skill 393a
Prefix *un-*

Listening and Speaking 393a
Announcement

Language Arts

Research and Inquiry 393b
Synthesize

Conventions 393c
Capital Letters

Spelling 393c
Vowel Sounds in *moon* and *foot*

Writing 393d
Notes

DAY 5

Get Ready to Read

Content Knowledge 393f
Review Oral Vocabulary
Monitor Progress
Check Oral Vocabulary

Phonics/Word Analysis 393i
Review Vowel Sounds /ü/ and /u̇/

Read and Comprehend

Text-Based Comprehension 393h
Review Fact and Opinion

Vocabulary Skill 393h
Review Prefix *un-*

Phonics/Word Analysis 393i
Review Vowel Sounds /ü/ and /u̇/

Literary Terms 393i
Review Word Choice

Assessment 393j, 393l
Monitor Progress
Fluency; Fact and Opinion

Language Arts

Research and Inquiry 393n
Communicate

Spelling 393o
Vowel Sounds in *moon* and *foot*, Test

Conventions 393o
Capital Letters

Writing 393p
Notes

Wrap Up Your Week! 393q

Access for All

What do I do in group time?
It's as easy as 1-2-3!

1 TEACHER-LED SMALL GROUPS → 2 INDEPENDENT PRACTICE STATIONS → 3 INDEPENDENT READING

Small Group Time

Bridge to Common Core

SKILL DEVELOPMENT
- Vowel Sounds /ü/ and /ů/
- Fact and Opinion
- Questioning
- Prefix *un-*

DEEP UNDERSTANDING

This Week's Knowledge Goals

Students will understand that symbols
- remind us of our history
- remind us of our unity
- stand for freedom

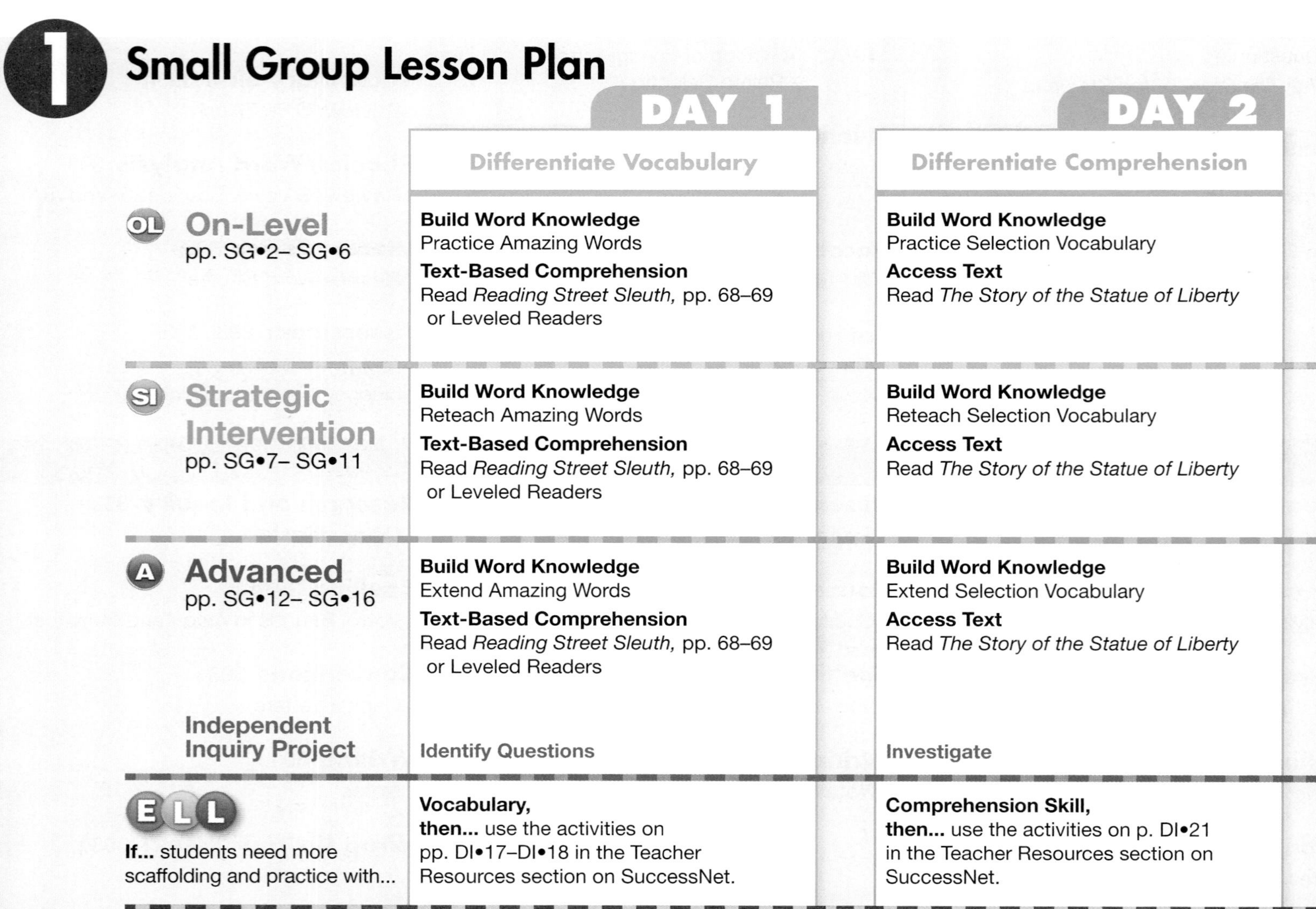

1 Small Group Lesson Plan

	DAY 1 Differentiate Vocabulary	DAY 2 Differentiate Comprehension
OL On-Level pp. SG•2– SG•6	**Build Word Knowledge** Practice Amazing Words **Text-Based Comprehension** Read *Reading Street Sleuth,* pp. 68–69 or Leveled Readers	**Build Word Knowledge** Practice Selection Vocabulary **Access Text** Read *The Story of the Statue of Liberty*
SI Strategic Intervention pp. SG•7– SG•11	**Build Word Knowledge** Reteach Amazing Words **Text-Based Comprehension** Read *Reading Street Sleuth,* pp. 68–69 or Leveled Readers	**Build Word Knowledge** Reteach Selection Vocabulary **Access Text** Read *The Story of the Statue of Liberty*
A Advanced pp. SG•12– SG•16	**Build Word Knowledge** Extend Amazing Words **Text-Based Comprehension** Read *Reading Street Sleuth,* pp. 68–69 or Leveled Readers	**Build Word Knowledge** Extend Selection Vocabulary **Access Text** Read *The Story of the Statue of Liberty*
Independent Inquiry Project	Identify Questions	Investigate
ELL **If...** students need more scaffolding and practice with...	**Vocabulary,** **then...** use the activities on pp. DI•17–DI•18 in the Teacher Resources section on SuccessNet.	**Comprehension Skill,** **then...** use the activities on p. DI•21 in the Teacher Resources section on SuccessNet.

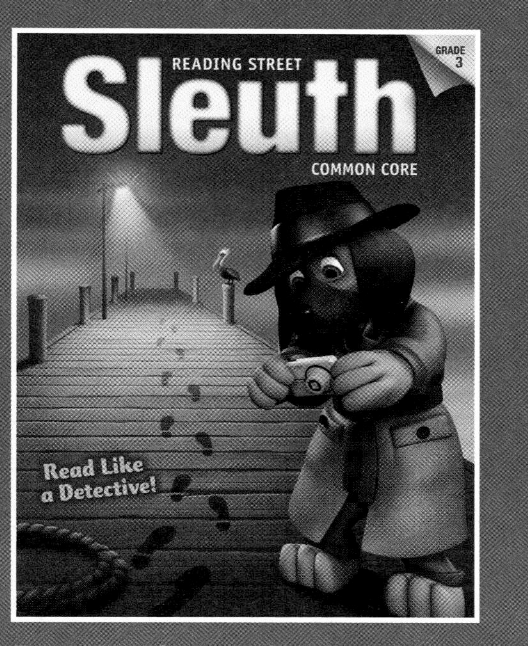

Reading Street Sleuth
- Provides access to grade-level text for all students
- Focuses on finding clues in text through close reading
- Builds capacity for complex text

Build Text-Based Comprehension

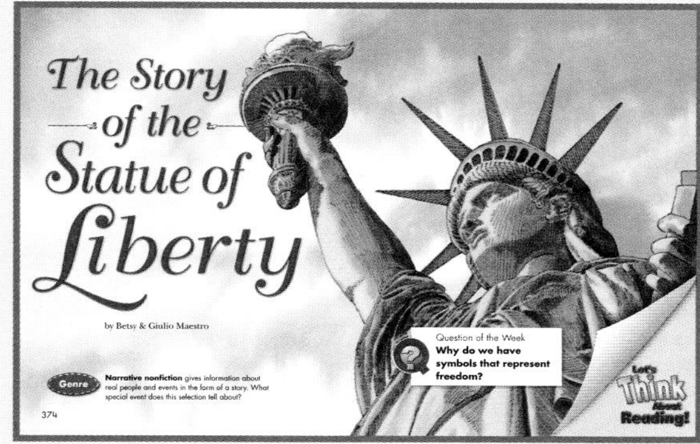

The Story of the Statue of Liberty

Optional Leveled Readers

Concept Literacy

Below-Level

On-Level

Advanced

ELL

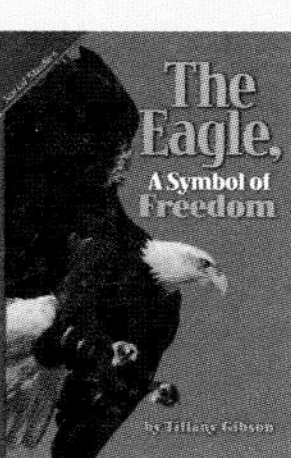
ELD

DAY 3	DAY 4	DAY 5
Differentiate Close Reading	**Differentiate Vocabulary**	**Differentiate Reteaching**
Reread to Develop Vocabulary **Close Reading** Read *The Story of the Statue of Liberty*	**Build Word Knowledge** Develop Language Using Amazing Words **Text-Based Comprehension** Read "A Nation of Immigrants"	**Practice Capital Letters** **Text-Based Comprehension** Reread *Reading Street Sleuth,* pp. 68–69 or Leveled Readers
Reread to Develop Vocabulary **Close Reading** Read *The Story of the Statue of Liberty*	**Build Word Knowledge** Review/Discuss Amazing Words **Text-Based Comprehension** Read "A Nation of Immigrants"	**Review Capital Letters** **Text-Based Comprehension** Reread *Reading Street Sleuth,* pp. 68–69 or Leveled Readers
Reread to Extend Vocabulary **Close Reading** Read *The Story of the Statue of Liberty* **Investigate**	**Build Word Knowledge** Extend Amazing Words and Selection Vocabulary **Text-Based Comprehension** Read "A Nation of Immigrants" **Organize**	**Extend Capital Letters** **Text-Based Comprehension** Reread *Reading Street Sleuth,* pp. 68–69 or Leveled Readers **Communicate**
Main Selection, **then...** use the activities on p. DI•22 in the Teacher Resources section on SuccessNet.	**Amazing Words,** **then...** use the Routine on pp. xxxvi–xxxvii in the *ELL Handbook.*	**Conventions and Writing,** **then...** use the Grammar Transition Lessons on pp. 312–386 in the *ELL Handbook.*

2 Independent Stations

Practice Last Week's Skills

Focus on these activities when time is limited.

ACCESS FOR ALL
- ● Below-Level Activities
- ▲ On-Level Activities
- ■ Advanced Activities

WORD WISE

Spell and use words in sentences.

OBJECTIVES
- Spell words with suffixes *-y, -ish, -hood,* and *-ment.*

MATERIALS
- *Word Wise* Flip Chart Activity 26, teacher-made word cards, paper, pencils

Letter Tile Drag and Drop

- ● Students write four words with suffixes *-y, -ish, -hood,* and *-ment;* write sentences using the words; and list other words with the suffixes.
- ▲ Students write eight words with suffixes *-y, -ish, -hood,* and *-ment;* write sentences using the words; and list other words with the suffixes.
- ■ Students write twelve words with suffixes *-y, -ish, -hood,* and *-ment;* write sentences using the words; and list other words with the suffixes.

WORD WORK

Identify and pronounce words.

OBJECTIVES
- Identify and pronounce words with suffixes *-y, -ish, -hood,* and *-ment*.

MATERIALS
- *Word Work* Flip Chart Activity 26, teacher-made word cards, paper, pencils

Letter Tile Drag and Drop

- ● Students write and say eight words and circle the suffix in each word.
- ▲ Students write and say ten words and circle the suffix in each word.
- ■ Students write and say twelve words and circle the suffix in each word.

LET'S WRITE!

Write to persuade.

OBJECTIVES
- Write a book review.

MATERIALS
- *Let's Write!* Flip Chart Activity 26, paper, pencils

Grammar Jammer

- ● Students write a three-sentence book review that states their opinion and includes details. They underline the book's title.
- ▲ Students write a book review that states their opinion and includes details. They tell the author and underline the title.
- ■ Students write a book review that introduces the book in an interesting way, summarizes it, and ends with a recommendation. They tell the author and underline the title.

WORDS TO KNOW

Determine word meanings.

OBJECTIVES
- Identify and define homonyms.

MATERIALS
- *Words to Know* Flip Chart Activity 26, teacher-made word cards, paper, pencils

Vocabulary Activities

- ● Students write three pairs of homonyms and then write a sentence for each pair to show the different meanings.
- ▲ Students write five pairs of homonyms and write a sentence for each pair to show the different meanings.
- ■ Students write ten pairs of homonyms on cards, turn the cards face down, and play a matching game with a partner.

READ FOR MEANING

Use comprehension skills.

OBJECTIVES

- Identify author's purpose.

MATERIALS

- *Read for Meaning* Flip Chart Activity 26, Leveled Readers, paper, pencils

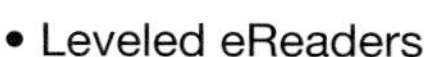
Pearson eText
- Leveled eReaders

Envision It! Animations

● Students read a book and write one sentence that tells the author's purpose and one sentence about a detail that supports their reasoning.

▲ Students read a book and write one sentence that tells the author's purpose and two sentences about details from the book that support their reasoning.

■ Students read a book and write a paragraph that tells the author's purpose and discusses details that support their reasoning.

GET FLUENT

Practice reading fluently with a partner.

OBJECTIVES

- Read aloud with appropriate phrasing.

MATERIALS

- *Get Fluent* Flip Chart Activity 26, Leveled Readers

Pearson eText
- Leveled eReaders

● Partners take turns reading aloud with appropriate phrasing from a Concept Literacy or Below-Level Reader and providing feedback.

▲ Partners take turns reading aloud with appropriate phrasing from an On-Level Reader and providing feedback.

■ Partners take turns reading aloud with appropriate phrasing from an Advanced Reader and providing feedback.

Manage the Stations

Use these management tools to set up and organize your Practice Stations:

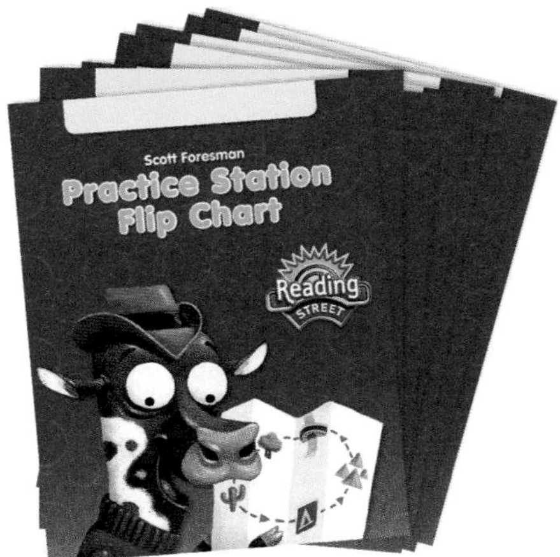

Practice Station Flip Charts

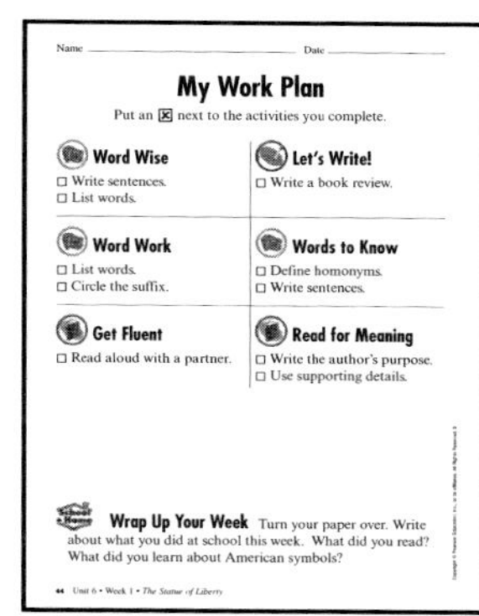
Name ______ Date ______

My Work Plan

Put an ☒ next to the activities you complete.

Word Wise
- ☐ Write sentences.
- ☐ List words.

Let's Write!
- ☐ Write a book review.

Word Work
- ☐ List words.
- ☐ Circle the suffix.

Words to Know
- ☐ Define homonyms.
- ☐ Write sentences.

Get Fluent
- ☐ Read aloud with a partner.

Read for Meaning
- ☐ Write the author's purpose.
- ☐ Use supporting details.

Wrap Up Your Week Turn your paper over. Write about what you did at school this week. What did you read? What did you learn about American symbols?

44 Unit 6 • Week 1 • *The Statue of Liberty*

Classroom Management Handbook for Differentiated Instruction Practice Stations, p. 44

3 Independent Reading

Students should select appropriate complex texts to read and write about independently every day before, during, and after school.

Suggestions for this week's independent reading:
- Fiction selections about life in a city
- Fiction selections about life in the country
- An information-rich Web site about cities

BOOK TALK Have partners discuss their independent reading for the week. Tell them to refer to their Reading Logs and paraphrase what each selection was about. Then have students focus on discussing one or more of the following:

Key Ideas and Details
- What is the theme or main idea of the text? What details support it?
- What conclusions did you draw from reading the text?

Craft and Structure
- Identify one example of figurative or technical language. What does it mean?
- What was the author's purpose for writing this text?

Integration of Ideas
- How did the illustrations in the text help you understand the meaning?
- How does this text compare and contrast with other texts on the same topic that you have read?

Pearson eText
- Student Edition
- Decodable Readers
- Leveled Readers

Trade Book Library

School or Classroom Library

DAY 1 at a Glance

Content Knowledge
Oral Vocabulary

Phonics/Word Analysis
Vowel Sounds /ü/ and /ù/

Text-Based Comprehension
Fact and Opinion
Questioning

Fluency
Rate

Selection Vocabulary

Research and Inquiry
Identify and Focus Topic

Spelling
Vowel Sounds in *moon* and *foot*

Conventions
Capital Letters

Handwriting
Cursive Letters *T* and *F*

Writing
Notes

Materials

- Student Edition
- Reader's and Writer's Notebook
- Decodable Reader

Bridge to Common Core

INTEGRATION OF KNOWLEDGE/IDEAS
This week, students will read, write, and talk about symbols of freedom.

Texts This Week

- "Let Freedom Ring"
- "Coming to America"
- "Emma and Liberty"
- *The Story of the Statue of Liberty*
- "A Nation of Immigrants"

Social Studies Knowledge Goals
Students will understand that symbols

- remind us of our history
- remind us of our unity
- stand for freedom

Street Rhymes!

Our country has symbols of freedom—
recognizable to you and me—
an American flag with stars and stripes—
the Statue of Liberty.

- To introduce this week's concept, read aloud the poem several times and ask students to join you.

Content Knowledge

Symbols of Freedom

CONCEPT TALK To explore the unit concept of Freedom, this week students will read, write, and talk about symbols that represent freedom. Write the Question of the Week—*Why do we have symbols that represent freedom?*—on the board.

Build Oral Language

TALK ABOUT SYMBOLS OF FREEDOM Have students turn to pp. 366–367 in their Student Editions. Look at each of the photos. Then use the prompts to guide discussion and create a concept map.

- Why is an impressive monument such as the Alamo a good symbol for freedom? (People fought and died for freedom at the Alamo.) Symbols often have important characteristics, such as an impressive history. Let's add *Characteristics* and *impressive* to our concept map.
- What important contributions does the American flag symbolize? (It can be a symbol of the sacrifices soldiers and others have made for our country.) Let's add *Contributions* to the concept map.
- How is the Liberty Bell a tribute to our nation? (It was made to ring out for freedom on July 4, 1776.) Let's add *Documents* and *Declaration of Independence* to the map.
- After discussing the photos, ask: Why do we have symbols that represent freedom?

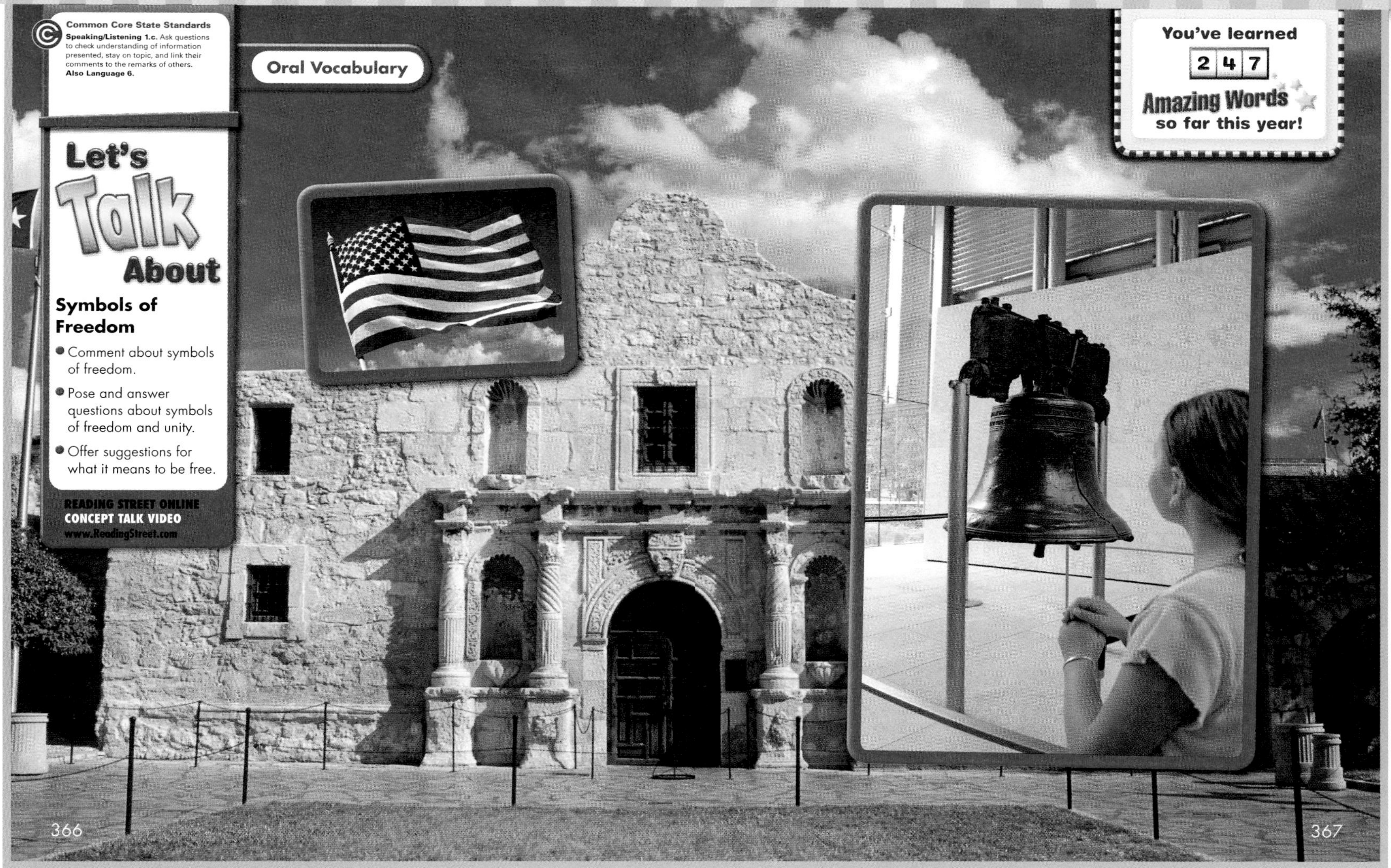

Common Core State Standards
Speaking/Listening 1.c. Ask questions to check understanding of information presented, stay on topic, and link their comments to the remarks of others.
Also Language 6.
Oral Vocabulary
You've learned
247
Amazing Words
so far this year!
Let's Talk About
Symbols of Freedom
• Comment about symbols of freedom.
• Pose and answer questions about symbols of freedom and unity.
• Offer suggestions for what it means to be free.
READING STREET ONLINE
CONCEPT TALK VIDEO
www.ReadingStreet.com
366
367
Student Edition, pp. 366–367

CONNECT TO READING Tell students that this week they will be reading about important symbols of freedom. Encourage students to add concept-related words to this week's concept map.

Why we have symbols that represent freedom
Characteristics
Documents
Contributions
impressive
Declaration of Independence

eStreet Interactive
www.ReadingStreet.com

- **Pearson eText**
  - Student Edition
- **Big Question Video**
- **Concept Talk Video**

ELL

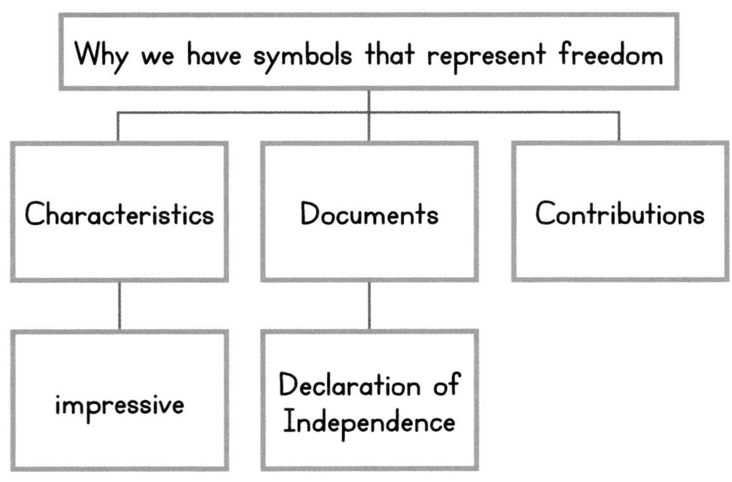

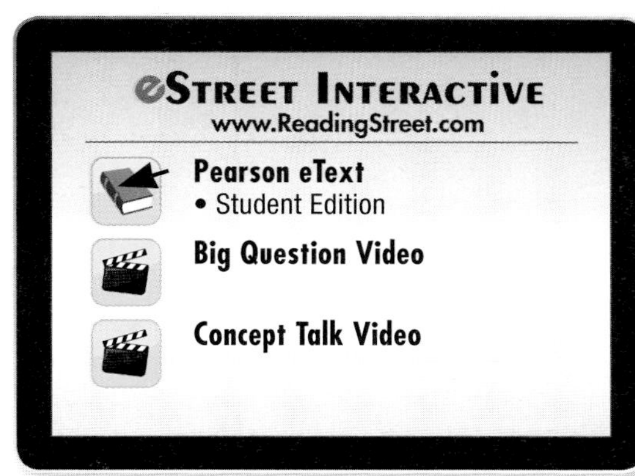

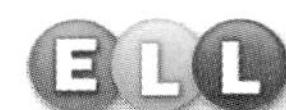

Preteach Concepts Use the Day 1 instruction on ELL Poster 26 to build knowledge, develop concepts, and build oral vocabulary.

ELL Support Additional ELL support and modified instruction are provided in the *ELL Handbook* and in the ELL Support Lessons on the *Teacher Resources DVD-ROM.*

Common Core State Standards

Language 4. Determine or clarify the meaning of unknown and multiple-meaning words and phrases based on grade 3 reading and content, choosing flexibly from a range of strategies. **Language 6.** Acquire and use accurately grade-appropriate conversational, general academic, and domain-specific words and phrases, including those that signal spatial and temporal relationships (e.g., *After dinner that night we went looking for them*). **Also Speaking/Listening 1.c.**

Amazing Words

You've learned 247 words so far.

You'll learn 010 words this week!

impressive	competition
tribute	recognizable
enlighten	disgrace
contribution	staggering
dedication	fund

Content Knowledge

Build Oral Vocabulary

INTRODUCE AMAZING WORDS "Let Freedom Ring" on p. 367b is about the Liberty Bell. Tell students to listen for this week's Amazing Words—*impressive*, *tribute*, *enlighten*, and *contribution*—as you read the Teacher Read Aloud on p. 367b.

Amazing Words Robust Vocabulary Routine

1. **Introduce** Write the word *impressive* on the board. Have students say the word aloud with you. In "Let Freedom Ring," we learn that the Liberty Bell is an *impressive* symbol of America even though it is cracked. Supply a student-friendly definition. (*Impressive* means "having an effect on.")
2. **Demonstrate** Have students answer questions to demonstrate understanding. Is coming to school on a bus *impressive?* Is winning a national spelling contest *impressive?*
3. **Apply** Ask students to name actions that would be *impressive.*
4. **Display the Word** Run your hand under the syllables *im-press-ive* as you read the word. Have students say the word again.

See p. OV•1 to teach *tribute, enlighten,* and *contribution.*

Routines Flip Chart

AMAZING WORDS AT WORK Reread "Let Freedom Ring" aloud. As students listen, have them notice how the Amazing Words are used in context. To build oral language, lead the class in a discussion about the meanings of the Amazing Words. Remind students to listen attentively to speakers and to build on the ideas of others in a discussion.

MONITOR PROGRESS Check Oral Vocabulary

During discussion, listen for students' use of Amazing Words.

If... students are unable to use the Amazing Words to discuss the concept,
then... use the Oral Vocabulary Routine in the Routines Flip Chart to demonstrate words in different contexts.

Teacher Read Aloud

MODEL FLUENCY As you read "Let Freedom Ring," model appropriate rate by reading at a speed that is appropriate to the text and will improve the listener's comprehension.

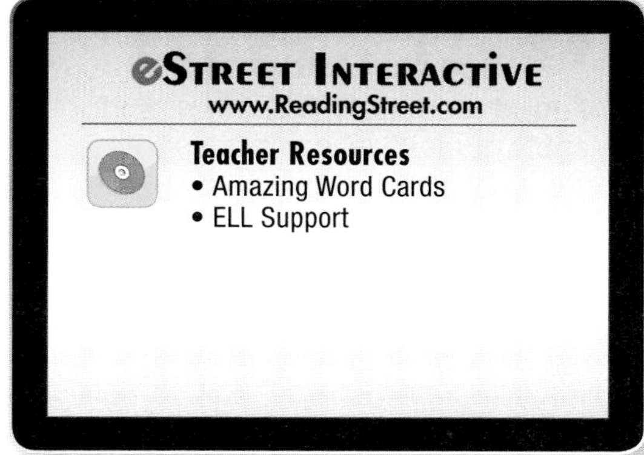

Let Freedom Ring

The most famous bell in the world has a big crack in it. The Liberty Bell tells the story of freedom, the freedom that was found in America. The crack destroyed the bell's sound, but its message still rings clear. The Liberty Bell makes Americans proud of the country they live in. It helps them remember that we live in a free land.

The Liberty Bell now rests in Philadelphia, Pennsylvania. That is where the Declaration of Independence was signed. That is where America became a free country. For many years, however, the bell traveled around the country. It took seven train trips and stopped at 400 cities! The Liberty Bell even traveled to seven of America's World's Fairs.

People read about the bell's travels in their city newspapers. When it would arrive on their streets, they would have big parades. Bands would play a tribute to the country, and people would sing songs to spread the bell's message of freedom. The songs were meant to enlighten America's children about our great nation's strength.

The Liberty Bell in Philadelphia is the third bell that was made. The first bell cracked the first time it was struck. Then someone made a new bell, using metal from the first one. But that bell had a problem too. So two more men made yet another bell. The third one was their contribution to our country. The bell weighs 13,000 pounds—1,000 pounds for each of the first 13 states.

This Liberty Bell has a big crack in it too. No one knows for sure when the crack happened. At first the crack was small and the bell still rang clearly. But the crack got bigger and bigger and the sound got worse and worse. Soon the bell fell silent. However, it was no less impressive. For years it hung in a building called Independence Hall. People from all over the world came to visit it every single day.

Later, the Liberty Bell was moved from Independence Hall to a new building in Philadelphia. The bell now hangs in Liberty Bell Center. The building is open all year so people can see the bell and learn about it. The story of the bell's travels is told in 12 different languages.

The Liberty Bell is only one of our country's symbols of freedom. These symbols are important because they make people think. They make people remember when and why Americans built a new nation. They make people feel proud that they can vote and govern themselves.

Until the Liberty Bell cracked, it rang every year—each July 4th on the birthday of our nation. It rang through the streets of Philadelphia for 61 years. But freedom still rings in the United States of America, and the Liberty Bell sends a message that is heard throughout the country.

ELL Support for Read Aloud Use the modified Read Aloud on p. DI•19 of the ELL Support lessons on the *Teacher Resources DVD-ROM* to prepare students to listen to "Let Freedom Ring."

Check Understanding Stop after reading each paragraph to discuss the content with students. Clarify understanding by asking questions such as Where is the Liberty Bell? Why was the Liberty Bell made? Why is the Liberty Bell important to Americans?

Common Core State Standards

Foundational Skills 3. Know and apply grade-level phonics and word analysis skills in decoding words. **Language 2.e.** Use conventional spelling for high-frequency and other studied words and for adding suffixes to base words (e.g., *sitting, smiled, cries, happiness*).

Skills Trace

Vowel Sounds /ü/ **and** /u̇/

Introduce U6W1D1

Practice U6W1D3; U6W1D4

Reteach/Review U6W1D5; U6W2D4

Assess/Test Weekly Test U6W1 Benchmark Test U6

KEY: U=Unit W=Week D=Day

Phonics

Teach/Model

Vowel Sounds /ü/ and /u̇/

CONNECT Write the words *rain* and *meat.* Ask students what they know about the vowel sounds in these words. (Two letters stand for one vowel sound.) Today you will learn how to spell and read words with the sound /ü/ as in the word *moon,* spelled *oo, ew, ue,* and *ui,* and /u̇/ as in the word *foot,* spelled *oo* and *u.*

USE SOUND-SPELLING CARDS Display Card 90. Point to *oo.* The sound /ü/ can be spelled *oo.* Repeat with Cards 68, 102, and 103 to show other spellings for /ü/: *ew, ue,* and *ui.* Have students say /ü/ several times as you point to *oo, ew, ue,* or *ui.* Follow the same procedure with Cards 89 and 101, the sound /u̇/, which can be spelled either *oo* or *u.*

MODEL Write *blew.* In this word, the letters *e* and *w* stand for the sound /ü/. Point to each spelling as you say its sound. Then blend the word: /b//l//ü/. Follow the same procedure to model blending the sounds in *cook,* /k//u̇//k/.

GROUP PRACTICE Continue the process. This time have students blend with you.

took	**book**	**flew**	**suit**	**tool**	**hook**
fruit	**grew**	**look**	**blue**	**fool**	**put**

REVIEW What do you know about reading these words? The letters *oo, ew, ue,* and *ui* stand for /ü/. The letters *oo* and *u* stand for /u̇/.

Guide Practice

MODEL Have students turn to p. 368 in their Student Editions. Each word on this page has the vowel sound /ü/ or /u̇/. The first word is *raccoon*. I hear /ü/ in the second syllable. In *raccoon*, /ü/ is spelled *oo.* When I say *threw,* I hear /ü/. In *threw,* /ü/ is spelled *ew.*

GROUP PRACTICE For each word in Words I Can Blend, ask for the sound of each letter or group of letters. Make sure that students identify the correct sounds for *oo, ew, ue, ui,* and *u.* Then have them blend the words.

Corrective feedback	**If...** students have difficulty blending a word, **then...** model blending the word, and ask students to blend it with you.

Phonics

Vowel Sounds in *moon* and *foot*

Words I Can Blend

raccoon
suit
threw
tissue
understood
input

Sentences I Can Read

1. A raccoon looks like a little bandit in its brown and black suit.
2. Megan threw the tissue in the wastebasket.
3. Has Tom understood how to input his address?

368

We took our new pooch Moochie from an animal rescue shelter. The folks there understood we were looking for a dog that would suit our whole family.

The minute we set foot in there, we could see the place was full of cool pets. And we knew Moochie was the pet for us when he pushed past the others and shook my hand.

Moochie does drool a little, and sometimes he chews up tissues, but when he snoozes on my bed, he suits me just fine.

Vowel Sounds in *moon* and *foot*: *oo, ew, ue, ui,* and *oo, u*

369

Student Edition, pp. 368–369

Apply

READ WORDS IN ISOLATION After students can successfully segment and blend the words on p. 368 in their Student Editions, point to words in random order and ask students to read them naturally.

READ WORDS IN CONTEXT Have students read each of the sentences on p. 368. Have them identify words in the sentences that have the vowel sounds /ü/ and /u̇/.

Pair students and have them take turns reading each of the sentences aloud.

Chorally read the I Can Read! passage on p. 369 with students. Then have them read the passage aloud to themselves.

ON THEIR OWN For additional practice, use *Reader's and Writer's Notebook*, p. 385.

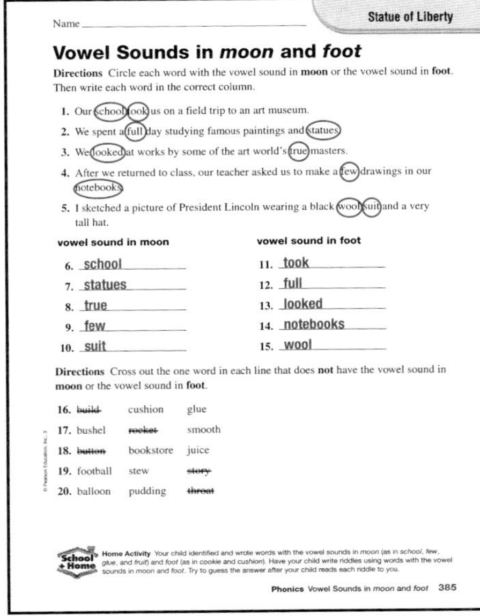

Name ____________ Statue of Liberty

Vowel Sounds in *moon* and *foot*

Directions Circle each word with the vowel sound in **moon** or the vowel sound in **foot**. Then write each word in the correct column.

1. Our (school) (took) us on a field trip to an art museum.
2. We spent a (full) day studying famous paintings and (statues).
3. We (looked) at works by some of the art world's (true) masters.
4. After we returned to class, our teacher asked us to make a (few) drawings in our (notebooks).
5. I sketched a picture of President Lincoln wearing a black (wool) (suit) and a very tall hat.

vowel sound in moon	vowel sound in foot
6. school	11. took
7. statues	12. full
8. true	13. looked
9. few	14. notebooks
10. suit	15. wool

Directions Cross out the one word in each line that does **not** have the vowel sound in **moon** or the vowel sound in **foot**.

16.	~~build~~	cushion	glue
17.	bushel	~~rocket~~	smooth
18.	~~button~~	bookstore	juice
19.	football	stew	~~story~~
20.	balloon	pudding	~~throat~~

School + Home **Home Activity** Your child identified and wrote words with the vowel sounds in *moon* (as in *school, few, glue,* and *fruit*) and *foot* (as in *cookie* and *cushion*). Have your child write riddles using words with the vowel sounds in *moon* and *foot*. Try to guess the answer after your child reads each riddle to you.

Phonics Vowel Sounds in *moon* and *foot* 385

Reader's and Writer's Notebook, p. 385

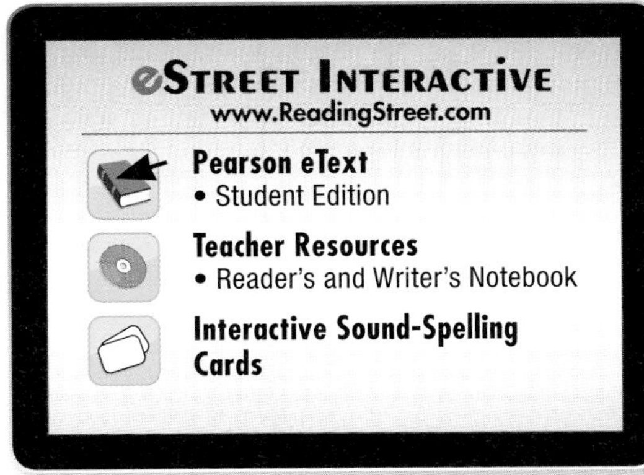

eStreet Interactive
www.ReadingStreet.com
Pearson eText
• Student Edition
Teacher Resources
• Reader's and Writer's Notebook
Interactive Sound-Spelling Cards

Common Core State Standards

Foundational Skills 3. Know and apply grade-level phonics and word analysis skills in decoding words. **Foundational Skills 3.d.** Read grade-appropriate irregularly spelled words. **Foundational Skills 4.** Read with sufficient accuracy and fluency to support comprehension. **Foundational Skills 4.a.** Read on-level text with purpose and understanding. **Speaking/Listening 5.** Create engaging audio recordings of stories or poems that demonstrate fluid reading at an understandable pace; add visual displays when appropriate to emphasize or enhance certain facts or details.

Decodable Reader 26A

If students need help, then...

Read *At the Zoo*

READ WORDS IN ISOLATION Have students turn to p. 121 of *Decodable Practice Readers 3.2*. Have students read each word.

Have students read the high-frequency words *was, to, a, some, wanted, could, said, do, you, the, friend, eye, of, live, they, one,* and *their* on the first page.

PREVIEW Have students read the title and preview the story. Tell them that they will read words with the vowel sound /ü/ spelled *oo, ew, ue,* and *ui* and the vowel sound /u̇/ spelled *oo* and *u.*

READ WORDS IN CONTEXT Pair students for reading and listen as they read. One student begins. Students read the entire story, switching readers after each page. Partners reread the story. This time the other student begins. Make sure students are monitoring their accuracy when they decode words.

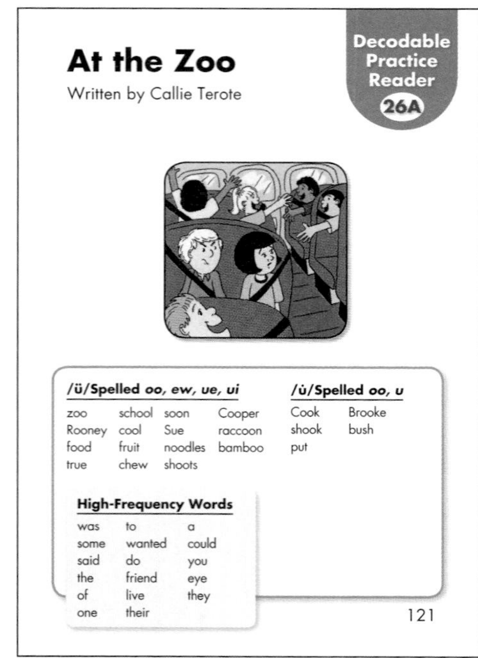

At the Zoo

Written by Callie Terote

Decodable Practice Reader 26A

/ü/Spelled *oo, ew, ue, ui*

zoo	school	soon	Cooper
Rooney	cool	Sue	raccoon
food	fruit	noodles	bamboo
true	chew	shoots	

/u̇/Spelled *oo, u*

Cook	Brooke
shook	bush
put	

High-Frequency Words

was	to	a
some	wanted	could
said	do	you
the	friend	eye
of	live	they
one	their	

121

Decodable Practice Reader 26A

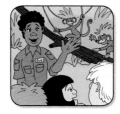

Josh dressed quickly. His long wait was almost over! Today was his class trip to City Zoo.

At nine sharp, a big school bus parked at Cook School. Josh and Brooke got on first. Soon everybody else joined them. Some children began playing wildly. Cooper jumped up on his seat. Ashley shouted loudly. Josh wasn't unruly. He just wanted to focus on zoo sights he'd see.

122

"Quiet, please!" Miss Rooney called.

At last Josh and Brooke could hear themselves think.

"I'm excited about seeing tigers," Brooke said happily. "They're the animals I like best. Which do you like best, Josh?"

123

"You will find out soon," Josh replied. He smiled shyly at Brooke. Josh didn't really like keeping secrets. But talking too much about the animal might bring bad luck. He hoped he'd find it playing outside. Last time, the animal had hidden in its cool, dark cave. Josh could hardly see his furry friend.

124

At City Zoo, a helpful zookeeper named Sue greeted Miss Rooney's class. She began showing the excited children zoo animals. They saw lions, tigers, camels, and monkeys. Josh liked them all. At each stop, Brooke asked, "Isn't that the animal you like best, Josh?" Each time, Josh replied, "No."

125

At long last Sue led everybody to the animal Josh liked best. Just as Josh had hoped, it sat outdoors. It was black and white and quite big. A big black mark circled each eye.

"It looks like a large raccoon!" Martin shouted.

"It looks like a gentle grizzly bear!" Ginny yelled.

126

"It's not a raccoon or a bear, but it has traits of both. It's a giant panda! Which food do you think Pete Panda likes most?" Sue asked.

"Fruit?" Kevin asked. Sue shook her head.

"Meat? Noodles?" Jane asked. Sue shook her head twice.

"Leaves from a lilac bush?" Kate asked.

Josh just had to speak up. "Bamboo," he said.

127

"That's true," Sue nodded. "Lots of bamboo trees grow in China where pandas live. Pandas chew bamboo shoots, or tiny branches. They chew bamboo leaves as well. Aren't pandas picky? Bamboo is one of the few foods they'll put in their mouths."

Soon everybody got back on the bus. "Now we all know which animal you like best, Josh," said Brooke. She gave Josh a high five. "Cool!"

128

Corrective feedback	**If...** students have difficulty decoding a word, **then...** refer them to the *Sound-Spelling Cards* to identify the sounds in the word. Then prompt them to blend the word. • What is the new word? • Is the new word a word you know? • Does it make sense in the story?

CHECK DECODING AND COMPREHENSION Have students retell the story to include characters, setting, and events. Then have students find words in the story that have the vowel sounds /ü/ and /u̇/ spelled *oo, ew, ue, ui, oo,* and *u.* Students should supply *zoo, Cooper, Sue, fruit, true, school, Rooney, raccoon, noodles, chew, soon, cool, food, bamboo, shoots, Cook, bush, Brooke, put,* and *shook.*

EXTRA PRACTICE Have students take turns recording the story as they read. Then ask each student to review his or her recording to identify areas to improve reading fluency.

Reread for Fluency

REREAD DECODABLE READER Have students reread *Decodable Practice Reader 26A* to develop automaticity decoding words with vowel sounds /ü/ and /u̇/.

Routine Oral Rereading

1. **Read** Have students read the entire book orally.
2. **Reread** To achieve optimal fluency, students should reread the text three or four times.
3. **Corrective Feedback** Listen as students read. Provide corrective feedback regarding their fluency and decoding.

Routines Flip Chart

Vowel Sounds /ü/ **and** /u̇/

Beginning Write several words with the vowel sound /ü/ from the *Decodable Practice Reader* on the board, such as *zoo, true, fruit,* and *chew.* Point to each word as you say it aloud. Then underline the letters that spell the sound /ü/ in each word. Repeat for the sound /u̇/, using words such as *bush, shook,* and *put.*

Intermediate After reading, have students find pairs of words with the vowel sound /ü/ or /u̇/ that are spelled the same. For example: *zoo* and *raccoon; Sue* and *true; bush* and *put; Cook* and *shook.*

Advanced After reading the story, have students choose four or five words with the vowel sound /ü/ or /u̇/ and write a sentence for each word.

Text-Based Comprehension

Fact and Opinion
Questioning

READ Remind students of the weekly concept—Symbols of Freedom. Have students read "Coming to America" on p. 371.

MODEL A CLOSE READ

The first paragraph has three statements of fact: your homeland is where you were born, immigrants are people who leave their homeland to come to another county, and America has been called a "Nation of Immigrants." I can prove that these are facts by checking them to verify they are true. At first, I didn't understand the nickname "nation of immigrants," so I asked a question and then read on to find the answer. The answer is in the second paragraph—Everyone who lives in America now once came, or has ancestors who came, from somewhere else.

TEACH Have students read p. 370. Explain that the skill of fact and opinion and the strategy of questioning are tools they can use to deepen understanding. Then have them use a graphic organizer like the one shown to identify statements of fact and opinion from the passage.

GUIDE PRACTICE Have students reread "Coming to America," using the callouts as guides. Then ask volunteers to respond to the questions in the callouts, citing specific examples from the text to support their answers.

Skill Facts are the definitions of *homeland* and *immigrants*. I could look them up in a dictionary or glossary to prove if they were true or false. Another fact is that America has been called a "nation of immigrants." I could look that up in reference books.

Strategy You can ask questions such as *When did people immigrate to the United States?*

APPLY Use *Reader's and Writer's Notebook,* p. 386 for additional practice with fact and opinion.

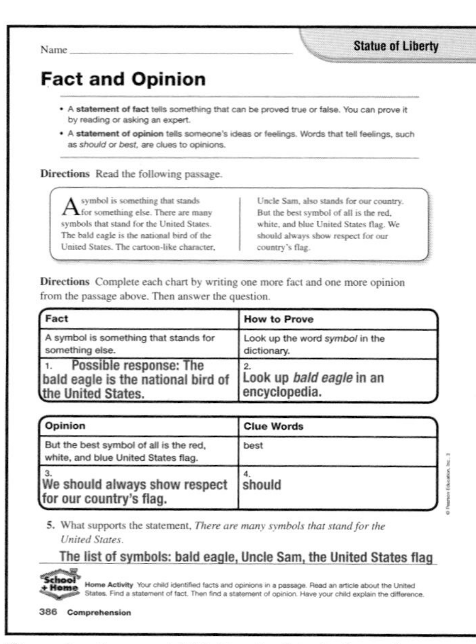

Name ____________ Statue of Liberty

Fact and Opinion

- A **statement of fact** tells something that can be proved true or false. You can prove it by reading or asking an expert.
- A **statement of opinion** tells someone's ideas or feelings. Words that tell feelings, such as *should* or *best*, are clues to opinions.

Directions Read the following passage.

A symbol is something that stands for something else. There are many symbols that stand for the United States. The bald eagle is the national bird of the United States. The cartoon-like character, Uncle Sam, also stands for our country. But the best symbol of all is the red, white, and blue United States flag. We should always show respect for our country's flag.

Directions Complete each chart by writing one more fact and one more opinion from the passage above. Then answer the question.

Fact	How to Prove
A symbol is something that stands for something else.	Look up the word *symbol* in the dictionary.
1. Possible response: The bald eagle is the national bird of the United States.	2. Look up *bald eagle* in an encyclopedia.

Opinion	Clue Words
But the best symbol of all is the red, white, and blue United States flag.	best
3. We should always show respect for our country's flag.	4. should

5. What supports the statement, *There are many symbols that stand for the United States.*

The list of symbols: bald eagle, Uncle Sam, the United States flag

School + Home **Home Activity** Your child identified facts and opinions in a passage. Read an article about the United States. Find a statement of fact. Then find a statement of opinion. Have your child explain the difference.

386 Comprehension

Reader's and Writer's Notebook, p. 386

Common Core State Standards

Informational Text 1. Ask and answer questions to demonstrate understanding of a text, referring explicitly to the text as the basis for the answers. **Informational Text 3.** Describe the relationship between a series of historical events, scientific ideas or concepts, or steps in technical procedures in a text, using language that pertains to time, sequence, and cause/effect. **Foundational Skills 4.** Read with sufficient accuracy and fluency to support comprehension. **Foundational Skills 4.b.** Read on-level prose and poetry orally with accuracy, appropriate rate, and expression on successive readings.

Skills Trace

Fact and Opinion

Introduce U4W3D1; U4W4D1; U6W1D1
Practice U1W4D2; U1W4D3; U4W3D2; U4W3D3; U4W4D2; U4W4D3; U6W1D2; U6W1D3; U6W3D3
Reteach/Review U4W3D5; U4W4D5; U6W1D5
Assess/Test Weekly Tests U4W3; U4W4; U6W1
Benchmark Tests U4
KEY: U=Unit W=Week D=Day

Academic Vocabulary 

statement of fact statement that can be proven true or false

statement of opinion statement that tells someone's ideas or feelings

Comprehension Support

Students may also turn to pp. EI•7 and EI•23 to review the skill and strategy if needed.

Common Core State Standards
Informational Text 1. Ask and answer questions to demonstrate understanding of a text, referring explicitly to the text as the basis for the answers.

Comprehension Skill

Fact and Opinion

- A statement of fact tells something that can be proven true or false. You can prove it by reading a reference source.
- A statement of opinion tells someone's ideas or feelings. Words that tell feelings, such as *should* or *best*, are clue words.
- Use what you learned about fact and opinion and a chart like the one below as you read "Coming to America." Then use the facts to draw a conclusion about immigrants in America.

Fact	How to Prove

Opinion	Clue Words

Comprehension Strategy

Questioning

Active readers use questions to help them understand what they read. While you read, ask literal questions to make sure you understand. You can also ask yourself questions using what you already know or have read to interpret, connect to, or evaluate what you are reading.

Coming to America

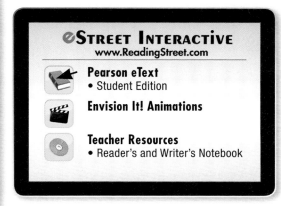

The country where you were born is called your *homeland*. People who leave their homeland and come to another country—such as America—are called *immigrants*. America has been called a "nation of immigrants." Why?

Everyone who lives in America now (except for Native Americans) once came from somewhere else. This may have happened a very long time ago in your family. Or maybe you and your family arrived here recently.

Immigrants leave their homeland for different reasons. Some came to America looking for religious freedom. Others came to escape war or hunger. But mostly, people came looking for a better life.

People came to America from all over the world, but together we are one nation!

Skill What are the statements of fact in the paragraph? How could you prove whether they are true or false?

Strategy Ask questions to make sure you understand the text, such as *What are the different reasons people immigrate?*

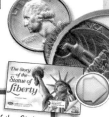

Your Turn!

Need a Review? See the *Envision It! Handbook* for more information about fact and opinion and questioning.

Let's Think About...

Ready to Try It? As you read *The Story of the Statue of Liberty*, use what you've learned about fact and opinion and asking questions to understand the text.

370 371

Student Edition, pp. 370–371

Model Fluent Reading

RATE Have students listen as you read paragraph 3 of "Coming to America" at an appropriate rate. Explain that when you are reading an expository text for comprehension, you slow down the rate of your reading so that all the points in the text are clear.

Routine Choral Reading

1. **Read** For "Coming to America," use paragraph 1 on p. 371.
2. **Model** Have students listen as you read the paragraph at an appropriate rate.
3. **Guide Practice** Have students read along with you.
4. **On Their Own** For optimal fluency, students should reread three or four times at an appropriate rate.

Routines Flip Chart

eStreet Interactive
www.ReadingStreet.com

Pearson eText
- Student Edition

Envision It! Animations

Teacher Resources
- Reader's and Writer's Notebook

ELL

Fact and Opinion Provide oral practice by having students state facts and opinions about the city or town where they live.

Common Core State Standards

Writing 7. Conduct short research projects that build knowledge about a topic. **Speaking and Listening 1.** Engage effectively in a range of collaborative discussions (one-on-one, in groups, and teacher-led) with diverse partners on grade 3 topics and texts, building on others' ideas and expressing their own clearly. **Language 4.** Determine or clarify the meaning of unknown and multiple-meaning words and phrases based on grade 3 reading and content, choosing flexibly from a range of strategies. **Language 6.** Acquire and use accurately grade-appropriate conversational, general academic, and domain-specific words and phrases, including those that signal spatial and temporal relationships (e.g., *After dinner that night we went looking for them*).

Selection Vocabulary

Use the following routine to introduce this week's tested selection vocabulary.

crown a metal head covering worn by someone with power

liberty freedom

models small copies of something

symbol an object, diagram, animal, or icon that stands for or represents something else

tablet a small, flat surface with something written on it

torch a long stick with material at one end that burns

unforgettable so good that you cannot forget it

unveiled removed a veil from; revealed

SEE IT/SAY IT Write *unforgettable*. Scan across the word with your finger as you say it: *un-for-get-ta-ble.*

HEAR IT Use the word in a sentence. The ride on the hot-air balloon was *unforgettable.*

DEFINE IT Elicit definitions from students. If you think a book is *unforgettable,* does that mean that it was interesting or that it was dull? Clarify or give a definition when necessary. Yes, that's right. If you think a book is unforgettable, that probably means it was interesting. Restate the word in student-friendly terms. Something *unforgettable* is something that you will always remember.

Team Talk What book have you read that is *unforgettable* to you? What made it that way? Turn and talk to your partner about this. Be prepared to explain your answer. Allow students time to discuss. Ask for examples. Rephrase their examples for usage when necessary or to correct misunderstandings.

MAKE CONNECTIONS Have students discuss the word. What do you find unforgettable? Favorite books? Favorite movies? A special time you had with your family or friends? Turn and talk to your partner about this. Then be prepared to share. Have students share. Rephrase their ideas for usage when necessary or to correct misunderstandings.

RECORD Have students write the word and its meaning.

Continue this routine to introduce the remaining words in this manner.

Corrective feedback	**If...** students are having difficulty understanding, **then...** review the definitions in small groups.

Research and Inquiry

Step 1 Identify and Focus Topic

TEACH Discuss the Question of the Week: *Why do we have symbols that represent freedom?* Tell students that they will each research one national symbol and why it represents freedom. They will present their findings to the class on Day 5 as an informational article.

Think Aloud **MODEL** I need to choose one national symbol to research. To help me decide, I'll brainstorm a list of questions about symbols that represent freedom. *What are some symbols of freedom? Which symbols are national symbols that represent freedom? What is the history and meaning of each symbol?*

GUIDE PRACTICE After students have formulated open-ended inquiry questions about the research topic, explain that tomorrow they will collect information from multiple sources of oral and written information, including reference texts, such as textbooks, and on-site inspections. To generate a research plan, help students identify keywords that will guide their search for relevant information.

ON THEIR OWN Have students work individually, in pairs, or in small groups to write an inquiry question.

Day 1 SMALL GROUP TIME • Differentiate Vocabulary, p. SG•1

OL On-Level	SI Strategic Intervention	A Advanced
• **Practice Vocabulary** Amazing Words • **Read** *Reading Street Sleuth,* pp. 68–69	• **Reteach Vocabulary** Amazing Words • **Read** *Reading Street Sleuth,* pp. 68–69	• **Extend Vocabulary** Amazing Words • **Read** *Reading Street Sleuth,* pp. 68–69 • **Introduce** Inquiry Project

eSTREET INTERACTIVE
www.ReadingStreet.com

Teacher Resources
- Envision It! Pictured Vocabulary Cards
- Tested Vocabulary Cards

21st Century Skills

Internet Guy *Don Leu*

Weekly Inquiry Project

STEP 1	Identify and Focus Topic
STEP 2	Navigate/Search
STEP 3	Analyze Information
STEP 4	Synthesize
STEP 5	Communicate

Academic Vocabulary

textbook a source of informational text, usually written about a specific topic

Multilingual Vocabulary Students can apply knowledge of their home languages to acquire new English vocabulary by using the Multilingual Vocabulary Lists (*ELL Handbook,* pp. 433–444).

If... students need more scaffolding and practice with **Vocabulary,** **then...** use the activities on pp. DI•17–DI•18 in the Teacher Resources section on SuccessNet.

Common Core State Standards

Language 2. Demonstrate command of the conventions of standard English capitalization, punctuation, and spelling when writing. **Language 2.a.** Capitalize appropriate words in titles. **Language 2.f.** Use spelling patterns and generalizations (e.g., word families, position-based spellings, syllable patterns, ending rules, meaningful word parts) in writing words.

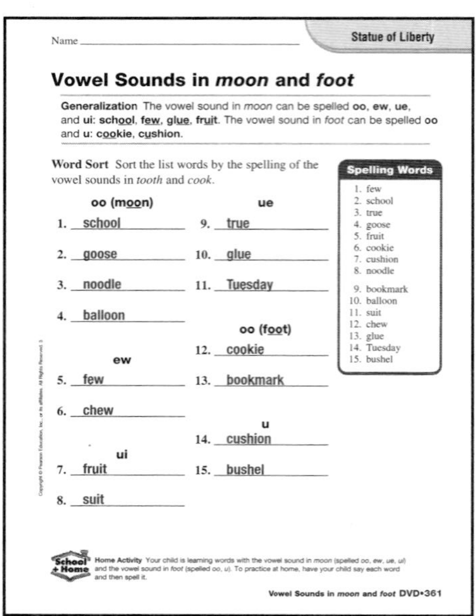

Name ______________ Statue of Liberty

Vowel Sounds in *moon* and *foot*

Generalization The vowel sound in *moon* can be spelled **oo, ew, ue,** and **ui: school, few, glue, fruit**. The vowel sound in *foot* can be spelled **oo** and **u: cookie, cushion.**

Word Sort Sort the list words by the spelling of the vowel sounds in *tooth* and *cook*.

oo (moon)
1. school
2. goose
3. noodle
4. balloon

ew
5. few
6. chew

ui
7. fruit
8. suit

ue
9. true
10. glue
11. Tuesday

oo (foot)
12. cookie
13. bookmark

u
14. cushion
15. bushel

Spelling Words
1. few
2. school
3. true
4. goose
5. fruit
6. cookie
7. cushion
8. noodle
9. bookmark
10. balloon
11. suit
12. chew
13. glue
14. Tuesday
15. bushel

School + Home **Home Activity** Your child is learning words with the vowel sound in *moon* (spelled *oo, ew, ue, ui*) and the vowel sound in *foot* (spelled *oo, u*). To practice at home, have your child say each word and then spell it.

Vowel Sounds in *moon* and *foot* DVD•361

Let's Practice It! TR DVD•361

Spelling Pretest

Vowel Sounds in *moon* and *foot*

INTRODUCE Some words have the same vowel sounds as in the words *moon* and *foot.*

PRETEST Say each word, read the sentence, and repeat the word.

1. few	I brought a **few** apples.
2. school	I forgot my backpack at **school.**
3. true	Is the answer **true** or false?
4. goose	The **goose** is on the pond.
5. fruit	I eat **fruit** as my snack.
6. cookie	Would you like a **cookie?**
7. cushion	The **cushion** is tied to the chair.
8. noodle	The **noodle** is long and skinny.
9. bookmark	Put the **bookmark** in the book.
10. balloon	I got a **balloon** at the party.
11. suit	Did Dad wear a **suit** to work?
12. chew	It is hard to **chew** taffy.
13. glue	Just a drop of **glue** is enough.
14. Tuesday	I was sick on **Tuesday.**
15. bushel	We need a **bushel** of apples.
Challenge words	
16. bamboo	Pandas like to eat **bamboo.**
17. mildew	The basement smelled of **mildew.**
18. soothe	She tried to **soothe** the crying baby.
19. barefoot	I like to go **barefoot** in the summer.
20. renewal	Spring is a time of **renewal.**

SELF-CORRECT Have students self-correct their pretests by rewriting misspelled words.

ON THEIR OWN Use *Let's Practice It!* p. 361 on the *Teacher Resources DVD-ROM.*

Conventions

Capital Letters

MAKE CONNECTIONS To focus attention on capital letters, write a sentence on the board with errors in capitalization, such as *I met susan at the library last wednesday where mr. green helped us find the book snowflake bentley.* Ask students what they notice about the sentence.

TEACH Display Grammar Transparency 26, and read aloud the explanation and examples in the box.

MODEL Model writing correctly the words that should have capital letters for items 1 and 2. Apply the rules for capital letters to show how you determined which words should be capitalized.

Capital Letters

Use **capital letters** for proper nouns and proper adjectives. Proper nouns and proper adjectives include names, names with initials, days of the week, months of the year, holidays, most words in book titles, and names of some famous periods in history. Titles for people and abbreviations of the titles should be capitalized when they are used with a person's name. Do not capitalize titles when they are used by themselves.

Incorrect	The fourth thursday in november is thanksgiving.
Correct	The fourth Thursday in November is Thanksgiving.
Incorrect	I read about a french sculptor named f. a. bartholdi.
Correct	I read about a French sculptor named F. A. Bartholdi.

Directions If a sentence has capitalization mistakes, write correctly the words that should have capital letters. If a sentence has no capitalization mistakes, write *C*.

1. Today mr. chang said Americans have many symbols of freedom.
   Mr. Chang
2. We eat special cakes at easter.
   Easter
3. We can display american flags from january to december.
   American; January; December
4. I read a book called *liberty's struggle,* which is about the revolutionary war.
   ***Liberty's Struggle;* Revolutionary War**
5. Bald eagles are also a symbol of freedom in the United States.
   C

Directions Write the sentences. Use capital letters correctly.

6. Last august my family visited Mount Rushmore.
   Last August my family visited Mount Rushmore.
7. In the summer, a ceremony is held there each night from monday through sunday.
   In the summer, a ceremony is held there each night from Monday through Sunday.

Unit 6 The Story of the Statue of Liberty Grammar **26**

Grammar Transparency 26, TR DVD

GUIDE PRACTICE Guide students to complete items 3–5. Record the correct responses on the transparency.

APPLY Have students read sentences 6 and 7 on the transparency and write them using capital letters correctly.

Handwriting

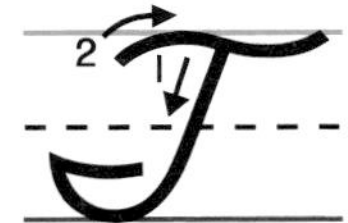

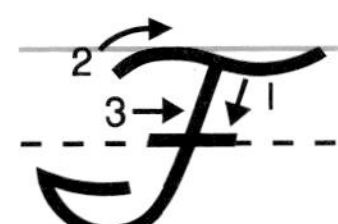

MODEL LETTER FORMATION AND SLANT Display capital cursive letters *T* and *F.* Follow the stroke instructions pictured to model letter formation. Explain that writing legibly means letters are the correct size, form, and slant. Point out that all letters should slant in the same direction. Model writing this sentence with proper letter slant: *Three students from Fairbanks won awards.*

GUIDE PRACTICE Have students write these sentences: *Fred and Tom went to school. Frieda lives in Toledo.* Circulate around the room, guiding students.

eSTREET INTERACTIVE
www.ReadingStreet.com

Teacher Resources
- Let's Practice It!
- Grammar Transparency
- Daily Fix-It Transparency

Daily Fix-It

1. The classes visits the Washington Monument on tuesday. *(visit; Tuesday)*
2. is the Statue of Liberty or the Washington Monument biggest? *(Is; bigger)*

Academic Vocabulary 

capital letters uppercase letters used at the beginning of proper nouns and proper adjectives

proper noun word that names a specific person, place, or thing; it is always capitalized

Identifying Vowel Sounds Have students write the words *moon* and *foot* on index cards. Have them practice saying each word correctly. Then read the following list of words aloud: *good, shoot, boot, stood, hook, blue, new, should, boo,* and *wood.* Have students hold up either *moon* or *foot,* indicating which vowel sound they hear.

Handwriting: Place Names To give students more practice writing capital cursive letters *T* and *F,* have them use an atlas to find names of countries, states, cities, or rivers that begin with *T* or *F.* Have them write these names in cursive.

Common Core State Standards

Writing 2.b. Develop the topic with facts, definitions, and details. **Writing 8.** Recall information from experiences or gather information from print and digital sources; take brief notes on sources and sort evidence into provided categories. **Also Language 2.a.**

Bridge to Common Core

TEXT TYPES AND PURPOSES

This week, students write notes about the most important ideas in a selection.

Informative/Explanatory Writing

Through reading and discussion, students will gain a deeper understanding of symbols of freedom. They will take notes on articles on this topic to help them retain the knowledge they gain.

Through the week, students will improve their range and content of writing through daily mini-lessons.

5-Day Plan

DAY 1	Read Like a Writer
DAY 2	Main Idea and Details
DAY 3	In Your Own Words
DAY 4	Revise: Adding
DAY 5	Proofread for Capitalization

Write Guy *by Jeff Anderson*

Trait-by-Trait: Organization

Organization is a trait of good writing, but let's not be so concerned with form that we forget about meaning. A student may develop a good way to communicate ideas that does not precisely follow the format we expect. There isn't only one way to reach the goal. And there isn't just one way to organize your writing. Reward creativity and help students see what other writers do in mentor texts.

Writing Zoom in on ©

Notes

Mini-Lesson Read Like a Writer

Introduce This week you will learn to take notes. Taking notes helps you keep track of and remember the most important information from an article or story. When you take notes, you write in your own words the information that you want to remember.

Prompt Think about the most important ideas in the selection. Now take notes on one part of the selection.

Trait Focus/Ideas

Mode Expository/Informative/Explanatory

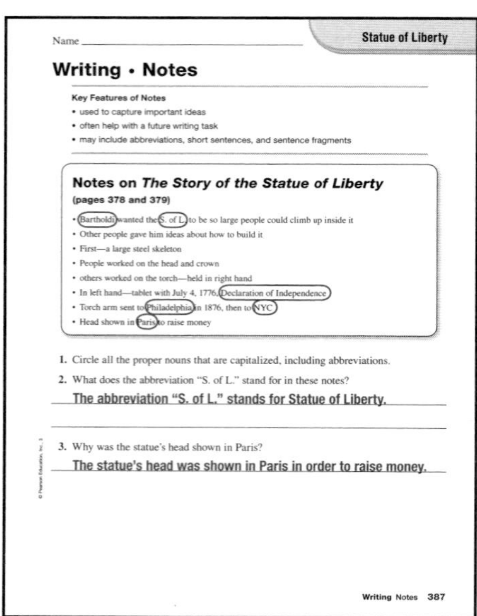

Name ____________ Statue of Liberty

Writing • Notes

Key Features of Notes
- used to capture important ideas
- often help with a future writing task
- may include abbreviations, short sentences, and sentence fragments

Notes on *The Story of the Statue of Liberty*
(pages 378 and 379)
- Bartholdi wanted the S. of L. to be so large people could climb up inside it
- Other people gave him ideas about how to build it
- First—a large steel skeleton
- People worked on the head and crown
- others worked on the torch—held in right hand
- In left hand—tablet with July 4, 1776, Declaration of Independence
- Torch arm sent to Philadelphia in 1876, then to NYC
- Head shown in Paris to raise money

1. Circle all the proper nouns that are capitalized, including abbreviations.
2. What does the abbreviation "S. of L." stand for in these notes?
   The abbreviation "S. of L." stands for Statue of Liberty.
3. Why was the statue's head shown in Paris?
   The statue's head was shown in Paris in order to raise money.

Writing Notes 387

Reader's and Writer's Notebook, p. 387

Examine Model Text Let's read an example of notes taken on the selection *The Story of the Statue of Liberty*. Have students read p. 387 of their *Reader's and Writer's Notebook*.

Key Features Notes focus on the most important facts and ideas in a selection. Have student volunteers read aloud each bulleted item in the model and tell why it is important.

Notes often help you with a future writing task. Ask students to list the kinds of writing tasks in which notes would be helpful (for example, research papers or tests).

Notes do not have to follow all the rules of writing. They may include abbreviations, short sentences, and sentence fragments. They may include key words. But it is still important that you spell and capitalize correctly. Remember, you may want to use your notes for a future writing task. Have students identify the proper nouns that must be spelled and capitalized correctly.

Review Key Features

Review the key features of notes with students. You may want to post the key features in the classroom or have students write them on note cards. As students take notes, they can refer to these key features.

Key Features of Notes

- used to capture the most important facts and ideas
- often help with a future writing task
- may include abbreviations, short sentences, and sentence fragments
- includes correct spelling and capitalization of proper nouns

Routine Quick Write for Fluency

Team Talk

1. **Talk** Have pairs take a few minutes to discuss the features of notes.
2. **Write** Each person writes one reason good notes are important.
3. **Share** Partners share their reasons with each other.

Routines Flip Chart

Read Like a Writer Remind students that notes help them keep track of important information. Select and reread aloud a paragraph from *The Story of the Statue of Liberty,* and guide students' note-taking by emphasizing important facts and ideas.

Wrap Up Your Day!

- **Content Knowledge** Reread "Street Rhymes!" on p. 366j to students. Ask them what they learned this week about symbols that represent freedom.
- **Oral Vocabulary** Have students use the Amazing Words they learned in context sentences.
- **Homework** Send home this week's Family Times newsletter on *Let's Practice It!* pp. 362–363 on the *Teacher Resources DVD-ROM*.

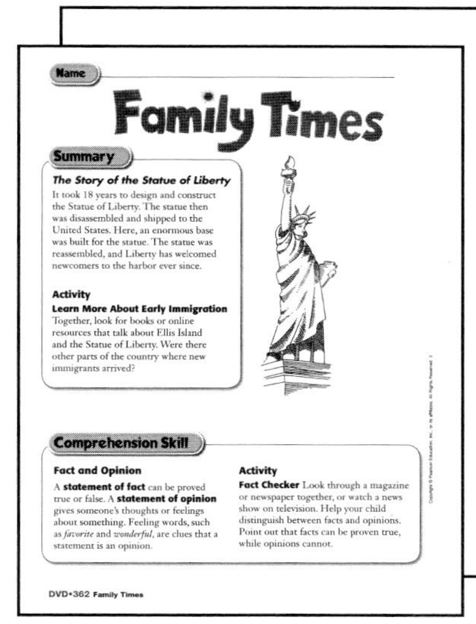

Let's Practice It!
TR DVD•362–363

Tell students that tomorrow they will read about a man who designed a famous symbol of freedom.

DAY 2 at a Glance

Content Knowledge
Oral Vocabulary

Phonics/Word Analysis
Vowel Sounds /ü/ and /u̇/

Literary Terms
Word Choice

Vocabulary Skill
Prefix *un-*

Fluency
Rate

Research and Inquiry
Navigate/Search

Conventions
Capital Letters

Spelling
Vowel Sounds in *moon* and *foot*

Writing
Notes

Materials

- Student Edition
- Reader's and Writer's Notebook

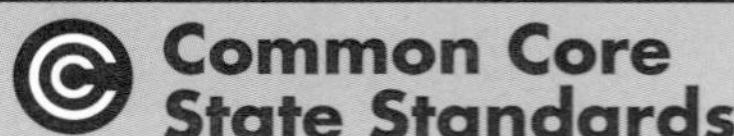

Common Core State Standards

Speaking/Listening 1. Engage effectively in a range of collaborative discussions (one-on-one, in groups, and teacher-led) with diverse partners on grade 3 topics and texts, building on others' ideas and expressing their own clearly. **Language 4.** Determine or clarify the meaning of unknown and multiple-meaning words and phrases based on grade 3 reading and content, choosing flexibly from a range of strategies. **Language 6.** Acquire and use accurately grade-appropriate conversational, general academic, and domain-specific words and phrases, including those that signal spatial and temporal relationships (e.g., *After dinner that night we went looking for them*). **Also Speaking/Listening 1.c.**

Content Knowledge

Symbols of Freedom

EXPAND THE CONCEPT Remind students of the weekly concept question—*Why do we have symbols that represent freedom?* Tell students that today they will begin reading *The Story of the Statue of Liberty.* As they read, encourage students to think about symbols of freedom.

Build Oral Language

TALK ABOUT SENTENCES AND WORDS Reread these sentences from the Read Aloud, "Let Freedom Ring."

At first the crack was small and the bell still rung clearly. But the crack got bigger and bigger and the sound got worse and worse. Soon the bell fell silent. However, it was no less impressive.

- What does *impressive* mean? (making an impression on, having an effect on)
- Why is it amazing that the Liberty Bell is so *impressive?* (It has an impact on people even though it can't make a sound.)
- How does the author's description help you visualize what happened to the Liberty Bell? (I can see the small crack getting bigger. I can hear the sound of the bell getting quieter. I can imagine it now, silent but still interesting because of its history.)

Team Talk Have students turn to a partner and discuss the following question. Then ask them to share their responses.

- Rephrase the text in short, simple sentences but without changing the basic meaning.

Build Oral Vocabulary

Amazing Words Robust Vocabulary Routine

1. **Introduce** Write the Amazing Word *dedication* on the board. Have students say it aloud with you. Relate *dedication* to the photographs on pp. 366–367 and "Let Freedom Ring." Why might the Liberty Bell or the other objects in the photographs have a *dedication* ceremony? Have students determine the definition of the word. (At a *dedication* ceremony, something or someone is named or honored.)
2. **Demonstrate** Have students answer questions to demonstrate understanding. Why might there be a *dedication* for a historical building? Why might there be a *dedication* for a new road or bridge? Why might a person give a speech at a *dedication* ceremony?
3. **Apply** Have students apply their understanding. Do you think a *dedication* ceremony was held when our school first opened? (Yes, because people would want to dedicate the school to education.)
4. **Display the Word** Run your hand under the word as you emphasize the syllables *ded-i-ca-tion.* Have students say the word.

See p. OV•1 to teach *competition.*

Routines Flip Chart

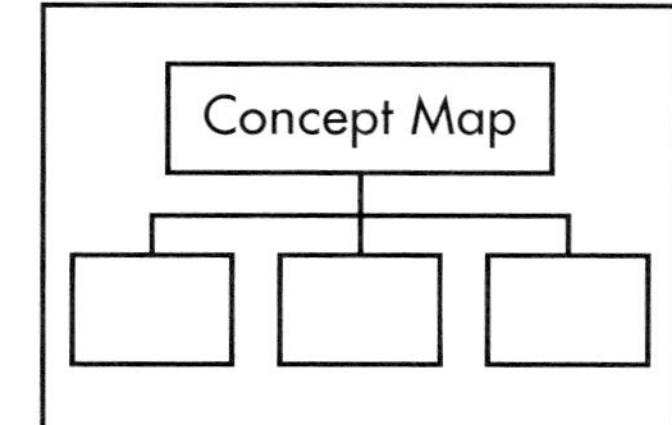

ADD TO THE CONCEPT MAP Use the photos on pp. 366–367 and the Read Aloud "Let Freedom Ring" to discuss why we have symbols that represent freedom and to talk about the Amazing Words *impressive, tribute, enlighten,* and *contribution*. Add these and other concept-related words to the concept map to develop students' knowledge of the topic. Discuss the photos and vocabulary to generate questions about the topic. Encourage students to build on others' ideas when they answer. Add words from the discussion to the concept map.

- What kinds of *contributions* might a symbol of freedom recognize?
- What is one *tribute* citizens can participate in to celebrate their freedom?
- How can the idea of freedom *enlighten* people? How does that help explain why there are many symbols that represent freedom?
- What might be *impressive* about a symbol of freedom?

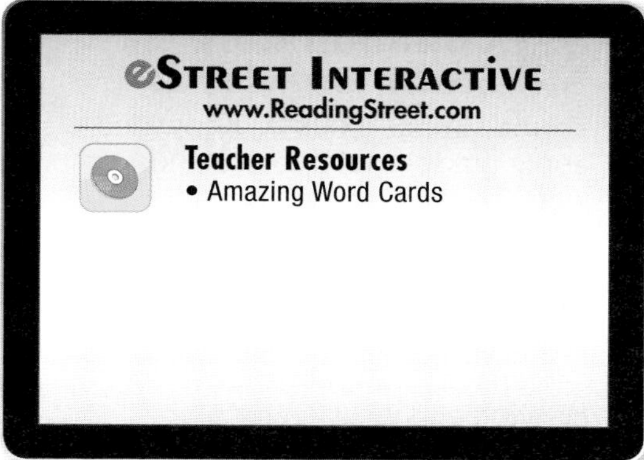

Amazing Words

impressive	competition
tribute	recognizable
enlighten	disgrace
contribution	staggering
dedication	fund

Reinforce Vocabulary Use the Day 2 instruction on ELL Poster 26 to teach lesson vocabulary and the lesson concept.

Cognates Point out that the Amazing Words *dedication* and *competition* have Spanish cognates, *dedicación* and *competición.*

Common Core State Standards

Foundational Skills 3. Know and apply grade-level phonics and word analysis skills in decoding words. **Language 1.a.** Explain the function of nouns, pronouns, verbs, adjectives, and adverbs in general and their functions in particular sentences. **Language 2.e.** Use conventional spelling for high-frequency and other studied words and for adding suffixes to base words (e.g., *sitting, smiled, cries, happiness*). **Language 3.a.** Choose words and phrases for effect.

Phonics

Vowel Sounds /ü/ and /u̇/

REVIEW Review the vowel sounds /ü/ and /u̇/ using *Sound-Spelling Cards* 68, 89, 90, 101, 102, and 103.

READ WORDS IN ISOLATION Display these words. Have the class blend the words. Then point to the words in random order and ask students to read them quickly.

clues **mood** **igloo** **pudding** **juice** **due** **crook** **wood**

Corrective feedback | Model blending decodable words and then ask students to blend them with you.

READ WORDS IN CONTEXT Display these sentences. Have the class read the sentences.

Team Talk Have pairs take turns reading the sentences naturally.

I read a **good book** today.

A shingle on the **roof** came **loose.**

I tested the water by **putting** my **foot** in the **pool.**

Don't Wait Until Friday

MONITOR PROGRESS Check Word Reading

Vowel Sounds /ü/ **and** /u̇/

FORMATIVE ASSESSMENT Write the following words and have the class read them. Notice which words students miss during the group reading. Call on individuals to read some of the words.

cook	**put**	**loon**	**glue**	**suit**	
tulip	**relax**	**rapid**	**music**	**pupil**	← Row 2 reviews words with V/CV and VC/V.
understood	**bamboo**	**unhook**	**trooper**	**scooter**	← Row 3 contrasts words with /ü/ and /u̇/.

Spiral Review

If... students cannot read words with vowel sounds /ü/ and /u̇/ at this point,
then... use the Day 1 Phonics lesson on p. 368a to reteach vowel sounds /ü/ and /u̇/. Use words from the *Decodable Practice Passages* (or *Reader*). Continue to monitor students' progress during the week. See the Skills Trace on p. 368a.

Literary Terms

Word Choice

TEACH Tell students that word choice refers to the specific words and phrases that authors choose to use in their writing. A writer's choice of words should be appropriate to the purpose of the text and for the audience. Writers can make their writing more interesting by choosing strong verbs, using memorable words and phrases, and including adjectives and adverbs that make ideas more specific.

Think Aloud **MODEL** Let's look at "Emma and Liberty" on p. 373. The first sentence in the second paragraph uses good word choice to tell us about what is happening in the story. Specific locations and adjectives tell us where Emma is. The phrase "breathless view" is a memorable phrase—only two words tell us what Emma is doing and what she is feeling at the same time.

GUIDE PRACTICE Find an example of good word choice in "Coming to America."

ON THEIR OWN Have students look for examples of good word choice in other selections of their Student Edition.

Common Core State Standards

Language 4.b. Determine the meaning of the new word formed when a known affix is added to a known word (e.g., *agreeable/disagreeable, comfortable/uncomfortable, care/careless, heat/preheat*). **Also Foundational Skills 4.b.**

Selection Vocabulary

crown a metal head covering worn by someone with power

liberty freedom

models small copies of something

symbol an object, diagram, animal, or icon that stands for or represents something else

tablet a small, flat surface with something written on it

torch a long stick with material at one end that burns

unforgettable so good that you cannot forget it

unveiled removed a veil from; revealed

Bridge to Common Core

VOCABULARY ACQUISITION AND USE

Examining word structure helps students determine the meanings of unknown words and enables them to acquire a broad range of academic and domain-specific words. By considering the meanings of prefixes, students demonstrate the ability to use their knowledge of word parts to determine word meanings on their own.

Vocabulary Support

Refer students to *Words!* on p. W•5 in the Student Edition for additional practice.

Vocabulary Skill

Prefix *un-*

READ Have students read "Emma and Liberty" on p. 373. Use the vocabulary skill and strategy as tools to build comprehension.

TEACH WORD STUCTURE Students can use what they know about prefixes to determine the meanings of unfamiliar words. When the prefix *un-* is added to the beginning of an adverb or adjective, it usually means "not." When it is added to the beginning of a verb, it means the opposite of the verb's meaning.

Think Aloud

MODEL Write on the board: *They pulled the cloth off, and as the statue was unveiled, we clapped.* I see the prefix *un-* in the word *unveiled.* I know that a prefix is added to the beginning of a root word and changes the meaning of the root word. When I cover *un-,* I see the root word is *veiled,* which means "covered." When *un-* is added to a verb, such as *veiled,* the new word usually means the opposite of the verb. So the word *unveiled* means "removed the cover."

GUIDE PRACTICE Write this sentence on the board: *The spectacular fireworks that lit up the sky were an unforgettable sight.* Have students determine the meaning of *unforgettable* using what they know about the prefix *un-* and root words. For additional support, use *Envision It! Pictured Vocabulary Cards* or *Tested Vocabulary Cards.*

ON THEIR OWN Have students reread "Emma and Liberty" on p. 373. Have them look at the words *remarkable, seen,* and *like* and consider what the words' meanings would be if the prefix *un-* were added to them. For additional practice, use *Reader's and Writer's Notebook,* p. 388.

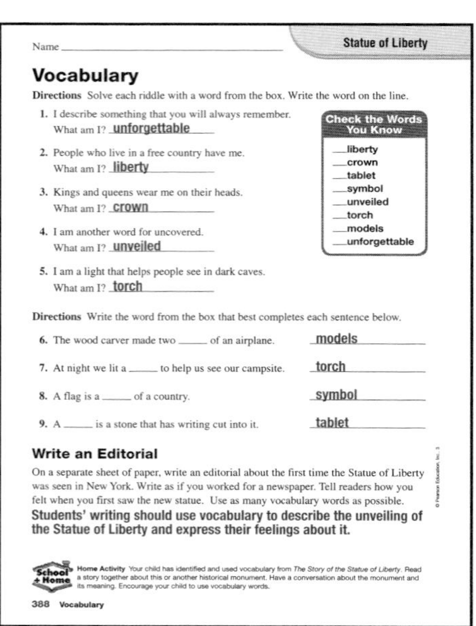
Name ____________ Statue of Liberty

Vocabulary

Directions Solve each riddle with a word from the box. Write the word on the line.

Check the Words You Know
__liberty
__crown
__tablet
__symbol
__unveiled
__torch
__models
__unforgettable

1. I describe something that you will always remember. What am I? unforgettable
2. People who live in a free country have me. What am I? liberty
3. Kings and queens wear me on their heads. What am I? crown
4. I am another word for uncovered. What am I? unveiled
5. I am a light that helps people see in dark caves. What am I? torch

Directions Write the word from the box that best completes each sentence below.

6. The wood carver made two ______ of an airplane. models
7. At night we lit a ______ to help us see our campsite. torch
8. A flag is a ______ of a country. symbol
9. A ______ is a stone that has writing cut into it. tablet

Write an Editorial

On a separate sheet of paper, write an editorial about the first time the Statue of Liberty was seen in New York. Write as if you worked for a newspaper. Tell readers how you felt when you first saw the new statue. Use as many vocabulary words as possible.
Students' writing should use vocabulary to describe the unveiling of the Statue of Liberty and express their feelings about it.

School + Home **Home Activity** Your child has identified and used vocabulary from *The Story of the Statue of Liberty*. Read a story together about this or another historical monument. Have a conversation about the monument and its meaning. Encourage your child to use vocabulary words.

388 Vocabulary

Reader's and Writer's Notebook, p. 388

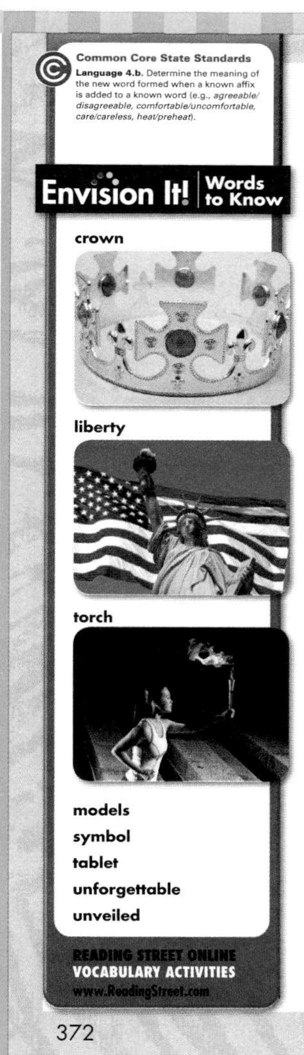

Vocabulary Strategy for

Prefix *un-*

Word Structure Prefixes can give you clues to the meanings of unfamiliar words. The prefix *un-* at the beginning of a word means "not ____." For example, *unpleasant* means "not pleasant." When *un-* is added to a verb, it usually means the reverse of the verb. For instance, *uncover* means "to remove a cover."

1. When you see an unfamiliar word with a prefix, cover up the prefix.
2. What does the base word mean without the prefix?
3. Add "not" in front of the word. Does this meaning make sense in the sentence?

Read "Emma and Liberty" on page 373. Look for words that have prefixes. Use your knowledge of prefixes to find the meanings of these words.

Words to Write Reread "Emma and Liberty." What symbols of freedom have you seen or heard about? Write about symbols of freedom. Use as many words from the Words to Know list as you can.

372

Emma and Liberty

Emma is visiting New York City. What she wants to see more than anything else is the remarkable Statue of Liberty. Emma knows everything about Liberty. She knows why the statue was made, who made it, and when it was unveiled. She knows how tall it is from its base to its crown, what its torch is made of, and what is written on the tablet. Emma has collected pictures of the statue and reproduced models of it. However, she has never seen the real Liberty.

From Battery Park in Lower Manhattan, Emma has a breathless view of the Statue of Liberty in the distance. She waits in line for the boat that will safely take her to the island. As the boat gets nearer, Emma imagines what it was like for the immigrants who sailed past Liberty as they arrived in America.

At last Emma is standing at Liberty's feet. She tilts her head back to look up at this symbol of freedom. It is an unforgettable moment.

Your Turn!

Need a Review? For additional help with prefixes, see *Words!*

Ready to Try It? Read *The Story of the Statue of Liberty* on pp. 374–385.

373

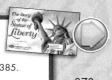

Student Edition, pp. 372–373

Reread for Fluency

RATE Read paragraph 1 of "Emma and Liberty" aloud at an appropriate rate. Tell students that you are reading the passage at a comfortable, steady pace. You read the passage just the way you speak.

Routine Choral Reading

1. **Read** For "Emma and Liberty," use paragraph 2 on p. 373.
2. **Model** Have students listen as you read the paragraph with appropriate rate and expression.
3. **Guide Practice** Have students read along with you.
4. **On Their Own** For optimal fluency, students should reread three or four times at an appropriate rate.

Routines Flip Chart

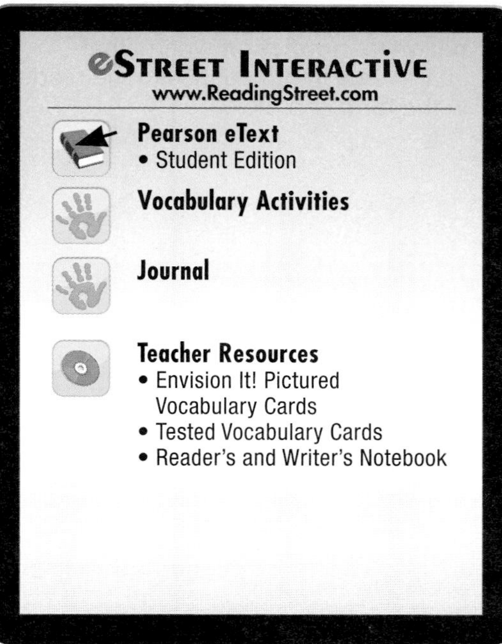

Text-Based Comprehension

Introduce Main Selection

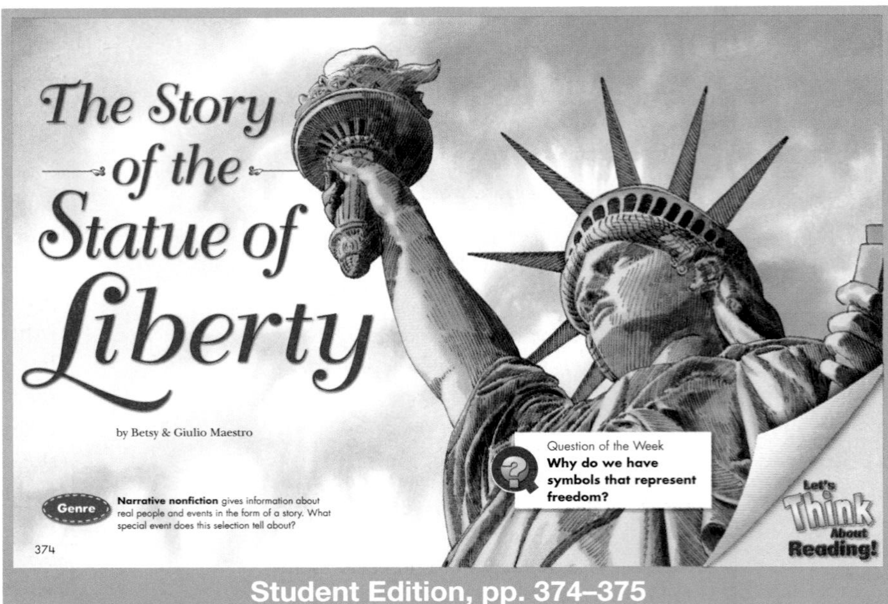

Student Edition, pp. 374–375

GENRE Tell students that **narrative nonfiction** is writing that shares true information with the reader in the form of a story. Narrative nonfiction tells about real people, places, and events. It often follows chronological order—the order in which events occurred. It sometimes has a beginning, middle, and end.

PREVIEW AND PREDICT Have students preview the title and illustrations in *The Story of the Statue of Liberty.* Be sure they notice the poem on the last page. Have students predict what they will find out as they read.

PURPOSE By analyzing *The Story of the Statue of Liberty,* a narrative nonfiction text, students will gain knowledge of symbols of freedom.

Common Core State Standards

Informational Text 1. Ask and answer questions to demonstrate understanding of a text, referring explicitly to the text as the basis for the answers. **Informational Text 10.** By the end of the year, read and comprehend informational texts, including history/social studies, science, and technical texts, at the high end of the grades 2–3 text complexity band independently and proficiently.

CRAFT AND STRUCTURE

Students analyze the selection's title and illustrations and think about how the components relate to each other. As they preview the selection and prepare to read, they come to see how purpose shapes the content and style of the text.

Academic Vocabulary

narrative nonfiction writing that shares true information with the reader in the form of a story

Strategy Response Log

Have students use p. 32 in the *Reader's and Writer's Notebook* to review and use the strategy of questioning.

Access Main Selection

READER AND TASK SUGGESTIONS	
Preparing to Read the Text	**Leveled Tasks**
• Review the strategy for using the prefix *un-* to determine the meanings of unknown words. • Discuss how authors sometimes deliver facts and details in the form of a story. • Remind students that they may need to read nonfiction more slowly to better understand the text.	• **Language Conventionality and Clarity** If students have difficulty following the sequence of the selection, have them identify signal words such as *first, then,* and *afterward*. • **Levels of Meaning • Analysis** Students may have trouble understanding the symbolism of parts of the Statue of Liberty. As they read the selection, have them note the different parts of the statue and why Bartholdi included each part.

See Text Complexity Measures for *The Story of the Statue of Liberty* on the tab at the beginning of this week.

READ Tell students that today they will read *The Story of the Statue of Liberty* for the first time. Use the Read for Understanding routine.

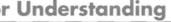

Routine Read for Understanding 

Deepen understanding by reading the selection multiple times.

1. **First Read**—If students need support, then use the **Access Text** notes to help them clarify understanding.
2. **Second Read**—Use the **Close Reading** notes to help students draw knowledge from the text.

Day 2 SMALL GROUP TIME • Differentiate Comprehension, p. SG•1

OL On-Level
- **Practice** Selection Vocabulary
- **Read** *The Story of the Statue of Liberty*

SI Strategic Intervention
- **Reteach** Selection Vocabulary
- **Read** *The Story of the Statue of Liberty*

A Advanced
- **Extend** Selection Vocabulary
- **Read** *The Story of the Statue of Liberty*
- **Investigate** Inquiry Project

eSTREET INTERACTIVE
www.ReadingStreet.com

Pearson eText
• Student Edition

AudioText CD

Teacher Resources
• Reader's and Writer's Notebook

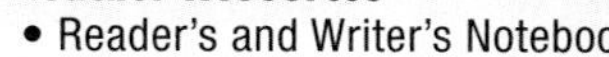
Background Building Audio CD

Access for All

 **Advanced**

Have students create a bulletin board for posting symbols and descriptions of what those symbols represent.

Build Background To build background, review the selection summary in English (*ELL Handbook,* p. 181). Use the Retelling Cards to provide visual support for the summary.

If... students need more scaffolding and practice with the **Comprehension Skill,**
then... use the activities on p. DI•21 in the Teacher Resources section on SuccessNet.

1ST READ

Access Text If students need help, then...

FACT AND OPINION Have students determine whether the following sentences are statements of fact or statements of opinion: *The Statue of Liberty stands on an island in New York Harbor.* (fact) *She is a beautiful sight to all who pass her by.* (opinion)

Think Aloud **MODEL** I could use a reference source to check if the first sentence is a fact. What word in the second sentence tells me that it might be a statement of opinion? *(beautiful)* A statement of opinion is someone's judgment, belief, or way of thinking. It cannot be proved true or false.

Let's Think About...

Before you read, ask questions. Look at the pictures and scan the highlighted words. Then focus on what you want to find out.

Questioning

1

The Statue of Liberty stands on an island in New York Harbor. She is a beautiful sight to all who pass by her. Each year, millions of visitors ride the ferry out to the island. They climb to the top of the statue and enjoy the lovely view.

A young French sculptor named Frédéric Auguste Bartholdi visited America in 1871. When he saw Bedloe's Island in New York Harbor, he knew it was just the right place for a statue he wanted to build.

Bartholdi had created many other statues and monuments, but this one was to be very special. It was to be a present from the people of France to the people of America, as a remembrance of the old friendship between the two countries.

Let's Think About...

As you read, keep asking yourself, "What does this mean?" and "Is this important? Why?"

Questioning

2

376

Student Edition, p. 376

2ND READ

Close Reading

ANALYSIS • TEXT EVIDENCE How was creating the Statue of Liberty similar to other projects that Frédéric Auguste Bartholdi had done? How was it different? Use evidence from the text in your response. (Frédéric Auguste Bartholdi had created many other statues and monuments. The Statue of Liberty project was different because it was a special gift from the people of France to the people of America as a remembrance of their friendship.)

ANALYSIS Help students generate text-based questions by providing the following question stem: Why did the sculptor Fréderíc Bartholdi ______?

ON THEIR OWN Have students reread pp. 376–377 to find more statements of fact about the Statue of Liberty and its creator. Have them discuss opinions people might have about the statue. For additional practice, use *Let's Practice It!* p. 364 on the *Teacher Resources DVD-ROM.*

When Bartholdi got back to Paris, he made sketches and some small models. The statue would be a woman whom he would call Liberty. She would be a symbol of the freedom in the New World. She would hold a lamp in her raised hand to welcome people who came to America. She would be *Liberty Enlightening the World.*

Let's Think About...

Ask yourself, "Who, what, where, why, how?" Questioning

3

377

Student Edition, p. 377

Let's Think About...

1. *What is the view like from the top? What other statues did Bartholdi create?*
2. *What is Bedloe's Island? Why is the friendship between America and France important?*
3. *Why is the statue modeled after a woman? Who is Bartholdi? What did he create? How did he get picked to make the statue?*

Common Core State Standards

Informational Text 1. Ask and answer questions to demonstrate understanding of a text, referring explicitly to the text as the basis for the answers. **Also Informational Text 8.**

Connect to Social Studies

Map Skills Have students locate New York City and Paris, France, on a world map. Ask them to estimate the distance between them. Explain that New York City is a city in the state of New York in the United States of America on the continent of North America. Paris is in the country of France on the continent of Europe. Use a ruler and map scale to figure out the approximate distance between the cities. (3,635 miles)

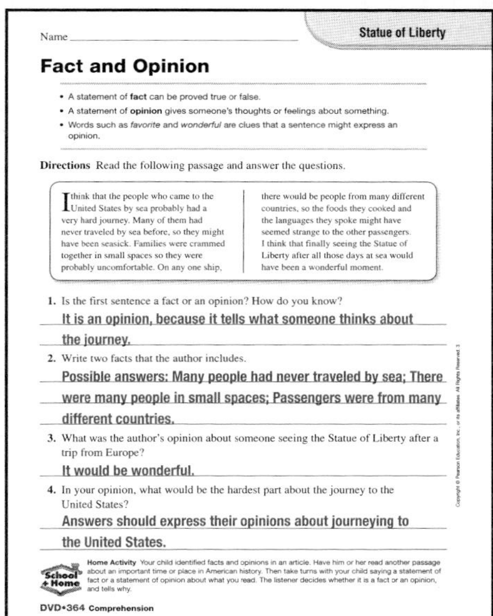

Name ______ Statue of Liberty

Fact and Opinion

- A statement of **fact** can be proved true or false.
- A statement of **opinion** gives someone's thoughts or feelings about something.
- Words such as *favorite* and *wonderful* are clues that a sentence might express an opinion.

Directions Read the following passage and answer the questions.

I think that the people who came to the United States by sea probably had a very hard journey. Many of them had never traveled by sea before, so they might have been seasick. Families were crammed together in small spaces so they were probably uncomfortable. On any one ship, there would be people from many different countries, so the foods they cooked and the languages they spoke might have seemed strange to the other passengers. I think that finally seeing the Statue of Liberty after all those days at sea would have been a wonderful moment.

1. Is the first sentence a fact or an opinion? How do you know?
   It is an opinion, because it tells what someone thinks about the journey.
2. Write two facts that the author includes.
   Possible answers: Many people had never traveled by sea; There were many people in small spaces; Passengers were from many different countries.
3. What was the author's opinion about someone seeing the Statue of Liberty after a trip from Europe?
   It would be wonderful.
4. In your opinion, what would be the hardest part about the journey to the United States?
   Answers should express their opinions about journeying to the United States.

School + Home **Home Activity** Your child identified facts and opinions in an article. Have him or her read another passage about an important time or place in American history. Then take turns with your child saying a statement of fact or a statement of opinion about what you read. The listener decides whether it is a fact or an opinion, and tells why.

DVD•364 Comprehension

Let's Practice It! TR•DVD•364

Access Content Discuss with students how the Statue of Liberty was designed. Ask students what they know about how a *sketch* or a *model* might be used. Provide an example of each design technique. Then have students sketch or make a clay model of a statue or building that they would like to build.

1ST READ

Access Text
If students need help, then...

Review **AUTHOR'S PURPOSE**
Remind students that the author's purpose is the reason or reasons that an author has for writing. Then ask students what the authors' purpose is on pp. 378–379.

Think Aloud **MODEL** The selection contains many facts and details, so I can tell that the authors' purpose is to inform, to describe the statue, and to tell how it was built. The authors are also writing to persuade readers that the Statue of Liberty is an impressive and important monument to freedom.

ON THEIR OWN Have students reread pp. 378–379. Ask them what details persuade the reader to value the Statue of Liberty as an important monument to freedom. For additional practice, use *Let's Practice It!* p. 365 on the *Teacher Resources DVD-ROM.*

The statue would be very large and very strong. Bartholdi wanted people to be able to climb up inside the statue and look out over the harbor from the crown and torch.

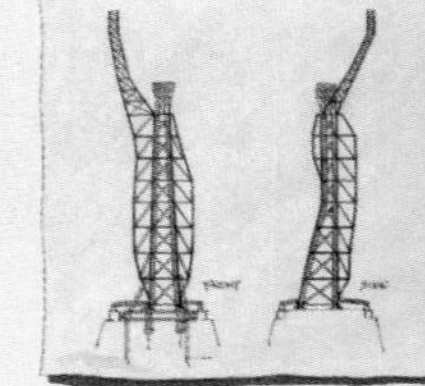

Many well-known artists, engineers, and craftsmen gave him ideas about how to build the statue. First, a huge skeleton was constructed from strong steel.

Many people worked together in a large workshop. Some worked on Liberty's head and crown. Others worked on her right hand, which would hold the torch.

In her left hand she would hold a tablet with the date July 4, 1776, written on it. This is when the Declaration of Independence was signed.

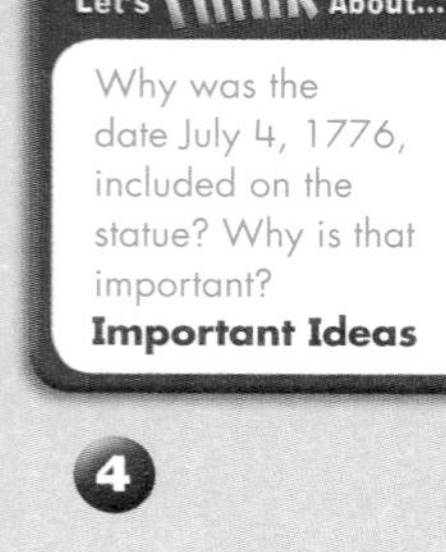

Let's Think About...

Why was the date July 4, 1776, included on the statue? Why is that important?
Important Ideas

4

378

Student Edition, p. 378

2ND READ

Close Reading

INFERENCE • TEXT EVIDENCE
Reread p. 378. Why do you think well-known artists, engineers, and craftsmen helped Bartholdi build the statue? Use evidence from the text to support your answer. (The Statue of Liberty was a well-known project at the time, so talented builders probably wanted to take part. It was also a symbol of freedom, an idea that the builders probably believed in.)

DEVELOP LANGUAGE Have students reread the second paragraph on p. 378. What does *constructed* mean? Name examples of other things *constructed* from steel.

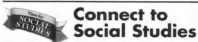

The arm holding the torch was sent to Philadelphia for America's 100th birthday celebration in 1876. Afterward, it stood in Madison Square in New York City for a number of years.

Liberty's head was shown at the World's Fair in Paris during this time. Visitors were able to climb inside and look around. In this way, money was raised to pay for the statue.

Let's **Think** About...

Why might the makers of the Statue of Liberty exhibit it in different parts and places for a few years?
Inferring

5

379

Student Edition, p. 379

Common Core State Standards

Informational Text 1. Ask and answer questions to demonstrate understanding of a text, referring explicitly to the text as the basis for the answers.

Connect to Social Studies

Declaration of Independence
Read a copy of the Declaration of Independence and discuss its meaning as a class.

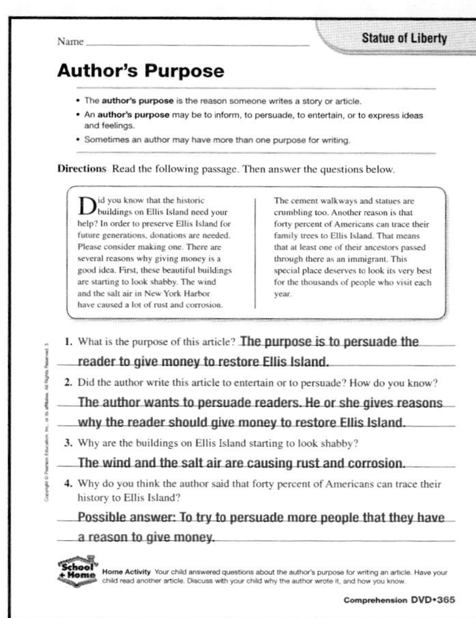

Name ______________ Statue of Liberty

Author's Purpose

- The **author's purpose** is the reason someone writes a story or article.
- An **author's purpose** may be to inform, to persuade, to entertain, or to express ideas and feelings.
- Sometimes an author may have more than one purpose for writing.

Directions Read the following passage. Then answer the questions below.

Did you know that the historic buildings on Ellis Island need your help? In order to preserve Ellis Island for future generations, donations are needed. Please consider making one. There are several reasons why giving money is a good idea. First, these beautiful buildings are starting to look shabby. The wind and the salt air in New York Harbor have caused a lot of rust and corrosion. The cement walkways and statues are crumbling too. Another reason is that forty percent of Americans can trace their family trees to Ellis Island. That means that at least one of their ancestors passed through there as an immigrant. This special place deserves to look its very best for the thousands of people who visit each year.

1. What is the purpose of this article? **The purpose is to persuade the reader to give money to restore Ellis Island.**
2. Did the author write this article to entertain or to persuade? How do you know? **The author wants to persuade readers. He or she gives reasons why the reader should give money to restore Ellis Island.**
3. Why are the buildings on Ellis Island starting to look shabby? **The wind and the salt air are causing rust and corrosion.**
4. Why do you think the author said that forty percent of Americans can trace their history to Ellis Island? **Possible answer: To try to persuade more people that they have a reason to give money.**

School + Home **Home Activity** Your child answered questions about the author's purpose for writing an article. Have your child read another article. Discuss with your child why the author wrote it, and how you know.

Comprehension DVD•365

Let's Practice It! p. 365

Let's Think About...

4 July 4, 1776 is the date of the signing of the Declaration of Independence. It is important because it stands for the beginning of liberty in America.

5 Exhibiting parts of the Statue of Liberty was a way for many people to see and learn about it. It also encouraged people to donate to help pay the expense.

Author's Purpose Remind students that the authors used the adjectives *large* and *strong* to persuade readers that the Statue of Liberty is an important monument. Have pairs of students discuss words they might use to persuade a friend that something is important.

1ST READ

Access Text

If students need help, then…

QUESTIONING Explain that good readers check their understanding by asking questions. Ask students what questions they have about how the Statue of Liberty was completed.

Think Aloud **MODEL** As I read, I think about questions I have about the text. For example, I'm not sure how the copper on the outside of the statue was held in place. I can go back and reread with that question in mind. Asking questions helps me monitor and clarify my understanding.

ON THEIR OWN Have students think of questions they have about the information on pp. 380–381. Then have them reread to answer the questions.

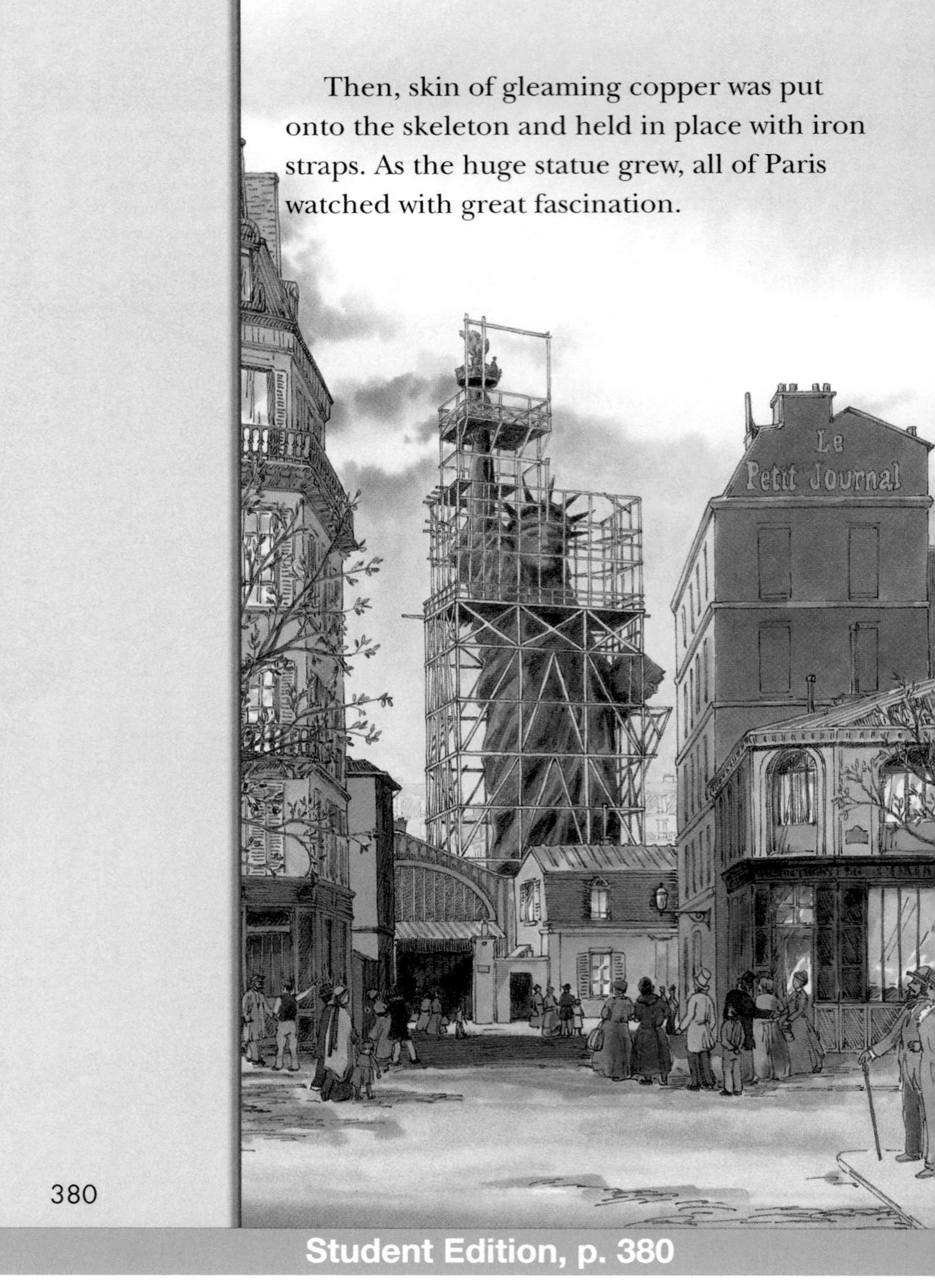

Then, skin of gleaming copper was put onto the skeleton and held in place with iron straps. As the huge statue grew, all of Paris watched with great fascination.
Le Petit Journal
380

Student Edition, p. 380

2ND READ

Close Reading

INFERENCE • TEXT EVIDENCE

Reread the last paragraph on page 381. After the statue was finished, workers took it apart. Why did they put the whole statue together if they were going to take it apart? (They needed to make sure all the parts fit together; they wanted the people in France to have a chance to see it before they shipped it to the United States.)

CHECK PREDICTIONS Have students look back at the predictions they made earlier and discuss whether they were accurate. Then have students preview the rest of the selection and either adjust their predictions accordingly or make new predictions.

Finally, in 1884, Liberty was completed. There was a big celebration in Paris. Many famous people came to see her. Only a few had the energy to climb all the way to the crown—168 steps!

Then began the hard work of taking Liberty apart for the long voyage across the Atlantic Ocean. Each piece was marked and packed into a crate. There were 214 crates in all. They were carried by train and then put on a ship to America.

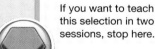

Let's Think About...

Why did they take the statue apart after it was finally finished?
Inferring

6

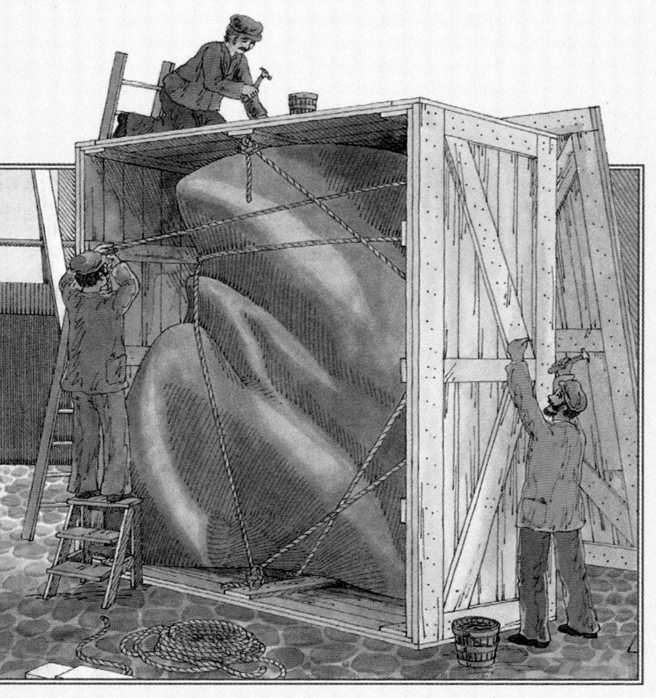

381

Student Edition, p. 381

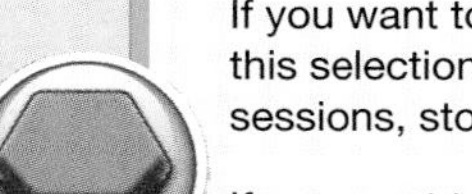

If you want to teach this selection in two sessions, stop here.

If you want to continue reading this selection, turn to p. 382–383.

Let's Think About...

6 It was much too big to ship in one piece so they had to take it apart and pack the pieces into crates.

Common Core State Standards

Informational Text 1. Ask and answer questions to demonstrate understanding of a text, referring explicitly to the text as the basis for the answers. **Also Informational Text 10.**

Access for All

SI Strategic Intervention

Review with students that asking *relevant* questions means asking questions about the most important information in the text.

A Advanced

Have students write three questions (one literal, one interpretive, and one evaluative) for discussion about the text they have read so far. Then have them discuss their questions with partners.

Monitor Comprehension Have students work in small groups to summarize the story events so far. Have them discuss questions they have about story events to clarify understanding. Use a graphic organizer to show the events.

Common Core State Standards

Writing 8. Recall information from experiences or gather information from print and digital sources; take brief notes on sources and sort evidence into provided categories. **Language 2.** Demonstrate command of the conventions of standard English capitalization, punctuation, and spelling when writing. **Language 2.f.** Use spelling patterns and generalizations (e.g., word families, position-based spellings, syllable patterns, ending rules, meaningful word parts) in writing words.

Bridge to Common Core

RESEARCH TO BUILD AND PRESENT KNOWLEDGE

On Day 2 of the weeklong research project, students gather relevant information based on their focused questions from Day 1. They consult informational texts as well as digital sources, assessing the credibility of each one. This process enables students to demonstrate an understanding of the subject under investigation. As students access online information, they should always note their sources for a Work Cited page.

Research and Inquiry

Step 2 Navigate/Search

TEACH Have students generate a research plan for gathering information about their topics. Suggest that students use multiple sources of written and oral information to gather facts for their informational article. Have students review their inquiry questions and decide on the best sources for answers to their questions: reference texts, online sources, or an on-site inspection. Have students search reference sources and the Internet using their questions and keywords. Remind them to skim and scan each source and use headings and other text features to locate information about their topic.

Think Aloud **MODEL** When looking for information about symbols that represent freedom, I can go to our town hall and see the American flag that is raised outside. I can also interview town officials and historians about the flag and other symbols that represent our town history and find out why they stand for freedom. I can use the information I learn from my on-site inspection to form keywords that can help me search for more information in reference texts and on the Internet.

GUIDE PRACTICE Have students review the reference texts they identified. Show them how to use an index to find information in a textbook or other reference text. Explain that indexes list keywords in alphabetical order and give the number of the page where the keyword or topic can be found. Using an index is an important way to locate information in a reference text quickly.

ON THEIR OWN Have students continue their review of reference texts, taking notes as they find relevant information.

Conventions

Capital Letters

TEACH Remind students that names of particular people, places, and things, as well as the first word in a sentence or greeting, begin with capital letters. Abbreviations, official titles, and initials in a person's name should also be capitalized.

GUIDE PRACTICE Write these sentences: *every year, on the fourth of july, the united states of america celebrates its independence. It is officer michael jones' favorite holiday.* Then explain which letters should be capitalized. *Every* should be capitalized. It is the first word in the sentence. *Fourth* and *July* should be capitalized. They are important words in the name of a holiday. *United, States,* and *America* should be capitalized. They are important words in the name of a country. *Officer Michael Jones* should be capitalized because it is a person's name with an official title that appears directly before the name.

Have students list proper nouns, titles, and abbreviations that are capitalized in the first part of *The Story of the Statue of Liberty*. Have students explain why capital letters were used.

ON THEIR OWN For additional practice, use *Reader's and Writer's Notebook,* p. 389.

Spelling

Vowel Sounds in *moon* and *foot*

TEACH Remind students that their spelling words for this week have the vowel sounds in *moon* spelled *oo, ew, ue,* or *ui* and *foot* spelled *oo* or *u*. Model how to spell words with these vowel sounds. Listen to the sounds in *school:* /s/ /k/ /ü/ /l/. I'll write the letters for the first two sounds, /s/ /k/. Then I'll write the letters for the next sound, /ü/. Then I'll write the letter for the final sound, /l/. I spelled the sounds in *school, s-c-h-o-o-l.*

GUIDE PRACTICE Have students write each spelling word and underline the vowels that make the vowel sound in *moon* or *foot.*

ON THEIR OWN For more practice, use *Reader's and Writer's Notebook,* p. 390.

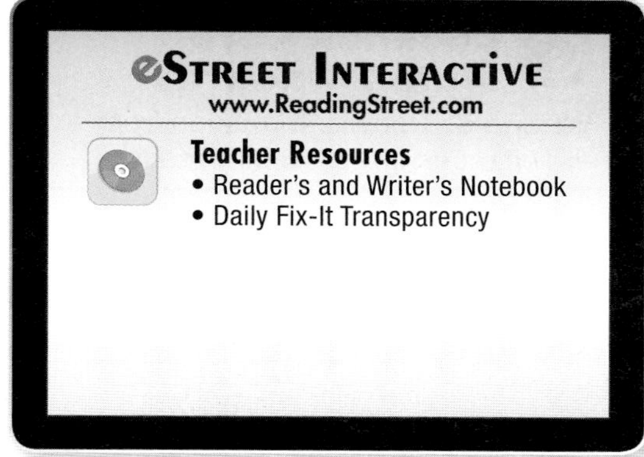

eSTREET INTERACTIVE
www.ReadingStreet.com
Teacher Resources
• Reader's and Writer's Notebook
• Daily Fix-It Transparency

Daily Fix-It

3. Maria and her daugter came to the United States in november. *(daughter; November)*
4. The Statue of Liberty greated Maria and she. *(greeted; her)*

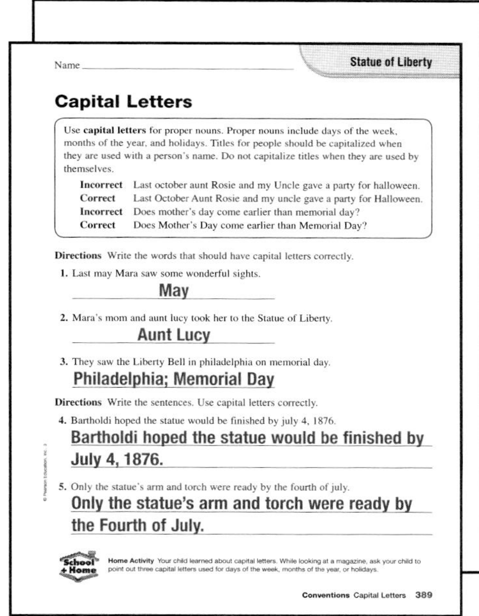

Name ______ Statue of Liberty

Capital Letters

Use **capital letters** for proper nouns. Proper nouns include days of the week, months of the year, and holidays. Titles for people should be capitalized when they are used with a person's name. Do not capitalize titles when they are used by themselves.

Incorrect	Last october aunt Rosie and my Uncle gave a party for halloween.
Correct	Last October Aunt Rosie and my uncle gave a party for Halloween.
Incorrect	Does mother's day come earlier than memorial day?
Correct	Does Mother's Day come earlier than Memorial Day?

Directions Write the words that should have capital letters correctly.

1. Last may Mara saw some wonderful sights.
   May
2. Mara's mom and aunt lucy took her to the Statue of Liberty.
   Aunt Lucy
3. They saw the Liberty Bell in philadelphia on memorial day.
   Philadelphia; Memorial Day

Directions Write the sentences. Use capital letters correctly.

4. Bartholdi hoped the statue would be finished by july 4, 1876.
   Bartholdi hoped the statue would be finished by July 4, 1876.
5. Only the statue's arm and torch were ready by the fourth of july.
   Only the statue's arm and torch were ready by the Fourth of July.

School + Home **Home Activity** Your child learned about capital letters. While looking at a magazine, ask your child to point out three capital letters used for days of the week, months of the year, or holidays.

Conventions Capital Letters 389

Reader's and Writer's Notebook, pp. 389–390

Conventions To provide students with practice on capitalization, use the modified grammar lessons in the *ELL Handbook* and Grammar Jammer online at: www.ReadingStreet.com

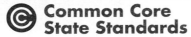

Common Core State Standards

Writing 8. Recall information from experiences or gather information from print and digital sources; take brief notes on sources and sort evidence into provided categories. **Also Informational Text 2., Writing 2.**

Notes

Writing Trait: Focus/Ideas

INTRODUCE THE PROMPT Remind students that the selection they are reading this week, *The Story of the Statue of Liberty,* is an example of narrative nonfiction. It tells a story, so it is a narrative. It tells a true story, so it is nonfiction. Narrative nonfiction often includes many details about the topic. These details support—or give more information about—the main ideas.

Writing Prompt

Think about the most important ideas in the selection. Now take notes on one part of the selection.

SELECT A TOPIC

To help students practice taking simple notes, tell or display a short story about eating breakfast. Have students list only the important information. Remind students that they do not need to write complete sentences. Jane had a good breakfast. She had cereal and toast. She drank a glass of orange juice. Then she ate a banana and threw the peel in the trash. When she looked at the clock, it was time to leave for school. She grabbed her backpack and went to school.

Corrective feedback Circulate around the room as students begin to write notes about the story. Confer briefly with students who seem to be having trouble. Ask them what important information in the story supports the main idea that Jane had a good breakfast.

Mini-Lesson Main Idea and Details

- When you take notes, you write only the most important information. A Main Idea and Details chart can help you identify the most important information. Display the graphic organizer and show students where to write the main idea of a section and where to write the supporting details.
- Read aloud the first two paragraphs on p. 378. Point out that "The statue would be very large and strong" is a main idea.
- Point out that the next sentence tells why Bartholdi wanted the statue to be so large and strong, so this is a supporting detail.

Have students use the Main Idea and Details chart on p. 391 of their *Reader's and Writer's Notebook* to continue adding details to their notes.

Routine Quick Write for Fluency

Team Talk

1. **Talk** Have pairs talk about why it is important to identify the main ideas and supporting details in an article or story.
2. **Write** Each student writes a sentence telling why he or she should include main ideas and supporting details in his or her notes.
3. **Share** Pairs read one another's writing and share what they wrote.

Routines Flip Chart

eStreet Interactive
www.ReadingStreet.com

Teacher Resources
- Reader's and Writer's Notebook
- Graphic Organizer

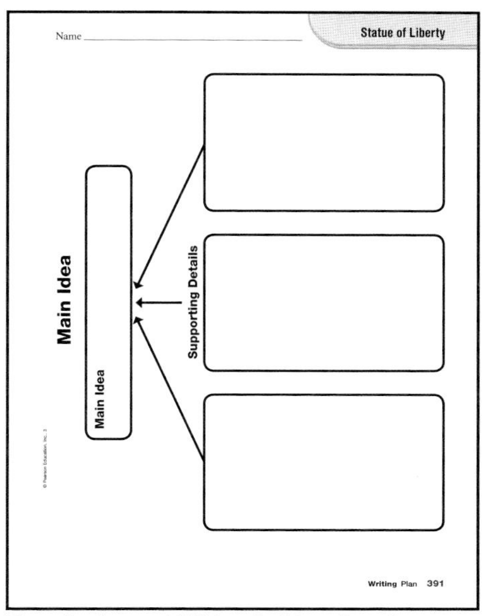
Name ____________ Statue of Liberty

Main Idea

Main Idea

Supporting Details

Writing Plan 391

Reader's and Writer's Notebook, p. 391

Wrap Up Your Day!

- ✓ **Content Knowledge** What did you learn about symbols of freedom?
- ✓ **Text-Based Comprehension** Tell one fact about how the Statue of Liberty was constructed.

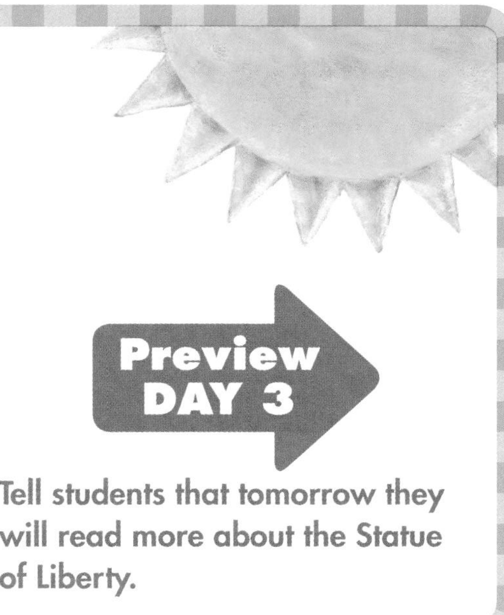

Tell students that tomorrow they will read more about the Statue of Liberty.

DAY 3 at a Glance

Content Knowledge
Oral Vocabulary

Phonics/Word Analysis
Vowel Sounds /ü/ and /ů/

Text-Based Comprehension
Fact and Opinion
Questioning

Fluency
Rate

Research and Study Skills
Time Line

Research and Inquiry
Analyze Information

Conventions
Capital Letters

Spelling
Vowel Sounds in *moon* and *foot*

Writing
Notes

Materials

- Student Edition
- Reader's and Writer's Notebook
- Retelling Cards
- Decodable Reader

Common Core State Standards

Speaking/Listening 1. Engage effectively in a range of collaborative discussions (one-on-one, in groups, and teacher led) with diverse partners on grade 3 topics and texts, building on others' ideas and expressing their own clearly. **Language 6.** Acquire and use accurately grade-appropriate conversational, general academic, and domain-specific words and phrases, including those that signal spatial and temporal relationships (e.g., *After dinner that night we went looking for them*). **Also Speaking/Listening 1.c.**

Content Knowledge

Symbols of Freedom

EXPAND THE CONCEPT Remind students of the weekly concept question—*Why do we have symbols that represent freedom?* Discuss how the question relates to *The Story of the Statue of Liberty.* Encourage students to think about why a recognizable symbol of freedom such as the Statue of Liberty is so powerful.

Build Oral Language

TALK ABOUT SENTENCES AND WORDS Reread these sentences from Student Edition, p. 380.

Then, skin of gleaming copper was put onto the skeleton and held in place with iron straps. As the huge statue grew, all of Paris watched with great fascination.

- What words does the author use to make the statue seem like a human body? What words tell that it is different than a human body? Have students turn to a partner to share. (The author describes the statue's skin and skeleton, which is like a human body, and says the statue grew, which is also like a human body. However, the statue's skin is made of copper and held on by iron straps; the statue is huge, and it grew while everyone watched.)
- Why does the author say "all of Paris" watched the statue being built? Is this the truth? (This is a generalization. The author says this because most people were interested in watching the statue being built, and the statue was huge, so it would be hard to miss and hard not to watch.)
- What does *gleaming* mean? (to flash or reflect light) What are some synonyms of *gleaming*? (shimmering, brilliant) What does *fascination* mean? (intensely interested) What are some synonyms of *fascination*? (interest, curiosity)

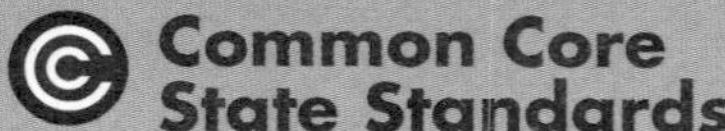

Team Talk Have students work with a partner to replace key words in the sentences with synonyms. Use the following sentence frame.

Then, skin of ______ copper was put onto the skeleton and held in place with iron straps. As the huge statue grew, all of Paris watched with great ______.

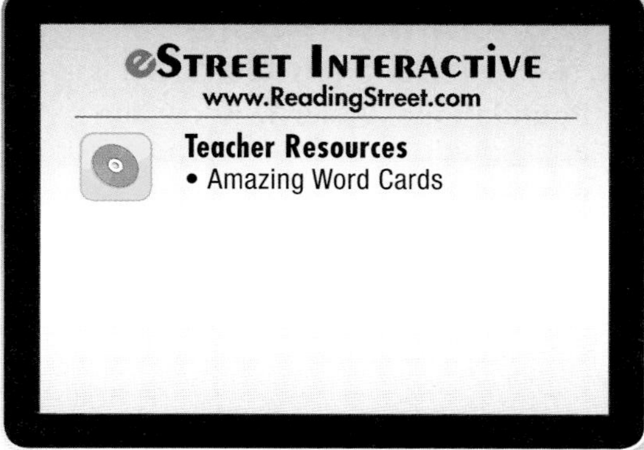

Build Oral Vocabulary

Amazing Words Robust Vocabulary Routine

1. **Introduce** Write the Amazing Word *recognizable* on the board. Have students say it aloud with you. Yesterday we learned that the Statue of Liberty is one of the most *recognizable* symbols of freedom. Have students determine the definition of the word. (Something that you know and can identify is *recognizable.*)
2. **Demonstrate** Have students answer questions to demonstrate understanding. Can you think of other symbols of freedom that are *recognizable* to many people? (American flag, bald eagle, Liberty Bell) What are the most *recognizable* symbolic features of the Statue of Liberty? (the tablet with July 4, 1776 on it; the lamp; the crown)
3. **Apply** Have students apply their understanding. What is a synonym for *recognizable?* *(familiar)*
4. **Display the Word** Students can identify the base word *recognize* and the suffix *-able*.

See p. OV•1 to teach *disgrace*.

Routines Flip Chart

ADD TO THE CONCEPT MAP Discuss the Amazing Words *dedication* and *competition*. Add these and other concept-related words to the concept map. Use the following questions to develop students' understanding of the concept.

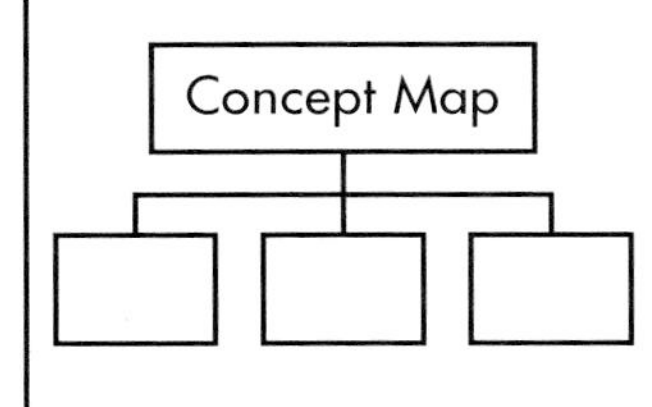

- Why is a celebration of a symbol, such as a *dedication* ceremony, important?
- At times, the United States has held *competitions* for artists or architects to design a symbol or monument to represent an important person or event. Why do you think designers would want to enter a *competition* to design a symbol for our country?

Amazing Words

impressive	competition
tribute	recognizable
enlighten	disgrace
contribution	staggering
dedication	fund

Expand Vocabulary Use the Day 3 instruction on ELL Poster 26 to help students expand vocabulary.

Common Core State Standards

Foundational Skills 3. Know and apply grade-level phonics and word analysis skills in decoding words. **Foundational Skills 3.d.** Read grade-appropriate irregularly spelled words.

Phonics

Vowel Sounds /ü/ and /u̇/

MODEL WORD BUILDING Now we are going to build words with the vowel sounds /ü/ and /u̇/. Write *cook* and blend it. Watch me change the *k* in *cook* to *l*. Model blending the new word, *cool*.

GUIDE PRACTICE Write *book* and have the class blend it with you. Have students spell *book* with their letter tiles. Monitor students' work.

Corrective feedback | For corrective feedback, model the correct spelling and have students correct their tiles.

- Change the *k* in *book* to *m*. Say the new word together.
- Change the *b* in *boom* to *l*. Say the new word together.
- Change the *m* in *loom* to *k*. Say the new word together.
- Change the *l* in *look* to *sh*. Say the new word together.

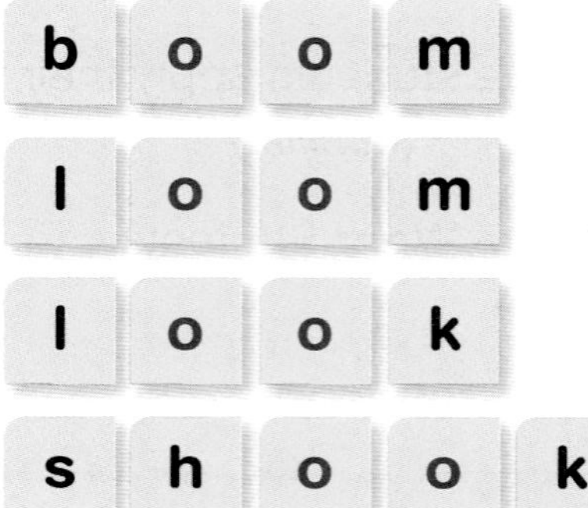

Fluent Word Reading

MODEL Write *shoot*. I know the sounds for *sh, oo,* and *t*. Blend them and read the word *shoot*.

GUIDE PRACTICE Write the words below. Say the sounds in your head for each spelling you see. When I point to the word, we'll read it together. Allow one second per sound previewing time for the first reading.

bloom	push	foot	blue	newt	ruin

ON THEIR OWN Have students read the list above three or four times until they can read one word per second.

Decodable Passage 26B

If students need help, then . . .

Read *Kat's Kite*

READ WORDS IN ISOLATION Have students turn to p. 129 in *Decodable Practice Readers 3.2* and find the first list of words. Each word in this list has the vowel sound /ü/, spelled *oo, ew, ue,* or *ui,* or the vowel sound /u̇/, spelled *oo* or *u.* Let's blend and read these words. Be sure that students identify the correct vowel sound in each word.

Next, have students read the high-frequency words.

PREVIEW Have students read the title and preview the story. Tell them that they will read words with vowel sounds /ü/ and /u̇/.

READ WORDS IN CONTEXT Chorally read the story along with students. Have students identify words in the story that have the vowel sounds /ü/ and /u̇/. Make sure that students are monitoring their accuracy when they decode words.

Team Talk Pair students and have them take turns reading the story aloud to each other. Monitor students as they read to check for proper pronunciation and appropriate pacing.

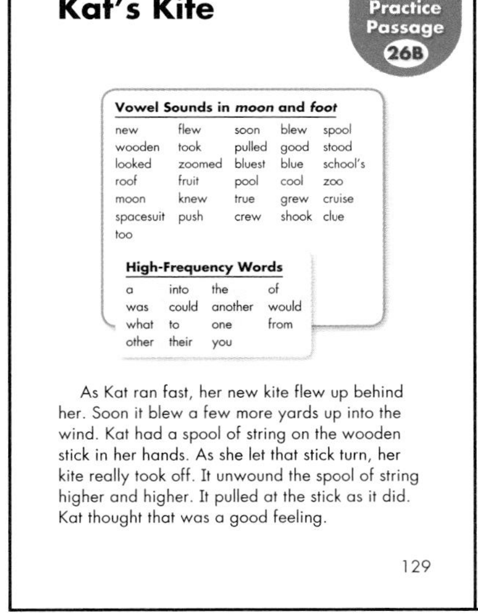

Kat's Kite

Decodable Practice Passage 26B

Vowel Sounds in *moon* and *foot*

new	flew	soon	blew	spool
wooden	took	pulled	good	stood
looked	zoomed	bluest	blue	school's
roof	fruit	pool	cool	zoo
moon	knew	true	grew	cruise
spacesuit	push	crew	shook	clue
too				

High-Frequency Words

a	into	the	of
was	could	another	would
what	to	one	from
other	their	you	

As Kat ran fast, her new kite flew up behind her. Soon it blew a few more yards up into the wind. Kat had a spool of string on the wooden stick in her hands. As she let that stick turn, her kite really took off. It unwound the spool of string higher and higher. It pulled at the stick as it did. Kat thought that was a good feeling.

129

Kat stood and looked as her kite zoomed up and down a bit in the bluest, blue sky. Then she sat on the ground and held the stick. Her kite looked as if it flew right over her school's roof now. That seemed far!

Kat wished she could tie on another spool of string. Then her kite could go higher and farther out. Might another spool help it fly over the fruit trees and swimming pool south of her school? That would be cool! Might a third spool of string make her kite reach high over the zoo? Might more spools help her kite reach the moon?

Kat knew that could not happen. But she knew what was true. She enjoyed the thrill of flying her kite!

As her kite danced high over her, Kat thought about flying. When she grew up, would she fly? Would she cruise the skies as a jet pilot? Would she put on a spacesuit and push a crew to the moon and stars? And would Kat one day look down from high? Would she see what her kite sees? Would she see other kids flying their kites in the sky below her?

The spool of string shook a bit. The kite quickly flew up and down in the sky. Was that a clue? Was her kite saying, "Yes, Kat, you will fly high too!"

130

Decodable Practice Passage 26B

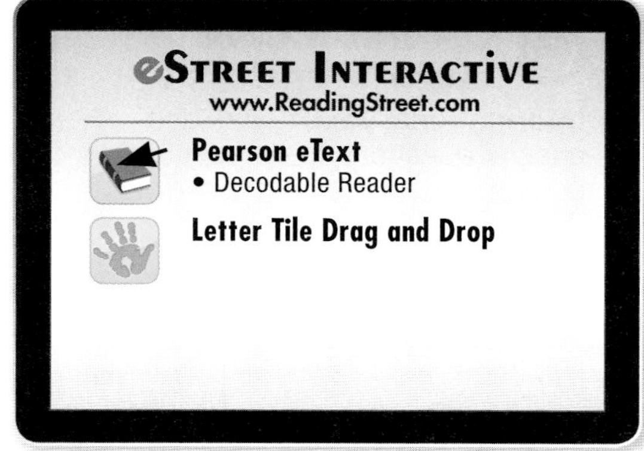

eSTREET INTERACTIVE
www.ReadingStreet.com
Pearson eText
• Decodable Reader
Letter Tile Drag and Drop

Access for All

Advanced

Have students work in pairs to choose four or five /ü/ and /u̇/ words to use in writing a paragraph. Have pairs exchange and read each other's paragraphs.

Common Core State Standards

Informational Text 1. Ask and answer questions to demonstrate understanding of a text, referring explicitly to the text as the basis for the answers. **Also Informational Text 2.**

Strategy Response Log

Have students write questions about the events of *The Story of the Statue of Liberty* on p. 32 in the *Reader's and Writer's Notebook.*

Text-Based Comprehension

Check Understanding

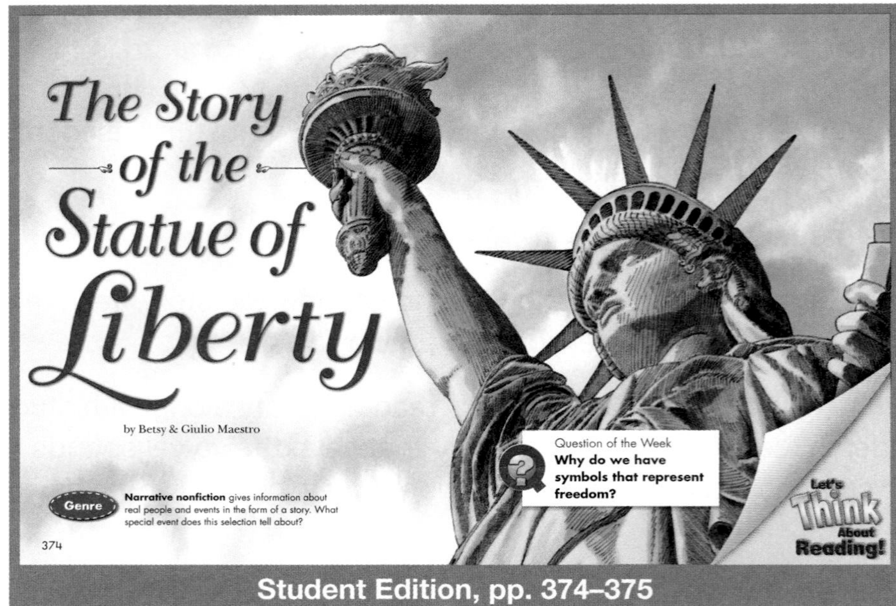

Student Edition, pp. 374–375

If... you chose to read *The Story of the Statue of Liberty* in two parts, **then...** use the following questions to monitor students' understanding of pp. 374–381 of the selection. Encourage students to cite evidence from the text.

INFERENCE Why do you think Bartholdi talked to engineers and craftsmen about the design before he started to build? (Because the statue was to be large enough for people to be able to climb up in it, Bartholdi needed to know the best way to build it and make it strong.) (p. 378)

ANALYSIS What details did Bartholdi include in the design of the Statue of Liberty to symbolize freedom? (The lamp is a symbol welcoming people to the United States and represents the freedom that enlightened the New World. Liberty also holds a tablet with the date July 4, 1776.) (pp. 377–378)

RETELL Have students retell pp. 378–381 of *The Story of the Statue of Liberty,* referring to details in the text. Remind them to use the correct sequence of events in their retellings.

Corrective feedback	**If...** students leave out important details, **then...** have students look back through the illustrations in the selection.

READ Use the **Access Text** and **Close Reading** notes to finish reading *The Story of the Statue of Liberty*.

If... you followed the Read for Understanding routine below,
then... ask students to retell the selection before you reread *The Story of the Statue of Liberty.*

RETELL Have students retell pp. 378–381 of *The Story of the Statue of Liberty,* referring to details in the text. Remind them to use the correct sequence of events in their retellings.

Corrective feedback	**If...** students leave out important details, **then...** have students look back through the illustrations in the selection.

READ Return to p. 376–377 and use the **2nd Read/Close Reading** notes to reread *The Story of the Statue of Liberty.*

Read Main Selection

Routine Read for Understanding

Deepen understanding by reading the selection multiple times.

1. **First Read**—If students need support, use the **Access Text** notes to help them clarify understanding.
2. **Second Read**—Use the **Close Reading** notes to help students draw knowledge from the text.

Day 3 SMALL GROUP TIME • Differentiate Close Reading, p. SG•1

OL On-Level	SI Strategic Intervention	
• **Reread** to Develop Vocabulary	• **Reread** to Develop Vocabulary	• **Reread** to Extend Vocabulary
• **Read** *The Story of the Statue of Liberty*	• **Read** *The Story of the Statue of Liberty*	• **Read** *The Story of the Statue of Liberty*
		• **Investigate** Inquiry Project

eSTREET INTERACTIVE
www.ReadingStreet.com

Pearson eText
• Student Edition

AudioText CD

Teacher Resources
• Reader's and Writer's Notebook

Check Retelling To support retelling, review the multilingual summary for *The Story of the Statue of Liberty* with the appropriate Retelling Cards to scaffold understanding.

If... students need more scaffolding and practice with the **Main Selection**,
then... use the activities on p. DI•22 in the Teacher Resources section on SuccessNet.

1ST READ

Access Text If students need help, then...

FACT AND OPINION Explain that good readers evaluate the statements of fact and opinion as they read. Ask students to evaluate statements of fact and opinion about why and how people paid for and felt about the statue.

Think Aloud **MODEL** The newspaper got people to donate money. That's a statement of fact because I could look in other reference sources to see if it is true. It is an opinion that there was "new excitement." Statements about how people felt cannot be proven true or false.

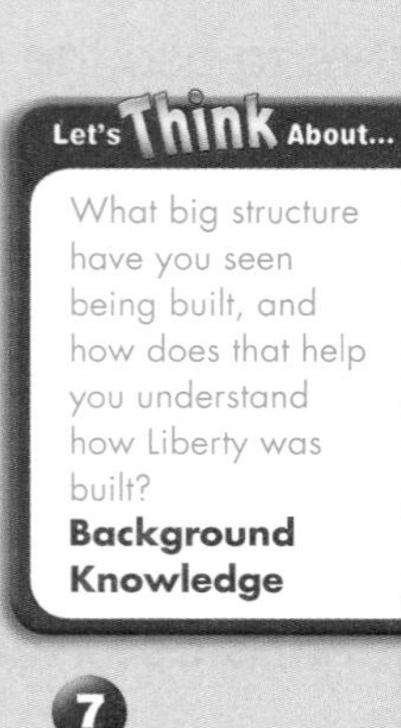

Let's Think About...
What big structure have you seen being built, and how does that help you understand how Liberty was built?
Background Knowledge

7

But in America people had lost interest in the Statue of Liberty. Money had run out and work on Bedloe's Island had stopped. The base for the statue was not finished. With the help of a large New York newspaper, the money was raised. People all over the country, including children, sent in whatever they could. By the time the ship reached New York in 1885, it was greeted with new excitement.

The work on the island went on, and soon the pedestal was completed. Piece by piece, the skeleton was raised. Then the copper skin was riveted in place. Liberty was put back together like a giant puzzle. The statue had been built not once, but twice!

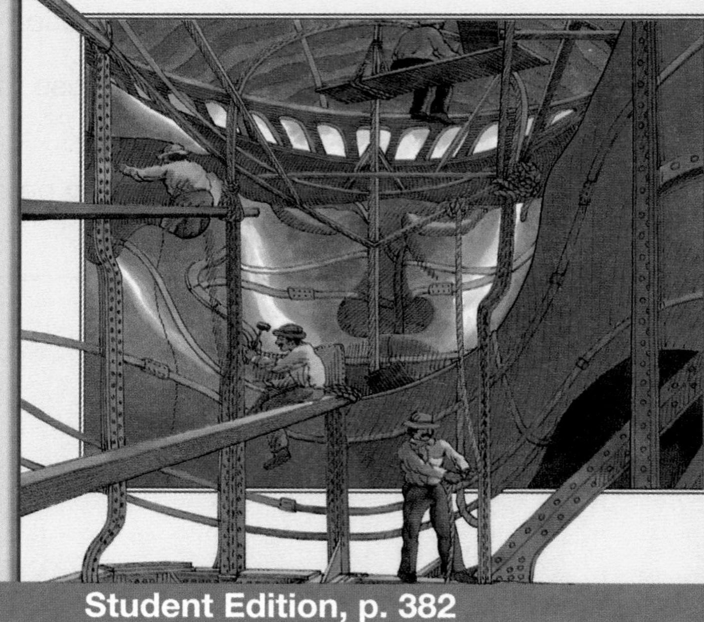

382

Student Edition, p. 382

2ND READ

Close Reading

ANALYSIS The authors explain that Liberty was put back together like a giant puzzle. How does the word *puzzle* help the reader visualize how Liberty was assembled? (It helps me understand that there were many pieces that fit together in a certain way to make the statue complete.)

ANALYSIS • TEXT EVIDENCE What details on page 382 tell how Liberty was put back together? (First the pedestal was completed. Then the skeleton was raised. Last, the copper skin was riveted into place.)

REREAD CHALLENGING TEXT Have students reread pp. 382–383 to clarify the sequence of events in this part of the selection. Students may need help keeping track of the events that led to the statue's unveiling.

ON THEIR OWN Have students discuss the last sentence on p. 382 to determine if it is a statement of fact or opinion.

At last, in 1886, Liberty was standing where she belonged. A wonderful celebration was held. Boats and ships filled the harbor. Speeches were read, songs were sung. Bartholdi himself unveiled Liberty's face and she stood, gleaming in all her glory, for everyone to see. There was a great cheer from the crowd. Then President Grover Cleveland gave a speech.

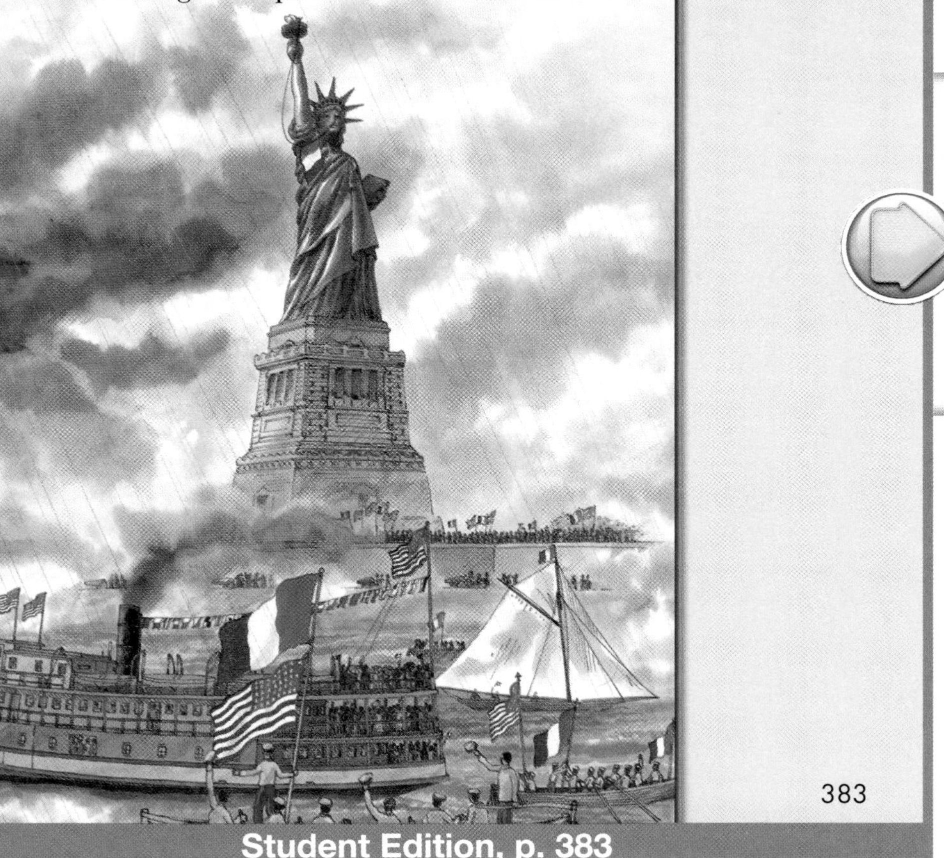

383

Student Edition, p. 383

Let's Think About...

7 Answers will vary but should include the ideas that it takes a lot of work to build something so big and that many people are involved in such a complex project.

Common Core State Standards

Informational Text 1. Ask and answer questions to demonstrate understanding of a text, referring explicitly to the text as the basis for the answers. **Also Informational Text 3.**

Access for All

 Strategic Intervention

Have students use a graphic organizer to map the sequence of events on p. 382.

 Advanced

Have students identify additional examples where the author's choice of a particular word enhances the meaning of the text. Then encourage them to point out examples where they could make a different word choice.

Connect to Social Studies

Ellis Island By the early 20th century, the Statue of Liberty was a well-known symbol to those arriving from Europe. Nearby Ellis Island was the entrance point for millions of immigrants to the United States. In 1924, the Statue of Liberty became a national monument. In 1965, Ellis Island was added to the Statue of Liberty National Monument.

Sequence Direct students' attention to the description of the unveiling of the Statue of Liberty on p. 383. Tell students that *sequence* is the order in which events occur. Have students act out the sequence of events at the celebration for the Statue of Liberty, using signal words, such as *first, next,* and *last* to announce each event.

1ST READ

Access Text If students need help, then...

PREFIX *un-* Tell students that the prefix *un-* means "not" or "the opposite of." Ask students to determine the meaning of the word *unlucky*.

Think Aloud **MODEL** I know that when people are *lucky,* good things come to them by chance. Since the prefix *un-* means "not" or "the opposite of," *unlucky* means "not lucky."

ON THEIR OWN Have partners list and define other words with the prefix *un-*. For additional practice, use *Reader's and Writer's Notebook,* p. 392.

CROSS-TEXT EVALUATION

Use a Strategy to Self-Check How did the Read Aloud "Let Freedom Ring" help you understand this selection?

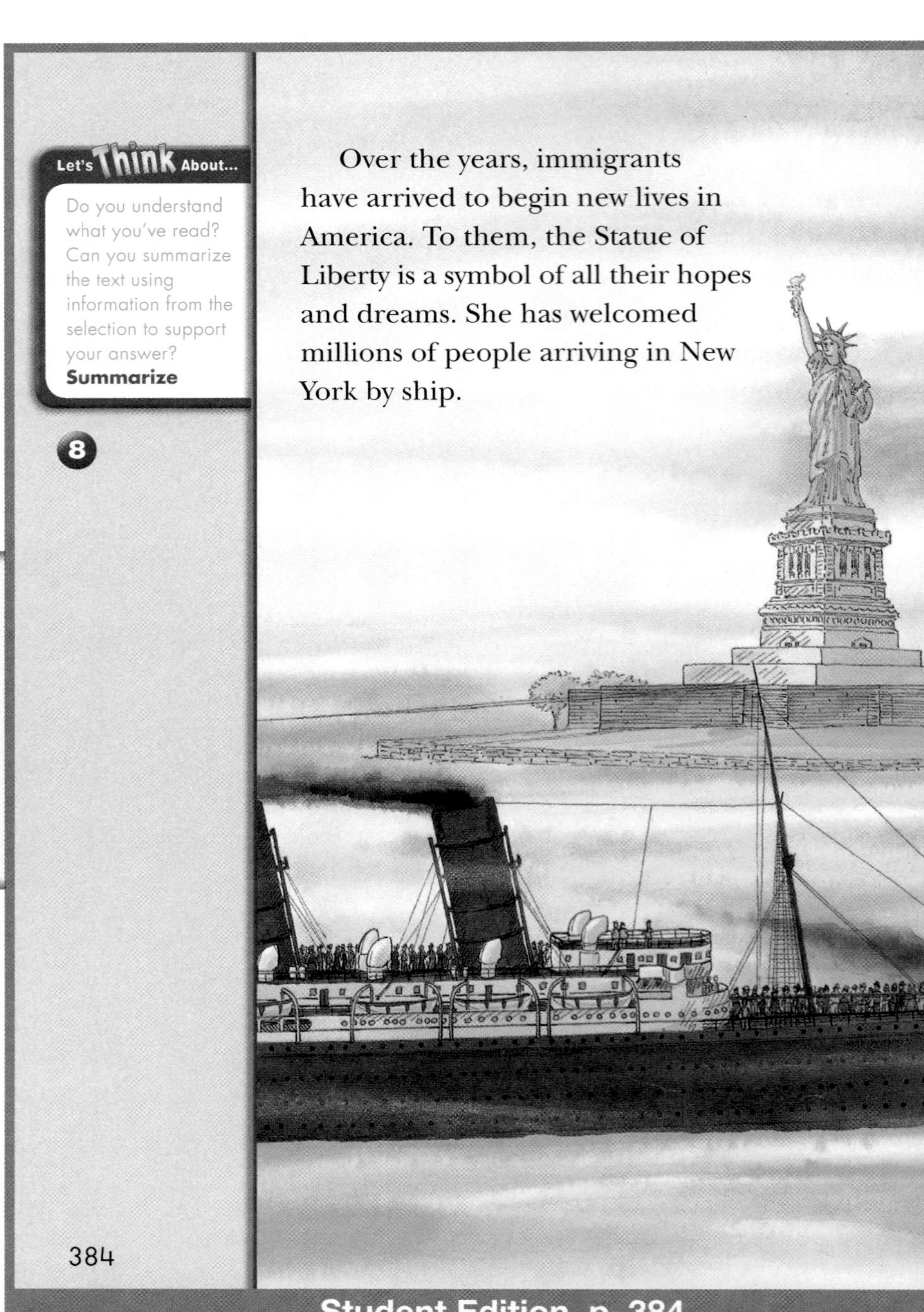

Let's Think About...
Do you understand what you've read? Can you summarize the text using information from the selection to support your answer?
Summarize
8
Over the years, immigrants have arrived to begin new lives in America. To them, the Statue of Liberty is a symbol of all their hopes and dreams. She has welcomed millions of people arriving in New York by ship.
384

Student Edition, p. 384

SYNTHESIS • TEXT EVIDENCE Using what you learned in this selection, tell why we have symbols that represent freedom. Have students cite examples from the text to support their responses.

2ND READ

Close Reading

EVALUATION • TEXT EVIDENCE The title of this selection is *The Story of the Statue of Liberty.* Using evidence from the text, tell why this selection is called a story even though it is not fiction. (The selection has facts, but it is told like a story.)

CHECK PREDICTIONS Have students return to the predictions they made earlier and confirm whether they were accurate.

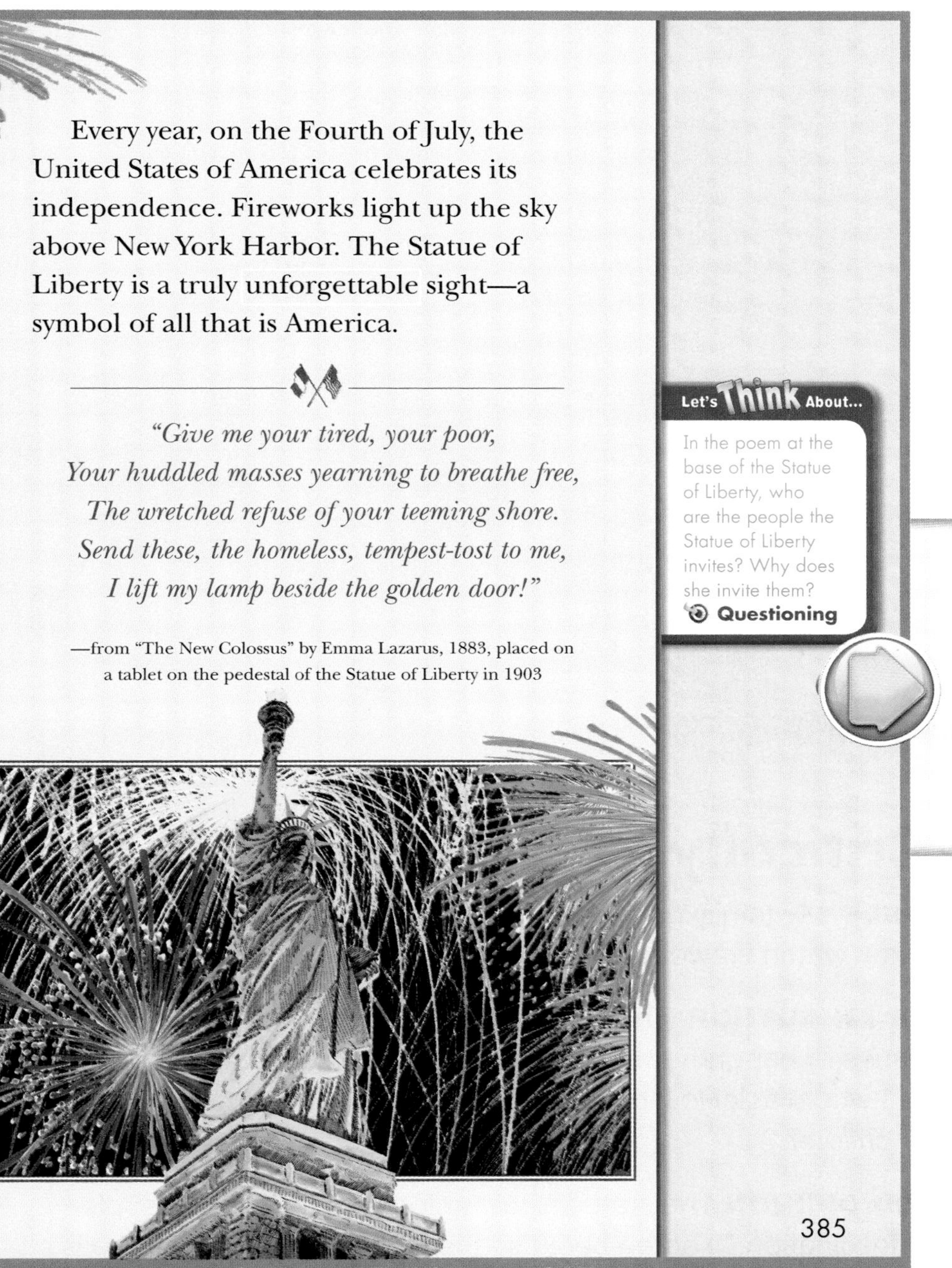

Every year, on the Fourth of July, the United States of America celebrates its independence. Fireworks light up the sky above New York Harbor. The Statue of Liberty is a truly unforgettable sight—a symbol of all that is America.

"Give me your tired, your poor,
Your huddled masses yearning to breathe free,
The wretched refuse of your teeming shore.
Send these, the homeless, tempest-tost to me,
I lift my lamp beside the golden door!"

—from "The New Colossus" by Emma Lazarus, 1883, placed on a tablet on the pedestal of the Statue of Liberty in 1903

Let's Think About...

In the poem at the base of the Statue of Liberty, who are the people the Statue of Liberty invites? Why does she invite them? **Questioning**

385

Student Edition, p. 385

Let's Think About...

8 Yes. A French sculptor made a statue to remember the friendship between France and America. Many people worked on the statue, and parts were displayed to raise money. It was taken apart and rebuilt in New York.

9 The poem invites the poor, the oppressed, and the homeless to come to America to find a better life.

Common Core State Standards

Informational Text 1. Ask and answer questions to demonstrate understanding of a text, referring explicitly to the text as the basis for the answers. **Language 4.b.** Determine the meaning of the new word formed when a known affix is added to a known word (e.g., *agreeable/disagreeable, comfortable/uncomfortable, care/careless, heat/preheat*). **Also Informational Text 10.**

Access for All

Strategic Intervention

Provide additional practice with using the prefix *un-* to figure out the meaning of a word. Use the following words: *unsafe, untie, unstoppable, unkind, unlock.*

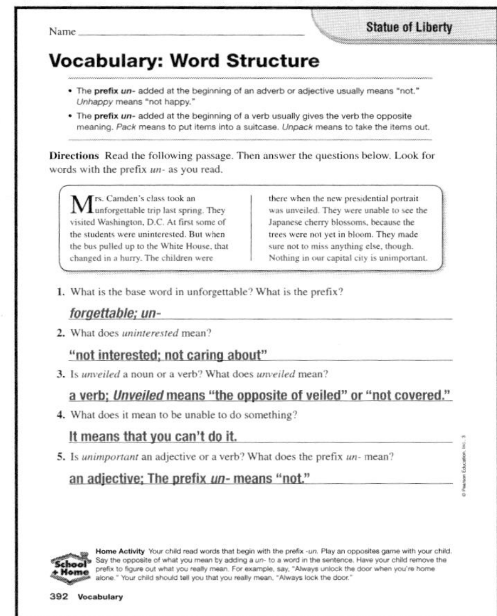

Name ____________ Statue of Liberty

Vocabulary: Word Structure

- The **prefix *un-*** added at the beginning of an adverb or adjective usually means "not." *Unhappy* means "not happy."
- The **prefix *un-*** added at the beginning of a verb usually gives the verb the opposite meaning. *Pack* means to put items into a suitcase. *Unpack* means to take the items out.

Directions Read the following passage. Then answer the questions below. Look for words with the prefix *un-* as you read.

Mrs. Camden's class took an unforgettable trip last spring. They visited Washington, D.C. At first some of the students were uninterested. But when the bus pulled up to the White House, that changed in a hurry. The children were there when the new presidential portrait was unveiled. They were unable to see the Japanese cherry blossoms, because the trees were not yet in bloom. They made sure not to miss anything else, though. Nothing in our capital city is unimportant.

1. What is the base word in unforgettable? What is the prefix?
   forgettable; un-
2. What does *uninterested* mean?
   "not interested; not caring about"
3. Is *unveiled* a noun or a verb? What does *unveiled* mean?
   a verb; *Unveiled* means "the opposite of veiled" or "not covered."
4. What does it mean to be unable to do something?
   It means that you can't do it.
5. Is *unimportant* an adjective or a verb? What does the prefix *un-* mean?
   an adjective; The prefix *un-* means "not."

Home Activity Your child read words that begin with the prefix -*un*. Play an opposites game with your child. Say the opposite of what you mean by adding a *un-* to a word in the sentence. Have your child remove the prefix to figure out what you really mean. For example, say, "Always unlock the door when you're home alone." Your child should tell you that you really mean, "Always lock the door."

© Pearson Education, Inc. 3

392 Vocabulary

Reader's and Writer's Notebook, p. 392

Monitor Comprehension Focus students' attention on the poem on p. 385. Guide students through the poem line by line. Discuss the words they know and help define unfamiliar words. Encourage students to ask questions to clarify meaning. Then have partners create an illustration that represents the meaning of the poem to confirm understanding.

Think Critically

1. In the story, the author writes about celebrating the Fourth of July. What do you do with your family, friends, and community to show your feelings about freedom? Text to Self
2. Read "Meet the Authors" on page 387. What is the topic in this selection? Why did the author write this story? What questions would you ask the authors about why they write? Think Like an Author
3. Look back at the story. Find some statements of opinion. Do you agree or disagree with any of the opinions? Tell why or why not using evidence from the text to support your answer. Fact and Opinion
4. What questions does the story bring up for you? Ask a literal, an interpretive, and an evaluative question and see if you or your classmates can answer them. Questioning
5. **Look Back and Write** Look back through the story to find what is interesting or important about the Statue of Liberty. Write a paragraph using facts and details to support this idea. Key Ideas and Details • Text Evidence

386

Meet the Authors

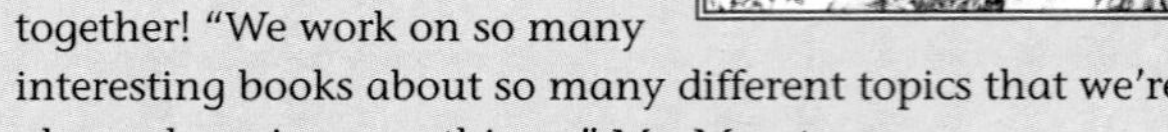

Betsy and Giulio Maestro

Betsy and Giulio Maestro are husband and wife. They have published more than 100 books together! "We work on so many interesting books about so many different topics that we're always learning new things," Ms. Maestro says.

Ms. Maestro wrote this story because she feels a special connection to the Statue of Liberty. Her grandmother saw the statue for the first time as she arrived at Ellis Island from Russia in 1918. Because Ms. Maestro grew up in New York City, she visited the Statue of Liberty many times. On a class field trip, she even climbed to the crown. Ms. Maestro feels the statue is "a symbol of human freedom and human rights throughout the world."

Read more books by Betsy and Giulio Maestro.

The New Americans: Colonial Times: 1620–1689

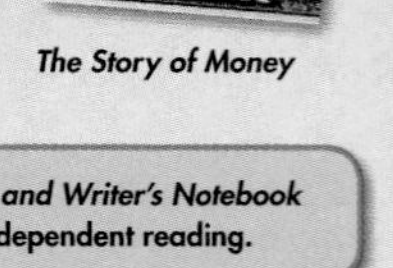

The Story of Money

Reading Log — Use the *Reader's and Writer's Notebook* to record your independent reading.

387

Student Edition, pp. 386–387

Common Core State Standards

Informational Text 1. Ask and answer questions to demonstrate understanding of a text, referring explicitly to the text as the basis for the answers. **Also Informational Text 2., Writing 2., Speaking/ Listening 4., Language 3.**

Bridge to Common Core

RANGE OF READING AND LEVEL OF TEXT COMPLEXITY

To increase students' capacity for reading and comprehending complex texts independently and proficiently, have them read other literary texts by Betsy and Giulio Maestro or about the social studies topic, symbols of freedom. After students read closely for a sustained period of time, they should record their reading in their Reading Logs.

Think Critically

1. **TEXT TO SELF** My family goes to a parade that honors soldiers. We wave American flags, watch fireworks, and wear red, white, and blue.
2. **THINK LIKE AN AUTHOR** The topic is the Statue of Liberty. Ms. Maestro wrote it because of her grandmother, who saw the statue when she arrived from Russia. I would ask *How do you decide what to write about? Why do you write for children?*
3. **FACT AND OPINION** The statue is an "unforgettable" sight; people watched "in fascination." I agree because the text says that the statue is large and the design includes many symbolic details. The statue must be a fascinating, unforgettable sight.
4. **QUESTIONING** literal: *Who made the statue?* interpretive: *Why is it an important symbol of freedom?* evaluative: *Is it a successful symbol of freedom?*
5. **LOOK BACK AND WRITE • TEXT EVIDENCE** To build writing fluency, allow 10–15 minutes.

Scoring Rubric Look Back and Write

TOP-SCORE RESPONSE A top-score response uses details from the selection to describe what is interesting or important about the Statue of Liberty.

A top-score response should include:

- The Statue of Liberty symbolizes the old friendship between France and the United States.
- Liberty holds a lamp that welcomes people to America.
- Millions of immigrants saw the statue as they arrived.

Retell

Have students work in pairs to retell the selection, using the retelling strip in the Student Edition or the Story Sort as prompts. Monitor students' retellings.

Scoring Rubric Narrative Retelling

	4	3	2	1
Connections	Makes connections and generalizes beyond the text	Makes connections to other events, stories, or experiences	Makes a limited connection to another event, story, or experience	Makes no connection to another event, story, or experience
Author's Purpose	Elaborates on author's purpose	Tells author's purpose with some clarity	Makes some connection to author's purpose	Makes no connection to author's purpose
Characters	Describes the main character(s) and any character development	Identifies the main character(s) and gives some information about them	Inaccurately identifies some characters or gives little information about them	Inaccurately identifies the characters or gives no information about them
Setting	Describes the time and location	Identifies the time and location	Omits details of time or location	Is unable to identify time or location
Plot	Describes the problem, goal, events, and ending using rich detail	Tells the problem, goal, events, and ending with some errors that do not affect meaning	Tells parts of the problem, goal, events, and ending with gaps that affect meaning	Retelling has no sense of story

Don't Wait Until Friday

MONITOR PROGRESS Check Retelling

If... students have difficulty retelling,

then... use the Retelling Cards/Story Sort to scaffold their retellings.

Plan to Assess Retelling

- ☑ **This week assess Strategic Intervention students.**
- ☐ **Week 2** Advanced
- ☐ **Week 3** Strategic Intervention
- ☐ **Week 4** On-Level
- ☐ **Week 5** Assess any students you have not yet checked during this unit.

Meet the Authors

Have students read about the authors Betsy and Giulio Maestro on p. 387. Ask them why the authors like writing together.

Read Independently

Have students enter their independent reading into their Reading Logs.

Common Core State Standards

Informational Text 7. Use information gained from illustrations (e.g., maps, photographs), and the words in a text to demonstrate understanding of the text (e.g., where, when, why, and how key events occur). **Foundational Skills 4.** Read with sufficient accuracy and fluency to support comprehension. **Foundational Skills 4.b.** Read on-level prose and poetry orally with accuracy, appropriate rate, and expression on successive readings.

Fluency

Rate

MODEL FLUENT READING Have students turn to p. 376 of *The Story of the Statue of Liberty.* Have students follow along as you read this page. Tell them that you will try to read about the Statue of Liberty just the way you speak. Vary your tone and volume, and don't read too fast or too slow.

GUIDE PRACTICE Have students follow along as you read the page again. Then have them reread the page as a group without you until they read the page at the correct rate. Ask questions to be sure students comprehend the text. Continue in the same way on p. 377.

Corrective feedback

If... students are having difficulty reading at an appropriate rate,
then... prompt:

- Do you think you need to slow down or read more quickly?
- Read the sentence more quickly. Now read it more slowly. Which helps you understand what you are reading?
- Tell me the sentence. Read it at the rate that would help me understand it.

Reread for Fluency

Routine Choral Reading

1. **Read** For *The Story of the Statue of Liberty,* use p. 379.
2. **Model** Have students listen as you read the page at an appropriate rate.
3. **Guide Practice** Have students read along with you.
4. **On Their Own** For optimal fluency, students should reread three or four times at an appropriate rate.

Routines Flip Chart

Research and Study Skills

Time Line

TEACH Tell students that time lines provide information about events in correct time order. A time line is a line with dates on it. An important event is usually described for each date. Display a time line and review that it presents information in time order. Then review information about time lines:

- The dates on a time line are in order from the earliest date to the latest date.
- Each date has information that goes along with it.
- Time lines are read from left to right or top to bottom.

Have students review the events in *The Story of the Statue of Liberty.* Have them look for dates in the text to make a time line. Work together as a class to make a time line that shows the dates and events in the story of how the statue was designed and built.

GUIDE PRACTICE Discuss these questions:

Why would someone want to make a time line? (Time lines can make information in a text easier to understand.)

How can you decide what time periods to use to divide your time line? (Think about the whole period you want to show and then divide it into equal amounts of time.)

Have students look at different time lines and discuss the information that each shows.

ON THEIR OWN Have students review the instructions and complete p. 393 of the *Reader's and Writer's Notebook.*

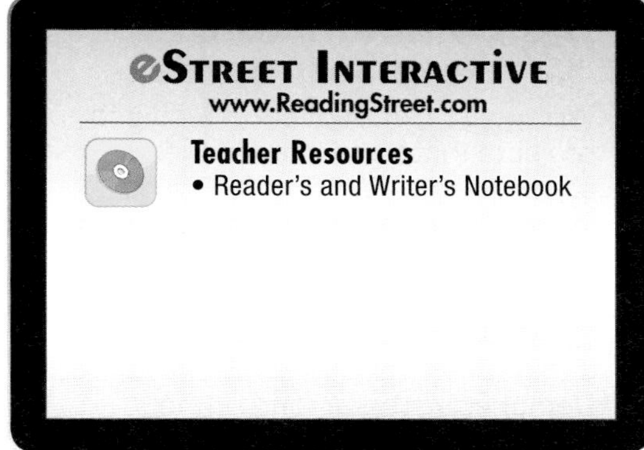

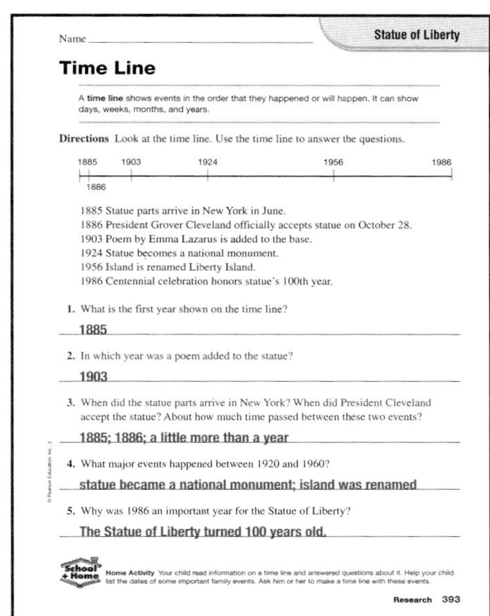
Name

Statue of Liberty

Time Line

A **time line** shows events in the order that they happened or will happen. It can show days, weeks, months, and years.

Directions Look at the time line. Use the time line to answer the questions.

1885 1886 1903 1924 1956 1986

1885 Statue parts arrive in New York in June.
1886 President Grover Cleveland officially accepts statue on October 28.
1903 Poem by Emma Lazarus is added to the base.
1924 Statue becomes a national monument.
1956 Island is renamed Liberty Island.
1986 Centennial celebration honors statue's 100th year.

1. What is the first year shown on the time line?
1885

2. In which year was a poem added to the statue?
1903

3. When did the statue parts arrive in New York? When did President Cleveland accept the statue? About how much time passed between these two events?
1885; 1886; a little more than a year

4. What major events happened between 1920 and 1960?
statue became a national monument; island was renamed

5. Why was 1986 an important year for the Statue of Liberty?
The Statue of Liberty turned 100 years old.

School + Home **Home Activity** Your child read information on a time line and answered questions about it. Help your child list the dates of some important family events. Ask him or her to make a time line with these events.

Research 393

Reader's and Writer's Notebook, p. 393

Professional Development: What ELL Experts Say About Accessing Content

"We can *scaffold* students' learning by modifying the input itself. [There] are a variety of ways of modifying the presentation of academic content to students so that they can more effectively gain access to the meaning....Visuals enable students to 'see' the basic concepts we are trying to teach much more effectively than if we rely only on words."
—Dr. Jim Cummins

Time Lines Point out that creating a time line may help students better understand events in stories or other texts. Encourage them to make time lines of their lives. Have them compare their time lines with those of partners to see how they are the same and how they differ.

Common Core State Standards

Writing 7. Conduct short research projects that build knowledge about a topic. **Writing 8.** Recall information from experiences or gather information from print and digital sources; take brief notes on sources and sort evidence into provided categories. **Language 2.** Demonstrate command of the conventions of standard English capitalization, punctuation, and spelling when writing. **Language 2.f.** Use spelling patterns and generalizations (e.g., word families, position-based spellings, syllable patterns, ending rules, meaningful word parts) in writing words.

Research and Inquiry

Step 3 Analyze Information

TEACH Tell students that today they will analyze their research findings. Suggest that students record the historical information about a symbol that they are collecting on a time line. Then explain that students may have to improve the focus of their research by returning to their on-site inspections to gather more information.

Think Aloud **MODEL** Originally I thought that the American flag was the only flag our town has that represents freedom. During my on-site inspection I learned that our town has other flags that represent other important historical events in our town. For example, there is a flag that shows the date that the town was incorporated. The flags represent our town's freedom and accomplishments. I will refocus my inquiry question to include this information from my on-site inspection. Now my inquiry question is *How do flags, including the American flag, represent the history and freedom of our town and our country?*

GUIDE PRACTICE Have students analyze their findings. They may need to refocus their inquiry question to better fit the information they found. Remind students that if they have difficulty improving their focus, they can do another on-site inspection and ask local experts for guidance.

Have students continue to take notes and to record the historical information they gather on a time line.

ON THEIR OWN Have small groups of students share their inquiry questions and time lines and evaluate the information they have gathered. Students should discuss whether they need to collect additional information to answer the inquiry question. Students can brainstorm additional ideas for locations for on-site inspections.

Conventions

Capital Letters

REVIEW Remind students that this week they learned about capitalization: proper nouns, days of the week, months of the year, people's titles, abbreviations, and the first word in a sentence or greeting are all capitalized.

CONNECT TO ORAL LANGUAGE Write the following letter on the board, omitting capital letters. Have students tell which words should begin with capital letters and why.

> **sat., dec. 5, 2011**
>
> **dear principal martinez,**
>
> **our family decided that we would visit the statue of liberty in new york. the statue is a symbol of freedom. the tablet in her hand is a symbol of the declaration of independence.**
>
> **your student,**
>
> **frederico**

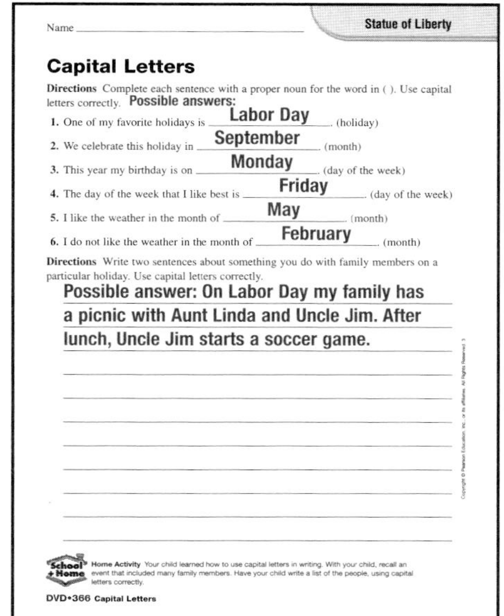

Name ______ Statue of Liberty

Capital Letters

Directions Complete each sentence with a proper noun for the word in ( ). Use capital letters correctly. **Possible answers:**

1. One of my favorite holidays is **Labor Day**. (holiday)
2. We celebrate this holiday in **September**. (month)
3. This year my birthday is on **Monday**. (day of the week)
4. The day of the week that I like best is **Friday**. (day of the week)
5. I like the weather in the month of **May**. (month)
6. I do not like the weather in the month of **February**. (month)

Directions Write two sentences about something you do with family members on a particular holiday. Use capital letters correctly.

Possible answer: On Labor Day my family has a picnic with Aunt Linda and Uncle Jim. After lunch, Uncle Jim starts a soccer game.

School + Home **Home Activity** Your child learned how to use capital letters in writing. With your child, recall an event that included many family members. Have your child write a list of the people, using capital letters correctly.

DVD•366 Capital Letters

Let's Practice It! TR DVD•366

ON THEIR OWN For additional support, use *Let's Practice It!* p. 366 on the *Teacher Resources DVD-ROM.*

Spelling

Vowel Sounds in *moon* and *foot*

FREQUENTLY MISSPELLED WORDS The words *through, took, would,* and *could* are words that students often misspell. Have students practice these words by writing the following sentences.

1. **I want to walk through the woods.**
2. **She took two cookies.**
3. **Would you please come in?**
4. **I could go for a bike ride, or I could go swimming.**

ON THEIR OWN For additional practice, use *Reader's and Writer's Notebook,* p. 394.

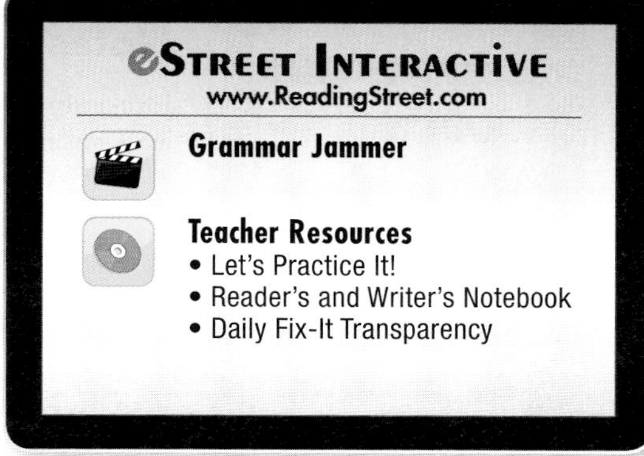

Access for All

Strategic Intervention

Have students keep track of proper nouns they hear, read, or say during the day. At the end of the day, have them write one sentence using each of the proper nouns, being careful to capitalize each one.

Daily Fix-It

5. Didnt you climb to the top of the statue on Toosday? *(Didn't; Tuesday)*
6. You cant go to the top anymore but you can go inside the base. *(can't; anymore, but)*

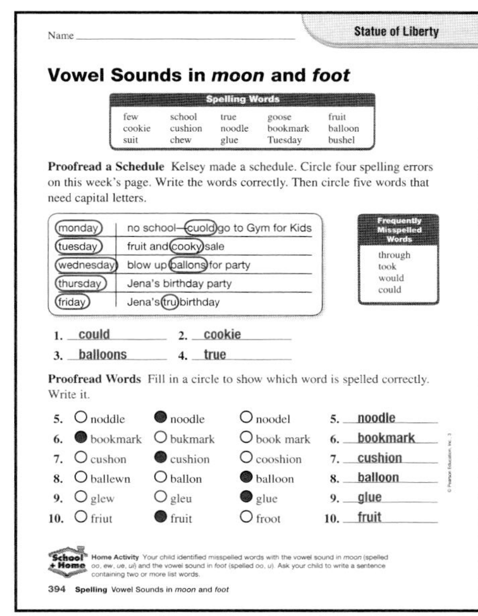

Name ______ Statue of Liberty

Vowel Sounds in *moon* and *foot*

Spelling Words				
few	school	true	goose	fruit
cookie	cushion	noodle	bookmark	balloon
suit	chew	glue	Tuesday	bushel

Proofread a Schedule Kelsey made a schedule. Circle four spelling errors on this week's page. Write the words correctly. Then circle five words that need capital letters.

monday	no school—cuold go to Gym for Kids
tuesday	fruit and cooky sale
wednesday	blow up ballons for party
thursday	Jena's birthday party
friday	Jena's tru birthday

Frequently Misspelled Words: through, took, would, could

1. **could** 2. **cookie**
3. **balloons** 4. **true**

Proofread Words Fill in a circle to show which word is spelled correctly. Write it.

5.	○ noddle	● noodle	○ noodel	5. **noodle**
6.	● bookmark	○ bukmark	○ book mark	6. **bookmark**
7.	○ cushon	● cushion	○ cooshion	7. **cushion**
8.	○ ballewn	○ ballon	● balloon	8. **balloon**
9.	○ glew	○ gleu	● glue	9. **glue**
10.	○ friut	● fruit	○ froot	10. **fruit**

School + Home **Home Activity** Your child identified misspelled words with the vowel sound in *moon* (spelled *oo, ew, ue, ui*) and the vowel sound in *foot* (spelled *oo, u*). Ask your child to write a sentence containing two or more list words.

394 **Spelling** Vowel Sounds in *moon* and *foot*

Reader's and Writer's Notebook, p. 394

Common Core State Standards
Writing 8. Recall information from experiences or gather information from print and digital sources; take brief notes on sources and sort evidence into provided categories. **Also Language 2.a.**

Let's Write It!

Key Features of Notes

- capture important ideas from a story or article
- often help with a future writing task
- may include abbreviations, short sentences, and sentence fragments

READING STREET ONLINE
GRAMMAR JAMMER
www.ReadingStreet.com

Expository

Notes

Taking **notes** helps you keep track of the most important information from an article or story. When you take notes, you write down in your own words the information that you want to make sure to remember. The student model on the next page is an example of note taking.

Writing Prompt Think about the most important ideas in *The Story of the Statue of Liberty*. Now write notes about one part of the selection.

Writer's Checklist

Remember, you should ...

- ✓ write down the most important facts and details in your own words.
- ✓ use short sentences, sentence fragments, and abbreviations.
- ✓ capitalize proper nouns, including geographical names and places.

388

Student Model

Notes on "The Story of the Statue of Liberty" (first three pages)

- the S. of L. was a gift from France to U.S., symbol of long friendship between the countries
- made by French sculptor—Frédéric Auguste Bartholdi
- built on Bedloe's Island, New York Harbor
- holds a lamp in one hand to light up the world with liberty
- holds tablet in other hand—July 4, 1776
- Bartholdi wanted statue big enough for people to climb up inside, look out over harbor
- got help from famous artists, engineers, craftsmen
- built huge skeleton out of steel
- started with statue's head and crown and her right hand

Use **capital letters** correctly to keep proper names and abbreviations clear.

Writing Trait Focus/Ideas Paraphrase the most important ideas.

Genre Notes help readers keep track of important information.

Conventions

Capital Letters

Capitalize days of the week, months of the year, countries, historical events, holidays, and other proper nouns.

389

Student Edition, pp. 388–389

Common Core State Standards

Writing 4. With guidance and support from adults, produce writing in which the development and organization are appropriate to task and purpose. **Writing 8.** Recall information from experiences or gather information from print and digital sources; take brief notes on sources and sort evidence into provided categories. **Language 2.** Demonstrate command of the conventions of standard English capitalization, punctuation, and spelling when writing. **Also Language 2.a., 3.**

Let's Write It!

WRITE NOTES Use pp. 388–389 in the Student Edition. Direct students to read the key features of notes, which appear on p. 388. Remind students that they can refer to the information in the Writer's Checklist as they write their own notes.

Read the student model on p. 389. Point out the key features of notes in the model.

CONNECT TO CONVENTIONS Remind students that the names of people, official places (for example, *the White House*), days, months, official historical events, holidays, and other proper nouns are always capitalized, even when taking notes. Also remind students that the book title uses capital letters.

Notes

Writer's Craft: Paraphrase

DISPLAY RUBRIC Display Scoring Rubric 26 from the *Teacher Resources DVD-ROM* and go over the criteria for each trait under each score. Then, using the model in the Student Edition, have student volunteers explain why the model should score a 4 for one of the traits. If a student says that the model should score below 4 for a particular trait, the student should offer support for that response. Remind students that this is the rubric that will be used to evaluate the notes they write.

Scoring Rubric Notes

	4	3	2	1
Focus/Ideas	Includes most important information from selection	Includes some important information from selection	Includes irrelevant information from selection	Does not include any important information from selection
Organization	Information is clear and orderly	Information is mostly clear and orderly	Information is somewhat clear and orderly	Information is neither clear nor orderly
Voice	Objective; no personal bias or opinions	Mostly objective; a little personal bias or opinions	Somewhat objective; some personal bias or opinions	Not objective; too much bias or personal information
Word Choice	Avoids unnecessary words and information	Uses some unnecessary words and information	Uses many unnecessary words; vague information	Notes are wordy and irrelevant
Sentences	Uses clear, short sentences and sentence fragments	Uses mostly clear, short sentences and sentence fragments	Uses somewhat clear, short sentences and fragments	Sentences are unclear or too long
Conventions	All proper nouns are capitalized	Most proper nouns are capitalized	Some proper nouns are capitalized	Few or no proper nouns are capitalized

MAIN IDEA AND DETAILS CHARTS Have students refer to the Main Idea and Details charts they created yesterday. If their charts are not complete, allow additional time for them to finish. Have students work in pairs if they are struggling to complete their charts.

WRITE You will use your Main Idea and Details charts to write the draft of your notes on the selection, *The Story of the Statue of Liberty.* When you are drafting, make sure to get the most important information down on paper. You will have time to revise tomorrow.

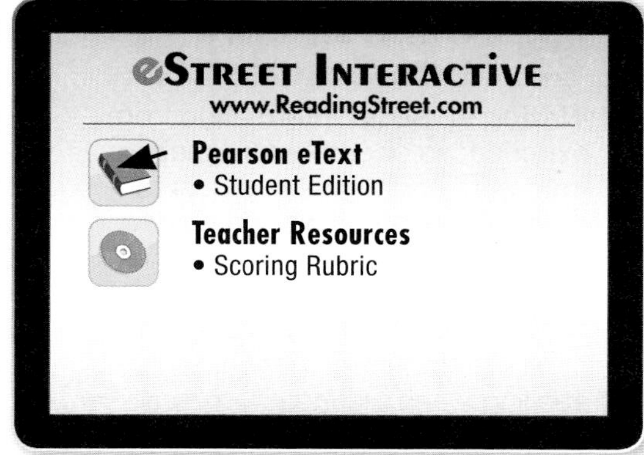

eStreet Interactive
www.ReadingStreet.com

Pearson eText
- Student Edition

Teacher Resources
- Scoring Rubric

Access for All

Point out to students that notes may differ for different purposes. For example, a research paper might require factual notes from several sources about a topic. Notes for a book review might include information about the author's opinions. Have students set a purpose for taking notes.

Key Features Make sure students understand the key features of notes by having them ask and answer the following questions orally: *What information should you write in your notes?* (I should write the most important information.) *What kind of sentences should you use?* (I should use short sentences or fragments.)

Common Core State Standards

Writing 8. Recall information from experiences or gather information from print and digital sources; take brief notes on sources and sort evidence into provided categories. **Language 2.** Demonstrate command of the conventions of standard English capitalization, punctuation, and spelling when writing.

Bridge to Common Core

RANGE OF WRITING

As students progress through the writing project, they routinely write for a range of tasks, purposes, and audiences. In this lesson, they learn the importance of putting the author's words into their own words. Taking notes also allows students to sort evidence into categories and later develop written work in which topics are supported with facts, details, and definitions.

Writing Zoom in on ©

Notes

Mini-Lesson In Your Own Words

■ **Introduce** Explain to students that when you take notes about a topic, you should paraphrase, or use your own words rather than the author's words. Paraphrasing means putting an idea in your own words. This way, if you use your notes for a future wrting project, you won't accidentally copy the author's words. Display the Note-Taking Tips for students. Remind them of the ways in which notes are different from other kinds of writing. Display Writing Transparency 26A.

Notes on *The Story of the Statue of Liberty*

(pages 380–381)

- To finish the statue, the skeleton was covered in copper
- The statue was put together in paris
- Liberty was finished in 1884
- Famous people celebrated
- Liberty has 168 steps up to her crown
- Pieces were packed for the trip across the Atlantic Ochen
- 214 crates were shipped to america

Unit 6 The Story of the Statue of Liberty Writing: Model **26A**

Writing Transparency 26A, TR DVD

Note-Taking Tips

✔ To get started, read one or two paragraphs of the selection. Think about what the most important information is. The important information can be main ideas or details.

✔ Use short sentences and sentence fragments in your notes.

✔ Remember to spell and capitalize all proper nouns correctly.

Think Aloud **MODEL** I'm going to take notes on pages 380–381 of the main selection. This part of the selection is about how the Statue of Liberty was finished in Paris. I think that how and where the statue was made is important information. I'll write this information in my own words in my notes.

Guide students through the next page of the selection, showing them where information appears in the text and in the notes. Then have students take notes on the remainder of the selection. Have students use the note-taking tips as a guide as they draft their notes. Remind them that their notes must include the most important information paraphrased, or written in their own words.

Routine Quick Write for Fluency **Team Talk**

1. **Talk** Pairs talk about what it means to put something in their own words.
2. **Write** Students write one or two sentences about what they like to do in the summer, using proper capitalization for names of people and places.
3. **Share** Pairs trade papers and try to restate their partner's sentences in their own words, retaining proper capitalization.

Routines Flip Chart

Access for All

SI Strategic Intervention

If students are having difficulty, have them work with a partner. One partner reads aloud a paragraph and then pauses while both students list important information in their notes. Then the other partner takes a turn reading aloud.

Wrap Up Your Day!

✔ **Content Knowledge** Have students discuss the importance of symbols of freedom such as the Stature of Liberty.

✔ **Text-Based Comprehension** Why is important to know which statements are fact and which are opinion? Encourage students to use evidence from the text to support their responses.

Preview DAY 4

Tell students that tomorrow they will read about people who have immigrated to the United States.

DAY 4 at a Glance

Content Knowledge
Oral Vocabulary

Phonics/Word Analysis
Review Suffixes

Social Studies in Reading
Textbook

Fluency
Rate

Vocabulary Skill
Prefix *un-*

Listening and Speaking
Announcement

Research and Inquiry
Synthesize

Conventions
Capital Letters

Spelling
Vowel Sounds in *moon* and *foot*

Writing
Notes

Materials

- Student Edition
- Reader's and Writer's Notebook
- Decodable Reader

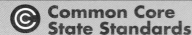

Common Core State Standards

Speaking/Listening 1. Engage effectively in a range of collaborative discussions (one-on-one, in groups, and teacher led) with diverse partners on grade 3 topics and texts, building on others' ideas and expressing their own clearly. **Language 6.** Acquire and use accurately grade-appropriate conversational, general academic, and domain-specific words and phrases, including those that signal spatial and temporal relationships (e.g., *After dinner that night we went looking for them*).

Content Knowledge

Symbols of Freedom

EXPAND THE CONCEPT Remind students of the weekly concept question, *Why do we have symbols that represent freedom?* Have students discuss symbols of freedom and why people have them.

Build Oral Language

Team Talk **TALK ABOUT SENTENCES AND WORDS** Ask students to reread these sentences from Student Edition, p. 385.

Give me your tired, your poor,
Your huddled masses yearning to breathe free,
The wretched refuse of your teeming shore.
Send these, the homeless, the tempest-tost to me,
I lift my lamp beside the golden door!

- What groups of people is the poem on the Statue of Liberty asking for? (the tired, the poor, those yearning to breathe free, the homeless, the tempest-tost) Who is being addressed in the poem? Who is "your"? What clues help you figure it out? Have students turn to a partner to share. (other countries; countries with too many people; countries without freedom; the poem mentions *shore,* which means another land; the poem is one country asking other countries to send the people who are downtrodden and perhaps unwanted.)
- What does *wretched* mean? (very unfortunate or unhappy, miserable) What are some synonyms of *wretched?* (miserable, unhappy) What does *refuse* mean? (items to be discarded; useless items) What are some synonyms of *refuse?* (rubbish, trash)
- *Teeming* means "overflowing." What is the shore overflowing with? (people) *Tempest* is an old word that means "storm." What do you think *tempest-tost* means? Why is that an appropriate phrase to have on this statue? Have students turn to a partner to share. (It means pounded by a storm; the statue is on an island welcoming people arriving by ship who may have encountered actual storms on their journey.)

Build Oral Vocabulary

Amazing Words Robust Vocabulary Routine

1. **Introduce** Write the Amazing Word *staggering* on the board. Have students say it aloud with you. Yesterday we read about how the Statue of Liberty was assembled on Bedloe's Island in New York. Why was building the Statue of Liberty a *staggering* accomplishment for that time? (It was a big accomplishment because the builders did not have the transportation options or the building tools that exist today.) Have students provide a definition of the word. (Something that is *staggering* is very surprising or huge.)
2. **Demonstrate** Have students answer questions to demonstrate understanding. Is collecting 50 pennies in a jar a *staggering* number of pennies? The White House has a table that can seat 140 guests. Is that a *staggering* number of guests for one table?
3. **Apply** Have students apply their understanding. When have you seen a *staggering* number of people?
4. **Display the Word** Write the word *staggering* on a card. Display it. Run your hand under the syllables *stag-ger-ing* as you read the word.

See p. OV•1 to teach *fund.*

Routines Flip Chart

ADD TO THE CONCEPT MAP Discuss the Amazing Words *recognizable* and *disgrace.* Add these and other concept-related words to the concept map. Use the following questions to develop students' understanding of the concept.

- What are some *recognizable* symbols of freedom?
- Why do people consider it a *disgrace* to damage or destroy a symbol?

Concept Map

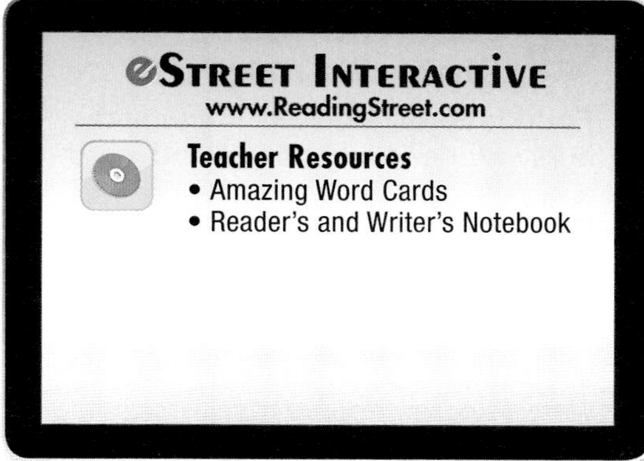

Amazing Words

impressive	competition
tribute	recognizable
enlighten	disgrace
contribution	staggering
dedication	fund

Strategy Response Log

Have students complete p. 32 in the *Reader's and Writer's Notebook.* Then have students work with a partner to answer the questions.

Produce Oral Language Use the Day 4 instruction on ELL Poster 26 to extend and enrich language.

Common Core State Standards

Foundational Skills 3. Know and apply grade-level phonics and word analysis skills in decoding words. **Foundational Skills 3.b.** Decode words with common Latin suffixes. **Language 4.b.** Determine the meaning of the new word formed when a known affix is added to a known word (e.g., *agreeable/disagreeable, comfortable/uncomfortable, care/careless, heat/preheat*).

Name ______ Statue of Liberty

Suffixes -y, -ish, -hood, -ment

Directions Read each word and circle the suffix. Write a definition of the word on the line.

1. scary that which scares a person
2. freakish like a freak
3. childish like a child
4. tasty that which tastes good
5. parenthood state of being a parent
6. employment state of being employed
7. neighborhood a place full of neighbors
8. arrangement something that has been arranged

Directions Add **-y, -ish, -hood,** or **-ment** to the base word in ( ) to best complete each sentence. Rewrite the sentence with the new word on the line.

9. A person enters (adult) around the age of eighteen.
adulthood
10. I went to bed early because I felt (fever).
feverish
11. Joe always felt (sleep) after tennis practice.
sleepy
12. The leaders made an (agree) to sign the peace treaty.
agreement
13. They have a (commit) to each other.
commitment
14. Tara has never told Kate a (false).
falsehood

School + Home **Home Activity** Your child defined and wrote words with the suffixes -y, -hood, -ish, and -ment. Help your child write a paragraph using some of the words with suffixes on this page.

Suffixes *-y, -ish, -hood, -ment* DVD•367

Let's Practice It! TR DVD•367

Phonics

Review Suffixes

REVIEW SUFFIXES To review last week's word analysis skill, write *fluffy, babyish, motherhood,* and *statement.* You studied words like these last week. What do you know about reading words with suffixes? (Read the base word first. Then read the suffix. Put the parts together to read the word.) What is the base word in the first word? *(fluff)* What is the suffix? *(-y)* Let's read the whole word: *fluffy.* Remember, the suffix *-y* means "like or having the quality of." Continue in the same way for the other words. Remind students that the suffix *-ish* means "like"; *-hood* means "state or condition"; and *-ment* means "act of."

Corrective feedback

If... students are unable to answer the questions about suffixes,
then... refer them to *Sound-Spelling Cards* 168, 170, 174, and 177.

GUIDE PRACTICE Display a three-column chart. I'll write a word in the first column. Write *chilly.* Then I will read the base word and write that word in the second column. Write *chill.* I will write the suffix in the third column. Write *y.* Let's put the parts together to read the word. *(chilly)* Continue writing words and having students read the base word, the suffix, and then the word.

Word	Base	Suffix
chilly	chill	-y
sisterhood	sister	-hood
selfish	self	-ish
government	govern	-ment
speedy	speed	-y
amusement	amuse	-ment

ON THEIR OWN For additional practice, use *Let's Practice It!* p. 367 on the *Teacher Resources DVD-ROM.*

Fluent Word Reading

Spiral Review

READ WORDS IN ISOLATION Display these words. Tell students that they can decode some words on this list. Explain that other words they should know because they appear often in reading.

Have students read the list three or four times until they can read at the rate of two to three seconds per word.

Word Reading

two	**eight**	**reins**	**reindeer**	**people**
neighbor's	**height**	**receipt**	**full**	**were**
many	**sleigh**	**thought**	**bought**	**ought**
all	**have**	**caused**	**seized**	**caught**

Corrective feedback

If... students have difficulty reading whole words,
then... have them use sound-by-sound blending for decodable words or chunking for words that have word parts, or have them say and spell high-frequency words.

If... students cannot read fluently at a rate of two to three seconds per word,
then... have pairs practice the list until they can read it fluently.

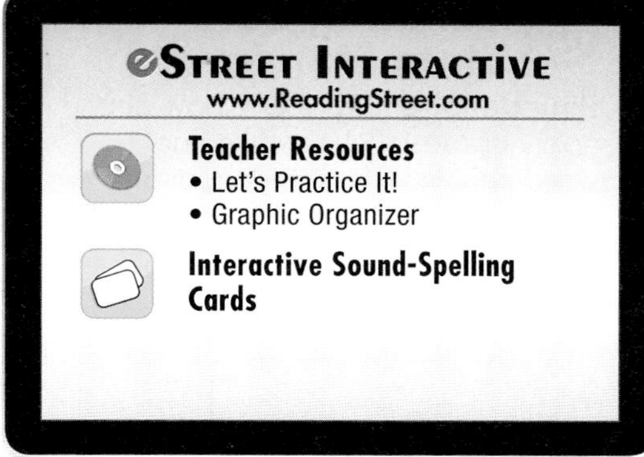

Access for All

Strategic Intervention

To assist students having difficulty decoding words with long *a* spelled *ei* or *eigh,* focus on one spelling at a time. Write words with long *a* spelled *ei,* such as *rein, vein,* and *veil.* Have students read the words with you and identify the letters that spell the vowel sound. Repeat with long *a* spelled *eigh (eight, weight, neighbor, sleigh).*

Spiral Review

These activities review

- previously taught high-frequency words *full, have, many, people, two, were.*
- words with long *a, e,* or *i* spelled *ei* or *eigh;* words with /ȯ/ spelled *a, au, aw, al, augh, ough.*

Fluent Word Reading Have students listen to a more fluent reader say the words. Then have them repeat the words.

Common Core State Standards

Foundational Skills 3. Know and apply grade-level phonics and word analysis skills in decoding words. **Foundational Skills 3.d.** Read grade-appropriate irregularly spelled words. **Foundational Skills 4.** Read with sufficient accuracy and fluency to support comprehension.

Fluent Word Reading

READ WORDS IN CONTEXT Display these sentences. Call on individuals to read a sentence. Then randomly point to review words and have students read them. To help you monitor word reading, high-frequency words are underlined and decodable words are italicized.

MONITOR PROGRESS Sentence Reading

We *all ought* to find what our *height* is.
Do you <u>have</u> a *receipt* for the <u>two</u> things you *bought*?
We <u>were</u> excited to see *eight reindeer* pulling a *sleigh* <u>full</u> of toys.
Dad *seized* the *reins* and *caught* our *neighbor's* horse.
She *thought* the ice *caused* <u>many</u> <u>people</u> to slip.

If… students are unable to read an underlined high-frequency word,
then… read the word for them and spell it, having them echo you.
If… students have difficulty reading an italicized decodable word,
then… guide them in using sound-by-sound blending or chunking.

Reread for Fluency

Have students reread the sentences to develop automaticity decoding words.

Routine Oral Rereading

1. **Read** Have students read all the sentences orally.
2. **Reread** To achieve optimal fluency, students should reread the sentences three or four times.
3. **Corrective Feedback** Listen as students read. Provide corrective feedback regarding their fluency and decoding.

Routines Flip Chart

Decodable Passage 26C

If students need help, then...

Read *Balloons!*

READ WORDS IN ISOLATION Have students turn to p. 131 in *Decodable Practice Readers 3.2* and find the first list of words. Each word in this list has the vowel sound /ü/, spelled *oo, ew, ue, ui,* or /u̇/, spelled *oo* and *u.* Let's blend and read these words. Be sure that students identify the correct vowel sound in each word.

Next, have students read the high-frequency words.

PREVIEW Have students read the title and preview the story. Tell them that they will read words with vowel sounds /ü/ and /u̇/.

READ WORDS IN CONTEXT Chorally read the story with students. Have students identify words in the story that have the vowel sounds /ü/ and /u̇/. Make sure that students are monitoring their accuracy when they decode words.

Team Talk Pair students and have them take turns reading the story aloud to each other. Monitor students as they read to check for proper pronunciation and appropriate pacing.

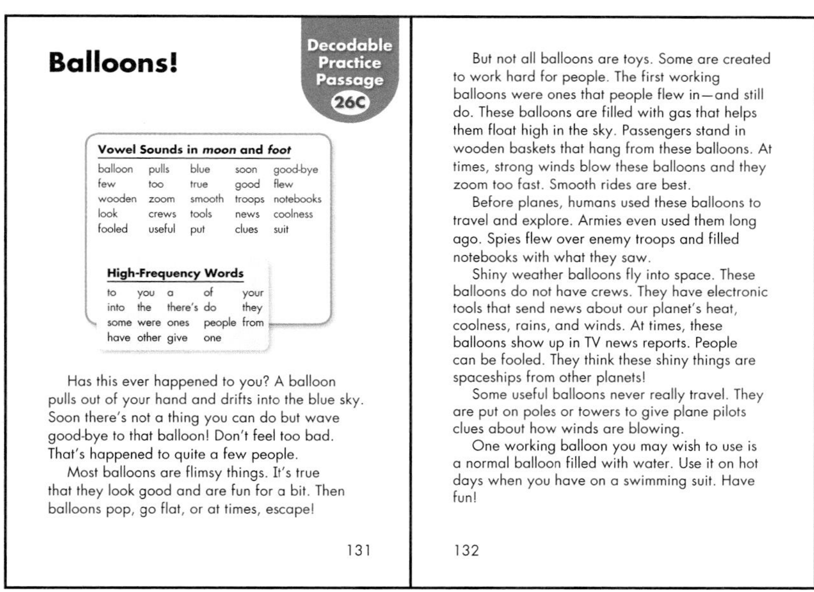

Balloons!

Decodable Practice Passage 26C

Vowel Sounds in *moon* and *foot*

balloon	pulls	blue	soon	good-bye
few	too	true	good	flew
wooden	zoom	smooth	troops	notebooks
look	crews	tools	news	coolness
fooled	useful	put	clues	suit

High-Frequency Words

to	you	a	of	your
into	the	there's	do	they
some	were	ones	people	from
have	other	give	one	

Has this ever happened to you? A balloon pulls out of your hand and drifts into the blue sky. Soon there's not a thing you can do but wave good-bye to that balloon! Don't feel too bad. That's happened to quite a few people.

Most balloons are flimsy things. It's true that they look good and are fun for a bit. Then balloons pop, go flat, or at times, escape!

131

But not all balloons are toys. Some are created to work hard for people. The first working balloons were ones that people flew in—and still do. These balloons are filled with gas that helps them float high in the sky. Passengers stand in wooden baskets that hang from these balloons. At times, strong winds blow these balloons and they zoom too fast. Smooth rides are best.

Before planes, humans used these balloons to travel and explore. Armies even used them long ago. Spies flew over enemy troops and filled notebooks with what they saw.

Shiny weather balloons fly into space. These balloons do not have crews. They have electronic tools that send news about our planet's heat, coolness, rains, and winds. At times, these balloons show up in TV news reports. People can be fooled. They think these shiny things are spaceships from other planets!

Some useful balloons never really travel. They are put on poles or towers to give plane pilots clues about how winds are blowing.

One working balloon you may wish to use is a normal balloon filled with water. Use it on hot days when you have on a swimming suit. Have fun!

132

Decodable Practice Passage 26C

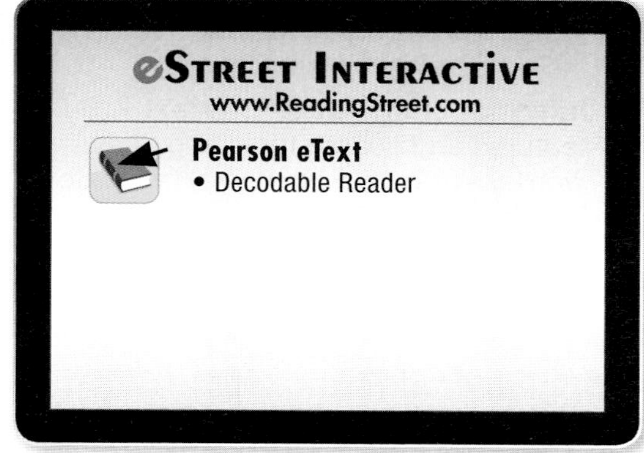

Access for All

Advanced

Have students write their own sentences using some of the decodable words in the sentences on p. 390e.

Common Core State Standards

Informational Text 5. Use text features and search tools (e.g., key words, sidebars, hyperlinks) to locate information relevant to a given topic efficiently.

Bridge to Common Core

KEY IDEAS AND DETAILS

Reading a textbook to find out more about immigrants will lead students to build a foundation of knowledge. By reading the textbook pages closely, students will be able to determine the central ideas and summarize the key details of the information presented.

Social Studies in Reading

Textbook

INTRODUCE Explain to students that what we read is structured differently depending on the author's reasons for writing and what kind of information he or she wishes to convey. Different types of texts are called genres. Tell them that a textbook is one genre.

DISCUSS THE GENRE Remind students that a textbook is a type of reference source, and a reference source is a type of expository text. Remind students that a textbook can be about any subject taught in school.

GROUP PRACTICE Display a T-chart like the one shown below. Label the columns *Graphic Source or Text Feature* and *Purpose.* Ask the following questions:

- What text features are in most textbooks? (tables of contents, chapters, heads, subheads)
- Why does a textbook have a table of contents? (It helps the reader find information.)
- Why do many textbooks include graphic sources, such as charts? (Graphic sources can make information easier for readers to understand.)
- How can graphic sources help when you preview a textbook? (They let you know what kind of information you will find in the book before you begin reading.)

Graphic Source or Text Feature	Purpose
table of contents	helps find information
chart	makes information clear

Team Talk Have students work in pairs to discuss and list the parts of a textbook and their purposes. Ask them to share their lists with the class.

READ Tell students that they will now read about why, how, and when immigrants came to the United States. Have students think about why their ancestors may have come to the United States.

Academic Vocabulary

textbook a reference source usually written about a specific topic

ELL

Graphic Organizer Provide support to students when creating a T-chart. Show them different textbooks so they can understand the different elements in this genre.

Day 4 SMALL GROUP TIME • Differentiate Vocabulary, p. SG•1

OL On-Level	SI Strategic Intervention	A Advanced
• **Develop** Language Using Amazing Words • **Read** "A Nation of Immigrants"	• **Review/Discuss** Amazing Words • **Read** "A Nation of Immigrants"	• **Extend** Amazing Words and Selection Vocabulary • **Read** "A Nation of Immigrants" • **Organize** Inquiry Project

ELL

If... students need more scaffolding and practice with the **Amazing Words,**
then... use the Routine on pp. xxxvi–xxxvii in the *ELL Handbook.*

Common Core State Standards
Informational Text 5. Use text features and search tools (e.g., key words, sidebars, hyperlinks) to locate information relevant to a given topic efficiently.

Social Studies in Reading

Genre
Textbook

- A textbook is a source of information, usually written about a specific topic.
- Textbooks use text features to help readers locate and remember the information.
- Textbook authors often use graphic sources, such as charts, to organize information visually.
- As you read "A Nation of Immigrants," think about how the chart and photos relate to the text.

A Nation of Immigrants

For decades, immigrants have come to the United States from almost every other country in the world. Some people wanted freedom or better opportunities. Some came because there was very little food in their home country. Some came to find jobs or to work on farms. Others came because they had no choice.

Ellis Island

Many ships that came from Europe arrived first at Ellis Island, in New York Harbor. Many immigrants from Asia arrived at Angel Island, in San Francisco Bay. Immigrants also entered through other cities, such as Boston, Massachusetts; Galveston, Texas; and New Orleans, Louisiana.

REVIEW What were some reasons immigrants came to the United States?

390

Times When Many Immigrants Came

Time Period	Where Many Were From
Before 1820	United Kingdom, countries of Western Africa, such as those now known as Ghana, Togo, Benin, Nigeria, and Cameroon
1820–1860	Ireland, Germany, United Kingdom, France, Canada
1861–1890	Germany, United Kingdom, Ireland, Canada, Norway/Sweden
1891–1920	Italy, Austria/Hungary, Russia, United Kingdom, Germany
1961–1990	Mexico, Philippines, Canada, Korea, Cuba

Angel Island

Let's Think About...

How do the text features and graphic sources help you learn the important ideas? **Textbook**

Let's Think About...

Reading Across Texts Immigrants from which countries would have been the first to see the new Statue of Liberty on Bedloe's Island? How do you know?

Writing Across Texts Imagine that you are one of those immigrants. Write a journal entry telling your impression of the Statue of Liberty.

391

Student Edition, pp. 390–391

Common Core State Standards

Informational Text 5. Use text features and search tools (e.g., key words, sidebars, hyperlinks) to locate information relevant to a given topic efficiently. **Informational Text 7.** Use information gained from illustrations (e.g., maps, photographs), and the words in a text to demonstrate understanding of the text (e.g., where, when, why, and how key events occur).

Access Text

TEACH Genre: Textbook Have students preview "A Nation of Immigrants" on pp. 390–391. Have them identify and discuss the text features and graphics in the text. Ask students: What does the chart on page 391 tell you? How does the chart organize the information?

Corrective feedback
If... students are unable to identify the topic of the chart and how the information is organized,
then... model how to interpret information in a chart.

MODEL The title tells me that the chart gives information about when immigrants came to the United States. The chart organizes information in rows and columns. What is the heading of the first column? (Time Period) That column shows the periods of time when immigrants came. What is the heading of the other column? (Where Many Were From) The other column shows the countries that immigrants came from during each time period.

ON THEIR OWN Have students work in pairs to continue previewing text features and graphics. Have pairs tell about the features that they identify.

Close Reading

ANALYSIS • TEXT EVIDENCE Immigrants coming to the United States is an effect. What were some causes? (lack of jobs, opportunities, or food where they lived, lack of freedom)

EVALUATION Is this sentence a statement of fact or opinion? *Many immigrants from Asia arrived at Angel Island in San Francisco Bay.* How do you know? (The sentence is a statement of fact because it can be proved true or false.)

ANALYSIS What questions can you ask to help you better understand the text? (Why did some people have "no choice" about coming? Why did many people from Western Africa come before 1820?)

Genre

LET'S THINK ABOUT... As you read "A Nation of Immigrants," use Let's Think About in the Student Edition to help students focus on the features of a textbook.

1 The photos and captions show what Ellis Island and Angel Island look like. The chart gives additional information about when immigrants came to the United States and where they came from.

Reading and Writing Across Texts

Have students review p. 383 to locate the date that the Statue of Liberty was completed on Bedloe's Island. (1886) Then have them look at the chart to find the time period that includes the date. Before they write, have students review *The Story of the Statue of Liberty* for details about the statue's design and think about what they have learned about why immigrants came.

Access for All

 Strategic Intervention

Review the concept of cause and effect. Give students additional examples of cause and effect. Then have pairs write a cause-and-effect statement.

 Advanced

Tell students that genealogy is the study of family ancestors. Have students talk to family members about their ancestors and use the information to create a genealogical chart (family tree).

Connect to Social Studies

Island of Hope For many years, Ellis Island was the chief immigration station for the United States. Between 1892 and 1954, over twelve million immigrants entered the United States via the Ellis Island station.

Visual Learning: Graphic Sources Provide extra practice with interpreting textbook graphics. Call on volunteers to tell what they know about different graphics in their textbooks. Point out the key features of each type of graphic. Then focus students' attention on the chart on p. 391 and say: A chart has rows and columns. There is information in each space. The columns are labeled with headings. What are the headings on this chart? What do the headings tell you?

Vocabulary

Prefix *un-*

Word Structure Use your knowledge of the structure of words to understand the meanings of words. You can figure out the meaning of a word with a prefix if you know what the base word and the prefix both mean. The prefix *un-* means "not" or "the opposite of."

Practice It! Using a sheet of paper, predict the meanings of the following words, based on your understanding of the prefix *un-*: *unhappy, unfamiliar, unkind, unlike, unfinished, unforgettable.*

Fluency

Rate

Rate is an important skill for comprehending what you read. You can improve the rate at which you read by reading a text more than once. Then you can use a rate that matches the mood of the text.

Practice It! With a classmate, practice reading aloud page 381 of *The Story of the Statue of Liberty.* Read the page a second time. Did your rate improve? How quickly should you read to match the mood of the text?

392

Listening and Speaking

Get Ready For Middle School: When making an announcement, use formal language.

Announcement

In an announcement, give information about a certain topic to inform or persuade listeners.

Practice It! Prepare an announcement about a new sculpture that is being put up in your city or town. Your announcement should be two minutes long. Include all the information a listener would need to find the new sculpture and attend the unveiling.

Tips

Listening . . .
- Listen attentively.
- Ask relevant questions.

Speaking . . .
- Speak at an appropriate pace.
- Use verbal cues.

Teamwork . . .
- Ask and answer questions about the differences between radio and TV announcements.
- Give suggestions for ways to influence or enhance the message.

393

Student Edition, pp. 392–393

Common Core State Standards

Foundational Skills 4.b. Read on-level prose and poetry orally with accuracy, appropriate rate, and expression on successive readings. **Speaking/Listening 4.** Report on a topic or text, tell a story, or recount an experience with appropriate facts and relevant, descriptive details, speaking clearly at an understandable pace. **Language 4.b.** Determine the meaning of the new word formed when a known affix is added to a known word (e.g., *agreeable/disagreeable, comfortable/uncomfortable, care/careless, heat/preheat*). **Also Speaking/Listening 1.b.**

Fluency

Rate

GUIDE PRACTICE Use the Fluency activity as an assessment tool. Make sure the reading passage is at least 200 words in length. As students read, make sure their reading rate is appropriate for the text.

Don't Wait Until Friday **MONITOR PROGRESS** Check Fluency

FORMATIVE ASSESSMENT As students reread, monitor their progress toward their individual fluency goals.
Current Goal: 110–120 words correct per minute
End–of–Year Goal: 120 words correct per minute

If... students cannot read fluently at a rate of 110–120 words correct per minute,
then... have students practice with text at their independent levels.

Vocabulary Skill

Prefix *un-*

TEACH PREFIX *un-* • WORD STRUCTURE Tell students that they can use their knowledge of word structure to understand the meanings of words. If they know the meaning of the base word and the meaning of the prefix or suffix, they can figure out the word's meaning. Write *unknown* on the board. Cover *un-* and ask students to tell the meaning of *known.* Explain that the prefix *un-* means "not" or "the opposite of." Write *not known* on the board.

GUIDE PRACTICE Have students work in pairs to write the base words for *unhappy, unfamiliar, unkind, unlike, unfinished,* and *unforgettable.* Have them discuss the meaning of each base word and how *un-* changes the meaning of the base word.

ON THEIR OWN Walk around the room as partners discuss what the prefix *un-* adds to the base word. Check to make sure that partners correctly predict the meaning of each word.

Listening and Speaking

Announcement

TEACH Tell students that they will make an announcement about a new sculpture. Explain that their announcement should name the sculpture and the artist who created it and explain why it was created. Encourage students to use descriptive words and offer complimentary opinions about the sculpture. Suggest that students conclude their announcements by explaining when and where the unveiling will take place.

GUIDE PRACTICE Remind students to be aware of the nonverbal cues they use when they are speaking, including facial expressions and body language. Encourage them to speak coherently, employing eye contact, speaking rate, volume, enunciation, and conventions of language to communicate their ideas effectively. Remind students to listen attentively when others are speaking.

ON THEIR OWN Have students write their announcements. Have them time themselves when they practice reading the announcements to be sure they are about two minutes long.

Announcement

Tell students that they should deliver oral presentations that employ conventions of language to communicate ideas effectively. Their presentation should use standard English, appropriate grade-level vocabulary, and grammatically correct sentences. Speakers should also use parts of speech correctly and observe usage rules.

Bridge to Common Core

PRESENTATION OF KNOWLEDGE/ IDEAS

As students make their announcements, they should build anticipation for the statue. They should use appropriate phrasing and present their descriptions in an organized way, focusing first on the physical characteristics of the statue and then offering their opinions of it. They might include media, such as appropriate music.

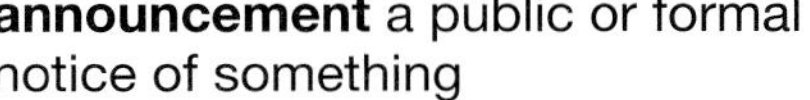

Academic Vocabulary

announcement a public or formal notice of something

Word Structure Review roots, prefixes, and suffixes. Write words on the board and help students identify the roots. Then have volunteers circle the prefixes and underline the suffixes in the word. Finally, have students use the words in sentences that show they understand the words' meanings.

Common Core State Standards

Writing 6. With guidance and support from adults, use technology to produce and publish writing (using keyboarding skills) as well as to interact and collaborate with others. **Writing 10.** Write routinely over extended time frames (time for research, reflection, and revision) and shorter time frames (a single sitting or a day or two) for a range of discipline-specific tasks, purposes, and audiences. **Language 2.** Demonstrate command of the conventions of standard English capitalization, punctuation, and spelling when writing. **Language 2.f.** Use spelling patterns and generalizations (e.g., word families, position-based spellings, syllable patterns, ending rules, meaningful word parts) in writing words.

Research and Inquiry

Step 4 Synthesize

TEACH Have students synthesize their research findings and results. Explain that when they synthesize, they combine relevant ideas from multiple sources of oral and written information to create an answer to their inquiry questions. Remind students that they can record historical information about symbols that they gather in a time line. Review how to choose relevant information from a number of sources and organize it logically. After students have reviewed their material, have them synthesize information by combining the most important pieces of information from reference texts and on-site inspections into a short paragraph.

GUIDE PRACTICE Have students use a word processing program or poster board to prepare for their presentations on Day 5. If students are using a time line, check to see that students are recording information in chronological order. Students' time lines should include the most important information from multiple sources, including reference texts and their on-site inspections.

ON THEIR OWN Have students write a brief informational article about their research findings. Then have them organize and combine information for their presentations.

Conventions

Capital Letters

TEST PRACTICE Remind students that grammar skills, such as recognizing and using correct capitalization, are often assessed on important tests. Remind students that proper nouns such as names of days of the week, months of the year, holidays, and historical periods; geographical place names; titles before names; abbreviations; and the first word in a sentence or greeting are capitalized.

ON THEIR OWN For additional practice, use *Reader's and Writer's Notebook,* p. 395.

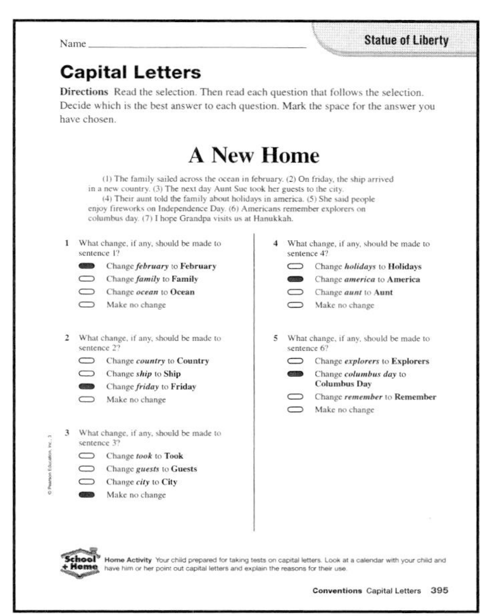

Name ____________ Statue of Liberty

Capital Letters

Directions Read the selection. Then read each question that follows the selection. Decide which is the best answer to each question. Mark the space for the answer you have chosen.

A New Home

(1) The family sailed across the ocean in february. (2) On friday, the ship arrived in a new country. (3) The next day Aunt Sue took her guests to the city.

(4) Their aunt told the family about holidays in america. (5) She said people enjoy fireworks on Independence Day. (6) Americans remember explorers on columbus day. (7) I hope Grandpa visits us at Hanukkah.

1 What change, if any, should be made to sentence 1?
- ● Change *february* to **February**
- ○ Change *family* to **Family**
- ○ Change *ocean* to **Ocean**
- ○ Make no change

2 What change, if any, should be made to sentence 2?
- ○ Change *country* to **Country**
- ○ Change *ship* to **Ship**
- ● Change *friday* to **Friday**
- ○ Make no change

3 What change, if any, should be made to sentence 3?
- ○ Change *took* to **Took**
- ○ Change *guests* to **Guests**
- ○ Change *city* to **City**
- ● Make no change

4 What change, if any, should be made to sentence 4?
- ○ Change *holidays* to **Holidays**
- ● Change *america* to **America**
- ○ Change *aunt* to **Aunt**
- ○ Make no change

5 What change, if any, should be made to sentence 6?
- ○ Change *explorers* to **Explorers**
- ● Change *columbus day* to **Columbus Day**
- ○ Change *remember* to **Remember**
- ○ Make no change

© Pearson Education, Inc., 3

School + Home **Home Activity** Your child prepared for taking tests on capital letters. Look at a calendar with your child and have him or her point out capital letters and explain the reasons for their use.

Conventions Capital Letters 395

Reader's and Writer's Notebook, p. 395

Spelling

Vowel Sounds in *moon* and *foot*

PRACTICE SPELLING STRATEGY Supply pairs of students with index cards on which the spelling words have been written. Have one student read a word while the other writes it. Then have students switch roles. Have them use the cards to check their spelling and correct any misspelled words.

ON THEIR OWN For additional practice, use *Let's Practice It!* p. 368 on the *Teacher Resources DVD-ROM.*

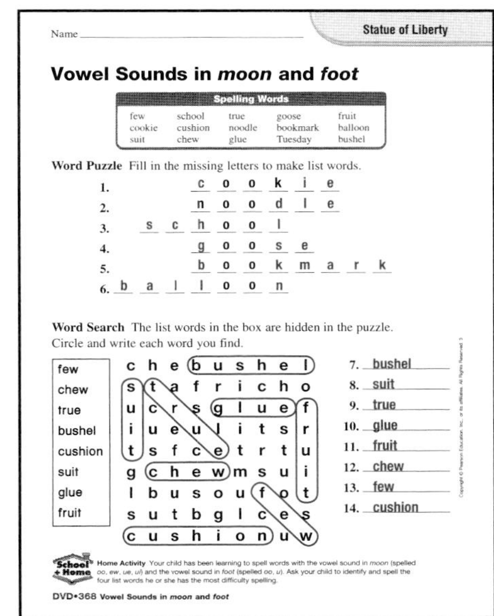

Name ____________ Statue of Liberty

Vowel Sounds in *moon* and *foot*

Spelling Words				
few	school	true	goose	fruit
cookie	cushion	noodle	bookmark	balloon
suit	chew	glue	Tuesday	bushel

Word Puzzle Fill in the missing letters to make list words.

1. c o o k i e
2. n o o d l e
3. s c h o o l
4. g o o s e
5. b o o k m a r k
6. b a l l o o n

Word Search The list words in the box are hidden in the puzzle. Circle and write each word you find.

few
chew
true
bushel
cushion
suit
glue
fruit

c h e b u s h e l
s t a f r i c h o
u c r s g l u e f
i u e u l i t s r
t s f c e t r t u
g c h e w m s u i
l b u s o u f o t
s u t b g l c e s
c u s h i o n u w

7. bushel
8. suit
9. true
10. glue
11. fruit
12. chew
13. few
14. cushion

Copyright © Pearson Education, Inc., or its affiliates. All Rights Reserved. 3

School + Home **Home Activity** Your child has been learning to spell words with the vowel sound in *moon* (spelled *oo, ew, ue, ui*) and the vowel sound in *foot* (spelled *oo, u*). Ask your child to identify and spell the four list words he or she has the most difficulty spelling.

DVD•368 Vowel Sounds in *moon* and *foot*

Let's Practice It! TR DVD•368

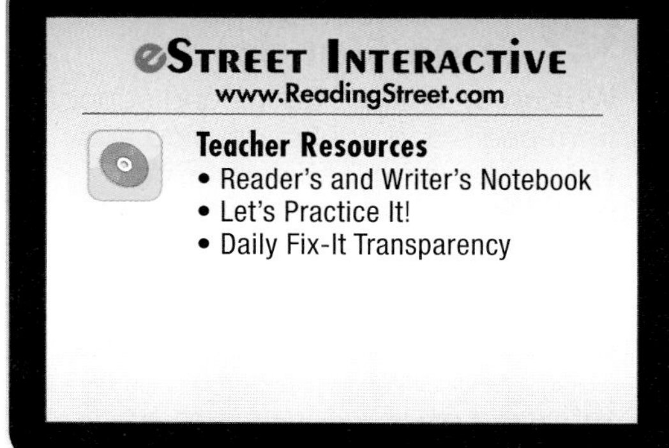

Daily Fix-It

7. Fue people had saw the Statue of Liberty until 1886. *(Few; seen)*
8. The statues torch shines over every one. *(statue's; everyone)*

Bridge to Common Core

CONVENTIONS OF STANDARD ENGLISH

As students correctly use capital letters, they are demonstrating command of the conventions of standard English. Your guidance will help them apply correct grammar, usage, and spelling to convey meaning when they speak and write.

Common Core State Standards

Writing 5. With guidance and support from peers and adults, develop and strengthen writing as needed by planning, revising, and editing. **Also Writing 8., 10.**

Write Guy *by Jeff Anderson*

Experiment *and* Use What You Know!

Encourage students to experiment or stretch themselves to try new things with spelling, punctuation, and grammar. Though they shouldn't "worry" about it when drafting, they can make an attempt to use all that they know. Reward students when they reach to spell a word.

Writing

Notes

Mini-Lesson Revise: Adding

- Yesterday we took notes on the selection, *The Story of the Statue of Liberty.* Today we will reread the selection and add any information to our notes we may have missed the first time. The goal is to make your notes clearer, more complete, and more accurate.
- Display Writing Transparency 26B. Remind students that revising does not include corrections of grammar and mechanics. Tell them that this will be done during the lesson as they proofread their work. Then introduce the revising strategy of adding.
- As I reread pp. 380–381, I can see that it wasn't just famous people who celebrated. I'll change that note so it just says "People celebrated." I can also see that I left out how the statue was taken apart to be shipped. That is important, so I'll add another bullet point with this information.

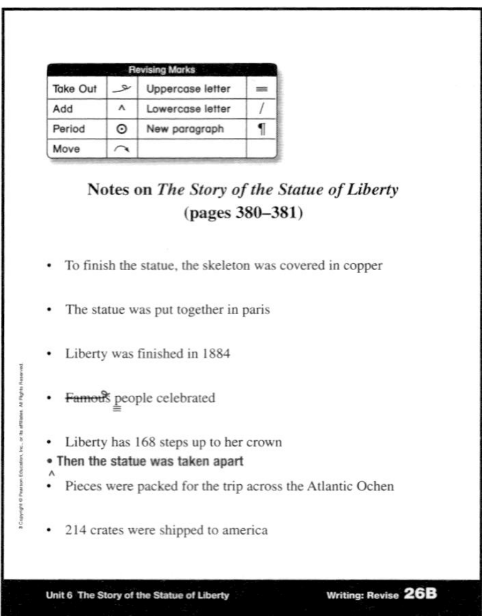

Revising Marks			
Take Out	⤼	Uppercase letter	≡
Add	^	Lowercase letter	/
Period	⊙	New paragraph	¶
Move	⌒		

Notes on *The Story of the Statue of Liberty* (pages 380–381)

- To finish the statue, the skeleton was covered in copper
- The statue was put together in paris
- Liberty was finished in 1884
- ~~Famous~~ people celebrated
- Liberty has 168 steps up to her crown
- **Then the statue was taken apart**
- Pieces were packed for the trip across the Atlantic Ochen
- 214 crates were shipped to america

Unit 6 The Story of the Statue of Liberty Writing: Revise **26B**

Writing Transparency 26B, TR DVD

Tell students that as they revise, they should look for places where they might add information to make their notes clearer and more accurate. Display the Revising Tips for students.

Revising Tips

- ✔ Make sure that all the important information is included in your notes.
- ✔ Check to make sure your original notes are correct, especially dates.
- ✔ Check the spellings of proper nouns.

PEER CONFERENCING • PEER REVISION Have students work with a partner to review their notes. Partners should read each other's notes and suggest information that should be added or correct information that is inaccurate.

Have students finish checking their notes for accuracy and completeness. They should use the suggestions their partner wrote during Peer Revision as well as the key features of notes to guide their revision. Be sure that students are using the revising strategy of adding.

Corrective feedback Circulate around the room to monitor and confer with students as they revise. Remind any students correcting errors that they will have time to edit tomorrow. They should be working on content today.

eStreet Interactive
www.ReadingStreet.com
Teacher Resources
- Writing Transparency

Routine Quick Write for Fluency

1. **Talk** Pairs talk about what they learned about the Statue of Liberty.
2. **Write** Each student writes a paragraph telling three things he or she learned about the statue from the selection.
3. **Share** Pairs read their paragraphs to each other and then check each other's paragraphs for important ideas and correct information, such as dates.

Routines Flip Chart

ELL

Identifying Important Information
Help students identify important information that they may have missed in their notes. Read aloud the text on which students have taken notes. Ask students to call out important people, places, objects, or events. Then have them include short sentences or phrases containing these words.

Wrap Up Your Day!

- ✔ **Content Knowledge** Have students discuss how people feel when they see symbols of freedom.
- ✔ **Oral Vocabulary** Monitor students' use of oral vocabulary as they respond to this question: *Why is Ellis Island recognizable as a tribute to immigrants?*
- ✔ **Text Features** Discuss how the chart helps students understand the chronology of the immigration to the United States.

Preview DAY 5

Remind students to think about why we have symbols to represent freedom.

DAY 5 at a Glance

Content Knowledge

Text-Based Comprehension
Review Fact and Opinion

Vocabulary Skill
Review Prefix *un-*

Phonics/Word Analysis
Review Vowel Sounds /ü/ and /u̇/

Literary Terms
Review Word Choice

Assessment
Fluency
Comprehension

Research and Inquiry
Communicate

Spelling
Vowel Sounds in *moon* and *foot*

Conventions
Capital Letters

Writing
Notes

Materials

- Student Edition
- Weekly Test
- Reader's and Writer's Notebook

Bridge to Common Core

INTEGRATION OF KNOWLEDGE/IDEAS

This week, students have integrated content presented in diverse media and analyzed how different texts address similar topics. They have developed knowledge about why people have symbols that represent freedom to expand the unit topic of Freedom.

Social Studies Knowledge Goals

Students have learned that symbols

- remind us of our history
- remind us of our unity
- stand for freedom

Content Knowledge

Symbols of Freedom

REVIEW THE CONCEPT Have students look back at the reading selections to find examples that best demonstrate why we have symbols that represent freedom.

Build Oral Language

REVIEW AMAZING WORDS Display and review this week's concept map. Remind students that this week they have learned ten Amazing Words related to symbols of freedom. Have students use the Amazing Words and the concept map to answer the Question of the Week, *Why do we have symbols that represent freedom?*

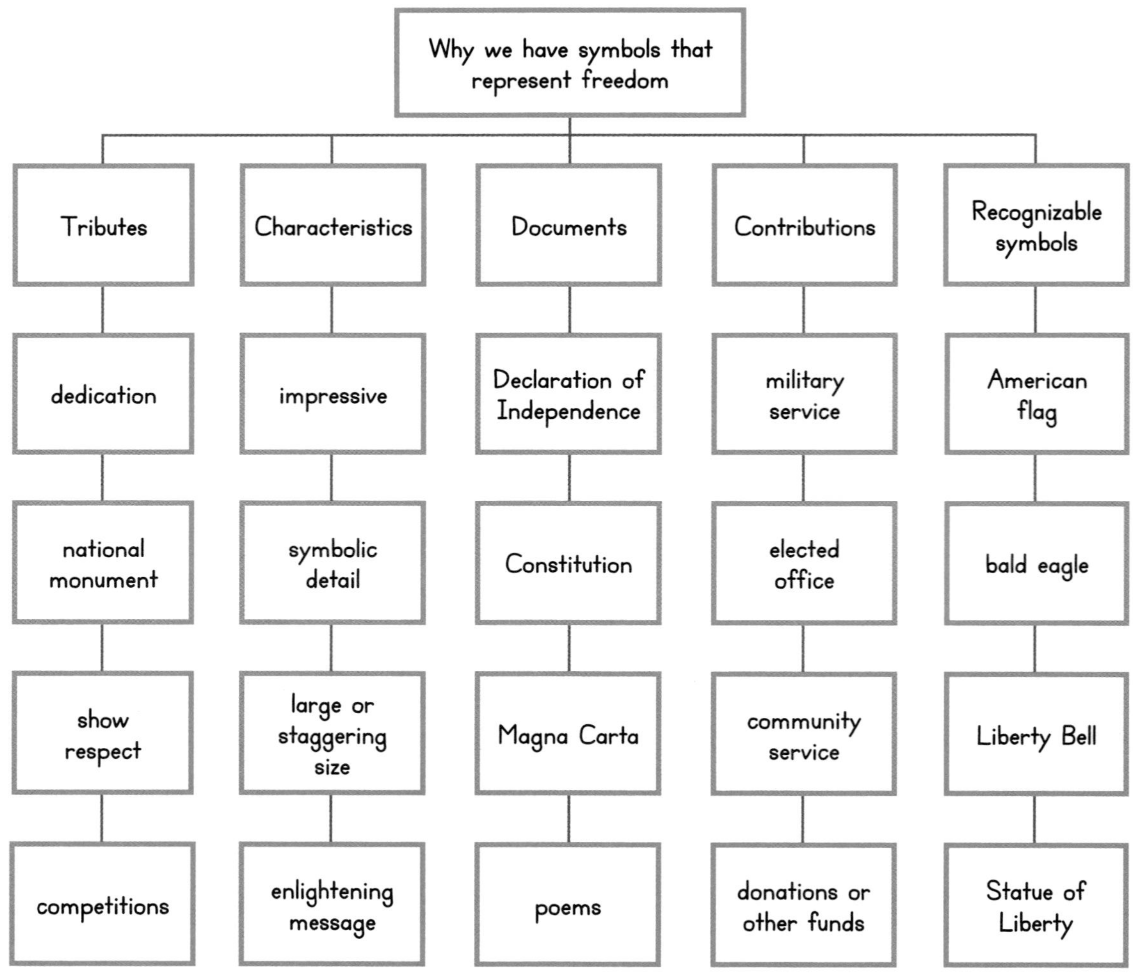

Build Oral Vocabulary

Team Talk **CONNECT TO AMAZING IDEAS** Have pairs of students discuss how the Question of the Week connects to the question for this unit of study, *What does freedom mean?* Tell students to use the concept map and what they have learned from this week's discussions and reading selections to form an Amazing Idea—a realization or "big idea" about Freedom. Remind partners to give suggestions that build on each other's ideas. Then ask each pair to share its Amazing Idea with the class.

Amazing Ideas might include these key concepts:

- Freedom allows people to do, say, and think what they want.
- Symbols that represent freedom remind us of the contributions and sacrifices people have made to protect this idea.

WRITE ABOUT IT Have students write a few sentences about their Amazing Idea, beginning with "This week I learned . . ."

It's Friday

MONITOR PROGRESS

Check Oral Vocabulary

FORMATIVE ASSESSMENT Have individuals use this week's Amazing Words to describe symbols that represent freedom. Monitor students' abilities to use the Amazing Words and note which words you need to reteach.

If... students have difficulty using the Amazing Words,

then... reteach using the Robust Vocabulary Routine on pp. 367a, 372b, 382b, 390b, and OV•1.

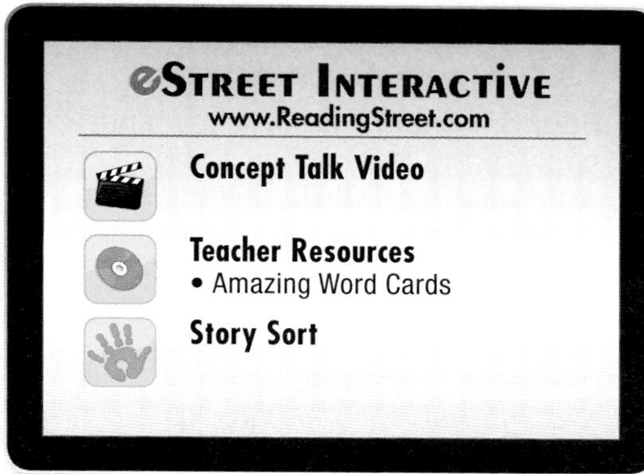

Amazing Words

impressive	competition
tribute	recognizable
enlighten	disgrace
contribution	staggering
dedication	fund

Check Concept and Language Use the Day 5 instruction on ELL Poster 26 to monitor students' understanding of the lesson concept.

Common Core State Standards

Foundational Skills 3. Know and apply grade-level phonics and word analysis skills in decoding words. **Language 4.b.** Determine the meaning of the new word formed when a known affix is added to a known word (e.g., *agreeable/ disagreeable, comfortable/ uncomfortable, care/ careless, heat/preheat*). **Also Informational Text 8., Language 3.a.**

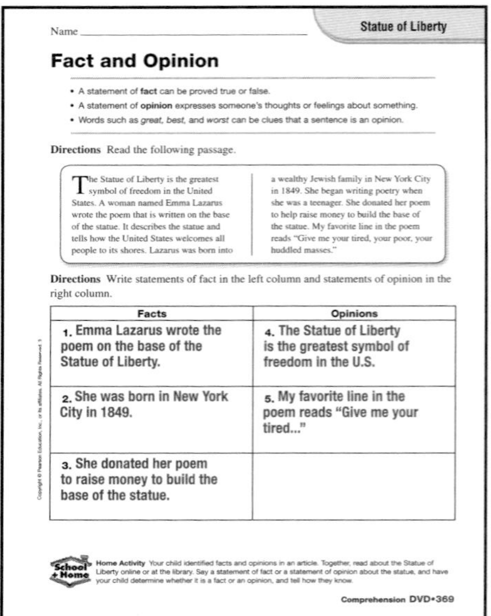

Name ____________________ Statue of Liberty

Fact and Opinion

- A statement of **fact** can be proved true or false.
- A statement of **opinion** expresses someone's thoughts or feelings about something.
- Words such as *great, best,* and *worst* can be clues that a sentence is an opinion.

Directions Read the following passage.

The Statue of Liberty is the greatest symbol of freedom in the United States. A woman named Emma Lazarus wrote the poem that is written on the base of the statue. It describes the statue and tells how the United States welcomes all people to its shores. Lazarus was born into a wealthy Jewish family in New York City in 1849. She began writing poetry when she was a teenager. She donated her poem to help raise money to build the base of the statue. My favorite line in the poem reads "Give me your tired, your poor, your huddled masses."

Directions Write statements of fact in the left column and statements of opinion in the right column.

Facts	Opinions
1. Emma Lazarus wrote the poem on the base of the Statue of Liberty.	4. The Statue of Liberty is the greatest symbol of freedom in the U.S.
2. She was born in New York City in 1849.	5. My favorite line in the poem reads "Give me your tired..."
3. She donated her poem to raise money to build the base of the statue.	

School + Home **Home Activity** Your child identified facts and opinions in an article. Together, read about the Statue of Liberty online or at the library. Say a statement of fact or a statement of opinion about the statue, and have your child determine whether it is a fact or an opinion, and tell how they know.

Comprehension DVD•369

Let's Practice It! TR DVD•369

Selection Vocabulary

crown a metal head covering worn by someone with power

liberty freedom

models small copies of something

symbol an object, diagram, animal, or icon that stands for or represents something else

tablet a small, flat surface with something written on it

torch a long stick with material on one end that burns

unforgettable so good that you cannot forget it

unveiled removed a veil from; revealed

Text-Based Comprehension

Review Fact and Opinion

TEACH Review the definitions of fact and opinio
dents that a statement of fact tells something thai e
and a statement of opinion tells someone's ideas
support, have students review p. EI•7 on fact and

GUIDE PRACTICE Have student pairs find examp
and opinion in *The Story of the Statue of Liberty*. Ha
statement of fact can be proved true or false and hov -
ion tells an idea or feeling.

ON THEIR OWN For additional practice with fact and
Let's Practice It! p. 369 on the *Teacher Resources DVD*

Vocabulary Skill

Review Prefix *un-*

TEACH Remind students that they can use what they know about word structure and the prefix *un-* to figure out the meaning of a word. Review that the prefix *un-* added to the beginning of an adverb or adjective usually means "not." When *un-* is added to a verb, it usually means "the opposite of."

GUIDE PRACTICE Review with students how to use word structure to determine the meaning of *unhappiness*. Guide students to identify the root, prefix, and suffix in the word and use the meanings of the word parts to define the word.

ON THEIR OWN Have students use word structure to determine the meaning of *unveiled*. Then have them use the word correctly in a sentence. Have volunteers share their sentences.

Phonics

Review  Vowel Sounds /ü/ and /u̇/

TEACH Write the following sentences on the board. Have students read each one, first quietly to themselves and then aloud as you track the print.

1. **Mom gave us fruit for our snack after school.**
2. **I spilled a few noodles on the book.**
3. **A goose flew south on a chilly Tuesday morning.**
4. **Drew put blueberries on his cereal.**
5. **Sue told us the good news.**

Team Talk Have students discuss with a partner which words have the vowel sound /ü/ and which words have the vowel sound /u̇/, and ask them to identify the letter or letters that spell each sound. Then call on individuals to share with the class.

Literary Terms

Review Word Choice

TEACH Have students reread "Emma and Liberty" on p. 373. Remind students that word choice refers to the specific words and phrases that authors choose to use in their writing.

GUIDE PRACTICE Discuss why the author chose to use the words *breathless view* when writing about how the statue can be seen from Battery Park. Have students find other examples of specific word choices the author made to appeal to the reader's senses.

ON THEIR OWN Have students create a word web that shows specific word choices the author made to tell the reader what Emma does and how she feels. Have students discuss the word choices as they build the word webs.

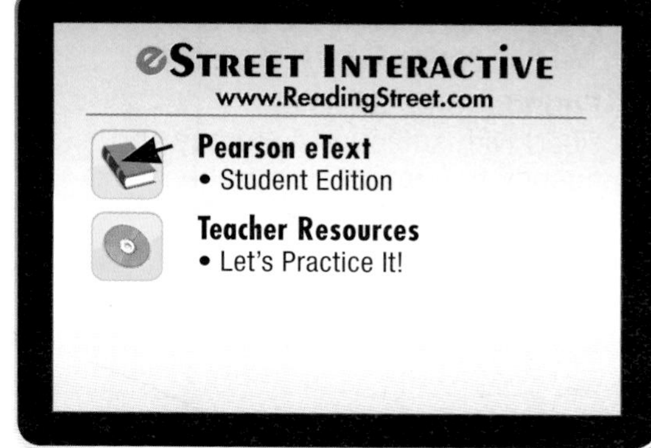

ELL

Fact and Opinion Provide support for students for distinguishing statements of fact from statements of opinion. Look at their statements together and ask questions such as

- Does this statement have information that can be proved true?
- Does this statement tell a feeling?
- Are there any clue words in the sentence that tells you it is an opinion?

Articulation Tip If students have trouble pronouncing words with vowel sounds /ü/ and /u̇/, demonstrate how to pronounce them by slowly repeating words. Have students pay close attention to the movement of your mouth when saying the words. Have students practice saying the words until they develop confidence.

Common Core State Standards

Foundational Skills 4. Read with sufficient accuracy and fluency to support comprehension. **Foundational Skills 4.b.** Read on-level prose and poetry orally with accuracy, appropriate rate, and expression on successive readings.

Plan to Assess Fluency

- ☑ **Week 1 This week assess Advanced students.**
- ☐ **Week 2** Strategic Intervention
- ☐ **Week 3** On-Level
- ☐ **Week 4** Strategic Intervention
- ☐ **Week 5** Assess any students you have not yet checked during this unit.

Set individual goals for students to enable them to reach the year-end goal.

- Current Goal: 110–120 WCPM
- Year-End Goal: 120 WCPM

Assessment

Monitor Progress

FLUENCY Make two copies of the fluency passage on p. 393k. As the student reads the text aloud, mark mistakes on your copy. Also mark where the student is at the end of one minute. To check the student's comprehension of the passage, have him or her retell what was read. To figure words correct per minute (WCPM), subtract the number of mistakes from the total number of words read in one minute.

RATE

Corrective feedback

If... students cannot read fluently at a rate of 110–120 WCPM,
then... make sure they practice with text at their independent reading level. Provide additional fluency practice by pairing nonfluent readers with fluent readers.

If... students already read at 120 WCPM,
then... have them read a book of their choice independently.

ELL

If... students need more scaffolding and practice with **Conventions and Writing,**
then... use the Grammar Transition Lessons on pp. 312–386 in the *ELL Handbook.*

Day 5 SMALL GROUP TIME • Differentiate Reteaching, p. SG•1

OL On-Level

- **Practice** Capital Letters
- **Reread** *Reading Street Sleuth,* pp. 68–69

SI Strategic Intervention

- **Review** Capital Letters
- **Reread** *Reading Street Sleuth,* pp. 68–69

A Advanced

- **Extend** Capital Letters
- **Reread** *Reading Street Sleuth,* pp. 68–69
- **Communicate** Inquiry Project

Name ______________________________

Grace's Place

Grace's class was putting on a play about famous places in the 12
United States. Each student was to choose his or her favorite place 24
and dress up to look like that place. Grace didn't know which place to 38
choose. 39

Her friend Nora was very tall. She was going to be the 51
Washington Monument. She was going to get a white suit and make a 64
pointy white hat with paper and glue. Grace couldn't think of anything 76
as good as that. 80

Grace had only a few days left to choose her place. She still had 94
no idea what to be. Grace went into her room and looked around. 107
She saw a crown from when she had dressed up as a princess. Then 121
she saw a flashlight that she had bought for camp. She looked in her 135
closet and saw a green dress that her mom had made her. She saw 149
her notebook on her desk. 154

Grace got an idea! She got all of the things together. 165

On the night of the play, all of Grace's friends showed up as 178
different famous places. There was a Mount Rushmore, a Craters of 189
the Moon, a White House, and of course the Washington Monument. 200
Grace unveiled her outfit last. 205

Grace's green dress became a gown. Her flashlight became a 215
torch, and her notebook became a tablet. She put the crown on top of 229
her head. 231

Grace was the Statue of Liberty! 237

MONITOR PROGRESS

- **Check Fluency**

Common Core State Standards

Informational Text 1. Ask and answer questions to demonstrate understanding of a text, referring explicitly to the text as the basis for the answers. **Foundational Skills 4.** Read with sufficient accuracy and fluency to support comprehension.

Assessment

Monitor Progress

For a written assessment of Vowel Sounds /ü/ and /u̇/, Fact and Opinion, and Selection Vocabulary, use Weekly Test 26, pp. 151–156.

FACT AND OPINION Use "The Pony Express" on p. 393m to check students' understanding of fact and opinion.

1. Is this sentence a statement of fact or opinion? *There were no telephones, email, or television.* How do you know? (I know it is a statement of fact because it is possible to prove whether those things existed before the 1850s.)
2. Is this sentence a statement of fact or opinion? *Pony Express riders were the bravest of all Americans alive in those days.* How do you know? (I know it is a statement of opinion because it tells a feeling. The word *bravest* is also a clue that it is an opinion.)
3. Name two facts you learned about the Pony Express in this passage. (The route was 1,800 miles long. Horses carried saddle bags filled with mail.)

Corrective feedback	**If...** students are unable to answer the comprehension questions, **then...** use the Reteach lesson in *First Stop*.

Name ______________________________

The Pony Express

Through much of American history, there wasn't an easy way to deliver mail around the country. There were no telephones, email, or televisions. It took a long time for information to get from one place to another.

By the 1850s, the telegraph started to be used. It allowed printed messages to be sent from place to place. Telegraph wires stretched across distant parts of America, but it took many, many years to get poles and wires up all over. In 1860, the Pony Express began to carry messages to some places where telegraph lines did not yet reach.

How did the Pony Express work? Horses and riders made up the Pony Express. The horses carried saddlebags filled with mail. A rider and horse started at one station and raced to the next. Then a new rider and horse would take the saddlebag and ride to the next station farther away.

The Pony Express could carry mail from Missouri to California in about 10 days. The route used was about 1,800 miles long. There were more than 150 stations along the way.

Pony Express riders were the bravest of all Americans alive in those days. Riders traveled alone on dangerous trails. They raced through icy rivers and along high cliffs. And Pony Express horses were America's fastest. They had to be in order to get the mail across those long distances.

In America's history, the Pony Express was one of the most important methods ever of getting and sending information.

MONITOR PROGRESS

- **Fact and Opinion**

Common Core State Standards

Speaking/Listening 1.a. Come to discussions prepared, having read or studied required material; explicitly draw on that preparation and other information known about the topic to explore ideas under discussion. **Speaking/Listening 4.** Report on a topic or text, tell a story, or recount an experience with appropriate facts and relevant, descriptive details, speaking clearly at an understandable pace. **Language 2.** Demonstrate command of the conventions of standard English capitalization, punctuation, and spelling when writing. **Language 2.a.** Capitalize appropriate words in titles. **Language 2.f.** Use spelling patterns and generalizations (e.g., word families, position-based spellings, syllable patterns, ending rules, meaningful word parts) in writing words. **Also Speaking/Listening 1.b.**

Research and Inquiry

Step 5 Communicate

PRESENT IDEAS Have students share their inquiry results by presenting their information and giving a brief talk on their research and on-site inspections. Have students display any time lines they created on Day 3.

SPEAKING Remind students how to be good speakers and how to communicate effectively with their audience.

- Respond to relevant questions with appropriate details.
- Speak clearly and loudly.
- Keep eye contact with audience members.
- Speak at an appropriate rate so that audience members can easily understand the ideas communicated.

LISTENING Review with students these tips for being a good listener.

- Wait until the speaker has finished before raising your hand to ask a relevant question or make a comment.
- Be polite, even if you disagree.

LISTEN TO IDEAS Have students listen attentively to the research results. Have them make pertinent comments, closely related to the topic.

Spelling Test

Vowel Sounds in *moon* and *foot*

To administer the spelling test, refer to the directions, words, and sentences on p. 371c.

Conventions

Capital Letters

MORE PRACTICE Remind students that days of the week, months of the year, people's titles, book titles, abbreviations, and the first word in a sentence or greeting are all capitalized.

GUIDE PRACTICE Write the following sentences on the board. Have students tell which words should begin with capital letters and why.

senator smith was on the committee.

does mr. mercer live in your neighborhood?

the harlem renaissance is an interesting period in history.

We read the book the story of the statue of liberty.

ON THEIR OWN Write these sentences. Have students look back in *The Story of the Statue of Liberty* to find the correct capitalized words to fill in the blanks. Students should complete *Let's Practice It!* p. 370 on the *Teacher Resources DVD-ROM*.

1. **It was to be a present from the people of ______ to the people of America, as a remembrance of the old friendship between the two countries.** (France)
2. **Afterward, it stood in Madison Square in ______ for a number of years.** (New York City)
3. **As the huge statue grew, all of ______ watched with great fascination.** (Paris)

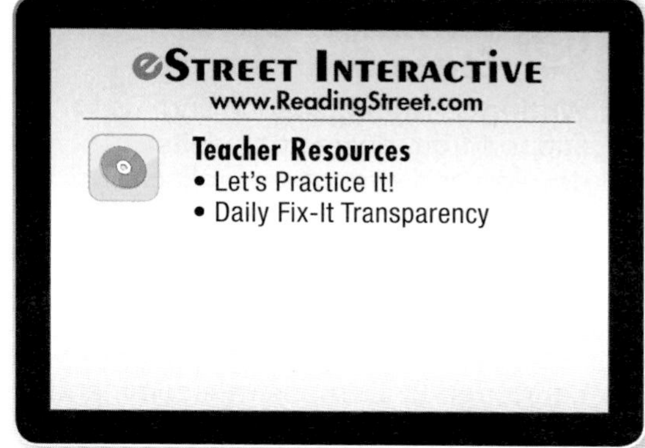

Daily Fix-It

9. When the Statue of Liberty was finaly presented, president Grover Cleveland gave a speech. *(finally; President)*
10. Mr. and mrs. Adams watched fireworks expload in the harbor. *(Mrs.; explode)*

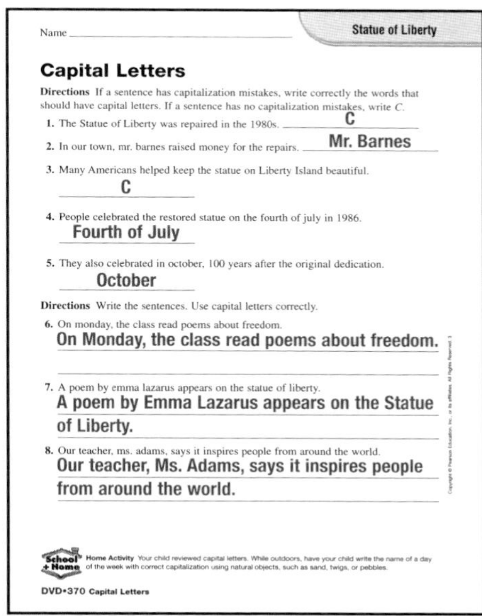

Name ______ Statue of Liberty

Capital Letters

Directions If a sentence has capitalization mistakes, write correctly the words that should have capital letters. If a sentence has no capitalization mistakes, write *C*.

1. The Statue of Liberty was repaired in the 1980s. **C**
2. In our town, mr. barnes raised money for the repairs. **Mr. Barnes**
3. Many Americans helped keep the statue on Liberty Island beautiful. **C**
4. People celebrated the restored statue on the fourth of july in 1986. **Fourth of July**
5. They also celebrated in october, 100 years after the original dedication. **October**

Directions Write the sentences. Use capital letters correctly.

6. On monday, the class read poems about freedom. **On Monday, the class read poems about freedom.**
7. A poem by emma lazarus appears on the statue of liberty. **A poem by Emma Lazarus appears on the Statue of Liberty.**
8. Our teacher, ms. adams, says it inspires people from around the world. **Our teacher, Ms. Adams, says it inspires people from around the world.**

School + Home **Home Activity** Your child reviewed capital letters. While outdoors, have your child write the name of a day of the week with correct capitalization using natural objects, such as sand, twigs, or pebbles.

DVD•370 Capital Letters

Let's Practice It! TR DVD•370

Common Core State Standards

Writing 5. With guidance and support from peers and adults, develop and strengthen writing as needed by planning, revising, and editing. **Language 1.** Demonstrate command of the conventions of standard English grammar and usage when writing or speaking. **Language 2.** Demonstrate command of the conventions of standard English capitalization, punctuation, and spelling when writing.

Teacher Note

Writing Self-Evaluation Make copies of the Writing Self-Evaluation Guide on p. 39 of the *Reader's and Writer's Notebook* and hand them out to students.

Bridge to Common Core

PRODUCTION AND DISTRIBUTION OF WRITING

Over the course of the week, students have developed and strengthened their ability to take notes through planning, revising, editing, and writing in their own words. The final drafts are clear and coherent notes in which the organization and style are appropriate for the purpose of recording details to craft main idea statements or to share with partners.

Writing

Zoom in on ©

Notes

REVIEW REVISING Remind students that yesterday they worked on revising their notes. Today they will proofread their notes.

Mini-Lesson Proofread

Proofread for Capitalization

- **Teach** When we proofread, we look closely at our work, searching for errors in mechanics, such as spelling, capitalization, and punctuation, and grammar. Today we will focus on using capitalization.

- **Model** Let's look at the notes we revised yesterday. Display Writing Transparency 26C. Explain that you will look for errors in the spelling and capitalization of proper nouns. If you are unsure of a spelling, model how to check the spelling in the selection. I see a problem. My notes say that the pieces of the statue went across the *Atlantic Ochen*. Something doesn't look right. I'm going to check the selection to make sure I spelled this right. I can see that the second word should be spelled *O-c-e-a-n*.

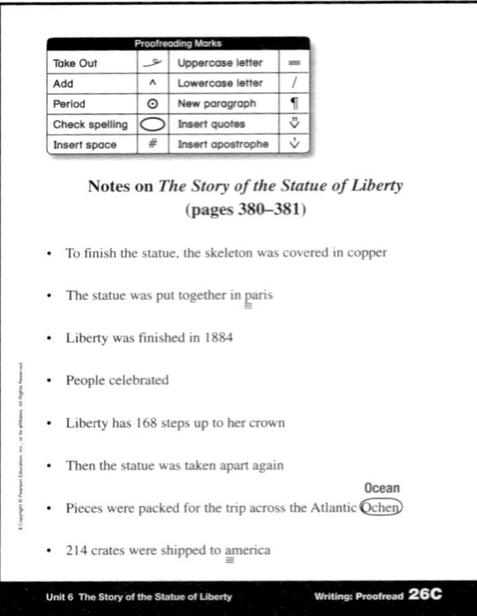

Proofreading Marks			
Take Out	⟿	Uppercase letter	≡
Add	^	Lowercase letter	/
Period	⊙	New paragraph	¶
Check spelling	◯	Insert quotes	∜
Insert space	#	Insert apostrophe	∛

Notes on *The Story of the Statue of Liberty* (pages 380–381)

- To finish the statue, the skeleton was covered in copper
- The statue was put together in paris
- Liberty was finished in 1884
- People celebrated
- Liberty has 168 steps up to her crown
- Then the statue was taken apart again
- Pieces were packed for the trip across the Atlantic Ochen (Ocean)
- 214 crates were shipped to america

Unit 6 The Story of the Statue of Liberty — Writing: Proofread 26C

Writing Transparency 26C, TR DVD

Continue to point out spelling and capitalization problems. Remind students that notes do not have to be in complete sentences. They can use sentences, sentence fragments, or a mixture of both. Then have students proofread their own notes.

PROOFREAD Display the Proofreading Tips. Ask students to proofread their notes, using the Proofreading Tips and paying particular attention to the spelling and capitalization of proper nouns. Circulate around the room answering students' questions. When students have finished editing their own work, have pairs proofread one another's notes.

Proofreading Tips

- ✔ Check to make sure that all proper nouns are capitalized and spelled correctly.
- ✔ Don't worry about punctuation.
- ✔ Remember, notes can be sentences or sentence fragments.

PRESENT Have students incorporate revisions and proofreading edits into their notes to create a final draft.

Then students may either compare their notes with a partner's or write a short summary of the selection based on their notes. When students have finished, have each complete the Writing Self-Evaluation Guide.

Routine Quick Write for Fluency **Team Talk**

1. **Talk** Pairs discuss what they learned about taking notes.
2. **Write** Students write a sentence explaining one or two things that are important to remember when taking notes.
3. **Share** Students read their own sentences to their partners.

Routines Flip Chart

Wrap Up Your Week!

Symbols of Freedom

Why do we have symbols that represent freedom?

In The Story of the Statue of Liberty and "A Nation of Immigrants," we learned that symbols remind us of the importance of our freedom.

Team Talk Have students recall their Amazing Ideas about symbols of freedom and use these ideas to help them demonstrate their understanding of the Question of the Week.

Next Week's Concept

Granting Freedom

What does it mean to grant freedom?

Poster Preview Prepare students for next week by using Week 2 ELL Poster 27. Read the Talk-Through to introduce the concept and vocabulary. Ask students to identify and describe actions in the art.

Selection Summary Send home the summary of next week's selection, *Happy Birthday Mr. Kang,* in English and in students' home languages, if available in the *ELL Handbook*. Students can read the summary with family members.

What does it mean to grant freedom? Tell students that next week they will read a story about a man who learns the true meaning of freedom.

Preview Next Week

Assessment Checkpoints for the Week

Weekly Assessment

Use pp. 151–156 of *Weekly Tests* to check:

- ✔ **Phonics** Vowel Sounds /ü/ and /u̇/
- ✔ **Comprehension** Fact and Opinion
- ✔ Review **Comprehension** Author's Purpose
- ✔ **Selection Vocabulary**

crown	**symbol**	**unforgettable**
liberty	**tablet**	**unveiled**
models	**torch**	

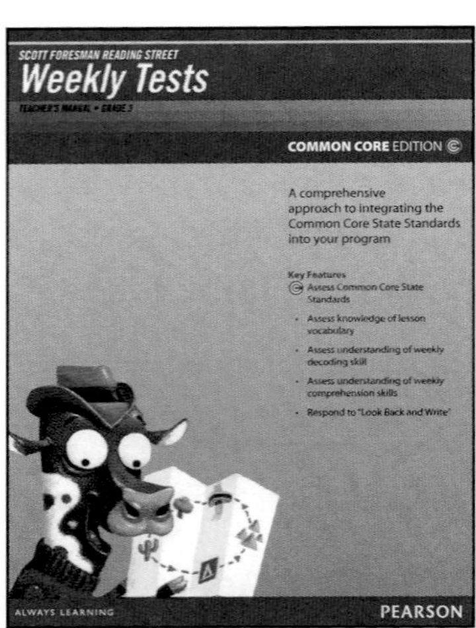

Weekly Tests

Differentiated Assessment

Advanced

On-Level

Strategic Intervention

Use pp. 151–156 of *Fresh Reads for Fluency and Comprehension* to check:

- ✔ **Comprehension** Fact and Opinion

- ✔ Review **Comprehension** Author's Purpose
- ✔ **Fluency** Words Correct Per Minute

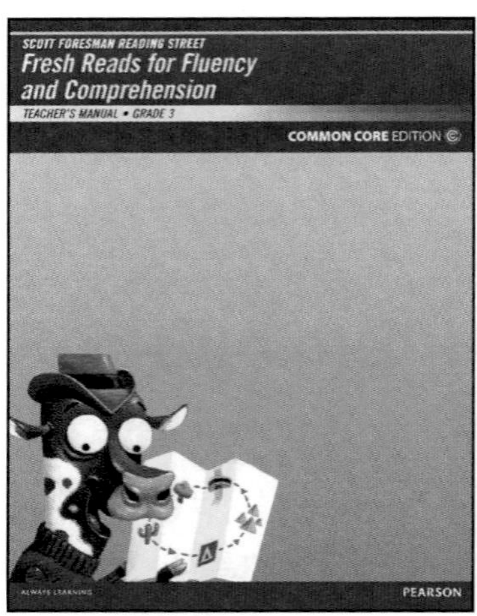

Fresh Reads for Fluency and Comprehension

Managing Assessment

Use *Assessment Handbook* for:

- ✔ **Weekly Assessment Blackline Masters for Monitoring Progress**
- ✔ **Observation Checklists**
- ✔ **Record-Keeping Forms**
- ✔ **Portfolio Assessment**

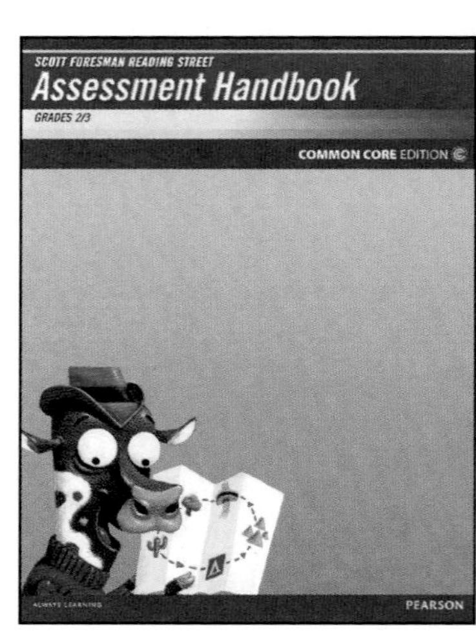

Assessment Handbook

TEACHER NOTES

TEACHER NOTES

DAY 1 Differentiate Vocabulary

- **Word Knowledge** Amazing Words
- **Read** "America's National Bird"
- **Inquiry** Identify Questions

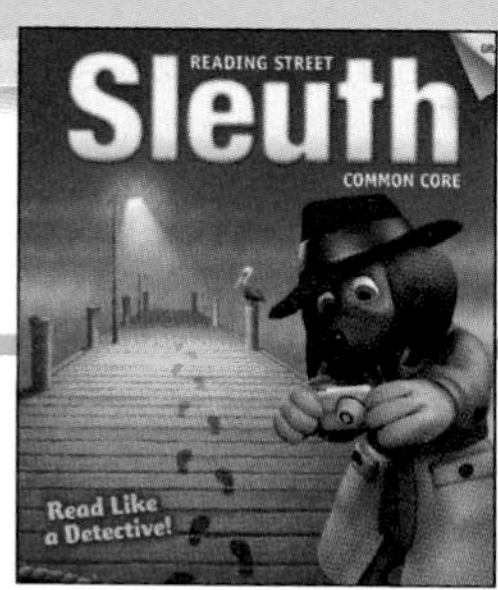

"America's National Bird," pp. 68–69

DAY 2 Differentiate Comprehension

- **Word Knowledge** Selection Vocabulary
- **Access Text** Read *The Story of the Statue of Liberty*
- **Inquiry** Investigate

DAY 3 Differentiate Close Reading

- **Word Knowledge** Develop Vocabulary
- **Close Reading** Read *The Story of the Statue of Liberty*
- **Inquiry** Investigate

DAY 4 Differentiate Vocabulary

- **Word Knowledge** Amazing Words
- **Read** "A Nation of Immigrants"
- **Inquiry** Organize

DAY 5 Differentiate Reteaching

- **Conventions** Capital Letters
- **Reread** "America's National Bird" or Leveled Readers
- **Inquiry** Communicate

Teacher Guides and Student pages can be found in the Leveled Reader Database.

Place English Language Learners in the groups that correspond to their reading abilities.
If... students need scaffolding and practice,
then... use the ELL Notes on the instructional pages.

Independent Practice

Independent Practice Stations

See pp. 366h and 366i for Independent Stations.

Pearson Trade Book Library

See the Leveled Reader Database for lesson plans and student pages.

Reading Street Digital Path

Independent Practice Activities are available in the Digital Path.

Independent Reading

See p. 366i for independent reading suggestions.

On-Level

Common Core State Standards

Informational Text 1. Ask and answer questions to demonstrate understanding of a text, referring explicitly to the text as the basis for the answers. **Informational Text 3.** Describe the relationship between a series of historical events, scientific ideas or concepts, or steps in technical procedures in a text, using language that pertains to time, sequence, and cause/effect. **Foundational Skills 4.** Read with sufficient accuracy and fluency to support comprehension. **Speaking/ Listening 1.** Engage effectively in a range of collaborative discussions (one-on-one, in groups, and teacher led) with diverse partners on grade 3 topics and texts, building on others' ideas and expressing their own clearly. **Language 4.** Determine or clarify the meaning of unknown and multiple-meaning words and phrases based on grade 3 reading and content, choosing flexibly from a range of strategies. **Also Language 6.**

Independent Reading Options

Trade Book Library

eSTREET INTERACTIVE
www.ReadingStreet.com

Teacher Guides are available on the Leveled Reader Database.

If... students need more scaffolding and practice with **Vocabulary,** **then...** use the activities on pp. DI•17–DI•18 in the Teacher Resources section on SuccessNet.

1 Build Word Knowledge

Practice Amazing Words

DEFINE IT Elicit the definition for the word *impressive* from students. Ask: How would you describe something that is *impressive* to another student? (Possible response: Something that is *impressive* is amazing or inspiring.) Clarify or give a definition when necessary. Continue with the words *tribute* and *contribution*.

Team Talk **TALK ABOUT IT** Have students internalize meanings. Ask: How can you group the Amazing Words together in a sentence? (Possible response: The Statue of Liberty is an *impressive tribute* from France and a great *contribution* to American landmarks.) Allow time for students to play with the words. Review the concept map with students. Discuss other words they can add to the concept map.

2 Text-Based Comprehension

Read

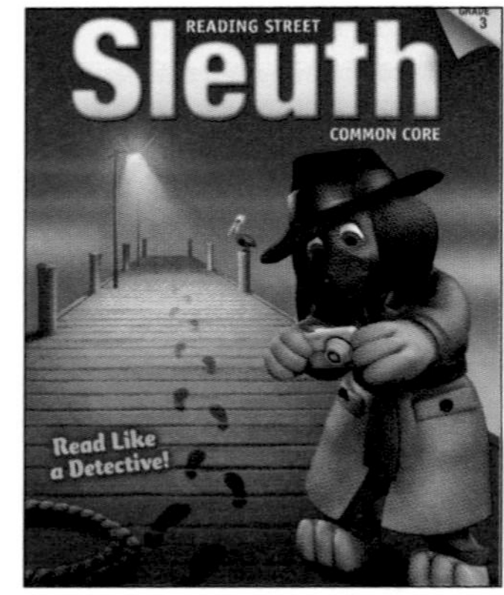

READ ALOUD "America's National Bird" Have partners read "America's National Bird" from *Reading Street Sleuth* on pp. 68–69.

ACCESS TEXT Discuss the Sleuth Work section with students before they work on it. Remind students that they can use these steps with other texts they read.

Gather Evidence Talk together about Benjamin Franklin's argument against the American bald eagle as our country's national symbol. Have partners work together to make a list of details from the text that supports this discussion.

Ask Questions Talk together about questions students wrote. Invite students to share where they would look for more information about the mammal they chose.

Make Your Case Have students share their opinions with a partner. Encourage discussion about the most convincing arguments made by each student.

On-Level

1 Build Word Knowledge

Practice Selection Vocabulary

crown	liberty	models	symbol
tablet	torch	unforgettable	unveiled

DEFINE IT Discuss the definition for the word *symbol* with students. Ask: How would you describe a *symbol* to another student? (Possible response: A *symbol* is something that stands for something else. The American flag is a symbol of freedom.) Continue with the remaining words.

TALK ABOUT IT Have pairs use the selection vocabulary in sentences to internalize meaning. Ask: How can you group the selection vocabulary together in a sentence? (Possible response: The Statue of Liberty, with its *torch* and *crown,* is an *unforgettable symbol* of *liberty*.) Allow time for students to play with the words and then share their sentences.

2 Read

The Story of the Statue of Liberty

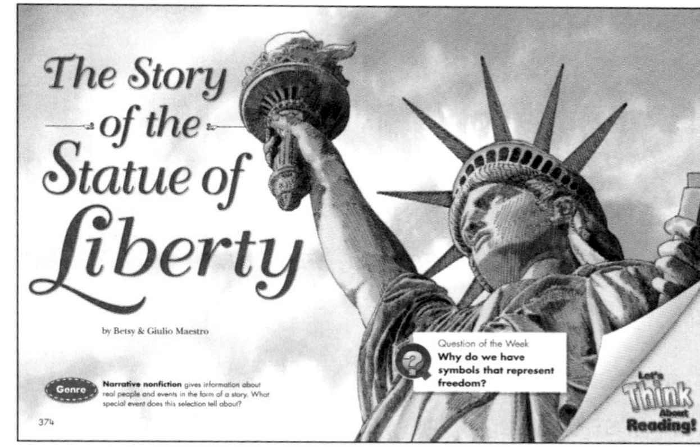

If you read *The Story of the Statue of Liberty* during whole group time, then use the following instruction.

ACCESS TEXT Reread p. 378.
Ask questions to check understanding. Why did Bartholdi want the statue to be so large and strong? (He wanted people to be able to climb up inside it.) Was the Statue of Liberty easy or difficult to build? How do you know? (It was difficult because many workers built its different parts.) Why is the date on the statue's tablet important? (It is July 4, 1776, which is the day when America declared its independence.)

Have students identify sections from today's reading that they did not completely understand. Reread them aloud and clarify misunderstandings.

If you are reading *The Story of the Statue of Liberty* during small group time, then return to pp. 376–381a to guide the reading.

SMALL GROUP TIME

More Reading for Group Time

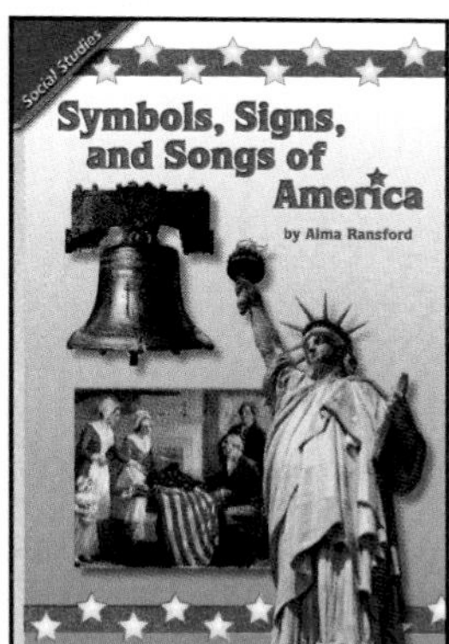

ON-LEVEL

Review
- Fact and Opinion
- Questioning
- Selection Vocabulary

Use this suggested Leveled Reader or other text at students' instructional level.

eStreet Interactive
www.ReadingStreet.com

Use the Leveled Reader Database for lesson plans and student pages for *Symbols, Signs, and Songs of America.*

On-Level

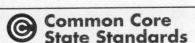

Common Core State Standards

Informational Text 1. Ask and answer questions to demonstrate understanding of a text, referring explicitly to the text as the basis for the answers. **Informational Text 7.** Use information gained from illustrations (e.g., maps, photographs), and the words in a text to demonstrate understanding of the text (e.g., where, when, why, and how key events occur). **Language 4.a.** Use sentence-level context as a clue to the meaning of a word or phrase. **Language 6.** Acquire and use accurately grade-appropriate conversational, general academic, and domain-specific words and phrases, including those that signal spatial and temporal relationships (e.g., *After dinner that night we went looking for them*).

1 Build Word Knowledge

Develop Vocabulary

REREAD FOR VOCABULARY Reread the second paragraph on p. 382. Introduce: Let's read this paragraph to find out what *pedestal* means. To help students understand the word *pedestal,* ask questions related to context, such as On what object is a statue often placed? Look at the illustration on page 383. What is directly underneath the statue? Have students use online sources to find out more information about a pedestal.

2 Read

The Story of the Statue of Liberty

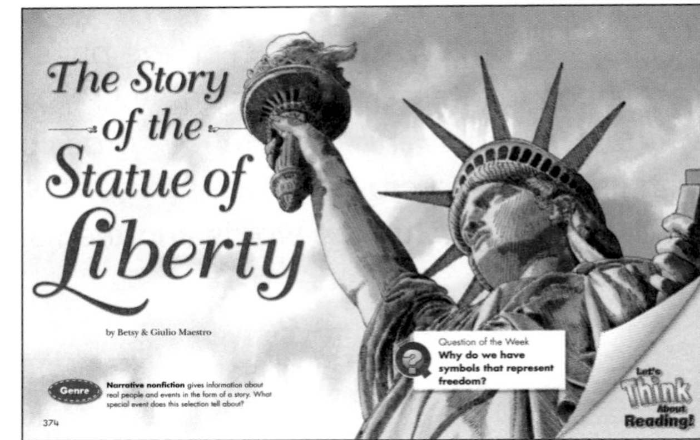

If you read *The Story of the Statue of Liberty* during whole group time, then use the following instruction.

CLOSE READING Read pp. 382–383. Have students search through the text to find words or phrases that express feelings or actions. As a class, make a list on the board. (*lost interest, excitement, celebration, speeches were read, songs were sung, great cheer*)

Ask: How did Americans' feelings change about the statue once they saw it? (At first, Americans had lost interest, but then they became excited and had a big celebration when the statue was finally finished.)

If you are reading *The Story of the Statue of Liberty* during small group time, then return to pp. 382–385a to guide the reading.

If... students need more scaffolding and practice with the **Main Selection, then...** use the activities on p. DI•22 in the Teacher Resources section on SuccessNet.

On-Level

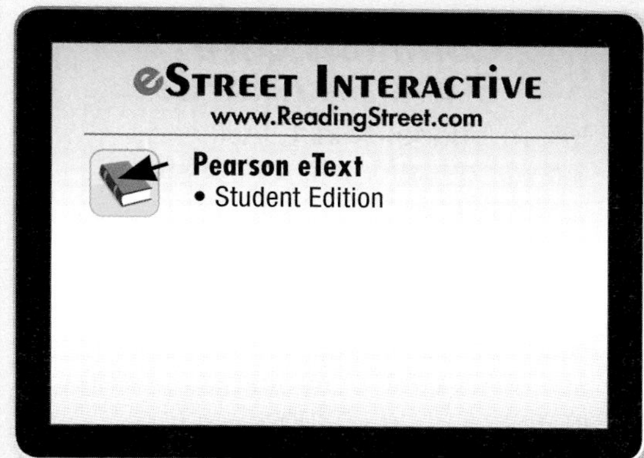

1 Build Word Knowledge

Practice Amazing Words

impressive	tribute	enlighten	contribution	dedication
competition	recognizable	disgrace	staggering	fund

Team Talk **LANGUAGE DEVELOPMENT** Have students practice building more complex sentences. Display a sentence starter and have students add oral phrases or clauses using the Amazing Words. For example: The statue was _______. (The statue was *impressive* / and a *recognizable tribute* / to *freedom*.) Guide students to add at least three phrases or clauses per sentence.

2 Read

"A Nation of Immigrants"

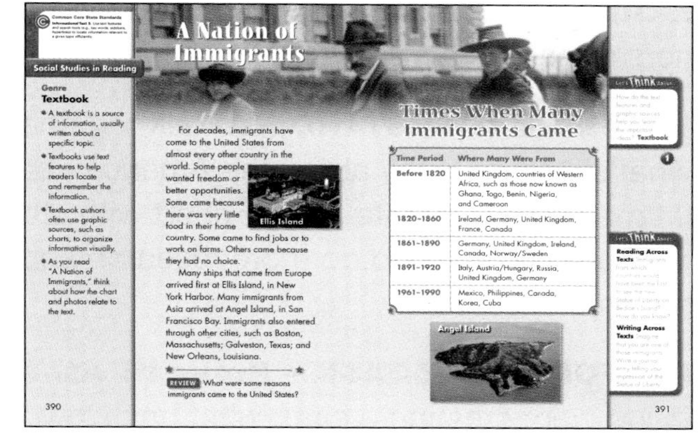

BEFORE READING Read aloud the genre information about textbooks on p. 390. Help students preview and set a purpose for reading.

- What features do you see that are different from those in stories you have read? (photographs, captions, a chart)
- What does the chart show? (dates when people from different countries came to the United States)

DURING READING Have students read along with you. Ask:

- Why do you think the author used a chart to show information? (The chart makes the long lists of dates and countries easier to read and understand.)
- How is the textbook similar to and different from *The Story of the Statue of Liberty*? (Both give facts and details. The textbook material is shorter and includes photographs, captions, and a chart. The narrative nonfiction selection contains opinions and illustrations.)

AFTER READING Have students share their reactions to "A Nation of Immigrants." Then have them use dates from *The Story of the Statue of Liberty* to create a time line that could appear in a textbook article about the Statue of Liberty.

SMALL GROUP TIME

Independent Reading Options

Trade Book Library

eStreet Interactive
www.ReadingStreet.com

Teacher Guides are available on the Leveled Reader Database.

On-Level

Common Core State Standards

Informational Text 1. Ask and answer questions to demonstrate understanding of a text, referring explicitly to the text as the basis for the answers. **Informational Text 3.** Describe the relationship between a series of historical events, scientific ideas or concepts, or steps in technical procedures in a text, using language that pertains to time, sequence, and cause/effect. **Foundational Skills 4.** Read with sufficient accuracy and fluency to support comprehension. **Writing 1.** Write opinion pieces on topics or texts, supporting a point of view with reasons. **Speaking/Listening 1.** Engage effectively in a range of collaborative discussions (one-on-one, in groups, and teacher led) with diverse partners on grade 3 topics and texts, building on others' ideas and expressing their own clearly. **Also Language 4.**

More Reading for Group Time

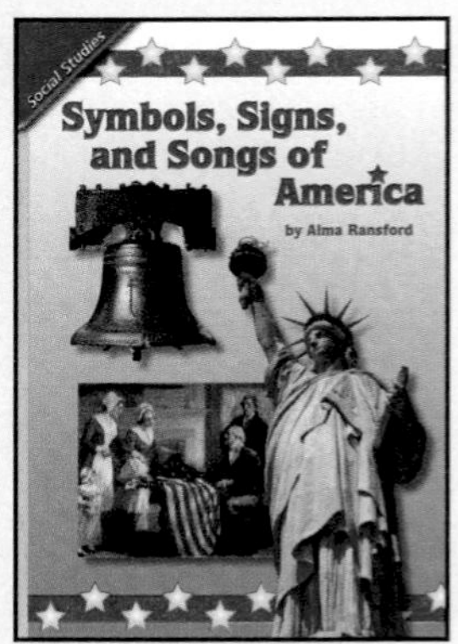

ON-LEVEL

Review
- Fact and Opinion
- Questioning
- Selection Vocabulary

Use this suggested Leveled Reader or other text at students' instructional level.

eSTREET INTERACTIVE
www.ReadingStreet.com

Use the Leveled Reader Database for lesson plans and student pages for *Symbols, Signs, and Songs of America.*

1 Build Word Knowledge

Practice Capital Letters

IDENTIFY Have students read the instruction at the bottom of p. 389 to review capitalization. Discuss with students how capital letters are used at the beginning of proper nouns. Have students work with partners to reread the model notes and find examples of how the author used capital letters. Allow time for students to share and discuss the examples.

2 Text-Based Comprehension

Read

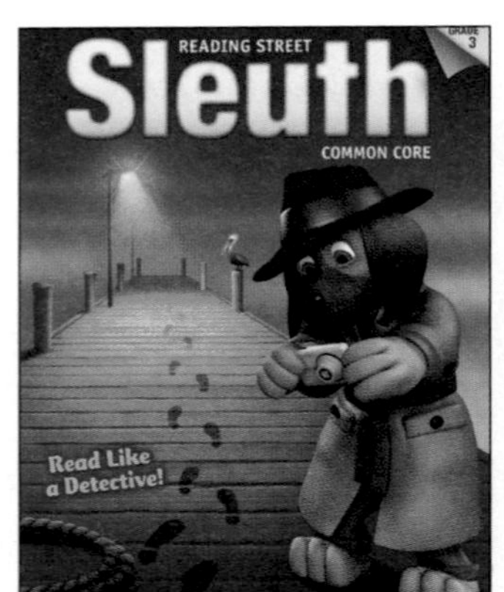

REREAD "America's National Bird" Have partners reread "America's National Bird."

EXTEND UNDERSTANDING Talk together about what students know about the American bald eagle. If time permits, create a KWL chart with students, encouraging them to do more research about our national symbol.

PERFORMANCE TASK • Prove It! Ask students: If you were creating a club, what animal would you use to symbolize the values of your club? Have them write a paragraph to support their reasons for choosing this animal and draw a picture to represent their symbol. Remind students to put their most convincing reason first in the paragraph and their least convincing reason last.

COMMUNICATE Have partners share their choice of animal for their club. Invite partners to discuss a trait of each animal and how it connects with the club's values.

Strategic Intervention

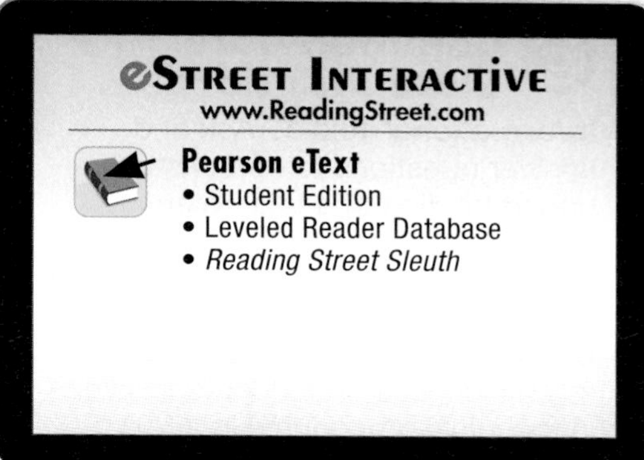

1 Build Word Knowledge

Reteach Amazing Words

Repeat the definition of the word. We learned that something that is *impressive* is amazing or inspiring. Then use the word in a sentence. The statue was so *impressive* that people from around the world came to see it.

Team Talk **TALK ABOUT IT** Have students take turns using the word *impressive* in a sentence. Continue this routine to practice the Amazing Words *tribute* and *contribution*. Review the concept map with students. Discuss other words they can add to the concept map.

Corrective feedback	**If...** students need more practice with the Amazing Words, **then...** use visuals from the Student Edition or online sources to clarify meaning.

2 Text-Based Comprehension

Read

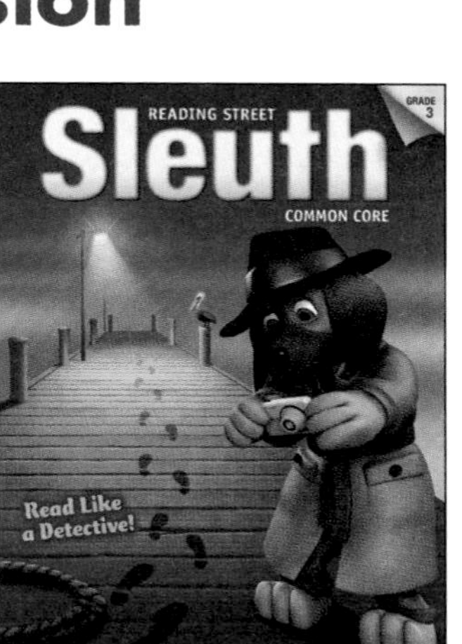

READ "America's National Bird" Have students track the print as you read "America's National Bird" from *Reading Street Sleuth* on pp. 68–69.

ACCESS TEXT Discuss the Sleuth Work section with students and provide support as needed as they work on it.

Gather Evidence Talk together about Benjamin Franklin's argument against the American bald eagle as our country's national symbol. Work together to make a list of details from the text that support this discussion.

Ask Questions Have students work with a partner to choose a mammal to be our country's symbol. Invite partners to write questions they would use to guide research on their mammal. Invite students to share where they would look for more information about the mammal they chose.

Make Your Case Have students work with someone on the same side of the issue. As students work together to write a paragraph supporting their opinions, encourage them to list the most convincing reasons first followed by the less convincing reasons.

SMALL GROUP TIME

More Reading for Group Time

CONCEPT LITERACY

Practice
Concept Words

BELOW-LEVEL

Review
- Fact and Opinion
- Questioning
- Selection Vocabulary

Use these suggested Leveled Readers or other text at students' instructional level.

eStreet Interactive
www.ReadingStreet.com

Use the Leveled Reader Database for lesson plans and student pages for *The Statue of Liberty* and *The Statue of Liberty: A Gift from France.*

Common Core State Standards

Informational Text 1. Ask and answer questions to demonstrate understanding of a text, referring explicitly to the text as the basis for the answers. **Informational Text 3.** Describe the relationship between a series of historical events, scientific ideas or concepts, or steps in technical procedures in a text, using language that pertains to time, sequence, and cause/effect. **Language 4.a.** Use sentence-level context as a clue to the meaning of a word or phrase. **Also Language 6.**

1 Build Word Knowledge

Reteach Selection Vocabulary

DEFINE IT Describe *models* to a friend. Give a definition when necessary. Restate the word in student-friendly terms and clarify meaning with a visual. *Models* are small copies of bigger things. Page 377 shows two models of the Statue of Liberty.

crown	liberty	models	symbol
tablet	torch	unforgettable	unveiled

Team Talk **TALK ABOUT IT** Have you ever seen models, such as model airplanes or cars? Turn and talk to your partner about this. Allow time for students to discuss. Ask for examples. Rephrase students' examples for usage when necessary or to correct misunderstandings. Continue with the remaining words.

Corrective feedback | **If...** students need more practice with selection vocabulary, **then...** use the *Envision It! Pictured Vocabulary Cards.*

2 Read

The Story of the Statue of Liberty

If you read *The Story of the Statue of Liberty* during whole group time, then use the instruction below.

ACCESS TEXT Reread the paragraphs on p. 378. Ask questions to check understanding. Why did Bartholdi want the statue to be very large and very strong? (so people could climb up inside it) What part of the statue was built first? (a huge skeleton of steel) How was the statue built? (Many different people worked on it. Each group worked on different parts of it.) Why is the date on the statue's tablet important? (It is July 4, 1776, the day when the Declaration of Independence was signed.)

If you are reading *The Story of the Statue of Liberty* during small group time, then return to pp. 376–381a to guide the reading.

Independent Reading Options

Trade Book Library

eStreet Interactive
www.ReadingStreet.com

Teacher Guides are available on the Leveled Reader Database.

Strategic Intervention

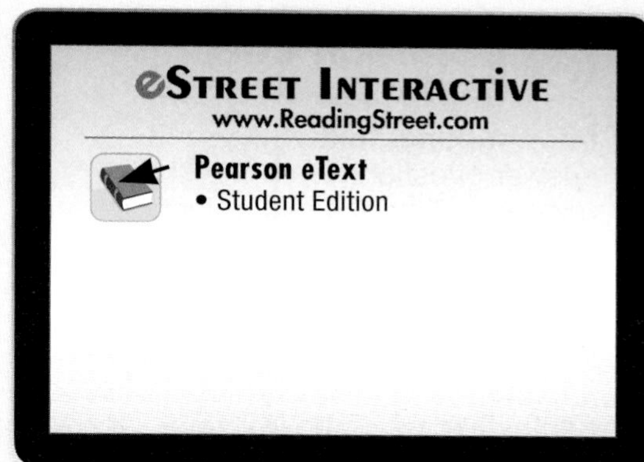

1 Build Word Knowledge

Develop Vocabulary

REREAD FOR VOCABULARY Reread the second paragraph on p. 382. Let's read this paragraph to find out what *pedestal* means. To help students understand the word *pedestal,* ask questions related to context, such as What was finished first? What was raised on top of it? How does the picture on page 383 help you understand what a pedestal is?

Corrective feedback	**If...** students have difficulty understanding the word *pedestal,* **then...** have students use the Internet to find images of other statues and point out how they stand on pedestals.

2 Read

The Story of the Statue of Liberty

If you read *The Story of the Statue of Liberty* during whole group time, then use the instruction below.

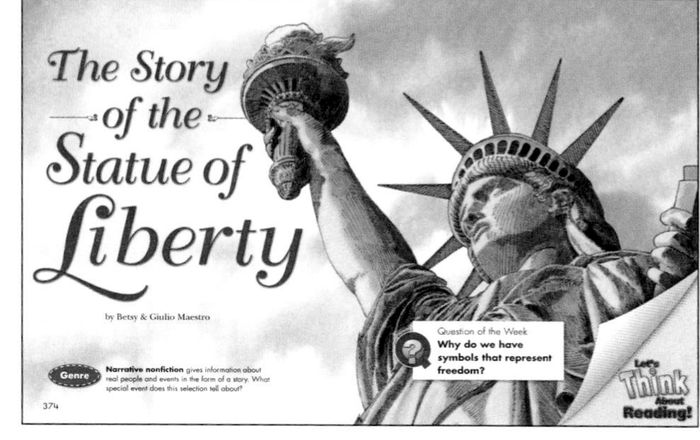

CLOSE READING Read pp. 382–383. Have students search through the text to find time-order words. Make a list of the words in the order they appear. (*By the time, soon, Then, At last, Then*)

Now use the time-order words you identified to retell the process of rebuilding the statue in the United States. (By the time the ship with the statue reached the United States, people were excited. Soon the pedestal was built. The skeleton was raised. Then the skin was attached to the statue. At last, the statue was put together and then people celebrated. Then the president gave a speech.)

If you are reading *The Story of the Statue of Liberty* during small group time, then return to pp. 382–385a to guide the reading.

SMALL GROUP TIME

If... students need more scaffolding and practice with the **Main Selection,** **then...** use the activities on p. DI•22 in the Teacher Resources section on SuccessNet.

Common Core State Standards

Informational Text 1. Ask and answer questions to demonstrate understanding of a text, referring explicitly to the text as the basis for the answers. **Informational Text 7.** Use information gained from illustrations (e.g., maps, photographs), and the words in a text to demonstrate understanding of the text (e.g., where, when, why, and how key events occur). **Foundational Skills 4.** Read with sufficient accuracy and fluency to support comprehension. **Writing 1.** Write opinion pieces on topics or texts, supporting a point of view with reasons. **Language 2.** Demonstrate command of the conventions of standard English capitalization, punctuation, and spelling when writing. **Also Writing 10.**

1 Build Word Knowledge

Review Amazing Words

impressive	tribute	enlighten	contribution	dedication
competition	recognizable	disgrace	staggering	fund

Team Talk **LANGUAGE DEVELOPMENT** Have students practice building more complex sentences. Display a sentence starter and have students add oral phrases or clauses using the Amazing Words. For example: The dedication _______. (The *dedication* / of the workers / who built the *impressive* statue / was *staggering*.) Guide students to add at least two phrases or clauses per sentence.

Corrective feedback | **If...** students have difficulty using the Amazing Words orally, **then...** review the meaning of each of the words.

2 Read

"A Nation of Immigrants"

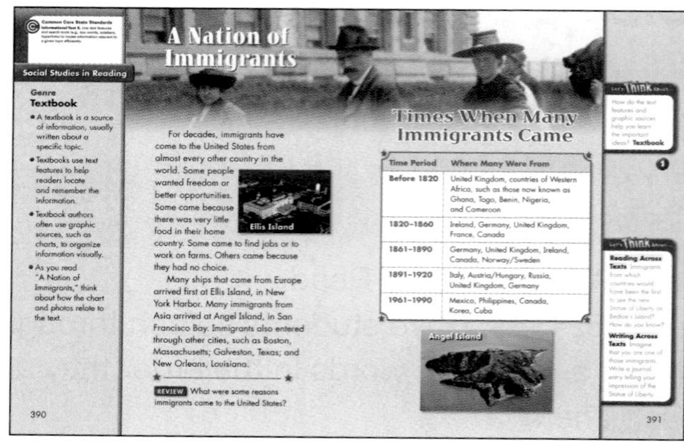

BEFORE READING Read aloud the genre information about textbooks on p. 390. Make sure students understand that a textbook is a source of information about any subject taught in school. Then have students preview the photographs and captions.

DURING READING Have students perform a choral reading of the selection. When you get to the chart, point out the headings. The headings in a chart help you know what kind of information the chart contains and how it is organized. What are the headings in this article? ("Time Period" and "Where Many Were From")

AFTER READING Have students share their reactions to the selection. Then guide them through the Reading Across Texts and Writing Across Texts activities. Why did immigrants come to the United States? (to find freedom, opportunity, or work; because they had no choice)

If... students need more scaffolding and practice with **Amazing Words**, **then...** use the Routine on pp. xxxvi–xxxvii in the *ELL Handbook*.

1 Build Word Knowledge

Review Capital Letters

IDENTIFY Choral read the instruction at the bottom of p. 389 with students to review how to use capital letters. Have students work with partners to reread the model notes on p. 389 and find examples of how the author used capital letters. Allow time for students to discuss the examples and correct any misunderstandings.

2 Text-Based Comprehension

Read

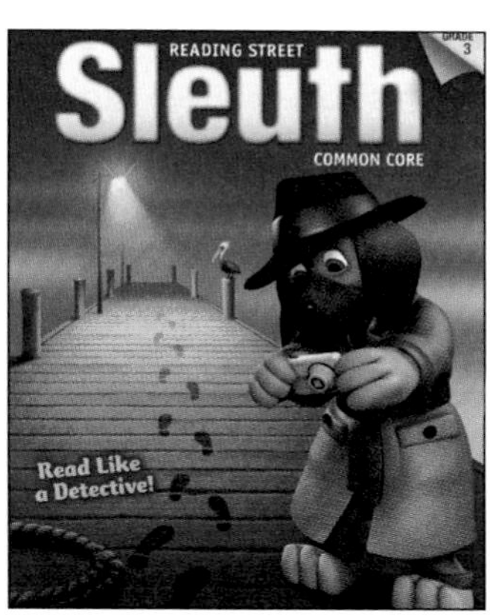

REREAD "America's National Bird" Have partners reread "America's National Bird," with partners alternating paragraphs.

EXTEND UNDERSTANDING Talk together about President John F. Kennedy's quote about the American bald eagle. Have students tell evidence that supports President Kennedy's opinion.

PERFORMANCE TASK • Prove It! Ask students: If you were creating a club, what animal would you use to symbolize the values of your club? Have students write a paragraph to support their reasons for choosing this animal and draw a picture to represent their symbol. Remind students to include facts and opinions in their paragraphs to support their choice.

COMMUNICATE Have partners share their paragraphs. Invite partners to identify the most convincing reasons in each student's paragraph.

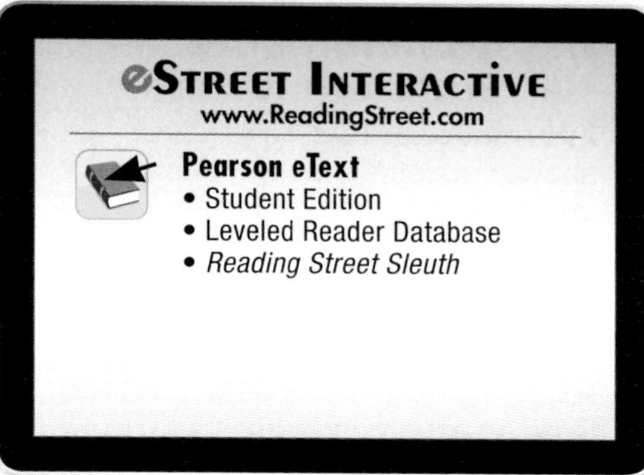

SMALL GROUP TIME

More Reading for Group Time

CONCEPT LITERACY

Practice
Concept Words

BELOW-LEVEL

Review
- Fact and Opinion
- Questioning
- Selection Vocabulary

Use these suggested Leveled Readers or other text at students' instructional level.

eStreet Interactive
www.ReadingStreet.com

Use the Leveled Reader Database for lesson plans and student pages for *The Statue of Liberty* and *The Statue of Liberty: A Gift from France.*

Advanced

Common Core State Standards

Informational Text 1. Ask and answer questions to demonstrate understanding of a text, referring explicitly to the text as the basis for the answers. **Informational Text 3.** Describe the relationship between a series of historical events, scientific ideas or concepts, or steps in technical procedures in a text, using language that pertains to time, sequence, and cause/effect. **Foundational Skills 4.** Read with sufficient accuracy and fluency to support comprehension. **Speaking/Listening 1.** Engage effectively in a range of collaborative discussions (one-on-one, in groups, and teacher led) with diverse partners on grade 3 topics and texts, building on others' ideas and expressing their own clearly. **Also Writing 7., 8.**

If... students need more scaffolding and practice with **Vocabulary,** **then...** use the activities on pp. DI•17–DI•18 in the Teacher Resources section on SuccessNet.

1 Build Word Knowledge

Extend Amazing Words

Team Talk Have students define *impressive.* Discuss other words for *impressive.* Continue with *tribute* and *contribution.* Have students use the words in sentences.

2 Text-Based Comprehension

Read

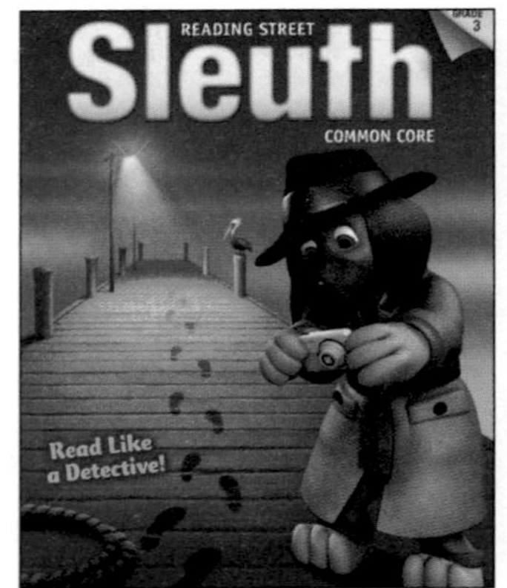

READ "America's National Bird" Have students read "America's National Bird" from *Reading Street Sleuth* on pp. 68–69.

ACCESS TEXT Discuss the Sleuth Work section with students before they work on it. Remind students that they can use these steps with other texts they read.

Gather Evidence Have students make a list of details from the text that supports Benjamin Franklin's argument. Encourage students to note these details as facts or opinions. Invite students to name the most convincing argument Franklin had.

Ask Questions Talk together about questions students wrote and where they might look for answers to their questions. If time permits, have students choose one question and begin researching to find the answer.

Make Your Case Have students share their opinions about our country's symbol. Encourage students to name the most convincing factual reason they stated in their paragraphs.

3 Inquiry: Extend Concepts

IDENTIFY QUESTIONS Have students think about questions they have about other American landmarks or national treasures, such as the Lincoln Memorial or the White House. Have students choose a landmark and use their questions to guide research and create an oral presentation with visuals about the building, its history, its symbolism, and its popularity. Throughout the week, they will gather information. On Day 5, they will present what they have learned.

Advanced

1 Build Word Knowledge

Extend Selection Vocabulary

Team Talk Have partners use the selection vocabulary in sentences to internalize their meanings. Have students use as many of the words as they can while making sure the sentence is grammatically correct. (Possible response: The *torch* and *tablet* of the Statue of Liberty are *unforgettable symbols* of freedom and *liberty.*) Continue with additional selection vocabulary.

crown	liberty	models	symbol
tablet	torch	unforgettable	unveiled

2 Read

The Story of the Statue of Liberty

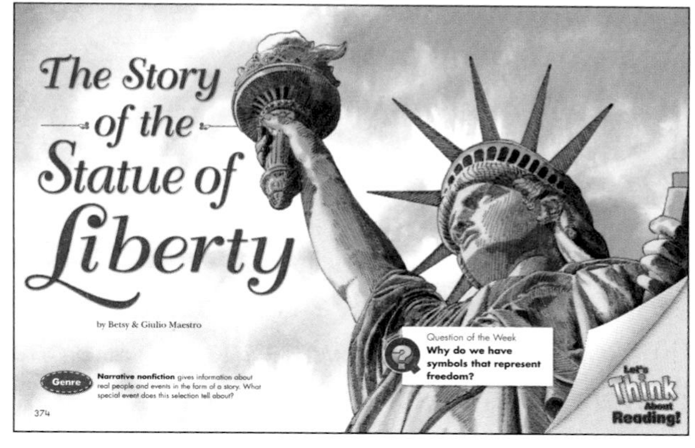

If you read *The Story of the Statue of Liberty* during whole group time, then use the instruction below.

ACCESS TEXT Reread p. 378.
Have students summarize the process of designing and building the statue. (The artist wanted the statue to be large enough for people to go inside. Many famous artists and craftspeople gave the artist ideas. Then many people worked together to build a huge skeleton and make some of the important parts, such as Liberty's head and crown and her left hand.) Ask: Why did the authors include these details in the selection? (They thought that readers might be interested in how the enormous statue was created.)

If you are reading *The Story of the Statue of Liberty* during small group time, then return to pp. 376–381a to guide the reading.

3 Inquiry: Extend Concepts

INVESTIGATE Encourage students to use materials at their independent reading levels or student-friendly search engines to identify relevant and credible sites to gather information about American historical landmarks or national treasures. Have students consider how they will present their information.

SMALL GROUP TIME

More Reading for Group Time

ADVANCED

Review
- Fact and Opinion
- Questioning

Use this suggested Leveled Reader or other text at students' instructional level.

eStreet Interactive
www.ReadingStreet.com

Use the Leveled Reader Database for lesson plans and student pages for *The French Connection.*

Advanced

Common Core State Standards

Informational Text 1. Ask and answer questions to demonstrate understanding of a text, referring explicitly to the text as the basis for the answers. **Informational Text 3.** Describe the relationship between a series of historical events, scientific ideas or concepts, or steps in technical procedures in a text, using language that pertains to time, sequence, and cause/effect. **Language 4.a.** Use sentence-level context as a clue to the meaning of a word or phrase. **Also Informational Text 7.**

1 Build Word Knowledge

Develop Vocabulary

REREAD FOR VOCABULARY Reread the first paragraph of p. 383. Let's read this paragraph to find out what *celebration* means. Discuss meaning and context with students.

2 Read

The Story of the Statue of Liberty

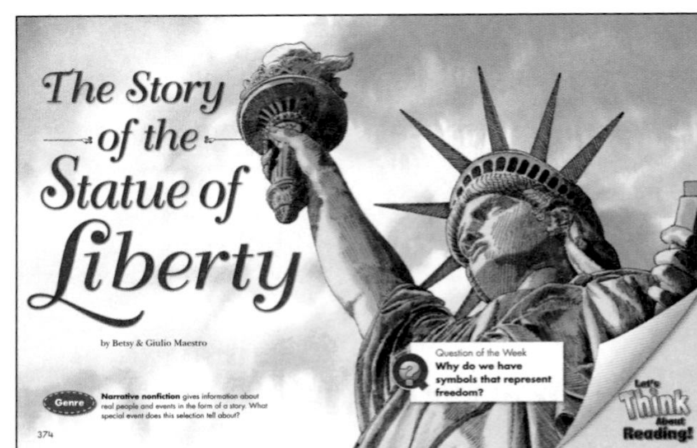

If you read *The Story of the Statue of Liberty* during whole group time, then use the instruction below.

CLOSE READING Read pp. 382–383. Have students create a T-chart with the heads **Time Order Words** and **Descriptive Words.** Have students search through the text to find time-order words and write them in the chart. Then have them find adjectives, or words that describe.

Time Order Words	Descriptive Words
By the time, soon, Then, At last, Then	large, new, giant, wonderful, great

Ask: What ideas are the authors developing on these pages? (They are telling how the statue got built in America and how people felt about it.) What do you notice about the descriptive words? (They are all positive. Many refer to the size of the statue to show how impressive it was.)

If you are reading *The Story of the Statue of Liberty* during small group time, then return to pp. 382–385a to guide the reading.

3 Inquiry: Extend Concepts

INVESTIGATE Provide time for students to investigate their topics in books or online. If necessary, help them locate information that is focused on their topics.

Independent Reading Options

Trade Book Library

eSTREET INTERACTIVE
www.ReadingStreet.com

Teacher Guides are available on the Leveled Reader Database.

ELL

If... students need more scaffolding and practice with the **Main Selection,** **then...** use the activities on p. DI•22 in the Teacher Resources section on SuccessNet.

Advanced

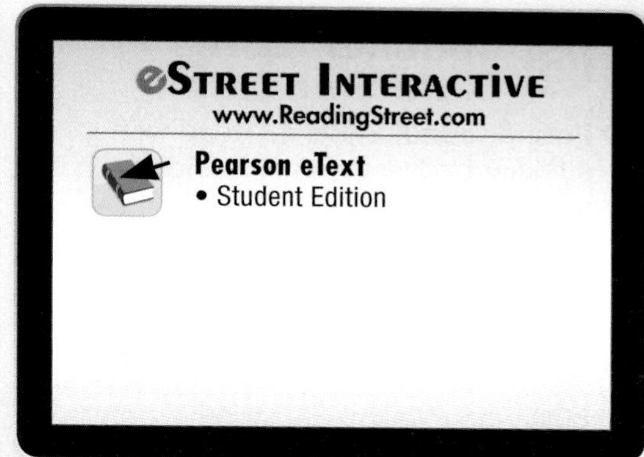

1 Build Word Knowledge

Extend Amazing Words and Selection Vocabulary

impressive	tribute	enlighten
contribution	dedication	competition
recognizable	disgrace	staggering
fund		

crown	liberty	models
symbol	tablet	torch
unforgettable	unveiled	

Team Talk Have students practice building more complex sentences. Display a sentence starter and have students add oral phrases or clauses using the Amazing Words and the selection vocabulary. Guide students to add at least three phrases or clauses per sentence.

2 Read

"A Nation of Immigrants"

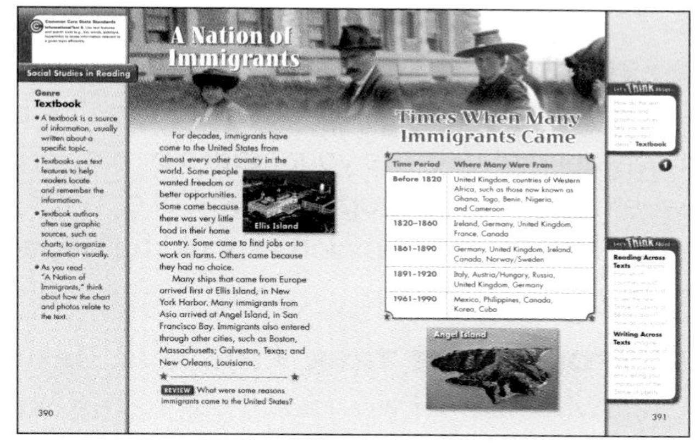

Social Studies in Reading

Genre
Textbook

- A textbook is a source of information, usually written about a specific topic.
- Textbooks use text features to help readers locate and remember the information.
- Textbook authors often use graphic sources, such as charts, to organize information visually.
- As you read "A Nation of Immigrants," think about how the chart and photos relate to the text.

A Nation of Immigrants

For decades, immigrants have come to the United States from almost every other country in the world. Some people wanted freedom or better opportunities. Some came because there was very little food in their home country. Some came to find jobs or to work on farms. Others came because they had no choice.

Many ships that came from Europe arrived first at Ellis Island, in New York Harbor. Many immigrants from Asia arrived at Angel Island, in San Francisco Bay. Immigrants also entered through other cities, such as Boston, Massachusetts; Galveston, Texas; and New Orleans, Louisiana.

Ellis Island

REVIEW What were some reasons immigrants came to the United States?

Times When Many Immigrants Came

Time Period	Where Many Were From
Before 1820	United Kingdom, countries of Western Africa, such as those now known as Ghana, Togo, Benin, Nigeria, and Cameroon
1820–1860	Ireland, Germany, United Kingdom, France, Canada
1861–1890	Germany, United Kingdom, Ireland, Canada, Norway/Sweden
1891–1920	Italy, Austria/Hungary, Russia, United Kingdom, Germany
1961–1990	Mexico, Philippines, Canada, Korea, Cuba

Angel Island

Textbook

Reading Across Texts

Writing Across Texts

390 391

BEFORE READING Have students read the genre information on textbooks on p. 390 and use the text features to set a purpose for reading.

DURING READING Have students read the selection. Point out the photographs, captions, and chart. Ask: How is a textbook different from narrative nonfiction, such as *The Story of the Statue of Liberty?* (A textbook uses visual aids to support and expand the text; narrative nonfiction provides information as a story.) As they read, have students consider how the text features increase understanding.

AFTER READING Have students discuss Reading Across Texts. Then have them do Writing Across Texts independently.

3 Inquiry: Extend Concepts

ORGANIZE INFORMATION Provide time for students to organize their information into a format that will effectively communicate their findings to their audience. Provide any necessary materials or computer time.

SMALL GROUP TIME

Independent Reading Options

Trade Book Library

eStreet Interactive
www.ReadingStreet.com
Teacher Guides are available on the Leveled Reader Database.

Advanced

Common Core State Standards

Foundational Skills 4. Read with sufficient accuracy and fluency to support comprehension. **Writing 1.** Write opinion pieces on topics or texts, supporting a point of view with reasons. **Speaking/Listening 4.** Report on a topic or text, tell a story, or recount an experience with appropriate facts and relevant, descriptive details, speaking clearly at an understandable pace. **Language 2.** Demonstrate command of the conventions of standard English capitalization, punctuation, and spelling when writing. **Also Writing 8.**

More Reading for Group Time

ADVANCED

Review

- Fact and Opinion
- Questioning

Use this suggested Leveled Reader or other text at students' instructional level.

eSTREET INTERACTIVE
www.ReadingStreet.com

Use the Leveled Reader Database for lesson plans and student pages for *The French Connection.*

1 Build Word Knowledge

Extend Capital Letters

IDENTIFY AND EXTEND Have partners read the instruction at the bottom of p. 389 and discuss how capital letters are used. Then have them reread the model notes and find examples of how the author used capital letters. Finally, have partners make lists of categories of proper nouns and practice correctly capitalizing the words.

2 Text-Based Comprehension

Read

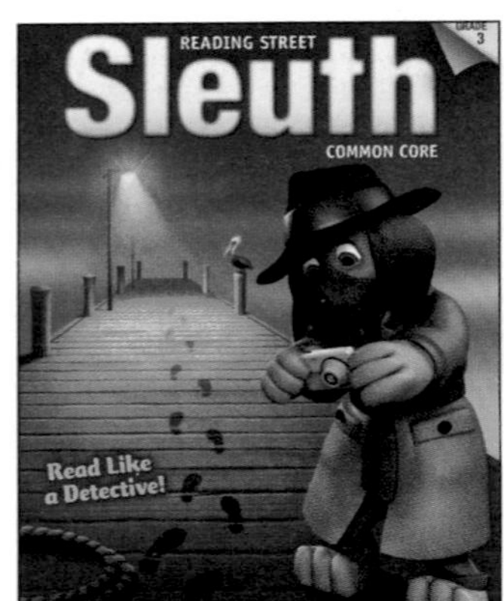

REREAD "America's National Bird" Have partners reread the selection and share their thoughts about the turkey as our national bird.

EXTEND UNDERSTANDING Talk together about your state's bird symbol. Consider why the bird may have been chosen as your state's bird symbol and whether it is an appropriate symbol or not. Remind students that their opinions should be backed up with convincing evidence.

PERFORMANCE TASK • Prove It! Ask students: If you were creating a club, what animal would you use to symbolize the values of your club? Have students write a paragraph to support their reasons for choosing this animal and draw a picture to represent their symbol. Remind students to provide specific details about how this animal symbolizes the values of their club.

COMMUNICATE Have small groups share their choices of animals for their clubs. Invite discussion about other animals that might symbolize a club's values.

3 Inquiry: Extend Concepts

COMMUNICATE Have students share their inquiry projects on American landmarks or national treasures with the rest of the class. Provide the following tips for presenting.

- Make eye contact with the audience and point to visuals as you speak.
- Speak slowly and pronounce names and places correctly.
- Explain any unfamiliar terms, events, or people.

Focus on Common Core State Standards ©

Main Selection, pp. 402–419

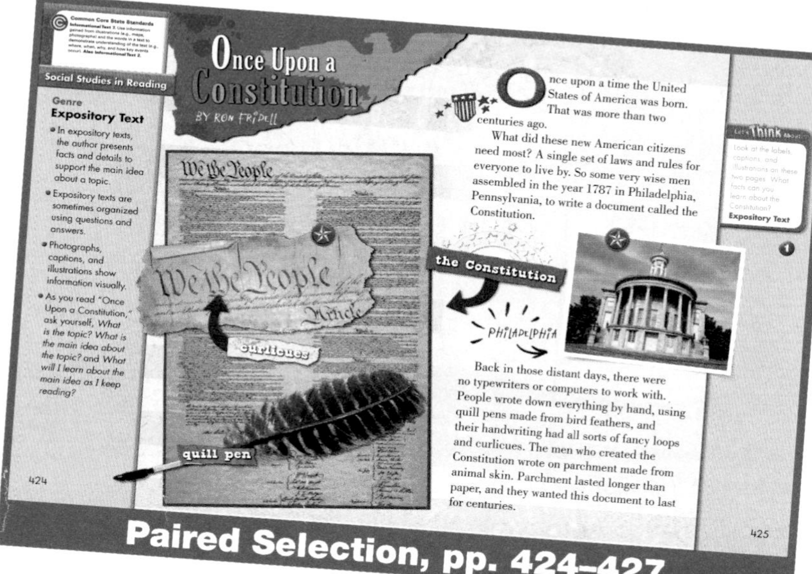

Paired Selection, pp. 424–427

Text-Based Comprehension

Cause and Effect
CCSS Informational Text 3.

Inferring
CCSS Informational Text 3.

Fluency

Appropriate Phrasing
CCSS Foundational Skills 4.

Writing and Conventions

Trait: Organization
CCSS Writing 4.

Writing Mini-Lesson: Poetry: Limerick
CCSS Writing 3., CCSS Language 3.

Conventions: Abbreviations
CCSS Language 1., CCSS Language 2.

Oral Vocabulary

Amazing Words

territory	affectionate
release	companion
loyal	nag
deserve	retrieve
manage	wandering

CCSS Language 6.

Selection Vocabulary

Antonyms
CCSS Language 4., CCSS Language 5.

Context Clues
CCSS Language 4., CCSS Language 4.a.

bows	foreign	perches
chilly	narrow	recipe
foolish		

Phonics and Spelling

Schwa
CCSS Foundational Skills 3., CCSS Language 2.f.

above	afraid
another	nickel
upon	sugar
animal	circus
paper	item
open	gallon
family	melon
travel	

Challenge Words

character	particular
cardinal	dinosaur
Oregon	

Listening and Speaking

Express an Opinion
CCSS Speaking/Listening 4.

Preview Your Week

What does it mean to grant freedom?

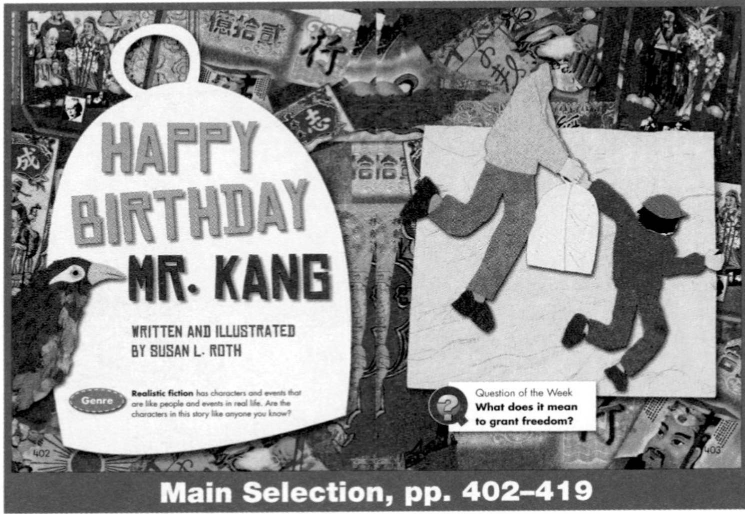

Main Selection, pp. 402–419

Genre: Realistic Fiction

Vocabulary: Antonyms

Text-Based Comprehension: Cause and Effect

Paired Selection, pp. 424–427

Social Studies in Reading

Genre: Expository Text

Build Content Knowledge

KNOWLEDGE GOALS

Students will understand that freedom

- can be granted to animals
- means pursuing interests
- can be granted through laws

THIS WEEK'S CONCEPT MAP

Develop a concept-related graphic organizer like the one below over the course of this week.

What it means to grant freedom

People can set wild animals free.

BUILD ORAL VOCABULARY

This week, students will acquire the following academic vocabulary/domain-specific words.

Amazing Words

territory	manage	nag
release	affectionate	retrieve
loyal	companion	wandering
deserve		

OPTIONAL CONCEPT-BASED READING Use the Digital Path to access readers offering different levels of text complexity.

Concept Literacy

Below-Level

On-Level

Advanced

ELL

ELD

This Week's Digital Resources

eStreet Interactive
www.ReadingStreet.com

Get Ready to Read

Concept Talk Video Use this video on the Digital Path to inspire interest and introduce the weekly concept of granting freedom.

Pearson eText Read the eText of the Student Edition pages on Pearson SuccessNet for comprehension and fluency support.

Envision It! Animations Use this colorful animation on the Digital Path to explain the target comprehension skill, Cause and Effect.

Read and Comprehend

Journal Use the Word Bank on the Digital Path to have students write sentences using this week's selection vocabulary words.

Background Building Audio CD This audio CD provides interesting background information about freedom to help students read and comprehend the weekly texts.

Pearson eText Read the eText of the main selection, *Happy Birthday Mr. Kang,* and the paired selection, "Once Upon a Constitution," with audio support on Pearson SuccessNet.

Vocabulary Activities A variety of interactive vocabulary activities on the Digital Path help students practice selection vocabulary and concept-related words.

Story Sort Use the Story Sort Activity on the Digital Path after reading *Happy Birthday Mr. Kang* to involve students in summarizing.

Language Arts

Grammar Jammer Opt for a stimulating animation on the Digital Path to provide an engaging grammar lesson that will capture students' attention.

Pearson eText Find the Student Edition eText of the Let's Write It! and Let's Learn It! pages with audio support on Pearson SuccessNet.

Additional Resources

Teacher Resources DVD-ROM Use the following resources on the TR DVD or on Pearson SuccessNet throughout the week:

- Amazing Word Cards
- Reader's and Writer's Notebook
- Writing Transparencies
- Daily Fix-It Transparencies
- Scoring Rubrics
- Grammar Transparencies
- ELL Support
- Let's Practice It!
- Graphic Organizers
- Vocabulary Cards

This Week's Skills

Phonics/Word Analysis
Schwa

Comprehension
Skill: Cause and Effect
Strategy: Inferring

Language
Vocabulary: Antonyms
Conventions: Abbreviations

Fluency
Appropriate Phrasing

Writing
Poetry: Limerick

5-Day Planner

DAY 1

Get Ready to Read

Content Knowledge 394j
Oral Vocabulary: *territory, release, loyal, deserve*

Monitor Progress
Check Oral Vocabulary

Phonics/Word Analysis 396a
Schwa
READ Decodable Reader 27A
Reread for Fluency

Read and Comprehend

Text-Based Comprehension 398c
Cause and Effect
Inferring

Fluency 398–399
Appropriate Phrasing

Selection Vocabulary 399a
bows, chilly, foolish, foreign, narrow, perches, recipe

Language Arts

Research and Inquiry 399b
Identify and Focus Topic

Spelling 399c
Schwa, Pretest

Conventions 399d
Abbreviations

Handwriting 399d
Cursive Letters *B, P,* and *R*

Writing 399e
Poetry: Limerick

DAY 2

Get Ready to Read

Content Knowledge 400a
Oral Vocabulary: *manage, affectionate*

Phonics/Word Analysis 400c
Schwa

Monitor Progress
Check Word Reading

Literary Terms 400d
Metaphor

Read and Comprehend

Vocabulary Skill 400e
Antonyms

Fluency 400–401
Appropriate Phrasing

Text-Based Comprehension 402–403
READ *Happy Birthday Mr. Kang* —1st Read

Language Arts

Research and Inquiry 411b
Navigate/Search

Conventions 411c
Abbreviations

Spelling 411c
Schwa

Writing 411d
Poetry: Limerick

DAY 3

Get Ready to Read

Content Knowledge 412a
Oral Vocabulary: *companion, nag*

Phonics/Word Analysis 412c
Fluent Word Reading
DECODE AND READ
Decodable Practice Passage 27B

Read and Comprehend

Text-Based Comprehension 412e
Cause and Effect
Inferring
READ *Happy Birthday Mr. Kang* —2nd Read
Monitor Progress
Check Retelling

Fluency 421b
Appropriate Phrasing

Language Arts

Research and Study Skills 421c
Maps

Research and Inquiry 421d
Analyze Information

Conventions 421e
Abbreviations

Spelling 421e
Schwa

Writing 422–423
Poetry: Limerick

DAY 4

Get Ready to Read

Content Knowledge 424a
Oral Vocabulary: *retrieve, wandering*

Phonics/Word Analysis 424c
Review Vowel Sounds /ü/ and /u̇/
Fluent Word Reading
DECODE AND READ
Decodable Practice Passage 27C

Read and Comprehend

Genre 424g
Expository Text
READ "Once Upon a Constitution" —Paired Selection

Fluency 428–429
Appropriate Phrasing
Monitor Progress Check Fluency

Vocabulary Skill 429a
Antonyms

Listening and Speaking 429a
Express an Opinion

Language Arts

Research and Inquiry 429b
Synthesize

Conventions 429c
Abbreviations

Spelling 429c
Schwa

Writing 429d
Poetry: Limerick

DAY 5

Get Ready to Read

Content Knowledge 429f
Review Oral Vocabulary
Monitor Progress
Check Oral Vocabulary

Read and Comprehend

Text-Based Comprehension 429h
Review Cause and Effect

Vocabulary Skill 429h
Review Antonyms

Phonics/Word Analysis 429i
Review Schwa

Literary Terms 429i
Review Metaphor

Assessment 429j, 429l
Monitor Progress
Fluency; Cause and Effect

Language Arts

Research and Inquiry 429n
Communicate

Spelling 429o
Schwa, Test

Conventions 429o
Abbreviations

Writing 429p
Poetry: Limerick

Wrap Up Your Week! 429q

Access for All

What do I do in group time?

It's as easy as 1-2-3!

1 TEACHER-LED SMALL GROUPS → 2 INDEPENDENT PRACTICE STATIONS → 3 INDEPENDENT READING

Small Group Time

SKILL DEVELOPMENT

- Schwa
- Cause and Effect
- Inferring
- Antonyms

DEEP UNDERSTANDING

This Week's Knowledge Goals

Students will understand that freedom
- can be granted to animals
- means pursuing interests
- can be granted through laws

1 Small Group Lesson Plan

	DAY 1 Differentiate Vocabulary	DAY 2 Differentiate Comprehension
OL **On-Level** pp. SG•18–SG•22	**Build Word Knowledge** Practice Amazing Words **Text-Based Comprehension** Read *Reading Street Sleuth,* pp. 70–71 or Leveled Readers	**Build Word Knowledge** Practice Selection Vocabulary **Access Text** Read *Happy Birthday Mr. Kang*
SI **Strategic Intervention** pp. SG•23–SG•27	**Build Word Knowledge** Reteach Amazing Words **Text-Based Comprehension** Read *Reading Street Sleuth,* pp. 70–71 or Leveled Readers	**Build Word Knowledge** Reteach Selection Vocabulary **Access Text** Read *Happy Birthday Mr. Kang*
A **Advanced** pp. SG•28–SG•32	**Build Word Knowledge** Extend Amazing Words **Text-Based Comprehension** Read *Reading Street Sleuth,* pp. 70–71 or Leveled Readers	**Build Word Knowledge** Extend Selection Vocabulary **Access Text** Read *Happy Birthday Mr. Kang*
Independent Inquiry Project	Identify Questions	Investigate
ELL **If...** students need more scaffolding and practice with...	**Vocabulary,** **then...** use the activities on pp. DI•42–DI•43 in the Teacher Resources section on SuccessNet.	**Comprehension Skill,** **then...** use the activities on p. DI•46 in the Teacher Resources section on SuccessNet.

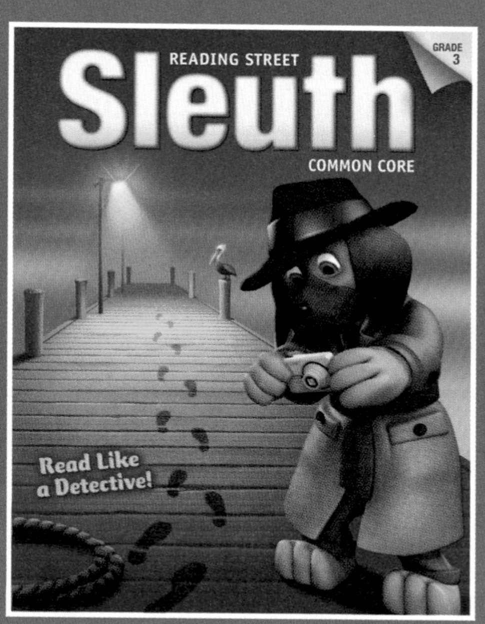

Reading Street Sleuth

- Provides access to grade-level text for all students
- Focuses on finding clues in text through close reading
- Builds capacity for complex text

Build Text-Based Comprehension

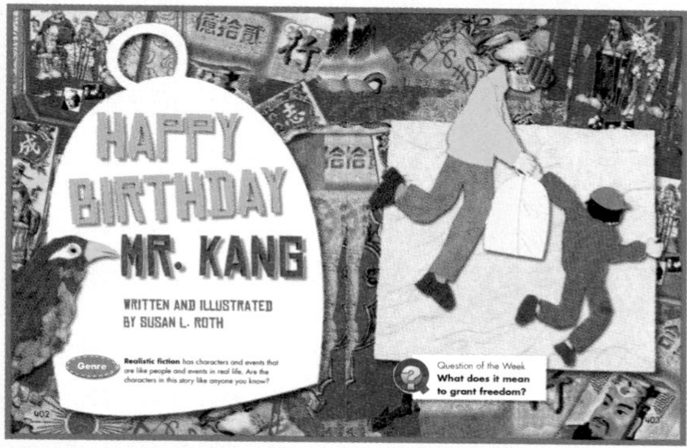

Happy Birthday Mr. Kang

Optional Leveled Readers

Concept Literacy

Below-Level

On-Level

Advanced

ELL

ELD

DAY 3	DAY 4	DAY 5
Differentiate Close Reading	**Differentiate Vocabulary**	**Differentiate Reteaching**
Reread to Develop Vocabulary **Close Reading** Read *Happy Birthday Mr. Kang*	**Build Word Knowledge** Develop Language Using Amazing Words **Text-Based Comprehension** Read "Once Upon a Constitution"	**Practice Abbreviations** **Text-Based Comprehension** Reread *Reading Street Sleuth,* pp. 70–71 or Leveled Readers
Reread to Develop Vocabulary **Close Reading** Read *Happy Birthday Mr. Kang*	**Build Word Knowledge** Review/Discuss Amazing Words **Text-Based Comprehension** Read "Once Upon a Constitution"	**Review Abbreviations** **Text-Based Comprehension** Reread *Reading Street Sleuth,* pp. 70–71 or Leveled Readers
Reread to Extend Vocabulary **Close Reading** Read *Happy Birthday Mr. Kang* Investigate	**Build Word Knowledge** Extend Amazing Words and Selection Vocabulary **Text-Based Comprehension** Read "Once Upon a Constitution" Organize	**Extend Abbreviations** **Text-Based Comprehension** Reread *Reading Street Sleuth,* pp. 70–71 or Leveled Readers Communicate
Main Selection, **then...** use the activities on p. DI•47 in the Teacher Resources section on SuccessNet.	**Amazing Words,** **then...** use the Routine on pp. xxxvi–xxxvii in the *ELL Handbook.*	**Conventions and Writing,** **then...** use the activities on pp. DI•49–DI•50 in the Teacher Resources section on SuccessNet.

2 Independent Stations

Practice Last Week's Skills

Focus on these activities when time is limited.

ACCESS FOR ALL
- Below-Level Activities
- On-Level Activities
- Advanced Activities

WORD WISE

Spell and use words in sentences.

OBJECTIVES
- Spell words with the vowel sounds in *moon* and *foot.*

MATERIALS
- *Word Wise* Flip Chart Activity 27, teacher-made word cards, paper and pencils

 **Letter Tile Drag and Drop**

- Students write five words and sentences using each word. Then they list other words with the vowel sounds.
- Students write seven words and sentences using each word. Then they list other words with the vowel sounds.
- Students write nine words and sentences using each word. Then they list other words with the vowel sounds.

WORD WORK

Identify and pronounce words.

OBJECTIVES
- Identify and pronounce words with the vowel sounds in *moon* and *foot.*

MATERIALS
- *Word Work* Flip Chart Activity 27, teacher-made word cards, paper and pencils

 **Letter Tile Drag and Drop**

- Students write and say eight words, circle the *moon* or *foot* vowel sound in each, and write a poem using some of the words.
- Students write and say ten words, circle the *moon* or *foot* vowel sound in each, and then write a silly, four- or eight-line poem, using some of the words.
- Students write and say twelve words, circle the *moon* or *foot* vowel sound in each, and write a silly, four- or eight-line poem, using some of the words.

LET'S WRITE!

Write to aid research.

OBJECTIVES
- Take notes while reading a nonfiction selection.

MATERIALS
- *Let's Write!* Flip Chart Activity 27, paper and pencils

 **Grammar Jammer**

- Students read a below-level book and take notes about the main idea and details, paraphrasing and including key words and phrases.
- Students read an on-level book and take notes about the main idea and details, paraphrasing and including key words and phrases.
- Students read an above-level book and take notes about the main idea and details, paraphrasing and including key words and phrases.

WORDS TO KNOW

Determine word meanings.

OBJECTIVES
- Identify the meaning of words with prefix *un-.*

MATERIALS
- *Words to Know* Flip Chart Activity 27, teacher-made word cards, paper and pencils

 **Vocabulary Activities**

- Students write four words, circle the prefix in each, use a dictionary to define each word, and write sentences using the words.
- Students write six words, circle the prefix in each, use a dictionary to define each word, and write sentences using the words.
- Students write eight words, use a dictionary to define each, and write a sentence for each word and each base word.

READ FOR MEANING

Use text-based comprehension skills.

OBJECTIVES

- Identify fact and opinion in a nonfiction selection.

MATERIALS

- *Read for Meaning* Flip Chart Activity 27, Leveled Readers, paper and pencils

Pearson eText
- Leveled eReaders

Envision It! Animations

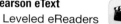

● Students read a book and write one sentence giving a fact from the selection and one sentence giving an opinion.

▲ Students read a book and write two sentences giving facts from the selection and two sentences giving opinions.

■ Students read a book and write a paragraph giving some of the facts and opinions the author includes.

GET FLUENT

Practice reading fluently with a partner.

OBJECTIVES

- Read aloud at an appropriate rate.

MATERIALS

- *Get Fluent* Flip Chart Activity 27, Leveled Readers

Pearson eText
- Leveled eReaders

● Partners take turns reading aloud at an appropriate rate from a Concept Literacy Reader or Below-Level Reader and providing feedback.

▲ Partners take turns reading aloud at an appropriate rate from an On-Level Reader and providing feedback.

■ Partners take turns reading aloud at an appropriate rate from an Advanced Reader and providing feedback.

Manage the Stations

Use these management tools to set up and organize your Practice Stations:

Practice Station Flip Charts

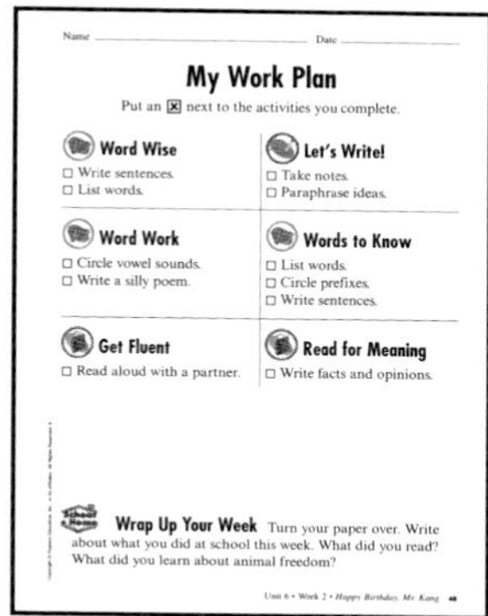
Name ____ Date ____

My Work Plan

Put an ☒ next to the activities you complete.

Word Wise
☐ Write sentences.
☐ List words.

Let's Write!
☐ Take notes.
☐ Paraphrase ideas.

Word Work
☐ Circle vowel sounds.
☐ Write a silly poem.

Words to Know
☐ List words.
☐ Circle prefixes.
☐ Write sentences.

Get Fluent
☐ Read aloud with a partner.

Read for Meaning
☐ Write facts and opinions.

Wrap Up Your Week Turn your paper over. Write about what you did at school this week. What did you read? What did you learn about animal freedom?

Classroom Management Handbook for Differentiated Instruction Practice Stations, p. 45

3 Independent Reading

Students should select appropriate complex texts to read and write about independently every day before, during, and after school.

Suggestions for this week's independent reading:
- Informational texts on last week's social studies topic: Symbols of freedom
- A high-quality magazine article about symbols of freedom
- An information-rich Web site about the statue of liberty and other symbols of freedom

BOOK TALK Have partners discuss their independent reading for the week. Tell them to refer to their Reading Logs and paraphrase what each selection was about. Then have students focus on discussing one or more of the following:

Key Ideas and Details
- What is the main idea of the text? What details support it?
- What conclusions did you draw as you read the text?

Craft and Structure
- How is the information in the text organized?
- What key words or phrases helped you identify the organizational structure?

Integration of Ideas
- Does the author state any claims or opinions? What are they?
- How well does the author support his or her claims or opinions?

Pearson eText
- Student Edition
- Decodable Readers
- Leveled Readers

Trade Book Library

School or Classroom Library

DAY 1 at a Glance

Content Knowledge
Oral Vocabulary

Phonics/Word Analysis
Schwa

Text-Based Comprehension
Cause and Effect
Inferring

Fluency
Appropriate Phrasing

Selection Vocabulary

Research and Inquiry
Identify and Focus Topic

Spelling
Schwa

Conventions
Abbreviations

Handwriting
Cursive Letters *B, P,* and *R*

Writing
Poetry: Limerick

Materials

- Student Edition
- Reader's and Writer's Notebook
- Decodable Reader

Bridge to Common Core

INTEGRATION OF KNOWLEDGE/IDEAS
This week, students will read, write, and talk about what it means to grant freedom.

Texts This Week
- "A Little Freedom"
- "A New Life"
- "Mr. Wang's Wonderful Noodles"
- *Happy Birthday Mr. Kang*
- "Once Upon a Constitution"

Social Studies Knowledge Goals
Students will understand that freedom
- can be granted to animals
- means pursuing interests
- can be granted through laws

Street Rhymes!

Should birds be in cages or fly free?
I would release them. Do you agree?
Should zoos be closed and animals set free?
What do you think? Now please tell me!

- To introduce this week's concept, read aloud the poem several times and ask students to join you.

Content Knowledge

Granting Freedom

CONCEPT TALK To further explore the unit concept of freedom, this week students will read, write, and talk about how freedom is granted. Write the Question of the Week, *What does it mean to grant freedom?,* on the board.

Build Oral Language

TALK ABOUT GRANTING FREEDOM Have students turn to pp. 394–395 in their Student Editions. Look at each of the photos. Then use the prompts to guide discussion and create a concept map.

- How is the man granting the shark freedom? (by letting it go to swim freely) It's now free to swim in its own *territory,* or area of the sea.
- What are the children in the other pictures doing? (letting a seal out of a box and an insect out of a jar) They are *releasing* the seal and the insect into the wild and letting them go *wandering* wherever they want to go.
- What do the shark, the seal, and the insect have in common? (They are all wild animals that people are letting go free.) Let's add *People can set wild animals free* to our concept map.

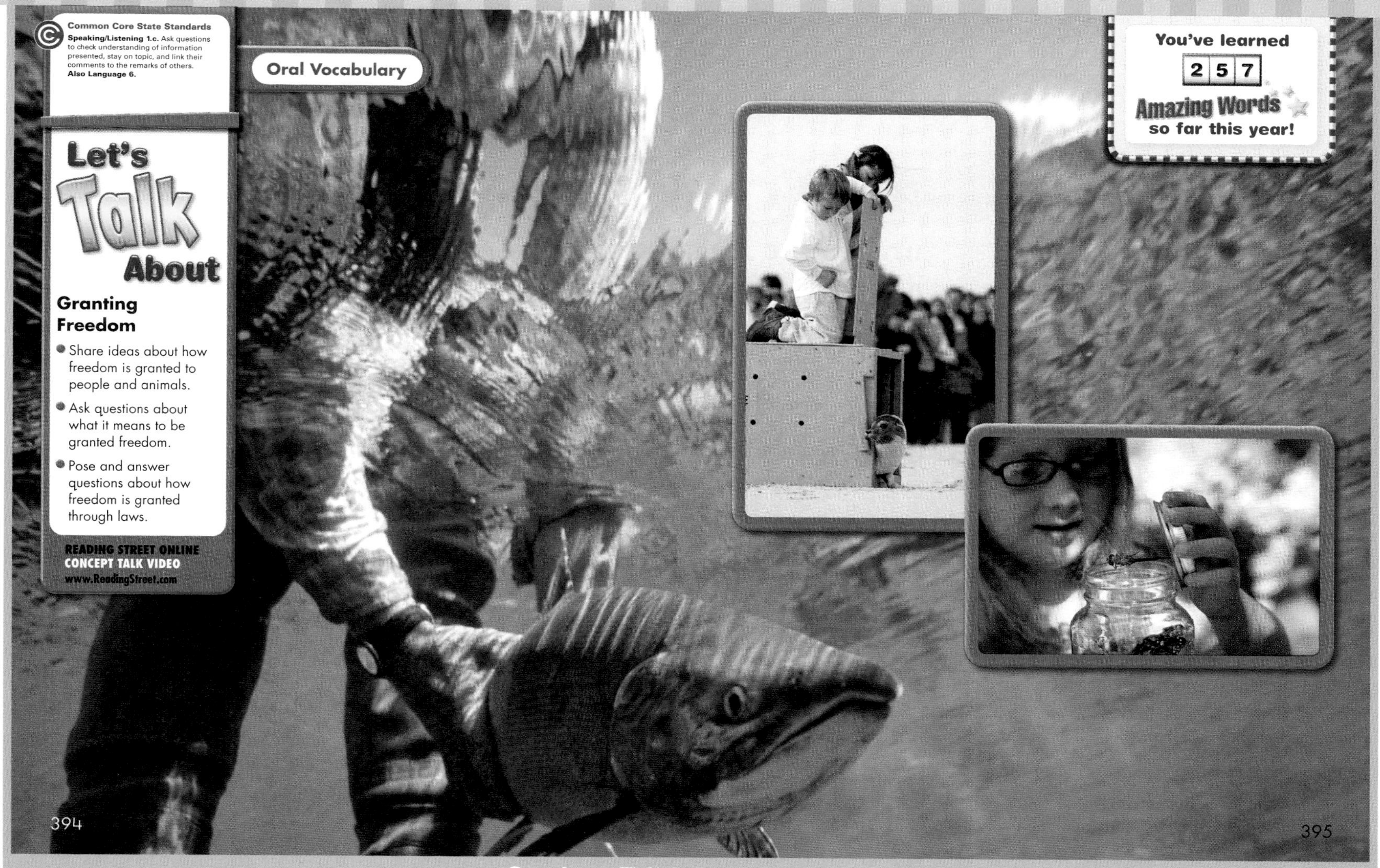

Common Core State Standards
Speaking/Listening 1.c. Ask questions to check understanding of information presented, stay on topic, and link their comments to the remarks of others. **Also Language 6.**

Oral Vocabulary

Let's Talk About

Granting Freedom

- Share ideas about how freedom is granted to people and animals.
- Ask questions about what it means to be granted freedom.
- Pose and answer questions about how freedom is granted through laws.

READING STREET ONLINE
CONCEPT TALK VIDEO
www.ReadingStreet.com

You've learned 257 Amazing Words so far this year!

394

395

Student Edition, pp. 394–395

CONNECT TO READING Tell students that this week they will be reading about different ways that freedom can be granted. Encourage students to add concept-related words to this week's concept map.

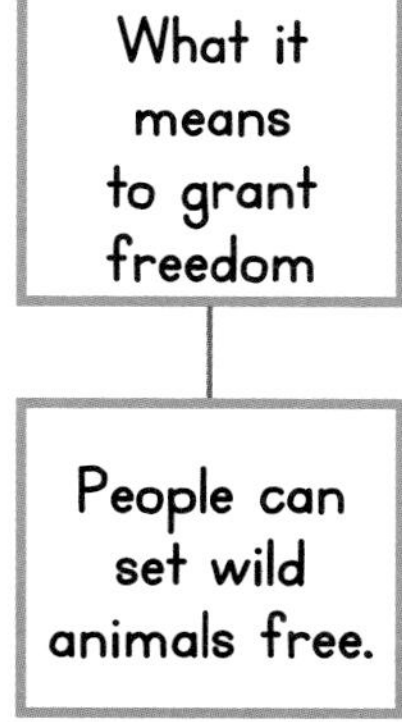

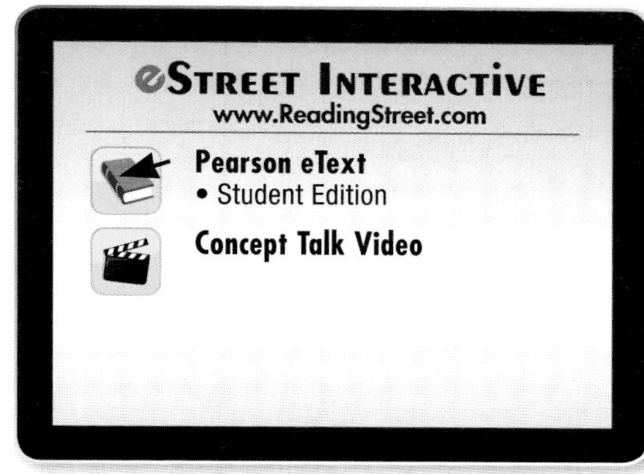

Preteach Concepts Use the Day 1 instruction on ELL Poster 27 to build knowledge, develop concepts, and build oral vocabulary.

ELL Support Additional ELL support and modified instruction is provided in the *ELL Handbook* and in the ELL Support Lessons found on the *Teacher Resources DVD-ROM.*

Common Core State Standards

Speaking/Listening 1. Engage effectively in a range of collaborative discussions (one-on-one, in groups, and teacher led) with diverse partners on grade 3 topics and texts, building on others' ideas and expressing their own clearly. **Speaking/Listening 2.** Determine the main ideas and supporting details of a text read aloud or information presented in diverse media and formats, including visually, quantitatively, and orally. **Language 4.** Determine or clarify the meaning of unknown and multiple-meaning word and phrases based on grade 3 reading and content, choosing flexibly from a range of strategies. **Language 6.** Acquire and use accurately grade-appropriate conversational, general academic, and domain-specific words and phrases, including those that signal spatial and temporal relationships (e.g., *After dinner that night we went looking for them*).

Amazing Words

You've learned 257 words so far.

You'll learn 010 words this week!

territory	affectionate
release	companion
loyal	nag
deserve	retrieve
manage	wandering

Content Knowledge

Zoom in on

Build Oral Vocabulary

INTRODUCE AMAZING WORDS "A Little Freedom" on p. 395b is about two robots that want to be set free. Tell students to listen for this week's Amazing Words—*territory, release, loyal,* and *deserve*—as you read the Teacher Read Aloud on p. 395b.

Amazing Words — Robust Vocabulary Routine

1. **Introduce** Write the word *territory* on the board. Have students say the word aloud with you. In "A Little Freedom," we learn that *territory* is somewhere you can stand. Are there any other context clues that tell me the meaning of this word? Supply a student-friendly definition.
2. **Demonstrate** Have students answer questions to demonstrate understanding. Where is a *territory* where sharks might live? How might a dog protect its *territory?*
3. **Apply** Ask students to think of examples of different *territories* and who or what might live in each one.
4. **Display the Word** Run your hand under the syllables *ter-ri-to-ry* as you read the word. Have students say the word again.

See p. OV•2 to teach *release, loyal,* and *deserve.*

Routines Flip Chart

AMAZING WORDS AT WORK Reread "A Little Freedom" aloud. As students listen, have them notice how the Amazing Words are used in context. To build oral vocabulary, lead the class in a discussion about the Amazing Words' meanings. Then have students state the main idea of the selection and give supporting details.

Check Oral Vocabulary

During discussion, listen for students' use of Amazing Words.

If... students are unable to use the Amazing Words in discussion,

then... use the Oral Vocabulary Routine in the Routines Flip Chart to demonstrate words in different contexts.

Teacher Read Aloud

MODEL FLUENCY As you read "A Little Freedom," model appropriate phrasing by grouping words in a meaningful way and paying attention to punctuation cues.

A Little Freedom

Ten-year-old Billy and Laury Norton have grown up under the care of two robots, JIL and JAK. Over the years, Billy and Laury have become quite fond of their robot friends. Tonight, JIL and JAK have an unusual request.

"Yes, JIL, JAK?" said Mr. Norton. He noticed the robots had been standing away from their usual territory near the children for several minutes. "Do you want something?"

JAK took one step forward. It seemed as though he were clearing his throat. "Dear Norton family," he began. "We would like our freedom. We would like you to release us."

"No-o-o-oo!" Bill and Laury wailed simultaneously.

"But why?" Mrs. Norton asked. "Don't you like us?"

"You're fine," answered JIL. "You've been very good employers."

"And of course we love Laury and Billy—," continued JAK.

"As much as robots can love," finished JIL.

"Well, then?" asked Mr. Norton.

JAK began, "Seven days ago, Billy mentioned freedom and how nice it is. And we've heard about freedom and read about it for years—"

JIL added, "Freedom of the press, freedom from slavery, religious freedom, freedom from underarm embarrassment—"

"'The land of the free, and the home of the brave.' It sounds like a nice thing, freedom," finished JAK.

"It's terribly important—to us humans," added Mr. Norton.

Billy said, "Our teacher Ms. Clive says our freedom is as important to us as the air we breathe."

Laury said, "But you can't be free—you're robots. And besides, we need you!"

"You're growing up, now," said JIL. "We're probably going to be too small for you in a year or so."

"And we know that we're out-of-date, technologically," added JAK. "We've been loyal to your family and served you for ten years, and we'd like to be free now."

"I guess you deserve it." Mrs. Norton looked back and forth between Billy and Laury and JIL and JAK. "But really," she said hesitatingly, "you belong to the children."

Laury and Billy seemed almost on the verge of tears.

"But—but—," began Billy.

"We'd miss you!" Laury burst out.

After a few days and a lot of thought, Billy and Laury finally agreed to set JAK and JIL free.

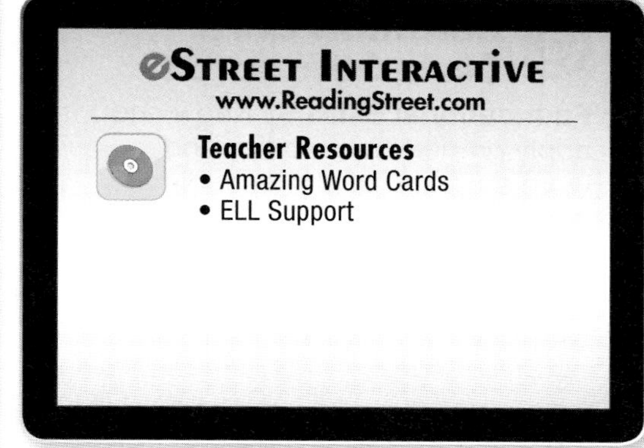

ELL Support for Read Aloud Use the modified Read Aloud on p. DI•44 of the ELL Support lessons on the *Teacher Resources DVD-ROM* to prepare students to listen to "A Little Freedom."

Check Understanding Stop after reading each paragraph to discuss the content with students. Clarify understanding by asking questions such as: What do the robots want? What kinds of freedoms do the robots want? Why might it be difficult for the owners to give the robots freedom?

Common Core State Standards

Foundational Skills 3. Know and apply grade-level phonics and word analysis skills in decoding words. **Foundational Skills 3.c.** Decode multisyllable words.

Skills Trace

Schwa

Introduce U6W2D1

Practice U6W2D2; U6W2D3

Reteach/Review U6W2D5; U6W3D4

Assess/Test Weekly Test U6W2
Benchmark Test U6

KEY: U=Unit W=Week D=Day

Vocabulary Support

You may wish to explain the meanings of these words.

almond a brown-skinned nut widely used in cooking

cardinal a North American songbird

Phonics/Word Analysis

Teach/Model

Schwa

CONNECT Write *termite* and *remote.* You can already read words like these that have more than one syllable. Read these words. Today you will learn to read multisyllabic words that have an unaccented syllable.

MODEL Write *affect.* I know that *affect* is a two-syllable word. When I read words that have more than one syllable, I know that at least one of the syllables is accented, or spoken with more force than the others. The syllable or syllables that are unaccented often have a vowel sound that is different from its normal sound. I can hear that sound in the first syllable of *affect.* The name for the vowel sound is *schwa.* This vowel sound can be spelled by any vowel. When I am not sure how to pronounce a multisyllabic word, I can say the schwa sound for the vowel in each syllable until I recognize the word.

GROUP PRACTICE Have students read the words below with you, and identify the unaccented syllable and schwa sound.

almond	**China**	**marble**	**cover**
circus	**April**	**occur**	**cardinal**

REVIEW What do you know about reading words with unaccented syllables? When you read a multisyllabic word, try stressing different syllables and using /ə/ in place of a vowel's normal sound until you recognize the word.

Guide Practice

MODEL Have students turn to p. 396 in their Student Editions. Each word on this page has an unaccented syllable with the schwa sound. The first word is *about.* I hear the schwa sound in the first syllable. The schwa sound is spelled *a.*

GROUP PRACTICE For each word in Words I Can Blend, ask students to segment the word parts. Make sure that students identify the correct sound for schwa in unaccented syllables. Then have them read the words.

Corrective feedback — **If...** students have difficulty reading a word, **then...** model reading the parts and then the whole word, and then ask students to read it with you.

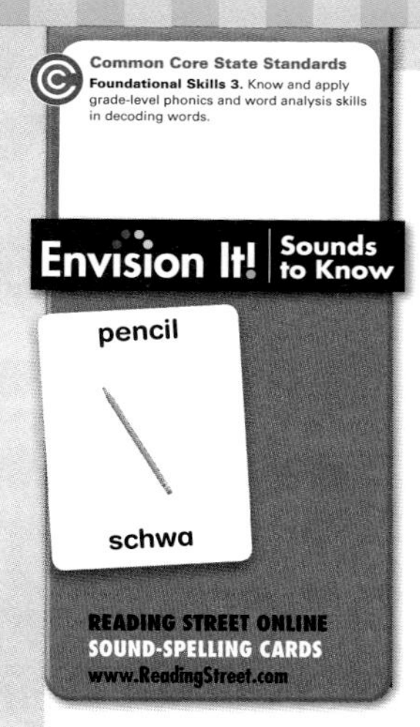

Phonics

Schwa

Words I Can Blend

about
benefit
difficult
popular
anonymous

Sentences I Can Read

1. The fire chief told us about the benefits of having a working smoke detector.
2. Red is a popular color.
3. The gift was anonymous.

396

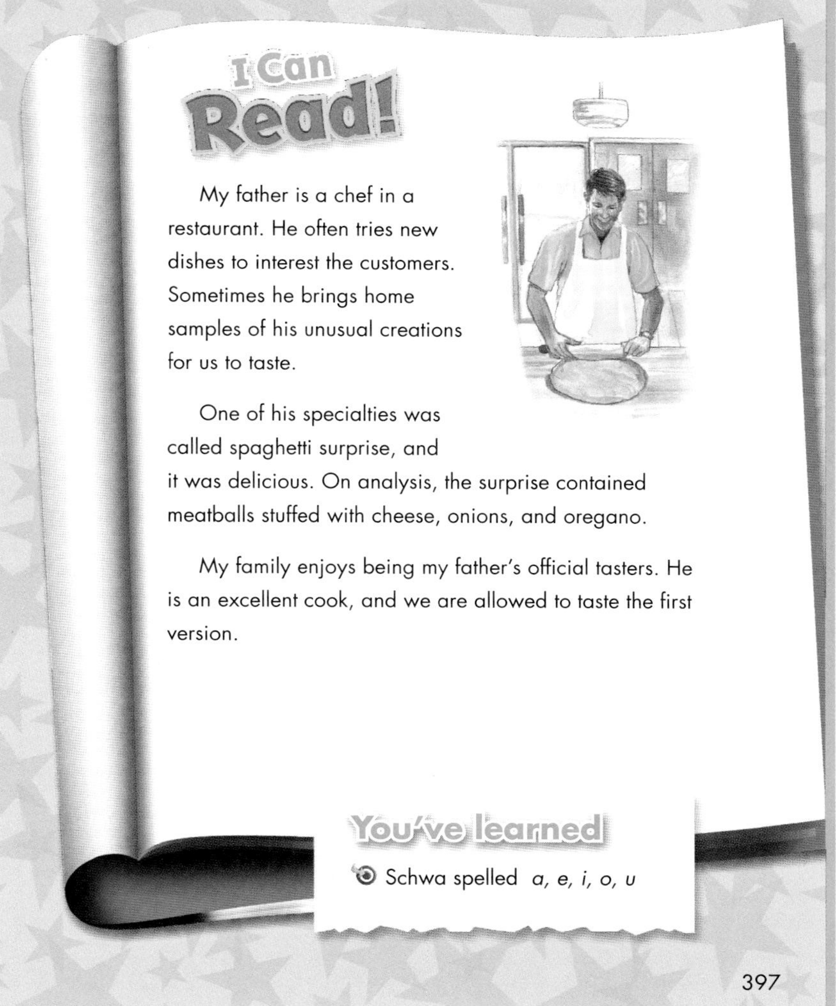

I Can Read!
My father is a chef in a restaurant. He often tries new dishes to interest the customers. Sometimes he brings home samples of his unusual creations for us to taste.
One of his specialties was called spaghetti surprise, and it was delicious. On analysis, the surprise contained meatballs stuffed with cheese, onions, and oregano.
My family enjoys being my father's official tasters. He is an excellent cook, and we are allowed to taste the first version.

You've learned

Schwa spelled *a, e, i, o, u*

397

Student Edition, pp. 396–397

Apply

READ WORDS IN ISOLATION After students can successfully segment and blend the words on p. 396 in their Student Editions, point to words in random order and ask students to read them naturally.

READ WORDS IN CONTEXT Have students read each of the sentences on p. 396. Have them identify words in the sentences that have the schwa sound.

 Pair students and have them take turns reading each of the sentences aloud.

Chorally read the I Can Read! passage on p. 397 with students. Then have them read the passage aloud to themselves.

ON THEIR OWN For additional practice, use *Reader's and Writer's Notebook,* p. 396.

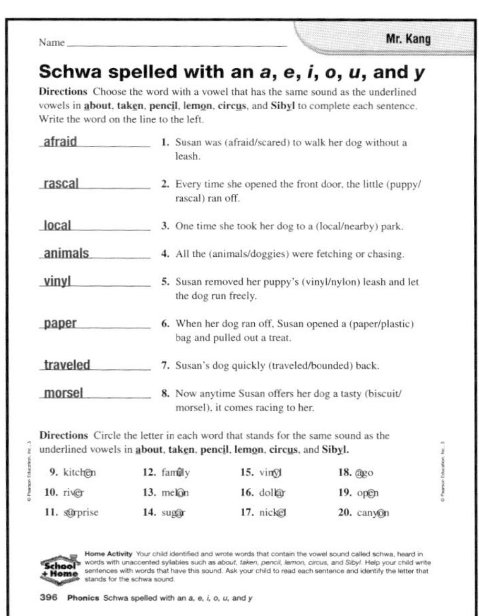

Name ______ Mr. Kang

Schwa spelled with an *a*, *e*, *i*, *o*, *u*, and *y*

Directions Choose the word with a vowel that has the same sound as the underlined vowels in **about**, **taken**, **pencil**, **lemon**, **circus**, and **Sibyl** to complete each sentence. Write the word on the line to the left.

afraid 1. Susan was (afraid/scared) to walk her dog without a leash.
rascal 2. Every time she opened the front door, the little (puppy/rascal) ran off.
local 3. One time she took her dog to a (local/nearby) park.
animals 4. All the (animals/doggies) were fetching or chasing.
vinyl 5. Susan removed her puppy's (vinyl/nylon) leash and let the dog run freely.
paper 6. When her dog ran off, Susan opened a (paper/plastic) bag and pulled out a treat.
traveled 7. Susan's dog quickly (traveled/bounded) back.
morsel 8. Now anytime Susan offers her dog a tasty (biscuit/morsel), it comes racing to her.

Directions Circle the letter in each word that stands for the same sound as the underlined vowels in **about**, **taken**, **pencil**, **lemon**, **circus**, and **Sibyl.**

9. kitchen	12. family	15. vinyl	18. ago
10. river	13. melon	16. dollar	19. open
11. surprise	14. sugar	17. nickel	20. canyon

Home Activity Your child identified and wrote words that contain the vowel sound called schwa, heard in words with unaccented syllables such as *about, taken, pencil, lemon, circus,* and *Sibyl.* Help your child write sentences with words that have this sound. Ask your child to read each sentence and identify the letter that stands for the schwa sound.

396 **Phonics** Schwa spelled with an *a, e, i, o, u,* and *y*

Reader's and Writer's Notebook, p. 396

Pronunciation Many languages do not have the schwa sound, so English language learners may have difficulty pronouncing and spelling the unstressed syllable in words such as *along* and *upon.* Provide additional practice with these words. Try having students clap the rhythm of the words to identify the syllables.

Common Core State Standards

Foundational Skills 3. Know and apply grade-level phonics and word analysis skills in decoding words. **Foundational Skills 3.c.** Decode multisyllable words. **Foundational Skills 3.d.** Read grade-appropriate irregularly spelled words. **Foundational Skills 4.** Read with sufficient accuracy and fluency to support comprehension. **Speaking/ Listening 5.** Create engaging audio recordings of stories or poems that demonstrate fluid reading at an understandable pace; add visual displays when appropriate to emphasize or enhance certain facts or details.

Decodable Reader 27A

If students need help, then...

Read *A Circus Life for Ben*

READ WORDS IN ISOLATION Have students turn to p. 133 in *Decodable Practice Readers 3.2.* Have students read each word.

Have students read the high-frequency words *a, was, to, water, some, said, everywhere, of, you, the, one, have, into, what, there, wanted, would, coming, been, they,* and *were* on the first page.

PREVIEW Have students read the title and preview the story. Tell them that they will read words with the schwa sound spelled *a, e, i, o, u,* and *y.*

READ WORDS IN CONTEXT Pair students for reading and listen as they read. One student begins. Students read the entire story, switching readers after each page. Partners reread the story. This time the other student begins. Make sure that students are monitoring their accuracy when they decode words.

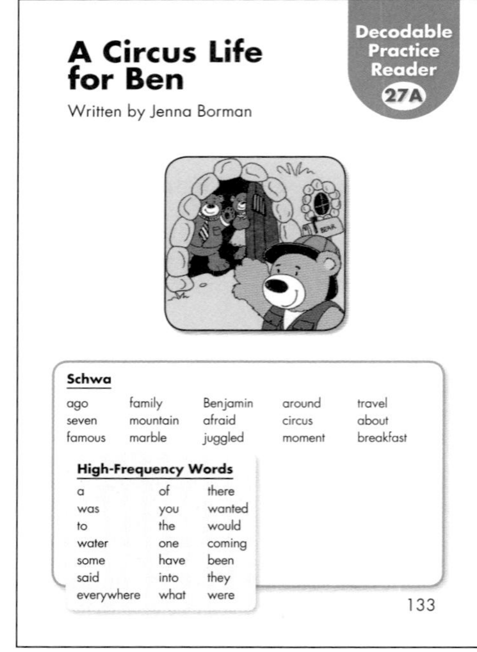

A Circus Life for Ben

Written by Jenna Borman

Decodable Practice Reader 27A

Schwa

ago	family	Benjamin	around	travel
seven	mountain	afraid	circus	about
famous	marble	juggled	moment	breakfast

High-Frequency Words

a	of	there
was	you	wanted
to	the	would
water	one	coming
some	have	been
said	into	they
everywhere	what	were

133

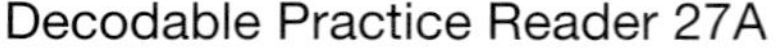

Decodable Practice Reader 27A

Long ago a family of bears lived in Berry Woods. There was Mama Bear, Papa Bear, and little Harry Benjamin Bear. It was a big name for a tiny bear. But Ben, as everybody called him, had big dreams.

Life was quiet in Berry Woods. It was way too quiet, if you asked Ben!

134

Ben wanted to travel around the world. He dreamed about sailing the seven seas. He would zip over bright blue water and see huge whales spout. He dreamed of climbing Earth's tallest mountain. He would plant his family's flag on it. He dreamed of exploring the darkest jungle. All wild animals would be afraid of him.

135

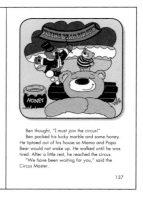

Then one day, Ben saw a poster. "A circus!" cried Ben. The Flying Bear Circus was coming to Berry Woods!

Ben liked everything about circuses. Now he dreamed about being a high-wire performer or a trapeze artist. He also dreamed about being a famous clown. A circus life was the life for Ben.

136

Ben thought, "I must join the circus!"

Ben packed his lucky marble and some honey. He tiptoed out of his house so Mama and Papa Bear would not wake up. He walked until he was tired. After a little rest, he reached the circus.

"We have been waiting for you," said the Circus Master.

137

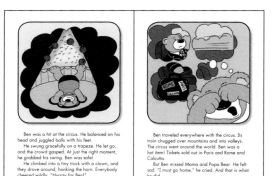

Ben was a hit at the circus. He balanced on his head and juggled balls with his feet.

He swung gracefully on a trapeze. He let go, and the crowd gasped. At just the right moment, he grabbed his swing. Ben was safe!

He climbed into a tiny truck with a clown, and they drove around, honking the horn. Everybody cheered wildly. "Hurray for Ben!"

138

Ben traveled everywhere with the circus. Its train chugged over mountains and into valleys. The circus went around the world. Ben was a hot item! Tickets sold out in Paris and Rome and Calcutta.

But Ben missed Mama and Papa Bear. He felt sad. "I must go home," he cried. And that is what he did.

139

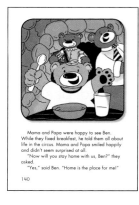

Mama and Papa were happy to see Ben. While they fixed breakfast, he told them all about life in the circus. Mama and Papa smiled happily and didn't seem surprised at all.

"Now will you stay home with us, Ben?" they asked.

"Yes," said Ben. "Home is the place for me!"

140

Corrective feedback	**If...** students have difficulty reading a word, **then...** refer them to the *Sound-Spelling Cards* to identify the word parts individually and then together to say the word. • What is the new word? • Is the new word a word you know? • Does it make sense in the story?

CHECK DECODING AND COMPREHENSION Have students retell the story to include characters, setting, and events. Then have students find words in the story that have the schwa sound. Students should supply *ago, around, mountain, about, juggled, family, travel, afraid, famous, moment, Benjamin, seven, circus, marble,* and *breakfast.*

EXTRA PRACTICE Have students take turns recording the story as they read. Then ask each student to review his or her recording to identify areas to improve reading fluency.

Reread for Fluency

REREAD DECODABLE READER Have students reread *Decodable Practice Reader 27A* to develop automaticity decoding words with the schwa sound.

Routine Oral Rereading

1. **Read** Have students read the entire book orally.
2. **Reread** To achieve optimal fluency, students should reread the text three or four times.
3. **Corrective Feedback** Listen as students read. Provide corrective feedback regarding their fluency and decoding.

Routines Flip Chart

Schwa

Beginning Write several words with the schwa sound from the *Decodable Practice Reader* on the board, such as *seven, famous, moment, family, afraid,* and *breakfast.* Point to each word as you read it aloud. Then underline the vowel in each unaccented syllable that stands for /ə/. Have students repeat the words with you.

Intermediate After reading, have students list the words in the story with the schwa sound. Have them sort the words according to the vowel that stands for /ə/. Ask students to compare their lists with a partner.

Advanced After reading the story, have students write about another adventure that Ben goes on. Ask students to use at least four words in their writing that have the schwa sound.

Common Core State Standards

Informational Text 3. Describe the relationship between a series of historical events, scientific ideas or concepts, or steps in technical procedures in a text, using language that pertains to time, sequence, and cause/effect. **Foundational Skills 4.** Read with sufficient accuracy and fluency to support comprehension. **Foundational Skills 4.b.** Read on-level prose and poetry orally with accuracy, appropriate rate, and expression on successive readings. **Also Informational Text 1.**

Skills Trace

Cause and Effect

Introduce U3W5D1; U4W5D1; U6W2D1
Practice U3W5D2; U3W5D3; U4W3D2; U4W5D2; U4W5D3; U5W1D2; U6W2D2; U6W2D3; U6W4D2; U6W4D3

Reteach/Review U3W5D5; U4W5D5; U6W2D5

Assess/Test Weekly Tests U3W5; U4W5; U6W2
Benchmark Test U6

KEY: U=Unit W=Week D=Day

Academic Vocabulary 

phrasing paying attention to punctuation when you read and pausing at appropriate places

Comprehension Support

Students may also turn to pp. EI•3 and EI•20 to review the skill and strategy if necessary.

Text-Based Comprehension

Cause and Effect
Inferring

READ Remind students of the weekly concept—Granting Freedom. Have students read "A New Life" on p. 399.

MODEL A CLOSE READ

Think Aloud What has caused immigrants to move to the United States? (They want to achieve their goals, to build better lives, and to experience freedom.) Can you identify any cause-and-effect clue words that show the relationship between immigrants coming to the United States and what causes them to do so? *(so, because)* I think immigrants can add to the richness of life in the United States. Making this inference helps me understand that, even though the population is increasing, the country will be more diverse.

TEACH Have students read p. 398. Explain that the skill of cause and effect and the strategy of inferring are tools they can use to deepen understanding of the text. Review the bulleted items and explanations on p. 398. Then have students use a graphic organizer like the one on p. 398 to identify cause and effect in the selection on p. 399.

GUIDE PRACTICE Have students reread "A New Life" using the callouts as guides. Then ask volunteers to respond to the questions in the callouts, citing specific examples from the text to support their answers.

Skill People have moved to the U.S. to build better lives for themselves and their families. People have moved to experience more freedom.
Strategy People bring their cultural heritage and new ideas with them.

APPLY Use *Reader's and Writer's Notebook* p. 397 for additional practice with cause and effect.

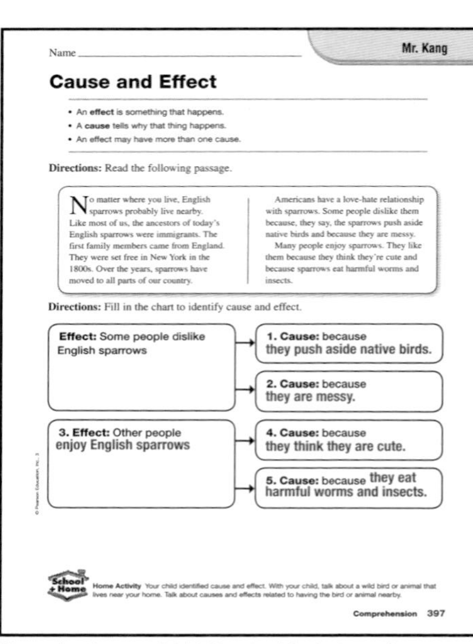
Name ____________ Mr. Kang

Cause and Effect

- An **effect** is something that happens.
- A **cause** tells why that thing happens.
- An effect may have more than one cause.

Directions: Read the following passage.

No matter where you live, English sparrows probably live nearby. Like most of us, the ancestors of today's English sparrows were immigrants. The first family members came from England. They were set free in New York in the 1800s. Over the years, sparrows have moved to all parts of our country.

Americans have a love-hate relationship with sparrows. Some people dislike them because, they say, the sparrows push aside native birds and because they are messy.

Many people enjoy sparrows. They like them because they think they're cute and because sparrows eat harmful worms and insects.

Directions: Fill in the chart to identify cause and effect.

Effect: Some people dislike English sparrows
1. Cause: because they push aside native birds.
2. Cause: because they are messy.
3. Effect: Other people enjoy English sparrows
4. Cause: because they think they are cute.
5. Cause: because they eat harmful worms and insects.

Home Activity Your child identified cause and effect. With your child, talk about a wild bird or animal that lives near your home. Talk about causes and effects related to having the bird or animal nearby.

Comprehension 397

Reader's and Writer's Notebook, p. 397

Comprehension Skill

Cause and Effect

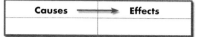

- An effect is something that happens.
- A cause is why that thing happens.
- An effect may have more than one cause.
- Use what you learned about cause and effect and a chart like the one below as you read "A New Life." Then write a short paragraph summarizing the cause-and-effect relationships.

Causes →	Effects

Comprehension Strategy

Inferring

As you read a selection, you make inferences, or decisions that make sense after you combine the details or facts the author has included with what you already know. When you come up with your own ideas based on information in a text, you are inferring.

A New Life

An *immigrant* is a person who has moved from one country into another. According to the U.S. Census Bureau, in 1990, the foreign-born population in the United States was about 19.8 million. By the year 2000, that number had grown to 37.2 million! Immigrants make up about 12.5 percent of the United States population.

There are many reasons that people have immigrated to the United States. Many people view the United States as a place where people can achieve any goal if they put their minds to it and work hard. Some come here because of the opportunities to build better lives for themselves and their families. Some move here so they can experience the freedom that the United States offers.

Skill What has caused some people to move to the United States?

Strategy What are some of the benefits of people immigrating to the United States?

Immigrants bring with them their cultural heritage, traditions, and new ideas. They have helped build the United States to make it what it is today.

Your Turn!

Need a Review? See the *Envision It! Handbook* for help with cause and effect and inferring.

Ready to Try It? As you read *Happy Birthday Mr. Kang*, use what you've learned about cause and effect and inferring to understand the text.

398 399

Student Edition, pp. 398–399

Model Fluent Reading

APPROPRIATE PHRASING Have students listen as you read the first paragraph of "A New Life." Explain that you will be careful to read with appropriate phrasing, which means that you will pay attention to all punctuation and pause at appropriate places.

Routine Oral Rereading

1. **Read** Have students read paragraph 1 of "A New Life" orally.
2. **Reread** To achieve optimal fluency, students should reread the text three or four times.
3. **Corrective Feedback** Have students read aloud without you. Encourage them to read carefully and look for punctuation marks that must be followed. Listen to make sure students pause at punctuation marks and where it makes sense, and provide feedback as needed.

Routines Flip Chart

ELL

Cause and Effect Have students stand. What did you do? Why did you do it? (We stood because you said to stand.) To figure out cause and effect in a story, you should think about key ideas: Rosa was doing well. The store was doing well. The Garcías were happy. Which sentence is the result of the other two sentences? (the last sentence)

Common Core State Standards

Writing 7. Conduct short research projects that build knowledge about a topic. **Speaking and Listening 1.** Engage effectively in a range of collaborative discussions (one-on-one, in groups, and teacher led) with diverse partners on grade 3 topics and texts, building on others' ideas and expressing their own clearly. **Language 4.** Determine or clarify the meaning of unknown and multiple-meaning words and phrases based on grade 3 reading and content, choosing flexibly from a range of strategies. **Language 6.** Acquire and use accurately grade-appropriate conversational, general academic, and domain-specific words and phrases, including those that signal spatial and temporal relationships (e.g., *After dinner that night we went looking for them*).

Selection Vocabulary

Use the following routine to introduce this week's tested selection vocabulary.

bows bends the head or body forward

chilly uncomfortably cold

foolish unwise; not making sense

foreign a place that is not your own country or homeland

narrow not wide

perches sits or rests on a bar, branch, or similar object

recipe ingredients and steps for making something to eat or drink

SEE IT/SAY IT Write *perches*. Scan across the word with your finger as you say it: *perch-es.*

HEAR IT Use the word in a sentence. My pet parakeet *perches* on a swing in its cage.

DEFINE IT Elicit definitions from students. How would you describe to another student what *perches* means? Clarify or give a definition when necessary. Yes, *perches* has almost the same meaning as *sits.* Restate the meaning of the word in student-friendly terms. *Perches* means to sit on a bar, a branch, or a similar object, such as a swing in a bird cage.

Team Talk Is an elephant an animal that *perches?* Why or why not? Turn and talk to your partner about this. Be prepared to explain your answer. Allow students time to discuss. Ask for examples. Rephrase their examples for usage when necessary or to correct misunderstandings.

MAKE CONNECTIONS Have students discuss the word. What animals do you know of that might *perch* in trees? Turn and talk to your partner about this. Then be prepared to share. Have students share. Rephrase their ideas for usage when necessary or to correct misunderstandings.

RECORD Have students write the word and its meaning.

Continue this routine to introduce the remaining words in this manner.

Corrective feedback	**If...** students are having difficulty understanding, **then...** review the definitions in small groups.

Research and Inquiry

Step 1 Identify and Focus Topic

TEACH Discuss the Question of the Week: *What does it mean to grant freedom?* Tell students they will research granting freedom to animals. They will write a newspaper article and present it to the class on Day 5.

Think Aloud **MODEL** I'll start by brainstorming a list of questions about different kinds of animals that might need to be granted freedom. Some possible questions could be *Where do baby chicks go after they have been hatched in a classroom? What happens to butterflies after a school butterfly release? What happens to an injured wild animal, such as a seal, after an oil spill once it has been nursed back to health?*

GUIDE PRACTICE After students have brainstormed inquiry questions, explain that tomorrow they will conduct online research of their questions. Help students identify keywords that will guide their search.

ON THEIR OWN Have students work individually, in pairs, or in small groups to write an inquiry question. Encourage them to generate their research topics from personal interests.

Day 1 SMALL GROUP TIME • Differentiate Vocabulary, p. SG•17

OL On-Level
- **Practice Vocabulary** Amazing Words
- **Read** *Reading Street Sleuth*, pp. 70–71

SI Strategic Intervention
- **Reteach Vocabulary** Amazing Words
- **Read** *Reading Street Sleuth*, pp. 70–71

A Advanced
- **Extend Vocabulary** Amazing Words
- **Read** *Reading Street Sleuth*, pp. 70–71
- **Introduce** Inquiry Project

eStreet Interactive
www.ReadingStreet.com

Teacher Resources
- Envision It! Pictured Vocabulary Cards
- Tested Vocabulary Cards

21st Century Skills

Internet Guy *Don Leu*

Weekly Inquiry Project

STEP 1	Identify and Focus Topic
STEP 2	Navigate/Search
STEP 3	Analyze Information
STEP 4	Synthesize
STEP 5	Communicate

Access for All

A Advanced

Have students brainstorm a list of keywords for their research and set a purpose for what they expect to find.

Multilingual Vocabulary Students can apply knowledge of their home languages to acquire new English vocabulary by using the Multilingual Vocabulary Lists (*ELL Handbook,* pp. 434–444).

ELL

If... students need more scaffolding and practice with **Vocabulary,** **then...** use the activities on pp. DI•42–DI•43 in the Teacher Resources section on SuccessNet.

Common Core State Standards

Language 1. Demonstrate command of the conventions of standard English grammar and usage when writing or speaking. **Language 2.** Demonstrate command of the conventions of standard English capitalization, punctuation, and spelling when writing. **Language 2.f.** Use spelling patterns and generalizations (e.g., word families, position-based spellings, syllable patterns, ending rules, meaningful word parts) in writing words.

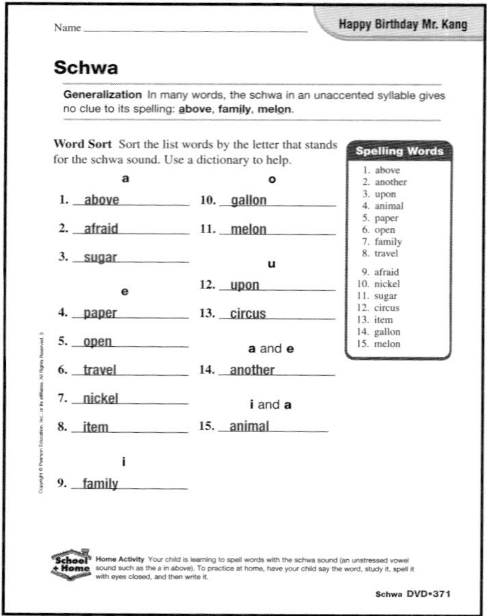

Name ______________ Happy Birthday Mr. Kang

Schwa

Generalization In many words, the schwa in an unaccented syllable gives no clue to its spelling: **above**, **family**, **melon**.

Word Sort Sort the list words by the letter that stands for the schwa sound. Use a dictionary to help.

a
1. above
2. afraid
3. sugar

e
4. paper
5. open
6. travel
7. nickel
8. item

i
9. family

o
10. gallon
11. melon

u
12. upon
13. circus

a and **e**
14. another

i and **a**
15. animal

Spelling Words
1. above
2. another
3. upon
4. animal
5. paper
6. open
7. family
8. travel
9. afraid
10. nickel
11. sugar
12. circus
13. item
14. gallon
15. melon

Home Activity Your child is learning to spell words with the schwa sound (an unstressed vowel sound such as the *a* in *above*). To practice at home, have your child say the word, study it, spell it with eyes closed, and then write it.

Schwa DVD•371

Let's Practice It! TR DVD•371

Spelling Pretest

Schwa

INTRODUCE Tell students to think of words with the *schwa* sound. *(oven, famous, stomach)* Remind them that the schwa is an unaccented syllable. This week we will spell words with the *schwa* sound.

PRETEST Say each word, read the sentence, and repeat the word.

1. above	Hold the ball **above** your head.
2. another	Would you like **another** muffin?
3. upon	Put your backpack **upon** the table.
4. animal	I saw a striped **animal** at the zoo.
5. paper	Can I borrow a sheet of **paper?**
6. open	I can't wait to **open** my present!
7. family	My brother is the youngest in the **family.**
8. travel	I would like to **travel** to the mountains.
9. afraid	Are you **afraid** of spiders?
10. nickel	The eraser costs a **nickel.**
11. sugar	Would you like **sugar** in your tea?
12. circus	We saw clowns at the **circus.**
13. item	Which **item** did you choose at the book fair?
14. gallon	Mom dropped the **gallon** of milk.
15. melon	Cantaloupe is my favorite **melon.**
Challenge words	
16. character	Mrs. Magoo is a **character** in a book.
17. cardinal	The **cardinal** is the state bird of Ohio.
18. Oregon	**Oregon** is a state in northwest United States.
19. particular	My sister is very **particular** about her room.
20. dinosaur	The museum has **dinosaur** bones on display.

SELF-CORRECT Have students self-correct their pretests by rewriting misspelled words.

ON THEIR OWN Use *Let's Practice It!* p. 371 on the *Teacher Resources DVD-ROM.*

Conventions

Abbreviations

MAKE CONNECTIONS On the board, write the names of several school staff members without using abbreviations, such as Mister Linden. Rewrite the names with abbreviations. Point out that each abbreviation stands for a longer word, begins with a capital letter, and ends with a period.

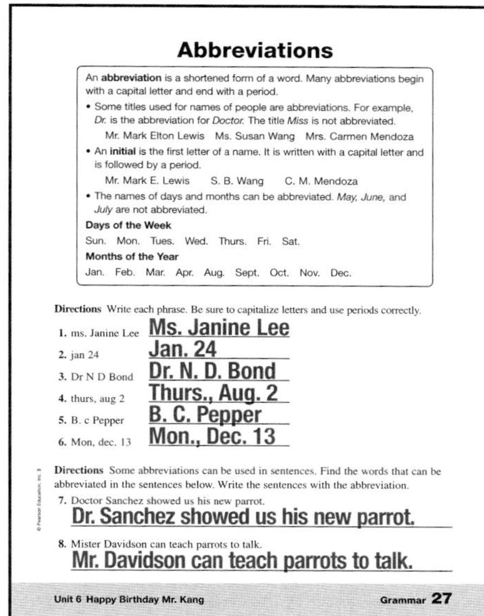

Abbreviations

An **abbreviation** is a shortened form of a word. Many abbreviations begin with a capital letter and end with a period.

- Some titles used for names of people are abbreviations. For example, *Dr.* is the abbreviation for *Doctor.* The title *Miss* is not abbreviated.
  Mr. Mark Elton Lewis   Ms. Susan Wang   Mrs. Carmen Mendoza
- An **initial** is the first letter of a name. It is written with a capital letter and is followed by a period.
  Mr. Mark E. Lewis   S. B. Wang   C. M. Mendoza
- The names of days and months can be abbreviated. *May, June,* and *July* are not abbreviated.

Days of the Week

Sun. Mon. Tues. Wed. Thurs. Fri. Sat.

Months of the Year

Jan. Feb. Mar. Apr. Aug. Sept. Oct. Nov. Dec.

Directions Write each phrase. Be sure to capitalize letters and use periods correctly.

1. ms. Janine Lee **Ms. Janine Lee**
2. jan 24 **Jan. 24**
3. Dr N D Bond **Dr. N. D. Bond**
4. thurs, aug 2 **Thurs., Aug. 2**
5. B. c Pepper **B. C. Pepper**
6. Mon, dec. 13 **Mon., Dec. 13**

Directions Some abbreviations can be used in sentences. Find the words that can be abbreviated in the sentences below. Write the sentences with the abbreviation.

7. Doctor Sanchez showed us his new parrot.
Dr. Sanchez showed us his new parrot.
8. Mister Davidson can teach parrots to talk.
Mr. Davidson can teach parrots to talk.

Unit 6 Happy Birthday Mr. Kang   Grammar **27**

Grammar Transparency 27, TR DVD

TEACH Display Grammar Transparency 27, and read aloud the explanation and examples. Point out the various abbreviations.

MODEL Model completing items 1 and 2. *Ms.* is an abbreviated title. It is pronounced /miz/. It begins with a capital letter and ends with a period.

GUIDE PRACTICE Guide students to complete items 3–6. Remind them to capitalize the first letter and to use periods correctly when writing abbreviations. Record the correct responses on the transparency.

APPLY Have students read sentences 7–8 on the transparency and write the abbreviation to correctly complete each sentence.

Handwriting

MODEL LETTER FORMATION AND SPACING Display the cursive uppercase letters *B, P,* and *R.* Follow the stroke instructions pictured to model letter formation. Explain that using proper letter spacing means that the letters in a word are evenly spaced with the same amount of space between letters. Model writing these words with proper letter spacing: *Rob's Birthday Party.*

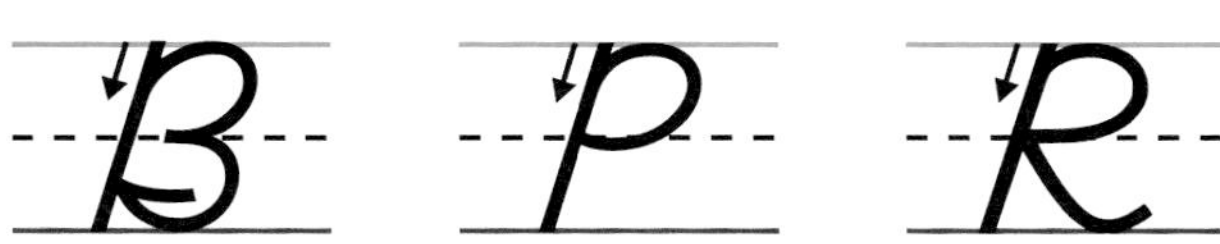

GUIDE PRACTICE Have students write these titles: *Play Ball, Rusty!, Band Plays Rock, Plain Red Box.* Circulate around the room, guiding students.

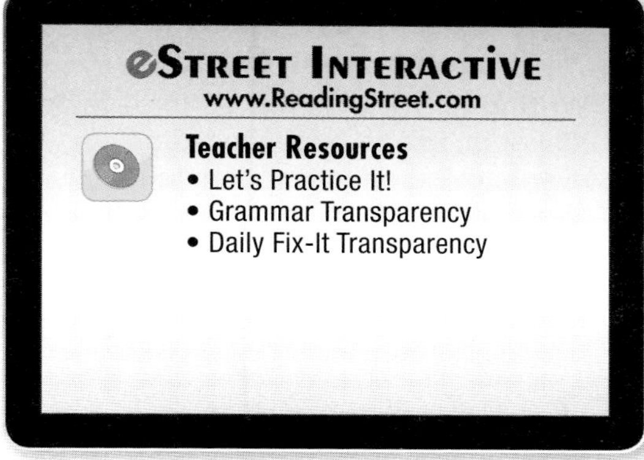

Daily Fix-It

1. Did Mr Kang's pet fly all the way from China. *(Mr.; China?)*
2. Most birds cant' traval across the ocean. *(can't; travel)*

Academic Vocabulary 

An **abbreviation** is a shortened form of a word.

A **period** is a punctuation mark that signals the end of a sentence or is placed at the end of an abbreviation.

Letter spacing is the distance between the letters in a word.

Spanish Cognates Tell Spanish-speaking students that the English word *abbreviate* shares the Latin root *brevis (short)* with the Spanish word *abreviar.*

Handwriting: Proper Nouns To provide practice in writing the cursive capital letters *B, P,* and *R,* have students write the names of people and places they know that begin with each letter.

Common Core State Standards

Writing 3. Write narratives to develop real or imagined experiences or events using effective technique, descriptive details, and clear event sequences. **Also Literature 5.**

Bridge to Common Core

TEXT TYPES AND PURPOSES

This week students write a limerick about the story *Happy Birthday Mr. Kang.*

Narrative Writing

Through reading and discussion, students will gain a deeper understanding of what it means to grant freedom. They will use this knowledge from the texts to write a limerick.

Throughout the week, students will improve the range and content of their writing through daily mini-lessons.

5-Day Plan

DAY 1	Read Like a Writer
DAY 2	Structure of a Limerick
DAY 3	Writer's Craft: Structure
DAY 4	Revise: Adding
DAY 5	Proofread for Abbreviations

Write Guy *by Jeff Anderson*

What Do You Notice?

When students are examining the model text, ask, "What do you notice?" By giving students the responsibility of commenting on what they find effective in the text, they build self-confidence and often begin to notice features of the writing they might not have otherwise. Eventually they will start trying them in their writing.

Poetry: Limerick

Mini-Lesson Read Like a Writer

Introduce This week you will write a **limerick.** A limerick is a form of poetry with five lines and a special rhyme and rhythm structure.

Prompt	Write a limerick about the story *Happy Birthday Mr. Kang.*
Trait	Organization
Mode	Narrative

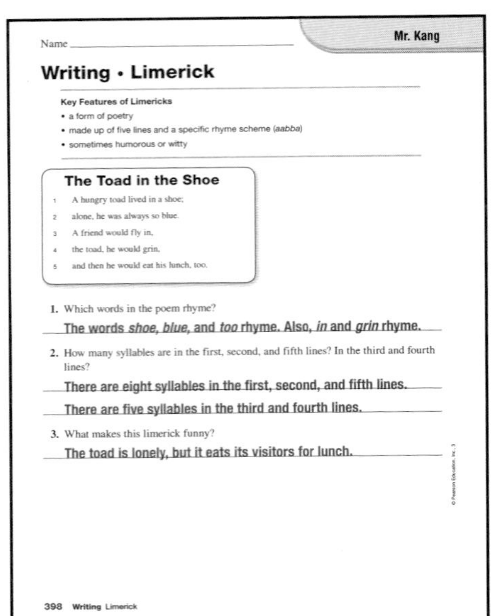

Name ____________ Mr. Kang

Writing • Limerick

Key Features of Limericks
- a form of poetry
- made up of five lines and a specific rhyme scheme (*aabba*)
- sometimes humorous or witty

The Toad in the Shoe

A hungry toad lived in a shoe;
alone, he was always so blue.
A friend would fly in,
the toad, he would grin,
and then he would eat his lunch, too.

1. Which words in the poem rhyme?
The words *shoe, blue,* and *too* rhyme. Also, *in* and *grin* rhyme.
2. How many syllables are in the first, second, and fifth lines? In the third and fourth lines?
There are eight syllables in the first, second, and fifth lines.
There are five syllables in the third and fourth lines.
3. What makes this limerick funny?
The toad is lonely, but it eats its visitors for lunch.

© Pearson Education, Inc. 3

398 Writing Limerick

Reader's and Writer's Notebook, p. 398

Examine Model Text Let's read an example of a limerick about a toad. Have students read "The Toad in the Shoe" on p. 398 of their *Reader's and Writer's Notebook.*

Key Features Limericks are poems made up of five lines and a fixed *a-a-b-b-a* rhyme scheme. Have students mark the *a-a-b-b-a* rhyme pattern on the model. Notice how lines 1, 2, and 5 rhyme. Have students identify the rhyming words *shoe, blue,* and *too.* Notice how lines 3 and 4 also rhyme. Have students identify the rhyming words *in* and *grin.*

Each line also has a set number of syllables with two or three accents per line. The accented syllables create rhythm, which is the beat you hear when a poem is read aloud. Lines 1, 2, and 5 not only rhyme but also have the same number of syllables and accents. Read the lines aloud and count the accented syllables. Lines 3 and 4 also have the same number of syllables and accents. Count aloud the accented syllables in lines 3 and 4.

Limericks are often called nonsense poems because they are sometimes humorous or witty. Ask students why the limerick is funny. (The toad is hungry and lonely, so when a "friend" visits, he eats it.)

eStreet Interactive

www.ReadingStreet.com

Teacher Resources

- Reader's and Writer's Notebook
- Let's Practice It!

Review Key Features

Review the key features of limericks with students. You may want to post the key features in the classroom for students to refer to as they work on their limericks.

Key Features of Limericks

- a form of poetry
- made up of five lines with a specific rhyme scheme *(a-a-b-b-a)*
- has rhythm created through the use of two or three accented syllables per line; each line contains a set number of syllables
- sometimes tells a humorous or witty story

Routine Quick Write for Fluency

Team Talk

1. **Talk** Pairs discuss the key features of limericks.
2. **Write** Each student writes a brief summary of the key features of limericks.
3. **Share** Partners read their summaries to each other.

Routines Flip Chart

Academic Vocabulary 

A **limerick** is a type of poem with five lines and a fixed rhythm and rhyme scheme.

ELL

Limerick Read the writing model aloud and help students understand it. Ask students to think about an experience that they have had that they could write about in a limerick.

Wrap Up Your Day!

- ✔ **Content Knowledge** Reread Street Rhymes! on p. 394j to students. Ask them what they learned today about what it means to grant freedom.
- ✔ **Oral Vocabulary** Have students use the Amazing Words they learned in context sentences.
- ✔ **Homework** Send home this week's Family Times newsletter on *Let's Practice It!* pp. 372–373 on the *Teacher Resources DVD-ROM.*

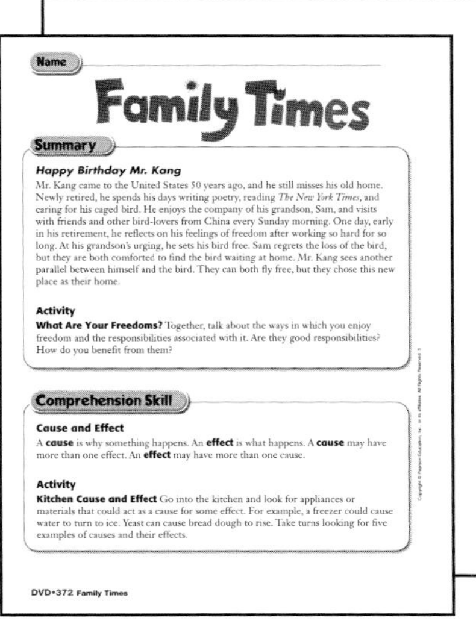

Name

Family Times

Summary

Happy Birthday Mr. Kang

Mr. Kang came to the United States 50 years ago, and he still misses his old home. Newly retired, he spends his days writing poetry, reading *The New York Times*, and caring for his caged bird. He enjoys the company of his grandson, Sam, and visits with friends and other bird-lovers from China every Sunday morning. One day, early in his retirement, he reflects on his feelings of freedom after working so hard for so long. At his grandson's urging, he sets his bird free. Sam regrets the loss of the bird, but they are both comforted to find the bird waiting at home. Mr. Kang sees another parallel between himself and the bird. They can both fly free, but they chose this new place as their home.

Activity

What Are Your Freedoms? Together, talk about the ways in which you enjoy freedom and the responsibilities associated with it. Are they good responsibilities? How do you benefit from them?

Comprehension Skill

Cause and Effect

A **cause** is why something happens. An **effect** is what happens. A **cause** may have more than one effect. An **effect** may have more than one cause.

Activity

Kitchen Cause and Effect Go into the kitchen and look for appliances or materials that could act as a cause for some effect. For example, a freezer could cause water to turn to ice. Yeast can cause bread dough to rise. Take turns looking for five examples of causes and their effects.

DVD•372 Family Times

Let's Practice It!
TR DVD•372–373

Preview DAY 2

Tell students that tomorrow they will read about what it means to grant freedom to someone or something.

DAY 2 at a Glance

Content Knowledge
Oral Vocabulary

Phonics/Word Analysis
Schwa

Literary Terms
Metaphor

Vocabulary Skill
Antonyms

Fluency
Appropriate Phrasing

Research and Inquiry
Navigate/Search

Conventions
Abbreviations

Spelling
Schwa

Writing
Poetry: Limerick

Materials

- Student Edition
- Reader's and Writer's Notebook
- Sound-Spelling Cards

Common Core State Standards

Speaking/Listening 1. Engage effectively in a range of collaborative discussions (one-on-one, in groups, and teacher led) with diverse partners on grade 3 topics and texts, building on others' ideas and expressing their own clearly. **Language 6.** Acquire and use accurately grade-appropriate conversational, general academic, and domain-specific words and phrases, including those that signal spatial and temporal relationships (e.g., *After dinner that night we went looking for them*).

Content Knowledge

Granting Freedom

EXPAND THE CONCEPT Remind students of the weekly concept question, *What does it mean to grant freedom?* Tell students that today they will begin reading *Happy Birthday Mr. Kang.* As they read, encourage students to think about what it means to grant freedom.

Build Oral Language

TALK ABOUT SENTENCES AND WORDS Reread the following sentences from the Read Aloud, "A Little Freedom."

We would like our freedom. We would like you to release us.

- The robots want to be *released*. What does it mean to *release* something or someone? (to let it go)
- What word in the first sentence is a clue to the meaning of the word *release?* (The word *freedom* is a clue to the meaning of *release.*)
- What are some synonyms or other ways to say "release us"? Have students share their responses.

Team Talk Have students turn to a partner and discuss the following question. Then ask them to share their responses.

- How could you combine the ideas in these two sentences into one sentence? (Possible response: *We would like you to release us because we would like our freedom.*)

Build Oral Vocabulary

Amazing Words Robust Vocabulary Routine

1. **Introduce** Write the Amazing Word *manage* on the board. Have students say it aloud with you. Relate *manage* to the photographs on pp. 394–395 and "A Little Freedom." What are some ways people *manage* to keep animals as pets? How do these ways compare with how the Nortons have *managed* to keep their robots for so long? Have students determine the definition of the word. When you *manage* something, you succeed in accomplishing it.
2. **Demonstrate** Have students answer questions to demonstrate understanding. How might a parent *manage* a crying baby? How could you *manage* to find your way around an unfamiliar place?
3. **Apply** Have students apply their understanding. What are some things you *manage* to do each day?
4. **Display the Word** Run your hand under the syllables *man-age*. Have students say the word.

See p. OV•2 to teach *affectionate.*

Routines Flip Chart

ADD TO THE CONCEPT MAP Use the photos on pp. 394–395 and the Read Aloud, "A Little Freedom," to talk about the Amazing Words *territory, release, loyal,* and *deserve*. Add the words to the concept map to develop students' knowledge of the topic. Discuss the following questions. Remind students to listen attentively to others, ask relevant questions, and make pertinent comments during the discussion.

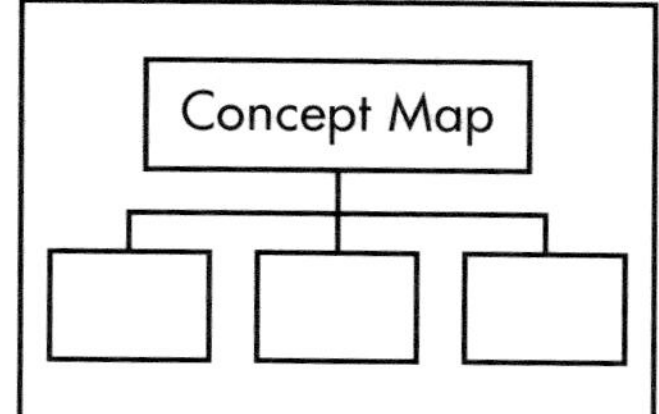

- Where are some *territories* into which people might *release* wild animals?
- Discuss how being *loyal* to a person might affect the actions of a wild animal or a servant robot after being set free.
- Give some examples why wild animals might *deserve* freedom.

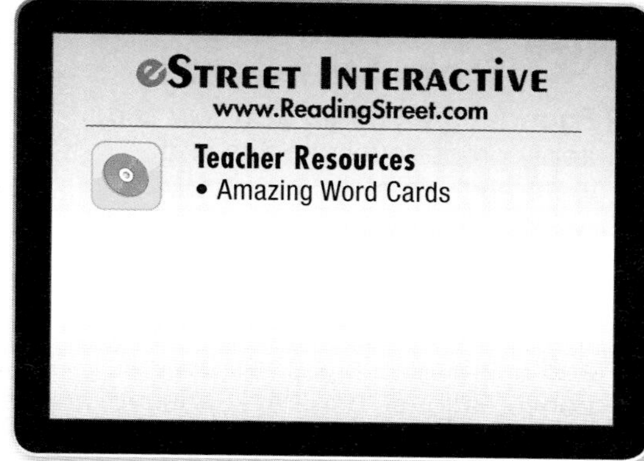

Amazing Words

territory	affectionate
release	companion
loyal	nag
deserve	retrieve
manage	wandering

Reinforce Vocabulary Use the Day 2 instruction on ELL Poster 27 to teach selection vocabulary and the lesson concept.

Common Core State Standards

Foundational Skills 3. Know and apply grade-level phonics and word analysis skills in decoding words. **Language 5.a.** Distinguish the literal and nonliteral meanings of words and phrases in context (e.g., *take steps*). **Language 6.** Acquire and use accurately grade-appropriate conversational, general academic, and domain-specific words and phrases, including those that signal spatial and temporal relationships (e.g., *After dinner that night we went looking for them*).

Phonics/Word Analysis

Schwa

REVIEW Review the schwa sound using *Sound-Spelling Card* 144.

READ WORDS IN ISOLATION Display these words. Have the class decode the words. Then point to the words in random order and ask students to read them quickly.

geologist	**taken**	**pencil**	**character**
robin	**commit**	**salad**	**another**

Corrective feedback | Model blending decodable words and then ask students to blend them with you.

READ WORDS IN CONTEXT Display these sentences. Have the class read the sentences.

Team Talk Have pairs take turns reading the sentences naturally.

Put the **paper upon** the table.
Which **item** did you **open?**
A bear is a **circus animal.**

Don't Wait Until Friday **MONITOR PROGRESS** **Check Word Reading**

Schwa

FORMATIVE ASSESSMENT Write the following words and have the class read them. Notice which words students miss during the group reading. Call on individuals to read some of the words.

open	**ripen**	**item**	**upon**	**sugar**
bugle	**handle**	**trouble**	**hurdle**	**sparkle**
redoing	**disliked**	**together**	**cardinal**	**rewrite**

Spiral Review
Row 2 reviews words with a consonant + *le.*
Row 3 contrasts multisyllabic words with and without the schwa sound.

If... students cannot read words with the sound of schwa at this point,
then... use the Day 1 Word Analysis lesson on p. 396a to reteach the schwa sound. Use words from the *Decodable Practice Passages* (or Reader). Continue to monitor students' progress using other instructional opportunities during the week. See the Skills Trace on p. 396a.

Literary Terms

Metaphor

TEACH Tell students that a metaphor is when two things that are not very much like each other, but are alike in at least one way, are compared without using the words *like* or *as.* A metaphor says that one thing is the other thing, not just that it is like the thing. A metaphor is used to help the reader visualize what something is like and to draw attention to a quality or qualities that it possesses.

Think Aloud **MODEL** Let's look at "A New Life," on p. 399. It says that immigrants have made the United States what it is today by bringing their cultures and traditions with them. I can use the metaphor "The United States is a melting pot" to help create an image of all the cultures coming together. The United States isn't really a melting pot, but the two are similar because both are places where things are mixed together.

GUIDE PRACTICE Find an example of a metaphor in the poem Mr. Kang writes on p. 407 of *Happy Birthday Mr. Kang.* Be sure to explain what comparison is being made and why the author (or Mr. Kang) might be making this comparison.

ON THEIR OWN Have students look for examples of metaphors in other selections in their Student Edition.

eStreet Interactive
www.ReadingStreet.com
Pearson eText
• Student Edition
Interactive Sound-Spelling Cards

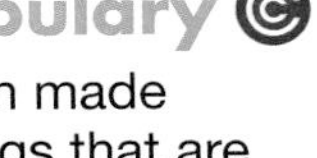

Academic Vocabulary

metaphor a comparison made between two unlike things that are alike in one way; metaphors do not use comparison words such as *like* or *as.*

Common Core State Standards

Language 4. Determine or clarify the meaning of unknown and multiple-meaning words and phrases based on grade 3 reading and content, choosing flexibly from a range of strategies. **Language 4.a.** Use sentence-level context as a clue to the meaning of a word or phrase. **Language 5.** Demonstrate understanding of word relationships and nuances in word meanings. **Also Foundational Skills 4.b., Language 4.d.**

Selection Vocabulary

bows bends the head or body forward

chilly uncomfortably cold

foolish unwise; not making sense

foreign a place that is not your own country or homeland

narrow not wide

perches sits or rests on a bar, branch, or similar object

recipe ingredients and steps for making something to eat or drink

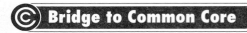

Bridge to Common Core

VOCABULARY ACQUISITION AND USE

Using context clues such as antonyms helps students determine the meanings of unknown words and enables them to acquire a broad range of academic and domain-specific words. By looking for antonyms as clues to word meaning, students demonstrate the ability to determine word meanings on their own.

Vocabulary Support

Refer students to *Words!* on p. W•2 in the Student Edition for additional practice.

Vocabulary Skill

Antonyms

READ Have students read "Mr. Wang's Wonderful Noodles" on p. 401. Use the vocabulary skill and strategy as tools to build comprehension.

TEACH CONTEXT CLUES Explain to students that they can use context clues to figure out the meaning of an unknown word. An author might have used antonyms, or words that have opposite meanings, in the text around the unfamiliar word.

Think Aloud

MODEL Write on the board: *The box was too wide to fit through the narrow doorway.* I can look for context clues to figure out the meaning of the word *narrow.* If I look in this sentence, I see the word *wide.* Something that is wide will not fit through something narrow. Something narrow is not wide, or has sides that are not very far apart.

GUIDE PRACTICE Write this sentence on the board: *Because the air was chilly, the girl put on a big coat to stay warm.* Have students determine the meaning of *chilly* using antonyms and context clues. Remind students that a thesaurus and some dictionaries list antonyms. For additional support, use *Envision It! Pictured Vocabulary Cards* or *Tested Vocabulary Cards.*

ON THEIR OWN Have students reread "Mr. Wang's Wonderful Noodles" on p. 401. Have them use a thesaurus or dictionary to find antonyms to help them define the selection vocabulary. For additional practice, use *Reader's and Writer's Notebook,* p. 399.

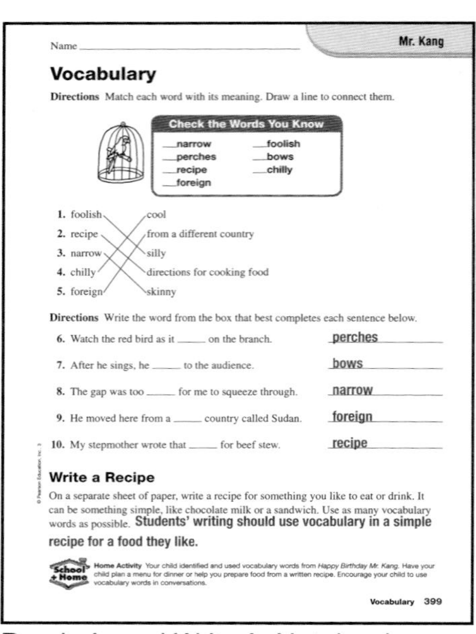

Name ______ Mr. Kang

Vocabulary

Directions Match each word with its meaning. Draw a line to connect them.

Check the Words You Know

__narrow __perches __recipe __foreign __foolish __bows __chilly

1. foolish — cool
2. recipe — from a different country
3. narrow — silly
4. chilly — directions for cooking food
5. foreign — skinny

Directions Write the word from the box that best completes each sentence below.

6. Watch the red bird as it ____ on the branch. perches
7. After he sings, he ____ to the audience. bows
8. The gap was too ____ for me to squeeze through. narrow
9. He moved here from a ____ country called Sudan. foreign
10. My stepmother wrote that ____ for beef stew. recipe

Write a Recipe

On a separate sheet of paper, write a recipe for something you like to eat or drink. It can be something simple, like chocolate milk or a sandwich. Use as many vocabulary words as possible. **Students' writing should use vocabulary in a simple recipe for a food they like.**

School + Home **Home Activity** Your child identified and used vocabulary words from *Happy Birthday Mr. Kang.* Have your child plan a menu for dinner or help you prepare food from a written recipe. Encourage your child to use vocabulary words in conversations.

Vocabulary 399

Reader's and Writer's Notebook, p. 399

Common Core State Standards
Language 4.a. Use sentence-level context as a clue to the meaning of a word or phrase. Also Language 4., 5.
Envision It! Words to Know
foreign
narrow
recipe
bows
chilly
foolish
perches
READING STREET ONLINE
VOCABULARY ACTIVITIES
www.ReadingStreet.com

Vocabulary Strategy for

Antonyms

Context Clues Sometimes you will read a word you don't know. The author may include an antonym for the word. An antonym is a word that means the opposite of another word. For example, *hot* is the opposite of *cold*. Look for an antonym to figure out the meaning of the word.

1. Look at the words around the unfamiliar word. The author may have used an antonym.
2. Do you recognize a word that seems to have the opposite meaning of the unfamiliar word?
3. Use the antonym to help you figure out the meaning of the unfamiliar word.

Read "Mr. Wang's Wonderful Noodles" on page 401. Look for antonyms to help you understand the meanings of unfamiliar words.

Words to Write Reread "Mr. Wang's Wonderful Noodles." Write about your favorite food. How does it taste? Why do you like it? Use words from the Words to Know list and antonyms in your story.

400

MR. WANG'S WONDERFUL Noodles

Mr. Wang is the best noodle maker in Shanghai, China. People who like wide, thick noodles may think people who like narrow, thin noodles are foolish. People who like narrow, thin noodles may think people who like wide, thick noodles are not very smart. But everyone agrees on one thing. Mr. Wang's noodles are the best.

One day, a stranger perches on a stool at the noodle shop. Mr. Wang bows his head in respect. The stranger says, "Mr. Wang, please bring your noodle recipe to the United States. Make noodles in my restaurant."

People stop slurping their noodles to listen to Mr. Wang's reply. The warm shop suddenly feels chilly.

Mr. Wang says, "Thank you. But I do not wish to go to a foreign land. I am happy making noodles in China."

Everyone heaves a sigh of relief. Everyone goes back to slurping Mr. Wang's wonderful noodles.

Your Turn!

Need a Review? For additional help with antonyms, see *Words!*

Ready to Try It? Read *Happy Birthday Mr. Kang*, pp. 402–419.

401

Student Edition, pp. 400–401

Reread for Fluency

APPROPRIATE PHRASING Read paragraph 2 of "Mr. Wang's Wonderful Noodles" aloud, modeling how to pause at punctuation marks and read dialogue. Tell students that in order to comprehend what they read, it is important to pause where it makes sense

Routine Oral Rereading

1. **Read** Have students read paragraph 2 of "Mr. Wang's Wonderful Noodles" orally.
2. **Reread** To achieve optimal fluency, students should reread the text three or four times.
3. **Corrective Feedback** Have students read aloud without you. Listen for appropriate phrasing and provide feedback.

Routines Flip Chart

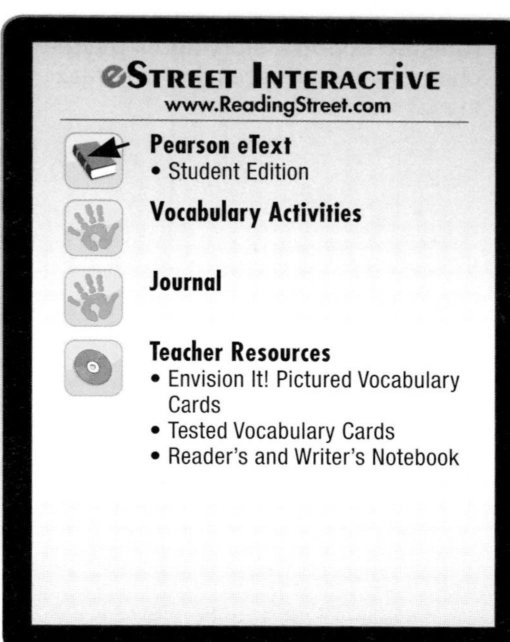

Common Core State Standards

Literature 7. Explain how specific aspects of a text's illustrations contribute to what is conveyed by the words in a story (e.g., create mood, emphasize aspects of a character or setting). **Literature 10.** By the end of the year, read and comprehend literature, including stories, dramas, and poetry, at the high end of the grades 2–3 text complexity band independently and proficiently.

Bridge to Common Core

CRAFT AND STRUCTURE

Students analyze the selection's title and illustrations and think about how portions of the text relate to the selection as a whole. As they preview the selection and prepare to read, they come to see how the genre shapes the content and style of the text.

Academic Vocabulary 

realistic fiction a story about made-up characters and places that could exist in real life

Strategy Response Log

Have students use p. 33 in the *Reader's and Writer's Notebook* to review the strategy of inferring. Then have them list their background knowledge of birds.

Text-Based Comprehension

Introduce Main Selection

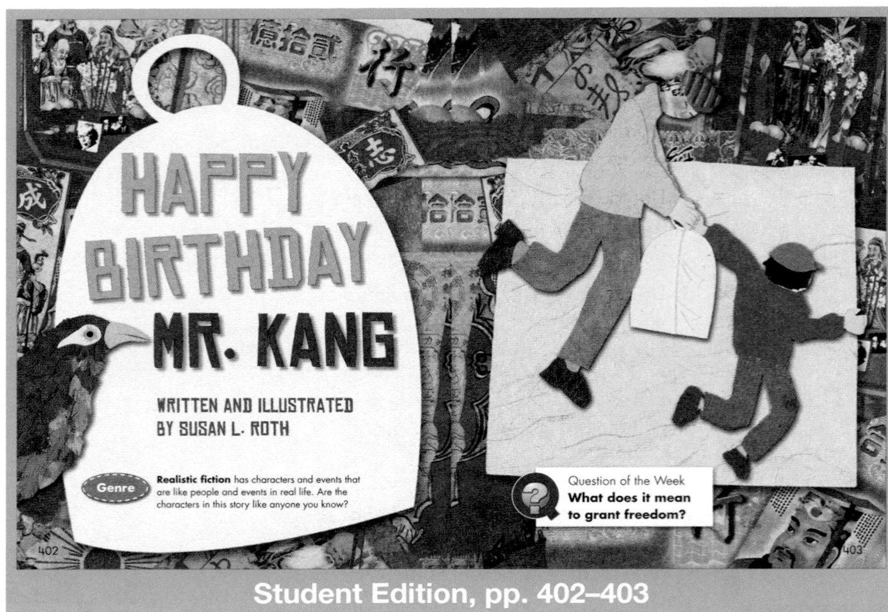

Student Edition, pp. 402–403

GENRE Remind students that **realistic fiction** is a made-up story that could happen in real life. Explain that while all fiction is made up, the characters in realistic fiction behave as real people (or animals) do and face real problems. The main character in *Happy Birthday Mr. Kang* is a Chinese immigrant who works for 50 years in a restaurant, cutting noodles.

PREVIEW AND PREDICT Have students read the title of the selection and the name of the author/illustrator. Ask them to use the title and the illustrations to predict what they think the story will be about.

PURPOSE By analyzing *Happy Birthday Mr. Kang,* a realistic fiction text, students will gain knowledge of what it means to grant freedom.

Access Main Selection

READER AND TASK SUGGESTIONS	
Preparing to Read the Text	**Leveled Tasks**
• Review the strategy of using antonyms as context clues. • Discuss how the author includes the main character's poems as part of the story. • Remind students that the story includes a combination of poetry and prose. They may need to read more slowly to better understand the text.	• **Levels of Meaning • Analysis** If students do not understand Mr. Kang's motivation in freeing his hua mei, have them read the last three paragraphs on p. 413 and tell how Mr. Kang compares himself to the bird. • **Theme and Knowledge Demands** Students may have difficulty relating to Mr. Kang's lifestyle and culture. Remind them to pay attention to the photographs of the neighborhood where he lives and the simple images in his poems.

See Text Complexity Measures for *Happy Birthday Mr. Kang* on the tab at the beginning of this week.

READ Tell students that today they will read *Happy Birthday Mr. Kang* for the first time. Use the Read for Understanding routine.

Routine Read for Understanding

Deepen understanding by reading the selection multiple times.

1. **First Read**— If students need support, then use the **Access Text** notes to help them clarify understanding.
2. **Second Read**—Use the **Close Reading** notes to help students draw knowledge from the text.

Day 2 SMALL GROUP TIME • Differentiate Comprehension, p. SG•17

OL On-Level	SI Strategic Intervention	A Advanced
• **Practice** Selection Vocabulary • **Read** *Happy Birthday Mr. Kang*	• **Reteach** Selection Vocabulary • **Read** *Happy Birthday Mr. Kang*	• **Extend** Selection Vocabulary • **Read** *Happy Birthday Mr. Kang* • **Investigate** Inquiry Project

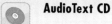

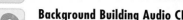

eSTREET INTERACTIVE
www.ReadingStreet.com

Pearson eText
• Student Edition

AudioText CD

Teacher Resources
• Reader's and Writer's Notebook

Background Building Audio CD

Access for All

 **Advanced**

Have students write a persuasive paragraph explaining why it is better to be either a pet bird in a safe cage or a free bird in the wild.

Build Background To build background, review the selection summary in English (*ELL Handbook,* p. 187). Use the Retelling Cards to provide visual support for the summary.

If... students need more scaffolding and practice with the **Comprehension Skill,**
then... use the activities on p. DI•46 in the Teacher Resources section on SuccessNet.

1 ST READ

Access Text If students need help, then...

CAUSE AND EFFECT Ask students what causes Mr. Kang to want to stop cooking. (He has been cooking every day for many years, so he is probably tired and wants to have time to do fun things.)

Think Aloud **MODEL** To figure out the cause and effect, I ask myself why Mr. Kang wants to stop cooking. This will give me the cause. (He has been cooking for many years.) What happens because he has been cooking for so many years? (He stops cooking on his 70th birthday.) This is the effect.

Student Edition, p. 404

Close Reading

INFERENCE • TEXT EVIDENCE What clues does the author give to show that birthdays are important in Mr. Kang's family? (The family has a party with cake and then makes sure that two of Mr. Kang's wishes come true.)

EVALUATION How do you know the story is a realistic story and not a fantasy? Give an example to support your answer. (A fantasy is a story about something that could not happen in real life, but events in this story could really happen. Mr. Kang could have come from China and lived in New York City.)

ON THEIR OWN Have students reread p. 405 to find another cause-and-effect relationship. For additional practice, use *Let's Practice It!* p. 374 on the *Teacher Resources DVD-ROM.*

Forty-three years before his grandson, Sam, was born in the New World, Mr. Kang left China and came to America. Every day he chopped scallions, wrapped dumplings, and pulled noodle dough into long and perfect strands for the hungry people who ate at the Golden Dragon Restaurant in New York City.

When Mr. Kang turned seventy, Mrs. Kang had a birthday party for him.

"Make a wish!" said Sam as Mr. Kang shut his eyes, puffed his cheeks, and blew out all the candles on his cake. Everyone clapped and shouted hurray.

"What was your wish?" Sam asked.

"Three wishes," said Mr. Kang. "I want to read *The New York Times* every day. I want to paint poems every day. And I want a bird, a *hua mei*, of my own. I'll feed him every day, and on Sundays I'll take him to Sara Delano Roosevelt Park on Delancey Street. Enough cooking."

"Good idea," said Mrs. Kang. "I'll cook for you, and the Golden Dragon Restaurant can get a new cook."

"Grandpa, why do you want a bird in a cage? There are birds all over the place outside," said Sam.

"Sam," said Mr. Kang. "This is not just an American bird in a cage. This is a Chinese bird. My grandfather had a hua mei in a cage. Now I want a hua mei in a cage. And sometimes you and I will take him to Sara Delano Roosevelt Park on Delancey Street together."

And so it is that every morning Mr. Kang finds *The New York Times* on his doorstep. Every morning he reads it while he drinks his tea and eats his sweet and fragrant almond cakes, warm from the oven.

405

Student Edition, p. 405

ANALYSIS • TEXT EVIDENCE How does the author use language that appeals to the senses to help the reader understand the experience of eating an almond cake? (To help the reader get a sense of the experience, the author describes how the cake feels warm from the oven, how it tastes sweet, and how it smells fragrant.)

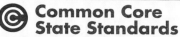

Common Core State Standards

Literature 1. Ask and answer questions to demonstrate understanding of a text, referring explicitly to the text as the basis for the answers. **Also Language 3.a.**

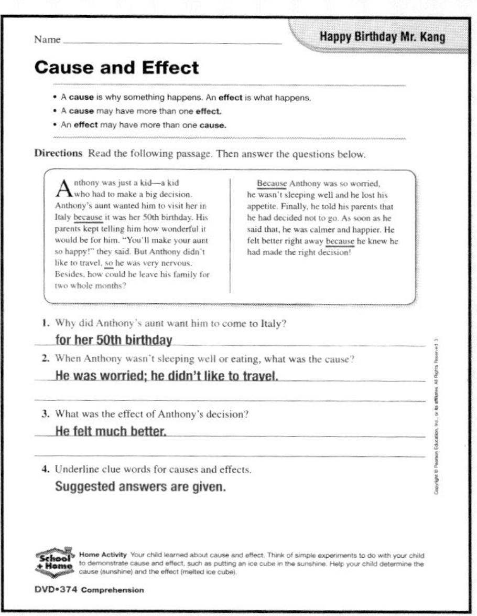

Name ______________________ **Happy Birthday Mr. Kang**

Cause and Effect

- A **cause** is why something happens. An **effect** is what happens.
- A **cause** may have more than one **effect.**
- An **effect** may have more than one **cause.**

Directions Read the following passage. Then answer the questions below.

Anthony was just a kid—a kid who had to make a big decision. Anthony's aunt wanted him to visit her in Italy because it was her 50th birthday. His parents kept telling him how wonderful it would be for him. "You'll make your aunt so happy!" they said. But Anthony didn't like to travel, so he was very nervous. Besides, how could he leave his family for two whole months?

Because Anthony was so worried, he wasn't sleeping well and he lost his appetite. Finally, he told his parents that he had decided not to go. As soon as he said that, he was calmer and happier. He felt better right away because he knew he had made the right decision!

1. Why did Anthony's aunt want him to come to Italy?
   for her 50th birthday
2. When Anthony wasn't sleeping well or eating, what was the cause?
   He was worried; he didn't like to travel.
3. What was the effect of Anthony's decision?
   He felt much better.
4. Underline clue words for causes and effects.
   Suggested answers are given.

Home Activity Your child learned about cause and effect. Think of simple experiments to do with your child to demonstrate cause and effect, such as putting an ice cube in the sunshine. Help your child determine the cause (sunshine) and the effect (melted ice cube).

DVD•374 Comprehension

Let's Practice It! TR DVD•374

Access for All

SI Strategic Intervention

If students need additional help identifying and understanding cause-and-effect relationships in this story, help them create a two-column graphic organizer that shows the cause-and-effect relationships. As they read, they should write down important events in the *effects* column and reasons for these events in the *causes* column.

Activate Prior Knowledge Create a two-column chart to record students' prior knowledge of what a pet owner must do to keep a pet bird safely. We're going to read about how Mr. Kang gets a pet bird to keep in a cage. What do you know about the reasons that pet owners keep pet birds in cages? What do you know about how birds might feel about being kept in cages? Record students' answers in the chart, adding to them as they read the selection.

1ST READ

Access Text If students need help, then...

ANTONYMS Remind students that antonyms are words that have opposite meanings. Ask students to use context clues to determine the meanings of the words *chilly* and *warm* on p. 407.

Think Aloud **MODEL** I see that the *chilly* wind makes icy tears. Ice is cold, so *chilly* must mean "cold." Then the *warm* memories melt the tears. Since hot things melt ice, *warm* must mean "hot." *Chilly* and *warm* are antonyms.

ON THEIR OWN For additional practice with antonyms, use *Reader's and Writer's Notebook*, p. 403.

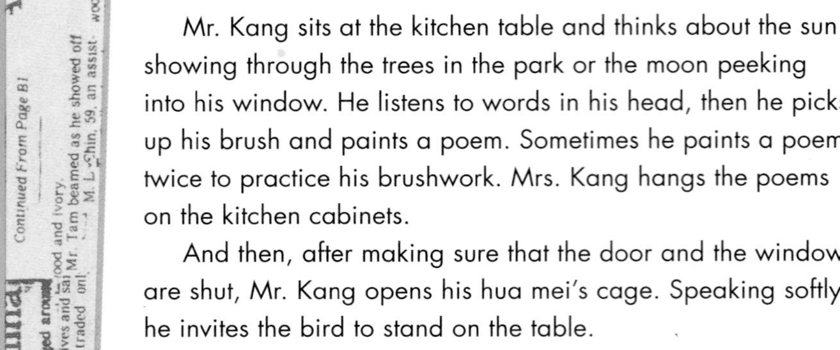

Mr. Kang sits at the kitchen table and thinks about the sun showing through the trees in the park or the moon peeking into his window. He listens to words in his head, then he picks up his brush and paints a poem. Sometimes he paints a poem twice to practice his brushwork. Mrs. Kang hangs the poems on the kitchen cabinets.

And then, after making sure that the door and the windows are shut, Mr. Kang opens his hua mei's cage. Speaking softly, he invites the bird to stand on the table.

Mr. Kang cleans the cage with a damp towel and dries it with a soft cloth. He takes out the hand-painted ceramic water bowl, rinses it, and puts it back in its stand, full of cool, clear water. He washes the hand-painted ceramic food bowl and puts it back, full of his own special recipe of millet coated with egg yolks and mixed with chopped meat. These days this is the only cooking Mr. Kang does.

Last, Mr. Kang takes a small piece of silk cloth, dampens it with water not too hot, not too cold, and gently wipes the sleek gray feathers of his bird. The hua mei walks right back into his cage. He prefers to give himself a bath.

"Never mind, Birdie," says Mr. Kang. "Instead of the bath, I'll read you my poem. I know you can understand. We both left our homeland. We still speak the old language."

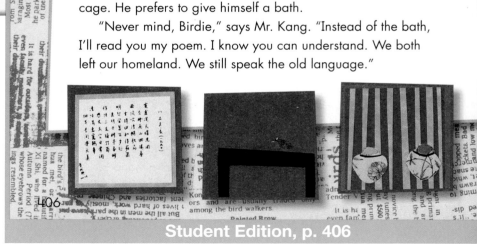

406

Student Edition, p. 406

2ND READ

Close Reading

INFERENCE • TEXT EVIDENCE

How does Mr. Kang feel about living in America? What evidence makes you think this? (He misses his old home, but he has seen things in America that he would never have seen if he had stayed in China. He thinks that people who have not left their homes look out of "narrow windows," while people who have left their homelands have seen more and look through "wide windows.")

REREAD CHALLENGING TEXT Have students reread Mr. Kang's poem on page 407. Students may need help understanding the figurative language such as *the icy tears on my cheek melt with memories of warm old days.*

DEVELOP LANGUAGE Have students reread the third paragraph on p. 406. What does *ceramic* mean? What other items might be made out of *ceramic*?

Rushing to the Golden Dragon
against a chilly wind,
the icy tears on my cheeks melt
with memories of warm old days.

Those who never left their home
stay safe, wrapped
in the arms of their motherfather land.
When they look out
their narrow windows,
they see their own kitchen gardens.
They know every plum tree, every kumquat,
every blade of grass, each gray pebble.

We who long ago tossed on cold waters
looking only straight ahead
watch our city mountains
from wide windows, tall rooftops.
Yet our old hearts hold old places.
We save, in old, grown heads,
a full-blown rose in summer,
the sound of bamboo leaves when
the wind is gentle,
the taste of mooncakes.

The hua mei sings his own melody back to Mr. Kang. Mr. Kang closes his eyes to listen.

"Beautiful, Birdie. You are a good poet and a good friend to me," says Mr. Kang.

407

Student Edition, p. 407

EVALUATION Why do you think the author inserted a poem that Mr. Kang wrote into this selection? (The poem shows Mr. Kang's thoughts and feelings.)

Common Core State Standards

Literature 1. Ask and answer questions to demonstrate understanding of a text, referring explicitly to the text as the basis for the answers. **Also Literature 3.**

Connect to Social Studies

Transportation Point out China and New York City on a world map or globe. Ask students on which continents they are located. In the late 1800s and early 1900s, people traveled from China to New York City by ship. They crossed the Pacific Ocean to North America and then traveled on land from the West Coast to the East Coast.

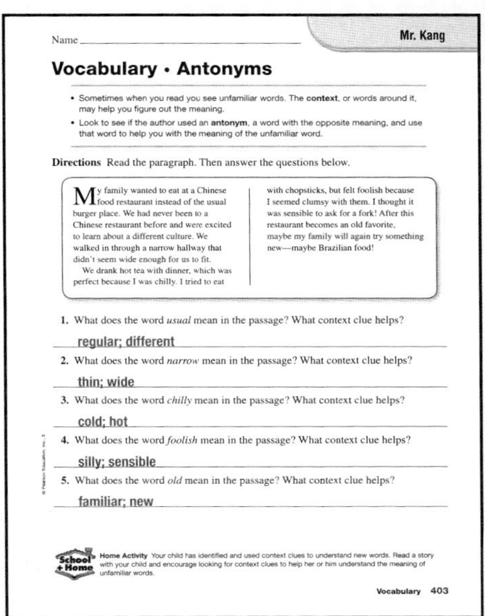

Name ______________ Mr. Kang

Vocabulary • Antonyms

- Sometimes when you read you see unfamiliar words. The **context**, or words around it, may help you figure out the meaning.
- Look to see if the author used an **antonym**, a word with the opposite meaning, and use that word to help you with the meaning of the unfamiliar word.

Directions Read the paragraph. Then answer the questions below.

My family wanted to eat at a Chinese food restaurant instead of the usual burger place. We had never been to a Chinese restaurant before and were excited to learn about a different culture. We walked in through a narrow hallway that didn't seem wide enough for us to fit.

We drank hot tea with dinner, which was perfect because I was chilly. I tried to eat with chopsticks, but felt foolish because I seemed clumsy with them. I thought it was sensible to ask for a fork! After this restaurant becomes an old favorite, maybe my family will again try something new—maybe Brazilian food!

1. What does the word *usual* mean in the passage? What context clue helps?
   regular; different
2. What does the word *narrow* mean in the passage? What context clue helps?
   thin; wide
3. What does the word *chilly* mean in the passage? What context clue helps?
   cold; hot
4. What does the word *foolish* mean in the passage? What context clue helps?
   silly; sensible
5. What does the word *old* mean in the passage? What context clue helps?
   familiar; new

School + Home **Home Activity** Your child has identified and used context clues to understand new words. Read a story with your child and encourage looking for context clues to help her or him understand the meaning of unfamiliar words.

Vocabulary 403

Reader's and Writer's Notebook, p. 403

Compound Words Help students identify compound words on this spread, such as *rooftops.* Have students draw a line between the two words in each compound.

Inferring Read aloud the second paragraph on p. 406. Why do you think Mr. Kang makes sure the door and window are shut? Have students use prior knowledge and information from the text to make an inference to answer the question. (Mr. Kang is about to open his bird's cage, and he does not want the bird to fly away.)

1ST READ

Access Text If students need help, then...

Review **THEME** Ask students to identify an important issue the story has presented so far. Then ask them what they think the theme might be at this point.

Think Aloud **MODEL** To figure out theme, I think about the important parts of the story and see how they go together. Mr. Kang stopped cooking so he would be free to do fun things. Now Sam is telling him to let his bird go free. The theme of this story will have something to do with being free.

Sam usually comes to visit on Saturdays. If Mr. Kang is cleaning the cage, then the hua mei sings to Sam. Sam holds out his finger, and the hua mei holds on tightly. They stare at each other, each without blinking.

"Did he really fly from China?" Sam asks one time.

"In an airplane," says Mr. Kang. "China is so far, even for a bird."

"You should let him go. Maybe he wants to fly home."

"I don't think he could without an airplane. Anyway, he's like me. Home is here with you. If he went home now, I think he would miss his Sundays on Delancey Street." Mr. Kang puts his arm around Sam's shoulders and hugs him.

"I have a very smart grandson," he sighs. "Maybe one day we can visit China together."

And this is how Mr. Kang spends his days, except for Sundays.

408

Student Edition, p. 408

2ND READ

Close Reading

ANALYSIS • TEXT EVIDENCE How does Sam feel about freedom? What detail supports this idea? (He thinks birds should be free to fly outside, not be locked up in cages. Sam suggests that Mr. Kang should let the hua mei fly home to China.)

EVALUATION Do you think Sam will convince Mr. Kang to let his bird go free? What makes you think that? (Mr. Kang said Sam is very smart. Mr. Kang must respect and value Sam's opinion. I predict that Mr. Kang will decide to let the bird go because Sam convinces him.)

ON THEIR OWN Have students reread pp. 405–407 to find more details that support the theme of the story. For additional practice, use *Let's Practice It!* p. 375 on the *Teacher Resources DVD-ROM.*

On Sundays Mr. Kang gets up when it's dark. He washes his face and puts on his clothes. When he is ready, he picks up the cage by the ring on top. The freshly ironed cover is tied shut, and the bird is still sleeping. As he opens the door to leave the apartment, Mrs. Kang is padding quickly behind him.

"Wait for me!" she calls.

"Shhhh!" says Mr. Kang, but he waits as she closes the door and turns her key.

Mr. Kang and his bird lead the way. He walks gingerly, holding onto the banister to steady himself as he goes down the stairs. Out the door, down the block, across the street he glides, to Sara Delano Roosevelt Park on Delancey Street.

Mrs. Kang follows, three steps behind. She sees her friends and slips away to join them.

Mr. Kang hangs the cage on the fence, stretches his arms, and breathes in the morning.

Mr. Lum arrives with a cage in each hand. "How are you, my friend? How is the bird?"

409

Student Edition, p. 409

EVALUATION How can you tell that Mr. Kang cares deeply for his bird? (He irons the sheet that he uses to cover the cage—that takes a lot of work!)

Common Core State Standards

Literature 1. Ask and answer questions to demonstrate understanding of a text, referring explicitly to the text as the basis for the answers. **Literature 2.** Recount stories, including fables, folktales, and myths from diverse cultures; determine the central message, lesson, or moral and explain how it is conveyed through key details in the text. **Literature 3.** Describe characters in a story (e.g., their traits, motivations, or feelings) and explain how their actions contribute to the sequence of events.

Access for All

SI Strategic Intervention

Have students use the illustration on p. 408 to describe how Mr. Kang, Sam, and the bird feel about one another.

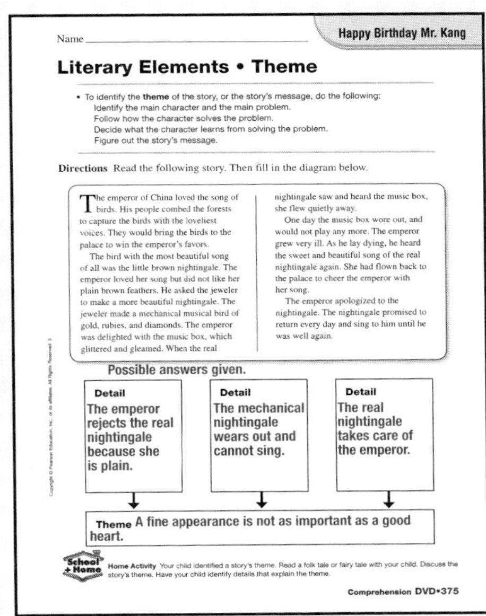

Name ____________ Happy Birthday Mr. Kang

Literary Elements • Theme

- To identify the **theme** of the story, or the story's message, do the following:
  Identify the main character and the main problem.
  Follow how the character solves the problem.
  Decide what the character learns from solving the problem.
  Figure out the story's message.

Directions Read the following story. Then fill in the diagram below.

The emperor of China loved the song of birds. His people combed the forests to capture the birds with the loveliest voices. They would bring the birds to the palace to win the emperor's favors.

The bird with the most beautiful song of all was the little brown nightingale. The emperor loved her song but did not like her plain brown feathers. He asked the jeweler to make a more beautiful nightingale. The jeweler made a mechanical musical bird of gold, rubies, and diamonds. The emperor was delighted with the music box, which glittered and gleamed. When the real nightingale saw and heard the music box, she flew quietly away.

One day the music box wore out, and would not play any more. The emperor grew very ill. As he lay dying, he heard the sweet and beautiful song of the real nightingale again. She had flown back to the palace to cheer the emperor with her song.

The emperor apologized to the nightingale. The nightingale promised to return every day and sing to him until he was well again.

Possible answers given.

Detail The emperor rejects the real nightingale because she is plain.

Detail The mechanical nightingale wears out and cannot sing.

Detail The real nightingale takes care of the emperor.

Theme A fine appearance is not as important as a good heart.

School + Home **Home Activity** Your child identified a story's theme. Read a folk tale or fairy tale with your child. Discuss the story's theme. Have your child identify details that explain the theme.

Comprehension DVD•375

Let'a Practice It! TR DVD•375

Inferring Read aloud the first paragraph on p. 408. What do you think the hua mei thinks about Sam? How can you tell? Have students think about what they have read and what they already know to answer the question. (The hua mei seems to like Sam because it sings to him and holds tightly to his finger.)

1ST READ

Access Text

If students need help, then…

INFERRING Ask students to infer why Mr. Kang greets Mr. Lum with this poem. (He is saying he enjoys their time in the park the way he enjoyed time with his grandfather.)

Think Aloud **MODEL** Mr. Kang's poem tells how seeing Mr. Lum reminds him of this past time. I know from my own life that sometimes friends have special ways of greeting each other. Mr. Lum seems to be a good friend; this is a way for Mr. Kang to greet him and tell him that.

ON THEIR OWN Have students reread the text on these pages. Ask them why Sam might want to accompany his grandfather to the park.

"We are enjoying the morning," smiles Mr. Kang.

"Mr. Lum!
When I see your cages
resting on the green ivy floor
of Sara Delano Roosevelt Park in New York,

I remember my arm is lifted up to hold
Grandfather's big hand
and that ivy is green
from the Shanghai sun
and that ginkgo tree is blowing
in the soft Shanghai breeze
and that heat in my breast
is from my sweet and fragrant almond cake.
Grandmother slipped it into my pocket,
and it is still there,
warm from her oven."

"Even when you speak a greeting to your friend you are painting a poem," says Mr. Lum. Mr. Kang bows his head.

Today is a special Sunday morning because Sam and Mr. Kang are going to the park together. Sam slept at his grandparents' house last night. It is still dark, and he is rubbing his eyes as he jumps from his bed. Just like Grandpa, he washes his face and puts on his clothes. Together, at dawn's first light, they lift the cage. The cover is still tied, the bird is still sleeping. Sam opens the front door. Grandpa steps out, and Grandma is there right behind him, just as she is every Sunday morning.

"Wait for me!" she says.

410

Student Edition, p. 410

2ND READ

Close Reading

ANALYSIS Why might Mrs. Kang put almond cakes in Sam's pocket? (When Mr. Kang was a boy with his grandfather, his grandmother put almond cakes in his pocket. It is probably now a family tradition.)

EVALUATION • TEXT EVIDENCE What kind of character is Mr. Kang? Use evidence from the text in your answer. (He is thoughtful; he expresses his feelings in his poems. He loves his grandson; he talks to him and spends time with him.)

CHECK PREDICTIONS Have students look back at the predictions they made earlier and discuss whether they were accurate. Then have students preview the rest of the selection and either adjust their predictions accordingly or make new predictions

"Shhhh!" say Mr. Kang and Sam, but they wait as she closes the door. Mrs. Kang takes one extra minute to slip two warm almond cakes into Sam's pocket. Then Sam and Mr. Kang lead the way down the stairs, out the front door, on to the corner, across the street, all the way to Sara Delano Roosevelt Park on Delancey Street.
411

Student Edition, p. 411

If you want to teach this selection in two sessions, stop here.

If you want to continue reading this selection, turn to page 412–413.

EVALUATION Why do you think Mr. Kang bows his head when Mr. Lum compliments his poem? (Mr. Kang may feel honored and pleased by his friend's kind words. He may also feel humble and embarrassed by the extra attention.)

Common Core State Standards

Literature 1. Ask and answer questions to demonstrate understanding of a text, referring explicitly to the text as the basis for the answers. **Literature 3.** Describe characters in a story (e.g., their traits, motivations, or feelings) and explain how their actions contribute to the sequence of events. **Also Literature 10.**

Access for All

SI Strategic Intervention

Have pairs of students work together to make inferences about Mr. Kang's relationship with his bird and how important this relationship is to him and his life after he retires as a cook.

A Advanced

Have students find information about kinds of birds people keep as pets in China and some activities people do with these pets. Then have students make inferences about the importance pet birds hold for people in China.

ELL

Antonyms Help students find a pair of antonyms on pp. 410–411, such as *dark/light* or *opens/closes.* Have students use context clues to create their own definitions for these words and to explain why they are antonyms.

Common Core State Standards

Informational Text 5. Use text features and search tools (e.g., key words, sidebars, hyperlinks) to locate information relevant to a given topic efficiently. **Writing 8.** Recall information from experiences or gather information from print and digital sources; take brief notes on sources and sort evidence into provided categories. **Language 2.** Demonstrate command of the conventions of standard English capitalization, punctuation, and spelling when writing. **Language 2.f.** Use spelling patterns and generalizations (e.g., word families, position-based spellings, syllable patterns, ending rules, meaningful word parts) in writing words.

Bridge to Common Core

RESEARCH TO BUILD AND PRESENT KNOWLEDGE

On Day 2 of the weeklong research project, students gather relevant information based on their focused questions from Day 1. They consult digital sources, assessing the credibility of each one. This process enables students to demonstrate an understanding of the subject under investigation.

Research and Inquiry

Step 2 Navigate/Search

TEACH Have students generate a research plan to gather relevant information. Suggest that students search the Internet using their inquiry questions and keywords. Tell them to skim and scan each site for information that helps answer their inquiry question or leads them to specific information that will be useful. Boldfaced or italicized words may be clues to what kind of information the Web site will provide. Have students look for other features, such as headings, illustrations, captions, or highlighting. Remind students to take notes as they gather information.

Think Aloud

MODEL When looking for information on how animals are granted freedom, I found: *After the seals were nursed back to health, they were released back into the wild.* I will use the keywords from this information, such as *health,* to lead me to more specific information. One fact I found using these keywords states, *Workers from wildlife rescue centers take care of sick seals until they are in good health again.*

GUIDE PRACTICE Have students continue their review of Web sites they identified. Explain that before accepting information from a Web site as reliable, students should check to see if the Web site contains spelling or grammatical errors. Remind them that Web addresses ending in *.gov, .org,* or *.edu* are more likely to have reliable information. Suggest they also check for the date when the Web site was last updated to make sure that the facts contained in the site are current.

ON THEIR OWN Have students write down Web addresses, authors, and the dates the Web sites were last updated to create a Works Cited page.

Conventions

Abbreviations

TEACH Write this sentence on the board: *"Mr. Kang," says Mrs. Kang, "did you forget about your three birthday wishes already?"* *Mr.* and *Mrs.* are abbreviated titles, which are capitalized and end with a period.

GUIDE PRACTICE Have students do the following:

- Write a list of adults they know whom they call by a title, such as neighbors, parents of friends, teachers, or doctors.
- Look up their birthdays on a calendar and write the date, including day of the week and month, using abbreviations.

ON THEIR OWN For additional practice, use *Reader's and Writer's Notebook,* p. 400.

Spelling

Schwa

TEACH The schwa in unaccented syllables can be spelled several different ways, but it always has the same sound. Model how to spell words with the schwa sound. The syllables in *another* are *a, no,* and *ther.* I spell the first syllable. If it is hard for me to spell the schwa sound, I'll check the spelling list. Then I write the second syllable. Then I write the last syllable. I may picture the word in my mind to help me spell *another, a-n-o-t-h-e-r.*

GUIDE PRACTICE Have students write each spelling word and underline the unaccented syllable. Tell them to identify the vowels that form the schwa sound.

ON THEIR OWN For additional practice, use *Reader's and Writer's Notebook,* p. 401.

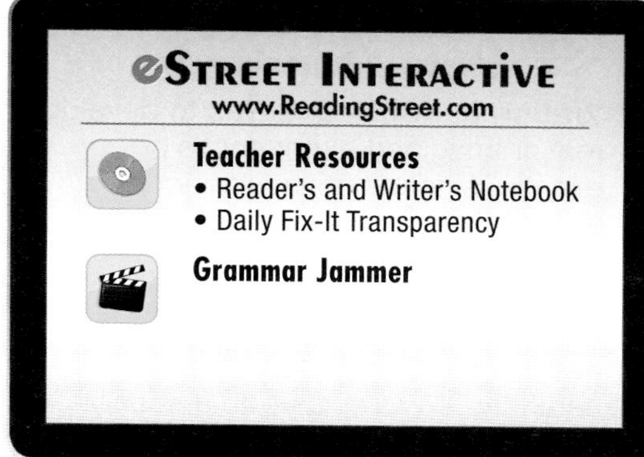

Daily Fix-It

3. I always look at the bird's in the cage in dr. Robinson's office. *(birds; Dr.)*
4. Ms. Sanchez and him clean the cage dayly. *(he; daily)*

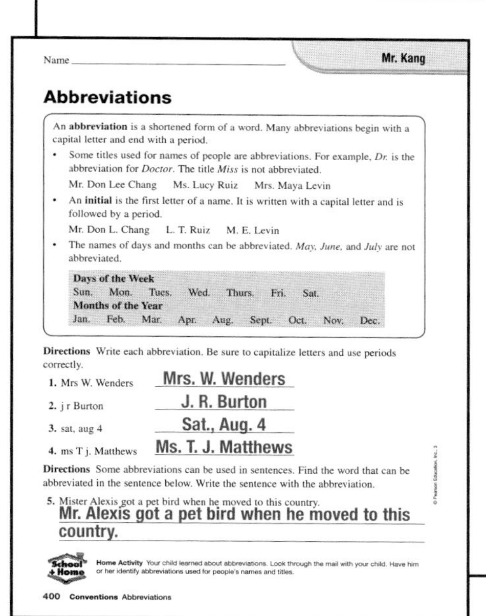

Name ____________ Mr. Kang

Abbreviations

An **abbreviation** is a shortened form of a word. Many abbreviations begin with a capital letter and end with a period.

- Some titles used for names of people are abbreviations. For example, *Dr.* is the abbreviation for *Doctor*. The title *Miss* is not abbreviated.
  Mr. Don Lee Chang Ms. Lucy Ruiz Mrs. Maya Levin
- An **initial** is the first letter of a name. It is written with a capital letter and is followed by a period.
  Mr. Don L. Chang L. T. Ruiz M. E. Levin
- The names of days and months can be abbreviated. *May, June,* and *July* are not abbreviated.

Days of the Week
Sun. Mon. Tues. Wed. Thurs. Fri. Sat.
Months of the Year
Jan. Feb. Mar. Apr. Aug. Sept. Oct. Nov. Dec.

Directions Write each abbreviation. Be sure to capitalize letters and use periods correctly.

1. Mrs W. Wenders **Mrs. W. Wenders**
2. j r Burton **J. R. Burton**
3. sat, aug 4 **Sat., Aug. 4**
4. ms T j. Matthews **Ms. T. J. Matthews**

Directions Some abbreviations can be used in sentences. Find the word that can be abbreviated in the sentence below. Write the sentence with the abbreviation.

5. Mister Alexis got a pet bird when he moved to this country.
Mr. Alexis got a pet bird when he moved to this country.

School + Home **Home Activity** Your child learned about abbreviations. Look through the mail with your child. Have him or her identify abbreviations used for people's names and titles.

400 **Conventions** Abbreviations

© Pearson Education, Inc. 3

Reader's and Writer's Notebook, pp. 400–401

Conventions To provide students with practice on abbreviations, use the modified grammar lessons in the *ELL Handbook* and Grammar Jammer online at: www.ReadingStreet.com

Common Core State Standards

Writing 3. Write narratives to develop real or imagined experiences or events using effective technique, descriptive details, and clear event sequences. **Writing 3.a.** Establish a situation and introduce a narrator and/or characters; organize an event sequence that unfolds naturally. **Writing 4.** With guidance and support from adults, produce writing in which the development and organization are appropriate to task and purpose. **Language 3.a.** Choose words and phrases for effect.

Poetry: Limerick

Writing Trait: Organization

INTRODUCE THE PROMPT Review the key features of limericks with students. Remind them that a limerick is a five-line poem that tells a silly, humorous story, has a fixed rhyme pattern, and each line contains a set number of syllables and accents that create rhythm. Remind students that they should think about these features as they are writing. Explain that they will begin the writing process for a limerick today. Read aloud the writing prompt.

Writing Prompt

Write a limerick about the story *Happy Birthday Mr. Kang*

SELECT A TOPIC

Today you will begin writing a limerick about the main selection, *Happy Birthday Mr. Kang.* Start by reading the selection carefully several times. As you read, keep a list of topics that you could write about. Let's start a list now. Display a T-chart and write the heading "Topics" at the top of the left column. Discuss with the class some key features and events of the story. Write these topics on the chart. Ask students for other suggestions from the story, adding viable topics to the list. Once you have a list of topics, think about how you can make that topic into a limerick. At the top of the right column, write the heading "Limerick Ideas" and brainstorm with students ways of making each topic into a limerick.

Topics	Limerick Ideas
Mr. Kang's three birthday wishes	
Mr. Kang writes poems/paints pictures with Sam	
Mr. Kang's bird from China	
Mr. Kang takes his bird to the park every Sunday	

Corrective feedback Circulate among students as they choose a topic to write about. Talk individually with students who are having difficulty understanding the assigment or making a choice. Ask students what their favorite part of the story was, and offer suggestions for making it into a limerick.

Mini-Lesson Structure of a Limerick

- Once you have chosen your topic and are ready to write, it's important to understand the structure of a limerick. Remember that a limerick has five lines. The rhyme scheme is *a-a-b-b-a.* Lines 1, 2, and 5 rhyme and lines 3 and 4 also rhyme.
- Limericks are written with a certain rhythm. The lines that rhyme should have the same number of syllables and two or three accented syllables per line. Read aloud the student model. Remind students to keep the rhythm in mind as they write.

  Now, use a T-chart to make lists of rhyming words to include in your limerick. You should have two lists—one list of rhyming words for the first, second, and fifth lines, and one list for the third and fourth lines. Have students begin their lists using the graphic organizer on p. 402 of their *Reader's and Writer's Notebook.*

Routine Quick Write for Fluency

Team Talk

1. **Talk** Have students discuss how they chose the rhyming words.
2. **Write** Each student should write a few sentences explaining his or her word choices.
3. **Share** Partners should read their writing to each other and then share their writing with other pairs.

Routines Flip Chart

eStreet Interactive
www.ReadingStreet.com

Teacher Resources
- Reader's and Writer's Notebook
- Graphic Organizer

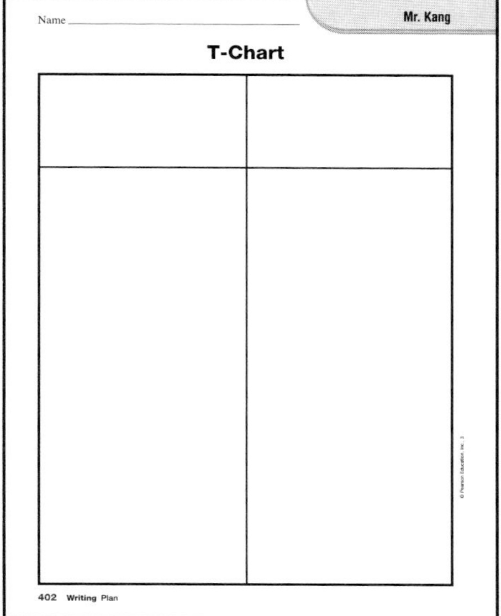

Reader's and Writer's Notebook, p. 402

Wrap Up Your Day!

- ✔ **Content Knowledge** *What did you learn about freedom?*
- ✔ **Text-Based Comprehension** *How does knowing how to identify the cause and effect of an event help you understand your reading?*

Tell students that tomorrow they will read more about why a person might feel that his or her pet deserves to be free.

DAY 3 at a Glance

Content Knowledge
Oral Vocabulary

Phonics/Word Analysis
Schwa

Text-Based Comprehension
Cause and Effect
Inferring

Fluency
Appropriate Phrasing

Research and Study Skills
Maps

Research and Inquiry
Analyze Information

Conventions
Abbreviations

Spelling
Schwa

Writing
Poetry: Limerick

Materials

- Student Edition
- Reader's and Writer's Notebook
- Retelling Cards
- Decodable Reader

Common Core State Standards

Speaking/Listening 1. Engage effectively in a range of collaborative discussions (one-on-one, in groups, and teacher led) with diverse partners on grade 3 topics and texts, building on others' ideas and expressing their own clearly. **Language 5.** Demonstrate understanding of word relationships and nuances in word meanings. **Language 6.** Acquire and use accurately grade-appropriate conversational, general academic, and domain-specific words and phrases, including those that signal spatial and temporal relationships (e.g., *After dinner that night we went looking for them*).

Content Knowledge

Granting Freedom

EXPAND THE CONCEPT Remind students of the weekly concept question, *What does it mean to grant freedom?* Discuss how the question relates to *Happy Birthday Mr. Kang*. Encourage students to think about why a person might think his or her pet companion deserves to be released into the wild.

Build Oral Language

TALK ABOUT SENTENCES AND WORDS Reread these sentences from Student Edition page 410, *Happy Birthday Mr. Kang.*

"Even when you speak a greeting to your friend you are painting a poem," says Mr. Lum. Mr. Kang bows his head.

- What does it mean to "speak a greeting"? (In effect, it means to say "Hello.")
- In what manner did Mr. Kang greet Mr. Lum? (with a poem)
- Why do you think Mr. Lum refers to Mr. Kang's greeting as "painting a poem"? (One reason may be that by choosing words and rhythm carefully, Mr. Kang paints a picture with words.)
- What is another way to describe a way someone could greet his or her friend? Have students share their suggestions.
- What is Mr. Kang showing by *bowing* his head? (He is acknowledging the compliment his friend Mr. Lum has just paid him.)
- What word is a homophone for *bows?* (*boughs*) What is another way to pronounce *b-o-w-s?* What is the meaning of this new word? (decorative knots fashioned with ribbon)

Team Talk Have students work with a partner to replace key words or phrases in the sentences with synonyms. Use the following sentence frame:

Even when you speak a greeting to your friend you are ________________," says Mr. Lum. Mr. Kang _______ his head.

Build Oral Vocabulary

Amazing Words Robust Vocabulary Routine

1. **Introduce** Write the word *companion* on the board. Have students say it with you. Yesterday, we read about a man who keeps a bird as a *companion*. Have students determine a definition of *companion*. (A *companion* is someone who spends time with another person.)

2. **Demonstrate** Have students answer questions to demonstrate understanding. What are some reasons that Mr. Kang's bird is a good *companion* for him? (The bird is a good *companion* for Mr. Kang because it reminds him of his homeland and his past. Also, the bird and Mr. Kang can spend fun time together being artists, with the bird singing and Mr. Kang writing poems.)

3. **Apply** Have students apply their understanding. What are some personality traits that someone might look for in a good *companion*?

4. **Display the Word** Run your hand under the syllables *com-pan-ion* as you read them.

See p. OV•2 to teach *nag*.

Routines Flip Chart

ADD TO THE CONCEPT MAP Discuss the Amazing Words *manage* and *affectionate*. Add these words to the concept map. Use the following questions to develop students' understanding of the concept. Add words generated in the discussion to the concept map.

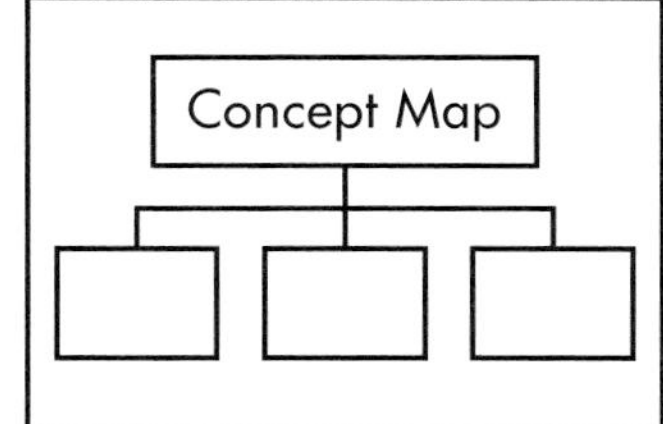

- Mr. Kang *manages* to keep his pet bird happy by taking very good care of it. Think of other ways that people *manage* pets to keep them content.
- Mr. Kang is *affectionate* with his pet bird as he takes care of it, and the bird is *affectionate* with Sam. What are some ways that people are *affectionate* with different kinds of pets for which they care?

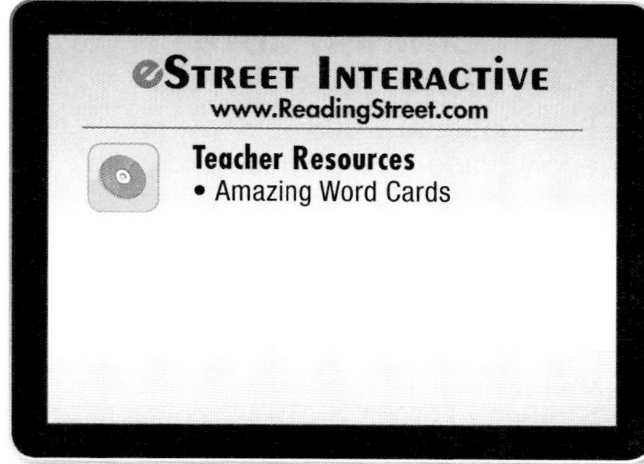

Amazing Words

territory	affectionate
release	companion
loyal	nag
deserve	retrieve
manage	wandering

Expand Vocabulary Use the Day 3 instruction on ELL Poster 27 to help students expand vocabulary.

Common Core State Standards

Foundational Skills 3. Know and apply grade-level phonics and word analysis skills in decoding words. **Foundational Skills 3.c.** Decode multisyllable words. **Foundational Skills 4.** Read with sufficient accuracy and fluency to support comprehension. **Foundational Skills 4.b.** Read on-level prose and poetry orally with accuracy, appropriate rate, and expression on successive readings.

Phonics/Word Analysis

Schwa

MODEL WORD SORTING Write *schwa* and *no schwa* as headings in a two-column chart. Now we are going to sort words. We'll put words with the schwa sound in the first column. Words without the schwa sound will go in the second column. I will start. Write *pretzel* and model how to read it, using the Teach/Model section on p. 396a. Since the second syllable in *pretzel* is an unaccented syllable, I will write *pretzel* in the first column. Model reading *nickel* and *redo* in the same way.

GUIDE PRACTICE Use the following words for the sort: *sister, meadow, profile, decorate, robin,* and *alarm*. Point to a word. Have students read the word, identify its syllables, and tell where it should be written on the chart.

Corrective feedback For corrective feedback, model identifying the syllables and whether or not they have the schwa sound.

schwa	no schwa
pretzel	redo
nickel	meadow
sister	profile
decorate	
robin	
alarm	

Fluent Word Reading

MODEL Write *family*. I know this word has three syllables: *fam-i-ly.* The middle syllable, *i,* is unaccented, so I say the schwa sound for the letter *i*. I read the word as *family*.

GUIDE PRACTICE Write the words below. Look for the word parts you know. When I point to the word, we'll read it together. Allow one second per word part previewing time for the first reading.

vitamin	envelope	balcony	camera	local	customer

ON THEIR OWN Have students read the list above three or four times, until they can read one word per second.

Decodable Passage 27B

If students need help, then...

Read *Sylvester's Notes*

READ WORDS IN ISOLATION Have students turn to p. 141 in *Decodable Practice Readers 3.2* and find the first list of words. Each word in this list has the schwa sound. Let's read these words. Be sure that students pronounce the vowel that stands for the schwa sound correctly.

Next, have students read the high-frequency words.

PREVIEW Have students read the title and preview the story. Tell them that they will read words that have the schwa sound.

READ WORDS IN CONTEXT Chorally read the story along with students. Have students identify words in the story that have the schwa sound. Make sure that students are monitoring their accuracy when they decode words.

Team Talk Pair students and have them take turns reading the story aloud to each other. Monitor students as they read to check for proper pronunciation and appropriate pacing.

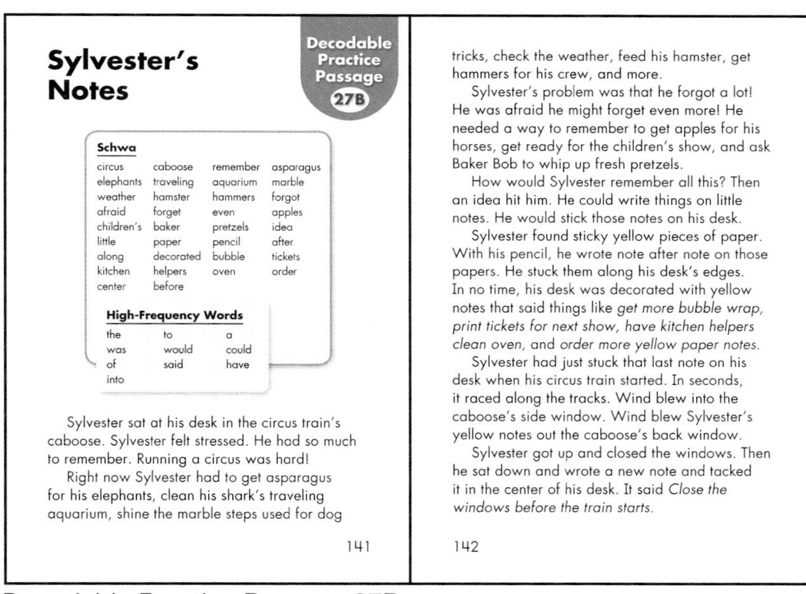

Decodable Practice Passage 27B

Sylvester's Notes

Decodable Practice Passage 27B

Schwa

circus	caboose	remember	asparagus
elephants	traveling	aquarium	marble
weather	hamster	hammers	forgot
afraid	forget	even	apples
children's	baker	pretzels	idea
little	paper	pencil	after
along	decorated	bubble	tickets
kitchen	helpers	oven	order
center	before		

High-Frequency Words

the	to	a
was	would	could
of	said	have
into		

Sylvester sat at his desk in the circus train's caboose. Sylvester felt stressed. He had so much to remember. Running a circus was hard!

Right now Sylvester had to get asparagus for his elephants, clean his shark's traveling aquarium, shine the marble steps used for dog

141

tricks, check the weather, feed his hamster, get hammers for his crew, and more.

Sylvester's problem was that he forgot a lot! He was afraid he might forget even more! He needed a way to remember to get apples for his horses, get ready for the children's show, and ask Baker Bob to whip up fresh pretzels.

How would Sylvester remember all this? Then an idea hit him. He could write things on little notes. He would stick those notes on his desk.

Sylvester found sticky yellow pieces of paper. With his pencil, he wrote note after note on those papers. He stuck them along his desk's edges. In no time, his desk was decorated with yellow notes that said things like *get more bubble wrap, print tickets for next show, have kitchen helpers clean oven,* and *order more yellow paper notes.*

Sylvester had just stuck that last note on his desk when his circus train started. In seconds, it raced along the tracks. Wind blew into the caboose's side window. Wind blew Sylvester's yellow notes out the caboose's back window.

Sylvester got up and closed the windows. Then he sat down and wrote a new note and tacked it in the center of his desk. It said *Close the windows before the train starts.*

142

Access for All

Help students divide each word in the list into syllables. Write each word on the board and show students how to indicate which syllable is stressed using an accent mark. For example, *pret´zel*. Then have children underline the vowel in the unstressed syllable that stands for the schwa sound.

Text-Based Comprehension

Check Understanding

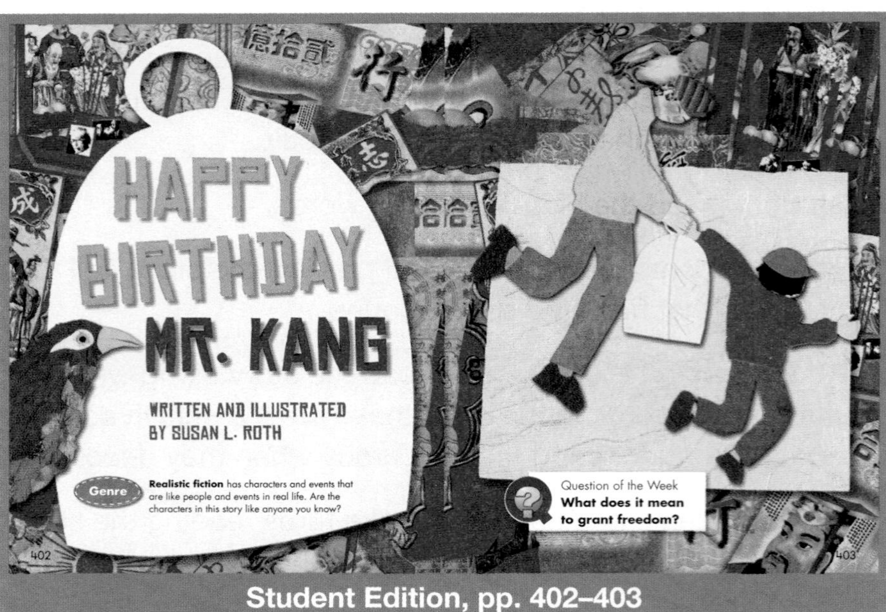

Student Edition, pp. 402–403

If... you chose to read *Happy Birthday Mr. Kang* in two parts, **then...** use the following questions to monitor students' understanding of pages 402–411 of the selection. Encourage students to cite evidence from the text.

ANALYSIS What causes Mr. Kang to want to read the newspaper every day, paint poems, and buy a bird? (He has retired. It has been his dream to do these things. Now that he is no longer working, he will do them.)

EVALUATION Why does the author provide details about how Mr. Kang takes care of his bird, such as the fact that the bird's water bowl is hand-painted and ceramic, that Mr. Kang cooks the bird's food himself, and that he bathes it with a silk cloth? (These details all show how much Mr. Kang treasures his bird.)

RETELL Have students retell pp. 404–411 of *Happy Birthday Mr. Kang,* summarizing the plot's main events.

Corrective feedback	**If...** students leave out important details, **then...** have students look back through the illustrations in the selection.

READ Use the **Access Text** and **Close Reading** notes to finish reading *Happy Birthday Mr. Kang*.

Common Core State Standards

Literature 1. Ask and answer questions to demonstrate understanding of a text, referring explicitly to the text as the basis for the answers. **Literature 2.** Recount stories, including fables, folktales, and myths from diverse cultures; determine the central message, lesson, or moral and explain how it is conveyed through key details in the text. **Literature 10.** By the end of the year, read and comprehend literature, including stories, dramas, and poetry, at the high end of the grades 2–3 text complexity band independently and proficiently. **Speaking/Listening 4.** Report on a topic or text, tell a story, or recount an experience with appropriate facts and relevant, descriptive details, speaking clearly at an understandable pace.

Strategy Response Log

Have students use their background knowledge and clues from the text to make inferences about being free to do what you like. Use p. 33 in the *Reader's and Writer's Notebook* to list clues found in the text.

eSTREET INTERACTIVE
www.ReadingStreet.com

Pearson eText
• Student Edition

AudioText CD

Teacher Resources
• Reader's and Writer's Notebook

If... you followed the Read for Understanding routine below,
then... ask students to retell the selection before you reread *Happy Birthday Mr. Kang*.

RETELL Have students retell pp. 404–411 of *Happy Birthday Mr. Kang,* summarizing the plot's main events.

Corrective feedback	**If...** students leave out important details, **then...** have students look back through the illustrations in the selection.

READ Return to p. 404–405 and use the **2nd Read/Close Reading** notes to reread *Happy Birthday Mr. Kang*.

Read Main Selection

Routine Read for Understanding

Deepen understanding by reading the selection multiple times.

1. **First Read**—If students need support, then use the **Access Text** notes to help them clarify understanding.
2. **Second Read**—Use the **Close Reading** notes to help students draw knowledge from the text.

Check Retelling To support retelling, review the multilingual summary for *Happy Birthday Mr. Kang* with the appropriate Retelling Cards to scaffold understanding.

Day 3 SMALL GROUP TIME • Differentiate Close Reading, p. SG•17

OL On-Level
- **Reread** to Develop Vocabulary
- **Read** *Happy Birthday Mr. Kang*

SI Strategic Intervention
- **Reread** to Develop Vocabulary
- **Read** *Happy Birthday Mr. Kang*

A Advanced
- **Reread** to Develop Vocabulary
- **Read** *Happy Birthday Mr. Kang*
- **Investigate** Inquiry Project

If... students need more scaffolding and practice with the **Main Selection,**
then... use the activities on p. DI•47 in the Teacher Resources section on SuccessNet.

1ST READ

Access Text If students need help, then...

ANTONYMS Ask students to figure out the meaning of *foreign* on p. 412 and find an antonym. (A *foreign* land is one that is strange to a person. An antonym for *foreign* is *familiar*.)

Think Aloud **MODEL** Mr. Kang came to America from China, so the land where he is growing old is not his original land. I think *foreign* means "unfamiliar." I am sure this is correct, because Mr. Kang uses *strange* in the same way in his poem. An antonym for *foreign* would be *familiar*.

As usual, Mrs. Kang follows until she sees her friends. Sam sets the bird cage gently on the ground. Mr. Lum's cages are already hanging.

"Look who's here!" says Mr. Lum. "How are you, Sam? You're getting so big. How old are you?"

"Seven," says Sam.

"Only seven?" says Mr. Lum. "You're handling that cage better than a twelve-year-old would!"

Sam smiles.

"An old grandfather does not mind growing old in a foreign land with such a grandson," says Mr. Kang.

"I am happy in this strange land:
I see my grandson planted
in the new, rich earth,
growing straight and smart and tall.
I water him.
The sun shines on his
firm young leaves
as I watch for his flowers
and for his fruit."

412

Student Edition, p. 412

2ND READ

Close Reading

INFERENCE What happens on page 412 to make Sam smile? (Sam's grandfather compliments him on how well Sam handles the bird cage.)

SYNTHESIS • TEXT EVIDENCE What reasons does Mr. Kang give in his poem on page 412 for being happy? (His grandson is growing up in the new, rich earth of America. Sam is becoming smart and tall, and Mr. Kang delights in "watering" him and watching him blossom and grow.)

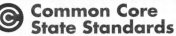

ON THEIR OWN Have students pick another word from pp. 412–413 and think of an antonym for it.

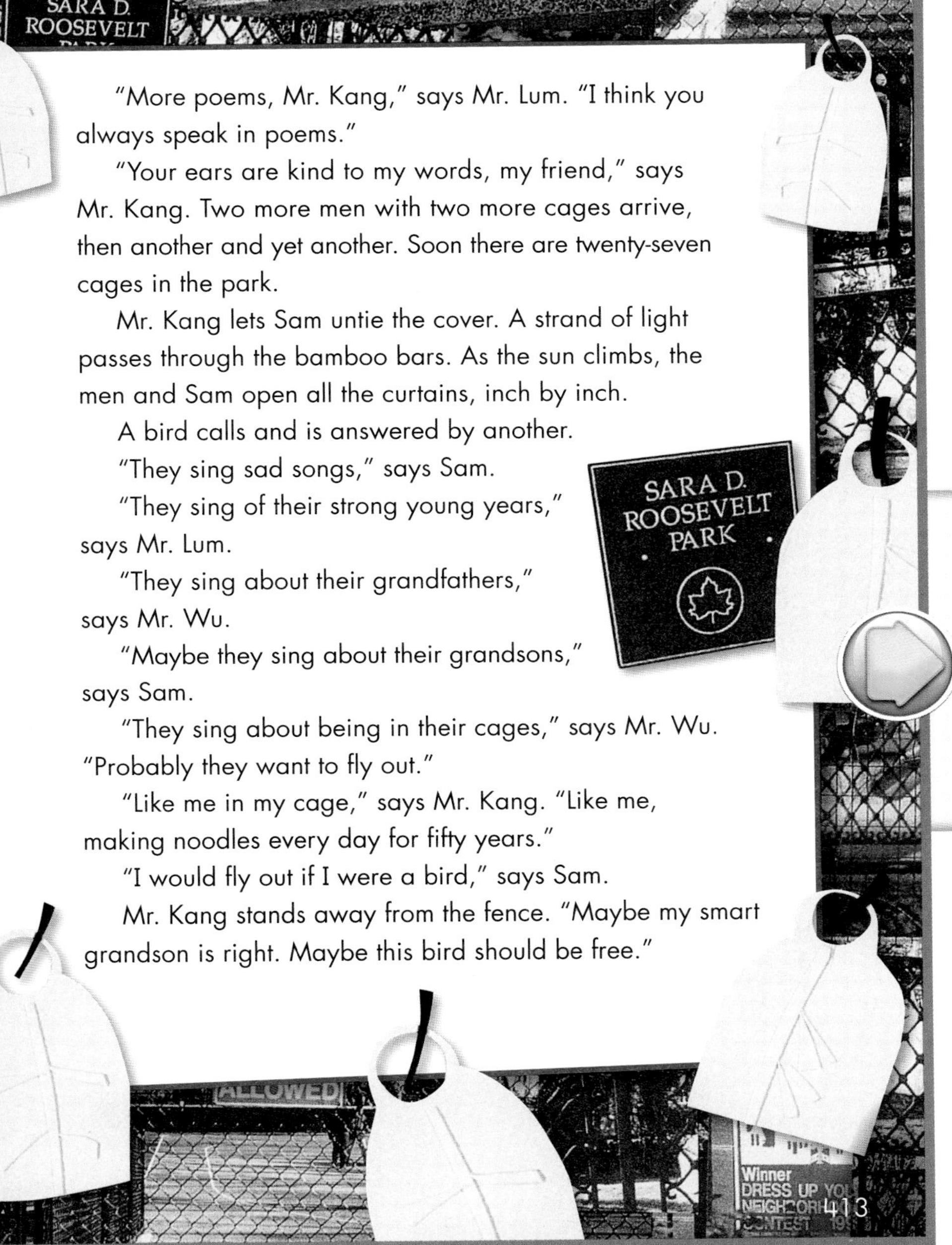
"More poems, Mr. Kang," says Mr. Lum. "I think you always speak in poems."

"Your ears are kind to my words, my friend," says Mr. Kang. Two more men with two more cages arrive, then another and yet another. Soon there are twenty-seven cages in the park.

Mr. Kang lets Sam untie the cover. A strand of light passes through the bamboo bars. As the sun climbs, the men and Sam open all the curtains, inch by inch.

A bird calls and is answered by another.

"They sing sad songs," says Sam.

"They sing of their strong young years," says Mr. Lum.

"They sing about their grandfathers," says Mr. Wu.

"Maybe they sing about their grandsons," says Sam.

"They sing about being in their cages," says Mr. Wu. "Probably they want to fly out."

"Like me in my cage," says Mr. Kang. "Like me, making noodles every day for fifty years."

"I would fly out if I were a bird," says Sam.

Mr. Kang stands away from the fence. "Maybe my smart grandson is right. Maybe this bird should be free."

Student Edition, p. 413

ANALYSIS What does Mr. Kang mean when he says that Mr. Lum's ears are kind to his words? (Mr. Lum has just complimented Mr. Kang for always speaking in poems. Mr. Kang is modestly replying that it's not his words that are poetry, but rather Mr. Lum's ears that are receiving them as poetry.)

Common Core State Standards

Literature 1. Ask and answer questions to demonstrate understanding of a text, referring explicitly to the text as the basis for the answers. **Literature 3.** Describe characters in a story (e.g., their traits, motivations, or feelings) and explain how their actions contribute to the sequence of events. **Literature 4.** Determine the meaning of words and phrases as they are used in a text, distinguishing literal from nonliteral language. **Also Language 5.a.**

Access for All

A Advanced

Have students identify examples of similes and metaphors on pp. 412–413. Then have them use these examples of figurative language as models for writing their own similes and metaphors about the process of growing up.

ELL

Inferring Read aloud the dialogue on p. 413 where each character explains what topic he thinks the birds are singing about. Ask students to use prior knowledge and what they have learned about each character to explain what the characters think the topics of the songs are and why they might think that.

1ST READ

Access Text If students need help, then...

INFERRING Ask students why they think Mr. Kang uses English after he lets his bird go free. (Speaking English shows his acceptance of a new way of thinking and his new life.)

Think Aloud **MODEL** I know that Mr. Kang cares deeply about his past in China. Mrs. Kang speaks Chinese to him here, so they must speak Chinese to each other often. By listening to Sam and speaking in English, Mr. Kang is showing that he is accepting American ways.

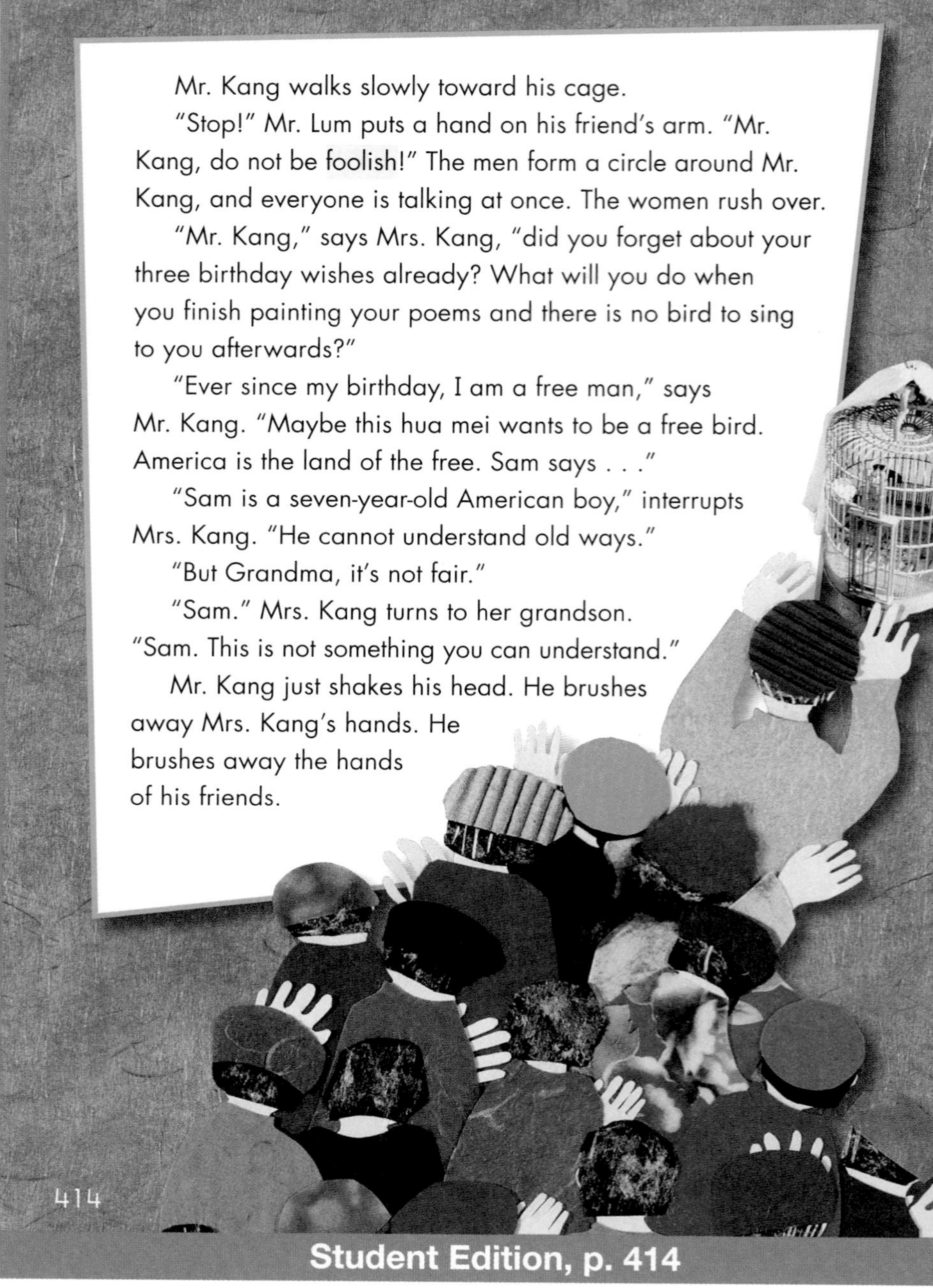

Mr. Kang walks slowly toward his cage.

"Stop!" Mr. Lum puts a hand on his friend's arm. "Mr. Kang, do not be foolish!" The men form a circle around Mr. Kang, and everyone is talking at once. The women rush over.

"Mr. Kang," says Mrs. Kang, "did you forget about your three birthday wishes already? What will you do when you finish painting your poems and there is no bird to sing to you afterwards?"

"Ever since my birthday, I am a free man," says Mr. Kang. "Maybe this hua mei wants to be a free bird. America is the land of the free. Sam says . . ."

"Sam is a seven-year-old American boy," interrupts Mrs. Kang. "He cannot understand old ways."

"But Grandma, it's not fair."

"Sam." Mrs. Kang turns to her grandson. "Sam. This is not something you can understand."

Mr. Kang just shakes his head. He brushes away Mrs. Kang's hands. He brushes away the hands of his friends.

414

Student Edition, p. 414

2ND READ

Close Reading

SYNTHESIS • TEXT EVIDENCE How does the way the other people feel about Mr. Kang letting his bird go free compare with the way Mr. Kang thinks about it? (The other people think it's a foolish idea to let the bird go, especially because Mr. Kang wanted it so much in the first place. They don't care whether it's fair to keep a bird in a cage as long as the bird's owner is happy. Sam and Mr. Kang think the bird should have a choice about where it lives.)

ANALYSIS Help students generate text-based questions by providing the following question stem: In the selection, what did Mr. Kang do when _______?

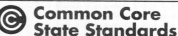

ON THEIR OWN Have students infer why Mrs. Kang thinks Sam doesn't understand why Mr. Kang shouldn't let his bird go free.

Suddenly Sam is frightened. What if Grandma is right? What if Grandpa is sorry after the hua mei flies away? What if the hua mei gets lost? What if he starves? What if he dies?

"Grandpa, wait," says Sam. But Grandpa does not hear. Mr. Kang cannot hear any voice except the voice inside his own head, inside his own heart. He opens the bamboo door.

Mr. Kang's hua mei perches on the threshold of his cage. Perhaps he thinks it's cage-cleaning time. He slowly steps out. He stops to sing a long, sweet note, turns his head to the breeze, and flies into the sky.

Mr. Kang takes off his cap and covers his heart with his hand. For a moment there is silence. Mrs. Kang bends her head and hugs herself. Her mouth is a thin straight line. "Oh, Mr. Kang," she whispers in Chinese. "What can you be thinking?" Sam starts to cry.

"Sam and I are going home to paint poems," says Mr. Kang loudly, in English.

He lifts his empty cage, takes Sam's hand, and together they walk out of the park. Onto the sidewalk, over to the corner, across the street, up the block they walk.

415

Student Edition, p. 415

INFERENCE • ANALYSIS Why does Sam cry when Mr. Kang releases the bird? (Sam is worried about the bird and wants to make sure it will be safe in the wild. He is also worried that his grandpa might regret the decision to let the bird go.)

Common Core State Standards

Literature 1. Ask and answer questions to demonstrate understanding of a text, referring explicitly to the text as the basis for the answers. **Literature 3.** Describe characters in a story (e.g., their traits, motivations, or feelings) and explain how their actions contribute to the sequence of events.

Access for All

SI Strategic Intervention

Have students compare how Sam feels about letting the bird go at the beginning of this spread with how he feels at the end. Ask them to explain why Sam's feelings change.

ELL

Metaphor Point out the metaphor on p. 415: *Her mouth is a thin, straight line*. Discuss how her mouth is not actually a line and how a metaphor makes a comparison without using *like* or *as*.

1ST READ

Access Text If students need help, then...

Review THEME Ask students how Mr. Kang's action of letting his bird fly free relates to this story's theme. (We should have freedom to make choices; Mr. Kang let his bird choose.)

Think Aloud **MODEL** To figure out the theme, I ask, "What is the message of this story?" The bird was free to fly away, but it returned. It was free to do this on its own. The theme is that we all should have freedom to decide where and how we live.

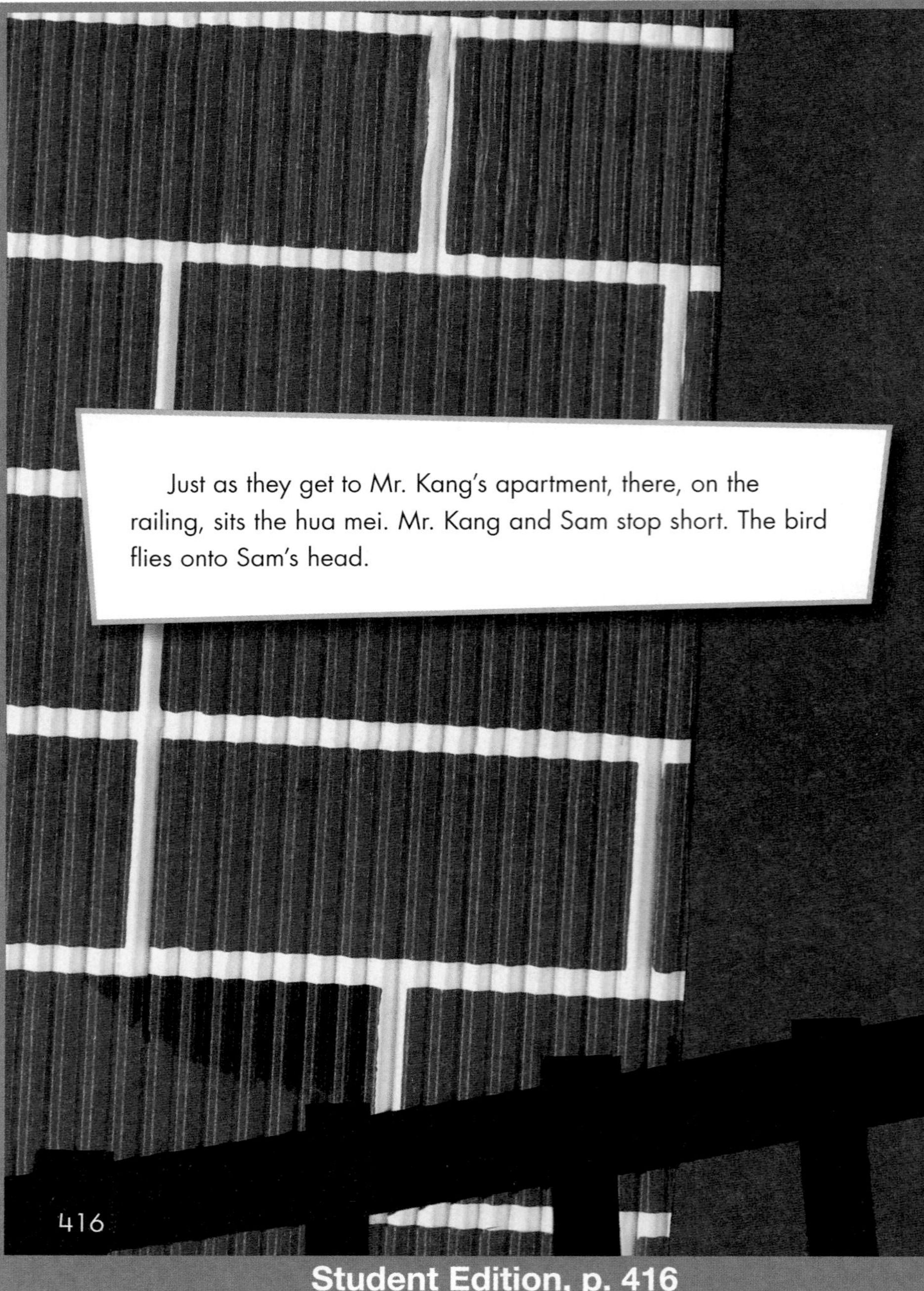

Just as they get to Mr. Kang's apartment, there, on the railing, sits the hua mei. Mr. Kang and Sam stop short. The bird flies onto Sam's head.
416

Student Edition, p. 416

2ND READ

Close Reading

EVALUATION Why do you think Mr. Kang's bird came back after being set free? How does this relate to the theme? (The bird was free to fly away, but it came back on its own. It is still free because it was free to make that choice. This relates to the theme because the bird has the freedom to decide where and how to live.)

ON THEIR OWN Have students paraphrase the theme in their own words.

Student Edition, p. 417

ANALYSIS What does the author mean when she says that Mr. Kang and Sam "stop short"? (It means they almost freeze because they are so startled.)

Common Core State Standards

Literature 2. Recount stories, including fables, folktales, and myths from diverse cultures; determine the central message, lesson, or moral and explain how it is conveyed through key details in the text. **Literature 3.** Describe characters in a story (e.g., their traits, motivations, or feelings) and explain how their actions contribute to the sequence of events. **Language 5.a.** Distinguish the literal and nonliteral meanings of words and phrases in context (e.g., *take steps*). **Also Literature 4.**

Access for All

A Advanced

Have students write a paragraph discussing what it means to be free and to allow others to be free.

Idioms Reread the sentence where Mr. Kang and Sam "stop short." Explain that when a person "stops short," he or she stops suddenly, taking a very short distance to do so. Have students stand up and act out walking and "stopping short."

1ST READ

Access Text

If students need help, then...

CAUSE AND EFFECT Ask students why Mrs. Kang starts smiling when she enters the kitchen.

Think Aloud **MODEL** I think back to what happened just before Mrs. Kang smiled. She walked into the kitchen, saw the bird, and then started to smile. I think she smiled because she was happy to see the bird back, too.

ON THEIR OWN Have students reread pp. 414–415 to find other related causes and effects.

CROSS-TEXT EVALUATION
Use a Strategy to Self-Check How did the Read Aloud "A Little Freedom" help you understand this selection?

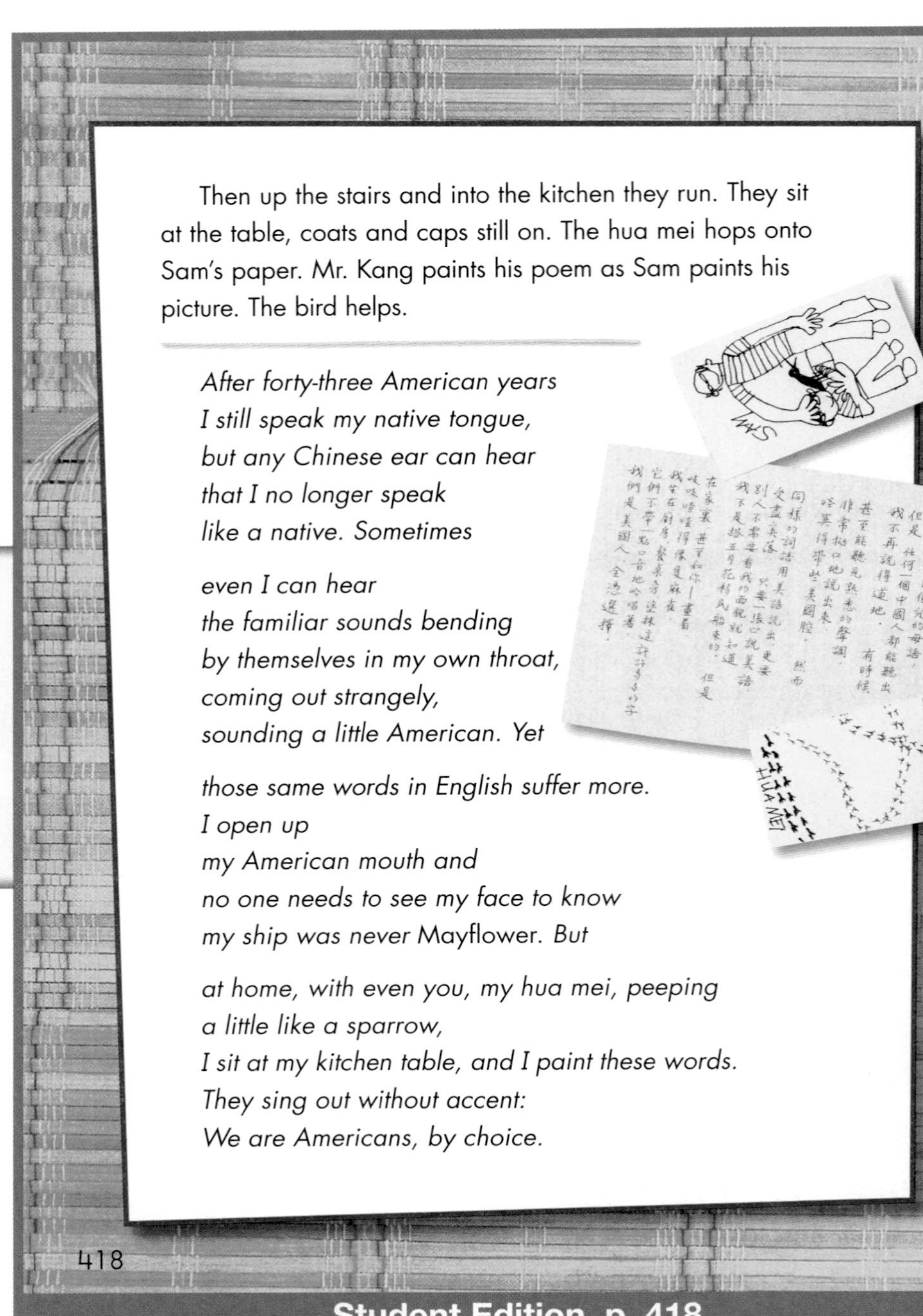

Then up the stairs and into the kitchen they run. They sit at the table, coats and caps still on. The hua mei hops onto Sam's paper. Mr. Kang paints his poem as Sam paints his picture. The bird helps.

After forty-three American years
I still speak my native tongue,
but any Chinese ear can hear
that I no longer speak
like a native. Sometimes

even I can hear
the familiar sounds bending
by themselves in my own throat,
coming out strangely,
sounding a little American. Yet

those same words in English suffer more.
I open up
my American mouth and
no one needs to see my face to know
my ship was never Mayflower. But

at home, with even you, my hua mei, peeping
a little like a sparrow,
I sit at my kitchen table, and I paint these words.
They sing out without accent:
We are Americans, by choice.

418

Student Edition, p. 418

2ND READ

Close Reading

EVALUATION • TEXT EVIDENCE Use evidence from the text to explain how Mr. Kang has changed. (Mr. Kang wanted a bird (*a hua mei*) for his birthday to keep up a tradition from his home country. Later, he realizes that like himself, the bird may long for freedom, so he decides to let the bird go free.)

SYNTHESIS • TEXT EVIDENCE Using what you learned in this selection, tell what we can learn about what it means to grant freedom. Have students cite examples from the text to support their responses.

CHECK PREDICTIONS Have students return to the predictions they made earlier and confirm whether they were accurate.

"This is your poem, Birdie," says Mr. Kang, "and Sam, it's your poem too."

Then Mr. Kang looks at Sam's painting. "My grandson is a great artist," he says. He hangs the paintings on the kitchen cabinet and sits back to admire them.

Mrs. Kang walks into the kitchen with her mouth still in that thin straight line, but there is the bird, and suddenly she is smiling.

"Today I'll cook for both of you, and for your hua mei," she says.

And she makes tea, and more sweet and fragrant almond cakes, warm from the oven.

419

Student Edition, p. 419

EVALUATION What reasons might the author have had for writing this story? (The author might have wanted to entertain readers but also to convince her audience how important it is to have the freedom to make our own choices and how people who live in America are lucky to have this freedom.)

Common Core State Standards

Literature 1. Ask and answer questions to demonstrate understanding of a text, referring explicitly to the text as the basis for the answers. **Literature 2.** Recount stories, including fables, folktales, and myths from diverse cultures; determine the central message, lesson, or moral and explain how it is conveyed through key details in the text. **Literature 3.** Describe characters in a story (e.g., their traits, motivations, or feelings) and explain how their actions contribute to the sequence of events. **Also Literature 10.**

Access for All

SI Strategic Intervention

To make sure students understand the meaning of Mr. Kang's last poem, have them write what it means to them.

A Advanced

Have students use Mr. Kang's poem as a model for writing a poem that celebrates how they feel about growing up in America.

Graphic Organizer Have students use a Venn diagram to compare and contrast Mr. Kang and his bird. Help them locate important details in the text and record them in the appropriate sections of the diagram.

Common Core State Standards
Literature 1. Ask and answer questions to demonstrate understanding of a text, referring explicitly to the text as the basis for the answers. **Also Literature 7., Writing 8.**

Think Critically

1. Compare this story to the historical fiction story *Me and Uncle Romie*. How are the two stories alike? How are they different? Text to Text
2. Find the most interesting illustration in the story. Pretend that you are the author. Explain why that illustration enhances your story. Think Like an Author
3. What caused Mr. Kang to change his mind about his *hua mei*? What was the effect? Cause and Effect
4. How do you know that Sam thinks the *hua mei* should be freed? Do you think Mr. Kang is happy he let the bird out of its cage? Use evidence from the story to explain your answer. Inferring
5. **Look Back and Write** What is special about Mr. Kang's birthday? Look back through the story and think about what Mr. Kang does during the days after his birthday. Write a response to the question, providing evidence to support your answer. Key Ideas and Details • Text Evidence

420

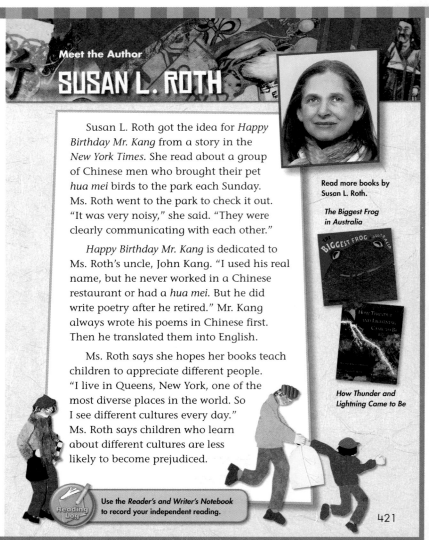

Meet the Author

SUSAN L. ROTH

Susan L. Roth got the idea for *Happy Birthday Mr. Kang* from a story in the *New York Times.* She read about a group of Chinese men who brought their pet *hua mei* birds to the park each Sunday. Ms. Roth went to the park to check it out. "It was very noisy," she said. "They were clearly communicating with each other."

Happy Birthday Mr. Kang is dedicated to Ms. Roth's uncle, John Kang. "I used his real name, but he never worked in a Chinese restaurant or had a *hua mei.* But he did write poetry after he retired." Mr. Kang always wrote his poems in Chinese first. Then he translated them into English.

Ms. Roth says she hopes her books teach children to appreciate different people. "I live in Queens, New York, one of the most diverse places in the world. So I see different cultures every day." Ms. Roth says children who learn about different cultures are less likely to become prejudiced.

Read more books by Susan L. Roth.

The Biggest Frog in Australia

How Thunder and Lightning Came to Be

Reading Log — Use the *Reader's and Writer's Notebook* to record your independent reading.

421

Student Edition, pp. 420–421

Common Core State Standards

Literature 1. Ask and answer questions to demonstrate understanding of a text, referring explicitly to the text as the basis for the answers. **Also Literature 7., Writing 2., Speaking/Listening 4., Language 3.**

Bridge to Common Core

RANGE OF READING AND LEVEL OF TEXT COMPLEXITY

To increase students' capacity for reading and comprehending complex texts independently and proficiently, have them read other literary texts by Susan L. Roth or material on the social studies topic, Freedom. After students read closely for a sustained period of time, they should record their reading in their Reading Logs.

Think Critically

1. **TEXT TO TEXT** They both tell about places, people, and events that are like real life. One tells about the past, and one tells about the present.
2. **THINK LIKE AN AUTHOR** On p. 418, the illustrator drew Sam's drawing, Mr. Kang's poem, and the bird's painting. These show how the characters share their time making art.
3. **CAUSE AND EFFECT** Cause: Sam helped Mr. Kang realize that the bird was not free. Effect: Mr. Kang let the bird go free so it could make its own choice.
4. **INFERRING** Sam says the birds' songs sound sad. Mr. Kang shows that he is happy with his decision by speaking English and holding Sam's hand.
5. **LOOK BACK AND WRITE • TEXT EVIDENCE** To build writing fluency, assign a 10–15 minute time limit.

Scoring Rubric Look Back and Write

TOP-SCORE RESPONSE A top-score response uses details to tell why Mr. Kang's birthday is special and how it influences future events in the plot.

A top-score response should include:

- Mr. Kang spent years not being free to do what he wanted.
- Mr. Kang announces on his birthday that his birthday wishes are to stop cooking and do what he wants.
- After his birthday, Mr. Kang does what he wants, including getting a Chinese bird as a companion.

Retell

Have students work in pairs to retell the selection, using the retelling strip in the Student Edition or the Story Sort as prompts. Monitor students' retellings.

Scoring Rubric Narrative Retelling

	4	3	2	1
Connections	Makes connections and generalizes beyond the text	Makes connections to other events, stories, or experiences	Makes a limited connection to another event, story, or experience	Makes no connection to another event, story, or experience
Author's Purpose	Elaborates on author's purpose	Tells author's purpose with some clarity	Makes some connection to author's purpose	Makes no connection to author's purpose
Characters	Describes the main character(s) and any character development	Identifies the main character(s) and gives some information about them	Inaccurately identifies some characters or gives little information about them	Inaccurately identifies the characters or gives no information about them
Setting	Describes the time and location	Identifies the time and location	Omits details of time or location	Is unable to identify time or location
Plot	Describes the problem, goal, events, and ending using rich detail	Tells the problem, goal, events, and ending with some errors that do not affect meaning	Tells parts of the problem, goal, events, and ending with gaps that affect meaning	Retelling has no sense of story

Don't Wait Until Friday

MONITOR PROGRESS Check Retelling

If... students have difficulty retelling,
then... use the Retelling Cards/Story Sort to scaffold their retellings.

Plan to Assess Retelling

- ☐ **Week 1** Strategic Intervention
- ☑ **This week assess Advanced students.**
- ☐ **Week 3** Strategic Intervention
- ☐ **Week 4** On-Level
- ☐ **Week 5** Assess any students you have not yet checked during this unit.

Meet the Author

Have students read about author Susan L. Roth on p. 421. Ask them how she expresses her beliefs about how to live freely in *Happy Birthday Mr. Kang*.

Read Independently

Have students enter their independent reading into their Reading Logs.

Common Core State Standards

Informational Text 7. Use information gained from illustrations (e.g., maps, photographs) and the words in a text to demonstrate understanding of the text (e.g., where, when, why, and how key events occur). **Foundational Skills 4.b.** Read on-level prose and poetry orally with accuracy, appropriate rate, and expression on successive readings.

Fluency

Appropriate Phrasing

MODEL FLUENT READING Have students turn to p. 412 of *Happy Birthday Mr. Kang*. Have students follow along as you read the dialogue at the top of this page. Tell them to notice where you pause for punctuation and listen carefully as you read the dialogue. Point out places where the text breaks naturally into groups of words, or phrases.

GUIDE PRACTICE Have students follow along as you read the page again. Then have them read the page as a group without you until they read with appropriate phrasing and with no mistakes. Ask questions to be sure students comprehend the text. Continue in the same way on p. 413.

Corrective feedback

If... students are having difficulty reading with appropriate phrasing,
then... prompt them as follows:

- Where can we break up this sentence? Which words are related?
- Read the sentence again. Pause after each group of words.
- Tell me the sentence. Now read it with pauses after each group of words.

Reread for Fluency

Routine Oral Rereading

1. **Read** Have students read the dialogue on p. 415 of *Happy Birthday Mr. Kang* orally.
2. **Reread** To achieve optimal fluency, students should reread the text three or four times.
3. **Corrective Feedback** Have students read aloud without you. Listen to ensure that words are read correctly with appropriate phrasing, and provide feedback.

Routines Flip Chart

Research and Study Skills

Maps

TEACH Ask students what kinds of texts use maps. Students may mention atlases, encyclopedias, newspapers, magazines, textbooks, or stories. Note that maps may show road systems, state boundaries, the geography of an area, weather, or products produced in an area. Show a map from a content-area text and use it to review these terms:

- Every map has a **legend,** or a key that explains the things the map shows. You must look at the legend before using the map for the first time.
- Each legend contains a **compass rose** that shows the directions north, south, east, and west on the map.
- Each legend has a **scale** that shows distance on the map and provides information such as how many inches equal a mile or a kilometer.
- Each legend contains **symbols,** or small pictures that show landmarks such as airports, schools, or campgrounds.

Provide groups with examples of different kinds of maps. Have each group show its map to the class, tell what kind of map it is, and use the legend to explain what it shows and how it is shown.

GUIDE PRACTICE Discuss these questions:

How do you know what the symbols on a map represent? (The legend explains the meanings of the symbols.)

How are maps alike or different? (They all show information about a place, but they show different kinds of information, such as area boundaries, geographical features, or man-made features such as roads or buildings.)

After groups describe their maps, ask specific questions about the information depicted on the map and how it is represented visually.

ON THEIR OWN Have students review and complete p. 404 of the *Reader's and Writer's Notebook*.

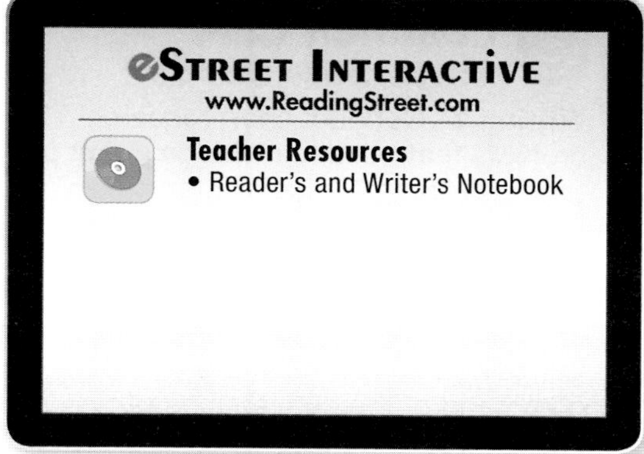

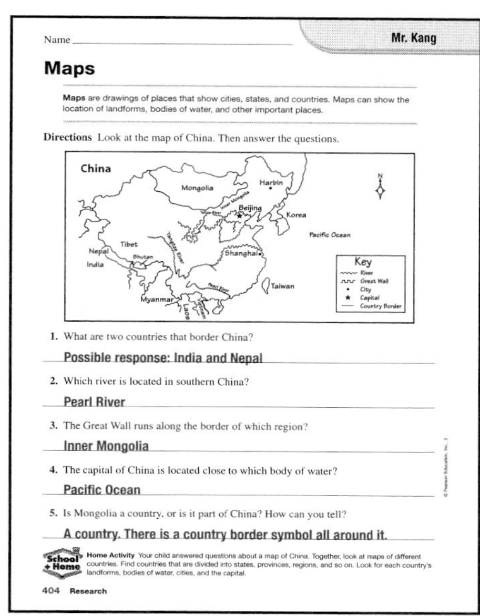

Name ______ Mr. Kang

Maps

Maps are drawings of places that show cities, states, and countries. Maps can show the location of landforms, bodies of water, and other important places.

Directions Look at the map of China. Then answer the questions.

1. What are two countries that border China?
   Possible response: India and Nepal
2. Which river is located in southern China?
   Pearl River
3. The Great Wall runs along the border of which region?
   Inner Mongolia
4. The capital of China is located close to which body of water?
   Pacific Ocean
5. Is Mongolia a country, or is it part of China? How can you tell?
   A country. There is a country border symbol all around it.

School + Home **Home Activity** Your child answered questions about a map of China. Together, look at maps of different countries. Find countries that are divided into states, provinces, regions, and so on. Look for each country's landforms, bodies of water, cities, and the capital.

404 Research

Reader's and Writer's Notebook, p. 404

Professional Development: What ELL Experts Say About Using Visuals "Visuals enable students to 'see' the basic concepts we are trying to teach more effectively than if we rely only on words. Among the visuals we can use are . . . maps."
—Dr. Jim Cummins

Maps Help students create and draw a classroom map that includes a legend with a scale, a compass rose, and symbols to represent typical classroom objects such as desks and bookcases.

Common Core State Standards

Writing 7. Conduct short research projects that build knowledge about a topic. **Writing 8.** Recall information from experiences or gather information from print and digital sources; take brief notes on sources and sort evidence into provided categories. **Language 2.** Demonstrate command of the conventions of standard English capitalization, punctuation, and spelling when writing. **Language 2.f.** Use spelling patterns and generalizations (e.g., word families, position-based spellings, syllable patterns, ending rules, meaningful word parts) in writing words. **Also Writing 10.**

Research and Inquiry

Step 3 Analyze Information

TEACH Tell students that today they will analyze their research findings. Have students sort the information from their notes into an outline. Remind students that an outline is a plan for writing. Then explain that information gathered from interviews with local experts may lead students to modify their inquiry questions.

Think Aloud **MODEL** Originally I thought that it would be easy for people to nurse animals back to health and release them into the wild if they were hurt by oil spills and other causes. When I talked to a local animal rescue worker, however, I found that sometimes people are not able to heal animals enough for them to be able to stay safe if they are returned to the wild. Now my inquiry question is *What must people do to be able to grant freedom to animals*?

GUIDE PRACTICE Have students analyze their findings. They may need to refocus their inquiry question to better fit the information they found. Remind students that if they have difficulty improving their focus they can ask a reference librarian or the local expert for guidance.

Remind students that they can use a map to provide a visual representation of their findings about places where animals might be released safely.

ON THEIR OWN Have students scan their information and decide if it is credible, reliable, and useful to their purposes. Suggest that they print out their research and highlight relevant information.

Conventions

Abbreviations

REVIEW Remind students that this week they learned about abbreviations. An abbreviation is a shortened version of a word.

- Certain titles, such as *Dr.* and *Mrs.*, are spelled as abbreviations.
- Days of the week and months of the year are often abbreviated.
- People's names are sometimes abbreviated as initials.
- Abbreviations often begin with a capital letter and end with a period.

CONNECT TO ORAL LANGUAGE Have students name the initials of each president.

Franklin D. Roosevelt (F.D.R.)
John F. Kennedy (J.F.K.)
Lyndon Baines Johnson (L.B.J.)

ON THEIR OWN For additional support, use *Let's Practice It!* p. 376 on the *Teacher Resources DVD-ROM*.

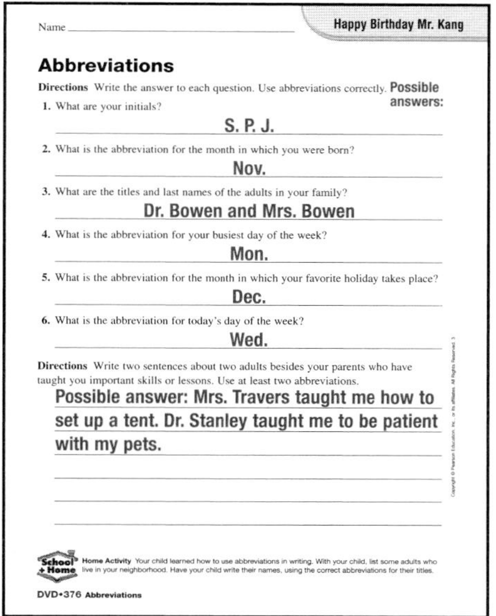
Name ______________ Happy Birthday Mr. Kang

Abbreviations

Directions Write the answer to each question. Use abbreviations correctly. Possible answers:

1. What are your initials? S. P. J.
2. What is the abbreviation for the month in which you were born? Nov.
3. What are the titles and last names of the adults in your family? Dr. Bowen and Mrs. Bowen
4. What is the abbreviation for your busiest day of the week? Mon.
5. What is the abbreviation for the month in which your favorite holiday takes place? Dec.
6. What is the abbreviation for today's day of the week? Wed.

Directions Write two sentences about two adults besides your parents who have taught you important skills or lessons. Use at least two abbreviations.

Possible answer: Mrs. Travers taught me how to set up a tent. Dr. Stanley taught me to be patient with my pets.

Home Activity Your child learned how to use abbreviations in writing. With your child, list some adults who live in your neighborhood. Have your child write their names, using the correct abbreviations for their titles.

DVD•376 Abbreviations

Let's Practice It! TR DVD•376

Spelling

Schwa

FREQUENTLY MISSPELLED WORDS The words *upon, again,* and *beautiful* are words that students often misspell. Think carefully before you write these words. Have students practice writing the words *upon, again,* and *beautiful* by writing sentences using each word.

ON THEIR OWN For additional practice, use *Reader's and Writer's Notebook,* p. 405.

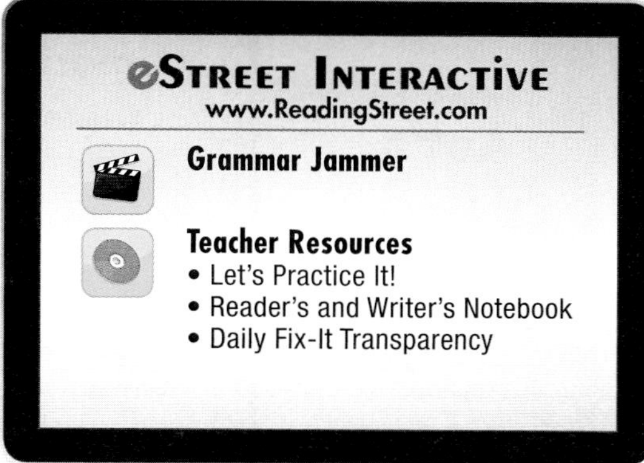

Access for All

Provide struggling students with extra practice working with abbreviations. Have each student write his or her name on a slip of paper and then exchange papers with a partner to identify each other's initials.

Daily Fix-It

5. This bird has bright fethers and it sings a cheerfull song. *(feathers, and; cheerful)*
6. It's musick makes me feel happy. *(Its; music)*

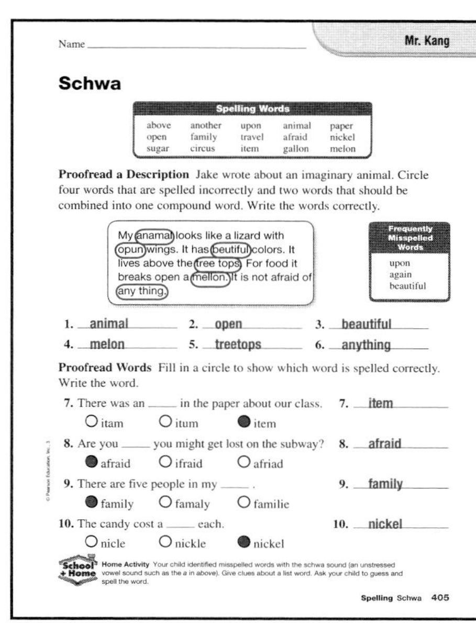
Name ______________ Mr. Kang

Schwa

Spelling Words

above	another	upon	animal	paper
open	family	travel	afraid	nickel
sugar	circus	item	gallon	melon

Proofread a Description Jake wrote about an imaginary animal. Circle four words that are spelled incorrectly and two words that should be combined into one compound word. Write the words correctly.

My anamal looks like a lizard with opun wings. It has beutiful colors. It lives above the tree tops. For food it breaks open a mellon. It is not afraid of any thing.

Frequently Misspelled Words: upon, again, beautiful

1. animal 2. open 3. beautiful
4. melon 5. treetops 6. anything

Proofread Words Fill in a circle to show which word is spelled correctly. Write the word.

7. There was an ____ in the paper about our class. ○ itam ○ itum ● item — 7. item
8. Are you ____ you might get lost on the subway? ● afraid ○ ifraid ○ afriad — 8. afraid
9. There are five people in my ____ . ● family ○ famaly ○ familie — 9. family
10. The candy cost a ____ each. ○ nicle ○ nickle ● nickel — 10. nickel

Home Activity Your child identified misspelled words with the schwa sound (an unstressed vowel sound such as the *a* in *above*). Give clues about a list word. Ask your child to guess and spell the word.

Spelling Schwa 405

Reader's and Writer's Notebook, p. 405

Common Core State Standards
Writing 4. With guidance and support from adults, produce writing in which the development and organization are appropriate to task and purpose. **Also Language 1., 2., 3., 3.a.**

Let's Write It!

Key Features of a Limerick

- a form of poetry
- made up of five lines and a specific rhyme scheme
- sometimes humorous or witty

READING STREET ONLINE
GRAMMAR JAMMER
www.ReadingStreet.com

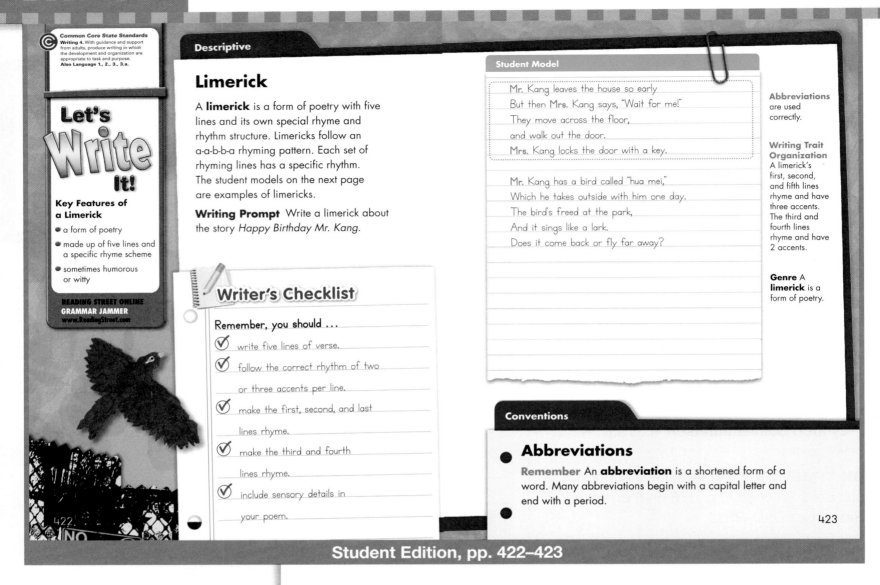

Descriptive

Limerick

A **limerick** is a form of poetry with five lines and its own special rhyme and rhythm structure. Limericks follow an a-a-b-b-a rhyming pattern. Each set of rhyming lines has a specific rhythm. The student models on the next page are examples of limericks.

Writing Prompt Write a limerick about the story *Happy Birthday Mr. Kang.*

Writer's Checklist

Remember, you should ...

- ✓ write five lines of verse.
- ✓ follow the correct rhythm of two or three accents per line.
- ✓ make the first, second, and last lines rhyme.
- ✓ make the third and fourth lines rhyme.
- ✓ include sensory details in your poem.

Student Model

Mr. Kang leaves the house so early
But then Mrs. Kang says, "Wait for me!"
They move across the floor,
and walk out the door.
Mrs. Kang locks the door with a key.

Mr. Kang has a bird called "hua mei,"
Which he takes outside with him one day.
The bird's freed at the park,
And it sings like a lark.
Does it come back or fly far away?

Abbreviations are used correctly.

Writing Trait Organization A limerick's first, second, and fifth lines rhyme and have three accents. The third and fourth lines rhyme and have 2 accents.

Genre A **limerick** is a form of poetry.

Conventions

Abbreviations

Remember An **abbreviation** is a shortened form of a word. Many abbreviations begin with a capital letter and end with a period.

Student Edition, pp. 422–423

Common Core State Standards

Writing 4. With guidance and support from adults, produce writing in which the development and organization are appropriate to task and purpose. **Language 2.** Demonstrate command of the conventions of standard English capitalization, punctuation, and spelling when writing. **Language 3.a.** Choose words and phrases for effect. **Also Writing 10., Language 1., 3.**

Let's Write It!

WRITE A LIMERICK Use pp. 422–423 in the Student Edition. Direct students to read the key features of a limerick, which appear on p. 422. Remind students that they can refer to the information in the Writer's Checklist as they write their own limericks.

Read the student models on p. 423. Point out that lines 1, 2, and 5 rhyme, as do lines 3 and 4. Read the models aloud so that students can identify the accents and hear the rhythm.

CONNECT TO CONVENTIONS Remind students that an abbreviation is a shortened form of a word that often begins with a capital letter and ends with a period. Point out the correct use of abbreviations in the models.

Poetry: Limerick

Writer's Craft: Structure

DISPLAY RUBRIC Display Scoring Rubric 27 from the *Teacher Resources DVD-ROM* and go over the criteria for each trait under each score. Then, using the model in the Student Edition, choose students to explain why the model should score a 4 for one of the traits. If a student suggests that the model should score below 4 for a particular trait, the student should offer support for that response. Remind students that this is the rubric that will be used to evaluate the limericks they write.

Scoring Rubric Limerick

	4	3	2	1
Focus/Ideas	Clear, focused limerick	Most details in limerick are clear	Some details in limerick unclear	Limerick lacks clarity and development
Organization	Correct use of limerick structure	Mostly correct use of the limerick structure	Some attempt to use limerick structure	No attempt to use limerick structure
Voice	Engaged, lively voice throughout	Writer engaged with topic	Writer not very engaged	Uninterested tone
Word Choice	Strong use of sensory details	Adequate use of sensory details	Weak use of sensory details	No use of sensory details
Sentences	Energetic; tied cleverly by rhythm and rhyme	Good balance between structure and rhyme scheme	Simple, but mostly connected by rhyme	Simple, error-filled; confused
Conventions	Few, if any, errors; correct use of abbreviations	Several minor errors; mostly correct use of abbreviations	Many errors; incorrect use of abbreviations	Numerous errors; no use of abbreviations

RHYMING WORD LIST Have students get out the lists of rhyming words that they worked on yesterday. If their lists are incomplete or if they have not yet chosen a topic, provide them additional time to do so.

WRITE You will use your lists of rhyming words as you write the first draft of your limerick. When you are drafting, don't worry if your limerick doesn't sound exactly how you want it. You will have a chance to revise it tomorrow.

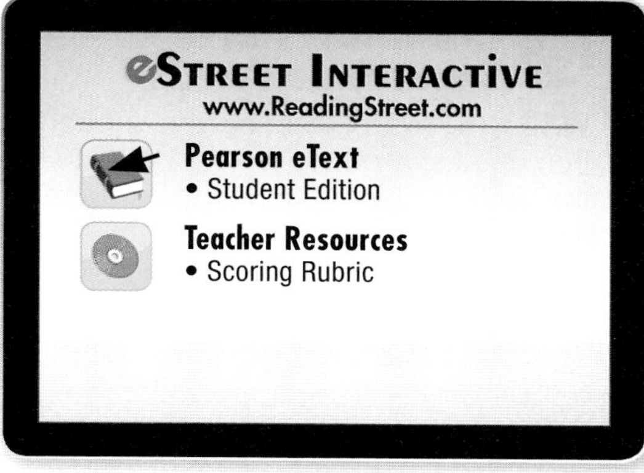

Advanced

Challenge students to include a variety of abbreviations in their limericks, such as the days of the week or months of the year.

Rhyming Words If beginning English language learners have difficulty identifying rhyming words, pair students with native English speakers. Have partners work together to develop lists of rhyming words. Instruct students to use a dictionary to find the meaning of unfamiliar words.

Common Core State Standards

Writing 4. With guidance and support from adults, produce writing in which the development and organization are appropriate to task and purpose. **Language 3.a.** Choose words and phrases for effect. **Also Writing 3., 10.**

Bridge to Common Core

RANGE OF WRITING

As students progress through the writing project, they routinely write for a range of tasks, purposes, and audiences. In this lesson, they learn the importance of the structure of a poem. They develop written work in which topics are supported with particular rhythms and structures.

Writing

Poetry: Limerick

Mini-Lesson Writer's Craft: Structure

■ **Introduce** Explain that rhythm is the beat heard when reading a poem aloud. The words you choose and the structure of the poem create rhythm. Remind students that a limerick has a set structure of five lines. Lines 1, 2, and 5 rhyme and have the same number of syllables and accents, or beats, and lines 3 and 4 rhyme and have the same number of syllables and beats. Display the Drafting Tips for students. Remind them that the goal of drafting is to get their ideas down in an organized way. Then display Writing Transparency 27A.

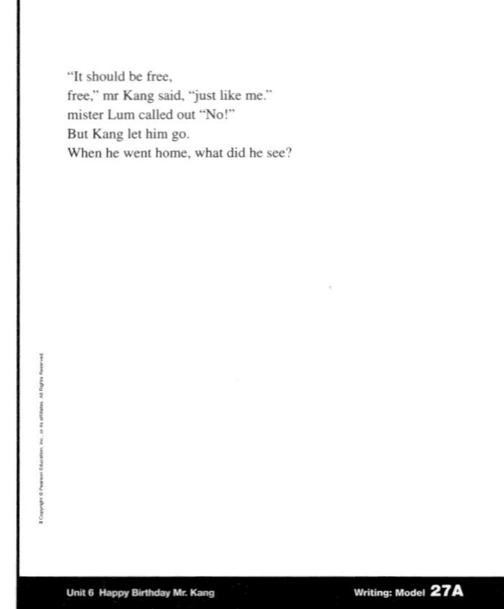
"It should be free,
free," mr Kang said, "just like me."
mister Lum called out "No!"
But Kang let him go.
When he went home, what did he see?

Unit 6 Happy Birthday Mr. Kang   Writing: Model **27A**

Writing Transparency 27A, TR DVD

Drafting Tips

- ✔ Review lists of rhyming words.
- ✔ Write with proper rhyme and rhythm—read lines aloud periodically to check for rhythm.
- ✔ Don't worry about grammar and mechanics while drafting. You'll have a chance to revise during the proofreading stage.

Think Aloud **MODEL** I am going to write my limerick about the story *Happy Birthday Mr. Kang*. When I draft, I develop my ideas. I won't worry about using correct grammar and mechanics right now, but I will make sure to choose words that create rhythm and rhyme. I will refer to my lists of rhyming words as I write.

Have students use the Drafting Tips as a guide as they draft their limericks. Remind students to include the key features of limericks in their writing.

Routine Quick Write for Fluency

Team Talk

1. **Talk** Pairs discuss how they created rhythm in their drafts.
2. **Write** Students write a sentence or two discussing the challenges of creating rhythm, using appropriate abbreviations.
3. **Share** Partners read each other's writing. Then partners check each other's writing for the correct use of abbreviations.

Routines Flip Chart

Access for All

A Advanced

Have partners review each other's limericks to ensure that proper rhyme and rhythm have been used. Monitor feedback partners provide to each other.

Wrap Up Your Day!

✔ **Content Knowledge** *What did you learn about what it might mean to set a pet free?*

✔ **Text-Based Comprehension** *How does knowing how to identify the cause and effect of an event help you understand your reading?* Encourage students to cite examples from the text.

Preview DAY 4

Tell students that tomorrow they will read about the freedoms given to us by the U.S. Constitution.

DAY 4 at a Glance

Content Knowledge
Oral Vocabulary

Phonics/Word Analysis
Review Vowel Sounds /ü/ and /u̇/

Social Studies in Reading
Expository Text

Fluency
Appropriate Phrasing

Vocabulary Skill
Antonyms

Listening and Speaking
Express an Opinion

Research and Inquiry
Synthesize

Conventions
Abbreviations

Spelling
Schwa

Writing
Poetry: Limerick

Materials

- Student Edition
- Reader's and Writer's Notebook
- Decodable Reader

Common Core State Standards

Speaking/Listening 1. Engage effectively in a range of collaborative discussions (one-on-one, in groups, and teacher led) with diverse partners on grade 3 topics and texts, building on others' ideas and expressing their own clearly. **Speaking/Listening 1.a.** Come to discussions prepared, having read or studied required material; explicitly draw on that preparation and other information known about the topic to explore ideas under discussion. **Language 6.** Acquire and use accurately grade-appropriate conversational, general academic, and domain-specific words and phrases, including those that signal spatial and temporal relationships (e.g., *After dinner that night we went looking for them*). **Also Language 4., 4.a.**

Content Knowledge

Granting Freedom

EXPAND THE CONCEPT Remind students of the weekly concept question, *What does it mean to grant freedom?* Have students discuss how laws and documents such as the United States Constitution grant people freedom.

Build Oral Language

Team Talk **TALK ABOUT SENTENCES AND WORDS** Ask students to reread the first sentence in the poem on p. 418.

After forty-three American years
I still speak my native tongue,
but any Chinese ear can hear
that I no longer speak
like a native.

- What part of speech is *native* in the term "native tongue"? (an adjective) What does *native* mean here? (It is used to indicate the language spoken in the place where one is born.) What would Mr. Kang's "native tongue" be? (Since Mr. Kang was born and raised in China, Chinese would be his native tongue.) What would be an antonym for *native* as it is used in the term "native tongue"? (*foreign*)
- What part of speech is *native* when Mr. Kang says "I no longer speak like a native"? (a noun) What does *native* mean here? (a person who was born and raised in a particular place) What would be an antonym for *native* as it is used here? (*foreigner*)
- How would you describe someone with a "Chinese ear"? (someone who speaks Chinese fluently and can tell when someone speaks Chinese with a "foreign accent")
- Applying your understanding of the different meanings of *native* and the term "Chinese ear," how can you restate this sentence in your own words? (Possible response: *After living in America for forty-three years, I still speak Chinese, but any Chinese-speaking person can tell that I now speak Chinese like a foreigner.*)

Build Oral Vocabulary

Amazing Words Robust Vocabulary Routine

1. **Introduce** Write the word *retrieve* on the board. Have students say it aloud with you. We read about how Mr. Kang did not have to *retrieve* his bird because it returned to his home on its own. What is something that a bird might *retrieve?* (It might *retrieve* its own food.) Have students determine a definition of *retrieve.* (When you *retrieve* something, you find it and then carry it back with you.)
2. **Demonstrate** Have students answer questions to demonstrate understanding. What is something you might have to *retrieve* from your bedroom?
3. **Apply** Have students apply their understanding. What word might be an antonym for *retrieve?*
4. **Display the Word** Run your finger under the word parts *re-trieve* as you read the word.

See p. OV•2 to teach *wandering.*

Routines Flip Chart

ADD TO THE CONCEPT MAP Discuss the Amazing Words *companion* and *nag*. Add these words to the concept map. Use the following questions to develop students' understanding of the concept. Add words generated in discussion to the concept map. Remind students to ask and answer questions with appropriate detail and to build on other students' answers.

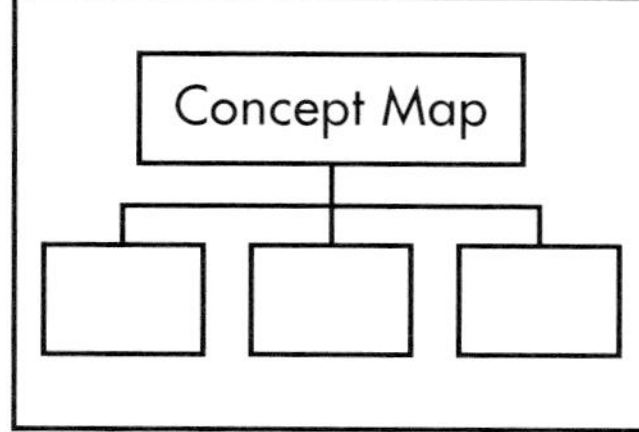

- Think about the ways that Mr. Kang's bird was a good *companion* to him. How might a person feel about the possibility of losing such a good *companion* by setting it free?
- Sam *nags* Mr. Kang to let the pet bird go free. When are some times that a person might *nag* others to do the right thing and let someone or something be free?

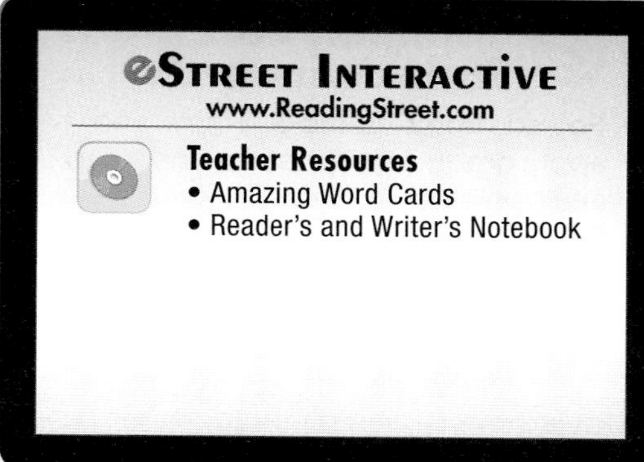

Amazing Words

territory	affectionate
release	companion
loyal	nag
deserve	retrieve
manage	wandering

Strategy Response Log

Have students interpret or make new inferences about *Happy Birthday Mr. Kang.* Then have them complete p. 33 in *Reader's and Writer's Notebook*.

ELL

Produce Oral Language Use the Day 4 instruction on ELL Poster 27 to extend and enrich language.

Common Core State Standards

Foundational Skills 3. Know and apply grade-level phonics and word analysis skills in decoding words. **Foundational Skills 3.c.** Decode multisyllable words. **Foundational Skills 3.d.** Read grade-appropriate irregularly spelled words.

Name ____________ Happy Birthday Mr. Kang

Vowel Sounds in *moon* and *foot*

Directions Each word below contains either the vowel sound heard in *moon* or the vowel sound heard in *foot*. Underline the letter or letters that stand for the vowel sound. Then write *moon* or *foot* on the line.

1. hook foot
2. moose moon
3. glue moon
4. suit moon
5. flew moon
6. wood foot
7. school moon
8. push foot

Directions Choose a word from above that completes each sentence.

9. Carla nailed a coat hook to the back of the door.
10. Dan took the shortest route to school.
11. You can use glue to fix the broken vase.
12. We need some dry wood to build a fire.
13. The airplane flew above the clouds.
14. We spotted a moose drinking from the lake.
15. Dad stopped by the tailor's to pick up his suit.
16. Rosa likes to push her brother on the swing.

School + Home **Home Activity** Your child identified and wrote words with the vowel sounds in *moon* and *foot*. Have your child write riddles using words with the vowel sounds in *moon* and *foot*. Try to guess each answer after your child reads each riddle to you.

Vowel Sounds in *moon* and *foot* DVD•377

Let's Practice It! TR DVD•377

Phonics/Word Analysis

Review Vowel Sounds /ü/ and /u̇/

REVIEW VOWEL SOUNDS /ü/ **AND** /u̇/ To review last week's phonics skill, write the following words: *school, took, full, statue, look, true, few, wool, suit, cushion, glue, smooth.* We studied different spellings for the sounds /ü/ and /u̇/. Let's review the spellings by looking at these words. Have students identify all the words with /ü/. *(school, statue, true, few, suit, glue, smooth)* What letters can stand for this sound? *(oo, ew, ue, ui)* Continue in the same way for words with /u̇/. *(took, full, look, wool, cushion)* Remind students that oo can stand for both /ü/ and /u̇/, so they must look at the context of the word to determine the sound.

Corrective feedback **If...** students are unable to answer the questions about the spellings of /ü/ and /u̇/, **then...** refer them to *Sound-Spelling Cards* 68, 89, 90, 101, 102, and 103.

GUIDE PRACTICE Display a two-column chart with the headings /ü/ and /u̇/. Write the following words on the board: *fruit, grew, took, bloom, push, shook, new, good, blue, hook.* Have students read the words and sort them into the correct column. Ask volunteers to underline the letters that stand for /ü/ or /u̇/ in each word.

/ü/	/u̇/
fruit	took
grew	push
bloom	shook
new	good
blue	hook

ON THEIR OWN For additional practice, use *Let's Practice It!* p. 377 on the *Teacher Resources DVD-ROM.*

Fluent Word Reading

Spiral Review

READ WORDS IN ISOLATION Display these words. Tell students that they can decode some words on this list. Explain that other words they should know because they appear often in reading.

Have students read the list three or four times until they can read at the rate of two to three seconds per word.

very	**because**	**neither**	**weight**	**clothes**
all	**warm**	**saw**	**always**	**from**
sunny	**childhood**	**friends**	**taught**	**receive**
stylish	**refreshment**	**eight**	**pretty**	**bought**

Corrective feedback

If... students have difficulty reading whole words,
then... have them use sound-by-sound blending for decodable words or chunking for words that have word parts, or have them say and spell high-frequency words.

If... students cannot read fluently at a rate of two to three seconds per word,
then... have pairs practice the list until they can read it fluently.

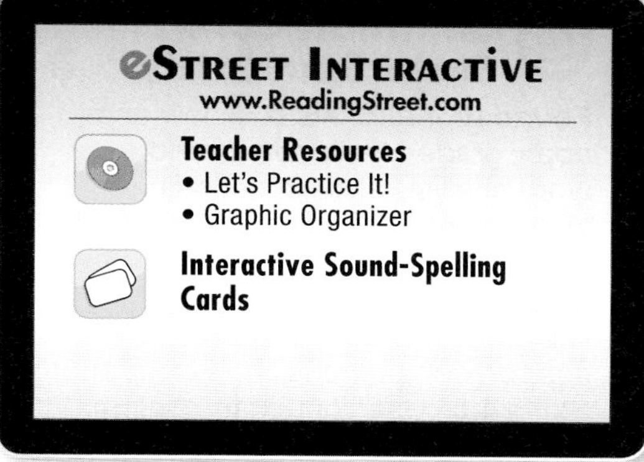

Access for All

Strategic Intervention

To assist students having difficulty with the vowel sounds /ü/ and /u̇/, focus on only one sound at a time. Assist students in writing words with /ü/ spelled *oo* on separate cards. Repeat with /ü/ words spelled *ew, ue,* and *ui* and /u̇/ words spelled *oo* and *u*.

Spiral Review

These activities review:

- previously taught high-frequency words *very, warm, friends, pretty, clothes, from.*
- vowel patterns *a, au, aw, al, augh, ough;* vowel patterns *ei, eigh;* suffixes *-y, -ish, -hood, -ment*.

Fluent Word Reading Have students listen to a more fluent reader say the words. Then have them repeat the words.

Common Core State Standards

Foundational Skills 3. Know and apply grade-level phonics and word analysis skills in decoding words. **Foundational Skills 3.d.** Read grade-appropriate irregularly spelled words. **Foundational Skills 4.** Read with sufficient accuracy and fluency to support comprehension. **Foundational Skills 4.c.** Use context to confirm or self-correct word recognition and understanding, rereading as necessary.

Fluent Word Reading

READ WORDS IN CONTEXT Display these sentences. Call on individuals to read a sentence. Then randomly point to review words and have students read them. To help you monitor word reading, high-frequency words are underlined and decodable words are italicized.

MONITOR PROGRESS Sentence Reading

Ice cream is a <u>very</u> good *refreshment* on a <u>warm</u> *sunny* day.
Mom *bought* <u>pretty</u>, *stylish* <u>clothes</u> <u>from</u> the boutique.
The *eight childhood* <u>friends</u> *saw* each other once a year.
Dad *taught all* of us to *always* say "thank you."
We did not *receive either* package *because* of its *weight*.

If... students are unable to read an underlined high-frequency word,
then... read the word for them and spell it, having them echo you.

If... students have difficulty reading an italicized decodable word,
then... guide them in using sound-by-sound blending or chunking.

Reread for Fluency

Have students reread the sentences to develop automaticity decoding words.

Routine Oral Rereading

1. **Read** Have students read all the sentences orally.
2. **Reread** To achieve optimal fluency, students should reread the sentences three or four times.
3. **Corrective Feedback** Listen as students read. Provide corrective feedback regarding their fluency and decoding.

Routines Flip Chart

Decodable Passage 27C

If students need help, then...

Read *Picnic Poster*

READ WORDS IN ISOLATION Have students turn to p. 143 in *Decodable Practice Readers 3.2* and find the first list of words. Each word in this list has the schwa sound. Let's read these words. Be sure that students pronounce the vowel that stands for the schwa sound correctly.

Next, have students read the high-frequency words.

PREVIEW Have students read the title and preview the story. Tell them that they will read words with the schwa sound.

READ WORDS IN CONTEXT Chorally read the story along with students. Have students identify words in the story that have the schwa sound. Make sure that students are monitoring their accuracy when they decode words.

Team Talk Pair students and have them take turns reading the story aloud to each other. Monitor students as they read to check for proper pronunciation and appropriate pacing.

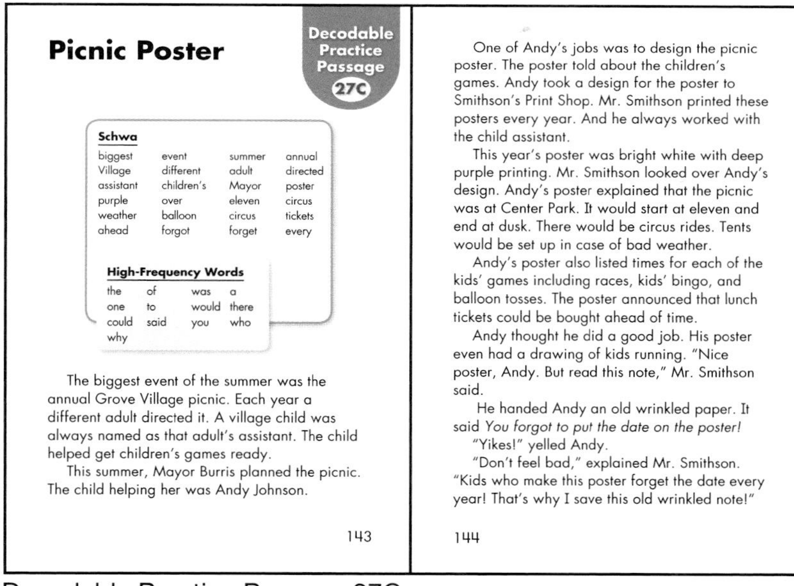

Picnic Poster

Decodable Practice Passage 27C

Schwa

biggest	event	summer	annual
Village	different	adult	directed
assistant	children's	Mayor	poster
purple	over	eleven	circus
weather	balloon	circus	tickets
ahead	forgot	forget	every

High-Frequency Words

the	of	was	a
one	to	would	there
could	said	you	who
why			

The biggest event of the summer was the annual Grove Village picnic. Each year a different adult directed it. A village child was always named as that adult's assistant. The child helped get children's games ready.

This summer, Mayor Burris planned the picnic. The child helping her was Andy Johnson.

143

One of Andy's jobs was to design the picnic poster. The poster told about the children's games. Andy took a design for the poster to Smithson's Print Shop. Mr. Smithson printed these posters every year. And he always worked with the child assistant.

This year's poster was bright white with deep purple printing. Mr. Smithson looked over Andy's design. Andy's poster explained that the picnic was at Center Park. It would start at eleven and end at dusk. There would be circus rides. Tents would be set up in case of bad weather.

Andy's poster also listed times for each of the kids' games including races, kids' bingo, and balloon tosses. The poster announced that lunch tickets could be bought ahead of time.

Andy thought he did a good job. His poster even had a drawing of kids running. "Nice poster, Andy. But read this note," Mr. Smithson said.

He handed Andy an old wrinkled paper. It said *You forgot to put the date on the poster!*

"Yikes!" yelled Andy.

"Don't feel bad," explained Mr. Smithson. "Kids who make this poster forget the date every year! That's why I save this old wrinkled note!"

144

Decodable Practice Passage 27C

Access for All

 Advanced

Have students write a short paragraph about a favorite memory using some of the decodable and high-frequency words found in the sentences on p. 424e.

Common Core State Standards

Informational Text 2. Determine the main idea of a text; recount the key details and explain how they support the main idea. **Informational Text 5.** Use text features and search tools (e.g., key words, sidebars, hyperlinks) to locate information relevant to a given topic efficiently. **Informational Text 7.** Use information gained from illustrations (e.g., maps, photographs), and the words in a text to demonstrate understanding of the text (e.g., where, when, why, and how key events occur). **Informational Text 10.** By the end of the year, read and comprehend informational texts, including history/social studies, science, and technical texts, at the high end of the grades 2–3 text complexity band independently and proficiently.

Bridge to Common Core

KEY IDEAS AND DETAILS

Reading expository text leads students to explicit information. By reading expository text and paying close attention to text features, such as details and illustrations, students will be able to determine the central ideas and summarize the key details of the information presented.

Social Studies in Reading

Expository Text

INTRODUCE Explain to students that what we read is structured differently depending on the author's reasons for writing and what kind of information he or she wishes to convey. Different types of texts are called genres. Expository text is one type of genre, and one purpose a writer might have for writing expository text is to inform an audience about a topic.

DISCUSS THE GENRE Discuss with students how authors write with different purposes in mind, such as to inform, to persuade, or to entertain. Ask students to share some examples of informative expository text they have read before. (Possible responses: biographies, encyclopedia articles, articles or books about things in nature)

GROUP PRACTICE Display the word web graphic organizer below. Label the center oval *Features that inform.* Help students brainstorm some features of expository text, such as facts, details, technical vocabulary, graphic sources such as photographs and illustrations, and text features such as labels. Record responses on the word web.

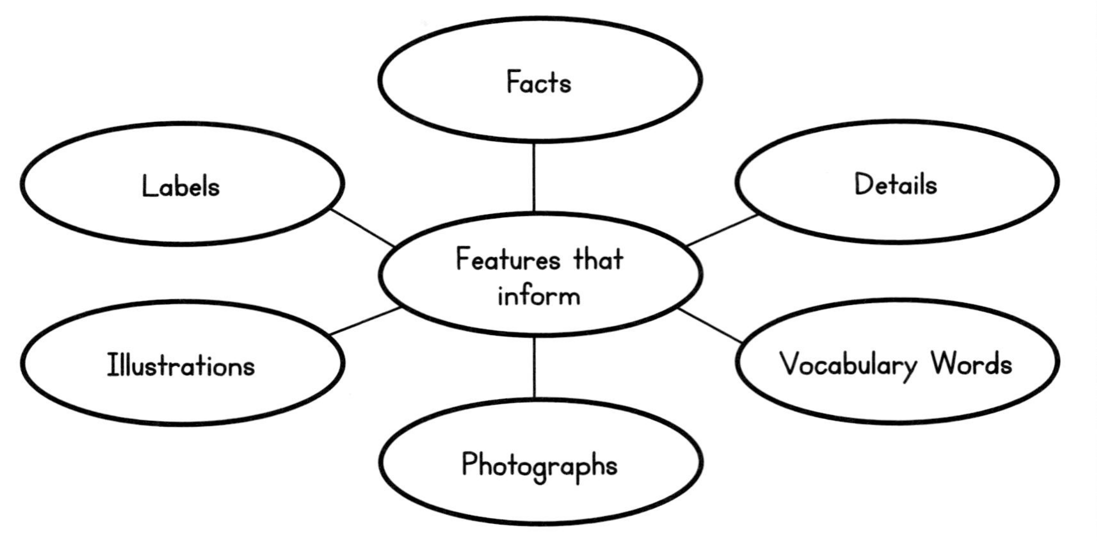

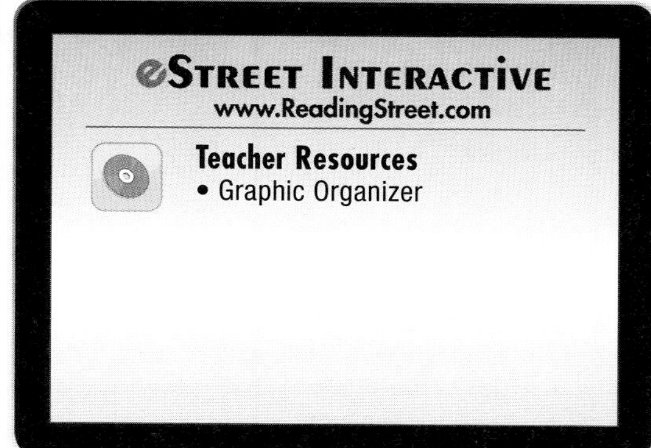

Team Talk Have students work in pairs to discuss how each text feature helps the author inform an audience about a topic. Invite them to share their ideas with the class. Encourage students to listen attentively and ask any relevant questions.

READ Tell students that they will now be reading an expository text whose purpose is to inform about the Constitution and the rights it grants. Have the class pay attention to how the author uses text features to inform.

Day 4 SMALL GROUP TIME • Differentiate Vocabulary, p. SG•17

OL On-Level
- **Develop** Amazing Words
- **Read** "Once Upon a Constitution"

SI Strategic Intervention
- **Review/Discuss** Amazing Words
- **Read** "Once Upon a Constitution"

A Advanced
- **Extend** Amazing Words and Selection Vocabulary
- **Read** "Once Upon a Constitution"
- **Organize** Inquiry Project

If... students need more scaffolding and practice with the **Amazing Words,**
then... use the Routine on pp. xxxvi–xxxvii in the *ELL Handbook.*

Common Core State Standards
Informational Text 7. Use information gained from illustrations (e.g., maps, photographs) and the words in a text to demonstrate understanding of the text (e.g., where, when, why, and how key events occur). **Also Informational Text 2.**

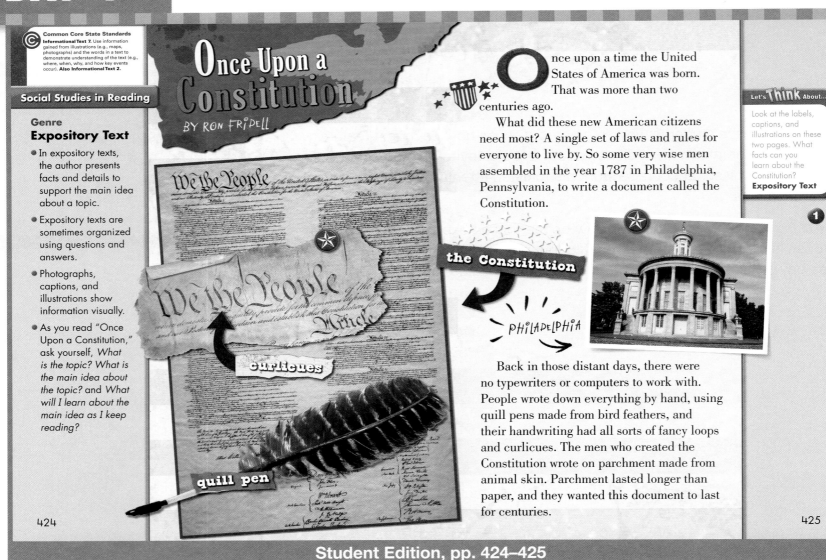

Social Studies in Reading

Genre

Expository Text

- In expository texts, the author presents facts and details to support the main idea about a topic.
- Expository texts are sometimes organized using questions and answers.
- Photographs, captions, and illustrations show information visually.
- As you read "Once Upon a Constitution," ask yourself, *What is the topic? What is the main idea about the topic?* and *What will I learn about the main idea as I keep reading?*

Once Upon a Constitution

BY RON FRIPELL

Once upon a time the United States of America was born. That was more than two centuries ago.

What did these new American citizens need most? A single set of laws and rules for everyone to live by. So some very wise men assembled in the year 1787 in Philadelphia, Pennsylvania, to write a document called the Constitution.

Back in those distant days, there were no typewriters or computers to work with. People wrote down everything by hand, using quill pens made from bird feathers, and their handwriting had all sorts of fancy loops and curlicues. The men who created the Constitution wrote on parchment made from animal skin. Parchment lasted longer than paper, and they wanted this document to last for centuries.

Let's Think About...

Look at the labels, captions, and illustrations on these two pages. What facts can you learn about the Constitution? **Expository Text**

1

424 425

Student Edition, pp. 424–425

Common Core State Standards

Informational Text 1. Ask and answer questions to demonstrate understanding of a text, referring explicitly to the text as the basis for the answers. **Informational Text 5.** Use text features and search tools (e.g., key words, sidebars, hyperlinks) to locate information relevant to a given topic efficiently. **Informational Text 7.** Use information gained from illustrations (e.g., maps, photographs) and the words in a text to demonstrate understanding of the text (e.g., where, when, why, and how key events occur). **Also Informational Text 9.**

Access Text

TEACH Genre: Expository Text Have students preview "Once Upon a Constitution" on pp. 424–425. Have them identify and describe any labels they see, noting any unusual fonts or text styles used. What purpose do these labels serve and how do they fulfill this purpose?

Corrective feedback | **If...** students are unable to identify the purpose of the labels and how they fulfill this purpose,
then... use the model to guide students in interpreting labels.

Think Aloud **MODEL** I see the words connected by arrows to the picture of the Constitution and the photo of Philadelphia. I think these words are telling me what I am looking at. To make it clear what exactly is being labeled, the arrows point to specific parts of the pictures and a different font is used for the labels for each graphic source.

ON THEIR OWN Have students work in pairs to think up another system of labeling the parts of a picture.

Close Reading

ANALYSIS Why did people write the Constitution? (Because the United States of America was a new country, it needed a single set of laws for everyone to follow.)

EVALUATION Why would it be important for the document to last for centuries? What clue in the text states this idea? (The men who wrote the Constitution wanted the laws to last a long time, so writing these laws on parchment that would hold up over time would show how strong the laws were too.)

Genre

LET'S THINK ABOUT... As you read "Once Upon a Constitution," use Let's Think About in the Student Edition to help students focus on the features of an expository text.

1 You can learn facts about how, when, and where the Constitution was written.

Team Talk Have partners find another expository article about the Constitution. Tell them to use a Venn diagram to compare and contrast the two texts. Encourage them to think about the main idea and details and how the information is presented in each.

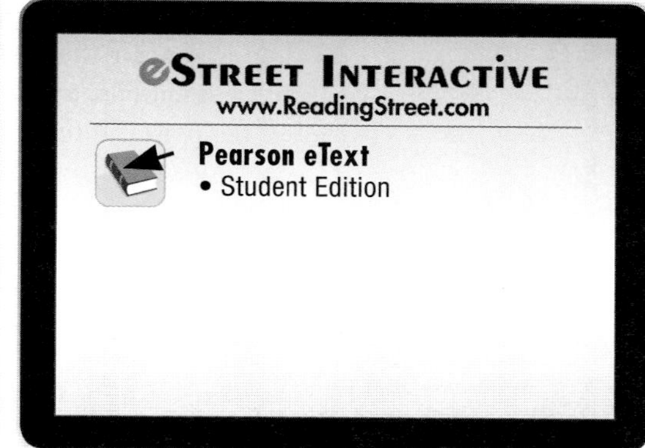

Access for All

SI Strategic Intervention
Give students extra practice with how the author presents information in a question and answer format. Have them pick out and rewrite, in simpler form, the questions the author asks and the answers he provides. Then have them write a short summary of the information contained in the reading.

A Advanced
Have students discuss reasons why it is important for a country to have one set of agreed-upon and clear laws for everyone to follow and what might happen to a country and its people if such a system of laws were not in place.

Social Studies Vocabulary Work with students to make a list of History-Social Science vocabulary words from this reading, such as *rights, democracy,* and *citizens*. Have students use context and dictionaries to write definitions for each.

Let's Think About...

How do the questions in the text introduce important ideas and details? **Expository Text**

2

So, what did this Constitution say? It told who made the laws and how. Back then in most nations, a monarch or emperor held all the power. If those rulers made careless decisions regarding the government, they would end up harming people. What kind of rulers would America have?

There would be no monarchs or emperors in the United States. Instead, in America, many people would contribute to creating the laws because the Constitution said so. It made the United States a democracy, a nation where the power belongs to its citizens.

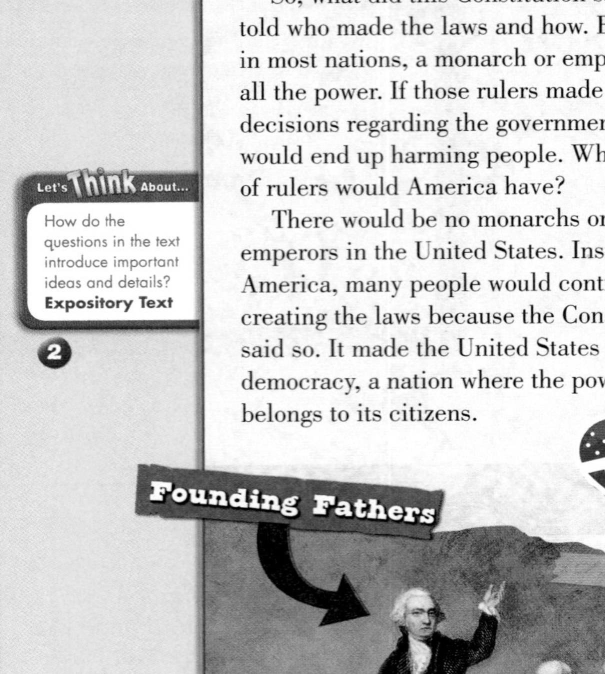

Was this Constitution a perfect document? It was a good beginning, but would require some perfecting. It talked about freedoms and liberties, but it didn't actually name them. So in 1791, a new part was added: the Bill of Rights. These ten amendments granted Americans basic rights, or freedoms.

One of those basic rights is freedom of speech. It means that people can tell others what they think and feel. The government cannot stop people from saying or writing whatever they want.

Another right is freedom of religion. The Constitution grants people the right to attend any church and worship any way they wish.

In the centuries that followed, more amendments were added to grant more rights and freedoms. Today, the Constitution still keeps Americans free and safe, just as it did once upon a time, more than two hundred years ago.

Let's Think About...

Reading Across Texts Mr. Kang says, "America is the land of the free." Do you think the Constitution and the Bill of Rights are important to Mr. Kang?

Writing Across Texts List some reasons for your answer. Then write a paragraph summarizing what you have learned.

426

427

Student Edition, pp. 426–427

Common Core State Standards

Informational Text 1. Ask and answer questions to demonstrate understanding of a text, referring explicitly to the text as the basis for the answers. **Informational Text 2.** Determine the main idea of a text; recount the key details and explain how they support the main idea. **Informational Text 8.** Describe the logical connection between particular sentences and paragraphs in a text (e.g., comparison, cause/effect, first/second/third in a sequence). **Writing 2.** Write informative/explanatory texts to examine a topic and convey ideas and information clearly.

Access Text

TEACH Genre: Expository Text Explain that to understand what an author is talking about in an informational article, the reader must be able to distinguish between main ideas and details. What is the main idea on these pages?

Corrective feedback

If... students are unable to distinguish the main idea from the details,
then... use the model to guide students in identifying the main idea.

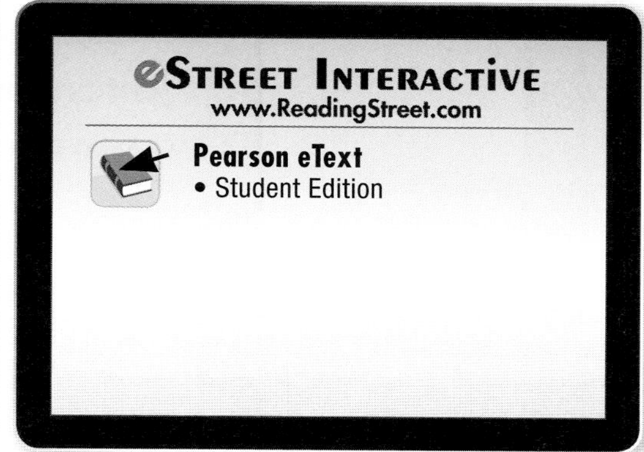

Think Aloud **MODEL** Authors include many pieces of information, so I need to figure out which piece of information is the most important, or the main idea. The questions the author asks give me clues as to what the author thinks are the most important ideas. They talk about what the Constitution says and how it works. The information about the specific freedoms is interesting, but I think the main idea of this article is that the Constitution is a single set of laws and rules for all Americans to live by.

ON THEIR OWN Have students identify and summarize details that support this main idea.

Close Reading ©

ANALYSIS How was the government of the new United States of America different from the way many other nations were ruled at the time? (Where other nations were ruled by monarchs or emperors who held all the power and could make decisions for everyone else, America gave power to its citizens and let many people help create its laws.)

INFERENCE Why was the Constitution only a beginning? (The people who wrote the Constitution couldn't predict what would happen to the country over time or imagine and write down every single freedom that would end up needing to be protected.)

Genre

LET'S THINK ABOUT... features of expository text.

2 The questions form the main ideas he will discuss. The author draws the reader's attention to these points and helps the reader understand what the most important ideas in this informational article are. The author then follows up with details about what words would ensure a fair government and what kind of leadership or government Americans would want.

Reading and Writing Across Texts

Have students consider whether they think the Constitution and Bill of Rights are important to Mr. Kang. Ask them to create a T-chart of facts about freedom learned from each selection to support their answers. Then have students write a paragraph summarizing what they have learned about freedom.

Connect to Social Studies

Constitutional Amendments
Amendments are changes or clarifications that are added to the Constitution. There have been 27 amendments to the U.S. Constitution. The first 10 were done collectively and are called the Bill of Rights. Other amendments include the 13th amendment to abolish slavery, the 22nd amendment to limit the length of time a president can serve, and the 26th amendment to set the voting age at 18.

Graphic Organizer Help students use a main idea and details graphic organizer to organize and record their ideas about the main idea and details in this informational article.

Vocabulary

Antonyms

Context Clues Remember that antonyms are words that have opposite meanings. Finding an antonym when reading is one way to figure out the meaning of an unfamiliar word.

Practice It! Read this tongue twister. Then find and list three antonym pairs:
Ned will go for wide, thick noodles. Nellie needs narrow, thin noodles. Neither Ned nor Nellie will nibble chilly noodles. Nellie won't wait for warm noodles either.

Fluency

Appropriate Phrasing

Pause when you come to a comma or a period when reading. When you read poetry, use punctuation, not line breaks, for grouping words together.

Practice It! Read aloud the poem on page 412, pausing at the end of lines. Then read the poem again, grouping together words using punctuation. Does this help you to better understand the poem?

428

Listening and Speaking

Get Ready For Middle School

Use appropriate strategies—ask questions, make comments—to keep a discussion going.

Express an Opinion

When you express an opinion, use facts and explanations to support your opinion and prove your point.

Practice It! Deliver a speech that expresses your opinion about a topic that is important in your community. First, brainstorm a list of several topics being discussed in your community. Topics may include a new playground or swimming pool.

Tips

Listening ...
- Sit quietly and listen.
- Draw a conclusion about what the speaker says.

Speaking ...
- Use appropriate persuasive techniques.
- Speak clearly and distinctly.
- Make eye contact.

Teamwork ...
- Ask questions and give detailed answers about the topic.

429

Student Edition, pp. 428–429

Common Core State Standards

Foundational Skills 4.b. Read on-level prose and poetry orally with accuracy, appropriate rate, and expression on successive readings. **Speaking/Listening 4.** Report on a topic or text, tell a story, or recount an experience with appropriate facts and relevant, descriptive details, speaking clearly at an understandable pace. **Language 4.a.** Use sentence-level context as a clue to the meaning of a word or phrase. **Also Foundational Skills 4., Speaking/Listening 1.b., Language 3., 4., 4.d.**

Fluency

Appropriate Phrasing

GUIDE PRACTICE Use the Student Edition activity as an assessment tool. Make sure the reading passage is at least 200 words in length. As students read, make sure they are reading at a natural rate.

Check Fluency

FORMATIVE ASSESSMENT As students reread, monitor their progress toward their individual fluency goals.
Current Goal: 110–120 words correct per minute
End-of-Year Goal: 120 words correct per minute

If... students cannot read fluently at a rate of 110–120 words correct per minute,

then... have students practice with text at their independent levels.

Vocabulary Skill

Antonyms

TEACH ANTONYMS • CONTEXT CLUES Write the following sentence on the board: *Jan liked quiet, so she left the house when Mark and his loud band began to practice.*

Discuss how *quiet/loud* are an antonym pair—words with opposite meanings. Note how students can use context clues to figure out the meaning of each word.

GUIDE PRACTICE Provide students with other sentences that contain antonym pairs such as *tall/short, fast/slow,* and *dark/light* and help students use context clues to identify and define each antonym pair.

ON THEIR OWN Walk around the room as students work with partners to make sure they can use context clues to identify and define the antonym pairs in the tongue twisters. Suggest that students use dictionaries and thesauruses to check their work.

Listening and Speaking

Express an Opinion

TEACH Tell students that to express their opinions effectively in a speech, they must gather evidence to support their view and organize the evidence in a logical manner. Point out the importance of listening to other viewpoints and asking questions when gathering evidence.

GUIDE PRACTICE As students prepare to present their speeches, remind them to make eye contact with their audience and to use appropriate speaking rate, volume, and enunciation to communicate their ideas. Tell them to use opinion phrases such as *I believe, I think,* and *my point of view* when presenting their thoughts about the topic.

ON THEIR OWN Have students present their speeches to the class. Invite the class to identify each speaker's opinion and evaluate how well the speaker convinced the audience to share this opinion. Tell students to listen attentively, ask relevant questions, and make pertinent comments.

Expressing an Opinion

Remind students that when presenting a speech that expresses an opinion, they should pick a viewpoint to support and explain it clearly with specific examples and details. Encourage them to use an organizational pattern that fits the information included in their speech. Tell listeners to identify the viewpoint being expressed, analyze the evidence the speaker uses to support this viewpoint, and then evaluate the worth of the overall opinion. Remind listeners that their judgment will be affected by their own viewpoint on the topic.

Bridge to Common Core

PRESENTATION OF KNOWLEDGE/ IDEAS

To prepare their speeches, students should gather evidence to support their views and organize the information in a logical manner, such as from least convincing to most convincing. As students give their speeches, they should adapt their speeches to engage their audiences as they state their viewpoints.

Common Core State Standards

Informational Text 7. Use information gained from illustrations (e.g., maps, photographs), and the words in a text to demonstrate understanding of the text (e.g., where, when, why, and how key events occur). **Writing 6.** With guidance and support from adults, use technology to produce and publish writing (using keyboarding skills) as well as to interact and collaborate with others. **Writing 10.** Write routinely over extended time frames (time for research, reflection, and revision) and shorter time frames (a single sitting or a day or two) for a range of discipline-specific tasks, purposes, and audiences. **Language 2.** Demonstrate command of the conventions of standard English capitalization, punctuation, and spelling when writing. **Language 2.f.** Use spelling patterns and generalizations (e.g., word families, position-based spellings, syllable patterns, ending rules, meaningful word parts) in writing words.

Research and Inquiry

Step 4 Synthesize

TEACH Have students synthesize their research findings and results. Suggest that students use a map to visually present information they found while researching. Students may choose to use a map to help show areas where animals might be granted their freedom and released. Review how to choose relevant information from a number of sources and organize it logically.

GUIDE PRACTICE Have students use a word processing program to create a short article for a school newspaper on Day 5. If students are using maps, check to see that they have included a legend that explains what all the symbols on the map mean and to include map parts such as a compass rose and a scale.

ON THEIR OWN Have students write a brief explanation of their research findings. Then have them organize and combine information and plan their presentations.

Conventions

Abbreviations

TEST PRACTICE Remind students that grammar skills, such as abbreviations, are often assessed on important tests. Remind students that an abbreviation is a shortened form of a word. It often begins with a capital letter and ends with a period.

ON THEIR OWN For additional practice, use *Reader's and Writer's Notebook,* p. 406.

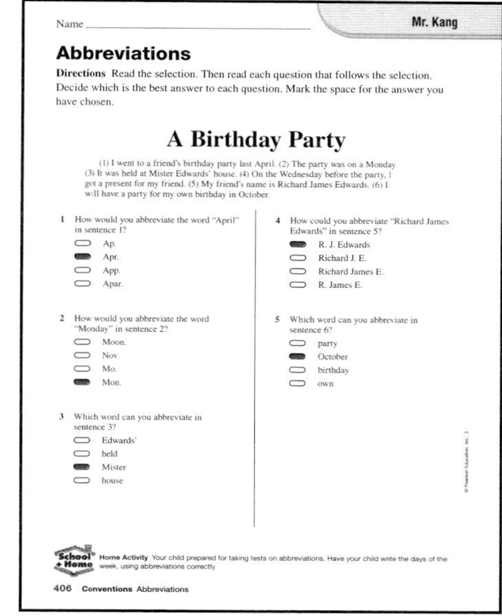

Name ______ **Mr. Kang**

Abbreviations

Directions Read the selection. Then read each question that follows the selection. Decide which is the best answer to each question. Mark the space for the answer you have chosen.

A Birthday Party

(1) I went to a friend's birthday party last April. (2) The party was on a Monday. (3) It was held at Mister Edwards' house. (4) On the Wednesday before the party, I got a present for my friend. (5) My friend's name is Richard James Edwards. (6) I will have a party for my own birthday in October.

1 How would you abbreviate the word "April" in sentence 1?
- Ap.
- Apr. (marked)
- App.
- Apar.

2 How would you abbreviate the word "Monday" in sentence 2?
- Moon.
- Nov.
- Mo.
- Mon. (marked)

3 Which word can you abbreviate in sentence 3?
- Edwards'
- held
- Mister (marked)
- house

4 How could you abbreviate "Richard James Edwards" in sentence 5?
- R. J. Edwards (marked)
- Richard J. E.
- Richard James E.
- R. James E.

5 Which word can you abbreviate in sentence 6?
- party
- October (marked)
- birthday
- own

© Pearson Education, Inc. 3

School + Home **Home Activity** Your child prepared for taking tests on abbreviations. Have your child write the days of the week, using abbreviations correctly.

406 **Conventions** Abbreviations

Reader's and Writer's Notebook, p. 406

Spelling

Schwa

PRACTICE SPELLING STRATEGY Supply pairs of students with index cards on which the spelling words have been written. Have one student read a word while the other writes it. Then have students switch roles. Have them use the cards to check their spelling and correct any misspelled words.

ON THEIR OWN For additional practice, use *Let's Practice It!* p. 378 on the *Teacher Resources DVD-ROM.*

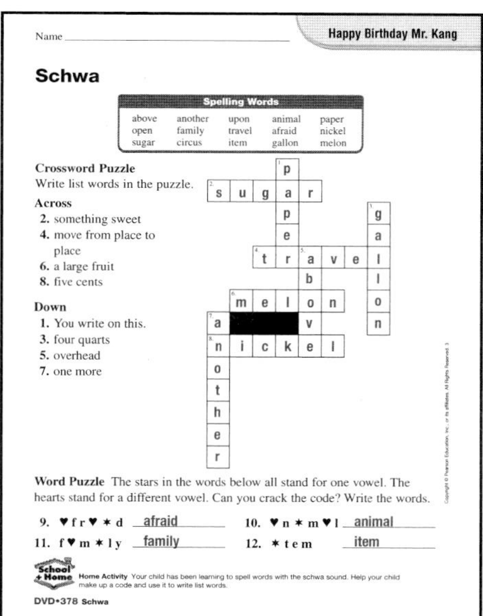

Name ______ **Happy Birthday Mr. Kang**

Schwa

Spelling Words				
above	another	upon	animal	paper
open	family	travel	afraid	nickel
sugar	circus	item	gallon	melon

Crossword Puzzle Write list words in the puzzle.

Across
2. something sweet — sugar
4. move from place to place — travel
6. a large fruit — melon
8. five cents — nickel

Down
1. You write on this. — paper
3. four quarts — gallon
5. overhead — above
7. one more — another

Word Puzzle The stars in the words below all stand for one vowel. The hearts stand for a different vowel. Can you crack the code? Write the words.

9. ♥ f r ♥ ∗ d afraid
10. ♥ n ∗ m ♥ l animal
11. f ♥ m ∗ l y family
12. ∗ t e m item

Copyright © Pearson Education, Inc., or its affiliates. All Rights Reserved. 3

School + Home **Home Activity** Your child has been learning to spell words with the schwa sound. Help your child make up a code and use it to write list words.

DVD•378 **Schwa**

Let's Practice It! TR DVD•378

eSTREET INTERACTIVE
www.ReadingStreet.com

Teacher Resources
- Reader's and Writer's Notebook
- Let's Practice It!
- Daily Fix-It Transparency

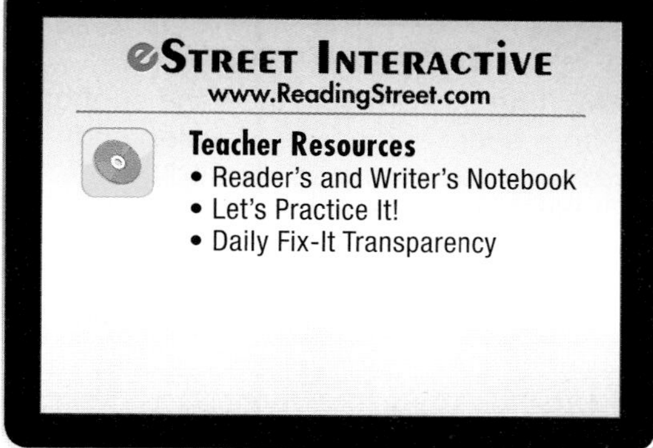

Daily Fix-It

7. The women was afriad the bird would fly away. *(were; afraid)*
8. The bird dissappeared on Feb 2. *(disappeared; Feb.)*

Bridge to Common Core

CONVENTIONS OF STANDARD ENGLISH

As students consider capitalization and punctuation when they write abbreviations, they are demonstrating command of the conventions of standard English. Your guidance will help them use correct grammar, usage, and spelling to convey meaning when they speak and write.

Common Core State Standards

Writing 5. With guidance and support from peers and adults, develop and strengthen writing as needed by planning, revising, and editing.

Write Guy *by Jeff Anderson*

Show Off—in a Good Way

Post students' successful sentences or short paragraphs. Celebrate them as writers. Select a sentence of the week, and write it large! Display it as a poster inside or outside the classroom door. Students learn from each others' successes.

Writing

Poetry: Limerick

Mini-Lesson Revise: Adding

- Yesterday we wrote limericks about the story *Happy Birthday Mr. Kang.* Today we will revise our drafts. The goal is to make your writing clearer and more interesting.
- Display Writing Transparency 27B. Remind students that revising does not include correcting grammar and mechanics. Tell them that this will be done during the lesson as they proofread their work. Then introduce the revising strategy of adding.
- When you revise, ask yourself, *What important information about the topic is missing?* Let's look at the first line of the limerick. What should be free, and why? I will revise the first line to read *This bird in its cage should be free.* Now I know that a bird should be free, and that it should be free because it is in a cage.

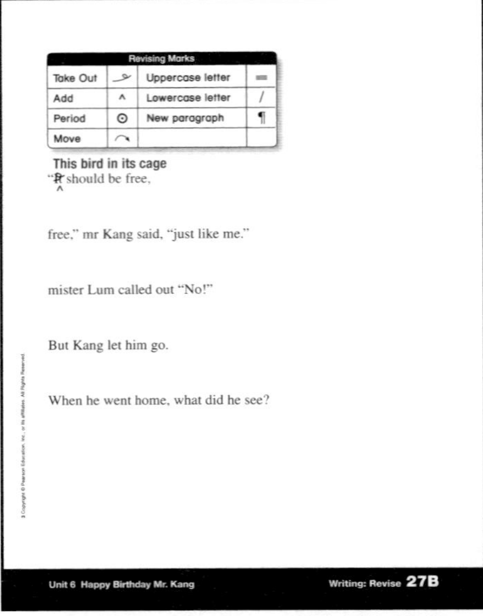

Revising Marks			
Take Out	⌐	Uppercase letter	═
Add	^	Lowercase letter	/
Period	⊙	New paragraph	¶
Move	⌒		

This bird in its cage
"~~It~~ should be free,

free," mr Kang said, "just like me."

mister Lum called out "No!"

But Kang let him go.

When he went home, what did he see?

Unit 6 Happy Birthday Mr. Kang Writing: Revise 27B

Writing Transparency 27B, TR DVD

Tell students that as they revise, they should also make sure they have the correct limerick format. Display the Revising Tips for students.

Revising Tips

- ✔ Make sure the ideas are clear and focused.
- ✔ Review writing to make sure that it maintains rhythm and includes rhyme.
- ✔ Add information to support the central idea and make writing more detailed.

PEER CONFERENCING • PEER REVISION Have pairs of students exchange papers for peer revision. Students should write two questions about the partner's writing. Tell students that their questions should focus on where the partner could revise by adding relevant information. Refer to the *Teacher Resources DVD-ROM* for more information about peer conferencing.

Have students revise their limericks using the questions their partner wrote during the peer revision as well as the key features of limericks to guide them. Be sure that students are using the revising strategy of adding.

Corrective feedback Circulate around the room to monitor and confer with students as they revise. Remind students correcting errors that they will have time to edit tomorrow. They should be working on content and organization today.

Routine Quick Write for Fluency

Team Talk

1. **Talk** Have pairs discuss Mr. Kang's character in *Happy Birthday Mr. Kang.*
2. **Write** Each student writes a brief description of Mr. Kang's character that includes rhyme.
3. **Share** Partners read each another's writing. Then partners check each other's writing for rhyme.

Routines Flip Chart

eStreet Interactive
www.ReadingStreet.com

Teacher Resources
- Writing Transparency

ELL

Creating Rhyme Beginning language learners may have trouble using the correct number of syllables in each line of their limericks. Allow these students to disregard the syllable pattern and focus instead on creating rhyme.

Wrap Up Your Day!

✔ **Content Knowledge** *What did you learn about the freedoms given to us by the U.S. Constitution?*

✔ **Oral Vocabulary** Monitor students' use of oral vocabulary as they respond to this question: *Should the U.S. Constitution protect the right to wander wherever we choose or retrieve things that belong to us? Why or why not?*

✔ **Text Features** *How did the illustrations help you understand the text?*

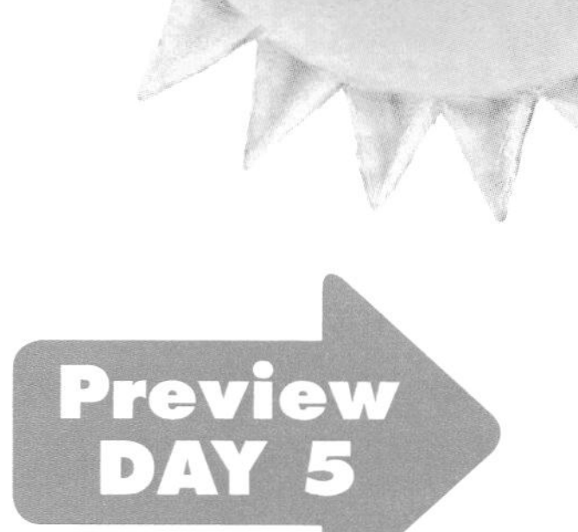

Preview DAY 5

Remind students to think about what it means to grant freedom.

DAY 5 at a Glance

Content Knowledge
Text-Based Comprehension
Review Cause and Effect
Vocabulary Skill
Review Antonyms
Phonics/Word Analysis
Review Schwa
Literary Terms
Review Metaphor
Assessment
Fluency
Comprehension
Research and Inquiry
Communicate
Spelling
Schwa
Conventions
Abbreviations
Writing
Poetry: Limerick

Materials

- Student Edition
- Weekly Test
- Reader's and Writer's Notebook

Bridge to Common Core

INTEGRATION OF KNOWLEDGE/IDEAS
This week, students have integrated content presented in diverse media and analyzed how different texts address similar topics. They have developed knowledge about granting freedom to expand the unit topic of Freedom.

Social Studies Knowledge Goals
Students have learned that freedom

- can be granted to animals
- means pursuing interests
- can be granted through laws

Content Knowledge

Granting Freedom

REVIEW THE CONCEPT Have students look back at the reading selections to find examples that best demonstrate what it means to grant freedom.

Build Oral Language

REVIEW AMAZING WORDS Display and review this week's concept map. Remind students that this week they have learned ten Amazing Words related to granting freedom. Have students use the Amazing Words and the concept map to answer the Question of the Week, *What does it means to grant freedom?*

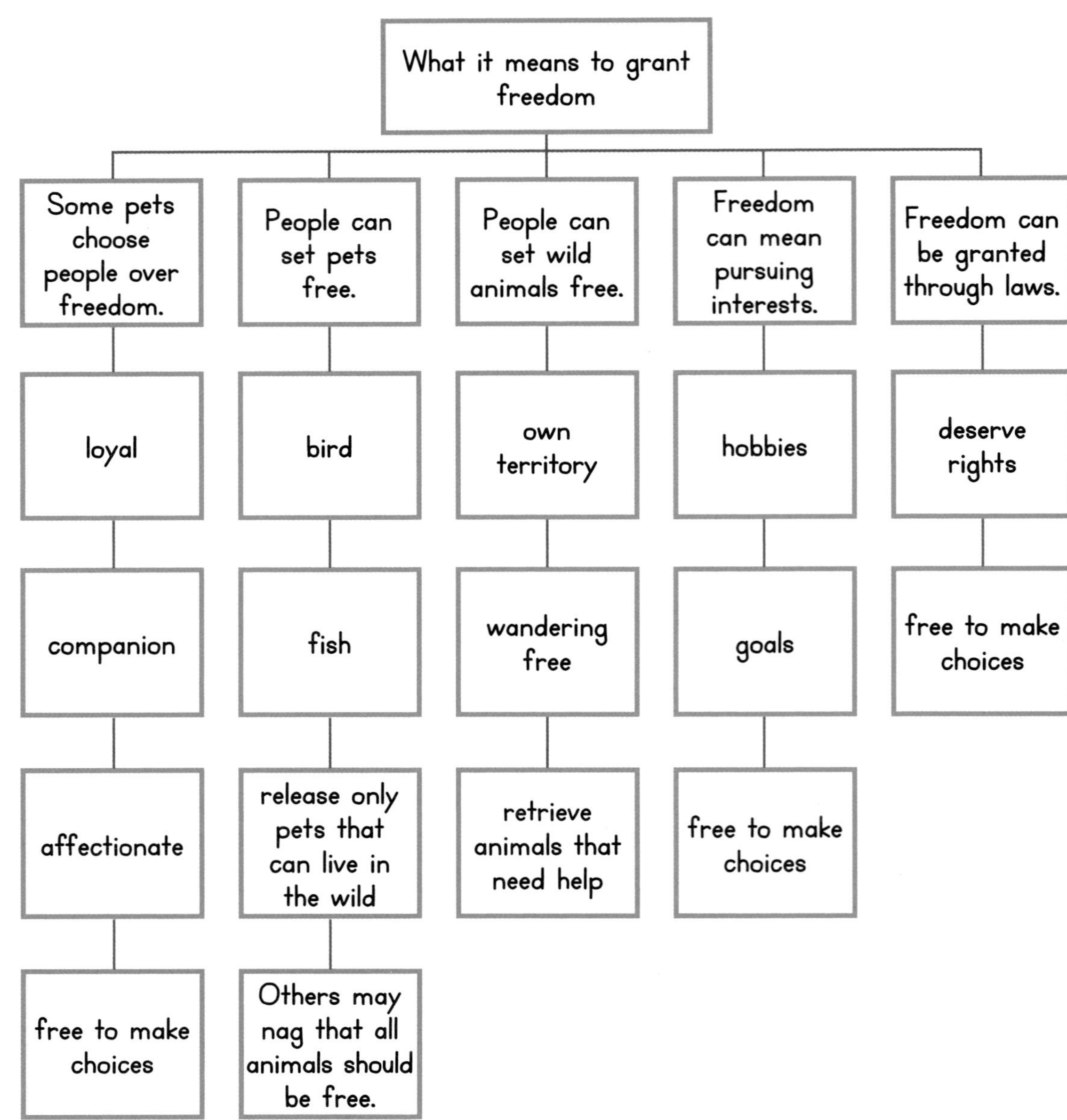

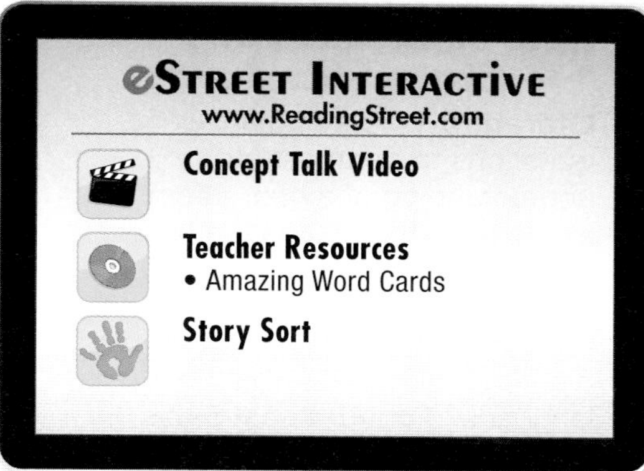

Build Oral Vocabulary

Team Talk **CONNECT TO AMAZING IDEAS** Have pairs of students discuss how the Question of the Week connects to the question for this unit of study: *What does freedom mean?* Tell students to use the concept map and what they have learned from this week's discussions and reading selections to form an Amazing Idea—a realization or "big idea" about Freedom. Remind partners to answer questions with appropriate detail and to give suggestions that build on each other's ideas. Then ask pairs to share their Amazing Ideas with the class.

Amazing Ideas might include these key concepts:

- Both people and animals can enjoy freedom.
- An important part of freedom is being able to make choices for yourself.
- Laws can protect people's freedom and the right to make choices for themselves.

WRITE ABOUT IT Have students write a few sentences about their Amazing Idea, beginning with "This week I learned . . ."

Amazing Words

territory	affectionate
release	companion
loyal	nag
deserve	retrieve
manage	wandering

It's Friday

MONITOR PROGRESS Check Oral Vocabulary

FORMATIVE ASSESSMENT Have individuals use this week's Amazing Words to describe how freedom can be granted. Monitor students' abilities to use the Amazing Words and note which words you need to reteach.

If... students have difficulty using the Amazing Words,

then... reteach using the Oral Vocabulary Routine, pp. 395a, 400b, 412b, 424b, OV•2.

Check Concepts and Language Use the Day 5 instruction on ELL Poster 27 to monitor students' understanding of the lesson concept.

Concept Map Work with students to add new words to the concept map.

Common Core State Standards

Literature 1. Ask and answer questions to demonstrate understanding of a text, referring explicitly to the text as the basis for the answers. **Literature 4.** Determine the meaning of words and phrases as they are used in a text, distinguishing literal from nonliteral language. **Foundational Skills 3.** Know and apply grade-level phonics and word analysis skills in decoding words. **Language 4.a.** Use sentence-level context as a clue to the meaning of a word or phrase. **Also Language 5.**

Text-Based Comprehension

Review Cause and Effect

TEACH Review the definition of cause and effect on p. 398. Remind students that an effect is something that happens and a cause is why that thing happens. Review how sometimes an effect may have more than one cause. For additional support have students review p. EI•3 on cause and effect.

GUIDE PRACTICE Have partners find a cause-and-effect relationship in *Happy Birthday Mr. Kang.* Then have pairs identify which is the cause and which is the effect and tell whether the effect has any other causes.

ON THEIR OWN For additional practice, use *Let's Practice It!* p. 379 on the *Teacher Resources DVD-ROM.*

Name ______________ Happy Birthday Mr. Kang

Cause and Effect

- A **cause** is why something happens. An **effect** is what happens.
- A **cause** may have more than one **effect.**
- An **effect** may have more than one **cause.**

Directions Read the following passage.

Rosa wanted to learn how to draw and paint, so she signed up for an art class. The first day, the students tried out all kinds of pens, pencils, and chalk, because the teacher said they weren't ready for paintbrushes yet. The class was fun because everyone helped each other and shared their ideas. At the end of class, the teacher told everyone to bring colored pencils next time. Because of that, Rosa bought a set of pencils and sharpened each one. Rosa knew she was going to learn a lot about art and she was really excited.

Directions Fill in the empty boxes in the two diagrams below.

CAUSES: Why did it happen?	EFFECTS: What happened?
The students weren't ready to paint.	1. **They used pens, pencils, and chalk.**
2. **Students helped each other and shared ideas.**	The art class was fun.
3. **Possible answer: The teacher told students to bring colored pencils.**	4. **Possible answer: Rosa bought a set of colored pencils and sharpened them.**

Home Activity Your child learned about cause and effect. Build a tower of blocks with your child. Have him or her pull out one of the bottom blocks and watch what happens. Have your child tell you why it happened (the cause) and what happened (the effect).

Comprehension DVD•379

Let's Practice It! TR DVD•379

Vocabulary Skill

Review Antonyms

TEACH Remind students that antonyms are words with opposite meanings.

GUIDE PRACTICE Using p. 407 of *Happy Birthday Mr. Kang,* review with students how to use context clues and antonyms to figure out the meaning of *chilly.*

ON THEIR OWN Have students work with a partner to write sentences using antonym pairs that include this week's selection vocabulary words. Partners can trade sentences and identify antonym pairs and context clues that help them determine each word's meaning.

Selection Vocabulary

bows bends the head or body forward
chilly uncomfortably cold
foolish unwise; not making sense
foreign from a place that is not your own country or homeland
narrow not wide
perches sits or rests on a bar, branch, or similar object
recipe ingredients and steps for making something to eat or drink

Phonics/Word Analysis

Review Schwa

TEACH Write the following sentences on the board. Have students read each one, first quietly to themselves and then aloud as you track the print.

1. **We stayed at a log cabin at the bottom of a canyon.**
2. **I like to put lots of lettuce in my salad.**
3. **Would you buy a pretzel for a nickel?**
4. **The firefighters saw that the garage was ablaze.**
5. **We will travel to seven cities this year.**

Team Talk Have students discuss with a partner which words have the schwa sound. Then call on individuals to identify the vowel in each word that stands for /ə/.

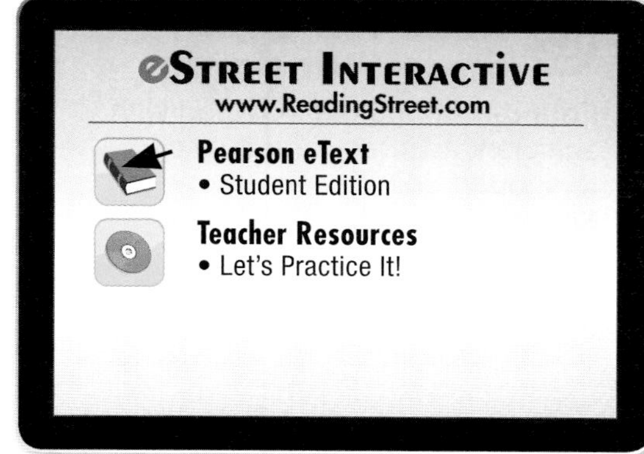

Literary Terms

Review Metaphor

TEACH Have students reread p. 412 of *Happy Birthday Mr. Kang,* focusing on Mr. Kang's poem. Remind students that a metaphor is when two unlike things are compared to each other, but without the use of the word *like* or *as.* Metaphors often use sensory words.

GUIDE PRACTICE Find an example of a metaphor in Mr. Kang's poem on this page. Discuss what two things the metaphor is comparing and why the author (and Mr. Kang) might be making this comparison. Have students find other examples of metaphors in this poem or in other parts of the selection and discuss them.

ON THEIR OWN Have students list examples of different metaphors from the selection and write a sentence or two explaining what each metaphor is comparing and why this comparison is being made. Tell students to identify words that appeal to the senses.

Articulation Tip If students have trouble pronouncing words with the sound of schwa, demonstrate how to pronounce them by slowly repeating words. Have students practice saying them until they develop confidence.

Metaphors If students have trouble identifying metaphors, work with them to identify examples of figurative language. How is each comparison made? Does it use the word *like* or *as*? Is it comparing two unlike things? What is being compared?

Common Core State Standards

Foundational Skills 4. Read with sufficient accuracy and fluency to support comprehension. **Foundational Skills 4.b.** Read on-level prose and poetry orally with accuracy, appropriate rate, and expression on successive readings.

Plan to Assess Fluency

- ☐ **Week 1** Advanced
- ☑ **This week assess Strategic Intervention students.**
- ☐ **Week 3** On-Level
- ☐ **Week 4** Strategic Intervention
- ☐ **Week 5** Assess any students you have not yet checked during this unit.

Set individual goals for students to enable them to reach the year-end goal.

- Current Goal: 110–120 WCPM
- Year-End Goal: 120 WCPM

Assessment

Monitor Progress

FLUENCY Make two copies of the fluency passage on p. 429k. As the student reads the text aloud, mark mistakes on your copy. Also mark where the student is at the end of one minute. To check the student's comprehension of the passage, have him or her retell what was read. To figure words correct per minute (WCPM), subtract the number of mistakes from the total number of words read in one minute.

RATE

Corrective feedback

If... students cannot read fluently at a rate of 110–120 WCPM,
then... make sure they practice with text at their independent reading level. Provide additional fluency practice by pairing nonfluent readers with fluent readers.

If... students already read at 120 WCPM,
then... have them read a book of their choice independently.

If... students need more scaffolding and practice with **Conventions and Writing,**
then... use the activities on pp. DI•49–DI•50 in the Teacher Resources section on SuccessNet.

Day 5 SMALL GROUP TIME • Differentiate Reteaching, p. SG•17

OL On-Level	SI Strategic Intervention	A Advanced
• **Practice** Abbreviations • **Reread** *Reading Street Sleuth,* pp. 70–71	• **Review** Abbreviations • **Reread** *Reading Street Sleuth,* pp. 70–71	• **Extend** Abbreviations • **Reread** *Reading Street Sleuth,* pp. 70–71 • **Communicate** Inquiry Project

Name ____________________

The Secret Recipe

When it's chilly out, I like to bake. My favorite recipe is a cookie 14
recipe that came from my aunt. When she is free, she travels. My aunt 28
says she found the recipe on one of her travels in a foreign country. 42
She bought a book that had the recipe. 50

When my aunt got home from that trip, she tried the cookie recipe. 63
It is very odd. Besides the other ingredients, she had to use a gallon 77
of milk. The recipe made more than seven dozen cookies. The cookies 89
baked for a long time in the oven. After a while, my aunt felt foolish. 104
Could this be right? When the cookies were done, though, we all 116
loved them. 118

Now, my family makes the cookies every year. We all have 129
different kinds of shapes we like to make. My brother likes animals. 141
He makes cats, dogs, bears, and tigers. Sometimes he makes so 152
many animals he could have his own circus. My cousin likes to make 165
stars. She also likes the color pink, so she colors all the stars pink. My 180
younger cousin likes to make dinosaurs. I like to make circles. I use the 194
bottom of a plastic drinking glass to get a perfect circle shape. 206

All of our friends like the cookies. They think they are the best 219
treats ever. My family laughs. We all know the secret. The famous 231
cookies have vinegar in them! 236

MONITOR PROGRESS

- **Check Fluency**

 **Common Core State Standards**

Informational Text 1. Ask and answer questions to demonstrate understanding of a text, referring explicitly to the text as the basis for the answers. **Informational Text 3.** Describe the relationship between a series of historical events, scientific ideas or concepts, or steps in technical procedures in a text, using language that pertains to time, sequence, and cause/effect. **Foundational Skills 4.** Read with sufficient accuracy and fluency to support comprehension. **Foundational Skills 4.a.** Read on-level text with purpose and understanding.

Assessment

Monitor Progress

For a written assessment of Schwa, Cause and Effect, and Selection Vocabulary, use Weekly Test 27, pp. 157–162.

CAUSE AND EFFECT Use "Yosuke Returns" on p. 429m to check students' understanding of cause and effect.

1. Given the choice, where was Yosuke the happiest to live? (Yosuke chose to return to his family instead of remaining free in the wild.)
2. Why do many parrots not survive in the wild? (They do not have the skills to survive alone without people to take care of them.)
3. What had to happen so that the vet could return Yosuke to his family? (He had to start talking and tell the vet his name and address.)

Corrective feedback	**If...** students are unable to answer the comprehension questions, **then...** use the Reteach lesson in *First Stop.*

Name ______________________________

Yosuke Returns

There are amazing stories of real lost pets and how they returned to their owners. For example, here's the entertaining tale of a parrot named Yosuke.

Yosuke lived with a Japanese family in a town near Tokyo. From his birth, Yosuke was raised as a pet. His human family took excellent care of him. Like many intelligent parrots, Yosuke was taught to repeat words and phrases. Yosuke could recite his name and address among other things.

One day Yosuke escaped from his cage. That probably wasn't too unusual, but he escaped from his family's house as well. Yosuke had flown to freedom!

The family searched, but couldn't find their Yosuke. How long could he survive without being fed and cared for?

Is a lost parrot happy to be free? There is no way to know what a parrot thinks. But most pet parrots don't have the skills to survive alone. They may not live very long once they have escaped. However, some birds figure out how to stay alive.

Yosuke was gone for two weeks when police noticed a gray parrot on the roof of a house. When they rescued the parrot, they didn't know it could talk. It said nothing to them. The police did know that the parrot needed help. They took it to a vet.

Once the parrot got a little care, it must have felt better. It started talking. It told the vet its name and address. It was Yosuke! Soon Yosuke was back home again.

MONITOR PROGRESS

- **Cause and Effect**

Common Core State Standards

Speaking/Listening 1.b. Follow agreed-upon rules for discussions (e.g., gaining the floor in respectful ways, listening to others with care, speaking one at a time about the topics and texts under discussion). **Speaking/Listening 3.** Ask and answer questions about information from a speaker, offering appropriate elaboration and detail. **Speaking/Listening 4.** Report on a topic or text, tell a story, or recount an experience with appropriate facts and relevant, descriptive details, speaking clearly at an understandable pace. **Language 2.** Demonstrate command of the conventions of standard English capitalization, punctuation, and spelling when writing. **Language 2.f.** Use spelling patterns and generalizations (e.g., word families, position-based spellings, syllable patterns, ending rules, meaningful word parts) in writing words. **Also Speaking/Listening 1.a.**

Research and Inquiry

Step 5 Communicate

PRESENT IDEAS Have students share their inquiry results by presenting their articles and giving a brief talk on their research. Have students display any graphic sources they created on Day 4.

SPEAKING Remind students how to be good speakers and how to communicate effectively with their audience.

- Respond to relevant questions with appropriate details.
- Speak clearly and loudly.
- Keep eye contact with audience members.

LISTENING Remind students of these tips for being a good listener.

- Wait until the speaker has finished before raising your hand to ask a relevant question.
- Be polite, even if you disagree.

LISTEN TO IDEAS Have students listen attentively to the various presentations. Have them make pertinent comments, closely related to the topic.

Spelling Test

Schwa

To administer the spelling test, refer to the directions, words, and sentences on p. 399c.

Conventions

Abbreviations

MORE PRACTICE Remind students of the week's conventions skill, abbreviations. Explain that an abbreviation is a shortened form of a word, and that it often begins with a capital letter and ends with a period.

GUIDE PRACTICE Write these sentences on the board and have students point to words that can be abbreviated. Invite volunteers to rewrite the sentences with abbreviations.

Mister Coleman's birthday party is on Saturday,
January 11. (Mr., Sat., Jan.)
Some birds fly south in October or November. (Oct., Nov.)
I am writing a report on Doctor Martin Luther King, Junior. (Dr., Jr.)

ON THEIR OWN Have students complete these sentence frames with relevant abbreviations. You may want to list common abbreviations on the board for students to refer to. Students should complete *Let's Practice It!* p. 380 on the *Teacher Resources DVD-ROM.*

1. **My teacher, _______ Wilman, was born in _______.**
2. **I am sick, so I am going to see _______ Carey.**
3. **_______ and _______ Lewis are my neighbors.**
4. **Today is _______ and the date is _______.**
5. **I was born on _______.**
6. **My friend was born on _______.**

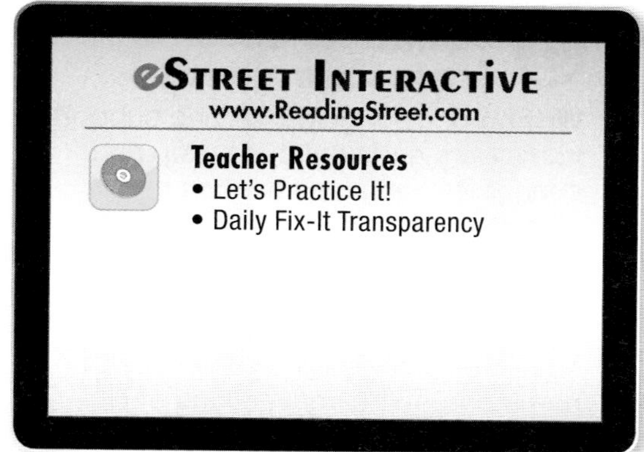

Daily Fix-It

9. The old man feel selfesh because the bird wants its freedom. *(feels; selfish)*
10. Can the bird live out side in the Winter safely? *(outside; winter)*

Name ______________________ Happy Birthday Mr. Kang

Abbreviations

Directions Write each sentence correctly. Use correct capitalization and periods for abbreviations.

1. Dr and mrs Hartz have many beautiful pet birds.
   Dr. and Mrs. Hartz have many beautiful pet birds.
2. They will display the birds at the home of mr and Ms Santos.
   They will display the birds at the home of Mr. and Ms. Santos.
3. I am going to see the birds with my friend c. j. Fox.
   I am going to see the birds with my friend C. J. Fox.
4. You can buy tickets at G B Watkins Department Store.
   You can buy tickets at G. B. Watkins Department Store.

Directions The following research notes have initials and abbreviations written incorrectly. Write each note. Correct mistakes in initials and abbreviations.

5. John j Audubon—bird painter
   John J. Audubon—bird painter
6. Born apr 1785
   Born Apr. 1785
7. Wrote book about animals with J Bachman
   Wrote book about animals with J. Bachman
8. Died jan 1851
   Died Jan. 1851

School + Home **Home Activity** Your child reviewed abbreviations. Scan a newspaper with your child and have your child identify abbreviations.

DVD•380 Abbreviations

Let's Practice It! TR DVD•380

Common Core State Standards

Writing 5. With guidance and support from peers and adults, develop and strengthen writing as needed by planning, revising, and editing. **Language 1.** Demonstrate command of the conventions of standard English grammar and usage when writing or speaking. **Language 2.** Demonstrate command of the conventions of standard English capitalization, punctuation, and spelling when writing. **Also Writing 10., Language 2.g.**

Teacher Note

Writing Self-Evaluation Make copies of the Writing Self-Evaluation Guide on p. 39 of the *Reader's and Writer's Notebook* and hand out to students.

Bridge to Common Core

PRODUCTION AND DISTRIBUTION OF WRITING

Over the course of the week, students have developed and strengthened their drafts through planning, revising, editing, and rewriting. The final drafts are clear and coherent limericks in which the organization and style are appropriate to the purpose and audience.

Writing Zoom in on ©

Poetry: Limerick

REVIEW REVISING Remind students that yesterday they revised their limericks, using the revising strategy adding to include important information about the topic. Today, students will proofread their writing.

Mini-Lesson Proofread

Proofread for Abbreviations

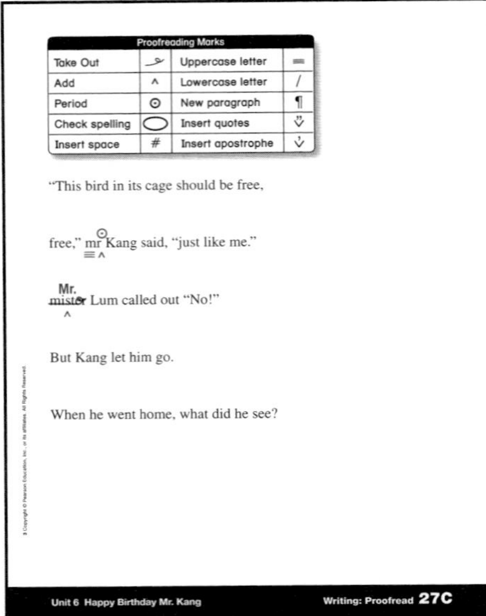

Proofreading Marks			
Take Out	⌐	Uppercase letter	═
Add	^	Lowercase letter	/
Period	⊙	New paragraph	¶
Check spelling	○	Insert quotes	∜
Insert space	#	Insert apostrophe	∜

"This bird in its cage should be free,

free," mr Kang said, "just like me."

Mr. mister Lum called out "No!"

But Kang let him go.

When he went home, what did he see?

Unit 6 Happy Birthday Mr. Kang Writing: Proofread 27C

Writing Transparency 27C, TR DVD

- **Teach** When we proofread, we look closely at our work, searching for errors in mechanics such as spelling, capitalization, punctuation, and grammar. Today we will focus on abbreviations.
- **Model** Let's look at the limerick we revised yesterday. Display Writing Transparency 27C and explain that you will look for errors in the use of abbreviations. In line 2, *mr* is not capitalized and the abbreviation needs to end with a period. In line 3, *mister* should be abbreviated. I will correct this by writing *Mr.* with an initial capital letter and ending it with a period. Then point out *Kang* in line 4. Explain that the writer intentionally left out the title in order to achieve the correct number of syllables in the line. Explain to students that they should reread their limericks a number of times, looking for errors in spelling, punctuation, capitalization, and grammar.

PROOFREAD Display the Proofreading Tips. Ask students to proofread their limericks, using the tips and paying attention to abbreviations. Circulate around the room answering students' questions. When students have finished editing their own work, have pairs proofread one another's limericks.

Proofreading Tips

- ✔ Be sure that all abbreviations are used correctly.
- ✔ Check for correct punctuation, capitalization, and grammar.
- ✔ Use a dictionary to check for correct spelling.
- ✔ Make sure that each line contains the correct number of syllables.

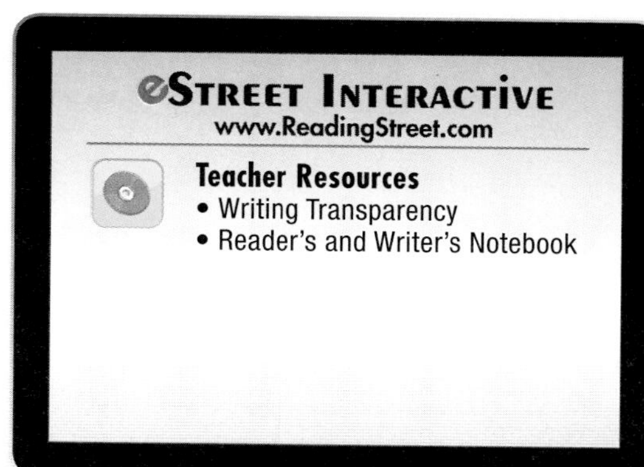

PRESENT Have students incorporate revisions and proofreading edits into their limericks to create a final draft.

Have students give an oral presentation of their limericks to the class. When students have finished, have each complete the Writing Self-Evaluation Guide.

Routine Quick Write for Fluency — Team Talk

1. **Talk** Pairs discuss what they learned about writing limericks.
2. **Write** Each student writes a paragraph summarizing what he or she learned.
3. **Share** Partners read their summaries to each other.

Routines Flip Chart

Wrap Up Your Week!

Granting Freedom

What does it mean to grant freedom?

In *Happy Birthday Mr. Kang* and "Once Upon a Constitution," we learned what freedom means to different groups of people and what it means to grant freedom.

Team Talk Have students recall their Amazing Ideas about freedom and use these ideas to help them demonstrate their understanding of the Question of the Week.

Next Week's Concept

Freedom of Expression

Why is freedom of expression important?

Poster Preview Prepare students for next week by using Week 3 ELL Poster 28. Read the Talk-Through to introduce the concept and vocabulary. Ask students to identify and describe actions in the art.

Selection Summary Send home the summary of next week's selection, *Talking Walls: Art for the People,* in English and in students' home languages, if available in the *ELL Handbook.* They can read the summary with family members.

Why is freedom of expression important? Read about how some artists express their beliefs in their art.

Preview Next Week

Assessment Checkpoints for the Week

Weekly Assessment

Use pp. 157–162 of *Weekly Tests* to check:

- ✔ **Phonics** Schwa
- ✔ **Comprehension** Cause and Effect
- ✔ Review **Comprehension** Literary Element: Theme
- ✔ **Selection Vocabulary**

bows	**narrow**
chilly	**perches**
foolish	**recipe**
foreign	

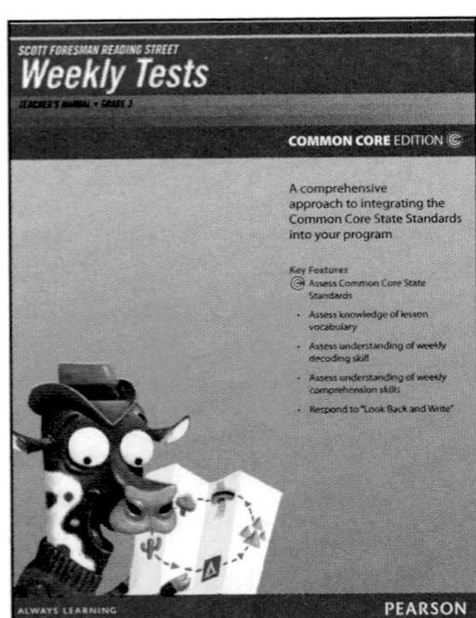

Weekly Tests

Differentiated Assessment

Advanced

On-Level

SI Strategic Intervention

Use pp. 157–162 of *Fresh Reads for Fluency and Comprehension* to check:

- ✔ **Comprehension** Cause and Effect
- ✔ Review **Comprehension** Literary Element: Theme

- ✔ **Fluency** Words Correct Per Minute

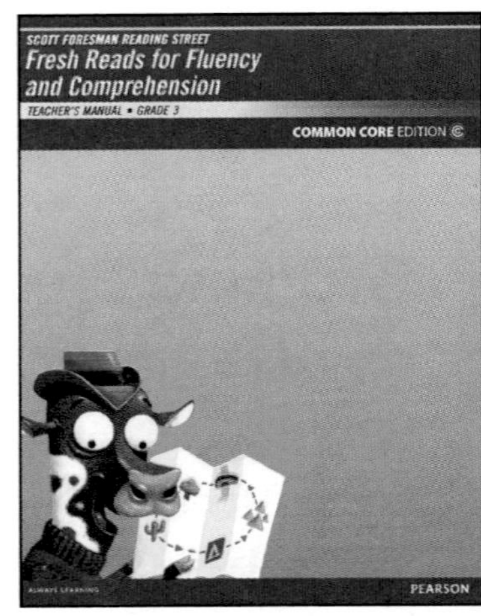

Fresh Reads for Fluency and Comprehension

Managing Assessment

Use *Assessment Handbook* for:

- ✔ **Weekly Assessment Blackline Masters for Monitoring Progress**
- ✔ **Observation Checklists**
- ✔ **Record-Keeping Forms**
- ✔ **Portfolio Assessment**

Assessment Handbook

TEACHER NOTES

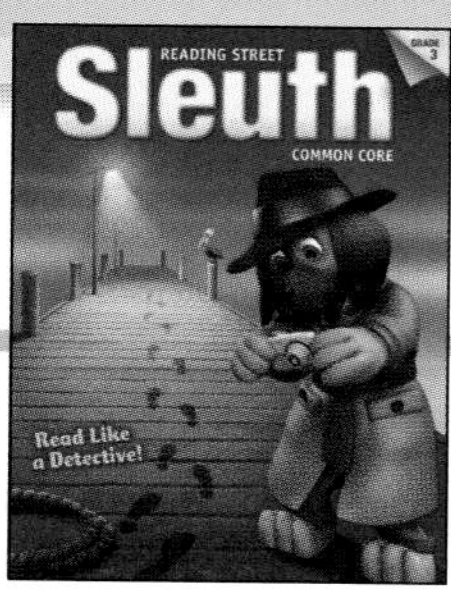

"Freedom for All," pp. 70–71

DAY 1 Differentiate Vocabulary

- **Word Knowledge** Amazing Words
- **Read** "Freedom for All"
- **Inquiry** Identify Questions

DAY 2 Differentiate Comprehension

- **Word Knowledge** Selection Vocabulary
- **Access Text** Read *Happy Birthday Mr. Kang*
- **Inquiry** Investigate

DAY 3 Differentiate Close Reading

- **Word Knowledge** Develop Vocabulary
- **Close Reading** Read *Happy Birthday Mr. Kang*
- **Inquiry** Investigate

DAY 4 Differentiate Vocabulary

- **Word Knowledge** Amazing Words
- **Read** "Once Upon a Constitution"
- **Inquiry** Organize

DAY 5 Differentiate Reteaching

- **Conventions** Abbreviations
- **Reread** "Freedom for All" or Leveled Readers
- **Inquiry** Communicate

Teacher Guides and Student pages can be found in the Leveled Reader Database.

Place English Language Learners in the groups that correspond to their reading abilities.
If... students need scaffolding and practice,
then... use the ELL Notes on the instructional pages.

Independent Practice

Independent Practice Stations

See pp. 394h and 394i for Independent Stations.

Pearson Trade Book Library

See the Leveled Reader Database for lesson plans and student pages.

Reading Street Digital Path

Independent Practice Activities are available in the Digital Path.

Independent Reading

See p. 394i for independent reading suggestions.

On-Level

Common Core State Standards

Literature 1. Ask and answer questions to demonstrate understanding of a text, referring explicitly to the text as the basis for the answers. **Literature 4.** Determine the meaning of words and phrases as they are used in a text, distinguishing literal from nonliteral language. **Informational Text 3.** Describe the relationship between a series of historical events, scientific ideas or concepts, or steps in technical procedures in a text, using language that pertains to time, sequence, and cause/effect. **Informational Text 6.** Distinguish their own point of view from that of the author of a text. **Foundational Skills 4.** Read with sufficient accuracy and fluency to support comprehension. **Language 4.** Determine or clarify the meaning of unknown and multiple-meaning words and phrases based on grade 3 reading and content, choosing flexibly from a range of strategies.

Independent Reading Options

Trade Book Library

eSTREET INTERACTIVE
www.ReadingStreet.com

Teacher Guides are available on the Leveled Reader Database.

If... students need more scaffolding and practice with **Vocabulary, then...** use the activities on pp. DI•42–DI•43 in the Teacher Resources section on SuccessNet.

1 Build Word Knowledge

Practice Amazing Words

DEFINE IT Elicit the definition for the word *territory* from students. Ask: How would you describe a *territory* to a friend? (Possible response: A *territory* is an area or somewhere you can stand.) Clarify or give a definition when necessary. Continue with the words *deserve* and *loyal*.

Team Talk **TALK ABOUT IT** Have students internalize meanings. Ask: How can you group the Amazing Words together in a sentence? (Possible response: The *loyal* dog that protected the *territory deserved* a treat.) Allow time for students to play with the words. Review the concept map with students. Discuss other words they can add to the concept map.

2 Text-Based Comprehension

Read

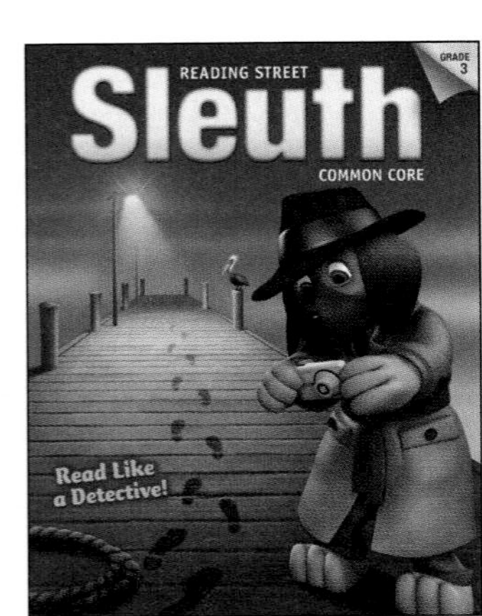

READ ALOUD "Freedom for All" Have partners read "Freedom for All" from *Reading Street Sleuth* on pp. 70–71.

ACCESS TEXT Discuss the Sleuth Work section with students before they work on it. Remind students that they can use these steps with other texts they read.

Gather Evidence Have partners revisit the text together, making a list of facts that tell why Abraham Lincoln is important. Remind students that facts can be proven true.

Ask Questions Have students share their questions with a partner. Together, discuss the kinds of questions students asked. Encourage students to share what triggered these questions.

Make Your Case Have students select a position on this issue. Encourage students who took the same side of the issue to work together to make a list of convincing reasons for supporting that side. Invite students to share their most convincing reasons with the group.

On-Level

1 Build Word Knowledge

Practice Selection Vocabulary

bows	chilly	foolish	foreign
narrow	perches	recipe	

DEFINE IT Discuss the definition for the word *foolish* with students. Ask: How would you describe *foolish* to another student? (Possible response: A *foolish* person is one who is silly or makes bad decisions.) Continue with the remaining words.

Team Talk **TALK ABOUT IT** Have pairs use the selection vocabulary in sentences to internalize meaning. Ask: How can you group the selection vocabulary words together in a sentence? (Possible response: It is *foolish* to think you can make a *foreign recipe* when you don't have the right ingredients.) Allow time for students to play with the words and then share their sentences.

2 Read

Happy Birthday Mr. Kang

If you read *Happy Birthday Mr. Kang* during whole group time, then use the following instruction.

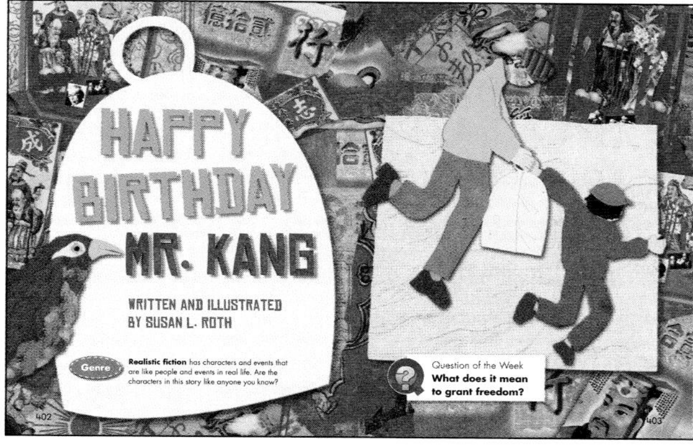

ACCESS TEXT Reread pp. 405–406. Ask questions to check understanding. Where is Mr. Kang from? (China) What does Mr. Kang wish for at his birthday party? (He wants to read the newspaper and paint poems every day, and he wants a bird of his own.) How have his mornings changed since he turned 70? (Before he turned 70, he went to work every day to cook at the Gold Dragon Restaurant. Now he reads the paper, cares for his bird, and drinks tea.)

Have students identify sections from today's reading that they did not completely understand. Reread them aloud and clarify misunderstandings.

If you are reading *Happy Birthday Mr. Kang* during small group time, then return to pp. 404–411a to guide the reading.

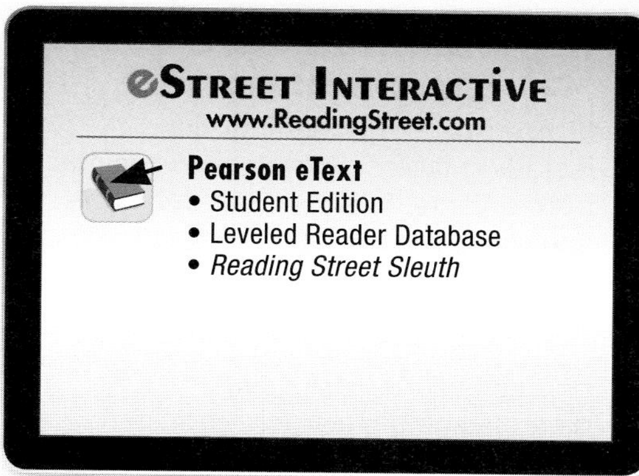

SMALL GROUP TIME

More Reading for Group Time

ON-LEVEL

Review
- Cause and Effect
- Inferring
- Selection Vocabulary

Use this suggested Leveled Reader or other text at students' instructional level.

eStreet Interactive
www.ReadingStreet.com

Use the Leveled Reader Database for lesson plans and student pages for *A Pet Bird.*

On-Level

Common Core State Standards

Literature 2. Recount stories, including fables, folktales, and myths from diverse cultures; determine the central message, lesson, or moral and explain how it is conveyed through key details in the text. **Literature 4.** Determine the meaning of words and phrases as they are used in a text, distinguishing literal from nonliteral language. **Language 4.** Determine or clarify the meaning of unknown and multiple-meaning words and phrases based on grade 3 reading and content, choosing flexibly from a range of strategies. **Also Informational Text 3., 5., Writing 4., Language 4.d., 6.**

1 Build Word Knowledge

Develop Vocabulary

REREAD FOR VOCABULARY Reread the fourth and fifth paragraphs on p. 414. Introduce: Let's read these paragraphs to find out what *interrupts* means. To help students understand the word *interrupts,* ask questions related to the context: Why is everyone talking all at once? How do Mrs. Kang's words affect Mr. Kang's talking? Have students use online sources to find out more information about the word *interrupt.*

2 Read

Happy Birthday Mr. Kang

If you read *Happy Birthday Mr. Kang* during whole group time, then use the following instruction.

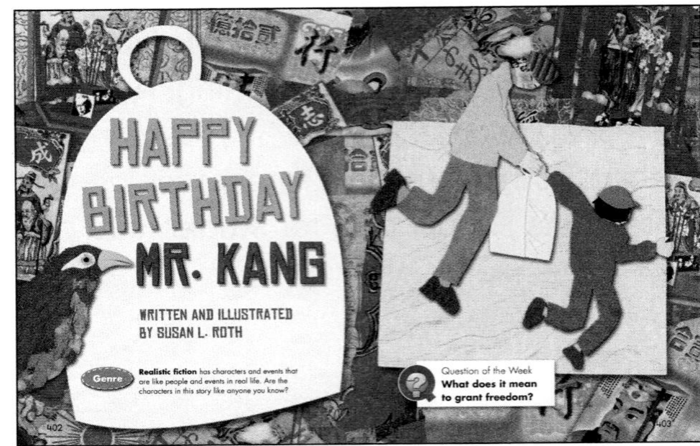

CLOSE READING Read pp. 414–415. Have students search through the text for sentences that show that Mr. Kang, Mrs. Kang, and Sam feel strongly about Mr. Kang's decision to free the bird. As a class, make a list of the sentences in the order they occur. ("Do not be foolish!"; "I am a free man"; "He cannot understand"; "But Grandma, it's not fair.")

Ask: Who thinks the bird should go free? Why? (Mr. Kang thinks it should go free because he is now free from working.) Who thinks it should stay in its cage? Why? (Mrs. Kang and Sam because it could get hurt and Mr. Kang would miss it)

If you are reading *Happy Birthday Mr. Kang* during small group time, then return to pp. 412–419a to guide the reading.

If... students need more scaffolding and practice with the **Main Selection, then...** use the activities on p. DI•47 in the Teacher Resources section on SuccessNet.

On-Level

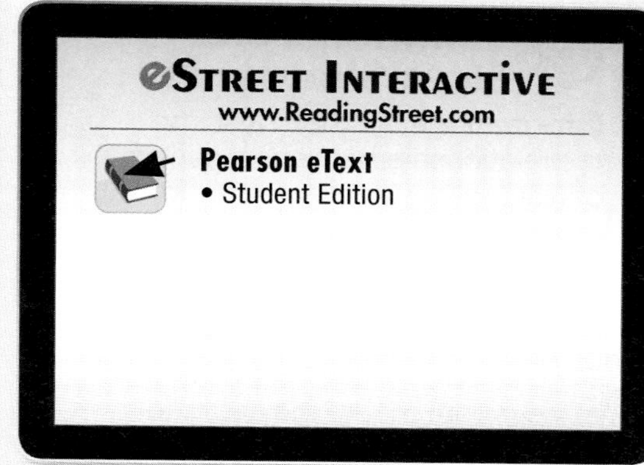

1 Build Word Knowledge

Practice Amazing Words

territory	release	loyal	deserve	manage
affectionate	companion	nag	retrieve	wandering

Team Talk **LANGUAGE DEVELOPMENT** Have students practice building more complex sentences. Display a sentence starter and have students add oral phrases or clauses using the Amazing Words. For example: His _______ companion _______. (His *loyal* and *affectionate* companion / went *wandering* with him / in the woods / on his *territory.*) Guide students to add at least three phrases or clauses per sentence.

2 Read

"Once Upon a Constitution"

BEFORE READING Read aloud the genre information about expository text on p. 424. Explain that expository text can help readers learn facts about a topic. Help students preview "Once Upon a Constitution" and set a purpose for reading. What features do you see that are different from most stories you have read? (photographs, arrows, and labels) Why do you think the opening words of the document are enlarged on the first page? (to show the importance of "We the People" in a democracy and to help explain the word *curlicue*)

DURING READING Have students read along with you. How does the author use the questions and answers? (Questions introduce main ideas; answers explain the ideas with supporting details.) How would a fictional story about the Constitution be different than the expository nonfiction? (A fictional story could have made-up characters, events, and details.)

AFTER READING Have students share their reactions to "Once Upon a Constitution." Then have them write a brief conversation between Mr. Kang and Sam in which the two discuss why the Constitution and Bill of Rights are important to them.

SMALL GROUP TIME

Independent Reading Options

Trade Book Library

eStreet Interactive
www.ReadingStreet.com
Teacher Guides are available on the Leveled Reader Database.

On-Level

Common Core State Standards

Informational Text 3. Describe the relationship between a series of historical events, scientific ideas or concepts, or steps in technical procedures in a text, using language that pertains to time, sequence, and cause/effect. **Informational Text 6.** Distinguish their own point of view from that of the author of a text. **Foundational Skills 4.** Read with sufficient accuracy and fluency to support comprehension. **Writing 4.** With guidance and support from adults, produce writing in which the development and organization are appropriate to task and purpose. **Language 2.** Demonstrate command of the conventions of standard English capitalization, punctuation, and spelling when writing. **Also Language 4.**

More Reading for Group Time

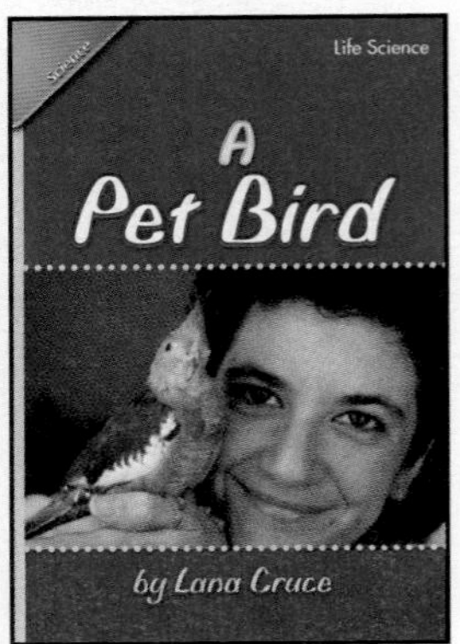

ON-LEVEL

Review
- Cause and Effect
- Inferring
- Selection Vocabulary

Use this suggested Leveled Reader or other text at students' instructional level.

eSTREET INTERACTIVE
www.ReadingStreet.com

Use the Leveled Reader Database for lesson plans and student pages for *A Pet Bird.*

1 Build Word Knowledge

Practice Abbreviations

IDENTIFY Ask a volunteer to read aloud the instruction on the bottom of p. 423 and discuss with students how to use abbreviations. Have students work in pairs to reread the model limericks and identify the abbreviations the writer used. Allow time for students to discuss their examples and correct any misunderstandings.

2 Text-Based Comprehension

Read

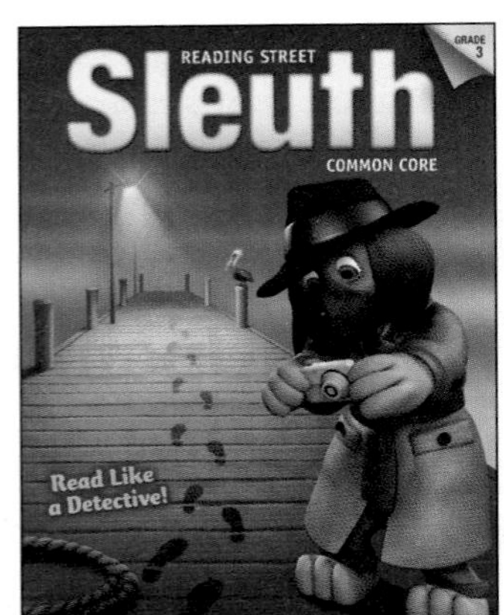

REREAD "Freedom for All" Have partners reread "Freedom for All."

EXTEND UNDERSTANDING Talk together about the history of slavery in our country.

PERFORMANCE TASK • Prove It! Have students write a poem about freedom. They can write about freedom in general, freedom in their own lives, or freedom as it pertains to the information in this article. Encourage students to use descriptive language in their poems.

COMMUNICATE Have groups share their poems with others. Invite discussion about the kinds of freedoms we have in our country today.

1 Build Word Knowledge

Reteach Amazing Words

Repeat the definition of the word *territory.* We learned that *territory* means a certain area someone owns or something lives in. Then use the word in a sentence. The dog protected its owner's *territory.*

Team Talk **TALK ABOUT IT** Have partners take turns using the word *territory* in a sentence. Continue this routine to practice the Amazing Words *deserve* and *loyal.* Review the concept map with students. Discuss other words they can add to the concept map.

Corrective feedback	**If...** students need more practice with the Amazing Words, **then...** use visuals from the Student Edition or online sources to clarify meaning.

2 Text-Based Comprehension

Read

READ "Freedom for All" Have partners track the print as you read "Freedom for All" from *Reading Street Sleuth* on pp. 70–71.

ACCESS TEXT Discuss the Sleuth Work section with students and provide support as needed as they work on it. Remind students that they can use these steps with other texts they read.

Gather Evidence Revisit the text together, finding facts that tell why Abraham Lincoln is important. Remind students that facts can be proven true while opinions are based on one's feelings.

Ask Questions Talk together about the kinds of questions students asked and the kinds of answers students are looking for: fact or opinion based. Encourage students to share what triggered these questions for them.

Make Your Case Have students select a position on this issue. Encourage small groups who took the same side of the issue to work together, listing reasons that support that side. Invite a spokesperson from each group to share their most convincing reason with the other groups.

SMALL GROUP TIME

More Reading for Group Time

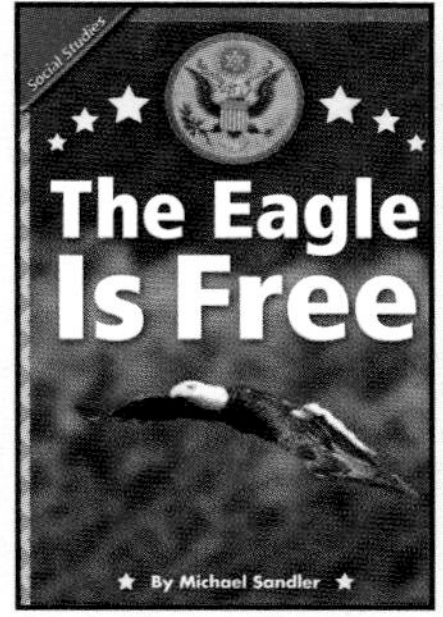

CONCEPT LITERACY

Practice
Concept Words

BELOW-LEVEL

Review
- Cause and Effect
- Inferring
- Selection Vocabulary

Use these suggested Leveled Readers or other text at students' instructional level.

eStreet Interactive
www.ReadingStreet.com

Use the Leveled Reader Database for lesson plans and student pages for *The Eagle Is Free* and *New York's Chinatown.*

Common Core State Standards

Literature 1. Ask and answer questions to demonstrate understanding of a text, referring explicitly to the text as the basis for the answers. **Literature 2.** Recount stories, including fables, folktales, and myths from diverse cultures; determine the central message, lesson, or moral and explain how it is conveyed through key details in the text. **Literature 4.** Determine the meaning of words and phrases as they are used in a text, distinguishing literal from nonliteral language. **Language 4.a.** Use sentence-level context as a clue to the meaning of a word or phrase. **Language 6.** Acquire and use accurately grade-appropriate conversational, general academic, and domain-specific words and phrases, including those that signal spatial and temporal relationships (e.g., *After dinner that night we went looking for them*).

Independent Reading Options

Trade Book Library

eStreet Interactive
www.ReadingStreet.com

Teacher Guides are available on the Leveled Reader Database.

1 Build Word Knowledge

Reteach Selection Vocabulary

bows	chilly	foolish
foreign	narrow	perches
recipe		

DEFINE IT Describe the word *perches* to a friend. Give a definition when necessary. Restate the word in student-friendly terms and clarify meaning with a visual. *Perches* means sits on a thin, high place, as birds do in trees. Page 407 shows the hua mei as it perches.

Team Talk **TALK ABOUT IT** Have you ever seen bird as it perches? Turn and talk to your partner about this. Allow time for students to discuss. Ask for examples. Rephrase students' examples for usage when necessary or to correct misunderstandings. Continue with the remaining words.

Corrective feedback	**If...** students need more practice with selection vocabulary, **then...** use the *Envision It! Pictured Vocabulary Cards.*

2 Read

Happy Birthday Mr. Kang

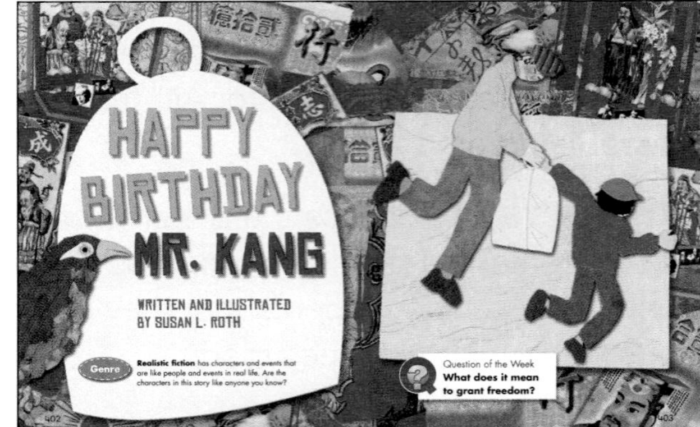

If you read *Happy Birthday Mr. Kang* during whole group time, then use the instruction below.

ACCESS TEXT Reread pp. 405–406. Ask questions to check understanding. Where does Mr. Kang live? (New York) Where did he live before that? (China) What does Mr. Kang wish for at his birthday? (to read the newspaper and paint poems every day and to have a bird) Do his wishes come true? How do you know? (Yes. After Mr. Kang turns 70, he reads the newspaper, drinks tea, eats cake, paints poems, and cares for his bird.)

Have students identify sections they did not understand. Reread them aloud. Clarify the meaning of each section to build understanding.

If you are reading *Happy Birthday Mr. Kang* during small group time, then return to pp. 404–411a to guide the reading.

Strategic Intervention

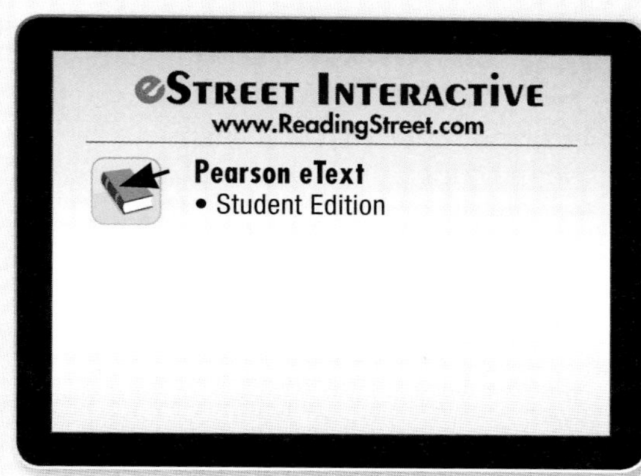

1 Build Word Knowledge

Develop Vocabulary

REREAD FOR VOCABULARY Read aloud the fourth and fifth paragraphs on p. 414. Have students follow as you read. Let's read this paragraph to find out what *interrupts* means. To help students understand the word *interrupts,* ask questions related to the context: What do the three dots at the end of paragraph five mean? Who is talking first? Then who starts talking? What happens when everyone talks at once?

Corrective feedback	**If...** students have difficulty understanding the word *interrupts,* **then...** guide students to use online sources, such as a dictionary or thesaurus, to find the meaning of the word.

2 Read

Happy Birthday Mr. Kang

If you read *Happy Birthday Mr. Kang* during whole group time, then use the instruction below.

CLOSE READING Read pp. 414–415. Have students search through the text for all the different arguments that Mrs. Kang and Sam make against letting the bird go free. As a class, make a list of the arguments in the order they occur. (Mr. Kang should remember his birthday wishes. He won't have anything to listen to after he paints his poems. Sam does not understand about the bird. The bird might go hungry or die. Sam worries Mr. Kang will be sad if the bird flies away.)

Why doesn't Mr. Kang listen to Mrs. Kang and Sam? (He thinks that the bird should be free, just as he is now free from working.)

If you are reading *Happy Birthday Mr. Kang* during small group time, then return to pp. 412–419a to guide the reading.

If... students need more scaffolding and practice with the **Main Selection,** **then...** use the activities on p. DI•47 in the Teacher Resources section on SucccessNet.

Strategic Intervention

Common Core State Standards

Informational Text 2. Determine the main idea of a text; recount the key details and explain how they support the main idea. **Informational Text 4.** Determine the meaning of general academic and domain-specific words and phrases in a text relevant to a grade 3 topic or subject area. **Foundational Skills 4.** Read with sufficient accuracy and fluency to support comprehension. **Writing 4.** With guidance and support from adults, produce writing in which the development and organization are appropriate to task and purpose **Language 2.** Demonstrate command of the conventions of standard English capitalization, punctuation, and spelling when writing. **Also Informational Text 3., Language 6.**

1 Build Word Knowledge

Review Amazing Words

territory	release	loyal	deserve	manage
affectionate	companion	nag	retrieve	wandering

Team Talk **LANGUAGE DEVELOPMENT** Have partners practice building more complex sentences. Display a sentence starter and have students add oral phrases or clauses using the Amazing Words. Guide students to add at least two phrases or clauses per sentence.

Corrective feedback | **If...** students have difficulty using the Amazing Words orally, **then...** review the meaning of each of the words.

2 Read

"Once Upon a Constitution"

Social Studies in Reading

Genre
Expository Text
- In expository texts, the author presents facts and details to support the main idea about a topic.
- Expository texts are sometimes organized using questions and answers.
- Photographs, captions, and illustrations show information visually.
- As you read "Once Upon a Constitution," ask yourself, *What is the topic? What is the main idea about the topic?* and *What will I learn about the main idea as I keep reading?*

Once Upon a Constitution
BY RON FRIDELL

Once upon a time the United States of America was born. That was more than two centuries ago.

What did these new American citizens need most? A single set of laws and rules for everyone to live by. So some very wise men assembled in the year 1787 in Philadelphia, Pennsylvania, to write a document called the Constitution.

Back in those distant days, there were no typewriters or computers to work with. People wrote down everything by hand, using quill pens made from bird feathers, and their handwriting had all sorts of fancy loops and curlicues. The men who created the Constitution wrote on parchment made from animal skin. Parchment lasted longer than paper, and they wanted this document to last for centuries.

Think...
Look at the labels, captions, and illustrations on these two pages. What facts can you learn about the Constitution?
Expository Text

424 425

BEFORE READING Read aloud the genre information about expository text on p. 424. Make sure students understand that in expository text, the author presents facts and details to support the main idea. Then have students find the arrows on the first three pages and read the labels.

DURING READING Help students do a choral reading of the article. Ask questions to help students recognize explicit and implicit causes and effects, such as "What happened because Americans needed laws and rules?"

AFTER READING Have students share their reactions to the selection. Then guide them through the Reading Across Texts and Writing Across Texts activities.

- What American rights and freedoms does Mr. Kang enjoy? (saying what he thinks and feels; living and working where and when he chooses; practicing Chinese traditions)
- Why does Mr. Kang change his mind about setting his bird free? (Sam reminds his grandfather that he had felt caged before he stopped cooking.)

If... students need more scaffolding and practice with **Amazing Words, then...** use the Routine on pp. xxxvi–xxxvii in the *ELL Handbook.*

1 Build Word Knowledge

Review Abbreviations

IDENTIFY Chorally read the instruction on the bottom of p. 423 to review how to use abbreviations. Have students work in pairs to reread the model limericks on p. 423 and identify the abbreviations the writer used. Allow time for students to discuss their examples and correct any misunderstandings.

2 Text-Based Comprehension

Read

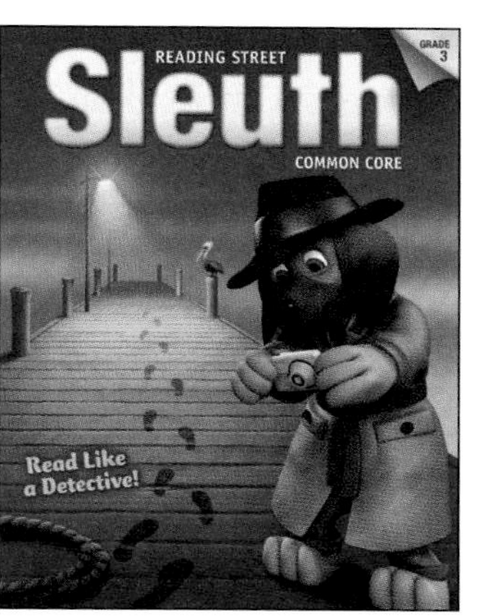

REREAD "Freedom for All" Have partners reread "Freedom for All" alternating paragraphs.

EXTEND UNDERSTANDING Talk together about the differing opinions of the Northern and Southern states regarding slavery.

PERFORMANCE TASK • Prove It! Have students write a poem about freedom. They can write about freedom in general, freedom in their own lives, or freedom as it pertains to the information in this article. Remind students that poems do not always rhyme.

COMMUNICATE Have students share their poems with a partner. Encourage partners to summarize the message of each other's poem.

SMALL GROUP TIME

More Reading for Group Time

CONCEPT LITERACY

Practice
Concept Words

BELOW-LEVEL

Review
- Cause and Effect
- Inferring
- Selection Vocabulary

Use these suggested Leveled Readers or other text at students' instructional level.

eStreet Interactive
www.ReadingStreet.com

Use the Leveled Reader Database for lesson plans and student pages for *The Eagle Is Free* and *New York's Chinatown.*

A Advanced

Common Core State Standards

Literature 1. Ask and answer questions to demonstrate understanding of a text, referring explicitly to the text as the basis for the answers. **Literature 4.** Determine the meaning of words and phrases as they are used in a text, distinguishing literal from nonliteral language. **Informational Text 1.** Ask and answer questions to demonstrate understanding of a text, referring explicitly to the text as the basis for the answers. **Informational Text 6.** Distinguish their own point of view from that of the author of a text. **Foundational Skills 4.** Read with sufficient accuracy and fluency to support comprehension. **Writing 7.** Conduct short research projects that build knowledge about a topic.

If... students need more scaffolding and practice with **Vocabulary, then...** use the activities on pp. DI•42–DI•43 in the Teacher Resources section on SuccessNet.

1 Build Word Knowledge

Extend Amazing Words

Team Talk Have students define *territory.* Discuss other words that have a similar meaning to *territory.* Continue with *deserve* and *loyal.*

2 Text-Based Comprehension

Read

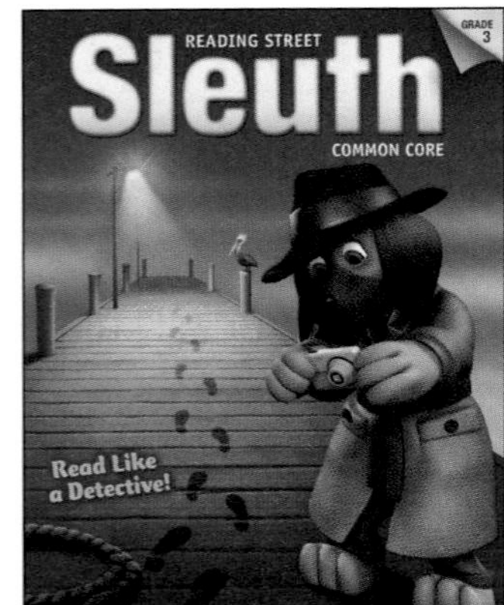

READ "Freedom for All" Have partners read "Freedom for All" from *Reading Street Sleuth* on pp. 70–71.

ACCESS TEXT Discuss the Sleuth Work section with students before they work on it. Remind students that they can use these steps with other texts they read.

Gather Evidence Remind students that facts can be proven true. Have students share facts from the text that tell why Abraham Lincoln is so important.

Ask Questions Have students share their questions with the group. Together, discuss the kinds of questions students asked. Encourage students to talk about why they would like to know the answers to their questions.

Make Your Case Ask students to select a position on this issue and make a list of convincing reasons. Remind them that facts and opinions can back up their point of view. If time permits, invite discussion about which facts best support each side of the issue.

3 Inquiry: Extend Concepts

IDENTIFY QUESTIONS Have students think about questions they have about unusual animals that people keep in their homes. Students should use these questions to create an informative poster about a particular animal that people keep as pets or companions. Throughout the week, students will gather information. On Day 5, they will present what they have learned.

Advanced

1 Build Word Knowledge

Extend Selection Vocabulary

Team Talk Have partners use the selection vocabulary in sentences to internalize their meanings. Have students use as many of the words as they can while making sure the sentence is grammatically correct. (Possible response: On *chilly* mornings, birds sit close together on *narrow perches* to keep warm.) Continue with additional selection vocabulary.

bows	chilly	foolish	foreign
narrow	perches	recipe	

2 Read

Happy Birthday Mr. Kang

If you read *Happy Birthday Mr. Kang* during whole group time, then use the instruction below.

ACCESS TEXT Reread pp. 405–406. Have students compare and contrast Mr. Kang's morning routines before and after his birthday. (Before: He got up every morning to go cook in a restaurant. After: He reads a newspaper, drinks tea, eats cake, paints poetry, and listens to and cares for his bird.) Why does the author describe Mr. Kang's mornings before and after his birthday? (to show how hard he worked; to show how free and relaxed he is now; to show a contrast between work and resting)

If you are reading *Happy Birthday Mr. Kang* during small group time, then return to pp. 404–411a to guide the reading.

3 Inquiry: Extend Concepts

INVESTIGATE Encourage students to use materials at their independent reading levels or student-friendly search engines to identify relevant and credible sites to gather information about unusual animals people keep as pets. Have students consider how they will present their information.

SMALL GROUP TIME

More Reading for Group Time

ADVANCED

Review
- Cause and Effect
- Inferring

Use this suggested Leveled Reader or other text at students' instructional level.

eStreet Interactive
www.ReadingStreet.com

Use the Leveled Reader Database for lesson plans and student pages for *China's Special Gifts to the World.*

Advanced

Common Core State Standards

Literature 2. Recount stories, including fables, folktales, and myths from diverse cultures; determine the central message, lesson, or moral and explain how it is conveyed through key details in the text. **Literature 4.** Determine the meaning of words and phrases as they are used in a text, distinguishing literal from nonliteral language. **Informational Text 8.** Describe the logical connection between particular sentences and paragraphs in a text (e.g., comparison, cause/effect, first/second/third in a sequence). **Also Informational Text 4.**

1 Build Word Knowledge

Develop Vocabulary

REREAD FOR VOCABULARY Reread the fifth paragraph on p. 414. Let's read this paragraph to find out what *interrupts* means. Discuss meaning and context with students.

2 Read

Happy Birthday Mr. Kang

If you read *Happy Birthday Mr. Kang* during whole group time, then use the instruction below.

CLOSE READING Read pp. 414–415. Have students create a T-chart with the headings **For** and **Against.** Have students search through the text for arguments for and against letting the bird go and complete the chart.

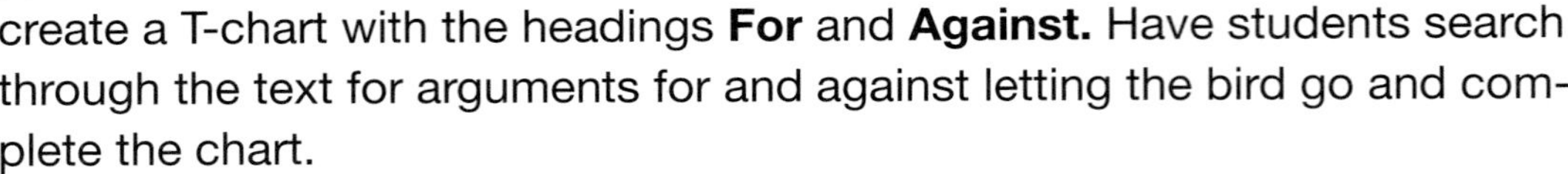

For	Against
The bird should be free, just as Mr. Kang is free from working.	Mr. Kang won't have anything to listen to after he paints his poems.
It's not fair to keep the bird in a cage.	The bird might go hungry or die on its own.

What idea is the author developing here? (There are good reasons for keeping the bird in its cage and good reasons for letting it go.) Which argument wins? Why? (Mr. Kang's because it is his bird and he thinks the bird should be free.)

If you are reading *Happy Birthday Mr. Kang* during small group time, then return to pp. 412–419a to guide the reading.

3 Inquiry: Extend Concepts

INVESTIGATE Provide time for students to investigate their topics in books or online. If necessary, help them locate information that is focused on their topics.

Independent Reading Options

Trade Book Library

eStreet Interactive
www.ReadingStreet.com

Teacher Guides are available on the Leveled Reader Database.

If... students need more scaffolding and practice with the **Main Selection, then...** use the activities on p. DI•47 in the Teacher Resources section on SuccessNet.

Advanced

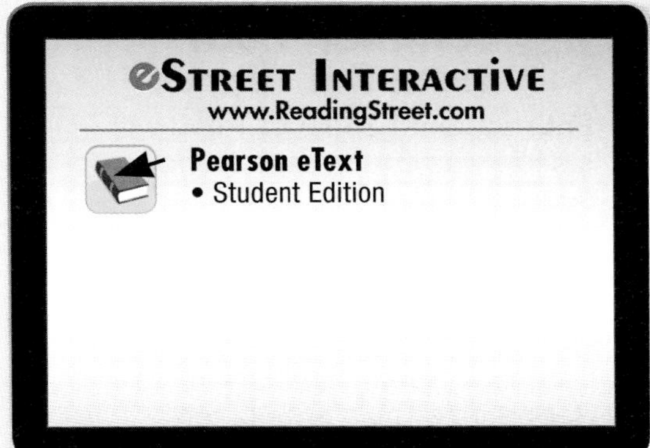

1 Build Word Knowledge

Extend Amazing Words and Selection Vocabulary

territory	release	loyal
deserve	manage	affectionate
companion	retrieve	wandering

nag	bows	chilly
foolish	foreign	narrow
perches	recipe	

Team Talk Have students practice building more complex sentences. Display a sentence starter and have students add oral phrases or clauses using the Amazing Words and the selection vocabulary. Guide students to add at least three phrases or clauses per sentence.

2 Read

"Once Upon a Constitution"

BEFORE READING Have students read the panel information on expository text on p. 424. Then have students use the text features to set a purpose for reading.

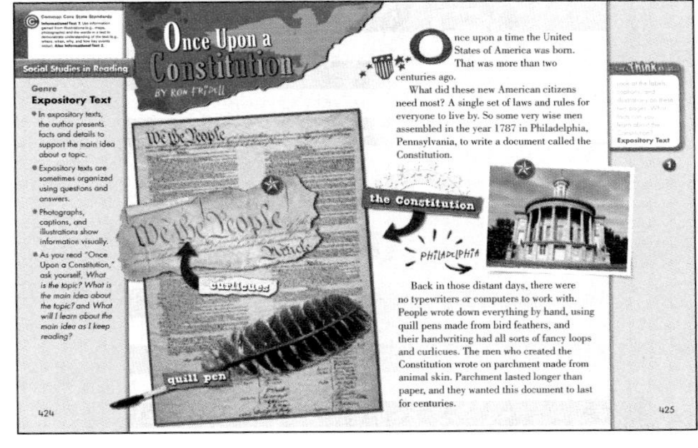

DURING READING Point out that the article is organized into three sections. What pattern does the author repeat in each section? (Each section begins with a question that introduces the main idea, followed by an answer that explains the main idea and gives supporting details.) Why do you think the author used this organization? (It prepares the reader for what is to follow.)

AFTER READING Have students discuss Reading Across Texts. Then have them do Writing Across Texts independently.

3 Inquiry: Extend Concepts

ORGANIZE INFORMATION Provide time for students to organize their information into a format that will effectively communicate their findings to their audience. Provide any necessary materials, such as poster board, markers and other supplies, or computer time.

SMALL GROUP TIME

Independent Reading Options

Trade Book Library

eStreet Interactive
www.ReadingStreet.com
Teacher Guides are available on the Leveled Reader Database.

Advanced

Common Core State Standards

Foundational Skills 4. Read with sufficient accuracy and fluency to support comprehension. **Writing 4.** With guidance and support from adults, produce writing in which the development and organization are appropriate to task and purpose. **Speaking/Listening 4.** Report on a topic or text, tell a story, or recount an experience with appropriate facts and relevant, descriptive details, speaking clearly at an understandable pace. **Language 2.** Demonstrate command of the conventions of standard English capitalization, punctuation, and spelling when writing.

More Reading for Group Time

ADVANCED

Review

- Cause and Effect
- Inferring

Use this suggested Leveled Reader or other text at students' instructional level.

eSTREET INTERACTIVE
www.ReadingStreet.com

Use the Leveled Reader Database for lesson plans and student pages for *China's Special Gifts to the World.*

1 Build Word Knowledge

Extend Abbreviations

IDENTIFY AND EXTEND Have students read the instruction on the bottom of p. 423 and encourage them to explain how to use abbreviations. Have students work in pairs to reread the model limericks and identify the abbreviations the writer used. Then ask students to write their own limericks, making sure they include abbreviations. Allow time for students to discuss their work and correct any misunderstandings.

2 Text-Based Comprehension

Read

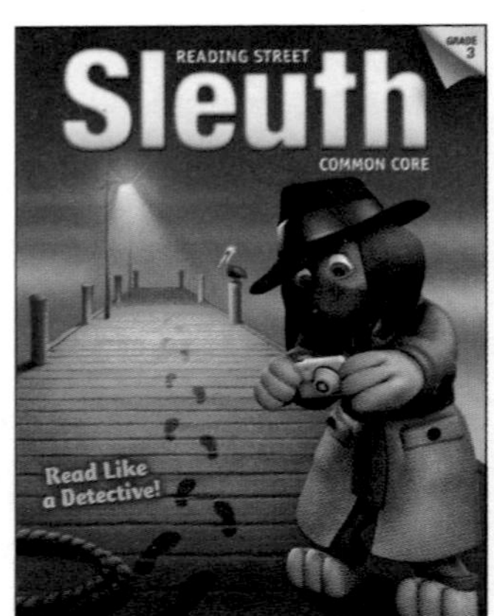

REREAD "Freedom for All" Have partners reread the selection. Have partners discuss how the slaves must have felt about Abraham Lincoln's Emancipation Proclamation.

EXTEND UNDERSTANDING Talk together about how the country might have been different if Lincoln had not freed the slaves.

PERFORMANCE TASK • Prove It! Have students write a poem about freedom. They can write about freedom in general, freedom in their own lives, or freedom as it pertains to the information in this article. Encourage students to make sure their poem has a central message supported by details.

COMMUNICATE Have students share their poems with a small group. Invite discussion about the kinds of messages each poem shared.

3 Inquiry: Extend Concepts

COMMUNICATE Have students share their inquiry projects on unusual animals that people keep in their homes with the rest of the class. Provide the following tips for presenting.

- Use gestures to communicate information, ideas, or actions.
- Make eye contact when answering questions.
- Point to your visuals and explain unfamiliar terms.

Focus on Common Core State Standards

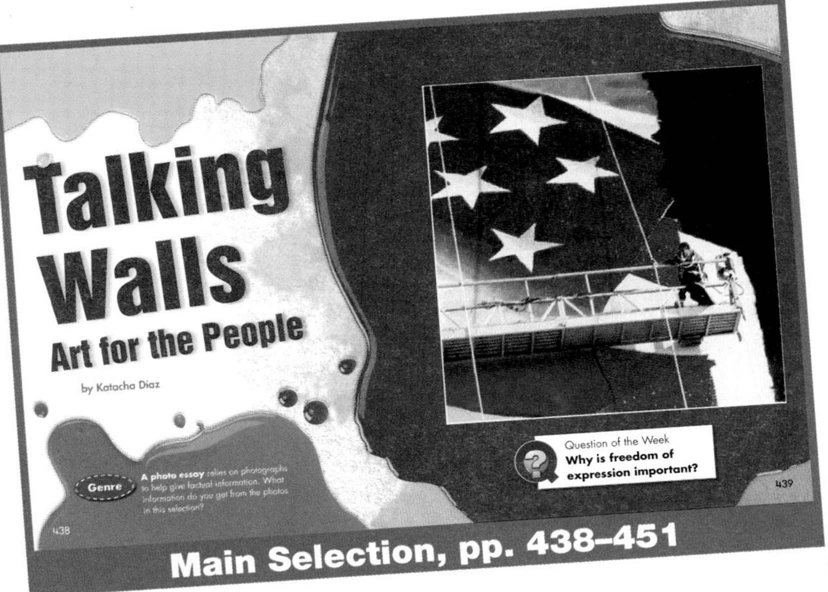

Talking Walls

Art for the People

by Katacha Diaz

Question of the Week

Why is freedom of expression important?

Genre

438 439

Main Selection, pp. 438–451

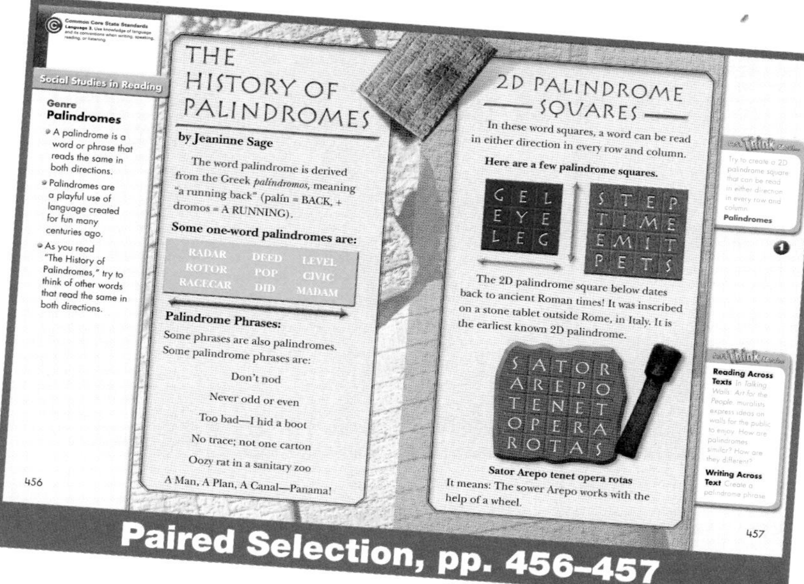

Social Studies in Reading

Genre

Palindromes

- A palindrome is a word or phrase that reads the same in both directions.
- Palindromes are a playful use of language created for fun many centuries ago.
- As you read "The History of Palindromes," try to think of other words that read the same in both directions.

THE HISTORY OF PALINDROMES

by Jeaninne Sage

The word palindrome is derived from the Greek *palindromos,* meaning "a running back" (palin = BACK, + dromos = A RUNNING).

Some one-word palindromes are:

RADAR DEED LEVEL
ROTOR POP CIVIC
RACECAR DID MADAM

Palindrome Phrases:

Some phrases are also palindromes. Some palindrome phrases are:

Don't nod

Never odd or even

Too bad—I hid a boot

No trace; not one carton

Oozy rat in a sanitary zoo

A Man, A Plan, A Canal—Panama!

2D PALINDROME SQUARES

In these word squares, a word can be read in either direction in every row and column.

Here are a few palindrome squares.

G E L / E Y E / L E G

S T E P / T I M E / E M I T / P E T S

The 2D palindrome square below dates back to ancient Roman times! It was inscribed on a stone tablet outside Rome, in Italy. It is the earliest known 2D palindrome.

S A T O R / A R E P O / T E N E T / O P E R A / R O T A S

Sator Arepo tenet opera rotas

It means: The sower Arepo works with the help of a wheel.

456 457

Paired Selection, pp. 456–457

Text-Based Comprehension

Graphic Sources

CCSS Informational Text 7.

Important Ideas

CCSS Informational Text 2.

Fluency

Accuracy

CCSS Foundational Skills 4., CCSS Foundational Skills 4.b.

Writing and Conventions

Trait: Word Choice

CCSS Language 3.a.

Writing Mini-Lesson: Description

CCSS Writing 2.a., CCSS Writing 2.b.

Conventions: Combining Sentences

CCSS Language 1.h., CCSS Language 1.i.

Oral Vocabulary

Amazing Words

creative	lecture
expressive	significant
emotion	pause
artistic	view
exquisite	lyrics

CCSS Language 6.

Selection Vocabulary

Unknown Words

CCSS Language 4., CCSS Language 4.d.

Dictionary/Glossary

CCSS Language 4.d.

encourages	native	social
expression	settled	support
local		

Phonics and Spelling

Final Syllables

CCSS Foundational Skills 3., CCSS Foundational Skills 3.b., CCSS Language 2.e.

question	vacation
creature	mansion
furniture	fiction
division	feature
collision	sculpture
action	vision
direction	celebration
culture	

Challenge Words

fascination	possession
legislature	declaration
manufacture	

Media Literacy

Talk Show

CCSS Speaking/Listening 3.

Preview Your Week

Why is freedom of expression important?

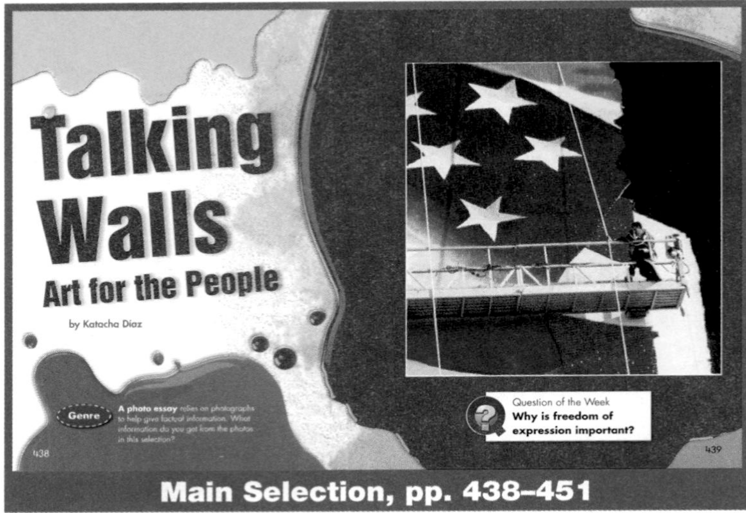

Main Selection, pp. 438–451

Genre: Photo Essay

Vocabulary: Unknown Words

Text-Based Comprehension: Graphic Sources

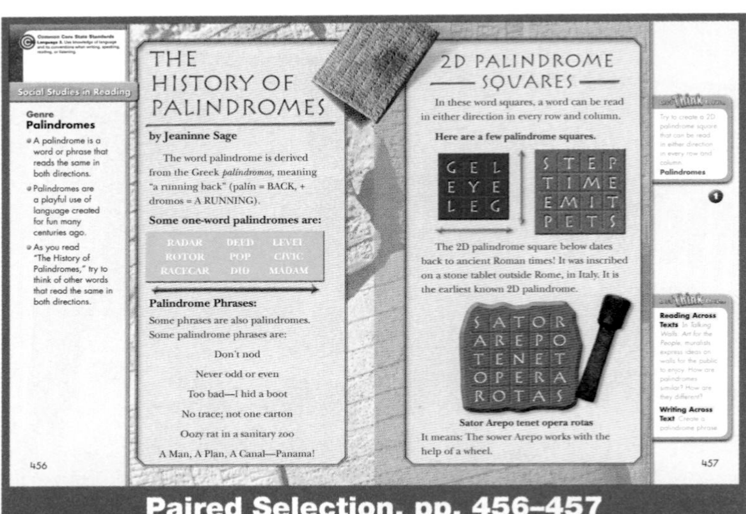

Paired Selection, pp. 456–457

Social Studies in Reading

Genre: Palindromes

Build Content Knowledge

KNOWLEDGE GOALS
Students will understand that freedom of expression

- allows us to express ideas or feelings
- can spread a message

THIS WEEK'S CONCEPT MAP
Develop a concept-related graphic organizer like the one below over the course of this week.

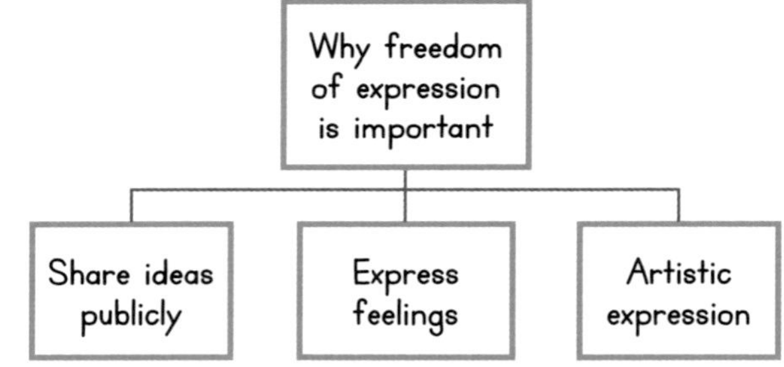

BUILD ORAL VOCABULARY
This week, students will acquire the following academic vocabulary/domain-specific words.

Amazing Words

creative	exquisite	pause
expressive	lecture	view
emotion	significant	lyrics
artistic		

OPTIONAL CONCEPT-BASED READING Use the Digital Path to access readers offering different levels of text complexity.

Concept Literacy

Below-Level

On-Level

Advanced

ELL

ELD

This Week's Digital Resources

eStreet Interactive

www.ReadingStreet.com

Get Ready to Read

Concept Talk Video Use this video on the Digital Path to build momentum and introduce the weekly concept of freedom of expression.

Pearson eText Read the eText of the Student Edition pages on Pearson SuccessNet for comprehension and fluency support.

Envision It! Animations Use this engaging animation on the Digital Path to explain the target comprehension skill, Graphic Sources.

Read and Comprehend

Journal Use the Word Bank on the Digital Path to have students write sentences using this week's selection vocabulary words.

Background Building Audio CD This audio CD provides essential background information about freedom to help students read and comprehend the weekly texts.

Pearson eText Read the eText of the main selection, *Talking Walls: Art for the People,* and the paired selection, "The History of Palindromes," with audio support on Pearson SuccessNet.

Vocabulary Activities A variety of interactive vocabulary activities on the Digital Path help students practice selection vocabulary and concept-related words.

Story Sort Use the Story Sort Activity on the Digital Path after reading *Talking Walls: Art for the People* to involve students in summarizing.

Language Arts

Grammar Jammer Choose a fun animation on the Digital Path to provide an engaging grammar lesson that will capture students' attention.

Pearson eText Find the Student Edition eText of the Let's Write It! and Let's Learn It! pages with audio support on Pearson SuccessNet.

Additional Resources

Teacher Resources DVD-ROM Use the following resources on the TR DVD or on Pearson SuccessNet throughout the week:

- Amazing Word Cards
- Reader's and Writer's Notebook
- Writing Transparencies
- Daily Fix-It Transparencies
- Scoring Rubrics
- Grammar Transparencies
- ELL Support
- Let's Practice It!
- Graphic Organizers
- Vocabulary Cards

This Week's Skills

Phonics/Word Analysis
Final Syllables

Comprehension
Skill: Graphic Sources
Strategy: Important Ideas

Language
Vocabulary: Unknown Words
Conventions: Combining Sentences

Fluency
Accuracy

Writing
Description

5-Day Planner

DAY 1

Get Ready to Read

Content Knowledge 430j
Oral Vocabulary: *creative, expressive, emotion, artistic*

Monitor Progress
Check Oral Vocabulary

Phonics/Word Analysis 432a
Final Syllables
READ Decodable Reader 28A
Reread for Fluency

Read and Comprehend

Text-Based Comprehension 434a
Graphic Sources
Important Ideas

Fluency 434–435
Accuracy

Selection Vocabulary 435a
encourages, expression, local, native, settled, social, support

Language Arts

Research and Inquiry 435b
Identify and Focus Topic

Spelling 435c
Final Syllables, Pretest

Conventions 435d
Combining Sentences

Handwriting 435d
Cursive Letters *G, S,* and *I*

Writing 435e
Description

DAY 2

Get Ready to Read

Content Knowledge 436a
Oral Vocabulary: *exquisite, lecture*

Phonics/Word Analysis 436c
Final Syllables

Monitor Progress
Check Word Reading

Literary Terms 436d
Personification

Read and Comprehend

Vocabulary Skill 436e
Unknown Words

Fluency 436–437
Accuracy

Text-Based Comprehension 438–439
READ *Talking Walls: Art for the People*—1st Read

Language Arts

Research and Inquiry 445b
Navigate/Search

Conventions 445c
Combining Sentences

Spelling 445c
Final Syllables

Writing 445d
Description

DAY 3

Get Ready to Read

Content Knowledge 446a
Oral Vocabulary: *significant, pause*

Phonics/Word Analysis 446c
Final Syllables
Fluent Word Reading
DECODE AND READ
Decodable Practice Passage 28B

Monitor Progress
Check Word Reading

Read and Comprehend

Text-Based Comprehension 446e
Graphic Sources
Important Ideas
READ *Talking Walls: Art for the People*—2nd Read

Monitor Progress
Check Retelling

Fluency 453b
Accuracy

Language Arts

Research and Study Skills 453c
Alphabetical Order

Research and Inquiry 453d
Analyze Information

Conventions 453e
Combining Sentences

Spelling 453e
Final Syllables

Writing 454–455
Description

DAY 4

Get Ready to Read

Content Knowledge 456a
Oral Vocabulary: *view, lyrics*

Phonics/Word Analysis 456c
Review Schwa
Fluent Word Reading
DECODE AND READ
Decodable Practice Passage 28C

Read and Comprehend

Genre 456g
Palindromes
READ "The History of Palindromes"—Paired Selection

Fluency 458–459
Accuracy

Monitor Progress Check Fluency

Vocabulary Skill 459a
Unknown Words

Media Literacy 459a
Talk Show

Language Arts

Research and Inquiry 459b
Synthesize

Conventions 459c
Combining Sentences

Spelling 459c
Final Syllables

Writing 459d
Description

DAY 5

Get Ready to Read

Content Knowledge 459f
Review Oral Vocabulary

Monitor Progress
Check Oral Vocabulary

Read and Comprehend

Text-Based Comprehension 459h
Review Graphic Sources

Vocabulary Skill 459h
Review Unknown Words

Phonics/Word Analysis 459i
Review Final Syllables

Literary Terms 459i
Review Personification

Assessment 459j, 459l

Monitor Progress
Fluency; Graphic Sources

Language Arts

Research and Inquiry 459n
Communicate

Spelling 459o
Final Syllables, Test

Conventions 459o
Combining Sentences

Writing 459p
Description

Wrap Up Your Week! 459q

Access for All

What do I do in group time?

It's as easy as 1-2-3!

1 TEACHER-LED SMALL GROUPS → 2 INDEPENDENT PRACTICE STATIONS → 3 INDEPENDENT READING

Small Group Time

SKILL DEVELOPMENT

- Final Syllables
- Graphic Sources
- Important Ideas
- Unknown Words

DEEP UNDERSTANDING

This Week's Knowledge Goals

Students will understand that freedom of expression

- allows us to express ideas or feelings
- can spread a message

1 Small Group Lesson Plan

	DAY 1 Differentiate Vocabulary	DAY 2 Differentiate Comprehension
On-Level (OL) pp. SG•34–SG•38	**Build Word Knowledge** Practice Amazing Words **Text-Based Comprehension** Read *Reading Street Sleuth,* pp. 72–73 or Leveled Readers	**Build Word Knowledge** Practice Selection Vocabulary **Access Text** Read *Talking Walls: Art for the People*
Strategic Intervention (SI) pp. SG•39–SG•43	**Build Word Knowledge** Reteach Amazing Words **Text-Based Comprehension** Read *Reading Street Sleuth,* pp. 72–73 or Leveled Readers	**Build Word Knowledge** Reteach Selection Vocabulary **Access Text** Read *Talking Walls: Art for the People*
Advanced (A) pp. SG•44–SG•48	**Build Word Knowledge** Extend Amazing Words **Text-Based Comprehension** Read *Reading Street Sleuth,* pp. 72–73 or Leveled Readers	**Build Word Knowledge** Extend Selection Vocabulary **Access Text** Read *Talking Walls: Art for the People*
Independent Inquiry Project	Identify Questions	Investigate
ELL **If...** students need more scaffolding and practice with...	**Vocabulary,** **then...** use the activities on pp. DI•67–DI•68 in the Teacher Resources section on SuccessNet.	**Comprehension Skill,** **then...** use the activities on p. DI•71 in the Teacher Resources section on SuccessNet.

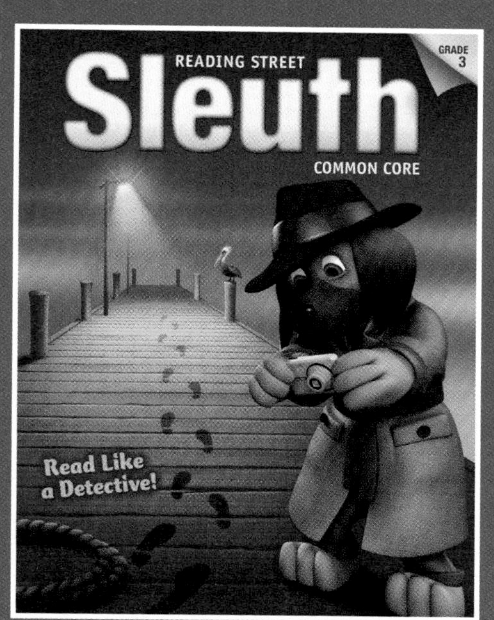

Reading Street Sleuth

- Provides access to grade-level text for all students
- Focuses on finding clues in text through close reading
- Builds capacity for complex text

Build Text-Based Comprehension

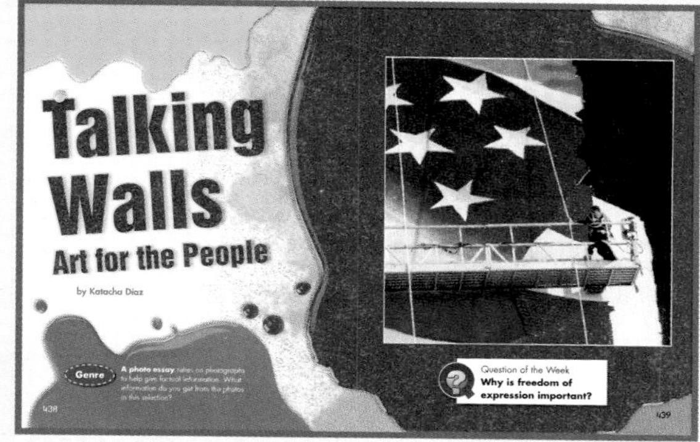

Talking Walls: Art for the People

Optional Leveled Readers

Concept Literacy

Below-Level

On-Level

Advanced

ELL

ELD

DAY 3 Differentiate Close Reading	DAY 4 Differentiate Vocabulary	DAY 5 Differentiate Reteaching
Reread to Develop Vocabulary **Close Reading** Read *Talking Walls: Art for the People*	**Build Word Knowledge** Develop Language Using Amazing Words **Text-Based Comprehension** Read "The History of Palindromes"	**Practice Combining Sentences** **Text-Based Comprehension** Reread *Reading Street Sleuth,* pp. 72–73 or Leveled Readers
Reread to Develop Vocabulary **Close Reading** Read *Talking Walls: Art for the People*	**Build Word Knowledge** Review/Discuss Amazing Words **Text-Based Comprehension** Read "The History of Palindromes"	**Review Combining Sentences** **Text-Based Comprehension** Reread *Reading Street Sleuth,* pp. 72–73 or Leveled Readers
Reread to Extend Vocabulary **Close Reading** Read *Talking Walls: Art for the People* Investigate	**Build Word Knowledge** Extend Amazing Words and Selection Vocabulary **Text-Based Comprehension** Read "The History of Palindromes" Organize	**Extend Combining Sentences** **Text-Based Comprehension** Reread *Reading Street Sleuth,* pp. 72–73 or Leveled Readers Communicate
Main Selection, **then...** use the activities on p. DI•72 in the Teacher Resources section on SuccessNet.	**Amazing Words,** **then...** use the Routine on pp. xxxvi–xxxvii in the *ELL Handbook.*	**Conventions and Writing,** **then...** use the Grammar Transition Lessons on pp. 312–386 in the *ELL Handbook.*

2 Independent Stations

Practice Last Week's Skills

★ Focus on these activities when time is limited.

ACCESS FOR ALL
- ● Below-Level Activities
- ▲ On-Level Activities
- ■ Advanced Activities

WORD WISE

Spell and use words in sentences.

OBJECTIVES

- Spell words with schwa spelled with an *a, e, i, o, u,* and *y.*

MATERIALS

- *Word Wise* Flip Chart Activity 28, teacher-made word cards, paper and pencils

 **Letter Tile Drag and Drop**

● Students write five words, write a sentence with each word, and then list other words with the *schwa* sound spelled with an *a, e, i, o, u,* or *y.*

▲ Students write seven words, write a sentence with each word, and then list other words with the *schwa* sound spelled with an *a, e, i, o, u,* or *y.*

■ Students write nine words, write a sentence with each word, and then list other words with the *schwa* sound spelled with an *a, e, i, o, u,* or *y.*

WORD WORK

Identify and pronounce words.

OBJECTIVES

- Identify and pronounce words with schwa sound spelled with an *a, e, i, o, u,* and *y.*

MATERIALS

- *Word Work* Flip Chart Activity 28, dictionary, paper and pencils

 **Letter Tile Drag and Drop**

● Students list five dictionary words with the schwa sound. Students write their pronunciations and circle the schwa.

▲ Students list eight dictionary words with the schwa sound. Students write their pronunciations and circle the schwa.

■ Students find, list, and say ten dictionary words with the schwa sound (four with the schwa in the first syllable, four in the last, and two in the middle). Students write the pronunciations and circle the schwa.

LET'S WRITE!

Write poetry.

OBJECTIVES

- Write a limerick.

MATERIALS

- *Let's Write!* Flip Chart Activity 28, paper and pencils

 **Grammar Jammer**

● Students write a funny limerick. The first, second, and fifth lines should rhyme. The third line should rhyme with the fourth line.

▲ Students write a humorous limerick, underline the rhyming words in the first, second, and fifth lines, and circle the rhymes in the third and fourth lines.

■ Students write a funny limerick and include rebuses, or pictures, for some of the rhyming words in the poem.

WORDS TO KNOW

Determine word meanings.

OBJECTIVES

- Identify and define antonyms.

MATERIALS

- *Words to Know* Flip Chart Activity 28, teacher-made word cards, paper and pencils

 **Vocabulary Activities**

● Students choose three pairs of antonyms, use a dictionary to check word meanings, and write sentences for the words.

▲ Students choose five pairs of antonyms, use a dictionary to check word meanings, and write sentences for the words.

■ Students choose seven pairs of antonyms, write a sentence for each pair to show the opposite meanings, and list other words and their antonyms.

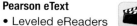

READ FOR MEANING

Use comprehension skills.

OBJECTIVES

- Identify cause and effect.

MATERIALS

- *Read for Meaning* Flip Chart Activity 28, Leveled Readers, paper and pencils

 **Pearson eText**
- Leveled eReaders

 **Envision It! Animations**

● Students read a book, write one sentence telling an event that happened, and write one sentence telling what caused it to happen.

▲ Students read a book, make a two-column chart labeled *Cause* and *Effect,* and list at least two events and their causes.

■ Students read a book, make a two-column chart with the headings *Cause* and *Effect,* and fill in the chart with examples from the text.

GET FLUENT

Practice reading fluently with partners.

OBJECTIVES

- Read aloud with appropriate phrasing.

MATERIALS

- *Get Fluent* Flip Chart Activity 28, Leveled Readers

 **Pearson eText**
- Leveled eReaders

● Partners take turns reading aloud with appropriate phrasing from a Concept Literacy Reader or Below-Level Reader and providing feedback.

▲ Partners take turns reading aloud with appropriate phrasing from an On-Level Reader and providing feedback.

■ Partners take turns reading aloud with appropriate phrasing from an Advanced Reader and providing feedback.

Manage the Stations

Use these management tools to set up and organize your Practice Stations:

Practice Station Flip Charts

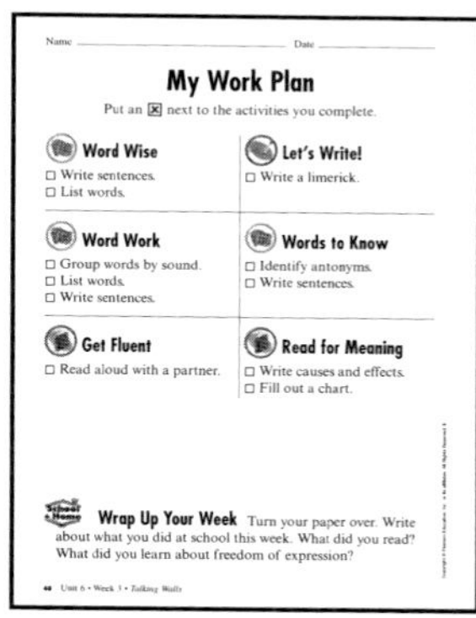

Name ______ Date ______

My Work Plan

Put an ☒ next to the activities you complete.

Word Wise
- ☐ Write sentences.
- ☐ List words.

Let's Write!
- ☐ Write a limerick.

Word Work
- ☐ Group words by sound.
- ☐ List words.
- ☐ Write sentences.

Words to Know
- ☐ Identify antonyms.
- ☐ Write sentences.

Get Fluent
- ☐ Read aloud with a partner.

Read for Meaning
- ☐ Write causes and effects.
- ☐ Fill out a chart.

Wrap Up Your Week Turn your paper over. Write about what you did at school this week. What did you read? What did you learn about freedom of expression?

46 Unit 6 • Week 3 • *Talking Walls*

Classroom Management Handbook for Differentiated Instruction Practice Stations, p. 46

3 Independent Reading

Students should select appropriate complex texts to read and write about independently every day before, during, and after school.

Suggestions for this week's independent reading:

- Informational texts on last week's social studies topic: What it means to grant freedom
- Nonfiction selections about what it means to grant freedom
- A nonfiction book by a favorite author

BOOK TALK Have partners discuss their independent reading for the week. Tell them to refer to their Reading Logs and paraphrase what each selection was about. Then have students focus on discussing one or more of the following:

Key Ideas and Details

- What does the text say explicitly or directly about its topic?
- State the text's main idea in your own words.

Craft and Structure

- How do the body paragraphs relate to the introductory paragraph?
- What ideas in the body paragraphs support the main idea in the introduction?

Integration of Ideas

- What is the author's point of view? What does he or she think about the topic?
- What words or phrases help you identify the author's point of view?

 **Pearson eText**
- Student Edition
- Decodable Readers
- Leveled Readers

 **Trade Book Library**

 **School or Classroom Library**

DAY 1 at a Glance

Content Knowledge
Oral Vocabulary

Phonics/Word Analysis
Final Syllables

Text-Based Comprehension
Graphic Sources
Important Ideas

Fluency
Accuracy

Selection Vocabulary

Research and Inquiry
Identify and Focus Topic

Spelling
Final Syllables

Conventions
Combining Sentences

Handwriting
Cursive Letters *G, S,* and *I*

Writing
Description

Materials

- Student Edition
- Reader's and Writer's Notebook
- Decodable Reader

Bridge to Common Core

INTEGRATION OF KNOWLEDGE/IDEAS
This week, students will read, write, and talk about freedom of expression.

Texts This Week

- "Toothpicks, Bottles, Tin, and Rocks"
- "Ancient Cave Murals"
- "Class Art"
- *Talking Walls: Art for the People*
- "The History of Palindromes"

Social Studies Knowledge Goals
Students will understand that freedom of expression

- allows us to express ideas or feelings
- can spread a message

Street Rhymes!

Writing poems and stories
is an artistic thing to do.
It also is creative [important] to
express your point of view.
What can you write that's inside of you?

- To introduce this week's concept, read aloud the poem several times and ask students to join you.

Content Knowledge

Freedom of Expression

CONCEPT TALK To further explore the unit concept of Freedom, this week students will read, write, and talk about freedom of expression. Write the Question of the Week on the board, *Why is freedom of expression important?*

Build Oral Language

TALK ABOUT FREEDOM OF EXPRESSION Have students turn to pp. 430–431 in their Student Editions. Look at each of the photos. Then use the prompts to guide discussion and create a concept map.

- Why is it important for the boy to be able to speak in front of his class? (Freedom of speech is important so the boy can share his ideas.) Freedom of expression allows us to *share ideas publicly.* Let's add this to our concept map.
- What emotion are the children in the large photo on pp. 430–431 expressing? (enthusiasm/joy) Freedom of expression allows us to *express feelings.* Let's add this to the concept map.
- Which photos show artistic expression? (the photos of the girls singing and playing the piano and the boy reading his writing) Let's add *Artistic expression* to our concept map.
- After discussing the photos, ask: Why is freedom of expression important?

Common Core State Standards
Speaking/Listening 1.c. Ask questions to check understanding of information presented, stay on topic, and link their comments to the remarks of others. **Also Language 6.**

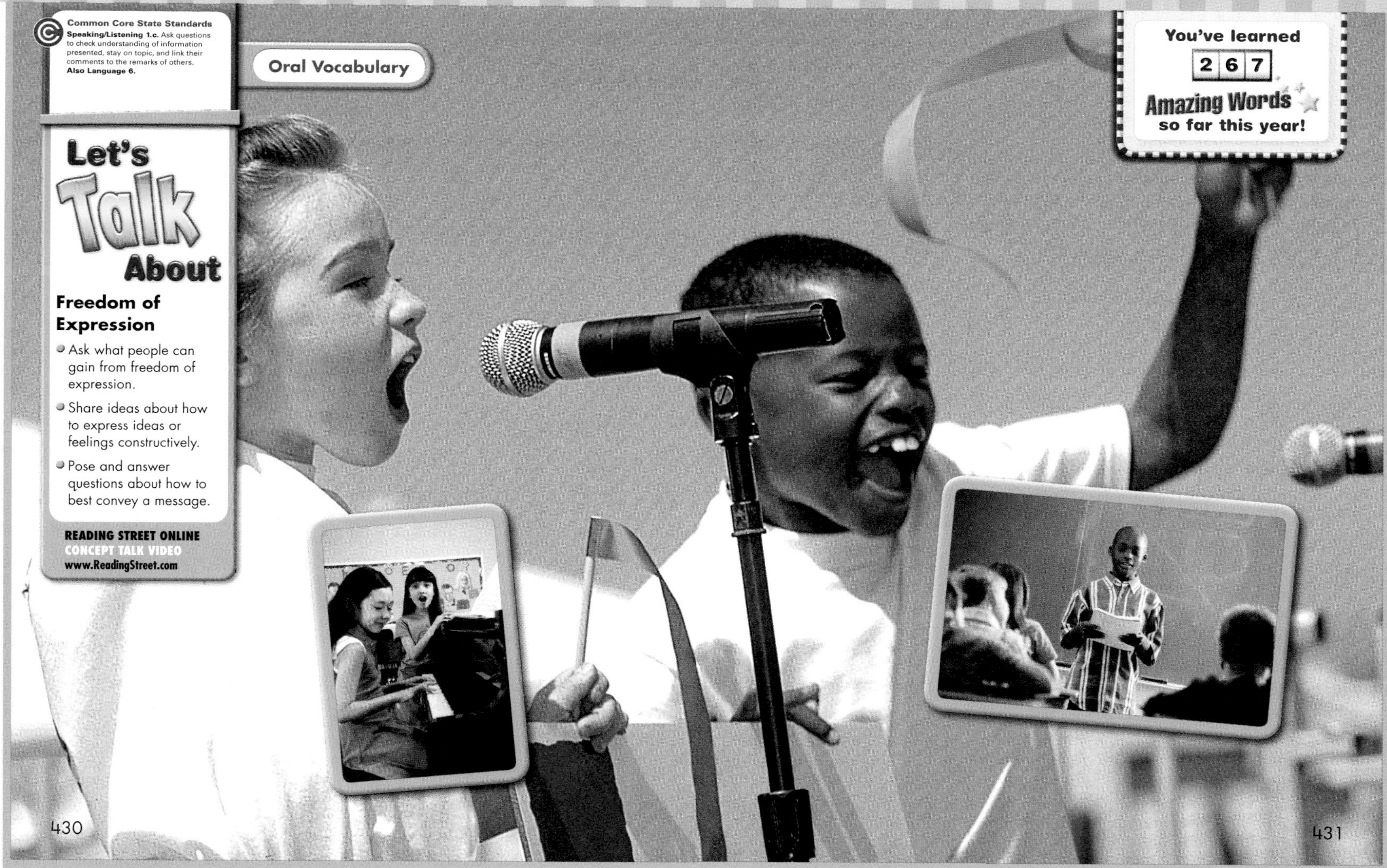

Oral Vocabulary
Let's Talk About
Freedom of Expression
Ask what people can gain from freedom of expression.
Share ideas about how to express ideas or feelings constructively.
Pose and answer questions about how to best convey a message.
READING STREET ONLINE
CONCEPT TALK VIDEO
www.ReadingStreet.com
You've learned
2 6 7
Amazing Words
so far this year!
430
431
Student Edition, pp. 430–431

CONNECT TO READING Tell students that this week they will be reading about why freedom of expression is important. Throughout the week, encourage students to add concept-related words to this week's concept map.

Why freedom of expression is important
Share ideas publicly
Express feelings
Artistic expression

eSTREET INTERACTIVE
www.ReadingStreet.com
- **Pearson eText**
  - Student Edition
- **Concept Talk Video**

ELL

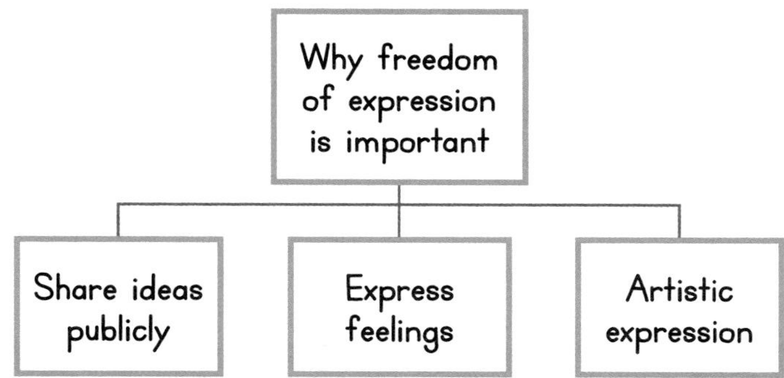

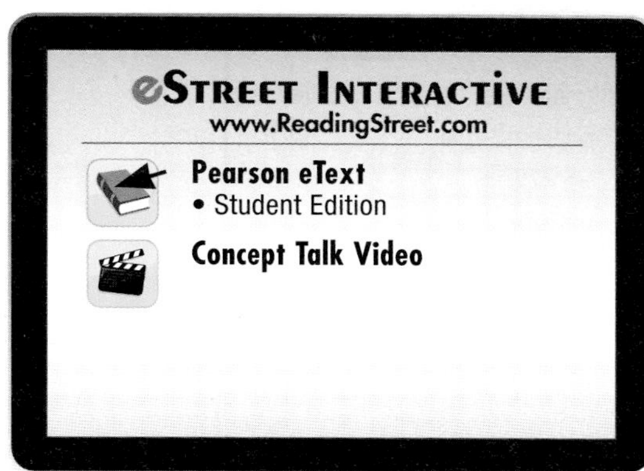

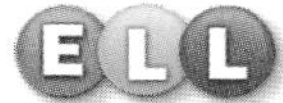

Preteach Concepts Use the Day 1 instruction on ELL Poster 28 to build knowledge, develop concepts, and build oral vocabulary.

ELL Support Additional ELL support and modified instruction are provided in the *ELL Handbook* and in the ELL Support lessons found on the *Teacher Resources DVD-ROM.*

Common Core State Standards

Speaking/Listening 1. Engage effectively in a range of collaborative discussions (one-on-one, in groups, and teacher led) with diverse partners on grade 3 topics and texts, building on others' ideas and expressing their own clearly. **Speaking/Listening 2.** Determine the main ideas and supporting details of a text read aloud or information presented in diverse media and formats, including visually, quantitatively, and orally. **Language 4.** Determine or clarify the meaning of unknown and multiple-meaning words and phrases based on grade 3 reading and content, choosing flexibly from a range of strategies. **Language 6.** Acquire and use accurately grade-appropriate conversational, general academic, and domain-specific words and phrases, including those that signal spatial and temporal relationships (e.g., *After dinner that night we went looking for them*).

Amazing Words

You've learned 267 words so far.

You'll learn 010 words this week!

creative	lecture
expressive	significant
emotion	pause
artistic	view
exquisite	lyrics

Content Knowledge

Build Oral Vocabulary

INTRODUCE AMAZING WORDS "Toothpicks, Bottles, Tin, and Rocks" on p. 431b is about artistic expression. Tell students to listen for this week's Amazing Words—*creative, expressive, emotion,* and *artistic*—as you read.

Amazing Words Robust Vocabulary Routine

1. **Introduce** Write the word *creative* on the board. Have students say the word aloud with you. In the story, we learn that the artists have all been *creative* in making their art forms. What does *creative* mean? Supply a student-friendly definition. *Creative* means having the power to create things or ideas.
2. **Demonstrate** Have students answer questions to demonstrate understanding. What *creative* material does Wayne Kusy use in his art? Why do artists need to be *creative?*
3. **Apply** Ask students what elements they might find in a *creative* story.
4. **Display the Word** Run your hand under the syllables *cre-a-tive* as you read the word. Have students say the word again.

See p. OV•3 to teach *expressive, emotion,* and *artistic.*

Routines Flip Chart

AMAZING WORDS AT WORK Reread "Toothpicks, Bottles, Tin, and Rocks" aloud. As students listen, have them notice how the Amazing Words are used in context. To build oral vocabulary, lead the class in a discussion about the Amazing Words' meanings. Then have students state the main idea of the selection and give supporting details.

Check Oral Vocabulary

During discussion, listen for students' use of Amazing Words.

If... students are unable to use the Amazing Words in discussion,
then... use the Oral Vocabulary Routine in the Routines Flip Chart to demonstrate words in different contexts.

Teacher Read Aloud

MODEL FLUENCY As you read "Toothpicks, Bottles, Tin, and Rocks," model accuracy with smooth, fluent reading.

Toothpicks, Bottles, Tin, and Rocks

Close your eyes and picture an artist at work. What do you see? Do you see someone brushing paints on a canvas or molding clay? Many artists use paints or clay, but some become very creative with their materials.

Whenever Wayne Kusy sees a toothpick, he thinks of a huge ship. To Wayne, a toothpick is not just a sliver of wood. It's a way for him to express himself. Wayne has been making model ships out of toothpicks since he was ten years old. He includes tiny details on his ships, such as portholes, stairways, and even lifeboats with teeny oars for rowing. Wayne once used 75,000 toothpicks to build a ten-foot model of the famous ocean liner *Titanic.*

In the art world, Wayne Kusy is known as an outsider artist. That means that he never went to art school. Outsider artists often work with unlikely materials, such as recycled trash, chunks of cardboard, burnt matchsticks, used chewing gum, and hunks of scrap metal.

Tressa Prisbrey, known as "Grandma," spent 25 years turning old bottles into something she calls Bottle Village. For many years, Grandma collected old bottles. She decided to make walls of bottles held together with concrete. Those walls eventually turned into a quirky village with buildings, gardens, shrines, walkways, and even wishing wells.

Through the years Grandma added all sorts of other expressive objects to her village, including doll heads, TV screens, and car headlights—all recovered from the garbage dump.

Grandma's Bottle Village has been declared a historical treasure by the United States government. It never made Grandma rich, but that was fine with her. The emotion people felt while walking through her whimsical village was enough for her.

Charlie Lucas is another artist who spends lots of time at the dump. But instead of bottles, Charlie looks for scrap metal. He makes sculptures and statues out of the metal that others have thrown away. That's why people call him the "Tin Man."

Charlie's yard has metal sculptures of enormous birds and prehistoric dinosaurs, and even a big rusty handmade airplane. People from all around the world buy Charlie's art and exhibit his sculptures in museums. But Charlie still says his sculptures are his toys. "If I called them anything else, I wouldn't know what I was talking about," said the Tin Man.

Artists like Wayne, Grandma, and the Tin Man see toothpicks, bottles, and tin in brand-new ways. They use these everyday objects to make artistic creations that amaze us all.

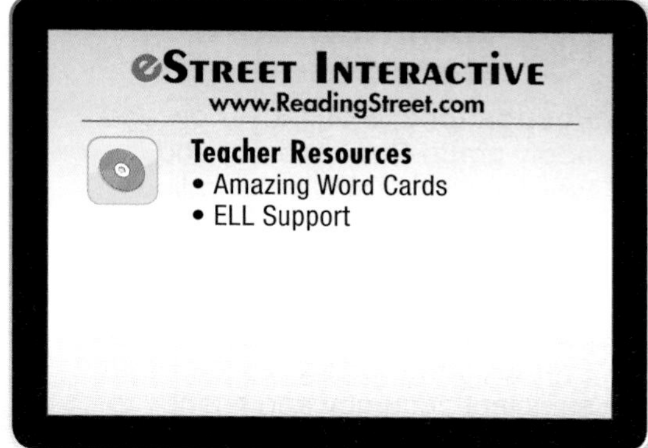

ELL Support for Read Aloud Use the modified Read Aloud on p. DI•69 of the ELL Support lessons on the *Teacher Resources DVD-ROM* to prepare students to listen to "Toothpicks, Bottles, Tin, and Rocks."

Support Listening Comprehension Before listening, have small groups of students discuss what they know about different types of art, such as sculptures. Of what are sculptures made? Where have students seen sculptures before? Share with the group. After listening, have students compare those experiences to what they heard in the Read Aloud.

Common Core State Standards

Foundational Skills 3. Know and apply grade-level phonics and word analysis skills in decoding words. **Foundational Skills 3.b.** Decode words with common Latin suffixes. **Foundational Skills 3.c.** Decode multisyllable words. **Foundational Skills 4.** Read with sufficient accuracy and fluency to support comprehension.

Skills Trace

Final Syllables

Introduce U6W3D1

Practice U6W3D3; U6W3D4

Reteach/Review U6W3D5; U6W4D4

Assess/Test Weekly Test U6W3
Benchmark Test U6

KEY: U=Unit W=Week D=Day

Vocabulary Support

You may wish to explain the meanings of these words.

culture the beliefs, practices, and customs of a particular people

native a person born in a certain place or country

adventure an exciting series of events

Word Analysis

Teach/Model

Final Syllables

REVIEW Write *childhood* and *babyish.* You already can read words like these. Each is a base word with an ending. Read these words. Today you will learn to read words with final syllables *-tion, -ion, -ture, -ive,* and *-ize.*

MODEL Write *collection. Collection* is a three-syllable word. I recognize the syllable *-tion.* When I see this word, I break it into parts. Cover the *-tion.* When I cover the *-tion,* I recognize the word *collect.* Uncover the *-tion.* Then I read the word ending: *-tion.* I put these parts together to read the word *collection.* Word endings change how a word is used. For example, to *collect* something is to gather something. *I collect toy cars.* A *collection* is a group of similar objects. *My toy car collection won a prize.*

GROUP PRACTICE Continue the process. This time have students read the words with you. Identify each final syllable.

culture	**active**	**realize**	**adventure**	**education**
native	**summarize**	**celebration**	**direction**	**expression**

REVIEW What do you know about reading words with these final syllables? When you recognize one of these final syllables, break the word into parts, read each part, and then put the parts together to read the whole word.

Guide Practice

MODEL Have students turn to p. 432 in their Student Editions. Each word on this page has one of the above final syllables. The first word is *contraction.* I recognize the ending *-tion,* and I recognize the first part: *contrac.* I put the parts together and read the whole word: *contraction.*

GROUP PRACTICE For each word in Words I Can Blend, ask for the word parts. Make sure that students identify the final syllables. Then have them read the words.

Corrective feedback

If... students have difficulty reading a word,
then... model reading the parts and then the whole word, and then ask students to read it with you.

Phonics

Final Syllables *-tion, -ion, -ture, -ive, -ize*

Words I Can Blend

contraction
cushion
puncture
festive
specialize

Sentences I Can Read

1. The word *I'll* is a contraction.
2. The scissors created a puncture mark on the cushion.
3. Party planners specialize in festive occasions.

432

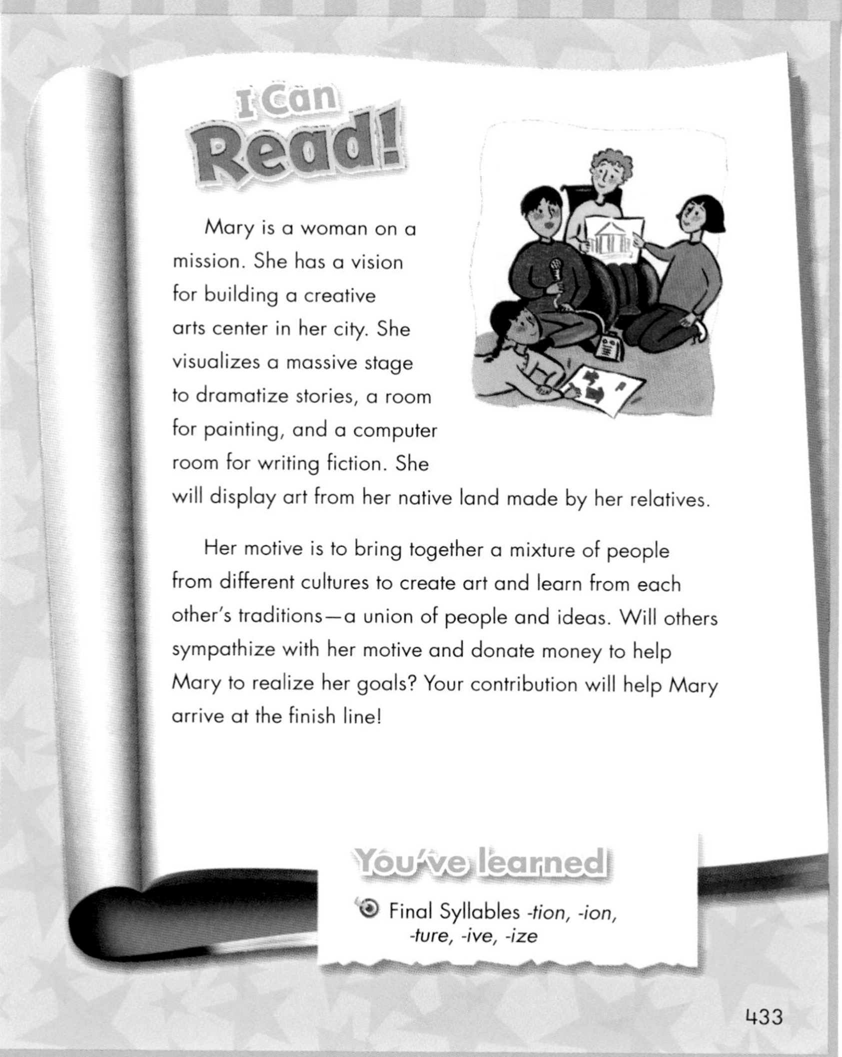

I Can Read!

Mary is a woman on a mission. She has a vision for building a creative arts center in her city. She visualizes a massive stage to dramatize stories, a room for painting, and a computer room for writing fiction. She will display art from her native land made by her relatives.

Her motive is to bring together a mixture of people from different cultures to create art and learn from each other's traditions—a union of people and ideas. Will others sympathize with her motive and donate money to help Mary to realize her goals? Your contribution will help Mary arrive at the finish line!

You've learned

Final Syllables *-tion, -ion, -ture, -ive, -ize*

433

Student Edition, pp. 432–433

Apply

READ WORDS IN ISOLATION After students can successfully combine the words parts to read the words on p. 432 in their Student Editions, point to words in random order and ask students to read them naturally.

READ WORDS IN CONTEXT Have students read each of the sentences on p. 432. Have them identify words in the sentences that have final syllables *-tion, -ion, -ture, -ive,* and *-ize.*

Team Talk Pair students and have them take turns reading each of the sentences aloud.

Chorally read the I Can Read! passage on p. 433 with the students. Then have them read the passage aloud to themselves.

ON THEIR OWN For additional Practice, use the *Reader's and Writer's Notebook* p. 407.

Name ______ Talking Walls

Syllables with *-tion, -sion, -ture, -ive, -ize*

Directions Circle the correctly spelled word in each pair.

1. commosion (commotion)
2. (invasion) invation
3. generasion (generation)
4. posision (position)
5. relaxasion (relaxation)
6. (division) divisition
7. vacasion (vacation)
8. explotion (explosion)

Directions Add -ture, -ive, or -ize to complete each word below. Write the complete word on the line. (HINT: there is only one correct choice for each word.)

9. pas pasture
10. act active
11. rup rupture
12. mass massive
13. maxim maximize
14. real realize
15. cap capture
16. adven adventure

Directions Choose four words from the above list and write a sentence for each word.

17. Sentences will vary.
18. ______
19. ______
20. ______

Home Activity Your child identified and wrote words that end with the syllables -tion, -sion, -ture, -ive, and -ize. Work together to write sentences using the words from the page above. Ask your child to underline the final syllable in the words used from this page.

Phonics Syllables -tion, -sion, -ture, -ive, -ize 407

Reader's and Writer's Notebook, p. 407

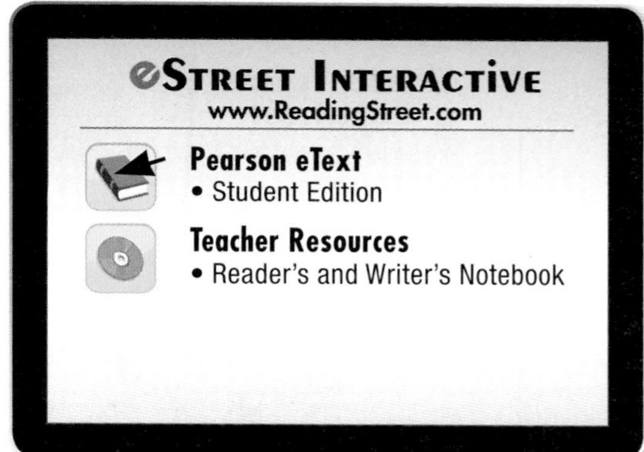

Final Syllables The suffix *-tion* has similar forms in other languages, including French (*-tion*), Spanish (*-scion, -sión*), Haitian Creole (*-syon*), and Portuguese (*ção*). For example, the English word *direction* is *direction* in French, *dirección* in Spanish, *direksyon* in Haitian Creole, and *direção* in Portuguese.

Common Core State Standards

Foundational Skills 3. Know and apply grade-level phonics and word analysis skills in decoding words. **Foundational Skills 3.b** Decode words with common Latin suffixes. **Foundational Skills 3.d.** Read grade-appropriate irregularly spelled words. **Foundational Skills 4.** Read with sufficient accuracy and fluency to support comprehension. **Speaking/Listening 5.** Create engaging audio recordings of stories or poems that demonstrate fluid reading at an understandable pace; add visual displays when appropriate to emphasize or enhance certain facts or details. **Also Literature 2., Foundational Skills 3.c.**

Decodable Reader 28A

If students need help, then...

Read *Chase Takes a Vacation*

READ WORDS IN ISOLATION Have students turn to p. 145 in *Decodable Practice Readers* 3.2. Have students read each word.

Have students read the high-frequency words *was, the, wasn't, a, would, have, of, to, only, could, gone, there, said, very, wanted,* and *water* on the first page.

PREVIEW Have students read the title and preview the story. Tell them that they will read words with final syllables *-tion, -ion, -ture, -ive,* and *-ize.*

READ WORDS IN CONTEXT Pair students for reading and listen as they read. One student begins. Students read the entire story, switching readers after each page. Partners reread the story. This time the other student begins. Make sure that students are monitoring their accuracy when they decode words.

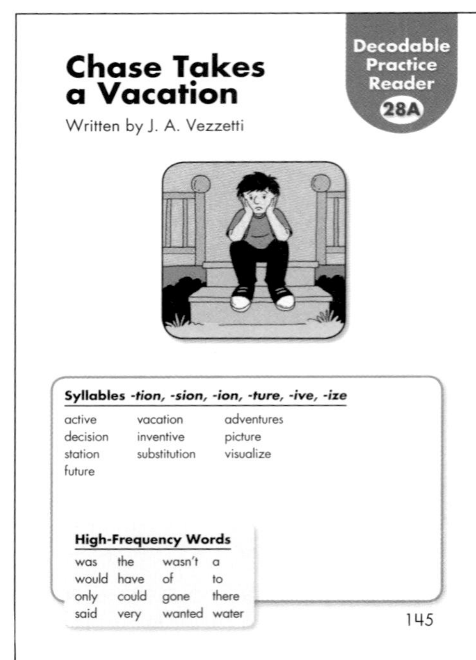

Chase Takes a Vacation

Written by J. A. Vezzetti

Decodable Practice Reader 28A

Syllables *-tion, -sion, -ion, -ture, -ive, -ize*

active	vacation	adventures
decision	inventive	picture
station	substitution	visualize
future		

High-Frequency Words

was	the	wasn't	a
would	have	of	to
only	could	gone	there
said	very	wanted	water

145

Decodable Practice Reader 28A

Henry Tucker was the unhappiest boy in Port Town. His cat Chase had disappeared six weeks ago. At first Henry wasn't worried. Chase was active and often took a vacation, but he always came back in a few days. Henry thought that Chase would have lots of good stories to tell about his adventures—if only Chase could talk!

146

After Chase had been gone for three days, Henry made a decision to search. First he looked carefully in all the places that Chase might hide. Chase wasn't in the shed in the garden or in the maple tree by the fence. He wasn't under the porch of the red house on Vine Street.

147

Chase wasn't in the boxes behind the bookstore or by the food market. He wasn't in the tall grass or under the hedges around the pond.

Next Henry was inventive. He posted signs all over town. The signs had the word *Missing,* a picture of Chase, and a phone number. Henry waited by the phone, but no one called.

148

As the days went by, Henry grew discouraged. His dad took him to the police station and the animal pound. There were lots of cats there, but no Chase. Dad said, "Maybe you want to get another cat."

A substitution for Chase? Henry could not visualize that. Chase was much too special a cat.

149

Henry thought about Chase all the time. He recalled that Chase often sat on Henry's desk while he worked. Chase gracefully tucked his paws and watched Henry with big green eyes. Now the desk looked empty. At night in bed Chase would curl up right next to Henry. It was a bit uncomfortable at first, but Henry got used to it. Now his bed felt very lonely.

150

Cat ownership was often hard and messy, but all that Henry recalled now was Chase purring and rubbing on his legs. Henry had disliked it when Chase misbehaved. Now Henry wished that Chase would come back and misbehave as much as he wanted. Henry slumped lower on the steps. The future did not look bright.

151

Suddenly Chase reappeared in the yard. Unprepared for this sight, Henry didn't move. Then he grabbed and hugged the cat tightly. Chase squirmed free and licked his ruffled fur. He looked at Henry as if to say, "How about refreshments?"

Henry smiled and refilled the food and water dishes. Chase was home.

152

Corrective feedback	**If...** students have difficulty reading a word, **then...** refer them to the *Sound-Spelling Cards* to identify the word parts individually and then together to say the word. • What is the new word? • Is the new word a word you know? • Does it make sense in the story?

CHECK DECODING AND COMPREHENSION Have students retell the story to include characters, setting, and events. Then have students find words in the story that have final syllables *-tion, -ion, -ture, -ive,* and *-ize.* Students should find *active, vacation, adventures, decision, inventive, picture, station, substitution, visualize,* and *future.*

EXTRA PRACTICE Have students take turns recording the story as they read. Then ask each student to review his or her recording to identify areas to improve reading fluency.

Reread for Fluency

REREAD DECODABLE READER Have students reread *Decodable Practice Reader 28A* to develop automaticity decoding words with final syllables *-tion, -ion, -ture, -ive,* and *-ize.*

Routine Oral Rereading

1. **Read** Have students read the entire book orally.
2. **Reread** To achieve optimal fluency, students should reread the text three or four times.
3. **Corrective Feedback** Listen as students read. Provide corrective feedback regarding their fluency and decoding.

Routines Flip Chart

Final Syllables

Beginning Have students make a set of flashcards with the *-tion, -ion, -ture, -ive,* and *-ize* words from the *Decodable Practice Reader: active, decision, station, future, vacation, inventive, substitution, adventures, picture,* and *visualize.* Have students work with a partner to gain fluency in reading the words by using the flashcards.

Intermediate After reading, have students orally use each of the words with these syllables from the *Decodable Practice Reader* in a sentence.

Advanced After reading, have students write about a future adventure they would like to have. Remind them to use words with final syllables *-tion, -ion, -ture, -ive,* and *-ize* and high-frequency words from the *Decodable Practice Reader* in their writing.

Common Core State Standards

Informational Text 2. Determine the main idea of a text; recount the key details and explain how they support the main idea. **Informational Text 7.** Use information gained from illustrations (e.g., maps, photographs), and the words in a text to demonstrate understanding of the text (e.g., where, when, why, and how key events occur). **Foundational Skills 4.** Read with sufficient accuracy and fluency to support comprehension. **Foundational Skills 4.b.** Read on-level prose and poetry orally with accuracy, appropriate rate, and expression on successive readings.

Skills Trace

Graphic Sources

Introduce U3W3D1; U4W2D1; U6W3D1
Practice U3W3D2; U3W3D3; U4W1D3; U4W2D2; U4W2D3; U6W3D2; U6W3D3
Reteach/Review U3W3D5; U4W2D5; U6W3D5
Assess/Test Weekly Tests U3W3; U4W2; U6W3
Benchmark Tests
KEY: U=Unit W=Week D=Day

Academic Vocabulary

accuracy reading without errors or mistakes

chart a diagram or table showing information

Comprehension Support

Students may also turn to pp. EI•10, EI•11, and EI•19 to review the skill and strategy if necessary.

Text-Based Comprehension

Graphic Sources
Important Ideas

READ Remind students of the weekly concept—Freedom of Expression. Have students read "Ancient Cave Murals" on p. 435.

MODEL A CLOSE READ

Think Aloud: Graphic sources are ways of showing information in a way you can see. The photo of the cave paintings is a graphic source—it shows what the murals look like. The color wheel is another graphic source. One important idea in this article is that two or more colors of paint can be mixed together to make a different color. The color wheel helped me to see how the primary colors can be mixed to get many other colors.

TEACH Have students read p. 434. Explain that the skill of graphic sources and the strategy of determining important ideas are tools they can use to deepen understanding of the text. Review the bulleted items and explanations on p. 434. Have students explain the multistep directions for making green paint on p. 435.

GUIDE PRACTICE Have students reread "Ancient Cave Murals" using the callouts as guides. Then ask volunteers to respond to the questions in the callouts, citing specific examples from the text to support their answers.

Skill Orange, yellow, black, white, gray
Strategy There are only three primary colors.
Skill Red and yellow

APPLY Use *Reader's and Writer's Notebook* p. 408 for additional practice with Cause and Effect.

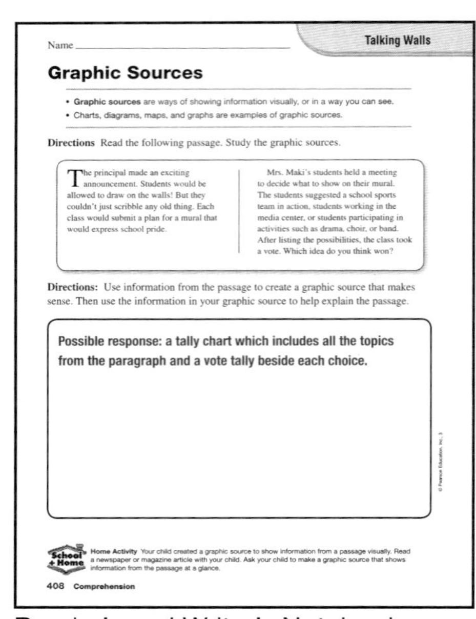

Name ____________ Talking Walls

Graphic Sources

- **Graphic sources** are ways of showing information visually, or in a way you can see.
- Charts, diagrams, maps, and graphs are examples of graphic sources.

Directions Read the following passage. Study the graphic sources.

The principal made an exciting announcement. Students would be allowed to draw on the walls! But they couldn't just scribble any old thing. Each class would submit a plan for a mural that would express school pride.

Mrs. Maki's students held a meeting to decide what to show on their mural. The students suggested a school sports team in action, students working in the media center, or students participating in activities such as drama, choir, or band. After listing the possibilities, the class took a vote. Which idea do you think won?

Directions: Use information from the passage to create a graphic source that makes sense. Then use the information in your graphic source to help explain the passage.

Possible response: a tally chart which includes all the topics from the paragraph and a vote tally beside each choice.

Home Activity Your child created a graphic source to show information from a passage visually. Read a newspaper or magazine article with your child. Ask your child to make a graphic source that shows information from the passage at a glance.

408 Comprehension

Reader's and Writer's Notebook, p. 408

Comprehension Skill

Graphic Sources

- Graphic sources are ways of showing information visually, or in a way you can see. They provide additional information to the text.
- Charts, photos, diagrams, and maps are all graphic sources.
- Use what you learned about graphic sources as you read "Ancient Cave Murals." Then, using the procedural text and the color wheel, write a paragraph explaining the steps to make purple paint.

Comprehension Strategy

Important Ideas

Active readers look for graphic sources and text features that often present important ideas. An author's most important ideas can be emphasized in graphic sources. Graphic sources help readers better understand the text.

Ancient Cave Murals

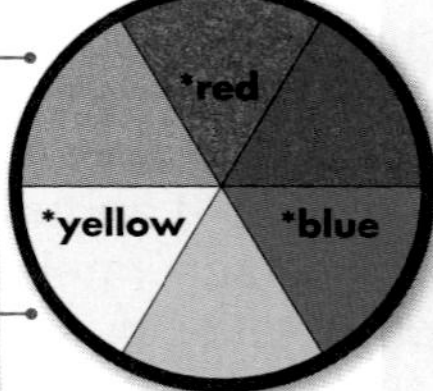

In 1940, four teenage boys discovered a cave covered with murals of animals. People had painted the murals about 17,000 years ago. Scientists studied the cave paintings and found that the ancient artists made their paint using pigment, which is a powder that gives paint its color. They were able to make very few colors of paint.

There are only three primary colors that, along with black and white, make all other colors. Today we can buy or make any color of paint we want!

How to Make Green Paint

1. Choose yellow and blue paint pigment.
2. Add water or oil and mix it together.
3. Add black or white pigment to make the green darker or lighter.
4. Add more blue or more yellow until you have a green you like!

Skill What colors do you see in the murals?

Strategy What important idea is shown by the color wheel?

*primary color

Skill What colors would you add together to make orange? Try it in art class!

Your Turn!

Need a Review? See the *Envision It! Handbook* for information about graphic sources and important ideas.

Ready to Try It? As you read *Talking Walls,* use what you've learned about graphic sources and important ideas to understand the text.

Student Edition, pp. 434–435

Model Fluent Reading

ACCURACY Have students listen as you read paragraph 1 of "Ancient Cave Murals" with accuracy. Explain that you will read each individual word correctly. Tell students that if any of the words were unknown, you would have looked them up before you began reading.

Routine Choral Reading

1. **Select a Passage** Use paragraph 1 of "Ancient Cave Murals."
2. **Model** Have students listen as you read with accuracy.
3. **Guide Practice** Have students read along with you.
4. **On Their Own** For optimal fluency, students should reread three or four times with accuracy.

Routines Flip Chart

eStreet Interactive
www.ReadingStreet.com
Pearson eText
• Student Edition
Envision It! Animations
Teacher Resources
• Reader's and Writer's Notebook

ELL

Graphic Sources Provide practice in having students use a map to locate cities and countries. Have students answer the question: Why are maps useful when reading about a place?

Common Core State Standards

Writing 7. Conduct short research projects that build knowledge about a topic. **Speaking/Listening 1.** Engage effectively in a range of collaborative discussions (one-on-one, in groups, and teacher led) with diverse partners on grade 3 topics and texts, building on others' ideas and expressing their own clearly. **Language 4.** Determine or clarify the meaning of unknown and multiple-meaning words and phrases based on grade 3 reading and content, choosing flexibly from a range of strategies. **Language 6.** Acquire and use accurately grade-appropriate conversational, general academic, and domain-specific words and phrases, including those that signal spatial and temporal relationships (e.g., *After dinner that night we went looking for them*).

Selection Vocabulary

Use the following routine to introduce this week's tested selection vocabulary.

encourages increases confidence
expression act of putting into words or visual medium
local of a certain place
native belonging to you because of your birth
settled made a home in a new place
social about people as a group
support to help or assist; to back

SEE IT/SAY IT Write *support*. Scan across the word with your finger as you say it: *sup-port*.

HEAR IT Use the word in a sentence. My family gave me their *support* to finish my project.

DEFINE IT Elicit definitions from students. How would you describe to another student what *support* means? Clarify or give a definition when necessary. Yes, when you *support* someone, you help the person. Restate the meaning of the word in student-friendly terms. *Support* means to give someone help or assistance. *Support* can also mean to encourage or cheer someone on.

Team Talk If people ask you for *support,* should you always give it? Be prepared to explain your answer. Allow students time to discuss. Ask for examples. Rephrase their examples for usage when necessary or to correct misunderstandings.

MAKE CONNECTIONS Have students discuss the word. When have you *supported* someone? When has someone *supported* you? Turn and talk to your partner about this. Then be prepared to share. Have students share. Rephrase their ideas for usage when necessary or to correct misunderstandings.

RECORD Have students write the word and its meaning.

Continue this routine to introduce the remaining words in this manner.

Corrective feedback | **If...** students are having difficulty understanding,
then... review the definitions in small groups.

Research and Inquiry

Step 1 Identify and Focus Topic

TEACH Discuss the Question of the Week: *Why is freedom of expression important?* Tell students they will research why freedom of expression is important. They will write a review or definition to present to the class on Day 5.

Think Aloud **MODEL** I'll start by brainstorming a list of questions about freedom of expression. I know that the First Amendment of the Constitution deals with free speech. Possible related questions could be *What does free speech mean? How can people express themselves nonverbally? What are some symbolic expressions of freedom?*

GUIDE PRACTICE After students have brainstormed inquiry questions, suggest they list them on a chart. Then explain that tomorrow they will conduct online research using their questions. Help students identify keywords that will guide their search.

ON THEIR OWN Have students work individually, in pairs, or in small groups to write an inquiry question.

Day 1 SMALL GROUP TIME • Differentiate Vocabulary, p. SG•33

OL On-Level
- **Practice** Vocabulary Amazing Words
- **Read** *Reading Street Sleuth,* pp. 72–73

SI Strategic Intervention
- **Reteach** Vocabulary Amazing Words
- **Read** *Reading Street Sleuth,* pp. 72–73

A Advanced
- **Extend** Vocabulary Amazing Words
- **Read** *Reading Street Sleuth,* pp. 72–73
- **Introduce** Inquiry Project

eStreet Interactive
www.ReadingStreet.com

Teacher Resources
- Envision It! Pictured Vocabulary Cards
- Tested Vocabulary Cards

21st Century Skills
Internet Guy *Don Leu*

Weekly Inquiry Project

STEP 1	Identify and Focus Topic
STEP 2	Navigate/Search
STEP 3	Analyze Information
STEP 4	Synthesize
STEP 5	Communicate

Multilingual Vocabulary Students can apply knowledge of their home languages to acquire new English vocabulary by using the Multilingual Vocabulary Lists (*ELL Handbook,* pp. 433–444).

ELL

If... students need more scaffolding and practice with **Vocabulary,**
then... use the activities on pp. DI•67–DI•68 in the Teacher Resources section on SuccessNet.

Common Core State Standards

Language 1.h. Use coordinating and subordinating conjunctions. **Language 1.i.** Produce simple, compound, and complex sentences. **Language 2.e.** Use conventional spelling for high-frequency and other studied words and for adding suffixes to base words (e.g., *sitting, smiled, cries, happiness*). **Language 2.f.** Use spelling patterns and generalizations (e.g., word families, position-based spellings, syllable patterns, ending rules, meaningful word parts) in writing words.

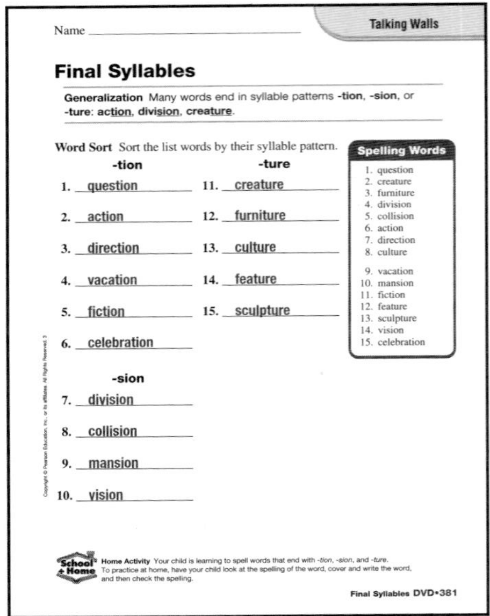

Name ____________ Talking Walls

Final Syllables

Generalization Many words end in syllable patterns **-tion**, **-sion**, or **-ture**: **action**, **division**, **creature**.

Word Sort Sort the list words by their syllable pattern.

-tion

1. question
2. action
3. direction
4. vacation
5. fiction
6. celebration

-sion

7. division
8. collision
9. mansion
10. vision

-ture

11. creature
12. furniture
13. culture
14. feature
15. sculpture

Spelling Words

1. question
2. creature
3. furniture
4. division
5. collision
6. action
7. direction
8. culture
9. vacation
10. mansion
11. fiction
12. feature
13. sculpture
14. vision
15. celebration

School + Home **Home Activity** Your child is learning to spell words that end with *-tion*, *-sion*, and *-ture*. To practice at home, have your child look at the spelling of the word, cover and write the word, and then check the spelling.

Final Syllables DVD•381

Let's Practice It! TR DVD•381

Spelling Pretest

Final Syllables *-ion, -ure*

INTRODUCE Tell students to think of words with the final syllables *-ion* and *-ure.* This week we will spell words with the syllables *-ion* and *-ure.*

PRETEST Say each word, read the sentence, and repeat the word.

1. question	She had a **question** for the teacher.
2. creature	A rabbit is a tiny **creature.**
3. furniture	We moved the **furniture** out of the room.
4. division	We learned about **division** in math.
5. collision	Two cars just had a **collision!**
6. action	There was a lot of **action** in the play.
7. direction	Do you know what **direction** we are traveling?
8. culture	I studied Chinese **culture** and food.
9. vacation	Where would you like to travel on **vacation?**
10. mansion	The **mansion** had a pool and a tennis court.
11. fiction	Where are the **fiction** books in the library?
12. feature	What **feature** of the game is your favorite?
13. sculpture	The **sculpture** is in the museum garden.
14. vision	The nurse checked my **vision.**
15. celebration	We had a **celebration** for my graduation.
Challenge words	
16. fascination	We listened to the story in **fascination.**
17. legislature	The **legislature** passed the law yesterday.
18. manufacture	At the factory, they **manufacture** light bulbs.
19. possession	They took **possession** of the new house.
20. declaration	I made a **declaration** that I would be a writer.

SELF-CORRECT Have students self-correct their pretests by rewriting misspelled words.

ON THEIR OWN Use *Let's Practice It!* p. 381 on the *Teacher Resources DVD-ROM.*

Conventions

Combining Sentences

MAKE CONNECTIONS Write short sentences on sentence strips and demonstrate how to combine the two sentences to create a single sentence. Then write short sentences on index cards and pair students to combine them. Be sure some are sentences that can be combined with *and,* while others are sentences that have common subjects.

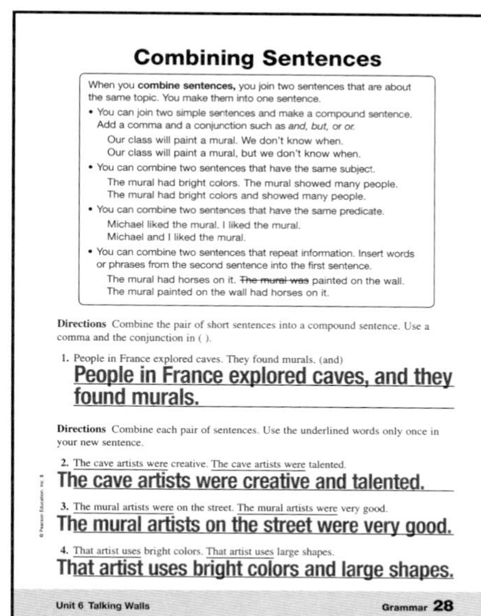

Combining Sentences

When you **combine sentences,** you join two sentences that are about the same topic. You make them into one sentence.

- You can join two simple sentences and make a compound sentence. Add a comma and a conjunction such as *and, but,* or *or.*
  Our class will paint a mural. We don't know when.
  Our class will paint a mural, but we don't know when.
- You can combine two sentences that have the same subject.
  The mural had bright colors. The mural showed many people.
  The mural had bright colors and showed many people.
- You can combine two sentences that have the same predicate.
  Michael liked the mural. I liked the mural.
  Michael and I liked the mural.
- You can combine two sentences that repeat information. Insert words or phrases from the second sentence into the first sentence.
  The mural had horses on it. ~~The mural was~~ painted on the wall.
  The mural painted on the wall had horses on it.

Directions Combine the pair of short sentences into a compound sentence. Use a comma and the conjunction in ( ).

1. People in France explored caves. They found murals. (and)
   People in France explored caves, and they found murals.

Directions Combine each pair of sentences. Use the underlined words only once in your new sentence.

2. The cave artists were creative. The cave artists were talented.
   The cave artists were creative and talented.
3. The mural artists were on the street. The mural artists were very good.
   The mural artists on the street were very good.
4. That artist uses bright colors. That artist uses large shapes.
   That artist uses bright colors and large shapes.

Unit 6 Talking Walls Grammar 28

Grammar Transparency 28, TR DVD

TEACH Display Grammar Transparency 28, and read aloud the explanation and examples in the box. Explain that repeated words and ideas in sentences are clues that the sentences can be combined.

MODEL Model combining sentences by completing number 1. Point out that the two sentences have the same subject *(People in France; They)* and so can be combined.

GUIDE PRACTICE Guide students to complete item 2. Remind them to use the underlined words only once in each new sentence. Record the correct responses on the transparency.

APPLY Have students read sentences 3–4 on the transparency and combine the pairs of sentences to form grammatically correct sentences.

Handwriting

MODEL LETTER FORMATION AND SPACING Display the capital cursive letters *G, S,* and *I.* Follow the stroke instructions pictured to model letter formation. Explain that writing legibly means words are spaced correctly. Model writing this sentence with appropriate spacing between words: *Greg goes sailing with Sue and Iris.* Make sure the letters aren't too light, dark, or jagged.

GUIDE PRACTICE Have students write these sentences: *Stop singing! I give Giselle eggs. Ina is in India.* Circulate around the room, guiding students.

Daily Fix-It

1. Carlos and Maria created a mural about they're cullture. *(their; culture)*
2. The class helped Carlos and she with the desine. *(her; design)*

Options for Grammar Support: Coordinating Conjunctions Display these pairs of sentences:

I like to play soccer.
I enjoy watching baseball.

I want to play soccer.
I need to do my homework first.

Read each sentence aloud. Explain to students that each set of sentences can be combined using a conjunction and a comma. Write *and* and *but* on the board. Identify them as conjunctions. Explain that *and* joins two sentences that are similar. *But* joins sentences that are different. Help students use *and* to join the first set of sentences and *but* to join the second set.

Common Core State Standards

Writing 2. Write informative/explanatory texts to examine a topic and convey ideas and information clearly. **Writing 2.a.** Introduce a topic and group related information together; include illustrations when useful to aiding comprehension. **Language 3.a.** Choose words and phrases for effect.

Bridge to Common Core

TEXT TYPES AND PURPOSES

This week students write a description of a piece of art.

Informative/Explanatory Writing

Through reading and discussion, students will gain a deeper understanding of freedom of expression. They will use this knowledge from the texts to write a description of their own.

Through the week, students will improve the range and content of their writing through daily mini-lessons.

5-Day Plan

DAY 1	Read Like a Writer
DAY 2	Main Idea and Details
DAY 3	Choosing Descriptive Words
DAY 4	Revise: Consolidating
DAY 5	Proofread for Voice

Write Guy *by Jeff Anderson*

Details, Details

Ask students to notice details in mentor text—but not just any details. Rather than pointing out many details, select a detail that is beyond the obvious. *(It was hot* versus *The sun melted my crayons that sat on the long window sill in the kitchen.)* What evocative description reveals something new to readers? With guidance, students can learn how to include *details that matter* rather than obvious details or simply longer and longer lists of details.

Writing

Zoom in on ©

Description

Mini-Lesson Read Like a Writer

Introduce This week you will write a description. Your description will be nonfiction. A description explains what a person, place, or thing is like, so the reader can imagine it.

Prompt	Think about a piece of art that you know from the selection or your own life. Describe it, using sensory details.
Trait	Word Choice
Mode	Expository/Informative/Explanatory

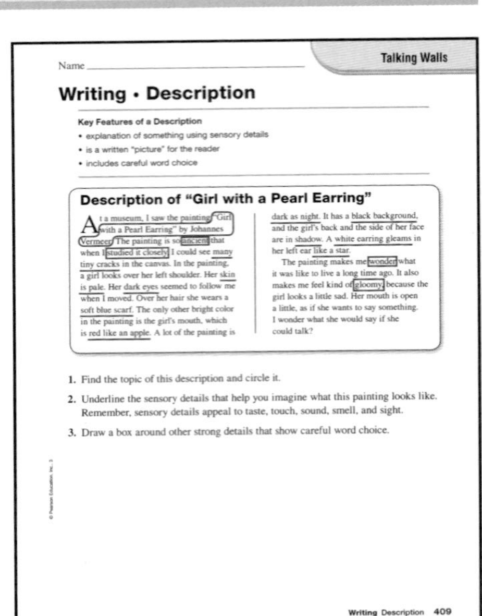

Name ______ Talking Walls

Writing • Description

Key Features of a Description
- explanation of something using sensory details
- is a written "picture" for the reader
- includes careful word choice

Description of "Girl with a Pearl Earring"

At a museum, I saw the painting "Girl with a Pearl Earring" by Johannes Vermeer. The painting is so ancient that when I studied it closely I could see many tiny cracks in the canvas. In the painting, a girl looks over her left shoulder. Her skin is pale. Her dark eyes seemed to follow me when I moved. Over her hair she wears a soft blue scarf. The only other bright color in the painting is the girl's mouth, which is red like an apple. A lot of the painting is dark as night. It has a black background, and the girl's back and the side of her face are in shadow. A white earring gleams in her left ear like a star.

The painting makes me wonder what it was like to live a long time ago. It also makes me feel kind of gloomy because the girl looks a little sad. Her mouth is open a little, as if she wants to say something. I wonder what she would say if she could talk?

1. Find the topic of this description and circle it.
2. Underline the sensory details that help you imagine what this painting looks like. Remember, sensory details appeal to taste, touch, sound, smell, and sight.
3. Draw a box around other strong details that show careful word choice.

Writing Description 409

Reader's and Writer's Notebook, p. 409

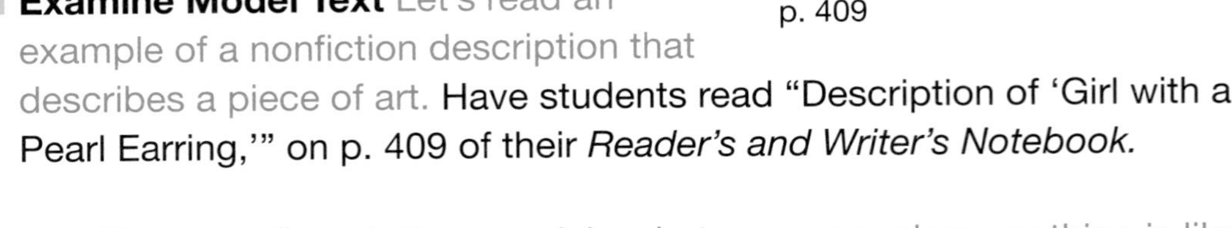

Examine Model Text Let's read an example of a nonfiction description that describes a piece of art. Have students read "Description of 'Girl with a Pearl Earring,'" on p. 409 of their *Reader's and Writer's Notebook.*

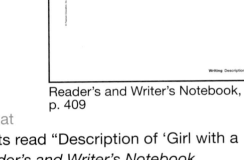

Key Features Descriptions explain what a person, place, or thing is like. What is being described here? Find the topic of this description and circle it. Point out to students that the topic sentence appears at the beginning of a description and that everything else in the description is a supporting detail that tells the reader something about that topic.

Descriptions help readers visualize something by using vivid words that appeal to the senses—taste, touch, smell, hearing, and sight. A description is full of strong details, such as the size, color, shape, smell, and texture of the person, place, or thing. Help students identify and underline sensory details in the model.

Good description contains vivid language. Writing a good description means choosing your words carefully. Have students draw a box around other strong details in the model that show careful word choice.

eSTREET INTERACTIVE
www.ReadingStreet.com

Teacher Resources
- Reader's and Writer's Notebook
- Let's Practice It!

Review Key Features

Review the key features of a description with students. You may want to have students write the key features on index cards to tape to their desktops to refer to as they work on their descriptive passages.

Key Features of a Description
- uses sensory details to explain something
- is a written "picture" for the reader
- includes careful precise word choice

Routine Quick Write for Fluency

Team Talk

1. **Talk** Students choose a person or object in the classroom and describe it to a partner, using sensory details.
2. **Write** Students write their descriptions without identifying the person or object they are describing.
3. **Share** Students read their descriptions out loud to a new partner and have that partner guess what or who it is they are describing.

Routines Flip Chart

Visual Learning Invite students to talk about which mural from the selection is their favorite. Help them describe the murals.

Wrap Up Your Day!

- ✓ **Content Knowledge** Reread "Street Rhymes!" on p. 430j to students. Ask them what they learned today about the importance of freedom of expression.
- ✓ **Oral Vocabulary** Have students use the Amazing Words they learned in context sentences.
- ✓ **Homework** Send home this week's Family Times newsletter on *Let's Practice It!* pp. 382–383 on the *Teacher Resources DVD-ROM.*

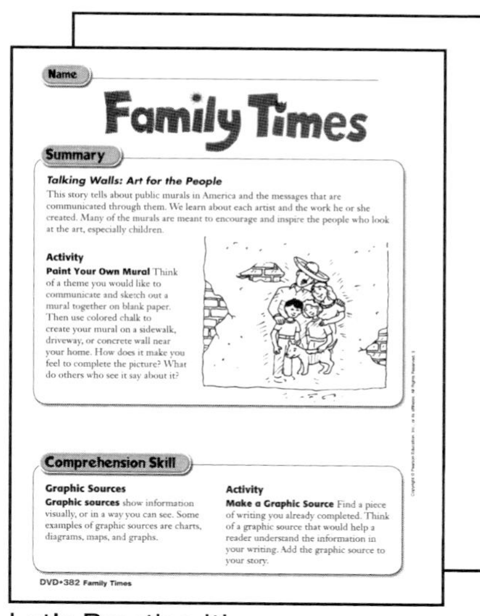

Name

Family Times

Summary

Talking Walls: Art for the People

This story tells about public murals in America and the messages that are communicated through them. We learn about each artist and the work he or she created. Many of the murals are meant to encourage and inspire the people who look at the art, especially children.

Activity

Point Your Own Mural Think of a theme you would like to communicate and sketch out a mural together on blank paper. Then use colored chalk to create your mural on a sidewalk, driveway, or concrete wall near your home. How does it make you feel to complete the picture? What do others who see it say about it?

Comprehension Skill

Graphic Sources

Graphic sources show information visually, or in a way you can see. Some examples of graphic sources are charts, diagrams, maps, and graphs.

Activity

Make a Graphic Source Find a piece of writing you already completed. Think of a graphic source that would help a reader understand the information in your writing. Add the graphic source to your story.

DVD•382 Family Times

Let's Practice It!
TR DVD•382–383

Preview DAY 2

Tell students that tomorrow they will read about talking walls.

DAY 2 at a Glance

Content Knowledge
Oral Vocabulary

Phonics/Word Analysis
Final Syllables

Literary Terms
Personification

Vocabulary Skill
Unknown Words

Fluency
Accuracy

Research and Inquiry
Navigate/Search

Conventions
Combining Sentences

Spelling
Final Syllables

Writing
Description

Materials

- Student Edition
- Reader's and Writer's Notebook

Common Core State Standards

Speaking/Listening 1. Engage effectively in a range of collaborative discussions (one-on-one, in groups, and teacher led) with diverse partners on grade 3 topics and texts, building on others' ideas and expressing their own clearly. **Language 4.** Determine or clarify the meaning of unknown and multiple-meaning words and phrases based on grade 3 reading and content, choosing flexibly from a range of strategies. **Language 6.** Acquire and use accurately grade-appropriate conversational, general academic, and domain-specific words and phrases, including those that signal spatial and temporal relationships (e.g., *After dinner that night we went looking for them*).

Content Knowledge

Freedom of Expression

EXPAND THE CONCEPT Remind students of the weekly concept question, *Why is freedom of expression important?* Tell students that today they will begin reading *Talking Walls: Art for the People*. As they read, encourage students to think about what freedom of expression means.

Build Oral Language

TALK ABOUT SENTENCES AND WORDS Reread this sentence from the Read Aloud, "Toothpicks, Bottles, Tin, and Rocks."

Through the years Grandma added all sorts of other expressive objects to her village, including doll heads, TV screens, and car headlights—all recovered from the garbage dump.

- Grandma adds *expressive* objects to her artistic village. What does *expressive* mean? (meaningful; vivid)
- Based on the sentence, how does Grandma feel about items such as doll heads, TV screens, and car headlights? (She thinks they are interesting and valuable.)
- How do Grandma's choices of *expressive* objects show that artists have freedom? (Artists can use any kinds of materials to create art, even things that other people think are garbage.)

Team Talk Have students turn to a partner and discuss the following question. Then ask them to share their responses.

- What is the shortest version of this sentence you can make without changing the basic meaning? (Possible response: Over the years Grandma recovered various expressive objects from the garbage to add to her village.)

Build Oral Vocabulary

Amazing Words Robust Vocabulary Routine

1. **Introduce** Write the Amazing Word *exquisite* on the board. Have students say it aloud with you. Relate *exquisite* to "Toothpicks, Bottles, Tin, and Rocks." What makes Wayne Kusy's creations *exquisite?* Have students determine the definition of the word. (*Exquisite* means lovely, beautiful, excellent, or of high quality.)
2. **Demonstrate** Have students answer questions to demonstrate understanding. Which is *exquisite,* an old jacket or a painting of a sunset? What would make a day at school *exquisite?*
3. **Apply** Have students apply their understanding. Make a list of things you think are *exquisite*.
4. **Display the Word** Run your hand under the syllables *ex-qui-site* as you read the word.

See p. OV•3 to teach *lecture.*

Routines Flip Chart

ADD TO THE CONCEPT MAP Use the photos on pp. 430–431 and the Read Aloud, "Toothpicks, Bottles, Tin, and Rocks," to talk about the Amazing Words: *emotion, artistic, creative,* and *expressive*. Add these and other concept-related words to the concept map to develop students' knowledge of the topic. Discuss the photos and vocabulary to generate questions about the topic. Encourage students to build upon the ideas of others.

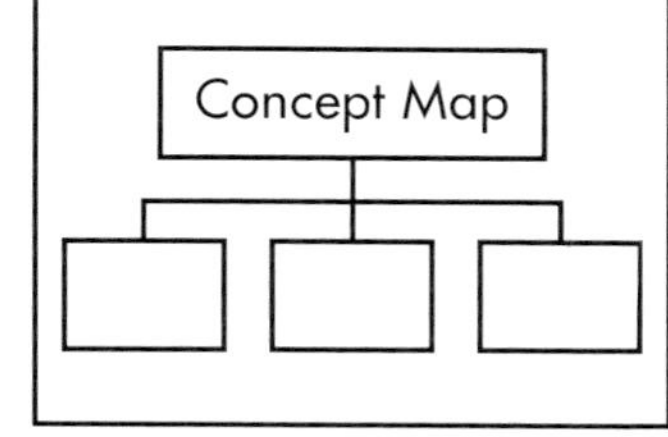

- Why is freedom of expression important to someone who is *artistic* or *creative?*
- What *expressive* creations have you made?
- What *emotion* comes to mind when you think of freedom?

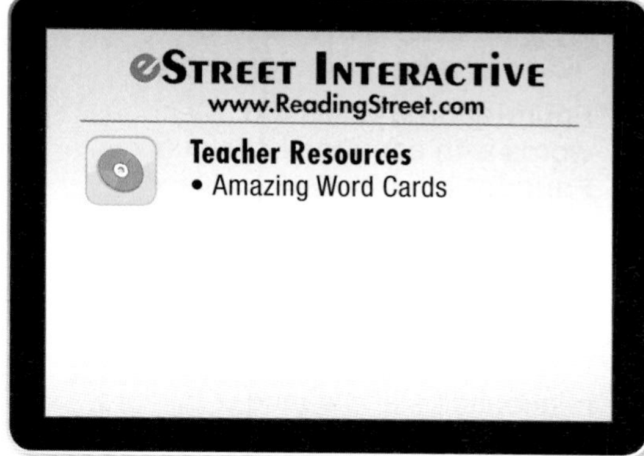

Amazing Words

creative	lecture
expressive	significant
emotion	pause
artistic	view
exquisite	lyrics

Reinforce Vocabulary Use the Day 2 instruction on ELL Poster 28 to teach lesson vocabulary and the lesson concept.

Common Core State Standards

Foundational Skills 3.b. Decode words with common Latin suffixes. **Foundational Skills 3.c.** Decode multisyllable words. **Language 3.** Use knowledge of language and its conventions when writing, speaking, reading, or listening. **Language 5.** Demonstrate understanding of word relationships and nuances in word meanings. **Language 5.a.** Distinguish the literal and nonliteral meanings of words and phrases in context (e.g., *take steps*). **Language 6.** Acquire and use accurately grade-appropriate conversational, general academic, and domain-specific words and phrases, including those that signal spatial and temporal relationships (e.g., *After dinner that night we went looking for them*).

Word Analysis

Final Syllables

REVIEW Review the final syllables *-tion, -ion, -ture, -ive,* and *-ize,* pointing out that these word parts appear at the end of words.

READ WORDS IN ISOLATION Display these words. Have the class read the words. Then point to the words in random order and ask students to read them quickly.

fiction	**expansion**	**signature**	**comprehension**
structure	**reflective**	**reactive**	**agonize**

Corrective feedback | Model reading the word parts and then ask students to read the whole word with you.

READ WORDS IN CONTEXT Display these sentences. Have the class read the sentences.

Team Talk Have pairs take turns reading the sentences naturally.

They stayed in a **mansion** on their **vacation.**

Since Dad had bad **vision,** he could not see the **sculpture.**

I did not **realize** that Lynn is not a **native** of this area.

Check Word Reading

FORMATIVE ASSESSMENT Write the following words and have the class read them. Notice which words students miss during the group reading. Call on individuals to read some of the words.

expansion	**exhaustion**	**adventure**	**active**	**Spiral Review**
football	**homework**	**scarecrow**	**earring**	← Row 2 reviews compound words.
lifeboat	**champion**	**brainstorm**	**nature**	← Row 3 contrasts compound words with words with final syllables *-tion, -ion, -ture, -ive,* and *-ize*.

If... students cannot read words with common syllables at this point,

then... use the Day 1 Word Analysis lesson on p. 432a to reteach final syllables *-tion, -ion, -ture, -ive,* and *-ize*. Use words from the *Decodable Practice Passages* (or Reader). Continue to monitor students' progress using other instructional opportunities during the week. See the Skills Trace on p. 432a.

Literary Terms

Personification

TEACH Tell students that personification is a figure of speech in which human traits are given to animals or objects. Personification is used in fiction and nonfiction to make things seem more real and make writing livelier.

MODEL Let's look at "Ancient Cave Murals" on p. 435. I don't see an example of personification in this passage. Since the passage is about murals, can you think of a way to personify these paintings? (Answers will vary.)

GUIDE PRACTICE Have students find an example of personification in *Talking Walls: Art for the People*. Ask them to think about the title. Ask them if walls actually talk.

ON THEIR OWN Have students find examples of personification in other selections of their Student Edition.

Academic Vocabulary 

personification a figure of speech in which human traits are given to animals or to inanimate objects or abstract ideas

Common Core State Standards

Foundational Skills 4.b. Read on-level prose and poetry orally with accuracy, appropriate rate, and expression on successive readings. **Language 4.d** Use glossaries or beginning dictionaries, both print and digital, to determine or clarify the precise meaning of key words and phrases. **Also Foundational Skills 4., Language 4.**

Selection Vocabulary

encourages increases confidence

expression act of putting into words or visual medium

local of a certain place

native belonging to you because of your birth

settled made a home in a new place

social about people as a group

support to help or assist; to back

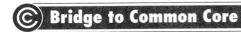

Bridge to Common Core

VOCABULARY ACQUISITION AND USE

Using context clues as well as dictionaries and glossaries helps students determine the meanings of unknown words and enables them to acquire a broad range of academic and domain-specific words. By considering the meanings of context clues and using resources to confirm or determine word meanings, students demonstrate the ability to determine word meanings on their own.

Vocabulary Support

Refer students to *Words!* on p. W•14 in the Student Edition for additional practice.

Vocabulary Skill

Unknown Words

READ Have students read "Class Art" on p. 437. Use the vocabulary skill and strategy as tools to build comprehension.

TEACH DICTIONARY/GLOSSARY Tell students that when they encounter an unknown word, they should use a dictionary or glossary to look up the meaning. Explain how a dictionary or glossary can help students understand the meaning, syllabication, and pronunciation of unknown words.

MODEL Write on the board: *Our town's cultural celebration encourages people to share their customs.* I can't figure out the meaning of *encourages* by using context clues, so I'll look in a dictionary or glossary. When I look up *encourages* in the dictionary, the definition is "increases confidence." Now I understand that the town's cultural celebration increases people's confidence in sharing their customs. Each word in a dictionary or glossary is divided into syllables, and the pronunciation of each word is shown in parentheses right after it. The pronunciation key helps me understand the pronunciations.

GUIDE PRACTICE Write this sentence on the board: *Volunteers develop art projects in their local neighborhoods*. Have students determine the meaning of *local* using context clues. If they are unable to define the word, have them look up the word in a dictionary or glossary. Have students determine the syllabication and pronunciation of *local*. For additional support, use *Envision It! Pictured Vocabulary Cards* or *Tested Vocabulary Cards*.

ON THEIR OWN Have students reread "Class Art" on p. 437. Have them use a dictionary or glossary to make a list of definitions for the Words to Know. For additional practice, use *Reader's and Writer's Notebook* p. 410.

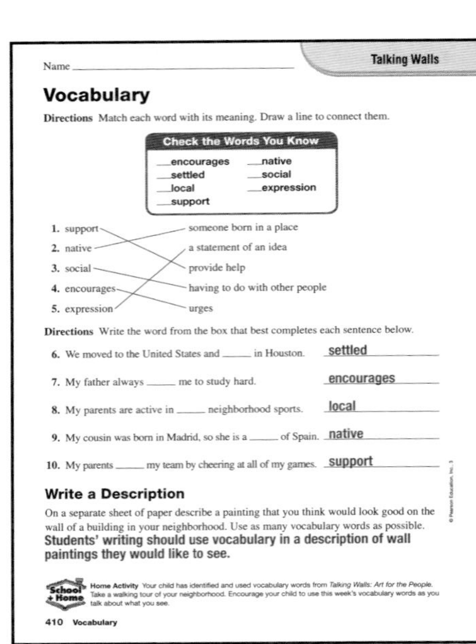

Name ______ Talking Walls

Vocabulary

Directions Match each word with its meaning. Draw a line to connect them.

Check the Words You Know

___encourages ___native
___settled ___social
___local ___expression
___support

1. support — provide help
2. native — someone born in a place
3. social — having to do with other people
4. encourages — urges
5. expression — a statement of an idea

Directions Write the word from the box that best completes each sentence below.

6. We moved to the United States and ______ in Houston. **settled**
7. My father always ______ me to study hard. **encourages**
8. My parents are active in ______ neighborhood sports. **local**
9. My cousin was born in Madrid, so she is a ______ of Spain. **native**
10. My parents ______ my team by cheering at all of my games. **support**

Write a Description

On a separate sheet of paper describe a painting that you think would look good on the wall of a building in your neighborhood. Use as many vocabulary words as possible. **Students' writing should use vocabulary in a description of wall paintings they would like to see.**

School + Home **Home Activity** Your child has identified and used vocabulary words from *Talking Walls: Art for the People*. Take a walking tour of your neighborhood. Encourage your child to use this week's vocabulary words as you talk about what you see.

410 Vocabulary

Reader's and Writer's Notebook, p. 410

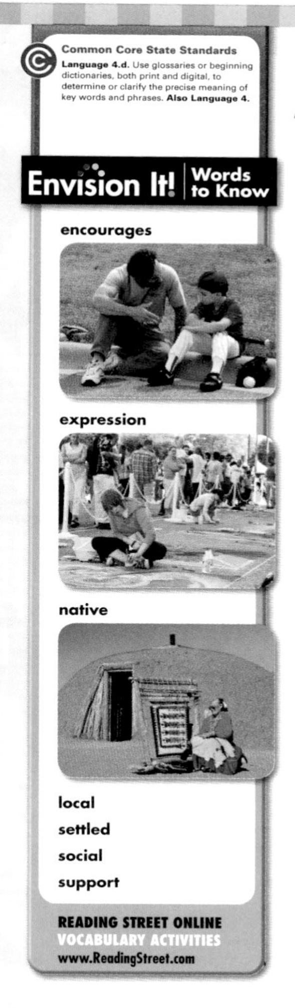
Common Core State Standards
Language 4.d. Use glossaries or beginning dictionaries, both print and digital, to determine or clarify the precise meaning of key words and phrases. **Also Language 4.**

Envision It! Words to Know

encourages

expression

native

local

settled

social

support

READING STREET ONLINE
VOCABULARY ACTIVITIES
www.ReadingStreet.com

Vocabulary Strategy for

Unknown Words

Dictionary/Glossary When you read an unknown word, ask yourself if it's a noun, verb, or adjective. Knowing what part of speech a word is can help you find and understand its meaning. Then use a dictionary or glossary to find the correct meaning and how the word is pronounced.

1. Use the first letter in the word to find it in the dictionary or glossary.
2. Look at the pronunciation key and each syllable to pronounce the word correctly.
3. Read the definitions of the word. Choose a meaning for the correct part of speech.
4. Try your meaning in the sentence. Does it make sense? If not, try another meaning.

Read "Class Art" on page 437. Use a dictionary or glossary to find the meanings and pronunciations of the Words to Know.

Words to Write Reread "Class Art." Sort the Words to Know into three groups: nouns, adjectives, and verbs, according to how each is used in the selection.

436

Class Art

Ms. Ramsey's students are excited. They are planning to paint a mural on one wall in their classroom. Ms. Ramsey encourages the students to talk about what they will paint on the mural. Everyone has a different idea. Julio's family came to the United States from Mexico. He wants to paint something about his native country. Mary wants to paint something about the community's history. Her family settled here a long, long time ago. Gerrard thinks the mural should show the social life of the people who live in the community. Diana thinks the mural should be more about global, not local, issues. It should show how the community is part of the world. How can the students get all these ideas on one mural? Ms. Ramsey points out that the mural should be an expression of the group's interests and beliefs. She says that with a little planning, the students can paint a mural that will support everyone's ideas.

Your Turn!

Need a Review? For additional help with unknown words, see *Words!*

Ready to Try It? Read *Talking Walls: Art for the People* on pp. 438–451.

437

Student Edition, pp. 436–437

Reread for Fluency

ACCURACY Read the first half of "Class Art" aloud, making sure you accurately read each individual word. Tell students that you are reading the passage with accuracy, focusing on understanding what you are reading.

Routine Choral Reading

1. **Select a Passage** Read the first half of "Class Art" aloud.
2. **Model** Have students listen as you read with accuracy.
3. **Guide Practice** Have students read along with you.
4. **On Their Own** For optimal fluency, students should reread three or four times with accuracy.

Routines Flip Chart

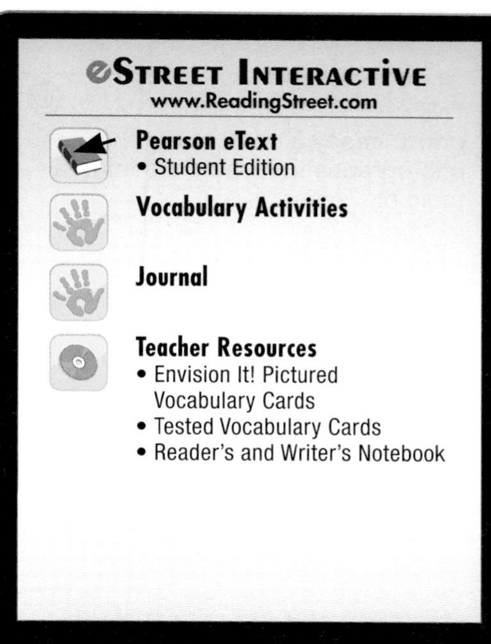
eStreet Interactive
www.ReadingStreet.com

Pearson eText
- Student Edition

Vocabulary Activities

Journal

Teacher Resources
- Envision It! Pictured Vocabulary Cards
- Tested Vocabulary Cards
- Reader's and Writer's Notebook

Common Core State Standards

Informational Text 7. Use information gained from illustrations (e.g., maps, photographs) and the words in a text to demonstrate understanding of the text (e.g., where, when, why, and how key events occur). **Informational Text 10.** By the end of the year, read and comprehend informational texts, including history/social studies, science, and technical texts, at the high end of the grades 2–3 text complexity band independently and proficiently.

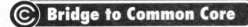

Bridge to Common Core

CRAFT AND STRUCTURE

Students analyze the selection's title and photographs and think about how the components relate to each other and to the selection as a whole. As they preview the selection and prepare to read, they come to see how genre and purpose shape the content and style of the text.

Academic Vocabulary 

photo essay a collection of photographs that share a common topic or theme

Strategy Response Log

Have students use p. 34 in the *Reader's and Writer's Notebook* to identify the characteristics of a photo essay.

Text-Based Comprehension

Introduce Main Selection

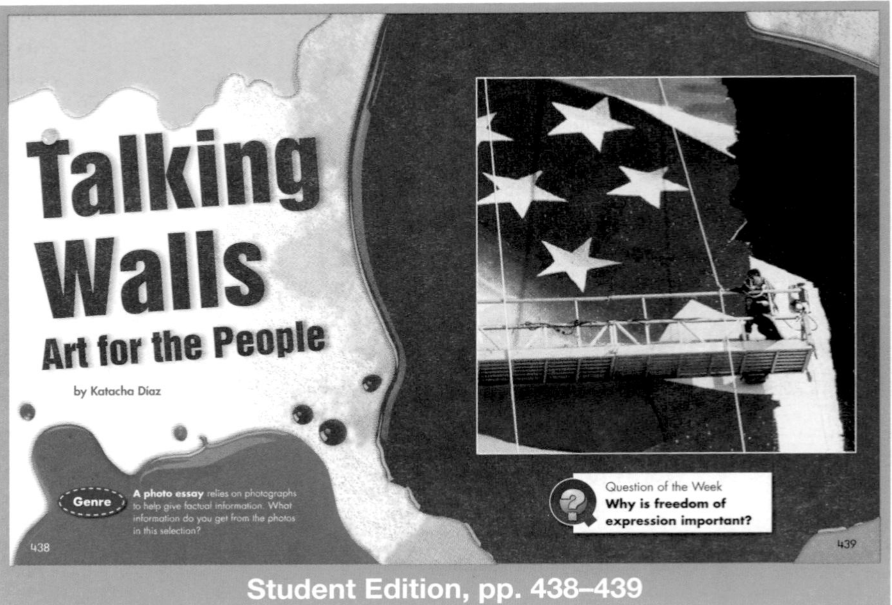

Student Edition, pp. 438–439

GENRE Tell students that a **photo essay** is a collection of photographs that share a common topic or theme. A photo essay has text to tell about the events and people in the photographs. The essay might have an introduction that explains the topic or purpose of the photo essay. Also, each photo may have a caption that gives additional information about it.

PREVIEW AND PREDICT Have students preview the title, photographs, and photo captions for *Talking Walls: Art for the People*. Ask students to predict what they will discover as they read.

PURPOSE By analyzing *Talking Walls: Art for the People,* a photo essay, students will gain knowledge of why freedom of expression is important.

Access Main Selection

READER AND TASK SUGGESTIONS	
Preparing to Read the Text	**Leveled Tasks**
• Review how to use a dictionary to learn the parts of speech and meanings of unknown words. • Discuss how authors sometimes use photographs to deliver information. • Remind students that this is a nonfiction selection. They may need to read more slowly to better understand the text.	• **Structure** Remind students that in this selection, much of the information is provided through photographs. As they read, they should connect the photographs to what is written in the text. • **Levels of Meaning • Evaluation** Students may have difficulty understanding the murals in the photo essay. Explain that murals often tell a story. Have students look at the mural on p. 445 and tell how a young girl could be like a tree.

See Text Complexity Measures for *Talking Walls: Art for the People* on the tab at the beginning of this week.

READ Tell students that today they will read *Talking Walls: Art for the People* for the first time. Use the Read for Understanding routine.

Routine Read for Understanding

Deepen understanding by reading the selection multiple times.

1. **First Read**—If students need support, then use the **Access Text** notes to help them clarify understanding.
2. **Second Read**—Use the **Close Reading** notes to help students draw knowledge from the text.

Day 2 SMALL GROUP TIME • Differentiate Comprehension, p. SG•33

OL On-Level	SI Strategic Intervention	A Advanced
• **Practice** Selection Vocabulary • **Read** *Talking Walls: Art for the People*	• **Reteach** Selection Vocabulary • **Read** *Talking Walls: Art for the People*	• **Extend** Selection Vocabulary • **Read** *Talking Walls: Art for the People* • **Investigate** Inquiry Project

eStreet Interactive
www.ReadingStreet.com

Pearson eText
• Student Edition

AudioText CD

Teacher Resources
• Reader's and Writer's Notebook

Background Building Audio CD

Access for All

Advanced

Brainstorm a list of things you might see on public murals.

Build Background To build background, review the selection summary in English (*ELL Handbook*, p. 193). Use the Retelling Cards to provide visual support for the summary.

If... students need more scaffolding and practice with the **Comprehension Skill,**
then... use the activities on p. DI•71 in the Teacher Resources section on SuccessNet.

1ST READ

Access Text If students need help, then…

UNKNOWN WORDS Have students look at the highlighted words on p. 440. Ask them to look up each word in the glossary in the back of this book or in a dictionary and write its definition.

Think Aloud **MODEL** The first word I see is *native.* That is a new word for me. My dictionary has *native* on a page with the guide words *nationalism* and *naturalize*. The definition given that fits the context of the sentence is "related to the place of one's birth."

Immigrants travel to America from all over the world. They leave behind homes and villages in their native countries for the promise of a better life and for the freedom this country has to offer.

The people in America enjoy many different kinds of freedom, including the freedom of artistic expression. Writers, musicians, dancers, and artists are free to speak their minds through their art—in any way they choose. Do you know that some painters use walls as their canvas? These painted walls are called murals and are often painted in public places for all the people of the community to see.

Muralists are asked by a town, school, or business to create a work of art on a wall. Muralists paint many different kinds of murals. Some are inside, some are outside. Some tell the history of a town and everyday life of the people who settled there. Others show special celebrations and community festivals. Still others depict symbols of American freedom and democracy at work. All are great examples of artistic expression at its best.

"Community of Music," Long Beach, California ▸

440

Student Edition, p. 440

2ND READ

Close Reading

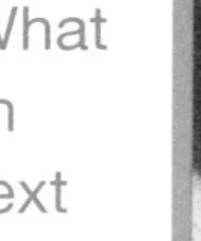

SYNTHESIS • TEXT EVIDENCE What is the main idea of the last paragraph on page 440? Cite details from the text that support this main idea. (Main idea: Muralists paint many different kinds of murals. Supporting details: Some are inside, some are outside; some tell the history of a town, others tell of the everyday life of the people who settled there; yet others show special celebrations and community festivals or symbols of American freedom and democracy at work.)

ON THEIR OWN Have students reread pp. 440–441 and use classroom dictionaries to check the meaning of other unknown words. For additional practice with unknown words, see *Reader's and Writer's Notebook* p. 414.

Student Edition, p. 441

ANALYSIS How are muralists different from other kinds of painters? How are they alike? (Muralists paint on walls, often in public places, instead of on canvas. Like other kinds of painters, muralists enjoy freedom of expression and use their art as a form of expression.)

Common Core State Standards

Informational Text 1. Ask and answer questions to demonstrate understanding of a text, referring explicitly to the text as the basis for the answers. **Informational Text 2.** Determine the main idea of a text; recount the key details and explain how they support the main idea. **Language 4.d.** Use glossaries or beginning dictionaries, both print and digital, to determine or clarify the precise meaning of key words and phrases. **Also Informational Text 10.**

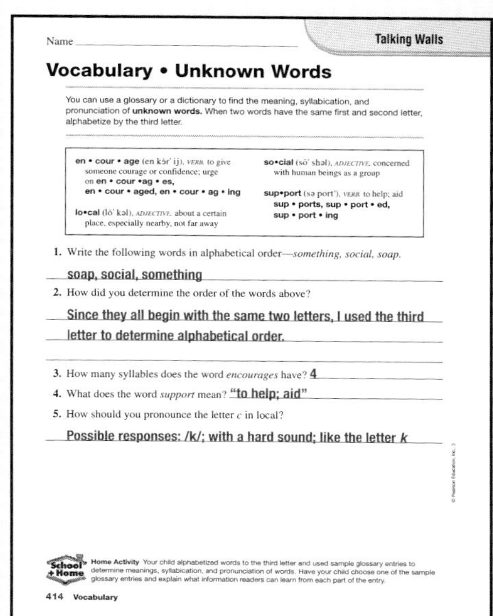
Name ______ Talking Walls

Vocabulary • Unknown Words

You can use a glossary or a dictionary to find the meaning, syllabication, and pronunciation of **unknown words.** When two words have the same first and second letter, alphabetize by the third letter.

en • cour • age (en kėr′ ij), *VERB.* to give someone courage or confidence; urge on **en • cour •ag • es, en • cour • aged, en • cour • ag • ing**

lo•cal (lō′ kəl), *ADJECTIVE.* about a certain place, especially nearby, not far away

so•cial (sō′ shəl), *ADJECTIVE.* concerned with human beings as a group

sup•port (sə port′), *VERB.* to help; aid **sup • ports, sup • port • ed, sup • port • ing**

1. Write the following words in alphabetical order—*something, social, soap.*
   soap, social, something
2. How did you determine the order of the words above?
   Since they all begin with the same two letters, I used the third letter to determine alphabetical order.
3. How many syllables does the word *encourages* have? 4
4. What does the word *support* mean? "to help; aid"
5. How should you pronounce the letter *c* in local?
   Possible responses: /k/; with a hard sound; like the letter *k*

© Pearson Education, Inc., 3

Home Activity Your child alphabetized words to the third letter and used sample glossary entries to determine meanings, syllabication, and pronunciation of words. Have your child choose one of the sample glossary entries and explain what information readers can learn from each part of the entry.

414 Vocabulary

Reader's and Writer's Notebook, p. 414

Connect to Social Studies

Communities Murals often bring members of a community together. What kind of mural would you expect to see in your community?

Activate Prior Knowledge Begin a word web with the word *mural* in the center. Have students activate their prior knowledge by adding related words to the word web. Record students' answers on the web, adding to it as they read the selection.

1ST READ

Access Text If students need help, then...

GRAPHIC SOURCES Have students look at the photograph and caption on p. 442. Then ask students how these graphic sources help them better understand the text in the first paragraph.

Think Aloud **MODEL** As I read, I can ask myself what information these graphic sources provide that may not be in the text. The photograph and caption on p. 442 help me see where this mural appears—on the side of a meat market in Los Angeles.

ON THEIR OWN For additional practice, see *Let's Practice It!* p. 384 on the *Teacher Resources DVD-ROM*.

Immigrant

On the walls of a meat market in Los Angeles is a mural about immigrants painted by Hector Ponce. It tells the history of the people who live in the Pico and Hoover neighborhood. This mural, titled "Immigrant," shows the Statue of Liberty just beyond reach and Latin American immigrants working hard to provide for their families. Do you see a woman with young children, a man selling bags of oranges, a seamstress, and a man looking for cans to recycle?

Hector Ponce, the artist, came from El Salvador more than 15 years ago. He says, "My mural shows what's in the hearts of many people who come to this country looking for a better life."

▲ "Immigrant," Los Angeles, California ►

442

Student Edition, p. 442

2ND READ

Close Reading

INFERENCE • TEXT EVIDENCE
What clue in the text tells you that muralist Hector Ponce was an immigrant? Why do you think that information was included in this photo essay? (The first sentence of the last paragraph tells us that Hector Ponce came to the United States from El Salvador. This facts shows that he knows what it is like to be a Latin American immigrant.)

DEVELOP LANGUAGE Have students reread the first paragraph on p. 442 and look at the photographs on p. 443. What is a *seamstress?* What are some examples of the kinds of things a *seamstress* might produce?

Student Edition, p. 443

EVALUATION Why did Hector Ponce include the Statue of Liberty in his mural "Immigrant"? (The Statue of Liberty is a symbol of freedom known by many around the world. Including the Statue of Liberty in the mural shows that the people are hoping for freedom and liberty in America.)

Common Core State Standards

Informational Text 1. Ask and answer questions to demonstrate understanding of a text, referring explicitly to the text as the basis for the answers. **Informational Text 7.** Use information gained from illustrations (e.g., maps, photographs) and the words in a text to demonstrate understanding of the text (e.g., where, when, why, and how key events occur). **Also Informational Text 10.**

Connect to Social Studies

Art and Culture Artists often create images that reflect their cultures. They can depict the world around them or paint scenes from their history or mythology. Hector Ponce uses art to show the everyday lives of immigrants. Have students look at the murals on pp. 442–443. Ask why they think Hector Ponce painted these murals.

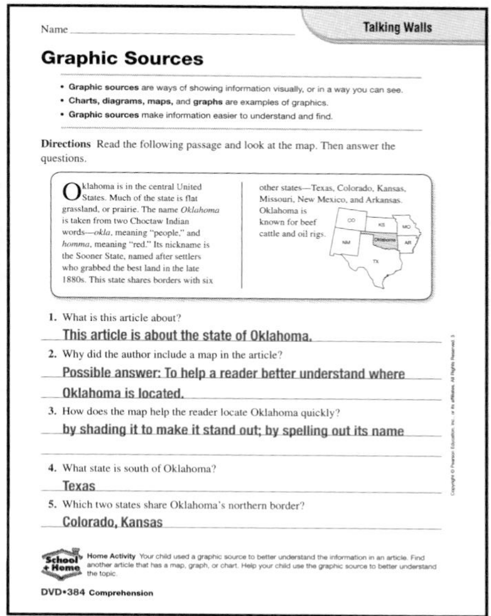

Name ______ Talking Walls

Graphic Sources

- **Graphic sources** are ways of showing information visually, or in a way you can see.
- **Charts, diagrams, maps,** and **graphs** are examples of graphics.
- **Graphic sources** make information easier to understand and find.

Directions Read the following passage and look at the map. Then answer the questions.

Oklahoma is in the central United States. Much of the state is flat grassland, or prairie. The name *Oklahoma* is taken from two Choctaw Indian words—*okla*, meaning "people," and *homma*, meaning "red." Its nickname is the Sooner State, named after settlers who grabbed the best land in the late 1880s. This state shares borders with six other states—Texas, Colorado, Kansas, Missouri, New Mexico, and Arkansas. Oklahoma is known for beef cattle and oil rigs.

1. What is this article about?
   This article is about the state of Oklahoma.
2. Why did the author include a map in the article?
   Possible answer: To help a reader better understand where Oklahoma is located.
3. How does the map help the reader locate Oklahoma quickly?
   by shading it to make it stand out; by spelling out its name
4. What state is south of Oklahoma?
   Texas
5. Which two states share Oklahoma's northern border?
   Colorado, Kansas

School + Home **Home Activity** Your child used a graphic source to better understand the information in an article. Find another article that has a map, graph, or chart. Help your child use the graphic source to better understand the topic.

DVD•384 Comprehension

Let's Practice It! TR DVD•384

Vocabulary: Idioms Focus students' attention on the expression "what's in the hearts" on p. 442. This is an idiom that means "what people feel." Ask students to share "what's in their hearts" when they think about the freedoms they have today.

1ST READ

Access Text © If students need help, then…

Review FACT AND OPINION Have students tell which is fact or opinion: *Before artist Joshua Sarantitis creates a mural, he talks with the people of the community.* (fact) *It's a good thing Joshua Sarantitus talks with members of the community.* (opinion)

Think Aloud **MODEL** How could I check or verify whether the first sentence is a fact? (ask the artist) What can I conclude from this fact? (that the murals reflect real life) What words in the second sentence tell me that this might be an opinion? *(It's a good thing)*

ON THEIR OWN Have students reread p. 444 to find more statements of fact about Joshua Sarantitis's murals. For additional practice with fact and opinion, see *Let's Practice It!* p. 385 on the *Teacher Resources DVD-ROM*.

Reach High and You Will Go Far

Before artist Joshua Sarantitis creates a mural, he talks with the people of the community. He listens to their stories about the neighborhood. He interprets their stories by making sketches, and then he makes plans for the painting of the mural.

Over the years, Sarantitis has created many public murals across America, including "Reach High and You Will Go Far." This mural honors the hopes and dreams of the many children who live in a downtown neighborhood in Philadelphia. The painting is beautiful. It shows a young girl with her arms held high. Her hands and fingers become a tree rising over the building. The artist fashioned the top of the tree as a billboard extending above the roof to show how people can grow and change. The mural encourages children to reach for the future through education.

444

Student Edition, p. 444

ANALYSIS Help students generate text-based questions by providing the following question stem: In the selection, how do murals ________?

2ND READ

Close Reading ©

ANALYSIS Find one more statement of opinion on page 444. How do you know it is an opinion? (*The painting is beautiful.* It is the author's feeling or judgment that the painting is beautiful. It can't be proved true or false.)

CHECK PREDICTIONS Have students look back at the predictions they made earlier and discuss whether they were accurate. Then have students preview the rest of the selection and either adjust their predictions accordingly or make new predictions.

Student Edition, p. 445

If you want to teach this selection in two sessions, stop here.

If you want to continue reading this selection, turn to p. 446–447.

EVALUATION • TEXT EVIDENCE What evidence in the text and photograph on page 445 supports the statement that "Reach High and You Will Go Far" is a mural that "encourages children to reach for the future"? (It shows a young girl reaching up, with her hands and fingers becoming a tree. We see the roots of the tree extending from her arms up through her hands to support the tree. The treetop is on a billboard rising over the mural to symbolize how people can grow and change.)

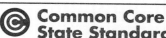

Common Core State Standards

Informational Text 1. Ask and answer questions to demonstrate understanding of a text, referring explicitly to the text as the basis for the answers. **Informational Text 7.** Use information gained from illustrations (e.g., maps, photographs) and the words in a text to demonstrate understanding of the text (e.g., where, when, why, and how key events occur). **Also Informational Text 2., 10.**

Access for All

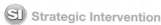

Strategic Intervention

Arrange students in small groups. Have groups write statements of fact and opinion about the mural "Reach High and You Will Go Far." Groups can share their statements. Other groups can decide which statements are fact and which are opinions.

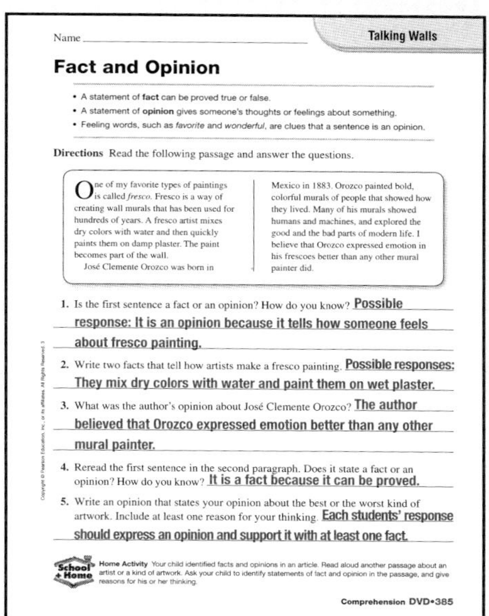

Name ______________ Talking Walls

Fact and Opinion

- A statement of **fact** can be proved true or false.
- A statement of **opinion** gives someone's thoughts or feelings about something.
- Feeling words, such as *favorite* and *wonderful*, are clues that a sentence is an opinion.

Directions Read the following passage and answer the questions.

One of my favorite types of paintings is called *fresco*. Fresco is a way of creating wall murals that has been used for hundreds of years. A fresco artist mixes dry colors with water and then quickly paints them on damp plaster. The paint becomes part of the wall.

José Clemente Orozco was born in Mexico in 1883. Orozco painted bold, colorful murals of people that showed how they lived. Many of his murals showed humans and machines, and explored the good and the bad parts of modern life. I believe that Orozco expressed emotion in his frescoes better than any other mural painter did.

1. Is the first sentence a fact or an opinion? How do you know? **Possible response: It is an opinion because it tells how someone feels about fresco painting.**
2. Write two facts that tell how artists make a fresco painting. **Possible responses: They mix dry colors with water and paint them on wet plaster.**
3. What was the author's opinion about José Clemente Orozco? **The author believed that Orozco expressed emotion better than any other mural painter.**
4. Reread the first sentence in the second paragraph. Does it state a fact or an opinion? How do you know? **It is a fact because it can be proved.**
5. Write an opinion that states your opinion about the best or the worst kind of artwork. Include at least one reason for your thinking. **Each students' response should express an opinion and support it with at least one fact.**

School + Home **Home Activity** Your child identified facts and opinions in an article. Read aloud another passage about an artist or a kind of artwork. Ask your child to identify statements of fact and opinion in the passage, and give reasons for his or her thinking.

Comprehension DVD•385

Let's Practice It! TR DVD•385

Vocabulary: Compound Words Have students find a compound word on p. 444 *(neighborhood, downtown, billboard)*. In pairs, have students look at one of the sentences with these words. Have students use context clues to determine the meaning of the words. Have students restate the meanings to the class.

Common Core State Standards

Informational Text 5. Use text features and search tools (e.g., key words, sidebars, hyperlinks) to locate information relevant to a given topic efficiently. **Writing 8.** Recall information from experiences or gather information from print and digital sources; take brief notes on sources and sort evidence into provided categories. **Language 1.h.** Use coordinating and subordinating conjunctions. **Language 1.i.** Produce simple, compound, and complex sentences. **Language 2.f.** Use spelling patterns and generalizations (e.g., word families, position-based spellings, syllable patterns, ending rules, meaningful word parts) in writing words.

Bridge to Common Core

RESEARCH TO BUILD AND PRESENT KNOWLEDGE

On Day 2 of the weeklong research project, students gather relevant information based on their focused questions from Day 1. They consult digital sources, using bolded and italicized words to locate relevant information. They evaluate the credibility and relevance of each Web site. This process enables students to demonstrate an understanding of the subject under investigation.

Research and Inquiry

Step 2 Navigate/Search

TEACH Have students generate a research plan for gathering relevant information about their research questions. Encourage them to search the Internet using their inquiry questions and keywords. Tell them to skim and scan each site for information that helps answer their inquiry question or leads them to specific information that will be useful. Bolded or italicized words may be clues to the kind of information the Web site will provide. Have students look for other features, such as headings, illustrations, captions, or highlighting. Remind students to take notes as they gather information.

Think Aloud **MODEL** When searching for information on the importance of freedom of expression, I found links to the First Amendment. I will scan and bookmark Web sites that contain information on the First Amendment because I know that this amendment deals with freedom of speech.

GUIDE PRACTICE Have students continue their review of Web sites they identified. Have students weed out any Web sites that are out of date or that are not relevant to their inquiry question.

ON THEIR OWN Have students write down Web addresses, authors, and the dates the Web sites were last updated and create a Works Cited page.

Conventions

Combining Sentences

TEACH One way to learn about compound sentences is to know how to identify them when you read. Write this sentence: *My cat likes to play at night, and he is always running and meowing at my feet.* Have students break it into two sentences.

GUIDE PRACTICE Have students identify the compound sentence in the following paragraph:

> **Parents, students, and teachers enjoy art. Teachers provide art materials, and students make creative art projects. Parents come to school and enjoy the art that students create.**

Have students identify sentences in *Talking Walls: Art for the People* that can be broken into two simple sentences. (p. 440: *These painted walls are called murals and are often painted in public places for all the people in the community to see.*)

ON THEIR OWN For additional practice, use *Reader's and Writer's Notebook,* p. 411.

Spelling

Final Syllables *-ion, -ure*

TEACH Remind students that their spelling words have the final syllables *-ion* and *-ure*. Model how to spell those words. The parts in *creature* are *crea* and *ture*. First, I write the first syllable, *crea*. Then I write the second syllable, *ture*. Then I spell *creature, c-r-e-a-t-u-r-e*.

GUIDE PRACTICE Have students write each spelling word and underline the final syllables.

ON THEIR OWN For additional practice, use *Reader's and Writer's Notebook,* p. 412.

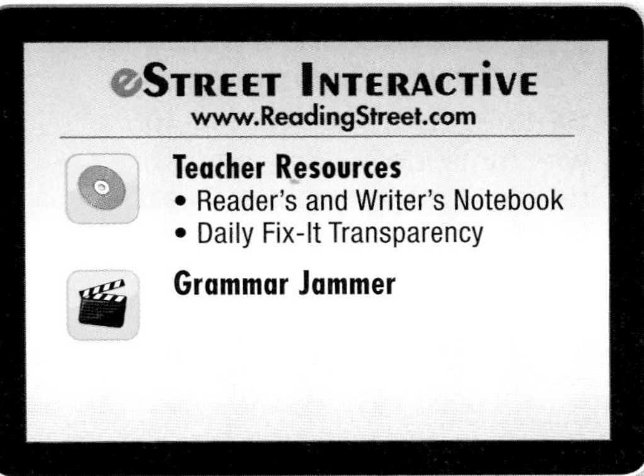

Daily Fix-It

3. The classes paints the mural on a large wall of the shcool. *(paint; school)*
4. We didnt know what great artests we had. *(didn't; artists)*

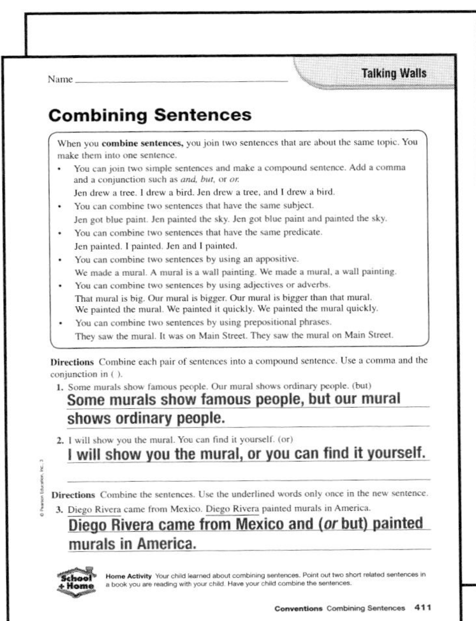

Name ____________ Talking Walls

Combining Sentences

When you **combine sentences,** you join two sentences that are about the same topic. You make them into one sentence.

- You can join two simple sentences and make a compound sentence. Add a comma and a conjunction such as *and, but,* or *or.*
  Jen drew a tree. I drew a bird. Jen drew a tree, and I drew a bird.
- You can combine two sentences that have the same subject.
  Jen got blue paint. Jen painted the sky. Jen got blue paint and painted the sky.
- You can combine two sentences that have the same predicate.
  Jen painted. I painted. Jen and I painted.
- You can combine two sentences by using an appositive.
  We made a mural. A mural is a wall painting. We made a mural, a wall painting.
- You can combine two sentences by using adjectives or adverbs.
  That mural is big. Our mural is bigger. Our mural is bigger than that mural.
  We painted the mural. We painted it quickly. We painted the mural quickly.
- You can combine two sentences by using prepositional phrases.
  They saw the mural. It was on Main Street. They saw the mural on Main Street.

Directions Combine each pair of sentences into a compound sentence. Use a comma and the conjunction in ( ).

1. Some murals show famous people. Our mural shows ordinary people. (but)
   Some murals show famous people, but our mural shows ordinary people.
2. I will show you the mural. You can find it yourself. (or)
   I will show you the mural, or you can find it yourself.

Directions Combine the sentences. Use the underlined words only once in the new sentence.

3. Diego Rivera came from Mexico. Diego Rivera painted murals in America.
   Diego Rivera came from Mexico and (*or* but) painted murals in America.

School + Home **Home Activity** Your child learned about combining sentences. Point out two short related sentences in a book you are reading with your child. Have your child combine the sentences.

Conventions Combining Sentences 411

Reader's and Writer's Notebook, pp. 411–412

Conventions To provide students with practice on combining sentences, use the modified grammar lessons in the *ELL Handbook* and the Grammar Jammer online at: www.ReadingStreet.com

Language Transfer: Clauses Students may have difficulty recognizing the clauses in a compound sentence. Give them additional practice finding the subject and verb within each independent clause.

Common Core State Standards

Writing 2.b. Develop the topic with facts, definitions, and details. **Language 3.a.** Choose words and phrases for effect. **Language 4.a.** Use sentence-level context as a clue to the meaning of a word or phrase. **Language 5.** Demonstrate understanding of word relationships and nuances in word meanings. **Language 5.b.** Identify real-life connections between words and their use (e.g., describe people who are *friendly* or *helpful*).

Writing

Description

Writer's Craft: Sensory Details

INTRODUCE THE PROMPT Review the key features of a description. Remind students that a description explains what something is like. A description uses words that appeal to the senses—taste, touch, smell, hearing, and sight. Point out that when describing a piece of art, a writer might use many sensory images that appeal to sight and touch, rather than taste, smell, or hearing.

Writing Prompt

Think about a piece of art that you know from the selection or your own life. Describe it, using sensory details.

SELECT A TOPIC

First, I'm going to look through the photos in *Talking Walls: Art for the People*. Let's see how these murals make us feel and what details make us feel that way. I'm going to write these details in a chart.

Display a three-column chart. Fill in the descriptions based on student responses. But my favorite piece of art is a collage my friend Ori made of a cat. It makes me feel really happy. Have students complete their own charts.

Name of Art	My Feeling	Sensory Details
"Community of Music"	magical, mysterious	green grass, blue and purple rocks, shadows, straight, tall people
"Dreams of Flight"	light, like I want to move	animals and a plane flying, people swinging and jumping
My friend Ori's collage	happy	bright colors, bottle caps for eyes, glitter, bumpy yarn for fur

GATHER INFORMATION Remind students that they can do research to help them find additional images of artwork. Have students keep this chart, as they will refer to it again tomorrow as they draft.

Corrective feedback If students seem to have trouble finding a piece of art that interests them, help them look through print resources and Web sites of different styles of visual art to find a piece of art that evokes strong emotion.

eStreet Interactive
www.ReadingStreet.com

Teacher Resources
- Reader's and Writer's Notebook
- Graphic Organizer

Mini-Lesson Main Idea and Details

- Knowing your main idea helps you keep your composition focused. When you know your main idea, you can make sure that each one of your details supports that idea. I've decided that my topic will be my friend Ori's cat collage, because I like it so much. I will use a chart to organize the details I will use to describe Ori's collage. Draw a main idea chart, but draw only two boxes for supporting details. In the Main Idea box, I will write, *My friend Ori made a collage of a cat.*
- I will use the sensory details from my earlier chart to describe Ori's collage. In the first box, I will describe how it looks: *It has bright colors, bottle caps for eyes, glitter, and yarn fur*. In the second box, I will describe how it makes me feel: *It makes me feel happy*.

  Have students begin their own chart using the form on p. 413 of their *Reader's and Writer's Notebook*.

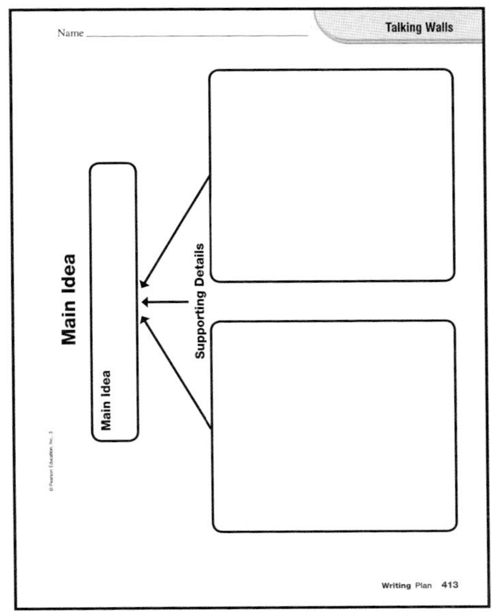

Reader's and Writer's Notebook, p. 413

Routine Quick Write for Fluency

Team Talk

1. **Talk** Pairs of students exchange images of the art they will be describing.
2. **Write** Students brainstorm a list of words and phrases that describe their partner's piece of art.
3. **Share** Students read their lists to each other. Make clear that students can use their partner's list to help them write their description.

Routines Flip Chart

Wrap Up Your Day!

- ✓ **Content Knowledge** Have students discuss how artists express themselves by painting murals.
- ✓ **Text-Based Comprehension** *How do the photographs help you understand the selection?*

Preview DAY 3

Tell students that tomorrow they will read more about interesting murals.

DAY 3 at a Glance

Content Knowledge
Oral Vocabulary

Phonics/Word Analysis
Final Syllables

Text-Based Comprehension
Graphic Sources
Important Ideas

Fluency
Accuracy

Research and Study Skills
Alphabetical Order

Research and Inquiry
Analyze Information

Conventions
Combining Sentences

Spelling
Final Syllables

Writing
Description

Materials

- Student Edition
- Reader's and Writer's Notebook
- Retelling Cards
- Decodable Reader

Common Core State Standards

Speaking/Listening 1. Engage effectively in a range of collaborative discussions (one-on-one, in groups, and teacher led) with diverse partners on grade 3 topics and texts, building on others' ideas and expressing their own clearly. **Language 6.** Acquire and use accurately grade-appropriate conversational, general academic, and domain-specific words and phrases, including those that signal spatial and temporal relationships (e.g., *After dinner that night we went looking for them*).

Content Knowledge

Freedom of Expression

EXPAND THE CONCEPT Remind students of the weekly concept question, *Why is freedom of expression important?* Discuss how the question relates to *Talking Walls: Art for the People*. Encourage students to think about artists and why they value freedom of expression.

Build Oral Language

TALK ABOUT SENTENCES AND WORDS Reread this sentence from Student Edition p. 440.

The people in America enjoy many different kinds of freedom, including the freedom of artistic expression.

- What is the base word in the word *artistic?* *(art)* So you know this word has something to do with art. What are some different forms of art? (paintings, sculpture, music, dance)
- What is the base word in the word *expression?* *(express)* What does it mean to "express your feelings"? (to translate your feelings into actions, for example, talking about them or doing something to convey them)
- Adding *-ion* to a verb can turn it into a noun. For example, if we add *-ion* to the verbs *discuss* and *subtract,* we get the nouns *discussion* and *subtraction*. So *expression* is a noun.
- The word *artistic* is being used to describe the noun *expression*. What do we call a word used to describe a noun? (adjective)

Team Talk Have students work in pairs to discuss the following question.

- Using what you now know, how would you explain the term *artistic expression* in your own words? (Possible response: using some kind of art form to show your thoughts, ideas, and/or feelings)

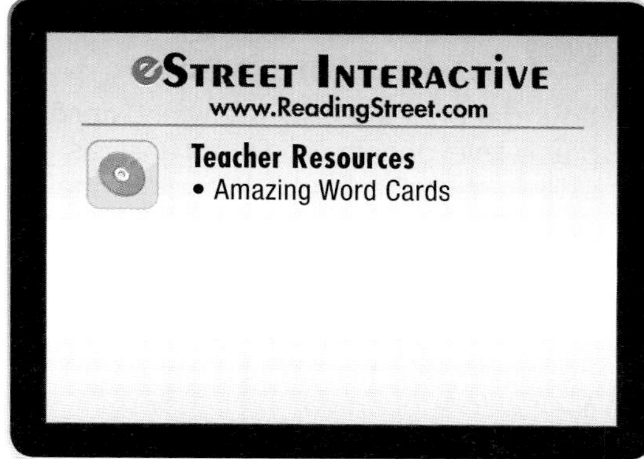

Build Oral Vocabulary

Amazing Words — Robust Vocabulary Routine

1. **Introduce** Write the word *significant* on the board. Have students say it with you. Yesterday we read about and looked at photos of some *significant* murals. Have students determine a definition of *significant*. (*Significant* means having importance.)
2. **Demonstrate** Have students answer questions to demonstrate understanding. How is an artist's personal life *significant* to what they paint? (Many artists paint murals showing where they came from or where they now live.)
3. **Apply** Have students apply their understanding. What is a synonym for *significant?*
4. **Display the Word** Run your hand under the word parts *sig-nif-i-cant* as you read the word.

See p. OV•3 to teach *pause*.

Routines Flip Chart

ADD TO THE CONCEPT MAP Discuss the Amazing Words *exquisite* and *lecture*. Add these and other concept-related words to the concept map. Use the following questions to develop students' understanding of the concept. Add words generated in the discussion to the concept map.

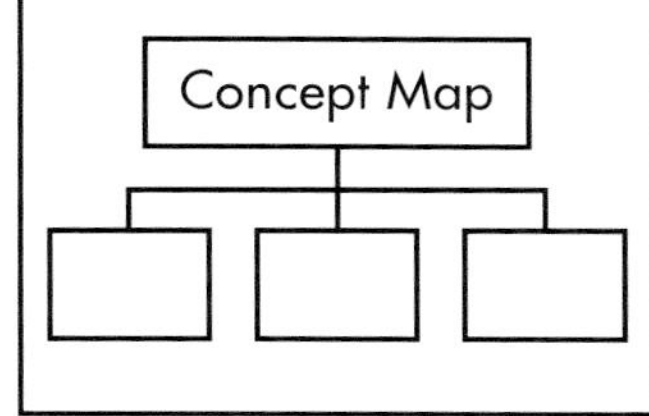

- Many of the murals in the story have *exquisite* details and colors. Think about what *exquisite* means. What makes freedom of expression *exquisite?*
- Think about the artists and why they painted the murals they did. If these artists were going to prepare a *lecture* for an art class, what would they say?

Amazing Words

creative	lecture
expressive	significant
emotion	pause
artistic	view
exquisite	lyrics

Expand Vocabulary Use the Day 3 instruction on ELL Poster 28 to help students expand vocabulary.

Common Core State Standards

Foundational Skills 3. Know and apply grade-level phonics and word analysis skills in decoding words. **Foundational Skills 3.b.** Decode words with common Latin suffixes. **Foundational Skills 3.d.** Read grade-appropriate irregularly spelled words. **Foundational Skills 4.** Read with sufficient accuracy and fluency to support comprehension. **Foundational Skills 4.b.** Read on-level prose and poetry orally with accuracy, appropriate rate, and expression on successive readings.

Word Analysis

Final Syllables

MODEL WORD SORTING Write *-tion, -ion, -ture, -ive,* and *-ize* as heads in a five-column chart. Now we are going to sort words. We'll put words with the syllable *-tion* in the first column. Words with the syllable *-ion* will go in the second column. Words with the syllable *-ture* will go in the third column, words with the syllable *-ive* will go in the fourth column, and words with the syllable *-ize* will go in the last column. I will start. Write *structure* and model how to read it, using the Teach/Model section on p. 432a. *Structure* ends with the final syllable *-ture,* so I will write *structure* in the third column. Model reading *expansion* and *subtraction* in the same way.

GUIDE PRACTICE Use practice words from the activity on p. 432a for the word sort. Point to a word. Have students read the word, identify its parts, and tell where it should be written on the chart.

Corrective feedback | For corrective feedback, model reading each word the same way you read *structure.*

-tion	-ion	-ture	-ive	-ize
subtraction	expansion	structure	active	realize
education	expression	culture	native	summarize
celebration		adventure		
direction				

Fluent Word Reading

MODEL Write *motorize.* I recognize the syllable *-ize* at the end. I combine that with the two other syllables *mo-tor* to read the whole word, *motorize.*

GUIDE PRACTICE Write the words below. Look for the word parts you know. When I point to the word, we'll read it together. Allow one second per word part previewing time for the first reading.

mature	civilize	positive	confusion	intervention	nature

ON THEIR OWN Have students read the list above three or four times, until they can read one word per second.

Decodable Passage 28B

If students need help, then…

Read *Talkative Millie*

READ WORDS IN ISOLATION Have students turn to p. 153 in *Decodable Practice Readers 3.2* and find the first list of words. Each word in this list has the final syllable *-tion, -ion, -ture, -ive,* or *-ize.* Let's read these words. Be sure that students pronounce each final syllable correctly.

Next, have students read the high-frequency words.

PREVIEW Have students read the title and preview the story. Tell them that they will read words with final syllables *-tion, -ion, -ture, -ive,* and *-ize.*

READ WORDS IN CONTEXT Chorally read the story along with the students. Have students identify words in the story with final syllables *-tion, -ion, -ture, -ive,* and *-ize.* Make sure that students are monitoring their accuracy when they decode words.

Team Talk Pair students and have them take turns reading the story aloud to each other. Monitor students as they read to check for proper pronunciation and appropriate pacing.

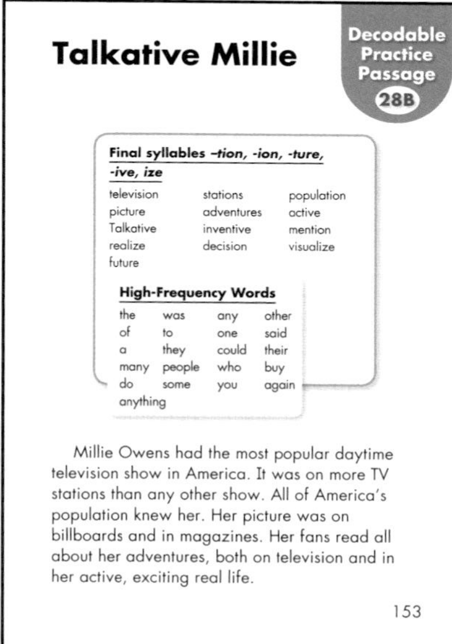

Talkative Millie

Decodable Practice Passage 28B

Final syllables *-tion, -ion, -ture, -ive, ize*

television	stations	population
picture	adventures	active
Talkative	inventive	mention
realize	decision	visualize
future		

High-Frequency Words

the	was	any	other
of	to	one	said
a	they	could	their
many	people	who	buy
do	some	you	again
anything			

Millie Owens had the most popular daytime television show in America. It was on more TV stations than any other show. All of America's population knew her. Her picture was on billboards and in magazines. Her fans read all about her adventures, both on television and in her active, exciting real life.

153

On Mondays, Millie Owens's show was always about cooking. Talkative Millie joked and told stories as she showed her fans how to prepare her new favorite dish.

One Monday, Millie baked an inventive new kind of casserole. When she lifted the hot dish out of the oven, Millie happened to mention that her oven mitts looked worn out. Talkative Millie did not even realize she had said it.

But across America, hundreds of thousands of Millie's fans realized she did. And most of those fans made a decision. They decided to send Millie new oven mitts. Fans could visualize Millie using their oven mitts on TV.

A few fans made oven mitts and sent them to Millie. Many, many fans bought mitts and sent them. Soon TV stations across America had boxes and boxes of mitts for Millie. For weeks, truckloads of mitts arrived at Millie's studio. People who really needed new oven mitts could not buy them. Stores had run out!

Millie did not know what to do with those mitts. She sent some to needy people, but the rest she saved. You can see them in Millie Owens's Museum of Oven Mitts!

And in the future, talkative Millie will never again mention on TV anything she might need!

154

Decodable Practice Passage 28B

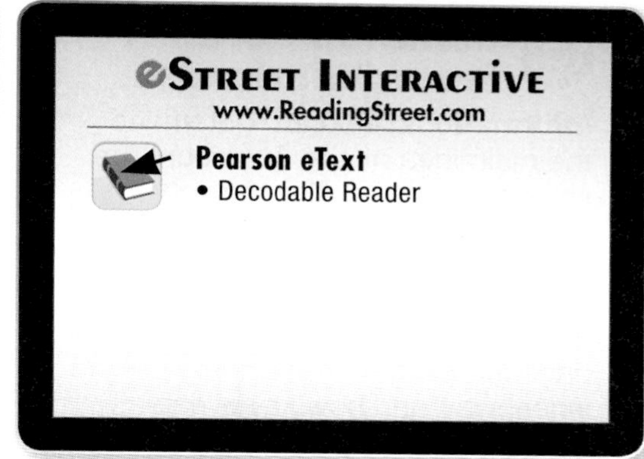

eStreet Interactive
www.ReadingStreet.com

Pearson eText
- Decodable Reader

Access for All

Advanced

Have students choose four words from the word sort activity and write a paragraph about school. Have students trade paragraphs with a partner and identify the words used that have final syllables *-tion, -ion, -ture, -ive,* and *-ize.*

Text-Based Comprehension

Check Understanding

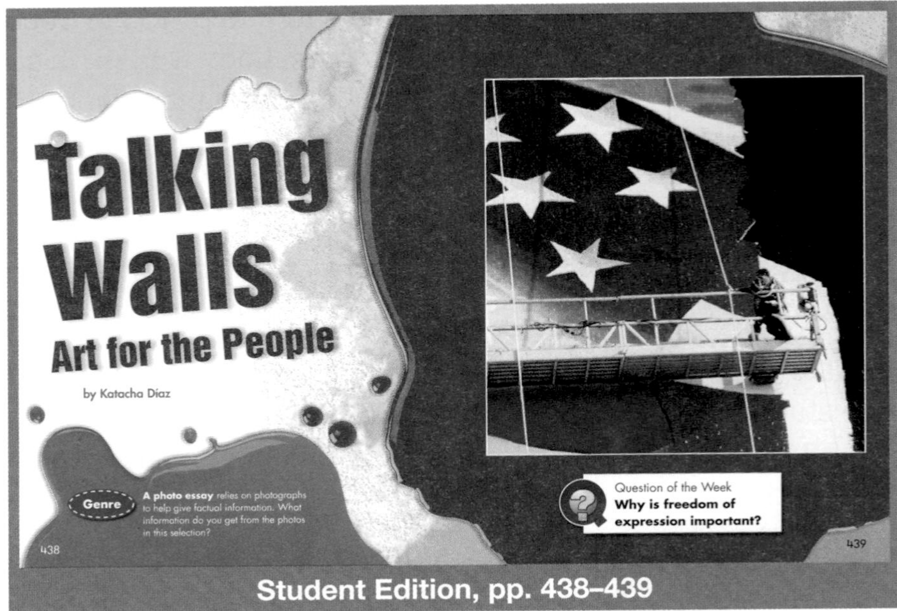

Student Edition, pp. 438–439

If... you chose to read *Talking Walls: Art for the People* in two parts, **then...** use the following questions to monitor students' understanding of pp. 438–445 of the selection. Encourage students to cite evidence from the text.

EVALUATION What are a few of the most important ideas the author wanted to share in the first part of this selection? How do you know? (Artists paint many different kinds of murals. The murals tell about different things such as about the neighborhoods and history of the people who live there. The illustrations help me realize the most important ideas.)

INFERENCE Use what you have learned about murals to define the word *canvas*. Check your definition in a dictionary or glossary. (*Canvas* means "something you paint on." I arrived at this definition because the text says muralists use walls as a canvas.)

RETELL Have students retell *Talking Walls: Art for the People.* Ask students to use details and name specific information in the graphic sources that helps them retell the text.

Corrective feedback	**If...** students leave out important details, **then...** have them look back through the illustrations and photographs in the selection.

READ Use the **Access Text** and **Close Reading** notes to finish reading *Talking Walls: Art for the People.*

Common Core State Standards

Informational Text 2. Determine the main idea of a text; recount the key details and explain how they support the main idea. **Informational Text 7.** Use information gained from illustrations (e.g., maps, photographs), and the words in a text to demonstrate understanding of the text (e.g., where, when, why, and how key events occur). **Speaking/Listening 4.** Report on a topic or text, tell a story, or recount an experience with appropriate facts and relevant, descriptive details, speaking clearly at an understandable pace.

Strategy Response Log

Have students revisit p. 34 in their *Reader's and Writer's Notebook* to add additional information about photo essays.

If... you followed the Read for Understanding routine below,
then... ask students to retell the selection before you reread *Talking Walls: Art for the People*.

RETELL Have students retell *Talking Walls: Art for the People*. Ask students to use details and name specific information in the graphic sources that helps them retell the text.

Corrective feedback	**If...** students leave out important details, **then...** have them look back through the illustrations and photographs in the selection.

READ Return to p. 440–441 and use the **2nd Read/Close Reading** notes to reread *Talking Walls: Art for the People.*

Read Main Selection

Routine Read for Understanding

Deepen understanding by reading the selection multiple times.

1. **First Read**—If students need support, then use the **Access Text** notes to help them clarify understanding.
2. **Second Read**—Use the **Close Reading** notes to help students draw knowledge from the text.

Day 3 SMALL GROUP TIME • Differentiate Close Reading, p. SG•33

OL On-Level

- **Reread** to Develop Vocabulary
- **Read** *Talking Walls: Art for the People*

SI Strategic Intervention

- **Reread** to Develop Vocabulary
- **Read** *Talking Walls: Art for the People*

A Advanced

- **Reread** to Extend Vocabulary
- **Read** *Talking Walls: Art for the People*
- **Investigate** Inquiry Project

eSTREET INTERACTIVE
www.ReadingStreet.com

- **Pearson eText**
  - Student Edition
- **AudioText CD**
- **Teacher Resources**
  - Reader's and Writer's Notebook

Check Retelling To support retelling, review the multilingual summary for *Talking Walls: Art for the People* with the appropriate Retelling Cards to scaffold understanding.

If... students need more scaffolding and practice with the **Main Selection,**
then... use the activities on p. DI•72 in the Teacher Resources section on SuccessNet.

1ST READ

Access Text

If students need help, then…

IMPORTANT IDEAS Ask students to state one important idea from the first paragraph on p. 446.

MODEL I know that important ideas are the facts and details that the author most wants me to learn from the text. When I read the first paragraph, I read many details about Paul Botello, but the most important idea the author wants me to know is that he creates and paints murals. What do you think the most important idea is in paragraph 2 on p. 446?

A Shared Hope

Paul Botello was 8 years old when he began helping his older brother, David, paint murals. Paul loved painting murals and was inspired to become an artist like his brother. When Paul graduated from high school, he went on to college to study art. Today he creates and paints murals, and he teaches art too!

Paul painted a special mural called "A Shared Hope" for an elementary school in Los Angeles, California. Most of the students at Esperanza School are immigrants from Central America. The mural speaks to the schoolchildren. It tells them that education is the key to success.

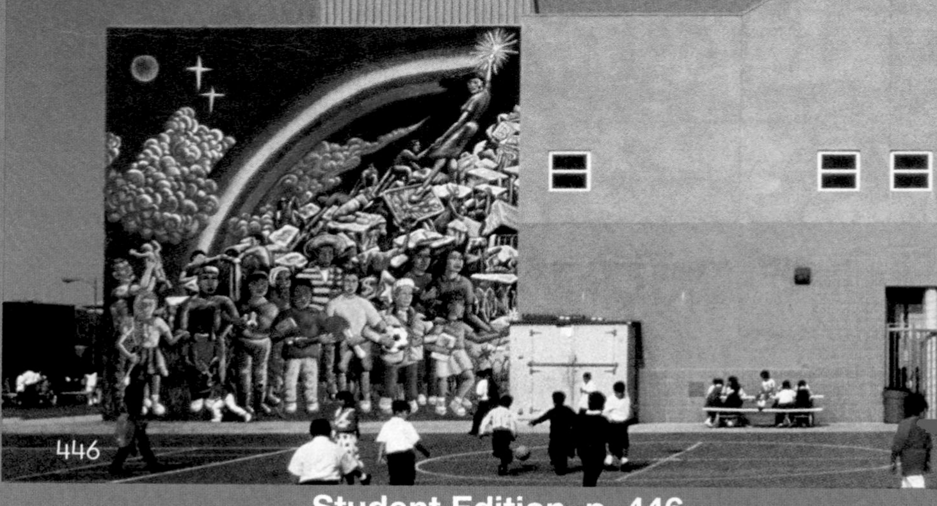

446

Student Edition, p. 446

2ND READ

Close Reading

EVALUATION • TEXT EVIDENCE

Why is "A Shared Hope" a good title for this mural? Use evidence from the text and the mural to support your answer. (It's a good title because its message is that children, with support from parents and teachers, can obtain a better life through education. The mural shows one line of children with objects symbolizing what they hope to do in the future. Their parents are standing behind them. Also shown is a second line of children being pulled up the building blocks of life by a teacher who is creating a rainbow as she climbs.)

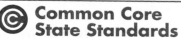

ON THEIR OWN Have students find the important ideas in the text on p. 447. Remind them that there can be more than one important idea.

At the top of the mural, a teacher helps guide her students over the building blocks of life. Students are standing at the bottom of the painting holding objects that symbolize their future. Their parents stand behind to help guide and support them. Teachers, students, and parents from the school posed for the artist and his assistants as they created the mural.

"Education, hope, and immigration are my themes," says Paul Botello. "People immigrate to the United States because they hope for a better life. Through education, a better life can be accomplished."

"A Shared Hope," Los Angeles, California

447

Student Edition, p. 447

ANALYSIS What does the author mean when she says that the mural "speaks to the schoolchildren"? (She means that, when the children see the mural, they learn an important message.)

Common Core State Standards

Informational Text 1. Ask and answer questions to demonstrate understanding of a text, referring explicitly to the text as the basis for the answers. **Informational Text 7.** Use information gained from illustrations (e.g., maps, photographs) and the words in a text to demonstrate understanding of the text (e.g., where, when, why, and how key events occur). **Also Informational Text 10., Language 5.a.**

Access for All

 **Advanced**

One of Paul Botello's important ideas is that education is the key to success. In small groups, have students discuss this idea and tell whether or not they agree with it.

Connect to Social Studies

Freedom of Speech One freedom of all Americans is the freedom of speech. Many people think that is our most important right. Discuss the effect of freedom of speech: How does it benefit our country? How does it not benefit our country? Make a list to discuss as a class.

Fact and Opinion Provide oral practice by having students share facts and opinions about their favorite artists or musicians. Then write these sentences on the board and read them aloud. Have students tell whether each sentence is a fact or an opinion; then support their answers.

- It would be fun to be an art teacher.
- "A Shared Hope" is the name of a mural on a building in Los Angeles.
- It's a good idea to paint murals for children.

1ST READ

Access Text If students need help, then...

UNKNOWN WORDS Tell students that the word *speak* has several meanings. Have students use a dictionary or glossary to determine the meaning of the word *speak* as it is used on p. 448, paragraph 3.

Think Aloud **MODEL** When I look up the word *speak* in a dictionary it gives two meanings: "to talk" and "to express opinions and ideas." Which meaning do you think the author means? ("to express opinions and ideas")

Dreams of Flight

David Botello—the older brother of Paul—loved to paint and dreamed of becoming an artist. When he was in the third grade, he and his art partner, Wayne Healy, painted a mural of a dinosaur in art class. Little did David know that that dinosaur mural was the first of many murals he would paint with Wayne.

Years later, the childhood friends, now both artists, decided to go into business together painting murals. David and Wayne often create and paint murals together, but not always.

David painted a large mural called "Dreams of Flight" at Estrada Courts, a public housing project in Los Angeles. He says, "I've always wanted this mural to speak to the children who see it, and to say, 'Your dreams can come true.'"

ARTIST	LOCATION	TITLE
Hector Ponce	Los Angeles, California	"Immigrant"
Joshua Sarantitis	Philadelphia, Pennsylvania	"Reach High and You Will Go Far"
Paul Botello	Los Angeles, California	"A Shared Hope"
Allyn Cox	U.S. Capitol, Washington, D.C.	"Declaration of Independence, 1776"

448

Student Edition, p. 448

2ND READ

Close Reading

ANALYSIS • TEXT EVIDENCE
How were dreams important to David Botello? Use evidence from the text to support your answer. (As a child, David dreamed of being an artist. When he painted "Dreams of Flight," he wanted it to tell children that if they work hard and followed their dreams, their dreams just might come true.)

REREAD CHALLENGING TEXT Have students reread the chart at the bottom of p. 448. Have them use the information to form a factual sentence. Some students may need to hear an example before being able to form a sentence on their own.

ON THEIR OWN Have students use a dictionary to figure out the meaning of the word *originally* on p. 449, paragraph 1.

It's interesting to note that when the artist repainted the mural seventeen years after it was originally completed, he changed one of the children from a boy to a girl. Much had changed over the years, and the artist wanted all children to know that girls can dream of flying model airplanes too. It is the artist's hope that over time the mural will inspire many of the children who see it to work hard and follow their dreams.

"Dreams of Flight," Los Angeles, California

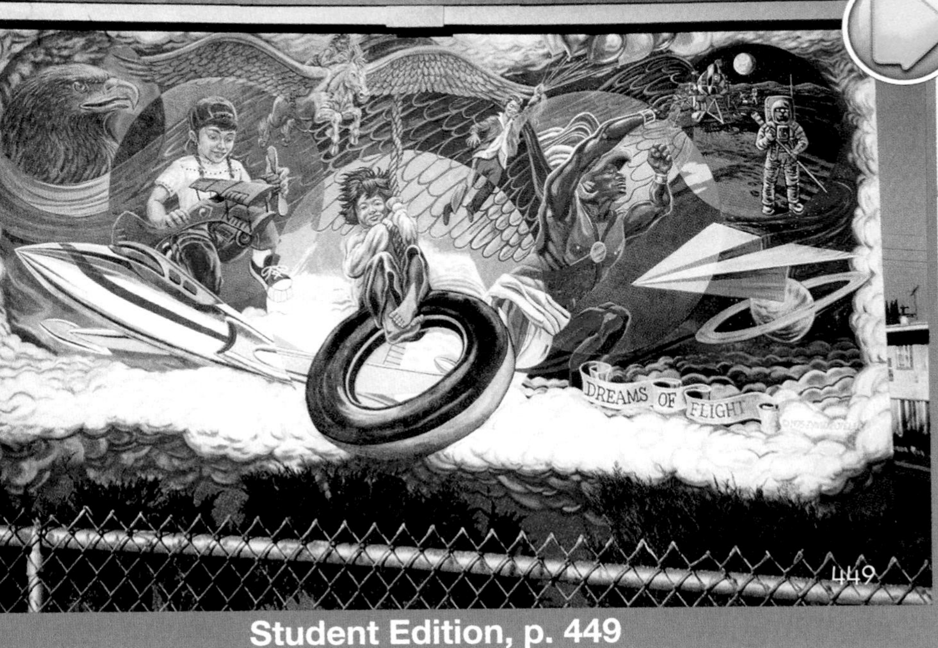

449

Student Edition, p. 449

ANALYSIS Is the first sentence on page 449 a statement of fact or an opinion? Explain how you can tell. (The sentence is an opinion. The words *It's interesting to note* show the author's belief.)

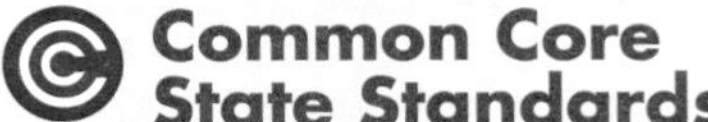

Common Core State Standards

Informational Text 1. Ask and answer questions to demonstrate understanding of a text, referring explicitly to the text as the basis for the answers. **Language 4.** Determine or clarify the meaning of unknown and multiple-meaning words and phrases based on grade 3 reading and content, choosing flexibly from a range of strategies. **Language 4.d.** Use glossaries or beginning dictionaries, both print and digital, to determine or clarify the precise meaning of key words and phrases. **Also Informational Text 10.**

Access for All

SI Strategic Intervention

Have students describe what the people in the mural "Dreams of Flight" are doing.

1ST READ

Access Text
If students need help, then...

GRAPHIC SOURCES Have students explain what they can tell about the mural on p. 450 just by looking at the photo.

Think Aloud **MODEL** Graphic sources help me get information presented visually. I see that the picture on page 450 shows an important event that took place a long time ago. Reading the caption confirms this.

ON THEIR OWN Have students look at the photo and caption at the top of p. 451. Ask what they learn from the caption.

CROSS-TEXT EVALUATION
Use a Strategy to Self-Check How did "Class Art" on p. 437 help you understand this selection?

Talking Walls

Cities, large and small, invite artists to paint special murals in public places for everyone to see. Murals are talking walls; they speak to the people.

Community murals tell stories of personal, political, and social beliefs of the local residents. Some murals inspire or amuse us, while others stir our hearts.

"Declaration of Independence, 1776" was painted by Allyn Cox in the United States Capitol, Washington, D.C.

450

Student Edition, p. 450

2ND READ

Close Reading

EVALUATION Reread the last sentence on page 450. Why does the author use the words *stir our hearts?* (to tell that some murals touch people very deeply)

SYNTHESIS • TEXT EVIDENCE Using what you learned in this selection, tell why freedom of expression is important. Have students cite examples from the text to support their responses.

CHECK PREDICTIONS Have students return to the predictions they made earlier and confirm whether they were accurate.

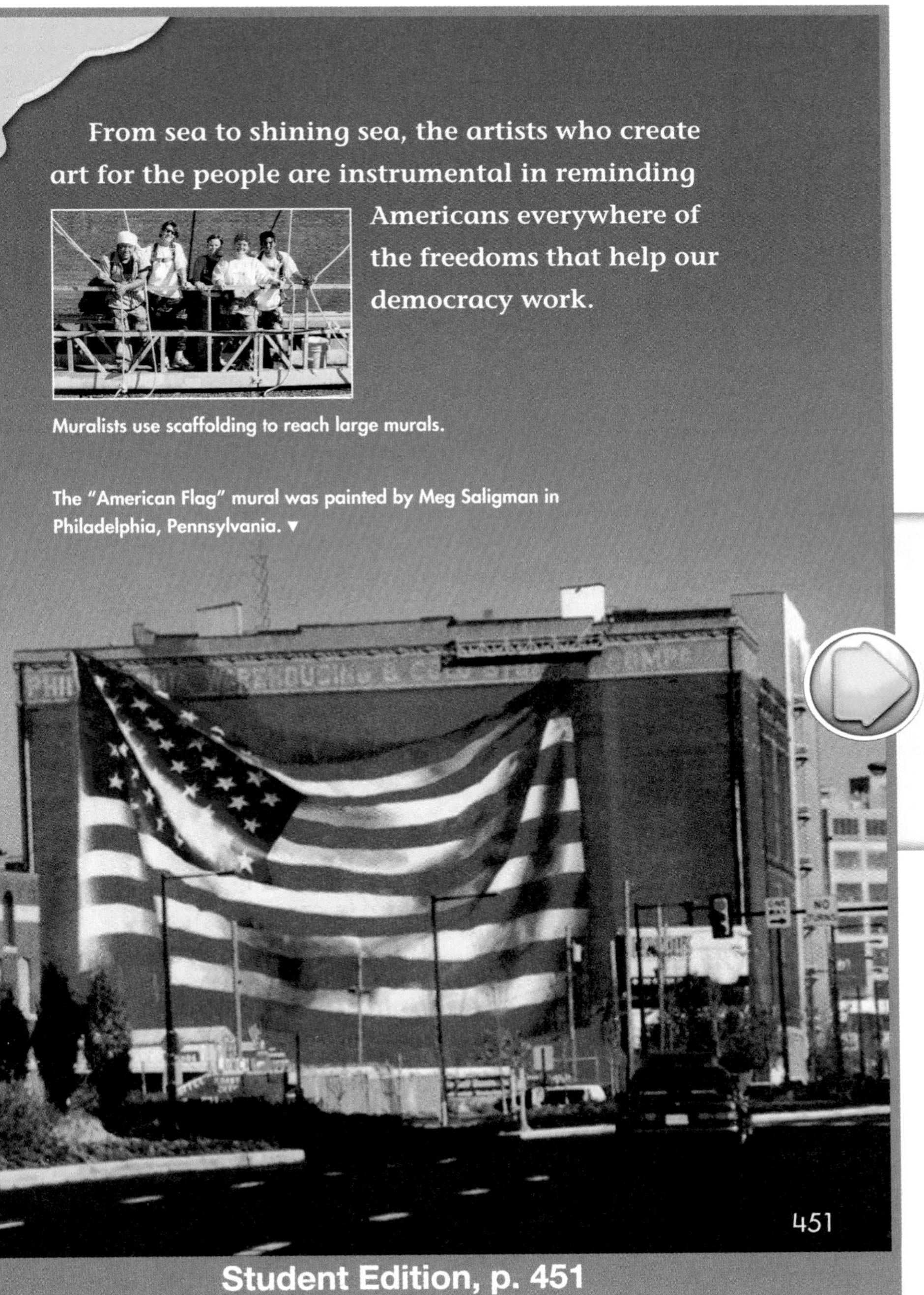

From sea to shining sea, the artists who create art for the people are instrumental in reminding Americans everywhere of the freedoms that help our democracy work.

Muralists use scaffolding to reach large murals.

The "American Flag" mural was painted by Meg Saligman in Philadelphia, Pennsylvania. ▼

451

Student Edition, p. 451

INFERENCE What conclusion can you draw about how the author of *Talking Walls: Art for the People* feels about the murals in the story? (The author likes the murals and thinks they remind Americans of the freedoms in our country.)

Common Core State Standards

Informational Text 1. Ask and answer questions to demonstrate understanding of a text, referring explicitly to the text as the basis for the answers. **Informational Text 7.** Use information gained from illustrations (e.g., maps, photographs) and the words in a text to demonstrate understanding of the text (e.g., where, when, why, and how key events occur). **Also Informational Text 10.**

Access for All

SI Strategic Intervention

Have children work in small groups to create their own mural symbolizing freedom.

A Advanced

Ask students to compare and contrast all of the murals in the story. Have them create a T-chart detailing their findings.

Professional Development: Shelter Instruction "English language learners benefit when teachers shelter, or make comprehensible their literacy instruction. One way to do this is to use consistent, simplified, clearly enunciated, and slower-paced oral language to explain literacy concepts or activities."—Dr. Georgia Earnest García

Common Core State Standards
Informational Text 1. Ask and answer questions to demonstrate understanding of a text, referring explicitly to the text as the basis for the answers. **Also Informational Text 2., 5., Writing 8.**

Envision It! Retell

READING STREET ONLINE
STORY SORT
www.ReadingStreet.com

Think Critically

1. The author uses a map to illustrate several mural locations in the United States. See if there is a mural in your city. If you were a muralist, where might you paint a mural? What would you paint a mural to celebrate? Text to Self
2. The subtitle of this selection is *Art for the People*. Why do you think the author used this subtitle? What topics does the author write about and why? Read "Meet the Author" on page 453 to find out. Think Like an Author
3. Look back at pages 448–449. What are the graphic sources on these pages? What information do they convey to the reader? Graphic Sources
4. What are the three most important ideas in the story? Explain your answers using evidence from the story. Important Ideas
5. **Look Back and Write** Look back at each artist and mural in the selection. Think about the reasons why the artists painted the murals. What do the murals represent, or stand for? Provide evidence to support your answer.
Key Ideas and Details • Text Evidence

452

Meet the Author

Katacha Díaz

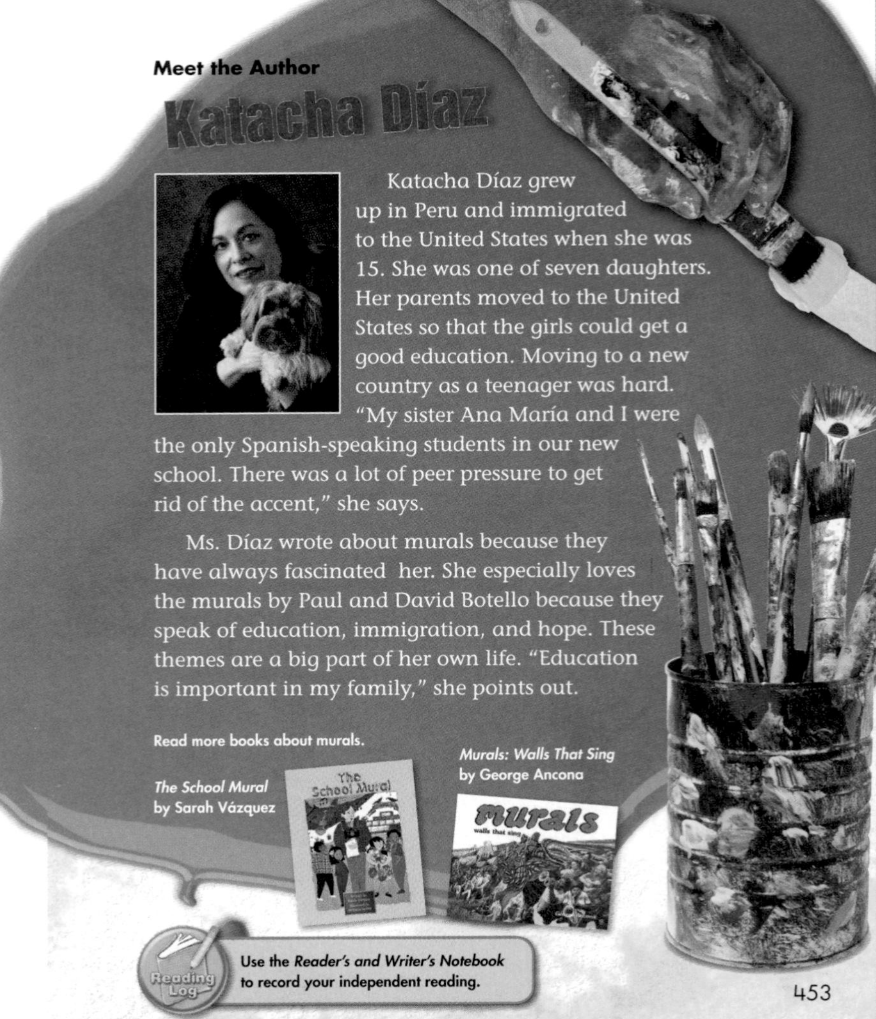

Katacha Díaz grew up in Peru and immigrated to the United States when she was 15. She was one of seven daughters. Her parents moved to the United States so that the girls could get a good education. Moving to a new country as a teenager was hard. "My sister Ana María and I were the only Spanish-speaking students in our new school. There was a lot of peer pressure to get rid of the accent," she says.

Ms. Díaz wrote about murals because they have always fascinated her. She especially loves the murals by Paul and David Botello because they speak of education, immigration, and hope. These themes are a big part of her own life. "Education is important in my family," she points out.

Read more books about murals.

The School Mural by Sarah Vázquez

Murals: Walls That Sing by George Ancona

Reading Log

Use the *Reader's and Writer's Notebook* to record your independent reading.

453

Student Edition, pp. 452–453

Common Core State Standards

Informational Text 1. Ask and answer questions to demonstrate understanding of a text, referring explicitly to the text as the basis for the answers. **Also Informational Text 2., 5., Writing 8.**

Bridge to Common Core

RANGE OF READING AND LEVEL OF TEXT COMPLEXITY

To increase students' capacity for reading and comprehending complex texts independently and proficiently, have them read other literary texts by Katacha Díaz or about the social studies topic, Freedom of Expression. After students read closely for a sustained period of time, they should record their reading in their Reading Logs.

Think Critically

1. **TEXT TO SELF** If I were a muralist, I would paint a mural of the sporting arena downtown. The mural would celebrate my hometown team.
2. **THINK LIKE AN AUTHOR** The author used the subtitle *Art for the People* because all of the murals are intended to share messages with people and to be enjoyed by people. The author writes about education, immigration, and hope because those things are important to her.
3. **GRAPHIC SOURCES** A photo and a chart; the photo conveys exactly what the mural looks like; the chart lists the artists, locations, and titles of some of the murals.
4. **IMPORTANT IDEAS** Muralists paint many different kinds of murals; murals tell about people, history, celebrations, and freedom; muralists use artistic expression to share their ideas through their artwork.
5. **LOOK BACK AND WRITE • TEXT EVIDENCE** To build writing fluency, assign a 10–15 minute time limit.

Scoring Rubric Look Back and Write

TOP-SCORE RESPONSE A top-score response uses details to tell about several of the murals and muralists in the story.

A top-score response should include:

- Some of the murals represent people in their neighborhoods and where they came from.
- Some of the murals represent hopes for the future.
- Some of the murals show symbols of American freedom.

Retell

Have students work in pairs to retell the selection, using the retelling strip in the Student Edition or the Story Sort as prompts. Monitor students' retellings.

Scoring Rubric Expository Retelling

	4	3	2	1
Connections	Makes connections and generalizes beyond the text	Makes connections to other events, texts, or experiences	Makes a limited connection to another event, text, or experience	Makes no connection to another event, text, or experience
Author's Purpose	Elaborates on author's purpose	Tells author's purpose with some clarity	Makes some connection to author's purpose	Makes no connection to author's purpose
Topic	Describes the main topic	Identifies the main topic with some details early in retelling	Identifies the main topic	Retelling has no sense of topic
Important Ideas	Gives accurate information about events, steps, and ideas using details and key vocabulary	Gives accurate information about events, steps, and ideas with some detail and key vocabulary	Gives limited or inaccurate information about events, steps, and ideas	Gives no information about events, steps, and ideas
Conclusions	Draws conclusions and makes inferences to generalize beyond the text	Draws conclusions about the text	Is able to tell some learnings about the text	Is unable to draw conclusions or make inferences about the text

Don't Wait Until Friday

MONITOR PROGRESS Check Retelling

If... students have difficulty retelling,

then... use the Retelling Cards/Story Sort to scaffold their retellings.

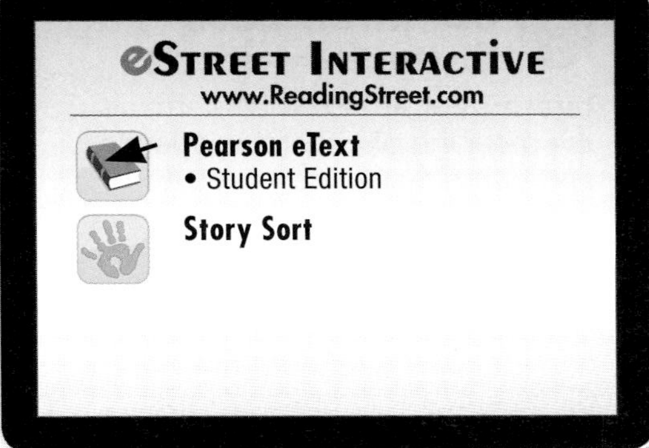

Plan to Assess Retelling

- ☐ **Week 1** Strategic Intervention
- ☐ **Week 2** Advanced
- ☑ **This week assess On-Level students.**
- ☐ **Week 4** On-Level
- ☐ **Week 5** Assess any students you have not yet checked during this unit.

Meet the Author

Have students read about author Katacha Díaz on p. 453. Ask how she expresses her respect for artists in *Talking Walls: Art for the People.*

Read Independently

Have students enter their independent reading into their Reading Logs.

Common Core State Standards

Informational Text 4. Determine the meaning of general academic and domain-specific words and phrases in a text relevant to a grade 3 topic or subject area. **Foundational Skills 4.** Read with sufficient accuracy and fluency to support comprehension. **Foundational Skills 4.b.** Read on-level prose and poetry orally with accuracy, appropriate rate, and expression on successive readings.

Fluency

Accuracy

MODEL FLUENT READING Have students turn to p. 448 of *Talking Walls: Art for the People.* Have students follow along as you read this page. Tell them to listen to how you read each word, including the names of the artists, with accuracy. Be sure to pronounce words clearly and pause at commas.

GUIDE PRACTICE Have students follow along as you read the page again. Then have them reread the page as a group without you until they read with no mistakes. Ask questions to be sure students comprehend the text. Continue in the same way on p. 449.

Corrective feedback

If... students are having difficulty reading with accuracy,
then... prompt them as follows:

- Did you read every word? Where do you see difficult words?
- How can you read with better accuracy?
- Read the sentence again. Read carefully and do not miss any words. Pause when you see commas.

Reread for Fluency

Routine Choral Reading

1. **Select a Passage** For *Talking Walls: Art for the People,* use p. 447.
2. **Model** Have students listen as you read accurately with no errors.
3. **Guide Practice** Have students read along with you.
4. **On Their Own** For optimal fluency, students should reread three or four times with accuracy.

Routines Flip Chart

Research and Study Skills

Alphabetical Order

TEACH Ask students what kind of information appears in alphabetical order. Students may mention dictionary or glossary entries, books in a library, and people's names in a telephone or address book. Tell students that being able to alphabetize will help them find information quickly. Have students look in the Glossary of their Student Edition and use it to review the following:

- Alphabetical order means that information is arranged or listed in the order of the letters of the alphabet.
- In glossaries, words are listed alphabetically.
- To put words in alphabetical order, look at their first letters. If the first letters are the same, look at their second letters. If the second letters are the same, look at their third letters and so on.

Have students read some of the entries in the Glossary, noticing that all of the words are listed in alphabetical order.

GUIDE PRACTICE Discuss these questions:

Which word would come first in a glossary—*plenty* or *plug?* *(plenty)*

How did you determine which word came first? (alphabetized by using the third letter in each word)

Ask students to use alphabetical order to find specific words in the Glossary.

ON THEIR OWN Have students review and complete p. 415 of the *Reader's and Writer's Notebook.*

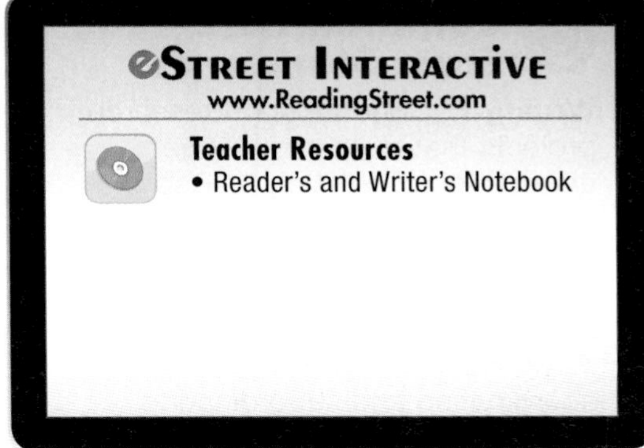

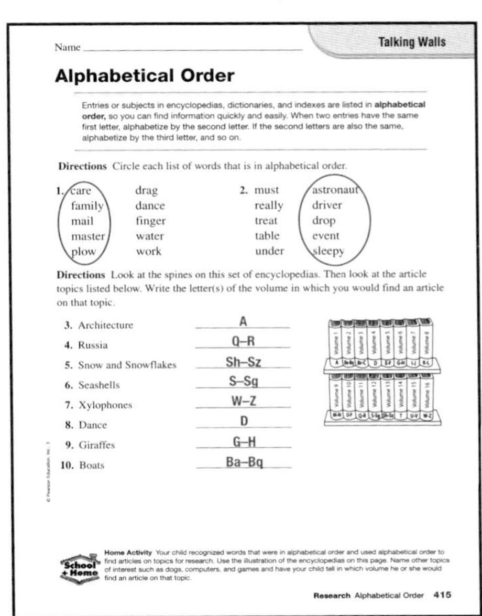

Name ____________

Talking Walls

Alphabetical Order

Entries or subjects in encyclopedias, dictionaries, and indexes are listed in **alphabetical order,** so you can find information quickly and easily. When two entries have the same first letter, alphabetize by the second letter. If the second letters are also the same, alphabetize by the third letter, and so on.

Directions Circle each list of words that is in alphabetical order.

1. care, family, mail, master, plow (circled) | drag, dance, finger, water, work
2. must, really, treat, table, under | astronaut, driver, drop, event, sleepy (circled)

Directions Look at the spines on this set of encyclopedias. Then look at the article topics listed below. Write the letter(s) of the volume in which you would find an article on that topic.

3. Architecture A
4. Russia Q–R
5. Snow and Snowflakes Sh–Sz
6. Seashells S–Sg
7. Xylophones W–Z
8. Dance D
9. Giraffes G–H
10. Boats Ba–Bq

Home Activity Your child recognized words that were in alphabetical order and used alphabetical order to find articles on topics for research. Use the illustration of the encyclopedias on this page. Name other topics of interest such as dogs, computers, and games and have your child tell in which volume he or she would find an article on that topic.

Research Alphabetical Order 415

Reader's and Writer's Notebook, p. 415

Access for All

 **Advanced**

Give students a list of their classmates' first and last names. Challenge students to write the names in alphabetical order. Remind students to use each person's last name.

Common Core State Standards

Writing 7. Conduct short research projects that build knowledge about a topic. **Writing 8.** Recall information from experiences or gather information from print and digital sources; take brief notes on sources and sort evidence into provided categories. **Language 1.h.** Use coordinating and subordinating conjunctions. **Language 1.i.** Produce simple, compound, and complex sentences. **Language 2.f.** Use spelling patterns and generalizations (e.g., word families, position-based spellings, syllable patterns, ending rules, meaningful word parts) in writing words.

Research and Inquiry

Step 3 Analyze Information

TEACH Tell students they will analyze the information they collected on Day 2. Based on the information gathered, they may need to refocus their original inquiry question and collect information from reference texts.

Think Aloud **MODEL** When I began my research I thought that freedom of expression and freedom of speech were the same thing. Then I learned that freedom of expression is not only freedom of saying things but also includes sharing information or ideas in other ways. I will refocus my inquiry question to include this information. My revised question is *In what ways are people granted the freedom to express themselves verbally and nonverbally?*

GUIDE PRACTICE Have students analyze their findings. They may need to refocus their inquiry question to better fit the information they found. Remind students that if they have difficulty improving their focus, they can ask a reference librarian or a local expert for guidance.

Remind students that keywords will be listed in alphabetical order in the back of most reference texts.

ON THEIR OWN Have students work with a partner to summarize their research findings. Partners should comment on whether the research fully supports and answers the inquiry question.

Conventions

Combining Sentences

REVIEW Recall that sentences can be combined in the following instances:

- when two simple sentences can make a compound sentence
- when two sentences have the same subject
- when two sentences have the same predicate
- when two sentences repeat information

CONNECT TO ORAL LANGUAGE Have students identify repeated information in the pair of simple sentences below. Then have them combine the sentences.

> **Stephanie lives in the city. She visits the country.** (Stephanie lives in the city, and she visits the country.)

ON THEIR OWN For additional support, use *Let's Practice It!* p. 386 on the *Teacher Resources DVD-ROM.*

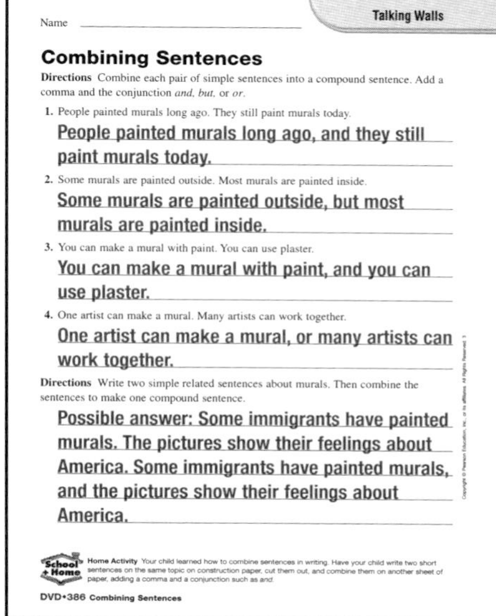

Name ______ Talking Walls

Combining Sentences

Directions Combine each pair of simple sentences into a compound sentence. Add a comma and the conjunction *and, but,* or *or.*

1. People painted murals long ago. They still paint murals today.
   People painted murals long ago, and they still paint murals today.
2. Some murals are painted outside. Most murals are painted inside.
   Some murals are painted outside, but most murals are painted inside.
3. You can make a mural with paint. You can use plaster.
   You can make a mural with paint, and you can use plaster.
4. One artist can make a mural. Many artists can work together.
   One artist can make a mural, or many artists can work together.

Directions Write two simple related sentences about murals. Then combine the sentences to make one compound sentence.

Possible answer: Some immigrants have painted murals. The pictures show their feelings about America. Some immigrants have painted murals, and the pictures show their feelings about America.

School + Home **Home Activity** Your child learned how to combine sentences in writing. Have your child write two short sentences on the same topic on construction paper, cut them out, and combine them on another sheet of paper, adding a comma and a conjunction such as *and.*

DVD•386 Combining Sentences

Let's Practice It! TR DVD•386

Spelling

Final Syllables *-ion, -ure*

FREQUENTLY MISSPELLED WORDS The words *we're* and *were* can be confusing to spell. Think carefully before you write these words. Think of which word means *we are.* I'll read several sentences. Think about which word correctly completes each sentence, and then write the sentence.

1. **The movie _______ seeing starts at 7:00.** (we're)
2. **They _______ late for class.** (were)
3. **What _______ you saying?** (were)
4. **_______ leaving early in the morning.** (We're)

ON THEIR OWN For additional practice, use *Reader's and Writer's Notebook,* p. 416.

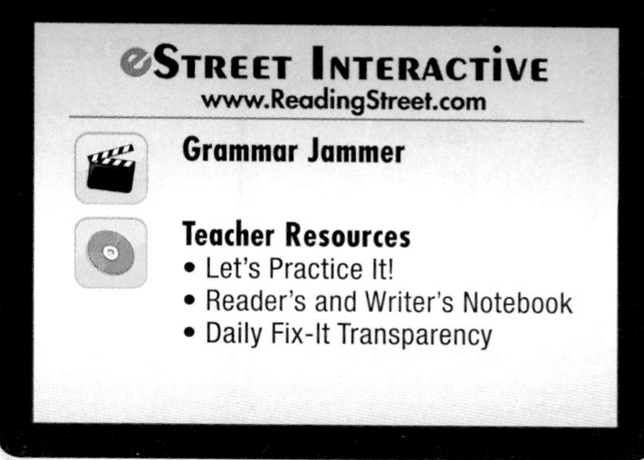

Daily Fix-It

5. The class's mural feachures a celebration, and is painted in bright colors. *(features; celebration and)*
6. The mural is the most biggest piece of art in the neighbor hood. *(the biggest; neighborhood)*

Access for All

Strategic Intervention

Help students draw graphic organizers that show two boxes at the left of the page with arrows pointing to one box on the right of the page. Provide two simple, related sentences for students to write in the boxes on the left. Guide them in combining the two sentences to make one sentence in the box on the right.

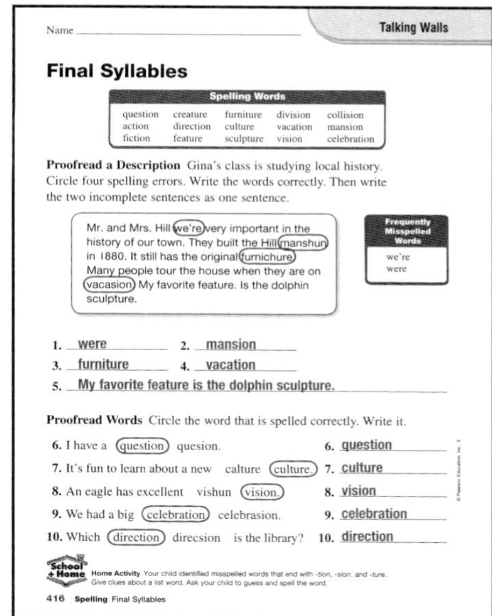

Name ______ Talking Walls

Final Syllables

Spelling Words				
question	creature	furniture	division	collision
action	direction	culture	vacation	mansion
fiction	feature	sculpture	vision	celebration

Proofread a Description Gina's class is studying local history. Circle four spelling errors. Write the words correctly. Then write the two incomplete sentences as one sentence.

Mr. and Mrs. Hill we're very important in the history of our town. They built the Hill manshun in 1880. It still has the original furnichure. Many people tour the house when they are on vacasion. My favorite feature. Is the dolphin sculpture.

Frequently Misspelled Words: we're, were

1. were 2. mansion
3. furniture 4. vacation
5. My favorite feature is the dolphin sculpture.

Proofread Words Circle the word that is spelled correctly. Write it.

6. I have a question quesion. 6. question
7. It's fun to learn about a new calture culture. 7. culture
8. An eagle has excellent vishun vision. 8. vision
9. We had a big celebration celebrasion. 9. celebration
10. Which direction direcsion is the library? 10. direction

School + Home **Home Activity** Your child identified misspelled words that end with *-tion, -sion,* and *-ture.* Give clues about a list word. Ask your child to guess and spell the word.

416 Spelling Final Syllables

Reader's and Writer's Notebook, p. 416

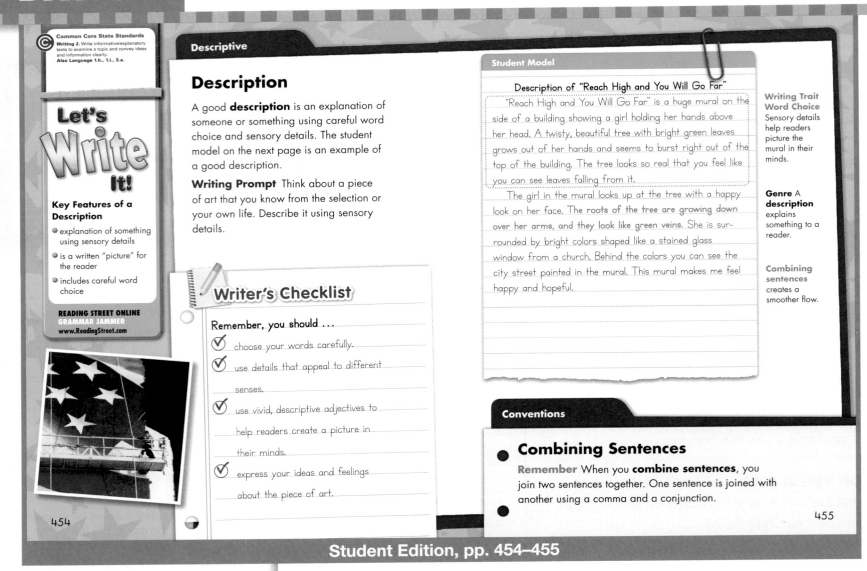

Common Core State Standards
Writing 2. Write informative/explanatory texts to examine a topic and convey ideas and information clearly. **Also Language 1.h., 1.i., 3.a.**

Let's Write It!

Key Features of a Description

- explanation of something using sensory details
- is a written "picture" for the reader
- includes careful word choice

READING STREET ONLINE
GRAMMAR JAMMER
www.ReadingStreet.com

Descriptive

Description

A good **description** is an explanation of someone or something using careful word choice and sensory details. The student model on the next page is an example of a good description.

Writing Prompt Think about a piece of art that you know from the selection or your own life. Describe it using sensory details.

Writer's Checklist

Remember, you should ...

- ✓ choose your words carefully.
- ✓ use details that appeal to different senses.
- ✓ use vivid, descriptive adjectives to help readers create a picture in their minds.
- ✓ express your ideas and feelings about the piece of art.

454

Student Model

Description of "Reach High and You Will Go Far"

"Reach High and You Will Go Far" is a huge mural on the side of a building showing a girl holding her hands above her head. A twisty, beautiful tree with bright green leaves grows out of her hands and seems to burst right out of the top of the building. The tree looks so real that you feel like you can see leaves falling from it.

The girl in the mural looks up at the tree with a happy look on her face. The roots of the tree are growing down over her arms, and they look like green veins. She is surrounded by bright colors shaped like a stained glass window from a church. Behind the colors you can see the city street painted in the mural. This mural makes me feel happy and hopeful.

Writing Trait Word Choice Sensory details help readers picture the mural in their minds.

Genre A **description** explains something to a reader.

Combining sentences creates a smoother flow.

Conventions

Combining Sentences

Remember When you **combine sentences**, you join two sentences together. One sentence is joined with another using a comma and a conjunction.

455

Student Edition, pp. 454–455

Common Core State Standards

Writing 2. Write informative/explanatory texts to examine a topic and convey ideas and information clearly. **Language 3.** Use knowledge of language and its conventions when writing, speaking, reading, or listening. **Language 3.a.** Choose words and phrases for effect. **Also Language 1.h., 1.i.**

Let's Write It!

WRITE A DESCRIPTION Use pp. 454–455 in the Student Edition. Direct students to read the key features of description, which appear on p. 454. Remind students that they can refer to the information in the Writer's Checklist as they write their own descriptions.

Read the student model on p. 455. Point out the sensory details and the careful word choice in the model that help the reader imagine what the mural looks like.

CONNECT TO CONVENTIONS Remind students that combining sentences means joining two sentences that contain some of the same information. Point out how some of the sentences in the model may have started out as two simple sentences.

Description

Writing Trait: Word Choice

DISPLAY RUBRIC Display Scoring Rubric 28 from the *Teacher Resources DVD-ROM* and go over the criteria for each trait under each score. Then, using the model in the Student Edition, choose students to explain why the model should score a 4 for one of the traits. If a student suggests that the model should score below 4 for a particular trait, the student should offer support for that response. Remind students that this is the rubric that will be used to evaluate their descriptions.

Scoring Rubric Description

	4	3	2	1
Focus/Ideas	Clear focus and description of a person, place, or thing	Fairly clear focus and description of a person, place, or thing	Little focus on a person, place, or thing	No focus or description of a person, place, or thing
Organization	Clear main idea; strong use of details	Unclear main idea; adequate use of details	No main idea; unclear use of details	No attempt at main idea; no organization of details
Voice	Writer is clearly interested in what is being described	Some evidence of interest in what is being described	Little evidence of interest in what is being described	No interest in what is being described
Word Choice	Strong use of vivid words that appeal to the senses	Some vivid words that appeal to the senses	Little attempt to use vivid words; descriptions do not appeal to the senses	Incorrect or limited word choice; no detailed descriptions
Sentences	Clear sentences of various lengths and types	Sentences of a few lengths and types	Little attempt at various lengths and types of sentences	No attempt at various lengths and types of sentences
Conventions	Few errors; all short sentences combined; correct use of commas	Several minor errors; most short sentences are combined; fair use of commas	Many errors; few short sentences combined; weak use of commas	Numerous errors; no short sentences combined; no use of commas

MAIN IDEA WEB Explain that students will use the main idea webs they worked on yesterday to help draft their descriptions. If they have not completed their webs, have them work in groups or with partners to brainstorm sensory details or other descriptive language to complete their webs.

WRITE You will use your main idea web to help you write the draft of your description. Remember that your draft is only the beginning of your composition. Drafting is the time to get your ideas down on paper. You will have time to revise your description tomorrow.

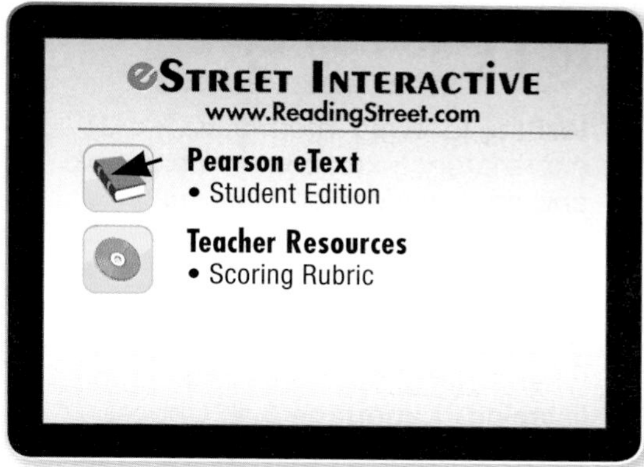

Access for All

 **Advanced**

Have students do Internet and library research to find other art by the same artist or that is similar to that art in several ways. Have them write a short comparison of the two works of art.

Main Idea Web Have students use their main idea and supporting details webs to talk to a partner as if their partner is the artist. Tell students to tell the "artist" their ideas and feelings about the mural or other artwork they admire. Answer any questions students may have before they begin to write.

Common Core State Standards

Writing 2. Write informative/explanatory texts to examine a topic and convey ideas and information clearly. **Writing 2.b.** Develop the topic with facts, definitions, and details. **Language 3.** Use knowledge of language and its conventions when writing, speaking, reading, or listening. **Language 3.a.** Choose words and phrases for effect.

Bridge to Common Core

RANGE OF WRITING

As students progress through the writing project, they routinely write for a range of tasks, purposes, and audiences. In this lesson, they learn the importance of choosing powerful descriptive words. They develop written work in which topics are developed with vivid descriptions.

Writing

Description

Mini-Lesson Choosing Descriptive Words

■ **Introduce** Explain to students that writing a good description means choosing words that help the reader imagine what something is like. Words that appeal to the senses—taste, touch, smell, hearing, and sight—are descriptive words. Adjectives and active verbs are descriptive words. With descriptive words, a noun such as *pencil* becomes *the sharp red pencil.* Display the Drafting Tips for students. Remind them that the focus of drafting is to get their ideas down in an organized way. Then display Writing Transparency 28A.

Drafting Tips

- ✔ Use your main idea web to help organize your paragraphs. Write one paragraph for each supporting idea.
- ✔ Choose words that appeal to the senses, adjectives, and active verbs to describe the piece of art.
- ✔ Remember that you will have a chance to check spelling, grammar, and mechanics later in the writing process.

Think Aloud **MODEL** I'm going to write the first paragraph of my description. My title will be "Description of Ori's Cat Collage." My first sentence will be my main idea: *My friend Ori made a collage of a cat.* When I draft, I think more about my topic and expand on the ideas I wrote in my web during the planning stage. I think of ways I can best describe the collage so that readers can imagine what it is like. I'll compare the green yarn to grass so readers can see it.

Description of Ori's Cat collage

My friend Ori made a collage of a cat. it hangs on the wall at her apartment. It hangs over the sofa. The cats fur is made of swirls of bumpy yarn. The yarn is bright greene, like grass in spring. A thin line of sky blue yarn outline the cat's plump body. The cat's silver bottle cap eyes shine out at you. They sparkle with a coating of Silver glitter. The cat's front paws are made of white yarn, and its whiskers is made of stiff white pipe cleaners that stick out from the picture.

The cat's bright green fur and white paws stand out against the black cardboard background. Crouching there with its tail wrapped around its body, it looks like it might leap right out at you. Looking at the collage makes me feel happy and energetic.

Unit 6 Talking Walls: Art for the People Writing: Model **28A**

Writing Transparency 28A, TR DVD

Read the draft on the transparency aloud, emphasizing your choice of descriptive words and phrases over more ordinary words and phrases. For example, you might consider the word *fat* before choosing the word *plump.* Direct students to use the drafting tips to guide them as they write their drafts.

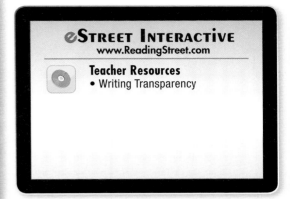

eSTREET INTERACTIVE
www.ReadingStreet.com

Teacher Resources
- Writing Transparency

Routine Quick Write for Fluency

Team Talk

1. **Talk** Pairs of students discuss the descriptive words they've chosen to include in their compositions.
2. **Write** Students write a sentence describing something, using some of the words they chose and correct comma use.
3. **Share** Students read their partner's paragraph and check for correct use of commas.

Routines Flip Chart

Access for All

A Advanced

Have students choose three sentences from their drafts and use a thesaurus to write as many different versions of that sentence as they can. The sentence variations should retain the same meaning while at the same time displaying different descriptive words and sentence structures.

Wrap Up Your Day!

✔ **Content Knowledge** Have students discuss the themes of the mural "A Shared Hope."

✔ **Text-Based Comprehension** *How do the captions help you understand the selection?* Encourage students to cite examples from the text.

Preview DAY 4

Tell students that tomorrow they will read about a playful use of language that was created long ago.

DAY 4 at a Glance

Content Knowledge
Oral Vocabulary

Phonics/Word Analysis
Review Schwa

Science in Reading
Palindromes

Fluency
Accuracy

Vocabulary Skill
Unknown Words

Media Literacy
Talk Show

Research and Inquiry
Synthesize

Conventions
Combining Sentences

Spelling
Final Syllables

Writing
Description

Materials

- Student Edition
- Reader's and Writer's Notebook
- Amazing Word Cards

Common Core State Standards

Speaking/Listening 1. Engage effectively in a range of collaborative discussions (one-on-one, in groups, and teacher led) with diverse partners on grade 3 topics and texts, building on others' ideas and expressing their own clearly. **Language 4.** Determine or clarify the meaning of unknown and multiple-meaning words and phrases based on grade 3 reading and content, choosing flexibly from a range of strategies. **Language 6.** Acquire and use accurately grade-appropriate conversational, general academic, and domain-specific words and phrases, including those that signal spatial and temporal relationships (e.g., *After dinner that night we went looking for them*).

Content Knowledge

Freedom of Expression

EXPAND THE CONCEPT Remind students of the weekly concept question, *Why is freedom of expression important?* Have students discuss how art and speech can allow us to freely express ourselves.

Build Oral Language

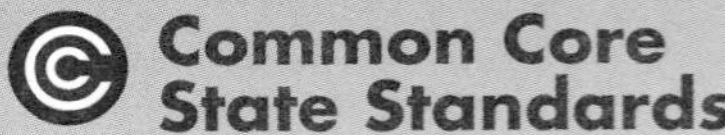

TALK ABOUT SENTENCES AND WORDS Ask students to reread the paragraph at the top of p. 451. Have them share with their partner their answers to the questions below.

From sea to shining sea, the artists who create art for the people are instrumental in reminding Americans everywhere of the freedoms that help our democracy work.

- What does the author mean by "from sea to shining sea"? (all across the country)
- What does the word *create* mean? (to make or produce)
- What is the base word in *instrumental? (instrument)* What is another word for *instrument? (tool)* So if something is *instrumental to something,* it is acting as a tool.
- Apply your understanding of "from sea to shining sea," *create,* and *instrumental* to restate this sentence in your own words. (Possible response: All across the country, artists who produce art for the people help remind Americans everywhere of the freedoms that help our democracy work.)

Build Oral Vocabulary

Amazing Words Robust Vocabulary Routine

1. **Introduce** Write the word *view* on the board. Have students say it aloud with you. We read about David Botello's *view* of the world. How did he want children to *view* the world? (Dreams can come true if you work hard.) Have students determine the definition of *view.* (A *view* is a way of looking at or thinking about something.)

2. **Demonstrate** Have students answer questions to demonstrate understanding. What is Paul Botello's *view* of education? (He thinks that people can have a better life through education.)

3. **Apply** Have students apply their understanding. How would your *view* of education affect how much you studied?

4. **Display the Word** Point out the sounds in *view* and have students blend them.

See p. OV•3 to teach *lyrics.*

Routines Flip Chart

ADD TO THE CONCEPT MAP Discuss the Amazing Words *significant* and *pause*. Add these and other concept-related words to the concept map. Use the following questions to develop students' understanding of the concept. Add words generated in discussion to the concept map.

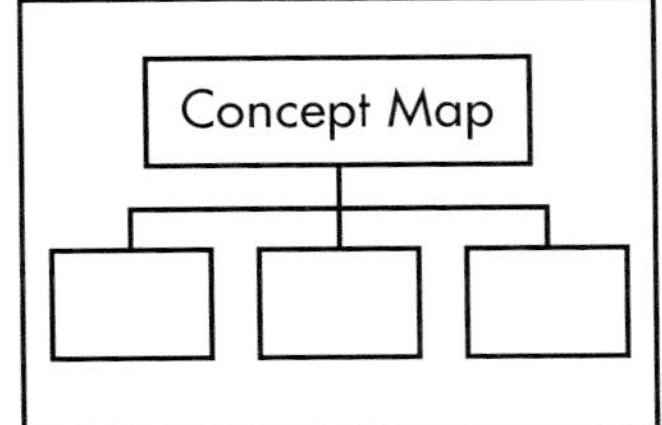

- Think about all of the different murals. What *significant* messages did the artists express through their art?
- What mural makes you *pause* the most to think about what freedom means to you?

Amazing Words

creative	lecture
expressive	significant
emotion	pause
artistic	view
exquisite	lyrics

Strategy Response Log

Have students review the characteristics of a photo essay on p. 34 of the *Reader's and Writer's Notebook.* Then have them compare *Talking Walls: Art for the People* to another example of a photo essay that they have read or know about.

Produce Oral Language Use the Day 4 instruction on ELL Poster 28 to extend and enrich language.

Common Core State Standards

Foundational Skills 3. Know and apply grade-level phonics and word analysis skills in decoding words. **Foundational Skills 3.c.** Decode multisyllable words. **Foundational Skills 3.d.** Read grade-appropriate irregularly spelled words.

Name ______________ Talking Walls

Schwa Spelled with an *a, e, i, o, u,* and *y*

Directions Each word below has a missing letter that stands for the vowel sound called schwa. Write the word correctly on the line.

1. penc_l	pencil	9. mess_ge	message
2. music_l	musical	10. sil_nt	silent
3. list_n	listen	11. _gree	agree
4. col_r	color	12. cous_n	cousin
5. surf_ce	surface	13. pres_nt	present
6. vin_l	vinyl	14. bott_m	bottom
7. playf_l	playful	15. im_ge	image
8. art_cle	article	16. circ_s	circus

Directions Choose the best word to complete each sentence. Write the word on the line.

nickel instant helpful control

17. Jake is helpful to his grandmother.
18. The light flashed and disappeared in an instant.
19. We cannot control the weather.
20. Pam found a nickel on the sidewalk.

School + Home **Home Activity** Your child wrote words that contain the vowel sound called schwa, which is heard in unaccented syllables, such as *about, taken, ribbon,* and *virus.* Have your child choose five words from this page. Then write these words on a separate sheet of paper and divide them into syllables. Have your child circle the unaccented syllable in each word.

Schwa Spelled with an *a, e, i, o, u,* and *y* DVD•387

Let's Practice It! TR DVD•387

Word Analysis

Review Schwa

REVIEW SCHWA To review unaccented syllables with the schwa sound, write *cardinal, robin, commit, method, cabin, letter, pretzel, circus, holiday,* and *ablaze.* You learned that unaccented syllables with schwa can be spelled with any vowel. Let's review the schwa sound by looking at these words. In what words is the schwa sound spelled *a*? *(cardinal, ablaze)* Continue in the same way for words with schwa spelled *e (letter, pretzel), i (robin, cabin, holiday), o (commit, method),* and *u (circus).* Remind students that they can divide words into syllables and then try the schwa sounds for each vowel in a word until they recognize the word.

Corrective feedback	**If...** students are unable to answer the questions about the schwa sound, **then...** refer them to *Sound-Spelling Card* 144.

GUIDE PRACTICE Display a two-column chart with the heads *Schwa* and *No schwa.* Write the following words on the board: *sister, Sunday, ago, popcorn, famous, family, rabbit, marble, walking, seesaw.* Let's read the words. Listen for the unaccented syllable to determine if you hear the schwa sound. Write each word in the appropriate column. Then have students read the words. Ask volunteers to underline the vowel that stands for the schwa sound in words in the first column.

Schwa	No schwa
sister	Sunday
ago	popcorn
famous	rabbit
family	walking
marble	seesaw

ON THEIR OWN For additional practice, use *Let's Practice It!,* p. 387 on the *Teacher Resources DVD-ROM.*

Fluent Word Reading

Spiral Review

READ WORDS IN ISOLATION Display these words. Tell students that they can already decode some words on this list. Explain that they should know other words because they appear often in reading.

Have students read the list three or four times until they can read at the rate of two to three seconds per word.

Word Reading

ceiling	**true**	**livelihood**	**payment**	**put**
brownish	**neighbor**	**one**	**the**	**sure**
of	**full**	**book**	**any**	**new**
look	**everything**	**school**	**suit**	**messy**

Corrective feedback

If... students have difficulty reading whole words,
then... have them use sound-by-sound blending for decodable words or chunking for words that have word parts, or have them say and spell high-frequency words.

If... students cannot read fluently at a rate of two to three seconds per word,
then... have pairs practice the list until they can read it fluently.

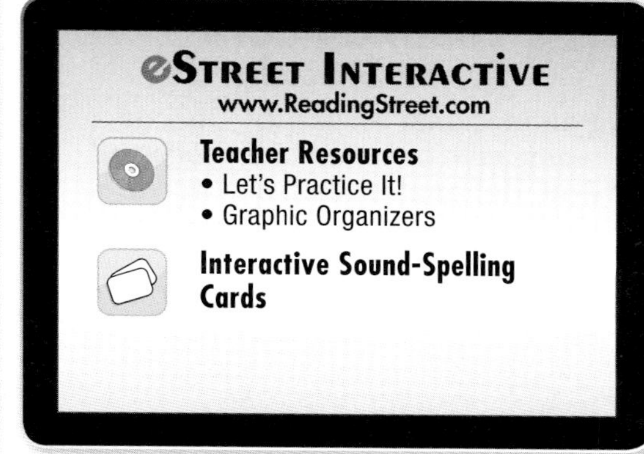

eStreet Interactive
www.ReadingStreet.com
Teacher Resources
• Let's Practice It!
• Graphic Organizers
Interactive Sound-Spelling Cards

Access for All

SI Strategic Intervention

To assist students having difficulty with the schwa sound, have them write the vowels *a, e, i, o, u,* and *y* on separate cards. Under each vowel, have students write a cue word in which the schwa sound is represented by that vowel. For example: *a* (*about*), *e* (*cover*), *i* (*decimal*), *o* (*harmony*), *u* (*medium*), *y* (*oxygen*). Encourage students to refer to these cue cards as they attempt to decode other words with the schwa sound.

Spiral Review

These activities review:

- previously taught high-frequency words *of, everything, one, the, any, sure.*
- vowel patterns *ei, eigh*; suffixes *-y, -ish, -hood, -ment*; spellings of /ü/, /u̇/.

Fluent Word Reading Have students listen to a more fluent reader say the words. Then have them repeat the words.

Common Core State Standards

Foundational Skills 3.b. Decode words with common Latin suffixes. **Foundational Skills 3.c.** Decode multisyllable words. **Foundational Skills 3.d.** Read grade-appropriate irregularly spelled words. **Foundational Skills 4.** Read with sufficient accuracy and fluency to support comprehension. **Foundational Skills 4.c.** Use context to confirm or self-correct word recognition and understanding, rereading as necessary.

Fluent Word Reading

READ WORDS IN CONTEXT Display these sentences. Call on individuals to read a sentence. Then randomly point to review words and have students read them. To help you monitor word reading, high-frequency words are underlined and decodable words are italicized.

MONITOR PROGRESS Sentence Reading

Are you sure I need a *new suit* for *school?*

***Look* up at the *brownish* spot on the *ceiling*.**

My *neighbor* did not receive *payment* for one *book*.

Is it *true* that Dad's *livelihood* depends on selling everything?

Do not *put* any cans *full* of *messy* paint on the table.

If... students are unable to read an underlined high-frequency word,
then... read the word for them and spell it, having them echo you.

If... students have difficulty reading an italicized decodable word,
then... guide them in using sound-by-sound blending or chunking.

Reread for Fluency

Have students reread the sentences to develop automaticity decoding words.

Routine Oral Rereading

1. **Read** Have students read all the sentences orally.
2. **Reread** To achieve optimal fluency, students should reread the sentences three or four times.
3. **Corrective Feedback** Listen as students read. Provide corrective feedback regarding their fluency and decoding.

Routines Flip Chart

Decodable Passage 28C

If students need help, then...

Read *Lester's Pictures*

READ WORDS IN ISOLATION Have students turn to p. 155 in *Decodable Practice Readers 3.2* and find the first list of words. Each word in this list has the final syllable *-tion, -ion, -ture, -ive,* or *-ize.* Let's read these words. Be sure that students pronounce each final syllable correctly.

Next, have students read the high-frequency words.

PREVIEW Have students read the title and preview the story. Tell them that they will read words with final syllables *-tion, -ion, -ture, -ive,* and *-ize.*

READ WORDS IN CONTEXT Chorally read the story along with students. Have students identify words in the story with final syllables *-tion, -ion, -ture, -ive,* and *-ize.* Make sure that students are monitoring their accuracy when they decode words.

Team Talk Pair students and have them take turns reading the story aloud to each other. Monitor students as they read to check for proper pronunciation and appropriate pacing.

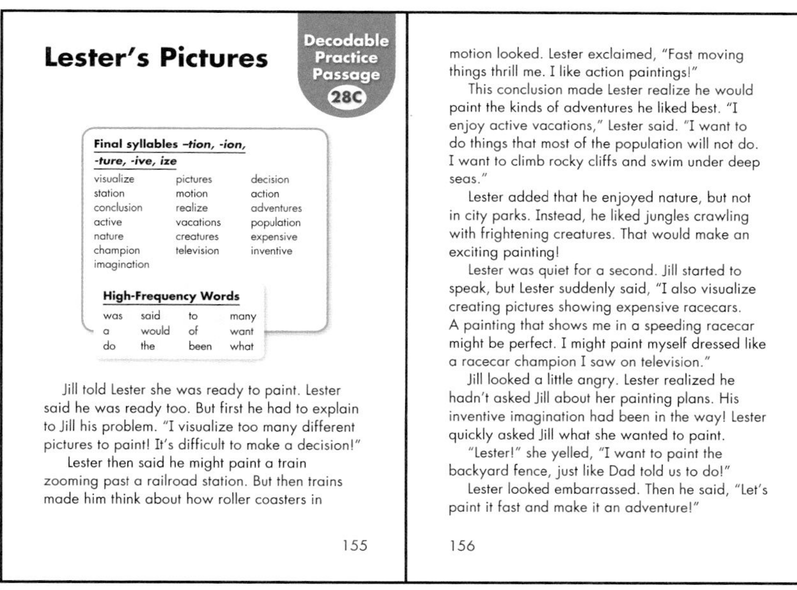

Lester's Pictures

Decodable Practice Passage 28C

Final syllables -tion, -ion, -ture, -ive, ize

visualize	pictures	decision
station	motion	action
conclusion	realize	adventures
active	vacations	population
nature	creatures	expensive
champion	television	inventive
imagination		

High-Frequency Words

was	said	to	many
a	would	of	want
do	the	been	what

Jill told Lester she was ready to paint. Lester said he was ready too. But first he had to explain to Jill his problem. "I visualize too many different pictures to paint! It's difficult to make a decision!"

Lester then said he might paint a train zooming past a railroad station. But then trains made him think about how roller coasters in

155

motion looked. Lester exclaimed, "Fast moving things thrill me. I like action paintings!"

This conclusion made Lester realize he would paint the kinds of adventures he liked best. "I enjoy active vacations," Lester said. "I want to do things that most of the population will not do. I want to climb rocky cliffs and swim under deep seas."

Lester added that he enjoyed nature, but not in city parks. Instead, he liked jungles crawling with frightening creatures. That would make an exciting painting!

Lester was quiet for a second. Jill started to speak, but Lester suddenly said, "I also visualize creating pictures showing expensive racecars. A painting that shows me in a speeding racecar might be perfect. I might paint myself dressed like a racecar champion I saw on television."

Jill looked a little angry. Lester realized he hadn't asked Jill about her painting plans. His inventive imagination had been in the way! Lester quickly asked Jill what she wanted to paint.

"Lester!" she yelled, "I want to paint the backyard fence, just like Dad told us to do!"

Lester looked embarrassed. Then he said, "Let's paint it fast and make it an adventure!"

156

Decodable Practice Passage 28C

Access for All

A Advanced

Have students write a letter to a neighbor using some of the decodable and high-frequency words found in the sentences on p. 456e.

Common Core State Standards

Informational Text 4. Determine the meaning of general academic and domain-specific words and phrases in a text relevant to a grade 3 topic or subject area. **Speaking/Listening 1.** Engage effectively in a range of collaborative discussions (one-on-one, in groups, and teacher led) with diverse partners on grade 3 topics and texts, building on others' ideas and expressing their own clearly. **Language 6.** Acquire and use accurately grade-appropriate conversational, general academic, and domain-specific words and phrases, including those that signal spatial and temporal relationships (e.g., *After dinner that night we went looking for them*).

Bridge to Common Core

KEY IDEAS AND DETAILS

By reading the selection on the history of palindromes, students are introduced to this playful use of language created many centuries ago. By reading the text closely, students can determine the central ideas and summarize key supporting details of the information presented.

Social Studies in Reading

Palindromes

INTRODUCE Explain to students that what we read is structured differently depending on the author's reasons for writing and what kind of information he or she wishes to convey. Different types of text are called genres. Tell students that palindrome is one type of genre.

DISCUSS THE GENRE Discuss with students what is special about a palindrome. For example, ask: What do you notice about palindromes? (Possible response: The word or phrase reads the same forward or backward.) Why do you think people invented palindromes so long ago and still use them today? (Possible response: People invented them to have fun with language.)

GROUP PRACTICE Display a concept map like the one below. Write the word *Palindromes* in the middle circle. Brainstorm with students palindromes they are familiar with. In addition to words and phrases, numbers can also be palindromes. Add students' suggestions to the concept map.

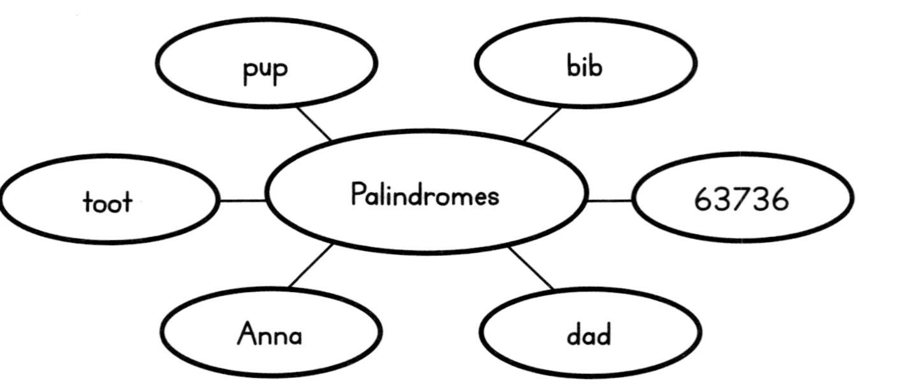

Team Talk Then have students work in pairs to discuss and list other palindromes. They may conduct an online search to find other examples. Ask them to share their lists with the class.

READ Tell students that they will now read about the history of palindromes. Ask students to find additional examples of palindromes in the text.

Academic Vocabulary

palindromes words or phrases that are spelled the same backward and forward

Day 4 SMALL GROUP TIME • Differentiate Vocabulary, p. SG•33

OL On-Level	SI Strategic Intervention	A Advanced
• **Develop** Language Using Amazing Words • **Read** "The History of Palindromes"	• **Review/Discuss** Amazing Words • **Read** "The History of Palindromes"	• **Extend** Amazing Words and Selection Vocabulary • **Read** "The History of Palindromes" • **Organize** Inquiry Project

If... students need more scaffolding and practice with the **Amazing Words,**
then... use the Routine on pp. xxxvi–xxxvii in the *ELL Handbook.*

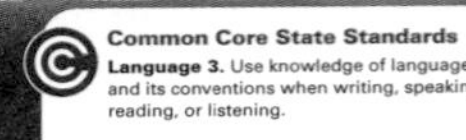

Common Core State Standards
Language 3. Use knowledge of language and its conventions when writing, speaking, reading, or listening.

Social Studies in Reading

Genre
Palindromes

- A palindrome is a word or phrase that reads the same in both directions.
- Palindromes are a playful use of language created for fun many centuries ago.
- As you read "The History of Palindromes," try to think of other words that read the same in both directions.

THE HISTORY OF PALINDROMES

by Jeaninne Sage

The word palindrome is derived from the Greek *palíndromos,* meaning "a running back" (palín = BACK, + dromos = A RUNNING).

Some one-word palindromes are:

RADAR	DEED	LEVEL
ROTOR	POP	CIVIC
RACECAR	DID	MADAM

Palindrome Phrases:

Some phrases are also palindromes. Some palindrome phrases are:

Don't nod

Never odd or even

Too bad—I hid a boot

No trace; not one carton

Oozy rat in a sanitary zoo

A Man, A Plan, A Canal—Panama!

456

2D PALINDROME SQUARES

In these word squares, a word can be read in either direction in every row and column.

Here are a few palindrome squares.

The 2D palindrome square below dates back to ancient Roman times! It was inscribed on a stone tablet outside Rome, in Italy. It is the earliest known 2D palindrome.

Sator Arepo tenet opera rotas

It means: The sower Arepo works with the help of a wheel.

Let's Think About...

Try to create a 2D palindrome square that can be read in either direction in every row and column. **Palindromes**

1

Let's Think About...

Reading Across Texts In *Talking Walls: Art for the People,* muralists express ideas on walls for the public to enjoy. How are palindromes similar? How are they different?

Writing Across Text Create a palindrome phrase.

457

Student Edition, pp. 456–457

Common Core State Standards

Informational Text 4. Determine the meaning of general academic and domain-specific words and phrases in a text relevant to a grade 3 topic or subject area. **Informational Text 10.** By the end of the year, read and comprehend informational texts, including history/social studies, science, and technical texts, at the high end of the grades 2–3 text complexity band independently and proficiently. **Language 2.** Demonstrate command of the conventions of standard English capitalization, punctuation, and spelling when writing. **Also Informational Text 9.**

Access Text

TEACH Genre: Palindrome Explain that there are different types of palindromes. Ask: What do you think a 2D palindrome square is?

Corrective feedback **If...** students are unable to explain a 2D palindrome square, **then...** use the model to guide students in explaining this type of palindrome.

MODEL 2D palindrome squares are a set of squares in which a word can be read in either direction in every row and column. 2D palindromes date back to ancient Roman times.

ON THEIR OWN Have partners show each other how the words in the 2D palindrome square can be read in either direction.

Close Reading

ANALYSIS Why are the palindromes shown on p. 457 called "2D palindromes"? (The squares form words in 2 dimensions: across the rows and down the columns.)

SYNTHESIS Palindromes are playful uses of language. What other playful uses of language are similar to palindromes? (onomatopoeia, alliteration, rhyme)

Genre

LET'S THINK ABOUT... As you read "The History of Palindromes," use Let's Think About in the Student Edition to help students focus on the features of a palindrome.

1 Students should create a 2D palindrome square that can be read in either direction in every row and column. Have students start from the top left corner of the square. You may want to provide them with a bank of short words to try using.

Reading and Writing Across Texts

Students may respond that palindromes and murals are different because some murals do not contain any words at all and palindromes are all words. They are similar in that both require a lot of planning and creativity. Once students have written their palindromes, have them create illustrations to go with them. Have students work together to combine their work and publish a book of palindromes that can be read by the class.

Team Talk Have partners find another text about palindromes, such as an encyclopedia entry. Tell them to use a Venn diagram to compare and contrast the two texts. Encourage them to think about the main idea and details of each text as well as how the information is presented.

Access for All

SI Strategic Intervention
Have students work with a partner to read each word in every row and column on the 2D palindrome squares. Have partners write each word they read and then compare all of the words on their list.

A Advanced
Have students use the library or Internet to learn about other ancient palindromes. Have them share their findings with the class and discuss the words and messages the palindromes contain.

Cognates The Spanish word *historia* may be familiar to Spanish speakers as the cognate for *history.*

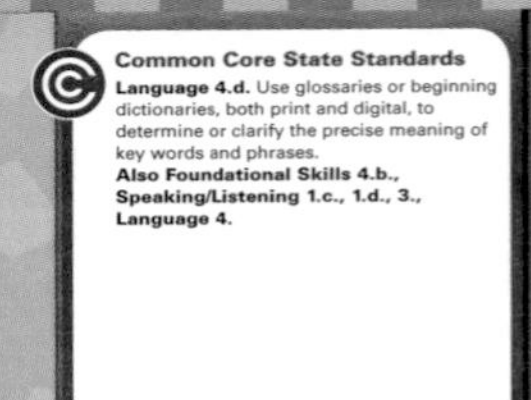
Common Core State Standards
Language 4.d. Use glossaries or beginning dictionaries, both print and digital, to determine or clarify the precise meaning of key words and phrases.
Also Foundational Skills 4.b., Speaking/Listening 1.c., 1.d., 3., Language 4.

Let's Learn It!

READING STREET ONLINE
ONLINE STUDENT EDITION
www.ReadingStreet.com

Vocabulary

Unknown Words

Dictionary/Glossary Use a dictionary or glossary to find the meanings of unknown words. If a word has multiple definitions, choose the meaning that fits in the context of what you are reading.

Practice It! Choose three unknown words from *Talking Walls.* Put the words into alphabetical order, using the letters in the third or fourth place in each word if necessary. Look them up in a dictionary or glossary. Write the correct meaning of each word as used in the selection.

Fluency

Accuracy

The more accurately you read a text, the greater your understanding will be. As you read, focus on reading each word as it appears.

Practice It! With a partner, practice reading the story aloud. How many words did you misread? Reread the section. Did your accuracy improve?

Media Literacy

Get Ready For Middle School

Use strategies—restate ideas and ask for clarification—to keep discussions going.

Talk Show

A talk show is hosted by a person who chats informally with guests who know about a subject or have done something noteworthy.

Practice It! Have a class talk show about the kind of murals you would paint and why. Take turns being the host, interviewing two classmates about their murals in front of the audience. How would communication change if the talk show were in an online format?

Tips

Listening ...
- Ask relevant questions and share your opinions.
- Listen attentively to others.

Speaking ...
- Speak loudly and clearly.
- Use appropriate verbal cues.

Teamwork ...
- Ask open-ended questions about the murals, and answer with detail.

458 459

Student Edition, pp. 458–459

Common Core State Standards

Foundational Skills 4.b. Read on-level prose and poetry orally with accuracy, appropriate rate, and expression on successive readings. **Speaking/Listening 1.d.** Explain their own ideas and understanding in light of the discussion. **Speaking/Listening 3.** Ask and answer questions about information from a speaker, offering appropriate elaboration and detail. **Language 4.d.** Use glossaries or beginning dictionaries, both print and digital, to determine or clarify the precise meaning of key words and phrases. **Also Speaking/Listening 1.c., Language 4.**

Fluency

Accuracy

GUIDE PRACTICE Use the Student Edition activity as an assessment tool. Make sure the reading passage is at least 200 words in length. Walk around to make sure students are reading the text accurately to enhance comprehension.

Don't Wait Until Friday **MONITOR PROGRESS** **Check Fluency**

FORMATIVE ASSESSMENT As students reread, monitor their progress toward their individual fluency goals.

Current Goal: 110–120 words correct per minute

End-of-Year Goal: 120 words correct per minute

If... students cannot read fluently at a rate of 110–120 words correct per minute,

then... have students practice with text at their independent levels.

Vocabulary Skill

Unknown Words

TEACH DICTIONARY/GLOSSARY Write these words on the board: *success, symbolize,* and *depict.* Remind students that the words in a dictionary or glossary appear in alphabetical order. To alphabetize, use the first letter in each word. If the first letters are the same, use the second letters, and so on.

GUIDE PRACTICE Have children alphabetize the words *success, symbolize,* and *depict.* Then have them look up each word in a dictionary or glossary and write a definition.

ON THEIR OWN Walk around the room as students work. Make sure they have correctly alphabetized the words. Check to see that students can quickly and accurately locate the words using a dictionary or glossary. Ask students to point out how each word is divided into syllables and make sure they pronounce each word correctly.

Media Literacy

Talk Show

TEACH Have students work in groups of three to stage talk shows using the Look Back and Write on p. 452. One student from each group will act as the host of the talk show and should prepare interview questions to ask during the show. The other two students will portray artists, while the rest of the class will pose as the audience. The artists will explain why they painted their murals and what their murals represent, or stand for. Remind students to monitor their speaking rate and volume, speak coherently, employ eye contact, and enunciate clearly to communicate their ideas effectively. Students should rehearse their roles together.

GUIDE PRACTICE Be sure students follow the oral instructions above to prepare for their talk shows. Have students restate the instructions to classmates. Remind the students posing as the audience to listen attentively to each speaker.

ON THEIR OWN Have students conduct the talk show interviews. After each talk show, have students discuss how communication would change if the talk show were in an online format.

Talk Show

Tell students that each talk show host should prepare questions ahead of time and share them with the artists. The questions should be about things the host thinks would interest the audience, as well as about the artist's reason for painting each mural and what each mural stands for. Encourage the artists to reread the *Talking Walls: Art for the People* text to find answers to the questions before the interview. As each mural is discussed, have the artists display that picture in the text.

Bridge to Common Core

COMPREHENSION AND COLLABORATION

As both interviewers and interviewees, students participate effectively in a range of conversations and collaborations with diverse partners. They also evaluate a speaker's point of view and reasoning and respond accordingly, building on others' ideas and expressing their own clearly and persuasively.

Common Core State Standards

Writing 2. Write informative/explanatory texts to examine a topic and convey ideas and information clearly. **Writing 6.** With guidance and support from adults, use technology to produce and publish writing (using keyboarding skills) as well as to interact and collaborate with others. **Language 1.i.** Produce simple, compound, and complex sentences. **Language 2.e.** Use conventional spelling for high-frequency and other studied words and for adding suffixes to base words (e.g., *sitting, smiled, cries, happiness*). **Language 2.f.** Use spelling patterns and generalizations (e.g., word families, position-based spellings, syllable patterns, ending rules, meaningful word parts) in writing words. **Also Language 1.h.**

Research and Inquiry

Step 4 Synthesize

TEACH Have students synthesize their research findings and results. Remind students that when they synthesize, they combine relevant ideas and information from different sources to develop answers to their inquiry questions. Have students explain how using alphabetical order helped them organize their research.

GUIDE PRACTICE Have students use a word-processing program to create a short review of the First Amendment or write a definition of freedom of expression. Have students revise their review or definition so that it is clear and grammatically correct.

ON THEIR OWN Have students write a brief explanation of their research findings. Then have them organize and combine information for their presentation. Have students create a Works Cited page from their notes, including the Web addresses, authors, and the dates the Web sites were last updated for each search.

Conventions

Combining Sentences

TEST PRACTICE Remind students that grammar skills, such as combining sentences, are often assessed on important tests. Remind students that they can combine sentences in the following ways:

- combine subjects
- combine predicates
- join two simple sentences with a comma and a conjunction
- join sentences that provide information about the same topic

ON THEIR OWN For additional practice, use *Reader's and Writer's Notebook,* p. 417.

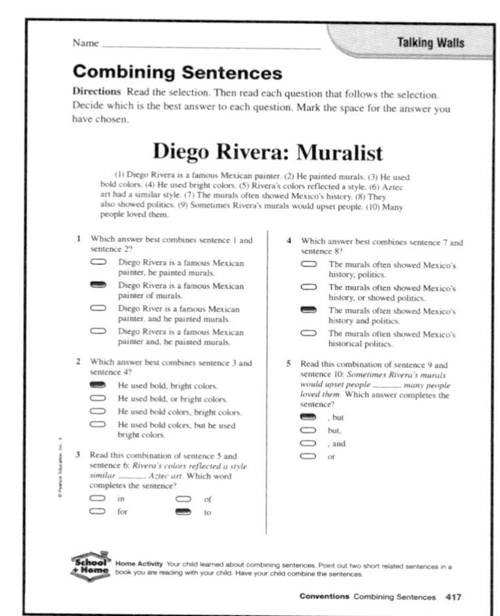

Name ______ Talking Walls

Combining Sentences

Directions Read the selection. Then read each question that follows the selection. Decide which is the best answer to each question. Mark the space for the answer you have chosen.

Diego Rivera: Muralist

(1) Diego Rivera is a famous Mexican painter. (2) He painted murals. (3) He used bold colors. (4) He used bright colors. (5) Rivera's colors reflected a style. (6) Aztec art had a similar style. (7) The murals often showed Mexico's history. (8) They also showed politics. (9) Sometimes Rivera's murals would upset people. (10) Many people loved them.

1 Which answer best combines sentence 1 and sentence 2?
- Diego Rivera is a famous Mexican painter, he painted murals.
- Diego Rivera is a famous Mexican painter of murals. (marked)
- Diego River is a famous Mexican painter, and he painted murals.
- Diego Rivera is a famous Mexican painter and, he painted murals.

2 Which answer best combines sentence 3 and sentence 4?
- He used bold, bright colors. (marked)
- He used bold, or bright colors.
- He used bold colors, bright colors.
- He used bold colors, but he used bright colors.

3 Read this combination of sentence 5 and sentence 6: *Rivera's colors reflected a style similar ______ Aztec art.* Which word completes the sentence?
- in
- for
- of
- to (marked)

4 Which answer best combines sentence 7 and sentence 8?
- The murals often showed Mexico's history, politics.
- The murals often showed Mexico's history, or showed politics.
- The murals often showed Mexico's history and politics. (marked)
- The murals often showed Mexico's historical politics.

5 Read this combination of sentence 9 and sentence 10: *Sometimes Rivera's murals would upset people ______ many people loved them.* Which answer completes the sentence?
- , but (marked)
- but,
- , and
- or

School + Home **Home Activity** Your child learned about combining sentences. Point out two short related sentences in a book you are reading with your child. Have your child combine the sentences.

Conventions Combining Sentences 417

Reader's and Writer's Notebook, p. 417

Spelling

Final Syllables *-ion, -ure*

PRACTICE SPELLING STRATEGY Supply pairs of students with index cards on which the spelling words have been written. Have one student read a word while the other writes it. Then have students switch roles. Have them use the cards to check their spelling and correct any misspelled words.

ON THEIR OWN For additional practice, use *Let's Practice It!* p. 388 on the *Teacher Resources DVD-ROM.*

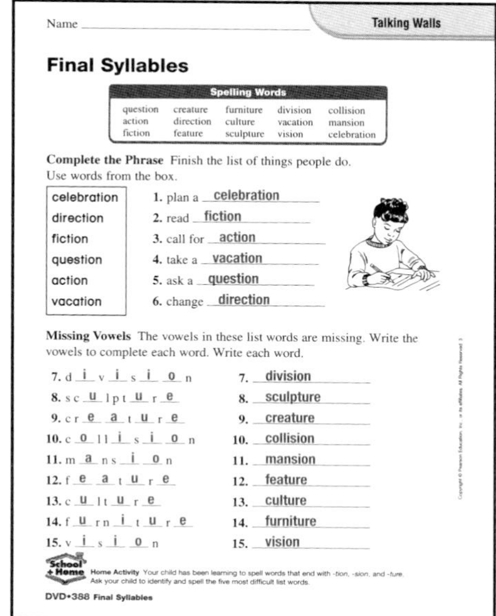

Name ______ Talking Walls

Final Syllables

Spelling Words				
question	creature	furniture	division	collision
action	direction	culture	vacation	mansion
fiction	feature	sculpture	vision	celebration

Complete the Phrase Finish the list of things people do. Use words from the box.

celebration, direction, fiction, question, action, vacation

1. plan a celebration
2. read fiction
3. call for action
4. take a vacation
5. ask a question
6. change direction

Missing Vowels The vowels in these list words are missing. Write the vowels to complete each word. Write each word.

7. d i v i s i o n — 7. division
8. s c u l p t u r e — 8. sculpture
9. c r e a t u r e — 9. creature
10. c o l l i s i o n — 10. collision
11. m a n s i o n — 11. mansion
12. f e a t u r e — 12. feature
13. c u l t u r e — 13. culture
14. f u r n i t u r e — 14. furniture
15. v i s i o n — 15. vision

School + Home **Home Activity** Your child has been learning to spell words that end with *-tion, -sion,* and *-ture.* Ask your child to identify and spell the five most difficult list words.

DVD•388 Final Syllables

Let's Practice It! TR DVD•388

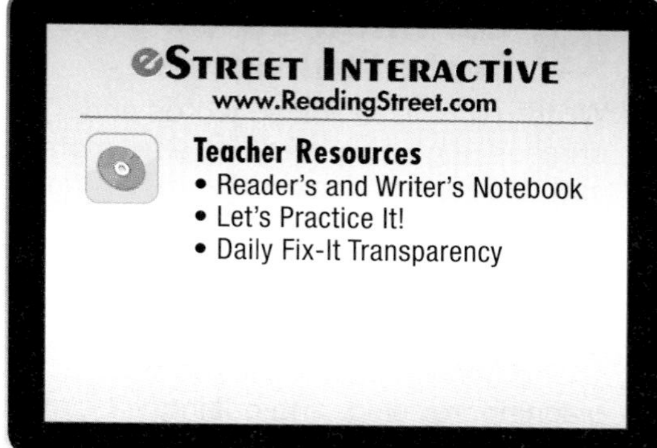

Daily Fix-It

7. Carlos begun a sculpchure to go with the mural. *(began; sculpture)*
8. He is making it out of clay and he will finish it next tuesday. *(clay, and; Tuesday)*

Bridge to Common Core

CONVENTIONS OF STANDARD ENGLISH

As students use correct punctuation and capitalization when combining sentences, they are demonstrating command of the conventions of standard English. Your guidance will help them use correct grammar, usage, and spelling to convey meaning when they speak and write.

Common Core State Standards

Writing 2.c. Use linking words and phrases (e.g., *also, another, and, more, but*) to connect ideas within categories of information. **Writing 2.d.** Provide a concluding statement or section. **Writing 5.** With guidance and support from peers and adults, develop and strengthen writing as needed by planning, revising, and editing. **Language 1.h.** Use coordinating and subordinating conjunctions. **Language 1.i.** Produce simple, compound, and complex sentences.

Write Guy *by Jeff Anderson*

Focus Your Editing

In the editing process, students can easily get bogged down by everything that needs to be fixed. Editing one aspect at a time helps students focus their efforts and concentrate on one task, while making it easier for you as a teacher to fully explain and reteach the concept, moving students toward correctness. Sometimes less really is more.

Description

Mini-Lesson Revise: Consolidating

- Yesterday we wrote a description about a piece of art. Today we will revise our drafts. The goal is to make your writing clearer, more interesting, and more informative.
- Display Writing Transparency 28B. Remind students that revising does not include corrections of grammar and mechanics. Tell them that this will be done later, when they proofread their work. Then introduce the revising strategy of consolidating.
- When you revise, you look for places where you have repeated words or ideas. In those places, you can consolidate, or combine, information. Look for sentences that contain the same words or information and combine them.

Revising Marks			
Take Out	⌒	Uppercase letter	═
Add	^	Lowercase letter	/
Period	⊙	New paragraph	¶
Move	⌒		

Description of Ori's Cat collage

My friend Ori made a collage of a cat. it hangs on the wall at her apartment. ~~It hangs~~ over the sofa. The cats fur is made of swirls of bumpy yarn. ~~The yarn~~ [that] is bright greene, like grass in spring. A thin line of sky blue yarn outline the cat's plump body. ~~The cat's~~ [and its] silver bottle cap eyes shine out at you. ~~They sparkle~~ [sparkling] with a coating of Silver glitter. The cat's front paws are made of white yarn, and its whiskers is made of stiff white pipe cleaners that stick out from the picture.

Unit 6 Talking Walls: Art for the People Writing: Revise 28B

Writing Transparency 28B, TR DVD

Remind students that as they revise, they should look for additional ways to make their writing clearer and more interesting, including adding sensory details that support the main idea.

Revising Tips

- ✔ Make sure all your supporting details refer to the main idea.
- ✔ Look for even more places to use strong adjectives, verbs, and words that appeal to the senses.
- ✔ Consolidate information that is repeated in your description by combining sentences.
- ✔ Make sure your concluding statement summarizes your main idea.

eStreet Interactive
www.ReadingStreet.com

Teacher Resources
- Writing Transparency

PEER CONFERENCING • PEER REVISION Have pairs of students exchange papers for peer revision. Students should write two questions about the partner's writing. Tell students that their questions should focus on where the partner could revise by adding relevant information. Refer to the *Teacher Resources DVD-ROM* for more information about peer conferencing.

Have students revise using the comments they collected during the peer revision as well as the key features of description and the revising tips. Check to make sure students are using the revising strategy of consolidating.

Corrective feedback Circulate around the room to monitor and confer with students as they revise. Remind students correcting errors that they will have time to edit tomorrow. They should be working on content and organization today.

Routine Quick Write for Fluency **Team Talk**

1. **Talk** Pairs of students discuss what it might be like to live in a country where there is no freedom of expression.
2. **Write** Students write briefly about what it might be like to live in a country where there is no freedom of expression.
3. **Share** Students read their writings aloud to their partners. Partners then check each other's writing for descriptive words.

Routines Flip Chart

Support Revision Have students listen for choppy sentences while they or a partner reads their story aloud. Once students have made their revisions, have them read their stories aloud again.

Wrap Up Your Day!

- ✔ **Content Knowledge** *What did you learn about palindromes?*
- ✔ **Oral Vocabulary** Monitor students' use of oral vocabulary as they respond: *Do you need to be an artistic and creative person to create palindromes?*
- ✔ **Text Features** Discuss how the palindrome squares help students understand text.

Preview DAY 5

Remind students to think about why freedom of expression is important.

DAY 5 at a Glance

Content Knowledge
Text-Based Comprehension
Review Graphic Sources

Vocabulary Skill
Review Unknown Words

Phonics/Word Analysis
Review Final Syllables

Literary Terms
Review Personification

Assessment
Fluency
Comprehension

Research and Inquiry
Communicate

Spelling
Final Syllables

Conventions
Combining Sentences

Writing
Description

Materials

- Student Edition
- Weekly Test
- Reader's and Writer's Notebook

Bridge to Common Core

INTEGRATION OF KNOWLEDGE/IDEAS

This week, students have integrated content presented in diverse media and analyzed how different texts address similar topics. They have developed knowledge about the importance of freedom of expression to expand the unit topic of Freedom.

Social Studies Knowledge Goals

Students have learned that freedom of expression

- allows us to express ideas or feelings
- can spread a message

Content Knowledge

Freedom of Expression

REVIEW THE CONCEPT Have students look back at the reading selections to find examples that best demonstrate why freedom of expression is important.

Build Oral Language

REVIEW AMAZING WORDS Display and review this week's concept map. Remind students that this week they have learned ten Amazing Words related to freedom of expression. Have students use the Amazing Words and the concept map to answer the Question of the Week, *Why is freedom of expression important?*

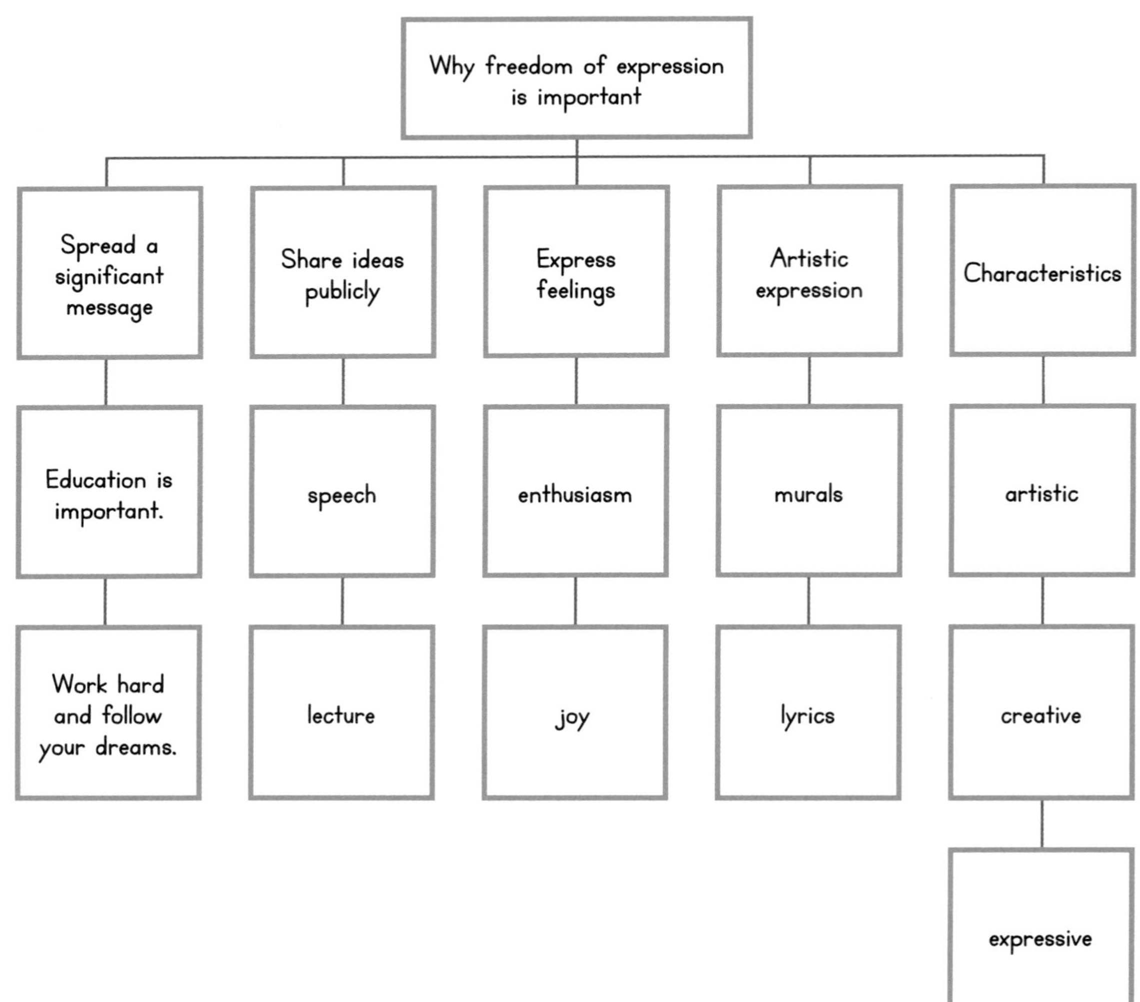

Build Oral Vocabulary

Think Aloud **CONNECT TO AMAZING IDEAS** Have pairs of students discuss how the Question of the Week connects to the question for this unit of study: *What does freedom mean?* Tell students to use the concept map and what they have learned from this week's discussions and reading selections to form an Amazing Idea—a realization or "big idea" about Freedom. Remind partners to answer questions with appropriate detail and to give suggestions that build on each other's ideas. Then ask pairs to share their Amazing Ideas with the class.

Amazing Ideas might include these key concepts:

- Freedom enables people to speak and act freely.
- People express themselves in many different ways.
- Freedom of expression is not something you should take for granted.

WRITE ABOUT IT Have students write a few sentences about their Amazing Idea, beginning with "This week I learned . . ."

It's Friday

MONITOR PROGRESS Check Oral Vocabulary

FORMATIVE ASSESSMENT Have individuals use this week's Amazing Words to describe the importance of freedom of expression. Monitor students' abilities to use the Amazing Words and note which words you need to reteach.

If... students have difficulty using the Amazing Words,

then... reteach using the Oral Vocabulary Routine, pp. 431a, 436b, 446b, 456b, OV•3.

Amazing Words

creative	lecture
expressive	significant
emotion	pause
artistic	view
exquisite	lyrics

Check Concepts and Language Use the Day 5 instruction on ELL Poster 28 to monitor students' understanding of the lesson concept.

Concept Map Work with students to add new words to the concept map.

Common Core State Standards

Informational Text 4. Determine the meaning of general academic and domain-specific words and phrases in a text relevant to a grade 3 topic or subject area. **Informational Text 7.** Use information gained from illustrations (e.g., maps, photographs) and the words in a text to demonstrate understanding of the text (e.g., where, when, why, and how key events occur). **Foundational Skills 3.b.** Decode words with common Latin suffixes. **Language 4.d.** Use glossaries or beginning dictionaries, both print and digital, to determine or clarify the precise meaning of key words and phrases. **Also Foundational Skills 3.**

Name ____________ Talking Walls

Graphic Sources

- **Graphic sources** are ways of showing information visually, or in a way you can see. Graphic sources make information easier to find and understand.
- **Charts, diagrams, maps,** and **graphs** are examples of graphic resources.

Directions Read the following chart. Then answer the questions.

U.S. Museums

Museum	Location	What You Can See or Hear	Museum Store?
Museum of Modern Art	New York City, NY	modern art, sculpture, photography	yes
National Air and Space Museum	Washington, D.C.	largest collection of aircraft in the world	yes
California State Railroad Museum	Sacramento, CA	railroad artifacts, locomotives	yes
Rock and Roll Hall of Fame	Cleveland, OH	photographs, guitars, early recordings	yes

1. What is the topic of this chart?
different museums in the United States
2. What can you see or hear at the National Air and Space Museum?
the largest collection of aircraft in the world
3. Which museum is located in Cleveland, Ohio?
the Rock and Roll Hall of Fame
4. Which museum sounds most interesting to you? Why? Students should include information from the chart to support their answer.

School + Home **Home Activity** Your child used a graphic source to understand information about different kinds of museums. With your child, create a similar chart that gives information about something that interests him or her. Invite another family member to locate information about the topic in the chart.

Comprehension DVD•389

Let's Practice It! TR DVD•389

Selection Vocabulary

encourages increases confidence

expression act of putting into words or visual medium

local of a certain place

native belonging to you because of your birth

settled made a home in a new place

social about people as a group

support to help or assist; to back

Text-Based Comprehension

Review Graphic Sources

TEACH Review the definition of graphic sources on p. 434. Remind students that graphic sources are ways of showing information visually. They provide additional information about the text and help readers better understand what they are reading. For additional support have students review pp. EI•10–EI•11 on graphic sources.

GUIDE PRACTICE Have student pairs find an example of a graphic source in *Talking Walls: Art for the People*. Then have pairs tell what information they learned from the graphic source.

ON THEIR OWN For additional practice, use *Let's Practice It!* p. 389 on the *Teacher Resources DVD-ROM*.

Vocabulary Skill

Review Unknown Words

TEACH Remind students to use a dictionary or a glossary to help them understand the meanings, syllabication, and pronunciation of unknown words.

GUIDE PRACTICE Review with students how to find the correct meaning, syllabication, and pronunciation of *support* using a dictionary. Tell students that some words have more than one definition listed.

ON THEIR OWN Have students use a dictionary or glossary to look up the meaning of a lesson vocabulary word. Then ask students to write a sentence that demonstrates the correct meaning of the word. Have partners read their sentences to verify that they can pronounce the word correctly.

Word Analysis

Review Final Syllables

TEACH Write the following sentences on the board. Have students read each one, first quietly to themselves and then aloud as you track the print.

1. **They began construction on the massive mansion.**
2. **Did you bring your permission slip for our outdoor adventure night?**
3. **We will learn about the culture and celebrations of Native Americans.**
4. **The oversized invention wouldn't fit in the convention hall.**
5. **Which direction is the furniture store from here?**

Team Talk Have partners identify and underline the final syllables *-tion, -ion, -ture, -ive,* and *-ize* in the words in the sentences. Then point to underlined words at random and have the group read them together.

Literary Terms

Review Personification

TEACH Have students reread pp. 446–451 of *Talking Walls: Art for the People*. Remind students that when an animal or object is personified, it is given human traits. Students should look for verbs that describe actions normally done by people.

GUIDE PRACTICE Point out the last sentence in the second paragraph of the "A Shared Hope" section of *Talking Walls: Art for the People*. Discuss with students how the author personifies the mural. (The mural *tells* children that education is the key to success.) Have students find another example of personification in the "Dreams of Flight" section and discuss.

ON THEIR OWN Point out the example of personification in the title *Talking Walls: Art for the People*. Have students put *talking walls* in the center of a word web and complete the web by adding circles that tell what the talking walls "say" to people.

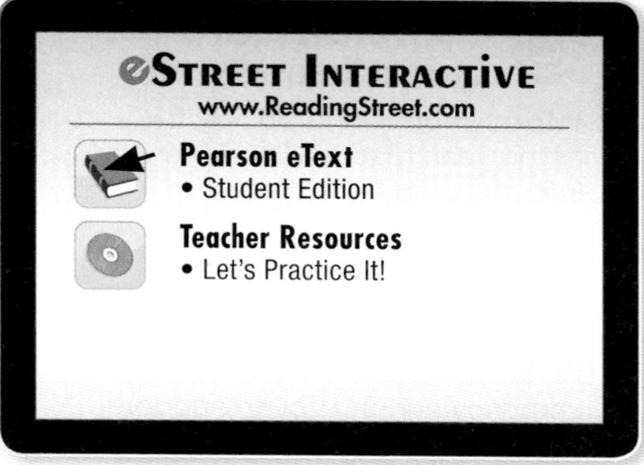

Graphic Sources Provide practice by having students find examples of graphic sources in other selections in their Student Edition. Discuss how each graphic source helps students better understand what they are reading.

Common Core State Standards

Informational Text 10. By the end of the year, read and comprehend informational texts, including history/social studies, science, and technical texts, at the high end of the grades 2–3 text complexity and independently and proficiently. **Foundational Skills 4.** Read with sufficient accuracy and fluency to support comprehension. **Foundational Skills 4.b.** Read on-level prose and poetry orally with accuracy, appropriate rate, and expression on successive readings.

Plan to Assess Fluency

- ☐ **Week 1** Advanced
- ☐ **Week 2** Strategic Intervention
- ☑ **This week assess On-Level students.**
- ☐ **Week 4** Strategic Intervention
- ☐ **Week 5** Assess any students you have not yet checked during this unit.

Set individual goals for students to enable them to reach the year-end goal.

- Current Goal: 110–120 WCPM
- Year-End Goal: 120 WCPM

Assessment

Monitor Progress

FLUENCY Make two copies of the fluency passage on p. 459k. As the student reads the text aloud, mark mistakes on your copy. Also mark where the student is at the end of one minute. To check the student's comprehension of the passage, have him or her retell what was read. To figure words correct per minute (WCPM), subtract the number of mistakes from the total number of words read in one minute

RATE

Corrective feedback	**If...** students cannot read fluently at a rate of 110–120 WCPM, **then...** make sure they practice with text at their independent reading level. Provide additional fluency practice by pairing nonfluent readers with fluent readers. **If...** students already read at 120 WCPM, **then...** have them read a book of their choice independently.

ELL

If... students need more scaffolding and practice with **Conventions and Writing,**
then... use the Grammar Transition Lessons on pp. 312–386 in the *ELL Handbook*.

Day 5 SMALL GROUP TIME • Differentiate Reteaching, p. SG•33

OL On-Level
- **Practice** Combining Sentences
- **Reread** *Reading Street Sleuth*, pp. 72–73

SI Strategic Intervention
- **Review** Combining Sentences
- **Reread** *Reading Street Sleuth*, pp. 72–73

A Advanced
- **Extend** Combining Sentences
- **Reread** *Reading Street Sleuth*, pp. 72–73
- **Communicate** Inquiry Project

Name ______________________________

Tips for Taking Great Travel Pictures

One of our freedoms is the freedom to travel, and it is fun to take 15
pictures when you do. They will help you remember your trips. For 27
your next trip, you can take great pictures too. Just follow these easy 40
directions. 41

At times, a close-up shot is best. Let's say you are taking a picture 55
of a sculpture. Use the zoom feature on your camera. That will let you 69
capture small details. The zoom also works well for taking shots of 81
nature. Use it to snap a picture of a native plant or a single tree. 96

Sometimes you may want to take a picture of something in motion. 108
You must be fast to take an action picture. Frame your picture first. 121
Make sure you are very still. Then use a fast shutter speed. If you do 136
this, you can take good shots of nature or people in motion. 148

You might want to take shots of the people you meet. Let's say you 162
are at a local celebration. Always ask before taking your shot. You 174
may think you are just being social. However, others might think you 186
are rude. Even if a person encourages you to take pictures, still ask. 199
Then you will not make anyone angry. 206

Follow these rules. If you do, you will take great pictures. You will 219
be able to look at them and remember your trip. 229

MONITOR PROGRESS

- **Check Fluency**

Common Core State Standards

Informational Text 1. Ask and answer questions to demonstrate understanding of a text, referring explicitly to the text as the basis for the answers. **Informational Text 7.** Use information gained from illustrations (e.g., maps, photographs) and the words in a text to demonstrate understanding of the text (e.g., where, when, why, and how key events occur). **Foundational Skills 4.** Read with sufficient accuracy and fluency to support comprehension. **Foundational Skills 4.b.** Read on-level prose and poetry orally with accuracy, appropriate rate, and expression on successive readings. **Also Informational Text 10.**

Assessment

Monitor Progress

For a written assessment of Final Syllables, Graphic Sources, and Selection Vocabulary, use Weekly Test 28, pp. 167–172.

GRAPHIC SOURCES Use "A Small Town Votes" on p. 459m to check students' understanding of graphic sources.

1. Why was there an election in Smithson? (to determine whether or not a new highway would be built)
2. Based on the chart, did the majority of people vote for or against the highway being built? (The majority of people voted for the highway to be built.)
3. Based on the map, would the new highway be more on the east or west side of the town? (more on the west side of town)

Corrective feedback

If... students are unable to answer the comprehension questions,
then... use the Reteach lesson in *First Stop*.

Name ____

A Small Town Votes

There was an election in the town of Smithson. Voters had to decide whether or not to approve a new highway that would go through town.

Some citizens wanted the highway because it would make travel around Smithson easier. Many also thought the highway would aid the town's businesses.

Other citizens did not want the highway because they were afraid it would mean too much traffic in their local neighborhood. Many of these citizens were also concerned about the expense of building a new highway.

The voting took place on a Tuesday in April. The chart and map show how people voted and where the new highway would go.

	East Smithson	West Smithson
Number of citizens	345	388
Number of yes votes	250	156
Number of no votes	95	232

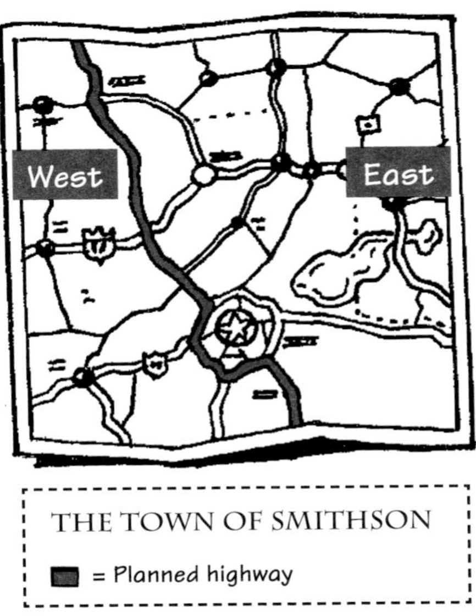

THE TOWN OF SMITHSON

■ = Planned highway

MONITOR PROGRESS

- **Graphic Sources**

Common Core State Standards

Speaking/Listening 1.a. Come to discussions prepared, having read or studied required material; explicitly draw on that preparation and other information known about the topic to explore ideas under discussion. **Speaking/Listening 4.** Report on a topic or text, tell a story, or recount an experience with appropriate facts and relevant, descriptive details, speaking clearly at an understandable pace. **Language 1.h.** Use coordinating and subordinating conjunctions. **Language 1.i.** Produce simple, compound, and complex sentences. **Language 2.e.** Use conventional spelling for high-frequency and other studied words and for adding suffixes to base words (e.g., *sitting, smiled, cries, happiness*). **Also Speaking/Listening 1.b., 1.c., 1.d., 3.**

Research and Inquiry

Step 5 Communicate

PRESENT IDEAS Have students share their inquiry results by presenting their information and giving a brief talk on their research. Have students display the review or definition they created on Day 4.

SPEAKING Remind students how to be good speakers and how to communicate effectively with their audience.

- Respond to relevant questions with appropriate details.
- Speak coherently about the topic.
- Speak clearly and loudly.
- Keep eye contact with audience members.

LISTENING Remind students of these tips for being a good listener.

- Wait until the speaker has finished before raising your hand to ask a relevant question.
- Be polite, even if you disagree.

LISTEN TO IDEAS Have students listen attentively to the various presentations of inquiry results. Have them make pertinent comments, closely related to the topic.

Spelling Test

Final Syllables *-ion, -ure*

To administer the spelling test, refer to the directions, words, and sentences on p. 435c.

Conventions

Combining Sentences

MORE PRACTICE Remind students that combining sentences improves choppy or repetitive writing.

GUIDE PRACTICE Have students write two simple sentences describing a favorite art project.

I painted a picture of a turtle. I used green and blue paint.

Have students exchange papers with a partner and combine the sentences. *(I painted a picture of a blue and green turtle.)*

ON THEIR OWN Write the pairs of simple sentences below. Direct students to look back in *Talking Walls: Art for the People* to find the sentences combined. Discuss with students which sentence from the selection is a compound sentence. Students should complete *Let's Practice It!* p. 390 on the *Teacher Resources DVD-ROM*.

1. **Muralists are asked by a town to create a work of art on a wall. They are asked by a school or business.** (*Muralists are asked by a town, school, or business to create a work of art on a wall*. p. 440)
2. **He interprets their stories by making sketches. He makes plans for the painting of the mural.** (*He interprets their stories by making sketches, and then he makes plans for the painting of the mural*. p. 444)
3. **Paul loved painting murals. Paul was inspired to become an artist like his brother.** (*Paul loved painting murals and was inspired to become an artist like his brother*. p. 446)

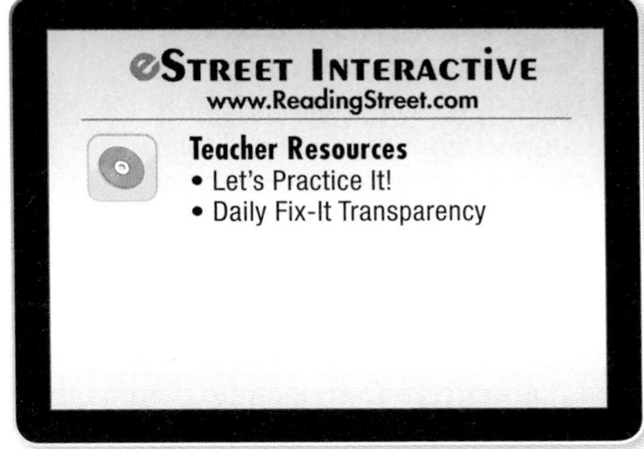

Daily Fix-It

9. The mural was a success and the class will paint unother soon. *(success, and; another)*
10. What subjeck will they choose for the next mural. *(subject; mural?)*

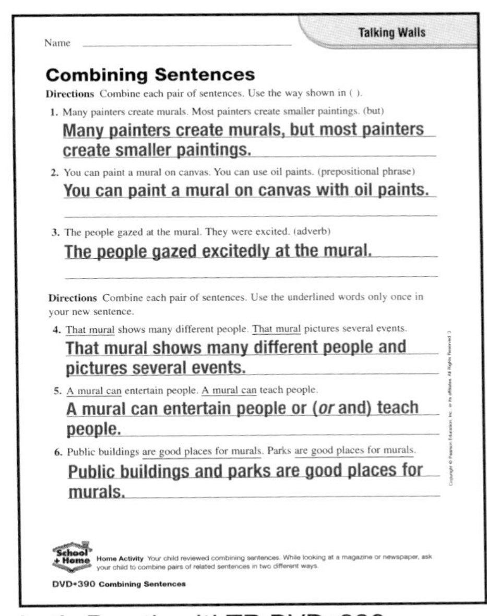

Name ____________ Talking Walls

Combining Sentences

Directions Combine each pair of sentences. Use the way shown in ( ).

1. Many painters create murals. Most painters create smaller paintings. (but)
   Many painters create murals, but most painters create smaller paintings.
2. You can paint a mural on canvas. You can use oil paints. (prepositional phrase)
   You can paint a mural on canvas with oil paints.
3. The people gazed at the mural. They were excited. (adverb)
   The people gazed excitedly at the mural.

Directions Combine each pair of sentences. Use the underlined words only once in your new sentence.

4. That mural shows many different people. That mural pictures several events.
   That mural shows many different people and pictures several events.
5. A mural can entertain people. A mural can teach people.
   A mural can entertain people or (*or* and) teach people.
6. Public buildings are good places for murals. Parks are good places for murals.
   Public buildings and parks are good places for murals.

School + Home **Home Activity** Your child reviewed combining sentences. While looking at a magazine or newspaper, ask your child to combine pairs of related sentences in two different ways.

DVD•390 Combining Sentences

Let's Practice It! TR DVD•390

Common Core State Standards

Writing 5. With guidance and support from peers and adults, develop and strengthen writing as needed by planning, revising, and editing. **Language 1.** Demonstrate command of the conventions of standard English grammar and usage when writing or speaking. **Language 2.** Demonstrate command of the conventions of standard English capitalization, punctuation, and spelling when writing. **Language 3.a.** Choose words and phrases for effect. **Also Writing 10.**

Teacher Note

Writing Self-Evaluation Make copies of the Writing Self-Evaluation Guide on p. 39 of the *Reader's and Writer's Notebook* and hand them out to students.

Bridge to Common Core

PRODUCTION AND DISTRIBUTION OF WRITING

Over the course of the week, students have developed and strengthened their drafts through planning, revising, editing, and rewriting. The final drafts are clear and coherent descriptions in which the organization and style are appropriate to the purpose and audience.

Writing

Description

REVIEW REVISING Remind students that yesterday they revised their descriptions of artwork, paying particular attention to consolidating by combining sentences. Today they will edit and proofread their descriptions.

Mini-Lesson Proofread

Proofread for Voice

- **Teach** When we proofread, we look closely at our work, searching for errors in mechanics, spelling, and grammar. Today we will also focus on voice, which communicates to the reader how the writer feels about the topic.

- **Model** Let's look at the description of Ori's cat collage. What words and phrases tell you that I am interested in my topic? Point out that *grass in spring, shine,* and *sparkling* tell the reader that the writer is excited about the collage. In the second paragraph, the writer uses the words *happy* and *energetic* to describe the nature of that interest. I tried to use words that would show how much I like the cat collage. But the part that says *it looks like it might leap right out at you* doesn't fit with the voice in the rest of the description. I think I'll change it to something more positive, like *it looks like it might want to play*. I'll reread my description a few more times, looking for other errors. Explain to students that they should do the same, and encourage them to keep the voice consistent.

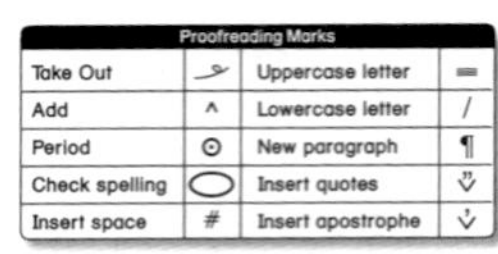

Proofreading Marks			
Take Out	⟶	Uppercase letter	═
Add	^	Lowercase letter	/
Period	⊙	New paragraph	¶
Check spelling	◯	Insert quotes	∛
Insert space	#	Insert apostrophe	∜

Description of Ori's Cat collage

My friend Ori made a collage of a cat. it hangs on the wall at her apartment, over the sofa. The cats fur is made of swirls of bumpy yarn that is bright greene like grass in spring. A thin line of sky blue yarn outline the cat's plump body and its silver bottle cap eyes shine out at you, sparkling with a coating of Silver glitter. The cat's front paws are made of white yarn, and its whiskers is made of stiff white pipe cleaners that stick out from the picture.

The cat's bright green fur and white paws stand out against the black cardboard background. Crouching there with its tail wrapped around its body, it looks like it might leap right out at you. Looking at the collage makes me feel happy and energetic.

Unit 6 Talking Walls: Art for the People Writing: Proofread 28C

Writing Transparency 28C, TR DVD

PROOFREAD Display the Proofreading Tips. Ask students to proofread their compositions, using the tips and paying particular attention to voice. Circulate around the room answering students' questions. When students have finished editing their own work, have pairs proofread one another's descriptions.

Proofreading Tips

- ✔ Use words and phrases that show you are interested in your topic.
- ✔ Check for correct spelling, punctuation, capitalization, and grammar.
- ✔ Be sure that compound sentences have a comma and a conjunction.

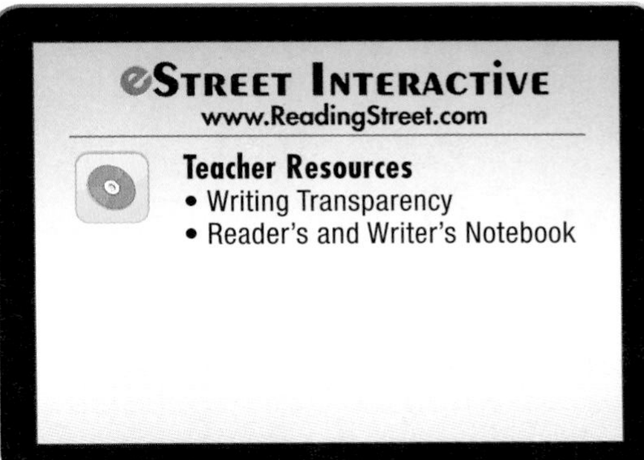

PRESENT Have students incorporate revisions and proofreading edits into their descriptions to create a final draft. Have students display their descriptions along with a photocopy or a student reproduction of the piece of art they are describing. Invite parents or other students to tour the display, while students act as gallery hosts. Collect the images and descriptions in a class book.

Routine Quick Write for Fluency — Team Talk

1. **Talk** Pairs discuss the purpose of murals.
2. **Write** Students write for two or three minutes on the effects murals have on the public.
3. **Share** Students exchange writing with their partners, who read it aloud.

Routines Flip Chart

Wrap Up Your Week!

Freedom of Expression

Why is freedom of expression important?

In *Talking Walls: Art for the People* and "The History of Palindromes," we learned how people express themselves through both art and language.

Team Talk Have students recall their Amazing Ideas about freedom and use these ideas to help them demonstrate their understanding of the Question of the Week.

Next Week's Concept

Rules and Laws Are Important to Freedom

Why are rules and laws important to freedom?

Poster Preview Prepare students for next week by using Week 4 ELL Poster 29. Read the Talk-Through to introduce the concept and vocabulary.

Selection Summary Send home the summary of next week's selection, *Two Bad Ants,* in English and in students' home languages, if available in the *ELL Handbook*.

Why are rules and laws important to freedom? Next week you will be reading about two ants that make an unfortunate decision.

Preview Next Week

Assessment Checkpoints for the Week

Weekly Assessment

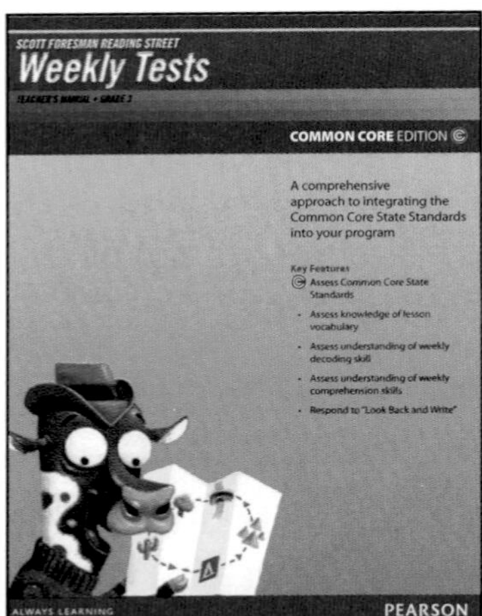

Weekly Tests

Use pp. 167–172 of *Weekly Tests* to check:

- ✔ **Phonics** Final Syllables
- ✔ **Comprehension** Graphic Sources
- ✔ Review **Comprehension** Fact and Opinion
- ✔ **Selection Vocabulary**

encourages	**settled**
expression	**social**
local	**support**
native	

Differentiated Assessment

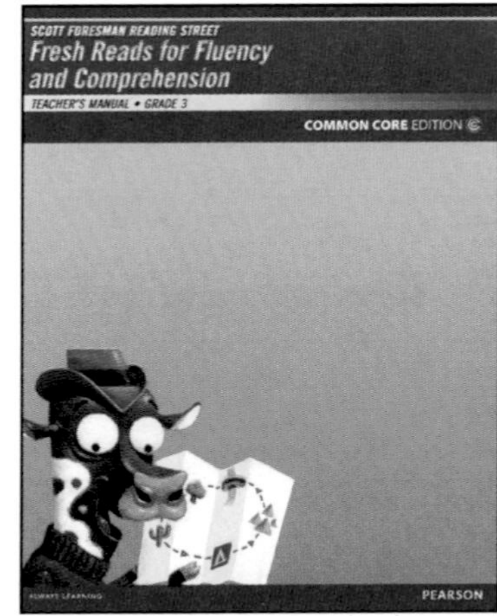

Fresh Reads for Fluency and Comprehension

Advanced

On-Level

SI
Strategic Intervention

Use pp. 167–172 of *Fresh Reads for Fluency and Comprehension* to check:

- ✔ **Comprehension** Graphic Sources

- ✔ Review **Comprehension** Fact and Opinion

- ✔ **Fluency** Words Correct Per Minute

Managing Assessment

Assessment Handbook

Use *Assessment Handbook* for:

- ✔ **Weekly Assessment Blackline Masters for Monitoring Progress**
- ✔ **Observation Checklists**
- ✔ **Record-Keeping Forms**
- ✔ **Portfolio Assessment**

TEACHER NOTES

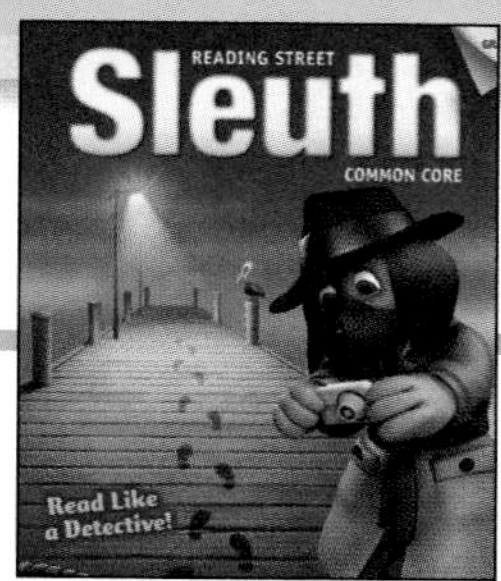

"A Performance in a Flash," pp. 72–73

DAY 1 Differentiate Vocabulary

- **Word Knowledge** Amazing Words
- **Read** "A Performance in a Flash"
- **Inquiry** Identify Questions

DAY 2 Differentiate Comprehension

- **Word Knowledge** Selection Vocabulary
- **Access Text** Read *Talking Walls: Art for the People*
- **Inquiry** Investigate

DAY 3 Differentiate Close Reading

- **Word Knowledge** Develop Vocabulary
- **Close Reading** Read *Talking Walls: Art for the People*
- **Inquiry** Investigate

DAY 4 Differentiate Vocabulary

- **Word Knowledge** Amazing Words
- **Read** "The History of Palindromes"
- **Inquiry** Organize

DAY 5 Differentiate Reteaching

- **Conventions** Combining Sentences
- **Reread** "A Performance in a Flash" or Leveled Readers
- **Inquiry** Communicate

Teacher Guides and Student pages can be found in the Leveled Reader Database.

Place English Language Learners in the groups that correspond to their reading abilities.
If... students need scaffolding and practice,
then... use the ELL Notes on the instructional pages.

Independent Practice

Independent Practice Stations

See pp. 430h and 430i for Independent Stations.

Pearson Trade Book Library

See the Leveled Reader Database for lesson plans and student pages.

Reading Street Digital Path

Independent Practice Activities are available in the Digital Path.

Independent Reading

See p. 430i for independent reading suggestions.

On-Level

Common Core State Standards

Informational Text 2. Determine the main idea of a text; recount the key details and explain how they support the main idea. **Informational Text 4.** Determine the meaning of general academic and domain-specific words and phrases in a text relevant to a grade 3 topic or subject area. **Informational Text 7.** Use information gained from illustrations (e.g., maps, photographs), and the words in a text to demonstrate understanding of the text (e.g., where, when, why, and how key events occur). **Foundational Skills 4.** Read with sufficient accuracy and fluency to support comprehension. **Language 4.** Determine or clarify the meaning of unknown and multiple-meaning words and phrases based on grade 3 reading and content, choosing flexibly from a range of strategies.

Independent Reading Options

Trade Book Library

eStreet Interactive
www.ReadingStreet.com

Teacher Guides are available on the Leveled Reader Database.

If... students need more scaffolding and practice with **Vocabulary, then...** use the activities on pp. DI•67–DI•68 in the Teacher Resources section on SuccessNet.

1 Build Word Knowledge

Practice Amazing Words

DEFINE IT Elicit the definition for the word *creative* from students. Ask: How would you describe a *creative* person to another student? (Possible response: A *creative* person is one who has imagination and comes up with new and original ideas.) Clarify or give a definition when necessary. Continue with the words *artistic* and *expressive.*

Team Talk **TALK ABOUT IT** Have partners internalize meanings. Ask: How can you group the Amazing Words together in a sentence? (Possible response: The beautiful and *expressive* works were done by a *creative* and *artistic* painter.) Allow time for students to play with the words. Review the concept map with students. Discuss other words they can add to the concept map.

2 Text-Based Comprehension

Read

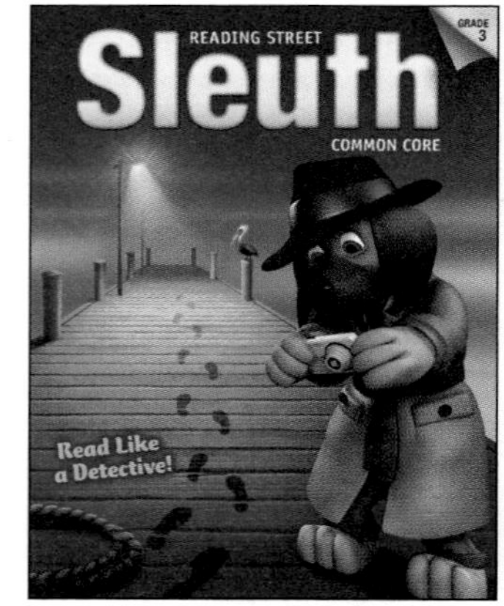

READ ALOUD "A Performance in a Flash" Have partners read "A Performance in a Flash" from *Reading Street Sleuth* on pp. 72–73.

ACCESS TEXT Discuss the Sleuth Work section with students before they work on it. Remind students that they can use these steps with other texts they read.

Gather Evidence Have partners take notes of text evidence. Invite students to share the evidence they found in the article.

Ask Questions Talk together about the questions students wrote. Invite discussion about how students might research the answers to their questions other than talking with Bill Wasik.

Make Your Case Have students share their paragraphs with the group, pointing out their most convincing reasons for their opinions. Invite discussion about how cited examples helped or hindered their arguments.

On-Level

1 Build Word Knowledge

Practice Selection Vocabulary

encourages	expression	local	native
settled	social	support	

DEFINE IT Discuss the definition for the word *support* with students. Ask: How would you describe *support* to another student? (Possible response: *Support* is something that holds up something or helps out someone. For example, friends *support,* or help, each other in times of need.) Continue with the remaining words.

Team Talk **TALK ABOUT IT** Have pairs use the selection vocabulary in sentences to internalize meaning. Ask: How can you group the selection vocabulary words together in a sentence? (Possible response: The city council *encourages* citizens to *support* their *local* police.) Allow time for students to play with the words and then share their sentences.

2 Read

Talking Walls: Art for the People

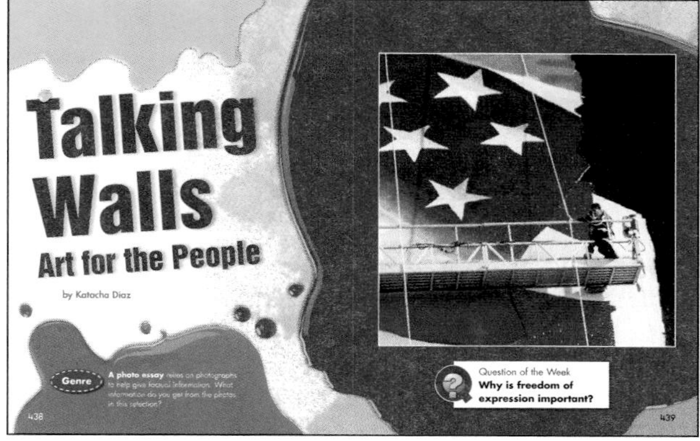

If you read *Talking Walls: Art for the People* during whole group time, then use the following instruction.

ACCESS TEXT Reread p. 440.
Ask questions to check understanding. What freedom do artists have? (to speak their minds or express their ideas through art) What can murals show? (celebrations, festivals, symbols of freedom) Why are murals a great example of artistic expression? (They reveal what the artists think or believe in a way that everyone can see and enjoy.)

Have students identify sections from today's reading that they did not completely understand. Reread them aloud and clarify misunderstandings.

If you are reading *Talking Walls: Art for the People* during small group time, then return to pp. 440–445a to guide the reading.

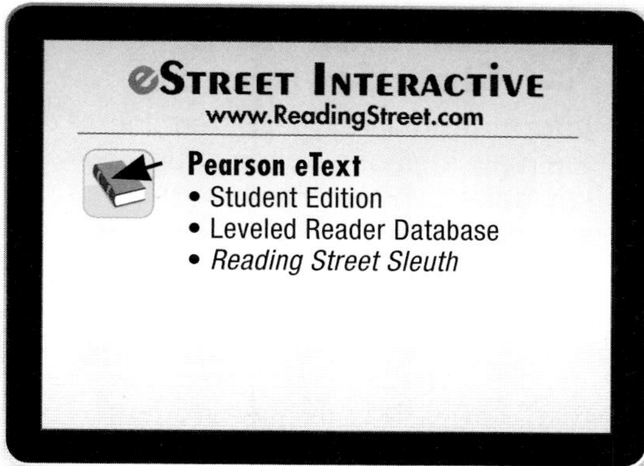

SMALL GROUP TIME

More Reading for Group Time

ON-LEVEL

Review
- Graphic Sources
- Important Ideas
- Selection Vocabulary

Use this suggested Leveled Reader or other text at students' instructional level.

eStreet Interactive
www.ReadingStreet.com

Use the Leveled Reader Database for lesson plans and student pages for *Lily's Adventure Around the World.*

On-Level

Common Core State Standards

Informational Text 2. Determine the main idea of a text; recount the key details and explain how they support the main idea. **Informational Text 7.** Use information gained from illustrations (e.g., maps, photographs), and the words in a text to demonstrate understanding of the text (e.g., where, when, why, and how key events occur). **Language 4.** Determine or clarify the meaning of unknown and multiple-meaning words and phrases based on grade 3 reading and content, choosing flexibly from a range of strategies. **Language 6.** Acquire and use accurately grade-appropriate conversational, general academic, and domain-specific words and phrases, including those that signal spatial and temporal relationships (e.g., *After dinner that night we went looking for them*).

1 Build Word Knowledge

Develop Vocabulary

REREAD FOR VOCABULARY Reread the second paragraph on p. 450. Introduce: Let's read this paragraph to find out what the word *residents* means. To help students understand the word *residents,* ask questions related to the context, such as: What are people who live in cities and towns called? How do murals tell stories of the local people? Have students use online sources to find out more information about the meaning of *residents.*

2 Read

Talking Walls: Art for the People

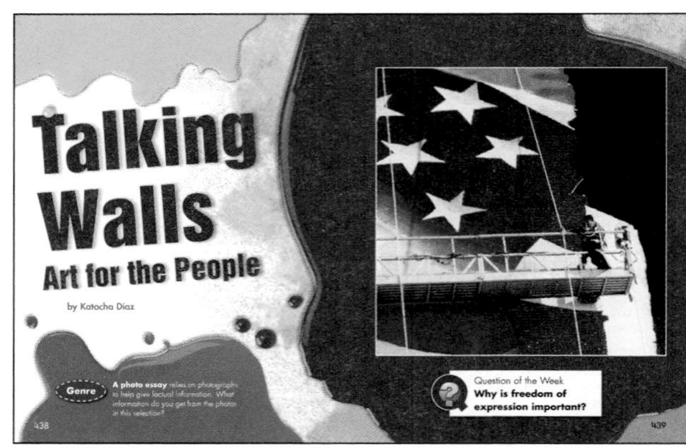

If you read *Talking Walls: Art for the People* during whole group time, then use the following instruction.

CLOSE READING Read pp. 448–449. Have students search through the text to find references to David's different murals. As a class, make a list of the murals David created, in the order they are described. (mural of dinosaurs; "Dreams of Flight," and a repainting of "Dreams of Flight")

Ask: How did David change the second "Dreams of Flight" to make it different from the first one? Why did he do this? (He changed one of the children from a boy to a girl in order to show that girls could dream of flying model airplanes, too.)

If you are reading *Talking Walls: Art for the People* during small group time, then return to pp. 446–451a to guide the reading.

If... students need more scaffolding and practice with the **Main Selection,** **then...** use the activities on p. DI•72 in the Teacher Resources section on SuccessNet.

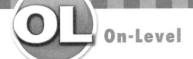

On-Level

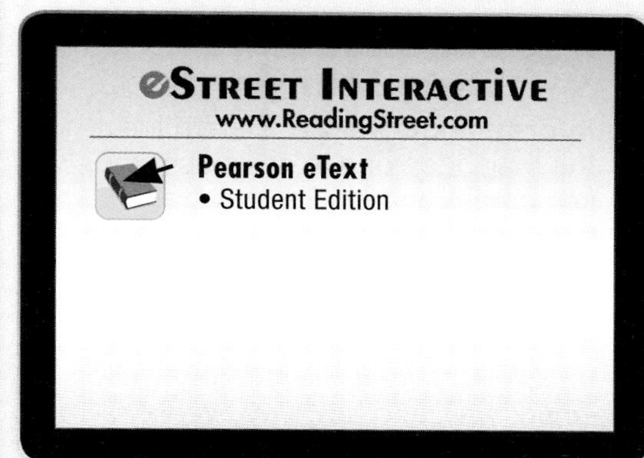

1 Build Word Knowledge

Practice Amazing Words

creative	expressive	emotion	artistic	exquisite
lecture	significant	pause	view	lyrics

Team Talk **LANGUAGE DEVELOPMENT** Have partners practice building more complex sentences. Display a sentence starter and have students add oral phrases or clauses using the Amazing Words. For example: The _______ lyrics _______. (The *expressive lyrics* / of the song / caused listeners / to *pause* / and experience a *significant emotion.*) Guide students to add at least three phrases or clauses per sentence.

2 Read

"The History of Palindromes"

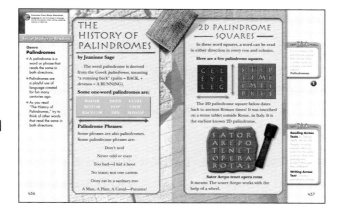

BEFORE READING Read aloud the genre information about palindromes on p. 456. Ask: How might a palindrome be a form of self-expression? (It is a use of language through which a person might playfully express an idea.) Help students preview the selection and set a purpose for reading.

DURING READING Have students read with you while tracking along with the print. Ask:

- How is this selection different from *Talking Walls: Art for the People?* (It is shorter. It doesn't give as much information. It has a more formal style.)
- How do the arrows help you understand the text? (They show that the palindrome squares can be read from left to right and from top to bottom.)

AFTER READING Have students share their reaction to "The History of Palindromes." Then have them search classroom books or the Internet for palindromes or palindrome phrases. Tell them to list the examples they find and then display their lists in the classroom.

SMALL GROUP TIME

Independent Reading Options

Trade Book Library

eStreet Interactive
www.ReadingStreet.com

Teacher Guides are available on the Leveled Reader Database.

On-Level

Common Core State Standards

Informational Text 2. Determine the main idea of a text; recount the key details and explain how they support the main idea. **Informational Text 7.** Use information gained from illustrations (e.g., maps, photographs), and the words in a text to demonstrate understanding of the text (e.g., where, when, why, and how key events occur). **Foundational Skills 4.** Read with sufficient accuracy and fluency to support comprehension. **Writing 5.** With guidance and support from peers and adults, develop and strengthen writing as needed by planning, revising, and editing. **Language 4.** Determine or clarify the meaning of unknown and multiple-meaning words and phrases based on grade 3 reading and content, choosing flexibly from a range of strategies. **Also Language 1.h., 1.i.**

More Reading for Group Time

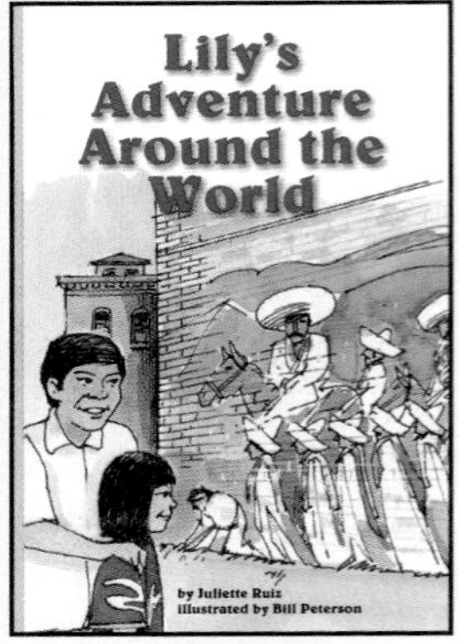

ON-LEVEL

Review

- Graphic Sources
- Important Ideas
- Selection Vocabulary

Use this suggested Leveled Reader or other text at students' instructional level.

eStreet Interactive
www.ReadingStreet.com

Use the Leveled Reader Database for lesson plans and student pages for *Lily's Adventure Around the World.*

1 Build Word Knowledge

Practice Combining Sentences

IDENTIFY Choral read the bottom of p. 455 with students and discuss sentence combining, in which short sentences are combined into longer ones. Have partners reread the model description and identify how the author combined sentences. Allow time for students to discuss their examples and correct any misunderstandings.

2 Text-Based Comprehension

Read

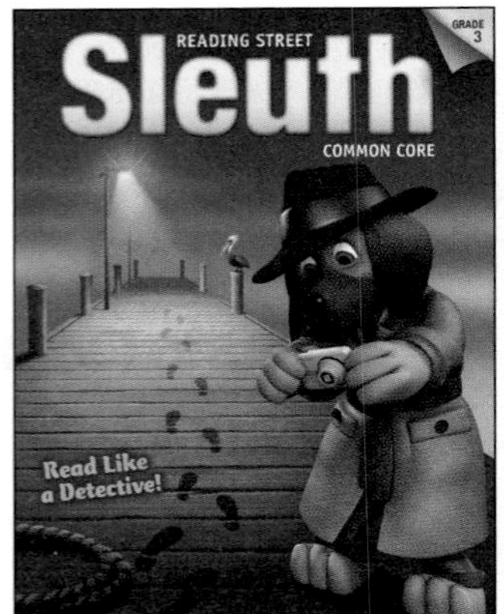

REREAD "A Performance in a Flash" Have partners reread "A Performance in a Flash."

EXTEND UNDERSTANDING Talk together about flash mobs and their impact on today's society. Invite students to share experiences they have had with flash mobs whether in person, on the Internet, or on TV.

PERFORMANCE TASK • Prove It! Have students work in groups. Ask groups to plan a surprise performance at school. Have them write a plan that includes what they will do, where they will perform, and how they will let others know about their plan. Remind students to be detail-oriented in their plans.

COMMUNICATE Have groups share their flash mob plans. Invite others to ask questions about missing details in the plan.

1 Build Word Knowledge

Reteach Amazing Words

Repeat the definition of the word. We learned that *creative* means having imagination and original or fresh ideas. Then use the word in a sentence. In art class, the teacher helps us be *creative*.

Team Talk **TALK ABOUT IT** Have students take turns using the word *creative* in a sentence. Continue this routine to practice the Amazing Words *artistic* and *expressive.* Review the concept map with students. Discuss other words they can add to the concept map.

Corrective feedback | **If...** students need more practice with the Amazing Words, **then...** use visuals from the Student Edition or online sources to clarify meaning.

2 Text-Based Comprehension

Read

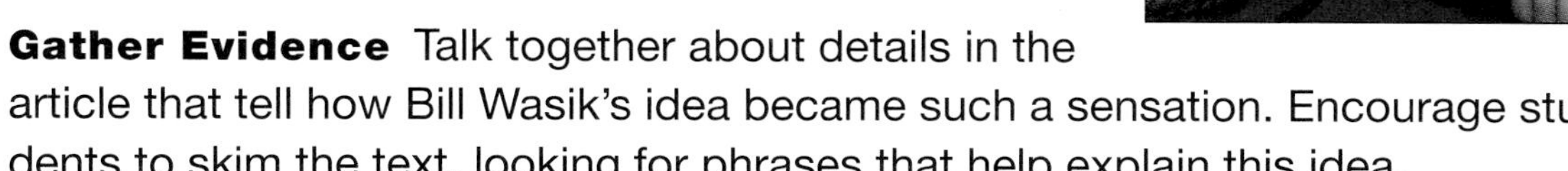

READ "A Performance in a Flash" Have students track the print as you read "A Performance in a Flash" from *Reading Street Sleuth* on pp. 72–73.

ACCESS TEXT Discuss the Sleuth Work section with students and provide support as needed as they work on it. Remind students that they can use these steps with other texts they read.

Gather Evidence Talk together about details in the article that tell how Bill Wasik's idea became such a sensation. Encourage students to skim the text, looking for phrases that help explain this idea.

Ask Questions Talk together about the questions students wrote. Invite discussion about how students might find answers to their questions if they can't talk with Bill Wasik.

Make Your Case Have students work with a partner on the same side of the issue. Before writing their paragraph, have students make two lists. One list names reasons for their side of the issue. The other list names examples to support their opinions. From these lists, students can work together to write their paragraphs. If time permits, have them share their most convincing argument with another set of partners.

SMALL GROUP TIME

More Reading for Group Time

CONCEPT LITERACY

Practice
Concept Words

BELOW-LEVEL

Review
- Graphic Sources
- Important Ideas
- Selection Vocabulary

Use these suggested Leveled Readers or other text at students' instructional level.

eSTREET INTERACTIVE
www.ReadingStreet.com

Use the Leveled Reader Database for lesson plans and student pages for *Many Voices* and *One Forest, Different Trees.*

Common Core State Standards

Informational Text 2. Determine the main idea of a text; recount the key details and explain how they support the main idea. **Informational Text 7.** Use information gained from illustrations (e.g., maps, photographs), and the words in a text to demonstrate understanding of the text (e.g., where, when, why, and how key events occur). **Language 4.** Determine or clarify the meaning of unknown and multiple-meaning words and phrases based on grade 3 reading and content, choosing flexibly from a range of strategies.

1 Build Word Knowledge

Reteach Selection Vocabulary

encourages	expression	local
native	settled	social
support		

DEFINE IT Describe *local* to a friend. Give a definition when necessary. Restate the word in student-friendly terms and clarify meaning with a visual. See the photograph on the bottom of page 442. It shows a *local* mural. The mural reflects what is important to a community.

Team Talk **TALK ABOUT IT** Have you ever read a local newspaper? Turn and talk to your partner about this. Rephrase students' examples for usage when necessary or to correct misunderstandings.

Corrective feedback | **If...** students need more practice with selection vocabulary, **then...** use the *Envision It! Pictured Vocabulary Cards.*

2 Read

Talking Walls: Art for the People

If you read *Talking Walls: Art for the People* during whole group time, then use the instruction below.

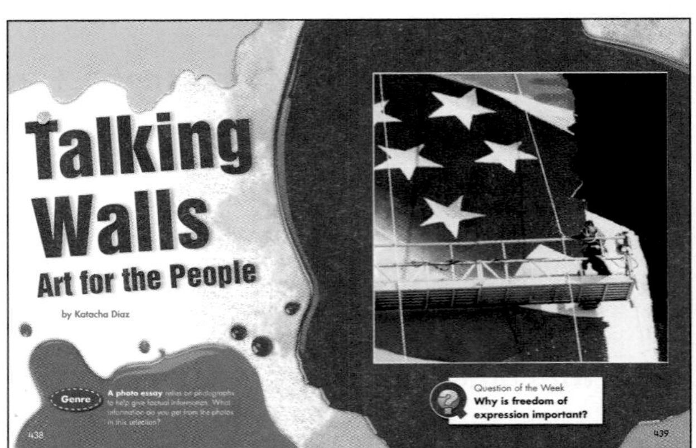

ACCESS TEXT Reread p. 440.
Ask questions to check understanding. Why do immigrants come to America? (for freedoms this country offers) What is freedom of expression? (It is the ability to express your ideas freely.) Why do you think murals are a way to express ideas or feelings? (They reveal what the artists think or believe in a way that everyone can see and enjoy.)

Have students identify sections they did not understand. Reread them aloud. Clarify the meaning of each section to build understanding.

If you are reading *Talking Walls: Art for the People* during small group time, then return to pp. 440–445a to guide the reading.

Independent Reading Options

Trade Book Library

eSTREET INTERACTIVE
www.ReadingStreet.com
Teacher Guides are available on the Leveled Reader Database.

Strategic Intervention

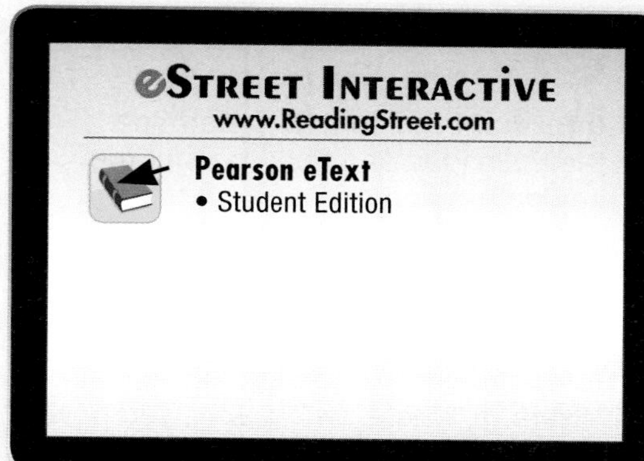

1 Build Word Knowledge

Develop Vocabulary

REREAD FOR VOCABULARY Reread the second paragraph on p. 450. Introduce: Let's read this paragraph to find out what *residents* means. To help students understand the word *residents,* ask questions related to the context, such as: Whose stories get told in the murals? Who enjoys the murals after they are painted? What word helps you understand the meaning of *residents?*

Corrective feedback | **If...** students have difficulty understanding the word *residents,* **then...** lead them in an analysis of word parts and remind them to use a dictionary to find the word's meaning.

2 Read

Talking Walls: Art for the People

If you read *Talking Walls: Art for the People* during whole group time, then use the instruction below.

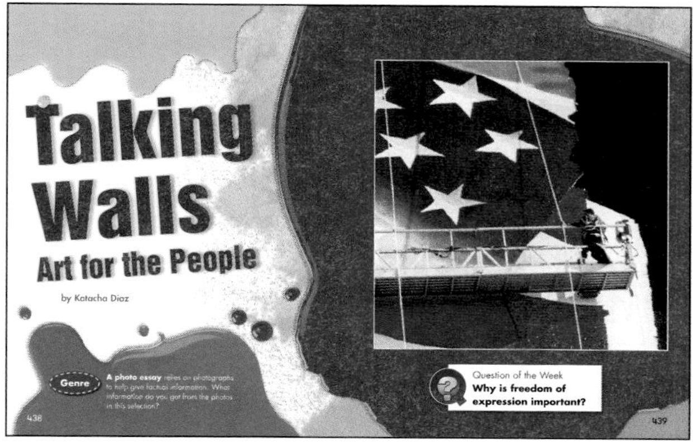

CLOSE READING Read pp. 448–449. Have students search through the text to find time references that help readers know the sequence of events. As a class, make a list of these words and phrases in the order they occur. *(When he was in the third grade, Years later, seventeen years after, over time)*

Now use the times you listed to retell what happened to David Botello. (When David was in the third grade, he painted a dinosaur mural. Years later, he painted a mural called "Dreams of Flight." Seventeen years after he painted that mural, he repainted it. He hopes that the mural will inspire people over time.)

If you are reading *Talking Walls: Art for the People* during small group time, then return to pp. 446–451a to guide the reading.

SMALL GROUP TIME

If... students need more scaffolding and practice with the **Main Selection, then...** use the activities on p. DI•72 in the Teacher Resources section on SuccessNet.

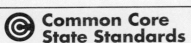

Strategic Intervention

Common Core State Standards

Informational Text 2. Determine the main idea of a text; recount the key details and explain how they support the main idea. **Informational Text 7.** Use information gained from illustrations (e.g., maps, photographs), and the words in a text to demonstrate understanding of the text (e.g., where, when, why, and how key events occur). **Foundational Skills 4.** Read with sufficient accuracy and fluency to support comprehension. **Writing 5.** With guidance and support from peers and adults, develop and strengthen writing as needed by planning, revising, and editing. **Language 1.h.** Use coordinating and subordinating conjunctions. **Language 1.i.** Produce simple, compound, and complex sentences. **Also Language 4.**

1 Build Word Knowledge

Review Amazing Words

creative	expressive	emotion	artistic	exquisite
lecture	significant	pause	view	lyrics

Team Talk **LANGUAGE DEVELOPMENT** Have partners practice building more complex sentences. Display a sentence starter and have students add oral phrases or clauses using the Amazing Words. For example: The _______ lyrics _______. (The *creative* songwriter wrote *lyrics* / that were *expressive* / and filled with *emotion*.) Guide students to add at least two phrases or clauses per sentence.

Corrective feedback | **If...** students have difficulty using the Amazing Words orally, **then...** review the meaning of each of the words.

2 Read

"The History of Palindromes"

BEFORE READING Read aloud the genre information about palindromes on p. 456. Which of the following words is a palindrome—*live, solos,* or *wallow?* *(solos)*

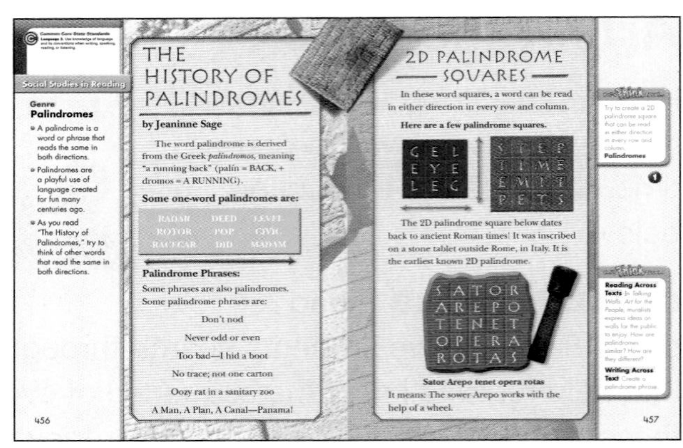
Social Studies in Reading

Genre
Palindromes
- A palindrome is a word or phrase that reads the same in both directions.
- Palindromes are a playful use of language created for fun many centuries ago.
- As you read "The History of Palindromes," try to think of other words that read the same in both directions.

THE HISTORY OF PALINDROMES

by Jeaninne Sage

The word palindrome is derived from the Greek *palindromos,* meaning "a running back" (palín = BACK, + dromos = A RUNNING).

Some one-word palindromes are:

RADAR DEED LEVEL
ROTOR POP CIVIC
RACECAR DID MADAM

Palindrome Phrases:

Some phrases are also palindromes. Some palindrome phrases are:

Don't nod

Never odd or even

Too bad—I hid a boot

No trace; not one carton

Oozy rat in a sanitary zoo

A Man, A Plan, A Canal—Panama!

456

2D PALINDROME SQUARES

In these word squares, a word can be read in either direction in every row and column.

Here are a few palindrome squares.

GEL
EYE
LEG

STEP
TIME
EMIT
PETS

The 2D palindrome square below dates back to ancient Roman times! It was inscribed on a stone tablet outside Rome, in Italy. It is the earliest known 2D palindrome.

SATOR
AREPO
TENET
OPERA
ROTAS

Sator Arepo tenet opera rotas

It means: The sower Arepo works with the help of a wheel.

Try to create a 2D palindrome square that can be read in either direction in every row and column. **Palindromes**

Reading Across Texts In Talking Walls: Art for the People, muralists express ideas on walls for the public to enjoy. How are palindromes similar? How are they different?

Writing Across Text Create a palindrome phrase.

457

DURING READING Have students locate and read the boldfaced headings.

- What are some examples of one-word palindromes on the first page? *(radar, deed, level)*
- What are some examples of palindrome phrases on the first page? (Don't nod; Never odd or even)
- What three words appear in the palindrome square at the top left of the second page? *(gel, leg, eye)*

AFTER READING Guide students through the Reading Across Texts and Writing Across Texts activities, prompting if necessary.

If... students need more scaffolding and practice with **Amazing Words, then...** use the Routine on pp. xxxvi–xxxvii in the *ELL Handbook.*

1 Build Word Knowledge

Review Combining Sentences

IDENTIFY Choral read the bottom of p. 455 with students to review sentence combining. Have partners reread the model description and identify how the author combined sentences. Allow time for students to discuss their examples and correct any misunderstandings.

2 Text-Based Comprehension

Read

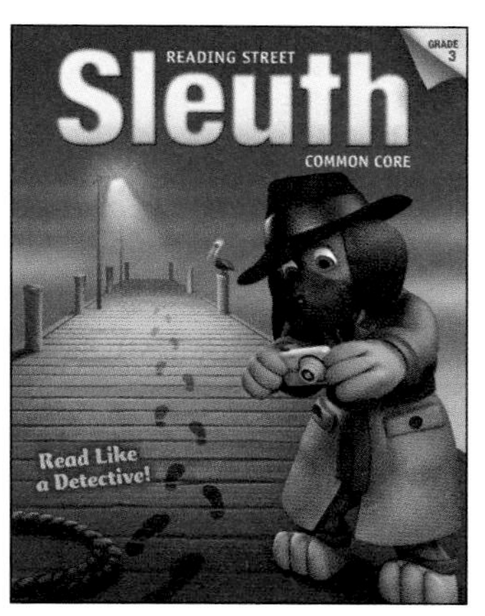

REREAD "A Performance in a Flash" Have partners reread "A Performance in a Flash," with partners alternating paragraphs.

EXTEND UNDERSTANDING Talk together about social experiments and what they tell us about our society. Invite students to share how they would feel if they were witness to a flash mob or part of a flash mob performance.

PERFORMANCE TASK • Prove It! Have students work in groups. Ask groups to plan a surprise performance at school. Have them write a plan that includes what they will do, where they will perform, and how they will let others know about their plan. Encourage students to revisit their plan, making sure *What?, Where?,* and *When?* are answered.

COMMUNICATE Have groups share their plan with others. Encourage students to discuss how they came to an agreement on what they will do and where they will perform.

SMALL GROUP TIME

More Reading for Group Time

CONCEPT LITERACY

Practice
Concept Words

BELOW-LEVEL

Review
- Graphic Sources
- Important Ideas
- Selection Vocabulary

Use these suggested Leveled Readers or other text at students' instructional level.

eStreet Interactive
www.ReadingStreet.com

Use the Leveled Reader Database for lesson plans and student pages for *Many Voices* and *One Forest, Different Trees.*

Advanced

Common Core State Standards

Informational Text 2. Determine the main idea of a text; recount the key details and explain how they support the main idea. **Informational Text 7.** Use information gained from illustrations (e.g., maps, photographs), and the words in a text to demonstrate understanding of the text (e.g., where, when, why, and how key events occur). **Foundational Skills 4.** Read with sufficient accuracy and fluency to support comprehension. **Also Writing 2.b., 7., Language 4.**

1 Build Word Knowledge

Extend Amazing Words

Team Talk Have partners define *creative.* Discuss synonyms for *creative.* Continue with *artistic* and *expressive.* Have students write sentences using each word.

2 Text-Based Comprehension

Read

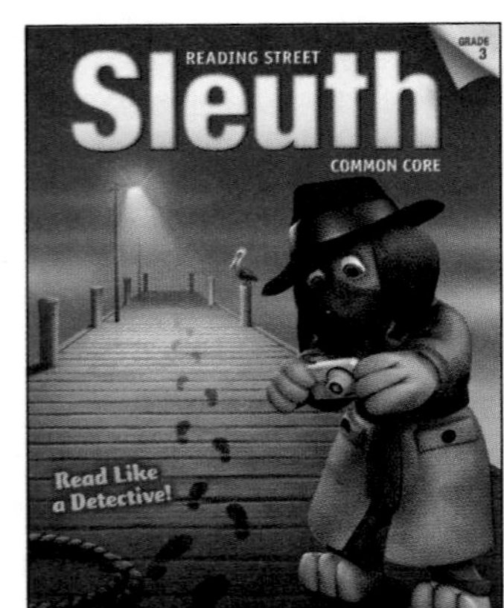

READ "A Performance in a Flash" Have students read "A Performance in a Flash" from Reading Street Sleuth on pp. 72–73.

ACCESS TEXT Discuss the Sleuth Work section with students before they work on it. Remind students that they can use these steps with other texts they read.

Gather Evidence Have students take notes of text evidence. Invite students to share the evidence they found in the article.

Ask Questions Have students share their most interesting question with the group. Talk together about how answers to their questions might help them organize their own flash mob.

Make Your Case Have students share their paragraphs with the group, pointing out how examples help support their arguments.

3 Inquiry: Extend Concepts

IDENTIFY QUESTIONS Have students think about questions they have about different kinds of art forms, such as paintings, sculptures, or drawings. Have students use these questions to find a work of art that interests them and to research the work or its artist. Students should prepare a poster or digital slide show about the artwork or artist. Throughout the week, they will gather information. On Day 5, they will present what they have learned.

If... students need more scaffolding and practice with **Vocabulary,** **then...** use the activities on pp. DI•67–DI•68 in the Teacher Resources section on SuccessNet.

Advanced

1 Build Word Knowledge

Extend Selection Vocabulary

Team Talk Have partners use the selection vocabulary in sentences to internalize their meanings. Have students use as many of the words as they can while making sure the sentence is grammatically correct. (Possible response: This mural is an *expression* of the *local* community's *social* values.) Continue with additional selection vocabulary.

encourages	expression	local	native
settled	social	support	

2 Read

Talking Walls: Art for the People

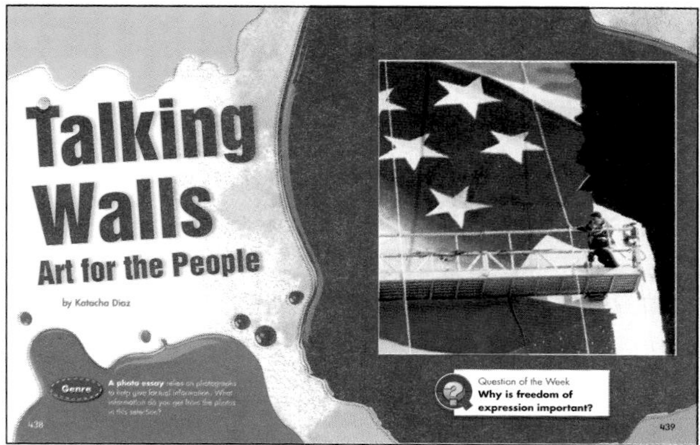

If you read *Talking Walls: Art for the People* during whole group time, then use the instruction below.

ACCESS TEXT Reread the paragraphs on p. 440. Discuss how America is different from some homelands of writers, musicians, dancers, and artists who come here. (In other places, people are not always free to express themselves through art. This country offers the chance for a better life and freedom.) Ask: What point is the author making about America? (The author seems to be saying that America is a place where creative and artistic people can express themselves in any form.)

If you are reading *Talking Walls: Art for the People* during small group time, then return to pp. 440–445a to guide the reading.

3 Inquiry: Extend Concepts

INVESTIGATE Encourage students to use materials at their independent reading levels or student-friendly search engines to identify relevant and credible sites to gather information about an artwork or artist that interests them. Have students consider how they will present their information.

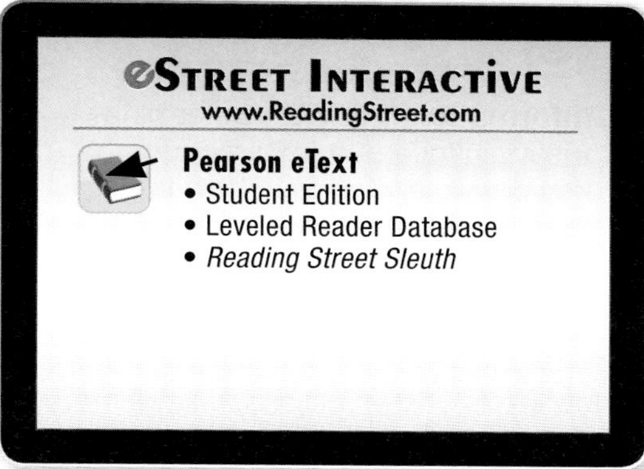

SMALL GROUP TIME

More Reading for Group Time

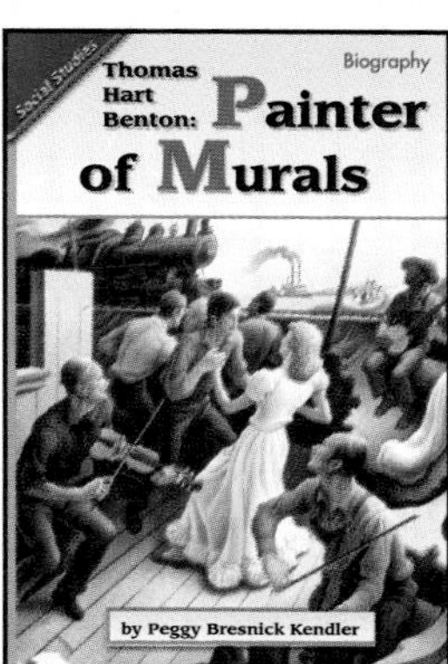

ADVANCED

Review
- Graphic Sources
- Important Ideas

Use this suggested Leveled Reader or other text at students' instructional level.

eStreet Interactive
www.ReadingStreet.com

Use the Leveled Reader Database for lesson plans and student pages for *Thomas Hart Benton: Painter of Murals.*

Advanced

Common Core State Standards

Informational Text 2. Determine the main idea of a text; recount the key details and explain how they support the main idea. **Informational Text 7.** Use information gained from illustrations (e.g., maps, photographs), and the words in a text to demonstrate understanding of the text (e.g., where, when, why, and how key events occur). **Writing 7.** Conduct short research projects that build knowledge about a topic. **Language 4.** Determine or clarify the meaning of unknown and multiple-meaning words and phrases based on grade 3 reading and content, choosing flexibly from a range of strategies.

1 Build Word Knowledge

Develop Vocabulary

REREAD FOR VOCABULARY Reread the second paragraph on p. 450. Let's read this paragraph to find out what *residents* means. Discuss meaning and context with students.

2 Read

Talking Walls: Art for the People

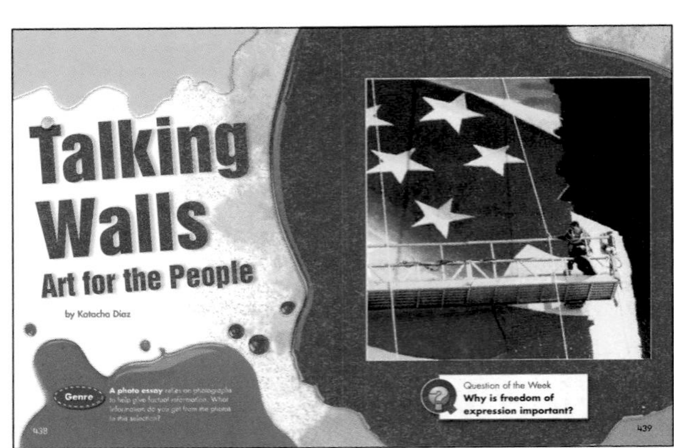

If you read *Talking Walls: Art for the People* during whole group time, then use the instruction below.

CLOSE READING Read pp. 448–449. Have students create a T-chart with the heads **Action Words** and **Time-Order Words.** Have students search through the text to find action words and to write them in the chart in the order they occur. Then find phrases that show time order or structure.

Action Words	Time-Order Words
loved, dreamed, painted, go, create, paint, repainted, completed, changed, wanted, dream, inspire, work, follow	When he was in the third grade, Years later, seventeen years after, over time

Ask: What do most of the action words tell you about David? (He feels strongly about his art. He is a busy, creative, and hopeful person.) What do the time-order words tell you about David's life? (He has been interested in art and painting for a long time—almost his entire life.)

If you are reading *Talking Walls: Art for the People* during small group time, then return to pp. 446–451a to guide the reading.

3 Inquiry: Extend Concepts

INVESTIGATE Provide time for students to investigate their topics in books or online. If necessary, help them locate information that is focused on their topics.

Independent Reading Options

Trade Book Library

eSTREET INTERACTIVE
www.ReadingStreet.com

Teacher Guides are available on the Leveled Reader Database.

ELL

If... students need more scaffolding and practice with the **Main Selection, then...** use the activities on p. DI•72 in the Teacher Resources section on SuccessNet.

Advanced

1 Build Word Knowledge

Extend Amazing Words and Selection Vocabulary

creative	expressive	emotion	lyrics
artistic	exquisite	lecture	
significant	pause	view	

encourages	expression	local
native	settled	social
support		

Team Talk Have partners practice building more complex sentences. Display a sentence starter and have students add oral phrases or clauses using the Amazing Words and the selection vocabulary.

2 Read

"The History of Palindromes"

BEFORE READING Review the panel information about palindromes on p. 456. Have students use the text features to set a purpose and then read "The History of Palindromes" on their own.

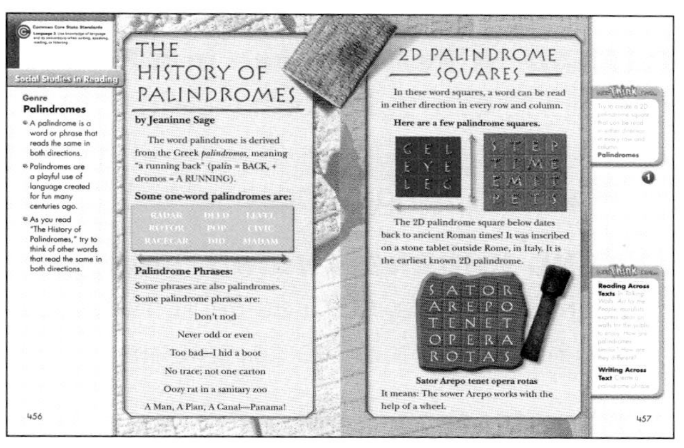

Social Studies in Reading

Genre
Palindromes

- A palindrome is a word or phrase that reads the same in both directions.
- Palindromes are a playful use of language created for fun many centuries ago.
- As you read "The History of Palindromes," try to think of other words that read the same in both directions.

THE HISTORY OF PALINDROMES

by Jeaninne Sage

The word palindrome is derived from the Greek *palíndromos,* meaning "a running back" (palín = BACK, + dromos = A RUNNING).

Some one-word palindromes are:

RADAR DEED LEVEL
ROTOR POP CIVIC
RACECAR DID MADAM

Palindrome Phrases:

Some phrases are also palindromes. Some palindrome phrases are:

Don't nod

Never odd or even

Too bad—I hid a boot

No trace; not one carton

Oozy rat in a sanitary zoo

A Man, A Plan, A Canal—Panama!

456

2D PALINDROME SQUARES

In these word squares, a word can be read in either direction in every row and column.

Here are a few palindrome squares.

GEL
EYE
LEG

STEP
TIME
EMIT
PETS

The 2D palindrome square below dates back to ancient Roman times! It was inscribed on a stone tablet outside Rome, in Italy. It is the earliest known 2D palindrome.

SATOR
AREPO
TENET
OPERA
ROTAS

Sator Arepo tenet opera rotas

It means: The sower Arepo works with the help of a wheel.

Palindromes

Reading Across Texts

Writing Across Text

457

DURING READING Encourage students to think creatively. For example, ask: Which of the palindrome phrases might serve as a headline for a newspaper story about a health problem? ("Oozy rat in a sanitary zoo") A warehouse robbery? ("No trace; not one carton")

AFTER READING Have students discuss Reading Across Texts. Then have them do Writing Across Texts independently. Why do you think palindromes were popular in ancient Rome and today? (They are fun, they make people think, and they sometimes make people laugh.) Have students create and share their own palindromes.

3 Inquiry: Extend Concepts

ORGANIZE INFORMATION Provide time for students to organize their information into a format that will effectively communicate their findings to their audience. Provide any necessary materials or computer time.

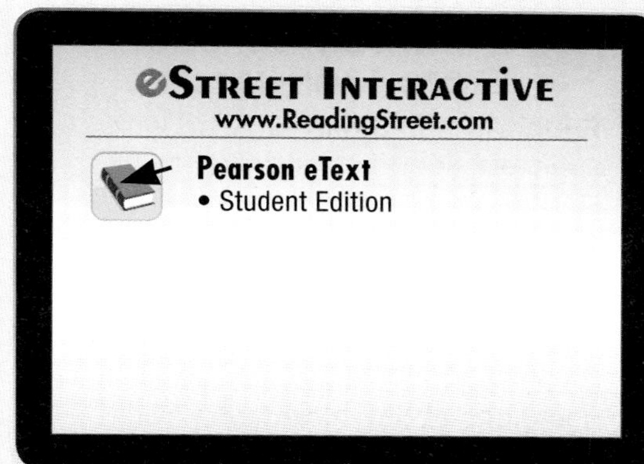

SMALL GROUP TIME

Independent Reading Options

Trade Book Library

eSTREET INTERACTIVE
www.ReadingStreet.com

Teacher Guides are available on the Leveled Reader Database.

Common Core State Standards

Foundational Skills 4. Read with sufficient accuracy and fluency to support comprehension. **Writing 5.** With guidance and support from peers and adults, develop and strengthen writing as needed by planning, revising, and editing. **Speaking/ Listening 3.** Ask and answer questions about information from a speaker, offering appropriate elaboration and detail. **Language 1.h.** Use coordinating and subordinating conjunctions. **Language 1.i.** Produce simple, compound, and complex sentences. **Also Writing 2.1., Speaking/Listening 4.**

More Reading for Group Time

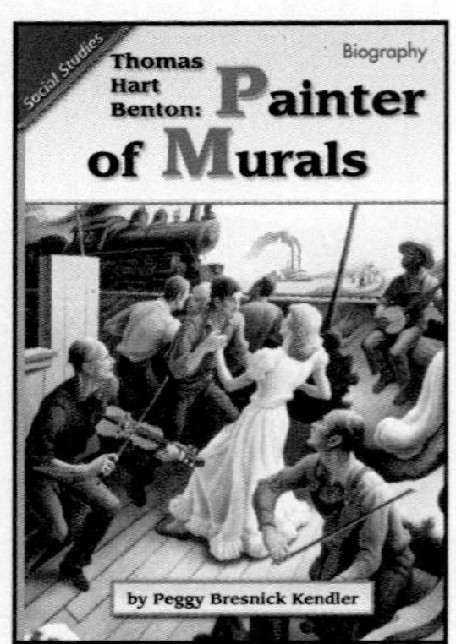

ADVANCED

Reviews
- Graphic Sources
- Important Ideas

Use this suggested Leveled Reader or other text at students' instructional level.

eStreet Interactive
www.ReadingStreet.com

Use the Leveled Reader Database for lesson plans and student pages for *Thomas Hart Benton: Painter of Murals.*

1 Build Word Knowledge

Extend Combining Sentences

IDENTIFY AND EXTEND Choral read the bottom of p. 455 with students and have them explain sentence combining, in which short sentences are combined into longer ones. Have partners reread the model description and identify how the author combined sentences. Allow time for students to discuss their examples and correct any misunderstandings.

2 Text-Based Comprehension

Read

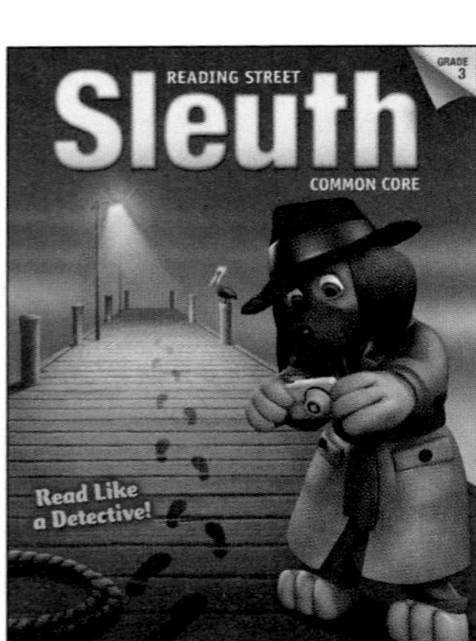

REREAD "A Performance in a Flash" Have partners reread "A Performance in a Flash." Have partners discuss the importance of media coverage for flash mob performances.

EXTEND UNDERSTANDING Talk together about how group efforts, such as flash mobs, can be put to use to help others in the community.

PERFORMANCE TASK • Prove It! Have students work in groups. Ask groups to plan a surprise performance at school. Have them write a plan that includes what they will do, where they will perform, and how they will let others know about their plan. If time permits, have students practice their surprise performance and share it with the class.

COMMUNICATE Have students share their plans with others. Invite discussion about the importance of letting others know the plan.

3 Inquiry: Extend Concepts

COMMUNICATE Have students share their inquiry projects on an artwork or artist with the rest of the class. Provide the following tips for presenting.

- Speak loudly and clearly and at an appropriate rate.
- Ask questions to make sure your audience understands the information.
- Define names correctly and explain any unfamiliar terms.

Focus on Common Core State Standards

Main Selection, pp. 468–485

Paired Selection, pp. 490–491

Text-Based Comprehension

Literary Elements: Plot and Theme
CCSS Literature 1., CCSS Literature 2

Story Structure
CCSS Literature 3.

Fluency

Rate
CCSS Foundational Skills 4.b.

Writing and Conventions

Trait: Conventions
CCSS Language 2.

Writing Mini-Lesson: Comic Book
CCSS Writing 3.a.

Conventions: Commas
CCSS Language 2.b.

Oral Vocabulary

Amazing Words

obey
responsibility
consequence
permission
citizen
fascinate
guilt
encounter
forbid
eerie

CCSS Language 6.

Selection Vocabulary

Prefixes and Suffixes *un-, dis-, -ful*
CCSS Foundational Skills 3.a.

Word Structure
CCSS Language 3.a.

crystal
disappeared
discovery
goal
journey
joyful
scoop
unaware

Phonics and Spelling

Prefixes, Suffixes, and Endings
CCSS Foundational Skills 3.a., CCSS Language 2.f.

leadership
impossibly
gracefully
refreshment
uncomfortable
overdoing
remarkable
carefully
unbearably
ownership
unacceptable
reappeared
unprepared
oncoming
misbehaving

Challenge Words

outrageous
incomprehensible
undoubtedly
independence
disadvantage

Listening and Speaking

Description
CCSS Speaking/Listening 4.

Preview Your Week

Why are rules and laws important to freedom?

Main Selection, pp. 468–485

Genre: Animal Fantasy

Vocabulary: Prefixes and Suffixes *un-, dis-, -ful*

Text-Based Comprehension: Literary Elements: Plot and Theme

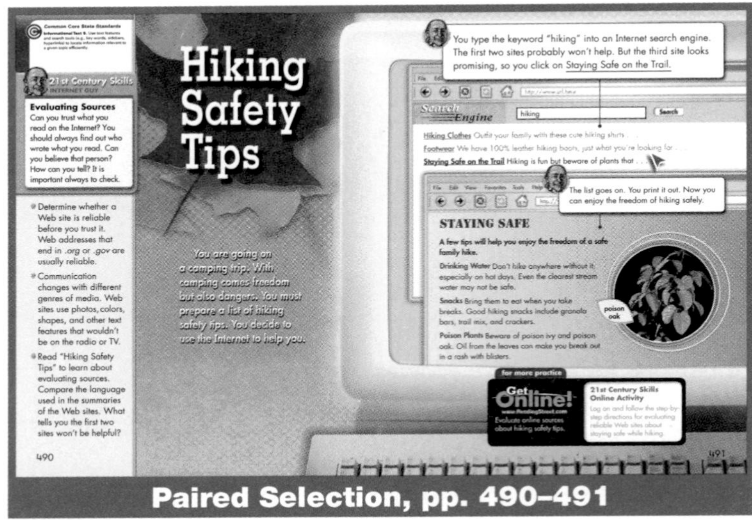

Paired Selection, pp. 490–491

21st Century Skills

Genre: Online Sources

Build Content Knowledge

KNOWLEDGE GOALS
Students will understand that rules and laws

- keep order
- keep us safe
- remind us to do the right thing

THIS WEEK'S CONCEPT MAP
Develop a concept-related graphic organizer like the one below over the course of this week.

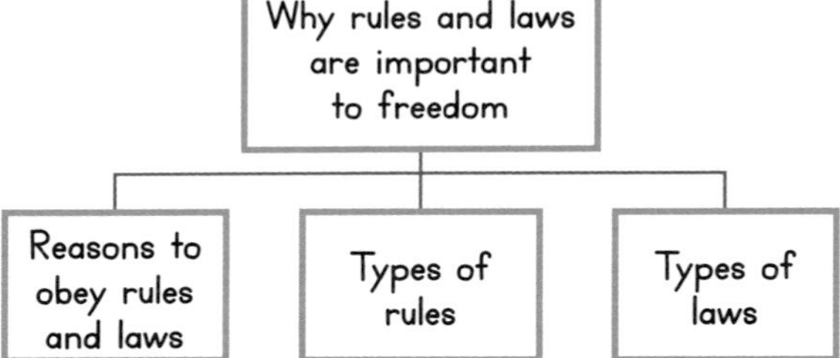

BUILD ORAL VOCABULARY
This week, students will acquire the following academic vocabulary/domain-specific words.

Amazing Words

obey	citizen	encounter
responsibility	fascinate	forbid
consequence	guilt	eerie
permission		

OPTIONAL CONCEPT-BASED READING Use the Digital Path to access readers offering different levels of text complexity.

Concept Literacy

Below-Level

On-Level

Advanced

ELL

ELD

This Week's Digital Resources

eStreet Interactive
www.ReadingStreet.com

Get Ready to Read

Concept Talk Video Use this video on the Digital Path to engage interest and introduce the weekly concept of freedom.

Pearson eText Read the eText of the Student Edition pages on Pearson SuccessNet for comprehension and fluency support.

Envision It! Animations Use this stimulating animation on the Digital Path to explain the target comprehension skill, Literary Elements: Plot and Theme.

Read and Comprehend

Journal Use the Word Bank on the Digital Path to have students write sentences using this week's selection vocabulary words.

Background Building Audio CD This audio CD provides important background information about freedom to help students read and comprehend the weekly texts.

Pearson eText Read the eText of the main selection, *Two Bad Ants,* and the paired selection, "Hiking Safety Tips," with audio support on Pearson SuccessNet.

Vocabulary Activities A variety of interactive vocabulary activities on the Digital Path help students practice selection vocabulary and concept-related words.

Story Sort Use the Story Sort Activity on the Digital Path after reading *Two Bad Ants* to involve students in summarizing.

Language Arts

Grammar Jammer Opt for a whimsical animation on the Digital Path to provide an engaging grammar lesson that will grab students' attention.

Pearson eText Find the Student Edition eText of the Let's Write It! and Let's Learn It! pages with audio support on Pearson SuccessNet.

Additional Resources

Teacher Resources DVD-ROM Use the following resources on the TR DVD or on Pearson SuccessNet throughout the week:

- Amazing Word Cards
- Reader's and Writer's Notebook
- Writing Transparencies
- Daily Fix-It Transparencies
- Scoring Rubrics
- Grammar Transparencies
- ELL Support
- Let's Practice It!
- Graphic Organizers
- Vocabulary Cards

This Week's Skills

Phonics/Word Analysis
- Prefixes *im-, in-*

Comprehension
- **Skill:** Literary Elements: Plot and Theme
- **Strategy:** Story Structure

Language
- **Vocabulary:** Prefixes and Suffixes *un-, dis-, -ful*

Conventions: Commas

Fluency
Rate

Writing
Comic Book

5-Day Planner

DAY 1

Get Ready to Read

Content Knowledge 460j
Oral Vocabulary: *obey, responsibility, consequence, permission*

Monitor Progress
Check Oral Vocabulary

Phonics/Word Analysis 462a
- Prefixes *im-, in-*

READ Decodable Reader 29A
Reread for Fluency

Read and Comprehend

Text-Based Comprehension 464a
- Literary Elements: Plot and Theme
- Story Structure

Fluency 464-465
Rate

Selection Vocabulary 465a
crystal, disappeared, discovery, goal, journey, joyful, scoop, unaware,

Language Arts

Research and Inquiry 465b
Identify and Focus Topic

Spelling 465c
Prefixes, Suffixes, and Endings, Pretest

Conventions 465d
Commas

Handwriting 465d
Cursive Letters *D, Q,* and *Z*

Writing 465e
Comic Book

DAY 2

Get Ready to Read

Content Knowledge 466a
Oral Vocabulary: *citizen, fascinate*

Phonics/Word Analysis 466c
- Prefixes *im-, in-*

Monitor Progress
Check Word Reading

Literary Terms 466d
Imagery

Read and Comprehend

Vocabulary Skill 466e
- Prefixes and Suffixes *un-, dis-, -ful*

Fluency 466–467
Rate

Text-Based Comprehension 468–469
READ *Two Bad Ants*—1st Read

Language Arts

Research and Inquiry 477b
Navigate/Search

Conventions 477c
Commas

Spelling 477c
Prefixes, Suffixes, and Endings

Writing 477d
Comic Book

DAY 3

Get Ready to Read

Content Knowledge 478a
Oral Vocabulary: *guilt, encounter*

Word Analysis 478c
Fluent Word Reading
DECODE AND READ
Decodable Practice Passage 29B

Read and Comprehend

Text-Based Comprehension 478e
Literary Elements: Plot and Theme
Story Structure
READ *Two Bad Ants*—2nd Read
Monitor Progress Check Retelling

Fluency 478b
Rate

Language Arts

Research and Study Skills 487c
Electronic Text

Research and Inquiry 487d
Analyze Information

Conventions 487e
Commas

Spelling 487e
Prefixes, Suffixes, and Endings

Writing 488–489
Comic Book

DAY 4

Get Ready to Read

Content Knowledge 490a
Oral Vocabulary: *forbid, eerie*

Phonics/Word Analysis 490c
Review Final Syllables
Fluent Word Reading
DECODE AND READ
Decodable Practice Passage 29C

Read and Comprehend

21st Century Skills 490g
Evaluating Online Sources
READ "Hiking Safety Tips"—Paired Selection

Fluency 492–493
Rate
Monitor Progress Check Fluency

Vocabulary Skill 493a
Prefixes and Suffixes *un-, dis-, -ful*

Listening and Speaking 493a
Description

Language Arts

Research and Inquiry 493b
Synthesize

Conventions 493c
Commas

Spelling 493c
Prefixes, Suffixes, and Endings

Writing 493d
Comic Book

DAY 5

Get Ready to Read

Content Knowledge 493f
Review Oral Vocabulary
Monitor Progress
Check Oral Vocabulary

Read and Comprehend

Text-Based Comprehension 493h
Review Literary Elements: Plot and Theme

Vocabulary Skill 493h
Review Prefixes and Suffixes *un-, dis-, -ful*

Phonics/Word Analysis 493i
Review Prefixes *im-, in-*

Literary Terms 493i
Review Imagery

Assessment 493j, 493l
Monitor Progress Fluency; Literary Elements: Plot and Theme

Language Arts

Research and Inquiry 493n
Communicate

Spelling 493o
Prefixes, Suffixes, and Endings, Test

Conventions 493o
Commas

Writing 493p
Comic Book

Wrap Up Your Week! 493q

Access for All

What do I do in group time?
It's as easy as 1-2-3!

1 TEACHER-LED SMALL GROUPS → 2 INDEPENDENT PRACTICE STATIONS → 3 INDEPENDENT READING

Small Group Time

SKILL DEVELOPMENT
- Prefixes *im-, in-*
- Literary Elements: Plot and Theme
- Story Structure
- Prefixes and Suffixes *un-, dis-, -ful*

DEEP UNDERSTANDING

This Week's Knowledge Goals

Students will understand that rules and laws
- keep order
- keep us safe
- remind us to do the right thing

1 Small Group Lesson Plan

	DAY 1 Differentiate Vocabulary	DAY 2 Differentiate Comprehension
OL On-Level pp. SG•50–SG•54	**Build Word Knowledge** Practice Amazing Words **Text-Based Comprehension** Read *Reading Street Sleuth,* pp. 74–75 or Leveled Readers	**Build Word Knowledge** Practice Selection Vocabulary **Access Text** Read *Two Bad Ants*
SI Strategic Intervention pp. SG•55–SG•59	**Build Word Knowledge** Reteach Amazing Words **Text-Based Comprehension** Read *Reading Street Sleuth,* pp. 74–75 or Leveled Readers	**Build Word Knowledge** Reteach Selection Vocabulary **Access Text** Read *Two Bad Ants*
A Advanced pp. SG•60–SG•64	**Build Word Knowledge** Extend Amazing Words **Text-Based Comprehension** Read *Reading Street Sleuth,* pp. 74–75 or Leveled Readers	**Build Word Knowledge** Extend Selection Vocabulary **Access Text** Read *Two Bad Ants*
Independent Inquiry Project	Identify Questions	Investigate
ELL **If...** students need more scaffolding and practice with...	**Vocabulary,** **then...** use the activities on pp. DI•92–DI•93 in the Teacher Resources section on SuccessNet.	**Comprehension Skill,** **then...** use the activities on p. DI•96 in the Teacher Resources section on SuccessNet.

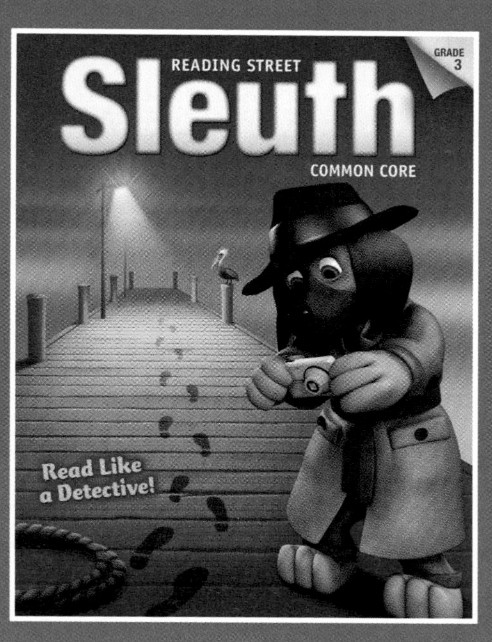

Reading Street Sleuth
- Provides access to grade-level text for all students
- Focuses on finding clues in text through close reading
- Builds capacity for complex text

Build Text-Based Comprehension

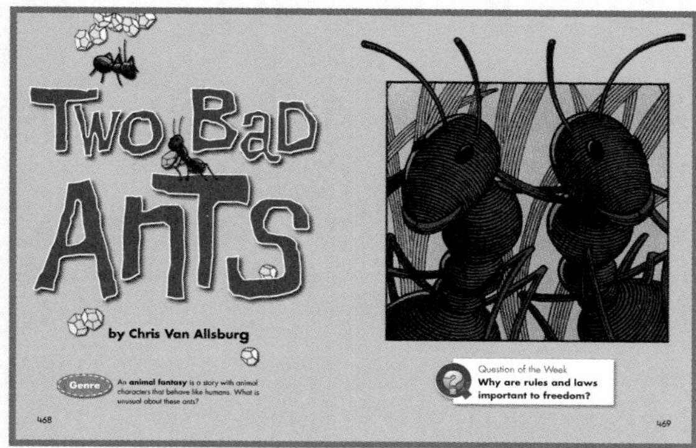

Two Bad Ants

Optional Leveled Readers

Concept Literacy

Below-Level

On-Level

Advanced

ELL

ELD

DAY 3 Differentiate Close Reading	DAY 4 Differentiate Vocabulary	DAY 5 Differentiate Reteaching
Reread to Develop Vocabulary **Close Reading** Read *Two Bad Ants*	**Build Word Knowledge** Develop Language Using Amazing Words **Text-Based Comprehension** Read "Hiking Safety Tips"	**Practice Commas** **Text-Based Comprehension** Reread *Reading Street Sleuth,* pp. 74–75 or Leveled Readers
Reread to Develop Vocabulary **Close Reading** Read *Two Bad Ants*	**Build Word Knowledge** Review/Discuss Amazing Words **Text-Based Comprehension** Read "Hiking Safety Tips"	**Review Commas** **Text-Based Comprehension** Reread *Reading Street Sleuth,* pp. 74–75 or Leveled Readers
Reread to Extend Vocabulary **Close Reading** Read *Two Bad Ants* **Investigate**	**Build Word Knowledge** Extend Amazing Words and Selection Vocabulary **Text-Based Comprehension** Read "Hiking Safety Tips" **Organize**	**Extend Commas** **Text-Based Comprehension** Reread *Reading Street Sleuth,* pp. 74–75 or Leveled Readers **Communicate**
Main Selection, **then...** use the activities on p. DI•97 in the Teacher Resources section on SuccessNet.	**Amazing Words,** **then...** use the Routine on pp. xxxvi–xxxvii in the *ELL Handbook.*	**Conventions and Writing,** **then...** use the activities on pp. DI•99–DI•100 in the Teacher Resources section on SuccessNet.

Independent Stations

Practice Last Week's Skills

Focus on these activities when time is limited.

ACCESS FOR ALL

- ● Below-Level Activities
- ▲ On-Level Activities
- ■ Advanced Activities

WORD WISE

Spell and use words in sentences.

OBJECTIVES

- Spell words with the final syllables *-tion, -ion, -ture, -ive, -ize.*

MATERIALS

- *Word Wise* Flip Chart Activity 29, teacher-made word cards, paper, pencils

Letter Tile Drag and Drop

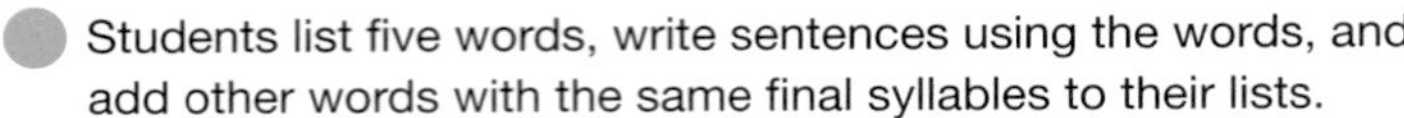

● Students list five words, write sentences using the words, and add other words with the same final syllables to their lists.

▲ Students write eight words, write sentences using the words, and identify other words with the same final syllables.

■ Students write ten words, write sentences using the words, and identify other words with the same final syllables.

WORD WORK

Identify and pronounce words.

OBJECTIVES

- Identify and pronounce words with the final syllables *-tion, -ion, -ture, -ive, -ize.*

MATERIALS

- *Word Work* Flip Chart Activity 29, teacher-made word cards, paper, pencils

Letter Tile Drag and Drop

● Students say and write eight words and then circle the final syllable in each word.

▲ Students write ten words, sort them in a five-column chart according to final syllables, and then say the words aloud.

■ Students make a five-column chart and then say and sort twelve words according to their final syllables.

LET'S WRITE!

Write a description.

OBJECTIVES

- Write a description about a place you have visited.

MATERIALS

- *Let's Write!* Flip Chart Activity 29, paper, pencils

Grammar Jammer

● Students write three sentences describing a place they have visited, using sensory words. They proofread their work.

▲ Students write a paragraph describing a place they have visited, using sensory words. They proofread their work.

■ Students write a description of a place they have visited, using sensory words. They proofread their work.

WORDS TO KNOW

Determine word meanings.

OBJECTIVES

- Identify the meanings of unknown words.

MATERIALS

- *Words to Know* Flip Chart Activity 29, dictionary, magazines, paper, pencils

Vocabulary Activities

● Students list three words found in a magazine, define them, and write a sentence using each word.

▲ Students list and define four words found in a magazine, identify the words' parts of speech, and then write a sentence for each word.

■ Students list five words from a magazine, use context and a dictionary to identify their meanings, and then write sentences using the words.

READ FOR MEANING

Use text-based comprehension skills.

OBJECTIVES

- Identify information presented in graphic sources.

MATERIALS

- *Read for Meaning* Flip Chart Activity 29, Leveled Readers, paper, pencils

 **Pearson eText**
- Leveled eReaders

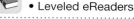

 **Envision It! Animations**

● Students choose one graphic source in a book and write a sentence telling what kind of graphic it is and what kind of information it explains.

▲ Students write one sentence about the graphic sources in a book. Then they write a sentence about one of the graphic sources.

■ Students write a sentence about the graphic sources in a book. Then they write a short paragraph about the types of information these sources explain.

GET FLUENT

Practice fluent reading with a partner.

OBJECTIVES

- Read aloud with accuracy.

MATERIALS

- *Get Fluent* Flip Chart Activity 29, Leveled Readers

 **Pearson eText**
- Leveled eReaders

● Students take turns reading aloud with accuracy from a Concept Reader or a Below-Level Reader and providing feedback.

▲ Students take turns reading aloud with accuracy from an On-Level Reader and providing feedback.

■ Students take turns reading aloud with accuracy from an Advanced Reader and providing feedback.

Manage the Stations

Use these management tools to set up and organize your Practice Stations:

Practice Station Flip Charts

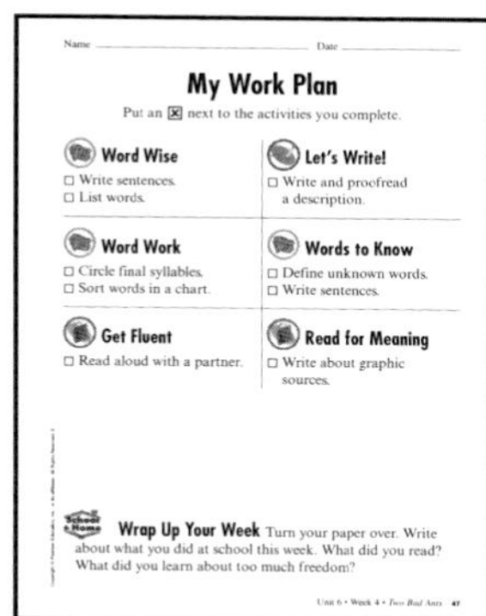

Name ______ Date ______

My Work Plan

Put an ☒ next to the activities you complete.

Word Wise
- ☐ Write sentences.
- ☐ List words.

Let's Write!
- ☐ Write and proofread a description.

Word Work
- ☐ Circle final syllables.
- ☐ Sort words in a chart.

Words to Know
- ☐ Define unknown words.
- ☐ Write sentences.

Get Fluent
- ☐ Read aloud with a partner.

Read for Meaning
- ☐ Write about graphic sources.

Wrap Up Your Week Turn your paper over. Write about what you did at school this week. What did you read? What did you learn about too much freedom?

Unit 6 • Week 4 • *Two Bad Ants* 47

Classroom Management Handbook for Differentiated Instruction Practice Stations, p. 47

3 Independent Reading

Students should select appropriate complex texts to read and write about independently every day before, during, and after school.

Suggestions for this week's independent reading:
- Informational text on last week's social studies topic: Why expressions of freedom are important
- Nonfiction selections about the importance of freedom of expression
- A high-quality newspaper article about the importance of freedom of expression

BOOK TALK Have partners discuss their independent reading for the week. Tell them to refer to their Reading Logs and paraphrase what each selection was about. Then have students focus on discussing one or more of the following:

Key Ideas and Details
- Summarize the key supporting details and ideas.
- Identify the main idea and explain how the key details support it.

Craft and Structure
- Identify interesting word choices. How do they shape the tone?
- What is the author's point of view? How do you know?

Integration of Ideas
- Compare this book to others you have read.
- What ideas do the two readings have in common?

 **Pearson eText**
- Student Edition
- Decodable Readers
- Leveled Readers

 **Trade Book Library**

 **School or Classroom Library**

DAY 1 at a Glance

Content Knowledge
Oral Vocabulary

Phonics/Word Analysis
Prefixes *im-*, *in-*

Text-Based Comprehension
Literary Elements: Plot and Theme
Story Structure

Fluency
Rate

Selection Vocabulary

Research and Inquiry
Identify and Focus Topic

Spelling
Prefixes, Suffixes, and Endings

Conventions
Commas

Handwriting
Cursive Letters *D, Q,* and *Z*

Writing
Comic Book

Materials

- Student Edition
- Reader's and Writer's Notebook
- Decodable Reader

Bridge to Common Core

INTEGRATION OF KNOWLEDGE/IDEAS

This week, students will read, write, and talk about the importance of rules and laws to freedom.

Texts This Week

- "Hannah Hopper's Hunt for Rules and Laws"
- "The Ant and the Beetle"
- "How Ants Find Food"
- *Two Bad Ants*
- "Hiking Safety Tips"

Social Studies Knowledge Goals

Students will understand that rules and laws

- keep order
- keep us safe
- remind us to do the right thing

Street Rhymes!

Citizens have laws that we must obey—
At school or on the street, at work or when we play.
Laws protect our rights and our freedoms too.
What are laws we follow, ones that we must do?

- To introduce this week's concept, read aloud the poem several times and ask students to join you.

Content Knowledge

Rules and Laws Are Important to Freedom

CONCEPT TALK To further explore the unit concept of Freedom, this week students will read, write, and talk about how rules and laws are important to freedom. Write the Question of the Week—*Why are rules and laws important to freedom?*—on the board.

Build Oral Language

TALK ABOUT RULES AND LAWS Have students turn to pp. 460–461 in their Student Editions. Look at each of the photos. Then use the prompts to guide discussion and create a concept map.

- What does the photo on page 460 show? (a courthouse) I know that people go to court to be punished if they break certain laws. Let's add *Types of laws* to our concept map.
- How does the crossing guard help us? (He keeps children safe.) Let's add *Reasons to obey rules and laws* to our concept map.
- What classroom rule are the children following? (raising their hands) Let's add *Types of rules* to the concept map.
- After discussing the photos, ask: Why are rules and laws important to freedom?

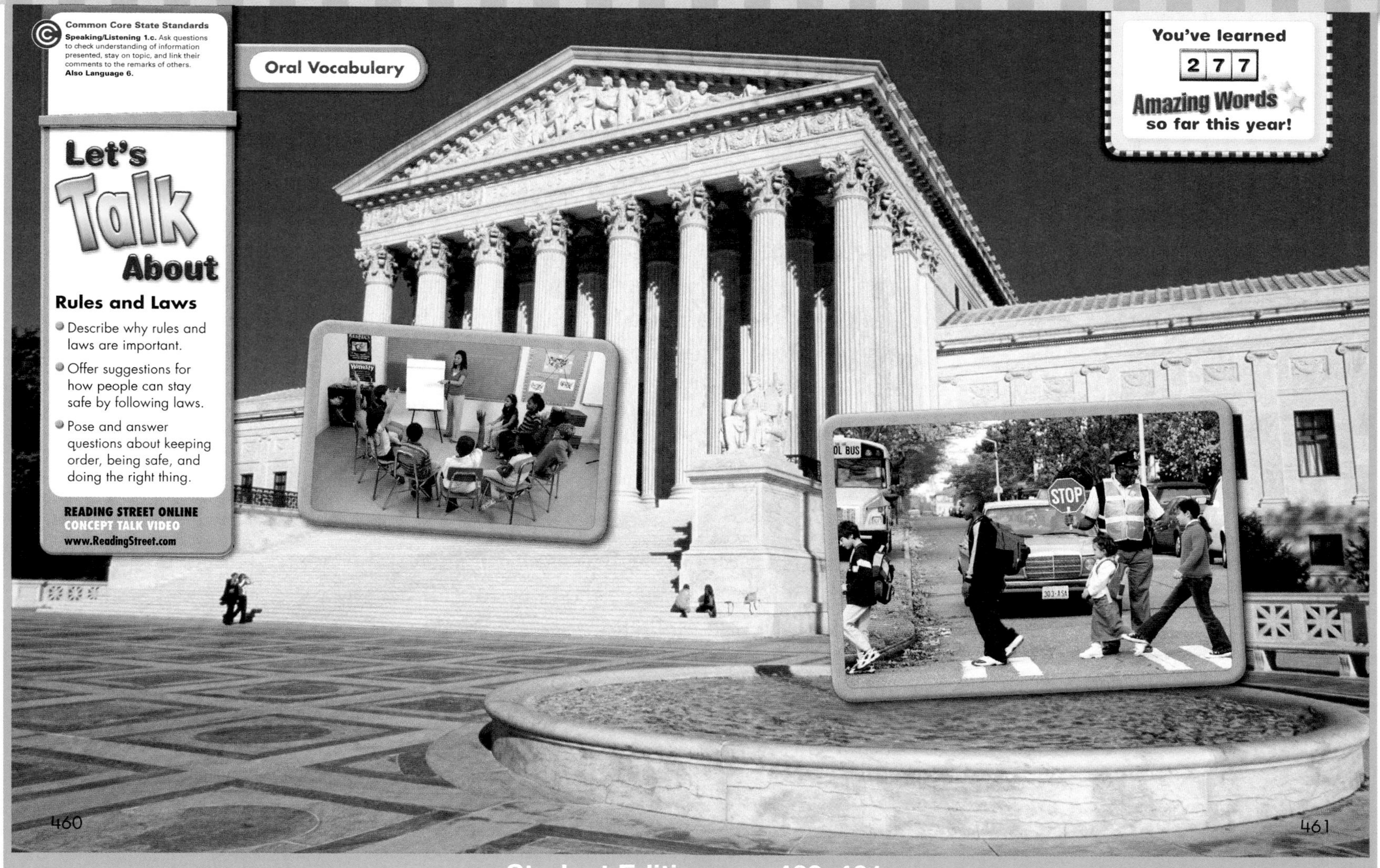

Common Core State Standards
Speaking/Listening 1.c. Ask questions to check understanding of information presented, stay on topic, and link their comments to the remarks of others.
Also Language 6.
Oral Vocabulary
Let's Talk About
Rules and Laws
Describe why rules and laws are important.
Offer suggestions for how people can stay safe by following laws.
Pose and answer questions about keeping order, being safe, and doing the right thing.
READING STREET ONLINE
CONCEPT TALK VIDEO
www.ReadingStreet.com
You've learned
2 7 7
Amazing Words
so far this year!
STOP
460
461
Student Edition, pp. 460–461

CONNECT TO READING Tell students that this week they will be reading about ways that rules and laws affect people's freedom and what can happen when rules are not followed. Throughout the week, encourage students to add concept-related words to this week's concept map.

Why rules and laws are important to freedom
Reasons to obey rules and laws
Types of rules
Types of laws

eSTREET INTERACTIVE
www.ReadingStreet.com

- **Pearson eText**
  - Student Edition
- **Concept Talk Video**

ELL

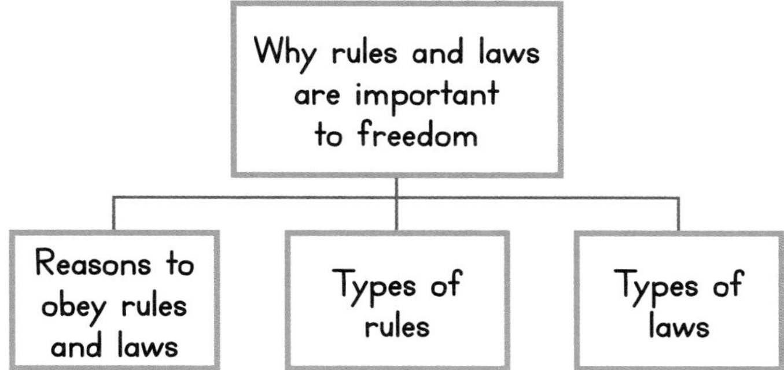

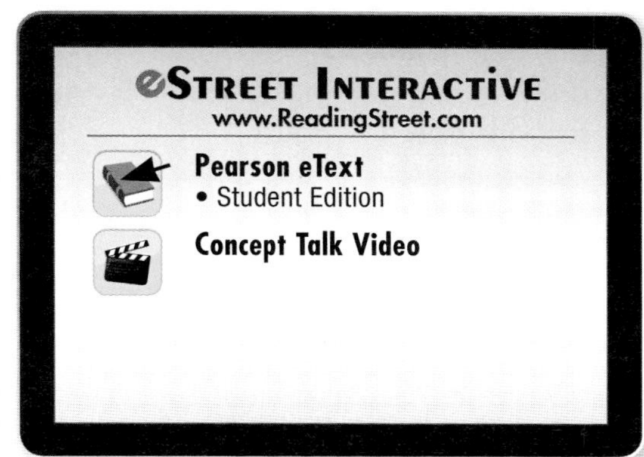

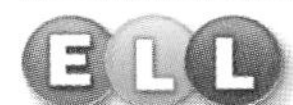

Preteach Concepts Use the Day 1 instruction on ELL Poster 29 to build knowledge, develop concepts, and build oral vocabulary.

ELL Support Additional ELL support and modified instruction are provided in the *ELL Handbook* and in the ELL Support lessons on the *Teacher Resources DVD-ROM.*

Common Core State Standards

Speaking/Listening 1. Engage effectively in a range of collaborative discussions (one-on-one, in groups, and teacher led) with diverse partners on grade 3 topics and texts, building on others' ideas and expressing their own clearly. **Speaking/Listening 2.** Determine the main ideas and supporting details of a text read aloud or information presented in diverse media and formats, including visually, quantitatively, and orally. **Language 4.** Determine or clarify the meaning of unknown and multiple-meaning words and phrases based on grade 3 reading and content, choosing flexibly from a range of strategies. **Language 6.** Acquire and use accurately grade-appropriate conversational, general academic, and domain-specific words and phrases, including those that signal spatial and temporal relationships (e.g., *After dinner that night we went looking for them*).

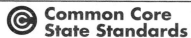

Amazing Words

You've learned 277 words so far.

You'll learn 010 words this week!

obey	fascinate
responsibility	guilt
consequence	encounter
permission	forbid
citizen	eerie

Content Knowledge

Build Oral Vocabulary

INTRODUCE AMAZING WORDS "Hannah Hopper's Hunt for Rules and Laws" on p. 461b is about a girl on a search for rules and laws that have been put in place around her community. Tell students to listen for this week's Amazing Words—*responsibility, obey, consequence,* and *permission*—as you read the Teacher Read Aloud on p. 461b.

Amazing Words — Robust Vocabulary Routine

1. **Introduce** Write the word *responsibility* on the board. Relate it to the selection. Hannah takes *responsibility* for her homework assignment. Supply a student-friendly definition: *Responsibility* means taking on a job and doing it without someone reminding you.
2. **Demonstrate** Have students answer questions to demonstrate understanding. What *responsibility* can you have at home? at school?
3. **Apply** Ask students to give a personal example of *responsibility.*
4. **Display the Word** Run your hand under the syllables *re-spon-si-bil-i-ty* as you read the word. Have students say the word again.

See p. OV•4 to teach *consequence, obey,* and *permission.*

Routines Flip Chart

AMAZING WORDS AT WORK Reread "Hannah Hopper's Hunt for Rules and Laws" aloud. As students listen, have them notice how the Amazing Words are used in context. To build oral vocabulary, lead the class in a discussion about Amazing Words' meanings. Then have students state the main idea of the selection and give supporting details.

MONITOR PROGRESS — Check Oral Vocabulary

During discussion, listen for students' use of Amazing Words.

If... students are unable to use the Amazing Words in discussion,

then... use the Oral Vocabulary Routine in the Routines Flip Chart to demonstrate words in different contexts.

Teacher Read Aloud

MODEL FLUENCY As you read "Hannah Hopper's Hunt for Rules and Laws," model appropriate rate by reading at a speed suitable for the text.

Hannah Hopper's Hunt for Rules and Laws

All the students in Miss Garcia's fourth-grade class wrote the same two words in their notebooks: *Rules and Laws.* Miss Garcia was about to assign their homework for the weekend. First, however, she explained the difference between rules and laws.

"Places like your school and home have rules to live by," said Miss Garcia. "Rules are made by groups of people, like school boards and families. 'Go to bed on time' is a rule at home."

"Laws are made by elected leaders," she continued. "It is every citizen's responsibility to follow rules and obey laws. A person who breaks a rule or a law faces a consequence."

"Your homework assignment for the weekend," said Miss Garcia, "is to be keen and alert observers. Each of you will make a list of rules and laws that you observe this weekend. As usual, the student with the longest list wins the mystery prize."

"Another challenge," thought Hannah Hopper. Hannah loved Miss Garcia's challenges. She looked over at Richard Jenkins. He almost always had the longest list, but Hannah hoped that this time she could win the mystery prize.

Later, Hannah was waiting at the bus stop after school when she spotted the **BUS PARKING ONLY** sign. Hannah added it to her list. She already had ten items: six rules and four laws. She knew she'd have to find a lot more to beat Richard Jenkins.

The next morning, Hannah asked her dad for permission to walk to town in search of more rules and laws. "Fine," Dad said, "as long as you return your overdue library books."

When Hannah arrived at the library, she noticed a sign outside that read: **NO BIKES ON SIDEWALK.** Hannah opened her notebook and wrote down the law. When she walked in the library doors, she immediately noticed how quiet it was. "Ah," thought Hannah, "another rule." After she paid her fine, Hannah added the rules about staying quiet in the library and paying fines for overdue books to her list.

For the rest of the weekend, Hannah listed the rules and laws that she saw in action. By Monday morning, she had filled seven pages of her notebook. But would her list be long enough to beat Richard Jenkins and win the mystery prize? Hannah felt butterflies in her stomach as she waited for Miss Garcia to announce the winner.

Finally, Miss Garcia stood up and said, "Congratulations, Hannah!" Hannah smiled as she accepted the prize—a magnifying glass to help with future observations!

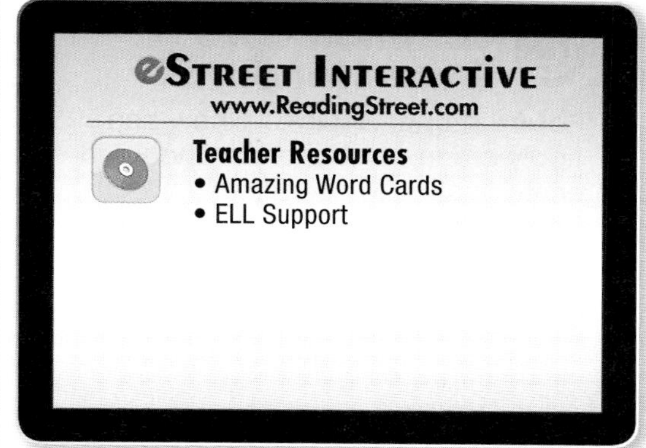

Check Understanding Stop reading after the third paragraph and discuss with students. Clarify understanding by asking questions such as What is the difference between a law and a rule? What is an example of a law? a rule?

ELL Support for Read Aloud Use the modified Read Aloud on p. DI•94 of the ELL Support lessons on the *Teacher Resources DVD-ROM* to prepare students to listen to "Hannah Hopper's Hunt for Rules and Laws."

Common Core State Standards

Foundational Skills 3. Know and apply grade-level phonics and word analysis skills in decoding words. **Foundational Skills 3.a.** Identify and know the meaning of the most common prefixes and derivational suffixes. **Also Language 4.b.**

Skills Trace

Prefixes *(im-, in-)*

Introduce U6W4D1

Practice U6W4D3; U6W4D4

Reteach/Review U6W4D5; U6W5D4

Assess/Test Weekly Test U6W4
Benchmark Test U6

KEY: U=Unit W=Week D=Day

Vocabulary Support

immobile not able to move or be moved

implode to burst inward

injustice an unfair action or treatment

Word Analysis

Teach/Model

Prefixes *im-, in-*

CONNECT Connect today's lesson to previously learned prefixes. Write *pre-pay* and *overhead*. You can already read words with prefixes like these. Let's read these words. Today you will learn to decode and read words with different prefixes.

MODEL Write *impure.* When I see the word *impure,* I recognize that it has a prefix. When I decode a word with a prefix, I break it into parts. First I identify the base word: *pure.* Then I identify the prefix: *im-.* Finally, I put the parts together and read the whole word: *impure.* The prefixes *im-* and *in-* both mean "not," so *impure* means "not pure."

Write *immature* and *incapable*. Model how to decode each multisyllabic word by applying knowledge of the prefixes *im-* and *in-* as with *impure.*

GROUP PRACTICE Continue the process. This time have students decode the words with you. Identify the prefix in each word and how it changes the meaning of the base word.

impatient	**inactive**	**incomplete**	**imperfect**	**impolite**	**incorrect**
immobile	**indefinite**	**incredible**	**implode**	**injustice**	**impossible**

REVIEW What do you know about reading words with prefixes? When I see a word with a prefix, I identify the prefix and the base word and then read the whole word.

Guide Practice

MODEL Have students turn to p. 462 in their Student Editions. Each word on this page has the prefix *im-* or *in-.* The first word is *impassable.* I see the prefix *im-* and the base word *passable.* I put them together and read the word: *impassable. Impassable* means "not able to be passed."

GROUP PRACTICE For each word in Words I Can Blend, ask for the prefix and the base word. Make sure that students identify the correct word parts. Then have them put the parts together and read the words.

Corrective feedback

If... students have difficulty reading a word,
then... model reading the parts and then the whole word, and then ask students to read it with you.

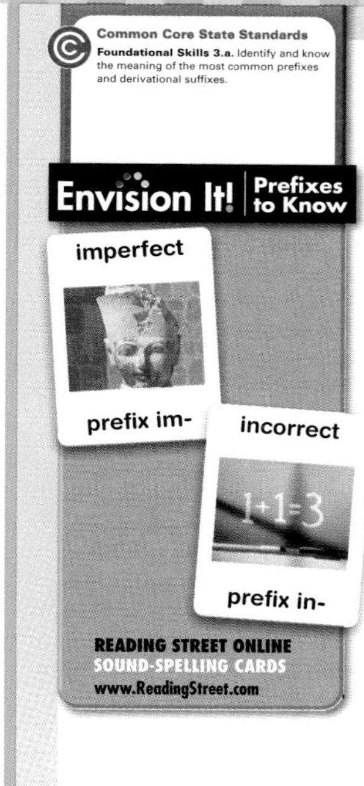

Common Core State Standards
Foundational Skills 3.a. Identify and know the meaning of the most common prefixes and derivational suffixes.
Envision It! Prefixes to Know
imperfect
prefix im-
incorrect
1+1=3
prefix in-
READING STREET ONLINE
SOUND-SPELLING CARDS
www.ReadingStreet.com

Phonics

Prefixes *im-, in-*

Words I Can Blend

im**passable**
im**practical**
in**convenient**
in**sensitive**
in**expensive**

Sentences I Can Read

1. The snow made the roads impassable.
2. It was impractical for me to come at such an inconvenient time.
3. Is it insensitive to ask if the price is inexpensive?

462

My family was hiking in snowshoes through the woods. We stopped to rest at the bottom of a hill that we felt incapable of climbing.

My brother and dad became impatient, so they kept going. Suddenly, my mom pointed to a large brown animal, immobile and inaudible, watching us from behind a tree. Was it a bear? Impossible! Aren't bears supposed to be inactive during the winter?

I didn't wait to find out. I charged up the hill. My mom, in a moment of indecision and fear, froze. She stared, immovable, as the bear snorted in her direction. Then the bear turned and walked away. My mom was immeasurably grateful!

Prefixes *im-, in-*

463

Student Edition, pp. 462–463

READ WORDS IN ISOLATION After students can successfully segment and blend the words on p. 462 in their Student Editions, point to words in random order and ask students to read them.

READ WORDS IN CONTEXT Have students read each of the sentences on p. 462. Have them identify words in the sentences that have the prefix *im-* or *in-*.

Team Talk Pair students and have them take turns reading the sentences aloud.

Chorally read the I Can Read! passage on p. 463 with students. Then have them read the passage aloud to themselves.

ON THEIR OWN For additional practice, use *Reader's and Writer's Notebook,* p. 418.

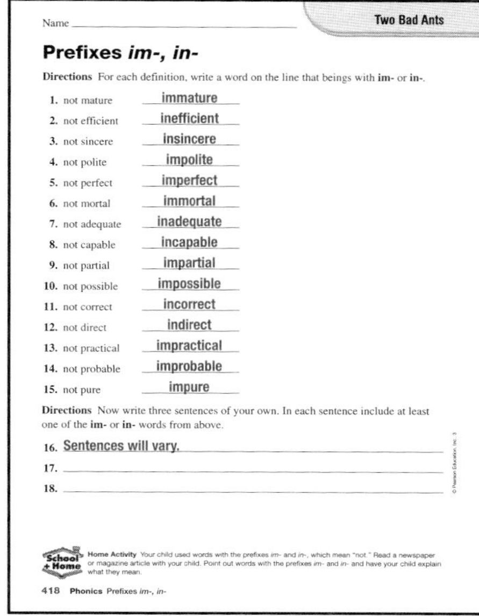

Name ______________ Two Bad Ants

Prefixes *im-, in-*

Directions For each definition, write a word on the line that beings with **im-** or **in-**.

1. not mature immature
2. not efficient inefficient
3. not sincere insincere
4. not polite impolite
5. not perfect imperfect
6. not mortal immortal
7. not adequate inadequate
8. not capable incapable
9. not partial impartial
10. not possible impossible
11. not correct incorrect
12. not direct indirect
13. not practical impractical
14. not probable improbable
15. not pure impure

Directions Now write three sentences of your own. In each sentence include at least one of the **im-** or **in-** words from above.

16. Sentences will vary.
17. ______________
18. ______________

© Pearson Education, Inc. 3

School + Home **Home Activity** Your child used words with the prefixes *im-* and *in-*, which mean "not." Read a newspaper or magazine article with your child. Point out words with the prefixes *im-* and *in-* and have your child explain what they mean.

418 **Phonics** Prefixes *im-, in-*

Reader's and Writer's Notebook, p. 418

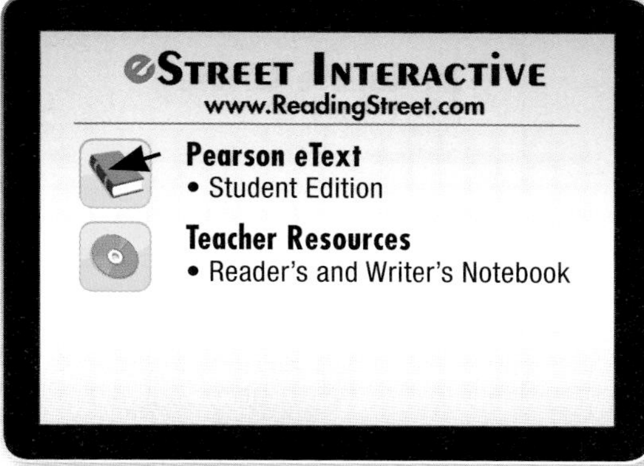

Prefixes Some students may have difficulty choosing between *in-*, *im-*, *dis-*, and *un-* to form the negative. When students use the incorrect prefix, model the correct prefix and have students repeat it.

Contrastive Analysis Chart See also the Contrastive Analysis Chart in the *First Stop* book.

Common Core State Standards

Foundational Skills 3. Know and apply grade-level phonics and word analysis skills in decoding words. **Foundational Skills 3.a.** Identify and know the meaning of the most common prefixes and derivational suffixes. **Foundational Skills 3.d.** Read grade-appropriate irregularly spelled words. **Foundational Skills 4.** Read with sufficient accuracy and fluency to support comprehension. **Foundational Skills 4.b.** Read on-level prose and poetry orally with accuracy, appropriate rate, and expression on successive readings. **Speaking/Listening 5.** Create engaging audio recordings of stories or poems that demonstrate fluid reading at an understandable pace; add visual displays when appropriate to emphasize or enhance certain facts or details.

Decodable Reader 29A

If students need help, then…

Read *Invisible Uncle Mycroft*

READ WORDS IN ISOLATION Have students turn to p. 157 in *Decodable Practice Readers 3.2.* Have students read each word.

Have students read the high-frequency words *to, a, they, what, was, the, would, their, could, one, said, of, you, wanted, buy, where, again,* and *your* on the first page.

PREVIEW Have students read the title and preview the story. Tell them that they will read words with the prefixes *im-* and *in-.*

READ WORDS IN CONTEXT Pair students for reading and listen as they read. One student begins. Students read the entire story, switching readers after each page. Partners reread the story. This time the other student begins. Make sure that students are monitoring their accuracy when they decode words.

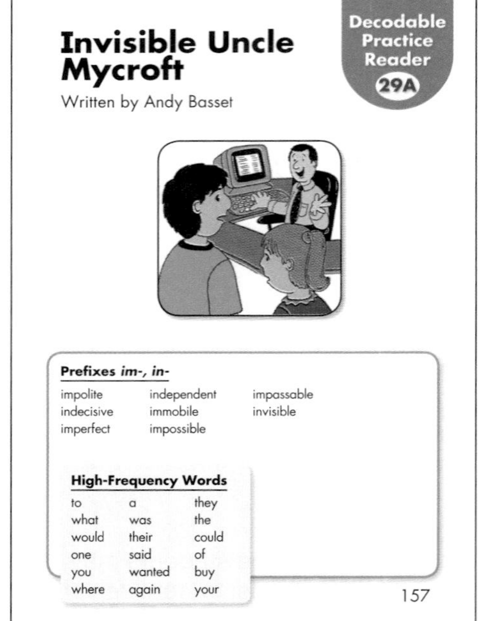

Decodable Practice Reader 29A

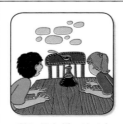

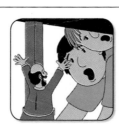

Invisible Uncle Mycroft

Written by Andy Basset

Prefixes *im-*, *in-*

impolite, independent, impassable
indecisive, immobile, invisible
imperfect, impossible

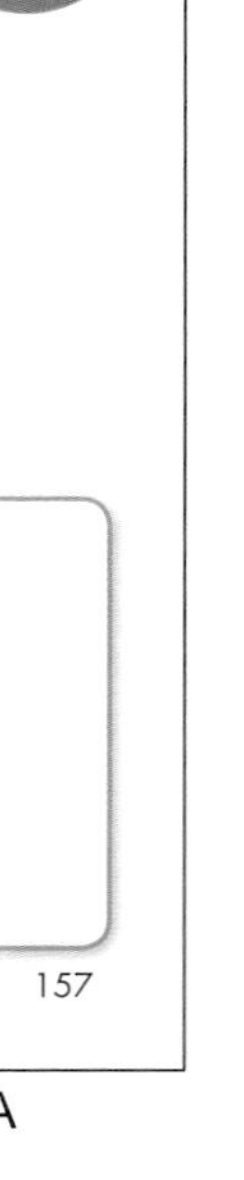

High-Frequency Words

to	a	they
what	was	the
would	their	could
one	said	of
you	wanted	buy
where	again	your

157

Decodable Practice Reader 29A

Uncle Mycroft had invited Brad and his sister Ella to spend a week with him. Brad and Ella had never met Uncle Mycroft. They didn't mean to be impolite, but they had lots of questions. Why did he ask to see them now? What was he like?

"My brother Mycroft is an inventor," Dad explained. "I speak to him by phone all the time, but I haven't seen him for twenty years."

158

This would be their first independent trip without Mom and Dad. They could not get away from work, so Ella and Brad traveled alone by bus.

They got a big surprise when they saw Uncle Mycroft's house. His house was old, and its walk was nearly impassable.

Brad sighed, and Ella took a deep breath. She wasn't indecisive. She rang the bell.

159

The door creaked open, but no one was in sight. All Brad and Ella saw was a room full of dusty furniture. They stood immobile.

"I'm over here, children," said a deep voice.

Brad and Ella looked in the direction of the voice. They saw an empty armchair.

"Don't be alarmed," said the voice. "You can't see me because I'm invisible!"

160

So that was why no one had seen Uncle Mycroft for twenty years!

A long time ago he had invented a potion that made a person invisible. The potion worked, but it was slightly imperfect. Uncle Mycroft had not found a way to reverse it. He wanted Brad and Ella to buy the things he needed for more tests.

161

All that week Brad and Ella went shopping for Uncle Mycroft. And all that week he tested his new potion. It seemed impossible to get right.

At last it was ready. Uncle Mycroft took a large spoonful. Nothing happened.

Suddenly Brad and Ella heard a small voice.

"It worked—well, sort of."

162

Brad and Ella gasped. Where was Uncle Mycroft this time?

"Look down, kids," called a cheerful voice.

They looked down and there was Uncle Mycroft. Yes, they could see him now. But he was just six inches tall.

"Not perfect, but a good start," said the tiny uncle.

163

At the end of the week, Brad and Ella told Uncle Mycroft that they'd visit him again whenever he needed them.

Mom and Dad met the kids at the bus station.

"Tell us all about your trip," Dad said. "What's Uncle Mycroft like now?"

"Well, right now he's kind of like you," Ella said, "but a little shorter."

164

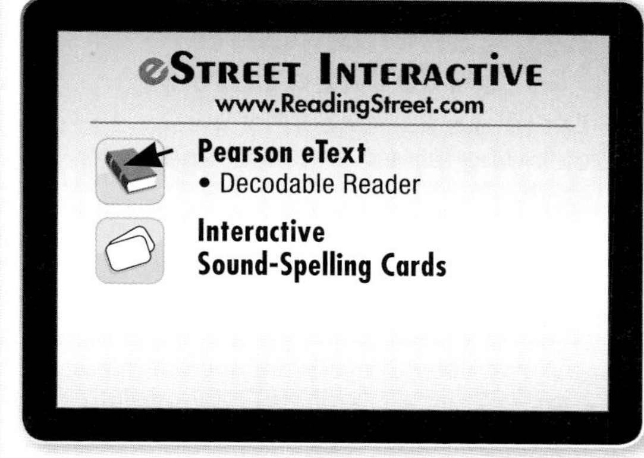

Corrective feedback	**If...** students have difficulty reading a word, **then...** refer them to the *Sound-Spelling Cards* to identify the word parts individually and then together to say the word. • What is the new word? • Is the new word a word you know? • Does it make sense in the story?

CHECK DECODING AND COMPREHENSION Have students retell the story to include characters, setting, and events. Then have students find words in the story that have the prefixes *im-* and *in-.* Students should supply *impolite, independent, impassable, indecisive, immobile, invisible, imperfect,* and *impossible.*

EXTRA PRACTICE Have students take turns recording the story as they read. Then ask each student to review his or her recording to identify areas to improve reading fluency.

Reread for Fluency

REREAD DECODABLE READER Have students reread *Decodable Practice Reader* 29A to develop automaticity decoding words with prefixes.

Routine Oral Rereading

1. **Read** Have students read the entire book orally.
2. **Reread** To achieve optimal fluency, students should reread the text three or four times.
3. **Corrective Feedback** Listen as students read. Provide corrective feedback regarding their fluency and decoding.

Routines Flip Chart

Prefixes *(im-, in-)*

Beginning Students may have difficulty decoding multisyllabic story words with the prefixes *im-* and *in-,* such as *impassable* and *independent.* If so, have them write each word and help them identify the base word by covering up both the prefix and the suffix in the word and then reading the whole word.

Intermediate Remind students that prefixes form separate syllables from the base word and that remembering this may help them to identify prefixes and base words. Write some words with the prefixes *im-* and *in-.* Have students take turns drawing lines to divide the syllables in each word.

Advanced After reading the story, have students list four or five words with prefixes from the story along with their base words. Then have students write pairs of sentences that illustrate the opposite meanings of each story word and its base word.

Common Core State Standards

Literature 2. Recount stories, including fables, folktales, and myths from diverse cultures; determine the central message, lesson, or moral and explain how it is conveyed through key details in the text. **Literature 3.** Describe characters in a story (e.g., their traits, motivations, or feelings) and explain how their actions contribute to the sequence of events. **Foundational Skills 4.** Read with sufficient accuracy and fluency to support comprehension. **Foundational Skills 4.b.** Read on-level prose and poetry orally with accuracy, appropriate rate, and expression on successive readings. **Also Literature 1.**

Skills Trace

Literary Elements: Plot and Theme

Introduce U1W1D1; U3W2D1; U6W4D1

Practice U1W1D2; U1W1D3; U1W2D3; U2W2D2; U2W2D3; U3W2D2; U3W2D3; U6W2D2; U6W2D3; U6W4D2; U6W4D3; U6W5D3

Reteach/Review U1W1D5; U3W2D5; U6W4D5

Assess/Test Weekly Tests U1W1; U3W2; U6W4
Benchmark Tests U1; U6

KEY: U=Unit W=Week D=Day

Comprehension Support

Students may also turn to pp. EI•13 and EI•24 to review the skill and strategy if needed.

Text-Based Comprehension

Literary Elements: Plot and Theme
Story Structure

READ Remind students of the weekly concept—Rules and Laws Are Important to Freedom. Have students read "The Ant and the Beetle" on p. 465.

MODEL A CLOSE READ

Think Aloud As I read, I think about the theme, or lesson of the story. What lesson does the author want to teach with this story? (Think before you act.) When I read, I ask myself what happens in the beginning, middle, and end of a story to help me summarize the story. What happens in the beginning, middle, and end of this story? (Beginning: Annie Ant steals a piece of cheese and meets a beetle who has a plan. Middle: The beetle tricks her. End: The beetle steals the cheese.)

TEACH Have students read p. 464. Explain that the skills of plot and theme and the strategy of story structure are tools they can use to deepen their understanding of a text. Review the bulleted items and explanations on p. 464. Then have students use a graphic organizer like the one shown to sequence the plot's main events and reveal the story structure.

GUIDE PRACTICE Have students look back at "The Ant and the Beetle," using the callouts as guides. Then ask volunteers to respond to the questions in the callouts, citing specific examples from the text to support their answers.

Strategy in time order
Skill A beetle uses flattery to trick an ant. Annie learns that she should think before she acts.

APPLY Use *Reader's and Writer's Notebook,* p. 419 for additional practice with plot and theme.

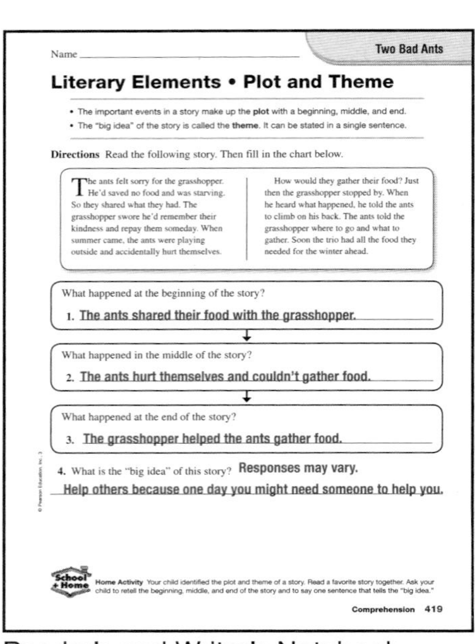

Name ____________ Two Bad Ants

Literary Elements • Plot and Theme

- The important events in a story make up the **plot** with a beginning, middle, and end.
- The "big idea" of the story is called the **theme**. It can be stated in a single sentence.

Directions Read the following story. Then fill in the chart below.

The ants felt sorry for the grasshopper. He'd saved no food and was starving. So they shared what they had. The grasshopper swore he'd remember their kindness and repay them someday. When summer came, the ants were playing outside and accidentally hurt themselves.

How would they gather their food? Just then the grasshopper stopped by. When he heard what happened, he told the ants to climb on his back. The ants told the grasshopper where to go and what to gather. Soon the trio had all the food they needed for the winter ahead.

What happened at the beginning of the story?
1. The ants shared their food with the grasshopper.

What happened in the middle of the story?
2. The ants hurt themselves and couldn't gather food.

What happened at the end of the story?
3. The grasshopper helped the ants gather food.

4. What is the "big idea" of this story? Responses may vary.
Help others because one day you might need someone to help you.

School + Home **Home Activity** Your child identified the plot and theme of a story. Read a favorite story together. Ask your child to retell the beginning, middle, and end of the story and to say one sentence that tells the "big idea."

Comprehension 419

Reader's and Writer's Notebook, p. 419

Comprehension Skill

Literary Elements: Plot and Theme

- The important events in the beginning, middle, and end of a story make up the plot.
- The theme is the "big idea" or lesson in the story.
- Use what you learned about plot and theme and a graphic organizer like the one below as you read "The Ant and the Beetle." Then write the theme of the story, using just one sentence.

Comprehension Strategy

Story Structure

Good readers look for what happens in the beginning, middle, and end of a story. Authors usually write in time order, using sequence words to show the order of events.

The Ant and the Beetle

Adapted from Aesop's "The Fox and the Crow"

Annie Ant stole a piece of cheese from an abandoned picnic and scrambled up on a rock. She was about to eat the cheese when she noticed a beetle nearby. The beetle had a plan.

"My, my, I have never seen such a beautiful ant," flattered the beetle. "From the tip of your antennae to the end of your abdomen, you are simply gorgeous!"

"Finally, someone appreciates my beauty!" Annie thought.

"You must be delicate," continued the beetle. "Surely you are not strong enough to help the other ants."

"Hmph!" said the insulted ant. To show him, Annie set down the cheese and lifted a huge rock over her head.

The beetle grabbed the cheese and began to scurry away. "Yes, you are strong, but you are also foolish."

Strategy Note the time order clues *about to* and *when*. How did the author structure this story?

Skill Summarize the plot. What lesson did Annie learn at the end of the story?

Your Turn!

Need a Review? See the *Envision It! Handbook* for help with plot and theme and story structure.

Ready to Try It? As you read *Two Bad Ants*, use what you've learned about plot, theme, and story structure to understand the text.

464 465

Student Edition, pp. 464–465

Model Fluent Reading

RATE Have students listen as you read paragraph two of "The Ant and The Beetle" at an appropriate rate. Explain that you will read at a pace similar to the speed you would use in normal conversation.

Routine Oral Rereading

1. **Select a Passage** Read paragraph two of "The Ant and the Beetle" aloud.
2. **Model** Have students listen to the rate at which you read.
3. **Guide Practice** Have students read along with you.
4. **On Their Own** For optimal fluency, students should reread three or four times using appropriate rate.

Routines Flip Chart

eStreet Interactive
www.ReadingStreet.com

Pearson eText
- Student Edition

Envision It! Animations

Teacher Resources
- Reader's and Writer's Notebook

ELL

Plot and Theme Provide practice for students by discussing the plot and theme of one or two familiar stories, fairy tales, or fables.

Common Core State Standards

Writing 7. Conduct short research projects that build knowledge about a topic. **Speaking/Listening 1.** Engage effectively in a range of collaborative discussions (one-on-one, in groups, and teacher-led) with diverse partners on grade 3 topics and texts, building on others' ideas and expressing their own clearly. **Language 4.** Determine or clarify the meaning of unknown and multiple-meaning words and phrases, based on grade 3 reading and content, choosing flexibly from a range of strategies. **Language 6.** Acquire and use accurately grade-appropriate conversational, general academic, and domain-specific words and phrases, including those that signal spatial and temporal relationships (e.g., *After dinner that night we went looking for them*).

Selection Vocabulary

Use the following routine to introduce this week's tested selection vocabulary.

crystal a solid, glass-like item
disappeared vanished from sight
discovery the action of finding something
goal an aim or desired result
journey a long trip
joyful feeling great happiness
scoop a spoon-shaped tool; the amount taken up by such a tool
unaware having no knowledge of something

SEE IT/SAY IT Write *disappeared*. Scan across the word with your finger as you say it: *dis-ap-peared.*

HEAR IT Use the word in a sentence. When the sun came out, the fog disappeared.

DEFINE IT Elicit definitions from students. How would you describe to another student what *disappeared* means? Clarify or give a definition when necessary. Yes, when something has *disappeared,* it means you can no longer see it. Restate the meaning of the word in student-friendly terms. *Disappeared* means that something you could see has gone away, so you can't see it anymore.

Team Talk If you have eaten all of your lunch, has your food *disappeared*? Why or why not? Turn and talk to your partner about this. Be prepared to explain your answer. Allow students time to discuss. Ask for examples. Rephrase their examples for usage when necessary or to correct misunderstandings.

MAKE CONNECTIONS Have students discuss the word. Has anything you owned ever *disappeared*? Turn and talk to your partner about this. Then be prepared to share. Have students share. Rephrase their ideas for usage when necessary or to correct misunderstandings.

RECORD Have students write the word and its meaning.

Continue this routine to introduce the remaining words in this manner.

Corrective feedback	**If...** students are having difficulty understanding, **then...** review the definitions in small groups.

Research and Inquiry

Step 1 Identify and Focus Topic

TEACH Discuss the Question of the Week: *Why are rules and laws important to freedom?* Tell students they will research the effect of rules and laws on freedom. They will write a letter about rules and laws to present to the class on Day 5.

Think Aloud **MODEL** I'll start by brainstorming a list of questions about rules and laws. I know that rules and laws keep people safe. Some possible questions could be *Who enforces rules and laws in different places? What happens if people do not follow rules and laws?* and *What kind of freedom could someone lose by not following rules and laws?*

GUIDE PRACTICE After students have brainstormed inquiry questions, explain that tomorrow they will conduct research using their questions. Help students identify keywords that will guide their search. Remind students that pull-down menus on Web sites can also be used as a way to identify additional keywords.

ON THEIR OWN Have students work individually, in pairs, or in small groups to write an inquiry question.

eStreet Interactive
www.ReadingStreet.com

Teacher Resources
- Envision It! Pictured Vocabulary Cards
- Tested Vocabulary Cards

21st Century Skills

Internet Guy *Don Leu*

Weekly Inquiry Project

STEP 1	Identify and Focus Topic
STEP 2	Navigate/Search
STEP 3	Analyze Information
STEP 4	Synthesize
STEP 5	Communicate

Academic Vocabulary

A **pull-down menu** appears on a Web site as a way to navigate to further information.

ELL

Multilingual Vocabulary Students can apply knowledge of their home languages to acquire new English vocabulary by using the Multilingual Vocabulary Lists (*ELL Handbook,* pp. 434–444).

Day 1 SMALL GROUP TIME • Differentiate Vocabulary, p. SG•49

OL On-Level
- **Practice Vocabulary** Amazing Words
- **Read** *Reading Street Sleuth,* pp. 74–75

SI Strategic Intervention
- **Reteach Vocabulary** Amazing Words
- **Read** *Reading Street Sleuth,* pp. 74–75

A Advanced
- **Extend Vocabulary** Amazing Words
- **Read** *Reading Street Sleuth,* pp. 74–75
- **Introduce** Inquiry Project

ELL

If... students need more scaffolding and practice with **Vocabulary,** **then...** use the activities on pp. DI•92–DI•93 in the Teacher Resources section on SuccessNet.

Common Core State Standards

Foundational Skills 3.a. Identify and know the meaning of the most common prefixes and derivational suffixes. **Language 2.** Demonstrate command of the conventions of standard English capitalization, punctuation, and spelling when writing. **Language 2.b.** Use commas in addresses. **Language 2.e.** Use conventional spelling for high-frequency and other studied words and for adding suffixes to base words (e.g., *sitting, smiled, cries, happiness*). **Language 2.f.** Use spelling patterns and generalizations (e.g., word families, position-based spellings, syllable patterns, ending rules, meaningful word parts) in writing words.

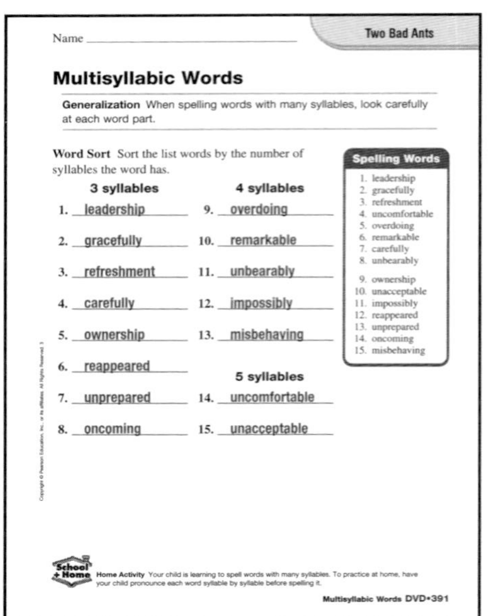

Name ______________ Two Bad Ants

Multisyllabic Words

Generalization When spelling words with many syllables, look carefully at each word part.

Word Sort Sort the list words by the number of syllables the word has.

3 syllables

1. leadership
2. gracefully
3. refreshment
4. carefully
5. ownership
6. reappeared
7. unprepared
8. oncoming

4 syllables

9. overdoing
10. remarkable
11. unbearably
12. impossibly
13. misbehaving

5 syllables

14. uncomfortable
15. unacceptable

Spelling Words

1. leadership
2. gracefully
3. refreshment
4. uncomfortable
5. overdoing
6. remarkable
7. carefully
8. unbearably
9. ownership
10. unacceptable
11. impossibly
12. reappeared
13. unprepared
14. oncoming
15. misbehaving

School + Home **Home Activity** Your child is learning to spell words with many syllables. To practice at home, have your child pronounce each word syllable by syllable before spelling it.

Multisyllabic Words DVD•391

Let's Practice It! TR DVD•391

Spelling Pretest

Prefixes, Suffixes, and Endings

INTRODUCE This week we will spell words with the prefixes *im-* and *in-*, or other prefixes, as well as suffixes and endings.

PRETEST Say each word, read the sentence, and repeat the word.

1. leadership	Our principal has great **leadership** skills.
2. impossibly	The puzzle was **impossibly** difficult.
3. gracefully	The dancer leapt **gracefully** on the stage.
4. refreshment	Lemonade is a good **refreshment.**
5. uncomfortable	I feel **uncomfortable** on stage.
6. overdoing	Were you **overdoing** your exercise?
7. remarkable	It's **remarkable** that a bird can fly so far.
8. carefully	The boy held the hamster **carefully.**
9. unbearably	It felt **unbearably** hot outside.
10. ownership	Someone claimed **ownership** of the lost pen.
11. unacceptable	It is **unacceptable** to cheat.
12. reappeared	The rabbit **reappeared** out of its hole.
13. unprepared	I was **unprepared** for how cold it was.
14. oncoming	Did you look for **oncoming** traffic?
15. misbehaving	My puppy is always **misbehaving**.
Challenge words	
16. outrageous	We found **outrageous** bargains at the market.
17. incomprehensible	Messy handwriting is **incomprehensible.**
18. undoubtedly	Gina is **undoubtedly** the best speller in our class.
19. independence	The United States fought for **independence** in the Revolutionary War.
20. disadvantage	A sore throat is a **disadvantage** to a singer.

SELF-CORRECT Have students self-correct their pretests by rewriting misspelled words.

ON THEIR OWN Use *Let's Practice It!* p. 391 on the *Teacher Resources DVD-ROM.*

Conventions

Commas

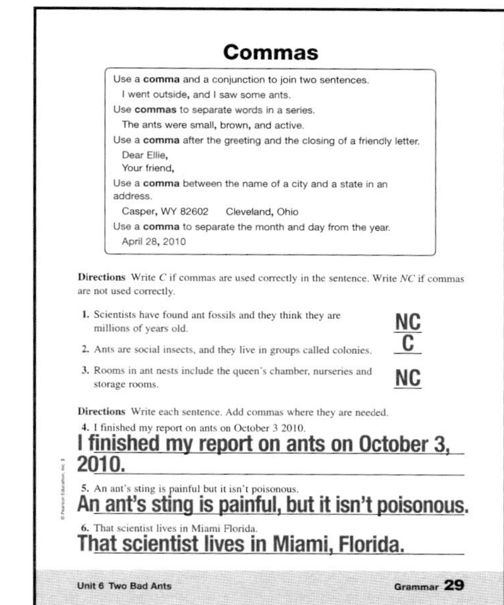

Commas

Use a **comma** and a conjunction to join two sentences.
I went outside, and I saw some ants.
Use **commas** to separate words in a series.
The ants were small, brown, and active.
Use a **comma** after the greeting and the closing of a friendly letter.
Dear Ellie,
Your friend,
Use a **comma** between the name of a city and a state in an address.
Casper, WY 82602 Cleveland, Ohio
Use a **comma** to separate the month and day from the year.
April 28, 2010

Directions Write *C* if commas are used correctly in the sentence. Write *NC* if commas are not used correctly.

1. Scientists have found ant fossils and they think they are millions of years old. NC
2. Ants are social insects, and they live in groups called colonies. C
3. Rooms in ant nests include the queen's chamber, nurseries and storage rooms. NC

Directions Write each sentence. Add commas where they are needed.

4. I finished my report on ants on October 3 2010.
I finished my report on ants on October 3, 2010.
5. An ant's sting is painful but it isn't poisonous.
An ant's sting is painful, but it isn't poisonous.
6. That scientist lives in Miami Florida.
That scientist lives in Miami, Florida.

Unit 6 Two Bad Ants Grammar 29

Grammar Transparency 29, TR DVD

MAKE CONNECTIONS To focus attention on commas, draw a rectangle on the board to represent an envelope. Write the school's address *without* commas separating the city and state. Ask students what is wrong with the address. Point out that a comma is always used between the names of a city and a state in an address.

TEACH Display Grammar Transparency 29. Point out the different uses for commas, such as in dates, addresses, letter greetings, and letter closings and between items in a series.

MODEL Model reading sentence 1 and writing *NC* to show that commas are not used correctly. Explain that this sentence needs a comma before the word *and* because it uses a conjunction to join two shorter sentences.

GUIDE PRACTICE Guide students to complete items 2–3. Remind them to write *C* if commas are used correctly and *NC* if they are not. Record the correct responses on the transparency.

APPLY Have students read sentences 4–6 on the transparency and add commas where they are needed to correctly write each sentence.

Handwriting

MODEL LETTER FORMATION AND WORD SPACING Display the capital cursive letters *D, Q,* and *Z.* Follow the stroke instructions pictured to model letter formation. Model writing the phrase: *Doc's Quiet Zone.* Make sure letters are evenly spaced and there is a finger's space between the words.

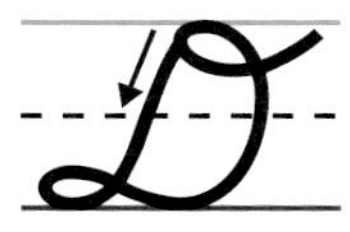 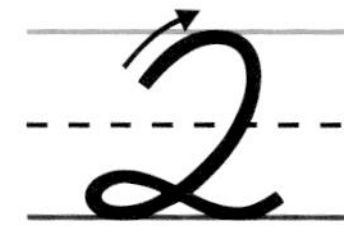 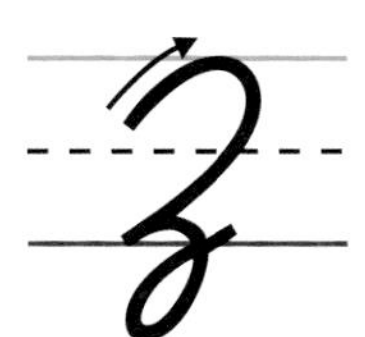

GUIDE PRACTICE Have students write these proper names: *Daring Daisy Doyle, Quiet Quentin Quan,* and *Zany Zachary Zinn.* Circulate around the room, guiding students.

Daily Fix-It

1. Dr Allen studys insects in his lab. *(Dr.; studies)*
2. He careful looks at ants, bees and butterflies. *(carefully; bees, and)*

Academic Vocabulary 

A **comma** is a punctuation mark used in a variety of ways: in compound sentences, between items in a series, in dates, and letter greetings and closings.

A **closing** is the concluding part of a letter. It is followed the letter writer's name or signature on the next line.

Word spacing is the space between two written words.

Language Transfer: Commas in Dates Conventions for writing dates vary in other languages, such as the abbreviations for the months of the year and the ordering of the year, month, and day. Write today's date on the board and have students choral read it, saying *comma* where the comma appears in the date. Ask students if they know of other ways of writing the date. Have them write and share examples with the class.

Handwriting: Proper Names Provide further practice with handwriting capital cursive letters *D, Q,* and *Z* with proper names, such as *Dexter, Dylan, Quincy,* and *Zoë.*

Common Core State Standards

Writing 3. Write narratives to develop real or imagined experiences or events using effective technique, descriptive details, and clear event sequences. **Writing 3.a.** Establish a situation and introduce a narrator and/or characters; organize an event sequence that unfolds naturally. **Writing 3.b.** Use dialogue and descriptions of actions, thoughts, and feelings to develop experiences and events or show the response of characters to situations.

Bridge to Common Core

TEXT TYPES AND PURPOSES

This week students write a comic book about the two ants in *Two Bad Ants.*

Narrative Writing

Through reading and discussion, students will gain a deeper understanding of why rules and laws are important to freedom. They will use this knowledge from the texts to write and support a narrative in the form of a comic book.

Through the week, students will improve their range and content of writing through daily mini-lessons.

5-Day Plan

DAY 1	Read Like a Writer
DAY 2	Develop a Story Sequence
DAY 3	Writing Effective Dialogue
DAY 4	Revise: Adding
DAY 5	Proofread for Commas

Write Guy *by Jeff Anderson*

Let's Use Books

Let's use books to solve problems! If a student wants to write dialogue, she can look at how the author of a recently read story wrote dialogue. Have the student ask herself, "What do I like about how these characters speak?" Young writers can use models.

Writing Zoom in on

Comic Book

Mini-Lesson Read Like a Writer

■ **Introduce** This week you will write a comic book. A comic book uses illustrations to help tell an imaginative story. Dialogue, or the words the characters say, is included in the illustrations.

Prompt Write a short comic book telling of a further adventure of the two ants in *Two Bad Ants.*

Trait Conventions

Mode Narrative

■ **Examine Model Text** Let's read an example of a comic book featuring these two ants. Have students read "The Crystal Palace Giant" on p. 420 of their *Reader's and Writer's Notebook.*

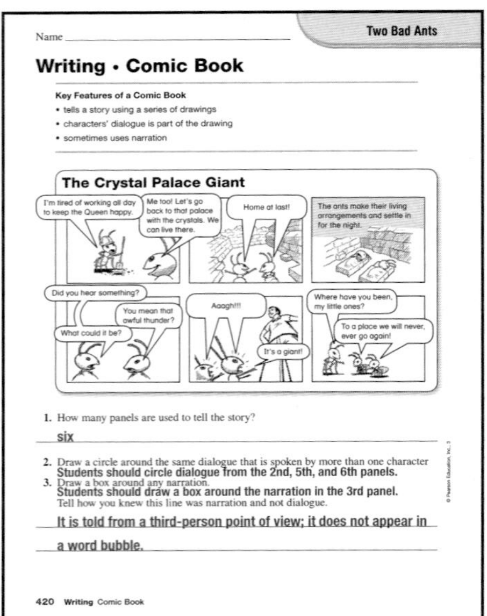

Name ____________ **Two Bad Ants**

Writing • Comic Book

Key Features of a Comic Book
- tells a story using a series of drawings
- characters' dialogue is part of the drawing
- sometimes uses narration

The Crystal Palace Giant

1. How many panels are used to tell the story?
   six
2. Draw a circle around the same dialogue that is spoken by more than one character
   Students should circle dialogue from the 2nd, 5th, and 6th panels.
3. Draw a box around any narration.
   Students should draw a box around the narration in the 3rd panel.
   Tell how you knew this line was narration and not dialogue.
   It is told from a third-person point of view; it does not appear in a word bubble.

420 Writing Comic Book

Reader's and Writer's Notebook, p. 420

■ **Key Features** Comic books tell a story using a series of drawings. Point to the first panel in the story and follow along with your finger until you get to the end. How many panels make up this comic book? (six)

Most comic books include dialogue. Dialogue appears in word bubbles, and the bubbles point to the characters who are talking. Which ant says, "Where have you been, my little ones?" (the Queen ant)

Some comic books include narration. Narration tells the story from a third-person point of view. The words do not appear in word bubbles because they are not words that a character says. Which panel features narration? (the third panel)

Comic books can also include captions and labels, which add details to the setting of the story. What has a label in this comic book? (the sugar jar) How does the label help tell the story? (The label tells us that the "crystals" the ants love are sugar crystals.)

Review Key Features

Review the key features of a comic book with students. You may want to post the key features in the classroom for students to refer to as they work on their comic books.

Key Features of a Comic Book

- tells a story using a series of drawings
- uses characters' dialogue as part of the drawing
- sometimes uses narration

Routine Quick Write for Fluency

Team Talk

1. **Talk** Have pairs discuss how drawings can be used to tell a story in a comic book.
2. **Write** Each student writes three sentences summarizing his or her ideas.
3. **Share** Partners read their sentences to one another.

Routines Flip Chart

eSTREET INTERACTIVE
www.ReadingStreet.com

Teacher Resources
- Reader's and Writer's Notebook
- Let's Practice It!

Academic Vocabulary 

Dialogue is a conversation between characters in a story. In a comic book, dialogue appears in word bubbles that point to the character who is speaking.

Visual Learning: Key Features of a Comic Book Display examples of comics. Invite students to read aloud a comic strip and retell the story for the group.

Wrap Up Your Day!

- **Content Knowledge** Reread "Street Rhymes!" on p. 460j to students. Ask them what they learned this week about why rules and laws are important to freedom.
- **Oral Vocabulary** Have students use the Amazing Words they learned in context sentences.
- **Homework** Send home this week's Family Times newsletter on *Let's Practice It!* pp. 392–393 on the *Teacher Resources DVD-ROM.*

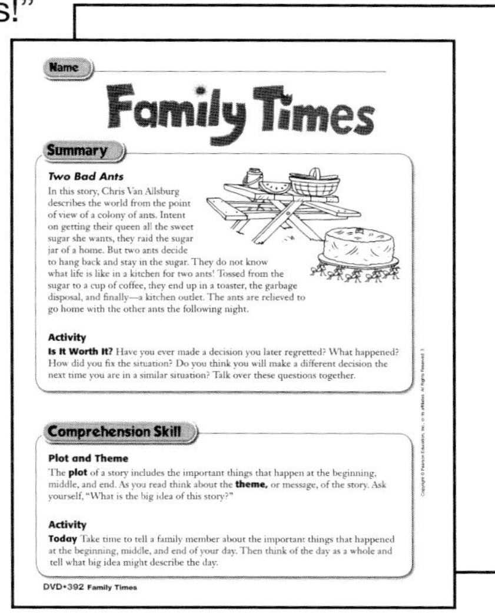

Name

Family Times

Summary

Two Bad Ants

In this story, Chris Van Allsburg describes the world from the point of view of a colony of ants. Intent on getting their queen all the sweet sugar she wants, they raid the sugar jar of a home. But two ants decide to hang back and stay in the sugar. They do not know what life is like in a kitchen for two ants! Tossed from the sugar to a cup of coffee, they end up in a toaster, the garbage disposal, and finally—a kitchen outlet. The ants are relieved to go home with the other ants the following night.

Activity

Is It Worth It? Have you ever made a decision you later regretted? What happened? How did you fix the situation? Do you think you will make a different decision the next time you are in a similar situation? Talk over these questions together.

Comprehension Skill

Plot and Theme

The **plot** of a story includes the important things that happen at the beginning, middle, and end. As you read think about the **theme,** or message, of the story. Ask yourself, "What is the big idea of this story?"

Activity

Today Take time to tell a family member about the important things that happened at the beginning, middle, and end of your day. Then think of the day as a whole and tell what big idea might describe the day.

DVD•392 Family Times

Let's Practice It! TR DVD•392–393

Preview DAY 2

Tell students that tomorrow they will read about why rules and laws are important to freedom.

DAY 2 at a Glance

Content Knowledge
Oral Vocabulary

Phonics/Word Analysis
Prefixes *im-*, *in-*

Literary Terms
Imagery

Vocabulary Skill
Prefixes and Suffixes *un-*, *dis-*, *-ful*

Fluency
Rate

Research and Inquiry
Navigate/Search

Conventions
Commas

Spelling
Prefixes, Suffixes, and Endings

Writing
Comic Book

Materials

- Student Edition
- Reader's and Writer's Notebook

Content Knowledge

Rules and Laws Are Important to Freedom

EXPAND THE CONCEPT Remind students of the weekly concept question, *Why are rules and laws important to freedom?* Tell students that today they will begin reading *Two Bad Ants*. As they read, encourage students to think about why rules and laws are important to freedom.

Build Oral Language

TALK ABOUT SENTENCES AND WORDS Reread this sentence from the Read Aloud, "Hannah Hopper's Hunt for Rules and Laws."

A person who breaks a rule or law faces a consequence.

- What does the phrase *breaks a law* mean? (does something a law says not to do)
- What is a *consequence*? (the result of doing something; a punishment)
- What kinds of *consequences* might there be when someone *breaks a law?* (go to jail, get a ticket)

Team Talk Have students turn to a partner and discuss the following question. Then ask them to share their responses.

- What sentence can you make that keeps the same ideas but presents them in a different order? (Possible response: There is a consequence for a person who breaks a rule or law.)

Common Core State Standards

Speaking/Listening 1. Engage effectively in a range of collaborative discussions (one-on-one, in groups, and teacher-led) with diverse partners on grade 3 topics and texts, building on others' ideas and expressing their own clearly. **Language 6.** Acquire and use accurately grade-appropriate conversational, general academic, and domain-specific words and phrases, including those that signal spatial and temporal relationships (e.g., *After dinner that night we went looking for them*).

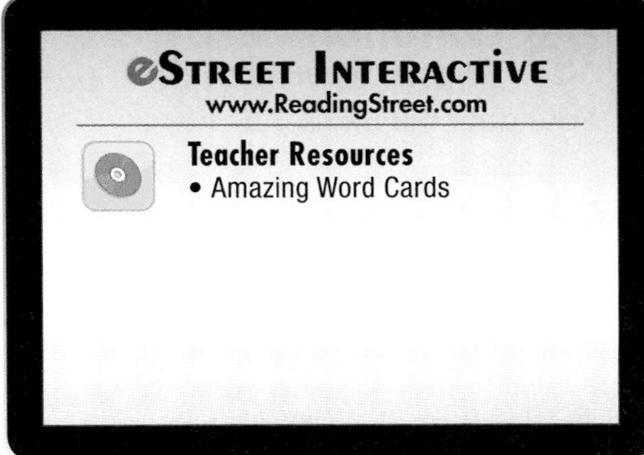

Build Oral Vocabulary

Amazing Words Robust Vocabulary Routine

1. **Introduce** Write the Amazing Word *citizen* on the board. Have students say it aloud with you. Relate *citizen* to the photographs on pp. 460–461 and "Hannah Hopper's Hunt for Rules and Laws." What kind of *citizen* is Hannah? What rights do *citizens* have? Have students determine the definition of the word. A *citizen* is a person who is a member of a country and has certain rights and privileges.
2. **Demonstrate** Have students answer questions to demonstrate understanding. What might a *citizen* do to stay safe? If you visit a new place, are you a *citizen*?
3. **Apply** Have students apply their understanding: What town, state, or country are you a *citizen* of?
4. **Display the Word** Run your hand under the word as you emphasize the syllables *cit-i-zen.* Have students say the word.

See p. OV•4 to teach *fascinate.*

Routines Flip Chart

ADD TO THE CONCEPT MAP Use the photos on pp. 460–461 and the Read Aloud, "Hannah Hopper's Hunt for Rules and Laws," to discuss how rules and laws are important to freedom and to talk about the Amazing Words *responsibility, obey, consequence,* and *permission.* Add these and other concept-related words to the concept map. Discuss the following questions. Encourage students to build on others' ideas when they answer. Add some of the words generated in the discussion to the concept map.

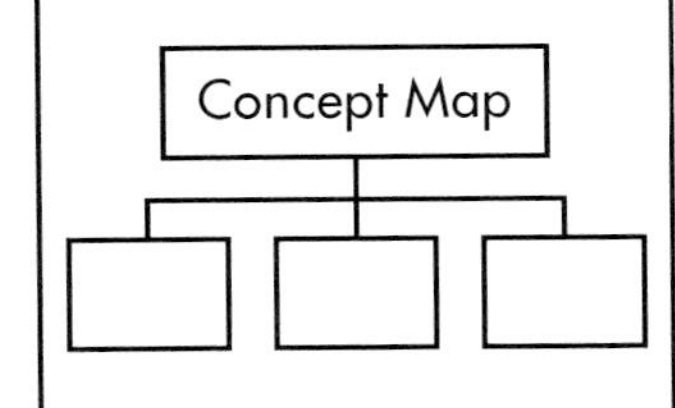

- Why is it the *responsibility* of good citizens to *obey* rules and laws?
- What are the *consequences* of obeying rules and laws?
- Why should people have *permission* to go against the rules?

Amazing Words

obey	fascinate
responsibility	guilt
consequence	encounter
permission	forbid
citizen	eerie

Reinforce Vocabulary Use the Day 2 instruction on ELL Poster 29 to teach lesson vocabulary and the lesson concept.

Cognates Point out that *fascinate,* one of today's Amazing Words, has a Spanish cognate, *fascinar*.

Common Core State Standards

Foundational Skills 3.a. Identify and know the meaning of the most common prefixes and derivational suffixes. **Language 3.a.** Choose words and phrases for effect. **Language 4.b.** Determine the meaning of the new word formed when a known affix is added to a known word (e.g., *agreeable/disagreeable, comfortable/uncomfortable, care/careless, heat/preheat*).

Word Analysis

Prefixes *im-, in-*

REVIEW Review the prefixes *im-* and *in-,* pointing out that prefixes are added to the beginning of base words.

READ WORDS IN ISOLATION Have the class read these words. Then point to the words in random order and ask students to read them quickly.

insoluble	**immortal**	**inedible**	**improbable**
impass	**incapable**	**impractical**	**invisible**

Corrective feedback Model reading the prefix and then the base word, and then ask students to read the word with you.

READ WORDS IN CONTEXT Have the class read these sentences.

Team Talk Have pairs take turns reading the sentences naturally.

It was **impossible** to move the heavy piano.

Eric was **indiscreet** in telling Abby about her surprise party.

The old vase at the museum was **imperfect**.

Don't Wait Until Friday **MONITOR PROGRESS** **Check Word Reading**

Prefixes *im-, in-*

FORMATIVE ASSESSMENT Have the class read these words. Notice which words students miss during the group reading. Call on individuals to read some of the words.

insanity	**immoral**	**incapable**	**immature**	**Spiral Review**
hopeful	**likely**	**childhood**	**graceful**	Row 2 reviews words with suffixes.
inactively	**immobilize**	**ungracefully**	**companion**	Row 3 contrasts words with prefixes and suffixes.

If... students cannot read words with prefixes *im-* and *in-* at this point,

then... use the Day 1 Word Analysis lesson on p. 462a to reteach these prefixes. Use words from the *Decodable Practice Passages* (or *Reader*). Continue to monitor students' progress. See the Skills Trace on p. 462a.

Literary Terms

Imagery

TEACH Tell students that imagery is the use of words that create a graphic visual experience and appeal to the senses. Explain that people use imagery in everyday conversations to describe things they experience. In literature, imagery can make characters and settings seem real and familiar to the reader.

MODEL Let's look at "The Ant and the Beetle" and "How Ants Find Food." The author uses imagery to describe the ants' black color and small size. What kind of imagery can you add to the author's description of ants? (Answers will vary.)

GUIDE PRACTICE Find an example of imagery in *Two Bad Ants* and point it out to students. Encourage students to think about how the author describes life from an ant's point of view. Talk about how this language helps the reader feel more familiar with the characters.

ON THEIR OWN Have students look for their own examples of imagery in *Two Bad Ants* or other selections in their Student Edition.

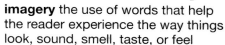

Academic Vocabulary

imagery the use of words that help the reader experience the way things look, sound, smell, taste, or feel

Common Core State Standards

Foundational Skills 3.a. Identify and know the meaning of the most common prefixes and derivational suffixes. **Foundational Skills 4.b.** Read on-level prose and poetry orally with accuracy, appropriate rate, and expression on successive readings. **Language 4.b.** Determine the meaning of the new word formed when a known affix is added to a known word (e.g., *agreeable/ disagreeable, comfortable/ uncomfortable, care/ careless, heat/ preheat*). **Also Language 4.d.**

Selection Vocabulary

crystal a solid, glass-like item

disappeared vanished from sight

discovery the action of finding something

goal an aim or desired result

journey a long trip

joyful feeling great happiness

scoop a spoon-shaped tool; the amount taken up by a such a tool

unaware having no knowledge of something

Bridge to Common Core

VOCABULARY ACQUISITION AND USE

Using word parts helps students determine the meanings of unknown words and enables them to acquire a broad range of academic and domain-specific words. By considering the meanings of prefixes and suffixes and using resources to confirm or determine word meanings, students demonstrate the ability to determine word meanings on their own.

Vocabulary Support

Refer students to *Words!* on p. W•14 in the Student Edition for additional practice.

Vocabulary Skill

Prefixes and Suffixes *un-, dis-, -ful*

READ Have students read "How Ants Find Food" on p. 467. Use the vocabulary skill and strategy as tools to build comprehension.

TEACH WORD STRUCTURE Tell students that when a prefix or suffix is added to a root word, the word meaning changes. Knowing what the prefix or suffix means can help determine the meanings of words.

Think Aloud **MODEL** Write on the board: *It is unusual for them to be distrustful.* I'm not sure of the meanings of the words *unusual* and *distrustful,* so I will look at their prefixes and suffixes. *Un-* is a prefix that means "not," *dis-* is a prefix that means "the opposite of," and *-ful* is a suffix that means "full of." Now I know that *unusual* means "not usual," and *distrustful* means "the opposite of full of trust."

GUIDE PRACTICE Write on the board: *We disagree about which painting is more beautiful*. Have students determine the meanings of the words *disagree* and *beautiful* using what they know about prefixes and suffixes. If they are unable to find the meanings of *disagree* and *beautiful* using word structure clues, have them look the words up in the dictionary. For additional support, use *Envision It! Pictured Vocabulary Cards* or *Tested Vocabulary Cards*.

ON THEIR OWN Have students reread "How Ants Find Food" on p. 467. Have them use clues about word structure to list the definitions of the selection vocabulary. For additional practice, use *Reader's and Writer's Notebook,* p. 421.

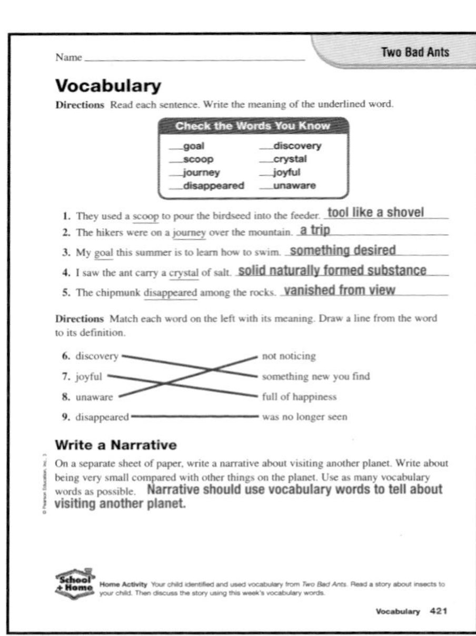

Name ________ Two Bad Ants

Vocabulary

Directions Read each sentence. Write the meaning of the underlined word.

Check the Words You Know

__goal	__discovery
__scoop	__crystal
__journey	__joyful
__disappeared	__unaware

1. They used a scoop to pour the birdseed into the feeder. tool like a shovel
2. The hikers were on a journey over the mountain. a trip
3. My goal this summer is to learn how to swim. something desired
4. I saw the ant carry a crystal of salt. solid naturally formed substance
5. The chipmunk disappeared among the rocks. vanished from view

Directions Match each word on the left with its meaning. Draw a line from the word to its definition.

6. discovery	not noticing
7. joyful	something new you find
8. unaware	full of happiness
9. disappeared	was no longer seen

Write a Narrative

On a separate sheet of paper, write a narrative about visiting another planet. Write about being very small compared with other things on the planet. Use as many vocabulary words as possible. Narrative should use vocabulary words to tell about visiting another planet.

School + Home **Home Activity** Your child identified and used vocabulary from *Two Bad Ants*. Read a story about insects to your child. Then discuss the story using this week's vocabulary words.

Vocabulary 421

Reader's and Writer's Notebook, p. 421

Common Core State Standards
Foundational Skills 3.a. Identify and know the meaning of the most common prefixes and derivational suffixes.
Envision It! Words to Know
crystal
discovery
scoop
disappeared
goal
journey
joyful
unaware
READING STREET ONLINE
VOCABULARY ACTIVITIES
www.ReadingStreet.com

Vocabulary Strategy for

Prefixes and Suffixes *un-, dis-,* and *-ful*

Word Structure When you see a word you don't know, look for a prefix or suffix. The prefixes *un-* or *dis-* make the word mean "not ____" or "opposite of ____." The suffix *-ful* makes a word mean "full of ____." Use *un-, dis-,* or *-ful* to figure out the meanings of words.

1. When you see an unfamiliar word with a prefix or suffix, put your finger over the prefix or suffix.
2. Look at the base word. Put the base word in the appropriate phrase: "not____," "opposite of ____," or "full of ____."
3. Try the new meaning in the sentence. Does it make sense?

Read "How Ants Find Food" on page 467. Look for words that have a prefix or suffix. Use the prefix or suffix to help you figure out the meanings of the words.

Words to Write Reread "How Ants Find Food." Write about the jobs a worker ant does. Use words from the Words to Know list in your writing.

466

How Ants Find Food

Ants are social insects. Like wasps and bees, they live in large groups called colonies. The queen ant lays all the eggs, and the worker ants build the nest, look for food, care for the eggs, and defend the nest.

Ants that look for food are called scouts. Their goal is to find food and report the locations to the ants back at the nest. Suppose a scout ant makes this discovery: someone has left out a scoop of sugar. The scout carries a sugar crystal back to the nest. On its return journey, the scout ant also leaves a scent trail leading from the food to the nest. When the other ants realize that the scout has found food, they become very excited. They seem joyful about the news.

Many ants follow the scout's trail back to the food. They swarm over the sugar, picking up all the crystals. In a short time, all of the sugar has disappeared, and so have the ants. It happens so quickly that often people are unaware that ants were ever there at all.

Your Turn!

Need a Review? For additional help with prefixes and suffixes, see *Words!*

Ready to Try It? Read *Two Bad Ants*, pp. 468–485.

467

Student Edition, pp. 466–467

Reread for Fluency

RATE Read the first paragraph of "How Ants Find Food" aloud, keeping a steady reading rate. Explain to students that paying attention to their reading rate, or speed, will help their reading sound natural. Students may need to slow their rate when reading informational text.

Routine Oral Rereading

1. **Select a Passage** Read paragraph 2 of "How Ants Find Food" aloud.
2. **Model** Have students listen to the rate at which you read.
3. **Guide Practice** Have students read along with you.
4. **On Their Own** For optimal fluency, students should reread three or four times using appropriate rate.

Routines Flip Chart

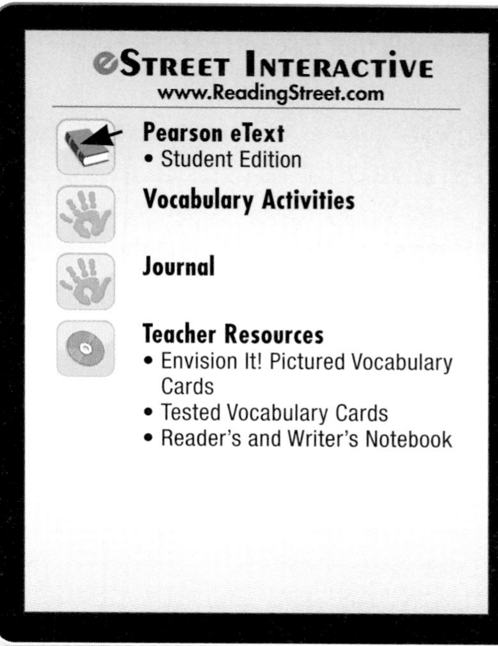

Common Core State Standards

Literature 7. Explain how specific aspects of a text's illustrations contribute to what is conveyed by the words in a story (e.g., create mood, emphasize aspects of a character or setting). **Literature 10.** By the end of the year, read and comprehend literature, including stories, dramas, and poetry, at the high end of the grades 2–3 text complexity band independently and proficiently.

CRAFT AND STRUCTURE

Students analyze the selection's title and illustrations and think about how the components relate to each other. As they preview the selection and prepare to read, they come to see how purpose shapes the content and style of the text.

Academic Vocabulary

animal fantasy a fictional story about animals that talk and act like people

Strategy Response Log

Have students use p. 35 in the *Reader's and Writer's Notebook* to identify the characteristics of an animal fantasy.

Text-Based Comprehension

Introduce Main Selection

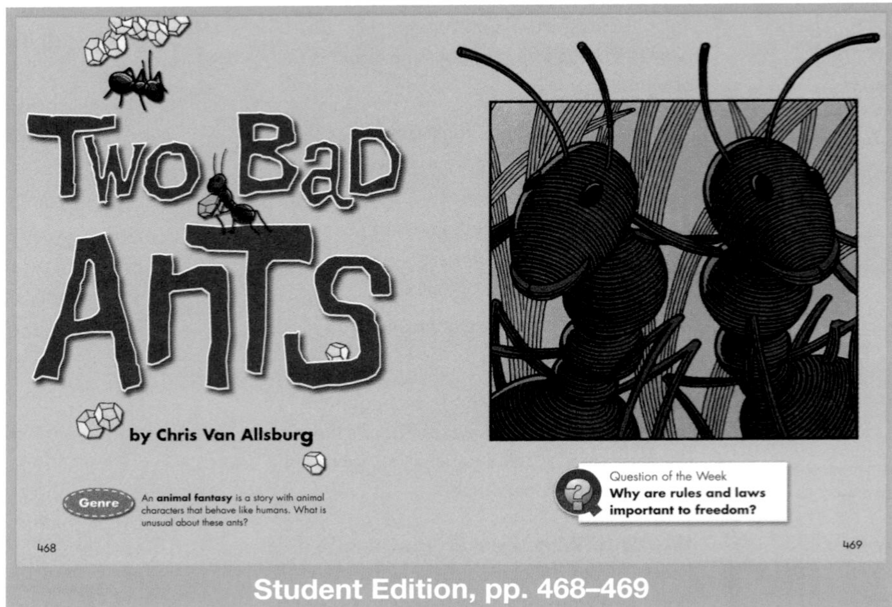

Student Edition, pp. 468–469

GENRE Explain that an **animal fantasy** has characters that are not people but are *personified* animals. They talk or live in homes like ours, have feelings like we do, or lead lives like we do. Explain that an animal fantasy is a form of fiction with a beginning, middle, and end. Tell students that an animal fantasy also has a plot and characters.

PREVIEW AND PREDICT Have students preview the title and illustrations to predict what they think the story will be about. Remind them that animals with human characteristics are a key feature of animal fantasies.

PURPOSE By analyzing *Two Bad Ants,* an animal fantasy, students will gain knowledge of the importance of rules and laws.

Access Main Selection

READER AND TASK SUGGESTIONS	
Preparing to Read the Text	**Leveled Tasks**
• Review the strategy of using word structure and prefixes and suffixes to determine word meaning. • Discuss how authors often make animals seem like humans in animal fantasies. • Remind students that as they encounter unfamiliar words, they should adjust their reading rate to ensure understanding.	• **Theme and Knowledge Demands** If students have difficulty understanding the story, have them imagine themselves as tiny people experiencing the adventures that the ants are experiencing for the first time. • **Language Conventionality and Clarity** The sentences and vocabulary may cause a problem for some students. Remind them to search for context and picture clues to help them understand difficult concepts.

See Text Complexity Measures for *Two Bad Ants* on the tab at the beginning of this week.

READ Tell students that today they will read *Two Bad Ants* for the first time. Use the Read for Understanding routine.

Routine Read for Understanding

Deepen understanding by reading the selection multiple times.

1. **First Read**—If students need support, then use the **Access Text** notes to help them clarify understanding.
2. **Second Read**—Use the **Close Reading** notes to help students draw knowledge from the text.

Day 2 SMALL GROUP TIME • Differentiate Comprehension, p. SG•49

OL On-Level
- **Practice** Selection Vocabulary
- **Read** *Two Bad Ants*

SI Strategic Intervention
- **Reteach** Selection Vocabulary
- **Read** *Two Bad Ants*

A Advanced
- **Extend** Selection Vocabulary
- **Read** *Two Bad Ants*
- **Investigate** Inquiry Project

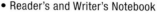

eSTREET INTERACTIVE
www.ReadingStreet.com

Pearson eText
- Student Edition

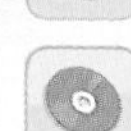

AudioText CD

Teacher Resources
- Reader's and Writer's Notebook

Background Building Audio CD

Access for All

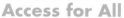

A Advanced

Have students think of other animal fantasies that they know. Ask them to recall the themes or plots of those stories.

Build Background Take a picture walk to frontload the selection, then review the selection summary (*ELL Handbook,* p. 199). Use the Retelling Cards to provide visual support for the summary.

If... students need more scaffolding and practice with the **Comprehension Skill,** **then...** use the activities on p. DI•96 in the Teacher Resources section on SuccessNet.

1ST READ

Access Text
If students need help, then...

PLOT Summarize the plot's main event on pp. 470–471. (The ants went on a trip because the queen wanted them to find more crystals for her.)

Think Aloud **MODEL** I know that the ants go on a long and dangerous journey to make the queen happy. This is important to the plot. I know the plot is a series of organized events that centers on a problem. So I know that the most important events of the story are related to the plot.

The news traveled swiftly through the tunnels of the ant world. A scout had returned with a remarkable discovery—a beautiful sparkling crystal. When the scout presented the crystal to the ant queen, she took a small bite, then quickly ate the entire thing.

She deemed it the most delicious food she had ever tasted. Nothing could make her happier than to have more, much more. The ants understood. They were eager to gather more crystals because the queen was the mother of them all. Her happiness made the whole ant nest a happy place.

470

Student Edition, p. 470

2ND READ

Close Reading

ANALYSIS What keeps the ants' nest running smoothly and makes it a great place for the ants to live? (the queen's happiness; working together)

EVALUATION • TEXT EVIDENCE How do you know the story is a fantasy story and not a realistic story? Support your answer with evidence from the text. (The characters of the story are ants, so this is an animal fantasy. The ants think and act like people when they show they are concerned about their queen's happiness.)

ON THEIR OWN Have students reread the last two sentences on p. 470 and discuss with a partner how the plot's main events so far might influence the future of the ants' lives. For additional practice, use *Let's Practice It!* p. 394 on the *Teacher Resources DVD-ROM*.

It was late in the day when they departed. Long shadows stretched over the entrance to the ant kingdom. One by one the insects climbed out, following the scout, who had made it clear—there were many crystals where the first had been found, but the journey was long and dangerous.

471

Student Edition, p. 471

INFERENCE • TEXT EVIDENCE Where do you think the problem of the story will arise? What evidence from the text makes you think so? (The problem will arise during the ants' journey. The text says that the journey is "long and dangerous," so that makes me think that something will happen.)

Common Core State Standards

Literature 1. Ask and answer questions to demonstrate understanding of a text, referring explicitly to the text as the basis for the answers.

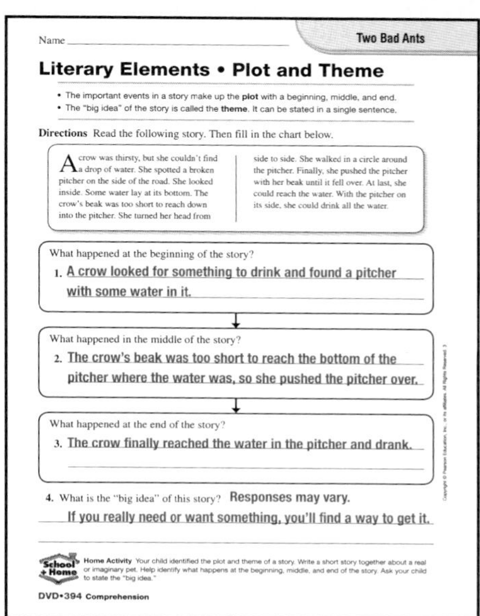

Name ______ Two Bad Ants

Literary Elements • Plot and Theme

- The important events in a story make up the **plot** with a beginning, middle, and end.
- The "big idea" of the story is called the **theme**. It can be stated in a single sentence.

Directions Read the following story. Then fill in the chart below.

A crow was thirsty, but she couldn't find a drop of water. She spotted a broken pitcher on the side of the road. She looked inside. Some water lay at its bottom. The crow's beak was too short to reach down into the pitcher. She turned her head from side to side. She walked in a circle around the pitcher. Finally, she pushed the pitcher with her beak until it fell over. At last, she could reach the water. With the pitcher on its side, she could drink all the water.

What happened at the beginning of the story?

1. A crow looked for something to drink and found a pitcher with some water in it.

What happened in the middle of the story?

2. The crow's beak was too short to reach the bottom of the pitcher where the water was, so she pushed the pitcher over.

What happened at the end of the story?

3. The crow finally reached the water in the pitcher and drank.

4. What is the "big idea" of this story? Responses may vary. If you really need or want something, you'll find a way to get it.

School + Home **Home Activity** Your child identified the plot and theme of a story. Write a short story together about a real or imaginary pet. Help identify what happens at the beginning, middle, and end of the story. Ask your child to state the "big idea."

DVD•394 Comprehension

Let's Practice It! TR DVD•394

Access for All

SI Strategic Intervention

Have students discuss what the crystal has to do with the plot of the story so far. Have students discuss the possibility of *not* having a crystal in the story. How different would the story be?

Access Content Remind students about the size of ants and how long it would take them to make a trip of any kind. Point out that a trip that we would consider short and easy is probably very long and dangerous for an ant.

1ST READ

Access Text If students need help, then...

STORY STRUCTURE Remind students that stories have a structure. The beginning sets up the story, the middle contains the problem, and the end shows how the problem was resolved. What happens at the beginning of this story that sets up what is to follow? (The ants leave their colony to find crystals for the queen.)

Think Aloud **MODEL** I know that in the beginning of The *Three Little Pigs,* the pigs had to make homes for themselves. In the middle, they each built a home, but a wolf tried to blow it down. In the end, only one pig was able to keep the wolf away.

They marched into the woods that surrounded their underground home. Dusk turned to twilight, twilight to night. The path they followed twisted and turned, every bend leading them deeper into the dark forest.

472

Student Edition, p. 472

2ND READ

Close Reading

ANALYSIS The ants will face some kind of problem in the story. How do you know that the problem has not arisen yet? (The story's title is *Two Bad Ants,* and the ants are still in a large group. The problem hasn't happened yet because the focus has to be on two ants, not on all of them.)

ANALYSIS Look back through the illustrations in this story. How can they help you summarize the plot's main events? (They show the ant bringing the crystal, the queen tasting the crystal, the line of ants leaving the hole, and the ants traveling through the woods.)

ON THEIR OWN Have students read pp. 472–473 and discuss how events in the beginning of the story continue to prepare the reader for a problem.

More than once the line of ants stopped and anxiously listened for the sounds of hungry spiders. But all they heard was the call of crickets echoing through the woods like distant thunder.

Dew formed on the leaves above. Without warning, huge cold drops fell on the marching ants. A firefly passed overhead that, for an instant, lit up the woods with a blinding flash of blue-green light.

473

Student Edition, p. 473

ANALYSIS • TEXT EVIDENCE Reread page 473. How does the imagery emphasize the size of the ants? (Tiny drops of dew that we would barely feel are "huge cold drops" to the ants, and the brief light of a firefly is a "blinding flash.")

Common Core State Standards

Literature 1. Ask and answer questions to demonstrate understanding of a text, referring explicitly to the text as the basis for the answers. **Literature 4.** Determine the meaning of words and phrases as they are used in a text, distinguishing literal from nonliteral language. **Literature 5.** Refer to parts of stories, dramas, and poems when writing or speaking about a text, using terms such as *chapter, scene,* and *stanza;* describe how each successive part builds on earlier sections. **Literature 7.** Explain how specific aspects of a text's illustrations contribute to what is conveyed by the words in a story (e.g., create mood, emphasize aspects of a character or setting). **Also Literature 3.**

Access for All

Strategic Intervention

Reread pp. 472–473 and discuss how the ants might be feeling and what impact this might have on the rest of the story.

Advanced

Ask students to talk about how the story might be different if it were not an animal fantasy. Would this story be possible if the characters were human? Why or why not? Have students discuss how the same theme might be covered in a story about humans.

Vocabulary Ask students to point out words that they do not understand. When possible, provide students with visual support for the word, or give synonyms or antonyms to clarify meaning.

1ST READ

Access Text If students need help, then...

Review CAUSE AND EFFECT Explain that on p. 474, the ants continued to climb no matter what because they had to get crystals for the queen. Ask students which is the cause and which is the effect.

Think Aloud **MODEL** I think about why the ants were climbing the wall, and I remember that they were on a mission to find crystals for the queen. That must be the cause because they wouldn't climb the wall at all if they didn't have a reason. So the effect is that they kept going no matter what.

At the edge of the forest stood a mountain. The ants looked up and could not see its peak. It seemed to reach right to the heavens. But they did not stop. Up the side they climbed, higher and higher.

The wind whistled through the cracks of the mountain's face. The ants could feel its force bending their delicate antennae. Their legs grew weak as they struggled upward. At last they reached a ledge and crawled through a narrow tunnel.

474

Student Edition, p. 474

2ND READ

Close Reading

SYNTHESIS • TEXT EVIDENCE What do you think the theme of the story is so far? What evidence from the text makes you think so? (The theme is that it's good to do things to please those you care about. The ants have gone on a journey far from their home. If they didn't care about the queen, they wouldn't have gone.)

ON THEIR OWN Have students find another example of cause and effect. For additional practice, use *Let's Practice It!* p. 395 on the *Teacher Resources DVD-ROM*.

When the ants came out of the tunnel they found themselves in a strange world. Smells they had known all their lives, smells of dirt and grass and rotting plants, had vanished. There was no more wind and, most puzzling of all, it seemed that the sky was gone.

They crossed smooth shiny surfaces, then followed the scout up a glassy, curved wall. They had reached their goal. From the top of the wall they looked below to a sea of crystals. One by one the ants climbed down into the sparkling treasure.

475

Student Edition, p. 475

INFERENCE On page 475, why did the ants think "that the sky was gone"? (They were inside a home, so all they could see above them was the room's ceiling.)

Common Core State Standards

Literature 1. Ask and answer questions to demonstrate understanding of a text, referring explicitly to the text as the basis for the answers. **Literature 3.** Describe characters in a story (e.g., their traits, motivations, or feelings) and explain how their actions contribute to the sequence of events. **Also Literature 2.**

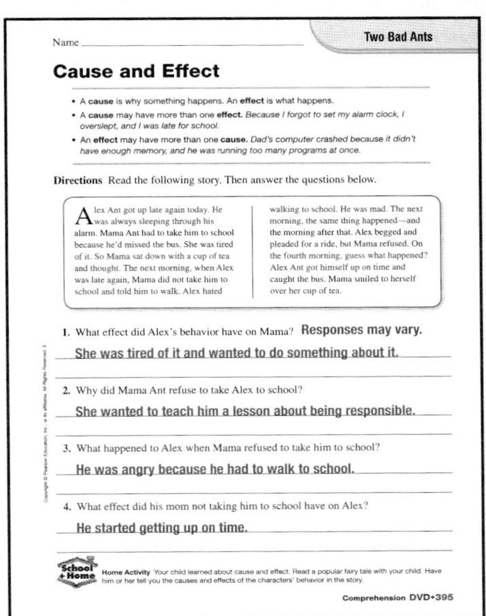

Name ________ Two Bad Ants

Cause and Effect

- A **cause** is why something happens. An **effect** is what happens.
- A **cause** may have more than one **effect**. *Because I forgot to set my alarm clock, I overslept, and I was late for school.*
- An **effect** may have more than one **cause**. *Dad's computer crashed because it didn't have enough memory, and he was running too many programs at once.*

Directions Read the following story. Then answer the questions below.

Alex Ant got up late again today. He was always sleeping through his alarm. Mama Ant had to take him to school because he'd missed the bus. She was tired of it. So Mama sat down with a cup of tea and thought. The next morning, when Alex was late again, Mama did not take him to school and told him to walk. Alex hated walking to school. He was mad. The next morning, the same thing happened—and the morning after that. Alex begged and pleaded for a ride, but Mama refused. On the fourth morning, guess what happened? Alex Ant got himself up on time and caught the bus. Mama smiled to herself over her cup of tea.

1. What effect did Alex's behavior have on Mama? **Responses may vary.**
 She was tired of it and wanted to do something about it.
2. Why did Mama Ant refuse to take Alex to school?
 She wanted to teach him a lesson about being responsible.
3. What happened to Alex when Mama refused to take him to school?
 He was angry because he had to walk to school.
4. What effect did his mom not taking him to school have on Alex?
 He started getting up on time.

Home Activity Your child learned about cause and effect. Read a popular fairy tale with your child. Have him or her tell you the causes and effects of the characters' behavior in the story.

Comprehension DVD•395

Let's Practice It! TR DVD•395

Access for All

A Advanced

Have pairs of students talk about what might happen next. Ask them to use what they know about how the ants feel about the queen and their knowledge of story structure to make a prediction about what happens.

Metaphor Point out the phrase "a sea of crystals" on p. 475. The phrase is called a *metaphor,* which is a figure of speech that is used to compare things. In this case, it is used to tell us how vast the amount of crystals looked to the tiny ants.

Plot Have students reread p. 474 and look at the illustration. Make sure students know that the "mountain" is actually the outside wall of a building. Point out that the ants climbing the wall is an event that contributes to the plot of the story.

1ST READ

Access Text If students need help, then...

PREFIXES AND SUFFIXES *un-, dis-, -ful* Remind students that the prefixes *un-* and *dis-* mean "not" or "the opposite of" and the suffix *-ful* means "full of." Point to *unnatural* on p. 476. Ask students what the word means.

Think Aloud **MODEL** I know that *un-* and *dis-* are prefixes. When I see these prefixes or the suffix *-ful*, I know they change the meaning of the whole word, so I look at the root and the prefix or suffix. I know that *helpful (help + ful)* means "full of help."

ON THEIR OWN Have students look for more examples of words with prefixes and suffixes and identify the affixes, base words, and meanings. For additional practice, use *Reader's and Writer's Notebook,* p. 425.

Quickly they each chose a crystal, then turned to start the journey home. There was something about this unnatural place that made the ants nervous. In fact they left in such a hurry that none of them noticed the two small ants who stayed behind.

"Why go back?" one asked the other. "This place may not feel like home, but look at all these crystals."

"You're right," said the other. "We can stay here and eat this tasty treasure every day, forever." So the two ants ate crystal after crystal until they were too full to move, and fell asleep.

476

Student Edition, p. 476

2ND READ

Close Reading

INFERENCE • TEXT EVIDENCE What clues tell you where the ants are? (They are in a sugar bowl—part of the word shows in the illustration on p. 476. This is confirmed when the two ants are scooped up and poured into a boiling brown lake that is probably coffee.)

ANALYSIS • TEXT EVIDENCE Why did the two ants decide not to leave? What evidence from the text makes you think so? (They wanted the rest of the crystals all to themselves. One ant said, "We can stay here and eat this tasty treat every day, forever.")

CHECK PREDICTIONS Have students look back at the predictions they made earlier and discuss whether they were accurate. Then have students preview the rest of the selection and either adjust their predictions accordingly or make new predictions.

If you want to teach this selection in two sessions, stop here.

If you want to continue reading this selection, turn to p. 478–479.

Daylight came. The sleeping ants were unaware of changes taking place in their new-found home. A giant silver scoop hovered above them, then plunged deep into the crystals. It shoveled up both ants and crystals and carried them high into the air.

The ants were wide awake when the scoop turned, dropping them from a frightening height. They tumbled through space in a shower of crystals and fell into a boiling brown lake.

477

Student Edition, p. 477

EVALUATION What part of the story are pages 476–477, and how is this part different from the pages you have already read? (These pages are part of the middle of the story. They are different from the beginning because this is where the problem arises that the characters must overcome.)

Common Core State Standards

Literature 1. Ask and answer questions to demonstrate understanding of a text, referring explicitly to the text as the basis for the answers. **Literature 3.** Describe characters in a story (e.g., their traits, motivations, or feelings) and explain how their actions contribute to the sequence of events. **Foundational Skills 3.a.** Identify and know the meaning of the most common prefixes and derivational suffixes. **Also Literature 5., 7., 10., Language 4.b.**

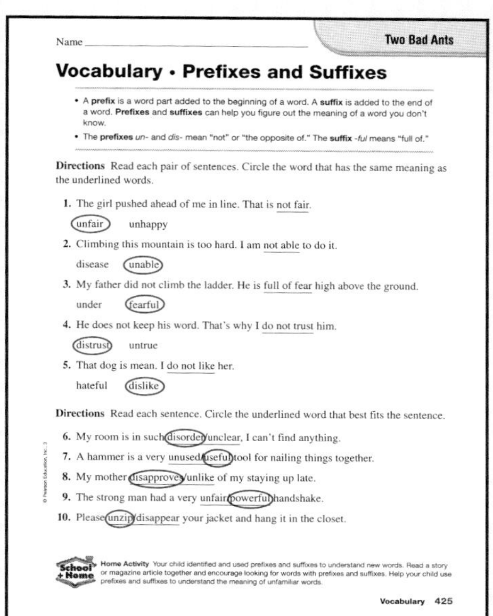

Name ____________ Two Bad Ants

Vocabulary • Prefixes and Suffixes

- A **prefix** is a word part added to the beginning of a word. A **suffix** is added to the end of a word. **Prefixes** and **suffixes** can help you figure out the meaning of a word you don't know.
- The **prefixes** *un-* and *dis-* mean "not" or "the opposite of." The **suffix** *-ful* means "full of."

Directions Read each pair of sentences. Circle the word that has the same meaning as the underlined words.

1. The girl pushed ahead of me in line. That is not fair.
   unfair unhappy
2. Climbing this mountain is too hard. I am not able to do it.
   disease unable
3. My father did not climb the ladder. He is full of fear high above the ground.
   under fearful
4. He does not keep his word. That's why I do not trust him.
   distrust untrue
5. That dog is mean. I do not like her.
   hateful dislike

Directions Read each sentence. Circle the underlined word that best fits the sentence.

6. My room is in such disorder/unclear, I can't find anything.
7. A hammer is a very unused/useful tool for nailing things together.
8. My mother disapproves/unlike of my staying up late.
9. The strong man had a very unfair/powerful handshake.
10. Please unzip/disappear your jacket and hang it in the closet.

School + Home **Home Activity** Your child identified and used prefixes and suffixes to understand new words. Read a story or magazine article together and encourage looking for words with prefixes and suffixes. Help your child use prefixes and suffixes to understand the meaning of unfamiliar words.

Vocabulary 425

Reader's and Writer's Notebook, p. 425

Access for All

SI Strategic Intervention

Ask students to discuss how knowing what happens in the beginning and middle of a story will help them make accurate predictions about how a story ends.

A Advanced

Why do you think these two ants are called "bad ants"? Discuss what they did that might be considered *bad* to the other ants and whether being greedy will get them into trouble.

ELL

Story Structure Have students point to the illustration that shows that the ants' decision might be a bad one. Ask students to use their own words to tell why this is an important point in the story.

Common Core State Standards

Writing 7. Conduct short research projects that build knowledge about a topic. **Writing 8.** Recall information from experiences or gather information from print and digital sources; take brief notes on sources and sort evidence into provided categories. **Language 2.** Demonstrate command of the conventions of standard English capitalization, punctuation, and spelling when writing. **Language 2.f.** Use spelling patterns and generalizations (e.g., word families, position-based spellings, syllable patterns, ending rules, meaningful word parts) in writing words. **Also Language 2.b., 2.e.**

Bridge to Common Core

RESEARCH TO BUILD AND PRESENT KNOWLEDGE

On Day 2 of the weeklong research project, students gather relevant information based on their focused questions from Day 1. They consult digital sources, using keywords to locate relevant information, and take notes as they gather information. This process enables students to demonstrate an understanding of the subject under investigation. As students access online information, they should always note their sources for a Works Cited page.

Research and Inquiry

Step 2 Navigate/Search

TEACH Have students generate a research plan for gathering information about their topic. Have students search the Internet using their inquiry questions and keywords. They can use keywords such as *rules, laws, consequences,* or *freedom* to begin their search. Remind students to take notes when they gather information, and note the Web site or source where they found the information.

Think Aloud

MODEL When looking for information on who enforces rules and laws at school, I found: *Teachers and principals have a big responsibility enforcing school rules*. I will use keywords from this information, such as *school rules* to lead me to more specific information. One article I found using these keywords is *"Kids have more freedom when they follow school rules."*

GUIDE PRACTICE Have students continue their review of sources they have identified. Explain that they don't have to read every word to tell whether they will be useful. Encourage them to skim and scan sources at first to judge whether they have the kind of information they are looking for. Remind them that some sources will be more useful to them than others, and some may not be helpful at all.

ON THEIR OWN Have students work with a partner to summarize their research findings. Partners should make suggestions for new avenues of research.

Conventions

Commas

TEACH Write this sentence on the board: *The ants found coffee water and toast in the kitchen.* Did the ants find *coffee* and *water* or did they find *coffee water?* Adding commas after *coffee* and *water* makes the writing clearer and easier to understand. Remind students that commas are used to join sentences with a conjunction and to separate items in a series. They are also used in dates, addresses, and letter greetings and closings.

GUIDE PRACTICE Write these sentences on the board without commas. Have students add commas where needed.

We found fruit, snacks, and toys in our treat bags.

Greg moved to Toledo, Ohio, on December 3rd, 2005.

Dad painted the fence, while Mom painted the front door.

Have students look for and read aloud sentences with commas in *Two Bad Ants*. (p. 486: *This place may not feel like home, but look at all these crystals*.)

ON THEIR OWN For additional practice, use *Reader's and Writer's Notebook,* p. 422.

Spelling

Prefixes, Suffixes, and Endings

TEACH Remind students that some of their spelling words for this week have prefixes, such as *im-* and *in-*. Model spelling words with prefixes. The parts in *improper* are *im* and *proper*. First I spell the prefix. Write *im*. Then I spell the base word. Write *proper*. Then I spell *improper,* i-m-p-r-o-p-e-r.

GUIDE PRACTICE Have students write each spelling word and underline any prefixes.

ON THEIR OWN For additional practice, use *Reader's and Writer's Notebook,* p. 423.

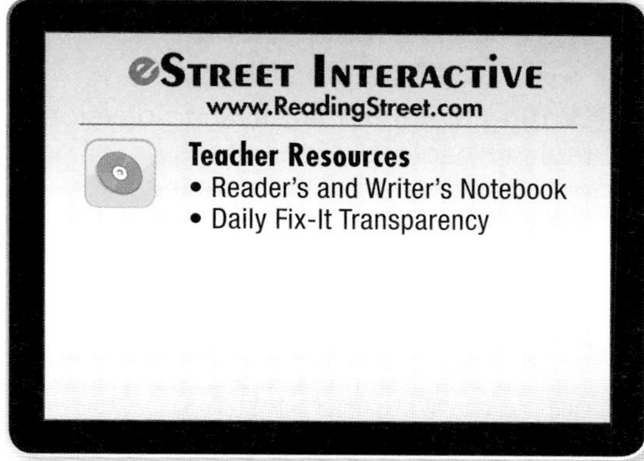

eStreet Interactive
www.ReadingStreet.com
Teacher Resources
• Reader's and Writer's Notebook
• Daily Fix-It Transparency

Daily Fix-It

3. Ants are remarkabel insects but sometimes they are pests. *(remarkable; insects,)*
4. They will go after the littlest crums in you're kitchen. *(crumbs; your)*

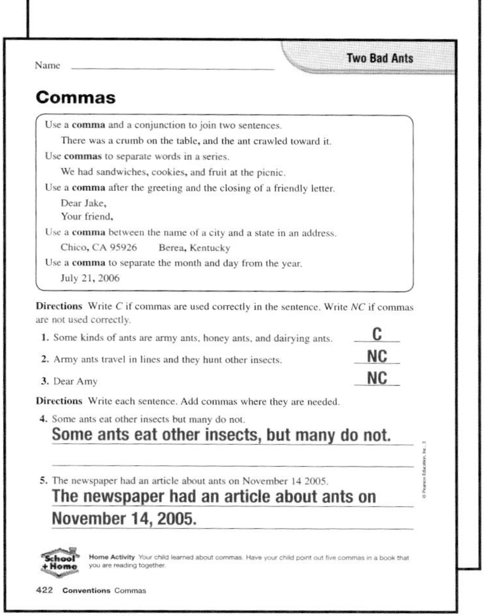

Name ______________ Two Bad Ants

Commas

Use a **comma** and a conjunction to join two sentences.
There was a crumb on the table, and the ant crawled toward it.
Use **commas** to separate words in a series.
We had sandwiches, cookies, and fruit at the picnic.
Use a **comma** after the greeting and the closing of a friendly letter.
Dear Jake,
Your friend,
Use a **comma** between the name of a city and a state in an address.
Chico, CA 95926 Berea, Kentucky
Use a **comma** to separate the month and day from the year.
July 21, 2006

Directions Write *C* if commas are used correctly in the sentence. Write *NC* if commas are not used correctly.

1. Some kinds of ants are army ants, honey ants, and dairying ants. **C**
2. Army ants travel in lines and they hunt other insects. **NC**
3. Dear Amy **NC**

Directions Write each sentence. Add commas where they are needed.

4. Some ants eat other insects but many do not.
Some ants eat other insects, but many do not.
5. The newspaper had an article about ants on November 14 2005.
The newspaper had an article about ants on November 14, 2005.

© Pearson Education, Inc. 3

School + Home **Home Activity** Your child learned about commas. Have your child point out five commas in a book that you are reading together.

422 **Conventions** Commas

Reader's and Writer's Notebook, pp. 422–423

Conventions To provide students with practice on commas, use the modified grammar lessons in the *ELL Handbook* and the Grammar Jammer online at: www.ReadingStreet.com.

Spelling: Prefixes Clarify the pronunciation and meaning of each spelling word. Demonstrate the meanings of *reappeared, uncomfortable, unprepared,* and *misbehaving* with motions and facial expressions.

Common Core State Standards

Writing 3. Write narratives to develop real or imagined experiences or events using effective technique, descriptive details, and clear event sequences. **Writing 3.a.** Establish a situation and introduce a narrator and/or characters; organize an event sequence that unfolds naturally. **Writing 4.** With guidance and support from adults, produce writing in which the development and organization are appropriate to task and purpose.

Comic Book

Writing Trait: Organization

INTRODUCE THE PROMPT Remind students that the selection, *Two Bad Ants,* features characters that they will write about in their comic books. Review the key features of a comic book. Remind students that they should think about these features as they plan their writing. Then explain that they will begin the writing process for a comic book today. Read aloud the writing prompt.

Writing Prompt

Write a short comic book telling of a further adventure of these two ants.

SELECT A TOPIC

To help select main events for our comic book, let's make a T-chart. We can list events that happened in *Two Bad Ants* in the first column. Then we can list further events that we might like to write about in the second column. Brainstorm with students events from the Main Selection. Add students' ideas to the chart. Then have students list ideas for the ants' further adventures in the second column.

Once you have finished listing possible events, select events that will best fit together to make a story and that can be told through illustrations and dialogue. Next, you will write and develop these events in a story sequence chart.

Main events in *Two Bad Ants*	Main event ideas for my comic book
Ants go to the house with the crystals.	Ants go to the "beach," a backyard sandlot.
Ants fall asleep in a sugar bowl.	Ants go ice-skating on an ice cube.
Ants fall into a cup of coffee.	Ants go on a vacation at the house.
	Ants write a postcard to their friends.

Corrective feedback Ask each student who is having difficulty to close his or her eyes and imagine being ant-sized and walking around a big home. Have the student tell what kinds of household items might appear fun, scary, or exciting to further develop the setting. Encourage the student to gather ideas based on your discussion.

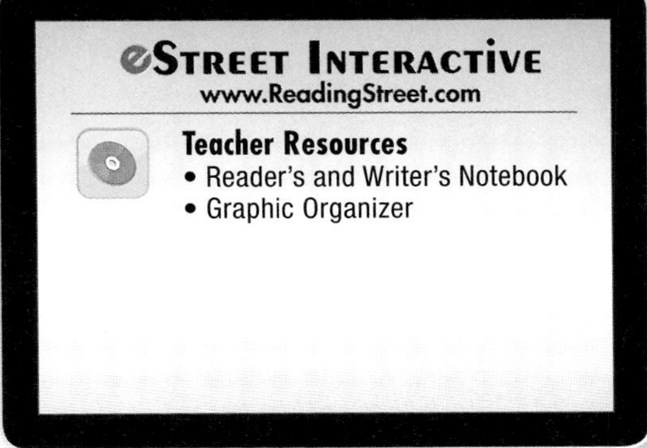

Mini-Lesson Develop a Story Sequence

- A story sequence chart helps you plan the layout for a comic book. I've decided to write about the ants on winter vacation. I'll call my comic book *Ants on Holiday*. Display a story sequence chart. Fill in the title, character, and setting boxes on the chart. Next I'll write the series of events.
- In Box 1, I'll write *The ants arrive at the house. A window shows it is snowing outside.* In Box 2, I'll write *The ants ski down a hill of sugar. They use matchsticks for skis.*
- In Box 3, I'll write *The ants go ice-skating. The rink is made up of just one ice cube.* In Box 4, I'll write *The ants write a postcard about their vacation.*

Have students begin their own story sequence chart using the form on p. 424 of their *Reader's and Writer's Notebook*.

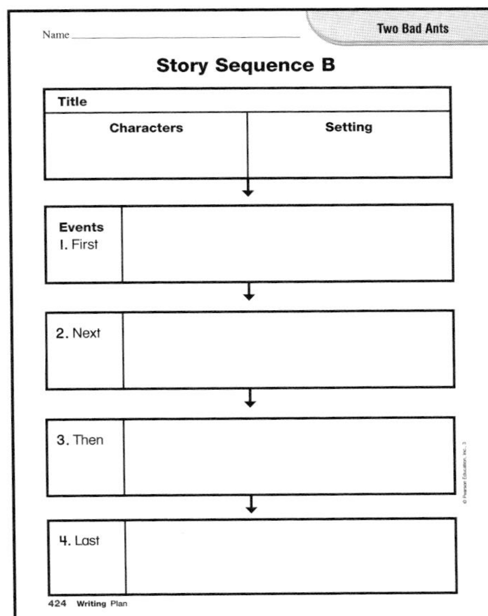
Name ____________ Two Bad Ants

Story Sequence B

Title

Characters | Setting

Events
1. First

2. Next

3. Then

4. Last

424 Writing Plan

Reader's and Writer's Notebook, p. 424

Routine Quick Write for Fluency

Team Talk

1. **Talk** Have pairs discuss how the story sequence chart helped them.
2. **Write** Each student writes a paragraph about the setting.
3. **Share** Students read their writing to a partner.

Routines Flip Chart

Wrap Up Your Day!

- ✓ **Content Knowledge** What did you learn about rules and laws and how they are important to freedom?
- ✓ **Text-Based Comprehension** What event causes the ants to set out on their journey?

Preview DAY 3

Tell students that tomorrow they will read more about how the ants make a decision that has difficult consequences.

DAY 3 at a Glance

Content Knowledge
Oral Vocabulary

Phonics/Word Analysis
Prefixes *im-*, *in-*

Text-Based Comprehension
Literary Elements: Plot and Theme
Story Structure

Fluency
Rate

Research and Study Skills
Electronic Text

Research and Inquiry
Analyze Information

Conventions
Commas

Spelling
Prefixes, Suffixes, and Endings

Writing
Comic Book

Materials

- Student Edition
- Reader's and Writer's Notebook
- Decodable Reader

Common Core State Standards

Speaking/Listening 1. Engage effectively in a range of collaborative discussions (one-on-one, in groups, and teacher-led) with diverse partners on grade 3 topics and texts, building on others' ideas and expressing their own clearly. **Language 6.** Acquire and use accurately grade-appropriate conversational, general academic, and domain-specific words and phrases, including those that signal spatial and temporal relationships (e.g., *After dinner that night we went looking for them*).

Content Knowledge

Rules and Laws Are Important to Freedom

EXPAND THE CONCEPT Remind students of the weekly concept question, *Why are rules and laws important to freedom?* Discuss how the question relates to *Two Bad Ants*. Encourage students to think about why the ants chose to break the rules.

Build Oral Language

TALK ABOUT SENTENCES AND WORDS Reread this sentence from Student Edition p. 471.

One by one the insects climbed out, following the scout, who had made it clear—there were many crystals where the first had been found, but the journey was long and dangerous.

- What is a *scout*? (someone who goes ahead of the main group to gather information on what lies ahead)
- What is a *journey*? (a long trip)
- If the journey is a dangerous one, why would it be important to follow the rules? (Following the rules will help keep the ants safe.)

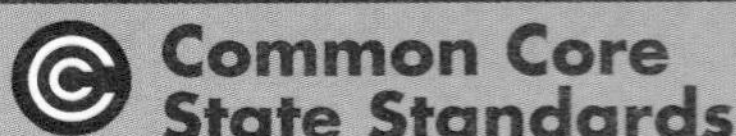

Have students work with a partner to create one sentence for each idea in the original sentence. Use the following sentence frames.

The ants climbed out _______.

The ants followed the _______.

The scout had made it clear that _______.

But the _______ was long and dangerous.

Build Oral Vocabulary

Amazing Words Robust Vocabulary Routine

1. **Introduce** Write the Amazing Word *guilt* on the board. Have students say it with you. In *Two Bad Ants,* the ants began to feel *guilt* about their decision to live away from their colony and collect crystals for themselves. Have students determine a definition of *guilt*. (*Guilt* means a feeling of shame and sadness after having done something.)

2. **Demonstrate** Have students answer questions to demonstrate understanding. When might people feel *guilt* after doing something? (A person might feel guilt after stealing, lying, or not following the rules.)

3. **Apply** Have students apply their understanding. Why do people feel *guilt* when they break a rule?

4. **Display the Word** Students can decode the sounds in *guilt* and blend them.

See p. OV•4 to teach *encounter.*

Routines Flip Chart

ADD TO THE CONCEPT MAP Discuss the Amazing Words *citizen* and *fascinate.* Add these words to the concept map. Use the following questions to develop students' understanding of the concept. Add words generated in the discussion to the concept map.

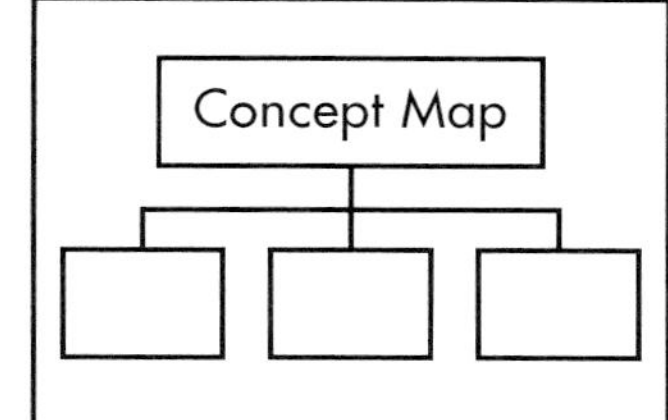

- Would you consider the two ants to be good *citizens* of their community?
- Why does the sugar *fascinate* the ants?

Amazing Words

obey	fascinate
responsibility	guilt
consequence	encounter
permission	forbid
citizen	eerie

Expand Vocabulary Use the Day 3 instruction on ELL Poster 29 to help students expand vocabulary.

Common Core State Standards

Foundational Skills 3.a. Identify and know the meaning of the most common prefixes and derivational suffixes. **Language 4.b.** Determine the meaning of the new word formed when a known affix is added to a known word (e.g., *agreeable/disagreeable, comfortable/uncomfortable, care/careless, heat/preheat*).

Word Analysis

Prefixes *im-, in-*

MODEL WORD SORTING Write *im-* and *in-* as heads on a two-column chart. Now we are going to sort words. We'll put words with the prefix *im-* in the first column. Words with the prefix *in-* will go in the second column. I will start. Write *incapable* and model how to read it, using the Teach/Model section on p. 462a. *Incapable* is made up of the prefix *in-* and the base word *capable,* so I will write *incapable* in the second column. Model reading *immaterial* and *insanity* in the same way.

GUIDE PRACTICE Use the practice words from the activity on p. 466c for the word sort. Point to a word. Have students read the word, identify its parts, and tell where it should be written on the chart.

Corrective feedback For corrective feedback, model reading the prefix and then the base word.

im-	in-
immaterial	incapable
impass	insanity
immortal	insoluble
improbable	inedible
impractical	incapable
	invisible

Fluent Word Reading

MODEL Write *indirect*. I know the prefix *in-*. I know the base word *direct*. I put them together and read the word *indirect*.

GUIDE PRACTICE Write the words below. Look for word parts you know. When I point to the word, we'll read it together. Allow one second per word part-previewing time for the first reading.

incorrect **impolite** **incomplete** **impass** **indefinite** **immobile**

ON THEIR OWN Have students read the list above three or four times until they can read one word per second.

Decodable Passage 29B

If students need help, then...

Read *Sadie's Size*

READ WORDS IN ISOLATION Have students turn to p. 165 in *Decodable Practice Readers 3.2* and find the first list of words. Each word in this list has a prefix. Let's read these words. Be sure that students identify the prefix in each word.

Next, have students read the high-frequency words.

PREVIEW Have students read the title and preview the story. Tell them that they will read words with the prefixes *im-* and *in-*.

READ WORDS IN CONTEXT Chorally read the story along with students. Have students identify words in the story that have the prefixes *im-* and *in-*. Make sure that students are monitoring their accuracy when they decode words.

Team Talk Pair students and have them take turns reading the story aloud to each other. Monitor students as they read to check for proper pronunciation and appropriate pacing.

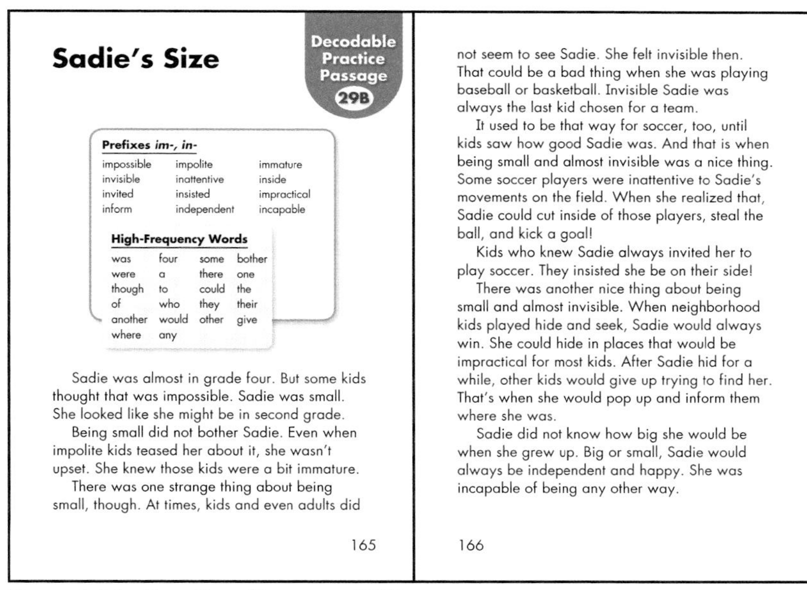

Sadie's Size

Decodable Practice Passage 29B

Prefixes *im-*, *in-*

impossible	impolite	immature
invisible	inattentive	inside
invited	insisted	impractical
inform	independent	incapable

High-Frequency Words

was	four	some	bother
were	a	there	one
though	to	could	the
of	who	they	their
another	would	other	give
where	any		

Sadie was almost in grade four. But some kids thought that was impossible. Sadie was small. She looked like she might be in second grade.

Being small did not bother Sadie. Even when impolite kids teased her about it, she wasn't upset. She knew those kids were a bit immature.

There was one strange thing about being small, though. At times, kids and even adults did not seem to see Sadie. She felt invisible then. That could be a bad thing when she was playing baseball or basketball. Invisible Sadie was always the last kid chosen for a team.

It used to be that way for soccer, too, until kids saw how good Sadie was. And that is when being small and almost invisible was a nice thing. Some soccer players were inattentive to Sadie's movements on the field. When she realized that, Sadie could cut inside of those players, steal the ball, and kick a goal!

Kids who knew Sadie always invited her to play soccer. They insisted she be on their side!

There was another nice thing about being small and almost invisible. When neighborhood kids played hide and seek, Sadie would always win. She could hide in places that would be impractical for most kids. After Sadie hid for a while, other kids would give up trying to find her. That's when she would pop up and inform them where she was.

Sadie did not know how big she would be when she grew up. Big or small, Sadie would always be independent and happy. She was incapable of being any other way.

165 166

Decodable Practice Passage 29B

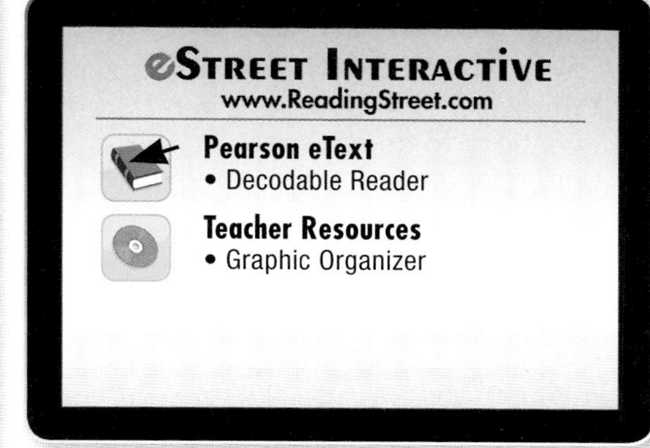

eStreet Interactive
www.ReadingStreet.com
Pearson eText
• Decodable Reader
Teacher Resources
• Graphic Organizer

Access for All

Advanced

Have students write sentences using a word from the chart in each sentence. The meaning of the word should be apparent from the context of the sentence. For example: *The rock was immobile because it was too heavy to move.*

Text-Based Comprehension

Check Understanding

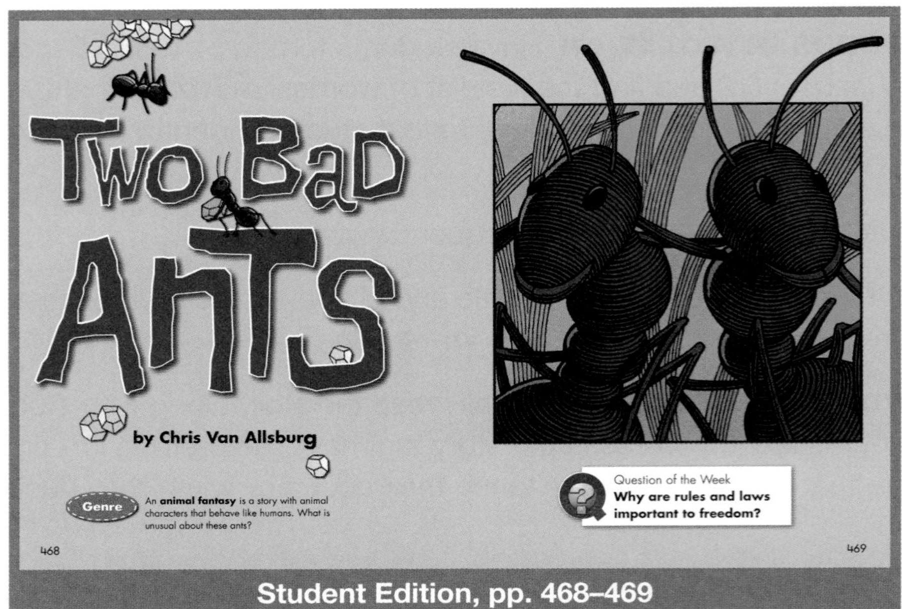

Student Edition, pp. 468–469

If... you chose to read *Two Bad Ants* in two parts,
then... use the following questions to monitor students' understanding of pp. 468–477 of the selection. Encourage students to cite evidence from the text.

ANALYSIS Why do you think the author chose to have animal characters with human characteristics to tell the story? (He thought people might be entertained by animal characters and that we would be able to identify with their human traits.)

EVALUATION How does the theme of the story teach the reader a lesson? Find a sentence that supports this. (The theme teaches the reader that it does not help to be greedy. A sentence on p. 476 that supports this theme is "There was something about this unnatural place that made the ants nervous." This makes me think the ants are wrong for choosing to stay there.)

RETELL Have students retell the part of *Two Bad Ants* in which the problem, or conflict, arises, referring to details in the text. Encourage students to use the text features in their retellings.

Corrective feedback	**If...** students leave out important details, **then...** have students look back through the illustrations in the selection.

READ Use the **Access Text** and **Close Reading** notes to finish reading *Two Bad Ants*.

Common Core State Standards

Literature 1. Ask and answer questions to demonstrate understanding of a text, referring explicitly to the text as the basis for the answers. **Literature 2.** Recount stories, including fables, folktales, and myths from diverse cultures; determine the central message, lesson, or moral and explain how it is conveyed through key details in the text. **Speaking/Listening 4.** Report on a topic or text, tell a story, or recount an experience with appropriate facts and relevant, descriptive details, speaking clearly at an understandable pace.

Strategy Response Log

Have students add story elements for *Two Bad Ants* to the plot map on p. 35 in the *Reader's and Writer's Notebook*.

If... you followed the Read for Understanding routine below,
then... ask students to retell the selection before you reread *Two Bad Ants*.

RETELL Have students retell the part of *Two Bad Ants* in which the problem, or conflict, arises, referring to details in the text. Encourage students to use the text features in their retellings.

Corrective feedback	**If...** students leave out important details, **then...** have them look back through the illustrations in the selection.

READ Return to p. 468–469 and use the **2nd Read/Close Reading** notes to reread *Two Bad Ants*.

Read Main Selection

Routine Read for Understanding

Deepen understanding by reading the selection multiple times.

1. **First Read**—If students need support, then use the **Access Text** notes to help them clarify understanding.
2. **Second Read**—Use the **Close Reading** notes to help students draw knowledge from the text.

Day 3 SMALL GROUP TIME • Differentiate Close Reading, p. SG•49

OL On-Level	SI Strategic Intervention	A Advanced
• **Reread** to Develop Vocabulary • **Read** *Two Bad Ants*	• **Reread** to Develop Vocabulary • **Read** *Two Bad Ants*	• **Reread** to Extend Vocabulary • **Read** *Two Bad Ants* • **Investigate** Inquiry Project

eSTREET INTERACTIVE
www.ReadingStreet.com

Pearson eText
• Student Edition

AudioText CD

Teacher Resources
• Reader's and Writer's Notebook

Check Retelling To support retelling, review the multilingual summary for *Two Bad Ants* with the appropriate Retelling Cards to scaffold understanding.

If... students need more scaffolding and practice with the **Main Selection,**
then... use the activities on p. DI•97 in the Teacher Resources section on SuccessNet.

1ST READ

Access Text If students need help, then...

PLOT AND THEME Paraphrase the theme of these pages and give some supporting details. (There are consequences for being greedy. The ants end up in danger in someone's coffee cup.)

Think Aloud **MODEL** The theme is the overall lesson or "big idea" of a story. To find the theme, I will ask myself, "What does the author want me to learn?" I know that the answer is not right there in the text. I will paraphrase the theme by thinking about the plot.

Then the giant scoop stirred violently back and forth. Crushing waves fell over the ants. They paddled hard to keep their tiny heads above water. But the scoop kept spinning the hot brown liquid.

Around and around it went, creating a whirlpool that sucked the ants deeper and deeper. They both held their breath and finally bobbed to the surface, gasping for air and spitting mouthfuls of the terrible, bitter water.

478

Student Edition, p. 478

2ND READ

Close Reading

SYNTHESIS How do the events on pages 478–479 relate to the story's theme? (They give a good example of the risks of greedy behavior.)

INFERENCE At this point in the story, how do you think the ants are feeling about their decision to stay behind? Why do you think this? (They wish they hadn't decided to separate from the group and stay behind. They are worried and scared because they are drowning in coffee.)

ON THEIR OWN Have students use the pictures to discuss the point of view of the ants and the fact that they live in a smaller universe than people do. Have them discuss how this point of view affects the theme of the story.

Then the lake tilted and began to empty into a cave. The ants could hear the rushing water and felt themselves pulled toward the pitch-black hole. Suddenly the cave disappeared and the lake became calm. The ants swam to the shore and found that the lake had steep sides.

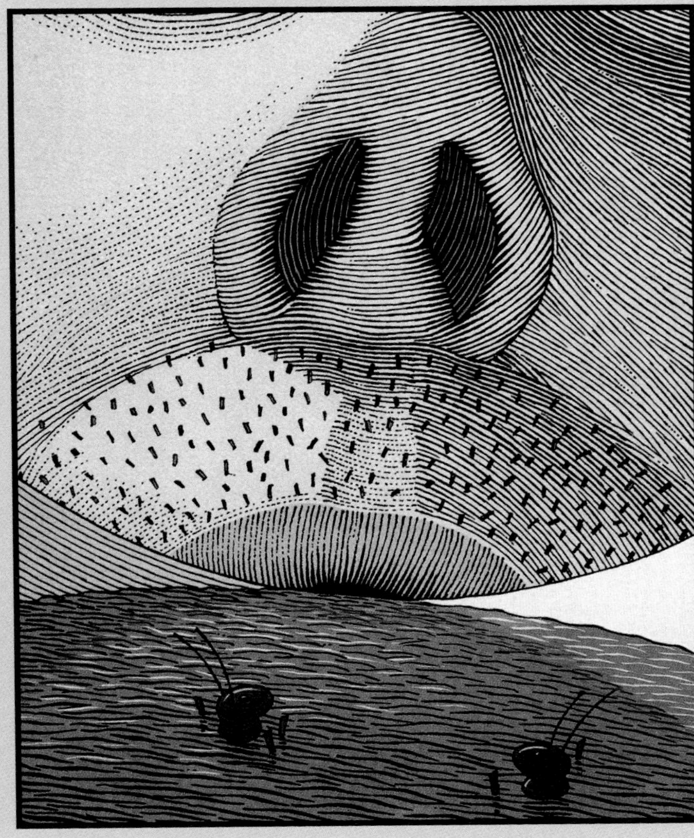

479

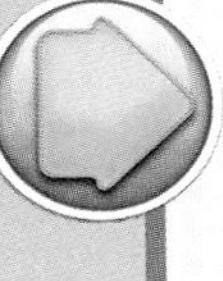

Student Edition, p. 479

ANALYSIS • TEXT EVIDENCE Read page 478. What words does the author use to emphasize the danger the ants are in? (The author uses words such as *violently*, *crushing*, *sucked*, and *gasping* to emphasize the danger.)

Common Core State Standards

Literature 1. Ask and answer questions to demonstrate understanding of a text, referring explicitly to the text as the basis for the answers. **Literature 2.** Recount stories, including fables, folktales, and myths from diverse cultures; determine the central message, lesson, or moral and explain how it is conveyed through key details in the text. **Literature 3.** Describe characters in a story (e.g., their traits, motivations, or feelings) and explain how their actions contribute to the sequence of events. **Literature 6.** Distinguish their own point of view from that of the narrator or those of the characters. **Also Literature 7.**

Access for All

SI Strategic Intervention

Ask students to describe the major events that occur on pp. 478–479. Have them discuss how these events help them understand the plot of the story.

Access Content As a group, identify what the brown liquid and scoop are on p. 478. Ask students to tell where they have seen each before and how they know what each is. Then ask them to talk about what is happening on p. 479 and if anything like that has ever happened to them.

1ST READ

Access Text If students need help, then…

STORY STRUCTURE How do we know that the events on pages 480–481 are still part of the middle and not part of the resolution? Summarize the main plot events on these two pages to see if they tell more of the conflict or the resolution.

Think Aloud **MODEL** When I read the words, I realize the ants are in danger again. They found a hiding place, but it became so hot that they were afraid they would be cooked. Then they were sent flying through the air. Clearly there are lots of problems and no solution yet.

They hurried down the walls that held back the lake. The frightened insects looked for a place to hide, worried that the giant scoop might shovel them up again. Close by they found a huge round disk with holes that could neatly hide them.

480

Student Edition, p. 480

2ND READ

Close Reading

SYNTHESIS • TEXT EVIDENCE Use evidence from the text to explain how the middle of the story is different from the beginning of the story. (The story begins with many ants going on a difficult trip, but there aren't any big problems, or conflicts. In the middle, two ants stay behind, and they run into a lot of trouble.)

EVALUATION Why do you think the author chose to put the characters in such dangerous situations? (It helps to support the theme by showing that the ants are getting into a lot of trouble because they were greedy.)

ON THEIR OWN Have students work in pairs to talk about how the events on pp. 480–481 relate to the structure of the story.

But as soon as they had climbed inside, their hiding place was lifted, tilted, and lowered into a dark space. When the ants climbed out of the holes, they were surrounded by a strange red glow. It seemed to them that every second the temperature was rising.

It soon became so unbearably hot that they thought they would soon be cooked. But suddenly the disk they were standing on rocketed upward, and the two hot ants went flying through the air.

481

Student Edition, p. 481

INFERENCE By the end of page 481, what might the two ants be thinking? Why do you think so? (They might think they could get badly hurt because they are very hot *and* flying.)

Common Core State Standards

Literature 1. Ask and answer questions to demonstrate understanding of a text, referring explicitly to the text as the basis for the answers. **Literature 3.** Describe characters in a story (e.g., their traits, motivations, or feelings) and explain how their actions contribute to the sequence of events. **Literature 5.** Refer to parts of stories, dramas, and poems when writing or speaking about a text, using terms such as *chapter, scene,* and *stanza;* describe how each successive part builds on earlier sections.

Inflectional Endings Point out one or two words that have inflectional ending *-ed* and explain that this ending means the action happened in the past. Ask students to find other examples of words with inflectional ending *-ed* on pp. 480–481.

1ST READ

Access Text If students need help, then...

Review CAUSE AND EFFECT Remind students that a cause is why something happens and an effect is what happens as a result. What caused the ants to fall down the waterfall into the wet, dark chamber?

Think Aloud **MODEL** I think about how the ants ended up in the wet, dark chamber. The cause was them reaching for a drink of water from the fountain, which was in fact water gushing from a faucet, and the effect was that the rushing water swept them off the faucet and into the dark, wet chamber.

ON THEIR OWN Ask students to review the events on pp. 482–483. Have them identify other cause-and-effect relationships and describe them.

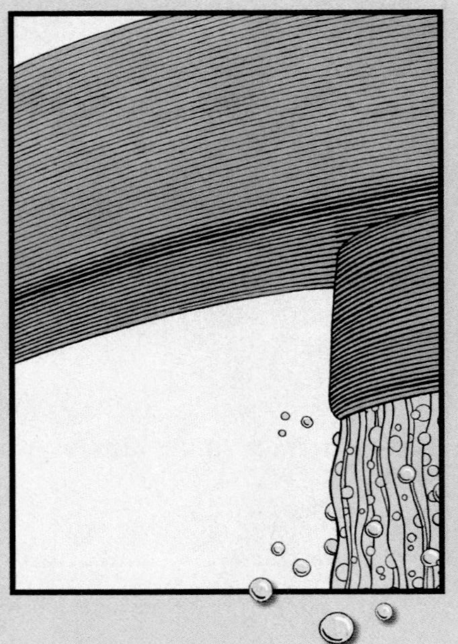

They landed near what seemed to be a fountain—a waterfall pouring from a silver tube. Both ants had a powerful thirst and longed to dip their feverish heads into the refreshing water. They quickly climbed along the tube.

As they got closer to the rushing water the ants felt a cool spray. They tightly gripped the shiny surface of the fountain and slowly leaned their heads into the falling stream. But the force of the water was much too strong.

482

Student Edition, p. 482

2ND READ

Close Reading

INFERENCE Why are the two ants so thirsty on page 482? (They were in the hot toaster, and the heat made them thirsty.)

ANALYSIS The picture on page 482 clearly shows a water faucet, but the author doesn't use the word *faucet*. What words does he use instead of *faucet?* (The author uses the words "a fountain—a waterfall pouring from a silver tube.")

ANALYSIS Help students generate text-based questions by providing the following question stem: In the selection, what happens after the two ants ______?

DEVELOP LANGUAGE Have students reread the the first sentence on p. 483. What does *plunged* mean? Describe situations where you might *plunge* into something.

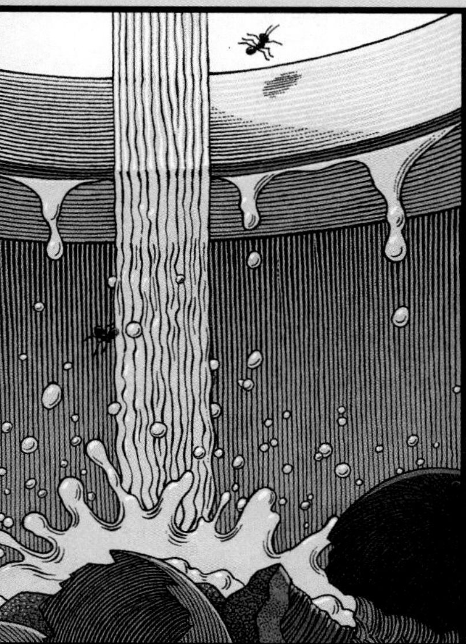

The tiny insects were pulled off the fountain and plunged down into a wet, dark chamber. They landed on half-eaten fruit and other soggy things. Suddenly the air was filled with loud, frightening sounds. The chamber began to spin.

The ants were caught in a whirling storm of shredded food and stinging rain. Then, just as quickly as it had started, the noise and spinning stopped. Bruised and dizzy, the ants climbed out of the chamber.

483

Student Edition, p. 483

INFERENCE • TEXT EVIDENCE What clues in the text and illustrations tell you that the "wet, dark chamber" was a garbage disposal? (The illustration shows the ants in a hole underneath the running water of the faucet. The text says the ants landed on half-eaten fruit and other soggy things. Then suddenly, the chamber began to spin, making loud noises and just as quickly, it stopped.)

Common Core State Standards

Literature 1. Ask and answer questions to demonstrate understanding of a text, referring explicitly to the text as the basis for the answers. **Literature 3.** Describe characters in a story (e.g., their traits, motivations, or feelings) and explain how their actions contribute to the sequence of events. **Literature 7.** Explain how specific aspects of a text's illustrations contribute to what is conveyed by the words in a story (e.g., create mood, emphasize aspects of a character or setting).

Access for All

Strategic Intervention

After students read pp. 482–483, ask them to use their own words to summarize what they read.

Access Content Make sure students understand that a garbage disposal grinds up pieces of unwanted or unused food and washes them down the drain. If students are not familiar with disposals, show them a picture of one and point out its parts.

1ST READ

Access Text If students need help, then...

PREFIXES AND SUFFIXES *un-, dis-, -ful* Ask students what the words *joyful* and *grateful* on p. 485 mean. (*joyful,* "full of joy"; *grateful,* "full of kindness or thanks")

Think Aloud **MODEL** When words use prefixes or suffixes, I can separate the word parts and find the root word. In *joyful,* the root word is *joy*. When *-ful* is added, the word's meaning changes.

ON THEIR OWN Have students list words from the text that have prefixes or suffixes. Have them discuss how the affix changes the meaning of the root word.

CROSS-TEXT EVALUATION

Use a Strategy to Self-Check How did "How Ants Find Food" on p. 467 help you understand this selection?

In daylight once again, they raced through puddles and up a smooth metal wall. In the distance they saw something comforting—two long, narrow holes that reminded them of the warmth and safety of their old underground home. They climbed up into the dark openings.

But there was no safety inside these holes. A strange force passed through the wet ants. They were stunned senseless and blown out of the holes like bullets from a gun. When they landed, the tiny insects were too exhausted to go on. They crawled into a dark corner and fell fast asleep.

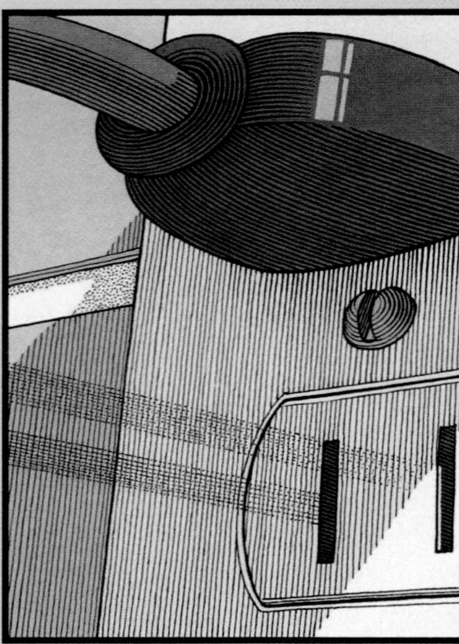

484

Student Edition, p. 484

2ND READ

Close Reading

ANALYSIS • TEXT EVIDENCE

Paraphrase the theme and supporting details of the story. (The theme of the story is that it does not pay to be greedy. The details that support the theme are the dangerous events that the ants went through in the house, such as being scooped into a mug of hot coffee, toasted in a toaster, ejected into the air along with the toast, and ending up in a garbage disposal.)

SYNTHESIS • TEXT EVIDENCE Using what you learned in this selection, tell why rules and laws are important to freedom. Have students cite examples from the text to support their responses.

CHECK PREDICTIONS Have students return to the predictions they made earlier and confirm whether they were accurate.

Night had returned when the battered ants awoke to a familiar sound—the footsteps of their fellow insects returning for more crystals. The two ants slipped quietly to the end of the line. They climbed the glassy wall and once again stood amid the treasure. But this time they each chose a single crystal and followed their friends home.

Standing at the edge of their ant hole, the two ants listened to the joyful sounds that came from below. They knew how grateful their mother queen would be when they gave her their crystals. At that moment, the two ants felt happier than they'd ever felt before. This was their home, this was their family. This was where they were meant to be.

485

Student Edition, p. 485

REREAD CHALLENGING TEXT Have students reread pp. 484–485 to clarify what is happening in this part of the story. Students may need help identifying the final obstacle the ants face and interpreting how all the problems are finally resolved.

Common Core State Standards

Literature 1. Ask and answer questions to demonstrate understanding of a text, referring explicitly to the text as the basis for the answers. **Literature 2.** Recount stories, including fables, folktales, and myths from diverse cultures; determine the central message, lesson, or moral and explain how it is conveyed through key details in the text. **Language 4.c.** Use a known root word as a clue to the meaning of an unknown word with the same root (e.g., *company, companion*). **Also Literature 10.**

Access for All

Have students work in teams to list all the words they know that have the prefix *un-* or *dis-* or the suffix *-ful*. Have teams compare lists.

A Advanced

Ask students to find information from classroom sources that tell about ants. Have them choose one interesting fact they learned and share it with the rest of the class.

Theme Be sure students understand the theme in the story: Greed doesn't pay. Have them discuss other stories with the same or a similar theme.

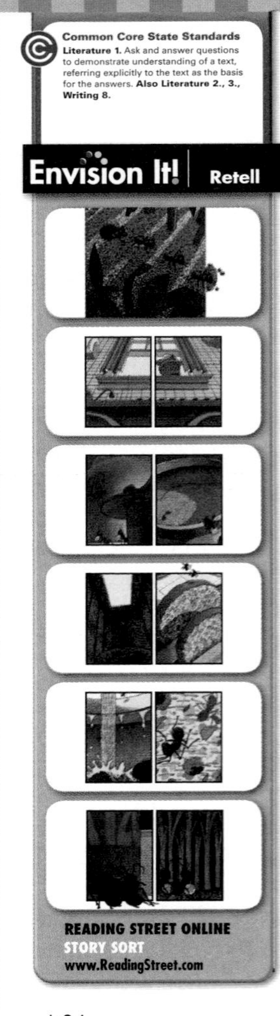

Think Critically

1. How is the ant world different from your world? How might ants describe a person? Text to World
2. How does the author and illustrator Chris Van Allsburg make you see the world the way ants see it? Use examples from the story in your answers. Think Like an Author
3. On page 476, the ants make a decision that leads to a huge problem for them. What is it, and how is it resolved? What can you learn from their adventures? Be sure to use details from the story to explain your answers. Plot and Theme
4. How did the author structure this story? What clue words help you know? Story Structure
5. **Look Back and Write** Look back at pages 477–479 to find "a boiling brown lake," "a giant scoop," and "a cave." Write a note to tell the ants what these things really are. Provide evidence from the story to support your answer. Key Ideas and Details • Text Evidence

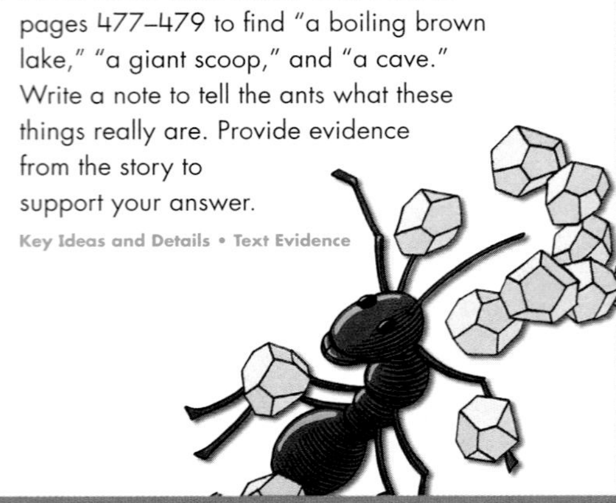

486

Meet the Author and Illustrator

Chris Van Allsburg

Chris Van Allsburg won the Caldecott Medal for his books *The Polar Express* and *Jumanji.* He is one of the best known children's book illustrators working today.

Mr. Van Allsburg says that in elementary school other kids thought it was cool if you could draw. But in junior high, he stopped drawing. He gave in to the peer pressure. Suddenly learning how to play football seemed more important.

Thankfully, Mr. Van Allsburg changed his mind. In college he decided to take some art classes. That decision changed his life. "I had a fever again," he says, "a fever to make art." He loved his art so much that he sometimes forgot his other classes, but he was being true to his nature.

Mr. Van Allsburg says that good stories contain a moral truth. Does *Two Bad Ants* say something about being true to your own nature? Mr. Van Allsburg thinks it does.

Read more books by Chris Van Allsburg.

The Wreck of the Zephyr

Just a Dream

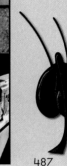

Reading Log — Use the *Reader's and Writer's Notebook* to record your independent reading.

487

Student Edition, pp. 486–487

Common Core State Standards

Literature 1. Ask and answer questions to demonstrate understanding of a text, referring explicitly to the text as the basis for the answers. **Also Literature 2., 3., 9., Writing 4., Speaking/Listening 4., Language 3.**

Bridge to Common Core

RANGE OF READING AND LEVEL OF TEXT COMPLEXITY

To increase students' capacity for reading and comprehending complex texts independently and proficiently, have them read other literary texts by Chris Van Allsburg or about the social studies topic, Rules and Laws. After students read closely for a sustained period of time, they should record their reading in their Reading Logs.

Think Critically

1. **TEXT TO TEXT** The ant world is different from ours because everything in our world seems big to ants. An ant might describe a person as a giant.
2. **THINK LIKE AN AUTHOR** The author doesn't use names from our world. Instead, the ants call sugar "crystals" because that's what it's like in their world.
3. **PLOT AND THEME** The ants decide to stay and collect more crystals. Problem: they are not safe there; resolution: they escape and return home.
4. **STORY STRUCTURE** The author structured the story in the order that things happened, using words such as "as soon as," "suddenly," and "night had returned."
5. **LOOK BACK AND WRITE • TEXT EVIDENCE** To build writing fluency, allow 10–15 minutes.

Team Talk Have students look for other selections by the author Chris Van Allsburg and write a paragraph comparing the plots, themes, or characters.

Scoring Rubric Look Back and Write

TOP-SCORE RESPONSE A top score response correctly describes the metaphors used and identifies illustrations that show the ants in each situation.

A top-score response should include:

- "a boiling brown lake" is a cup of coffee.
- "a giant scoop" is a spoon.
- "a cave" is a mouth.

Retell

Have students work in pairs to retell the selection, using the retelling strip in the Student Edition or the Story Sort as prompts. Monitor students' retellings.

Scoring Rubric Narrative Retelling

	4	3	2	1
Connections	Makes connections and generalizes beyond the text	Makes connections to other events, stories, or experiences	Makes a limited connection to another event, story, or experience	Makes no connection to another event, story, or experience
Author's Purpose	Elaborates on author's purpose	Tells author's purpose with some clarity	Makes some connection to author's purpose	Makes no connection to author's purpose
Characters	Describes the main character(s) and any character development	Identifies the main character(s) and gives some information about them	Inaccurately identifies some characters or gives little information about them	Inaccurately identifies the characters or gives no information about them
Setting	Describes the time and location	Identifies the time and location	Omits details of time or location	Is unable to identify time or location
Plot	Describes the problem, goal, events, and ending using rich detail	Tells the problem, goal, events, and ending with some errors that do not affect meaning	Tells parts of the problem, goal, events, and ending with gaps that affect meaning	Retelling has no sense of story

Don't Wait Until Friday

MONITOR PROGRESS Check Retelling

If... students have difficulty retelling,

then... use the Retelling Cards/Story Sort to scaffold their retellings.

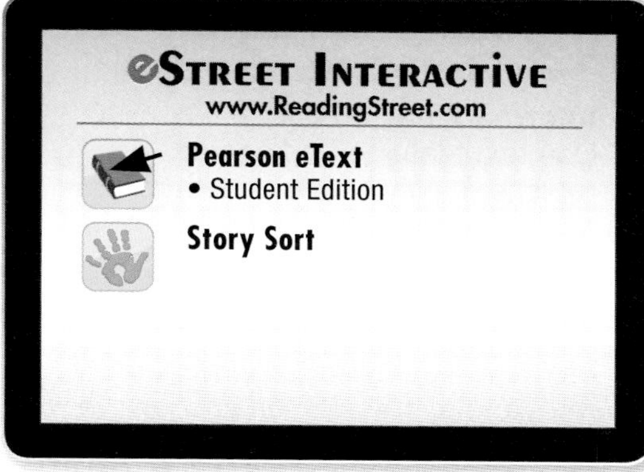

Plan to Assess Retelling

- ☐ **Week 1** Strategic Intervention
- ☐ **Week 2** Advanced
- ☐ **Week 3** Strategic Intervention
- ☑ **This week assess On-Level students.**
- ☐ **Week 5** Assess any students you have not yet checked during this unit.

Meet the Author

Ask students to read about author and illustrator Chris Van Allsburg on p. 487. Ask them how he got interested in art again in college.

Read Independently

Have students enter their independent reading information into their Reading Logs.

Retelling Use the Retelling Cards to discuss the selection with students. Place the cards in an incorrect order and have volunteers correct the mistake. Then have students explain where each card should go as they describe the sequence of the selection.

 **Common Core State Standards**

Informational Text 5. Use text features and search tools (e.g., key words, sidebars, hyperlinks) to locate information relevant to a given topic efficiently. **Foundational Skills 4.b.** Read on-level prose and poetry orally with accuracy, appropriate rate, and expression on successive readings. **Language 6.** Acquire and use accurately grade-appropriate conversational, general academic, and domain-specific words and phrases, including those that signal spatial and temporal relationships (e.g., *After dinner that night we went looking for them*).

Fluency

Rate

MODEL FLUENT READING Have students turn to p. 485 of *Two Bad Ants*. Ask students to follow along as you read the page. Tell them to pay special attention to the rate at which you read. Explain that you will be reading in a regular speaking voice and you will try not to read too quickly or too slowly.

GUIDE PRACTICE Have students follow along as you read the page again. Then have them reread the page as a group without you until they read at an appropriate rate and with no mistakes. Ask questions to be sure students comprehend the text. Continue in the same way on p. 486.

Corrective feedback

If... students are having difficulty reading at an appropriate rate,
then... prompt them as follows:

- Do you think you need to slow down or read more quickly?
- Read the sentence more quickly. Now read it more slowly. Which helps you understand what you are reading?
- Tell me the sentence. Read it at the rate that would help me understand it.

Routine Oral Rereading

1. **Select a Passage** Read paragraph 2 of *Two Bad Ants* aloud.
2. **Model** Have students listen to the rate at which you read.
3. **Guide Practice** Have students read along with you.
4. **On Their Own** For optimal fluency, students should reread three or four times using an appropriate rate.

Routines Flip Chart

Research and Study Skills

Electronic Text

TEACH Ask students where they have seen text in electronic form. Students may mention the Internet or a CD-ROM. Explain the characteristics of these forms of electronic text.

- CD-ROMs provide information on a computer disk that can only be viewed on a computer screen. Information from a CD-ROM can often be printed out like pages in a book.
- Computers connected to the Internet and a search engine can look up information quickly. The viewer will probably be given many choices when a topic is searched. The viewer must choose the items he or she wants to read.
- Electronic text is often used for research. The reader can skim and scan the electronic pages by scrolling down the page with a mouse. Not every word must be read. Text is often broken into smaller parts with subheads to make them easier to read.

GUIDE PRACTICE Have students research a topic of their choice on the Internet and with a CD-ROM from the library. Discuss these questions:

- How do you know what information an electronic text page on the Internet shows? (There may be heads and subheads, and the viewer may have searched the topic on a search screen.)
- How are electronic texts on the Internet and on a CD-ROM different? (Text on a CD-ROM is on a disk that must be inserted into the computer. Text on a Web site is found through a search engine on the Internet, which is a worldwide network of computers.)

After students share the results of their research topics, ask specific questions about the electronic text they used.

ON THEIR OWN Have students review and complete p. 426 of the *Reader's and Writer's Notebook*.

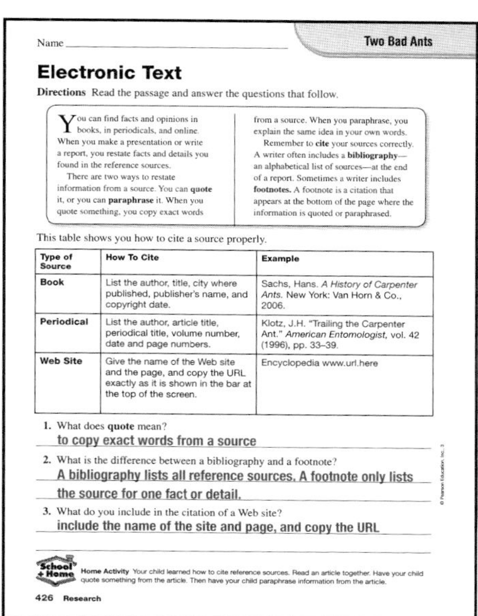

Name ______ Two Bad Ants

Electronic Text

Directions Read the passage and answer the questions that follow.

You can find facts and opinions in books, in periodicals, and online. When you make a presentation or write a report, you restate facts and details you found in the reference sources.

There are two ways to restate information from a source. You can **quote** it, or you can **paraphrase** it. When you quote something, you copy exact words from a source. When you paraphrase, you explain the same idea in your own words.

Remember to **cite** your sources correctly. A writer often includes a **bibliography**—an alphabetical list of sources—at the end of a report. Sometimes a writer includes **footnotes.** A footnote is a citation that appears at the bottom of the page where the information is quoted or paraphrased.

This table shows you how to cite a source properly.

Type of Source	How To Cite	Example
Book	List the author, title, city where published, publisher's name, and copyright date.	Sachs, Hans. *A History of Carpenter Ants.* New York: Van Horn & Co., 2006.
Periodical	List the author, article title, periodical title, volume number, date and page numbers.	Klotz, J.H. "Trailing the Carpenter Ant." *American Entomologist,* vol. 42 (1996), pp. 33–39.
Web Site	Give the name of the Web site and the page, and copy the URL exactly as it is shown in the bar at the top of the screen.	Encyclopedia www.url.here

1. What does **quote** mean?
to copy exact words from a source
2. What is the difference between a bibliography and a footnote?
A bibliography lists all reference sources. A footnote only lists the source for one fact or detail.
3. What do you include in the citation of a Web site?
include the name of the site and page, and copy the URL

School + Home **Home Activity** Your child learned how to cite reference sources. Read an article together. Have your child quote something from the article. Then have your child paraphrase information from the article.

426 Research

Reader's and Writer's Notebook, p. 426

Using Library Resources Remind students of any specific rules about using CD-ROMs or other electronic media in your library or classroom. Help students use or listen to the media while showing respect to others around them. Offer headphones if students are listening to media with sound, and allow students enough time to analyze the results of their electronic searches.

Common Core State Standards

Writing 7. Conduct short research projects that build knowledge about a topic. **Writing 8.** Recall information from experiences or gather information from print and digital sources; take brief notes on sources and sort evidence into provided categories. **Language 2.** Demonstrate command of the conventions of standard English capitalization, punctuation, and spelling when writing. **Language 2.f.** Use spelling patterns and generalizations (e.g., word families, position-based spellings, syllable patterns, ending rules, meaningful word parts) in writing words. **Also Writing 5., Language 2.b., 2.e.**

Research and Inquiry

Step 3 Analyze Information

TEACH Tell students that they will analyze their findings from the sources they read and might need to change the focus of their original inquiry question.

Think Aloud

MODEL When I started my research, I thought I would find out why people should follow rules and laws and how that affected their freedom. Now I am realizing that I can't really answer that question with my research. Now I realize that I must look at individual rules and laws and think about how they affect a person's freedom directly. So, now my inquiry question is *What might happen to someone in school who doesn't follow rules about cheating*?

GUIDE PRACTICE Have students analyze their findings. They may need to refocus their inquiry question to better fit the information they found. Remind students that if they have difficulty improving their focus, they can ask a reference librarian or a local expert for guidance.

Remind students that they can use additional sources to help them find the information they are looking for.

ON THEIR OWN Have students sort their information into categories such as *rule, reason for rule,* and *consequence for breaking the rule*.

Conventions

Commas

REVIEW Remind students that this week they learned that commas are used in dates, addresses, and letter greetings and closings. They are also used to join sentences with a conjunction and to separate the words in a series.

CONNECT TO ORAL LANGUAGE Write the following sentences on the board. Have students read aloud each sentence and pause when they come to a comma.

> **A kitchen should be neat, clean, and fresh.**
>
> **The woman picked up the cup, put it to her lips, and drank the coffee.**

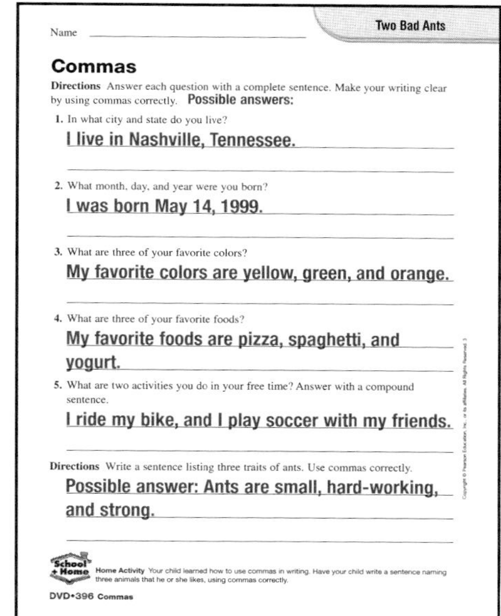

Name ____________ Two Bad Ants

Commas

Directions Answer each question with a complete sentence. Make your writing clear by using commas correctly. **Possible answers:**

1. In what city and state do you live?
   I live in Nashville, Tennessee.
2. What month, day, and year were you born?
   I was born May 14, 1999.
3. What are three of your favorite colors?
   My favorite colors are yellow, green, and orange.
4. What are three of your favorite foods?
   My favorite foods are pizza, spaghetti, and yogurt.
5. What are two activities you do in your free time? Answer with a compound sentence.
   I ride my bike, and I play soccer with my friends.

Directions Write a sentence listing three traits of ants. Use commas correctly.
Possible answer: Ants are small, hard-working, and strong.

School + Home **Home Activity** Your child learned how to use commas in writing. Have your child write a sentence naming three animals that he or she likes, using commas correctly.

DVD•396 Commas

Let's Practice It! TR DVD•396

ON THEIR OWN For additional support, use *Let's Practice It!* p. 396 on the *Teacher Resources DVD-ROM*.

Spelling

Prefixes, Suffixes, and Endings

FREQUENTLY MISSPELLED WORDS The words *everybody* and *everything* are words that students often misspell. The words *impossibly* and *uncomfortable* from your spelling list are also difficult to spell. I'm going to read a sentence. Choose the correct word to complete the sentence and then write it correctly.

1. **The tight jacket is an _______ fit.** (uncomfortable)
2. **_______ from class was invited to the party.** (Everybody)
3. **The geography quiz was _______ difficult.** (impossibly)
4. **We packed _______ we needed in the bag.** (everything)

ON THEIR OWN For additional practice, use *Reader's and Writer's Notebook,* p. 427.

Access for All

Display a map of Texas or the United States and ask students, one at a time, to close their eyes and point to a place on the map. Write the name of the city or town they pointed to, such as El Paso, Texas. Do not write the comma. Have students insert the comma where it belongs.

Daily Fix-It

5. We learned about ants's strenth, and it is amazing. *(ants'; strength)*
6. Did you know an ant can lift something ten times heavyer than its body. *(heavier; body?)*

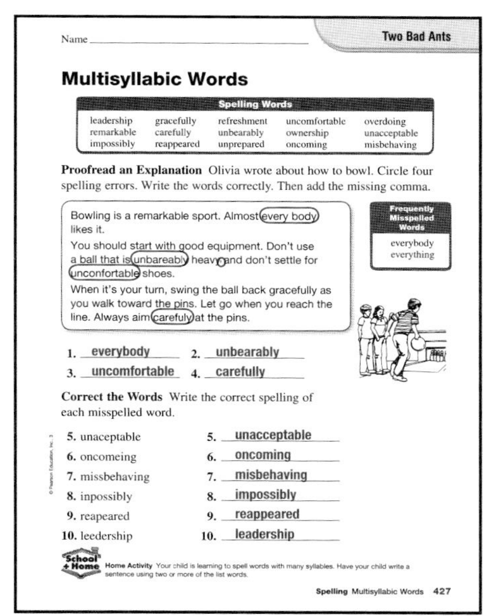

Name ____________ Two Bad Ants

Multisyllabic Words

Spelling Words				
leadership	gracefully	refreshment	uncomfortable	overdoing
remarkable	carefully	unbearably	ownership	unacceptable
impossibly	reappeared	unprepared	oncoming	misbehaving

Proofread an Explanation Olivia wrote about how to bowl. Circle four spelling errors. Write the words correctly. Then add the missing comma.

Bowling is a remarkable sport. Almost every body likes it.
You should start with good equipment. Don't use a ball that is unbareably heavy and don't settle for unconfortable shoes.
When it's your turn, swing the ball back gracefully as you walk toward the pins. Let go when you reach the line. Always aim carefuly at the pins.

Frequently Misspelled Words
everybody
everything

1. everybody 2. unbearably
3. uncomfortable 4. carefully

Correct the Words Write the correct spelling of each misspelled word.

5. unaceptable	5. unacceptable
6. oncomeing	6. oncoming
7. missbehaving	7. misbehaving
8. inpossibly	8. impossibly
9. reapeared	9. reappeared
10. leedership	10. leadership

School + Home **Home Activity** Your child is learning to spell words with many syllables. Have your child write a sentence using two or more of the list words.

Spelling Multisyllabic Words 427

Reader's and Writer's Notebook, p. 427

Common Core State Standards
Writing 3.a. Establish a situation and introduce a narrator and/or characters; organize an event sequence that unfolds naturally. **Also Language 2.**

Let's Write It!

Key Features of a Comic Book

- tells a story using a series of drawings
- characters' dialogue is part of the drawing
- sometimes uses narration

READING STREET ONLINE
GRAMMAR JAMMER
www.ReadingStreet.com

Narrative

Comic Book

In a **comic book**, drawings, or illustrations, are used to help tell the story. Characters' dialogue and any narration is included with the illustrations. The student model on the next page is an example of a comic book.

Writing Prompt Write a short comic book telling of a further adventure of these two ants.

Writer's Checklist

Remember, you should ...

- draw a sequence of pictures that show what the ants are doing.
- write dialogue in "word balloons."
- include details about the setting.
- tell a story with a beginning, middle, and end.
- use punctuation correctly, including commas in dates and in a series.

488

Student Model

Two Bad Ants, Act II

Commas, including the one in the date, are used correctly.

Writing Trait Conventions In a comic book, dialogue appears in a word bubble.

Genre A **comic book** is a series of drawings used to tell a story.

Conventions

Commas

Remember **Commas** separate words in a series. They also separate the month and day from the year in a date.

489

Student Edition, pp. 488–489

Common Core State Standards

Writing 3. Write narratives to develop real or imagined experiences or events using effective technique, descriptive details, and clear event sequences. **Writing 3.b.** Use dialogue and descriptions of actions, thoughts, and feelings to develop experiences and events or show the response of characters to situations. **Also Language 2.**

Let's Write It!

WRITE A COMIC BOOK Use pp. 488–489 in the Student Edition. Direct students to read the key features of a comic book, which appear on p. 488. Remind students that they can refer to the information in the Writer's Checklist as they write their own comic books.

Read the student model on p. 489. Point out how the drawings help tell the story in the model.

CONNECT TO CONVENTIONS Remind students that commas are used to separate the day and year in dates, as well as after the greeting and closing of a friendly letter. Point out the correct use of commas in the model.

Comic Book

Writer's Craft: Dialogue

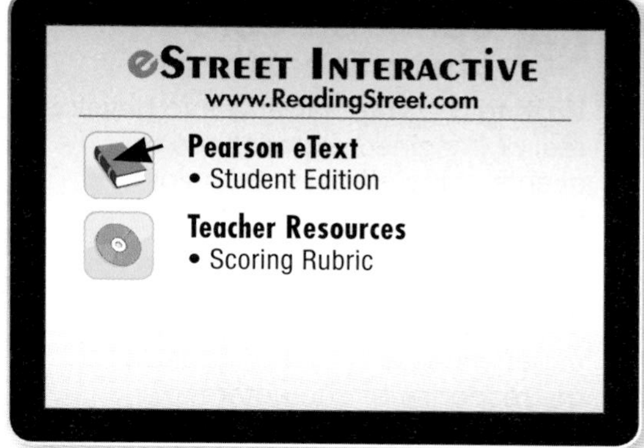

DISPLAY RUBRIC Display Scoring Rubric 29 from the *Teacher Resources DVD-ROM* and go over the criteria for each trait under each score. Then, using the model in the Student Edition, choose students to score the model for each trait. If a student says that the model should score below 4 for a particular trait, have the student support that response. Remind students that this is the rubric that will be used to evaluate the comic book they write.

Scoring Rubric Comic Book

	4	3	2	1
Focus/Ideas	Has clear plot focus; well-developed setting and characters	Has plot and some focus; has a setting and characters	Lacks plot and focus; poorly developed setting and characters	No plot; no focus; lacks plausible setting and characters
Organization	Correct use of comic book format	Use of comic book format	Incorrect use of comic book format	No attempt at using comic book format
Voice	Consistent voice appropriate to theme and purpose	Voice somewhat consistent and appropriate to theme and purpose	Inconsistent voice or voice inappropriate to theme and purpose	No attempt to create voice
Word Choice	Clear, concise character dialogue; reveals character traits; describes action	Somewhat clear dialogue; reveals some character traits; describes some action	Flat, unclear dialogue; does not reveal character; does not describe action	No attempt to create coherent dialogue
Sentences	Clear sentences of various lengths and types	Sentences of a few lengths and types	Sentences of similar length and type	No attempt at sentences of various lengths and types
Conventions	Few, if any, errors; correct use of commas	Several minor errors; mostly correct use of commas	Many errors; incorrect use of commas	Numerous errors; no or incorrect use of commas

STORY SEQUENCE CHART Have students refer to the story sequence charts they worked on yesterday. If necessary, allow additional class time for students to add details and complete their charts.

WRITE You will be using your story sequence chart as you write the first draft of your comic book. When you are drafting, just make a rough sketch of your drawings and do not worry if your writing does not sound exactly as you want it to. You will have a chance to finalize your drawings, as well as revise and proofread your writing, at a later stage.

Common Core State Standards

Writing 3. Write narratives to develop real or imagined experiences or events using effective technique, descriptive details, and clear event sequences. **Writing 3.b.** Use dialogue and descriptions of actions, thoughts, and feelings to develop experiences and events or show the response of characters to situations. **Writing 4.** With guidance and support from adults, produce writing in which the development and organization are appropriate to task and purpose.

Bridge to Common Core

RANGE OF WRITING

As students progress through the writing project, they routinely write for a range of tasks, purposes, and audiences. In this lesson, they learn the importance of writing vivid dialogue. They develop written work in which characters are developed through their dialogue.

Writing

Comic Book

Mini-Lesson Writing Effective Dialogue

■ **Introduce** Explain to students that the words in a comic book are mostly dialogue. Dialogue is anything that a character says aloud. It appears in word bubbles that point to the character who is speaking. Tell students that it is important to write dialogue that relates to their characters and drawings. For example, if a character is excited, the dialogue as well as the illustration should reflect this state of mind. Point out that good writers adjust their dialogue to reflect each individual character. Just as different people speak differently in real life, well-developed characters will speak differently from one another. Display Writing Transparency 29A.

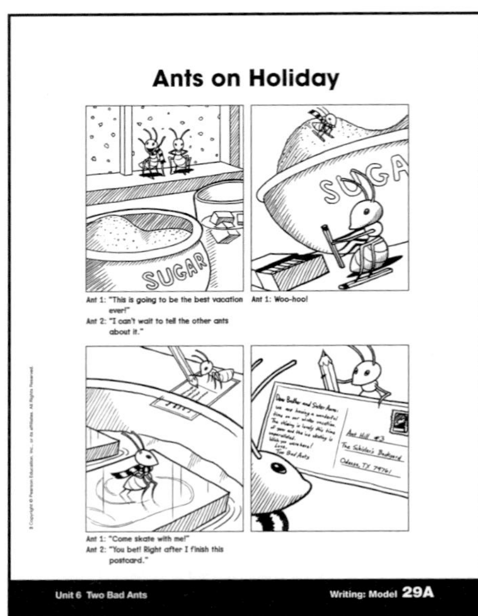

Writing Transparency 29A, TR DVD

Drafting Tips

✔ To get started, review your story sequence chart.

✔ Make sure your drawings and dialogue tell most of the story.

✔ Just make quick, rough sketches of your drawings at this point. You will have a chance to finalize illustrations later.

Think Aloud **MODEL** I'm going to write the dialogue for the first panel in my comic book. Since I want to show that the ants are on holiday, I'll have one of my ant characters talk about how excited it is to be on vacation. Also, I want to show that the ants are on a winter holiday. I will make a quick sketch of a large window and show that it is snowing outside. As I write, I will pay attention to what each ant is saying. I will write dialogue that expresses each ant's personality.

Direct students to use the drafting tips to guide them in developing their drafts. Remind them to make sure each panel in their comic book has an illustration that helps tell the story.

Writing Trait: Conventions

Point out to students that in addition to the comic convention of writing characters' dialogue in bubbles, they should follow many of the same conventions as they do for any kind of writing. Acknowledge that dialogue will likely contain informal language and might include sentence fragments. However, most of the standard capitalization and punctuation rules still apply.

- Begin all sentences with capital letters and end all sentences with punctuation marks.
- Capitalize all proper nouns and adjectives.
- Use punctuation to help readers understand what your characters are saying and feeling.

Routine Quick Write for Fluency

Team Talk

1. **Talk** Have partners discuss how to write effective dialogue.
2. **Write** Each student writes four to five lines of dialogue that includes commas used correctly.
3. **Share** Partners read each other's dialogue and check for correct use of commas.

Routines Flip Chart

Access for All

SI Strategic Intervention

Have students work together in groups of three to read aloud two or three sentences of dialogue from their comic books. Each student in the group can help make sure the dialogue sounds natural and matches the attitude of the character speaking.

Wrap Up Your Day!

✔ **Content Knowledge** What did you learn about rules and consequences?

✔ **Text-Based Comprehension** How do you know that the two bad ants learned their lesson? Encourage students to cite evidence from the text to support their responses.

Preview DAY 4

Tell students that tomorrow they will read about rules to follow to stay safe while hiking.

DAY 4
at a Glance

Content Knowledge
Oral Vocabulary

Phonics/Word Study
Review Final Syllables

21st Century Skills
Evaluating Online Sources

Fluency
Rate

Vocabulary Skill
Prefixes and Suffixes *un-, dis-, -ful*

Listening and Speaking
Description

Research and Inquiry
Synthesize

Conventions
Commas

Spelling
Prefixes, Suffixes, and Endings

Writing
Comic Book

Materials
- Student Edition
- Reader's and Writer's Notebook
- Decodable Reader

Common Core State Standards

Speaking/Listening 1. Engage effectively in a range of collaborative discussions (one-on-one, in groups, and teacher-led) with diverse partners on grade 3 topics and texts, building on others' ideas and expressing their own clearly. **Language 6.** Acquire and use accurately grade-appropriate conversational, general academic, and domain-specific words and phrases, including those that signal spatial and temporal relationships (e.g., *After dinner that night we went looking for them*).

Content Knowledge

Rules and Laws Are Important to Freedom

EXPAND THE CONCEPT Remind students of the weekly concept question, *Why are rules and laws important to freedom?* Have students discuss how following rules and laws can help keep them safe.

Build Oral Language

TALK ABOUT SENTENCES AND WORDS Have students reread the first sentence of the second paragraph on p. 483. Remind them this describes the scene in the garbage disposal. Then have them share with a partner their answers to the questions below.

The ants were caught in a whirling storm of shredded food and stinging rain.

- What noun is *whirling* describing? (*storm*) What is an antonym for *storm*? (*calm*)
- How does this help you understand what *whirling* means? (I know it has something to do with a storm. In a storm, the wind blows a lot so it probably has something to do with blowing or spinning around.)
- What does a garbage disposal do? (It grinds up the food that is put into it.) Given this, what do you think *shredded food* means? (food that has been torn up into shreds, or small pieces)
- If a bee stings you, what does it feel like? (painful, sharp) So what would *stinging rain* feel like? (It would feel painful when it touches your skin.)
- Have students replace the adjectives in the phrases *whirling storm, shredded food,* and *stinging rain* with synonyms.

Build Oral Vocabulary

Amazing Words Robust Vocabulary Routine

1. **Introduce** Write the Amazing Word *forbid* on the board. Have students say it aloud with you. We read about the way the ants did not follow the rules of their colony and stayed by themselves. Why do you think the queen ant might *forbid* this kind of behavior? (Tiny ants out on their own could get into a lot of danger.) Supply a student-friendly definition: *Forbid* means "to make a rule against, or not allow someone to do something."

2. **Demonstrate** Have students answer questions to demonstrate understanding. What else are the two ants doing that the queen would probably *forbid*? (They are not helping the other ants.)

3. **Apply** Have students apply their understanding. What kinds of things would a teacher *forbid* students to do?

4. **Display the Word** Point out the *r*-controlled /ôr/ in the first syllable of *forbid*.

See p. OV•4 to teach *eerie.*

Routines Flip Chart

ADD TO THE CONCEPT MAP Discuss the Amazing Words *guilt* and *encounter.* Add these and other concept-related words to the concept map. Use the following questions to develop students' understanding of the concept. Add words generated in the discussion to the concept map.

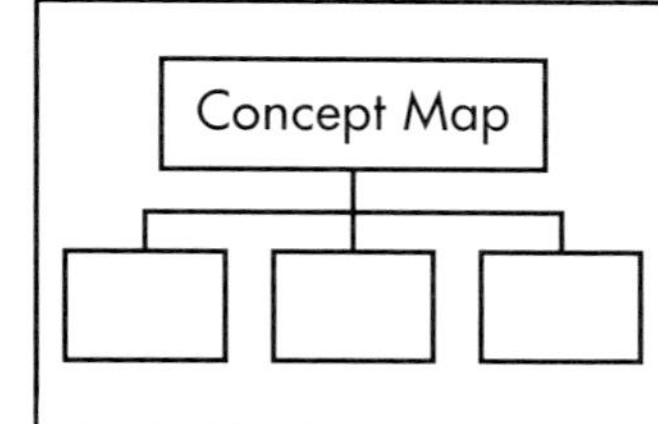

- How do you think the ants' *encounter* with the dangers of the kitchen could be thought of as a consequence for breaking the rules of the colony?
- At the end of the story, the ants felt much better about returning home. What kind of freedom did they give up so that they could stay safe and not feel *guilt?*

Amazing Words

obey	fascinate
responsibility	guilt
consequence	encounter
permission	forbid
citizen	eerie

Produce Oral Language Use the Day 4 instruction on ELL Poster 29 to extend and enrich language.

Common Core State Standards

Foundational Skills 3. Know and apply grade-level phonics and word analysis skills in decoding words. **Foundational Skills 3.b.** Decode words with common Latin suffixes. **Foundational Skills 3.c.** Decode multisyllable words. **Also Foundational Skills 3.d.**

Name ______________ Two Bad Ants

Final Syllables *-tion, -sion, -ture, -ive, -ize*

Directions Circle the correctly spelled word in each pair.

1. vacasion (vacation)
2. (submission) submition
3. extracsion (extraction)
4. ignision (ignition)
5. (provision) provition
6. (action) acsion
7. exploton (explosion)
8. mantion (mansion)

Directions Add **-ture**, **-ive**, or **-ize** to complete each word below. Write the complete word on the line. (HINT: there is only one correct choice for each word.)

9. rap rapture
10. pass passive
11. lec lecture
12. secret secretive
13. harmon harmonize
14. dramat dramatize
15. crea creature
16. real realize

Directions Choose four words from the above list and write a sentence using each word.

17. Sentences will vary.
18. ______________
19. ______________
20. ______________

School + Home **Home Activity** Your child identified and wrote words ending in -tion, -sion, -ture, -ive, and -ize. Read each correct word from the list. Have your child tell how many syllables are in the word.

Final Syllables *-tion, -sion, -ture, -ive, -ize* DVD•397

Let's Practice It! TR DVD•397

Word Analysis

Review Final Syllables

REVIEW FINAL SYLLABLES To review last week's word analysis skill, write *contraction, tension, picture, passive,* and *summarize.* You studied words with final syllables like these last week. What do you know about words with final syllables like these? (Recognizing a final syllable in a word can help you break the word into smaller parts and read more fluently.) Have students identify the letters that spell the final syllable in each word. What letters spell the final syllable in *contraction*? (*tion*) In *tension*? (*ion*) Continue in the same way for *picture* (*ture*), *passive* (*ive*), and *summarize* (*ize*).

Corrective feedback

If... students are unable to answer the questions about final syllables,
then... refer them to *Sound-Spelling Cards* 131, 132, 133, 135, and 136.

GUIDE PRACTICE Draw a five-column chart with the heads *-tion, -ion, -ture, -ive, -ize.* We will work together to place words with these final syllables in the chart. For example, words with the final syllable *-tion* as in *contraction* will go in the first column of the chart. Listen as I say each word. Then I will call on volunteers to tell me where to write the word in the chart. Say the words in the chart below in random order. Write each word in the appropriate column. Then have students read the words and ask volunteers to underline the letters that spell the final syllable in each word.

-tion	-ion	-ture	-ive	-ize
tradition	discussion	fixture	negative	popularize
inspiration	tension	pasture	positive	glamorize
condition	abrasion	fracture	reactive	magnetize

ON THEIR OWN For additional practice, use *Let's Practice It!* p. 397 on the *Teacher Resources DVD-ROM.*

Fluent Word Reading

Spiral Review

READ WORDS IN ISOLATION Display these words. Tell students that they can decode some words on this list. Explain that they should know other words because they appear often in reading.

Have students read the list three or four times until they can read at the rate of two to three seconds per word.

Word Reading

ago	cool	bamboo	food	been
the	travel	you	wanted	noodles
true	coming	seven	live	circus
to	a	everywhere	famous	could

Corrective feedback

If… students have difficulty reading whole words,
then… have them use sound-by-sound blending for decodable words or chunking for words that have word parts, or have them say and spell high-frequency words.

If… students cannot read fluently at a rate of two to three seconds per word,
then… have pairs practice the list until they can read it fluently.

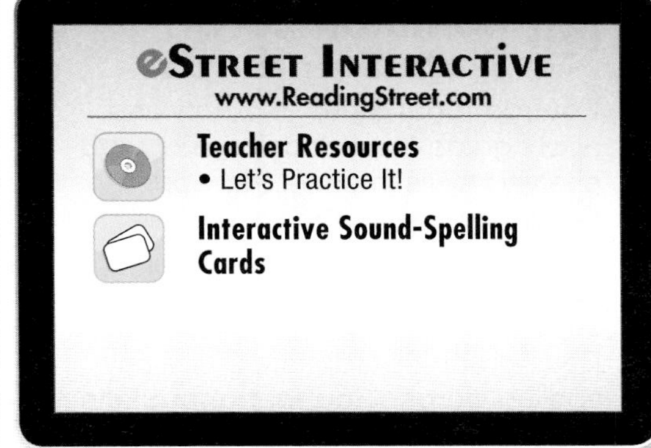

Access for All

Strategic Intervention

Explain that remembering final syllables will help with reading unfamiliar words. Review the final syllables *-tion, -ion, -ture, -ive, -ize.* Then write the following words and have students identify the final syllables and read the words together: *posture, fraction, session, selective,* and *organize.*

Spiral Review

These activities review

- previously taught high-frequency words *been, the, you, wanted, coming, live, to, a, everywhere, could.*
- vowel sounds /ü/ and /u̇/; schwa.

Fluent Word Reading Have students listen to a more fluent reader say the words. Then have them repeat the words.

Common Core State Standards

Foundational Skills 3. Know and apply grade-level phonics and word analysis skills in decoding words. **Foundational Skills 3.a.** Identify and know the meaning of the most common prefixes and derivational suffixes. **Foundational Skills 3.d.** Read grade-appropriate irregularly spelled words. **Foundational Skills 4.** Read with sufficient accuracy and fluency to support comprehension.

Fluent Word Reading

READ WORDS IN CONTEXT Display these sentences. Call on individuals to read a sentence. Then randomly point to review words and have students read them. To help you monitor word reading, high-frequency words are underlined and decodable words are italicized.

MONITOR PROGRESS Sentence Reading

I could not live without my dad's *famous noodles.*
Is it *true* that the panda's favorite *food* is *bamboo?*
The *circus* is coming to a town near you.
The weather has been *cool* everywhere we have gone.
I have wanted to *travel* to Greece since *seven* years *ago.*

If… students are unable to read an underlined high-frequency word,
then… read the word for them and spell it, having them echo you.

If… students have difficulty reading an italicized decodable word,
then… guide them in using sound-by-sound blending or chunking.

Reread for Fluency

Have students reread the sentences to develop automaticity decoding words.

Routine Oral Rereading

1. **Read** Have students read all the sentences orally.
2. **Reread** To achieve optimal fluency, students should reread the sentences three or four times.
3. **Corrective Feedback** Listen as students read. Provide corrective feedback regarding their fluency and decoding.

Routines Flip Chart

Decodable Passage 29C

If students need help, then...

Read *Ms. Impossible*

READ WORDS IN ISOLATION Have students turn to p. 167 in *Decodable Practice Readers 3.2* and find the first list of words. Each word in this list has a prefix. Let's read these words. Be sure that students identify the prefix in each word.

Next, have students read the high-frequency words.

PREVIEW Have students read the title and preview the story. Tell them that they will read words with the prefixes *im-* and *in-*.

READ WORDS IN CONTEXT Chorally read the story along with students. Have students identify words in the story that have the prefixes *im-* and *in-*. Make sure that students are monitoring their accuracy when they decode words.

Team Talk Pair students and have them take turns reading the story aloud to each other. Monitor students as they read to check for proper pronunciation and appropriate pacing.

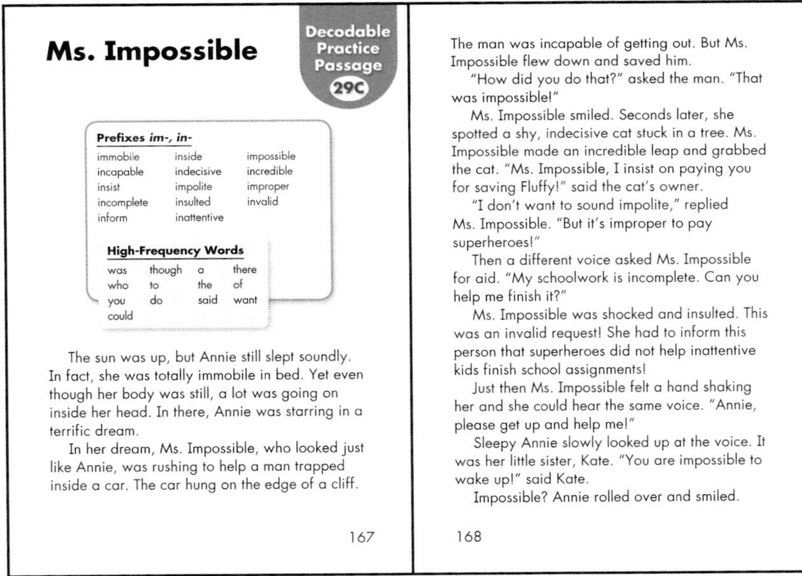

Ms. Impossible

Decodable Practice Passage 29C

Prefixes *im-*, *in-*

immobile	inside	impossible
incapable	indecisive	incredible
insist	impolite	improper
incomplete	insulted	invalid
inform	inattentive	

High-Frequency Words

was	though	a	there
who	to	the	of
you	do	said	want
could			

The sun was up, but Annie still slept soundly. In fact, she was totally immobile in bed. Yet even though her body was still, a lot was going on inside her head. In there, Annie was starring in a terrific dream.

In her dream, Ms. Impossible, who looked just like Annie, was rushing to help a man trapped inside a car. The car hung on the edge of a cliff.

167

The man was incapable of getting out. But Ms. Impossible flew down and saved him.

"How did you do that?" asked the man. "That was impossible!"

Ms. Impossible smiled. Seconds later, she spotted a shy, indecisive cat stuck in a tree. Ms. Impossible made an incredible leap and grabbed the cat. "Ms. Impossible, I insist on paying you for saving Fluffy!" said the cat's owner.

"I don't want to sound impolite," replied Ms. Impossible. "But it's improper to pay superheroes!"

Then a different voice asked Ms. Impossible for aid. "My schoolwork is incomplete. Can you help me finish it?"

Ms. Impossible was shocked and insulted. This was an invalid request! She had to inform this person that superheroes did not help inattentive kids finish school assignments!

Just then Ms. Impossible felt a hand shaking her and she could hear the same voice. "Annie, please get up and help me!"

Sleepy Annie slowly looked up at the voice. It was her little sister, Kate. "You are impossible to wake up!" said Kate.

Impossible? Annie rolled over and smiled.

168

Decodable Practice Passage 29C

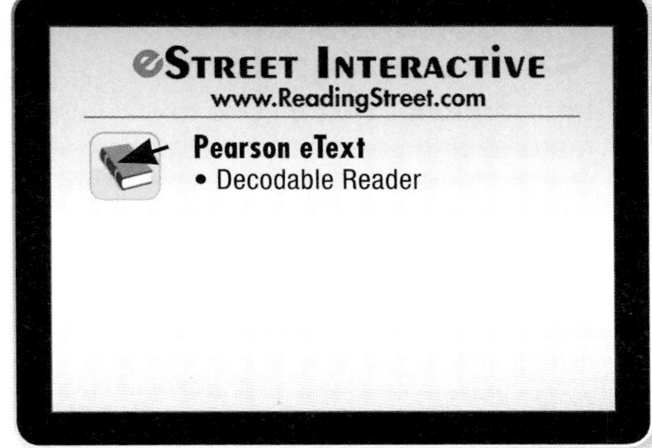

Access for All

Write the high-frequency words found in the sentences on p. 490e on note cards. Have students practice showing and reading the words on the cards to each other. Once they have mastered the words, have them quickly think of sentences using the words on the cards.

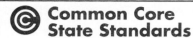

Common Core State Standards

Informational Text 5. Use text features and search tools (e.g., key words, sidebars, hyperlinks) to locate information relevant to a given topic efficiently.

KEY IDEAS AND DETAILS

Using online sources leads students to explicit information. By questioning the validity of online sources, students determine which information is reliable and which may be suspect.

21st Century Skills

Evaluating Online Sources

INTRODUCE Explain to students that not everything they find online will be reliable. Tell them that it is important to evaluate, or think about, everything they find online and decide if it is reliable and trustworthy.

DISCUSS EVALUATING ONLINE SOURCES Discuss with students why they should question some information they find online. For example, ask: Do you think it is possible to get information from the Internet that is not correct or reliable? Why? (Possible responses: Yes, because people are free to put whatever they want on the Internet, so it is likely that not everyone will have checked their facts correctly.) Explain: Books are checked carefully before they are printed, but many online sources do not need to be checked before they are posted. People should evaluate sources to make sure they come from places the reader has heard of or can trust. Let's take a closer look at the similarities and differences between online sources and print sources.

GROUP PRACTICE Display a graphic organizer like the one below. Fill in the Venn diagram as students respond to the following questions:

- How do you find online sources? (Possible response: search and read information on a computer by typing keywords into a search engine)
- How do you find print sources? (Possible responses: search in a library for printed books by their topics, use a card catalog or a computer database)
- How are these two sources alike? How are they different? (Possible responses: They both give information on many different topics. The information on a Web site may be more up-to-date.)

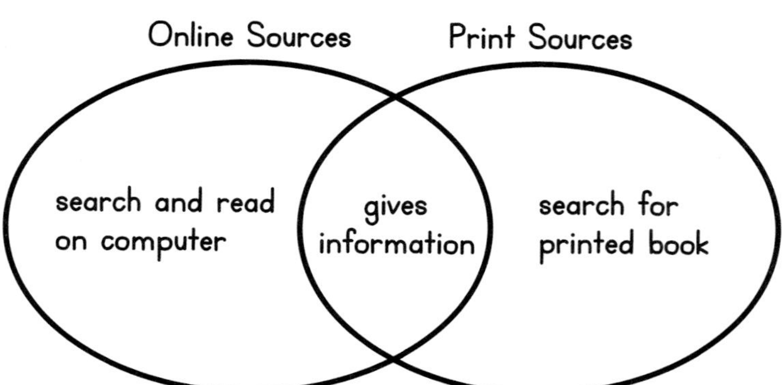

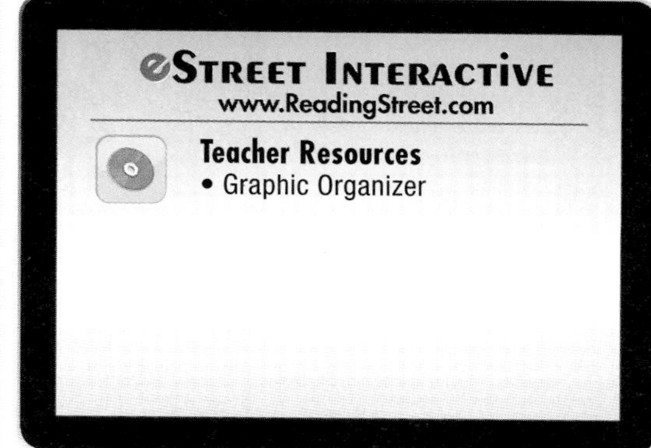

Team Talk Have students work in pairs to list the ways they can evaluate online information to make sure it is from a trusted source.

READ Tell students that they will now read about using online sources to find tips that are useful for a hiking trip. Have the class think about ways they can evaluate the sources.

Day 4 SMALL GROUP TIME • Differentiate Vocabulary, p. SG•49

OL On-Level

- **Develop** Language Using Amazing Words
- **Read** "Hiking Safety Tips"

SI Strategic Intervention

- **Review/Discuss** Amazing Words
- **Read** "Hiking Safety Tips"

A Advanced

- **Extend** Amazing Words and Selection Vocabulary
- **Read** "Hiking Safety Tips"
- **Organize** Inquiry Project

ELL

If... students need more scaffolding and practice with the **Amazing Words,**
then... use the Routine on pp. xxxvi–xxxvii in the *ELL Handbook.*

Common Core State Standards

Informational Text 5. Use text features and search tools (e.g., key words, sidebars, hyperlinks) to locate information relevant to a given topic efficiently.

21st Century Skills
INTERNET GUY

Evaluating Sources
Can you trust what you read on the Internet? You should always find out who wrote what you read. Can you believe that person? How can you tell? It is important always to check.

- Determine whether a Web site is reliable before you trust it. Web addresses that end in *.org* or *.gov* are usually reliable.
- Communication changes with different genres of media. Web sites use photos, colors, shapes, and other text features that wouldn't be on the radio or TV.
- Read "Hiking Safety Tips" to learn about evaluating sources. Compare the language used in the summaries of the Web sites. What tells you the first two sites won't be helpful?

490

Hiking Safety Tips

You are going on a camping trip. With camping comes freedom but also dangers. You must prepare a list of hiking safety tips. You decide to use the Internet to help you.

You type the keyword "hiking" into an Internet search engine. The first two sites probably won't help. But the third site looks promising, so you click on Staying Safe on the Trail.

Search Engine
hiking
Search

Hiking Clothes Outfit your family with these cute hiking shirts . . .
Footwear We have 100% leather hiking boots, just what you're looking for . . .
Staying Safe on the Trail Hiking is fun but beware of plants that . . .

The list goes on. You print it out. Now you can enjoy the freedom of hiking safely.

STAYING SAFE

A few tips will help you enjoy the freedom of a safe family hike.

Drinking Water Don't hike anywhere without it, especially on hot days. Even the clearest stream water may not be safe.

Snacks Bring them to eat when you take breaks. Good hiking snacks include granola bars, trail mix, and crackers.

Poison Plants Beware of poison ivy and poison oak. Oil from the leaves can make you break out in a rash with blisters.

poison oak

for more practice
Get Online!
www.ReadingStreet.com
Evaluate online sources about hiking safety tips.

21st Century Skills Online Activity
Log on and follow the step-by-step directions for evaluating reliable Web sites about staying safe while hiking.

491

Student Edition, pp. 490–491

Common Core State Standards

Informational Text 1. Ask and answer questions to demonstrate understanding of a text, referring explicitly to the text as the basis for the answers. **Informational Text 5.** Use text features and search tools (e.g., key words, sidebars, hyperlinks) to locate information relevant to a given topic efficiently.

Access Text

TEACH 21st Century Skills: Evaluating Online Sources Have students preview "Hiking Safety Tips" on pp. 490–491. Have them look at the types of Web sites that the search engine found. Then ask: Why are the first two on the list not helpful for someone who wants to find out how to stay safe on a hiking trip?

Corrective feedback	**If...** students are unable to evaluate which online sources are useful, **then...** use the model to guide students in evaluating online sources.

MODEL I can see that the first Web site gives information about finding the right hiking clothes to wear. While this might help you to stay safe by being covered and warm, it does not give safety tips to hikers. The second site is about what to wear on your feet. While this is also important, it is not a list of hiking tips.

ON THEIR OWN Have students work in pairs to come up with other words they could put into a search engine to get the results they wanted. If possible, allow students to try it on a search engine connected to the Internet.

Close Reading

ANALYSIS What is one benefit of using the Internet to find the latest information about a topic? What is one drawback? (The Internet is a fast way to search through a huge supply of information, but you have to carefully evaluate the source of any information to determine whether it is reliable.)

EVALUATION • TEXT EVIDENCE What do the first two search results on the list have in common? (They both are designed to sell things. They are both commercial.)

Get Online!

Evaluating Online Sources

FOR MORE PRACTICE Have students log on at www.ReadingStreet.com and follow the step-by-step directions for evaluating reliable Web sites about staying safe while hiking.

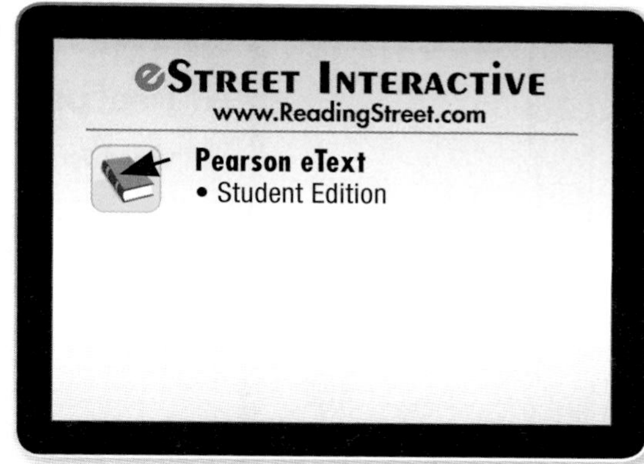

Access for All

A Advanced

Have students write the search words they would put into a search engine if they were looking for information about campgrounds in their area.

ELL

Summarize Ask students to summarize the selection "Hiking Safety Tips" by using their own words. If necessary, provide students with a sentence frame to get them started, such as *The selection was about ________.*

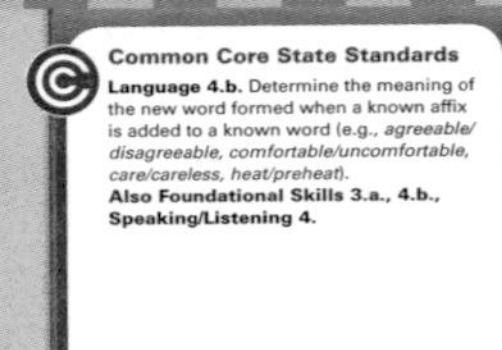

Let's Learn It!

READING STREET ONLINE
ONLINE STUDENT EDITION
www.ReadingStreet.com

Vocabulary

Prefixes and Suffixes

Word Structure Remember that prefixes and suffixes change the meanings of words. The prefixes *un-* or *dis-* at the beginning of a word make the word mean "not___" or "the opposite of___." The suffix *-ful* at the end of a word makes a word mean "full of___."

Practice It! Add *un-*, *dis-*, or *-ful* to as many of the following words as you can: *usual, like, mouth, care, natural, tidy, like, comfort, care, scoop*. Make a list of the new words. Tell what each word means.

Fluency

Rate

Remember that when you read aloud, read as fast as you would normally talk. To do this, you might need to reread a story aloud a few times and practice some of the difficult words and phrasing.

Practice It! Practice reading aloud *Two Bad Ants*, page 477. Listen for places where your rate slows down. What can you do to read them at a faster rate?

Listening and Speaking

Get Ready For Middle School: Speak loudly, clearly, and with expression.

Description

When giving a description, use words that tell how something looks, sounds, smells, tastes, or feels to create images in your listeners' minds.

Practice It! Describe your classroom from an ant's point of view. Begin with an exciting statement about what your classroom looks like. Then imagine the ant crawling to different areas in the room. Include details.

Listening . . .

- Comment about how effective the descriptions were.
- Paraphrase what the speaker says.

Speaking . . .

- Determine your purpose for speaking.
- Use expression.

Teamwork . . .

- Suggest creative ways to describe items.
- Build upon the ideas of others.

492 493

Student Edition, pp. 492–493

Common Core State Standards

Foundational Skills 3.a. Identify and know the meaning of the most common prefixes and derivational suffixes. **Foundational Skills 4.b.** Read on-level prose and poetry orally with accuracy, appropriate rate, and expression on successive readings. **Speaking/Listening 4.** Report on a topic or text, tell a story, or recount an experience with appropriate facts and relevant, descriptive details, speaking clearly at an understandable pace. **Language 3.** Use knowledge of language and its conventions when writing, speaking, reading, or listening. **Language 4.b.** Determine the meaning of the new word formed when a known affix is added to a known word (e.g., *agreeable/disagreeable, comfortable/uncomfortable, care/careless, heat/preheat*). **Also Speaking/Listening 1.b.**

Fluency

Rate

GUIDE PRACTICE Use the Fluency activity as an assessment tool. Make sure the reading passage is at least 200 words in length. Make sure students are reading at a speed that is appropriate to the text.

Check Fluency

FORMATIVE ASSESSMENT As students reread, monitor their progress toward their individual fluency goals.
Current Goal: 110–120 words correct per minute
End-of-Year Goal: 120 words correct per minute

If... students cannot read fluently at a rate of 110–120 words correct per minute,
then... have students practice with text at their independent levels.

Vocabulary Skill

Prefixes and Suffixes *un-, dis-, -ful*

TEACH PREFIXES AND SUFFIXES • WORD STRUCTURE Tell students that the structure, or makeup, of a word can give the reader clues about the word's meaning. Prefixes and suffixes are added to root words to change their meanings. The prefix *un-* or *dis-* at the beginning of a word makes the word mean "not" or "the opposite of _______." The suffix *-ful* at the end of a word makes the word mean "full of _______."

GUIDE PRACTICE Have students work in pairs and use their knowledge of word structure to write the meanings of the words *unhappy, disappear,* and *skillful.* Have them underline the prefix or suffix in each word.

ON THEIR OWN Have students practice by adding *un-, dis-,* or *-ful* to as many of the following words as possible and telling the words' meanings: *usual, like, hope, care, natural, tidy, comfort, harm.*

Listening and Speaking

Description

TEACH Tell students that a good description takes into account the entire environment around the narrator. Ask students to look around the classroom and think of how they would describe it. Then have them think of how they would describe the same classroom from an ant's point of view. Ask for volunteers to describe sections of the room from an ant's-eye view. Explain that thinking in this way improves their ability to describe details for the listener.

GUIDE PRACTICE Encourage students to list things in the classroom that they will talk about in their descriptions. Remind them that the more they plan ahead of time, the easier it will be for them to present their description to the listener. Remind them to speak coherently about their topic and use eye contact with the audience. Encourage them to speak with the correct rate, volume, or enunciation. When they are finished, point out the use of correct language conventions. Remind the students to listen attentively, ask relevant questions, and make pertinent comments.

ON THEIR OWN Have students present their descriptions to the class.

Describing

Remind students that they can practice their skills at describing by retelling events that happen during their day. After students return to the classroom from an event such as gym class, recess, or lunch, ask a volunteer to describe the events. Tell students that describing events effectively takes practice and that they cannot expect to give a perfect description during their first attempt.

Bridge to Common Core

PRESENTATION OF KNOWLEDGE/ IDEAS

As students present their descriptions, they give information and supporting details that help listeners follow the line of reasoning. The descriptions' organization, development, and style are appropriate to task, purpose, and audience.

Practice Pronunciation Assist pairs of students by modeling the correct pronunciation of words with prefixes and suffixes. Model the difference between the pronunciations of *un-* and *in-*. Pair students with mixed language proficiencies together to practice pronunciation and employ self-corrective techniques.

Common Core State Standards

Writing 2. Write informative/explanatory texts to examine a topic and convey ideas and information clearly. **Writing 2.b.** Develop the topic with facts, definitions, and details. **Language 2.** Demonstrate command of the conventions of standard English capitalization, punctuation, and spelling when writing. **Language 2.e.** Use conventional spelling for high-frequency and other studied words and for adding suffixes to base words (e.g., *sitting, smiled, cries, happiness*). **Also Language 2.b., 2.f.**

Research and Inquiry

Step 4 Synthesize

TEACH Have students synthesize their research findings and results. Have them review the information they sorted under the categories *rule, reason for the rule,* and *consequence of breaking the rule.* Have them note if they have all the information they need to write a letter about the importance of following rules.

GUIDE PRACTICE Have students imagine that they are writing a letter to convince someone not to break a school rule. They should write about what kind of freedom they would lose as a consequence of not following the rule.

ON THEIR OWN Have students write a brief explanation of their research findings. Then have them revise drafts of their letter to make sure that it is appropriate for the audience and the purpose (explaining the importance of following a rule). Also have them check for appropriate grammar and letter conventions.

Conventions

Commas

TEST PRACTICE Remind students that punctuation skills, such as correct use of commas, are often assessed on important tests. Remind students that commas are used for dates, addresses, and letter greetings and closings. They are also used to join sentences with a conjunction and to separate the words in a series.

ON THEIR OWN For additional practice, use *Reader's and Writer's Notebook,* p. 428.

Name ______ Two Bad Ants

Commas

Directions Read the selection. Then read each question that follows the selection. Decide which is the best answer to each question. Mark the space for the answer you have chosen.

Insect Communities

(1) Bees, wasps, termites and ants live in communities. (2) These insects work together to feed the community. (3) Other jobs in the community include builder soldier or, queen. (4) Communities are also called colonies. (5) They live in hives or nests. (6) Scientists study termite nests at the University of Kentucky in Lexington Kentucky.

1 What change, if any, should be made in sentence 1?
- ● Place a comma after ***termites***
- ○ Change ***Bees, wasps*** to **Bees and wasps**
- ○ Place a comma after ***and***
- ○ Make no change

2 Which change, if any, should be made in sentence 2?
- ○ Place a comma after ***insects***
- ○ Place a comma after ***work***
- ○ Place a comma after ***together***
- ● Make no change

3 Which change, if any, should be made in sentence 3?
- ○ Change ***builder soldier or, queen*** to **builder, soldier or queen.**
- ○ Change ***builder soldier or, queen*** to **builder soldier, or queen.**
- ● Change ***builder soldier or, queen*** to **builder, soldier, or queen.**
- ○ Make no change

4 Which answer correctly uses commas to combine sentence 4 and sentence 5?
- ○ Communities are also called colonies, they live in hives or nests.
- ○ Communities are also called colonies and live in hives or, nests.
- ○ Communities, also called colonies, live in hives, or nests.
- ● Communities are also called colonies, and they live in hives or nests.

5 What change, if any, should be made in sentence 6?
- ○ Place a comma after ***University of Kentucky***
- ● Place a comma after ***Lexington***
- ○ Place a comma after ***nests***
- ○ Make no change

School + Home **Home Activity** Your child prepared for taking tests on commas. Have your child show you some sentences from a school paper or ad and explain why they need commas or not.

428 **Conventions** Commas

Reader's and Writer's Notebook, p. 428

Spelling

Prefixes, Suffixes, and Endings

PRACTICE SPELLING STRATEGY Supply pairs of students with index cards on which the spelling words have been written. Have one student read a word while the other writes it. Then have students switch roles. Have them use the cards to check their spelling and correct any misspelled words.

ON THEIR OWN For additional practice, use *Let's Practice It!* p. 398 on the *Teacher Resources DVD-ROM.*

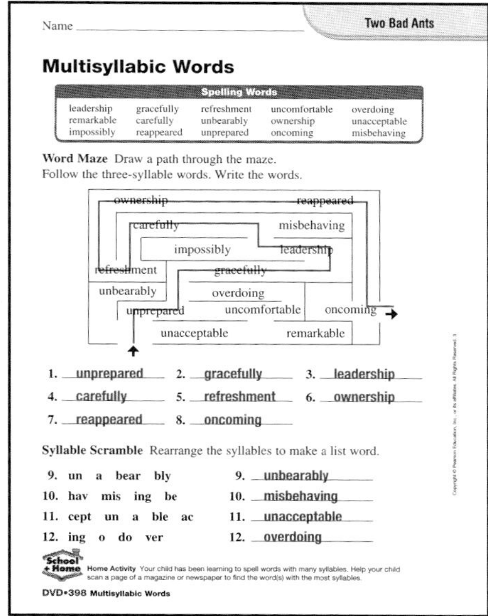

Name ______ Two Bad Ants

Multisyllabic Words

Spelling Words

leadership	gracefully	refreshment	uncomfortable	overdoing
remarkable	carefully	unbearably	ownership	unacceptable
impossibly	reappeared	unprepared	oncoming	misbehaving

Word Maze Draw a path through the maze. Follow the three-syllable words. Write the words.

1. unprepared 2. gracefully 3. leadership
4. carefully 5. refreshment 6. ownership
7. reappeared 8. oncoming

Syllable Scramble Rearrange the syllables to make a list word.

9. un a bear bly — 9. unbearably
10. hav mis ing be — 10. misbehaving
11. cept un a ble ac — 11. unacceptable
12. ing o do ver — 12. overdoing

School + Home **Home Activity** Your child has been learning to spell words with many syllables. Help your child scan a page of a magazine or newspaper to find the word(s) with the most syllables.

DVD•398 **Multisyllabic Words**

Let's Practice It! TR DVD•398

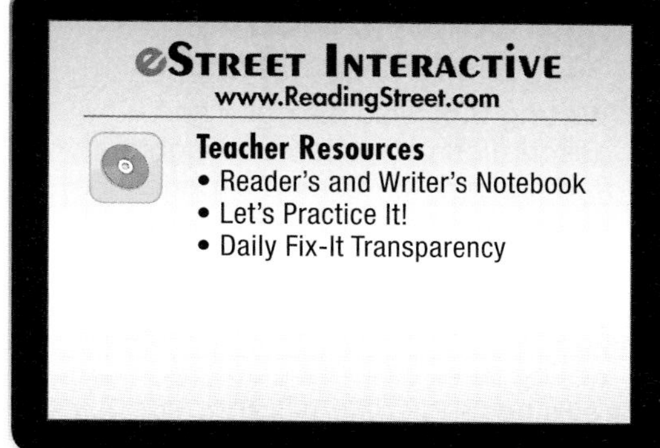

eStreet Interactive
www.ReadingStreet.com

Teacher Resources
- Reader's and Writer's Notebook
- Let's Practice It!
- Daily Fix-It Transparency

Daily Fix-It

7. The Masons and Marks went to a lake cabin for a vacasion on March 16 2008. *(vacation; 16,)*

8. The families was unprapared for the ants and other insects there. *(were; unprepared)*

Access for All

 Advanced

Have students pretend they are one of the characters in *Two Bad Ants.* Have them write a friendly letter from this character's perspective. Have partners exchange letters to check for correct use of commas in the greeting and closing.

Bridge to Common Core

CONVENTIONS OF STANDARD ENGLISH

As students consider comma usage when they write sentences, they are demonstrating command of the conventions of standard English. Your guidance will help them use correct grammar, usage, punctuation, and spelling to convey meaning when they speak and write.

Common Core State Standards

Writing 3.b. Use dialogue and descriptions of actions, thoughts, and feelings to develop experiences and events or show the response of characters to situations. **Writing 5.** With guidance and support from peers and adults, develop and strengthen writing as needed by planning, revising, and editing. **Language 3.a.** Choose words and phrases for effect.

Writing

Zoom in on

Comic Book

Mini-Lesson Revise: Adding

- Yesterday we wrote a comic book about the two ants from *Two Bad Ants.* Today we will revise our drafts. The goal is to make your writing clearer and more interesting.

- Display Writing Transparency 29B. Remind students that revising does not include corrections of grammar and mechanics. Tell them that this will be done during the lesson as they proofread their work. Then introduce the revising strategy of adding.

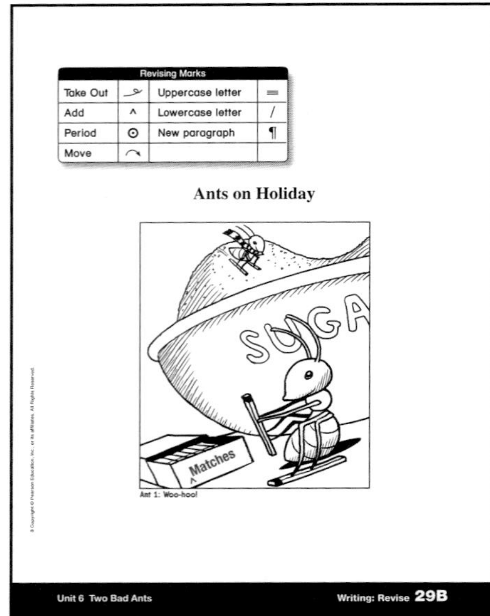

Revising Marks			
Take Out	⌒	Uppercase letter	═
Add	^	Lowercase letter	/
Period	⊙	New paragraph	¶
Move	⌒		

Ants on Holiday

Ant 1: Woo-hoo!

Unit 6 Two Bad Ants Writing: Revise **29B**

Writing Transparency 29B, TR DVD

- When you revise, ask yourself *What details about the setting, plot, or characters can I add to clarify my story? Can adding details introduce more humor or consistency?* Let's look at the second panel from our comic book. The drawing shows the ants using matchsticks for skis, but I'm not sure if this idea is clear enough for the reader. I can add the label *Matches* to my drawing. Also, I will add a scarf to the ant on skis since every other drawing shows this ant wearing a scarf.

Tell students that as they revise, not only should they look for places where they might add information to help make their comic books clearer and more interesting, but they should also make sure that they have included effective dialogue and reviewed their drawings.

Revising Tips

- ✔ Make sure drawings are consistent from one panel to the next.
- ✔ Add details to clarify and introduce humor to the comic book.
- ✔ Review writing and illustrations to make sure both are well organized and engaging.

PEER CONFERENCING • PEER REVISION Have students work in groups of three. Each student should write two to three questions on sticky notes about each of the other group members' comic books. Have them place the notes next to the corresponding panels. Have students focus on making the details in the draft clearer and more vivid.

Have students revise their drafts using their group members' questions from Peer Revision as well as the key features of a comic book to guide them. Be sure that students are using the revising strategy of adding.

Corrective feedback Circulate around the room to monitor students and confer with them as they revise. Remind students correcting errors that they will have time to edit and make finalized drawings tomorrow. They should be working on content and organization today.

Routine Quick Write for Fluency **Team Talk**

1. **Talk** Have pairs compare and contrast the adventures of the two ants in *Two Bad Ants* and their comic books.
2. **Write** Each student writes dialogue from the ants' perspective comparing the adventures.
3. **Share** Partners read each other's sentences and check that dialogue appears in word bubbles.

Routines Flip Chart

eStreet Interactive
www.ReadingStreet.com
Teacher Resources
- Writing Transparency

ELL

Modify the Prompt Allow beginning English speakers to work with a partner, dictating dialogue and narration as their partner records the sentences in word bubbles on separate sticky notes. In the revising step, have students choose the correct word bubble for each panel. Challenge them to add details to the writing to make their comic books clearer and to introduce humor.

Wrap Up Your Day!

- ✔ **Content Knowledge** What did you learn about hiking safety rules?
- ✔ **Oral Vocabulary** Monitor students' use of oral vocabulary as they respond: How do prefixes and suffixes change the meanings of words?
- ✔ **Story Structure** Discuss how knowing about conflict helps you understand text.

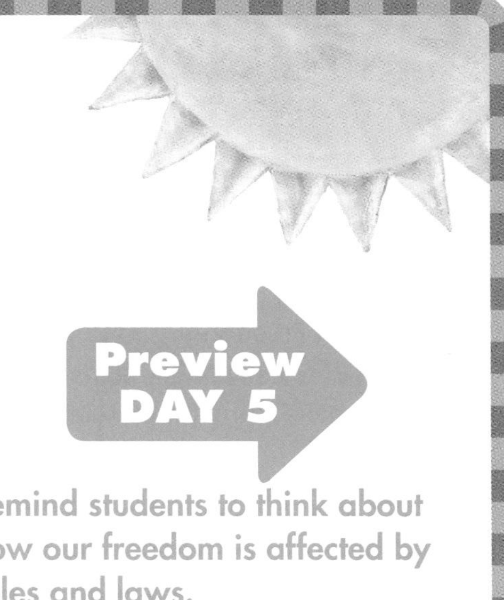

Remind students to think about how our freedom is affected by rules and laws.

DAY 5 at a Glance

Content Knowledge

Text-Based Comprehension
Review Literary Elements: Plot and Theme

Vocabulary Skill
Review Prefixes and Suffixes *un-, dis-, -ful*

Phonics/Word Analysis
Review Prefixes *im-, in-*

Literary Terms
Review Imagery

Assessment
Fluency
Comprehension

Research and Inquiry
Communicate

Spelling
Prefixes, Suffixes, and Endings

Conventions
Commas

Writing
Comic Book

Materials
- Student Edition
- Weekly Test
- Reader's and Writer's Notebook

Bridge to Common Core

INTEGRATION OF KNOWLEDGE/IDEAS
This week, students have integrated content presented in diverse media and analyzed how different texts address similar topics. They have developed knowledge about the importance of rules and laws to expand the unit topic of Freedom.

Social Studies Knowledge Goals
Students have learned that rules and laws
- keep order
- keep us safe
- remind us to do the right thing

Content Knowledge

Rules and Laws Are Important to Freedom

REVIEW THE CONCEPT Have students look back at the reading selections to find examples that best demonstrate the importance of rules and laws of freedom.

Build Oral Language

REVIEW AMAZING WORDS Display and review this week's concept map. Remind students that this week they have learned ten Amazing Words related to rules, laws, and freedom. Have students use the Amazing Words and the concept map to answer the question *Why are rules and laws important to freedom?*

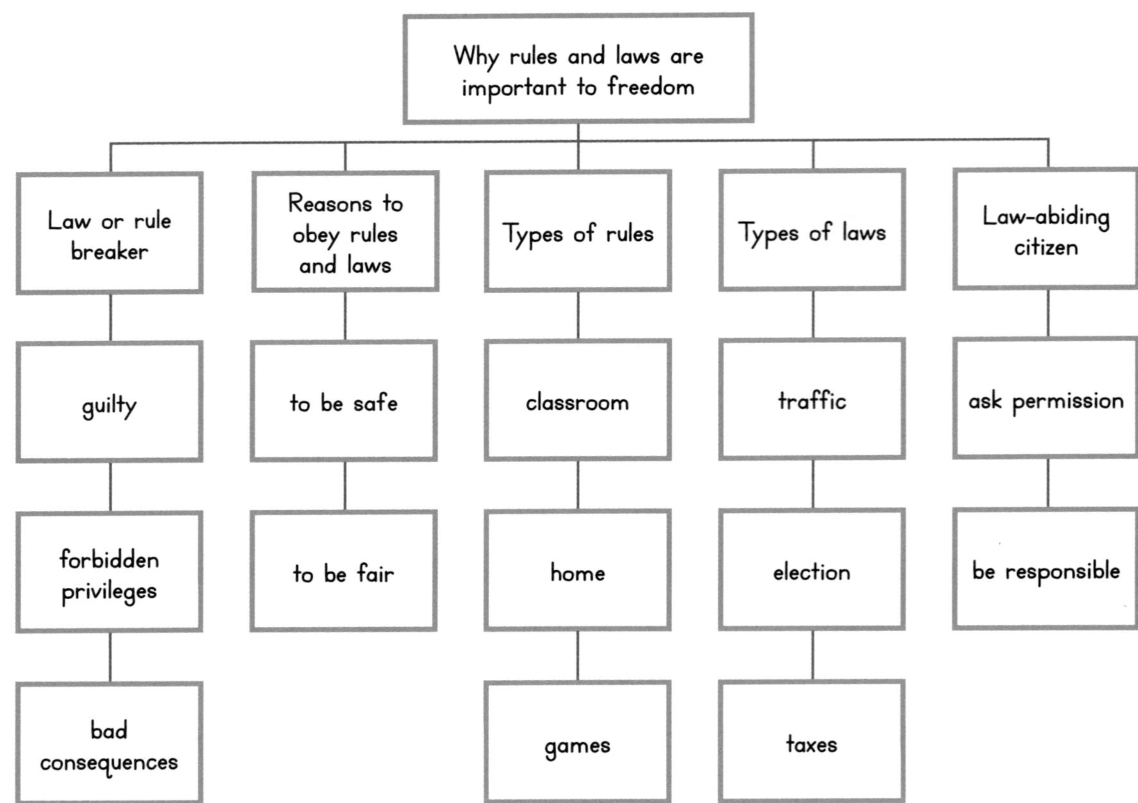

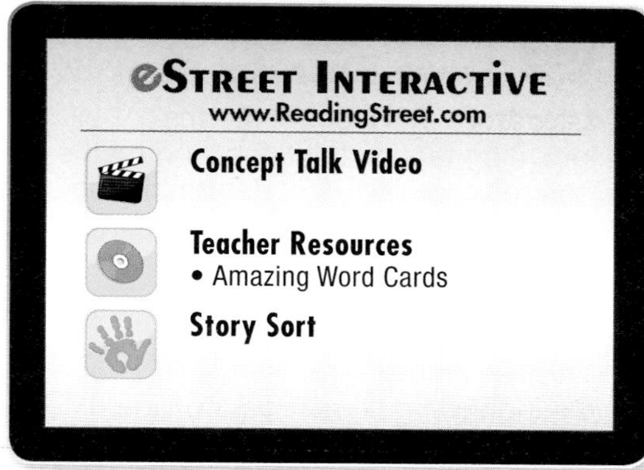

Build Oral Vocabulary

Team Talk **CONNECT TO AMAZING IDEAS** Have pairs of students discuss how the Question of the Week connects to the question for this unit of study: *What does freedom mean?* Tell students to use the concept map and what they have learned from this week's discussions and reading selections to form an Amazing Idea—a realization or "big idea" about Freedom. Remind partners to answer questions with appropriate detail and to give suggestions that build on each other's ideas. Then ask pairs to share their Amazing Ideas with the class.

Amazing Ideas might include these key concepts:

- Rules and laws are created so citizens can be protected.
- Freedom does not mean you can do whatever you want. You need to consider the needs of the community.
- There are often serious consequences if you do not follow rules and laws.

WRITE ABOUT IT Have students write a few sentences about their Amazing Idea, beginning with "This week I learned . . ."

Amazing Words

obey	fascinate
responsibility	guilt
consequence	encounter
permission	forbid
citizen	eerie

Check Oral Vocabulary

FORMATIVE ASSESSMENT Have individuals use this week's Amazing Words to describe freedom. Monitor students' abilities to use the Amazing Words and note which words you need to reteach.

If... students have difficulty using the Amazing Words,

then... reteach using the Oral Vocabulary Routine, pp. 461a, 466b, 478b, 490b, and OV•4.

Check Concepts and Language Use the Day 5 instruction on ELL Poster 29 to monitor students' understanding of the lesson concept.

Concept Map Work with students to add new words to the concept map.

Common Core State Standards

Literature 2. Recount stories, including fables, folktales, and myths from diverse cultures; determine the central message, lesson, or moral and explain how it is conveyed through key details in the text. **Literature 4.** Determine the meaning of words and phrases as they are used in a text, distinguishing literal from nonliteral language. **Foundational Skills 3.a.** Identify and know the meaning of the most common prefixes and derivational suffixes. **Language 4.b.** Determine the meaning of the new word formed when a known affix is added to a known word (e.g., *agreeable/disagreeable, comfortable/uncomfortable, care/careless, heat/preheat*). **Also Language 3.a.**

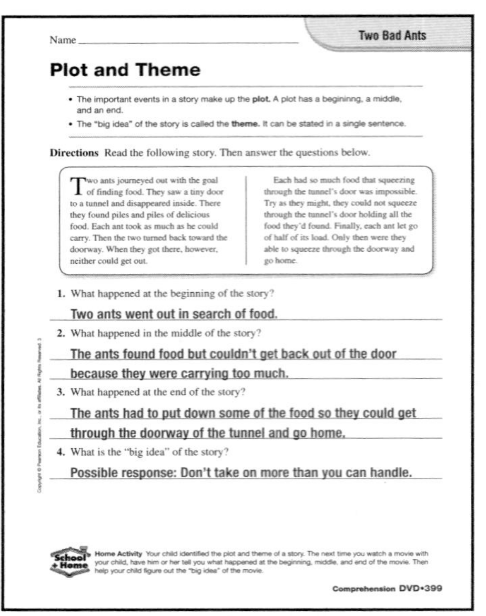

Name ______________ Two Bad Ants

Plot and Theme

- The important events in a story make up the **plot.** A plot has a beginning, a middle, and an end.
- The "big idea" of the story is called the **theme.** It can be stated in a single sentence.

Directions Read the following story. Then answer the questions below.

Two ants journeyed out with the goal of finding food. They saw a tiny door to a tunnel and disappeared inside. There they found piles and piles of delicious food. Each ant took as much as he could carry. Then the two turned back toward the doorway. When they got there, however, neither could get out.

Each had so much food that squeezing through the tunnel's door was impossible. Try as they might, they could not squeeze through the tunnel's door holding all the food they'd found. Finally, each ant let go of half of its load. Only then were they able to squeeze through the doorway and go home.

1. What happened at the beginning of the story?
   Two ants went out in search of food.
2. What happened in the middle of the story?
   The ants found food but couldn't get back out of the door because they were carrying too much.
3. What happened at the end of the story?
   The ants had to put down some of the food so they could get through the doorway of the tunnel and go home.
4. What is the "big idea" of the story?
   Possible response: Don't take on more than you can handle.

School + Home **Home Activity** Your child identified the plot and theme of a story. The next time you watch a movie with your child, have him or her tell you what happened at the beginning, middle, and end of the movie. Then help your child figure out the "big idea" of the movie.

Comprehension DVD•399

Let's Practice It! TR DVD•399

Selection Vocabulary

crystal a solid, glass-like item

disappeared vanished from sight

discovery the action of finding something

goal an aim or desired result

journey a long trip

joyful feeling great happiness

scoop a spoon-shaped tool; the amount taken up by such a tool

unaware having no knowledge of something

Text-Based Comprehension

Review Literary Elements: Plot and Theme

TEACH Review the definitions of plot and theme on p. 464. Explain that the plot of a story should be summarized by stating the beginning, middle, and end of the story. The theme should be told in one or two short sentences. For additional support have students review p. EI•13 on plot and theme.

GUIDE PRACTICE Have partners summarize the plot of *Two Bad Ants,* and paraphrase the theme and its supporting details. Have the partners work together to tell how the plot of the story is different from the theme of the story.

ON THEIR OWN For additional practice, use *Let's Practice It!* p. 399 on the *Teacher Resources DVD-ROM*.

Vocabulary Skill

Review Prefixes and Suffixes *un-, dis-, -ful*

TEACH Remind students that they can look at a word's prefix or suffix to help them find out the meaning of an unknown word.

GUIDE PRACTICE Review with students how to find the correct meaning of *unbelievable* using word structure clues. Explain that recalling the meaning of the prefix *un-* will help them determine the meaning of the word.

ON THEIR OWN Have students work with partners to list words for each other that can be defined by looking at prefixes or suffixes. Partners can trade lists and define the words based on their knowledge of the meanings of the prefixes *un-, dis-,* and the suffix *-ful.*

Word Analysis

Review Prefixes *im-, in-*

TEACH Write the following sentences on the board. Have students read each one, first quietly to themselves and then aloud as you track the print.

1. **It is *improper* to put *inedible* food in the fridge.**
2. **I spelled *impatient incorrectly* on the spelling test.**
3. **It's *improbable* that the law is *invalid*.**
4. **Isn't it *incredible* the way a building can be *imploded*?**
5. **I used an *incorrect* recipe, so dinner was *imperfect*.**

Team Talk Have students work with a partner to identify and underline the prefixes in the words. Then point to words at random and have the group read them together.

Literary Terms

Review Imagery

TEACH Have students reread *Two Bad Ants* on pp. 468–485. Remind students that imagery is the use of words that helps the reader experience the way things look, sound, smell, taste, or feel.

GUIDE PRACTICE Have students reread the first paragraph on p. 483. Ask students to supply words and phrases that the author uses to bring to mind the sights, sounds, and feelings of the garbage disposal. Have students point out other examples of imagery from the selection and talk about how these examples help the reader create a graphic visual image to aid comprehension.

ON THEIR OWN Have students make a Venn diagram to compare and contrast the experiences of an ant and a human living in a house. Have them compare and contrast what humans and ants would see, hear, smell, taste, or feel. Ask them to discuss what the story might have been like without the author's use of imagery.

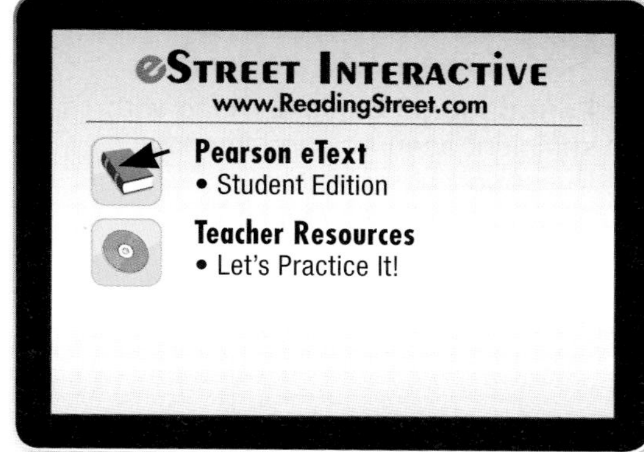

Articulation Tip The prefixes *im-* and *in-* look and sound very similar. Encourage students to enunciate when saying these prefixes so that it is clear which prefix they are saying.

Imagery If students have trouble with imagery, ask them to think of the school lunchroom and to describe the image they have in their heads. Remind them that describing words such as *big, crowded,* or *loud* should help them express a simple image to the listener.

Literary Elements: Plot If students have trouble identifying the plot of *Two Bad Ants,* write a definition on the board and brainstorm a sentence about the plot. For example: *plot: events in a story: two ants go on an adventure.*

Common Core State Standards

Foundational Skills 4. Read with sufficient accuracy and fluency to support comprehension. **Foundational Skills 4.b.** Read on-level prose and poetry orally with accuracy, appropriate rate, and expression on successive readings.

Plan to Assess Fluency

- ☐ **Week 1** Advanced
- ☐ **Week 2** Strategic Intervention
- ☐ **Week 3** On-Level
- ☑ **This week assess Strategic Intervention students.**
- ☐ **Week 5** Assess any students you have not yet checked during this unit.

Set individual goals for students to enable them to reach the year-end goal.

- Current Goal: 110–120 WCPM
- Year-End Goal: 120 WCPM

Assessment

Monitor Progress

FLUENCY Make two copies of the fluency passage on p. 493k. As the student reads the text aloud, mark mistakes on your copy. Also mark where the student is at the end of one minute. To check the student's comprehension of the passage, have him or her tell what was read. To figure words correct per minute (WCPM), subtract the number of mistakes from the total number of words read in one minute.

RATE

Corrective feedback

If... students cannot read fluently at a rate of 110–120 WCPM,
then... make sure they practice with text at their independent reading level. Provide additional fluency practice by pairing nonfluent readers with fluent readers.

If... students already read at 120 WCPM,
then... have them read a book of their choice independently.

If... students need more scaffolding and practice with **Conventions and Writing,**
then... use the activities on pp. DI•99–DI•100 in the Teacher Resources section on SuccessNet.

Day 5 SMALL GROUP TIME • Differentiate Reteaching, p. SG•49

OL On-Level
- **Practice** Commas
- **Reread** *Reading Street Sleuth,* pp. 74–75

SI Strategic Intervention
- **Review** Commas
- **Reread** *Reading Street Sleuth,* pp. 74–75

A Advanced
- **Extend** Commas
- **Reread** *Reading Street Sleuth,* pp. 74–75
- **Communicate** Inquiry Project

Name ____________________

The Case of the Missing Crystal

When Ned walked into the dining room, he gasped. A crystal 11
candlestick had disappeared! Who could have taken it? Ned wasn't 21
sure, but he was determined to find out. 29

Ned went to see Rosa. "Rosa," Ned asked, "Do you know where 41
the crystal candlestick is?" 45

"No, I sure don't, but I'll help you look for it," Rosa replied. 58

"I think some immature person has stolen it!" Ned told her 69
impatiently. "My goal is to catch the thief. I've already started an 81
informal list of possible suspects." 86

"Wow, that was fast!" Rosa smiled at Ned. She was unaware that 98
she was the only person on the list so far. 108

Rosa followed Ned on his journey through the house. In the 119
garage they saw broken crystal on the floor. 127

"Wow, I hope no one hurt themselves," Rosa said. "We'd better 138
tell Mom so that she can scoop up the pieces." 148

Ned wasn't paying attention. He was impolitely studying a muddy 158
patch in the corner. "This is an incredible clue," he muttered to himself. 171

"The thief was Rusty," he said. 177

Rusty was their dog. 181

"That's impossible!" Rosa cried. "Why would Rusty take a 190
candlestick?" 191

"I don't know," Ned said. "But he grabbed it off the table and ran 205
outside. Then he came back in and dropped it in the garage. I found a 220
muddy paw print that proves it!" 226

MONITOR PROGRESS

- **Check Fluency**

Common Core State Standards

Literature 2. Recount stories, including fables, folktales, and myths from diverse cultures; determine the central message, lesson, or moral and explain how it is conveyed through key details in the text. **Foundational Skills 4.** Read with sufficient accuracy and fluency to support comprehension.

Assessment

Monitor Progress

For a written assessment of Prefixes *im-, in-,* Plot and Theme, and Selection Vocabulary, use Weekly Test 29, pp. 169–174.

LITERARY ELEMENTS: PLOT AND THEME Use "A Field Trip" on p. 493m to check students' understanding of plot and theme.

1. Summarize the plot's main events. On a field trip, Rich and Felix want to go to the racecar exhibit instead of going to the dinosaur and Texas exhibits that their teacher told them to go to. However, they followed the rules and went only where they were supposed to go. Their teacher was proud of their actions. He let them choose the next exhibit for the class to visit.
2. What is the theme of the story? It pays to follow the rules and do the right thing instead of doing whatever you want.
3. What shows you that this is the theme of the story? It is the story's message or "big idea."

Corrective feedback	**If...** students are unable to answer the comprehension questions, **then...** use the Reteach lesson in *First Stop.*

Name ___

A Field Trip

As the bus pulled up to City Museum, Mr. Latham said to the seated third graders, "Now don't forget the rules for our field trip. Always stay with your assigned partner. For the first hour, feel free to visit the dinosaur exhibit and the Texas history room. Don't go to other exhibits until after we meet again at 10 o'clock."

Mr. Latham, the kids, and a few parents walked into the museum together. "I can enjoy dinosaurs and history," said Rich to his partner Felix. "But I'd really like to see the racecar exhibit."

"Me too," agreed Felix.

Rich and Felix didn't realize it, but Mr. Latham heard what they said. He knew they were good kids, yet he wondered if they might break the rules and sneak into the racecar exhibit. For the next hour, Mr. Latham had many students to watch, but now and then he checked to see where Rich and Felix were.

For 45 minutes, Rich and Felix roamed around the dinosaur exhibit. They really enjoyed it. Then they walked to the history room. They passed the big open doorway that led to the racecar exhibit. They peeked in a bit, but didn't go in. Instead, they walked into the history room and studied a model fort. Mr. Latham was proud of them.

At 10 o'clock, the class met. "Now we'll go to a different exhibit," said Mr. Latham. "Rich and Felix, will you pick one?"

"The racecar exhibit!" they both said.

Mr. Latham just smiled.

MONITOR PROGRESS

- **Literary Elements: Plot and Theme**

Common Core State Standards

Speaking/Listening 1.b. Follow agreed-upon rules for discussions (e.g., gaining the floor in respectful ways, listening to others with care, speaking one at a time about the topics and texts under discussion). **Speaking/Listening 4.** Report on a topic or text, tell a story, or recount an experience with appropriate facts and relevant, descriptive details, speaking clearly at an understandable pace. **Language 2.** Demonstrate command of the conventions of standard English capitalization, punctuation, and spelling when writing. **Language 2.f.** Use spelling patterns and generalizations (e.g., word families, position-based spellings, syllable patterns, ending rules, meaningful word parts) in writing words. **Also Language 2.b.**

Research and Inquiry

Step 5 Communicate

PRESENT IDEAS Have students share their inquiry results by presenting their letters and giving a brief talk on their research.

SPEAKING Remind students how to be good speakers and how to communicate effectively with their audience.

- Respond to relevant questions with appropriate details.
- Speak clearly and loudly.
- Keep eye contact with audience members.

LISTENING Remind students of these tips for being a good listener.

- Wait until the speaker has finished before raising your hand to ask a relevant question or make a comment.
- Be polite, even if you disagree.

LISTEN TO IDEAS Have students listen attentively to the various letters and research talks. Have them make pertinent comments, closely related to the topic.

Spelling Test

Prefixes, Suffixes, and Endings

To administer the spelling test, refer to the directions, words, and sentences on p. 465c.

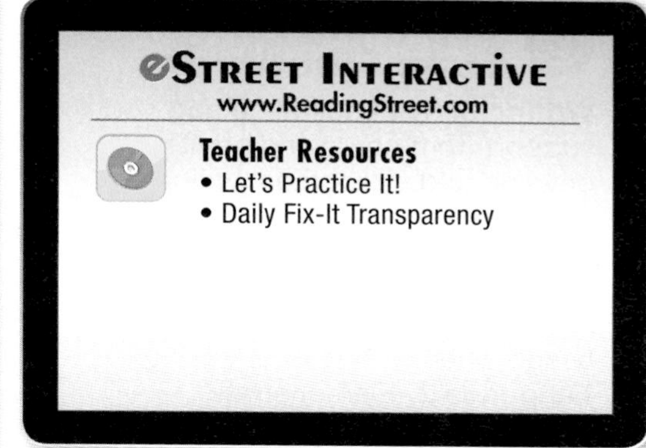

Conventions

Commas

MORE PRACTICE Remind students that commas are used for dates, addresses, and letter greetings and closings. They are also used to join sentences with a conjunction and to separate the words in a series.

GUIDE PRACTICE Write today's date (month, day, year) and the location of the school (city and state), omitting commas. Have students tell where the commas belong. Ask students to write tomorrow's date, the state capital, and the greeting and closing of a letter to a friend, using commas correctly.

ON THEIR OWN Write these sentences without commas. Have students rewrite the sentences, adding commas where needed. Students should complete *Let's Practice It!* p. 400 on the *Teacher Resources DVD-ROM.*

1. **We made milk, toast, and eggs for breakfast.**
2. **A bus can take us home, or Dad can pick us up.**
3. **We moved to a small house in San Antonio, Texas.**
4. **Sam made his bed, took out the garbage, and swept the kitchen floor.**
5. **My uncle was born August 19th, 1977.**

Daily Fix-It

9. Tommy found a anthill out side his house. *(an; outside)*
10. He staring at the tiny creetures for hours. *(was staring or stared; creatures)*

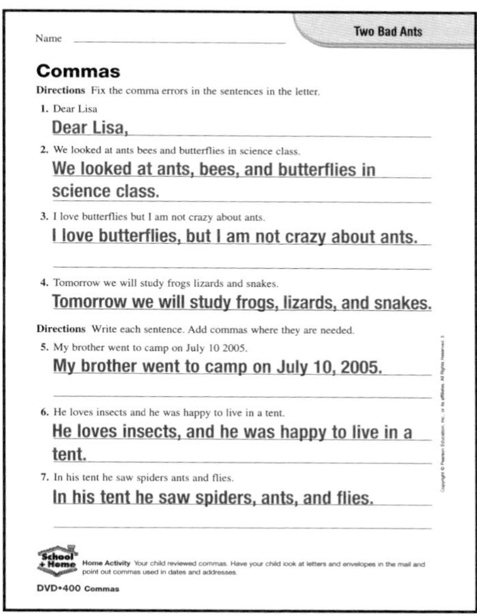
Name ______ Two Bad Ants

Commas

Directions Fix the comma errors in the sentences in the letter.

1. Dear Lisa
Dear Lisa,
2. We looked at ants bees and butterflies in science class.
We looked at ants, bees, and butterflies in science class.
3. I love butterflies but I am not crazy about ants.
I love butterflies, but I am not crazy about ants.
4. Tomorrow we will study frogs lizards and snakes.
Tomorrow we will study frogs, lizards, and snakes.

Directions Write each sentence. Add commas where they are needed.

5. My brother went to camp on July 10 2005.
My brother went to camp on July 10, 2005.
6. He loves insects and he was happy to live in a tent.
He loves insects, and he was happy to live in a tent.
7. In his tent he saw spiders ants and flies.
In his tent he saw spiders, ants, and flies.

School + Home **Home Activity** Your child reviewed commas. Have your child look at letters and envelopes in the mail and point out commas used in dates and addresses.

DVD•400 Commas

Let's Practice It! TR DVD•400

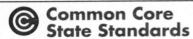

Common Core State Standards

Writing 5. With guidance and support from peers and adults, develop and strengthen writing as needed by planning, revising, and editing. **Language 1.** Demonstrate command of the conventions of standard English grammar and usage when writing or speaking. **Language 2.** Demonstrate command of the conventions of standard English capitalization, punctuation, and spelling when writing. **Language 2.g.** Consult reference materials, including beginning dictionaries, as needed to check and correct spellings. **Also Writing 10.**

Teacher Note

Writing Self-Evaluation Make copies of the Writing Self-Evaluation Guide on p. 39 of the *Reader's and Writer's Notebook* and hand out to students.

Bridge to Common Core

PRODUCTION AND DISTRIBUTION OF WRITING

Over the course of the week, students have developed and strengthened their drafts through planning, revising, editing, and rewriting. The final drafts are clear and coherent comic books in which the organization and style are appropriate to the purpose and audience.

Write Guy *by Jeff Anderson*

Focus Your Editing

In the editing process, students can easily get bogged down by everything that needs to be fixed. Editing one aspect at a time helps students focus their efforts and concentrate on one task, while making it easier for you as a teacher to fully explain and reteach the concept, moving students toward correctness. Sometimes less really is more.

Writing

Comic Book

REVIEW REVISING Remind students that yesterday they revised their comic books, paying particular attention to adding details for clarification and to introducing humor and consistency to make each panel more detailed and engaging. Today they will proofread their comic books.

Mini-Lesson Proofread

Proofread for Commas

- **Teach** When we proofread, we look closely at our work, searching for errors in mechanics such as spelling, capitalization, punctuation, and grammar. Today we will focus on correct use of commas.
- **Model** Display Writing Transparency 29C. I will look for sentences with a comma missing. I see a problem with the sentence *The skiing is lovely this time of year and the ice-skating is unparalleled.* We need a comma to separate the two parts of this compound sentence. I will add a comma after the word *year*. Now there is a comma before the joining word where the two sentences are combined. Point out that the greeting *Dear Brother and Sister Ants* should also be followed by a comma. Then explain to students that they should reread their comic books several times, each time looking for different types of errors: spelling, punctuation, capitalization, and grammar.

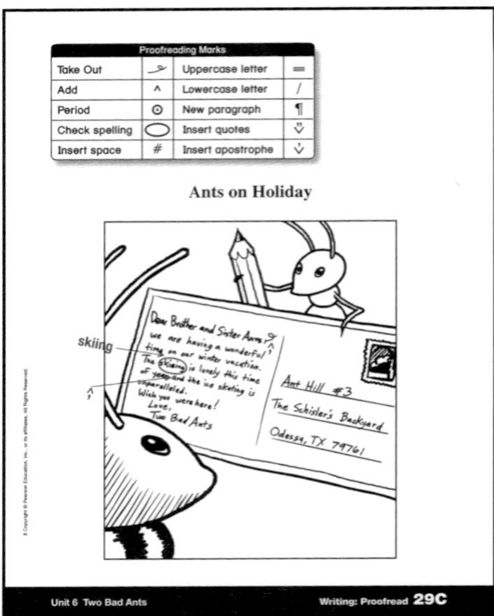

Writing Transparency 29C, TR DVD

PROOFREAD Display the Proofreading Tips. Ask students to proofread their comic books, using the Proofreading Tips and paying particular attention to correct use of commas. Circulate around the room answering students' questions. Then have pairs proofread one another's comic books.

Proofreading Tips

- ✔ Check for correct use of commas.
- ✔ Check for correct spelling, punctuation, capitalization, and grammar.
- ✔ Use a dictionary to check the spelling of difficult words.

eStreet Interactive
www.ReadingStreet.com

Teacher Resources
- Writing Transparency
- Reader's and Writer's Notebook

PRESENT Have students incorporate revisions and proofreading edits into their comic books to create a final draft. Have students draw the final illustrations for their comic books. After students have finished their comic books, make a class book that includes each student's work. Display the book at a silent reading station so that every student can read it. When students have finished, have each student complete the Writing Self-Evaluation Guide.

Routine Quick Write for Fluency **Team Talk**

1. **Talk** Pairs discuss what they learned about writing a comic book this week.
2. **Write** Each student writes a sentence summarizing what he or she learned.
3. **Share** Partners read their summaries to one another.

Routines Flip Chart

Wrap Up Your Week!

Rules and Laws Are Important to Freedom

Why are rules and laws important to freedom?

In *Two Bad Ants* and "Hiking Safety Tips," we learned that rules and laws are important to freedom because they help keep us safe.

Team Talk Have students recall their Amazing Ideas about freedom and use these ideas to help them demonstrate their understanding of the Question of the Week.

Next Week's Concept

Keeping Your Freedom

What is the best way to keep your freedom?

Poster Preview Prepare students for next week by using Week 5 ELL Poster 30. Read the Talk-Through to introduce the concept and vocabulary. Ask students to identify and describe actions in the art.

Selection Summary Send home the summary of the next week's selection, *Atlantis,* in English and in students' home languages, if available in the *ELL Handbook*. They can read the summary with family members.

What is the best way to keep your freedom? Next week you will read about what happened to the people of Atlantis.

Preview Next Week

Assessment Checkpoints for the Week

Weekly Assessment

Use pp. 169–174 of *Weekly Tests* to check:

- ✓ **Phonics/Word Analysis** Prefixes *im-, in-*
- ✓ **Comprehension** Literary Elements: Plot and Theme
- ✓ Review **Comprehension** Cause and Effect
- ✓ **Selection Vocabulary**

crystal	journey
disappeared	joyful
discovery	scoop
goal	unaware

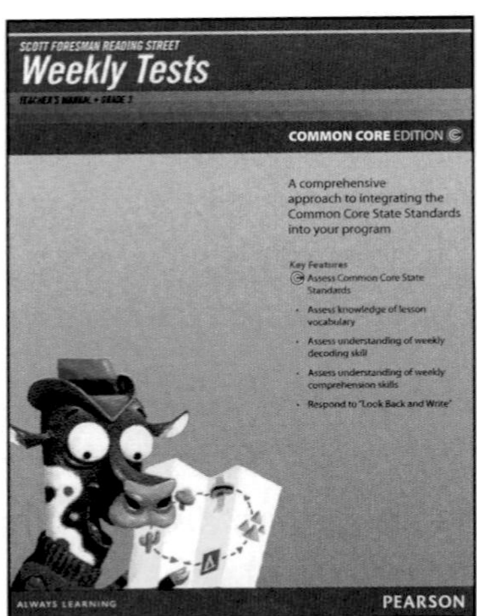

Weekly Tests

Differentiated Assessment

Advanced

On-Level

SI
Strategic Intervention

Use pp. 169–174 of *Fresh Reads for Fluency and Comprehension* to check:

- ✓ **Comprehension** Literary Elements: Plot and Theme
- ✓ Review **Comprehension** Cause and Effect
- ✓ **Fluency** Words Correct Per Minute

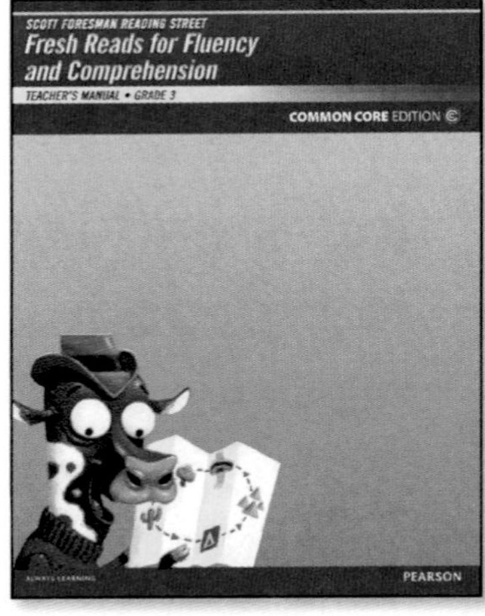

Fresh Reads for Fluency and Comprehension

Managing Assessment

Use *Assessment Handbook* for:

- ✓ **Weekly Assessment Blackline Masters for Monitoring Progress**
- ✓ **Observation Checklists**
- ✓ **Record-Keeping Forms**
- ✓ **Portfolio Assessment**

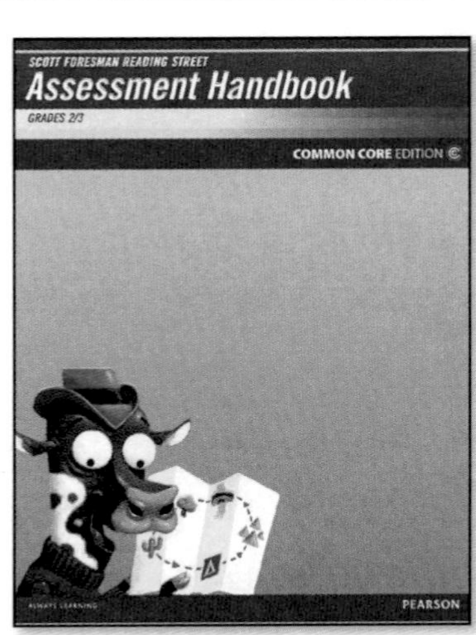

Assessment Handbook

TEACHER NOTES

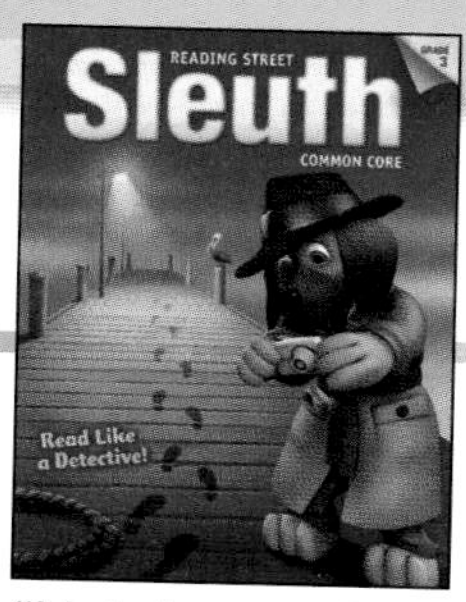

"Lin's Lesson," pp. 74–75

DAY 1 Differentiate Vocabulary

- **Word Knowledge** Amazing Words
- **Read** "Lin's Lesson"
- **Inquiry** Identify Questions

DAY 2 Differentiate Comprehension

- **Word Knowledge** Selection Vocabulary
- **Access Text** Read *Two Bad Ants*
- **Inquiry** Investigate

DAY 3 Differentiate Close Reading

- **Word Knowledge** Develop Vocabulary
- **Close Reading** Read *Two Bad Ants*
- **Inquiry** Investigate

DAY 4 Differentiate Vocabulary

- **Word Knowledge** Amazing Words
- **Read** "Hiking Safety Tips"
- **Inquiry** Organize

DAY 5 Differentiate Reteaching

- **Conventions** Commas
- **Reread** "Lin's Lesson" or Leveled Readers
- **Inquiry** Communicate

Teacher Guides and Student pages can be found in the Leveled Reader Database.

Place English Language Learners in the groups that correspond to their reading abilities.
If... students need scaffolding and practice,
then... use the ELL Notes on the instructional pages.

Independent Practice

Independent Practice Stations

See pp. 460h and 460i for Independent Stations.

Pearson Trade Book Library

See the Leveled Reader Database for lesson plans and student pages.

Reading Street Digital Path

Independent Practice Activities are available in the Digital Path.

Independent Reading

See p. 460i for independent reading suggestions.

On-Level

Common Core State Standards

Literature 1. Ask and answer questions to demonstrate understanding of a text, referring explicitly to the text as the basis for the answers. **Literature 3.** Describe characters in a story (e.g., their traits, motivations, or feelings) and explain how their actions contribute to the sequence of events. **Foundational Skills 4.** Read with sufficient accuracy and fluency to support comprehension. **Language 4.** Determine or clarify the meaning of unknown and multiple-meaning words and phrases based on grade 3 reading and content, choosing flexibly from a range of strategies. **Language 6.** Acquire and use accurately grade-appropriate conversational, general academic, and domain-specific words and phrases, including those that signal spatial and temporal relationships (e.g., *After dinner that night we went looking for them*).

Independent Reading Options

Trade Book Library

eStreet Interactive
www.ReadingStreet.com

Teacher Guides are available on the Leveled Reader Database.

If... students need more scaffolding and practice with **Vocabulary, then...** use the activities on pp. DI•92–DI•93 in the Teacher Resources section on SuccessNet.

1 Build Word Knowledge

Practice Amazing Words

DEFINE IT Elicit the definition for the word *responsibility* from students. Ask: How would you describe a *responsibility* to another student? (Possible response: A *responsibility* is something that you should do, like a duty.) Clarify or give a definition when necessary. Continue with the words *consequence* and *permission.*

Team Talk **TALK ABOUT IT** Have students internalize meanings. Ask: How can you group the Amazing Words together in a sentence? (Possible response: It's your *responsibility* to ask for *permission* or there might be *consequences.*) Allow time for students to play with the words. Review the concept map with students. Discuss other words they can add to the concept map.

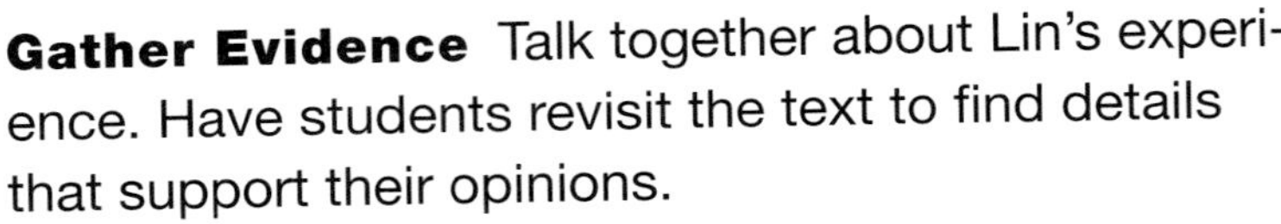

2 Text-Based Comprehension

Read

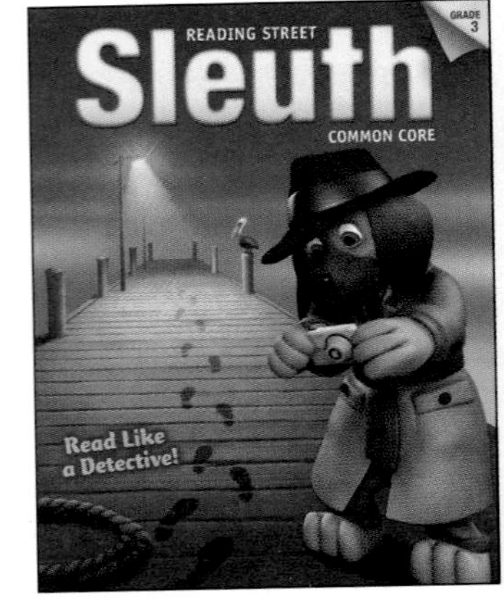

READ ALOUD "Lin's Lesson" Have partners read "Lin's Lesson" from *Reading Street Sleuth* on pp. 74–75.

ACCESS TEXT Discuss the Sleuth Work section with students before they work on it. Remind students that they can use these steps with other texts they read.

Gather Evidence Talk together about Lin's experience. Have students revisit the text to find details that support their opinions.

Ask Questions Have partners role-play, asking each other their questions. Talk together about whether questions are fact or opinion based.

Make Your Case Remind students that they can use their own personal experiences to support their opinions. Have students discuss their opinions with a partner. Encourage students to point out the other's most convincing reason.

On-Level

1 Build Word Knowledge

Practice Selection Vocabulary

crystal	disappeared	discovery	goal
journey	joyful	scoop	unaware

DEFINE IT Discuss the definition for the word *joyful* with students. Ask: How would you describe *joyful* to another student? (Possible response: Someone who is *joyful* is extremely happy.) Continue with the remaining words.

Team Talk **TALK ABOUT IT** Have pairs use the selection vocabulary in sentences to internalize meaning. Ask: How can you group the selection vocabulary words together in a sentence? (Possible response: The explorer's *discovery* of the rare *crystal* made him *joyful*.) Allow time for students to play with the words and then share their sentences.

2 Read

Two Bad Ants

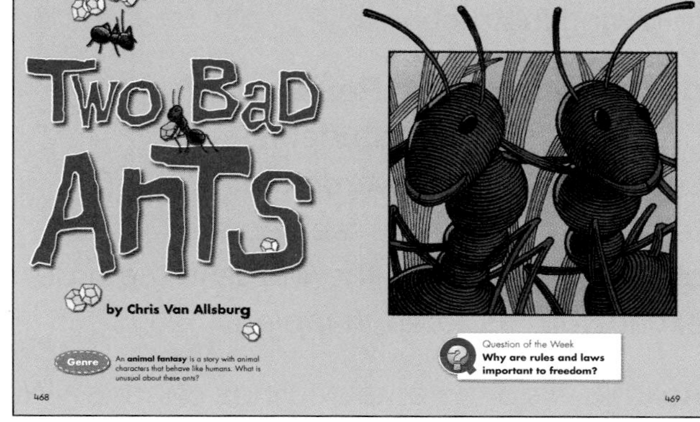

If you read *Two Bad Ants* during whole group time, then use the following instruction.

ACCESS TEXT Reread the paragraphs on pp. 475–476. Ask questions to check understanding. How is the world inside the kitchen different from the outside world? (The surfaces are smooth and shiny, and the smells are different. There is no sky in the kitchen.) What is the sparkling treasure that the ants take? (sugar from a sugar bowl) What happens to the two small ants? (They decide to stay and eat so much sugar they fall asleep.)

Have students identify sections from today's reading that they did not completely understand. Reread them aloud and clarify misunderstandings.

If you are reading *Two Bad Ants* during small group time, then return to pp. 470–477a to guide the reading.

SMALL GROUP TIME

More Reading for Group Time

ON-LEVEL

Reviews
- Plot and Theme
- Story Structure
- Selection Vocabulary

Use this suggested Leveled Reader or other text at student's instructional level.

eStreet Interactive
www.ReadingStreet.com

Use the Leveled Reader Database for lesson plans and student pages for *The Three Bears and Goldilocks.*

On-Level

Common Core State Standards

Literature 1. Ask and answer questions to demonstrate understanding of a text, referring explicitly to the text as the basis for the answers. **Informational Text 5.** Use text features and search tools (e.g., key words, sidebars, hyperlinks) to locate information relevant to a given topic efficiently. **Language 4.** Determine or clarify the meaning of unknown and multiple-meaning words and phrases based on grade 3 reading and content, choosing flexibly from a range of strategies. **Language 6.** Acquire and use accurately grade-appropriate conversational, general academic, and domain-specific words and phrases, including those that signal spatial and temporal relationships (e.g., *After dinner that night we went looking for them*).

1 Build Word Knowledge

Develop Vocabulary

REREAD FOR VOCABULARY Reread the paragraph of *Two Bad Ants* on p. 479. Let's read this paragraph and think about words with meanings similar to the word *disappeared.* To help students think of synonyms, ask them to complete the following sentence: If something has disappeared, then it is _______. (Possible responses: missing, lost, gone, vanished, or ended) Have students discuss how the different synonyms would change the meaning of the original sentence in the story.

2 Read

Two Bad Ants

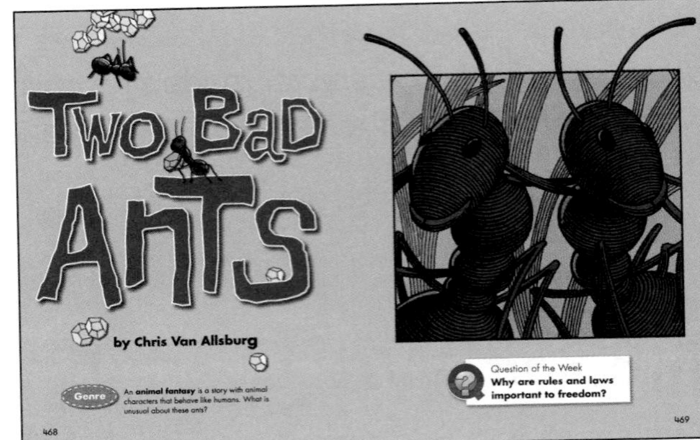

If you read *Two Bad Ants* during whole group time, then use the following instruction.

CLOSE READING Read pp. 484–485. Have students search the text for words that tell how the two ants feel. As a class, make a list of the words in the order they appear. (*stunned senseless, exhausted, battered, happier*)

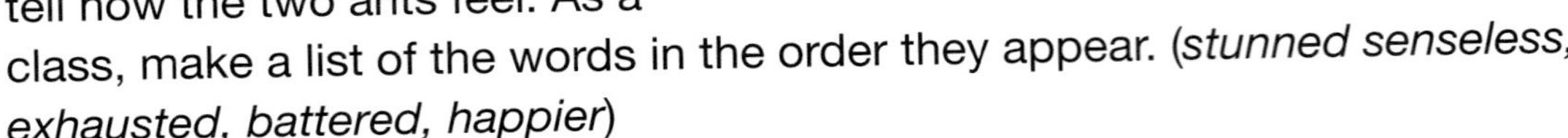

Ask: How do the ants' feelings change? Why do their feelings change? (The ants feel senseless, exhausted, and battered in the kitchen because it is dangerous and unfamiliar to them. They feel happier when they rejoin the other ants and return to their home.)

If you are reading *Two Bad Ants* during small group time, then return to pp. 478–485a to guide the reading.

If... students need more scaffolding and practice with the **Main Selection,** **then...** use the activities on p. DI•97 in the Teacher Resources section on SuccessNet.

On-Level

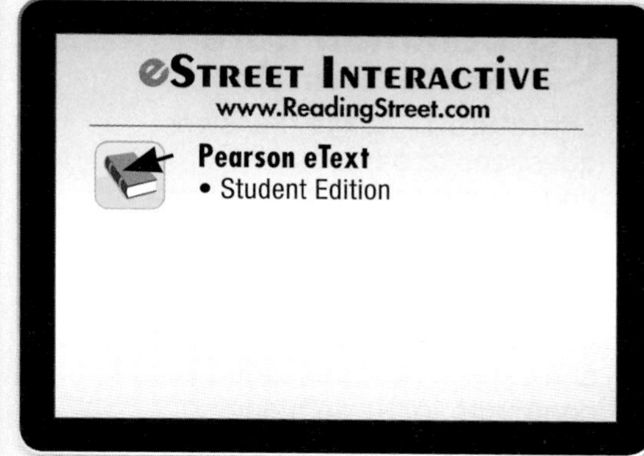

1 Build Word Knowledge

Practice Amazing Words

obey	responsibility	consequence	permission	citizen
fascinate	guilt	encounter	forbid	eerie

Team Talk **LANGUAGE DEVELOPMENT** Have students practice building more complex sentences. Display a sentence starter and have students add oral phrases or clauses using the Amazing Words. For example: There will be _______ because _______. (There will be *consequences* / because I did not *obey* my parents / and went / to the *eerie* haunted house / without their *permission.*) Guide students to add at least three phrases or clauses.

2 Read

"Hiking Safety Tips"

BEFORE READING Read aloud the genre information about evaluating sources on p. 490. Ask: What are some reasons that information on a site should not be trusted? (It might be old and contain outdated information. The person who wrote it knows little about the topic.) How can you make sure that information on a site is trustworthy? (You can check the information against another source or use sources that a teacher or librarian recommends.)

DURING READING Have students read along with you.

- What path did the user take to get from general to specific information? (typed a keyword into a search engine and then chose the link that had the most useful description)
- The site includes a picture of a poison oak plant. Why is it important to know what a poison oak plant looks like? (The text states that touching poison oak leaves can leave rashes and blistering. Hikers should know what the plant looks like so they can avoid it.)

AFTER READING Have students create a sketch of the front page of a Web site that gives safety tips for a favorite sport or hobby. Then have students complete the Get Online! activity.

Independent Reading Options

Trade Book Library

eStreet Interactive
www.ReadingStreet.com

Teacher Guides are available on the Leveled Reader Database.

On-Level

Common Core State Standards

Literature 1. Ask and answer questions to demonstrate understanding of a text, referring explicitly to the text as the basis for the answers. **Literature 3.** Describe characters in a story (e.g., their traits, motivations, or feelings) and explain how their actions contribute to the sequence of events. **Foundational Skills 4.** Read with sufficient accuracy and fluency to support comprehension. **Writing 3.** Write narratives to develop real or imagined experiences or events using effective technique, descriptive details, and clear event sequences. **Language 2.b.** Use commas in addresses. **Language 4.** Determine or clarify the meaning of unknown and multiple-meaning words and phrases based on grade 3 reading and content, choosing flexibly from a range of strategies.

More Reading for Group Time

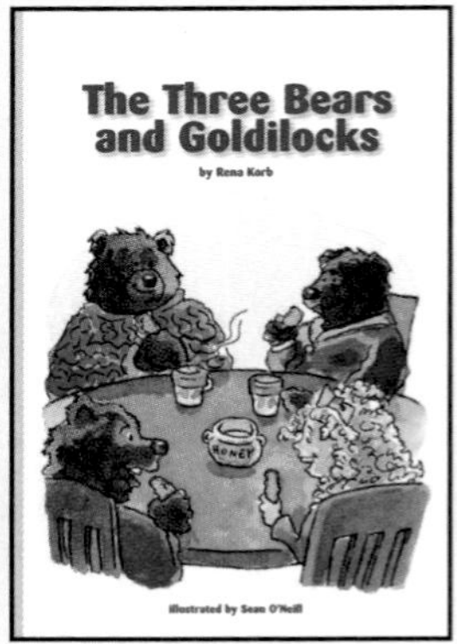

ON-LEVEL

Review
- Plot and Theme
- Story Structure
- Selection Vocabulary

Use this suggested Leveled Reader or other text at student's instructional level.

eStreet Interactive
www.ReadingStreet.com

Use the Leveled Reader Database for lesson plans and student pages for *The Three Bears and Goldilocks.*

1 Build Word Knowledge

Practice Commas

IDENTIFY Read aloud the Conventions note at the bottom of p. 489 and discuss the function of commas, such as in direct speech, items in a series, and in dates and addresses. Have partners reread the model comic book page to find examples of how the author used commas in the letter (date, salutation, and closing). Allow time for students to discuss their examples and correct any misunderstandings.

2 Text-Based Comprehension

Read

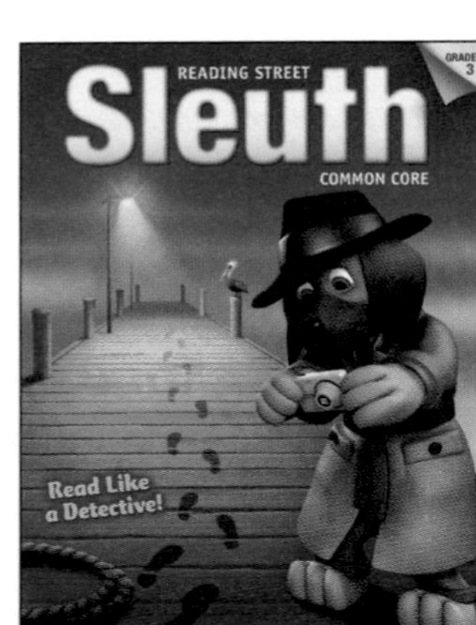

REREAD "Lin's Lesson" Have partners reread "Lin's Lesson."

EXTEND UNDERSTANDING Talk together about the kinds of rules students have at home. Encourage students to look at those rules from a different viewpoint after reading this story.

PERFORMANCE TASK • Prove It! Have students think about a time when they ignored one of the rules in their households. Ask them to write about it and include the consequences they paid for breaking that rule. Encourage students to share both facts and opinions about this experience.

COMMUNICATE Have pairs share their writing with each other. Encourage students to discuss similarities and differences between their experiences.

Strategic Intervention

1 Build Word Knowledge

Reteach Amazing Words

Repeat the definition of the word *responsibility.* We learned that *responsibility* is a duty or something that you should do. Then use the word in a sentence. It is my *responsibility* to walk the dog every day.

Team Talk **TALK ABOUT IT** Have students take turns using the word *responsibility* in a sentence. Continue this routine to practice the Amazing Words *consequence* and *permission.* Review the concept map with students. Discuss other words they can add to the concept map.

Corrective feedback | **If...** students need more practice with the Amazing Words, **then...** use visuals from the Student Edition or online sources to clarify meaning.

2 Text-Based Comprehension

Read

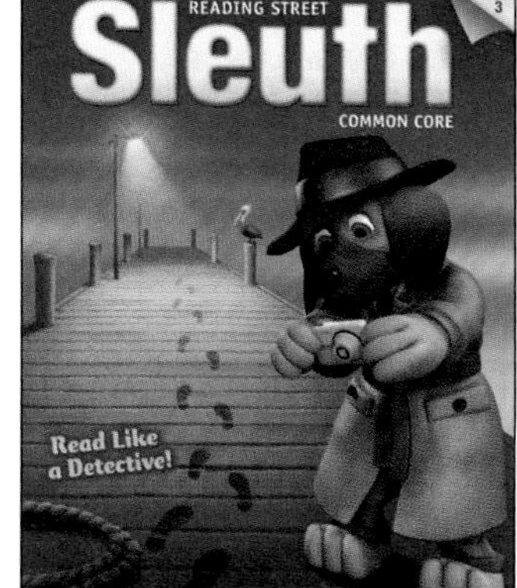

READ "Lin's Lesson" Have students track the print as you read "Lin's Lesson" from *Reading Street Sleuth* on pp. 74–75.

ACCESS TEXT Discuss the Sleuth Work section with students and provide support as needed as they work on it. Remind students that they can use these steps with other texts they read.

Gather Evidence Talk together about Lin's experience. Take a student poll as to whether Lin learned a lesson or not. Choosing the majority side, work together to find text details that support that opinion. List the details.

Ask Questions Talk together about what might happen at Lin's house a week after this experience. Then have pairs role-play asking and answering questions as Lin and his mom. As students role-play, encourage students to ask both factual and opinion questions.

Make Your Case Have students select a position on the issue. With a student who took the same side of the issue, have students work together to make a list of reasons to help justify their opinions.

More Reading for Group Time

CONCEPT LITERACY

Practice
Concept Words

BELOW-LEVEL

Review
• Plot and Theme
• Story Structure
• Selection Vocabulary

Use these suggested Leveled Readers or other text at students' instructional level.

eStreet Interactive
www.ReadingStreet.com

Use the Leveled Reader Database for lesson plans and student pages for *We Have Rules* and *Swimming in a School.*

SMALL GROUP TIME

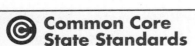

Common Core State Standards

Literature 1. Ask and answer questions to demonstrate understanding of a text, referring explicitly to the text as the basis for the answers. **Literature 3.** Describe characters in a story (e.g., their traits, motivations, or feelings) and explain how their actions contribute to the sequence of events. **Language 4.** Determine or clarify the meaning of unknown and multiple-meaning words and phrases based on grade 3 reading and content, choosing flexibly from a range of strategies. **Also Language 6.**

1 Build Word Knowledge

Reteach Selection Vocabulary

DEFINE IT Describe a *scoop* to a friend. Give a definition when necessary. Restate the word in student-friendly terms and clarify meaning with a visual. *Scoop* means a curved tool, like a spoon or shovel. Page 477 shows a scoop going into the sugar bowl.

crystal	disappeared	discovery	goal
journey	joyful	scoop	unaware

Team Talk **TALK ABOUT IT** Have you ever used or seen a scoop? Turn and talk to your partner about this. Rephrase students' examples for usage when necessary or to correct misunderstandings.

Corrective feedback | **If...** students need more practice with selection vocabulary, **then...** use the *Envision It! Pictured Vocabulary Cards.*

2 Read

Two Bad Ants

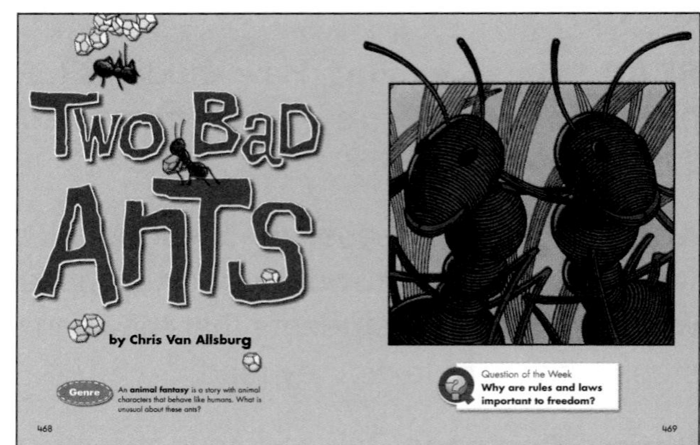

If you read *Two Bad Ants* during whole group time, then use the instruction below.

ACCESS TEXT Reread the paragraphs on pp. 475–476. Ask questions to check understanding. Where are the ants when they come out of the tunnel? (a kitchen) Why does it seem like a strange world? (The surfaces are smooth and shiny, and the smells are different. The kitchen has no sky.) What is the sparkling treasure that the ants wanted? (It is the sugar in a sugar bowl.) What happens to the two small ants? (They decide to stay in the bowl and eat so much sugar they fall asleep.)

Have students identify sections they did not understand. Reread them aloud. Clarify the meaning of each section to build understanding.

If you are reading *Two Bad Ants* during small group time, then return to pp. 468–477a to guide the reading.

Independent Reading Options

Trade Book Library

eStreet Interactive
www.ReadingStreet.com
Teacher Guides are available on the Leveled Reader Database.

Strategic Intervention

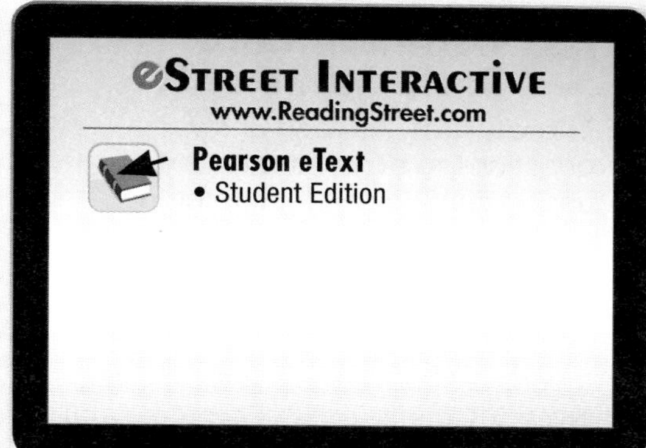

1 Build Word Knowledge

Develop Vocabulary

REREAD FOR VOCABULARY Reread the paragraph of *Two Bad Ants* on p. 479. Let's read this paragraph and think about synonyms for the word *disappeared*. To help students think of synonyms, ask students questions related to context: What is the cave? What happens to the cave? What happens when something disappears?

Corrective feedback	**If...** students have difficulty thinking of synonyms for the word *disappeared*, **then...** guide students to use online sources to find more information.

2 Read

Two Bad Ants

If you read *Two Bad Ants* during whole group time, then use the instruction below.

CLOSE READING Read pp. 484–485. Have students search the text for action words that tell what the ants are doing or what happens to them. As a class, make a list of the words in the order they appear. (raced, saw, reminded, climbed, passed, stunned, blown, landed, crawled, returned, returning, awoke, slipped, climbed, stood, chose, followed, listened, knew, gave, felt)

Now use the words you listed to tell what happened to the ants in this part of the story. (The two raced through the kitchen and then saw something familiar. They climbed into a wall socket but were stunned and blown out of the holes. When they landed, they were too exhausted to go on. That night the ants felt battered but when they awoke, they heard the other ants and slipped into line with them. They each chose a crystal and gave it to the queen. They were happy to be home.)

If you are reading *Two Bad Ants* during small group time, then return to pp. 478–485a to guide the reading.

SMALL GROUP TIME

If... students need more scaffolding and practice with the **Main Selection, then...** use the activities on p. DI•97 in the Teacher Resources section on SuccessNet.

Common Core State Standards

Literature 1. Ask and answer questions to demonstrate understanding of a text, referring explicitly to the text as the basis for the answers. **Informational Text 5.** Use text features and search tools (e.g., key words, sidebars, hyperlinks) to locate information relevant to a given topic efficiently. **Foundational Skills 4.** Read with sufficient accuracy and fluency to support comprehension. **Writing 3.** Write narratives to develop real or imagined experiences or events using effective technique, descriptive details, and clear event sequences. **Language 2.b.** Use commas in addresses. **Also Language 6.**

1 Build Word Knowledge

Review Amazing Words

obey	responsibility	consequence	permission	citizen
fascinate	guilt	encounter	forbid	eerie

Team Talk **LANGUAGE DEVELOPMENT** Have students practice building more complex sentences. Display a sentence starter and have students add oral phrases or clauses using the Amazing Words. For example: The encounter ______. (The *encounter* / with the police officer / reminded me / of my *responsibility* / to be a good *citizen* and *obey* the laws.) Guide students to add at least two phrases or clauses per sentence.

Corrective feedback | **If...** students have difficulty using the Amazing Words orally, **then...** review the meaning of each of the words.

2 Read

"Hiking Safety Tips"

BEFORE READING Read aloud the genre information on p. 490 about evaluating sources. Even if a source has information you can trust, it may not be exactly the information you are looking for. To read an online source, click on a link to its site. A link is often underlined or in blue type.

DURING READING Have students read along with you while tracking the print. Stop to point out each computer screen and the information it shows.

AFTER READING Have students share their reactions to the selection. Then guide them through the Get Online! activity.

- How can you evaluate Web sites about safe hiking? (Read the Web sites' summaries to help determine which might be helpful.)
- Which hiking tips would you give someone? (Carrying water with you will help to keep you from using water from nature that may not be pure.)

If... students need more scaffolding and practice with **Amazing Words, then...** use the Routine on pp. xxxvi–xxxvii in the *ELL Handbook.*

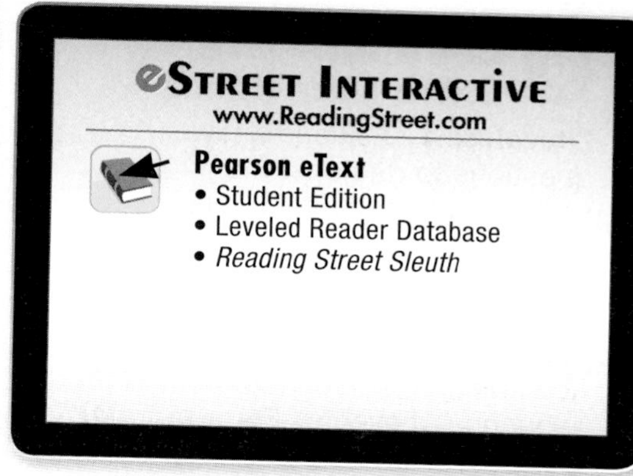

1 Build Word Knowledge

Review Commas

IDENTIFY Read aloud the Conventions note at the bottom of p. 489 to review how to use commas. Have partners reread the model comic book page to find examples of how the author used commas in the letter (date, salutation, and closing). Allow time for students to discuss their examples and correct any misunderstandings.

2 Text-Based Comprehension

Read

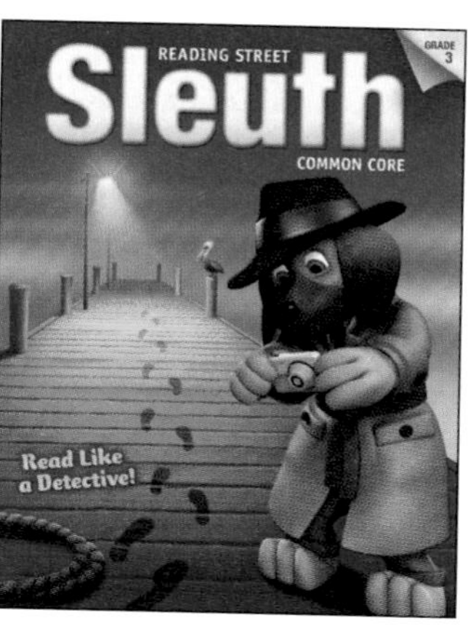

REREAD "Lin's Lesson" Have partners reread "Lin's Lesson," with partners alternating paragraphs.

EXTEND UNDERSTANDING Talk together about Lin's punishment. Encourage students to share their opinions as to whether or not they feel this was adequate punishment. Invite students to role-play as Lin's mom, sharing how they would have reacted to the news from Lin.

PERFORMANCE TASK • Prove It! Have students think about a time when they ignored one of the rules in their households. Ask them to write about it and include the consequences they paid for breaking that rule. Encourage students to tell not only what the consequences were but also how they felt about those consequences.

COMMUNICATE Have pairs share their writing with each other. Invite discussion about the feelings each student had about the consequences. Ask students to name other words that can be used to describe those feelings.

SMALL GROUP TIME

More Reading for Group Time

CONCEPT LITERACY

Practice
Concept Words

BELOW-LEVEL

Review
- Plot and Theme
- Story Structure
- Selection Vocabulary

Use these suggested Leveled Readers or other text at students' instructional level.

eStreet Interactive
www.ReadingStreet.com

Use the Leveled Reader Database for lesson plans and student pages for *We Have Rules* and *Swimming in a School.*

Advanced

Common Core State Standards

Literature 1. Ask and answer questions to demonstrate understanding of a text, referring explicitly to the text as the basis for the answers. **Literature 3.** Describe characters in a story (e.g., their traits, motivations, or feelings) and explain how their actions contribute to the sequence of events. **Foundational Skills 4.** Read with sufficient accuracy and fluency to support comprehension. **Writing 7.** Conduct short research projects that build knowledge about a topic. **Language 6.** Acquire and use accurately grade-appropriate conversational, general academic, and domain-specific words and phrases, including those that signal spatial and temporal relationships (e.g., *After dinner that night we went looking for them*).

1 Build Word Knowledge

Extend Amazing Words

Team Talk Have students define *responsibility.* Discuss other words for *responsibility.* Continue with *consequence* and *permission.* Have students use the words in sentences.

2 Text-Based Comprehension

Read

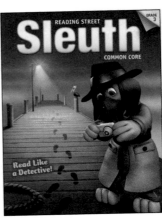

READ "Lin's Lesson" Have students read "Lin's Lesson" from *Reading Street Sleuth* on pp. 74–75.

ACCESS TEXT Discuss the Sleuth Work section with students before they work on it. Remind students that they can use these steps with other texts they read.

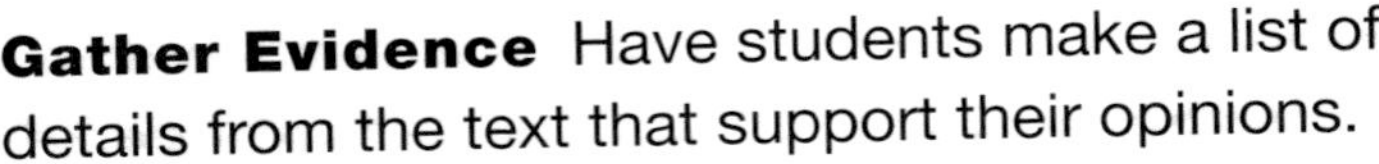

Gather Evidence Have students make a list of details from the text that support their opinions.

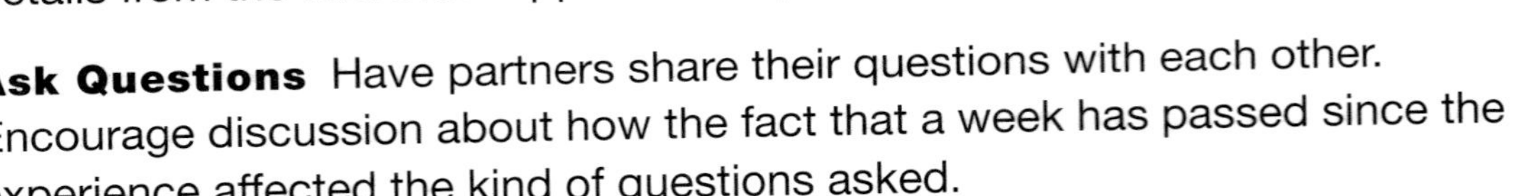

Ask Questions Have partners share their questions with each other. Encourage discussion about how the fact that a week has passed since the experience affected the kind of questions asked.

Make Your Case Have students discuss their opinions, sharing their own personal experiences to explain their opinions.

3 Inquiry: Extend Concepts

IDENTIFY QUESTIONS Have students think about questions they have about the responsibilities of being a good citizen and use these questions to create their own citizen's handbook with a checklist of activities that good citizens do. Throughout the week, they will gather information. On Day 5, they will present what they have learned.

If... students need more scaffolding and practice with **Vocabulary,** **then...** use the activities on pp. DI•92–DI•93 in the Teacher Resources section on SuccessNet.

Advanced

1 Build Word Knowledge

Extend Selection Vocabulary

Team Talk Have partners use the selection vocabulary in sentences to internalize their meanings. Have students use as many of the words as they can while making sure the sentence is grammatically correct. (Possible response: She was *unaware* of the *discovery* of the valuable *crystal* but felt *joyful* at the news.) Continue with additional selection vocabulary words.

crystal	disappeared	discovery	goal
journey	joyful	scoop	unaware

2 Read

Two Bad Ants

If you read *Two Bad Ants* during whole group time, then use the instruction below.

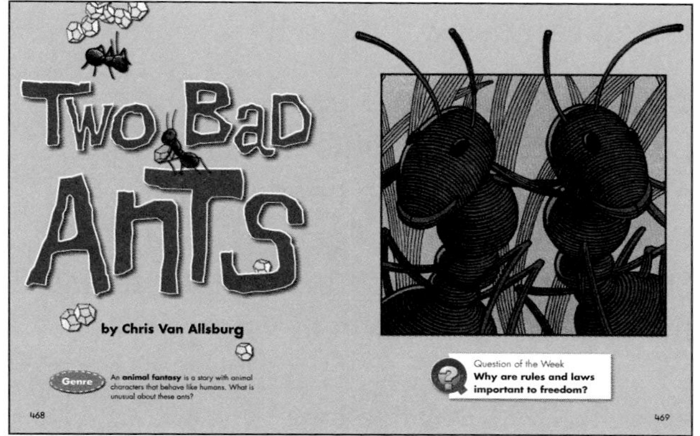

ACCESS TEXT Reread the paragraphs on pp. 475–476. Discuss the similarities and differences between the outside and inside worlds. (Similar: Both are challenging to travel over. Both must be traveled in order to reach the crystal. Different: The ants feel the wind and see the sky outside. Inside, there are no natural smells, wind, or sky above.) Ask: Why did the author compare the two places? (The author wants readers to experience inside and outside from an ant's perspective, or point of view, and to show how the inside world seems strange to the ants.)

If you are reading *Two Bad Ants* during small group time, then return to pp. 468–477a to guide the reading.

3 Inquiry: Extend Concepts

INVESTIGATE Encourage students to use materials at their independent reading levels or student-friendly search engines to identify relevant and credible sites to gather information about the responsibilities of citizenship. Have students consider how they will present their information.

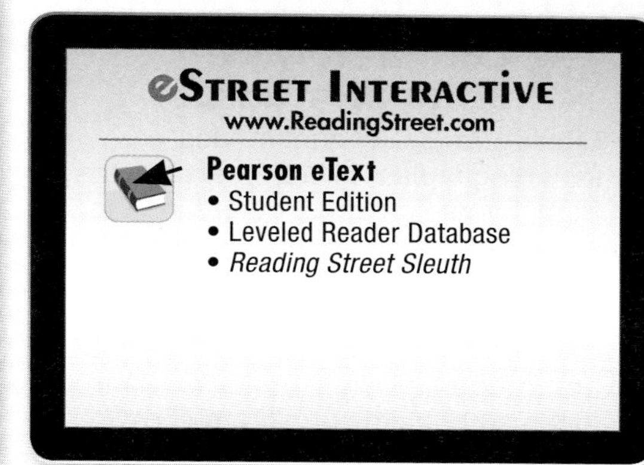

SMALL GROUP TIME

More Reading for Group Time

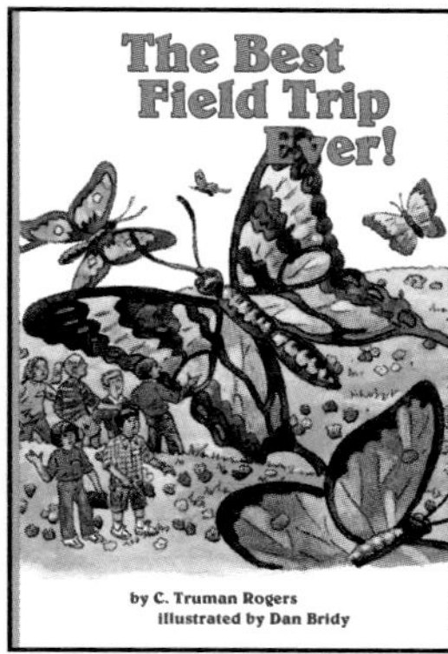

ADVANCED

Reviews
- Plot and Theme
- Story Structure

Use this suggested Leveled Reader or other text at student's instructional level.

eStreet Interactive
www.ReadingStreet.com

Use the Leveled Reader Database for lesson plans and student pages for *The Best Field Trip Ever!*

Advanced

Common Core State Standards

Literature 2. Recount stories, including fables, folktales, and myths from diverse cultures; determine the central message, lesson, or moral and explain how it is conveyed through key details in the text. **Language 3.a.** Choose words and phrases for effect. **Language 4.** Determine or clarify the meaning of unknown and multiple-meaning words and phrases based on grade 3 reading and content, choosing flexibly from a range of strategies. **Also Informational Text 7., Language 6.**

1 Build Word Knowledge

Develop Vocabulary

REREAD FOR VOCABULARY Reread the second paragraph on p. 481. Let's read this paragraph to find out what *unbearably* means. Discuss meaning and context with students.

2 Read

Two Bad Ants

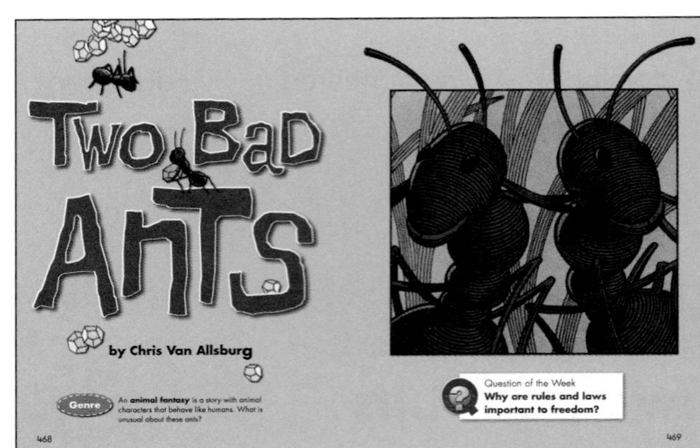

If you read *Two Bad Ants* during whole group time, then use the instruction below.

CLOSE READING Read pp. 484–485. Have students create a T-chart with the heads **Day Feelings** and **Night Feelings.** Have students search through the text to find feeling words and write them in the order they occur in the story.

Day Feelings	Night Feelings
senseless, exhausted, battered	joyful, grateful, never happier

Ask: What idea is the author developing? (The feeling words show how unhappy and tired the ants are in the kitchen and how happy they feel returning to the outside world with their fellow ants.) What lesson did the ants learn from their experience? (They learned that it is better to stay with their families and to be good ants.)

If you are reading *Two Bad Ants* during small group time, then return to pp. 478–485a to guide the reading.

3 Inquiry: Extend Concepts

INVESTIGATE Provide time for students to investigate their topics in books or online. If necessary, help them locate information that is focused on their topics.

Independent Reading Options

Trade Book Library

eStreet Interactive
www.ReadingStreet.com

Teacher Guides are available on the Leveled Reader Database.

If... students need more scaffolding and practice with the **Main Selection, then...** use the activities on p. DI•97 in the Teacher Resources section on SuccessNet.

Advanced

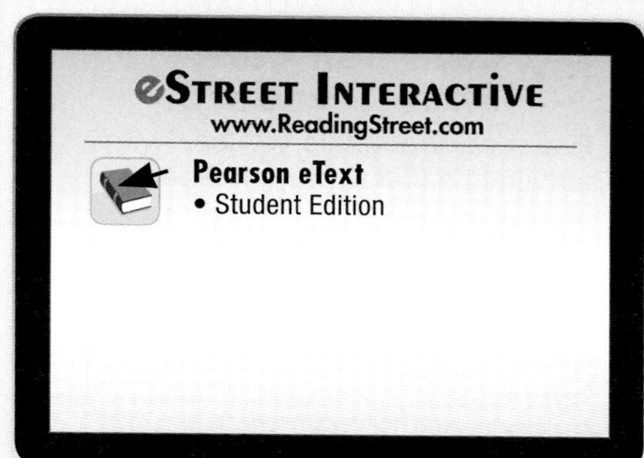

1 Build Word Knowledge

Extend Amazing Words and Selection Vocabulary

obey	responsibility	consequence
permission	citizen	fascinate
guilt	encounter	forbid
eerie		

crystal	disappeared	discovery
goal	journey	joyful
scoop	unaware	

Team Talk Have students practice building more complex sentences. Display a sentence starter and have students add oral phrases or clauses using the Amazing Words and the selection vocabulary. Guide students to add at least three phrases or clauses per sentence.

2 Read

"Hiking Safety Tips"

BEFORE READING Read the genre information on evaluating sources on p. 490. Ask students to use the text features to set a purpose for reading. Then have students read "Hiking Safety Tips" on their own.

DURING READING Point out that the user begins by typing a keyword into a search engine. How does the third link on the search engine results page—the link about staying late—differ from the first two links? (The first two seem to be advertisements, so they probably focus on selling things instead of providing helpful information.)

AFTER READING Have students complete the Get Online! activity.

3 Inquiry: Extend Concepts

ORGANIZE INFORMATION Provide time for students to organize their information into a format that will effectively communicate their findings to their audience. Provide any necessary materials, such as poster board, markers, and other supplies, or computer time.

SMALL GROUP TIME

Independent Reading Options

Trade Book Library

eStreet Interactive
www.ReadingStreet.com
Teacher Guides are available on the Leveled Reader Database.

Advanced

Common Core State Standards

Foundational Skills 4. Read with sufficient accuracy and fluency to support comprehension. **Writing 3.** Write narratives to develop real or imagined experiences or events using effective technique, descriptive details, and clear event sequences. **Speaking/Listening 4.** Report on a topic or text, tell a story, or recount an experience with appropriate facts and relevant, descriptive details, speaking clearly at an understandable pace. **Language 1.** Demonstrate command of the conventions of standard English grammar and usage when writing or speaking. **Language 2.b.** Use commas in addresses.

More Reading for Group Time

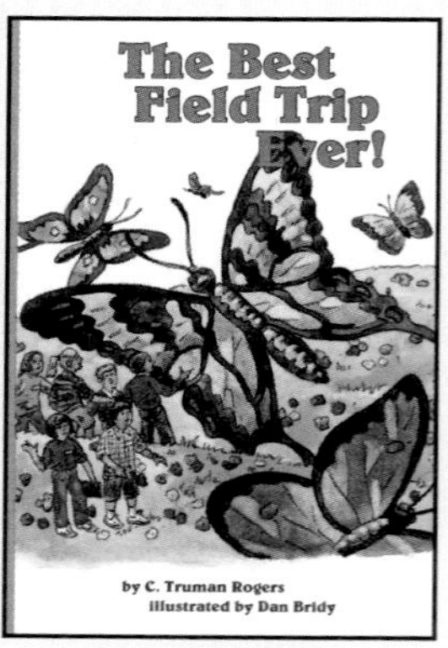

The Best Field Trip Ever!
by C. Truman Rogers
illustrated by Dan Bridy

ADVANCED

Review

- Plot and Theme
- Story Structure

Use this suggested Leveled Reader or other text at students' instructional level.

eStreet Interactive
www.ReadingStreet.com

Use the Leveled Reader Database for lesson plans and student pages for *The Best Field Trip Ever!*

1 Build Word Knowledge

Extend Commas

IDENTIFY AND EXTEND Have partners read the bottom of p. 489 to review the functions of commas, for example, in dates, addresses, and items in a series. Have partners reread the model comic book page to find examples of how the author used commas in the letter (date, salutation, and closing). Then ask partners to write their own letters, paying attention to comma usage. Have pairs exchange letters and check for the correct use of commas.

2 Text-Based Comprehension

Read

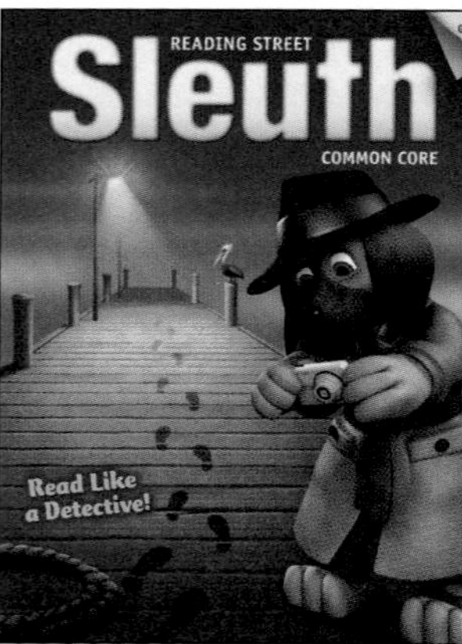

REREAD "Lin's Lesson" Have partners reread "Lin's Lesson." Have partners discuss what they would have done if they had awoken to ants crawling in their bedroom.

EXTEND UNDERSTANDING Talk together about how Lin might make a deal with his mom to still have food downstairs.

PERFORMANCE TASK • Prove It! Have students think about a time when they ignored one of the rules in their households. Ask them to write about it and include the consequences they paid for breaking that rule. Encourage students to tell what they learned from the experience.

COMMUNICATE Have students share their writing with a small group. Invite students to discuss the importance of rules.

3 Inquiry: Extend Concepts

COMMUNICATE Have students share their inquiry projects on the responsibilities of citizenship with the rest of the class. Provide the following tips for presenting.

- Speak loudly and clearly.
- Make eye contact with the audience and point to visuals as you speak.
- Use gestures to communicate ideas or emphasize key points.

Focus on Common Core State Standards

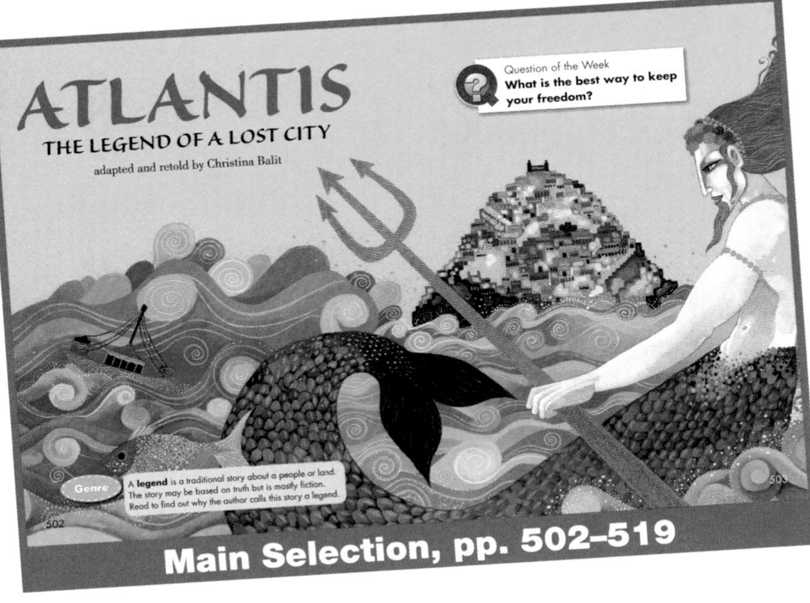
Main Selection, pp. 502–519

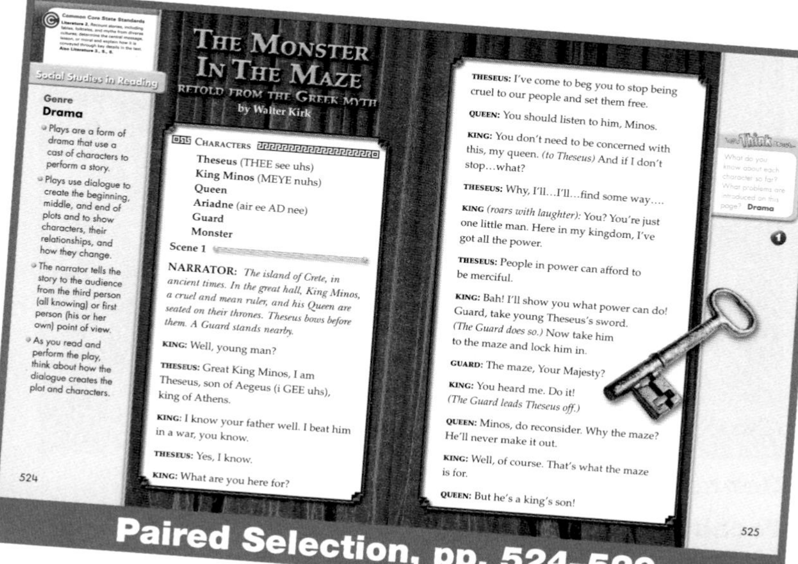
Paired Selection, pp. 524–529

Text-Based Comprehension

Generalize
CCSS Informational Text 1.

Inferring
CCSS Informational Text 1.,
CCSS Informational Text 2.

Fluency

Expression
CCSS Foundational Skills 4.b.

Writing and Conventions

Trait: Word Choice
CCSS Language 3.a.

Writing Mini-Lesson: Historical Fiction
CCSS Writing 3.a., CCSS Writing 3.b.

Conventions: Quotations and Parentheses
CCSS Language 2.c.

Oral Vocabulary

Amazing Words

witty
equality
justice
perish
demonstrate
mourn
blight
wept
violence

CCSS Language 6.

Selection Vocabulary

Homographs
CCSS Language 4.

Context Clues
CCSS Language 4., CCSS Language 4.a.

aqueducts
content
crouched
guidance
honor
pillar
thermal

Phonics and Spelling

Related Words
CCSS Foundational Skills 3.,
CCSS Language 2.f.

cloth
clothes
nature
natural
able
ability
mean
meant
deal
dealt
please
pleasant
sign
signal
signature

Challenge Words

equal
equation
equator
major
majority

Listening and Speaking

Song
CCSS Speaking/Listening 6.

Preview Your Week

What is the best way to keep your freedom?

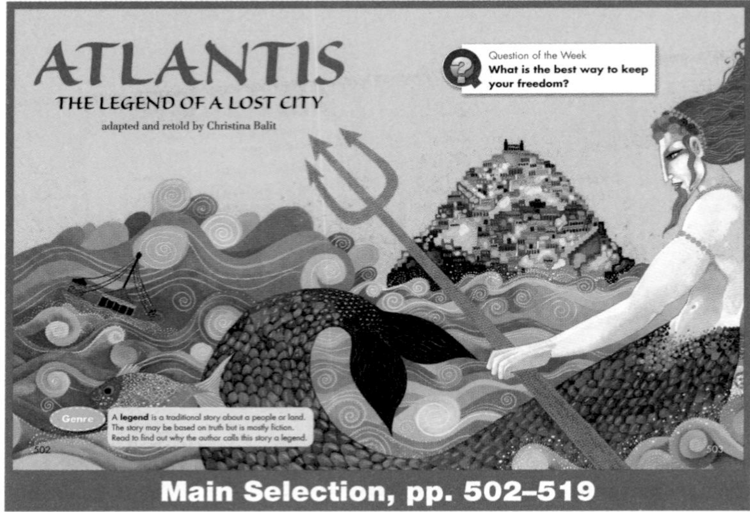
ATLANTIS
THE LEGEND OF A LOST CITY
adapted and retold by Christina Balit

Question of the Week
What is the best way to keep your freedom?

Genre A **legend** is a traditional story about a people or land. The story may be based on truth but is mostly fiction. Read to find out why the author calls this story a legend.

502 503

Main Selection, pp. 502–519

Social Studies in Reading

Genre
Drama
- Plays are a form of drama that use a cast of characters to perform a story.
- Plays use dialogue to create the beginning, middle, and end of plots and to show characters, their relationships, and how they change.
- The narrator tells the story to the audience from the third person (all knowing) or first person (his or her own) point of view.
- As you read and perform the play, think about how the dialogue creates the plot and characters.

THE MONSTER IN THE MAZE
RETOLD FROM THE GREEK MYTH
by Walter Kirk

CHARACTERS
Theseus (THEE see uhs)
King Minos (MEYE nuhs)
Queen
Ariadne (air ee AD nee)
Guard
Monster

Scene 1

NARRATOR: *The island of Crete, in ancient times. In the great hall, King Minos, a cruel and mean ruler, and his Queen are seated on their thrones. Theseus bows before them. A Guard stands nearby.*

KING: Well, young man?

THESEUS: Great King Minos, I am Theseus, son of Aegeus (i GEE uhs), king of Athens.

KING: I know your father well. I beat him in a war, you know.

THESEUS: Yes, I know.

KING: What are you here for?

THESEUS: I've come to beg you to stop being cruel to our people and set them free.

QUEEN: You should listen to him, Minos.

KING: You don't need to be concerned with this, my queen. *(to Theseus)* And if I don't stop…what?

THESEUS: Why, I'll…I'll…find some way….

KING *(roars with laughter)*: You? You're just one little man. Here in my kingdom, I've got all the power.

THESEUS: People in power can afford to be merciful.

KING: Bah! I'll show you what power can do! Guard, take young Theseus's sword. *(The Guard does so.)* Now take him to the maze and lock him in.

GUARD: The maze, Your Majesty?

KING: You heard me. Do it! *(The Guard leads Theseus off.)*

QUEEN: Minos, do reconsider. Why the maze? He'll never make it out.

KING: Well, of course. That's what the maze is for.

QUEEN: But he's a king's son!

Drama

524 525

Paired Selection, pp. 524–529

Genre: Legend
Vocabulary: Homographs
Text-Based Comprehension: Generalize

Social Studies in Reading
Genre: Drama

Build Content Knowledge

KNOWLEDGE GOALS
Students will understand that keeping freedom means
- defending it
- working together
- having necessary laws

THIS WEEK'S CONCEPT MAP
Develop a concept-related graphic organizer like the one below over the course of this week.

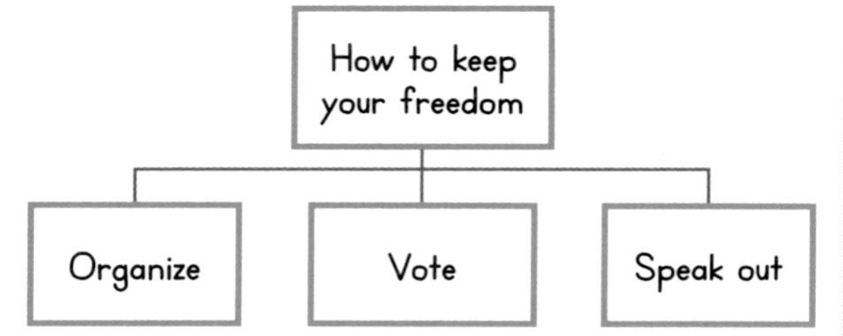

BUILD ORAL VOCABULARY
This week, students will acquire the following academic vocabulary/domain-specific words.

Amazing Words

witty	perish	blight
equality	demonstrate	wept
justice	mourn	violence

OPTIONAL CONCEPT-BASED READING Use the Digital Path to access readers offering different levels of text complexity.

Concept Literacy

Below-Level

On-Level

Advanced

ELL

ELD

This Week's Digital Resources

eStreet Interactive
www.ReadingStreet.com

Get Ready to Read

Concept Talk Video Use this video on the Digital Path to build momentum and introduce the weekly concept of keeping your freedom.

Pearson eText Read the eText of the Student Edition pages on Pearson SuccessNet for comprehension and fluency support.

Envision It! Animations Use this colorful animation on the Digital Path to explain the target comprehension skill, Generalize.

Read and Comprehend

Journal Use the Word Bank on the Digital Path to have students write sentences using this week's selection vocabulary words.

Background Building Audio CD This audio CD provides valuable background information about freedom to help students read and comprehend the weekly texts.

Pearson eText Read the eText of the main selection, *Atlantis,* and the paired selection, "The Monster in the Maze," with audio support on Pearson SuccessNet.

Vocabulary Activities A variety of interactive vocabulary activities on the Digital Path help students practice selection vocabulary and concept-related words.

Story Sort Use the Story Sort Activity on the Digital Path after reading *Atlantis* to involve students in summarizing.

Language Arts

Grammar Jammer Select a lighthearted animation on the Digital Path to provide an engaging grammar lesson that will capture students' attention.

Pearson eText Find the Student Edition eText of the Let's Write It! and Let's Learn It! pages with audio support on Pearson SuccessNet.

Additional Resources

Teacher Resources DVD-ROM Use the following resources on the TR DVD or on Pearson SuccessNet throughout the week:

- Amazing Word Cards
- Reader's and Writer's Notebook
- Writing Transparencies
- Daily Fix-It Transparencies
- Scoring Rubrics
- Grammar Transparencies
- ELL Support
- Let's Practice It!
- Graphic Organizers
- Vocabulary Cards

This Week's Skills

Phonics/Word Analysis
Related Words

Comprehension
Skill: Generalize
Strategy: Inferring

Language
Vocabulary: Homographs
Conventions: Quotations and Parentheses

Fluency
Expression

Writing
Historical Fiction

5-Day Planner

DAY 1

Get Ready to Read

Content Knowledge 494j
Oral Vocabulary: *witty, equality, justice, perish*

Monitor Progress
Check Oral Vocabulary

Phonics/Word Analysis 496a
Related Words
READ Decodable Reader 30A
Reread for Fluency

Read and Comprehend

Text-Based Comprehension 498a
Generalize
Inferring

Fluency 498–499
Expression

Selection Vocabulary 499a
aqueducts, content, crouched, guidance, honor, pillar, thermal,

Language Arts

Research and Inquiry 499b
Identify and Focus Topic

Spelling 499c
Related Words, Pretest

Conventions 499d
Quotations and Parentheses

Handwriting 499d
Cursive Letters *J*, *X*, and *L*

Writing 499e
Historical Fiction

DAY 2

Get Ready to Read

Content Knowledge 500a
Oral Vocabulary: *demonstrate, mourn*

Phonics/Word Analysis 500c
Related Words

Monitor Progress
Check Word Reading

Literary Terms 500d
Foreshadowing

Read and Comprehend

Vocabulary Skill 500e
Homographs

Fluency 500–501
Expression

Text-Based Comprehension 502–503
READ *Atlantis*—1st Read

Language Arts

Research and Inquiry 511b
Navigate/Search

Conventions 511c
Quotations and Parentheses

Spelling 511c
Related Words

Writing 511d
Historical Fiction

DAY 3

Get Ready to Read

Content Knowledge 512a
Oral Vocabulary: *blight, wept*

Word Analysis 512c
Related Words
Fluent Word Reading
DECODE AND READ
Decodable Practice Passage 30B

Read and Comprehend

Text-Based Comprehension 512e
Generalize
Inferring
READ *Atlantis*—2nd Read
Monitor Progress Check Retelling

Fluency 521b
Expression

Language Arts

Research and Study Skills 521c
Quote and Paraphrase Sources

Research and Inquiry 521d
Analyze Information

Conventions 521e
Quotations and Parentheses

Spelling 521e
Related Words

Writing 522–523
Historical Fiction

DAY 4

Get Ready to Read

Content Knowledge 524a
Oral Vocabulary: *violence*

Phonics/Word Analysis 524c
Review Prefixes *im-, in-*
Fluent Word Reading
DECODE AND READ
Decodable Practice Passage 30C

Read and Comprehend

Genre 524g
Drama
READ "The Monster in the Maze" —Paired Selection

Fluency 530–531
Expression
Monitor Progress Check Fluency

Vocabulary Skill 531a
Homographs

Listening and Speaking 531a
Song

Language Arts

Research and Inquiry 531b
Synthesize

Conventions 531c
Quotations and Parentheses

Spelling 531c
Related Words

Writing 531d
Historical Fiction

DAY 5

Get Ready to Read

Content Knowledge 531f
Review Oral Vocabulary
Monitor Progress
Check Oral Vocabulary

Read and Comprehend

Text-Based Comprehension 531h
Review Generalize

Vocabulary Skill 531h
Review Homographs

Word Analysis 531i
Review Related Words

Literary Terms 531i
Review Foreshadowing

Assessment 531j, 531l
Monitor Progress
Fluency; Generalize

Language Arts

Research and Inquiry 531n
Communicate

Spelling 531o
Related Words, Test

Conventions 531o
Quotations and Parentheses

Writing 531p
Historical Fiction

Wrap Up Your Week! 531q

Access for All

What do I do in group time?

It's as easy as 1-2-3!

1 TEACHER-LED SMALL GROUPS → 2 INDEPENDENT PRACTICE STATIONS → 3 INDEPENDENT READING

Small Group Time

Bridge to Common Core

SKILL DEVELOPMENT

- Related Words
- Generalize
- Inferring
- Homographs

DEEP UNDERSTANDING

This Week's Knowledge Goals

Students will understand that keeping freedom means

- defending it
- working together
- having necessary laws

1 Small Group Lesson Plan

	DAY 1 Differentiate Vocabulary	DAY 2 Differentiate Comprehension
OL On-Level pp. SG•107–SG•111	**Build Word Knowledge** Practice Amazing Words **Text-Based Comprehension** Read *Reading Street Sleuth,* pp. 76–77 or Leveled Readers	**Build Word Knowledge** Practice Selection Vocabulary **Access Text** Read *Atlantis*
SI Strategic Intervention pp. SG•101–SG•106	**Build Word Knowledge** Reteach Amazing Words **Text-Based Comprehension** Read *Reading Street Sleuth,* pp. 76–77 or Leveled Readers	**Build Word Knowledge** Reteach Selection Vocabulary **Access Text** Read *Atlantis*
A Advanced pp. SG•112–SG•115	**Build Word Knowledge** Extend Amazing Words **Text-Based Comprehension** Read *Reading Street Sleuth,* pp. 76–77 or Leveled Readers	**Build Word Knowledge** Extend Selection Vocabulary **Access Text** Read *Atlantis*
Independent Inquiry Project	Identify Questions	Investigate
ELL **If...** students need more scaffolding and practice with...	**Vocabulary,** **then...** use the activities on pp. DI•117–DI•118 in the Teacher Resources section on SuccessNet.	**Comprehension Skill,** **then...** use the activities on p. DI•121 in the Teacher Resources section on SuccessNet.

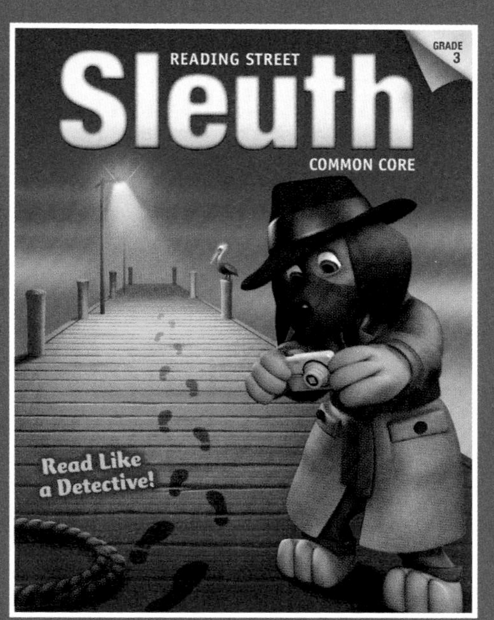

Reading Street Sleuth
- Provides access to grade-level text for all students
- Focuses on finding clues in text through close reading
- Builds capacity for complex text

Build Text-Based Comprehension

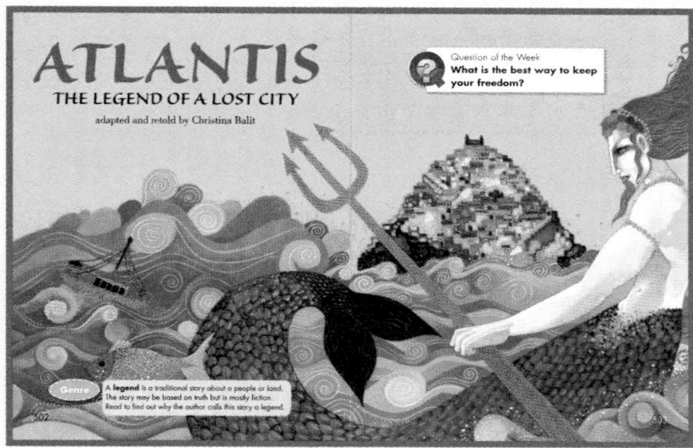

Atlantis

Optional Leveled Readers

Concept Literacy

Below-Level

On-Level

Advanced

ELL

ELD

DAY 3 Differentiate Close Reading	DAY 4 Differentiate Vocabulary	DAY 5 Differentiate Reteaching
Reread to Develop Vocabulary **Close Reading** Read *Atlantis*	**Build Word Knowledge** Develop Language Using Amazing Words **Text-Based Comprehension** Read "The Monster in the Maze"	**Practice Quotations and Parentheses** **Text-Based Comprehension** Reread *Reading Street Sleuth,* pp. 76–77 or Leveled Readers
Reread to Develop Vocabulary **Close Reading** Read *Atlantis*	**Build Word Knowledge** Review/Discuss Amazing Words **Text-Based Comprehension** Read "The Monster in the Maze"	**Review Quotations and Parentheses** **Text-Based Comprehension** Reread *Reading Street Sleuth,* pp. 76–77 or Leveled Readers
Reread to Extend Vocabulary **Close Reading** Read *Atlantis* **Investigate**	**Build Word Knowledge** Extend Amazing Words and Selection Vocabulary **Text-Based Comprehension** Read "The Monster in the Maze" **Organize**	**Extend Quotations and Parentheses** **Text-Based Comprehension** Reread *Reading Street Sleuth,* pp. 76–77 or Leveled Readers **Communicate**
Main Selection, **then...** use the activities on p. DI•122 in the Teacher Resources section on SuccessNet.	**Amazing Words,** **then...** use the Routine on pp. xxxvi–xxxvii in the *ELL Handbook.*	**Conventions and Writing,** **then...** use the Grammar Transition Lessons on pp. 312–386 in the *ELL Handbook.*

2 Independent Stations

Practice Last Week's Skills

Focus on these activities when time is limited.

ACCESS FOR ALL

- ● Below-Level Activities
- ▲ On-Level Activities
- ■ Advanced Activities

WORD WISE

Spell and use words in sentences.

OBJECTIVES

- Spell words with prefixes *im-* and *in-*.

MATERIALS

- *Word Wise* Flip Chart Activity 30, teacher-made word cards, paper and pencils

 **Letter Tile Drag and Drop**

● Students choose and write five words, write sentences with them, and then add other words with the prefixes to their lists.

▲ Students choose and write seven words, write sentences with them, and then add other words with the prefixes to their lists.

■ Students choose and write ten words, write sentences with them, and then think of other words with the prefixes and write sentences using them.

WORD WORK

Identify and pronounce words.

OBJECTIVES

- Identify and pronounce words with prefixes *im-* and *in-*.

MATERIALS

- *Word Work* Flip Chart Activity 30, teacher-made word cards, paper and pencils

 **Letter Tile Drag and Drop**

● Students choose six word cards and sort the words by prefix on a T-chart. Students say and write each word, circling the prefix.

▲ Students choose nine word cards and sort the words by prefix on a T-chart. Students say and write each word, circling the prefix.

■ Students choose twelve word cards and sort the words by prefix on a T-chart. Students say and write each word, circling the prefix.

LET'S WRITE!

Write with graphics.

OBJECTIVES

- Create a comic book.

MATERIALS

- *Let's Write!* Flip Chart Activity 30, paper, markers and pencils

 **Grammar Jammer**

● Partners write and illustrate a two-picture comic book about two characters, with a beginning, a middle, and an end.

▲ Partners write and illustrate a four-picture comic book about two characters, with a complete plot.

■ Partners write and illustrate a four- or six-picture comic book about two characters' adventures, with dialogue and a complete plot.

WORDS TO KNOW

Determine word meanings.

OBJECTIVES

- Determine the meaning of words with affixes *un-, dis-,* and *-ful*.

MATERIALS

- *Words to Know* Flip Chart Activity 30, newspaper, dictionary, paper and pencils

 **Vocabulary Activities**

● Students list six words with the affixes *un-, dis-,* and *-ful* from a magazine, check their meanings, and write a sentence with each word.

▲ Students list nine words with the affixes *un-, dis-,* and *-ful* from a magazine, check their meanings, and write a sentence with each word.

■ Students list twelve words with the affixes *un-, dis-,* and *-ful* from a magazine, check their meanings, and write a sentence with each word.

READ FOR MEANING

Use comprehension skills.

OBJECTIVES

- Identify plot and theme in a story.

MATERIALS

- *Read for Meaning* Flip Chart Activity 30, Leveled Readers, paper and pencils

 **Pearson eText**

- Leveled eReaders

 **Envision It! Animations**

● Students read a book and write three sentences about the plot. Then they write one sentence that tells the author's message or theme.

▲ Students read a book, summarize the plot, and write one sentence that tells the author's theme or message.

■ Students read a book and write a paragraph that describes the plot. Then they write another paragraph about the theme or message.

GET FLUENT

Practice fluent reading with a partner.

OBJECTIVES

- Read aloud at an appropriate rate.

MATERIALS

- *Get Fluent* Flip Chart Activity 30, Leveled Readers

 **Pearson eText**
- Leveled eReaders

● Students take turns reading aloud at an appropriate rate from a Concept Literacy Reader or Below-Level Reader and providing feedback.

▲ Students take turns reading aloud at an appropriate rate from an On-Level Reader and providing feedback.

■ Students take turns reading aloud at an appropriate rate from an Advanced Reader and providing feedback.

Manage the Stations

Use these management tools to set up and organize your Practice Stations:

Practice Station Flip Charts

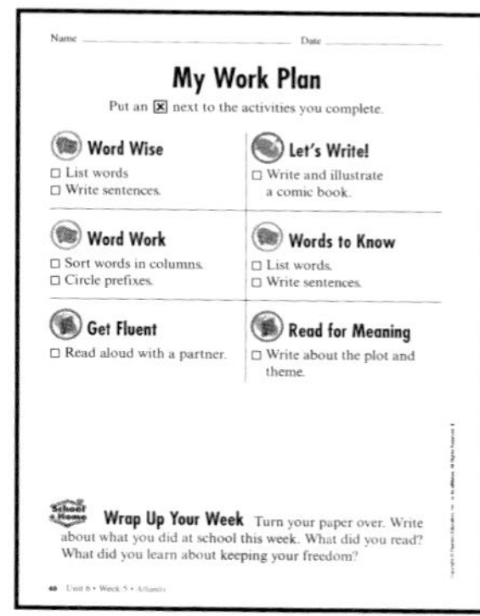
Name ____ Date ____

My Work Plan

Put an ☒ next to the activities you complete.

Word Wise
☐ List words.
☐ Write sentences.

Let's Write!
☐ Write and illustrate a comic book.

Word Work
☐ Sort words in columns.
☐ Circle prefixes.

Words to Know
☐ List words.
☐ Write sentences.

Get Fluent
☐ Read aloud with a partner.

Read for Meaning
☐ Write about the plot and theme.

Wrap Up Your Week Turn your paper over. Write about what you did at school this week. What did you read? What did you learn about keeping your freedom?

Classroom Management Handbook for Differentiated Instruction Practice Stations, p. 48

3 Independent Reading

Students should select appropriate complex texts to read and write about independently every day before, during, and after school.

Suggestions for this week's independent reading:

- Informational texts on last week's social studies topic: Why rules and laws are important to freedom
- Nonfiction selections about freedom
- An information-rich Web site about how rules and laws preserve freedom

BOOK TALK Have partners discuss their independent reading for the week. Tell them to refer to their Reading Logs and paraphrase what each selection was about. Then have students focus on discussing one or more of the following:

Key Ideas and Details
- Identify the main idea of the text. What details in the text support it?
- Identify a conclusion that the writer makes in the text. How well does he or she support it?

Craft and Structure
- Find at least three words with positive or negative connotations.
- What is the author's point of view about the topic? How do you know?

Integration of Ideas
- Compare and contrast the text to another text on the same topic.
- Explain how the two texts are similar and different.

 **Pearson eText**
- Student Edition
- Decodable Readers
- Leveled Readers

 **Trade Book Library**

 **School or Classroom Library**

DAY 1 at a Glance

Content Knowledge
Oral Vocabulary

Phonics/Word Analysis
Related Words

Text-Based Comprehension
Generalize
Inferring

Fluency
Expression

Selection Vocabulary

Research and Inquiry
Identify and Focus Topic

Spelling
Related Words

Conventions
Quotations and Parentheses

Handwriting
Cursive Letters *J, X, L*

Writing
Historical Fiction

Materials

- Student Edition
- Reader's and Writer's Notebook
- Decodable Reader

Bridge to Common Core

INTEGRATION OF KNOWLEDGE/IDEAS
This week, students will read, write, and talk about people keeping their freedom.

Texts This Week

- "Martin's Dream"
- "The Famous Thinker, Plato"
- "The Art of Architecture"
- *Atlantis: The Legend of a Lost City*
- "The Monster in the Maze"

Social Studies Knowledge Goals
Students will understand that keeping freedom means

- defending it
- working together
- having necessary laws

Street Rhymes!

This country is our home—a big community!
Freedom is a right we have—our identity.
This nation fought for freedom.
Think back historically.
We believe in justice and equality!

- To introduce this week's concept, read aloud the poem several times and ask students to join you.

Content Knowledge

Keeping Your Freedom

CONCEPT TALK To explore the unit concept of Freedom, this week students will read, write, and talk about keeping freedom. Write the Question of the Week on the board, *What is the best way to keep your freedom?*

Build Oral Language

TALK ABOUT KEEPING YOUR FREEDOM Have students turn to pp. 494–495 in their Student Edition. Look at each of the photos. Then, use the prompts to guide discussion and create a concept map.

- How are the people holding a meeting keeping their freedom? (They are organizing to share ideas.) When people organize, they work together to bring about change. Let's add *Organize* to the concept map.
- How are the people voting keeping their freedom? (By voting, people can have a say in what their government does.) By voting, people can determine who will govern them and how the money they pay in taxes will be spent. Let's add *Vote* to the concept map.
- How is Martin Luther King Jr. keeping his freedom? (He is speaking out to a large crowd.) Yes, Dr. King is speaking out about his beliefs. Let's add *Speak out* to the map.
- After discussing the photos, ask: What is the best way to keep your freedom?

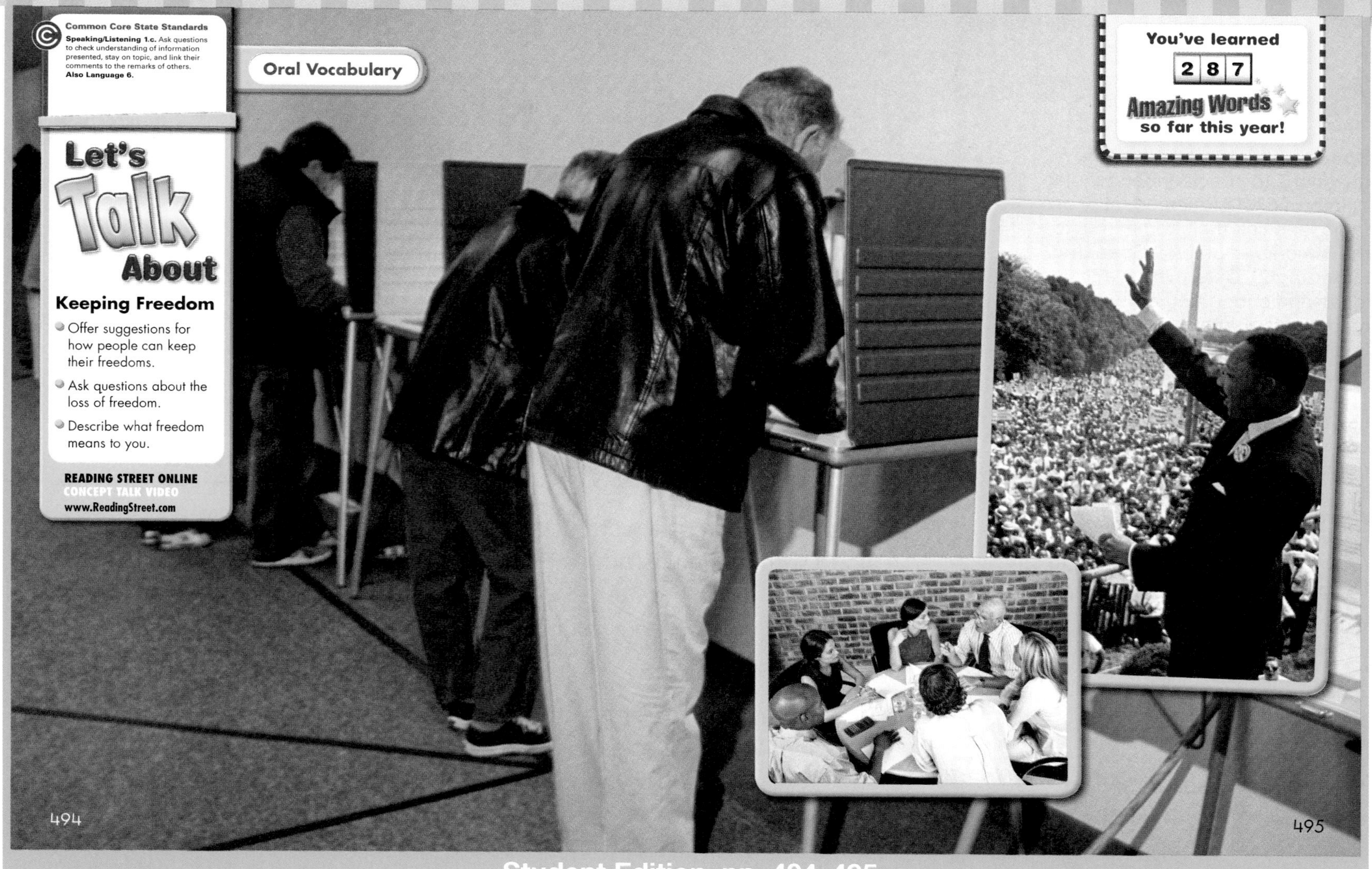

Common Core State Standards
Speaking/Listening 1.c. Ask questions to check understanding of information presented, stay on topic, and link their comments to the remarks of others.
Also Language 6.
Oral Vocabulary
Let's Talk About
Keeping Freedom
Offer suggestions for how people can keep their freedoms.
Ask questions about the loss of freedom.
Describe what freedom means to you.
READING STREET ONLINE
CONCEPT TALK VIDEO
www.ReadingStreet.com
You've learned
287
Amazing Words
so far this year!
494
495

Student Edition, pp. 494–495

CONNECT TO READING Tell students that this week they will be reading about ways that people try to keep their freedom. Encourage students to add concept-related words to this week's concept map.

How to keep your freedom
Organize
Vote
Speak out

eSTREET INTERACTIVE
www.ReadingStreet.com

- **Pearson eText**
  - Student Edition
- **Concept Talk Video**

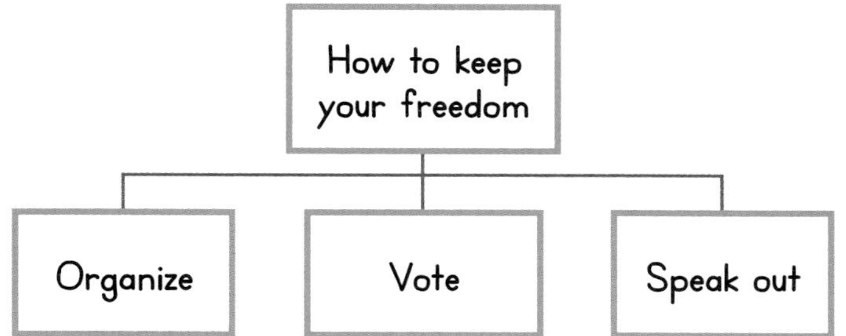

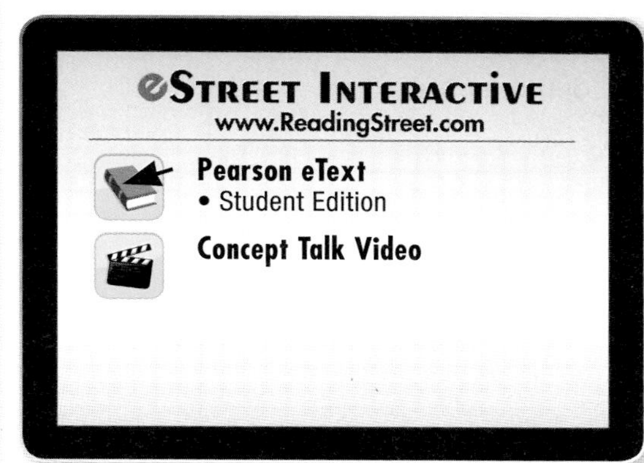

ELL

Preteach Concepts Use the Day 1 instruction on ELL Poster 30 to build knowledge, develop concepts, and build oral vocabulary.

ELL Support Additional ELL support and modified instruction is provided in the *ELL Handbook* and in the ELL Support lessons on the *Teacher Resources DVD-ROM.*

Common Core State Standards

Speaking/Listening 1.c. Ask questions to check understanding of information presented, stay on topic, and link their comments to the remarks of others. **Speaking/Listening 2.** Determine the main ideas and supporting details of a text read aloud or information presented in diverse media and formats, including visually, quantitatively, and orally. **Language 6.** Acquire and use accurately grade-appropriate conversational, general academic, and domain-specific words and phrases, including those that signal spatial and temporal relationships (e.g., *After dinner that night we went looking for them*). **Also Speaking/Listening 1., Language 4.**

Amazing Words

You've learned 287 words so far.

You'll learn 009 words this week!

witty	mourn
equality	blight
justice	wept
perish	violence
demonstrate	

Content Knowledge

Build Oral Vocabulary

INTRODUCE AMAZING WORDS "Martin's Dream" on p. 495b is about Dr. Martin Luther King Jr.'s dream of a better world. Tell students to listen for this week's Amazing Words—*witty, equality, justice,* and *perish*—as you read the Teacher Read Aloud on p. 495b.

Amazing Words — Robust Vocabulary Routine

1. **Introduce** Write the word *witty* on the board. Have students say the word aloud with you. In "Martin's Dream," we learn that *witty* describes a kind of comment. Does the author include any context clues that tell me the meaning of this word? *(funny)* Supply a student-friendly definition. *Witty* means "clever and amusing."
2. **Demonstrate** Have students answer questions to demonstrate understanding. What job requires a person to be *witty?* In what kind of situation should you not say something *witty?*
3. **Apply** Ask students to give a personal example of *witty*.
4. **Display the Word** Have students break the word between the two syllables, *wit-ty,* and say the word.

See p. OV•5 to teach *equality, justice,* and *perish.*

Routines Flip Chart

AMAZING WORDS AT WORK Reread "Martin's Dream" aloud. As students listen, have them notice how the Amazing Words are used in context. To build oral vocabulary, lead the class in a discussion about the Amazing Words' meanings. Then have students state the main idea of the selection and give supporting details.

Don't Wait Until Friday **MONITOR PROGRESS** **Check Oral Vocabulary**

During discussion, listen for students' use of Amazing Words.

If... students are unable to use the Amazing Words in discussion,

then... use the Oral Vocabulary Routine in the Routines Flip Chart to demonstrate words in different contexts.

Teacher Read Aloud

MODEL FLUENCY As you read "Martin's Dream," model appropriate expression by adjusting your voice to demonstrate lively, fluent reading.

Martin's Dream

How do you feel when someone treats you unfairly? Do you get angry? Do you try to be funny and make a witty comment? Or do you just walk away? We all respond differently to being mistreated, but injustice hurts everyone just the same.

It was the pain of injustice that started the civil rights movement in the 1950s. Civil rights are the basic rights of all citizens to be treated fairly and equally. Many people had different ideas about how to achieve civil rights, but one man's dream became the driving force behind this movement. That man was Martin Luther King Jr. On August 28, 1963, he and other civil rights leaders organized a march to the nation's capital. It was there that Martin gave his famous "I Have a Dream" speech.

On the steps of the Lincoln Memorial, in front of more than 200,000 people and millions more watching on TV, Martin Luther King Jr. spoke about his dream of equality. He began by telling his audience that even though President Abraham Lincoln had freed black slaves one hundred years earlier, black people still were not free. In many places, like Martin's hometown of Atlanta, Georgia, black people experienced discrimination every day.

In Atlanta, Martin had to use a separate water fountain from white people. He also had to give up his seat on a bus for a white person. But he did not let anger get the best of him. He had learned from his family to be dignified and not show his anger. Instead of acting with anger, Martin encouraged people of all backgrounds to work for peace and justice.

In his speech he said, "I have a dream that my four little children will one day live in a nation where they will not be judged by the color of their skin but by the content of their character."

The crowd was moved by Martin's words. People wept and cheered as they listened to his vision of a better America. They knew that they would have to work together to make this dream a reality.

The following year, Martin was present as President Johnson signed into law the Civil Rights Act of 1964. It would end segregation in public places. That same year, Martin Luther King Jr. was awarded the Nobel Peace Prize.

Although the civil rights movement made more progress over the next few years, it suffered its worst setback in 1968. Sadly, in that year Martin Luther King Jr. was shot and killed. People everywhere mourned the fallen leader. Many people were confused. Some people responded to the news with violence.

However, most people responded to the tragedy with a determination to make his dream a reality. Martin's dream did not perish. His vision and hope for a better world still live on to this day.

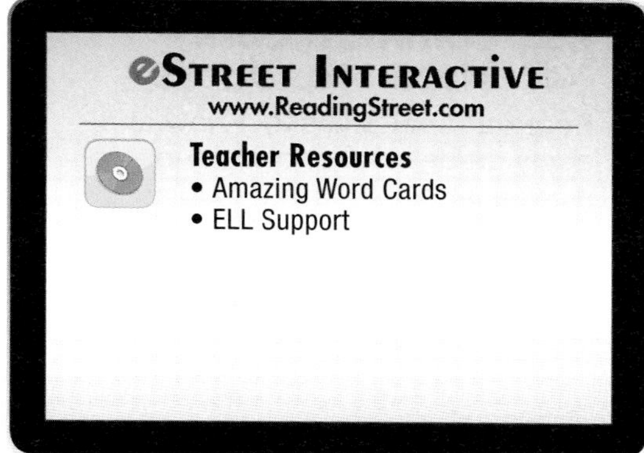

Support for Read Aloud Use the modified Read Aloud on p. D1•119 of the ELL Support lessons on the *Teacher Resources DVD-ROM* to prepare students to listen to "Martin's Dream."

Check Understanding After reading each paragraph, stop and discuss it with students. Clarify understanding by asking questions such as: *What are civil rights? What did Martin Luther King Jr. talk about in his speech?*

Common Core State Standards
Foundational Skills 3. Know and apply grade-level phonics and word analysis skills in decoding words. **Foundational Skills 3.c.** Decode multisyllable words. **Also Language 4.b., 4.c.**

Skills Trace

Related Words
Introduce U6W5D1
Practice U6W5D3; U6W5D4
Assess/Test Weekly Test U6W5 Benchmark Test U6
KEY: U=Unit W=Week D=Day

Vocabulary Support

You may wish to explain the meanings of these words.
courtesy polite behavior
courteous displaying good manners

Word Analysis

Teach/Model

Related Words

CONNECT Write *admire* and *admiration*. You can already read words like these. The second word looks like the first word, only the suffix *-ation* has been added. Read these words. Today you'll learn to decode and read words that are related or alike in some way.

MODEL Write *ability*. When I see an unfamiliar word like *ability*, I think about similar words I know. Often words that look and sound similar are related, so they have similar meanings. Write *able*. The first part of *ability* reminds me of *able*. I can use what I know about *able* to understand what *ability* means. If I think about related words and use context clues, I can often figure out a new word without looking it up.

GROUP PRACTICE Have students read *ability* with you. Then write the words below. Read the words and have students identify the related words and discuss how they are alike. Have students read the words.

courtesy	**courteous**	**describe**	**description**	**add**	**additional**
dine	**dinner**	**crumbs**	**crumbled**	**goal**	**goalie**

REVIEW What do you know about reading related words? Break an unknown word into parts. Then think about words that may be related and that will help you read and define the unknown word.

Guide Practice

MODEL Have students turn to p. 496 in their Student Editions. Each word on this page is related to another word. The first word is *compete*. I see that the next two words are *competitor* and *competition*. Those two words remind me of *compete*. Knowing the word *compete* will help me read and figure out the meanings of the related words *competitor* and *competition*.

GROUP PRACTICE For each word in Words I Can Blend, ask how the words are related and discuss their meanings. Then have students read all the related words.

Corrective feedback
If... students have difficulty reading a word,
then... model reading the parts of the word and then the whole word; then ask students to read it with you.

Common Core State Standards Foundational Skills 3. Know and apply grade-level phonics and word analysis skills in decoding words.
Envision It! Sounds to Know
sign
GRAND OPENING
signal
signature
READING STREET ONLINE
SOUND-SPELLING CARDS
www.ReadingStreet.com

Phonics

Related Words

Words I Can Blend

compete
competitor
competition

refresh
refreshment

Sentences I Can Read

1. Jenna is a strong competitor.
2. The three runners will compete in tomorrow's competition.
3. Let's refresh ourselves with some refreshment.

496

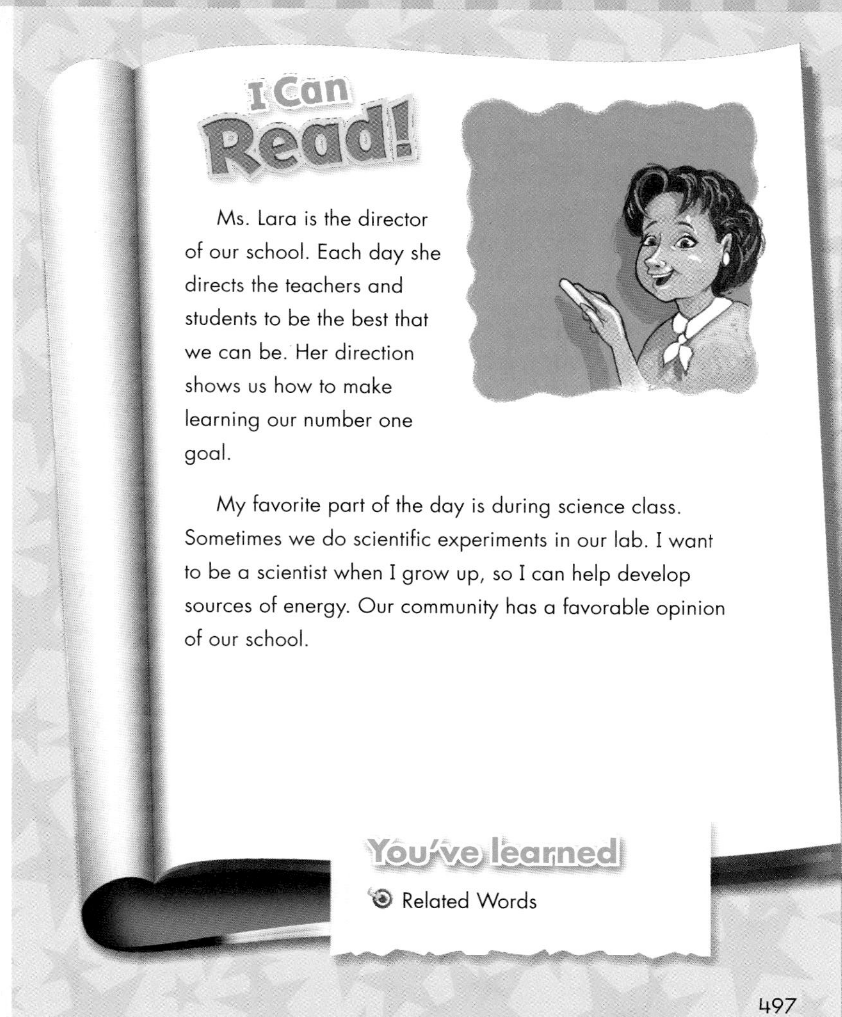

I Can Read!

Ms. Lara is the director of our school. Each day she directs the teachers and students to be the best that we can be. Her direction shows us how to make learning our number one goal.

My favorite part of the day is during science class. Sometimes we do scientific experiments in our lab. I want to be a scientist when I grow up, so I can help develop sources of energy. Our community has a favorable opinion of our school.

You've learned
Related Words

497

Student Edition, pp. 496–497

Apply

READ WORDS IN ISOLATION After students can successfully combine the word parts on p. 496 to read the words, point to words in random order and ask students to read them naturally.

READ WORDS IN CONTEXT Have students read each of the sentences on p. 496. Have them identify the related words in the sentences.

Team Talk Pair partners and have them take turns reading each of the sentences aloud.

Chorally read the I Can Read! passage on p. 497 with students. Then have them read the passage aloud to themselves.

ON THEIR OWN For additional practice, use *Reader's and Writer's Notebook* p. 429.

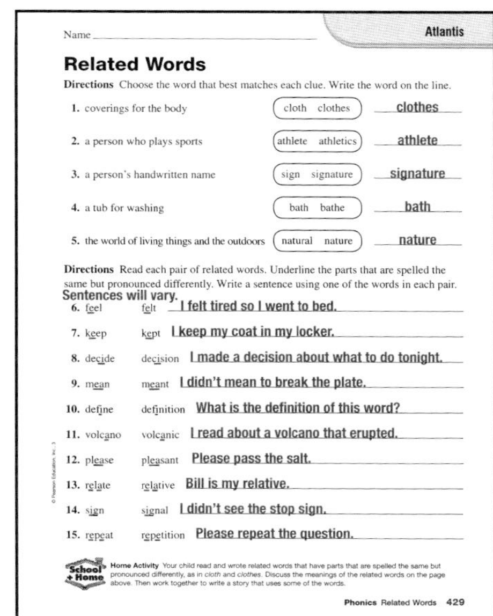

Name ______ Atlantis

Related Words

Directions Choose the word that best matches each clue. Write the word on the line.

1. coverings for the body (cloth clothes) clothes
2. a person who plays sports (athlete athletics) athlete
3. a person's handwritten name (sign signature) signature
4. a tub for washing (bath bathe) bath
5. the world of living things and the outdoors (natural nature) nature

Directions Read each pair of related words. Underline the parts that are spelled the same but pronounced differently. Write a sentence using one of the words in each pair.
Sentences will vary.

6. feel felt I felt tired so I went to bed.
7. keep kept I keep my coat in my locker.
8. decide decision I made a decision about what to do tonight.
9. mean meant I didn't mean to break the plate.
10. define definition What is the definition of this word?
11. volcano volcanic I read about a volcano that erupted.
12. please pleasant Please pass the salt.
13. relate relative Bill is my relative.
14. sign signal I didn't see the stop sign.
15. repeat repetition Please repeat the question.

Phonics Related Words 429

Reader's and Writer's Notebook, p. 429

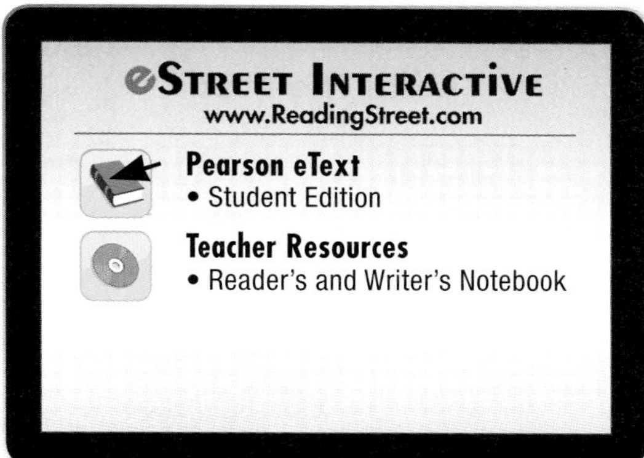

Support Phonics English learners will benefit from studying related words in English. Have students create word webs for related words and indicate whether each word in the web is a noun, verb, adjective, or adverb.

Contrastive Analysis Chart See also the Contrastive Analysis Chart in the *First Stop* book.

Common Core State Standards

Foundational Skills 3. Know and apply grade-level phonics and word analysis skills in decoding words. **Foundational Skills 3.d.** Read grade-appropriate irregularly spelled words. **Foundational Skills 4.** Read with sufficient accuracy and fluency to support comprehension. **Speaking/Listening 5.** Create engaging audio recordings of stories or poems that demonstrate fluid reading at an understandable pace; add visual displays when appropriate to emphasize or enhance certain facts or details. **Also Foundational Skills 3.c., 4.a.**

Decodable Reader 30A

If students need help, then...

Read *Mike the Medic*

READ WORDS IN ISOLATION Have students turn to p. 169 of *Decodable Practice Readers 3.2.* Have them read each word.

Have students read the high-frequency words *a, people, who, have, they, to, gives, the, many, where, one, anyone, their, clothes, sure, do,* and *very* on the first page.

PREVIEW Have students read the title and preview the story. Tell them that they will read words that are related words.

READ WORDS IN CONTEXT Pair students for reading and listen as they read. One student begins. Students read the entire story, switching readers after each page. Partners reread the story. This time the other student begins. Make sure students are monitoring their accuracy when they decode words.

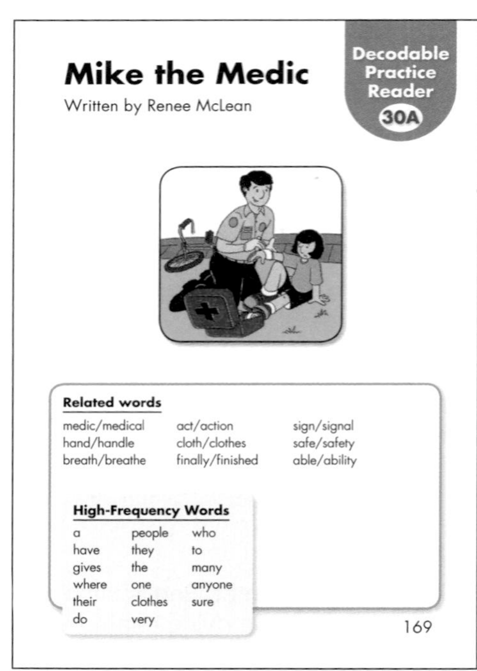

Mike the Medic

Written by Renee McLean

Decodable Practice Reader 30A

Related words

medic/medical	act/action	sign/signal
hand/handle	cloth/clothes	safe/safety
breath/breathe	finally/finished	able/ability

High-Frequency Words

a	people	who
have	they	to
gives	the	many
where	one	anyone
their	clothes	sure
do	very	

169

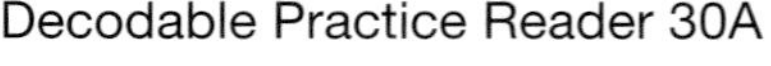
Decodable Practice Reader 30A

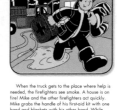

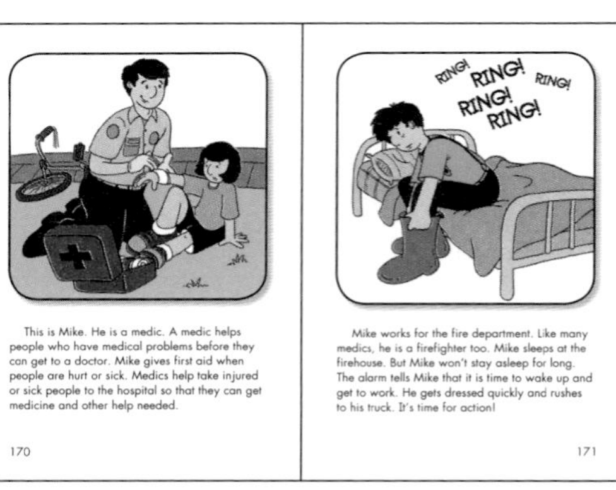

This is Mike. He is a medic. A medic helps people who have medical problems before they can get to a doctor. Mike gives first aid when people are hurt or sick. Medics help take injured or sick people to the hospital so that they can get medicine and other help needed.

170

Mike works for the fire department. Like many medics, he is a firefighter too. Mike sleeps at the firehouse. But Mike won't stay asleep for long. The alarm tells Mike that it is time to wake up and get to work. He gets dressed quickly and rushes to his truck. It's time for action!

171

The truck has lights and sirens that signal drivers to pull over to the side of the road. Bright, flashing lights and loud, wailing sirens are signs that this truck needs to get someplace fast. Cars pull over and stop to make way for this fire truck.

172

When the truck gets to the place where help is needed, the firefighters see smoke. A house is on fire! Mike and the other firefighters act quickly. Mike grabs the handle of his first-aid kit with one hand and blankets with his other hand. While other firefighters put out the fire, Mike checks to see if anyone is hurt.

173

Mike sees a family standing on the sidewalk. They look cold and frightened. Their clothes smell smoky and their faces are sooty. But everybody is safe. They had put cloth over their noses and mouths, which protected them from smoke. Mike checks them out and wraps blankets around them to keep them warm.

174

The fire is out at last. Now Mike helps the firefighters. Tim feels sick from heat and smoke. He cannot catch his breath. Mike puts a mask on his face to help him breathe clean air while he rests. Tim will see a doctor to make sure he is healthy and safe. Marla needs Mike's help too. She fell inside the house and cut her arm. Mike works hard looking after these brave safety workers.

175

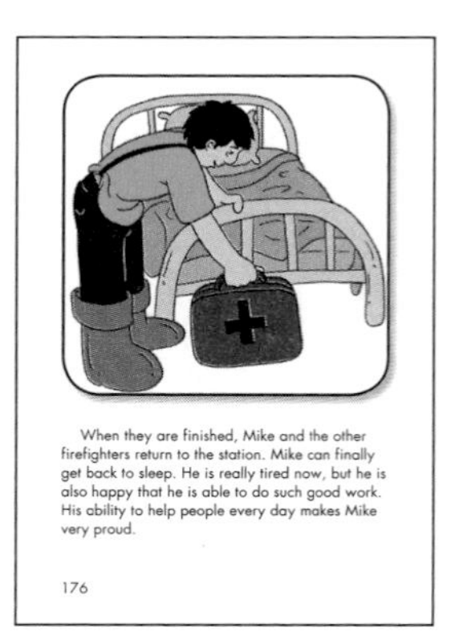

When they are finished, Mike and the other firefighters return to the station. Mike can finally get back to sleep. He is really tired now, but he is also happy that he is able to do such good work. His ability to help people every day makes Mike very proud.

176

Corrective feedback **If...** students have difficulty decoding a word, **then...** refer them to the *Sound-Spelling Cards* to identify the word parts. Have them read the word parts individually and then together to say the word.

- What is the new word?
- Is the new word a word you know?
- Does it make sense in the story?

CHECK DECODING AND COMPREHENSION Have students retell the story to include characters, setting, and events. Then have students find words in the story that are related words. Students should supply *medic/medical, act/action, sign/signal, hand/handle, cloth/clothes, safe/safety, breath/breathe, finally/finished, able/ability*.

EXTRA PRACTICE Have students take turns recording the story as they read. Then ask each student to review his or her recording to identify areas to improve reading fluency.

Reread for Fluency

REREAD DECODABLE READER Have students reread *Decodable Practice Reader 30A* to develop automaticity decoding words with related words.

Routine Oral Rereading

1. **Read** Have students read the entire practice reader orally.
2. **Reread** To achieve optimal fluency, students should reread the text three or four times.
3. **Corrective Feedback** Listen as students read. Provide corrective feedback regarding their fluency and decoding.

Routines Flip Chart

Related Words

Beginning Write the words *bath* and *bathes*. Read the words and talk with students about how they are related. Point out that even though the words are related and have parts that are spelled the same, they are pronounced differently. Have students read the words with you. Follow a similar procedure with the word pairs *cloth/clothes* and *close/closet*.

Intermediate After students have read the story, say a sentence using each word in one of the word pairs. Then call on volunteers to do the same with the other word pairs.

Advanced After reading the story, have partners look in the dictionary to find other words that are related to each word pair. Have them make a list of the words they find for each pair.

Common Core State Standards

Informational Text 1. Ask and answer questions to demonstrate understanding of a text, referring explicitly to the text as the basis for the answers. **Informational Text 2.** Determine the main idea of a text; recount the key details and explain how they support the main idea. **Also Foundational Skills 4.b.**

Skills Trace

Generalize

Introduce U3W4D1; U4W1D1; U6W5D1

Practice U3W4D2; U3W4D3; U3W5D2; U4W1D2; U4W1D3; U4W4D2; U6W5D2; U6W5D3

Reteach/Review U3W4D5; U4W1D5; U6W5D5

Assess/Test Weekly Tests U3W4; U4W1; U6W5
Benchmark Tests U4

KEY: U=Unit W=Week D=Day

Comprehension Support

Students may also turn to pp. EI•8 and EI•20 to review the skill and strategy if necessary.

Text-Based Comprehension

Generalize
Inferring

TEACH Remind students of the weekly concept—Keeping Your Freedom. Have students read "The Famous Thinker, Plato" on p. 499.

MODEL A CLOSE READ

Think Aloud

Today we're going to read about a great thinker named Plato. Have students follow along as you reread the last paragraph. Many of the sentences in the last paragraph are generalizations about what Plato's writings have in common. I see clue words, such as *many, mostly,* and *some,* that tell me that the author is making generalizations about Plato's writings. I read that Plato's school became a model for today's colleges and that his writings are still read and taught in school. I know that schools teach important lessons, so I can infer that Plato's school taught important lessons.

TEACH Have students read p. 498. Explain that the skill of generalizing and the strategy of inferring are tools they can use to deepen their understanding. Then have them use a graphic organizer like the one on p. 498 and identify generalizations from the passage.

GUIDE PRACTICE Have students reread "The Famous Thinker, Plato," using the callouts as guides. Then ask volunteers to respond to the questions in the callouts, citing specific examples from the text to support their answers.

Skill His ideas are still popular because people think his ideas make sense.
Strategy Students almost always study Plato's writings in school.

APPLY Use *Reader's and Writer's Notebook* p. 430 for additional practice with generalizing.

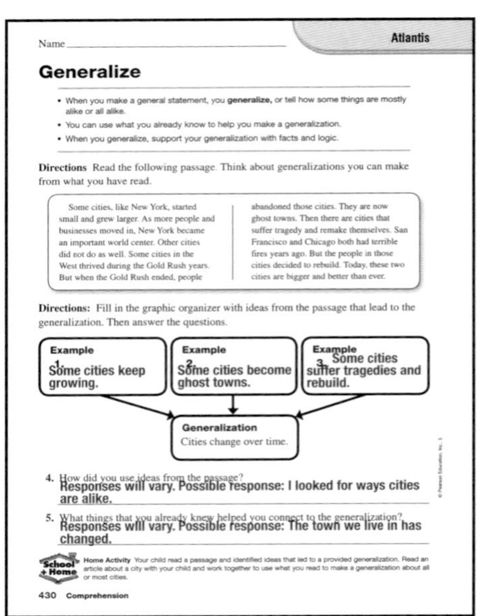

Name ______________ Atlantis

Generalize

- When you make a general statement, you **generalize,** or tell how some things are mostly alike or all alike.
- You can use what you already know to help you make a generalization.
- When you generalize, support your generalization with facts and logic.

Directions Read the following passage. Think about generalizations you can make from what you have read.

Some cities, like New York, started small and grew larger. As more people and businesses moved in, New York became an important world center. Other cities did not do as well. Some cities in the West thrived during the Gold Rush years. But when the Gold Rush ended, people abandoned those cities. They are now ghost towns. Then there are cities that suffer tragedy and remake themselves. San Francisco and Chicago both had terrible fires years ago. But the people in those cities decided to rebuild. Today, these two cities are bigger and better than ever.

Directions: Fill in the graphic organizer with ideas from the passage that lead to the generalization. Then answer the questions.

Example 1. Some cities keep growing.

Example 2. Some cities become ghost towns.

Example 3. Some cities suffer tragedies and rebuild.

Generalization Cities change over time.

4. How did you use ideas from the passage?
Responses will vary. Possible response: I looked for ways cities are alike.

5. What things that you already knew helped you connect to the generalization?
Responses will vary. Possible response: The town we live in has changed.

School + Home **Home Activity** Your child read a passage and identified ideas that led to a provided generalization. Read an article about a city with your child and work together to use what you read to make a generalization about all or most cities.

430 Comprehension

Reader's and Writer's Notebook, p. 430

Common Core State Standards
Informational Text 1. Ask and answer questions to demonstrate understanding of a text, referring explicitly to the text as the basis for the answers.
Also Informational Text 2.

Envision It! Skill Strategy

Skill

Strategy

READING STREET ONLINE
ENVISION IT! ANIMATIONS
www.ReadingStreet.com

Comprehension Skill

Generalize

- A general statement, or generalization, tells how some things are mostly or all alike.
- Key words, such as *always, never,* and *most,* signal a generalization.
- Be sure you can support your generalization with facts and logic.
- Use what you learned about generalizing and a graphic organizer like the one below as you read "The Famous Thinker, Plato." Then write a short paragraph explaining your generalization and support it with details from the text.

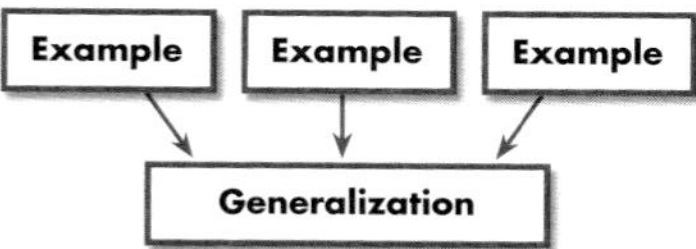

Comprehension Strategy

Inferring

Active readers use what they know and the ideas and clues in what they read to come up with their own ideas about what the author presents. Making inferences can help you understand the text better.

498

The Famous Thinker, Plato

One of the most famous thinkers of the ancient world was Plato. He was a Greek man who lived about 2,400 years ago. Plato was a student of another famous thinker, Socrates. Some ideas about our world today started with Plato and Socrates.

How did Plato learn so much? Besides studying many writings, Plato traveled far. He observed much on his journeys. Then Plato began a school of science and philosophy. Philosophy is the study of how our minds gather knowledge. This school became a model for today's colleges.

Many of Plato's writings have survived through history. He wrote mostly letters and dialogues. His writing covered many topics, including politics, nature, and happiness. In school, you will likely read some of Plato's famous writings. They have been part of many students' educations for hundreds of years.

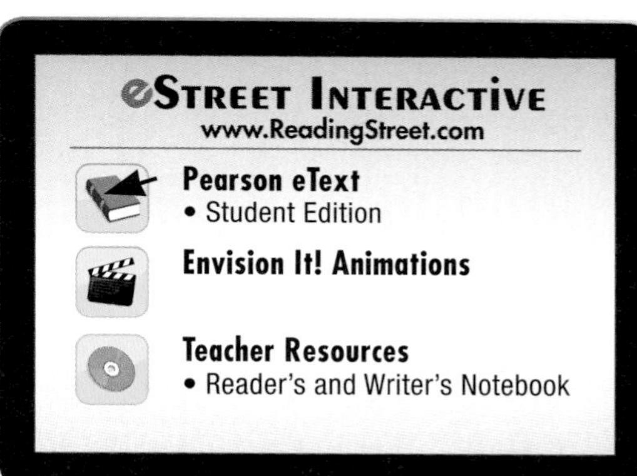

Strategy Why do you think that the teachings of Plato are still popular today?

Skill What generalization can you make about the writings of Plato? Use a key word, such as *always,* in your answer.

Your Turn!

Need a Review? See the *Envision It! Handbook* for more information about generalizing and inferring.

Ready to Try It? As you read *Atlantis: The Legend of a Lost City,* use what you've learned about generalizing and inferring to understand the text.

499

Student Edition, pp. 498–499

Model Fluent Reading

EXPRESSION Have students listen as you read paragraph 2 of "The Famous Thinker, Plato" with appropriate expression. Explain that you will adjust your voice level to stress important words and phrases.

Routine Oral Rereading

1. **Read** Have students read paragraph 2 of "The Famous Thinker, Plato" orally.
2. **Reread** To achieve optimal fluency, students should reread the text three or four times.
3. **Corrective Feedback** Have students read aloud without you. Provide feedback about their expression and encourage them to adjust their voice level to stress important words and phrases. Listen for use of appropriate expression.

Routines Flip Chart

eStreet Interactive
www.ReadingStreet.com

Pearson eText
- Student Edition

Envision It! Animations

Teacher Resources
- Reader's and Writer's Notebook

ELL

Generalize Have students state generalizations about their school. Then write the sentences below on the board. Have students identify which is a generalization.
- Plato began a school of science and philosophy.
- Plato wrote mostly letters and dialogues.
- Plato was a student of Socrates.

Common Core State Standards

Writing 7. Conduct short research projects that build knowledge about a topic. **Language 4.** Determine or clarify the meaning of unknown and multiple-meaning words and phrases based on grade 3 reading and content, choosing flexibly from a range of strategies. **Also Language 5.b.**

Selection Vocabulary

Use the following routine to introduce this week's tested selection vocabulary.

aqueducts channels for carrying water long distances
content satisfied
crouched stooped or bent down
guidance the act or process of guiding, or leading
honor treat with great respect; an expression of respect or affection
pillar an upright support for a building
thermal causing heat or warmth

SEE IT/SAY IT Write *guidance*. Scan across the word with your finger as you say it: *guid-ance.*

HEAR IT Use the word in a sentence. The teacher gave the students *guidance* during the exercise.

DEFINE IT Elicit definitions from students. How would you tell a friend what *guidance* means? Clarify or give a definition when necessary. Yes, it means to "guide" or "lead." Restate the word in student-friendly terms. So, *guidance* refers to leading or guiding someone.

Team Talk Is it always good to have *guidance?* Is there ever a time you might not want *guidance*? Turn and talk to your partner about this. Be prepared to explain your answer. Allow students time to discuss. Ask for examples. Rephrase their examples for usage when necessary or to correct misunderstandings.

MAKE CONNECTIONS Have students discuss the word. Have you ever given someone *guidance*? Why did you give *guidance*? Turn and talk to your partner about this. Then be prepared to share. Have students share. Rephrase their ideas for usage when necessary or to correct misunderstandings.

RECORD Have students write the word and its meaning.

Continue this routine to introduce the remaining words in this manner.

Corrective feedback | **If...** students are having difficulty understanding, **then...** review the definitions in small groups.

Research and Inquiry

Step 1 Identify and Focus Topic

TEACH Discuss the Question of the Week: *What is the best way to keep your freedom?* Tell students they will research the best way to keep their freedom. They will present their findings to the class on Day 5 as a journal entry.

Think Aloud **MODEL** I'll start by brainstorming a list of questions about the best way to keep my freedom. I know that if I want something to change, I must speak out about it. So I'll choose speaking out for causes I believe in. Some possible questions could be: *What famous people in history have spoken out for their beliefs? What response did they get? What was the final result of their action?*

GUIDE PRACTICE After students have formulated open-ended inquiry questions, explain that tomorrow they will consult a reference librarian about their questions.

ON THEIR OWN Have students work individually, in pairs, or in small groups to write an inquiry question.

Day 1 SMALL GROUP TIME • Differentiate Vocabulary, p. SG•65

OL On-Level

- **Practice Vocabulary** Amazing Words
- **Read** *Reading Street Sleuth,* pp. 76–77

SI Strategic Intervention

- **Reteach Vocabulary** Amazing Words
- **Read** *Reading Street Sleuth,* pp. 76–77

A Advanced

- **Extend Vocabulary** Amazing Words
- **Read** *Reading Street Sleuth,* pp. 76–77
- **Introduce** Inquiry Project

eSTREET INTERACTIVE
www.ReadingStreet.com

Teacher Resources

- Envision It! Pictured Vocabulary Cards
- Tested Vocabulary Cards

21st Century Skills

Internet Guy *Don Leu*

Weekly Inquiry Project

STEP 1	Identify and Focus Topic
STEP 2	Navigate/Search
STEP 3	Analyze Information
STEP 4	Synthesize
STEP 5	Communicate

Academic Vocabulary

journal a personal record of thoughts and events kept by an individual

Multilingual Vocabulary Students can apply knowledge of their home languages to acquire new English vocabulary by using the Multilingual Vocabulary Lists (*ELL Handbook,* pp. 433–444).

If... students need more scaffolding and practice with **Vocabulary,** **then...** use the activities on pp. DI•117–DI•118 in the Teacher Resources section on SuccessNet.

Common Core State Standards

Language 2.c. Use commas and quotation marks in dialogue. **Language 2.f.** Use spelling patterns and generalizations (e.g., word families, position-based spellings, syllable patterns, ending rules, meaningful word parts) in writing words. **Language 4.c.** Use a known root word as a clue to the meaning of an unknown word with the same root (e.g., *company, companion*). **Also Language 2.**

Spelling Pretest

Related Words

INTRODUCE This week we will spell related words. As you spell these words, remember to take the words apart (segment) in your mind and think about letter sounds, word parts, and syllables.

PRETEST Say each word, read the sentence, and repeat the word.

1. cloth	She used a **cloth** for dusting.
2. clothes	The mud ruined his **clothes.**
3. nature	We saw a lot of **nature** on our hike.
4. natural	The muffins had **natural** ingredients.
5. able	I was **able** to lift the heavy suitcase.
6. ability	I have the **ability** to run fast.
7. mean	What do you **mean**?
8. meant	Do you think he **meant** to leave his coat?
9. deal	We made a **deal** to help each other study.
10. dealt	Which card were you **dealt** first?
11. please	**Please** walk quietly down the hall.
12. pleasant	Mrs. Lopez is always **pleasant** and nice.
13. sign	There is a "For Sale" **sign** in front of my house.
14. signal	The traffic **signal** turned red.
15. signature	Did you forget your **signature** on your paper?
Challenge words	
16. equal	Martin Luther King Jr. fought for **equal** rights.
17. equation	Chad solved the math **equation.**
18. equator	It can get very hot at the **equator.**
19. major	Hunger is a **major** problem in some countries.
20. majority	The **majority** of fans cheer for the home team.

SELF-CORRECT Have students self-correct their pretests by rewriting misspelled words.

ON THEIR OWN Use *Let's Practice It!* page 401 on the *Teacher Resources DVD-ROM.*

Name ______ Atlantis

Related Words

Generalization Related words often have parts that are spelled the same but pronounced differently: cloth, clothes.

Word Sort Sort the list words by words you know how to spell and words you are learning to spell. Write every word.

words I know how to spell	words I'm learning to spell
1. Answers will vary.	9. Answers will vary.
2.	10.
3.	11.
4.	12.
5.	13.
6.	14.
7.	15.
8.	

Spelling Words
1. cloth
2. clothes
3. nature
4. natural
5. able
6. ability
7. mean
8. meant
9. deal
10. dealt
11. please
12. pleasant
13. sign
14. signal
15. signature

School + Home — Home Activity: Your child is learning to spell related words. To practice at home, have your child study each word that he or she wrote in the second column on this page, spell the word with eyes shut, and then write it.

Related Words DVD•401

Let's Practice It! TR DVD•401

Conventions

Quotations and Parentheses

MAKE CONNECTIONS Ask students if they've ever made air quotes when they were talking to someone. Have them give some examples and explain why they did that. Then tell them that in writing, they will also put quotations, or someone's exact words, in quotation marks.

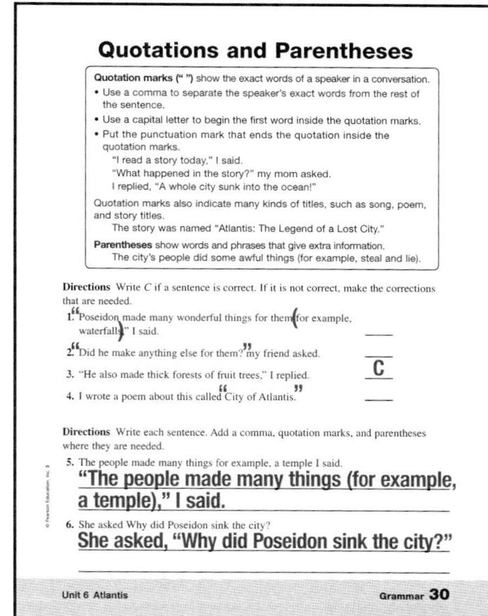

Quotations and Parentheses

Quotation marks (" ") show the exact words of a speaker in a conversation.
- Use a comma to separate the speaker's exact words from the rest of the sentence.
- Use a capital letter to begin the first word inside the quotation marks.
- Put the punctuation mark that ends the quotation inside the quotation marks.

"I read a story today," I said.
"What happened in the story?" my mom asked.
I replied, "A whole city sunk into the ocean!"

Quotation marks also indicate many kinds of titles, such as song, poem, and story titles.
The story was named "Atlantis: The Legend of a Lost City."

Parentheses show words and phrases that give extra information.
The city's people did some awful things (for example, steal and lie).

Directions Write *C* if a sentence is correct. If it is not correct, make the corrections that are needed.

1. "Poseidon made many wonderful things for them (for example, waterfalls)," I said. ____
2. "Did he make anything else for them?" my friend asked. ____
3. "He also made thick forests of fruit trees," I replied. **C**
4. I wrote a poem about this called "City of Atlantis." ____

Directions Write each sentence. Add a comma, quotation marks, and parentheses where they are needed.

5. The people made many things for example, a temple I said.
"The people made many things (for example, a temple)," I said.
6. She asked Why did Poseidon sink the city?
She asked, "Why did Poseidon sink the city?"

© Pearson Education, Inc. 3

Unit 6 Atlantis   Grammar 30

Grammar Transparency 30, TR DVD

TEACH Display Grammar Transparency 30, and read aloud the explanation and examples in the box. Point out the quotation marks and parentheses in the examples.

MODEL Model using quotation marks and parentheses to complete items 1 and 2. Apply the rules for quotations and parentheses to show why you inserted them.

GUIDE PRACTICE Guide students to complete items 3 and 4. Record the correct responses on the transparency.

APPLY Have students read sentences 5 and 6 on the transparency and add commas, quotation marks, and parentheses.

Handwriting

MODEL LETTER FORMATION AND JOINING OF CURSIVE STROKES Display the capital letters *J, X,* and *L*. Follow the stroke instructions pictured to model letter formation.

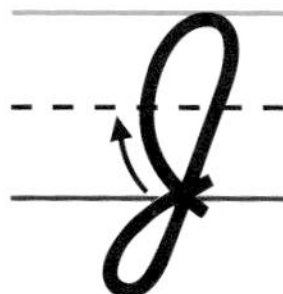

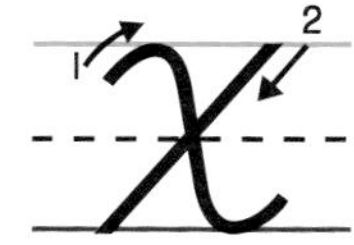

After you have written a cursive letter, do not raise your pencil. (*X* is an exception). Connect the end of one letter to the beginning of the next letter in the word. The connection should be a smooth curve. Model joining letters in this sentence: *Larry and Joseph studied Xerxes the Great*. Make sure the connections between letters are smooth and flowing.

GUIDE PRACTICE Have students write these sentences. *Xavier is my new friend. Last night, I had a tasty dinner. Jennifer and Jeremy sit in the first row.* Circulate around the room, guiding students.

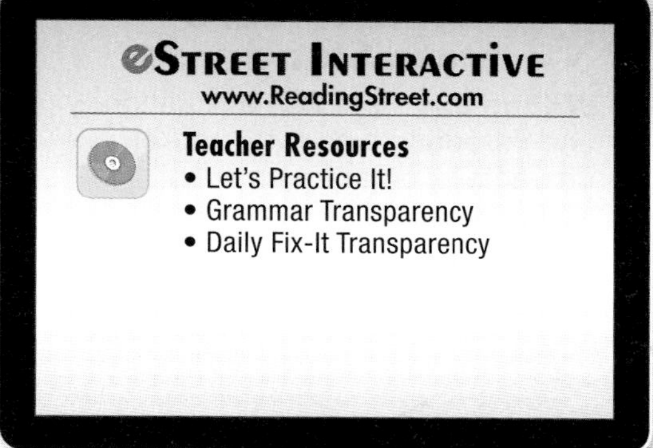

Daily Fix-It

1. Tina and me enjoy the naturel world in the desert. *(I; natural)*
2. Tina said "I thouht I saw a snake." *(said,; thought)*

Academic Vocabulary 

A **quotation** shows the exact words of a speaker.

Quotation marks enclose quotations, dialogue, and the titles of songs, poems, and short stories.

Parentheses enclose words that add extra details to the sentence.

Language Transfer Students might have difficulty distinguishing dialogue from the rest of a sentence. Show that words such as *said* and *replied* usually are found just before or after the dialogue, *outside* the quotation marks.

Common Core State Standards

Writing 3.a. Establish a situation and introduce a narrator and/or characters; organize an event sequence that unfolds naturally. **Also Writing 3., 5.**

Bridge to Common Core

TEXT TYPES AND PURPOSES

This week students will write two historical fiction narratives to practice writing for tests. They will adapt the form, organization, and content of their writing to communicate clearly to an external audience.

Narrative Writing

Through reading and discussing, students will gain a deeper understanding of how to keep our freedoms. They will use this knowledge from the texts to write historical fiction narratives that are cleanly developed; contain effective, well-chosen details; and have well-structured sequences of events.

Throughout the week, students will improve their range and content of writing through daily mini-lessons.

5-Day Plan

DAY 1	Read Like a Writer
DAY 2	Think About the Past
DAY 3	Evaluation
DAY 4	Historical Figures
DAY 5	Revise

Write Guy *by Jeff Anderson*

What Do You Notice?

When students are examining the model text, ask, "What do you notice?" By giving students the responsibility of commenting on what they find effective in the text, they build self-confidence and often begin to notice features of the writing they might not have otherwise. Eventually they will start trying them in their writing. Relish students' movement toward correctness and beauty.

Writing

Historical Fiction

Mini-Lesson Writing for Tests: Read Like a Writer

Introduce This week you will write an imaginative story in the form of historical fiction. Historical fiction is a type of story that is set in a real time or historical setting. Frequently some of the events are true. Historical fiction often has a mix of made-up characters and historical people, such as kings and queens.

Genre Historical Fiction

Trait Word Choice

Mode Narrative

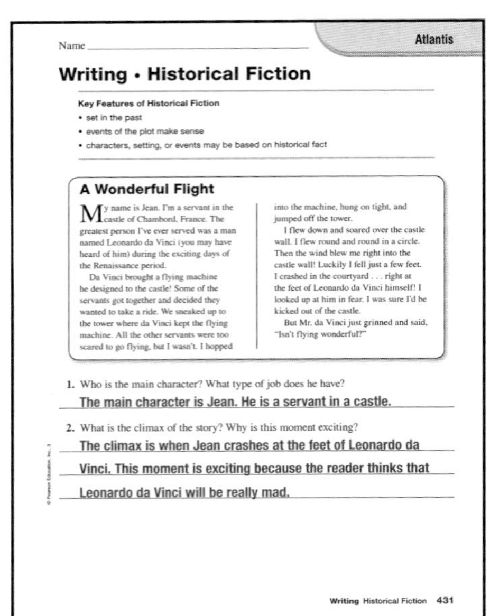

Name ______ Atlantis

Writing • Historical Fiction

Key Features of Historical Fiction
- set in the past
- events of the plot make sense
- characters, setting, or events may be based on historical fact

A Wonderful Flight

My name is Jean. I'm a servant in the castle of Chambord, France. The greatest person I've ever served was a man named Leonardo da Vinci (you may have heard of him) during the exciting days of the Renaissance period.

Da Vinci brought a flying machine he designed to the castle! Some of the servants got together and decided they wanted to take a ride. We sneaked up to the tower where da Vinci kept the flying machine. All the other servants were too scared to go flying, but I wasn't. I hopped into the machine, hung on tight, and jumped off the tower.

I flew down and soared over the castle wall. I flew round and round in a circle. Then the wind blew me right into the castle wall! Luckily I fell just a few feet. I crashed in the courtyard . . . right at the feet of Leonardo da Vinci himself! I looked up at him in fear. I was sure I'd be kicked out of the castle.

But Mr. da Vinci just grinned and said, "Isn't flying wonderful?"

1. Who is the main character? What type of job does he have?
The main character is Jean. He is a servant in a castle.

2. What is the climax of the story? Why is this moment exciting?
The climax is when Jean crashes at the feet of Leonardo da Vinci. This moment is exciting because the reader thinks that Leonardo da Vinci will be really mad.

© Pearson Education, Inc. 3

Writing Historical Fiction 431

Reader's and Writer's Notebook, p. 431

Examine Model Text Let's read an example of historical fiction written in response to a writing prompt on a test. Have students read "A Wonderful Flight" on p. 431 of their *Reader's and Writer's Notebook*.

Key Features Historical fiction is set in a real place. It might still exist today, or it might have fallen into ruin long ago. Have students circle the setting (Chambord, France). Point out the correct capitalization of this geographic location.

Frequently, some of the events are true. The fact that Leonardo da Vinci designed a flying machine is true, but the other information in the story is not.

Historical fiction takes place in a historical time period. A historical time period could be thousands of years ago or 20 years ago. Have students find the name of the time period during which the story is set. (the Renaissance) Remind students to capitalize the names of historical periods.

Historical fiction often uses a mix of historical people and fictional characters. What historical people can you find in this story? (Leonardo da Vinci) Which characters are fictional? (the main character, the other servants)

Review Key Features

Review the key features of historical fiction with students. You might want to post the key features in the classroom for students to refer to.

Key Features of Historical Fiction

- imaginary story often based on real events
- takes place in the past
- set in a real place
- uses a mix of historical and fictional characters

Routine Quick Write for Fluency

Team Talk

1. **Talk** Have pairs discuss the features of historical fiction.
2. **Write** Each student writes about mixing historical and fictional characters.
3. **Share** Partners read their sentences aloud to each other.

Routines Flip Chart

eStreet Interactive
www.ReadingStreet.com

Teacher Resources
- Reader's and Writer's Notebook
- Let's Practice It!

Model Text Read aloud the writing model "A Wonderful Flight" and help students understand it. Discuss with students the parts of the story that are historical and those that are fictional. Have students restate the events in the plot. List them on the board.

Wrap Up Your Day!

- **Concept Knowledge** Reread Street Rhymes! on p. 494j to students. Ask them what they learned today about the best ways to keep their freedom.
- **Oral Vocabulary** Have students use the Amazing Words they learned in context sentences.
- **Homework** Send home this week's Family Times newsletter on *Let's Practice It!* pp. 402–403 on the *Teacher Resources DVD-ROM*.

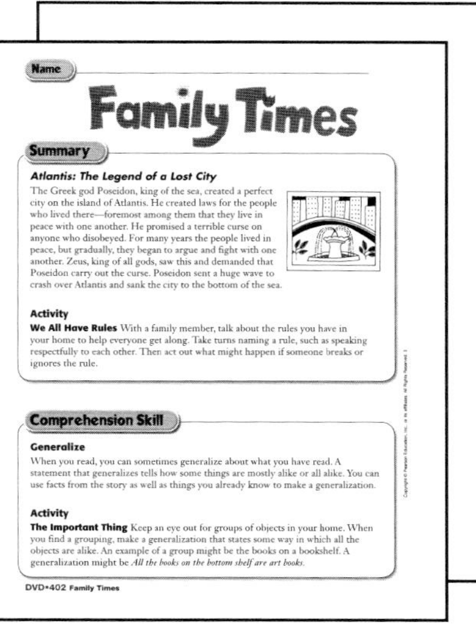

Name

Family Times

Summary

Atlantis: The Legend of a Lost City

The Greek god Poseidon, king of the sea, created a perfect city on the island of Atlantis. He created laws for the people who lived there—foremost among them that they live in peace with one another. He promised a terrible curse on anyone who disobeyed. For many years the people lived in peace, but gradually, they began to argue and fight with one another. Zeus, king of all gods, saw this and demanded that Poseidon carry out the curse. Poseidon sent a huge wave to crash over Atlantis and sank the city to the bottom of the sea.

Activity

We All Have Rules With a family member, talk about the rules you have in your home to help everyone get along. Take turns naming a rule, such as speaking respectfully to each other. Then act out what might happen if someone breaks or ignores the rule.

Comprehension Skill

Generalize

When you read, you can sometimes generalize about what you have read. A statement that generalizes tells how some things are mostly alike or all alike. You can use facts from the story as well as things you already know to make a generalization.

Activity

The Important Thing Keep an eye out for groups of objects in your home. When you find a grouping, make a generalization that states some way in which all the objects are alike. An example of a group might be the books on a bookshelf. A generalization might be *All the books on the bottom shelf are art books.*

DVD•402 Family Times

Let's Practice It!
TR DVD•402–403

Preview DAY 2

Tell students that tomorrow they will begin reading about a place called Atlantis.

DAY 2 at a Glance

Content Knowledge
Oral Vocabulary

Phonics/Word Analysis
Related Words

Literary Terms
Foreshadowing

Vocabulary Skill
Homographs

Fluency
Expression

Research and Inquiry
Navigate/Search

Conventions
Quotations and Parentheses

Spelling
Related Words

Writing
Historical Fiction

Materials

- Student Edition
- Reader's and Writer's Notebook

Common Core State Standards

Speaking/Listening 1. Engage effectively in a range of collaborative discussions (one-on-one, in groups, and teacher-led) with diverse partners on grade 3 topics and texts, building on others' ideas and expressing their own clearly. **Language 6.** Acquire and use accurately grade-appropriate conversational, general academic, and domain-specific words and phrases, including those that signal spatial and temporal relationships (e.g., *After dinner that night we went looking for them*).

Content Knowledge

Keeping Your Freedom

EXPAND THE CONCEPT Remind students of the weekly concept question, *What is the best way to keep your freedom?* Tell students that today they will begin reading *Atlantis: The Legend of a Lost City.* As they read, encourage students to think about different ways to keep freedom.

Build Oral Language

TALK ABOUT SENTENCES AND WORDS Reread these sentences from the Read Aloud, "Martin's Dream."

... Martin Luther King Jr. spoke about his dream of equality. He began by telling his audience that even though President Abraham Lincoln had freed black slaves one hundred years earlier, black people still were not.

- What does the word *equality* mean in this sentence? (to be treated the same as others)
- What does the word *dream* mean in the first sentence? (a wish)
- Do *equal* and *free* mean the same thing? (No, you can be free but still not treated equally.)

Team Talk Have students turn to a partner and discuss the following question. Then ask them to share their responses.

- Why do you think the author uses the word *dream* in the first sentence instead of the word *wish* or *hope?* (The word *dream* is stronger than *wish* or *hope;* it is a vision that Dr. King believes can one day happen.)

Build Oral Vocabulary

Amazing Words Robust Vocabulary Routine

1. **Introduce** Write the Amazing Word *demonstrate* on the board. Have students say it aloud with you. Relate *demonstrate* to the photographs on pp. 494–495 and "Martin's Dream." What are some ways that people *demonstrate* for a cause? (organize, march, speak out) What does our right to *demonstrate* say about our freedom? (Our freedom gives us the right to express our opinions.) Have students determine a definition of the word. Point out that *demonstrate* has multiple meanings. Students can use context clues to figure out the meaning. To *demonstrate* is to show support in public for a cause or person.

2. **Demonstrate** Have students answer questions to demonstrate understanding. How did Dr. King's followers *demonstrate*? (They gathered in Washington to hear him speak.) How might *demonstrating* make a difference? (Large crowds of people draw attention to a cause.)

3. **Apply** Have students apply their understanding. For what kind of cause would you like to *demonstrate*?

4. **Display the Word** Run your hand under the word as you emphasize the syllables *dem-on-strate.* Have students say the word.

See p. OV•5 to teach *mourn.*

Routines Flip Chart

ADD TO THE CONCEPT MAP Use the photos on p. 494–495 and the Read Aloud, "Martin's Dream," to discuss how we can keep our freedom and to talk about the Amazing Words *witty, equality, justice,* and *perish.* Add these and other concept-related words to the concept map to develop students' knowledge of the topic. Discuss the following questions. Encourage students to build on others' ideas when they answer. Add some of the words generated in the discussion to the concept map.

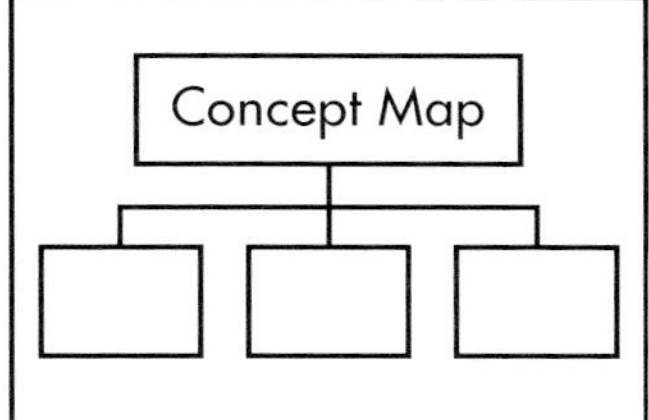

- How might you react if you hear a *witty* comment?
- What can you do to promote *justice* and *equality* in your community?
- Why must we not let our freedom *perish?*

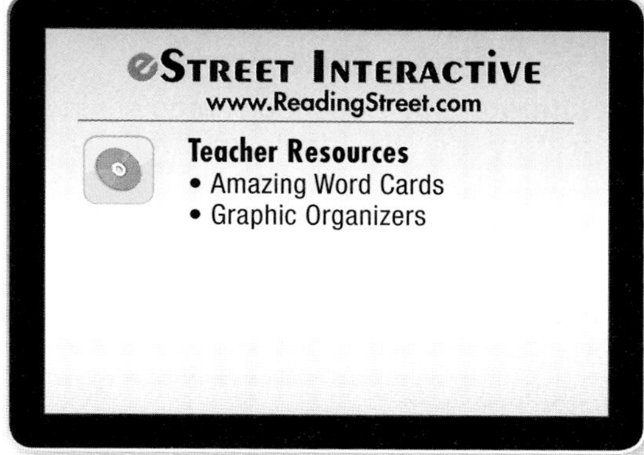

eSTREET INTERACTIVE
www.ReadingStreet.com
Teacher Resources
• Amazing Word Cards
• Graphic Organizers

Amazing Words

witty	mourn
equality	blight
justice	wept
perish	violence
demonstrate	

Connect to Social Studies

Dr. Martin Luther King Jr. Day Americans observe the third Monday in January as a national holiday to honor the birthday of civil rights leader Dr. Martin Luther King Jr. His actual birthday was January 15, 1929.

Reinforce Vocabulary Use the Day 2 instruction on ELL Poster 30 to teach lesson vocabulary and discuss the weekly concept.

Common Core State Standards

Literature 3. Describe characters in a story (e.g., their traits, motivations, or feelings) and explain how their actions contribute to the sequence of events. **Foundational Skills 3.** Know and apply grade-level phonics and word analysis skills in decoding words. **Also Foundational Skills 3.c., 5.**

Word Analysis

Related Words

REVIEW Review related words, pointing out that related words are words that have parts that look and sound similar.

READ WORDS IN ISOLATION Have the class read these words. Then point to these words in random order and ask students to read them quickly.

soft	define	final	keep
softener	definition	finish	keeper

Corrective feedback Model reading the pairs of related words, and then have students read the words with you.

READ WORDS IN CONTEXT Have the class read these sentences.

Team Talk Have pairs take turns reading the sentences naturally.

There was a **sign** warning us of the broken traffic **signal.**

I **feel** that the man **felt** bad about the traffic accident.

Carla used a lot of **cloth** to make her own **clothes.**

Check Word Reading

Related Words

FORMATIVE ASSESSMENT Write the following words and have the class read them. Notice which words students miss during the group reading. Call on individuals to read some of the words.

bath	**bathes**	**sign**	**signal**
fashion	**father**	**kitchen**	**machine**
incredible	**discredit**	**volunteer**	

Spiral Review
Row 2 reviews words with consonant digraphs.
Row 3 contrasts related words and words with consonant digraphs

If... students cannot read related words at this point,

then... use the Day 1 Word Analysis lesson on p. 496a to reteach related words. Use words from the *Decodable Practice Passages* (or Reader). Continue to monitor students' progress using other instructional opportunities during the week. See the Skills Trace on p. 496a.

Literary Terms

Foreshadowing

TEACH Tell students that foreshadowing is the use of hints and clues about what will happen later in a story. Explain that foreshadowing can help them predict what will happen.

Think Aloud **MODEL** Let's look at "The Art of Architecture" on page 501. The first paragraph of this story tells how as a little boy, Billy dreamed of becoming an architect. The second paragraph talks about Billy's later work as an architect. Do any sentences in the first paragraph provide foreshadowing or hints that Billy might someday become an architect? (The last sentence: *Ever since he could hold a crayon, he's been busy drawing houses with tall pillars and wide columns supporting giant roofs.*)

GUIDE PRACTICE Have students look for an example of foreshadowing as they read *Atlantis: The Legend of a Lost City.* Be sure to point out how foreshadowing can help students predict what will happen in the story.

ON THEIR OWN Have students look for examples of foreshadowing in other selections in their Student Edition.

Academic Vocabulary 

foreshadowing hints and clues about what will happen later in a story

Common Core State Standards

Language 4.a. Use sentence-level context as a clue to the meaning of a word or phrase. **Also Foundational Skills 4.b., 4.c., Language 4., 5., 5.c.**

Selection Vocabulary

aqueducts channels for carrying water long distances

content satisfied

crouched stooped or bent down

guidance the act or process of guiding, or leading

honor treat with great respect; an expression of respect or affection

pillar an upright support for a building

thermal causing heat or warmth

Bridge to Common Core

VOCABULARY ACQUISITION AND USE

Using context clues helps students determine the meaning of homographs and enables them to acquire a broad range of academic and domain-specific words. By clarifying definitions and pronunciations of homographs, they demonstrate the ability to gather vocabulary knowledge on their own.

Vocabulary Support

Refer students to *Words!* on p. W•10 in the Student Edition for additional practice.

Vocabulary Skill

Homographs

READ Have students read "The Art of Architecture" on p. 501. Use the vocabulary skill and strategy as tools to build comprehension.

Tell students that when they encounter a homograph, they should use context clues to determine its meaning and pronunciation. Explain how context clues can help students understand which meaning and pronunciation of a word fits the sentence.

MODEL Write on the board: *He knows that he will be happy and content with helping people make the best use of space.* I thought the word *content* meant "everything inside a box, a house, and so on." That meaning doesn't make sense here. *Content* must be a homograph. I'll look at other words in the sentence to figure out another meaning for *content.* The phrase *happy and content* in the sentence gives me a clue. I think *content* means "satisfied" or "pleased."

GUIDE PRACTICE Write this sentence on the board: *He helps people live better lives.* Explain that the word *live* has different meanings and pronunciations (/liv/ "to be alive; exist;" /līv/ "alive; living"). Have students use context clues to determine the meaning and pronunciation of *live* in this sentence. Repeat with *lives,* the last word of the sentence. For additional support, use *Envision It! Pictured Vocabulary Cards* or *Tested Vocabulary Cards.*

ON THEIR OWN Have students reread "The Art of Architecture" on p. 501. Have them find homographs and other Words to Know in the passage and use context clues to determine the meaning and pronunciation of each. For additional practice, use *Reader's and Writer's Notebook* p. 432.

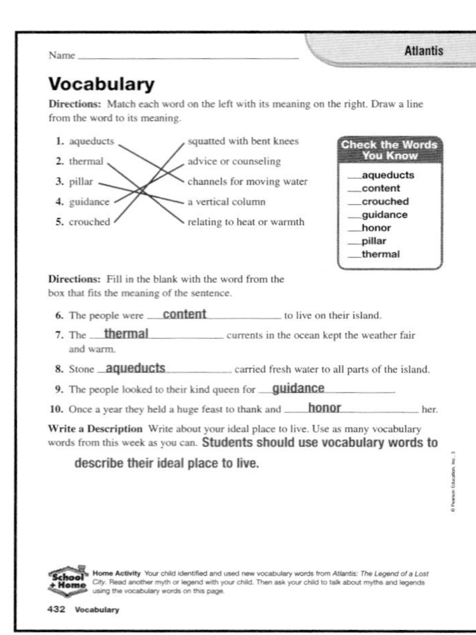

Name ____________ Atlantis

Vocabulary

Directions: Match each word on the left with its meaning on the right. Draw a line from the word to its meaning.

1. aqueducts — squatted with bent knees
2. thermal — advice or counseling
3. pillar — channels for moving water
4. guidance — a vertical column
5. crouched — relating to heat or warmth

Check the Words You Know
__aqueducts
__content
__crouched
__guidance
__honor
__pillar
__thermal

Directions: Fill in the blank with the word from the box that fits the meaning of the sentence.

6. The people were **content** to live on their island.
7. The **thermal** currents in the ocean kept the weather fair and warm.
8. Stone **aqueducts** carried fresh water to all parts of the island.
9. The people looked to their kind queen for **guidance**.
10. Once a year they held a huge feast to thank and **honor** her.

Write a Description Write about your ideal place to live. Use as many vocabulary words from this week as you can. **Students should use vocabulary words to describe their ideal place to live.**

School + Home **Home Activity** Your child identified and used new vocabulary words from *Atlantis: The Legend of a Lost City*. Read another myth or legend with your child. Then ask your child to talk about myths and legends using the vocabulary words on this page.

432 Vocabulary

Reader's and Writer's Notebook, p. 432

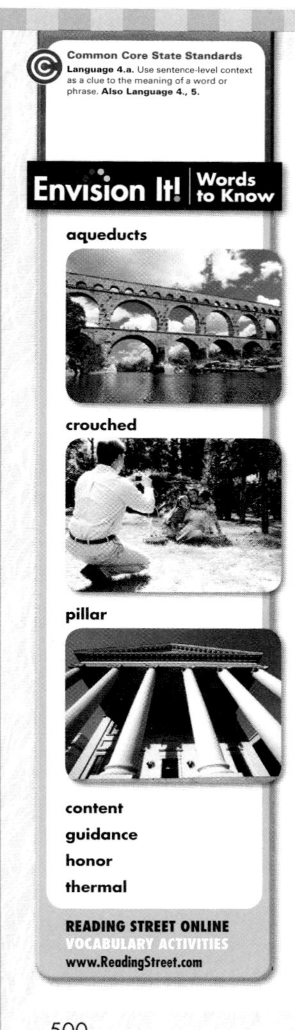

Common Core State Standards
Language 4.a. Use sentence-level context as a clue to the meaning of a word or phrase. Also Language 4., 5.
Envision It! Words to Know
aqueducts
crouched
pillar
content
guidance
honor
thermal
READING STREET ONLINE
VOCABULARY ACTIVITIES
www.ReadingStreet.com

Vocabulary Strategy for

Homographs

Context Clues Sometimes you may read a word you know, but the meaning doesn't make sense in the sentence. The word might be a homograph. Homographs are words that are spelled the same but have different pronunciations and meanings. For example, *lead* with a long *e* sound means to "go in front of," and *lead* with a short *e* sound means "a soft heavy metal."

1. If a word you know doesn't make sense in the sentence, it might be a homograph.
2. Look at the words around it. Can you figure out another meaning and pronunciation?
3. Try the new meaning in the sentence. Does it make sense?

Read "The Art of Architecture" on page 501. As you read, use context clues to find the meanings of homographs.

Words to Write Reread "The Art of Architecture." List the homographs and the other Words to Know, their pronunciations, including the syllables, and their meanings. Use a dictionary or glossary for help if needed. Then use those words to write a story about an ancient city.

500

The Art of Architecture

The aqueducts of Paris, which are tunnels that carry water from one place to another, are an example of the ancient art of architecture. When Billy visited Paris with his grandmother, he crouched on his knees on the bank of the Seine to take a photograph of the famous structures, which were built centuries ago during Roman rule. Under his grandmother's guidance, Billy is learning more about architecture. Billy wants to be an architect when he grows up, which would honor the work of both his grandmother and grandfather who met in architecture school and designed many buildings in his hometown of Dallas. Ever since he could hold a crayon, he's been drawing houses with tall pillars and wide columns supporting giant roofs.

Now that Billy is older, he knows that architects do more than just draw fancy buildings. He feels a responsibility to conserve resources, and he has been reading about using thermal insulation to keep heating costs down. Even though he likes the idea of designing world-famous high rises, he knows that he will be happy and content with helping people make the best use of space and live better lives.

Your Turn!

Need a Review? For additional help with homographs, see *Words!*

Ready to Try It? Read *Atlantis: The Legend of a Lost City* on pp. 502–519.

501

Student Edition, pp. 500–501

Reread for Fluency

EXPRESSION Read paragraph 1 of "The Art of Architecture" aloud, using changes of voice level for emphasis. Tell students that you are reading the passage with expression, paying special attention to the new vocabulary.

Routine Oral Rereading

1. **Read** Have students read paragraph 1 of "The Art of Architecture" orally.
2. **Reread** To achieve optimal fluency, students should reread the text three or four times.
3. **Corrective Feedback** Have students read aloud without you. Provide feedback about their expression and encourage them to adjust their voice level to stress important words and phrases. Listen for use of appropriate expression.

Routines Flip Chart

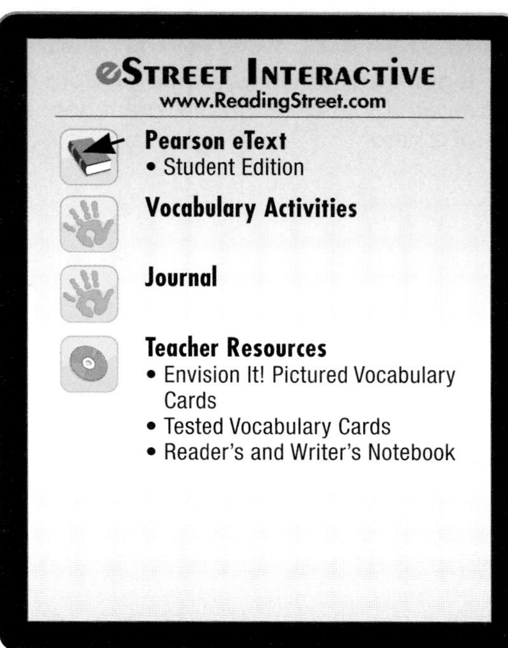

Text-Based Comprehension

Introduce Main Selection

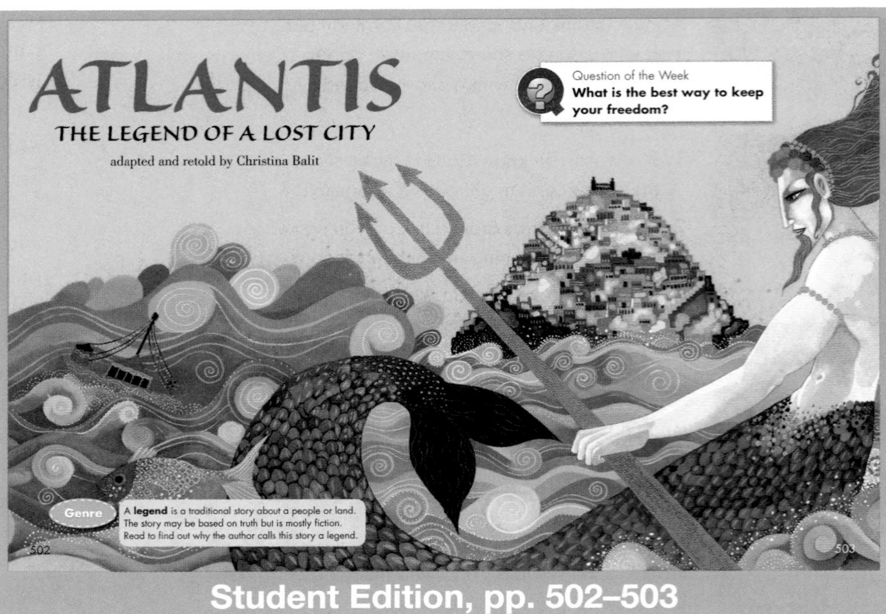

Student Edition, pp. 502–503

GENRE Explain that a **legend** is an old story passed by word of mouth that tells about the great deeds of a hero. The story of George Washington chopping down a cherry tree and tales of Big Foot are legends. Many Native American stories are legends. Often the events in a legend can't really happen, but legends are frequently based on some historical truth.

PREVIEW AND PREDICT Have students preview the title and illustrations in *Atlantis.* Have them predict what they will find out as they read.

PURPOSE By analyzing *Atlantis,* a legend, students will gain knowledge about keeping freedom.

Common Core State Standards

Literature 2. Recount stories, including fables, folktales, and myths from diverse cultures; determine the central message, lesson, or moral and explain how it is conveyed through key details in the text. **Literature 10.** By the end of the year, read and comprehend literature, including stories, dramas, and poetry, at the high end of the grades 2–3 complexity band independently and proficiently.

CRAFT AND STRUCTURE

Students analyze the structure of the selection and how its components relate to each other and the whole when they examine its genre. As they preview the title and illustrations of the selection and prepare to read, they come to see how purpose shapes the content and style of the text.

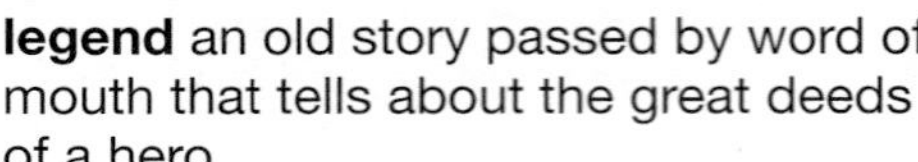

Academic Vocabulary

legend an old story passed by word of mouth that tells about the great deeds of a hero

Strategy Response Log

Have students use p. 36 in the *Reader's and Writer's Notebook* to identify the characteristics of a legend.

eStreet Interactive
www.ReadingStreet.com

Pearson eText
• Student Edition

AudioText CD

Teacher Resources
• Reader's and Writer's Notebook

Background Building Audio CD

Access Main Selection

READER AND TASK SUGGESTIONS	
Preparing to Read the Text	**Leveled Tasks**
• Provide students with a basic understanding of Greek gods and their power. • Discuss the features of a legend. • Remind students that they may need to adjust their reading rate and look for context clues to better understand the vocabulary in the selection.	• **Levels of Meaning • Evaluation** If students have difficulty understanding why the story of Atlantis is a legend, ask them to think about events in the selection that could really happen and events that could not really happen. • **Language Conventionality and Clarity** The complex structure of sentences in the selection may cause problems for some students. Remind them to break long sentences into smaller parts and identify the main action in each sentence.

See Text Complexity Measures for *Atlantis* on the tab at the beginning of this week.

READ Tell students that today they will read *Atlantis* for the first time. Use the Read for Understanding routine.

Routine Read for Understanding

Deepen understanding by reading the selection multiple times.

1. **First Read**—If students need support, then use the **Access Text** notes to help them clarify understanding.
2. **Second Read**—Use the **Close Reading** notes to help students draw knowledge from the text.

Day 2 SMALL GROUP TIME • Differentiate Comprehension, p. SG•65

OL On-Level	SI Strategic Intervention	A Advanced
• **Practice** Selection Vocabulary • **Read** *Atlantis*	• **Reteach** Selection Vocabulary • **Read** *Atlantis*	• **Extend** Selection Vocabulary • **Read** *Atlantis* • **Investigate** Inquiry Project

Access for All

Strategic Intervention

Work with students to set a purpose for reading, or if time permits, have students work with partners to set purposes.

A Advanced

Have students discuss why people tell legends.

Build Background To build background, review the summary selection in English (*ELL Handbook,* p. 205) Use the Retelling Cards to provide visual support for the summary.

If... students need more scaffolding and practice with the **Comprehension Skill,**
then... use the activities on p. DI•121 in the Teacher Resources section on SuccessNet.

1ST READ

Access Text If students need help, then...

GENERALIZE Write the following sentences on the board. Ask students to make a generalization about what people think about the island: *Few people visited the rocky island. No one bothered to give it a name.*

Think Aloud **MODEL** A generalization often sums up information or states the main idea. Words such as *few* and *most* are clues that a generalization is being made. I know *few* people visited the island; so I can say: The island wasn't important to *most* people. How else can you say that? (The island was important to few people.)

First there was Chaos. From Chaos sprang Earth and Heaven.

From them came the race of Titans; two of them, Cronus and Rhea, seized power and ruled over all. Their son Zeus overthrew them. Then he and his brothers divided up the world: to Zeus went the heavens, to Hades, the realms of the dead, while the seas and oceans went to mighty Poseidon, who promised to guard the waters with care.

Floating on one of Poseidon's emerald seas was a small rocky island. Few visited its shores and no one bothered to give it a name. But the sun rose warmly over it each morning and set sleepily behind it every night.

504

Student Edition, p. 504

2ND READ

Close Reading

INFERENCE • TEXT EVIDENCE Do you think Evenor, Leucippe, and Cleito are some of the people who think the island is not important? What statement in the story supports your answer? (No, they would not be part of that group. The last sentence on p. 505 tells us they live happily on the island, so they probably think it is important.)

EVALUATION After reading the first two pages, do you think this story is true or made up? Why? (Most of the story is made up because the characters are not real. We don't know for sure whether Atlantis or a similar city actually existed.)

ON THEIR OWN Have students reread pp. 504–505 to find clues to the generalization that many gods fought with each other. For additional practice, use *Let's Practice It!* p. 404 on the *Teacher Resources DVD-ROM.*

In the center of the island there stood a mountain, and at the foot of the mountain lived a man called Evenor and his wife, Leucippe. They lived happily together, working hard to tend the barren land, and brought up their daughter Cleito to honor all creatures.

505

Student Edition, p. 505

SYNTHESIS • TEXT EVIDENCE What clues tell you that Cleito is a kind character? (The text says that Cleito's parents raised her to honor all creatures. I know that when you honor something, you treat it kindly and with respect.)

Common Core State Standards

Literature 1. Ask and answer questions to demonstrate understanding of a text, referring explicitly to the text as the basis for the answers. **Literature 3.** Describe characters in a story (e.g., their traits, motivations, or feelings) and explain how their actions contribute to the sequence of events. **Also Literature 10.**

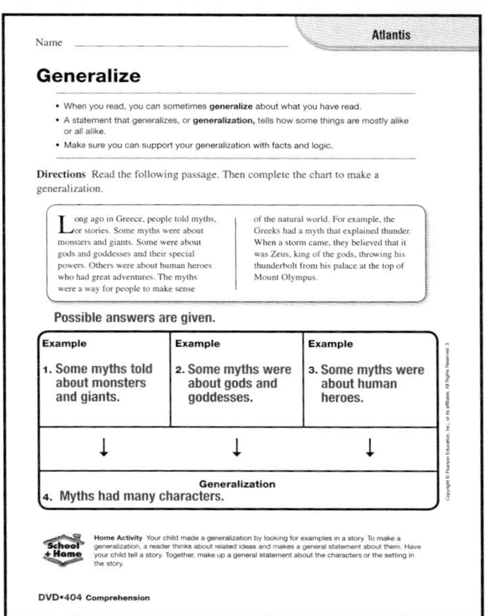

Name ______________________ Atlantis

Generalize

- When you read, you can sometimes **generalize** about what you have read.
- A statement that generalizes, or **generalization,** tells how some things are mostly alike or all alike.
- Make sure you can support your generalization with facts and logic.

Directions Read the following passage. Then complete the chart to make a generalization.

Long ago in Greece, people told myths, or stories. Some myths were about monsters and giants. Some were about gods and goddesses and their special powers. Others were about human heroes who had great adventures. The myths were a way for people to make sense of the natural world. For example, the Greeks had a myth that explained thunder. When a storm came, they believed that it was Zeus, king of the gods, throwing his thunderbolt from his palace at the top of Mount Olympus.

Possible answers are given.

Example	Example	Example
1. Some myths told about monsters and giants.	2. Some myths were about gods and goddesses.	3. Some myths were about human heroes.
↓	↓	↓

Generalization
4. Myths had many characters.

School + Home **Home Activity** Your child made a generalization by looking for examples in a story. To make a generalization, a reader thinks about related ideas and makes a general statement about them. Have your child tell a story. Together, make up a general statement about the characters or the setting in the story.

DVD•404 Comprehension

Let's Practice It! TR DVD•404

Activate Prior Knowledge Ask students to tell what they know about islands and why there might not be many people living on an island.

1ST READ

Access Text If students need help, then...

INFERRING Have students read the first paragraph on p. 506. Ask students how they know that a god doesn't usually look like a person. ("He took on human form" tells me he usually has a different form.)

Think Aloud **MODEL** Being able to make inferences helps me understand a story. I read that Poseidon took on human form. If I think about what I know and what the story tells me, I can infer that he changed what he looked like. He changed from what he usually looked like into what humans look like.

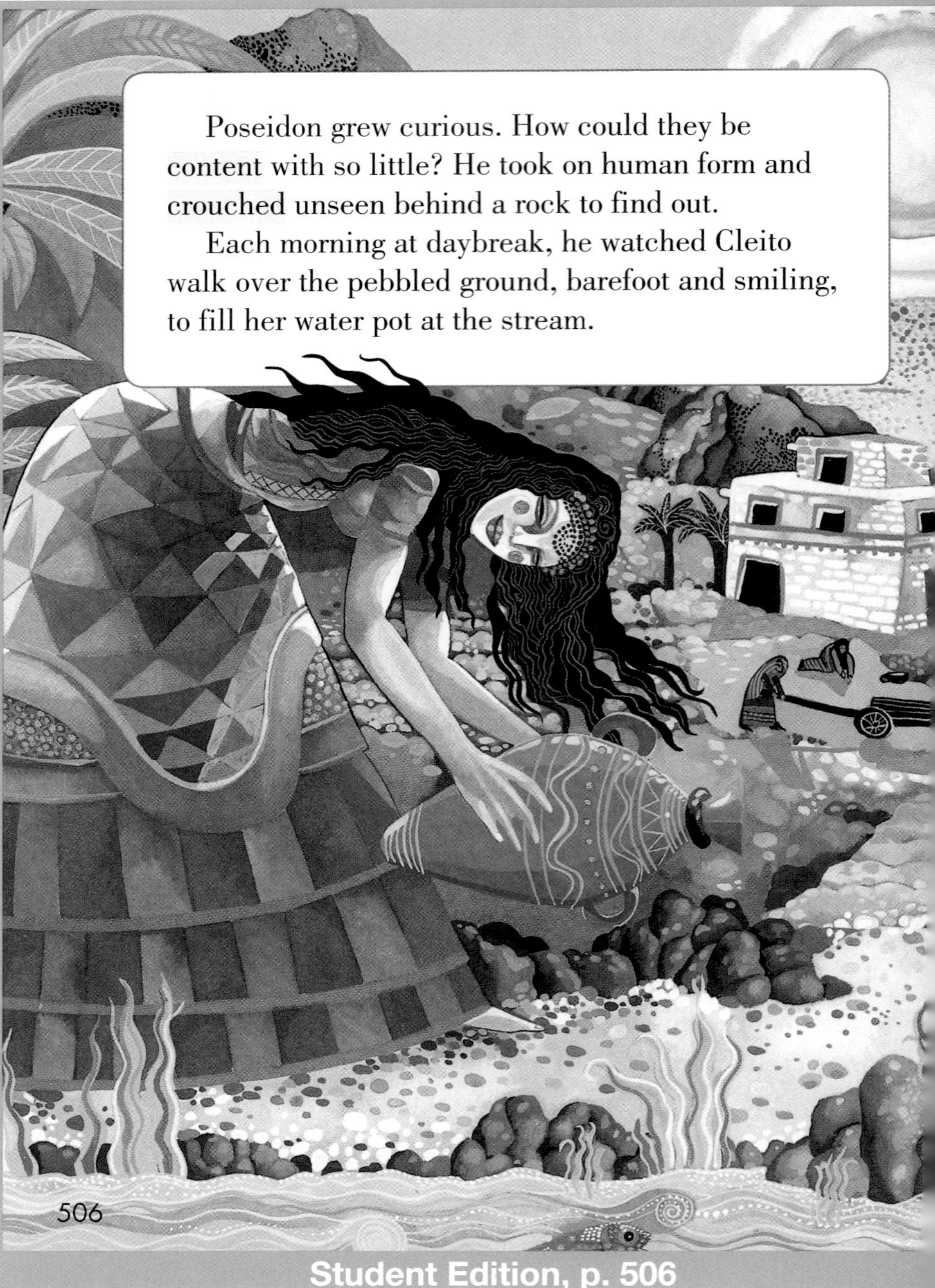

Poseidon grew curious. How could they be content with so little? He took on human form and crouched unseen behind a rock to find out.
Each morning at daybreak, he watched Cleito walk over the pebbled ground, barefoot and smiling, to fill her water pot at the stream.
506

Student Edition, p. 506

2ND READ

Close Reading

SYNTHESIS Do you think Cleito's parents would have let her marry Poseidon if they had known he was a god? What helped you decide that? (Probably not; the author tells us that Cleito's parents did not know that Poseidon was a god when they said Cleito could marry him, so it must be important to the story, and it implies that they would not have approved of the marriage.)

ANALYSIS Why did Poseidon watch Cleito every morning? (He was curious, so he watched her to find out why she was so happy all the time.) Why did he finally come out from behind the rock? (He thought she was beautiful, and he fell in love with her.)

ON THEIR OWN Have students reread pp. 506–507 to find additional places where they can make inferences. Ask them to explain why they think Poseidon decided to appear as a human.

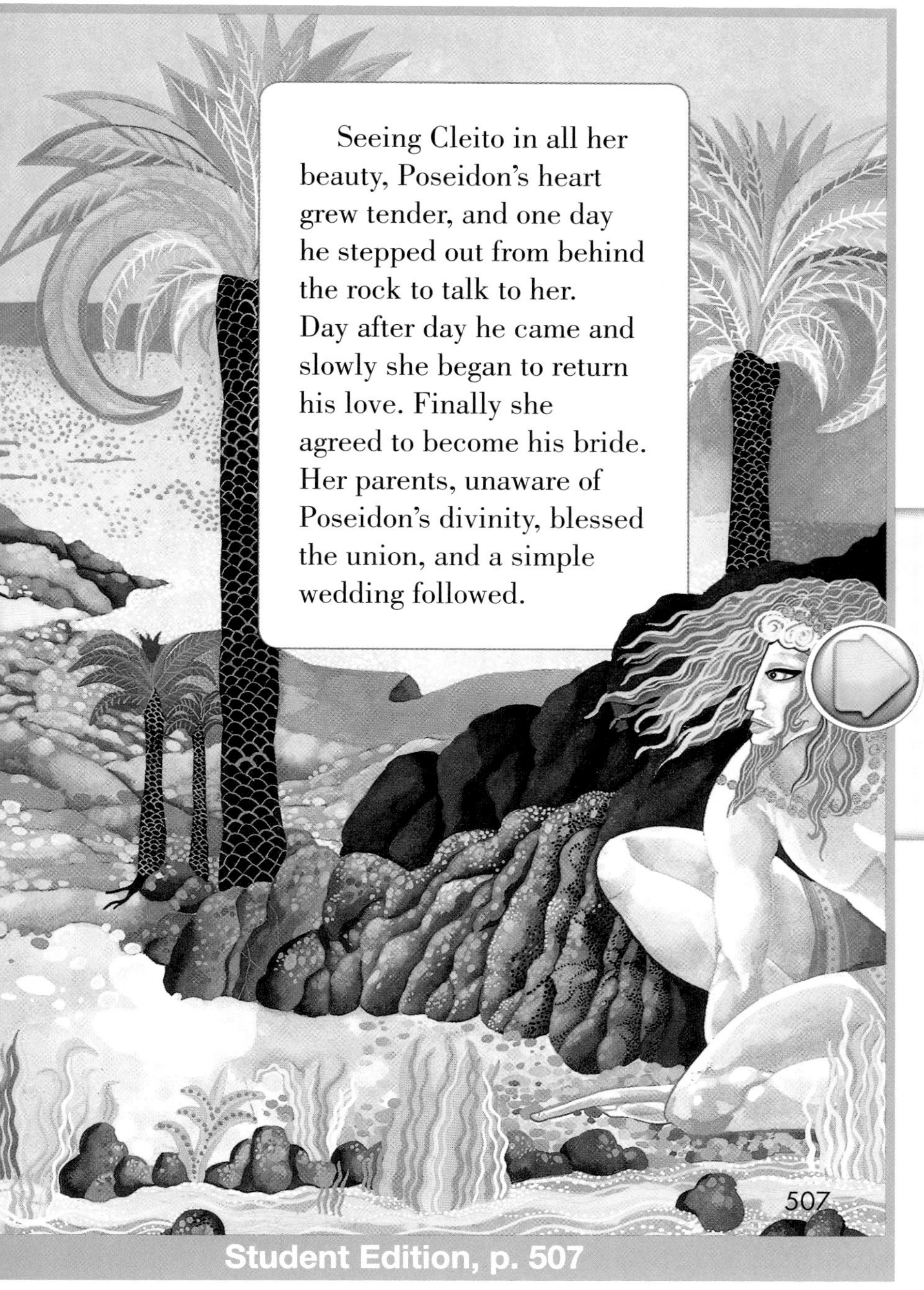

Seeing Cleito in all her beauty, Poseidon's heart grew tender, and one day he stepped out from behind the rock to talk to her. Day after day he came and slowly she began to return his love. Finally she agreed to become his bride. Her parents, unaware of Poseidon's divinity, blessed the union, and a simple wedding followed.
507

Student Edition, p. 507

Common Core State Standards

Literature 1. Ask and answer questions to demonstrate understanding of a text, referring explicitly to the text as the basis for the answers. **Literature 3.** Describe characters in a story (e.g., their traits, motivations, or feelings) and explain how their actions contribute to the sequence of events. **Also Literature 10.**

Access for All

SI Strategic Intervention

Have students work in pairs to reread pp. 506–507 and to identify the important events in the story so far.

ELL

Figurative Language Read aloud the first sentence on p. 507. Then explain to students that the phrase "Poseidon's heart grew tender" means that he became loving. When people are kind and loving we sometimes say they are tenderhearted or softhearted. Ask students to name other things that might make us tenderhearted.

1ST READ

Access Text
If students need help, then...

HOMOGRAPHS Have students reread the second sentence on p. 508. Ask them to find a homograph in the sentence. *(rose)* Remind students that homographs have the same spelling. Then ask them to give the correct definition of the word *rose* as it is used in this sentence.

Think Aloud **MODEL** The second sentence says that all the spirits of the sea rose to the surface to sing. I know the word *rose* can mean a flower. The word *rose* can be the past tense of *rise,* which means "to go up" or "to move up." In this sentence, the spirits of the sea end up at the water's surface, so the definition of *rose* must be "went up."

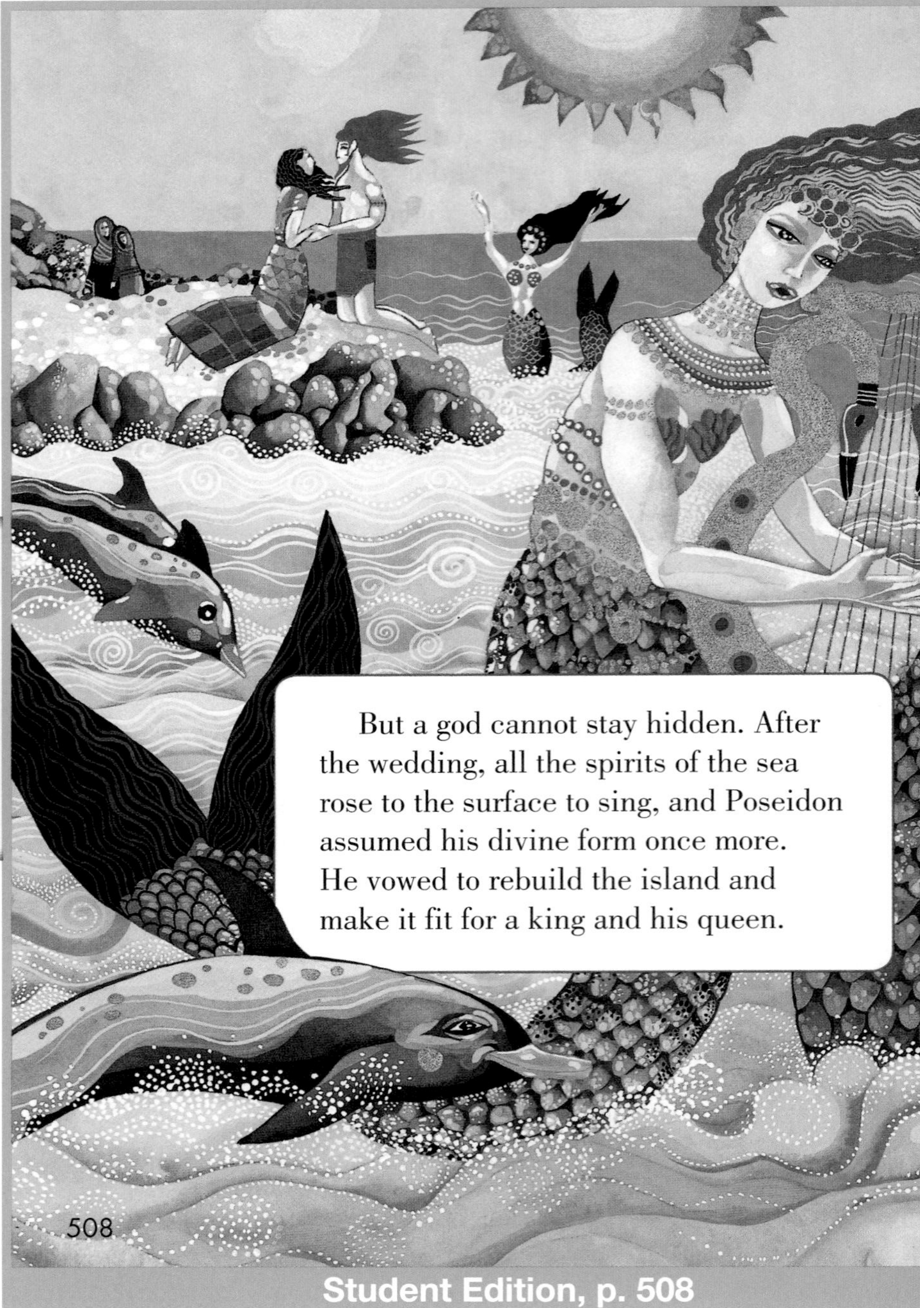

But a god cannot stay hidden. After the wedding, all the spirits of the sea rose to the surface to sing, and Poseidon assumed his divine form once more. He vowed to rebuild the island and make it fit for a king and his queen.
508

Student Edition, p. 508

2ND READ

Close Reading

EVALUATION Can we make the generalization that everyone was better off with the changes Poseidon made to the island? Why or why not? (No. It has not been said that anyone is better off with these changes. There are a lot more crops and resources, but Cleito and her family were happy when they had very little.)

ANALYSIS • TEXT EVIDENCE Help students generate text-based questions by providing the following question stem: In the selection, what did Poseidon do when _______?

ON THEIR OWN Have students read page 509 and look for other examples of homographs *(alternate).*

Poseidon used powers beyond human imagining to transform the isle into a paradise.

First, he arranged alternate circles of land and sea—three of land and three of water—to enclose the mountain. Within each circle of land a forest sprang up. Trees bloomed and grew heavy with fruits, and creatures multiplied.

Next, he made a network of canals, fed by waterfalls. Soon the island was yielding two crops each year—one watered by winter rains, the other irrigated by Poseidon's canals. The rich earth was carpeted with herbs and vegetables, and thick with healing roots; from its depths men dug out priceless yellow mountain copper. All things flourished on the sacred island.

509

Student Edition, p. 509

ANALYSIS • TEXT EVIDENCE Some language helps us visualize. The language creates a picture in our minds. What language does the author use on page 509 to create an image? What does this mean? (The author says that the "rich earth was carpeted with herbs and vegetables." The earth was thickly covered with herbs and vegetables.)

Common Core State Standards

Literature 1. Ask and answer questions to demonstrate understanding of a text, referring explicitly to the text as the basis for the answers. **Also Literature 3., 10., Language 4., 4.a., 5.**

Connect to Social Studies

Floating Gardens Poseidon's concentric rings of land and sea are similar to the floating gardens of the Aztec in Lake Xochimilco in Mexico. Although the Xochimilco islands were built in a freshwater lake, the Aztec also converted a saltwater bay in Lake Texcoco into a freshwater bay by using dikes and aqueducts. The floating islands are called *chinampas.*

ELL

Compound Words Point out the word *waterfalls* on p. 509. Remind students that a compound word is a single word made of two or more words. Ask them to identify the two words in the compound and tell what each word means. Then ask them what the compound means. Help them verify the definition in a dictionary.

1ST READ

Access Text

If students need help, then...

Review PLOT AND THEME Remind students that the story's plot describes the major events of the story. The plot drives the theme, or the big idea. Have students summarize and sequence events they have read about so far.

Think Aloud **MODEL** When I summarize and sequence the plot of a story, I describe the major events in the order in which they happen. What major event happens to the characters Cleito and Poseidon first? (They get married.) What major event happens next? (Poseidon transforms the island into a paradise.) These are plot events.

ON THEIR OWN Have students reread pp. 510–511 and use a graphic organizer to record what has happened so far in the story. For additional practice, use *Let's Practice It!* page 405 on the *Teacher Resources DVD-ROM.*

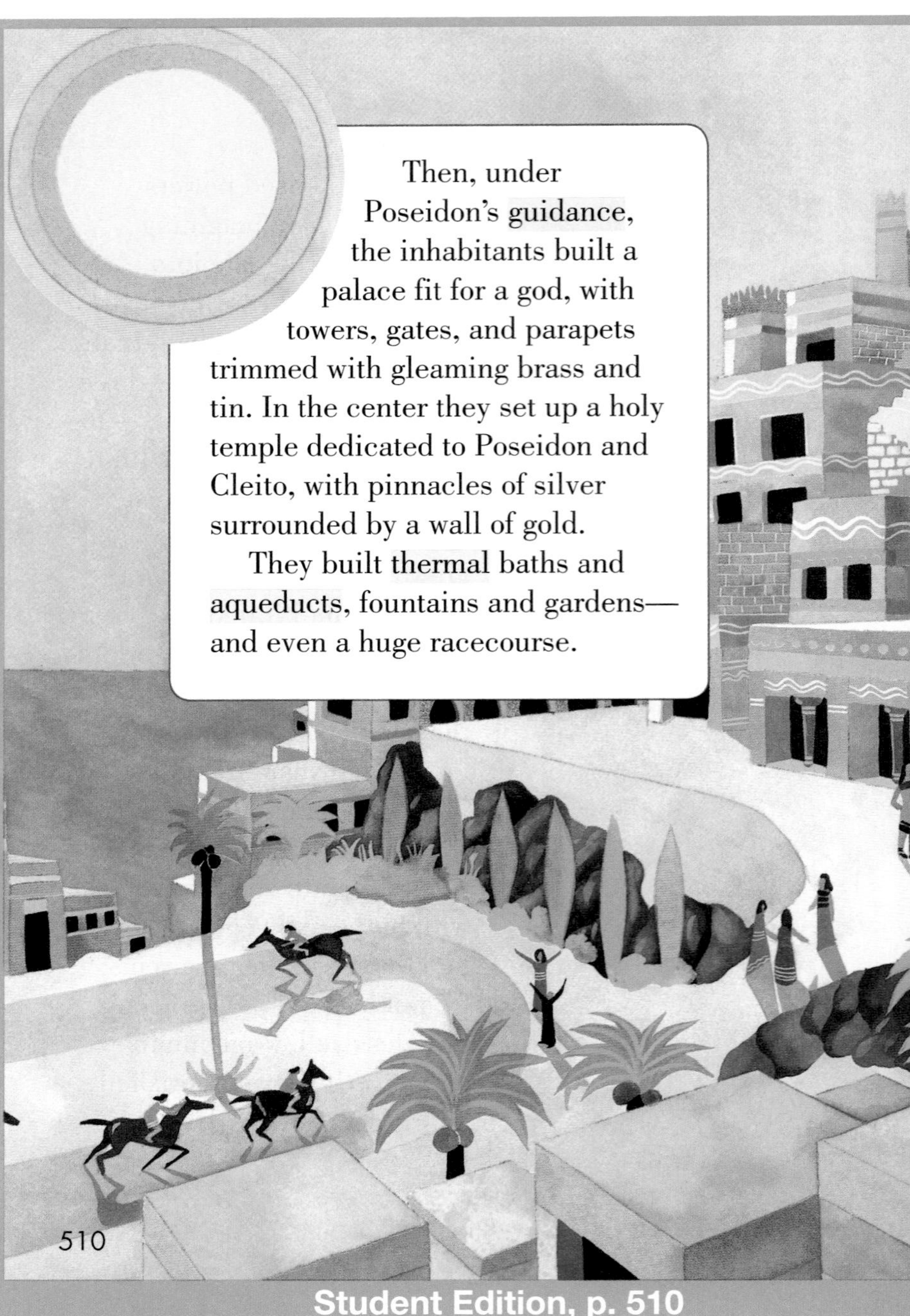

Then, under Poseidon's guidance, the inhabitants built a palace fit for a god, with towers, gates, and parapets trimmed with gleaming brass and tin. In the center they set up a holy temple dedicated to Poseidon and Cleito, with pinnacles of silver surrounded by a wall of gold.
They built thermal baths and aqueducts, fountains and gardens—and even a huge racecourse.
510

Student Edition, p. 510

2ND READ

Close Reading

EVALUATION • TEXT EVIDENCE In what ways is the island becoming fit for a king and his queen? What caused Poseidon to make these changes? Use details from the text to support your answer. (It is more beautiful. It provides more food and water, and there are a greater number of animals. Poseidon has just married Cleito and he wants to make her happy.)

ANALYSIS Why do you think Poseidon divided the island into ten parts? (He gave one part to each son so they wouldn't argue. Also, there were too many people for one person to be in charge of all of them. Each son would have a way to support his family.)

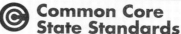

CHECK PREDICTIONS Have students look back at the predictions they made earlier and discuss whether they were accurate. Then have students preview the rest of the selection and either adjust their predictions accordingly or make new predictions.

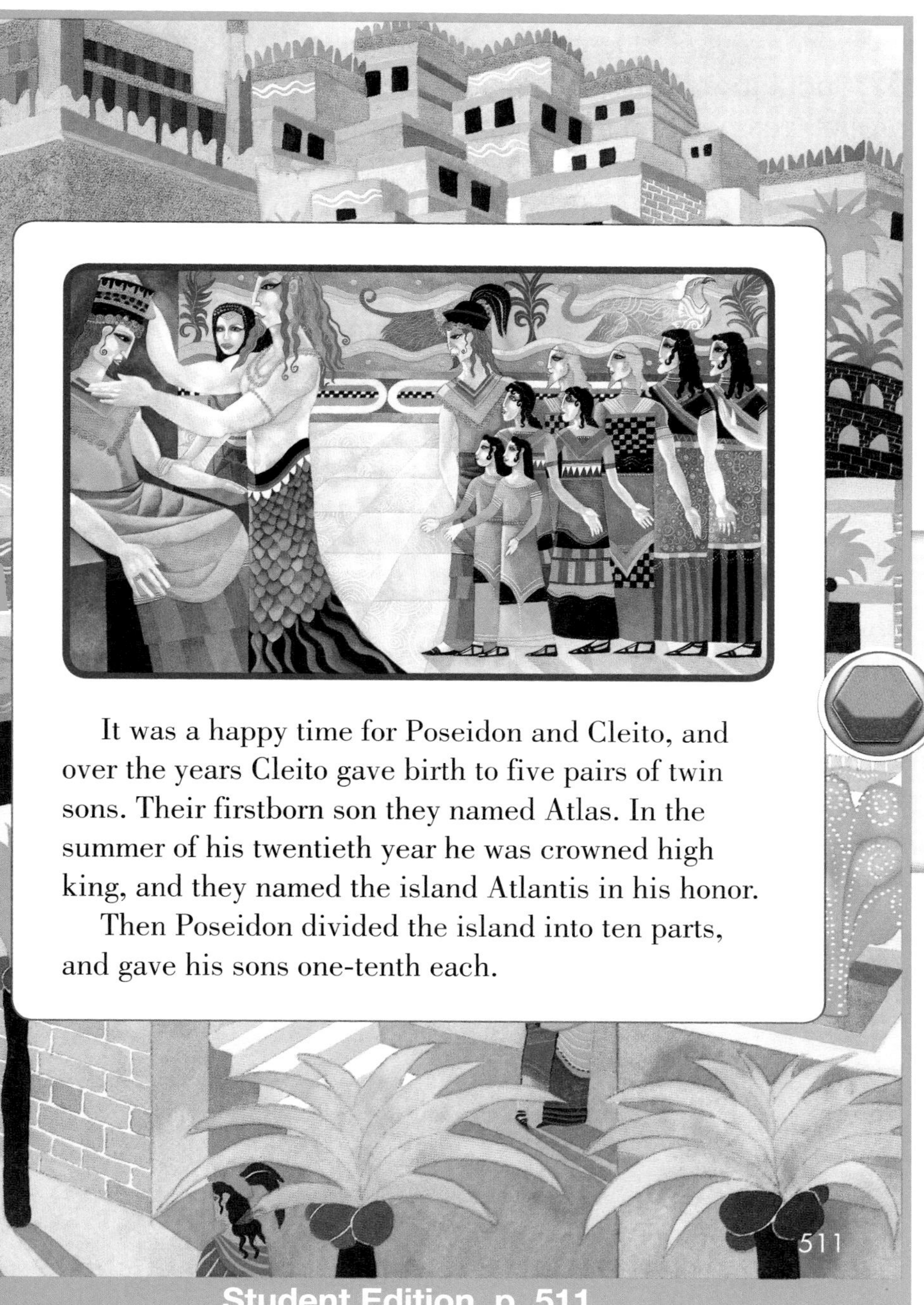

It was a happy time for Poseidon and Cleito, and over the years Cleito gave birth to five pairs of twin sons. Their firstborn son they named Atlas. In the summer of his twentieth year he was crowned high king, and they named the island Atlantis in his honor.

Then Poseidon divided the island into ten parts, and gave his sons one-tenth each.

511

Student Edition, p. 511

If you want to teach this selection in two sessions, stop here.

If you want to continue reading this selection, turn to page 512–513.

ANALYSIS Poseidon and Cleito have ten sons. What does Poseidon do for his firstborn son? Why? (He makes him king because it is traditional for the first son, or child, to become the ruler.)

Common Core State Standards

Literature 3. Describe characters in a story (e.g., their traits, motivations, or feelings) and explain how their actions contribute to the sequence of events. **Also Literature 1., 2., 10.**

Access for All

SI Strategic Intervention

Brainstorm with students about what they think Poseidon's palace, or any palace, should have to make it special.

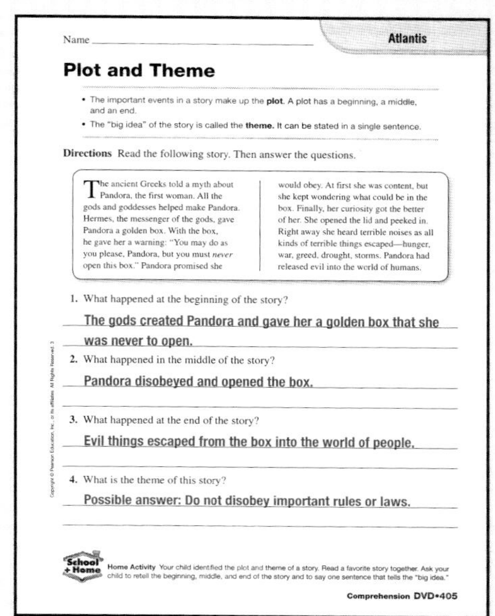

Name ____________ Atlantis

Plot and Theme

- The important events in a story make up the **plot**. A plot has a beginning, a middle, and an end.
- The "big idea" of the story is called the **theme.** It can be stated in a single sentence.

Directions Read the following story. Then answer the questions.

The ancient Greeks told a myth about Pandora, the first woman. All the gods and goddesses helped make Pandora. Hermes, the messenger of the gods, gave Pandora a golden box. With the box, he gave her a warning: "You may do as you please, Pandora, but you must *never* open this box." Pandora promised she would obey. At first she was content, but she kept wondering what could be in the box. Finally, her curiosity got the better of her. She opened the lid and peeked in. Right away she heard terrible noises as all kinds of terrible things escaped—hunger, war, greed, drought, storms. Pandora had released evil into the world of humans.

1. What happened at the beginning of the story?
   The gods created Pandora and gave her a golden box that she was never to open.
2. What happened in the middle of the story?
   Pandora disobeyed and opened the box.
3. What happened at the end of the story?
   Evil things escaped from the box into the world of people.
4. What is the theme of this story?
   Possible answer: Do not disobey important rules or laws.

School + Home **Home Activity** Your child identified the plot and theme of a story. Read a favorite story together. Ask your child to retell the beginning, middle, and end of the story and to say one sentence that tells the "big idea."

Comprehension DVD•405

Let's Practice It! TR DVD•405

ELL

Vocabulary Use the illustrations to clarify the meanings of words on pp. 510–511; for example, *palace, towers, parapets, pinnacles,* and *racecourse.* Then ask volunteers to use the words in oral sentences.

Professional Development: What ELL Experts Say About Using Visuals "Visuals enable students to 'see' the basic concepts we are trying to teach much more effectively than if we rely only on words. Among the visuals we can use are:

- *pictures/diagrams*
- *vocabulary cards*
- *real objects*
- *graphic organizers*
- *maps"*

—Jim Cummings

Common Core State Standards

Writing 7. Conduct short research projects that build knowledge about a topic. **Language 2.c.** Use commas and quotation marks in dialogue. **Language 2.f.** Use spelling patterns and generalizations (e.g., word families, position-based spellings, syllable patterns, ending rules, meaningful word parts) in writing words. **Also Language 4.**

Bridge to Common Core

RESEARCH TO BUILD AND PRESENT KNOWLEDGE

On Day 2 of the weeklong research project, students gather relevant information based on their focused questions from Day 1. They consult a reference librarian, who will help direct them to online and print resources. They scan the sources to identify text features that help them locate information. This process enables students to demonstrate an understanding of the subject under investigation.

Research and Inquiry

Step 2 Navigate/Search

TEACH Have students generate a research plan for gathering relevant information about their research questions. Encourage them to consult a reference librarian about their inquiry questions. The reference librarian will direct them to online searches and reference texts, such as encyclopedias. Tell students to skim and scan each text to identify results that helps answer their inquiry questions or leads them to specific information that will be useful. Text features such as bold and italicized print may provide clues to the kind of information each text provides. Also have students look at headings, illustrations, captions, and key words. Remind them to take notes as they gather information.

Think Aloud

MODEL When looking for information about famous people in history who have spoken out for different causes, I found: *Dr. Martin Luther King Jr. spoke out about civil rights for all Americans.* I will use key words from this text, such as *civil rights,* to lead me to more specific information. One fact I found using these key words states: *Congress passed the Civil Rights Act in 1964.*

GUIDE PRACTICE Have students continue their review of reference materials they identified. Remind them to keep in mind the inquiry questions they posed and continue to gather information that answers those questions.

ON THEIR OWN Encourage students to talk to a local history teacher to help them find answers to their inquiry questions.

ON THEIR OWN Have students reread pp. 504–505 to find clues to the generalization that many gods fought with each other. For additional practice, use *Let's Practice It!* p. 404 on the *Teacher Resources DVD-ROM.*

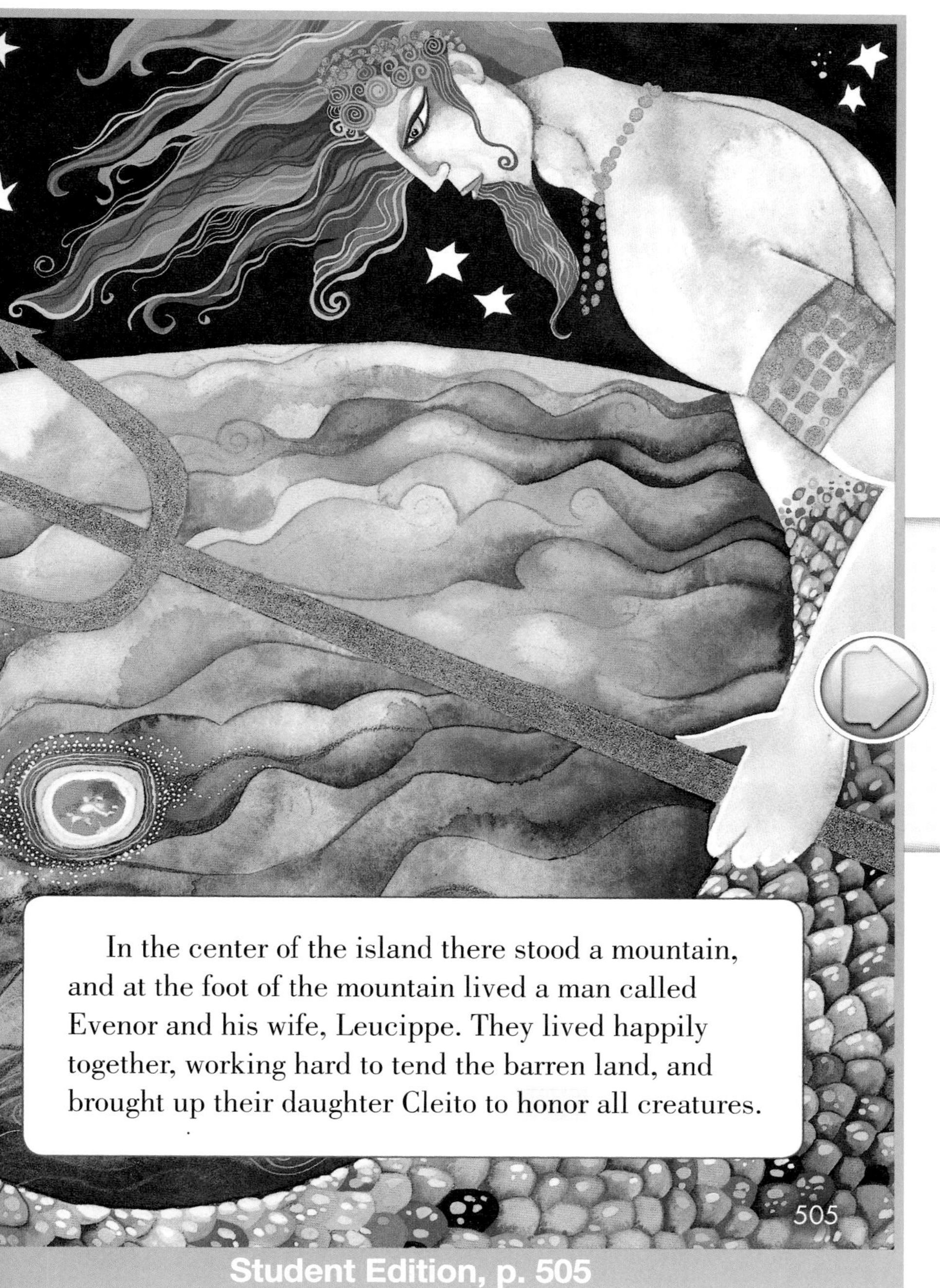

In the center of the island there stood a mountain, and at the foot of the mountain lived a man called Evenor and his wife, Leucippe. They lived happily together, working hard to tend the barren land, and brought up their daughter Cleito to honor all creatures.

505

Student Edition, p. 505

SYNTHESIS • TEXT EVIDENCE What clues tell you that Cleito is a kind character? (The text says that Cleito's parents raised her to honor all creatures. I know that when you honor something, you treat it kindly and with respect.)

Common Core State Standards

Literature 1. Ask and answer questions to demonstrate understanding of a text, referring explicitly to the text as the basis for the answers. **Literature 3.** Describe characters in a story (e.g., their traits, motivations, or feelings) and explain how their actions contribute to the sequence of events. **Also Literature 10.**

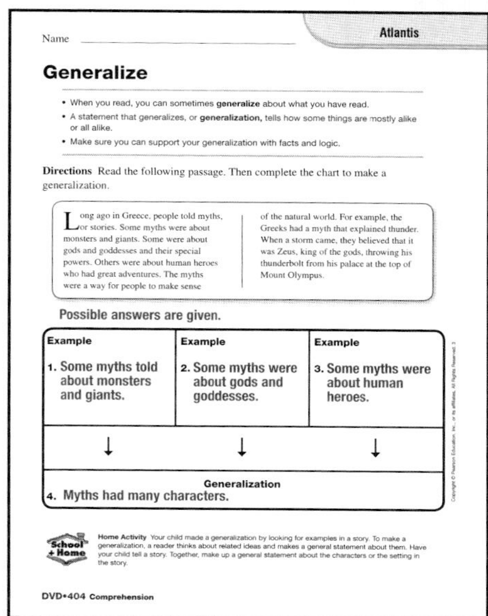

Name ______________ Atlantis

Generalize

- When you read, you can sometimes **generalize** about what you have read.
- A statement that generalizes, or **generalization,** tells how some things are mostly alike or all alike.
- Make sure you can support your generalization with facts and logic.

Directions Read the following passage. Then complete the chart to make a generalization.

Long ago in Greece, people told myths, or stories. Some myths were about monsters and giants. Some were about gods and goddesses and their special powers. Others were about human heroes who had great adventures. The myths were a way for people to make sense of the natural world. For example, the Greeks had a myth that explained thunder. When a storm came, they believed that it was Zeus, king of the gods, throwing his thunderbolt from his palace at the top of Mount Olympus.

Possible answers are given.

Example	Example	Example
1. Some myths told about monsters and giants.	2. Some myths were about gods and goddesses.	3. Some myths were about human heroes.
↓	↓	↓
Generalization 4. Myths had many characters.		

Home Activity Your child made a generalization by looking for examples in a story. To make a generalization, a reader thinks about related ideas and makes a general statement about them. Have your child tell a story. Together, make up a general statement about the characters or the setting in the story.

DVD•404 Comprehension

Let's Practice It! TR DVD•404

Activate Prior Knowledge Ask students to tell what they know about islands and why there might not be many people living on an island.

1ST READ

Access Text If students need help, then...

INFERRING Have students read the first paragraph on p. 506. Ask students how they know that a god doesn't usually look like a person. ("He took on human form" tells me he usually has a different form.)

Think Aloud **MODEL** Being able to make inferences helps me understand a story. I read that Poseidon took on human form. If I think about what I know and what the story tells me, I can infer that he changed what he looked like. He changed from what he usually looked like into what humans look like.

Poseidon grew curious. How could they be content with so little? He took on human form and crouched unseen behind a rock to find out.
Each morning at daybreak, he watched Cleito walk over the pebbled ground, barefoot and smiling, to fill her water pot at the stream.
506
Student Edition, p. 506

2ND READ

Close Reading

SYNTHESIS Do you think Cleito's parents would have let her marry Poseidon if they had known he was a god? What helped you decide that? (Probably not; the author tells us that Cleito's parents did not know that Poseidon was a god when they said Cleito could marry him, so it must be important to the story, and it implies that they would not have approved of the marriage.)

ANALYSIS Why did Poseidon watch Cleito every morning? (He was curious, so he watched her to find out why she was so happy all the time.) Why did he finally come out from behind the rock? (He thought she was beautiful, and he fell in love with her.)

Conventions

Quotations and Parentheses

TEACH Write these sentences on the board: *"Please pass the butter," said John. Many types of spiders live in the desert (for example, tarantulas and brown recluses).* Opening quotation marks go at the beginning of a speaker's words. If the dialogue is followed by a speaker tag, closing quotation marks go at the end of the dialogue after the comma, question mark, or exclamation mark. If there is no speaker tag, or if it is before the dialogue, the quotation marks follow the closing punctuation. The opening parenthesis goes before the extra information, and the closing parenthesis goes at the end, but before the punctuation mark.

GUIDE PRACTICE Write these sentences on the board, leaving out the parentheses and quotation marks. Have students add the punctuation.

My brother asked, "Where are Mom and Dad?"

I have many types of hats (baseball caps, sombreros).

ON THEIR OWN For more practice, use *Reader's and Writer's Notebook* p. 433.

Spelling

Related Words

TEACH Remind students that their spelling words for this week include related words. Model how to spell the related words *nature* and *natural,* pointing out the common letters *natur.*

GUIDE PRACTICE Have students write each spelling word, divide it into syllables, and underline the common letters in the related words.

ON THEIR OWN For more practice, use *Reader's and Writer's Notebook* p. 434.

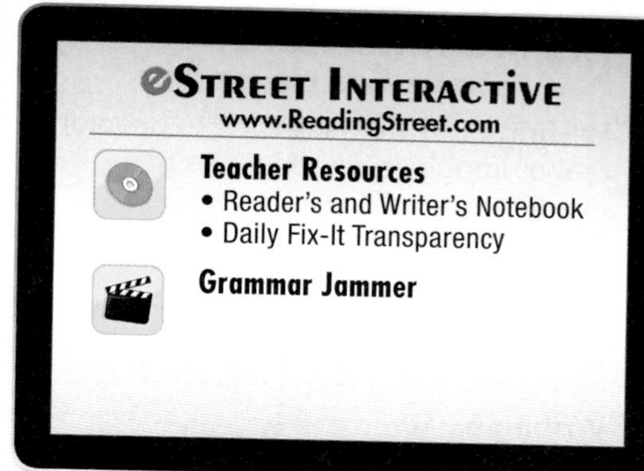

Daily Fix-It

3. Doesnt the warm sun in the desert feel pleasent? *(Doesn't; pleasant)*
4. The desert animels rests during the day. *(animals; rest)*

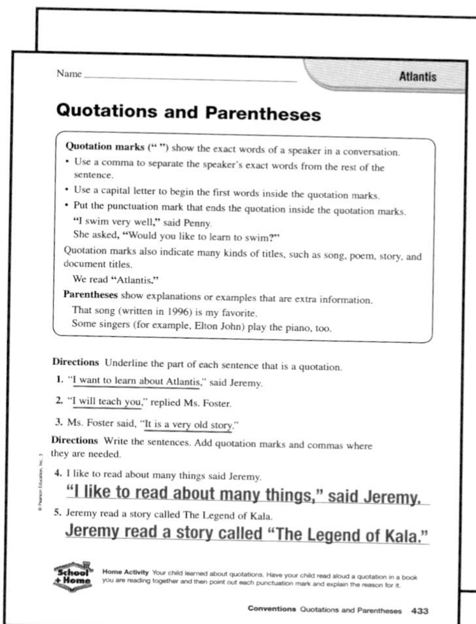

Name ______________ Atlantis

Quotations and Parentheses

Quotation marks (" ") show the exact words of a speaker in a conversation.
- Use a comma to separate the speaker's exact words from the rest of the sentence.
- Use a capital letter to begin the first words inside the quotation marks.
- Put the punctuation mark that ends the quotation inside the quotation marks.

"I swim very well," said Penny.
She asked, "Would you like to learn to swim?"

Quotation marks also indicate many kinds of titles, such as song, poem, story, and document titles.

We read "Atlantis."

Parentheses show explanations or examples that are extra information.

That song (written in 1996) is my favorite.
Some singers (for example, Elton John) play the piano, too.

Directions Underline the part of each sentence that is a quotation.

1. "I want to learn about Atlantis," said Jeremy.
2. "I will teach you," replied Ms. Foster.
3. Ms. Foster said, "It is a very old story."

Directions Write the sentences. Add quotation marks and commas where they are needed.

4. I like to read about many things said Jeremy.
"I like to read about many things," said Jeremy.
5. Jeremy read a story called The Legend of Kala.
Jeremy read a story called "The Legend of Kala."

School + Home **Home Activity** Your child learned about quotations. Have your child read aloud a quotation in a book you are reading together and then point out each punctuation mark and explain the reason for it.

Conventions Quotations and Parentheses 433

Reader's and Writer's Notebook, pp. 433–434

Conventions To provide students with practice on quotations and parentheses, use the modified grammar lessons in the *ELL Handbook* and the *Grammar Jammer* online at: www.ReadingStreet.com

Common Core State Standards

Writing 3. Write narratives to develop real or imagined experiences or events using effective technique, descriptive details, and clear event sequences. **Writing 3.a.** Establish a situation and introduce a narrator and/or characters; organize an event sequence that unfolds naturally. **Also Writing 5., 10.**

Writing

Historical Fiction

INTRODUCE THE PROMPT Review the key features of historical fiction. Remind students to think about these features as they plan their writing. Tell them that today they will practice writing for tests by creating a historical fiction story that addresses the prompt. Read aloud the writing prompt.

Writing Prompt

Write a historical fiction story about a voyage across the Atlantic Ocean.

Mini-Lesson Writing for Tests: Think About the Past

- Before you start writing, you need to decide when and where your story takes place. Because you will be writing historical fiction, you will have to think about the past to create your setting.
- Suggest that students ask themselves several questions when thinking about a setting for their historical fiction story. Draw a T-chart on the board. Write these questions in the left-hand column: *Does my story take place a few years ago, many years ago, or hundreds of years ago? Where does my story take place? What was life like in this time?* Encourage students to think of as many details as they can about their chosen setting. Write these details in the right-hand column.
- Have students think of some real people who lived during their chosen time. What were these people like? How did they dress? What problems did they have? What did they think about? Also have them think about what kinds of fictional characters might interact with the historical figures.
- Remember that a historical fiction story also has a plot. Have students come up with a problem for the characters to solve.
- Students can practice organizing their ideas aloud, discussing them with a partner until they are ready to write.

DISCUSS RUBRIC Have students look at the Scoring Rubric on p. 435 in the *Reader's and Writer's Notebook.* Remind students that this rubric will be used to evaluate their writing this week.

SAMPLE TEST Direct students to get paper and pencil ready to take a writing test. Display the writing prompt and give them appropriate time to write to the prompt. Remind students to allow themselves time after writing to make changes or additions to their stories.

Routine Quick Write for Fluency **Team Talk**

1. **Talk** Pairs discuss the historical setting of their stories.
2. **Write** Students write a sentence describing their setting.
3. **Share** Students read their sentences to their partner and then ask what other adjectives could be used in the story.

Routines Flip Chart

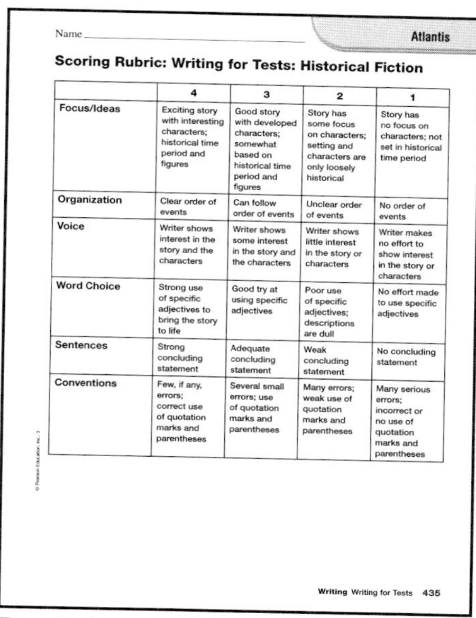

Name__________ Atlantis

Scoring Rubric: Writing for Tests: Historical Fiction

	4	3	2	1
Focus/Ideas	Exciting story with interesting characters; historical time period and figures	Good story with developed characters; somewhat based on historical time period and figures	Story has some focus on characters; setting and characters are only loosely historical	Story has no focus on characters; not set in historical time period
Organization	Clear order of events	Can follow order of events	Unclear order of events	No order of events
Voice	Writer shows interest in the story and the characters	Writer shows some interest in the story and the characters	Writer shows little interest in the story or characters	Writer makes no effort to show interest in the story or characters
Word Choice	Strong use of specific adjectives to bring the story to life	Good try at using specific adjectives	Poor use of specific adjectives; descriptions are dull	No effort made to use specific adjectives
Sentences	Strong concluding statement	Adequate concluding statement	Weak concluding statement	No concluding statement
Conventions	Few, if any, errors; correct use of quotation marks and parentheses	Several small errors; use of quotation marks and parentheses	Many errors; weak use of quotation marks and parentheses	Many serious errors; incorrect or no use of quotation marks and parentheses

Writing Writing for Tests 435

Reader's and Writer's Notebook, p. 435

Wrap Up Your Day!

- ✓ **Content Knowledge** *What have you learned about Atlantis so far?*
- ✓ **Text-Based Comprehension** *What generalization can you make about the island?*

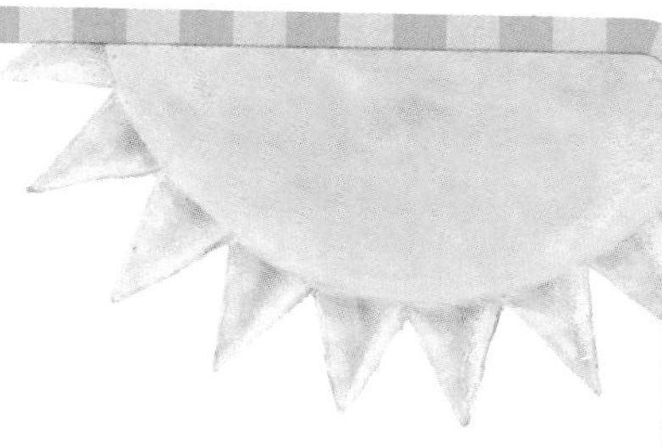

Tell students that tomorrow they will read more about Atlantis.

DAY 3 at a Glance

Content Knowledge
Oral Vocabulary

Phonics/Word Analysis
Related Words

Text-Based Comprehension
Generalize
Inferring

Fluency
Expression

Research and Study Skills
Quote and Paraphrase Sources

Research and Inquiry
Analyze Information

Conventions
Quotations and Parentheses

Spelling
Related Words

Writing
Historical Fiction

Materials

- Student Edition
- Reader's and Writer's Notebook
- Decodable Reader

Common Core State Standards

Speaking/Listening 1. Engage effectively in a range of collaborative discussions (one-on-one, in groups, and teacher-led) with diverse partners on grade 3 topics and texts, building on others' ideas and expressing their own clearly. **Language 6.** Acquire and use accurately grade-appropriate conversational, general academic, and domain-specific words and phrases, including those that signal spatial and temporal relationships (e.g., *After dinner that night we went looking for them*).

Content Knowledge

Keeping Your Freedom

EXPAND THE CONCEPT Remind students of the weekly concept question, *What is the best way to keep your freedom?* Discuss how the question relates to *Atlantis: The Legend of a Lost City.* Encourage students to think about how the people of Atlantis lost their freedom.

Build Oral Language

TALK ABOUT SENTENCES AND WORDS Reread the following sentences from Student Edition page 506, *Atlantis.*

Poseidon grew curious. How could they be content with so little? He took on human form and crouched unseen behind a rock to find out.

- What does the word *curious* mean? (eager to know)
- What does the word *content* mean in the first sentence? (happy)
- What does the word *crouched* mean? (stooped low with bent legs)
- What are some synonyms for *crouched?* (squatted, stooped)
- Why did the author choose the word *crouched?* (Answers will vary.)

Team Talk Have students work with a partner to replace words in the sentences without changing the meaning.

Poseidon grew ______. How could they be ______ with so little?
He took on human form and ______ unseen behind a rock to find out.

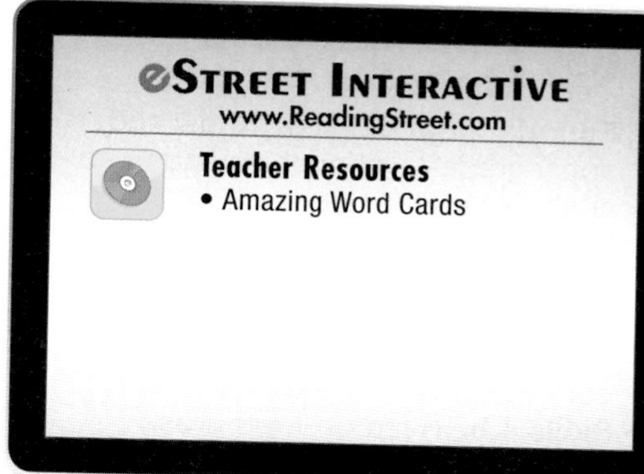

Build Oral Vocabulary

Amazing Words Robust Vocabulary Routine

1. **Introduce** Write the word *blight* on the board. Have students say it with you. Yesterday we learned that before Poseidon transformed Atlantis, little had grown on its land. The island was experiencing *blight.* Have students determine a definition of *blight.* (a ruined condition)
2. **Demonstrate** Have students answer questions to demonstrate understanding. How can you tell that the *blight* had ended after Poseidon used his powers? (Trees bloomed and grew heavy with fruits, and the earth was carpeted with herbs and vegetables.)
3. **Apply** Have students apply their understanding. What evidence of *blight* have you seen?
4. **Display the Word** Students can decode the sounds in *blight* and blend them.

See p. OV•5 to teach *wept.*

Routines Flip Chart

ADD TO THE CONCEPT MAP Discuss the Amazing Words *demonstrate* and *mourn.* Add these and other concept-related words to the concept map. Use the following questions to develop students' understanding of the concept. Add words generated in the discussion to the concept map.

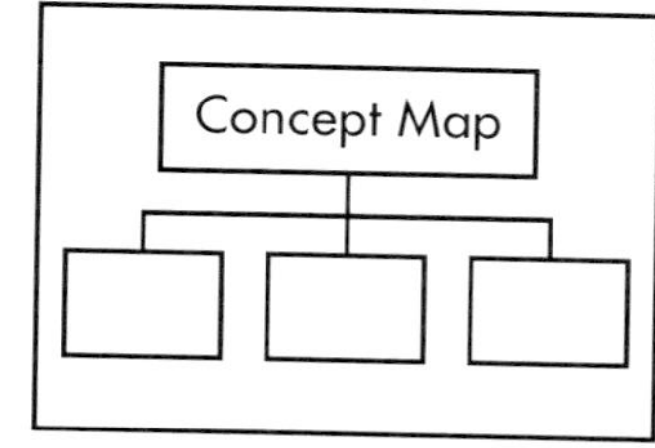

- People *demonstrate* to bring about change. How does this help them keep their freedom?
- Everyone *mourned* the loss of Martin Luther King Jr. when he was killed in 1968. How can we be sure that his dream lives on?

Amazing Words

witty	mourn
equality	blight
justice	wept
perish	violence
demonstrate	

Expand Vocabulary Use the Day 3 instruction on ELL Poster 30 to help students expand vocabulary.

Common Core State Standards

Foundational Skills 3. Know and apply grade-level phonics and word analysis skills in decoding words. **Foundational Skills 3.c.** Decode multisyllable words. **Foundational Skills 4.** Read with sufficient accuracy and fluency to support comprehension. **Foundational Skills 4.b.** Read on-level prose and poetry orally with accuracy, appropriate rate, and expression on successive readings. **Also Foundational Skills 4.a., 4.c., Language 2.e., 4., 4.c.**

Word Analysis

Related Words

MODEL WORD SORTING Write *Related Word 1* and *Related Word 2* as heads in a two-column chart. Now we are going to sort words. We'll write a word in the first column and write a related word in the second column. I will start. Write *nature* in the first column. When I see the word *nature,* I notice that it shares the letters *n-a-t-u-r* with the word *natural. Nature* and *natural* are related words. I will write *natural* in the second column.

GUIDE PRACTICE Use the practice words from the activities on p. 496a for the word sort. Point to a word. Have students read the word, identify its parts, and tell where it should be written on the chart.

Corrective feedback For corrective feedback, model breaking the word into parts and looking for similar letters in order to find the related words.

Related Word 1	Related Word 2
nature	natural
courtesy	courteous
describe	description
add	additional
dine	dinner
crumbs	crumbled
goal	goalie

Fluent Word Reading

MODEL Write *please* and *pleasant.* I know the word *please.* I see the letters *pleas* in both words. That helps me read the word *pleasant.*

GUIDE PRACTICE Write the words below. Look for word parts you know. When I point to a word, we'll read it together. Allow one second per word previewing time for the first reading.

bath **bathes** **nature** **natural** **signal** **signature**

ON THEIR OWN Have students read the list above three or four times, until they can read one word per second.

Decodable Passage 30B

If students need help, then...

Read *Finally Finished*

READ WORDS IN ISOLATION Have students turn to p. 177 in *Decodable Practice Reader 3.2* and find the first list of words. Each word in this list is related to another word. Let's decode and read these words. Be sure that students fluently read the related words.

Next, have students read the high-frequency words.

PREVIEW Have students read the title and preview the story. Tell them that they will read related words.

READ WORDS IN CONTEXT Chorally read the story along with the students. Have them identify related words in the story. Make sure that students are monitoring their accuracy when they decode words.

Team Talk Pair students and have them take turns reading the story aloud to each other. Monitor students as they read to check for proper pronunciation and appropriate pacing.

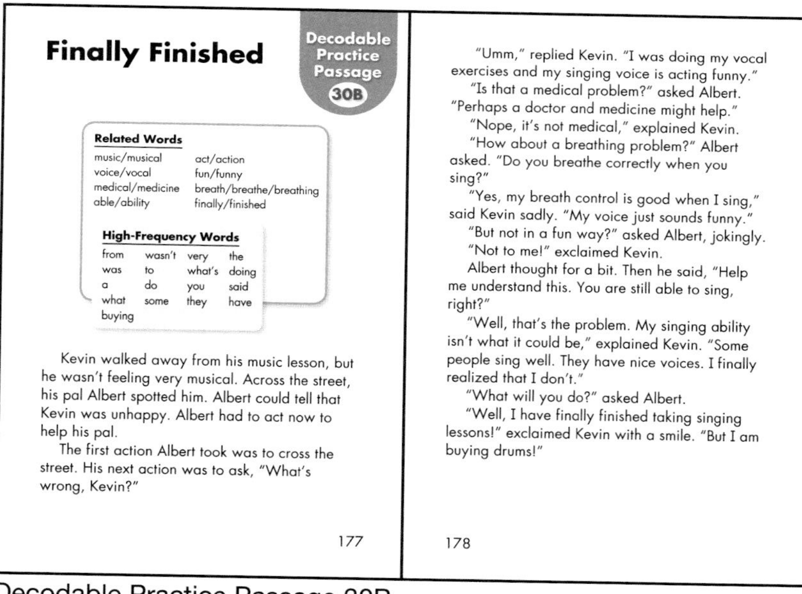

Finally Finished

Decodable Practice Passage 30B

Related Words

music/musical	act/action
voice/vocal	fun/funny
medical/medicine	breath/breathe/breathing
able/ability	finally/finished

High-Frequency Words

from	wasn't	very	the
was	to	what's	doing
a	do	you	said
what	some	they	have
buying			

Kevin walked away from his music lesson, but he wasn't feeling very musical. Across the street, his pal Albert spotted him. Albert could tell that Kevin was unhappy. Albert had to act now to help his pal.

The first action Albert took was to cross the street. His next action was to ask, "What's wrong, Kevin?"

177

"Umm," replied Kevin. "I was doing my vocal exercises and my singing voice is acting funny."

"Is that a medical problem?" asked Albert. "Perhaps a doctor and medicine might help."

"Nope, it's not medical," explained Kevin.

"How about a breathing problem?" Albert asked. "Do you breathe correctly when you sing?"

"Yes, my breath control is good when I sing," said Kevin sadly. "My voice just sounds funny."

"But not in a fun way?" asked Albert, jokingly.

"Not to me!" exclaimed Kevin.

Albert thought for a bit. Then he said, "Help me understand this. You are still able to sing, right?"

"Well, that's the problem. My singing ability isn't what it could be," explained Kevin. "Some people sing well. They have nice voices. I finally realized that I don't."

"What will you do?" asked Albert.

"Well, I have finally finished taking singing lessons!" exclaimed Kevin with a smile. "But I am buying drums!"

178

Decodable Practice Passage 30B

Pronunciation Students may have difficulty reading and saying related words because often the similar word parts look the same but sound different. Have students practice reading and pronouncing the related words in the chart as you point to each word.

Text-Based Comprehension

Check Understanding

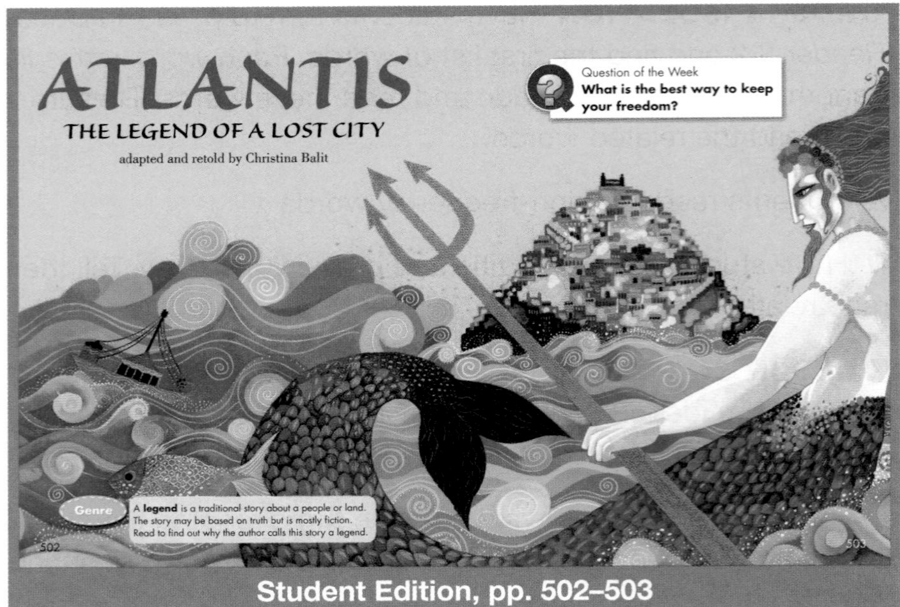

Student Edition, pp. 502–503

If... you chose to read *Atlantis* in two parts,
then... use the following questions to monitor students' understanding of pp. 502–511 of the selection. Encourage students to cite evidence from the text.

INFERENCE What does the description of Cleito's parents, Evenor and Leucippe, tell you about the kind of people they are? (They are hard workers, are happy with their lives, and realize the importance of treating everyone and everything fairly.) (p. 505)

SYNTHESIS What is a generalization that could be made about Poseidon and Cleito's palace? (Poseidon and Cleito's palace was the most beautiful building on the island.) (p. 510)

RETELL Have students retell the first part of *Atlantis,* summarizing information in the text in a logical order.

Corrective feedback	**If...** students leave out important details, **then...** have them look back through the illustrations in the selection.

READ Use the **Access Text** and **Close Reading** notes to finish reading *Atlantis: The Legend of a Lost City.*

Common Core State Standards

Literature 1. Ask and answer questions to demonstrate understanding of a text, referring explicitly to the text as the basis for the answers. **Literature 3.** Describe characters in a story (e.g., their traits, motivations, or feelings) and explain how their actions contribute to the sequence of events. **Also Literature 2.**

Strategy Response Log

Have students revisit p. 36 in the *Reader's and Writer's Notebook* to add more information about legends.

If... you followed the Read for Understanding routine below,
then... ask students to retell the selection before you reread *Atlantis.*

Corrective feedback	**If...** the students leave out important details, **then...** have them look back through the illustrations in the selection.

READ Return to p. 504–505 and use the **2nd Read/Close Reading** notes to reread *Atlantis.*

Read Main Selection

Routine Read for Understanding

Deepen understanding by reading the selection multiple times.

1. **First Read**—If students need support, then use the **Access Text** notes to help them clarify understanding.
2. **Second Read**—Use the **Close Reading** notes to help students draw knowledge from the text.

eSTREET INTERACTIVE
www.ReadingStreet.com

Pearson eText
- Student Edition

AudioText CD

Teacher Resources
- Reader's and Writer's Notebook

ELL

Check Retelling To support retelling, review the multilingual summary for *Atlantis* with the appropriate Retelling Cards to scaffold understanding.

Day 3 SMALL GROUP TIME • Differentiate Close Reading, p. SG•65

OL On-Level	SI Strategic Intervention	A Advanced
• **Reread** to Develop Vocabulary • **Read** *Atlantis*	• **Reread** to Develop Vocabulary • **Read** *Atlantis*	• **Reread** to Extend Vocabulary • **Read** *Atlantis* • **Investigate** Inquiry Project

If... students need more scaffolding and practice with the **Main Selection,**
then... use the activities on p. DI•122 in the Teacher Resources section on SuccessNet.

1ST READ

Access Text
If students need help, then...

INFERRING Explain that an author doesn't tell a reader everything. Good readers make inferences by using details from the story and what they already know. Have students reread p. 512 and infer what Poseidon thought about laws and judges.

Think Aloud **MODEL** I read that Poseidon made laws to make certain the people had peace. Where were the laws written? (on a stone pillar) Why would he do that? (He wanted everyone to see them.) He also used judges. So I can infer that he thought laws and judges are very important.

ON THEIR OWN Have students discuss what they know and don't know about Poseidon. What have they inferred about this character so far in the story? (That he has great power and good judgment.)

To ensure peace in his new island city, Poseidon set down laws in stone on a pillar of the temple. Chief among them was the commandment that no person should take up arms against another—with a terrible curse on anyone who disobeyed. Every five years, Atlas and the nine princes gathered by night beside the pillar to judge their people according to Poseidon's laws. The people of Atlantis became wise, gentle, and great-spirited. They were sober and kind, as the Creator had always wanted them to be. Above all, they lived in peace.

512

Student Edition, p. 512

2ND READ

Close Reading

SYNTHESIS • TEXT EVIDENCE Use ideas from the story and what you know about the ways people behave to make an inference about Poseidon. Why did Poseidon go back to his home at the bottom of the sea? (He was satisfied with his accomplishments. He believed that his sons and his people were safe and happy. He was comfortable leaving his sons in control.)

DEVELOP LANGUAGE Have students reread the first two sentences on p. 513. What does *thronged with* mean? What might a street be *thronged with*? a playground?

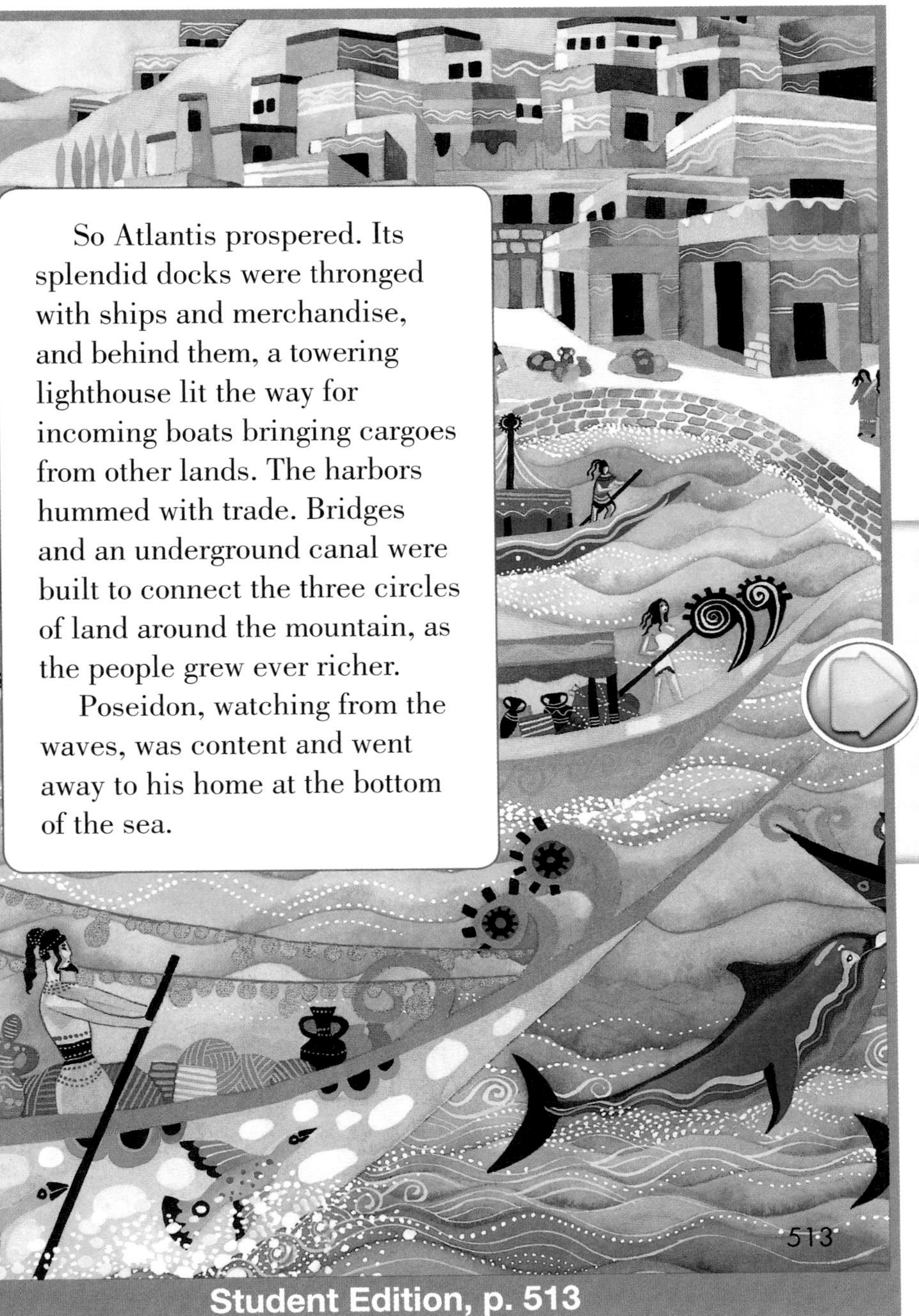

So Atlantis prospered. Its splendid docks were thronged with ships and merchandise, and behind them, a towering lighthouse lit the way for incoming boats bringing cargoes from other lands. The harbors hummed with trade. Bridges and an underground canal were built to connect the three circles of land around the mountain, as the people grew ever richer.

Poseidon, watching from the waves, was content and went away to his home at the bottom of the sea.

513

Student Edition, p. 513

ANALYSIS What effect did Poseidon's laws have on the people of Atlantis? How do you know? (Because of Poseidon's laws, people were kind and fair to one another. This is seen by how well they got along and are able to trade with others.)

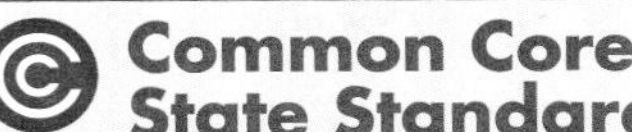

Literature 3. Describe characters in a story (e.g., their traits, motivations, or feelings) and explain how their actions contribute to the sequence of events. **Also Literature 1., 4., 10.**

Access for All

SI Strategic Intervention

The third sentence on p. 512 might confuse some students who are expecting ten princes. Remind students that one prince, Atlas, became the king.

Compound Words Have pairs of students locate the words *lighthouse, underground,* and *great-spirited.* Then have them use the meanings of the individual words that make up each compound and context clues to figure out the meaning of the compound.

1ST READ

Access Text If students need help, then...

Review THEME Remind students that the theme is the big idea of a story. It can be stated in a single sentence. Ask students to paraphrase the theme and supporting details so far.

Think Aloud **MODEL** Poseidon is punishing the people of Atlantis because they broke the law. The theme might be about the consequences of breaking laws or being greedy. What are some supporting details? (Poseidon made Atlantis a paradise. He told people not to hurt one another. They began to hurt each other. Poseidon punished them.)

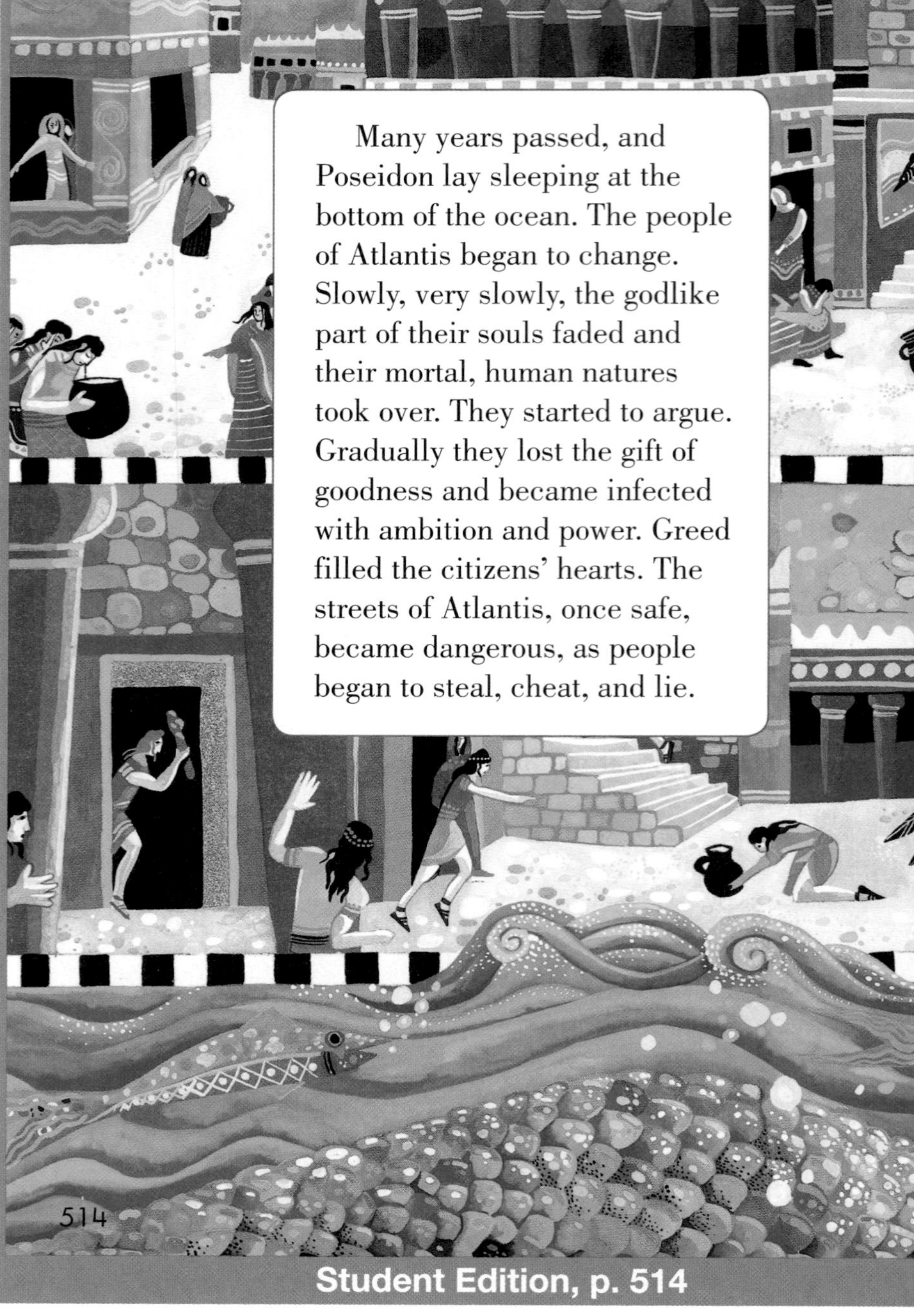
Many years passed, and Poseidon lay sleeping at the bottom of the ocean. The people of Atlantis began to change. Slowly, very slowly, the godlike part of their souls faded and their mortal, human natures took over. They started to argue. Gradually they lost the gift of goodness and became infected with ambition and power. Greed filled the citizens' hearts. The streets of Atlantis, once safe, became dangerous, as people began to steal, cheat, and lie.

514

Student Edition, p. 514

2ND READ

Close Reading

ANALYSIS • TEXT EVIDENCE How did Poseidon feel about having to carry out the curse? Support your answer with evidence from the text. (He felt terrible because he didn't want to do it, but he had no choice. The story says he weeps when he sees what has happened to his kingdom.)

REREAD CHALLENGING TEXT Have students reread p. 514 in order to better understand the descriptions used in explaining how the people of Atlantis changed. Students may need help with figurative language, such as "souls faded," "became infected with ambition and power," and "Greed filled the citizens' hearts."

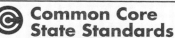

ON THEIR OWN Have students use their graphic organizer to record information about the theme of the story.

One day Zeus, god of gods, who ruled according to the law of the Creator, looked down from the heavens above. He saw the city walls crumbling with neglect, the empty temple, and, worst of all, people fighting one another. He roared out his anger.

The sound of his fury woke Poseidon. Rising to the surface of the waves, the sea-god looked out over his once-perfect kingdom—and wept.

Now he had no choice: he must carry out his terrible curse.

515

Student Edition, p. 515

ANALYSIS What was the cause of the streets of Atlantis no longer being safe? (People became greedy; they lost the gift of goodness; they began to steal, cheat, and lie.)

Common Core State Standards

Literature 1. Ask and answer questions to demonstrate understanding of a text, referring explicitly to the text as the basis for the answers. **Literature 2.** Recount stories, including fables, folktales, and myths from diverse cultures; determine the central message, lesson, or moral and explain how it is conveyed through key details in the text. **Literature 3.** Describe characters in a story (e.g., their traits, motivations, or feelings) and explain how their actions contribute to the sequence of events. **Also Literature 10.**

Access for All

 **Advanced**

Ask small groups of students to discuss what Poseidon might do to punish his people.

Summarizing Ask volunteers to summarize the plot to this point. Clarify any misunderstandings.

1ST READ

Access Text If students need help, then...

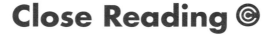

GENERALIZE Write: *Poseidon was always sad.* Explain that when we generalize, we make a broad statement. Ask students if this generalization is reasonable, and how they know. (No; we can identify times when Poseidon was not sad.)

Think Aloud **MODEL** At first I thought it was reasonable to say "Poseidon was always sad." That seemed like a valid generalization. Then I remembered that he was happy with his family and when he was transforming the island. How can I change this generalization to make it reasonable? (Poseidon is sometimes sad.)

Raising his trident, he stirred the seas into a wave that rose so high, it lashed the heavens. The wave vibrated with a roar that could be heard two thousand miles away, and the earth trembled in terror. Gathering its full force, the wave crashed upon the land, while burning rain and ashes blistered down from above.

In a single day and night, Atlantis was swallowed up by the sea.

Then there was silence. The city sank slowly to its new resting place on the ocean floor.

516

Student Edition, p. 516

2ND READ

Close Reading

INFERENCE • TEXT EVIDENCE

Think about what you know about legends as you reread the first paragraph on page 517. Then make an inference about what became of the people of Atlantis. Support your answer with evidence from the text. (They became the animals and fish who live in the sea. The story says they become "little more than creatures of the water." If they are able to live and breathe under water, then they must have developed special features, such as gills. In legends, it's possible for people to turn into animals and fish.)

ON THEIR OWN Have students reread pp. 515–516 and make a valid generalization about Zeus and his anger. (Zeus always gets angry when people disobey his laws.)

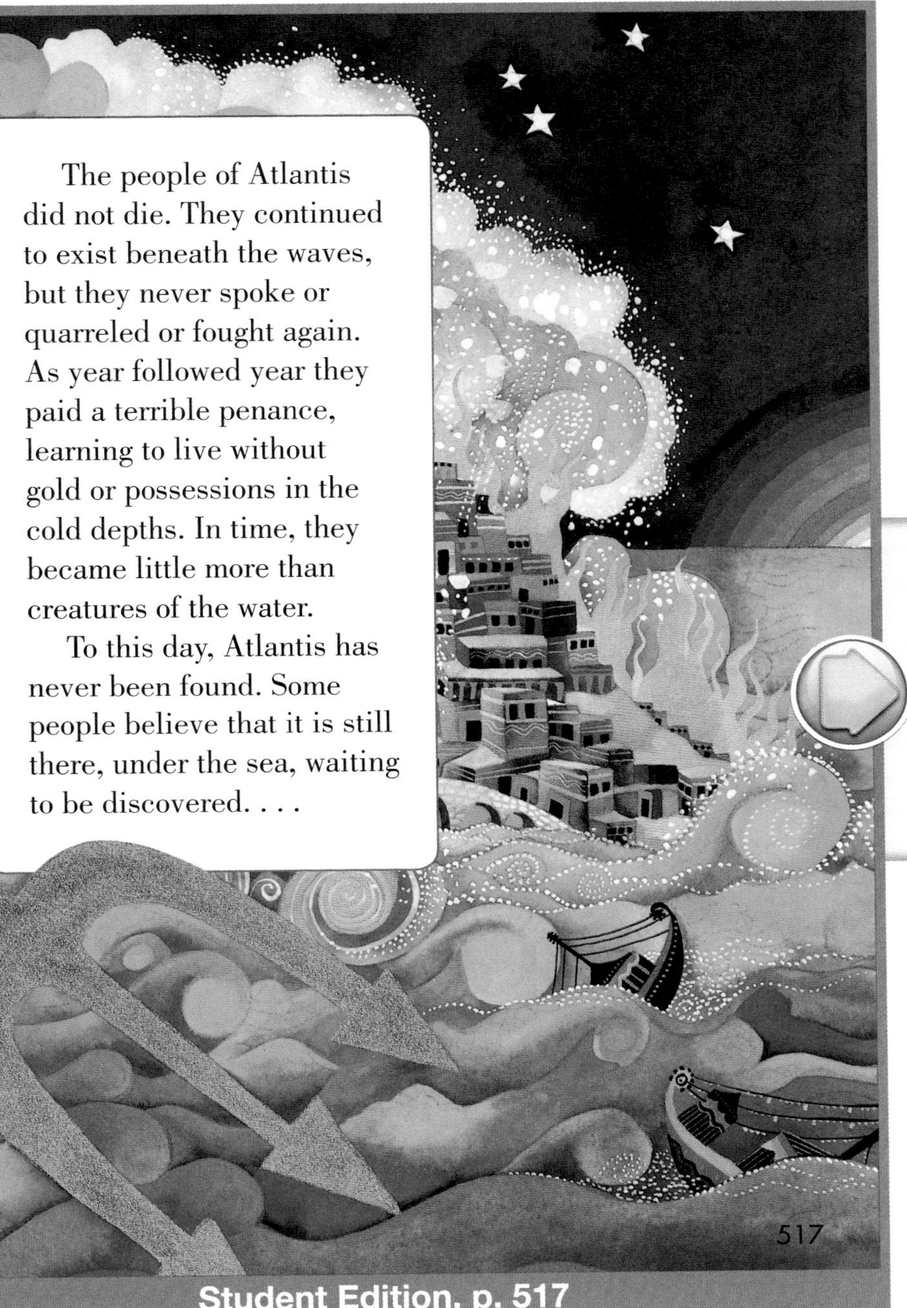
The people of Atlantis did not die. They continued to exist beneath the waves, but they never spoke or quarreled or fought again. As year followed year they paid a terrible penance, learning to live without gold or possessions in the cold depths. In time, they became little more than creatures of the water.

To this day, Atlantis has never been found. Some people believe that it is still there, under the sea, waiting to be discovered. . . .

517

Student Edition, p. 517

SYNTHESIS What valid generalization can you make about people disobeying Poseidon and punishment? (Sometimes when people broke Poseidon's laws, they were punished.)

Literature 1. Ask and answer questions to demonstrate understanding of a text, referring explicitly to the text as the basis for the answers. **Literature 3.** Describe characters in a story (e.g., their traits, motivations, or feelings) and explain how their actions contribute to the sequence of events. **Also Literature 10.**

Access for All

SI Strategic Intervention

Work with students in using a dictionary to determine the meanings of *trident, vibrated,* and *penance.* One way to emphasize the value of using one "difficult" word instead of several simpler words is to have students use the definition in place of the difficult word in the sentence.

Cognates Point out the words *fury* and *vibrated*, which have Spanish cognates—*furia* and *vibrar.*

1ST READ

Access Text If students need help, then...

HOMOGRAPHS Have students reread the first sentence on p. 519 and identify the homograph. (closer) Say the two pronunciations.

Think Aloud **MODEL** When I find a homograph, I have to use context clues to figure out which word is being used. What can *closer* mean? (nearer; one who closes) The sentence is about two bodies of land. Which word makes sense in the sentence? (nearer)

ON THEIR OWN For more practice, use *Reader's and Writer's Notebook* p. 436.

CROSS-TEXT EVALUATION
Use a Strategy to Self-Check How did the Read Aloud "Martin's Dream," help you understand this selection?

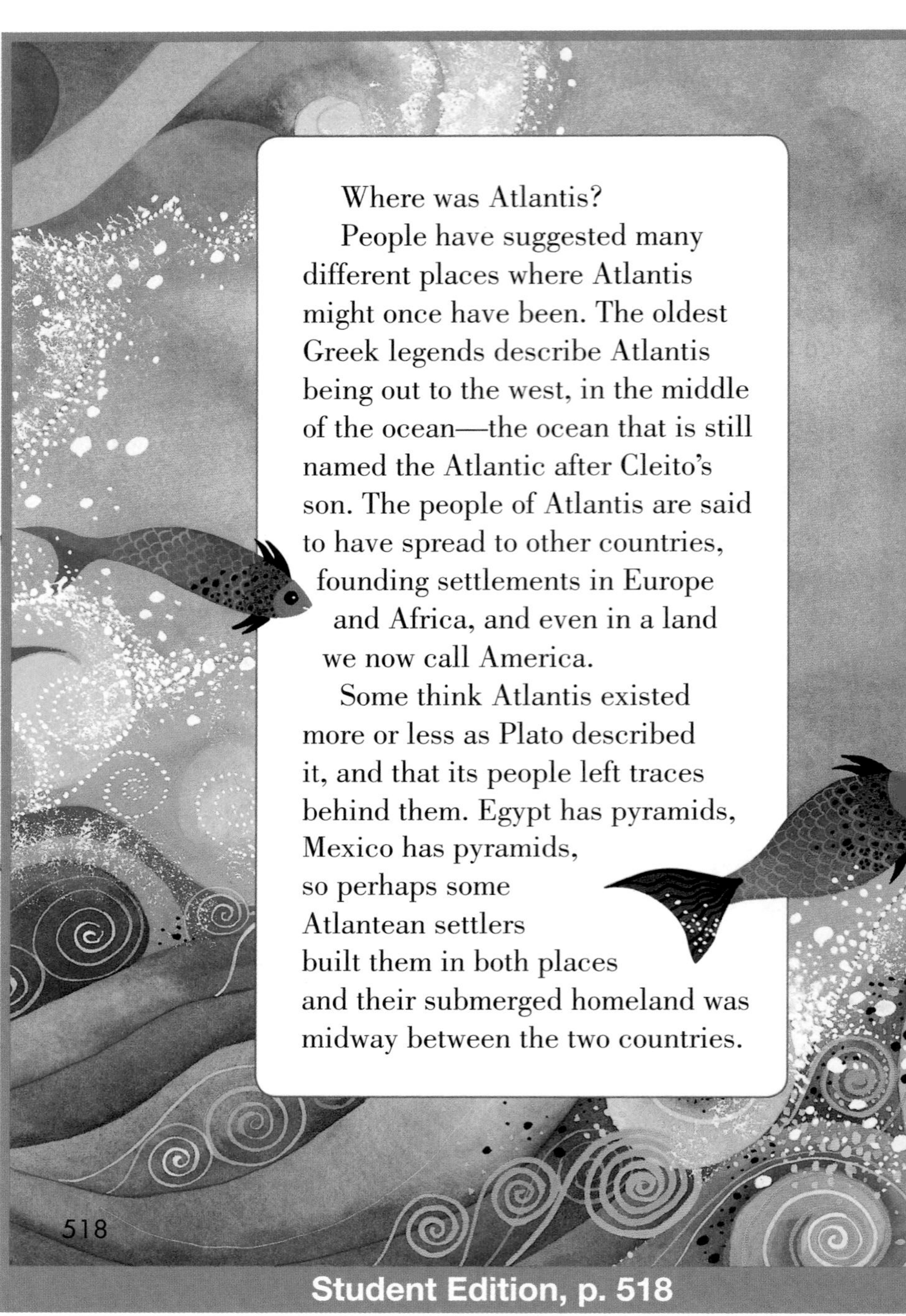

Where was Atlantis?

People have suggested many different places where Atlantis might once have been. The oldest Greek legends describe Atlantis being out to the west, in the middle of the ocean—the ocean that is still named the Atlantic after Cleito's son. The people of Atlantis are said to have spread to other countries, founding settlements in Europe and Africa, and even in a land we now call America.

Some think Atlantis existed more or less as Plato described it, and that its people left traces behind them. Egypt has pyramids, Mexico has pyramids, so perhaps some Atlantean settlers built them in both places and their submerged homeland was midway between the two countries.

518

Student Edition, p. 518

2ND READ

Close Reading

ANALYSIS Read the last sentence on page 519. Is this a valid generalization? Why or why not? (It is a valid generalization because it includes the qualifier "many" and it doesn't specify where Atlantis might have been.)

SYNTHESIS • TEXT EVIDENCE
Using what you learned in this selection, tell what we can learn about keeping freedom. Have students cite examples from the text to support their responses.

CHECK PREDICTIONS Have students return to the predictions they made and confirm whether they were accurate.

Others suggest that Atlantis was closer to America. The native inhabitants of the West Indies told early explorers that their islands were once part of a single landmass but that a disaster long ago shattered it. The fifth-century Greek philosopher Proclus, who wanted to convince his readers that Atlantis was real, writes, very mysteriously, as if he knew of the West Indies and their story.

Some people suggest that Atlantis was a part of Britain. Legend tells of a sunken land between Cornwall and the Isles of Scilly.

The theory taken most seriously is that the story is actually about the island of Crete, which was highly civilized and ruled over several smaller islands. One of them, Thera, was partially destroyed in about 1450 B.C.E. by a tremendous eruption, which also destroyed part of Crete, and its civilization never recovered.

With so much uncertainty, some argue that the story of Atlantis is not history at all but a myth warning us against conflict and power seeking. Yet the legend is so vivid that many will always believe Atlantis existed . . . somewhere.

519

Student Edition, p. 519

Common Core State Standards

Literature 1. Ask and answer questions to demonstrate understanding of a text, referring explicitly to the text as the basis for the answers. **Also Literature 4., 10., Language 4., 4.a., 5.**

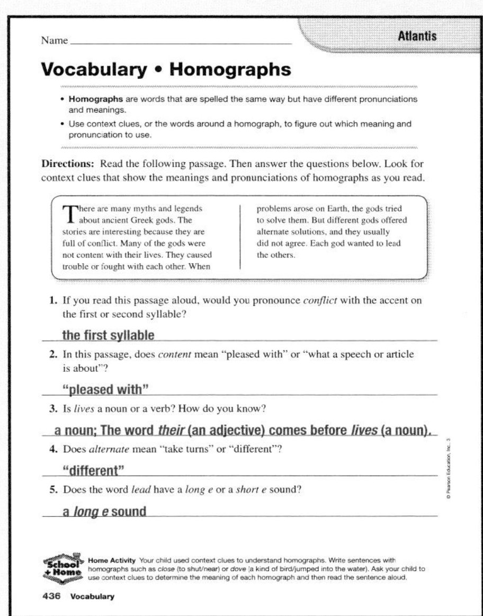

Name ____________ **Atlantis**

Vocabulary • Homographs

- **Homographs** are words that are spelled the same way but have different pronunciations and meanings.
- Use context clues, or the words around a homograph, to figure out which meaning and pronunciation to use.

Directions: Read the following passage. Then answer the questions below. Look for context clues that show the meanings and pronunciations of homographs as you read.

There are many myths and legends about ancient Greek gods. The stories are interesting because they are full of conflict. Many of the gods were not content with their lives. They caused trouble or fought with each other. When problems arose on Earth, the gods tried to solve them. But different gods offered alternate solutions, and they usually did not agree. Each god wanted to lead the others.

1. If you read this passage aloud, would you pronounce *conflict* with the accent on the first or second syllable?
   the first syllable
2. In this passage, does *content* mean "pleased with" or "what a speech or article is about"?
   "pleased with"
3. Is *lives* a noun or a verb? How do you know?
   a noun; The word *their* (an adjective) comes before *lives* (a noun).
4. Does *alternate* mean "take turns" or "different"?
   "different"
5. Does the word *lead* have a *long e* or a *short e* sound?
   a *long e* sound

School + Home **Home Activity** Your child used context clues to understand homographs. Write sentences with homographs such as *close* (to shut/near) or *dove* (a kind of bird/jumped into the water). Ask your child to use context clues to determine the meaning of each homograph and then read the sentence aloud.

436 Vocabulary

Reader's and Writer's Notebook p. 436

Connect to Social Studies

Origin of the Myth The story of Atlantis evidently originated in 355 B.C. with the philosopher Plato. He wrote of Atlantis in his book *Timaeus.*

Homographs Because homographs can be especially confusing to English language learners, find frequent opportunities to model using context clues to determine meaning. Whenever possible, use visuals and pantomime to clarify.

Think Critically

1. In the story, the author writes about the mythical lost city of Atlantis. Think about other myths you know, such as "Catch It and Run." How are the myths alike and different? Be sure to compare the settings; paraphrase the themes and supporting details; and describe the characters, their relationships, and the changes they undergo. Text to Text
2. The subtitle of this selection is *The Legend of a Lost City.* Why do you think the author used this subtitle? Why did the author use the word *legend* instead of *myth?* Think Like an Author
3. What generalization can you make about the gods in this story? What generalization can you make about people in this story? Generalize
4. Read page 514. What inference can you make about ambition and power? Explain your answer using evidence from the story. Inferring
5. **Look Back and Write** Look back at pages 518–519. Think about the reasons why the story was created. What does the story try to explain about the world? Provide evidence to support your answer. Key Ideas and Details • Text Evidence

520

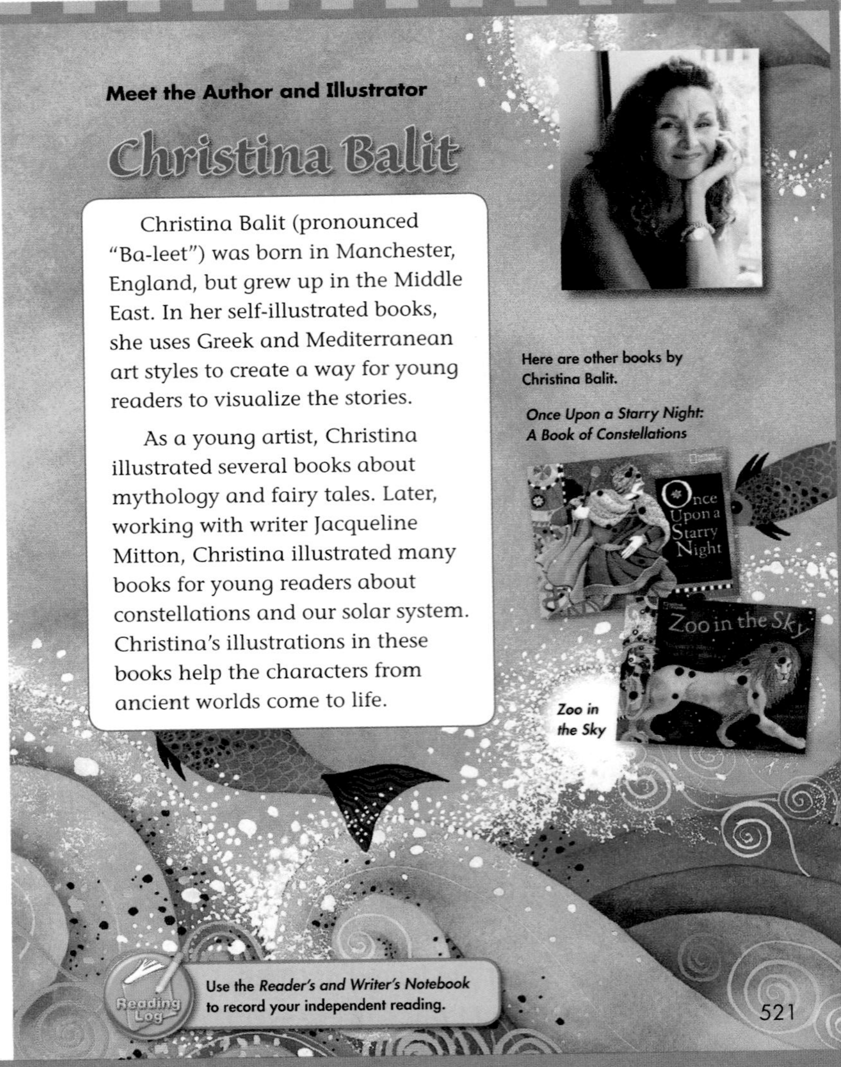
Meet the Author and Illustrator

Christina Balit

Christina Balit (pronounced "Ba-leet") was born in Manchester, England, but grew up in the Middle East. In her self-illustrated books, she uses Greek and Mediterranean art styles to create a way for young readers to visualize the stories.

As a young artist, Christina illustrated several books about mythology and fairy tales. Later, working with writer Jacqueline Mitton, Christina illustrated many books for young readers about constellations and our solar system. Christina's illustrations in these books help the characters from ancient worlds come to life.

Here are other books by Christina Balit.

Once Upon a Starry Night: A Book of Constellations

Zoo in the Sky

Use the *Reader's and Writer's Notebook* to record your independent reading.

521

Student Edition, pp. 520–521

Common Core State Standards

Literature 1. Ask and answer questions to demonstrate understanding of a text, referring explicitly to the text as the basis for the answers. **Also Literature 2., 3., Writing 4., 8., 10., Speaking/Listening 4.**

Bridge to Common Core

RANGE OF READING AND LEVEL OF TEXT COMPLEXITY

To increase students' capacity for reading and comprehending complex texts independently and proficiently, have them read other myths or legends. After students read closely for a sustained period of time, they should record their reading in their Reading Logs.

Think Critically

1. **TEXT TO TEXT** Student responses should include comparisons of the settings; paraphrases of the themes; and descriptions of the characters, their relationships, and the changes they undergo.
2. **THINK LIKE AN AUTHOR** The author believes Atlantis may have existed and that there is some truth to this story. Legends may be based on truth but are mostly fiction.
3. **GENERALIZE** All gods have great powers. At the beginning of the story, all of the people of Atlantis lived in peace.
4. **INFERRING** I can infer that ambition and power ruined Atlantis because I read that ambition and power made the people greedy.
5. **LOOK BACK AND WRITE** To build writing fluency, allow 10–15 minutes.

Scoring Rubric Look Back and Write

TOP-SCORE RESPONSE A top-score response uses details to tell about the lessons of the story.

A top-score response should include:

- The story was written to teach a lesson.
- It teaches that we can live peacefully together.
- It teaches that greed often has consequences.

Retell

Have students work in pairs to retell the selection, using the retelling strip in the Student Edition or the Story Sort as prompts. Monitor students' retellings.

Scoring Rubric Narrative Retelling

	4	3	2	1
Connections	Makes connections and generalizes beyond the text	Makes connections to other events, stories, or experiences	Makes a limited connection to another event, story, or experience	Makes no connection to another event, story, or experience
Author's Purpose	Elaborates on author's purpose	Tells author's purpose with some clarity	Makes some connection to author's purpose	Makes no connection to author's purpose
Characters	Describes the main character(s) and any character development	Identifies the main character(s) and gives some information about them	Inaccurately identifies some characters or gives little information about them	Inaccurately identifies the characters or gives no information about them
Setting	Describes the time and location	Identifies the time and location	Omits details of time or location	Is unable to identify time or location
Plot	Describes the problem, goal, events, and ending using rich detail	Tells the problem, goal, events, and ending with some errors that do not affect meaning	Tells parts of the problem, goal, events, and ending with gaps that affect meaning	Retelling has no sense of story

Don't Wait Until Friday

MONITOR PROGRESS Check Retelling

If... students have difficulty retelling,

then... use the Retelling Cards/Story Sort to scaffold their retellings.

Plan to Assess Retelling

- ☐ **Week 1** Strategic Intervention
- ☐ **Week 2** Advanced
- ☐ **Week 3** Strategic Intervention
- ☐ **Week 4** On-Level
- ☑ **This week assess any students you have not yet checked during this unit.**

Meet the Author

Have students read about author Christina Balit on p. 521. Ask them what art styles influence the illustrations in her books.

Read Independently

Have students enter their independent reading into their Reading Logs.

Common Core State Standards

Foundational Skills 4.b. Read on-level prose and poetry orally with accuracy, appropriate rate, and expression on successive readings. **Writing 8.** Recall information from experiences or gather information from print and digital sources; take brief notes on sources and sort evidence into provided categories.

Fluency

Expression

MODEL FLUENT READING Have students turn to p. 516 of *Atlantis: The Legend of a Lost City.* Have students follow along as you read this page. Tell them to listen to the expression of your voice as you read about how Poseidon carried out his terrible curse. Adjust your voice level to stress important words and phrases.

GUIDE PRACTICE Have the students follow along as you read the page again. Ask questions to be sure students comprehend the text. Then have them reread the page as a group without you until they read with the right expression and with no mistakes. Continue in the same way on p. 517.

Corrective feedback

If... students are having difficulty reading with the right expression,

then... prompt them as follows:

- Which word is a problem? Let's read it together.
- Read the sentence again to be sure you understand it.
- Tell me the sentence. Now read it as if you are speaking to me.

Reread for Fluency

Routine Oral Rereading

1. **Read** Have students read p. 514 of *Atlantis: The Legend of a Lost City* orally.
2. **Reread** To achieve optimal fluency, students should reread the text three or four times.
3. **Corrective Feedback** Have students read aloud without you. Provide feedback about their expression and encourage them to adjust their voice level to stress important words and phrases. Listen for use of appropriate expression.

Routines Flip Chart

Research and Study Skills

Quote and Paraphrase Sources

TEACH Ask students what they know about quoting and paraphrasing sources of information. Show them the same information as a direct quotation and as paraphrasing to review these terms:

- A **direct quotation** is anything quoted word-for-word. It can be something someone said, a statistic, or sentences from a book.
- A **quotation mark** is a punctuation mark placed at the beginning and end of a direct quotation.
- To **paraphrase** means to state something in your own words.
- To **plagiarize** is to take the ideas or exact words of someone else and present them as your own. Plagiarism is unlawful.
- To **cite** a source means to give credit to the person who came up with an idea or said something important.

Tell students that they should cite the source of their information within their writing. Write the following example on the board and discuss: *Albert Einstein, a famous scientist, once said, "Imagination is more important than knowledge."*

GUIDE PRACTICE Discuss these questions:

When should source information be cited? (whenever it is summarized, paraphrased, or quoted)

When should source information contain quotation marks? (when it consists of the exact words taken from a source)

ON THEIR OWN Have students review the instructions and complete p. 437 of the *Reader's and Writer's Notebook.*

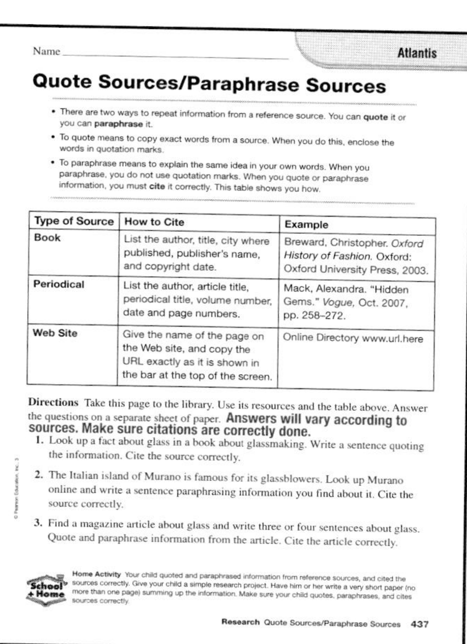

Name ______________________ **Atlantis**

Quote Sources/Paraphrase Sources

- There are two ways to repeat information from a reference source. You can **quote** it or you can **paraphrase** it.
- To quote means to copy exact words from a source. When you do this, enclose the words in quotation marks.
- To paraphrase means to explain the same idea in your own words. When you paraphrase, you do not use quotation marks. When you quote or paraphrase information, you must **cite** it correctly. This table shows you how.

Type of Source	How to Cite	Example
Book	List the author, title, city where published, publisher's name, and copyright date.	Breward, Christopher. *Oxford History of Fashion.* Oxford: Oxford University Press, 2003.
Periodical	List the author, article title, periodical title, volume number, date and page numbers.	Mack, Alexandra. "Hidden Gems." *Vogue,* Oct. 2007, pp. 258–272.
Web Site	Give the name of the page on the Web site, and copy the URL exactly as it is shown in the bar at the top of the screen.	Online Directory www.url.here

Directions Take this page to the library. Use its resources and the table above. Answer the questions on a separate sheet of paper. **Answers will vary according to sources. Make sure citations are correctly done.**

1. Look up a fact about glass in a book about glassmaking. Write a sentence quoting the information. Cite the source correctly.
2. The Italian island of Murano is famous for its glassblowers. Look up Murano online and write a sentence paraphrasing information you find about it. Cite the source correctly.
3. Find a magazine article about glass and write three or four sentences about glass. Quote and paraphrase information from the article. Cite the article correctly.

School + Home **Home Activity** Your child quoted and paraphrased information from reference sources, and cited the sources correctly. Give your child a simple research project. Have him or her write a very short paper (no more than one page) summing up the information. Make sure your child quotes, paraphrases, and cites sources correctly.

Research Quote Sources/Paraphrase Sources 437

Reader's and Writer's Notebook, p. 437

Quote and Paraphrase Sources Ask a volunteer to say something about a topic of interest. Write what he/she says as a direct quotation and as paraphrasing. Have students take turns reading both sentences aloud.

Common Core State Standards

Writing 8. Recall information from experiences or gather information from print and digital sources; take brief notes on sources and sort evidence into provided categories. **Language 2.c.** Use commas and quotation marks in dialogue. **Language 2.f.** Use spelling patterns and generalizations (e.g., word families, position-based spellings, syllable patterns, ending rules, meaningful word parts) in writing words.

Research and Inquiry

Step 3 Analyze Information

TEACH Tell students that today they will analyze their findings and may need to change the focus of their original inquiry question.

MODEL Originally I thought that speaking out was the best way to keep my freedom. Part of my research was to interview a local expert, such as a history professor, about the success people in history have had by speaking out for a cause. She told me that demonstrations, such as marches, also bring attention to a cause. I will refocus my inquiry question to include information from my local expert and from reference materials. Now my inquiry question is *Can I keep my freedom by speaking out and demonstrating for what I believe in?*

GUIDE PRACTICE Have students analyze their findings. They may need to refocus their inquiry question to better fit the information they found. Remind students that if they have difficulty improving their focus, they can ask local experts for guidance.

Remind students that whether they quote or paraphrase sources of information, they need to cite the source.

ON THEIR OWN Have students survey one another about the best way to keep their freedom. Students should then compare their research results to the survey they conducted in class.

Conventions

Quotations and Parentheses

REVIEW Remind students that this week they learned about quotations and parentheses.

- Quotations are a speaker's exact words.
- Quotation marks enclose dialogue and the titles of songs, poems, and stories.
- Parentheses enclose words that add extra, but not necessary, information to a sentence.

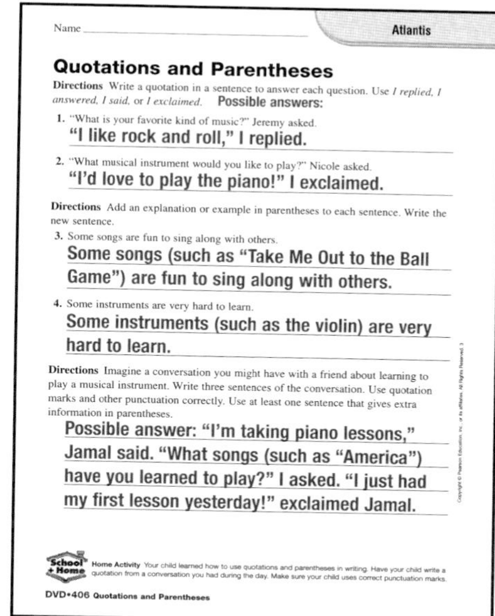

Name ____________ Atlantis

Quotations and Parentheses

Directions Write a quotation in a sentence to answer each question. Use *I replied, I answered, I said,* or *I exclaimed.* **Possible answers:**

1. "What is your favorite kind of music?" Jeremy asked.
   "I like rock and roll," I replied.
2. "What musical instrument would you like to play?" Nicole asked.
   "I'd love to play the piano!" I exclaimed.

Directions Add an explanation or example in parentheses to each sentence. Write the new sentence.

3. Some songs are fun to sing along with others.
   Some songs (such as "Take Me Out to the Ball Game") are fun to sing along with others.
4. Some instruments are very hard to learn.
   Some instruments (such as the violin) are very hard to learn.

Directions Imagine a conversation you might have with a friend about learning to play a musical instrument. Write three sentences of the conversation. Use quotation marks and other punctuation correctly. Use at least one sentence that gives extra information in parentheses.

Possible answer: "I'm taking piano lessons," Jamal said. "What songs (such as "America") have you learned to play?" I asked. "I just had my first lesson yesterday!" exclaimed Jamal.

School + Home **Home Activity** Your child learned how to use quotations and parentheses in writing. Have your child write a quotation from a conversation you had during the day. Make sure your child uses correct punctuation marks.

DVD•406 Quotations and Parentheses

Let's Practice It! TR DVD•406

CONNECT TO ORAL LANGUAGE Have the class complete these sentence frames orally.

"Come over here quickly!" Melissa ______.

The factory makes many types of cheese (for example, ______).

ON THEIR OWN For additional support, use *Let's Practice It!* page 406 on the *Teacher Resources DVD-ROM.*

Spelling

Related Words

FREQUENTLY MISSPELLED WORDS The words *want* and *whole* appear often in reading. They are also words that we frequently misspell. Think carefully before you write these words. Use letter sounds to help you spell them. I'm going to read a sentence. Choose the right word to complete the sentence, and then write it correctly.

1. **We bought a ______ pineapple at the store.** (whole)
2. **Did you ______ a ride home?** (want)
3. **What do you ______ for dinner?** (want)
4. **I finished reading the ______ book in one day.** (whole)

ON THEIR OWN For additional support, use the *Reader's and Writer's Notebook* p. 438.

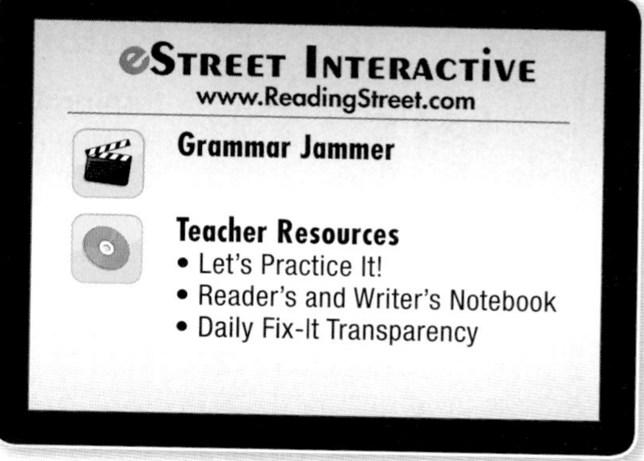

Daily Fix-It

5. Roadrunners are birds and they usual live in the desert. *(birds,; usually)*
6. Joe said, "Roadrunners are abel to run 15 miles per hour". *(able; hour.")*

Access for All

Strategic Intervention

Have students work in pairs to brainstorm different verbs to complete the first oral sentence frame. Then have them brainstorm types of cheese for the parenthetical information in the second oral sentence frame.

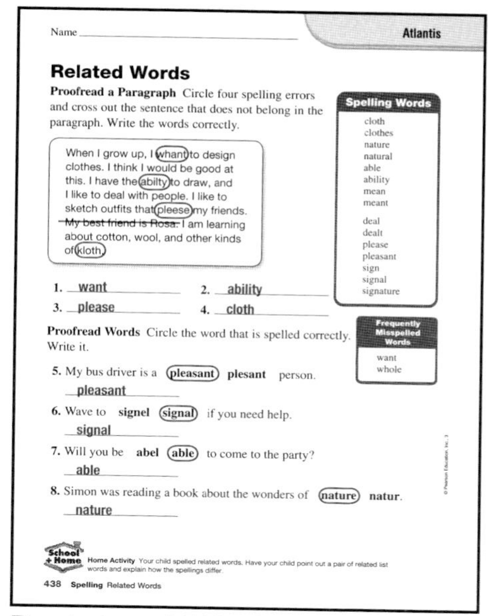

Name ____________ Atlantis

Related Words

Proofread a Paragraph Circle four spelling errors and cross out the sentence that does not belong in the paragraph. Write the words correctly.

When I grow up, I whant to design clothes. I think I would be good at this. I have the abilty to draw, and I like to deal with people. I like to sketch outfits that pleese my friends. ~~My best friend is Rosa.~~ I am learning about cotton, wool, and other kinds of kloth.

1. want 2. ability
3. please 4. cloth

Spelling Words: cloth, clothes, nature, natural, able, ability, mean, meant, deal, dealt, please, pleasant, sign, signal, signature

Frequently Misspelled Words: want, whole

Proofread Words Circle the word that is spelled correctly. Write it.

5. My bus driver is a **pleasant** **plesant** person. pleasant
6. Wave to **signel** **signal** if you need help. signal
7. Will you be **abel** **able** to come to the party? able
8. Simon was reading a book about the wonders of **nature** **natur**. nature

School + Home **Home Activity** Your child spelled related words. Have your child point out a pair of related list words and explain how the spellings differ.

438 Spelling Related Words

Reader's and Writer's Notebook, p. 438

Common Core State Standards
Writing 3. Write narratives to develop real or imagined experiences or events using effective technique, descriptive details, and clear event sequences. **Also Writing 3.a., 3.b., Language 2.c., 3.a.**

Let's Write It!

Key Features of Historical Fiction

- set in the past
- events of the plot make sense
- characters, setting, or events may be based on historical fact

READING STREET ONLINE
GRAMMAR JAMMER
www.ReadingStreet.com

Narrative

Historical Fiction

Historical fiction is realistic fiction that takes place in the past. The student model on the next page is an example of historical fiction.

Writing Prompt Write a historical fiction story about a voyage across the Atlantic Ocean.

Writer's Checklist

Remember, you should ...

- ✓ set your story in the past.
- ✓ include details about the characters and setting.
- ✓ build the plot to a climax.
- ✓ indent new paragraphs.
- ✓ capitalize geographical names and places, or historical periods.

522

Student Model

To America!

My name is Sal Valle. I was only nine years old in 1910 when my family moved from Italy to America. We sailed on an enormous ship with hundreds of others. The journey took a very long time, and the conditions were harsh. The living quarters were stuffy and crowded, and there was little food. When I got scared or sad, my mother would say to me, "Soon we will live in the most wonderful place. It won't be long now."

Many people got very ill during the journey, including my mother. I worried about her as she got sicker and sicker, but there wasn't much anyone could do (there was no medicine). We just had to wait and hope for the best. After weeks, she showed signs of improvement.

Then one morning, I awoke to the voice of a man telling us that they had spotted land. Hurray! I ran to my mother's bed excitedly and leaned down to her and said, "Just like you said, Mother. It won't be long now. Land has been sighted!"

Writing Trait Word choice Specific adjectives create interest.

Genre Historical fiction takes place in the past.

Quotations and parentheses are used correctly.

Conventions

Quotations and Parentheses

Quotation marks ("") show the exact words of a speaker. **Parentheses** are punctuation marks inserted into a sentence around a word or group of words to explain something or give additional information.

523

Student Edition, pp. 522–523

Common Core State Standards

Writing 3. Write narratives to develop real or imagined experiences or events using effective technique, descriptive details, and clear event sequences. **Writing 3.a.** Establish a situation and introduce a narrator and/or characters; organize an event sequence that unfolds naturally. **Also Writing 3.b., Language 2.c., 3., 3.a.**

Let's Write It!

WRITE HISTORICAL FICTION Use pp. 522–523 in the Student Edition. Direct students to read the key features of historical fiction that appear on p. 522. Remind students to read the information in the Writer's Checklist.

Read the student model on p. 523. Point out the key features of historical fiction in the model.

CONNECT TO CONVENTIONS Remind students that quotation marks are used to show the exact words of a speaker or to set off titles of stories, poems, and music. Also remind students that parentheses can be used to enclose words that add details that are not absolutely necessary to a sentence. Point out the correct use of quotation marks and parentheses in the model.

Historical Fiction

Writing for Tests: Evaluation

DISPLAY RUBRIC Have students return to the scoring rubric they looked at yesterday on p. 435 in their *Reader's and Writer's Notebook.* Then explain to students that they will use this rubric to evaluate the historical fiction stories they wrote yesterday.

Scoring Rubric Historical Fiction

	4	3	2	1
Focus/Ideas	Exciting story with interesting characters; historical time period and figures	Good story with developed characters; somewhat based on historical time period and figures	Story has some focus on characters; setting and characters are only loosely historical	Story has no focus on characters; not set in historical time period
Organization	Clear order of events	Can follow order of events	Unclear order of events	No order of events
Voice	Writer shows interest in the story and the characters	Writer shows some interest in the story and the characters	Writer shows little interest in the story or characters	Writer makes no effort to show interest in the story or characters
Word Choice	Strong use of specific adjectives to bring the story to life	Good try at using specific adjectives	Poor use of specific adjectives; descriptions are dull	No effort made to use specific adjectives
Sentences	Strong concluding statement	Adequate concluding statement	Weak concluding statement	No concluding statement
Conventions	Few, if any, errors; correct use of quotation marks and parentheses	Several small errors; use of quotation marks and parentheses	Many errors; weak use of quotation marks and parentheses	Many serious errors; incorrect or no use of quotation marks and parentheses

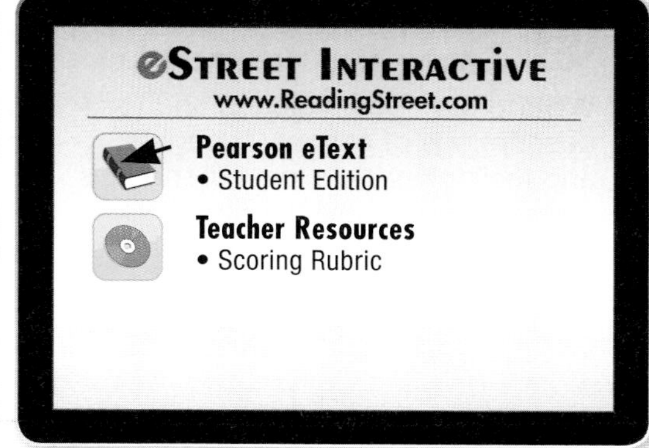

Key Features Have pairs of students take turns asking each other questions about their historical fiction stories: *When does your story take place? Who are the characters in your story? Do historical figures appear in your story? Is the story based on real events?*

Common Core State Standards

Writing 3.b. Use dialogue and descriptions of actions, thoughts, and feelings to develop experiences and events or show the response of characters to situations. **Language 3.a.** Choose words and phrases for effect. **Also Writing 3., 5., 10., Language 3.**

Bridge to Common Core

RANGE OF WRITING

Throughout the week, students produce writing in which the organization and style are appropriate to the task of writing for tests as they complete historical fiction narratives. They also develop and strengthen their revising and editing skills through self-evaluation.

Writing

Historical Fiction

Mini-Lesson Writing for Tests: Evaluation

- **Introduce** Explain that when you evaluate writing with a rubric, you are evaluating different traits in the writing. Have students read aloud a few of the six traits in the rubric.

- **Evaluate a Trait** Direct students to the fourth trait (row) in the rubric, word choice. We will focus on word choice. Remind students that word choice can make the difference between an exciting story that holds the reader's interest and a dull tale that does not. According to the rubric, we want to make sure that we evaluate our adjectives specifically. Adjectives help bring descriptions to life. We want to make sure we're using specific adjectives in order to make our descriptions clear and interesting. For example, the adjective *mad* could be replaced with the adjective *furious.* The adjective *cold* could be strengthened with the adjective *bitter.*

- Have students review their historical fiction narratives and circle all the adjectives. Then, using the rubric as a guide, have them evaluate their use of specific adjectives on a scale from 4 to 1.

- **Apply Scoring** Direct students to continue evaluating their historical fiction stories based on the other 5 traits in the rubric. Remind students that they might receive different number scores for each of the different traits, but that is all right. Lower or higher scores for different traits can help them see where their strengths lie, and where they might need to focus more attention and effort to improve areas of their writing.

Writing Trait: Word Choice

Review the importance of choosing the best possible words when writing. Good writers use specific nouns, vivid adjectives, and strong verbs. They replace vague, weak words, such as *thing, good,* and *take,* with precise, vivid words such as *suitcase, wonderful,* and *snatch.* They want their readers to be able to imagine exactly what is happening. Help students improve their word choices by writing sentences with vague, weak words and having them replace the words with more vivid, precise words.

Routine Quick Write for Fluency — Team Talk

1. **Talk** Pairs talk about how using specific adjectives can make descriptions in a narrative clearer and more interesting.
2. **Write** Students write one sentence using two specific adjectives.
3. **Share** Partners read each other's sentence aloud.

Routines Flip Chart

ELL

Evaluation Have students make a list of all the adjectives in their narratives.

Beginning Students brainstorm a replacement for two adjectives in their list.

Intermediate Students brainstorm a replacement for each adjective in their list.

Advanced Students brainstorm two or more replacements for each adjective in their list. Have students replace the adjectives in their narratives with the replacement adjectives.

Wrap Up Your Day!

✔ **Content Knowledge** Have students discuss the lessons taught by the myth of Atlantis.

✔ **Text-Based Comprehension** What generalization can you make about the legend of Atlantis? Encourage students to cite examples from the text.

Tell students that tomorrow they will read about a mythical monster.

DAY 4 at a Glance

- **Content Knowledge**
  Oral Vocabulary
- **Phonics/Word Analysis**
  Review Prefixes *im-*, *in-*
- **Social Studies in Reading**
  Drama
- **Fluency**
  Expression
- **Vocabulary Skill**
  Homographs
- **Listening and Speaking**
  Song
- **Research and Inquiry**
  Synthesize
- **Conventions**
  Quotations and Parentheses
- **Spelling**
  Related Words
- **Writing**
  Historical Fiction

Materials

- Student Edition
- Reader's and Writer's Notebook
- Decodable Reader

Common Core State Standards

Speaking/Listening 1. Engage effectively in a range of collaborative discussions (one-on-one, in groups, and teacher-led) with diverse partners on grade 3 topics and texts, building on others' ideas and expressing their own clearly. **Language 6.** Acquire and use accurately grade-appropriate conversational, general academic, and domain-specific words and phrases, including those that signal spatial and temporal relationships (e.g., *After dinner that night we went looking for them*). **Also Language 5.b.**

Content Knowledge

Keeping Your Freedom

EXPAND THE CONCEPT Remind students of the weekly concept question, *What is the best way to keep your freedom?* Have students discuss freedom and what it takes to keep it.

Build Oral Language

Team Talk **TALK ABOUT SENTENCES AND WORDS** Ask students to reread this sentence from the first paragraph of Student Edition p. 516.

The wave vibrated with a roar that could be heard two thousand miles away, and the earth trembled in terror.

- What does the word *vibrated* mean? (moved rapidly to and fro) What are some synonyms for the word *vibrated*? Have students turn to a partner to share. *(shake, tremble)*
- What does the word *trembled* mean? (shook because of fear, excitement, weakness, cold, and so on) Could the words *vibrated* and *trembled* be switched in the sentence so that the sentence still has the same meaning? (Yes, the meaning of the new sentence would be very close to the meaning of the original sentence.)
- What does the word *terror* mean? (great fear) What are some words that are related to *terror*? *(terrify, terrified, terrorize)*
- Using your understanding of the words *vibrated, trembled,* and *terror,* how can you restate the sentence in your own words? Have student pairs share their ideas. *(The wave shook with a roar that could be heard two thousand miles away, and the earth shivered in fright.)*
- Can the earth really tremble in terror? (no) Why do you think the author wrote that the earth trembled in terror? (Writing it this way makes the sentence more powerful; it gives the earth a human quality that the reader can relate to.)

Build Oral Vocabulary

Amazing Words Robust Vocabulary Routine

1. **Introduce** Write the Amazing Word *violence* on the board. Have students say it aloud with you. We read that as the people of Atlantis began to change, *violence* broke out in the city. What kinds of things did people do to each other? (They argued and fought. They began to steal, cheat, and lie.) Have students provide a definition of *violence*. (physical force that harms or injures)
2. **Demonstrate** Have students answer questions to demonstrate understanding. What *violence* occurred near the end of the story? (Poseidon stirred up the sea so that it would swallow up Atlantis.)
3. **Apply** Have students apply their understanding. What are some examples of *violence* caused by nature?
4. **Display the Word** Run your hand under the syllables, *vi-o-lence,* and have students read the word with you.

Routines Flip Chart

ADD TO THE CONCEPT MAP Discuss the Amazing Words *blight* and *wept.* Add these and other concept-related words to the concept map. Use the following questions to develop students' understanding of the concept. Add words generated in discussion to the concept map.

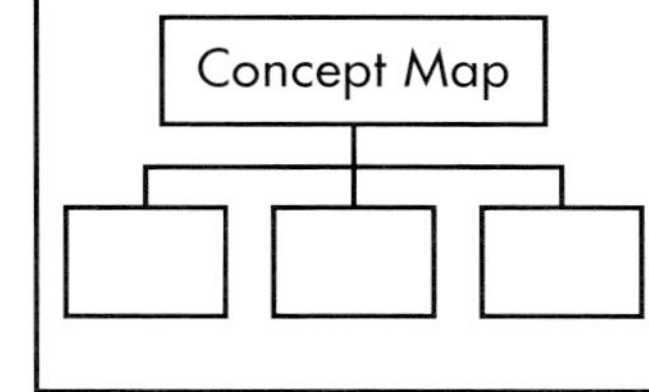

- Atlantis experienced two *blights*—one caused by nature and the other caused by people. What is needed to prevent people from causing *blight* in their communities?
- Poseidon *wept* when he discovered that his once-perfect kingdom had fallen into ruin. Have you ever *wept* when something you cared about turned out badly? Did weeping make you feel better?

Amazing Words

witty	mourn
equality	blight
justice	wept
perish	violence
demonstrate	

Strategy Response Log

Have students review the characteristics of legends on p. 36 of the *Reader's and Writer's Notebook.* Then have them compare *Atlantis* to another example of legend that they have read or know about.

Produce Oral Language Use the Day 4 instruction on ELL Poster 30 to extend and enrich language.

Word Analysis

Review Prefixes *im-*, *in-*

REVIEW SOUND-SPELLINGS To review last week's word analysis skill, write *invalid* and *impolite*. You studied words like these last week. What do you know about words like these that have the prefixes *im-* and *in-*? (The prefixes *im-* and *in-* can be added in front of a base word to make a new word.) Have students identify the base word in each word. What is the base word in *invalid*? *(valid)* In *impolite*? *(polite)* Remind students that the prefixes *im-* and *in-* can mean "not."

Corrective feedback | If students are unable to answer the questions about prefixes, refer them to *Sound-Spelling Cards* 153 and 154.

GUIDE PRACTICE Display a two-column chart with the heads *im-* and *in-*. We will work together to place words with the prefixes *im-* and *in-* in the chart. Listen as I say each word. For words with the prefix *im-*, moo like a cow; for *in-*, neigh like a horse. Write each word in the appropriate column. Then have students read the words. Call on volunteers to underline each base word.

im-	in-
impure	inaction
impassable	inexact
improper	incoherent
immobile	invisible

ON THEIR OWN For additional practice, use *Let's Practice It!* p. 407 on the *Teacher Resources DVD-ROM*.

Common Core State Standards

Foundational Skills 3.a. Identify and know the meaning of the most common prefixes and derivational suffixes. **Foundational Skills 3.c.** Decode multisyllable words. **Also Foundational Skills 3.**

Name ____________ Atlantis

Prefixes *im-*, *in-*

Directions Complete each word by adding the prefix *im-* or *in-*.

1. in complete
2. in visible
3. im material
4. im mobile
5. in direct
6 im pure
7. in sincere
8. im practical
9. im mortal
10. in sane
11. im partial
12. in capable
13. in correct
14. im possible
15. im moral
16. in accurate

Directions Now write four sentences of your own. In each sentence include at least one of the completed words from above.

17. Sentences will vary.

18. ____________

19. ____________

20. ____________

School + Home **Home Activity** Your child used words with the prefixes *im-* and *in-*, meaning "not." Work with your child to write other words that begin with these prefixes.

Prefixes *im-*, *in-* DVD•407

Let's Practice It! TR DVD•407

Fluent Word Reading

Spiral Review

READ WORDS IN ISOLATION Display these words. Tell students that they can already decode some words on this list. Explain that they should know other words because they appear often in reading.

Have students read the list three or four times until they can read at the rate of two to three seconds per word.

Word Reading

active	**ago**	**they**	**gone**	**was**
very	**decision**	**family**	**only**	**there**
could	**water**	**substitution**	**breakfast**	**visualize**
vacation	**afraid**	**have**	**picture**	**mountain**

Corrective feedback

If... students have difficulty reading whole words,
then... have them use sound-by-sound blending for decodable words or chunking for words that have word parts, or have them say and spell high-frequency words.

If... students cannot read fluently at a rate of two to three seconds per word,
then... have pairs practice the list until they can read it fluently.

Access for All

Strategic Intervention

Write the word *imperfect*. Remind students that a prefix can be added to the beginning of a base word to make a new word. Help students identify the base word *perfect* and the prefix *im-*. Have students write the words from the chart and identify the prefix and the base word in each word.

Spiral Review

These activities review:

- previously taught high-frequency words *they, gone, was, very, only, there, could, water, have.*
- schwa spelled with *a, e, i, o, u*, and *y;* final syllables (*-tion, -ion, -ture, -ive, -ize*).

Practice Pronunciation Incorrect pronunciation can lead to incorrect spelling. Have students listen as you say some words with the schwa sound, listening for the sound. Then have them say each word aloud as they write it.

Common Core State Standards

Foundational Skills 3. Know and apply grade-level phonics and word analysis skills in decoding words. **Foundational Skills 3.d.** Read grade-appropriate irregularly spelled words. **Foundational Skills 4.** Read with sufficient accuracy and fluency to support comprehension. **Foundational Skills 4.b.** Read on-level prose and poetry orally with accuracy, appropriate rate, and expression on successive readings. **Also Foundational Skills 4.a., 4.c., Language 2.e.**

Fluent Word Reading

READ WORDS IN CONTEXT Display these sentences. Call on individuals to read a sentence. Then randomly point to review words and have students read them. To help you monitor word reading, high-frequency words are underlined and decodable words are italicized.

MONITOR PROGRESS Sentence Reading

<u>There</u> <u>could</u> be no *substitution* for a good *breakfast*.
This *picture* helps me *visualize* the tallest *mountain*.
The *family* made a *decision* to *vacation* <u>only</u> near <u>water</u>.
<u>They</u> <u>have</u> been <u>very</u> *active* in planning the bake sale.
I'm *afraid* the ice cream <u>was</u> <u>gone</u> long <u>ago</u>.

If... students are unable to read an underlined high-frequency word,
then... read the word for them and spell it, having them echo you.

If... students have difficulty reading an italicized decodable word,
then... guide them in using sound-by-sound blending or chunking.

Reread for Fluency

Have students reread the sentences to develop automaticity decoding words.

Routine Oral Rereading

1. **Read** Have students read all the sentences orally.
2. **Reread** To achieve optimal fluency, students should reread the sentences three or four times.
3. **Corrective Feedback** Listen as students read. Provide corrective feedback regarding their fluency and decoding.

Routines Flip Chart

Decodable Passage 30C

If students need help, then...

Read *Desert Hiking*

READ WORDS IN ISOLATION Have students turn to p.179 in *Decodable Practice Readers 3.2* and find the first list of words. Each word in this list is related to another word. Let's read these words. Be sure that students identify the related words.

Next, have students read the high-frequency words.

PREVIEW Have students read the title and preview the story. Tell them that they will read words that are related to each other.

READ WORDS IN CONTEXT Chorally read the story along with the students. Have students identify the related words in the story. Make sure that students are monitoring their accuracy when they decode words.

Team Talk Pair students and have them take turns reading the story aloud to each other. As students read, monitor them to check for proper pronunciation and appropriate pacing.

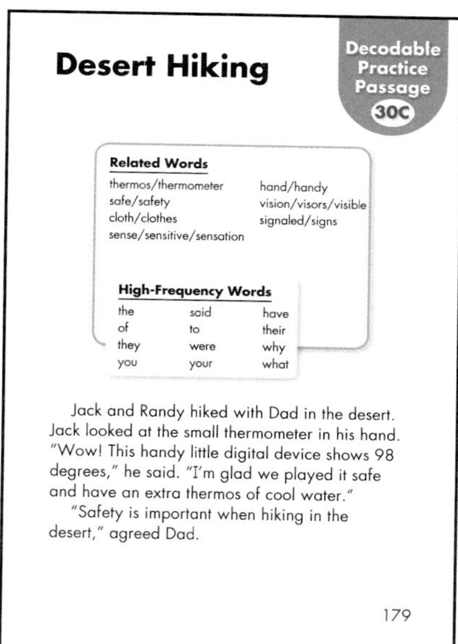

Desert Hiking

Decodable Practice Passage 30C

Related Words

thermos/thermometer
safe/safety
cloth/clothes
sense/sensitive/sensation
hand/handy
vision/visors/visible
signaled/signs

High-Frequency Words

the	said	have
of	to	their
they	were	why
you	your	what

Jack and Randy hiked with Dad in the desert. Jack looked at the small thermometer in his hand. "Wow! This handy little digital device shows 98 degrees," he said. "I'm glad we played it safe and have an extra thermos of cool water."

"Safety is important when hiking in the desert," agreed Dad.

179

"Looking at this little thermometer makes me feel even hotter," announced Jack. "I'm going to hide it out of my sight for a while."

Dad and his boys continued on their walk. They were glad they wore visors and sunglasses to protect their vision in the bright sun.

Suddenly Dad signaled the boys to stop and be silent. He pointed to a tiny lizard. The boys looked as the lizard scampered away.

"Hey," said Randy. "That's why we keep seeing signs along this trail with a picture of a lizard. The trail we're on is called Lizard Trail."

"We saw visible proof!" said Jack.

The hikers continued. "Whew," said Jack. "Even in the thin cloth of this hiking shirt, I sense that the temperature has climbed up."

"I feel it too," replied Randy. "My clothes are soaked with sweat. I'm too sensitive to heat. Why don't you check your thermometer, Jack?"

Jack pulled out the thermometer and said, "Great. It shows 75 degrees! That's better."

"What!" exclaimed Dad. "My body has a real sensation of higher heat, not lower."

"Well, that's probably because I hid the thermometer in the thermos of cool water," smiled Jack. "But just seeing this thermometer say 75 degrees makes me feel much cooler!"

180

Decodable Practice Passage 30C

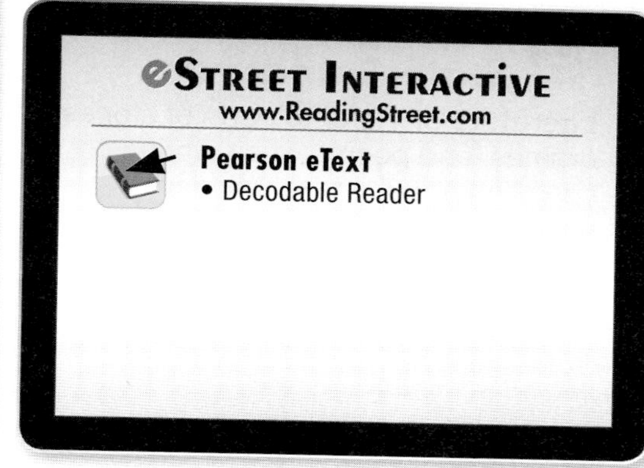

Pearson eText
- Decodable Reader

Access for All

A Advanced

Have students write a story using some of the high-frequency words that are underlined in the sentences on p. 524e.

Common Core State Standards

Literature 5. Refer to parts of stories, dramas, and poems when writing or speaking about a text, using terms such as *chapter, scene,* and *stanza;* describe how each successive part builds on earlier sections.

Bridge to Common Core

KEY IDEAS AND DETAILS

Examining the structure and features of dramas and myths enables students to determine what the text says explicitly and cite textual evidence to support conclusions. By reading the text closely, students can determine the central ideas and summarize key details, making logical inferences about lessons or morals.

Social Studies in Reading

Drama

INTRODUCE Explain to students that what we read is structured differently depending on the author's reasons for writing and what kind of information he or she wishes to convey. Different types of texts are called genres. Tell them that drama is one type of genre.

Discuss with students some of the dramas or plays they have seen and what they were like. Explain to students that many plays were first written as stories. Then ask students: Why might someone turn a story into a play? (Possible response: because people enjoy seeing actors perform a play live on stage) Explain: Any type of story—an adventure, a mystery, or a myth—can be written and performed as a play. But a play has a different structure or form than a story. Let's take a look at the form of a play and decide if a myth could be written as a play.

Display a diagram like the one below. Label the larger circle *Drama* and the smaller one *Myth*. Ask the following questions and add students' answers in the appropriate circle.

- What are the special features of a drama? (a list of characters, a description of the setting, divided into acts and scenes, characters perform the story, dialogue appears as script, dialogue creates plot)
- What are the special features of a myth? (a setting long ago, use of make-believe characters, themes include lessons or morals, fictional explanations for natural occurrences)
- Which features of a myth could be included in a play? (all features)

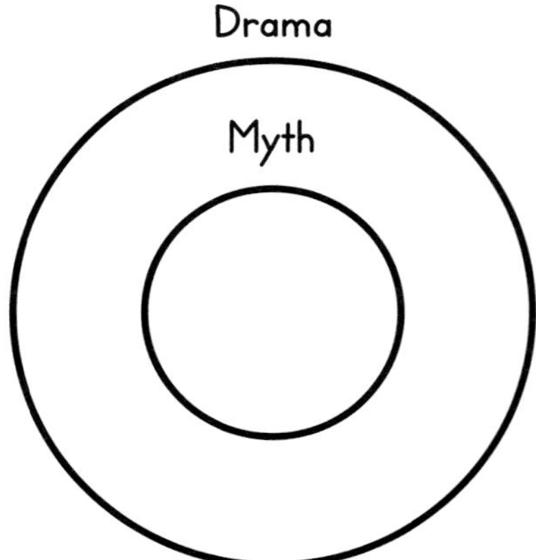

Team Talk Then have students work in small groups to summarize what they have learned about the ways that a myth could be incorporated into a drama.

READ Tell students that they will now read a drama about a prince and a monster. Have the class think about how the drama uses features of myths.

eSTREET INTERACTIVE
www.ReadingStreet.com

Teacher Resources
- Graphic Organizer

Day 4 SMALL GROUP TIME • Differentiate Vocabulary, p. SG•65

OL On-Level
- **Develop** Language Using Amazing Words
- **Read** "The Monster in the Maze"

SI Strategic Intervention
- **Review/Discuss** Amazing Words
- **Read** "The Monster in the Maze"

A Advanced
- **Extend** Amazing Words and Selection Vocabulary
- **Read** "The Monster in the Maze"
- **Organize** Inquiry Project

If... students need more scaffolding and practice with the **Amazing Words,**
then... use the Routine on pp. xxxvi–xxxvii in the *ELL Handbook.*

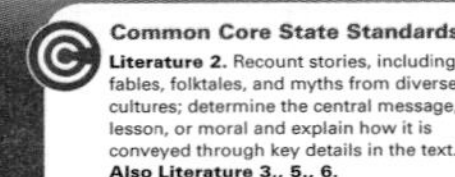

Common Core State Standards
Literature 2. Recount stories, including fables, folktales, and myths from diverse cultures; determine the central message, lesson, or moral and explain how it is conveyed through key details in the text. **Also Literature 3., 5., 6.**

Social Studies in Reading

Genre
Drama

- Plays are a form of drama that use a cast of characters to perform a story.
- Plays use dialogue to create the beginning, middle, and end of plots and to show characters, their relationships, and how they change.
- The narrator tells the story to the audience from the third person (all knowing) or first person (his or her own) point of view.
- As you read and perform the play, think about how the dialogue creates the plot and characters.

The Monster In The Maze

Retold from the Greek Myth

by Walter Kirk

Characters

Theseus (THEE see uhs)
King Minos (MEYE nuhs)
Queen
Ariadne (air ee AD nee)
Guard
Monster

Scene 1

NARRATOR: *The island of Crete, in ancient times. In the great hall, King Minos, a cruel and mean ruler, and his Queen are seated on their thrones. Theseus bows before them. A Guard stands nearby.*

KING: Well, young man?

THESEUS: Great King Minos, I am Theseus, son of Aegeus (i GEE uhs), king of Athens.

KING: I know your father well. I beat him in a war, you know.

THESEUS: Yes, I know.

KING: What are you here for?

THESEUS: I've come to beg you to stop being cruel to our people and set them free.

QUEEN: You should listen to him, Minos.

KING: You don't need to be concerned with this, my queen. *(to Theseus)* And if I don't stop…what?

THESEUS: Why, I'll…I'll…find some way….

KING *(roars with laughter):* You? You're just one little man. Here in my kingdom, I've got all the power.

THESEUS: People in power can afford to be merciful.

KING: Bah! I'll show you what power can do! Guard, take young Theseus's sword. *(The Guard does so.)* Now take him to the maze and lock him in.

GUARD: The maze, Your Majesty?

KING: You heard me. Do it! *(The Guard leads Theseus off.)*

QUEEN: Minos, do reconsider. Why the maze? He'll never make it out.

KING: Well, of course. That's what the maze is for.

QUEEN: But he's a king's son!

Let's Think About...
What do you know about each character so far? What problems are introduced on this page? **Drama**

1

524

525

Student Edition, pp. 524–525

Common Core State Standards

Literature 3. Describe characters in a story (e.g., their traits, motivations, or feelings) and explain how their actions contribute to the sequence of events. **Literature 5.** Refer to parts of stories, dramas, and poems when writing or speaking about a text, using terms such as *chapter, scene,* and *stanza;* describe how each successive part builds on earlier sections. **Also Literature 10., Language 4., 4.a., 4.d.**

Access Text

TEACH Drama Have students preview "The Monster in the Maze" on pp. 524–529. Explain to students that the structure an author uses helps communicate a message. Have them look at the structure of the play and discuss conventions such as speaker tags and stage directions. Then ask: How is the play structure different from the standard story structure?

Corrective feedback	**If...** students are unable to identify differences between the play structure and story structure, **then...** use the model to guide them.

MODEL The first difference I see is the way the characters are introduced. They are listed at the beginning of a play, and they are introduced within a story. Also, there isn't much description of the setting and the action in a play. How do I get that information? (from the characters, from the narrator)

ON THEIR OWN Have pairs of students write a brief conversation between two characters, using the play structure they see in the book.

Close Reading ©

ANALYSIS • TEXT EVIDENCE Reread p. 524. What is the setting of "The Monster in the Maze?" How do you know that? (The setting is the island of Crete a long time ago and the palace of King Minos. The Narrator tells us about the island of Crete and that the king and queen are sitting on their thrones.)

ANALYSIS Write on the board the homograph *bows* from p. 524. Ask volunteers to supply meanings for the word using context clues or a dictionary to clarify meanings and pronunciations. Then ask students what the word means as it is used in the story. (bends head or body as a sign of respect)

Genre

LET'S THINK ABOUT... As you read "The Monster in the Maze," use Let's Think About in the Student Edition to help students focus on the features of a drama.

1 The dialogue between the king and queen shows that the king is evil but the queen doesn't like what the king is doing. Theseus is the son of another king and he cares about his people. The king sends Theseus away to the maze.

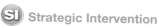

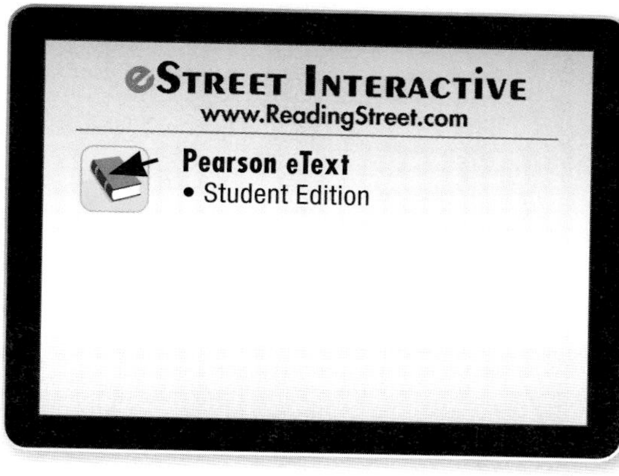

Access for All

 **Strategic Intervention**

Have students work in groups of three or four to read the first two pages of the play. Encourage them to express characterization through the way they speak.

 **Advanced**

Ask small groups to discuss Theseus's statement: *People in power can afford to be merciful*. Also, ask, *Does that statement imply anything about people who are not in power?*

Type Conventions Remind students that ellipses sometimes mean that words have been left out of a statement, and sometimes they indicate a statement that is interrupted or that the speaker is thinking, trying to think of what he or she wants to say. Have students find the ellipses on p. 525 and help them figure out how they are used.

Let's Think About...
Describe the King and Queen and their relationship. What questions would you ask them? **Drama**
2
Let's Think About...
What do you think will happen to Theseus and the people? **Drama**
3
526

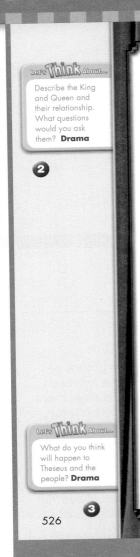

KING: So what? I'm the one who won the war.

QUEEN: So you keep reminding me.

Scene 2

NARRATOR: *The hallway and entrance to the maze. The Guard leads Theseus along.*

THESEUS: What is this maze you're taking me to?

GUARD: Oh, it's a terrible place, terrible place. It's like a gigantic puzzle that you walk through. No one ever escapes.

THESEUS: What happens to them?

GUARD: See, there's a monster who lives there. A horrible beast with the body of a man but the head of a bull.

THESEUS: That's…that's awful!

GUARD: Oh, yeah. Awful enough. That's why they built the maze, just for him. So he couldn't get loose. The maze is so complicated, you see. You can't find your way out. Well, here we are. The maze. In you go. I'd tell you to have a nice day, but you won't. *(He starts to leave.)*

THESEUS: No, wait! At least tell me…. *(But the Guard has gone.)* Well, here I am.

ARIADNE *(whispering from the shadows)*: Theseus! Over here!

THESEUS: What? Who's that? Why, it's a young woman! Who are you?

ARIADNE: I'm Ariadne, King Minos's daughter.

THESEUS: But what are you doing here? Isn't it dangerous?

ARIADNE: I don't think the monster ever found its way this far out. The maze really is complicated. And I'm here to save your life.

THESEUS: But you don't even know me.

ARIADNE: No, but I'm just sick of Father being so terrible to people, just because he's king and wants to show off.

THESEUS: I hear there's a monster.

ARIADNE: Yes. I've never seen him, but I've heard him howling, some nights. But here, I brought you a sword. You can kill the monster.

THESEUS: But what if I get lost in the maze?

ARIADNE: I've thought of that. Here. *(She hands him a ball of string.)*

Let's Think About...
Pretend that you are inviting a friend to the play and she asks you what the play is about. How would you summarize the plot for her so far? **Drama**

4

527

Student Edition, pp. 526–527

Common Core State Standards

Literature 1. Ask and answer questions to demonstrate understanding of a text, referring explicitly to the text as the basis for the answers. **Literature 5.** Refer to parts of stories, dramas, and poems when writing or speaking about a text, using terms such as *chapter, scene,* and *stanza;* describe how each successive part builds on earlier sections. **Also Literature 3., 10.**

Access Text

TEACH Drama On p. 527, we meet another important character in the story, Ariadne. Who is Ariadne and how do you know? (King Minos's daughter; she tells us in her second speech.) What does she think of her father and how do you know? (She thinks he's mean; she tells us in her fourth speech.)

Corrective feedback	**If...** students are unable to describe Ariadne, **then...** use the model to guide them in using dialogue to identify character elements.

Think Aloud **MODEL** Unless the author describes a character in a play, I know I have to find out about the character by what she does or says or by what others say about her. Ariadne tells us who she is when she says: *I'm Ariadne, King Minos's daughter*. Read Theseus's first speech on page 527. What does he say about her? *(Why, it's a young woman!)*

ON THEIR OWN Have pairs of students discuss what they know about the monster so far and have them identify statements to back up their ideas.

Close Reading ©

ANALYSIS Why would Ariadne say her first speech in a whisper? (She doesn't want her father to hear her. She doesn't want anyone to know she is helping Theseus.)

SYNTHESIS Why is Ariadne giving Theseus a ball of string and a sword? (The string will help him find his way back out of the maze. She might be afraid that the monster will try to kill Theseus.) Why does Theseus need to kill the monster? (The monster might kill Theseus if Theseus doesn't kill him first.)

Genre

LET'S THINK ABOUT... features of a drama.

2 The king and queen do not get along. The king does not listen to the queen. I would ask the king, *Why are you so cruel?* and the queen, *What can you do to stop the king from being cruel?*

3 I think that Theseus will slay the monster, defeat the king, and save his people.

4 The play is about a young man, Theseus, who wants King Minos to stop being cruel to his people. The king sends Theseus to the maze where he will be lost forever, and the king's daughter tries secretly to save Theseus.

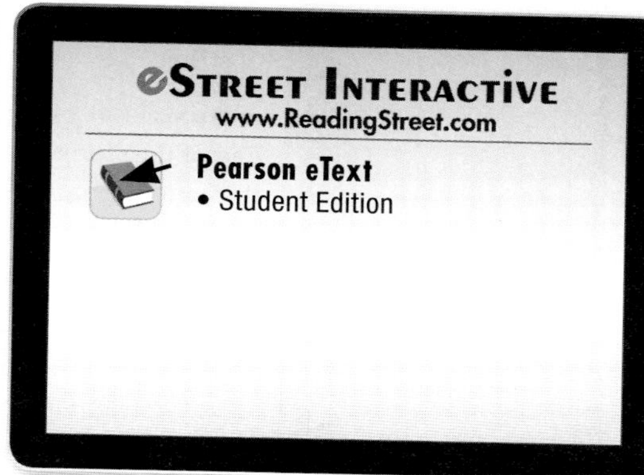

Access for All

 **Strategic Intervention**
Work with students on a graphic organizer that will help them keep track of the characters, the setting, and the elements of the plot.

 **Advanced**
Have students work in pairs to write a scene in which Ariadne tells her mother about helping Theseus.

Cognates Point out the Spanish cognates *complicado (complicated)* and *monstroso (monster)*.

Is the narrator of this play first person or third person? **Drama**

5

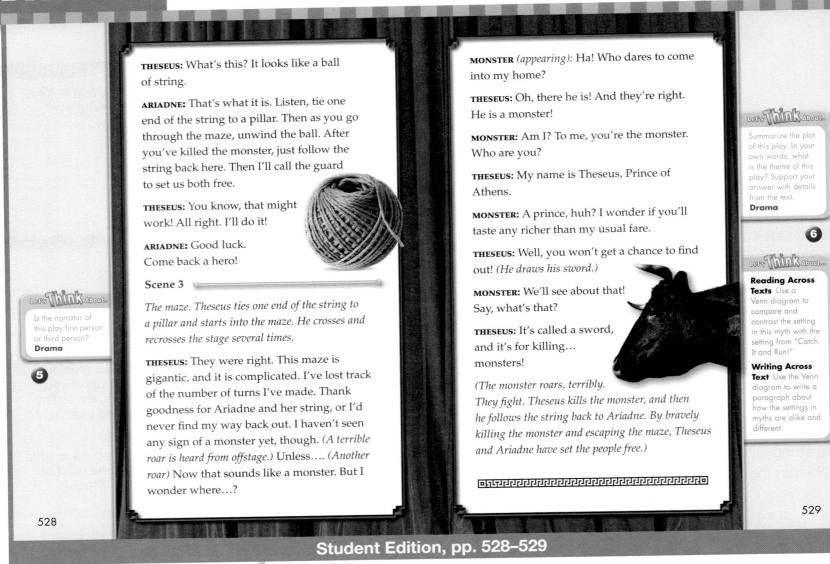

THESEUS: What's this? It looks like a ball of string.

ARIADNE: That's what it is. Listen, tie one end of the string to a pillar. Then as you go through the maze, unwind the ball. After you've killed the monster, just follow the string back here. Then I'll call the guard to set us both free.

THESEUS: You know, that might work! All right. I'll do it!

ARIADNE: Good luck. Come back a hero!

Scene 3

The maze. Theseus ties one end of the string to a pillar and starts into the maze. He crosses and recrosses the stage several times.

THESEUS: They were right. This maze is gigantic, and it is complicated. I've lost track of the number of turns I've made. Thank goodness for Ariadne and her string, or I'd never find my way back out. I haven't seen any sign of a monster yet, though. *(A terrible roar is heard from offstage.)* Unless…. *(Another roar)* Now that sounds like a monster. But I wonder where…?

528

MONSTER *(appearing)*: Ha! Who dares to come into my home?

THESEUS: Oh, there he is! And they're right. He is a monster!

MONSTER: Am I? To me, you're the monster. Who are you?

THESEUS: My name is Theseus, Prince of Athens.

MONSTER: A prince, huh? I wonder if you'll taste any richer than my usual fare.

THESEUS: Well, you won't get a chance to find out! *(He draws his sword.)*

MONSTER: We'll see about that! Say, what's that?

THESEUS: It's called a sword, and it's for killing… monsters!

(The monster roars, terribly. They fight. Theseus kills the monster, and then he follows the string back to Ariadne. By bravely killing the monster and escaping the maze, Theseus and Ariadne have set the people free.)

Let's Think About...

Summarize the plot of this play. In your own words, what is the theme of this play? Support your answer with details from the text. **Drama**

6

Let's Think About...

Reading Across Texts Use a Venn diagram to compare and contrast the setting in this myth with the setting from "Catch It and Run!"

Writing Across Text Use the Venn diagram to write a paragraph about how the settings in myths are alike and different.

529

Student Edition, pp. 528–529

Common Core State Standards

Literature 2. Recount stories, including fables, folktales, and myths from diverse cultures; determine the central message, lesson, or moral and explain how it is conveyed through key details in the text. **Literature 5.** Refer to parts of stories, dramas, and poems when writing or speaking about a text, using terms such as *chapter, scene,* and *stanza;* describe how each successive part builds on earlier sections. **Also Literature 3., 6., 10.**

Access Text

TEACH Drama What steps does Theseus have to take to solve his problem? (He must get through the maze, kill the monster, and get out of the maze.) What is the most exciting part of the story? (when Theseus faces the monster) What happens because Theseus solves his problem? (The people are set free.)

Corrective feedback	**If…** students are unable to identify elements of plot in drama, **then…** use the model to guide them.

Think Aloud **MODEL** I know that a drama has a plot and a story line, and that a plot has a beginning, middle, and end. In the beginning, I find out about the problem Theseus has to solve. The problem moves the story. In the middle, I find out how he solves the problem, and in the end, I find out what happens because he solved the problem.

ON THEIR OWN Have students discuss what they think happened when Theseus and Ariadne went back to King Minos.

Close Reading

ANALYSIS Why does Ariadne wait in the maze for Theseus? (She wants to help him so that he can kill the monster and find his way out of the maze.)

SYNTHESIS What do you know about the monster now that the story is finished? Use dialogue to support your answer. (He's half bull, half man. He lives in the maze. He thinks that he's normal and that Theseus is a monster. The monster tells Theseus this during their dialogue.)

Genre

LET'S THINK ABOUT... features of a drama.

5 The narrator of the play is third person.

6 Theseus visits King Minos to ask him to set his people free. Theseus is sent to the maze by the evil King. Ariadne helps Theseus kill the monster and escape. Then Theseus sets his people free. One theme is that we have to fight our own battles, but we don't always have to do it alone. Sometimes we can have freedom only by fighting for it.

Reading and Writing Across Texts

Have students work together to create lists of setting features for both myths before they begin filling out their Venn diagram. Next, have students write a paragraph about the similarities and differences they found.

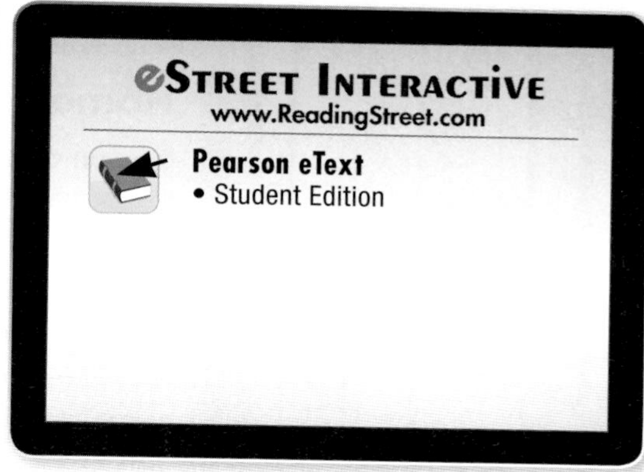

Connect to Social Studies

Greek Coast Crete is an island off the coast of Greece in the Mediterranean Sea. There is evidence that humans have lived on the island from at least 3000 B.C.

Graphic Organizer Provide support to students creating the Venn diagram. Show them how to label the organizer and have them work in groups to think of descriptions of the settings in each myth.

Let's Learn It!

READING STREET ONLINE
ONLINE STUDENT EDITION
www.ReadingStreet.com

Vocabulary

Homographs

Context Clues Homographs are words that are spelled the same, but have different meanings and pronunciations. You will need to use clues in the context of the word to understand which meaning and pronunciation is correct.

Practice It! Using a sheet of paper, write down two different definitions for each of the following homographs: *produce, lead, tear, invalid, moped.* Then write a sentence for each homograph.

Fluency

Expression

When you are reading aloud, change your voice to match the mood of what you are reading. Changing your volume, tone, emotion, and rhythm helps you express the meaning of the story. This makes the story more interesting and understandable.

Practice It! With a partner, read aloud page 516 of *Atlantis.* How should you use expression to make this page sound interesting?

530

Listening and Speaking

Get Ready For Middle School

Work productively with others.

Song

Songs are words sung to music. Songs have rhythm and sometimes rhyme. Their purpose is usually to express emotions or feelings.

Practice It! Look back at *Atlantis: The Legend of a Lost City.* Write a song that tells a story about the lost city of Atlantis. Set your lyrics to music or just speak them to the class. Listen when your classmates speak or sing their lyrics.

Tips

Listening . . .
- Face the speaker.
- Listen attentively to the lyrics.

Speaking . . .
- Have good posture and make eye contact.
- Use expression to show the mood of your song.

Teamwork . . .
- Give suggestions for writing lyrics.
- Build upon the ideas of others.

531

Student Edition, pp. 530–531

Common Core State Standards

Speaking/Listening 6. Speak in complete sentences when appropriate to task and situation in order to provide requested detail or clarification. **Language 4.** Determine or clarify the meaning of unknown and multiple-meaning word and phrases based on grade 3 reading and content, choosing flexibly from a range of strategies. **Language 4.a.** Use sentence-level context as a clue to the meaning of a word or phrase. **Also Foundational Skills 4.b., Speaking/Listening 4., Language 4.d., 5.**

Fluency

Expression

GUIDE PRACTICE Use the Fluency activity as an assessment tool. Make sure the reading passage is at least 200 words long. As students read aloud with partners, walk around to make sure their expression is appropriate.

Don't Wait Until Friday **MONITOR PROGRESS** **Check Fluency**

FORMATIVE ASSESSMENT As students reread, monitor progress toward their individual fluency goals. Current Goal: 110–120 words correct per minute. End-of-Year Goal: 120 words correct per minute.

If... students cannot read fluently at a rate of 110–120 words correct per minute,

then... have students practice with text at their independent levels.

Vocabulary Skill

Homographs

TEACH HOMOGRAPHS • CONTEXT CLUES Write this sentence on the board:

It is dangerous to work with old paints that contain ***lead.***

Point out that the word *lead* has different meanings and pronunciations. The word *lead* can refer to a poisonous, gray-colored metal or it can mean "to show the way." Have students use context clues to determine the meaning of *lead* in this sentence.

GUIDE PRACTICE Have students determine and write down two different definitions for each homograph on p. 530.

ON THEIR OWN Have students use a dictionary to find additional homographs. Then have them write sentences using the two different meanings of the homographs.

Listening and Speaking 

Song

TEACH Tell students that as they say their song lyrics, they should speak clearly and distinctly. Suggest that they speak at a rate that communicates their ideas effectively. If their lyrics rhyme, they should enunciate the rhyming words at the end of each line as well as any other key words. Students should also vary the volume of their speech for effect. Remind students to keep the conventions of grammar and vocabulary in mind as they write and deliver their song lyrics.

GUIDE PRACTICE Be sure students are making eye contact with members of their audience as they speak. Make sure they also use good posture. Remind students in the audience to face the speaker and listen attentively.

ON THEIR OWN Have students present their song lyrics to the class.

Song Lyrics

Remind students to be aware of their body language as they speak. Explain that appropriate hand gestures and facial expressions can enhance a speaker's delivery. They can also help to maintain audience interest and attention. Tell students to avoid behaviors that might be distracting.

Bridge to Common Core

PRESENTATION OF KNOWLEDGE/ IDEAS

As students present their song lyrics, they should use appropriate phrasing and speak at a rate that communicates their ideas effectively. Students should enunciate rhyming words and vary their speech for effect.

Homographs With a small group of students, use the homographs on p. 530 in sentences that reflect two different meanings. Point out the different pronunciations and have students repeat them after you. Ask students to use context clues to determine two different definitions. Have students write the definitions on a sheet of paper.

Common Core State Standards

Writing 2.a. Introduce a topic and group related information together; include illustrations when useful to aiding comprehension. **Language 2.c.** Use commas and quotation marks in dialogue. **Language 2.f.** Use spelling patterns and generalizations (e.g., word families, position-based spellings, syllable patterns, ending rules, meaningful word parts) in writing words. **Also Writing 2., 2.b., 4., 5., 6., 8., 10.**

Research and Inquiry

Step 4 Synthesize

TEACH Have students synthesize their research findings and results. Students should use quotation marks around direct quotations taken from reference texts and interviews. They should paraphrase any other information they use from a source and cite the source. Review how to choose relevant information from a number of sources and organize it logically. Remind students that a journal entry is a record of events and their thoughts about the events. Explain that the entry should be organized so that by the end they reach a logical conclusion.

GUIDE PRACTICE Have students use a word processing program to prepare for their presentations on Day 5. If students are using direct quotes, check to see that they have inserted quotation marks around the exact words. If they are paraphrasing information, check to make sure they have credited the source.

ON THEIR OWN Have students organize and combine information from their research into a journal entry. Remind them to use print and electronic resources to find and check correct spellings.

Conventions

Quotations and Parentheses

TEST PRACTICE Remind students that grammar skills, such as correct usage of quotation marks and parentheses, are often assessed on important tests. Remind students that quotation marks enclose a speaker's exact words and are also used in titles of songs, poems, and short stories. Parentheses enclose extra information.

ON THEIR OWN For additional practice, use *Reader's and Writer's Notebook* p. 439.

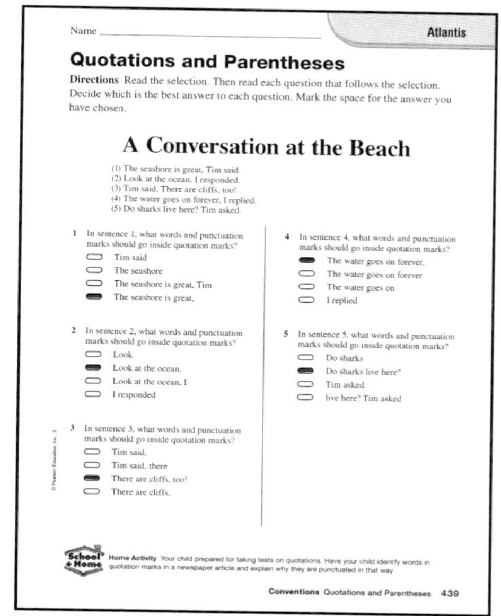

Name ______ Atlantis

Quotations and Parentheses

Directions Read the selection. Then read each question that follows the selection. Decide which is the best answer to each question. Mark the space for the answer you have chosen.

A Conversation at the Beach

(1) The seashore is great, Tim said.
(2) Look at the ocean, I responded.
(3) Tim said, There are cliffs, too!
(4) The water goes on forever, I replied.
(5) Do sharks live here? Tim asked.

1 In sentence 1, what words and punctuation marks should go inside quotation marks?
- Tim said
- The seashore
- The seashore is great, Tim
- The seashore is great,

2 In sentence 2, what words and punctuation marks should go inside quotation marks?
- Look
- Look at the ocean,
- Look at the ocean, I
- I responded

3 In sentence 3, what words and punctuation marks should go inside quotation marks?
- Tim said,
- Tim said, there
- There are cliffs, too!
- There are cliffs,

4 In sentence 4, what words and punctuation marks should go inside quotation marks?
- The water goes on forever,
- The water goes on forever
- The water goes on
- I replied

5 In sentence 5, what words and punctuation marks should go inside quotation marks?
- Do sharks
- Do sharks live here?
- Tim asked.
- live here? Tim asked

School + Home **Home Activity** Your child prepared for taking tests on quotations. Have your child identify words in quotation marks in a newspaper article and explain why they are punctuated in that way.

Conventions Quotations and Parentheses 439

Reader's and Writer's Notebook, p. 439

Spelling

Related Words

PRACTICE SPELLING STRATEGY

Related words have the same root word. For example, *sign, signal,* and *signature* are related. What is the root in each of these words? *(sign) Sign* comes from a Latin word that means "a sign, a symbol, or a mark." Have students identify the roots in the related words on their spelling list.

ON THEIR OWN For additional practice, use *Let's Practice It!* p. 408 on the *Teacher Resources DVD-ROM.*

Name ______ Atlantis

Related Words

Spelling Words				
cloth	clothes	nature	natural	able
ability	mean	meant	deal	dealt
please	pleasant	sign	signal	signature

Riddle Write the missing words. Then use the numbered letters to solve the riddle.

What has eighteen legs and catches flies?

1. You have a ___ smile. p l e a s a n t
2. I like being out in ___. n a t u r e
3. What do you ___? m e a n
4. Are you ___ to sit up? a b l e
5. Will you ___ help? p l e a s e

a baseball team

Hidden Words Each of the list words below contains a shorter list word related in spelling and meaning to the longer word. Circle the short word. Write both words.

6. clothes — 6. cloth, clothes
7. dealt — 7. deal, dealt
8. signature — 8. sign, signature
9. meant — 9. mean, meant
10. signal — 10. sign, signal

School + Home **Home Activity** Your child has been learning to spell related words. Pronounce a list word. Ask your child to name a related word and spell it.

DVD•408 Related Words

Let's Practice It! TR DVD•408

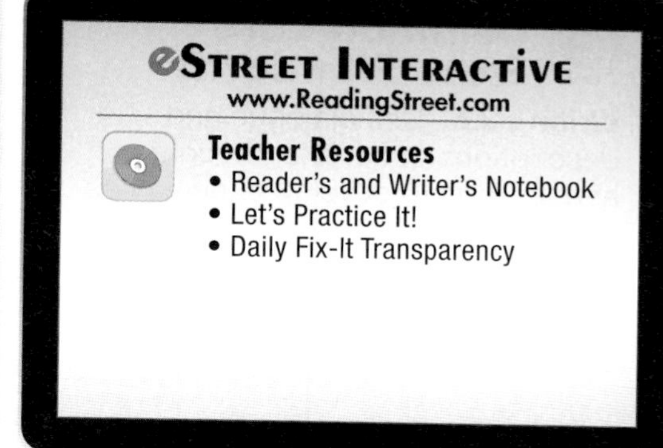

Daily Fix-It

7. Tina said, "I wonder if there are wolfs in the desert. *(wolves; desert.")*
8. Coyotes live in the desert and they are members of the dog family to. *(desert,; too)*

Bridge to Common Core

CONVENTIONS OF STANDARD ENGLISH

As students correctly use quotations and parentheses when writing, they are demonstrating command of the conventions of standard English. Your guidance will help them use correct grammar, usage, and spelling to convey meaning when they speak and write.

Common Core State Standards

Writing 3.b. Use dialogue and descriptions of actions, thoughts, and feelings to develop experiences and events or show the response of characters to situations. **Also Writing 3., 3.a., 4., 10.**

Write Guy *by Jeff Anderson*

Show Off—in a Good Way

Post students' successful sentences or short paragraphs. Celebrate students as writers. Select a sentence of the week, and write it large! Display it as a poster inside or outside the classroom door. Students learn from classmates' successes.

Writing

Historical Fiction

Mini-Lesson Writing for Tests: Historical Figures

- Yesterday we evaluated our test writing sample based on a scoring rubric. Today we will prepare to write in response to another writing prompt.

- Remind students that historical figures often appear in historical fiction. Suggest to students that using a historical figure as a main character is a great way to bring history to life. Abraham Lincoln is a famous president of the United States. What was he like to talk to? What kinds of things did he think about? How did he feel about the Civil War? Why did he make the famous decisions we read about in history books? Write students' responses on the board to create a character sketch of Abraham Lincoln as a character. Then, from the character sketch, have students write a sample paragraph from a story about Lincoln. Write a sample paragraph on the board. Discuss how the details in the sketch were used in the paragraph. Also, as a mechanics reminder, point out your use of correct paragraph indentation and tell students to follow that model when they write.

INTRODUCE NEW PROMPT Direct students to get paper and pencil ready to take a sample writing test. Display the new writing prompt for students. Read the prompt aloud. Tell students to spend some time thinking about the key features of historical fiction before beginning to write. Allow them appropriate time to write to the prompt. Remind students to allow themselves a couple of minutes after writing to reread what they've written and make changes or additions.

Prompt

Write a historical fiction narrative about three people who find a lost treasure.

Routine Quick Write for Fluency

Team Talk

1. **Talk** Pairs discuss the types of details they can use to bring their historical characters to life.
2. **Write** Students write three sentences describing a historical figure's thoughts when he or she made an important decision.
3. **Share** Students read their own sentences aloud. Then partners check each other's sentences for details about an actual historical figure.

Routines Flip Chart

Wrap Up Your Day!

- ✔ **Content Knowledge** Have students discuss the plot of the play.
- ✔ **Oral Vocabulary** Monitor students' use of oral vocabulary as they respond to this question: *Was it right or wrong for Theseus to use violence against the monster? Explain your answer.*
- ✔ **Story Structure** Discuss how the writer built the action to a climax in the play.

Preview DAY 5

Remind students to think about the best ways to keep their freedom.

DAY 5 at a Glance

Content Knowledge

Text-Based Comprehension
Review Generalize

Vocabulary Skill
Review Homographs

Phonics/Word Analysis
Review Related Words

Literary Terms
Review Foreshadowing

Assessment
Fluency
Comprehension

Research and Inquiry
Communicate

Spelling
Related Words

Conventions
Quotations and Parentheses

Writing
Historical Fiction

Materials

- Student Edition
- Weekly Test
- Reader's and Writer's Notebook

Bridge to Common Core

INTEGRATION OF KNOWLEDGE/IDEAS

This week, students have integrated content presented in diverse media and analyzed how different texts address similar topics. They have developed knowledge about the best way to keep their freedom to expand the unit topic of Freedom.

Social Studies Knowledge Goals

Students have learned that keeping freedom means

- defending it
- working together
- having necessary laws

Content Knowledge

Keeping Your Freedom

REVIEW THE CONCEPT Have students look back at the reading selections to find examples that demonstrate the best ways to keep your freedom.

Build Oral Language

REVIEW AMAZING WORDS Display and review this week's concept map. Remind students that this week they have learned nine Amazing Words related to freedom. Have students use the Amazing Words and the concept map to answer the Question of the Week, *What is the best way to keep your freedom?*

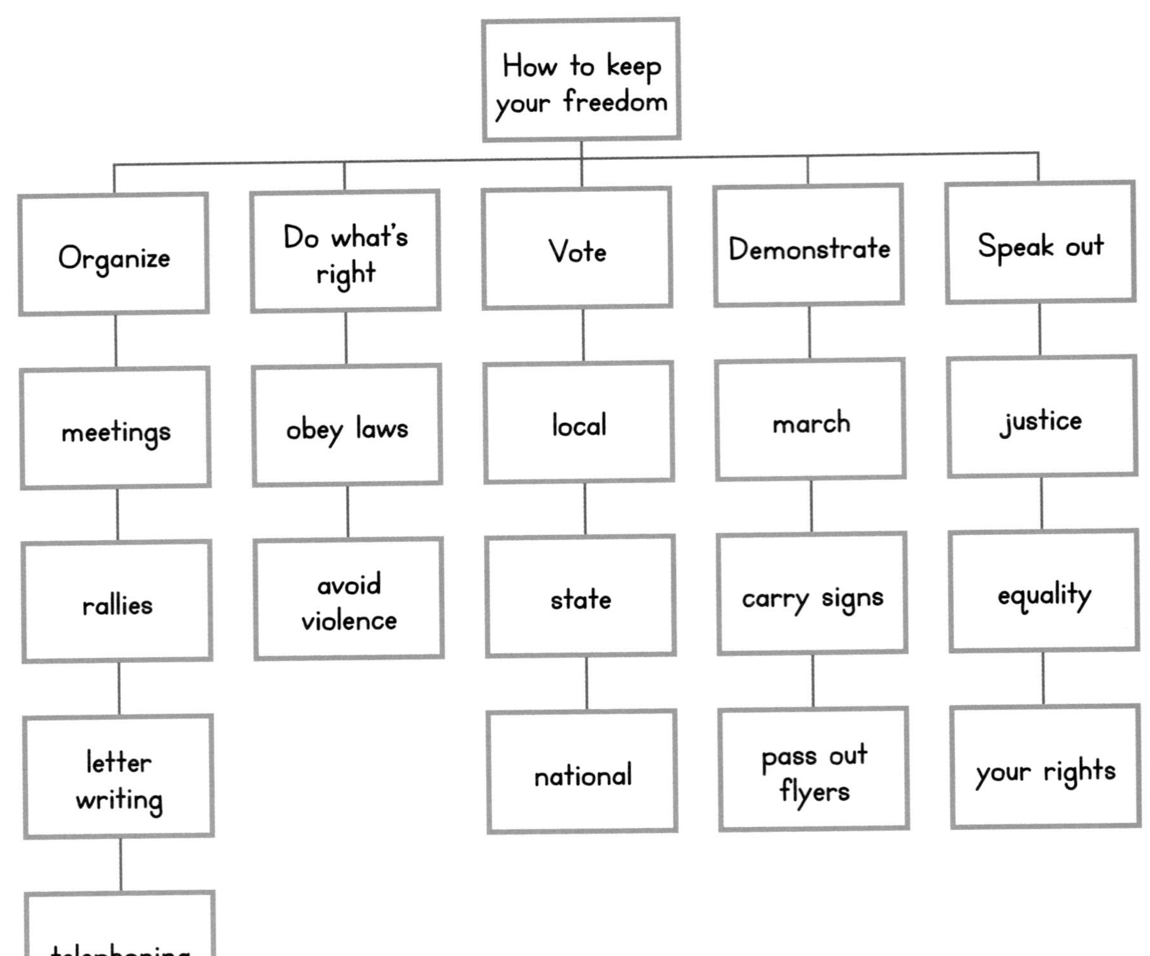

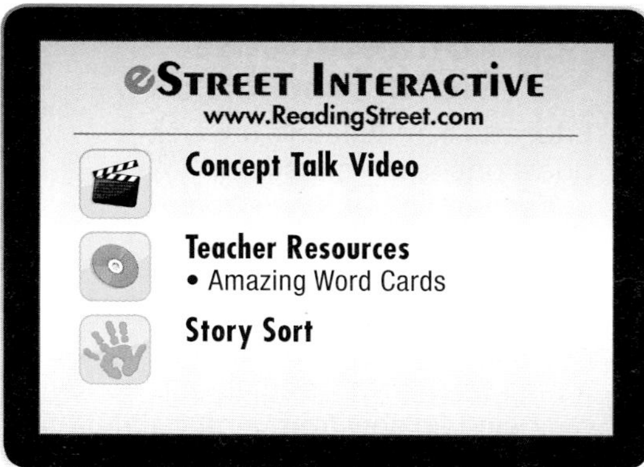

Build Oral Vocabulary

Team Talk **CONNECT TO AMAZING IDEAS** Have pairs of students discuss how the Question of the Week connects to the question for this unit of study: *What does freedom mean?* Tell students to use the concept map and what they have learned from this week's discussions and reading selections to form an Amazing Idea—a realization or "big idea" about Freedom. Remind partners to pose and answer questions with appropriate detail and to give suggestions that build on each other's ideas. Then ask pairs to share their Amazing Ideas with the class.

Amazing Ideas might include these key concepts:

- If we don't continue to defend our freedom, we could lose it.
- We must work together to keep our freedom.
- Laws are necessary to guarantee freedom.

WRITE ABOUT IT Have students write a few sentences about their Amazing Idea, beginning with "This week I learned . . ."

Amazing Words

witty
equality
justice
perish
demonstrate
mourn
blight
wept
violence

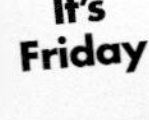

It's Friday

MONITOR PROGRESS Check Oral Vocabulary

FORMATIVE ASSESSMENT Have individuals use this week's Amazing Words to describe ways to keep your freedom. Monitor students' abilities to use the Amazing Words, and note which words you need to reteach.

If... students have difficulty using the Amazing Words,

then... reteach using the Oral Vocabuary Routine, pp. 495a, 500b, 512b, 524b, OV•5.

Check Concepts and Language Use the Day 5 instruction on ELL Poster 30 to monitor students' understanding of the lesson concept.

Common Core State Standards

Literature 1. Ask and answer questions to demonstrate understanding of a text, referring explicitly to the text as the basis for the answers. **Language 4.** Determine or clarify the meaning of unknown and multiple-meaning words and phrases based on grade 3 reading and content, choosing flexibly from a range of strategies. **Also Foundational Skills 3., Language 3., 4.a., 5.**

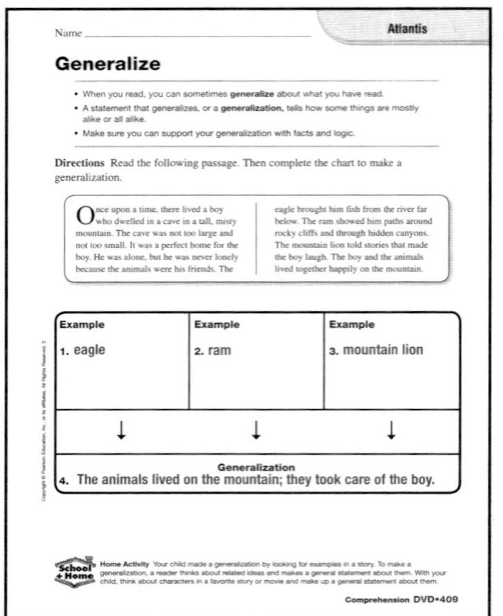

Name ______ **Atlantis**

Generalize

- When you read, you can sometimes **generalize** about what you have read.
- A statement that generalizes, or a **generalization,** tells how some things are mostly alike or all alike.
- Make sure you can support your generalization with facts and logic.

Directions Read the following passage. Then complete the chart to make a generalization.

Once upon a time, there lived a boy who dwelled in a cave in a tall, misty mountain. The cave was not too large and not too small. It was a perfect home for the boy. He was alone, but he was never lonely because the animals were his friends. The eagle brought him fish from the river far below. The ram showed him paths around rocky cliffs and through hidden canyons. The mountain lion told stories that made the boy laugh. The boy and the animals lived together happily on the mountain.

Example	Example	Example
1. eagle	2. ram	3. mountain lion
↓	↓	↓

Generalization

4. The animals lived on the mountain; they took care of the boy.

School + Home **Home Activity** Your child made a generalization by looking for examples in a story. To make a generalization, a reader thinks about related ideas and makes a general statement about them. With your child, think about characters in a favorite story or movie and make up a general statement about them.

Comprehension DVD•409

Let's Practice It! TR DVD•409

Selection Vocabulary

aqueducts channels for carrying water long distances

content satisfied

crouched stooped or bent down

guidance the act or process of guiding, or leading

honor treat with great respect; an expression of respect or affection

pillar an upright support for a building

thermal causing heat or warmth

Text-Based Comprehension

Review Generalize

TEACH Review the definition of *generalize*. Remind students that a generalization tells what some things have in common. Generalizations often contain clue words, such as *all, many, everyone,* and *never*. Remind students that they can use what they know about a topic to help them make a generalization. For additional support, have students review p. EI•8 on generalize.

GUIDE PRACTICE Have pairs find an example of a generalization in *Atlantis*. Then have them tell if the generalization they found is well supported in the passage.

ON THEIR OWN For additional practice with generalize, use *Let's Practice It!* page 409 on the *Teacher Resources DVD-ROM*.

Vocabulary Skill

Review Homographs

TEACH Remind students to use context clues to help them understand which meaning and pronunciation of a homograph should be used in a sentence.

GUIDE PRACTICE Review with students the two meanings and pronunciations of the word *content*. Help them determine which meaning and pronunciation should be used in the following sentence: *The family's puppy was not content to stay home*.

ON THEIR OWN Have students work with partners to write context sentences using the two different meanings and pronunciations of the homograph *content*. Partners can trade sentences and identify the context clues that help them determine which meaning and pronunciation to use.

Word Analysis

Review Related Words

TEACH Write the following sentences on the board. Have students read each one, first quietly to themselves and then aloud as you track the print.

1. **We will dine at a special place for my birthday dinner.**
2. **I crumbled the cracker into tiny crumbs.**
3. **The goalie has to keep the ball out of the goal.**
4. **The town historian studies our town's history.**
5. **It is natural for a science teacher to like nature.**

Team Talk Have students work with a partner to list the related words in the sentences. Also ask them to identify the common word parts. Then call on individuals to share with the class.

Literary Terms

Review Foreshadowing

TEACH Remind students that foreshadowing is the use of hints and clues about what will happen later in a story.

GUIDE PRACTICE Find an example of foreshadowing from p. 512 of *Atlantis: The Legend of a Lost City*. Discuss how the author uses foreshadowing and the impact it has on the story. Have students find other examples of foreshadowing from the selection and discuss.

ON THEIR OWN Have students list the examples of foreshadowing from the selection.

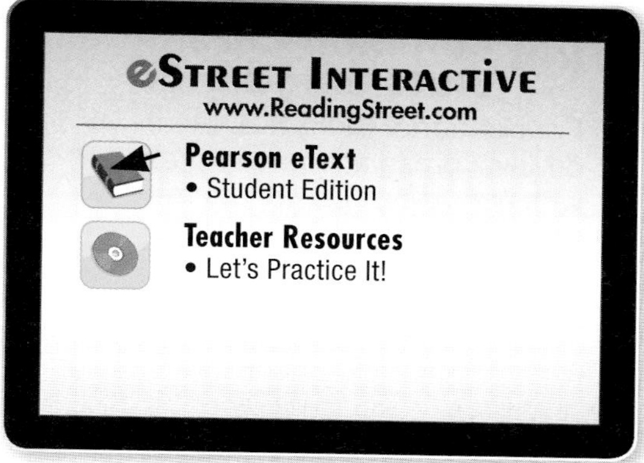

Generalize Read aloud p. 508 and the last paragraph of p. 509 of *Atlantis* to a small group of students as they follow along in their books. Tell them to look for a word that signals a generalization as you read. *(all)* Review other words that signal generalizations. *(most, some, many,* etc.*)*

Common Core State Standards

Foundational Skills 4.b. Read on-level prose and poetry orally with accuracy, appropriate rate, and expression on successive readings. **Also Foundational Skills 4., 4.a.**

Plan to Assess Fluency

- ☐ **Week 1** Advanced
- ☐ **Week 2** Strategic Intervention
- ☐ **Week 3** On-Level
- ☐ **Week 4** Strategic Intervention
- ☑ **This week assess any students you have not yet checked during this unit.**

Set individual goals for students to enable them to reach the year-end goal.

- Current Goal: 110–120 WCPM
- Year-End Goal: 120 WCPM

Assessment

Monitor Progress

FLUENCY Make two copies of the fluency passage on p. 531k. As the student reads the text aloud, mark mistakes on your copy. Also mark where the student is at the end of one minute. To figure words correct per minute (WCPM), subtract the number of mistakes from the total number of words read in one minute.

RATE

Corrective feedback

If... students cannot read fluently at a rate of 110–120 WCPM,
then... make sure they practice with text at their independent reading level. Provide additional fluency practice by pairing nonfluent readers with fluent readers.

If... students already read at 120 WCPM,
then... have them read a book of their choice independently.

ELL

If... students need more scaffolding and practice with **Conventions and Writing,**
then... use the activities on pp. DI•124–DI•125 in the Teacher Resources section on SuccessNet.

Day 5 SMALL GROUP TIME • Differentiate Reteaching, p. SG•65

OL On-Level
- **Practice** Quotations and Parentheses
- **Reread** *Reading Street Sleuth,* pp. 76–77

SI Strategic Intervention
- **Review** Quotations and Parentheses
- **Reread** *Reading Street Sleuth,* pp. 76–77

A Advanced
- **Extend** Quotations and Parentheses
- **Reread** *Reading Street Sleuth,* pp. 76–77
- **Communicate** Inquiry Project

Name ____________________

Liz's Great-Grandfather

Liz sat and watched TV with Gramps, her great-grandfather. He 10
had lived a long time and now needed help doing simple things like 23
getting dressed or eating. He felt bad about that, yet didn't complain. 35
He always said, "In my life, I've seen worse days." 45

Liz and Gramps watched a television program about World 54
War II. When Gramps was a young adult, he was a soldier and 67
fought in that war. Even now, Gramps didn't enjoy talking about it, 79
but Liz knew that he had survived many tough battles. 89

Now the program showed a battle. A voice on TV explained how 101
horrible the battle was and why it was so important in history. Gramps 114
pointed to the TV and said, "I was there." 123

Liz watched the program closely. She didn't understand all of it. 134
Still she could tell that the battle was terrible. Liz thought about how 147
Gramps always said, "I've seen worse days." She knew now that 158
those days were during the war. 164

As the program ended, the voice on TV said that the battle helped 177
America win the war. It helped keep Americans free. Liz looked at 189
Gramps. He had tears in his eyes. So did she. 199

MONITOR PROGRESS

- **Check Fluency**

Assessment

Common Core State Standards

Literature 1. Ask and answer questions to demonstrate understanding of a text, referring explicitly to the text as the basis for the answers.

Monitor Progress

For a written assessment of Related Words, Generalization, and Selection Vocabulary, use Weekly Test 30, pp. 175–180.

GENERALIZE Use "A History Mystery" on p. 531m to check students' understanding of generalizations.

1. What is the mystery surrounding Molly Pitcher? (Some people believe that Mary Hays may not have been Molly Pitcher. There's a mystery surrounding the true identity of Molly Pitcher.)

2. Which sentence in paragraph 2 is a generalization? How do you know? (*Many Americans thought battling for that freedom was worth the risk*. This generalization has the clue word *many* and makes a broad statement that applies to Americans.)

3. Is this sentence a generalization? *Molly Pitcher carried water to cool off cannons during battle*. How do you know? (No; it is a fact about Molly.)

Corrective feedback	**If...** students are unable to answer the comprehension questions, **then...** use the Reteach lesson in *First Stop*.

Name ____________________

A History Mystery

Sometimes history is a mystery! Take, for example, the famous story of Molly Pitcher. She was known as a Revolutionary War hero, but who was she really?

In the Revolutionary War, American colonies fought against Great Britain. America didn't have a big army, but Great Britain did. Could America win the war and become an independent country? Many Americans thought battling for that freedom was worth the risk.

In those days, only men were allowed to be soldiers. Women wanted to fight but were denied the opportunity. Some women did heroic things anyway. Molly Pitcher was certainly one of those women.

Molly Pitcher's husband was a soldier in charge of a huge gun called a cannon. In battles, cannons fire shell after shell. They would get so hot! They had to be cooled off. Molly Pitcher carried water to cool off cannons during battle. That was dangerous work!

During one battle, Molly Pitcher's husband was wounded. He couldn't fire his cannon. So Molly Pitcher did. She helped the American soldiers. She became a hero.

Here's the mystery. The wounded soldier's name was William Hays, and his wife's name was Mary. Where did Molly Pitcher come from? Molly was a nickname for Mary. And Mary carried pitchers of water to cool cannons. So Mary Hays became Molly Pitcher.

Some people say that Mary Hays wasn't Molly Pitcher. Several other women might have been Molly Pitcher. Which one? That's the mystery. But this isn't: Many women helped America win the Revolutionary War!

MONITOR PROGRESS

- **Generalize**

Research and Inquiry

Step 5 Communicate

PRESENT IDEAS Have students share their inquiry results by presenting their information and giving a brief talk on their research. Have students read aloud any quotes they collected on Day 3.

SPEAKING Remind students how to be good speakers and how to communicate effectively with their audience.

- Respond to relevant questions with appropriate details.
- Speak clearly and loudly.
- Speak at a natural pace.
- Keep eye contact with audience members.
- Use the conventions of language to communicate ideas effectively.

LISTENING Review with students these tips for being a good listener.

- Listen attentively to speakers.
- Wait until the speaker has finished before raising your hand to ask a relevant question.
- Make pertinent comments.
- Be polite, even if you disagree.

LISTEN TO IDEAS Have students listen attentively to the various quotes their classmates collected. Have them make pertinent comments, closely related to the topic.

Common Core State Standards

Speaking/Listening 4. Report on a topic or text, tell a story, or recount an experience with appropriate facts and relevant, descriptive details, speaking clearly at an understandable pace. **Language 2.c.** Use commas and quotation marks in dialogue. **Language 2.f.** Use spelling patterns and generalizations (e.g., word families, position-based spellings, syllable patterns, ending rules, meaningful word parts) in writing words. **Also Speaking/ Listening 1., 1.a., 1.b., 1.c., 3., 6.**

Spelling Test

Related Words

To administer the spelling test, refer to the directions, words, and sentences on p. 499c.

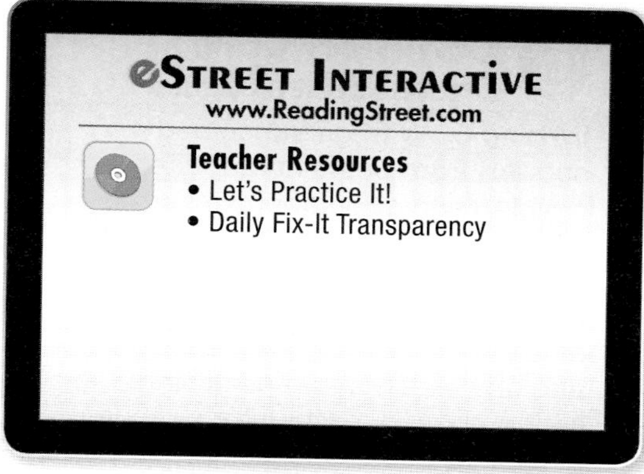

Conventions

Quotations and Parentheses

MORE PRACTICE Remind students that quotation marks enclose a speaker's exact words and are also used with titles of songs, poems, and stories. Remind them that parentheses enclose extra information.

GUIDE PRACTICE Write the following sentences on the board. Have the class tell you whether the sentences are punctuated correctly.

Vince cried "Help me"!

(incorrect; should be *Vince cried, "Help me!"*)

There are two planets)Mars and Jupiter(between Earth and Saturn.

(incorrect: should be *There are two planets (Mars and Jupiter) between Earth and Saturn.)*

ON THEIR OWN Write these sentences on the board. Have students fill in the blanks with their own words. Students should complete *Let's Practice It!* p. 410 on the *Teacher Resources DVD-ROM*.

1. **"Where's my _______?" asked Juan.**
2. **The class sang the song "_______."**
3. **"There are too many people here," said _______.**
4. **My parents had a few names in mind (_______, _______, and _______) for my new little sister.**
5. **The store sold many different types of rock music (for example, _______ and _______).**

Daily Fix-It

9. Coyotes, wolves and foxs are all members of the dog family. *(wolves,; foxes)*
10. Chris and him hear coyotes howling in the desert in july. *(he; July)*

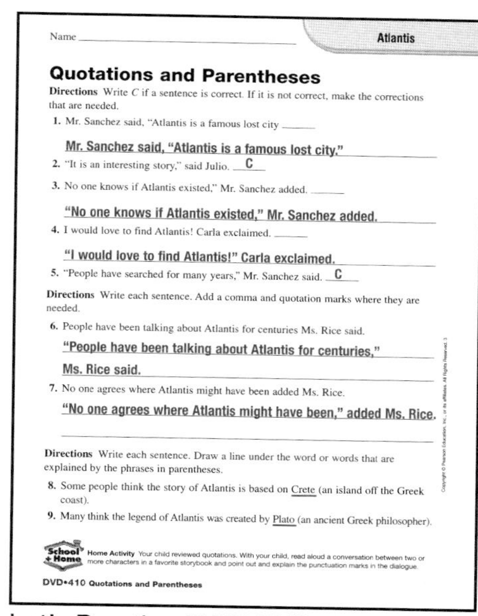
Name ______________ Atlantis

Quotations and Parentheses

Directions Write *C* if a sentence is correct. If it is not correct, make the corrections that are needed.

1. Mr. Sanchez said, "Atlantis is a famous lost city ______
   Mr. Sanchez said, "Atlantis is a famous lost city."
2. "It is an interesting story," said Julio. **C**
3. No one knows if Atlantis existed," Mr. Sanchez added. ______
   "No one knows if Atlantis existed," Mr. Sanchez added.
4. I would love to find Atlantis! Carla exclaimed. ______
   "I would love to find Atlantis!" Carla exclaimed.
5. "People have searched for many years," Mr. Sanchez said. **C**

Directions Write each sentence. Add a comma and quotation marks where they are needed.

6. People have been talking about Atlantis for centuries Ms. Rice said.
   "People have been talking about Atlantis for centuries," Ms. Rice said.
7. No one agrees where Atlantis might have been added Ms. Rice.
   "No one agrees where Atlantis might have been," added Ms. Rice.

Directions Write each sentence. Draw a line under the word or words that are explained by the phrases in parentheses.

8. Some people think the story of Atlantis is based on Crete (an island off the Greek coast).
9. Many think the legend of Atlantis was created by Plato (an ancient Greek philosopher).

School + Home **Home Activity** Your child reviewed quotations. With your child, read aloud a conversation between two or more characters in a favorite storybook and point out and explain the punctuation marks in the dialogue.

DVD•410 Quotations and Parentheses

Let's Practice It! TR DVD•410

Common Core State Standards

Writing 5. With guidance and support from peers and adults, develop and strengthen writing as needed by planning, revising, and editing. **Writing 10.** Write routinely over extended time frames (time for research, reflection, and revision) and shorter time frames (a single sitting or a day or two) for a range of discipline-specific tasks, purposes, and audiences. **Language 2.g.** Consult reference materials, including beginning dictionaries, as needed to check and correct spellings. **Also Writing 3., 3.d., 4.**

Teacher Note

Writing Self-Evaluation Make copies of the Writing Self-Evaluation Guide on p. 39 of the *Reader's and Writer's Notebook* and hand out to students.

Bridge to Common Core

PRODUCTION AND DISTRIBUTION OF WRITING

Throughout the week, students developed writing in which organization and style were appropriate to the task, purpose, and audience. Given opportunities to practice writing for shorter time frames, students expand their range and ability of writing.

Writing

Historical Fiction

REVIEW Remind students that yesterday they learned more about how to write about historical figures. Then they wrote to another prompt. Today they will evaluate their second writing sample.

Mini-Lesson Writing for Tests: Revise

- When we revise, we read through our work, looking for places where we can make our writing clearer and more interesting. We want to revise our writing before we turn in our test. We might find places in our writing that can be improved. Today we will focus on revising our concluding statements.

- Remind students that a concluding statement is the final sentence or group of sentences in a composition. The concluding statement often makes a final point. For example, in "A Wonderful Flight," the concluding statement was a surprising comment by Leonardo da Vinci. The main character expected da Vinci to be angry, but the scientist was actually amused. This kind of concluding statement can amuse the reader and help him or her remember your story. Can you end your historical fiction with a joke or other surprising statement?

DISPLAY Display the following Revising Tips for students.

Revising Tips

- ✔ Review writing to make sure that it is clear and engaging.
- ✔ Review the concluding statement to see if you can make it memorable in some way to the reader.
- ✔ Use a dictionary to check spelling.

EVALUATE Have students spend a few minutes editing and revising the sample test writing they wrote on Day 4, paying particular attention to the concluding statement. When students have finished editing in the allotted time, have them use the Scoring Rubric from their *Reader's and Writer's Notebook,* p. 435, that they used on Day 3. This time they should use it to evaluate the sample test writing they just revised.

Routine Quick Write for Fluency **Team Talk**

1. **Talk** Pairs discuss what they learned about historical fiction.
2. **Write** Students write three sentences explaining what they learned about writing historical fiction.
3. **Share** Students read their sentences to their partners.

Routines Flip Chart

Wrap Up Your Week!

Keeping Your Freedom

What is the best way to keep your freedom?

In *Atlantis* and "The Monster in the Maze," we learned about how people in legends and myths kept their freedom.

Team Talk Have students recall their Amazing Ideas about freedom. Then have students use these ideas to help them demonstrate their understanding of the Question of the Week.

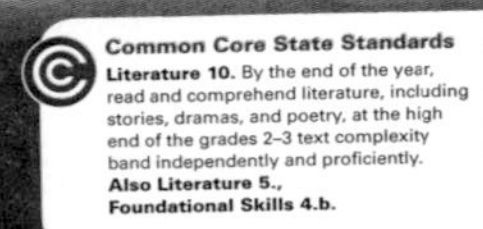

Common Core State Standards
Literature 10. By the end of the year, read and comprehend literature, including stories, dramas, and poetry, at the high end of the grades 2–3 text complexity band independently and proficiently. **Also Literature 5., Foundational Skills 4.b.**

Poetry

- **Free verse poems** have little or no **rhyme** or regular **rhythm,** but they can use many comparisons and sensory words. In some free verse poems, the lines do not start with a capital letter.
- **Imagery** is one of the most important elements of any kind of poem. Sensory words help you to see, hear, feel, taste, or smell in your mind what is being described.
- **Lyrical poems** usually rhyme and use **cadence**, or rhythm that repeats itself. Lyrical poems have the form and musical quality of a song. (The words to songs are called "lyrics.")

532

Words Free as Confetti

by Pat Mora

Come, words, come in your every color.
I'll toss you in storm or breeze.
I'll say, say, say you,
taste you sweet as plump plums,
bitter as old lemons.
I'll sniff you, words, warm
as almonds or tart as apple-red,
feel you green
and soft as new grass,
lightwhite as dandelion plumes,
or thorngray as cactus,
heavy as black cement,
cold as blue icicles,
warm as *abuelita's* yellowlap.
I'll hear you, words, loud as searoar's
purple crash, hushed
as *gatitos* curled in sleep,
as the last goldlullaby.

I'll see you long and dark as tunnels,
bright as rainbows,
playful as chestnutwind.
I'll watch you, words,
rise and dance and spin.
I'll say, say, say you
in English,
in Spanish,
I'll find you.
Hold you.
Toss you.
I'm free too.
I say *yo soy libre,*
I am free
free, free,
free as confetti.

Let's Think About...
Is "Words Free as Confetti" a **free verse** poem or a **lyrical** poem? How do you know? 1

Let's Think About...
Why do you think "Words Free as Confetti" uses both English and Spanish to create **imagery**? 2

Let's Think About...
Identify examples of sensory language for all five senses. What comparisons create graphic visual images for you? 3

533

Student Edition, pp. 532–533

Common Core State Standards

Literature 10. By the end of the year, read and comprehend literature, including stories, dramas, and poetry, at the high end of the grades 2–3 text complexity band independently and proficiently. **Also Literature 5., Foundational Skills 4.b.**

Academic Vocabulary

free verse poems poems with little or no rhyme or regular rhythm

Poetry

Free Verse Poems

TEACH Review the definition of free verse poems on p. 532. Remind students that free verse poems have little or no rhyme and that the rhythm is similar to the way people talk. Point out that writers use comparisons and sensory words in free verse poems. Explain that unlike most poems, the first word in each line does not always begin with a capital letter.

GUIDE PRACTICE Read aloud the first five lines of the poem. Ask students how this poem is different from many poems they have heard. Then ask students: Do you think a free verse poem would be easier or harder to write than another kind of poem? Why or why not?

ON THEIR OWN Remind students that free verse poems use comparisons. Point out that some comparisons use the word *as.* Have partners find examples of comparisons in the poem. Have them tell how each example creates a picture in their mind.

Imagery

TEACH Review the definition of imagery on p. 532. Remind students that writers use imagery to help readers form pictures in their minds. When readers can see, hear, feel, taste, smell, and touch the image in their minds, they get a clearer understanding of what is happening.

GUIDE Ask students to find examples in the poem that tell how the writer thinks things look, taste, smell, feel, and sound.

ON THEIR OWN Have students write how they think different images in the poem look, taste, smell, feel, or sound.

Let's Think About...

1 The poem is a free verse poem. It has no rhyme or regular rhythm and many lines do not start with a capital letter.

2 The author uses both English and Spanish to show that words in every language are wonderful. There is a different cadence to Spanish words that adds interest to the poem.

3 **sight:** *plump, green, long, dark, bright;* **taste:** *sweet, bitter, tart;* **smell:** *sniff;* **touch:** *soft, heavy, cold, warm;* **sound:** *loud, crash, hushed*. Graphic visual images are created for me by the phrases *bitter as old lemons, soft as new grass, hushed as* gatitos *curled in sleep,* and *bright as rainbows*.

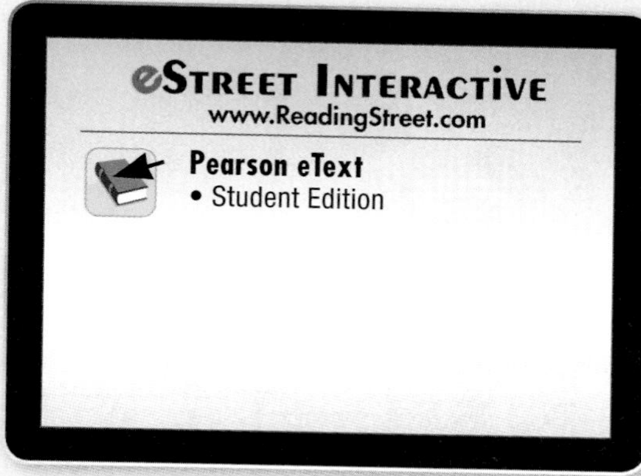

Academic Vocabulary

imagery the use of words that help the reader experience the way things look, sound, smell, taste, or feel

Access for All

 Strategic Intervention

Create a five-column chart with the heads *See, Hear, Feel, Taste,* and *Smell*. Ask students to name sensory words that belong in each column. Discuss how each word creates a picture in the mind.

 Advanced

Explain that authors sometimes invent, or make up, words to express certain ideas. Point out the words *thorngray, yellowlap, searoar, goldlullaby,* and *chestnutwind* in the poem. Ask students what they think the words mean. Then have students write invented words of their own.

Multilingual Vocabulary Write the words *abuelita's, gatitos,* and *yo soy libre* on a chart. Ask Spanish speakers to read the words aloud and tell what they mean. Write the meanings on the chart. Reread the lines of the poem in which these words occur. Ask volunteers to substitute the English word for its Spanish counterpart.

The Star-Spangled Banner

by Francis Scott Key

Oh say, can you see, by the dawn's
early light,
What so proudly we hailed at the twilight's
last gleaming—
Whose broad stripes and bright stars,
through the perilous fight,
O'er the ramparts we watched were so
gallantly streaming!
And the rocket's red glare, the bombs
bursting in air,
Gave proof through the night that our flag
was still there;
Oh! say, does that star-spangled banner
yet wave
O'er the land of the free, and the home
of the brave!

534

I Watched an Eagle Soar

by Virginia Driving Hawk Sneve

Grandmother,
I watched an eagle soar
high in the sky
until a cloud covered him up.
Grandmother,
I still saw the eagle
behind my eyes.

535

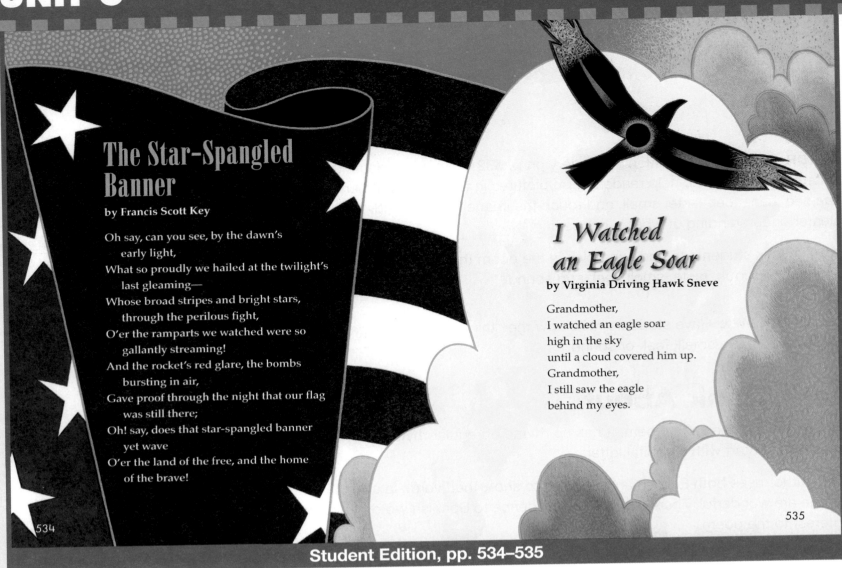

Student Edition, pp. 534–535

Common Core State Standards

Literature 10. By the end of the year, read and comprehend literature, including stories, dramas, and poetry, at the high end of the grades 2–3 text complexity band independently and proficiently. **Also Literature 5., Foundational Skills 4.b.**

Poetry

Lyrical Poems

TEACH Review the definition of lyrical poems on p. 532. Tell students that unlike free verse poems, lyrical poems rhyme and have cadence, a beat that repeats itself line after line. Lyrical poems often describe things and might sound like a song. Write *lyrical* and *lyrics* on the board and compare the words. Ask students to define the word *lyrics*.

GUIDE PRACTICE Point out that the lyrical poem "The Star-Spangled Banner" is also the first verse of a famous song—our national anthem. Tell students that you will read the poem rather than sing it. Have students listen for the rhyming words and the rhythm of the poem. Have them clap for each accented syllable. Then have students describe the characteristics of the poem.

ON THEIR OWN Point out that all the poems in this unit have to do with freedom. Have students write a pair of lines about a freedom they cherish. Tell students to include rhyme and rhythm.

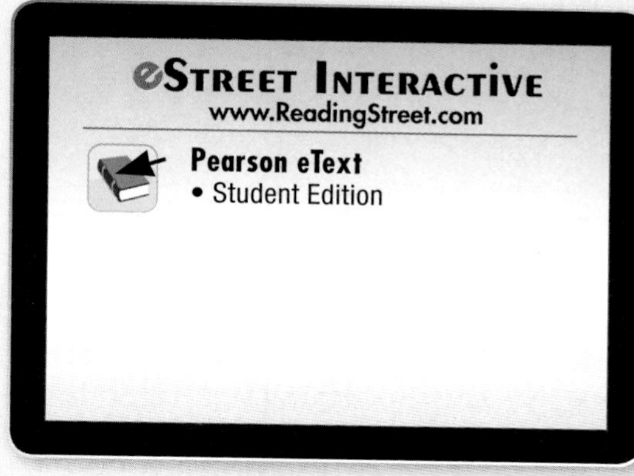

Close Reading

ANALYSIS Why do you think the title of the poem is "The Star-Spangled Banner"? What does the flag represent? (*Banner* is another way to say *flag*. Our flag has stars, so it is "star-spangled." The flag represents courage and freedom.)

EVALUATION In "The Star-Spangled Banner," what does the poet describe that you can picture in your mind? (the flag at night; the battle; the flag still waving in the morning)

ANALYSIS What makes "I Watched an Eagle Soar," a free verse poem? (It does not rhyme or have a regular rhythm. Some of the lines do not begin with a capital letter.)

Practice Fluent Reading

EXPRESSION Have students take turns reading "I Watched an Eagle Soar" in groups of three of four. As they read, have students imagine they are addressing an important adult in their lives. Encourage them to use a tone that is both respectful and excited.

Writing Poetry

Explain to students that an *anthem* is a song of praise or tribute. Then have students work in groups to write their own poetic tribute to the American flag. Tell students to include rhyme and meter in their writing. Allow students to illustrate their poems and display them in the classroom.

Access for All

SI Strategic Intervention

Provide students with the words to another song about freedom, such as "My Country 'Tis of Thee." Read the words aloud and discuss why the song could be considered a lyrical poem. Have students identify the rhyming words and the rhythm of the song.

A Advanced

Tell students that a symbol is a person, place, event, or object that has a meaning in itself but suggests other meanings as well. Remind students that "The Star-Spangled Banner" and "I Watched an Eagle Soar" are both about American symbols. Have students brainstorm other American symbols. Then have them choose one symbol to learn more about. Have students write a short poem about it.

Imagery Display an American flag or a picture of one. On the board, begin a concept map with *American flag* in the middle circle. Ask students to name words that describe the flag. Add the words to the map. Discuss with students how each word helps them "see" the flag.

Assessment Checkpoints for the Week

Weekly Assessment

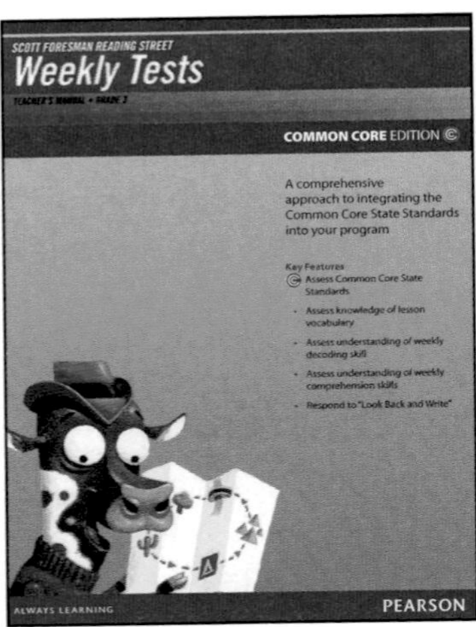

Weekly Tests

Use pp. 175–180 of *Weekly Tests* to check:

- ✔ **Phonics/Word Analysis** Related Words
- ✔ **Comprehension** Generalize
- ✔ Review **Comprehension** Literary Elements: Plot and Theme
- ✔ **Selection Vocabulary**

aqueducts	**crouched**	**honor**	**thermal**
content	**guidance**	**pillar**	

Differentiated Assessment

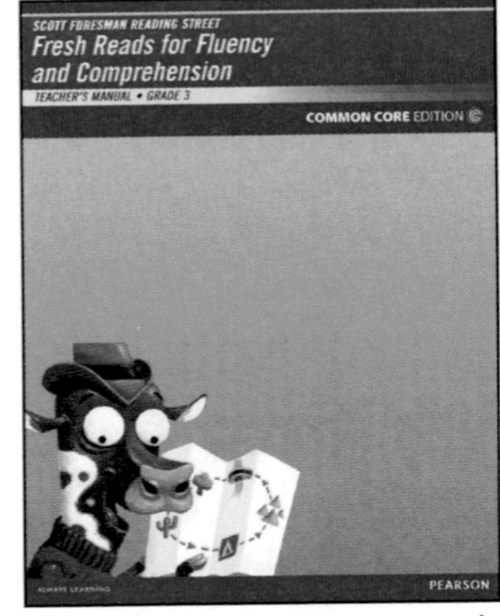

Fresh Reads for Fluency and Comprehension

Advanced

On-Level

Strategic Intervention

Use pp. 175–180 of *Fresh Reads for Fluency and Comprehension* to check:

- ✔ **Comprehension** Generalize
- ✔ Review **Comprehension** Literary Elements: Plot and Theme
- ✔ **Fluency** Words Correct Per Minute

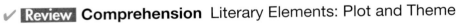

Managing Assessment

Assessment Handbook

Use *Assessment Handbook* to check:

- ✔ **Weekly Assessment Blackline Masters for Monitoring Progress**
- ✔ **Observation Checklists**
- ✔ **Record-Keeping Forms**
- ✔ **Portfolio Assessment**

TEACHER NOTES

TEACHER NOTES

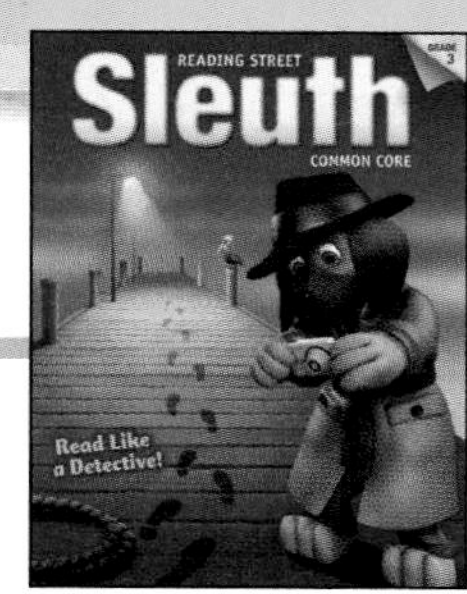

"A Community Spring Break," pp. 76–77

DAY 1 Differentiate Vocabulary

- **Word Knowledge** Amazing Words
- **Read** "A Community Spring Break"
- **Inquiry** Identify Questions

DAY 2 Differentiate Comprehension

- **Word Knowledge** Selection Vocabulary
- **Access Text** Read *Atlantis*
- **Inquiry** Investigate

DAY 3 Differentiate Close Reading

- **Word Knowledge** Develop Vocabulary
- **Close Reading** Read *Atlantis*
- **Inquiry** Investigate

DAY 4 Differentiate Vocabulary

- **Word Knowledge** Amazing Words
- **Read** "The Monster in the Maze"
- **Inquiry** Organize

DAY 5 Differentiate Reteaching

- **Conventions** Quotations and Parentheses
- **Reread** "A Community Spring Break" or Leveled Readers
- **Inquiry** Communicate

Teacher Guides and Student pages can be found in the Leveled Reader Database.

Place English Language Learners in the groups that correspond to their reading abilities.
If... students need scaffolding and practice,
then... use the ELL Notes on the instructional pages.

Independent Practice

Independent Practice Stations

See pp. 494h and 494i for Independent Stations.

Pearson Trade Book Library

See the Leveled Reader Database for lesson plans and student pages.

Reading Street Digital Path

Independent Practice Activities are available in the Digital Path.

Independent Reading

See p. 494i for independent reading suggestions.

On-Level

Common Core State Standards

Literature 1. Ask and answer questions to demonstrate understanding of a text, referring explicitly to the text as the basis for the answers. **Literature 3.** Describe characters in a story (e.g., their traits, motivations, or feelings) and explain how their actions contribute to the sequence of events. **Foundational Skills 4.** Read with sufficient accuracy and fluency to support comprehension. **Language 4.** Determine or clarify the meaning of unknown and multiple-meaning words and phrases based on grade 3 reading and content, choosing flexibly from a range of strategies. **Also Informational Text 1., 10., Language 6.**

Independent Reading Options

Trade Book Library

eSTREET INTERACTIVE
www.ReadingStreet.com

Teacher Guides are available on the Leveled Reader Database.

If... students need more scaffolding and practice with **Vocabulary, then...** use the activities on pp. DI•117–DI•118 in the Teacher Resources section on SuccessNet.

1 Build Word Knowledge

Practice Amazing Words

DEFINE IT Elicit the definition for the word *witty* from students. Ask: How would you describe someone who is *witty* to another student? (Possible response: Someone who is *witty* is very clever or funny.) Clarify or give a definition when necessary. Continue with the words *justice* and *equality.*

Team Talk **TALK ABOUT IT** Have partners internalize meanings. Ask: How can you group the Amazing Words together in a sentence? (Possible response: A person should not try to be *witty* when talking about *justice* or *equality.*) Allow time for students to play with the words. Review the concept map with students. Discuss other words they can add to the concept map.

2 Text-Based Comprehension

Read

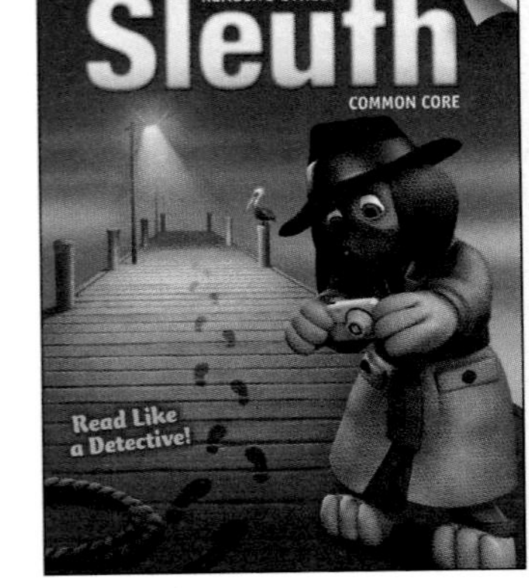

READ ALOUD "A Community Spring Break" Have partners read "A Community Spring Break" from *Reading Street Sleuth* on pp. 76–77.

ACCESS TEXT Discuss the Sleuth Work section with students before they work on it. Remind students that they can use these steps with other texts they read.

Gather Evidence Have partners work together to list good citizen qualities that are evident in the text and from their own experiences. Invite students to state the two qualities they feel are most important and tell why.

Ask Questions Have students share the question that is first on their list to get answered. Discuss community sources that students can use to help answer their questions.

Make Your Case Encourage students to make a list of reasons to support their opinion. Using that list, have students write their paragraphs. If time permits, invite students to share their paragraphs with a partner.

On-Level

1 Build Word Knowledge

Practice Selection Vocabulary

aqueducts	content	crouched	guidance
honor	pillar	thermal	

DEFINE IT Discuss the definition for the word *pillar* with students. Ask: How would you describe a *pillar* to another student? (Possible response: A *pillar* is a tall column on a building that holds up the roof.) Continue with the remaining words.

Team Talk **TALK ABOUT IT** Have pairs use the selection vocabulary in sentences to internalize meaning. Ask: How can you group the selection vocabulary words together in a sentence? (Possible response: Paintings of the ancient city show an *aqueduct* and buildings with *pillars.*) Allow time for students to play with the words and then share their sentences.

2 Read

Atlantis

If you read *Atlantis* during whole group time, then use the following instruction.

ACCESS TEXT Reread pp. 508–509. Ask questions to check understanding. Why does Poseidon change the island? (He wants to make it special for his new bride.) How does Poseidon improve the island? (He changes it from a barren, rocky place into a beautiful paradise, with forests, waterfalls, and rich farmland.)

Have students identify sections from today's reading that they did not completely understand. Reread them aloud and clarify misunderstandings.

If you are reading *Atlantis* during small group time, then return to pp. 504–511a to guide the reading.

SMALL GROUP TIME

More Reading for Group Time

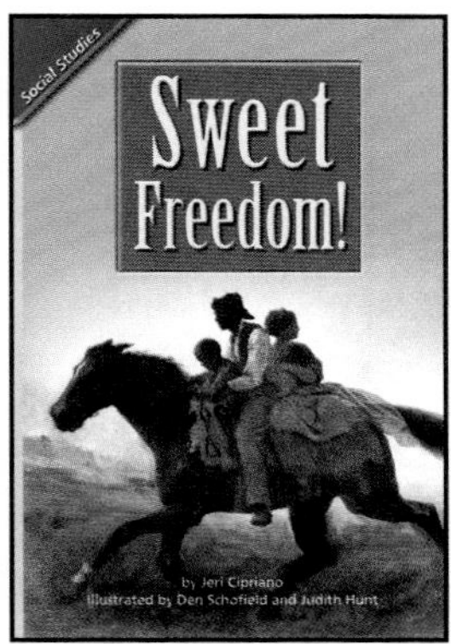

ON-LEVEL

Review
- Generalize
- Inferring
- Selection Vocabulary

Use this suggested Leveled Reader or other text at students' instructional level.

eStreet Interactive
www.ReadingStreet.com

Use the Leveled Reader Database for lesson plans and student pages for *Sweet Freedom!*

Common Core State Standards

Literature 1. Ask and answer questions to demonstrate understanding of a text, referring explicitly to the text as the basis for the answers. **Literature 3.** Describe characters in a story (e.g., their traits, motivations, or feelings) and explain how their actions contribute to the sequence of events. **Language 4.** Determine or clarify the meaning of unknown and multiple-meaning words and phrases based on grade 3 reading and content, choosing flexibly from a range of strategies. **Language 4.a.** Use sentence-level context as a clue to the meaning of a word or phrase. **Also Writing 4., 10., Language 6.**

1 Build Word Knowledge

Develop Vocabulary

REREAD FOR VOCABULARY Reread the first paragraph on p. 513. Let's read this paragraph to find out what *prospered* means. To help students understand the word *prospered,* ask questions related to the context, such as: What is life like in Atlantis? Why do the people of Atlantis grow richer? Have students use online sources to find out more information about the word *prospered.*

2 Read

Atlantis

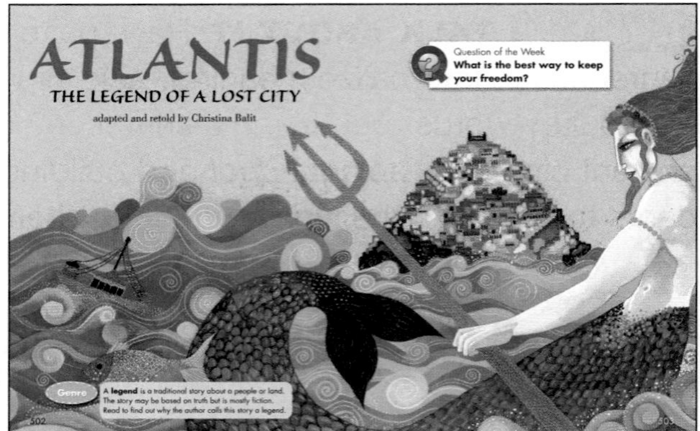

If you read *Atlantis* during whole group time, then use the following instruction.

CLOSE READING Read pp. 514–515. Have students search through the text to find references to words that show time order. As a class, make a list of the words in the order they occur. (*many years passed, gradually, one day, now*)

Ask: What happens to the people of Atlantis while Poseidon sleeps? (The people change. They argue and become greedy.) What does Poseidon do when he wakes? (Poseidon cries and then carries out his curse on the city.)

If you are reading *Atlantis* during small group time, then return to pp. 512–519a to guide the reading.

If... students need more scaffolding and practice with the **Main Selection, then...** use the activities on p. DI•122 in the Teacher Resources section on SuccessNet.

On-Level

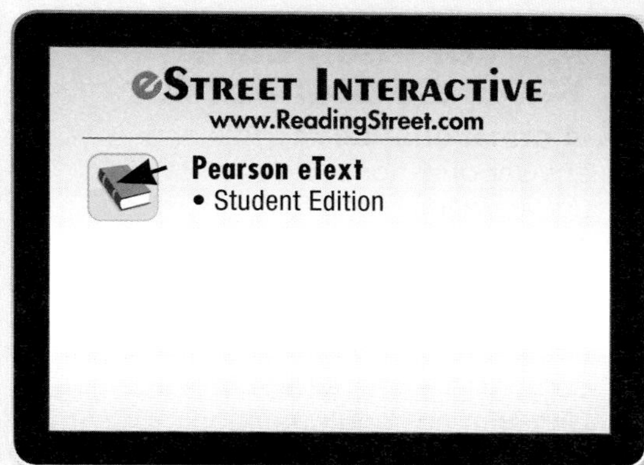

eStreet Interactive
www.ReadingStreet.com

Pearson eText
- Student Edition

1 Build Word Knowledge

Practice Amazing Words

witty	equality	justice	perish	demonstrate
mourn	blight	wept	violence	

Team Talk **LANGUAGE DEVELOPMENT** Have partners practice building more complex sentences. Display a sentence starter and have students add oral phrases or clauses using the Amazing Words. For example: The _______ violence _______. (The sudden *violence* / caused many people / to *perish* / and many *wept* / at the *blight* / on their city.) Guide students to add at least three phrases or clauses per sentence.

2 Read

"The Monster in the Maze"

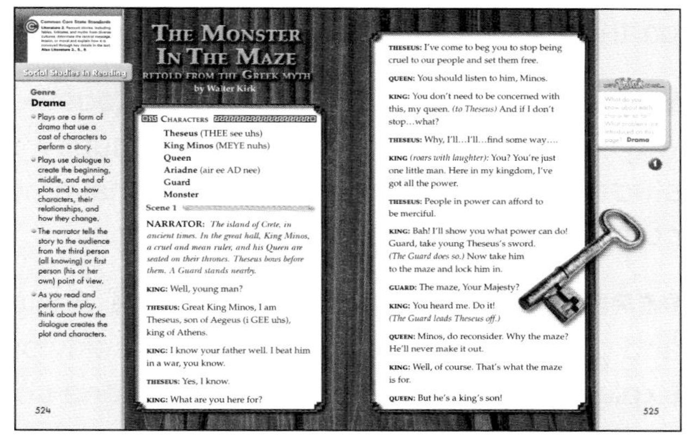

Social Studies in Reading

Genre
Drama

- Plays are a form of drama that use a cast of characters to perform a story.
- Plays use dialogue to create the beginning, middle, and end of plots and to show characters, their relationships, and how they change.
- The narrator tells the story to the audience from the third person (all knowing) or first person (his or her own) point of view.
- As you read and perform the play, think about how the dialogue creates the plot and characters.

THE MONSTER IN THE MAZE
RETOLD FROM THE GREEK MYTH
by Walter Kirk

CHARACTERS
Theseus (THEE see uhs)
King Minos (MEYE nuhs)
Queen
Ariadne (air ee AD nee)
Guard
Monster

Scene 1

NARRATOR: *The island of Crete, in ancient times. In the great hall, King Minos, a cruel and mean ruler, and his Queen are seated on their thrones. Theseus bows before them. A Guard stands nearby.*

KING: Well, young man?

THESEUS: Great King Minos, I am Theseus, son of Aegeus (i GEE uhs), king of Athens.

KING: I know your father well. I beat him in a war, you know.

THESEUS: Yes, I know.

KING: What are you here for?

524

THESEUS: I've come to beg you to stop being cruel to our people and set them free.

QUEEN: You should listen to him, Minos.

KING: You don't need to be concerned with this, my queen. *(to Theseus)* And if I don't stop…what?

THESEUS: Why, I'll…I'll…find some way….

KING *(roars with laughter)*: You? You're just one little man. Here in my kingdom, I've got all the power.

THESEUS: People in power can afford to be merciful.

KING: Bah! I'll show you what power can do! Guard, take young Theseus's sword. *(The Guard does so.)* Now take him to the maze and lock him in.

GUARD: The maze, Your Majesty?

KING: You heard me. Do it! *(The Guard leads Theseus off.)*

QUEEN: Minos, do reconsider. Why the maze? He'll never make it out.

KING: Well, of course. That's what the maze is for.

QUEEN: But he's a king's son!

525

BEFORE READING Read aloud the genre information on p. 524. Then help students preview "The Monster in the Maze" and set a purpose for reading. Ask: What clues can you get from the title? (A monster is usually bad or terrible. The play might be about something or someone who is bad.) Who are the characters in this play? (Theseus, King Minos, Queen, a guard, Ariadne, the narrator, and the monster) What is the purpose of the narrator's first speech? (It tells readers or audience members where the play takes place, who the characters are, and what they are like.)

DURING READING Have students perform the play. Ask: What kind of person is the queen? (She is a kind and sensible person who thinks that King Minos should not be so cruel to Theseus. Instead, she thinks they should respect him, especially because he is a king's son.) How do you know? (The things she says show readers and audience members what she is like.)

AFTER READING Have students share their reactions to "The Monster in the Maze." Then have them write a paragraph comparing and contrasting Poseidon and King Minos.

SMALL GROUP TIME

Independent Reading Options

Trade Book Library

eStreet Interactive
www.ReadingStreet.com

Teacher Guides are available on the Leveled Reader Database.

On-Level

Common Core State Standards

Informational Text 1. Ask and answer questions to demonstrate understanding of a text, referring explicitly to the text as the basis for the answers. **Foundational Skills 4.** Read with sufficient accuracy and fluency to support comprehension. **Language 2.c.** Use commas and quotation marks in dialogue. **Language 4.** Determine or clarify the meaning of unknown and multiple-meaning words and phrases based on grade 3 reading and content, choosing flexibly from a range of strategies. **Also Informational Text 10., Writing 7., Speaking/ Listening 1.**

More Reading for Group Time

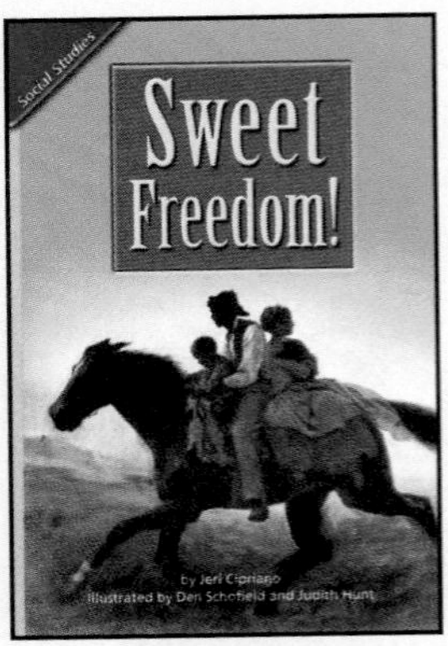

ON-LEVEL

Review

- Generalize
- Inferring
- Selection Vocabulary

Use this suggested Leveled Reader or other text at students' instructional level.

eStreet Interactive
www.ReadingStreet.com

Use the Leveled Reader Database for lesson plans and student pages for *Sweet Freedom!*

1 Build Word Knowledge

Practice Quotations and Parentheses

IDENTIFY Have a volunteer read the text at the bottom of p. 523 and discuss with students how to use quotations and parentheses. Have students reread the model historical fiction to find examples of how the author used quotations and parentheses. Allow time for students to discuss their examples and correct any misunderstandings.

2 Text-Based Comprehension

Read

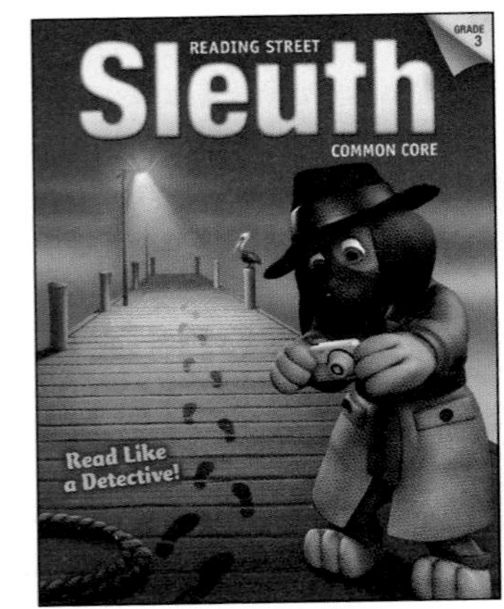

REREAD "A Community Spring Break" Have partners reread "A Community Spring Break."

EXTEND UNDERSTANDING Talk together about ways students can help in the community. Encourage students to share experiences they have had with community volunteerism.

PERFORMANCE TASK • Prove It! Assign partners and give each pair an outline of a weekly calendar. Explain that they will plan activities for a community spring break. Have them brainstorm ideas of ways they can improve their community or help others where they live. Tell them that they should have one activity for each day. Encourage students to note the goal for each day's activity.

COMMUNICATE Have each pair present their calendar to another pair and explain how these activities will improve their community. Invite discussion about what parts of the community will be improved upon with these activities.

Strategic Intervention

1 Build Word Knowledge

Reteach Amazing Words

Repeat the definition of the word. We learned that *witty* means clever or funny. Then use the word in a sentence. The actor surprised the reporter with his witty answers.

Team Talk **TALK ABOUT IT** Have partners take turns using the word *witty* in a sentence. Continue this routine to practice the Amazing Words *justice* and *equality.* Review the concept map with students. Discuss other words they can add to the concept map.

Corrective feedback	**If...** students need more practice with the Amazing Words, **then...** use visuals from the Student Edition or online sources to clarify meaning.

2 Text-Based Comprehension

Read

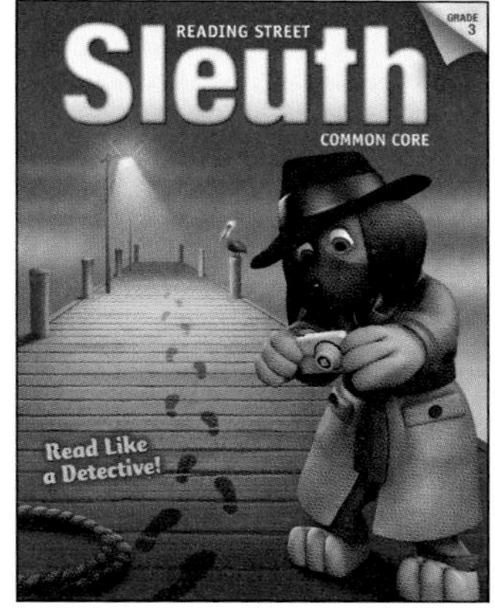

READ "A Community Spring Break" Have students track the print as you read "A Community Spring Break" from *Reading Street Sleuth* on pp. 76–77.

ACCESS TEXT Discuss the Sleuth Work section with students and provide support as needed as they work on it. Remind students that they can use these steps with other texts they read.

Gather Evidence Talk together about being a good citizen. With students, skim the text, finding evidence that names some of these qualities. Have students add to the list with their own experiences of good citizenship.

Ask Questions Have students work with a partner to make a list of questions they will need to research as planners of a community spring break. If time permits, have students choose one question to begin researching.

Make Your Case Remind students that they can support their opinions with both facts and opinions based on personal experiences. Have students list at least two reasons in their paragraph that support their opinion.

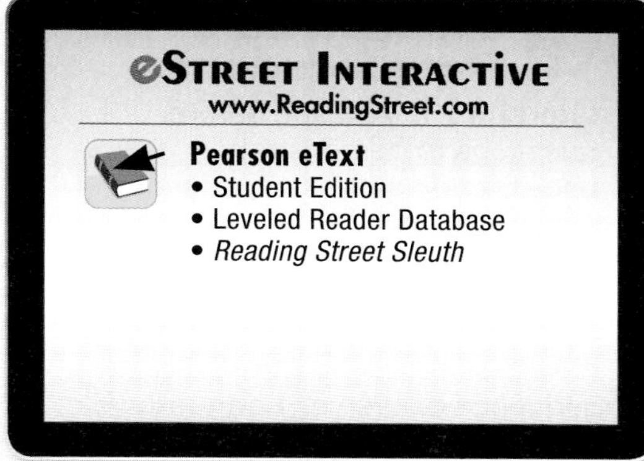

SMALL GROUP TIME

More Reading for Group Time

CONCEPT LITERACY

Practice
Concept Words

BELOW-LEVEL

Review
- Generalize
- Inferring
- Selection Vocabulary

Use these suggested Leveled Readers or other text at students' instructional level.

eSTREET INTERACTIVE
www.ReadingStreet.com

Use the Leveled Reader Database for lesson plans and student pages for *Freedom For All!* and *Greek Myths.*

Strategic Intervention

Common Core State Standards

Literature 1. Ask and answer questions to demonstrate understanding of a text, referring explicitly to the text as the basis for the answers. **Literature 3.** Describe characters in a story (e.g., their traits, motivations, or feelings) and explain how their actions contribute to the sequence of events. **Language 4.** Determine or clarify the meaning of unknown and multiple-meaning words and phrases based on grade 3 reading and content, choosing flexibly from a range of strategies. **Language 4.a.** Use sentence-level context as a clue to the meaning of a word or phrase. **Also Literature 2., Language 5.b., 6.**

1 Build Word Knowledge

Reteach Selection Vocabulary

DEFINE IT Describe a *pillar* to a friend. Give a definition when necessary. Restate the word in student-friendly terms and clarify meaning with a visual. A *pillar* is a column or post that decorates a building or helps hold up the roof. Page 510 shows two pillars.

aqueducts	content	crouched	guidance
honor	pillar	thermal	

Team Talk **TALK ABOUT IT** Have you ever seen a building with pillars? Turn and talk to your partner about this. Allow time for students to discuss. Ask for examples. Rephrase students' examples for usage when necessary or to correct misunderstandings. Continue with the remaining words.

Corrective feedback | **If...** students need more practice with selection vocabulary, **then...** use the *Envision It! Pictured Vocabulary Cards.*

2 Read

Atlantis

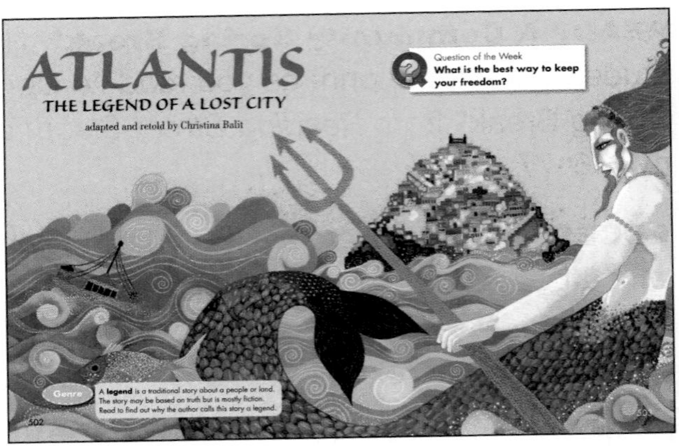

If you read *Atlantis* during whole group time, then use the instruction below.

ACCESS TEXT Reread the paragraphs on pp. 508–509. Ask questions to check understanding. What does Poseidon do after the wedding? (He changes into his divine form.) What does he promise everyone? (that he will rebuild the island) Why does he promise this? (He wants to make it special for his new bride.) How does Poseidon improve the island? (He changes it from a barren, rocky place into a beautiful paradise, with forests, waterfalls, and rich farmland.)

Have students identify sections they did not understand. Reread them aloud. Clarify the meaning of each section to build understanding.

If you are reading *Atlantis* during small group time, then return to pp. 504–511a to guide the reading.

Independent Reading Options

Trade Book Library

eSTREET INTERACTIVE
www.ReadingStreet.com

Teacher Guides are available on the Leveled Reader Database.

Strategic Intervention

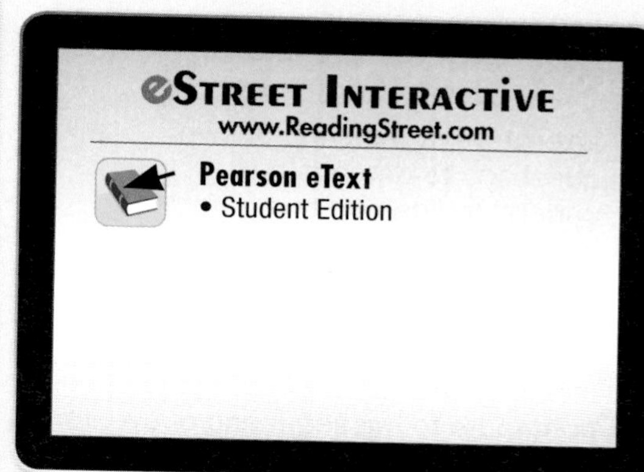

1 Build Word Knowledge

Develop Vocabulary

REREAD FOR VOCABULARY Reread the first paragraph on p. 513. Let's read this paragraph to find out what *prospered* means. To help students understand the word *prospered,* ask questions related to the context, such as: What activities does the author describe in this paragraph? How do these activities help the people of Atlantis grow "ever richer"?

Corrective feedback	**If...** students have difficulty understanding the word *prospered,* **then...** guide students to use online sources to find more information.

2 Read

Atlantis

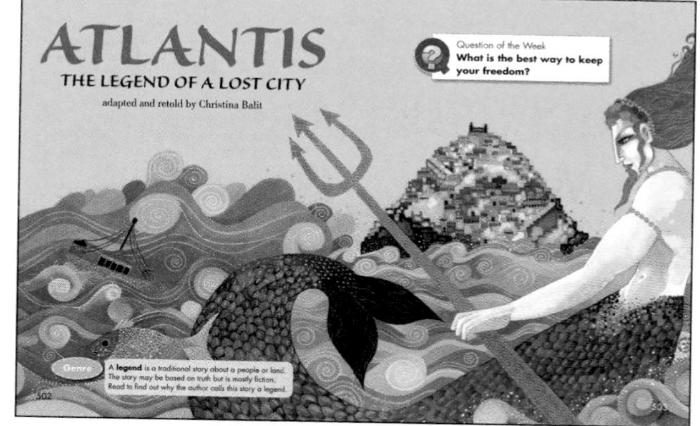

If you read *Atlantis* during whole group time, then use the instruction below.

CLOSE READING Read pp. 514–515. Have students search through the text to find references to words that show time order. As a class, make a list of the words in the order they occur. (*many years passed, while, gradually, one day, now*)

Now use the time words you listed to retell what happened in this part of the story. (Many years passed, and while Poseidon slept, the people of Atlantis gradually became greedy and mean. One day, Zeus saw how bad Atlantis had become, and he roared angrily. Now Poseidon had to carry out his curse on the city.)

If you are reading *Atlantis* during small group time, then return to pp. 512–519a to guide the reading.

SMALL GROUP TIME

ELL

If... students need more scaffolding and practice with the **Main Selection,** **then...** use the activities on p. DI•122 in the Teacher Resources section on SuccessNet.

Strategic Intervention

Common Core State Standards

Literature 1. Ask and answer questions to demonstrate understanding of a text, referring explicitly to the text as the basis for the answers. **Literature 3.** Describe characters in a story (e.g., their traits, motivations, or feelings) and explain how their actions contribute to the sequence of events. **Foundational Skills 4.** Read with sufficient accuracy and fluency to support comprehension. **Speaking/Listening 3.** Ask and answer questions about information from a speaker, offering appropriate elaboration and detail. **Language 2.c.** Use commas and quotation marks in dialogue. **Also Writing 10., Speaking/Listening 1., Language 4., 6.**

1 Build Word Knowledge

Review Amazing Words

witty	equality	justice	perish	demonstrate
mourn	blight	wept	violence	

Team Talk **LANGUAGE DEVELOPMENT** Have students practice building more complex sentences. Display a sentence starter and have students add oral phrases or clauses using the Amazing Words.

Corrective feedback | **If...** students have difficulty using the Amazing Words orally, **then...** review the meaning of each of the words.

2 Read

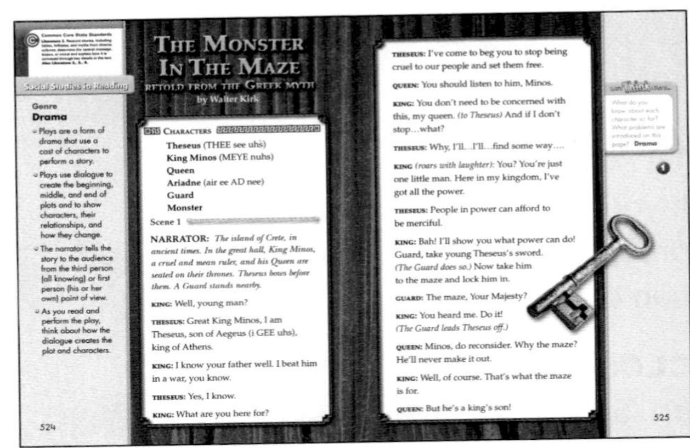

"The Monster in the Maze"

BEFORE READING Read aloud the genre information about drama on p. 524. Then have students locate the list of characters for "The Monster in the Maze." Read the names aloud together. Show students how to use the pronunciation keys to *Theseus, King Minos,* and *Ariadne* correctly.

DURING READING Have students perform a choral reading of the selection. Before you begin, point out the narrator's first speech. Why does the author begin the play with this speech for the narrator? (The narrator's first speech sets the scene, introduces the main characters, and offers some information about their personalities.)

AFTER READING Have students share their reactions. Then guide them through the Reading Across Texts and Writing Across Texts activities.

- How are the characters in the selections alike? (The people of Atlantis and King Minos have wealth and become bad.)
- How do the endings of the selections differ? (Poseidon destroys Atlantis because its people become bad; in the play, Theseus defeats the monster, and the people are set free.)

If... students need more scaffolding and practice with **Amazing Words, then...** use the Routine on pp. xxxvi–xxxvii in the *ELL Handbook.*

1 Build Word Knowledge

Review Quotations and Parentheses

IDENTIFY Choral read the text at the bottom of p. 523 with students to review how to use quotations and parentheses. Have students reread the model historical fiction to find examples of how the author used quotations and parentheses. Allow time for students to discuss their examples and correct any misunderstandings.

2 Text-Based Comprehension

Read

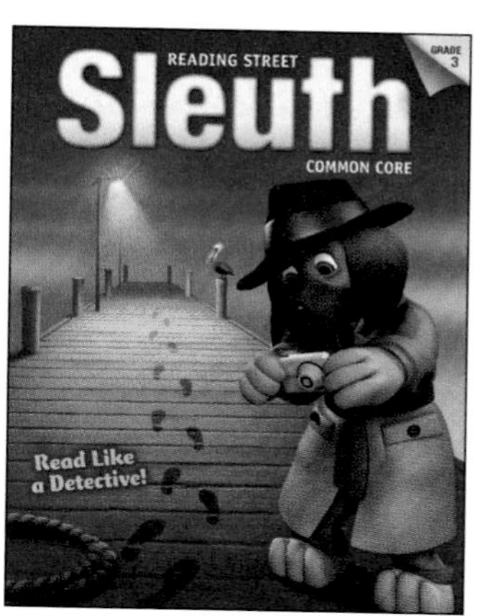

REREAD "A Community Spring Break" Have partners reread "A Community Spring Break," with partners alternating paragraphs.

EXTEND UNDERSTANDING Talk together about the kinds of community activities mentioned in the story. Encourage students to share any similar experiences they have had.

PERFORMANCE TASK • Prove It! Assign partners and give each pair an outline of a weekly calendar. Explain that they will plan activities for a community spring break. Have them brainstorm ideas of ways they can improve their community or help others where they live. Tell them that they should have one activity for each day. Encourage students to plan activities that help different groups of people each day.

COMMUNICATE Have each pair present their calendar and explain how these activities will improve their community. Invite discussion among students about which activities they most want to participate in and why.

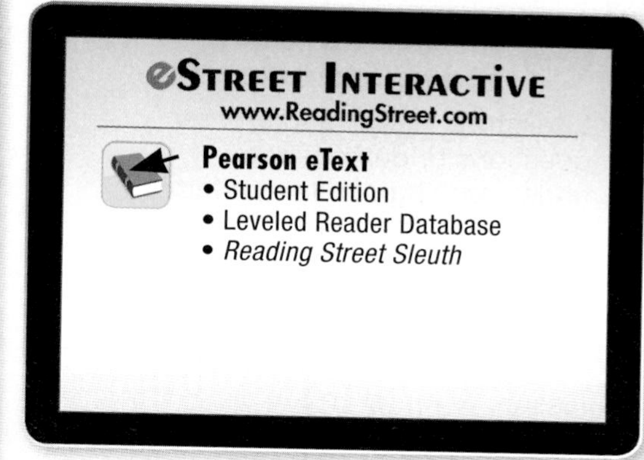

SMALL GROUP TIME

More Reading for Group Time

CONCEPT LITERACY
Practices
Concept Words

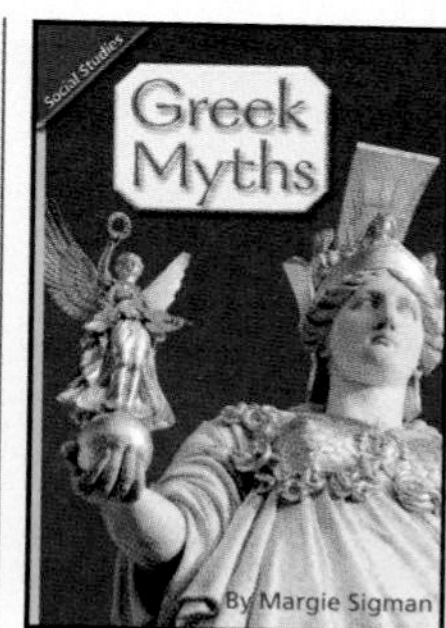

BELOW-LEVEL
Review
- Generalize
- Inferring
- Selection Vocabulary

Use these suggested Leveled Readers or other text at students' instructional level.

eSTREET INTERACTIVE
www.ReadingStreet.com

Use the Leveled Reader Database for lesson plans and student pages for *Freedom For All!* and *Greek Myths.*

Advanced

Common Core State Standards

Literature 1. Ask and answer questions to demonstrate understanding of a text, referring explicitly to the text as the basis for the answers. **Literature 2.** Recount stories, including fables, folktales, and myths from diverse cultures; determine the central message, lesson, or moral and explain how it is conveyed through key details in the text. **Foundational Skills 4.** Read with sufficient accuracy and fluency to support comprehension. **Writing 7.** Conduct short research projects that build knowledge about a topic. **Also Informational Text 1., 10., Language 6.**

1 Build Word Knowledge

Extend Amazing Words

Team Talk Have partners define *witty.* Discuss other names for *witty.* Continue with *justice* and *equality.*

2 Text-Based Comprehension

Read

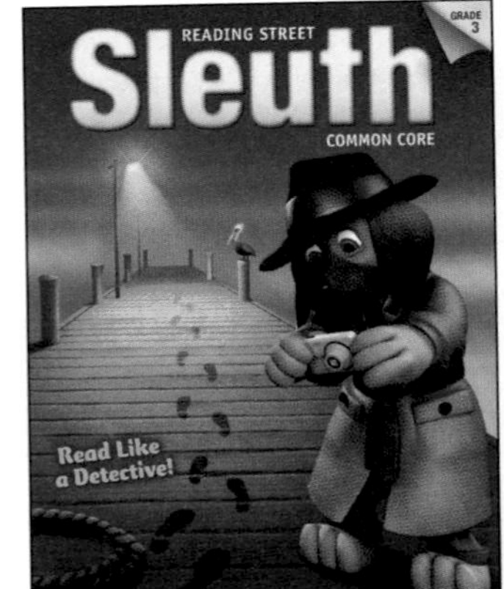

READ "A Community Spring Break" Have students read "A Community Spring Break" from *Reading Street Sleuth* on pp. 76–77.

ACCESS TEXT Discuss the Sleuth Work section with students before they work on it. Remind students that they can use these steps with other texts they read.

Gather Evidence Have students list qualities of good citizens, using both evidence from the story and their own experiences. Encourage students to expand upon their list, telling why each quality they noted is helpful.

Ask Questions Have students share their questions. If time permits, have pairs begin researching their questions as they plan a community spring break.

Make Your Case Encourage students to write a paragraph, listing their reasons from most important to least important.

3 Inquiry: Extend Concepts

IDENTIFY QUESTIONS Have students think about questions they have about Atlantis and use these questions to create a story about the city's origins and destruction, map its location, and draw images of the buildings and people. Throughout the week, they will gather information. On Day 5, they will present what they have learned.

If... students need more scaffolding and practice with **Vocabulary, then...** use the activities on pp. DI•117–DI•118 in the Teacher Resources section on SuccessNet.

Advanced

1 Build Word Knowledge

Extend Selection Vocabulary

Team Talk Have partners use the selection vocabulary in sentences to internalize their meanings. Have students use as many of the words as they can while making sure the sentence is grammatically correct. (Possible response: The people of Atlantis *crouched* near the *pillar* of the temple and asked Poseidon for *guidance*.) Continue with additional selection vocabulary words.

aqueducts	content	crouched	guidance
honor	pillar	thermal	

2 Read

Atlantis

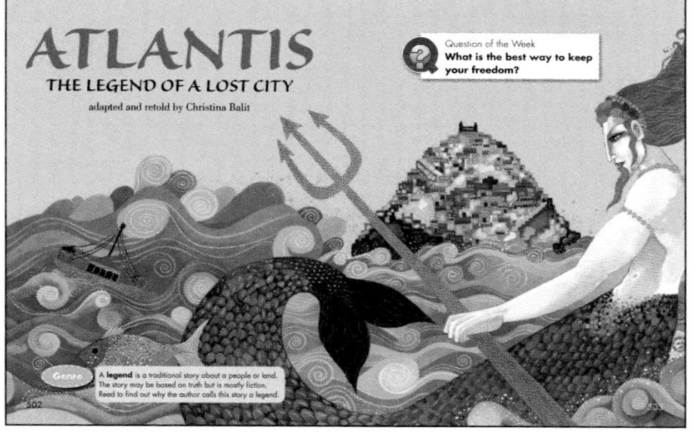

If you read *Atlantis* during whole group time, then use the instruction below.

ACCESS TEXT Reread the paragraphs on pp. 508–509. Discuss what the island was like before and after Poseidon changes it. (Before: It was a barren, rocky little island with a mountain. After: It was a network of islands and sea, with forests, waterfalls, and gardens.) Ask: What were the results of the changes? (The forests he created gave the people fruit and more creatures. The canals helped water the crops, so the island yielded two crops every year. All things flourished on the island.)

If you are reading *Atlantis* during small group time, then return to pp. 504–511a to guide the reading.

3 Inquiry: Extend Concepts

INVESTIGATE Encourage students to use materials at their independent reading levels or student-friendly search engines to identify relevant and credible sites to gather information about the city of Atlantis. Have students consider how they will present their information.

SMALL GROUP TIME

More Reading for Group Time

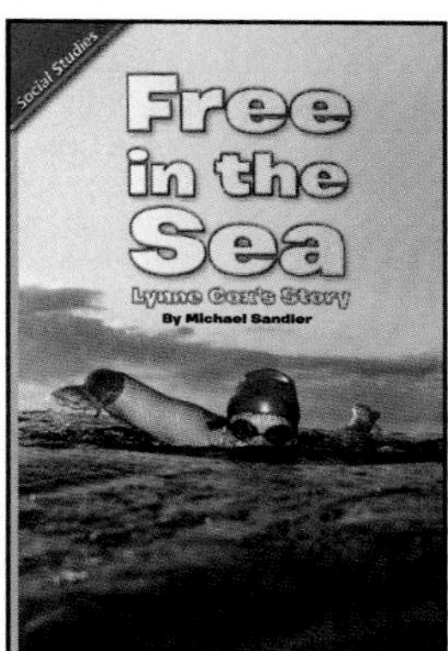

ADVANCED

Review
- Generalize
- Inferring

Use this suggested Leveled Reader or other text at students' instructional level.

eSTREET INTERACTIVE
www.ReadingStreet.com

Use the Leveled Reader Database for lesson plans and student pages for *Free in the Sea.*

Advanced

Common Core State Standards

Literature 1. Ask and answer questions to demonstrate understanding of a text, referring explicitly to the text as the basis for the answers. **Literature 3.** Describe characters in a story (e.g., their traits, motivations, or feelings) and explain how their actions contribute to the sequence of events. **Writing 7.** Conduct short research projects that build knowledge about a topic. **Language 4.a.** Use sentence-level context as a clue to the meaning of a word or phrase. **Also Literature 5., Language 4., 6.**

1 Build Word Knowledge

Develop Vocabulary

REREAD FOR VOCABULARY Reread the first paragraph on p. 513. Let's read this paragraph to find out what *prospered* means. Discuss the meaning and context with students.

2 Read

Atlantis

If you read *Atlantis* during whole group time, then use the instruction below.

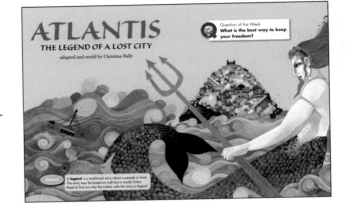

CLOSE READING Read pp. 514–515. Have students create a T-chart with the heads **Humans** and **Gods.** Have students search through the text to find references to what the humans do and how the gods react.

Humans	Gods
began to change	looked down from the heavens
started to argue	roared out his anger
lost the gift of goodness	looked out over the kingdom
became infected with ambition and power	wept
began to steal, cheat, lie	had to carry out a curse

Ask: What idea is the author developing? (While the gods are away, the humans become bad, which makes the gods angry.) Why do you think the author says that the gods roared with anger and wept? (It shows that the gods have feelings. Even though they are very powerful, they are like humans.)

If you are reading *Atlantis* during small group time, then return to pp. 512–519a to guide the reading.

3 Inquiry: Extend Concepts

INVESTIGATE Provide time for students to investigate their topics in books or online. If necessary, help them locate information that is focused on their topics.

Independent Reading Options

Trade Book Library

eSTREET INTERACTIVE
www.ReadingStreet.com

Teacher Guides are available on the Leveled Reader Database.

ELL

If... students need more scaffolding and practice with the **Main Selection, then...** use the activities on p. DI•122 in the Teacher Resources section on SuccessNet.

Advanced

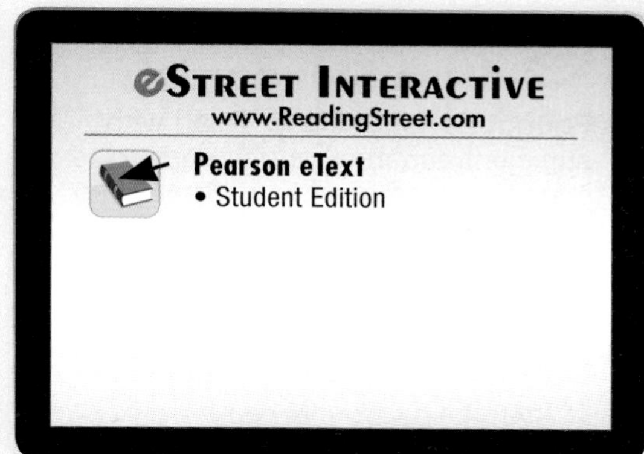

1 Build Word Knowledge

Extend Amazing Words and Selection Vocabulary

witty	equality	justice
perish	demonstrate	mourn
blight	wept	violence

aqueducts	content	crouched
guidance	honor	pillar
thermal		

Team Talk Have students practice building more complex sentences. Display a sentence starter and have students add oral phrases or clauses using the Amazing Words and the selection vocabulary. Guide students to add at least three phrases or clauses per sentence.

2 Read

"The Monster in the Maze"

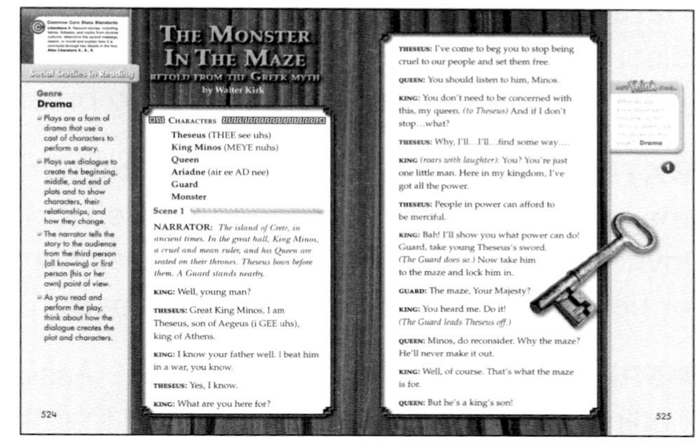

BEFORE READING Read the panel information on dramas on p. 524. Ask students to use the text features to set a purpose for reading. Then have students read the selection on their own.

DURING READING Point out that a play usually begins with a list of characters. Explain that those characters will be saying the lines of dialogue in the play. How is this play similar to the legend you just read? (Students may say that both include events that could never happen in real life. Both take place long ago, and both include dramatic events.)

AFTER READING Have students discuss Reading Across Texts. Then have them do Writing Across Texts independently.

3 Inquiry: Extend Concepts

ORGANIZE INFORMATION Provide time for students to organize their information into a format that will effectively communicate their findings to their audience. Provide any necessary materials, such as posterboard, markers and other supplies, or computer time.

SMALL GROUP TIME

Independent Reading Options

Trade Book Library

eStreet Interactive
www.ReadingStreet.com

Teacher Guides are available on the Leveled Reader Database.

Common Core State Standards

Foundational Skills 4. Read with sufficient accuracy and fluency to support comprehension. **Speaking/Listening 3.** Ask and answer questions about information from a speaker, offering appropriate elaboration and detail. **Speaking/Listening 4.** Report on a topic or text, tell a story, or recount an experience with appropriate facts and relevant, descriptive details, speaking clearly at an understandable pace. **Language 2.c.** Use commas and quotation marks in dialogue.

More Reading for Group Time

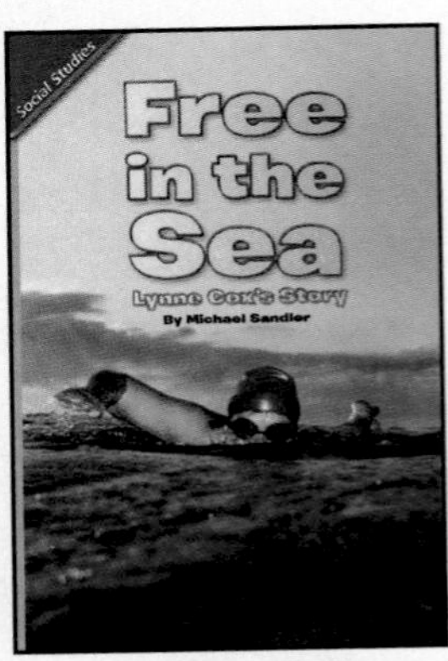

ADVANCED

Review
- Generalize
- Inferring

Use this suggested Leveled Reader or other text at students' instructional level.

eStreet Interactive
www.ReadingStreet.com

Use the Leveled Reader Database for lesson plans and student pages for *Free in the Sea*.

1 Build Word Knowledge

Extend Quotations and Parentheses

IDENTIFY AND EXTEND Have students read the text at the bottom of p. 523. Discuss how to use quotations (for dialogue) and parentheses (for less important information). Have students write several sentences, each using quotations and parentheses. Allow time for students to discuss their examples and correct any misunderstandings.

2 Text-Based Comprehension

Read

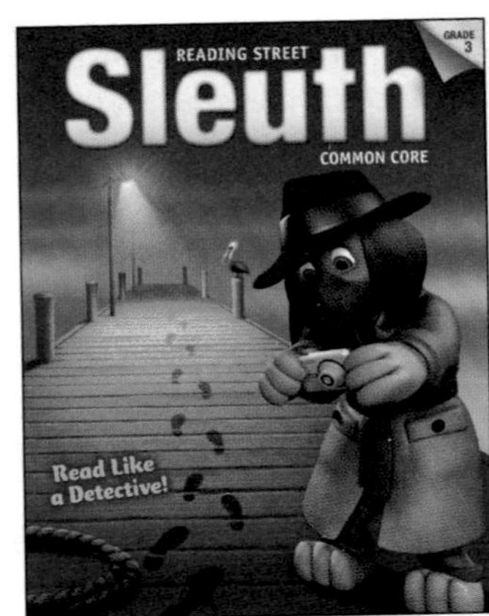

REREAD "A Community Spring Break"
Have partners reread the selection. Have partners discuss what story characters may have learned from participating in the community spring break.

EXTEND UNDERSTANDING Talk together about the importance of volunteering in one's community. Invite discussion about ways the class can volunteer or help the community on a regular basis.

PERFORMANCE TASK • Prove It! Assign partners and give each pair an outline of a weekly calendar. Explain that they will plan activities for a community spring break. Have them brainstorm ideas of ways they can improve their community or help others where they live. Tell them that they should have one activity for each day.

COMMUNICATE Have each pair present their calendar and explain how these activities will improve their community. Invite discussion about how students can "recruit" volunteers to help with each of these activities.

3 Inquiry: Extend Concepts

COMMUNICATE Have students share their inquiry projects on the city of Atlantis with the rest of the class. Provide the following tips for presenting.

- Match your tone of voice and your pitch to your content.
- Make eye contact with the audience and point to visuals as you speak.
- Pronounce names correctly and explain any unfamiliar terms.

Preview Your Week

What does freedom mean?

DAY 1

Student Edition, pp. 374–375

Genre: Narrative Nonfiction

Phonics: Vowel Sounds /ü/ and /ů/

Text-Based Comprehension: Fact and Opinion

DAY 2

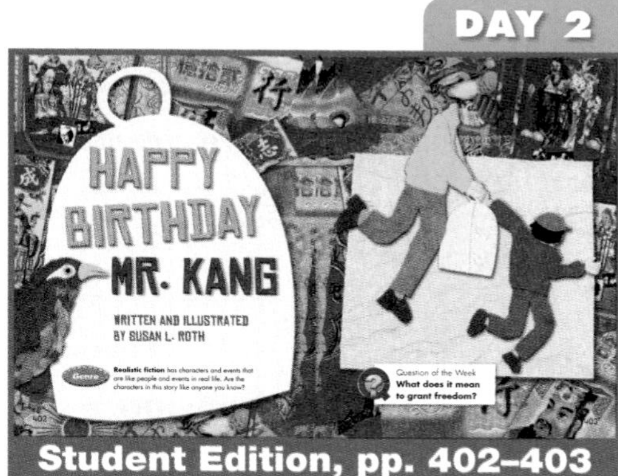

Student Edition, pp. 402–403

Genre: Realistic Fiction

Phonics: Schwa

Text-Based Comprehension: Cause and Effect

DAY 3

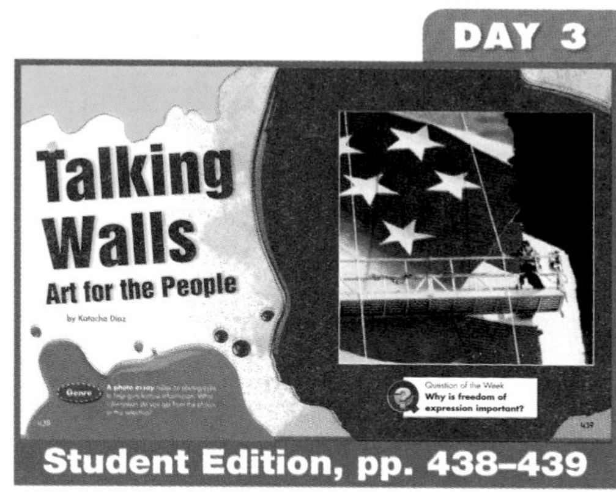

Student Edition, pp. 438–439

Genre: Photo Essay

Phonics: Final Syllables

Text-Based Comprehension: Graphic Sources

DAY 4

Student Edition, pp. 468–469

Genre: Animal Fantasy

Phonics: Prefixes *im-*, *in-*

Text-Based Comprehension: Literary Elements: Plot and Theme

DAY 5

Student Edition, pp. 502–503

Genre: Legend

Phonics: Related Words

Text-Based Comprehension: Generalize

Reinforce Content Knowledge

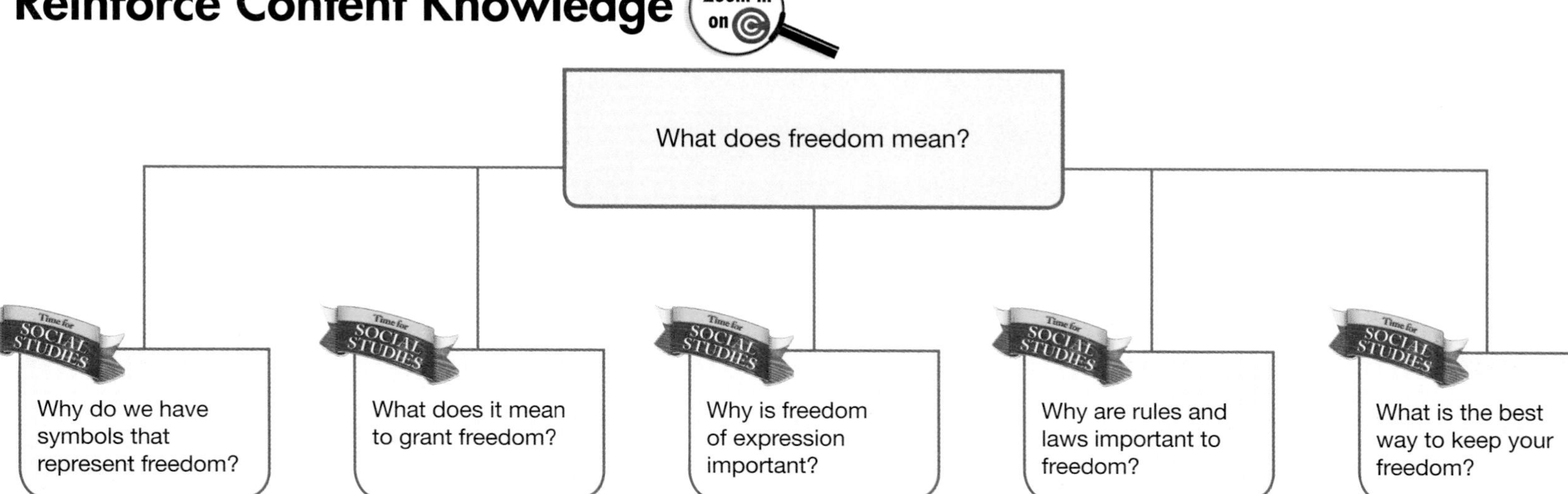

5-Day Planner

DAY 1 Review Week 1

Get Ready to Read

Content Knowledge UR•6
Oral Vocabulary: *impressive, tribute, enlighten, contribution, dedication, competition, recognizable, disgrace, staggering, fund*

Read and Comprehend

Text-Based Comprehension UR•8–13
Fact and Opinion

Vocabulary Skill UR•10–13
Prefix *un-*

Fluency UR•13
Rate

Language Arts

Phonics UR•14
Vowel Sounds /ü/ and /u̇/

Spelling UR•14
Vowel Sounds /ü/ and /u̇/ as in *moon* and *foot*

Conventions UR•15
Capital Letters

Wrap Up Week 1 Review! UR•15

DAY 2 Review Week 2

Get Ready to Read

Content Knowledge UR•16
Oral Vocabulary: *territory, release, loyal, deserve, manage, affectionate, companion, nag, retrieve, wandering*

Read and Comprehend

Text-Based Comprehension UR•18–23
Cause and Effect

Vocabulary Skill UR•20–23
Antonyms

Fluency UR•23
Appropriate Phrasing

Language Arts

Word Analysis UR•24
Schwa

Spelling UR•24
Schwa

Conventions UR•25
Abbreviations

Wrap Up Week 2 Review! UR•25

DAY 3 Review Week 3

Get Ready to Read

Content Knowledge UR•26
Oral Vocabulary: *creative, expressive, emotion, artistic, exquisite, lecture, significant, pause, view, lyrics*

Read and Comprehend

Text-Based Comprehension UR•28–33
Graphic Sources

Vocabulary Skill UR•30–33
Unknown Words

Fluency UR•33
Accuracy

Language Arts

Word Analysis UR•34
Final Syllables

Spelling UR•34
Final Syllables

Conventions UR•35
Combining Sentences

Wrap Up Week 3 Review! UR•35

DAY 4 Review Week 4

Get Ready to Read

Content Knowledge UR•36
Oral Vocabulary: *responsibility, consequence, obey, permission, citizen, fascinate, guilt, encounter, forbid, eerie*

Read and Comprehend

Text-Based Comprehension UR•38–43
Literary Elements: Plot and Theme

Vocabulary Skill UR•40–43
Prefixes and Suffixes *un-, dis-, -ful*

Fluency UR•43
Rate

Language Arts

Phonics UR•44
Prefixes *im-, in-*

Spelling UR•44
Prefixes, Suffixes, and Endings

Conventions UR•45
Commas

Wrap Up Week 4 Review! UR•45

DAY 5 Review Week 5

Get Ready to Read

Content Knowledge UR•46
Oral Vocabulary: *equality, justice, witty, perish, mourn, demonstrate, wept, blight, violence*

Read and Comprehend

Text-Based Comprehension UR•48–53
Generalize

Vocabulary Skill UR•50–53
Homographs

Fluency UR•53
Expression

Language Arts

Phonics UR•54
Related Words

Spelling UR•54
Related Words

Conventions UR•55
Quotations and Parentheses

Wrap Up Week 5 Review! UR•55

Access for All

Small Group Lesson Plan

★ Focus on these activities when time is limited.

	DAY 1 Review Week 1 pages UR•6–UR•15	DAY 2 Review Week 2 pages UR•16–UR•25
OL On-Level	**Review** ★ • Fact and Opinion • Prefixes • Read with Appropriate Rate ★ • Quick Write for Fluency	**Review** ★ • Cause and Effect • Antonyms • Read with Appropriate Phrasing ★ • Quick Write for Fluency
SI Strategic Intervention	**Reteach and Review** • Content Knowledge • Oral Vocabulary ★ • Vowel Sounds /ü/ and /u̇/ ★ • Fact and Opinion • Prefixes • Read with Appropriate Rate • Spelling ★ • Capital Letters ★ • Quick Write for Fluency	**Reteach and Review** • Content Knowledge • Oral Vocabulary ★ • Schwa ★ • Cause and Effect • Antonyms • Read with Appropriate Phrasing • Spelling ★ • Abbreviations ★ • Quick Write for Fluency
A Advanced	**Extend** ★ • Fact and Opinion • Prefixes ★ • Quick Write for Fluency	**Extend** ★ • Cause and Effect • Antonyms ★ • Quick Write for Fluency
ELL	**Reteach and Review** • Content Knowledge • Oral Vocabulary • ELL Poster ★ • Vowel Sounds /ü/ and /u̇/ ★ • Fact and Opinion • Prefixes • Read with Appropriate Rate • Spelling • Capital Letters ★ • Quick Write for Fluency	**Reteach and Review** • Content Knowledge • Oral Vocabulary • ELL Poster ★ • Schwa ★ • Cause and Effect • Antonyms • Read with Appropriate Phrasing • Spelling ★ • Abbreviations ★ • Quick Write for Fluency

DAY 3 Review Week 3	DAY 4 Review Week 4	DAY 5 Review Week 5
pages UR•26–UR•35	pages UR•36–UR•45	pages UR•46–UR•55
Review ★ • Graphic Sources • Unknown Words • Read with Accuracy ★ • Quick Write for Fluency	**Review** ★ • Literary Elements: Plot and Theme • Prefixes and Suffixes *un-, dis-, -ful* • Read with Appropriate Rate ★ • Quick Write for Fluency	**Review** ★ • Generalize • Homographs • Read with Expression ★ • Quick Write for Fluency
Reteach and Review • Content Knowledge • Oral Vocabulary ★ • Final Syllables ★ • Graphic Sources • Unknown Words • Read with Accuracy • Spelling ★ • Combining Sentences ★ • Quick Write for Fluency	**Reteach and Review** • Content Knowledge • Oral Vocabulary ★ • Prefixes *im-, in-* ★ • Literary Elements: Plot and Theme • Prefixes and Suffixes *un-, dis-, -ful* • Read with Appropriate Rate • Spelling ★ • Commas ★ • Quick Write for Fluency	**Reteach and Review** • Content Knowledge • Oral Vocabulary ★ • Related Words ★ • Generalize • Homographs • Read with Expression • Spelling ★ • Quotations and Parentheses ★ • Quick Write for Fluency
Extend ★ • Graphic Sources • Unknown Words ★ • Quick Write for Fluency	**Extend** ★ • Literary Elements: Plot and Theme • Prefixes and Suffixes *un-, dis-, -ful* ★ • Quick Write for Fluency	**Extend** ★ • Generalize • Homographs ★ • Quick Write for Fluency
Reteach and Review • Content Knowledge • Oral Vocabulary • ELL Poster ★ • Final Syllables ★ • Graphic Sources • Unknown Words • Read with Accuracy • Spelling ★ • Combining Sentences ★ • Quick Write for Fluency	**Reteach and Review** • Content Knowledge • Oral Vocabulary • ELL Poster ★ • Prefixes *im-, in-* ★ • Literary Elements: Plot and Theme • Prefixes and Suffixes *un-, dis-, -ful* • Read with Appropriate Rate • Spelling ★ • Commas ★ • Quick Write for Fluency	**Reteach and Review** • Content Knowledge • Oral Vocabulary • ELL Poster ★ • Related Words ★ • Generalize • Homographs • Read with Expression • Spelling ★ • Quotations and Parentheses ★ • Quick Write for Fluency

Review Week 1

Content Knowledge
Review Oral Vocabulary

Text-Based Comprehension
Review Fact and Opinion

Selection Vocabulary
Review Prefix *un-*

Fluency
Rate

Phonics/Word Analysis
Review Vowel Sounds /ü/ and /ù/

Spelling
Review Vowel Sounds in *moon* and *foot*

Conventions
Review Capital Letters

Writing
Quick Write for Fluency

Materials

- Student Edition
- Retelling Cards
- Reader's and Writer's Notebook

Common Core State Standards

Speaking/Listening 1. Engage effectively in a range of collaborative discussions (one-on-one, in groups, and teacher-led) with diverse partners on grade 3 topics and texts, building on others' ideas and expressing their own clearly. **Language 6.** Acquire and use accurately grade-appropriate conversational, general academic, and domain-specific words and phrases, including those that signal spatial and temporal relationships (e.g., *After dinner that night we went looking for them*).

Content Knowledge

Symbols of Freedom

REVISIT THE CONCEPT Today students will explore how the question for this unit of study connects to *The Story of the Statue of Liberty.* Remind students of the Question of the Week, *Why do we have symbols that represent freedom?*

Build Oral Language

DISCUSS FREEDOM Remind students of the question for this unit of study, *What does freedom mean?* Use the prompts and the concept map from Week 1 to discuss why symbols of freedom are important.

- Why are recognizable symbols of freedom important?
- How are symbols a tribute to freedom?
- How do you feel when you see a symbol of freedom such as the flag or the Liberty Bell?

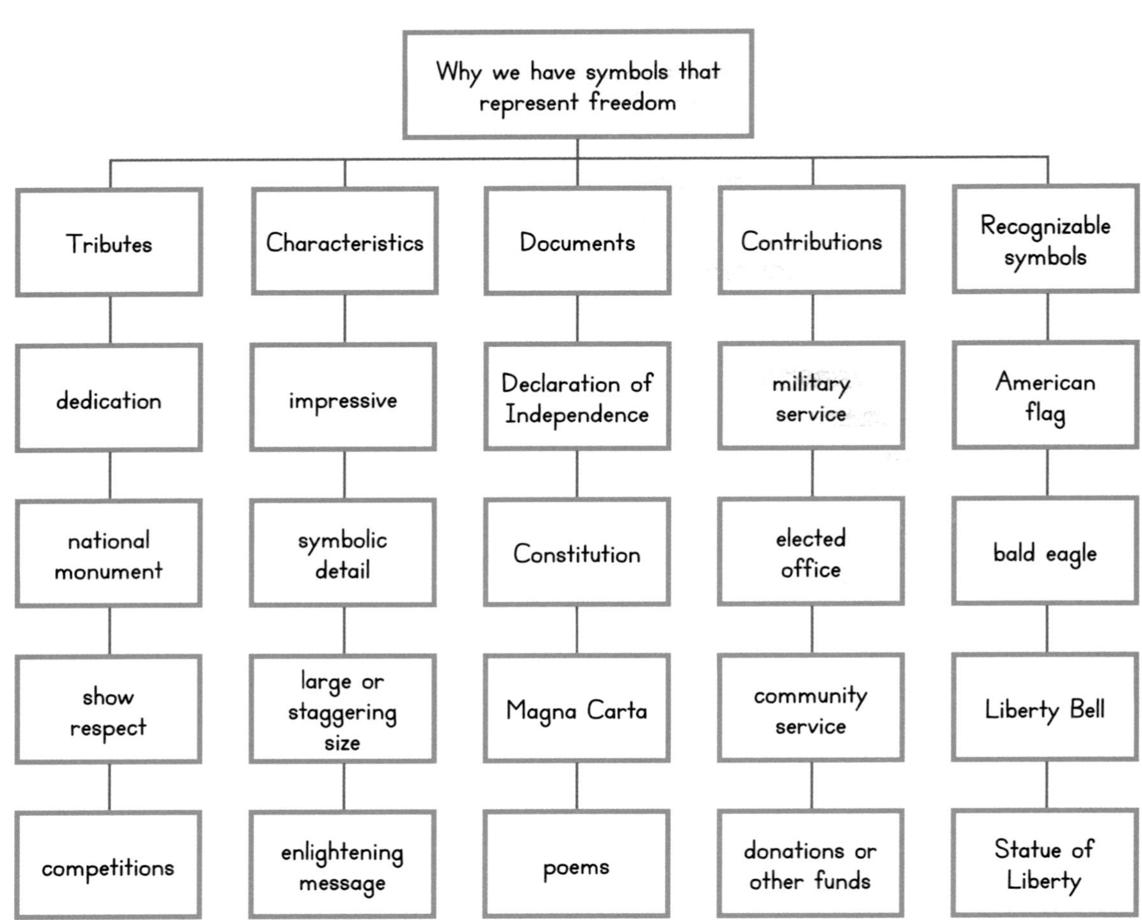

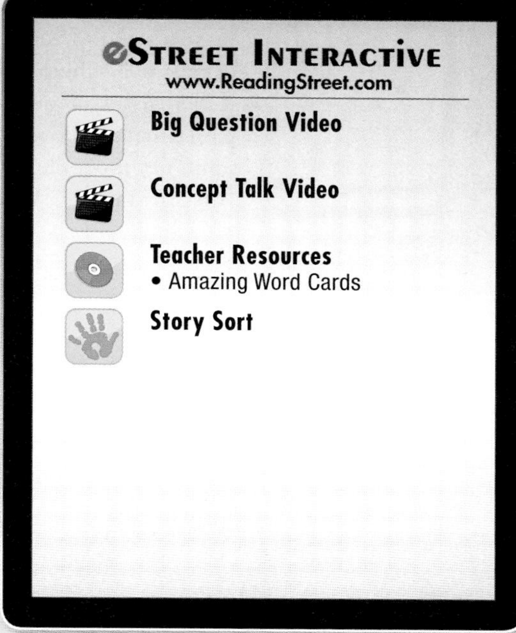

Build Oral Vocabulary

REVIEW AMAZING WORDS Display the Amazing Words for *The Story of the Statue of Liberty.* Remind students that the words are related to the week's concept.

Amazing Words — Robust Vocabulary Routine

1. **Review** Ask students for definitions of the words, starting at the top of the list. Listen for accurate definitions. Prompt students to connect the words to the unit concept of Freedom whenever possible.
2. **Demonstrate** Have students use two or more Amazing Words in the same sentence. Guide the discussion by providing an example that shows the meaning of each word. The *dedication* on the monument paid *tribute* to the soldiers the statue honored. Follow this pattern to cover as many of the ten words as possible.
3. **Apply** Assign the words in random order and have students come up with more new sentences for them. To show that you are becoming more comfortable using these Amazing Words, think up more new sentences for them.

Routines Flip Chart

AMAZING WORDS AT WORK Have students use the Retelling Cards/Story Sort for *The Story of the Statue of Liberty* to talk about the Amazing Words.

CONNECT TO READING Tell students that today they will be rereading passages from *The Story of the Statue of Liberty* and reading "The 54th Regiment." As they read, ask students to think about symbols of freedom.

Amazing Words

impressive	competition
tribute	recognizable
enlighten	disgrace
contribution	staggering
dedication	fund

Build Background Use ELL Poster 26 to review the Week 1 lesson concept and to practice oral language. Point out and read the question: *Why do we have symbols that represent freedom?*

Let's Think About...

Do you understand what you've read? Can you summarize the text using information from the selection to support your answer? **Summarize**

8

Over the years, immigrants have arrived to begin new lives in America. To them, the Statue of Liberty is a symbol of all their hopes and dreams. She has welcomed millions of people arriving in New York by ship.

384

Every year, on the Fourth of July, the United States of America celebrates its independence. Fireworks light up the sky above New York Harbor. The Statue of Liberty is a truly unforgettable sight—a symbol of all that is America.

"Give me your tired, your poor,
Your huddled masses yearning to breathe free,
The wretched refuse of your teeming shore.
Send these, the homeless, tempest-tost to me,
I lift my lamp beside the golden door!"

—from "The New Colossus" by Emma Lazarus, 1883, placed on a tablet on the pedestal of the Statue of Liberty in 1903

Let's Think About...

In the poem at the base of the Statue of Liberty, who are the people the Statue of Liberty invites? Why does she invite them? **Questioning**

9

385

Student Edition, pp. 384–385

Common Core State Standards

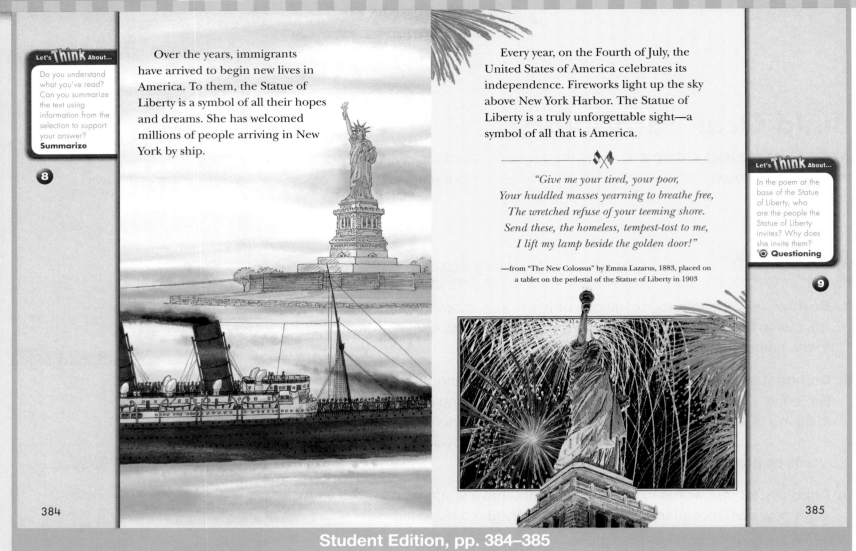

Informational Text 1. Ask and answer questions to demonstrate understanding of a text, referring explicitly to the text as the basis for the answers. **Informational Text 4.** Determine the meaning of general academic and domain-specific words and phrases in a text relevant to a grade 3 topic or subject area. **Speaking/Listening 4.** Report on a topic or text, tell a story, or recount an experience with appropriate facts and relevant, descriptive details, speaking clearly at an understandable pace.

Access Text

REVIEW FACT AND OPINION Review the definitions of fact and opinion on p. 370. Remind students that you can prove a statement of fact true or false by asking an expert or looking up the fact in a reference source. A statement of opinion tells someone's ideas or feelings. You can use clue words such as *should* or *better* to identify feelings.

GUIDE PRACTICE Have students reread p. 385 of *The Story of the Statue of Liberty* and identify facts and opinions. Provide prompts such as: Is the first sentence about the Fourth of July a statement of fact or an opinion? (fact) Is "the Statue of Liberty is a truly unforgettable sight" a statement of fact or an opinion? (opinion) Then have students write one fact and one opinion about the Statue of Liberty. Have volunteers share their sentences with the class.

ON THEIR OWN Have students look back at p. 384 of *The Story of the Statue of Liberty* and identify a statement of fact or of opinion.

Close Reading ©

EVALUATION Reread page 384 of *The Story of the Statue of Liberty.* Does the sentence "To them, the Statue of Liberty is a symbol of all their hopes and dreams" express a statement of fact or an opinion? Explain why. The sentence expresses an opinion, or an idea, that the writer has about how immigrants feel about the Statue of Liberty. While many immigrants may see the statue as a symbol of their hopes and dreams, you cannot prove true or false that all immigrants feel that way.

SYNTHESIS How is the Statue of Liberty "a symbol of all that is America"? The Statue of Liberty stands as a symbol welcoming immigrants to America. The United States and Americans have always welcomed people from all backgrounds into the country. The Statue of Liberty represents the freedom, acceptance, and success that people find in the United States.

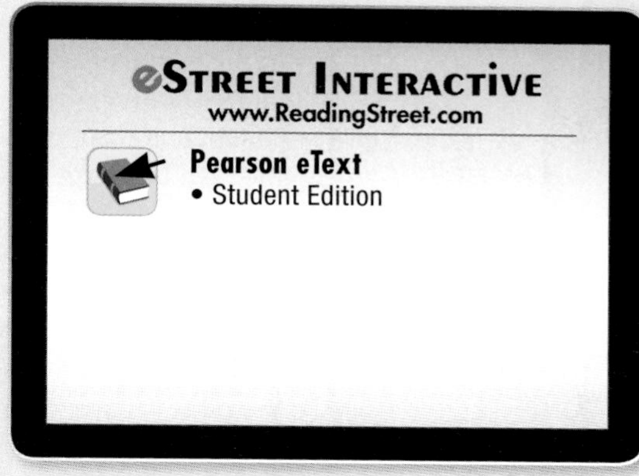

Access for All

SI Strategic Intervention

Make a T-chart with the headings *Fact* and *Opinion.* Review *The Story of the Statue of Liberty* with students and guide them to identify statements of fact and of opinion. Write them in the chart.

A Advanced

Explain to students that not all statements of fact are true. Have them choose a statement of fact in the selection and check at least two sources to see if it is true.

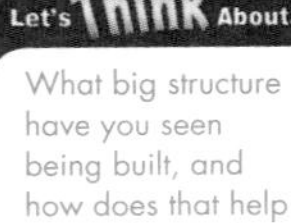

What big structure have you seen being built, and how does that help you understand how Liberty was built? **Background Knowledge**

But in America people had lost interest in the Statue of Liberty. Money had run out and work on Bedloe's Island had stopped. The base for the statue was not finished. With the help of a large New York newspaper, the money was raised. People all over the country, including children, sent in whatever they could. By the time the ship reached New York in 1885, it was greeted with new excitement.

The work on the island went on, and soon the pedestal was completed. Piece by piece, the skeleton was raised. Then the copper skin was riveted in place. Liberty was put back together like a giant puzzle. The statue had been built not once, but twice!

382

At last, in 1886, Liberty was standing where she belonged. A wonderful celebration was held. Boats and ships filled the harbor. Speeches were read, songs were sung. Bartholdi himself unveiled Liberty's face and she stood, gleaming in all her glory, for everyone to see. There was a great cheer from the crowd. Then President Grover Cleveland gave a speech.

383

Student Edition, pp. 382–383

Common Core State Standards

Informational Text 1. Ask and answer questions to demonstrate understanding of a text, referring explicitly to the text as the basis for the answers. **Foundational Skills 3.** Know and apply grade-level phonics and word analysis skills in decoding words. **Foundational Skills 3.a.** Identify and know the meaning of the most common prefixes and derivational suffixes. **Language 4.a.** Use sentence-level context as a clue to the meaning of a word or phrase. **Language 4.b.** Determine the meaning of the new word formed when a known affix is added to a known word (e.g., *agreeable/disagreeable, comfortable/uncomfortable, care/careless, heat/preheat*).

Access Text

REVIEW PREFIX *UN-* Remind students that prefixes are letters added to the beginning of a word that change the meaning of the word. Review the definitions of the prefix *un-* on p. 372. Remind students that prefixes can give you clues to the meanings of unfamiliar words.

GUIDE PRACTICE Read aloud p. 383 of *The Story of the Statue of Liberty.* Point out the word *unveiled* in the fifth sentence. Cover the prefix *un-* and ask, What does the base word *veiled* mean? *Veiled* means "covered." In this word, the prefix *un-* means "do the opposite of." What is the meaning of the word *unveiled?* to remove a cover

ON THEIR OWN Use *Let's Practice It!* p. 414 on the *Teacher Resources DVD-ROM* for additional practice with vocabulary.

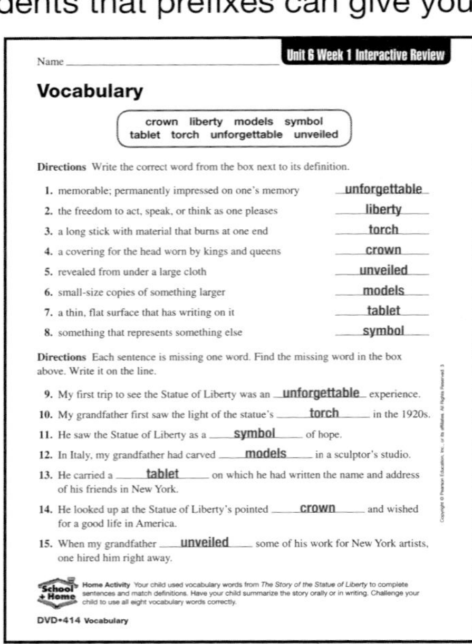

Name ____________ **Unit 6 Week 1 Interactive Review**

Vocabulary

crown liberty models symbol
tablet torch unforgettable unveiled

Directions Write the correct word from the box next to its definition.

1. memorable; permanently impressed on one's memory unforgettable
2. the freedom to act, speak, or think as one pleases liberty
3. a long stick with material that burns at one end torch
4. a covering for the head worn by kings and queens crown
5. revealed from under a large cloth unveiled
6. small-size copies of something larger models
7. a thin, flat surface that has writing on it tablet
8. something that represents something else symbol

Directions Each sentence is missing one word. Find the missing word in the box above. Write it on the line.

9. My first trip to see the Statue of Liberty was an unforgettable experience.
10. My grandfather first saw the light of the statue's torch in the 1920s.
11. He saw the Statue of Liberty as a symbol of hope.
12. In Italy, my grandfather had carved models in a sculptor's studio.
13. He carried a tablet on which he had written the name and address of his friends in New York.
14. He looked up at the Statue of Liberty's pointed crown and wished for a good life in America.
15. When my grandfather unveiled some of his work for New York artists, one hired him right away.

Home Activity Your child used vocabulary words from *The Story of the Statue of Liberty* to complete sentences and match definitions. Have your child summarize the story orally or in writing. Challenge your child to use all eight vocabulary words correctly.

DVD•414 Vocabulary

Let's Practice It! TR DVD•414

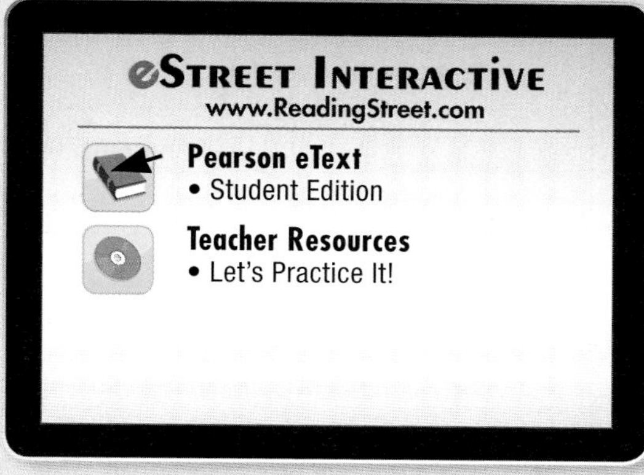

Close Reading

DEVELOP LANGUAGE Use your knowledge of prefixes and word structure to help you determine the meaning of the word *unstoppable.* Use the word in a sentence. The prefix is *un-,* the base word with the suffix *-able* is *stoppable.* The prefix *un-* means "not" or "do the opposite of." *Stoppable* means "capable of being stopped." *Unstoppable* means "not capable of being stopped." *The speeding car was unstoppable.*

EVALUATION Read the last paragraph on page 382. Is the sentence "The statue had been built not once, but twice!" a statement of fact or of opinion? How do you know? The sentence is a statement of fact because you can prove that it is either true or false.

INFERENCE Why do you think that people contributed to the fund to complete the base for the Statue of Liberty? People contributed to the fund because they thought it was important to support and protect symbols of freedom.

EVALUATION Read the description of the celebration for the Statue of Liberty on page 383. Does the celebration seem appropriate for the occasion? Yes, the celebration is grand and exciting. It is appropriate for the unveiling of a national symbol of freedom.

Access for All

SI Strategic Intervention

Guide students to use their knowledge of the prefix *un-* to determine the meaning of these words: *unfold, unlucky, unskilled.*

A Advanced

Have students look in a dictionary or glossary to find five unfamiliar words with the prefix *un-*. Have them use their knowledge of how *un-* changes the meaning of a word to determine the meaning of each word. Have them confirm their definition in the dictionary or glossary. Then have them use each word in a sentence.

Name ______________ **Unit 6 Week 1 Interactive Review**

Read the story.
Answer the questions.

The 54th Regiment

In the 1860s, the Civil War tore the United States apart. Slavery was on everyone's mind. In the North, African Americans were free. In the South, they were still slaves.

Many African Americans in the North felt that it was important to fight against the South and get rid of slavery. They wanted to join the North's army, known as the Union Army.

At first, because of an old law, African Americans were not allowed to join the Union Army. Then, in 1863, things changed. African American soldiers were allowed to enlist. Over the next several years, more than 180,000 African Americans would fight for the Union Army. Perhaps the most famous of these soldiers fought in the 54th Regiment.

The 54th Regiment was a unit made up entirely of African American soldiers. Even in the army, these soldiers had to face a lot of prejudice and hatred. But in July of 1863, the soldiers of the 54th got a chance to prove their worth.

The Union Army wanted to capture Fort Wagner in South Carolina. On July 18, the 54th Regiment led the attack on the fort. The soldiers charged at the fort as their enemies fired shot after shot at them. Out of 600 men, 116 were killed, including the leader, Colonel Robert Shaw.

Home Activity Your child identified a statement of fact and a statement of opinion in a nonfiction text. Read a short newspaper article with your child and take turns identifying statements of fact. Then ask your child to find a statement of opinion in the article.

Name ______________ **Unit 6 Week 1 Interactive Review**

The battle for Fort Wagner was lost, but the 54th Regiment's great bravery impressed other Union troops. Many of the 54th Regiment's soldiers received medals. They went on to fight in other battles.

One battle they fought and won was with their own army. African American soldiers were paid less than white soldiers in the Union Army. The men of the 54th Regiment thought this was unfair. They protested to the government and refused to take their pay unless it was equal to that of white soldiers.

Other African American regiments heard about the 54th Regiment and began to do the same thing. Finally, in 1864, the 54th and other African American regiments began receiving equal pay.

1. Find a statement of fact in the passage that tells something about the men in the 54th Regiment. Write the statement.

   Possible response: The 54th Regiment was a unit made up entirely of African American soldiers.

2. Reread the second paragraph. Write an opinion the men in the 54th Regiment had. Underline the word that helps you know this is an opinion.

   Many African Americans in the North felt it was important to fight against the South and get rid of slavery.

3. In paragraph 5, it says that Colonel Robert Shaw was killed during the attack on Fort Wagner. How can you prove that this is a statement of fact?

   Possible response: I can look in a reference book to see if it is true or false.

Let's Practice It! TR DVD•415–416

Common Core State Standards

Informational Text 1. Ask and answer questions to demonstrate understanding of a text, referring explicitly to the text as the basis for the answers. **Foundational Skills 4.b.** Read on-level prose and poetry orally with accuracy, appropriate rate, and expression on successive readings. **Speaking/Listening 1.c.** Ask questions to check understanding of information presented, stay on topic, and link their comments to the remarks of others. **Language 4.b.** Determine the meaning of the new word formed when a known affix is added to a known word (e.g., *agreeable/disagreeable, comfortable/ uncomfortable, care/careless, heat/ preheat*).

Access Text

Have students read "The 54th Regiment" and respond to the questions.

REVIEW FACT AND OPINION Find a statement of fact in the passage that tells something about the men in the 54th Regiment. The 54th Regiment was a unit made up entirely of African American soldiers.

Remind students that a statement of fact tells something that can be proved true or false by asking an expert or looking up the fact in a reference source.

REVIEW QUESTIONING What is a literal, an interpretive, and an evaluative question you can ask about the text? Literal: When were African Americans allowed to enlist? Interpretive: Why did the soldiers face prejudice and hatred? Evaluative: Was it a good idea to let African Americans join the Union Army?

Remind students that active readers use questioning to help them monitor and adjust their comprehension. Readers should ask themselves questions as they read to seek clarification and make sure they understand the events, facts, or details in a text.

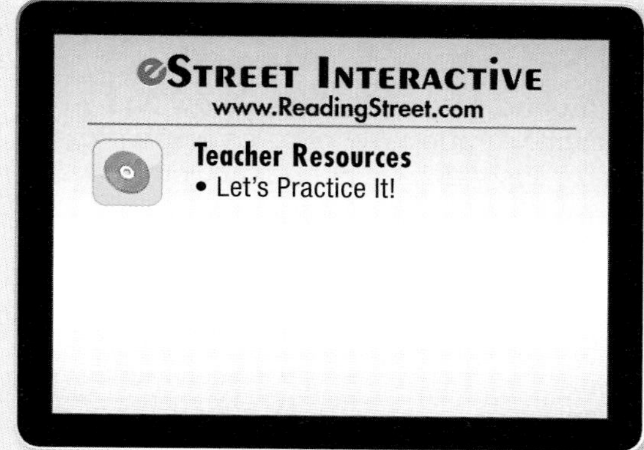

REVIEW PREFIX *UN-* Read aloud the second paragraph on p. 416. Point out the word *unfair* in the third sentence. Cover the prefix *un-* and ask, What does the base word *fair* mean? just In this word, the prefix *un-* means "not." What is the meaning of the word *unfair*? not just

Remind students that a prefix is a word part added to the beginning of a word that changes the meaning of the word. The prefix *un-* can mean "not" or "do the opposite of." Remind students that prefixes can give you clues to the meanings of unfamiliar words.

REVIEW FACT AND OPINION Reread the third paragraph on page 415. Find a statement of opinion. Write the statement and underline the words that help you know that it is a statement of opinion. Perhaps the most famous of these soldiers fought in the 54th Regiment.

Remind students that a statement of opinion tells someone's ideas or feelings. You can use clue words such as *best, most,* or *should* to identify feelings.

Reread for Fluency

MODEL FLUENT READING Remind students that when they read, it is important to read at an appropriate rate. Model reading the first paragraph of "The 54th Regiment" on p. 415 at an appropriate rate.

Routine Paired Reading

1. **Reading 1 Begins** Students read the entire text, switching readers at the end of each page.
2. **Reading 2 Begins** Partners reread the text. This time the other student begins.
3. **Reread** For optimal fluency, have partners continue to read three or four times.
4. **Corrective Feedback** Listen to students read and provide corrective feedback regarding their rate.

Routines Flip Chart

Common Core State Standards

Foundational Skills 3. Know and apply grade-level phonics and word analysis skills in decoding words. **Also Writing 2., 2.b., Language 2., 2.a., 2.f.**

Name ____________ **Unit 6 Week 1 Interactive Review**

Vowel Sounds in *moon* and *foot*

Directions Each word below contains either the vowel sound in *moon* or the vowel sound in *foot*. Underline the letter or letters that stand for these vowel sounds. Then circle the word with the same vowel sound.

1. renew — (moon) foot
2. overlook — moon (foot)
3. stupid — (moon) foot
4. input — moon (foot)
5. understood — moon (foot)
6. pollute — (moon) foot
7. clueless — (moon) foot
8. kazoo — (moon) foot
9. juicy — (moon) foot
10. childhood — moon (foot)

Directions Each sentence below contains a pair of words in ( ). Circle the word that best completes the sentence. If the word has the same vowel sound as in *moon*, write *moon* on the line. If it has the same vowel sound as in *foot*, write *foot*.

11. The tablet in the (crook, reach) of the Statue of Liberty's left arm is the Declaration of Independence. foot
12. The Statue of Liberty is a landmark of (New York, Chicago). moon
13. It's nice to buy a (meal, souvenir) so you can always remember your trip. moon
14. (Did, Would) you like to visit the Statue of Liberty next year? foot
15. A famous photo shows singer John Lennon giving a peace (salute, concert) on Liberty Island. moon

School + Home **Home Activity** Have your child choose five words from the first exercise and write a sentence using each word. Have your child identify the words that sound like *foot* or *moon*.

Vowel Sounds in *moon* and *foot* DVD•413

Let's Practice It! TR DVD•413

Name ____________ **Unit 6 Week 1 Interactive Review**

Vowel Sounds in *moon* and *foot*

Spelling Words				
few	school	true	goose	fruit
cookie	cushion	noodle	bookmark	balloon
suit	chew	glue	Tuesday	bushel

Word Clues Read the two meaning clues. Write the list word that the clues tell about.

1. a group of fish / place where students learn — 1. school
2. a pillow / to pad — 2. cushion
3. a sticky paste / to paste something — 3. glue
4. a toy filled with air / to get bigger — 4. balloon
5. matched pieces of clothing / to please or satisfy — 5. suit

Meaning Connections Change the underlined word or words to a list word. Write the word.

6. I ate a chocolate chip sweet treat. — 6. cookie
7. A bird that honks chased me. — 7. goose
8. Darla put a paper placeholder in the book. — 8. bookmark
9. On the day after Monday, it rained. — 9. Tuesday
10. We bought apples, grapes, and pears. — 10. fruit
11. I saw a piece of pasta in my soup. — 11. noodle
12. I chomp on raw carrots for a snack. — 12. chew
13. The farmer put corn in the 32-quart basket. — 13. bushel
14. What she said was not false. — 14. true
15. Not many people can be called heroes. — 15. Few

School + Home **Home Activity** Your child spelled words with the vowel sound in *moon* (spelled *oo, ew, ue, ui*) and in *foot* (spelled *oo, u*). Play Tic-Tac-Toe. One person chooses a word for the other person to spell. If the person spells the word correctly, he or she marks an X or an O on the grid.

440 Spelling

Reader's and Writer's Notebook, pp. 440–441

Phonics

REVIEW VOWEL SOUNDS /ü/ **AND** /u̇/ Review the /ü/ and /u̇/ spelling patterns *(oo, ew, ue, ui)* and *(oo, u)*, using *Sound-Spelling Cards* 68, 89, 90, 101, 102, and 103.

Use *Let's Practice It!* p. 413 on the *Teacher Resources DVD-ROM.*

READ WORDS IN ISOLATION Point out that students know how to blend these words. Have students read the words together. Allow several seconds previewing time for the first reading.

READ WORDS IN CONTEXT Point out that there are many words in the sentences that students already know. Have students read the sentences together.

Corrective feedback

If... students have difficulty reading the sounds /ü/ and /u̇/, **then...** guide them in using sound-by-sound blending. Have students read all the words repeatedly until they can read the words fluently. Then have students read each sentence repeatedly until they can read the sentences fluently.

Spelling

REVIEW VOWEL SOUNDS IN *moon* AND *foot* Write *few, suit,* and *cookie.* Point out that *few* and *suit* have the sound /ü/, while *cookie* has the sound /u̇/. Remind students that they have learned to spell words with the sounds /ü/ and /u̇/.

SPELLING STRATEGY Review words with the vowel sounds in *moon* and *foot* by having students follow the spelling strategy for spelling these words.

Step 1: Mark the letters that give you a problem, such as *ui* in *fruit*.

Step 2: Find words you know with the same letters. *(suit)*

Step 3: Use your problem words and the words you know in a phrase or sentence. *(I keep fruit in the pocket of my suit.)*

ON THEIR OWN Use p. 440 of the *Reader's and Writer's Notebook* for additional practice with spelling words with the vowel sounds in *moon* and *foot*.

Conventions

REVIEW CAPITAL LETTERS Review the use of **capital letters** for proper nouns.

GUIDE PRACTICE Have students circle words that should be capitalized and then write the words.

1. **We celebrate the united states freedom on the fourth of july.** (United States, Fourth of July)
2. **Our librarian, mr. hsu, has books on immigrants.** (Mr. Hsu)

ON THEIR OWN For additional practice use the *Reader's and Writer's Notebook,* p. 441.

Routine Quick Write for Fluency

Team Talk

1. **Talk** Have pairs discuss why the Statue of Liberty is a symbol of freedom.
2. **Write** Each student writes a paragraph about the statue from an immigrant's perspective, using correct capitalization.
3. **Share** Partners read one another's paragraphs, checking for correct capitalization of proper nouns, dates, and geographical places.

Routines Flip Chart

Writing Workshop

Use the writing process lesson on pp. WP•1–WP•10 for this week's writing instruction.

Wrap Up Week 1 Review!

- ✔ **Content Knowledge** *Why are symbols of freedom important?*
- ✔ **Fact and Opinion** *Share one fact and one opinion about the Statue of Liberty.*
- ✔ **Prefix *un-*** *How does the prefix* un- *change the meaning of a word?*
- ✔ **Homework** Send home this week's Family Times newsletter on *Let's Practice It!* pp. 411–412 on the *Teacher Resources DVD-ROM.*

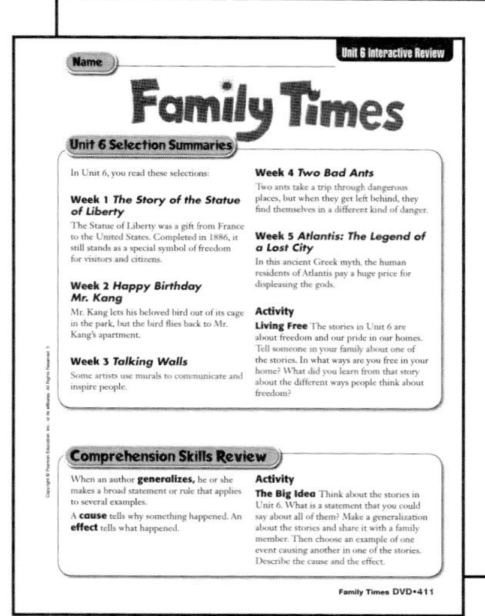

Unit 6 Interactive Review

Name

Family Times

Unit 6 Selection Summaries

In Unit 6, you read these selections:

Week 1 *The Story of the Statue of Liberty*
The Statue of Liberty was a gift from France to the United States. Completed in 1886, it still stands as a special symbol of freedom for visitors and citizens.

Week 2 *Happy Birthday Mr. Kang*
Mr. Kang lets his beloved bird out of its cage in the park, but the bird flies back to Mr. Kang's apartment.

Week 3 *Talking Walls*
Some artists use murals to communicate and inspire people.

Week 4 *Two Bad Ants*
Two ants take a trip through dangerous places, but when they get left behind, they find themselves in a different kind of danger.

Week 5 *Atlantis: The Legend of a Lost City*
In this ancient Greek myth, the human residents of Atlantis pay a huge price for displeasing the gods.

Activity
Living Free The stories in Unit 6 are about freedom and our pride in our homes. Tell someone in your family about one of the stories. In what ways are you free in your home? What did you learn from that story about the different ways people think about freedom?

Comprehension Skills Review

When an author **generalizes,** he or she makes a broad statement or rule that applies to several examples.

A **cause** tells why something happened. An **effect** tells what happened.

Activity
The Big Idea Think about the stories in Unit 6. What is a statement that you could say about all of them? Make a generalization about the stories and share it with a family member. Then choose an example of one event causing another in one of the stories. Describe the cause and the effect.

Family Times DVD•411

Let's Practice It!
TR DVD•411–412

Tell students that tomorrow they will review *Happy Birthday Mr. Kang.*

Content Knowledge
Review Oral Vocabulary

Text-Based Comprehension
Review Cause and Effect

Selection Vocabulary
Review Antonyms

Fluency
Appropriate Phrasing

Phonics/Word Analysis
Review Schwa

Spelling
Review Schwa

Conventions
Review Abbreviations

Writing
Quick Write for Fluency

Materials

- Student Edition
- Retelling Cards
- Reader's and Writer's Notebook

Common Core State Standards

Speaking/Listening 1. Engage effectively in a range of collaborative discussions (one-on-one, in groups, and teacher-led) with diverse partners on grade 3 topics and texts, building on others' ideas and expressing their own clearly. **Language 4.** Determine or clarify the meaning of unknown and multiple-meaning words and phrases based on grade 3 reading and content, choosing flexibly from a range of strategies. **Language 6.** Acquire and use accurately grade-appropriate conversational, general academic, and domain-specific words and phrases, including those that signal spatial and temporal relationships (e.g., *After dinner that night we went looking for them*).

Content Knowledge

Granting Freedom

REVISIT THE CONCEPT Today students will explore how the question for this unit of study connects to *Happy Birthday Mr. Kang*. Remind students of the Question of the Week, *What does it mean to grant freedom?*

Build Oral Language

DISCUSS FREEDOM Remind students of the question for this unit of study, *What does freedom mean?* Use the prompts and the concept map from Week 2 to discuss how understanding freedom can help us understand when, why, and how to grant people and animals freedom.

- How can people grant freedom to other people and animals?
- When is a good time to release an animal companion, and when is not?
- Who deserves to be free and why?
- What does freedom mean to you?

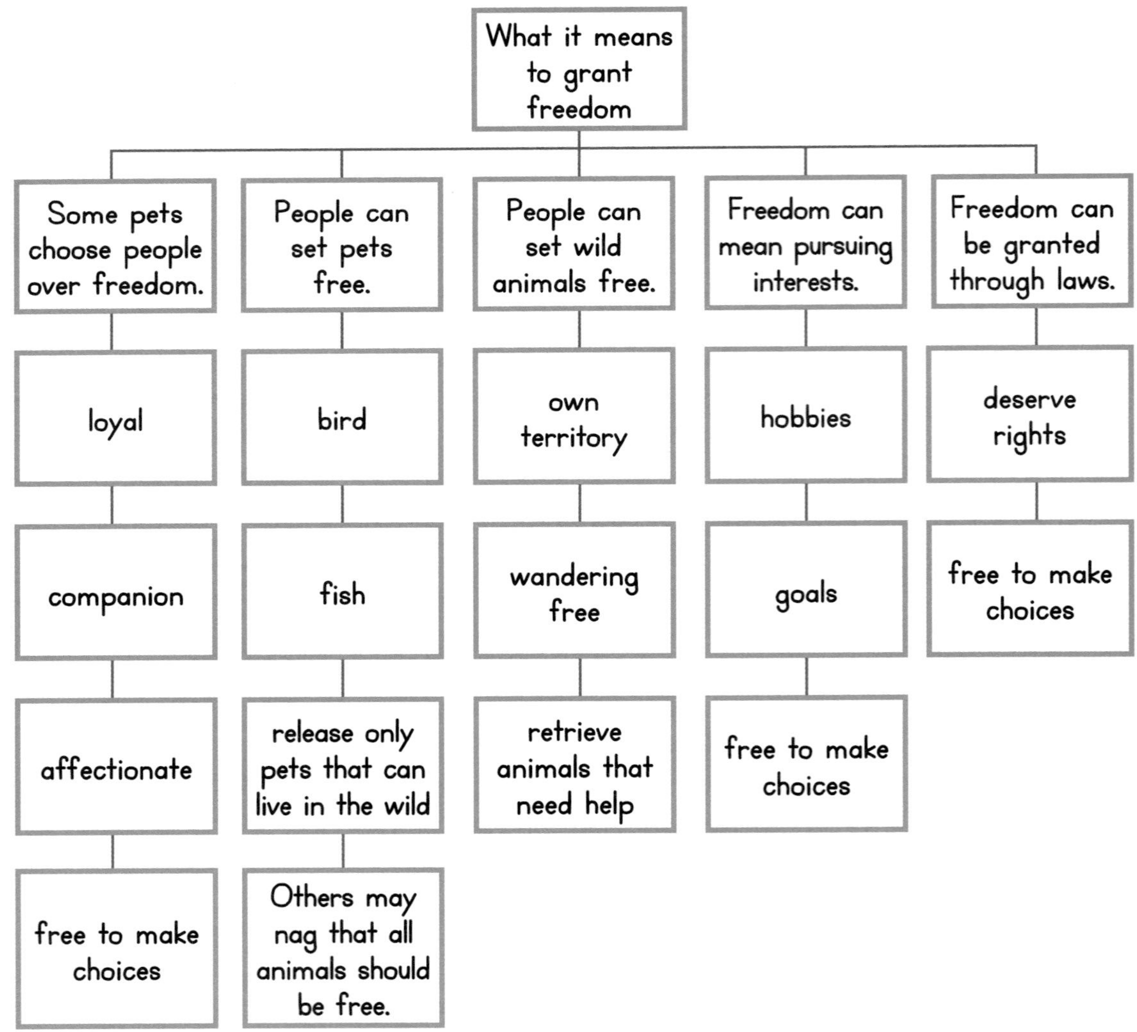

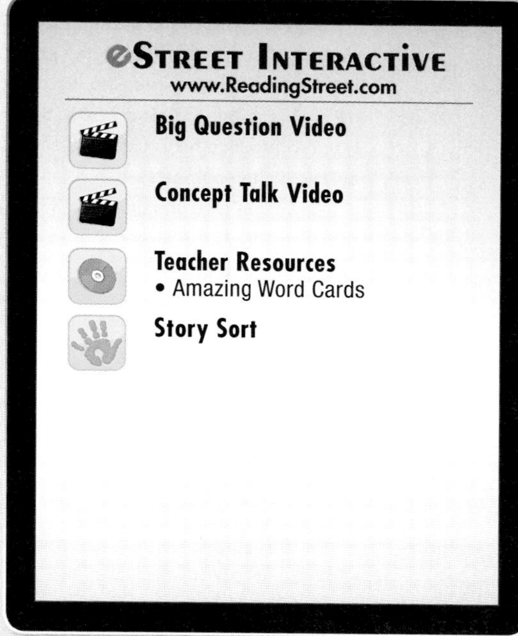

Build Oral Vocabulary

REVIEW AMAZING WORDS Display the Amazing Words for *Happy Birthday Mr. Kang*. Remind students that the words are related to the week's concept.

Amazing Words — Robust Vocabulary Routine

1. **Review** Ask students for definitions of the words, starting at the top of the list. Listen for accurate definitions. Prompt students to connect the words to the unit concept of Freedom whenever possible.
2. **Demonstrate** Have students use two or more Amazing Words in the same sentence. Lead the discussion by providing an example that shows the meaning of each word. The owner found her dog *wandering* around the wild *territory* behind the woods. Follow this pattern to the end of the list, covering as many of the ten words as possible.
3. **Apply** Assign the words in random order and have students provide more new sentences for them. To show that you are becoming more comfortable using these Amazing Words, think up more new sentences for them.

Routines Flip Chart

AMAZING WORDS AT WORK Have students use the Retelling Cards/Story Sort for *Happy Birthday Mr. Kang* to talk about the Amazing Words.

CONNECT TO READING Tell students that today they will be rereading passages from *Happy Birthday Mr. Kang* and reading "Margaret." As they read, ask students to think about what it means to a person or animal to be granted freedom.

Amazing Words

territory	affectionate
release	companion
loyal	nag
deserve	retrieve
manage	wandering

ELL

Build Background Use ELL Poster 27 to review the Week 2 lesson concept and to practice oral language. Point out and read the question: *What does it mean to grant freedom?*

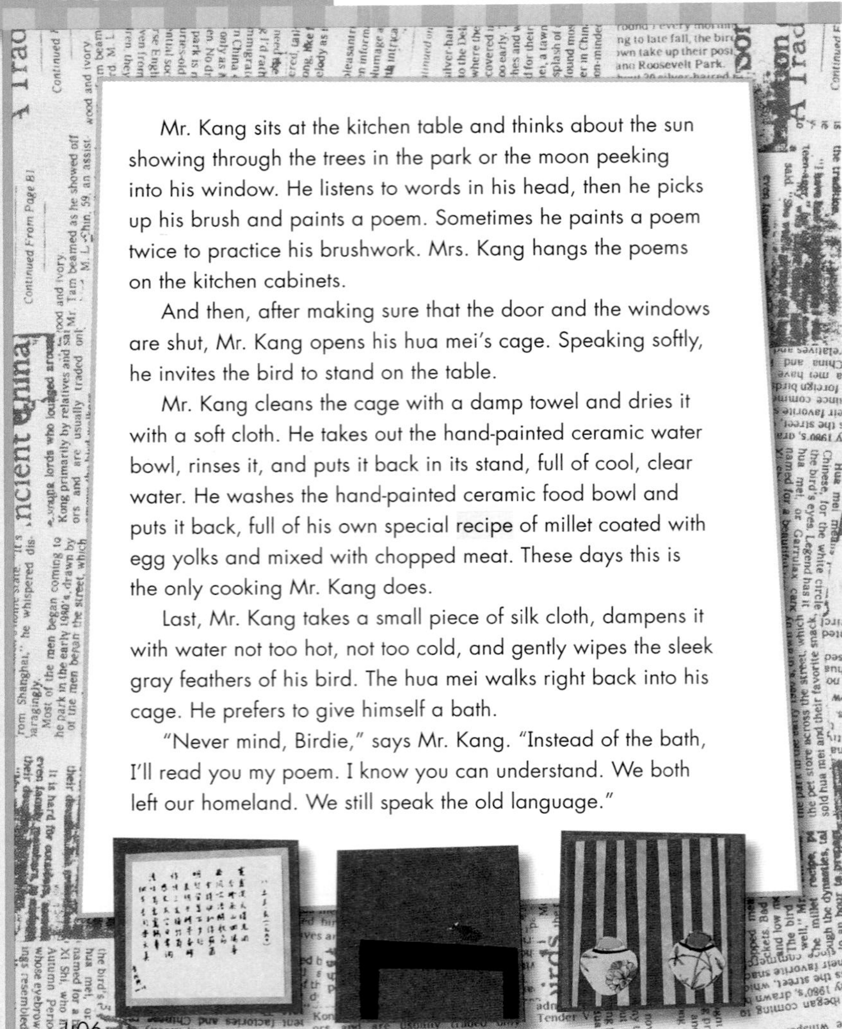

Mr. Kang sits at the kitchen table and thinks about the sun showing through the trees in the park or the moon peeking into his window. He listens to words in his head, then he picks up his brush and paints a poem. Sometimes he paints a poem twice to practice his brushwork. Mrs. Kang hangs the poems on the kitchen cabinets.

And then, after making sure that the door and the windows are shut, Mr. Kang opens his hua mei's cage. Speaking softly, he invites the bird to stand on the table.

Mr. Kang cleans the cage with a damp towel and dries it with a soft cloth. He takes out the hand-painted ceramic water bowl, rinses it, and puts it back in its stand, full of cool, clear water. He washes the hand-painted ceramic food bowl and puts it back, full of his own special recipe of millet coated with egg yolks and mixed with chopped meat. These days this is the only cooking Mr. Kang does.

Last, Mr. Kang takes a small piece of silk cloth, dampens it with water not too hot, not too cold, and gently wipes the sleek gray feathers of his bird. The hua mei walks right back into his cage. He prefers to give himself a bath.

"Never mind, Birdie," says Mr. Kang. "Instead of the bath, I'll read you my poem. I know you can understand. We both left our homeland. We still speak the old language."

406

Rushing to the Golden Dragon
against a chilly wind,
the icy tears on my cheeks melt
with memories of warm old days.

Those who never left their home
stay safe, wrapped
in the arms of their motherfather land.
When they look out
their narrow windows,
they see their own kitchen gardens.
They know every plum tree, every kumquat,
every blade of grass, each gray pebble.

We who long ago tossed on cold waters
looking only straight ahead
watch our city mountains
from wide windows, tall rooftops.
Yet our old hearts hold old places.
We save, in old, grown heads,
a full-blown rose in summer,
the sound of bamboo leaves when
the wind is gentle,
the taste of mooncakes.

The hua mei sings his own melody back to Mr. Kang. Mr. Kang closes his eyes to listen.

"Beautiful, Birdie. You are a good poet and a good friend to me," says Mr. Kang.

407

Student Edition, pp. 406–407

Common Core State Standards

Literature 1. Ask and answer questions to demonstrate understanding of a text, referring explicitly to the text as the basis for the answers. **Literature 3.** Describe characters in a story (e.g., their traits, motivations, or feelings) and explain how their actions contribute to the sequence of events. **Speaking/Listening 1.d.** Explain their own ideas and understanding in light of the discussion.

Access Text

REVIEW CAUSE AND EFFECT Review the definitions of *cause* and *effect* on p. 398. Remind students that an effect is something that happens. A cause is why that thing happens. An effect may have more than one cause.

GUIDE PRACTICE Have students reread the first paragraph on p. 406. Ask students to identify an example of a cause-and-effect relationship. (The cause is that Mr. Kang wants to practice his brushwork. The effect is that sometimes he paints a poem twice.)

ON THEIR OWN Have students work together to identify other cause-and-effect relationships on pp. 406–407.

Close Reading

ANALYSIS Why do Mr. Kang and the hua mei both speak the old language? They come from the same homeland—China.

EVALUATION Why does Mr. Kang paint poems? to express his thoughts and feelings about things What thoughts and feelings does his poem on page 407 express? It describes his homesickness and sadness.

ANALYSIS How would you describe Mr. Kang's feelings for his new home and the one he left behind? Mr. Kang appreciates the new life he has made in America, but he still keeps the memory of things he loved in his homeland. He is both sad and happy.

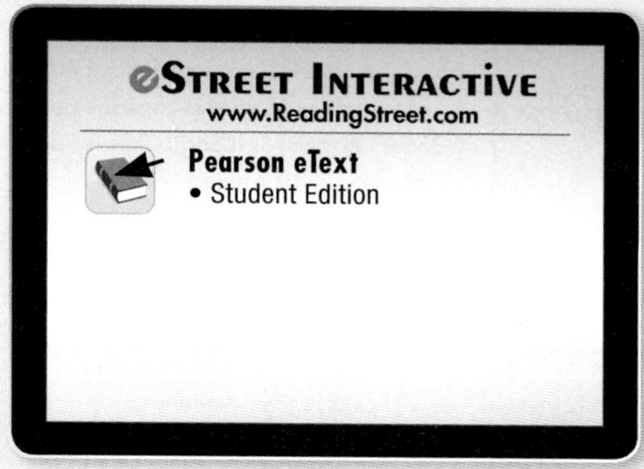

Access for All

SI Strategic Intervention

Have students make a T-chart with *Cause* in the left column and *Effect* in the right column. Tell students to list causes and effects as they read.

A Advanced

Have students predict what future effects hua mei's return might have on the relationship between hua mei, Sam, and Mr. Kang.

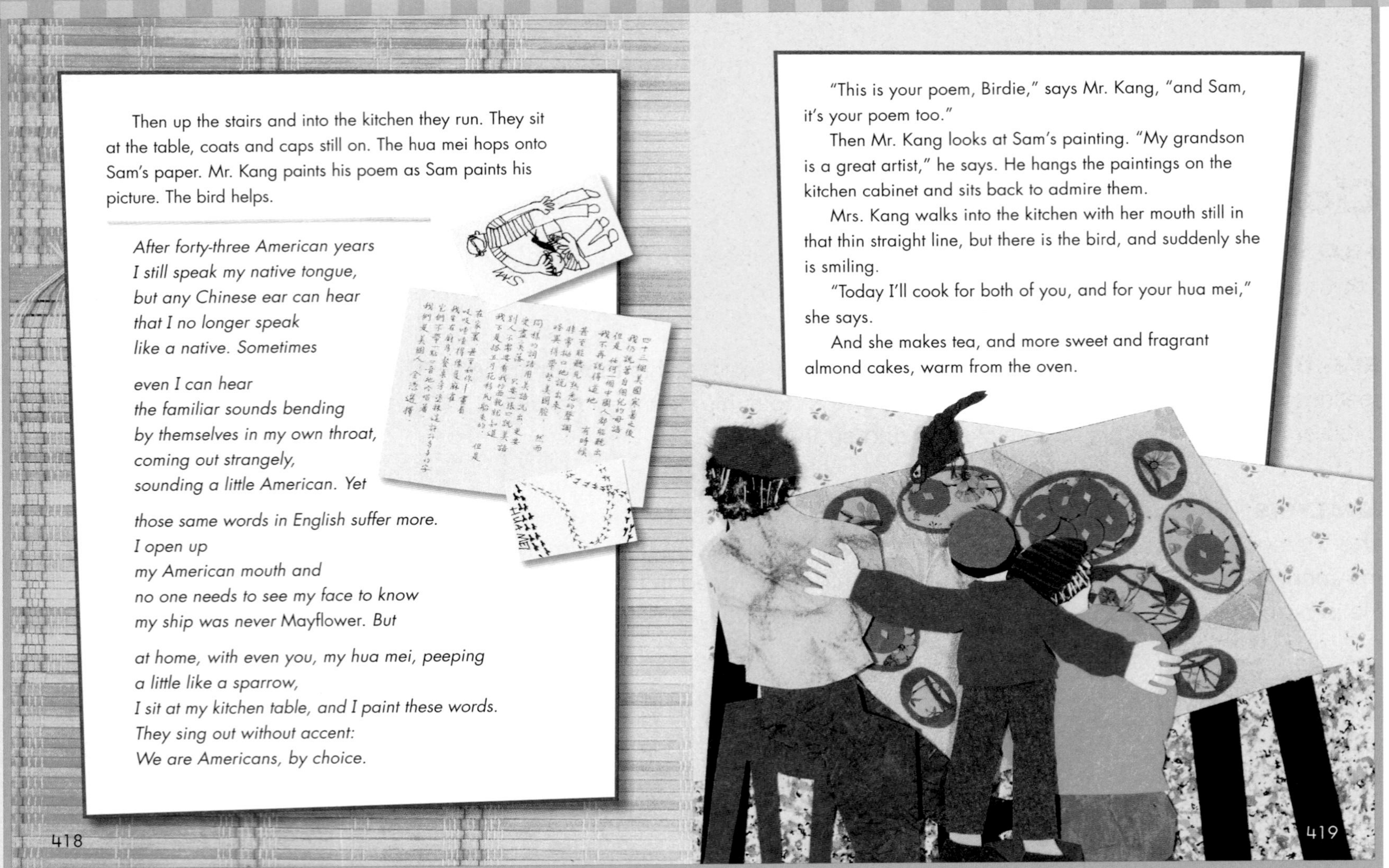

Then up the stairs and into the kitchen they run. They sit at the table, coats and caps still on. The hua mei hops onto Sam's paper. Mr. Kang paints his poem as Sam paints his picture. The bird helps.

After forty-three American years
I still speak my native tongue,
but any Chinese ear can hear
that I no longer speak
like a native. Sometimes

even I can hear
the familiar sounds bending
by themselves in my own throat,
coming out strangely,
sounding a little American. Yet

those same words in English suffer more.
I open up
my American mouth and
no one needs to see my face to know
my ship was never Mayflower. But

at home, with even you, my hua mei, peeping
a little like a sparrow,
I sit at my kitchen table, and I paint these words.
They sing out without accent:
We are Americans, by choice.

418

"This is your poem, Birdie," says Mr. Kang, "and Sam, it's your poem too."

Then Mr. Kang looks at Sam's painting. "My grandson is a great artist," he says. He hangs the paintings on the kitchen cabinet and sits back to admire them.

Mrs. Kang walks into the kitchen with her mouth still in that thin straight line, but there is the bird, and suddenly she is smiling.

"Today I'll cook for both of you, and for your hua mei," she says.

And she makes tea, and more sweet and fragrant almond cakes, warm from the oven.

419

Student Edition, pp. 418–419

Common Core State Standards

Literature 3. Describe characters in a story (e.g., their traits, motivations, or feelings) and explain how their actions contribute to the sequence of events. **Literature 4.** Determine the meaning of words and phrases as they are used in a text, distinguishing literal from nonliteral language. **Language 4.** Determine or clarify the meaning of unknown and multiple-meaning words and phrases based on grade 3 reading and content, choosing flexibly from a range of strategies. **Language 5.** Demonstrate understanding of figurative language, word relationships and nuances in word meanings.

Access Text

REVIEW ANTONYMS Review the meaning of antonyms on p. 400. Remind students that they can often use context clues such as antonyms to figure out the meaning of an unfamiliar word.

GUIDE PRACTICE Point out *familiar* on p. 418. Ask students to look around this word for words that have the opposite meaning. *(strangely)* Have students think of a definition for the opposite of *strange*. (not strange; known) Have students substitute this meaning in the sentence to see if it works. Have students write a sentence using the antonyms *familiar* and *strange* to show they understand the meaning of both words.

ON THEIR OWN Use *Let's Practice It!* p. 418 on the *Teacher Resources DVD-ROM* for additional practice with voacabulary.

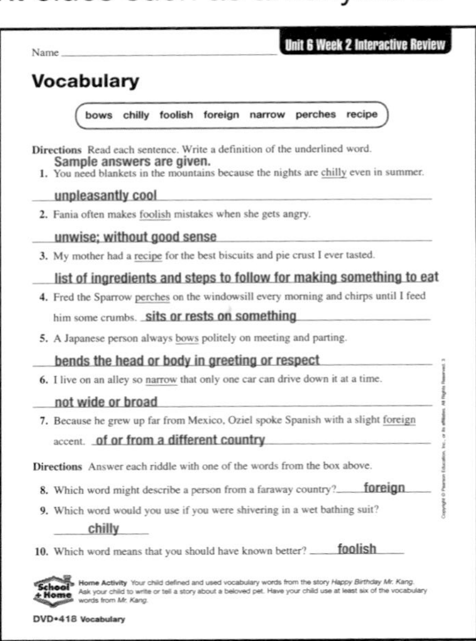

Name ______ **Unit 6 Week 2 Interactive Review**

Vocabulary

bows chilly foolish foreign narrow perches recipe

Directions Read each sentence. Write a definition of the underlined word. Sample answers are given.

1. You need blankets in the mountains because the nights are chilly even in summer. unpleasantly cool
2. Fania often makes foolish mistakes when she gets angry. unwise; without good sense
3. My mother had a recipe for the best biscuits and pie crust I ever tasted. list of ingredients and steps to follow for making something to eat
4. Fred the Sparrow perches on the windowsill every morning and chirps until I feed him some crumbs. sits or rests on something
5. A Japanese person always bows politely on meeting and parting. bends the head or body in greeting or respect
6. I live on an alley so narrow that only one car can drive down it at a time. not wide or broad
7. Because he grew up far from Mexico, Oziel spoke Spanish with a slight foreign accent. of or from a different country

Directions Answer each riddle with one of the words from the box above.

8. Which word might describe a person from a faraway country? foreign
9. Which word would you use if you were shivering in a wet bathing suit? chilly
10. Which word means that you should have known better? foolish

School + Home **Home Activity** Your child defined and used vocabulary words from the story *Happy Birthday Mr. Kang*. Ask your child to write or tell a story about a beloved pet. Have your child use at least six of the vocabulary words from *Mr. Kang*.

DVD•418 Vocabulary

Let's Practice It! TR DVD•418

Close Reading

DEVELOP LANGUAGE Have students reread p. 415 in the selection and find antonyms to help them figure out the meaning of *silence* in the fourth paragraph. (The antonym *loudly* in the fifth paragraph indicates that *silence* means *"quiet."*)

ANALYSIS Why might hua mei peep a little like a sparrow? Just as Mr. Kang's way of speaking has been affected by living in America, so, too, has hua mei's voice become more American.

INFERENCE When Mr. Kang lets hua mei go free, the story says that he can only hear the voice inside his own head and own heart. What voice is the author talking about? Mr. Kang is hearing his conscience that tells him the right thing to do.

EVALUATION In this story, hua mei decides to return to Mr. Kang. Do you think it is a good thing that hua mei returns? Why or why not? Yes, it is a good thing because Mr. Kang would be sad without hua mei.

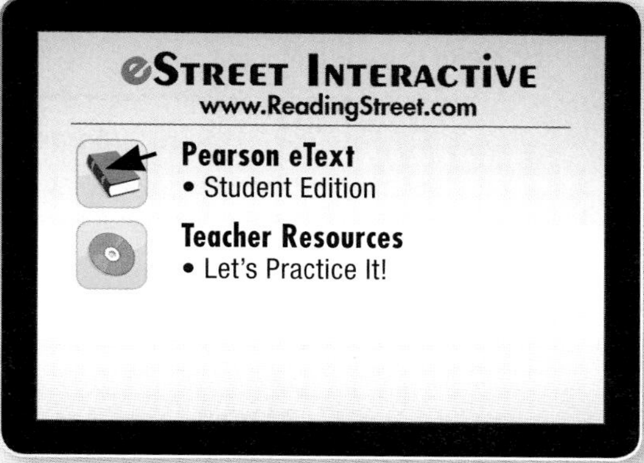

Access for All

SI Strategic Intervention
Have students practice using pairs of simple antonyms, such as *open/shut, warm/cold,* and *up/down*, together in sentences.

A Advanced
Have students use dictionaries and thesauruses to find antonyms for unfamiliar words in the story that are not accompanied by an antonym, such as *suffer* (p. 418) or *admire* (p. 419).

Name ______________________ **Unit 6 Week 2 Interactive Review**

Read the story. Then follow the directions and answer the questions.

Margaret

My mother always enjoys telling me stories about my great-great-great grandmother. Her name was Margaret and she was born a slave. She grew up on a plantation in the South, until the Civil War gave her freedom.

According to my mom, Margaret never stopped cherishing her freedom. Since she was free, she could finally go to school and learn to read and write. She began keeping a journal, which my mother still has today.

My mother says Margaret was just one in a long line of strong, free women, and that I will be one too, when I grow up. It sounds good to me! I would love to lead a life like Margaret's.

When the Civil War ended, Margaret had no place to live. So she moved north to Chicago. There she started a business baking pies and selling them to men working downtown. Because her pies were so good, she made lots of money. Soon she had enough to buy a little house for herself.

Then she met her husband, Richard. They got married and lived in her little house. That's where my great-great grandmother was born.

Soon, Margaret and Richard had five children. Richard worked on the railroad and Margaret kept making pies. Because of the money she earned selling those pies, all of their children got to go to college.

Name ______________________ **Unit 6 Week 2 Interactive Review**

The pies come up a lot in Margaret's journal. Apparently, she learned to make them from her mama on the plantation. But right before the Civil War, her mama was sold, and Margaret never saw her again.

Margaret wrote that making pies brought her mama back to her. She imagined her mama, free like her, baking in her kitchen, just as Margaret was. So she poured all of her love for her mama into her delicious pies.

Sometimes, when I close my eyes, I can smell those pies and taste the love she put into them. My mother says that love is still in me today.

1. Underline a sentence in the second paragraph that shows a cause-and-effect relationship. Circle the cause and effect signal word. **Answers are given.**
2. What caused Margaret to gain her freedom?
   The Civil War gave Margaret her freedom.
3. What were two effects of Margaret's successful pie business?
   She made enough money to buy a house and to send all her kids through college.

School + Home **Home Activity** Your child identified cause-and-effect relationships in the story. Have your child identify a cause-and-effect relationship in your family.

Let's Practice It! TR DVD•419–420

Common Core State Standards

Literature 1. Ask and answer questions to demonstrate understanding of a text, referring explicitly to the text as the basis for the answers. **Foundational Skills 3.** Know and apply grade-level phonics and word analysis skills in decoding words. **Foundational Skills 4.b.** Read on-level prose and poetry orally with accuracy, appropriate rate, and expression on successive readings. **Language 4.a.** Use sentence-level context as a clue to the meaning of a word or phrase. **Also Foundational Skills 4.**

Access Text

Have students read "Margaret" and respond to the questions.

REVIEW CAUSE AND EFFECT What were two effects of Margaret's successful pie business? She made enough money to buy a house and to send all her kids through college.

Tell students that sometimes there can be more than one effect from a single cause. There can sometimes be more than one cause for a single effect. Sometimes one cause and one effect can lead to another cause and effect.

REVIEW INFERRING Why do you think the pies come up a lot in Margaret's journal? They probably come up a lot because they were important to her. Not only did they help Margaret make money so she could give things to her family, but they also reminded her of her mama.

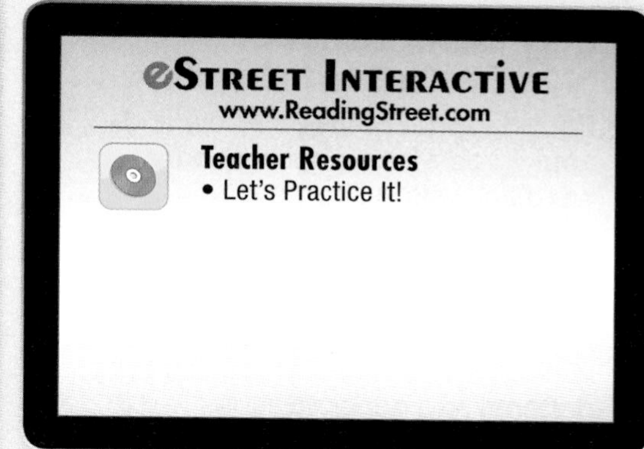

REVIEW ANTONYMS Which word near the word *slave* is an antonym that can help you figure out the meaning of the word *slave* in the first paragraph? What is the meaning of the word *slave*? The word *free* in the second paragraph is an antonym that helps me figure out the meaning of the word *slave*. The paragraph talks about Margaret gaining her freedom, which tells me she was not free before. That helps me understand that a *slave* is someone who is not free.

Remind students that when they find unfamiliar words in their reading, they can look for antonyms, or words with opposite meanings, and use them to figure out the meaning of the unfamiliar word.

REVIEW CAUSE AND EFFECT What caused Margaret to gain her freedom? The Civil War gave Margaret her freedom.

Underline the sentence that gives the reason why Margaret could finally get an education. (Since she was free, she could finally go to school and learn to read and write.)

Reread for Fluency

MODEL FLUENT READING Read the first four paragraphs of "Margaret" on p. 419 aloud, using appropriate phrasing as you read. Explain to students that the way we speak affects how listeners understand what we are saying.

Routine Oral Rereading

1. **Read** Have students read "Margaret" orally.
2. **Reread** To achieve optimal fluency, students should reread the text three or four times.
3. **Corrective Feedback** Listen as students read. Provide corrective feedback regarding their oral reading, paying special attention to appropriate phrasing.

Routines Flip Chart

Common Core State Standards

Foundational Skills 3. Know and apply grade-level phonics and word analysis skills in decoding words. **Language 2.** Demonstrate command of the conventions of standard English capitalization, punctuation, and spelling when writing. **Language 2.f.** Use spelling patterns and generalizations (e.g., word families, position-based spellings, syllable patterns, ending rules, meaningful word parts) in writing words. **Also Writing 2.a., 2.b.**

Name ____________ **Unit 6 Week 2 Interactive Review**

Schwa Spelled with an *a, e, i, o, u,* and *y*

Directions Each word below has a missing letter that makes the schwa sound. Write the word correctly on the line.

1. _bove ____above____
2. min_s ____minus____
3. less_n ____lesson____
4. plan_t ____planet____
5. an_mal ____animal____
6. _lone ____alone____
7. din_saur ____dinosaur____
8. _ pon ____upon____
9. vin_l ____vinyl____
10. bask_t ____basket____

Directions Each sentence below contains a pair of words in ( ). Circle the word that has a schwa sound in an unaccented syllable.

11. I stopped at the candy store to buy some (caramels, gumdrops).
12. The blue (armchair, sofa) is our cat's favorite place to nap.
13. My dad enjoys watching baseball on (Tuesdays, television).
14. Jill plays the (clarinet, oboe) in our school band.
15. We buy fruits and vegetables from a (local, nearby) farmer.
16. Kyoko learned to play the (piano, trumpet) when she was six.
17. My mother likes to spread (butter, jelly) on her toast in the morning.
18. The rocking horse has a (joyful, silly) expression painted on its face.
19. Rose requested a new (camera, suitcase) for her birthday.
20. (Friday, Tomorrow) is the last day to enter the contest.

School + Home **Home Activity** Your child identified and wrote words that contain the schwa sound in unaccented syllables. Play a game with your child in which you take turns writing original sentences about a favorite activity. Identify words with the schwa sound in each other's sentences. Players get one point for each correct identification.

Schwa Spelled with an *a, e, i, o, u,* and *y* DVD•417

Let's Practice It! TR DVD•417

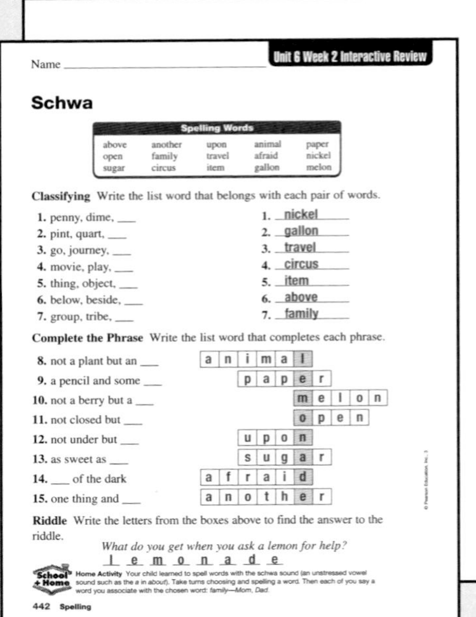
Name ____________ **Unit 6 Week 2 Interactive Review**

Schwa

Spelling Words				
above	another	upon	animal	paper
open	family	travel	afraid	nickel
sugar	circus	item	gallon	melon

Classifying Write the list word that belongs with each pair of words.

1. penny, dime, ___ — 1. nickel
2. pint, quart, ___ — 2. gallon
3. go, journey, ___ — 3. travel
4. movie, play, ___ — 4. circus
5. thing, object, ___ — 5. item
6. below, beside, ___ — 6. above
7. group, tribe, ___ — 7. family

Complete the Phrase Write the list word that completes each phrase.

8. not a plant but an ___ a n i m a l
9. a pencil and some ___ p a p e r
10. not a berry but a ___ m e l o n
11. not closed but ___ o p e n
12. not under but ___ u p o n
13. as sweet as ___ s u g a r
14. ___ of the dark a f r a i d
15. one thing and ___ a n o t h e r

Riddle Write the letters from the boxes above to find the answer to the riddle.

What do you get when you ask a lemon for help?
l e m o n a d e

School + Home **Home Activity** Your child learned to spell words with the schwa sound (an unstressed vowel sound such as the *a* in *about*). Take turns choosing and spelling a word. Then each of you say a word you associate with the chosen word: *family*—*Mom, Dad.*

442 Spelling

Reader's and Writer's Notebook, pp. 442–443

Word Analysis

REVIEW SCHWA Review the schwa in unaccented syllables using *Sound-Spelling Card* 144.

Use *Let's Practice It!* p. 417 on the *Teacher Resources DVD-ROM.*

READ WORDS IN ISOLATION Point out that students know how to read these words. Have students read the words together. Allow several seconds previewing time for the first reading.

READ WORDS IN CONTEXT Point out that there are many words in the sentences that students already know. Have students read the sentences together.

Corrective feedback	**If...** students have difficulty reading words with schwa, **then...** guide them in using the word parts strategy. Have students read all the words repeatedly until they can read the words fluently. Then have students read each sentence repeatedly until they can read the sentences fluently.

Spelling

REVIEW SCHWA Write *animal, family,* and *nickel*. Point out that these words have the schwa sound. Remind students that they have learned to spell words with schwa.

SPELLING STRATEGY Review words with schwa by having students follow the spelling strategy for spelling these words.

Step 1: Ask yourself: Which part of the word gives me a problem?

Step 2: Underline your problem part.

Step 3: Picture the word. Focus on the problem part.

Step 4: Say the whole word.

ON THEIR OWN Use p. 442 of the *Reader's and Writer's Notebook* for additional practice with spelling words with schwa.

Conventions

REVIEW ABBREVIATIONS An **abbreviation** is a shortened form of a word. Many abbreviations begin with a capital letter and end with a period.

GUIDE PRACTICE Write the following sentences. Have students identify the abbreviation in each sentence.

1. My birthday is **Sept.** 20.
2. **Mrs.** Helmer said I can bring treats to class.
3. Then on **Sat.,** I will have a party!

ON THEIR OWN For additional practice use the *Reader's and Writer's Notebook,* p. 443.

Routine Quick Write for Fluency — Team Talk

1. **Talk** Have pairs discuss the freedoms granted in *Happy Birthday Mr. Kang* and "Once Upon a Constitution."
2. **Write** Students write a few sentences about a freedom they have been granted, using abbreviations where appropriate.
3. **Share** Partners read their sentences to one another, checking for the correct use of any abbreviations.

Routines Flip Chart

eStreet Interactive
www.ReadingStreet.com

Teacher Resources
- Reader's and Writer's Notebook
- Let's Practice It!

Interactive Sound-Spelling Cards

Writing Workshop

Use the writing process lesson on pp. WP•1–WP•10 for this week's writing instruction.

Wrap Up Week 2 Review!

- ✔ **Content Knowledge** *How can we give the people around us more freedom?*
- ✔ **Cause and Effect** *If opening a birdcage is a cause, what is one likely effect?*
- ✔ **Antonyms** *What is the relationship between words that are antonyms?*

Preview DAY 3

Tell students that tomorrow they will review *Talking Walls: Art for the People.*

Review Week 3

Content Knowledge
Review Oral Vocabulary

Text-Based Comprehension
Review Graphic Sources

Selection Vocabulary
Review Unknown Words

Fluency
Accuracy

Phonics/Word Analysis
Review Final Syllables

Spelling
Review Final Syllables

Conventions
Review Combining Sentences

Writing
Quick Write for Fluency

Materials

- Student Edition
- Retelling Cards
- Reader's and Writer's Notebook

Common Core State Standards

Speaking/Listening 1. Engage effectively in a range of collaborative discussions (one-on-one, in groups, and teacher-led) with diverse partners on grade 3 topics and texts, building on others' ideas and expressing their own clearly. **Language 4.** Determine or clarify the meaning of unknown and multiple-meaning words and phrases based on grade 3 reading and content, choosing flexibly from a range of strategies. **Language 6.** Acquire and use accurately grade-appropriate conversational, general academic, and domain-specific words and phrases, including those that signal spatial and temporal relationships (e.g., *After dinner that night we went looking for them*).

Content Knowledge

Freedom of Expression

REVISIT THE CONCEPT Today students will explore how the question for this unit of study connects to *Talking Walls: Art for the People*. Remind students of the Question of the Week, *Why is freedom of expression important?*

Build Oral Language

DISCUSS FREEDOM Remind students of the question for this unit of study, *What does freedom mean?* Use the prompts and the concept map from Week 3 to discuss why freedom of expression is important to each one of us.

- What emotions does freedom of expression bring about?
- What significant events have helped ensure that people can freely express themselves?
- How would your life be different without freedom of expression?

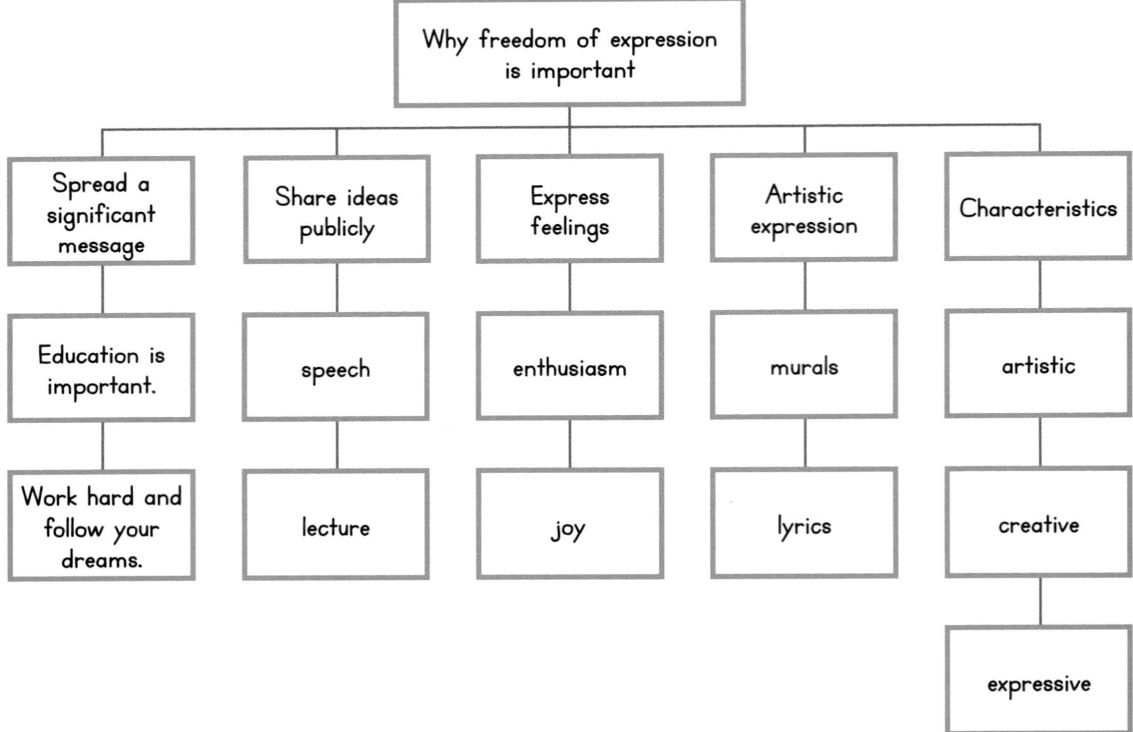

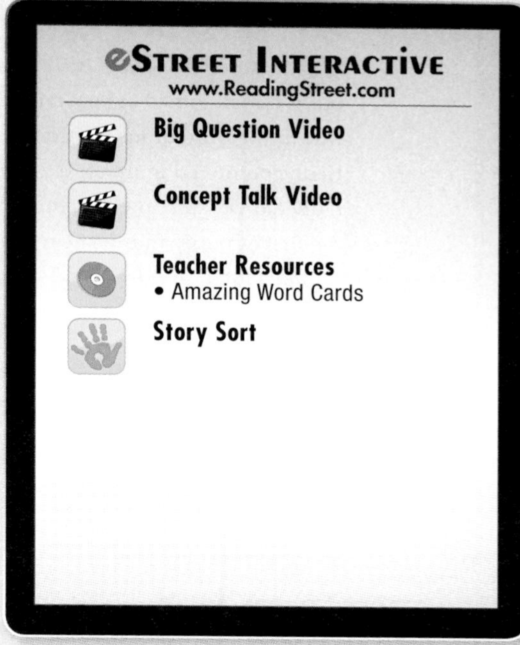

Build Oral Vocabulary

REVIEW AMAZING WORDS Display the Amazing Words for *Talking Walls: Art for the People.* Remind students that the words are related to the week's concept.

Amazing Words — Robust Vocabulary Routine

1. **Review** Ask students for definitions of the words, starting at the top of the list. Listen for accurate definitions with appropriate detail. Prompt students to connect the words to the unit concept of Freedom whenever possible.
2. **Demonstrate** Have students use two or more Amazing Words in the same sentence. Guide the discussion by providing an example that shows the meaning of each word. I wanted to *view* the mural again to take in all of the *exquisite* details. Follow this pattern to the end of the list, covering as many of the ten words as possible.
3. **Apply** Assign the words in random order and have students come up with more new sentences for them. To show that you are becoming more comfortable using these Amazing Words, think up more new sentences for them.

Routines Flip Chart

AMAZING WORDS AT WORK Have students use the Retelling Cards/Story Sort for *Talking Walls: Art for the People* to talk about the Amazing Words.

CONNECT TO READING Tell students that today they will be rereading passages from *Talking Walls: Art for the People* and reading "Cave Paintings." As they read, ask students to think about how artists value freedom of expression.

Amazing Words

creative	lecture
expressive	significant
emotion	pause
artistic	view
exquisite	lyrics

ELL

Build Background Use ELL Poster 28 to review the Week 3 lesson concept and to practice oral language. Point out and read the question: *Why is freedom of expression important?*

Dreams of Flight

David Botello—the older brother of Paul—loved to paint and dreamed of becoming an artist. When he was in the third grade, he and his art partner, Wayne Healy, painted a mural of a dinosaur in art class. Little did David know that that dinosaur mural was the first of many murals he would paint with Wayne.

Years later, the childhood friends, now both artists, decided to go into business together painting murals. David and Wayne often create and paint murals together, but not always.

David painted a large mural called "Dreams of Flight" at Estrada Courts, a public housing project in Los Angeles. He says, "I've always wanted this mural to speak to the children who see it, and to say, 'Your dreams can come true.'"

ARTIST	LOCATION	TITLE
Hector Ponce	Los Angeles, California	"Immigrant"
Joshua Sarantitis	Philadelphia, Pennsylvania	"Reach High and You Will Go Far"
Paul Botello	Los Angeles, California	"A Shared Hope"
Allyn Cox	U.S. Capitol, Washington, D.C.	"Declaration of Independence, 1776"

448

It's interesting to note that when the artist repainted the mural seventeen years after it was originally completed, he changed one of the children from a boy to a girl. Much had changed over the years, and the artist wanted all children to know that girls can dream of flying model airplanes too. It is the artist's hope that over time the mural will inspire many of the children who see it to work hard and follow their dreams.

"Dreams of Flight," Los Angeles, California

449

Student Edition, pp. 448–449

Common Core State Standards

Informational Text 1. Ask and answer questions to demonstrate understanding of a text, referring explicitly to the text as the basis for the answers. **Informational Text 7.** Use information gained from illustrations (e.g., maps, photographs) and the words in a text to demonstrate understanding of the text (e.g., where, when, why, and how key events occur).

Access Text

REVIEW GRAPHIC SOURCES Review the definition of graphic sources on p. 434. Remind students that graphic sources show information visually. They support the text by providing additional information. Charts, photos, diagrams, maps, and graphs are all graphic sources.

GUIDE PRACTICE Have students identify the chart on p. 448. Ask them what information is shown in the chart and how it adds to their understanding of the text. Be sure they understand that charts like this are one way of organizing the information in a text.

ON THEIR OWN Have students look at the photograph on p. 449 and discuss how the effect would be different if the photograph did not show the wire fence in front of the mural.

Close Reading ©

INFERENCE • TEXT EVIDENCE What clues in the text and the photo tell you why David Botello titled the mural at Estrada Courts "Dreams of Flight"? He painted this mural at a public housing project in Los Angeles, a place where many poor families lived. His mural shows many things related to flying—careers, hobbies, activities, imaginary creatures. He wanted to inspire children in the projects to dream big and soar high.

ANALYSIS • TEXT EVIDENCE When David Botello repainted his mural seventeen years later, he changed one of the children from a boy to a girl. Why? On what page do you find the answer? On p. 449, the artist explains that he changed the boy to a girl because he wanted to show girls also realizing their dreams.

INFERENCE What was the world probably like seventeen years earlier, when the artist first painted his mural with only boys flying model airplanes? It was a world in which people did not expect girls to be interested in model airplanes.

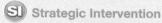

Access for All

SI Strategic Intervention

Using a map of the United States, have students locate the community where each mural in the story appears.

A Advanced

Have students create a T-chart listing all of the murals in the first column and their personal interpretation of them in the second column.

A Shared Hope

Paul Botello was 8 years old when he began helping his older brother, David, paint murals. Paul loved painting murals and was inspired to become an artist like his brother. When Paul graduated from high school, he went on to college to study art. Today he creates and paints murals, and he teaches art too!

Paul painted a special mural called "A Shared Hope" for an elementary school in Los Angeles, California. Most of the students at Esperanza School are immigrants from Central America. The mural speaks to the schoolchildren. It tells them that education is the key to success.

At the top of the mural, a teacher helps guide her students over the building blocks of life. Students are standing at the bottom of the painting holding objects that symbolize their future. Their parents stand behind to help guide and support them. Teachers, students, and parents from the school posed for the artist and his assistants as they created the mural.

"Education, hope, and immigration are my themes," says Paul Botello. "People immigrate to the United States because they hope for a better life. Through education, a better life can be accomplished."

"A Shared Hope," Los Angeles, California

446 447

Student Edition, pp. 446–447

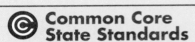

Common Core State Standards

Informational Text 1. Ask and answer questions to demonstrate understanding of a text, referring explicitly to the text as the basis for the answers. **Informational Text 2.** Determine the main idea of a text; recount the key details and explain how they support the main idea. **Informational Text 7.** Use information gained from illustrations (e.g., maps, photographs) and the words in a text to demonstrate understanding of the text (e.g., where, when, why, and how key events occur). **Foundational Skills 3.** Know and apply grade-level phonics and word analysis skills in decoding words. **Language 4.d.** Use glossaries or beginning dictionaries, both print and digital, to determine or clarify the precise meaning of key words and phrases.

Access Text

REVIEW UNKNOWN WORDS Review using a dictionary or glossary to find the meanings and pronunciations of any unknown words on p. 436. Remind students to look at the pronunciation key and the syllables in a dictionary or glossary entry to see how to pronounce a word correctly. They should also use information in the definition about part of speech to choose the meaning of the word that makes sense in the sentence.

GUIDE PRACTICE Point out the word *success* in the last line on p. 446. Have students use a dictionary or glossary to figure out the meaning of this word, its pronunciation, and its syllabication.

ON THEIR OWN Use *Let's Practice It!* p. 422 on the *Teacher Resources DVD-ROM* for additional practice with vocabulary.

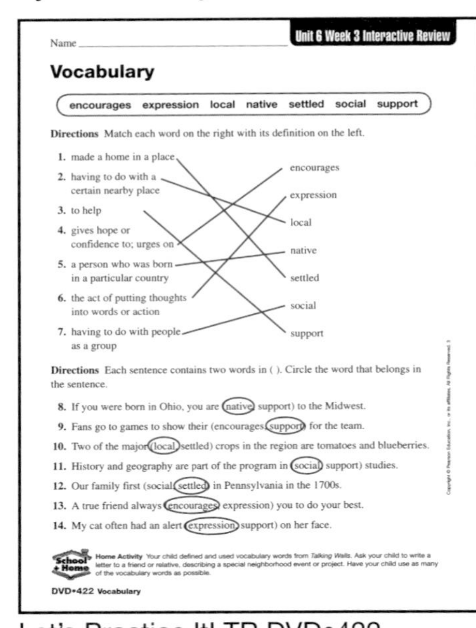

Name ______________ **Unit 6 Week 3 Interactive Review**

Vocabulary

encourages expression local native settled social support

Directions Match each word on the right with its definition on the left.

1. made a home in a place — settled
2. having to do with a certain nearby place — local
3. to help — support
4. gives hope or confidence to; urges on — encourages
5. a person who was born in a particular country — native
6. the act of putting thoughts into words or action — expression
7. having to do with people as a group — social

Directions Each sentence contains two words in ( ). Circle the word that belongs in the sentence.

8. If you were born in Ohio, you are (native, support) to the Midwest.
9. Fans go to games to show their (encourages, support) for the team.
10. Two of the major (local, settled) crops in the region are tomatoes and blueberries.
11. History and geography are part of the program in (social, support) studies.
12. Our family first (social, settled) in Pennsylvania in the 1700s.
13. A true friend always (encourages, expression) you to do your best.
14. My cat often had an alert (expression, support) on her face.

School + Home **Home Activity** Your child defined and used vocabulary words from *Talking Walls*. Ask your child to write a letter to a friend or relative, describing a special neighborhood event or project. Have your child use as many of the vocabulary words as possible.

DVD•422 Vocabulary

Let's Practice It! TR DVD•422

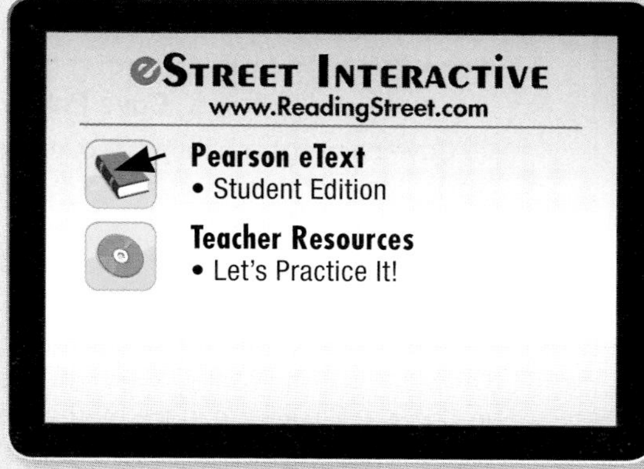

Close Reading ©

DEVELOP LANGUAGE What is the meaning of the word *immigrate* in the second paragraph on page 447? Use a dictionary or glossary to find the definition, pronunciation, and syllabication. Then make up a sentence of your own using *immigrate*. Meaning: "to come to a foreign country or region to live there." Pronunciation: /im//ə//grāt/. The accent is on the first syllable. Sentence: *Ian wants to immigrate to the United States because he wants to be free.*

ANALYSIS What information does the photo on pages 446–447 provide that is not in the text? The photo shows many details not mentioned in the text such as the rainbow and what the students, teachers, and parents look like. It also shows that the mural faces the playground where children will see it every day.

EVALUATION In your own words, explain what is the message of the mural "A Shared Hope." Teachers, parents, and students all need to support good education for children because education is the key to the success of those children.

INFERENCE How old was Paul Botello when he began helping his brother paint murals? He was 8 years old. What does the fact that he started painting at a young age tell you about Botello? He was creative and interested in art even as a young child.

Access for All

SI Strategic Intervention

Have students choose a word from the passage that they don't know, look it up in a dictionary or glossary, and find its meaning, pronunciation, and syllabication.

A Advanced

Ask students to read the second sentence on p. 447. Have students make up their own definition for the word *symbolize*. Then have students look this word up in a dictionary and compare the dictionary definition to their own definition.

Name ______________ **Unit 6 Week 3 Interactive Review**

Read the picture essay. **Answer** the questions.

Cave Paintings

Cave paintings are found all over the world. Many of them were made by people who lived in prehistoric times. Today, we study the details in cave paintings to understand how ancient people lived.

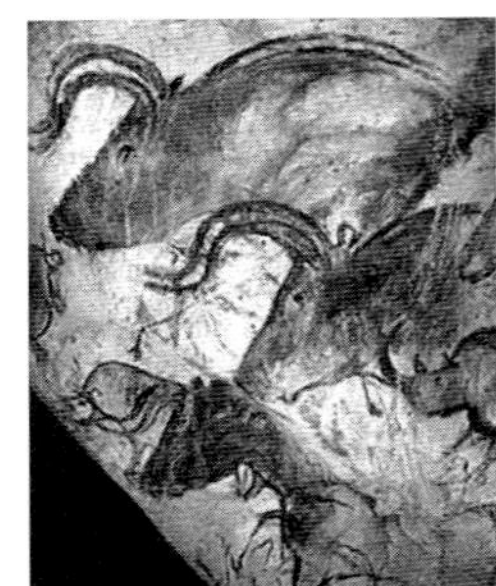
Painting 1

This painting is like one found in Chauvet Cave in France. The paintings in Chauvet Cave were made more than 30,000 years ago! The animals with horns are *aurochs*, giant oxen that are now extinct. These paintings were discovered in 1994 by three cave explorers.

Painting 2

This painting is like one found in Cueva de Las Manos, or Cave of the Hands, in Argentina. Since most of the hands are left hands, we think that the painters were right-handed!

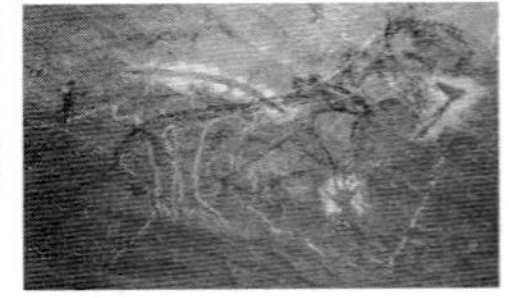
Painting 3

This painting of a kangaroo may be more than 2,000 years old. It is like one found in an Australian cave. Most cave paintings in Australia were done by ancient Aborigines, the first people there. Like other ancient people, Aborigines used paintings to record stories and ideas.

Name ______________ **Unit 6 Week 3 Interactive Review**

1. What does the first painting show?
   a painting like one found in Chauvet Cave in France
2. Look at the second painting. Write a caption, or label, for what you see.
   Possible response: This painting shows people's hands.
3. Why do you think the writer included paintings in this story?
   Possible response: to give readers a better idea of what cave paintings look like

School + Home **Home Activity** Your child used graphic sources to understand concepts in a nonfiction story. Look at an illustrated book with your child, and discuss the information contained in the photographs, charts, or maps.

Let's Practice It! TR DVD•423–424

Common Core State Standards

Informational Text 2. Determine the main idea of a text; recount the key details and explain how they support the main idea. **Informational Text 7.** Use information gained from illustrations (e.g., maps, photographs) and the words in a text to demonstrate understanding of the text (e.g., where, when, why, and how key events occur). **Language 4.** Determine or clarify the meaning of unknown and multiple-meaning words and phrases based on grade 3 reading and content, choosing flexibly from a range of strategies. **Language 4.d.** Use glossaries or beginning dictionaries, both print and digital, to determine or clarify the precise meaning of key words and phrases. **Also Foundational Skills 4., 4.b.**

Access Text

Have students read "Cave Paintings" and respond to the questions.

REVIEW GRAPHIC SOURCES Why do you think the writer included photographs in this story? to give readers a better idea of what cave paintings look like

Remind students that graphic sources such as photographs, maps, charts, and graphs show readers information in a visual way. Graphic sources help readers see what is written about in the text.

REVIEW IMPORTANT IDEAS What important ideas about cave paintings are conveyed in the first paragraph? Cave paintings are found all over the world; people who lived in prehistoric times made cave paintings; the paintings help us understand how ancient people lived.

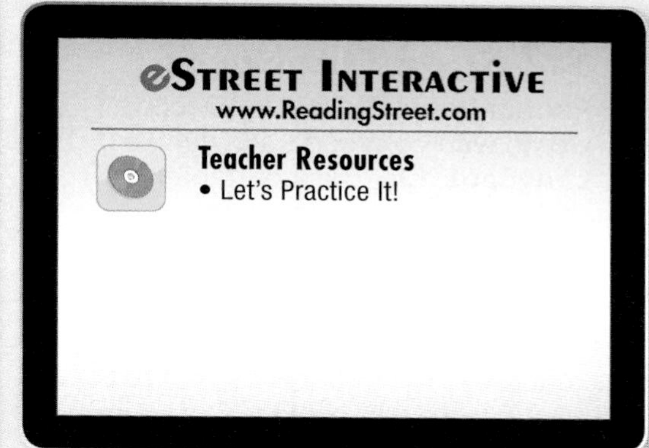

REVIEW UNKNOWN WORDS What is the meaning of the word *extinct* in the second paragraph? something that no longer exists

Review with students how to use a dictionary or glossary to find the meaning and pronunciation of unknown words. To find the word *extinct*, students would look under the letter *e*, find the pronunciation key for the word, and read to find a definition that fits the context of the sentence. Have students find another unknown word in the passage and tell how they would find its pronunciation and meaning.

REVIEW GRAPHIC SOURCES What does the first photograph show? a painting like one found in Chauvet Cave in France

Reread for Fluency

MODEL FLUENT READING Have students listen as you read the first three paragraphs of "Cave Paintings" on p. 423 aloud with accuracy. Explain that you will read each individual word correctly. Tell students that if any of the words were unknown, you would have looked them up before you began reading.

Routine Oral Rereading

1. **Select a Passage** Use paragraph four of "Cave Paintings."
2. **Model** Have students listen as you read with accuracy.
3. **Read** Have students read along with you.
4. **Reread** For optimal fluency, students should reread the text three or four times with accuracy.
5. **Corrective Feedback** Listen as students read. Provide corrective feedback regarding their oral reading, paying special attention to accuracy.

Routines Flip Chart

Common Core State Standards

Foundational Skills 3.b. Decode words with common Latin suffixes. **Language 1.h.** Use coordinating and subordinating conjunctions. **Language 1.i.** Produce simple, compound, and complex sentences. **Language 2.e.** Use conventional spelling for high-frequency and other studied words and for adding suffixes to base words (e.g., *sitting, smiled, cries, happiness*). **Also Writing 2.c., 10.**

Name ________ **Unit 6 Week 3 Interactive Review**

Final Syllables *-tion, -sion, -ture, -ive, -ize*

Directions Each sentence has a pair of words in ( ). Circle the word that is spelled correctly and completes the sentence.

1. We spent our (vacasion, vacation) driving through New England and Canada.
2. Answer every test (quession, question) as accurately as you can.
3. (Ficsion, Fiction) means "stories that come from a writer's imagination."
4. My sister has a huge (collecsion, collection) of valuable old books.
5. My mother promised to make a (decision, decition) about camp by tomorrow.
6. I think long (division, divition) is the hardest subject in math.
7. The famous Bayeux Tapestry shows the French (invasion, invation) of England.
8. When the director saw that everyone was ready, he called out ("Acsion!," "Action!")
9. Totah blocked my chess piece into a difficult (posision, position) on the board.
10. His nice manners made a good (impression, impretion) on everyone there.

Directions Add **-ture, -ive,** or **-ize** to complete each word below. Write the complete word on the line. (HINT: there is only one correct choice for each word.)

11. lec **lecture**
12. pic **picture**
13. dramat **dramatize**
14. real **realize**
15. na **nature**
16. secret **secretive**
17. crea **creature**
18. mass **massive**
19. act **active**
20. terror **terrorize**

School + Home **Home Activity** Your child identified and wrote words that contain the syllables -tion, -sion, -ture, -ive, and -ize. Read a newspaper article on a favorite subject with your child. Have your child identify and define words that contain these five common syllables.

Final Syllables *-tion, -sion, -ture, -ive, -ize* DVD•421

Let's Practice It! TR DVD•421

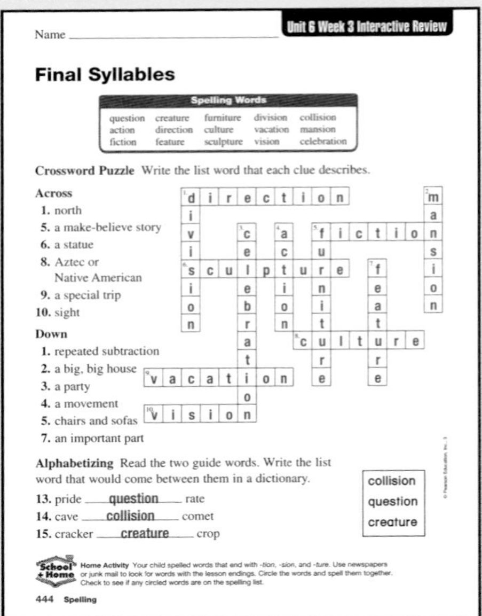

Name ________ **Unit 6 Week 3 Interactive Review**

Final Syllables

Spelling Words

question	creature	furniture	division	collision
action	direction	culture	vacation	mansion
fiction	feature	sculpture	vision	celebration

Crossword Puzzle Write the list word that each clue describes.

Across
1. north
5. a make-believe story
6. a statue
8. Aztec or Native American
9. a special trip
10. sight

Down
1. repeated subtraction
2. a big, big house
3. a party
4. a movement
5. chairs and sofas
7. an important part

Alphabetizing Read the two guide words. Write the list word that would come between them in a dictionary.

collision
question
creature

13. pride **question** rate
14. cave **collision** comet
15. cracker **creature** crop

School + Home **Home Activity** Your child spelled words that end with *-tion, -sion,* and *-ture.* Use newspapers or junk mail to look for words with the lesson endings. Circle the words and spell them together. Check to see if any circled words are on the spelling list.

444 Spelling

Reader's and Writer's Notebook, p. 444

Word Analysis

REVIEW FINAL SYLLABLES *-tion, -ion, -ture, -ive, -ize* Review final syllables *-tion, -ion, -ture, -ive,* and *-ize* using *Sound Spelling Cards* 131, 132, 133, 135, and 136.

Use *Let's Practice It!* p. 421 on the *Teacher Resources DVD-ROM.*

READ WORDS IN ISOLATION Point out that students know how to read these words. Have students read the words together. Allow several seconds previewing time for the first reading.

READ WORDS IN CONTEXT Point out that there are many words in the sentences that students already know. Have students read the sentences together.

Corrective feedback

If... students have difficulty reading words with final syllables, **then...** guide them in using the word parts strategy. Have students read all the words repeatedly until they can read the words fluently. Then have students read each sentence repeatedly until they can read the sentences fluently.

Spelling

REVIEW FINAL SYLLABLES *-ion, -ure* Write *question, division,* and *creature.* Point out that these words contain the final syllables *-ion* and *-ure.* Remind students that they have learned how to spell words with these final syllables.

SPELLING STRATEGY Review words with the final syllables *-ion* or *-ure* by having students follow the spelling strategy for spelling these words.

Step 1: Draw a line between the base word and its final syllable.

Step 2: Study the word one part at a time.

Step 3: Read the whole word.

ON THEIR OWN Use p. 444 of the *Reader's and Writer's Notebook* for additional practice with spelling words with the final syllables *-ion* or *-ure.*

Conventions

REVIEW COMBINING SENTENCES When you combine sentences, you join two choppy sentences that have the same subject, and predicate, or are about the same topic.

GUIDE PRACTICE Read the following sentences. Have the students combine the sentences to make a compound sentence.

1. **We visited the museum. We saw many items on display.**
2. **I want to paint a picture. I want to make a sculpture.**

ON THEIR OWN For additional practice use the *Reader's and Writer's Notebook,* p. 445.

Routine Quick Write for Fluency **Team Talk**

1. **Talk** Have pairs use *Talking Walls* and "The History of Palindromes" to discuss how both words and art can be used to express ideas.
2. **Write** Each student writes a paragraph about why freedom of expression is important, combining short sentences where appropriate.
3. **Share** Partners read one another's paragraphs and check for combined sentences.

Routines Flip Chart

eSTREET INTERACTIVE
www.ReadingStreet.com

Teacher Resources
- Reader's and Writer's Notebook
- Let's Practice It!

Interactive Sound-Spelling Cards

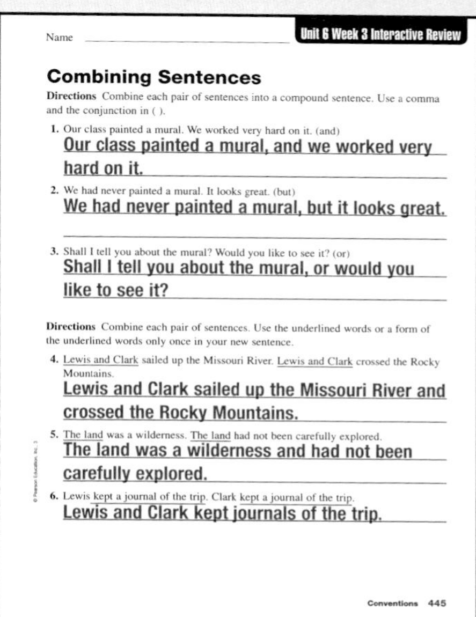
Name ______________ **Unit 6 Week 3 Interactive Review**

Combining Sentences

Directions Combine each pair of sentences into a compound sentence. Use a comma and the conjunction in ( ).

1. Our class painted a mural. We worked very hard on it. (and)
Our class painted a mural, and we worked very hard on it.
2. We had never painted a mural. It looks great. (but)
We had never painted a mural, but it looks great.
3. Shall I tell you about the mural? Would you like to see it? (or)
Shall I tell you about the mural, or would you like to see it?

Directions Combine each pair of sentences. Use the underlined words or a form of the underlined words only once in your new sentence.

4. Lewis and Clark sailed up the Missouri River. Lewis and Clark crossed the Rocky Mountains.
Lewis and Clark sailed up the Missouri River and crossed the Rocky Mountains.
5. The land was a wilderness. The land had not been carefully explored.
The land was a wilderness and had not been carefully explored.
6. Lewis kept a journal of the trip. Clark kept a journal of the trip.
Lewis and Clark kept journals of the trip.

Conventions 445

Reader's and Writer's Notebook, p. 445

Writing Workshop

Use pp. WP•1–WP•10 for this week's writing instruction.

Wrap Up Week 3 Review!

- ✔ **Content Knowledge** *How do you express yourself?*
- ✔ **Graphic Sources** *How can diagrams, maps, or charts help clarify ideas?*
- ✔ **Unknown Words** *What resources can you use to figure out the meaning of unknown words?*

Preview DAY 4

Tell students that tomorrow they will review *Two Bad Ants.*

Review Week 4

Content Knowledge
Review Oral Vocabulary

Text-Based Comprehension
Review Literary Elements: Plot and Theme

Selection Vocabulary
Review Prefixes and Suffixes, *un-, dis-, -ful*

Fluency
Rate

Phonics/Word Analysis
Review Prefixes *im-, in-*

Spelling
Review Prefixes, Suffixes, and Endings

Conventions
Review Commas

Writing
Quick Write for Fluency

Materials
- Student Edition
- Retelling Cards
- Reader's and Writer's Notebook

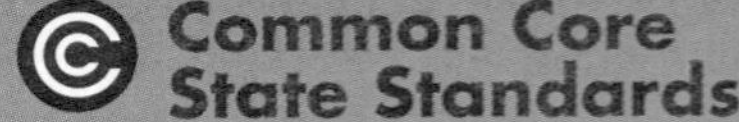

Common Core State Standards

Speaking/Listening 1. Engage effectively in a range of collaborative discussions (one-on-one, in groups, and teacher led) with diverse partners on grade 3 topics and texts, building on others' ideas and expressing their own clearly. **Language 6.** Acquire and use accurately grade-appropriate conversational, general academic, and domain-specific words and phrases, including those that signal spatial and temporal relationships (e.g., *After dinner that night we went looking for them*).

Content Knowledge

Rules and Laws are Important to Freedom

REVISIT THE CONCEPT Today students will explore how the question for this unit of study connects to *Two Bad Ants*. Remind students of the Question of the Week, *Why are rules and laws important to freedom?*

Build Oral Language

DISCUSS FREEDOM Remind students of the question for this unit of study, *What does freedom mean?* Use the prompts and the concept map from Week 4 to discuss why rules and laws are important to freedom.

- Does having freedom mean you can do anything you want? Why or why not?
- What kinds of consequences do you expect when you do not obey classroom rules?
- How does sharing the responsibility for classroom chores help everyone in the class have more freedom?

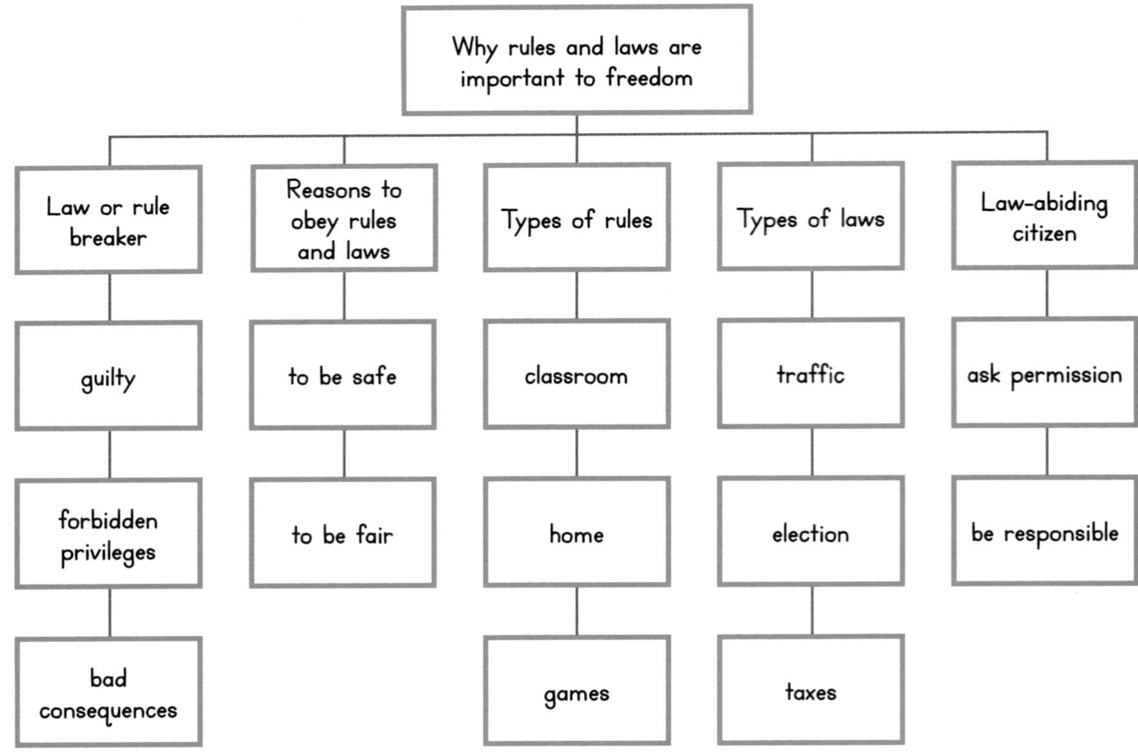

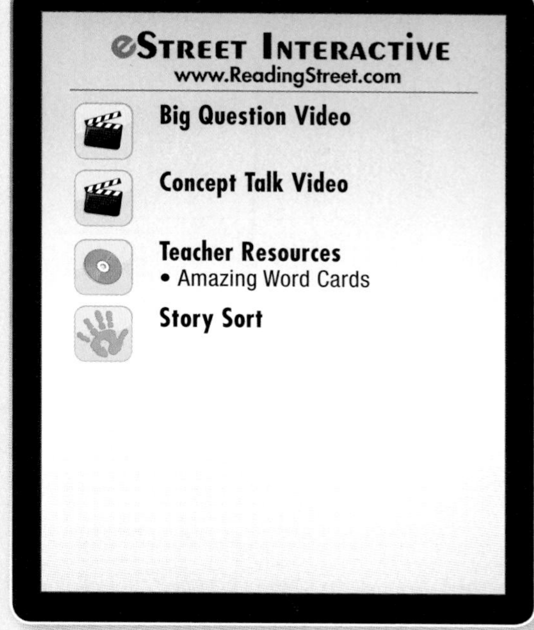

Build Oral Vocabulary

REVIEW AMAZING WORDS Display the Amazing Words for *Two Bad Ants.* Remind students that the words are related to the week's concept.

Amazing Words Robust Vocabulary Routine

1. **Review** Ask students for definitions of the words, starting at the top of the list. Listen for accurate definitions. Prompt students to connect the words to the unit concept of Freedom whenever possible.
2. **Demonstrate** Have students use two or more Amazing Words in the same sentence. Guide the discussion by providing an example that shows the meaning of each word. Each *citizen* of our town, no matter what his or her age, has a *responsibility* to *obey,* or follow, laws. Follow this pattern to the end of the list, covering as many of the ten words as possible.
3. **Apply** Assign the words in random order and have students come up with more new sentences for them. To show that you are becoming more comfortable using these Amazing Words, think up more new sentences for them.

Routines Flip Chart

AMAZING WORDS AT WORK Have students use the Retelling Cards/Story Sort for *Two Bad Ants* to talk about the Amazing Words.

CONNECT TO READING Tell students that today they will be rereading passages from *Two Bad Ants* and reading "The Wrong Colors." As they read, ask students to think about what the characters learned about rules and freedom.

Amazing Words

obey	fascinate
responsibility	guilt
consequence	encounter
permission	forbid
citizen	eerie

Build Background Use ELL Poster 29 to review the Week 4 lesson concept and to practice oral language. Point out and read the question: *Why are rules and laws important to freedom?*

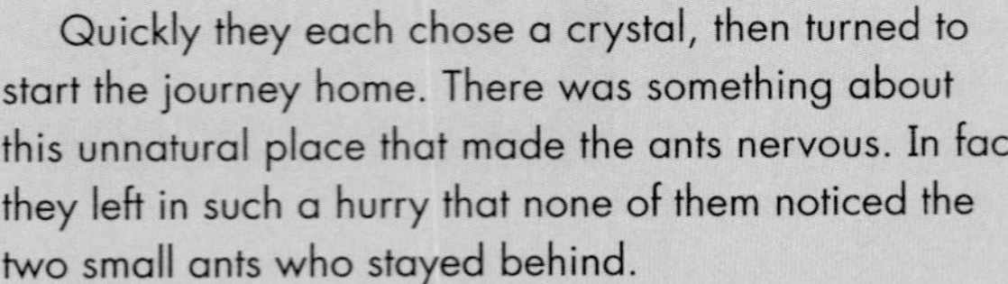

Quickly they each chose a crystal, then turned to start the journey home. There was something about this unnatural place that made the ants nervous. In fact they left in such a hurry that none of them noticed the two small ants who stayed behind.

"Why go back?" one asked the other. "This place may not feel like home, but look at all these crystals."

"You're right," said the other. "We can stay here and eat this tasty treasure every day, forever." So the two ants ate crystal after crystal until they were too full to move, and fell asleep.

476

Daylight came. The sleeping ants were unaware of changes taking place in their new-found home. A giant silver scoop hovered above them, then plunged deep into the crystals. It shoveled up both ants and crystals and carried them high into the air.

The ants were wide awake when the scoop turned, dropping them from a frightening height. They tumbled through space in a shower of crystals and fell into a boiling brown lake.

477

Student Edition, pp. 476–477

Common Core State Standards

Literature 1. Ask and answer questions to demonstrate understanding of a text, referring explicitly to the text as the basis for the answers. **Literature 2.** Recount stories, including fables, folktales, and myths from diverse cultures; determine the central message, lesson, or moral and explain how it is conveyed through key details in the text. **Literature 4.** Determine the meaning of words and phrases as they are used in a text, distinguishing literal from nonliteral language.

Access Text

REVIEW LITERARY ELEMENTS: PLOT AND THEME Review the definitions of plot and theme on p. 464. Remind students that the plot is made up of the important events in the beginning, middle, and end of a story. The theme is the big idea of the story.

GUIDE PRACTICE Have students reread p. 476 and identify the event on this page that is important to the plot of this story. (The two ants decide not to return with the other ants.) Why is this event important to the story? This event changes the course of the story. The two ants become the central characters and the story becomes about them.

ON THEIR OWN Have students reread p. 477 of *Two Bad Ants* and describe the events that affect the plot.

Close Reading ©

ANALYSIS What unstated rule did the two ants break? What were the consequences of their actions? They were not supposed to leave the group. They put themselves in danger of being killed or hurt.

EVALUATION The two ants in this story make a choice to stay in the unnatural place. Was the decision a good decision or a bad one? Why? It was a bad decision because staying in the place put the ants in danger.

INFERENCE What do you think the "boiling brown lake" is? Why do you think so? (The boiling brown lake is probably a cup of coffee or tea. The ants are in a sugar bowl, and some people put sugar in their coffee or tea.

Access for All

SI Strategic Intervention

Have students discuss what is happening on pp. 476–477. Encourage them to look at the illustrations to help them understand that the ants are in a canister of sugar. A spoon is scooping up sugar for a cup of tea or coffee and has also scooped up the ants. Ask: *What happens last on these pages?* (The spoon drops the ants into a cup of very hot coffee or tea.)

A Advanced

Have partners discuss how the author presents ants as a group and as individuals. Then have them create a T-chart to list similarities and differences.

Then the giant scoop stirred violently back and forth. Crushing waves fell over the ants. They paddled hard to keep their tiny heads above water. But the scoop kept spinning the hot brown liquid.

Around and around it went, creating a whirlpool that sucked the ants deeper and deeper. They both held their breath and finally bobbed to the surface, gasping for air and spitting mouthfuls of the terrible, bitter water.

478

Then the lake tilted and began to empty into a cave. The ants could hear the rushing water and felt themselves pulled toward the pitch-black hole. Suddenly the cave disappeared and the lake became calm. The ants swam to the shore and found that the lake had steep sides.

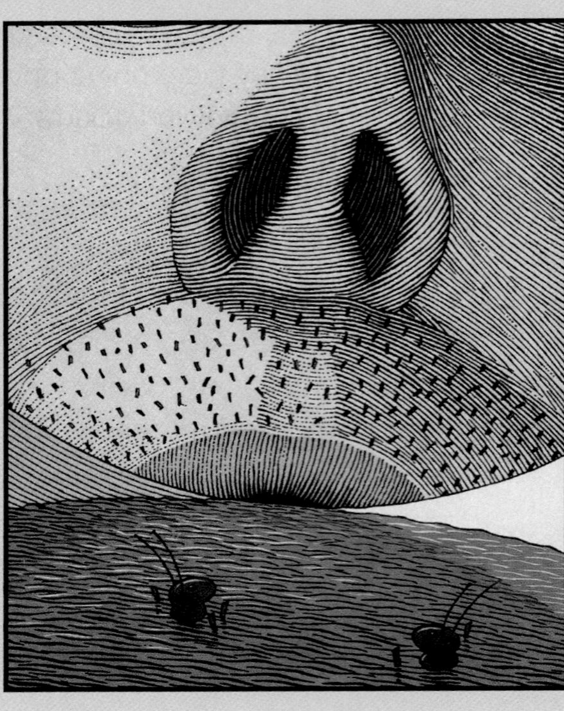

479

Student Edition, pp. 478–479

Common Core State Standards

Literature 1. Ask and answer questions to demonstrate understanding of a text, referring explicitly to the text as the basis for the answers. **Foundational Skills 3.a.** Identify and know the meaning of the most common prefixes and derivational suffixes. **Language 4.b.** Determine the meaning of the new word formed when a known affix is added to a known word (e.g., *agreeable/disagreeable, comfortable/uncomfortable, care/careless, heat/preheat*).

Access Text

REVIEW PREFIXES AND SUFFIXES *UN-, DIS-, -FUL* Review prefixes and suffixes on p. 466. Tell students that knowing prefixes and suffixes can help them figure out the meaning of unknown words. Remind them that the prefixes *un-* and *dis-* make a word mean "not" or "opposite" of the word. The suffix *-ful* makes a word mean "full of" something.

GUIDE PRACTICE Point out *mouthfuls* on p. 478 and *disappeared* on p. 479. Have students identify the base words, endings, suffixes, and prefixes in these words. Have students tell what each prefix means and how it changes the meaning of each base word.

ON THEIR OWN Use *Let's Practice It!* p. 426 on the *Teacher Resources DVD-ROM* for additional practice with words with vocabulary.

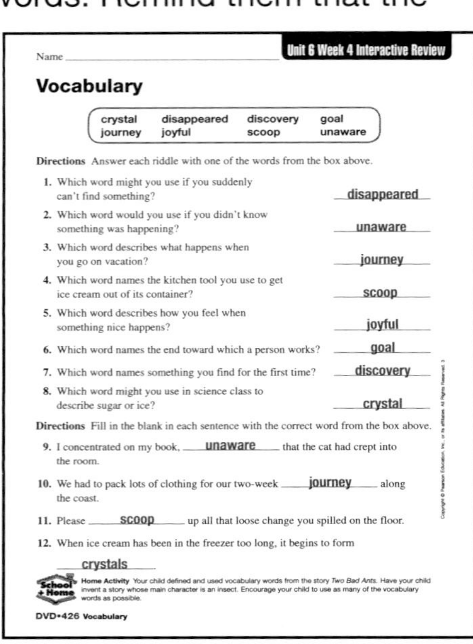
Name ____________ **Unit 6 Week 4 Interactive Review**

Vocabulary

crystal, disappeared, discovery, goal, journey, joyful, scoop, unaware

Directions Answer each riddle with one of the words from the box above.

1. Which word might you use if you suddenly can't find something? disappeared
2. Which word would you use if you didn't know something was happening? unaware
3. Which word describes what happens when you go on vacation? journey
4. Which word names the kitchen tool you use to get ice cream out of its container? scoop
5. Which word describes how you feel when something nice happens? joyful
6. Which word names the end toward which a person works? goal
7. Which word names something you find for the first time? discovery
8. Which word might you use in science class to describe sugar or ice? crystal

Directions Fill in the blank in each sentence with the correct word from the box above.

9. I concentrated on my book, unaware that the cat had crept into the room.
10. We had to pack lots of clothing for our two-week journey along the coast.
11. Please scoop up all that loose change you spilled on the floor.
12. When ice cream has been in the freezer too long, it begins to form crystals.

Home Activity Your child defined and used vocabulary words from the story *Two Bad Ants*. Have your child invent a story whose main character is an insect. Encourage your child to use as many of the vocabulary words as possible.

DVD•426 Vocabulary

Let's Practice It! TR DVD•426

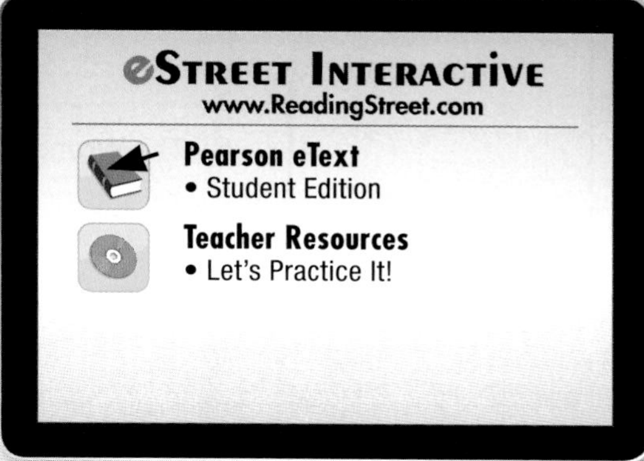

Close Reading ©

DEVELOP LANGUAGE Think of words with the prefix *un-* that describe the way the two ants might have felt on pages 478–479. Use a dictionary to add to your list. *uncomfortable, unhappy, unlucky, unprepared*

EVALUATION Why do you think the author didn't identify the scoop as a spoon, the hot brown liquid as coffee or tea, and the cave as a mouth? He is presenting the story through the ants' eyes. The ants wouldn't know what these things are called.

INFERENCE • TEXT EVIDENCE Do you think the person in the story noticed the ants in the coffee? How do you know? Give examples from the text to support your answer. No. The person took a drink and then set the cup back down. That's why on p. 479 the "lake became calm." Most likely, if the person had seen the ants in the coffee, he would have dumped out his cup.

EVALUATION Compare a group of ants to human soldiers. Why is it important that both groups follow rules and obey their leaders? Ants and soldiers both follow leaders and have to follow the rules. It is important because the rules are there to protect the group. An ant or a soldier who does not follow the rules can put himself or herself and others in danger.

Access for All

SI Strategic Intervention

Have students work with partners to list five words that have the prefix *dis-* or the suffix *-ful*. Have students use a dictionary to help them think of words. Then have partners make up a sentence using each word.

A Advanced

Have students write a short story that includes at least one word with the prefix *un-*, at least one word with the prefix *dis-*, and at least one word with the suffix *–ful.*

Name ____________ **Unit 6 Week 4 Interactive Review**

Read the story.
Answer the questions.

The Wrong Colors

Zoe the Zebra was upset—very, very upset—and her father was trying to console her.

"Honey, it's okay," her father said, patting her gently on the back. "All of us are unique and special in some way."

"Unique?" Zoe sniffed. "You don't know what unique really is. You have black and white stripes, just as pretty as can be. I'm the only zebra in the world that's striped brown and yellow!"

"Honey," her father began again, but Zoe interrupted as if she hadn't heard him.

"You said I would grow out of it, but I'm almost grown-up now, and look at me. I'm still brown and yellow."

Suddenly, Zoe's father had an idea. "You should go visit Geri. She's very wise and she'll be able to help you."

Geri the Giraffe lived with her herd not far from Zoe, so Zoe went to see her. When Zoe got there, Geri was busy eating some leaves from the top of a tree. Zoe looked up to where Geri towered above her.

"So let me get this straight," Geri said, her mouth full of leaves. "You're upset because you're brown and yellow. Honey, let me tell you, I think brown and yellow are terrific colors."

Name ____________ **Unit 6 Week 4 Interactive Review**

"That's because you're a giraffe," Zoe pointed out. "You're supposed to be brown and yellow."

Geri thought for a minute. "I think there's someone you should meet. Come with me."

Geri led Zoe back to the giraffe herd. There, sitting apart from the others, was a young giraffe about Zoe's age, looking very glum.

Geri made the introductions. "Zoe, this is Gina, and Gina, this is Zoe. I think you two might hit it off."

Zoe looked at Gina and burst out laughing. Gina was a black and white giraffe. They were a perfect pair. So Zoe and Gina became the best of friends, and Zoe never complained about her colors again.

1. Why is Zoe unhappy at the beginning of the story?

Zoe is unhappy because she is brown and yellow instead of black and white like the other zebras.

2. What happened to make Zoe happy at the end of the story?

Zoe met Gina, a black and white giraffe, and they became friends.

3. What do you think is the theme of this story?

Possible answer: Friends make difficult things in life easier.

Home Activity Your child analyzed the plot of a story and identified the theme. Read a short story with your child. Have your child tell you the theme of the story and what happened at the beginning, middle, and end.

Let's Practice It! TR DVD•427–428

Common Core State Standards

Literature 1. Ask and answer questions to demonstrate understanding of a text, referring explicitly to the text as the basis for the answers. **Literature 2.** Recount stories, including fables, folktales, and myths from diverse cultures; determine the central message, lesson, or moral and explain how it is conveyed through key details in the text. **Literature 3.** Describe characters in a story (e.g., their traits, motivations, or feelings) and explain how their actions contribute to the sequence of events. **Foundational Skills 3.a.** Identify and know the meaning of the most common prefixes and derivational suffixes. **Foundational Skills 4.b.** Read on-level prose and poetry orally with accuracy, appropriate rate, and expression on successive readings.

Access Text

Have students read "The Wrong Colors" and respond to the questions.

REVIEW LITERARY ELEMENTS: PLOT AND THEME What is Geri's solution to Zoe's problem? She takes Zoe to meet a giraffe that has a similar problem as Zoe's.

Remind students that the important events in the beginning, middle, and end of a story make up the plot.

REVIEW STORY STRUCTURE What happens at the beginning of this story that sets up what is to follow? What happens in the middle? What happens in the end that resolves the problem? In the beginning, Zoe the Zebra explains how she feels about her unusual coloring to her father. In the middle, Zoe talks to her friend Geri the Giraffe. In the end, Zoe meets a young giraffe that also has unusual coloring. They become best friends and never worry about their unusual colors again.

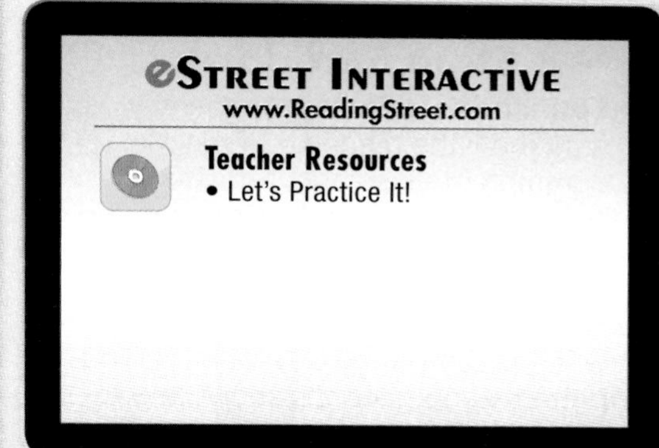

REVIEW PREFIXES AND SUFFIXES *UN-, DIS-, -FUL* What is the prefix in the word *unhappy*? What does this prefix mean? *un-;* not How can you change "mouth full of leaves" to use a word with the suffix *-ful?* mouthful of leaves

REVIEW LITERARY ELEMENTS: PLOT AND THEME Which words best describe the theme of the story: sharing love, accepting differences, or giving advice? Why? Accepting differences is the theme because once Zoe sees someone else in her same situation, she doesn't feel so alone and accepts who she is.

Explain to students that the theme of a story is its overall big idea. To find the theme, students should ask themselves, "What does the author want me to learn?" The answer will not be right there in the text. Readers will have to put the theme into their own words by thinking about the plot.

Reread for Fluency

MODEL FLUENT READING Have students listen as you read the first three paragraphs of "The Wrong Colors" at an appropriate rate. Explain that you will read at a pace similar to the speed you would use in normal conversation.

Routine Oral Rereading

1. **Select a Passage** Read the first three paragraphs of "The Wrong Colors" aloud.
2. **Model** Have students listen to the rate at which you read.
3. **Read** Have students read along with you.
4. **Reread** For optimal fluency, students should reread the text three or four times using appropriate rate.
5. **Corrective Feedback** Listen as students read. Provide corrective feedback regarding their oral reading, paying special attention to rate.

Routines Flip Chart

Common Core State Standards

Foundational Skills 3.a. Identify and know the meaning of the most common prefixes and derivational suffixes. **Language 2.** Demonstrate command of the conventions of standard English capitalization, punctuation, and spelling when writing. **Language 2.f.** Use spelling patterns and generalizations (e.g., word families, position-based spellings, syllable patterns, ending rules, meaningful word parts) in writing words. **Also Writing 2., Language 1.i.**

Name ______ **Unit 6 Week 4 Interactive Review**

Prefixes *im-, in-*

Directions Each sentence contains a word in ( ) that is missing the prefix *im-* or *in-*. Add the correct prefix and write the word on the line.

1. H.G. Wells once wrote a famous novel about an (visible) man. invisible
2. It isn't safe to drink water that is (pure) from pollution. impure
3. The potter always sold her (perfect) pieces for lower prices. imperfect
4. It's (polite) to walk past people without saying "excuse me." impolite
5. Gods and goddesses of Greek mythology are also called (mortals). immortals
6. My best friend is (capable) of unkindness or sarcasm. incapable
7. Science fiction stories often describe (possible) events. impossible
8. She was fired because her methods were so (efficient). inefficient
9. We drove along an (direct) route through the mountains. indirect
10. Umpires in a baseball game must be (partial). impartial

Directions For each definition, supply a word that begins with *im-* or *-in*. Write the word on the line.

11. wrong incorrect
12. not truly meant; not believable insincere
13. not clever or good at doing things inept
14. not likely to happen improbable
15. crazy; not reasonable insane
16. not grown-up; not adult immature

Home Activity Your child wrote words that contain the prefixes *im-* and *in-*, meaning "not." Have your child find and read an article about butterflies or beetles. Have him or her summarize the article for you, using some words that begin with *im-* and *in-*.

Prefixes *im-, in-* DVD•425

Let's Practice It! TR DVD•425

Name ______ **Unit 6 Week 5 Interactive Review**

Multisyllabic Words

Spelling Words				
leadership	gracefully	refreshment	uncomfortable	overdoing
remarkable	carefully	unbearably	ownership	unacceptable
impossibly	reappeared	unprepared	oncoming	misbehaving

Word Building Read the word in dark type. Add the part or parts to the given word. Write the list word you make.

1. **grace** + suffix + suffix gracefully
2. prefix + **appear** + ending reappeared
3. **remark** + suffix remarkable
4. prefix + **comfort** + suffix uncomfortable
5. prefix + **accept** + suffix unacceptable
6. **care** + suffix + suffix carefully
7. prefix + **prepare** + ending unprepared
8. prefix + **fresh** + suffix refreshment
9. **lead** + suffix + suffix leadership
10. **own** + suffix + suffix ownership

Finish the Phrase Circle the list word that completes each phrase. Write it. Say the word. Write in the box the number of syllables you hear in the word.

11. (unprepared unbearably) hot unbearably 4
12. (overdoing reappeared) it a bit overdoing 4
13. (oncoming unprepared) traffic oncoming 3
14. (leadership misbehaving) puppy misbehaving 4
15. (impossibly carefully) difficult problem impossibly 4

Total 19

Syllable Addition Add the numbers in the boxes. If you get 19, you did a great job!

Home Activity Your child is learning to spell words with many syllables. Together, say each word and clap the syllables. Let your child pick the three words he or she finds most difficult. Have your child write them and spell them to you.

446 Spelling

Reader's and Writer's Notebook, p. 446

Word Analysis

REVIEW PREFIXES *IM-, IN-* Review prefixes *im-* and *in-* using *Sound-Spelling Cards* 153 and 154.

Use *Let's Practice It!* p. 425 on the *Teacher Resources DVD-ROM.*

READ WORDS IN ISOLATION Point out that students know how to read these words. Have students read the words together. Allow several seconds previewing time for the first reading.

READ WORDS IN CONTEXT Point out that there are many words in the sentences that students already know. Have students read the sentences together.

Corrective feedback

If... students have difficulty reading words with prefixes *im-* and *in-,*
then... guide them in using the word parts strategy. Have students read all the words repeatedly until they can read the words fluently. Then have students read each sentence repeatedly until they can read the sentences fluently.

Spelling

REVIEW PREFIXES, SUFFIXES, AND ENDINGS Write *impossibly, incomprehensible,* and *independence.* Point out that these words have prefixes. Remind students that they have learned how to spell words with prefixes.

SPELLING STRATEGY Review words with prefixes, suffixes, and endings by having students follow the spelling strategy for spelling these words.

Step 1: Draw a line between the base word and its prefix.
Step 2: Study the word one part at a time.
Step 3: Read the whole word.

ON THEIR OWN Use p. 446 of the *Reader's and Writer's Notebook* for additional practice with spelling words with prefixes, suffixes, and endings.

Conventions

REVIEW COMMAS Review the proper use of **commas** with students.

GUIDE PRACTICE Write the following sentences, omitting the commas. Have students add commas where appropriate.

1. **Ants were climbing on the sidewalk, grass, and shrubs.**
2. **I saw fire ants in Houston, Texas.**
3. **We went to the Insect Museum on August 8, 1999.**
4. **The ants dug a tunnel, but it collapsed.**

ON THEIR OWN For additional practice use the *Reader's and Writer's Notebook,* p. 447.

Routine Quick Write for Fluency

Team Talk

1. **Talk** Have pairs use what they learned in "Hiking Safety Tips" to give some safety tips to the pair of ants in *Two Bad Ants*.
2. **Write** Each student writes a few sentences summarizing their safety tips, using commas where appropriate.
3. **Share** Partners read one another's sentences and check for the correct use of commas.

Routines Flip Chart

eStreet Interactive
www.ReadingStreet.com

Teacher Resources
- Reader's and Writer's Notebook
- Let's Practice It!

Interactive Sound-Spelling Cards

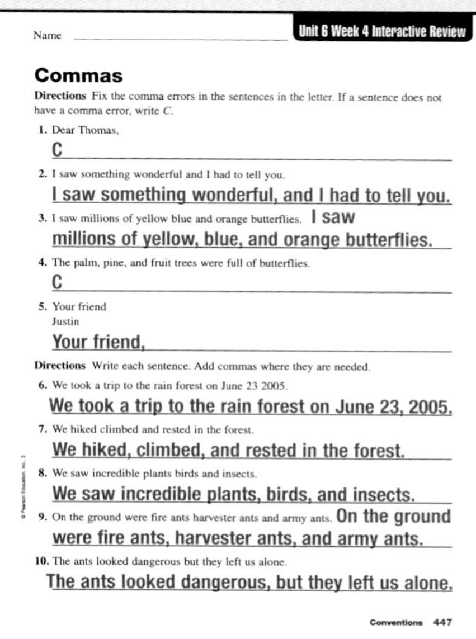

Name ______ Unit 6 Week 4 Interactive Review

Commas

Directions Fix the comma errors in the sentences in the letter. If a sentence does not have a comma error, write *C*.

1. Dear Thomas,
   C
2. I saw something wonderful and I had to tell you.
   I saw something wonderful, and I had to tell you.
3. I saw millions of yellow blue and orange butterflies. I saw millions of yellow, blue, and orange butterflies.
4. The palm, pine, and fruit trees were full of butterflies.
   C
5. Your friend
   Justin
   Your friend,

Directions Write each sentence. Add commas where they are needed.

6. We took a trip to the rain forest on June 23 2005.
   We took a trip to the rain forest on June 23, 2005.
7. We hiked climbed and rested in the forest.
   We hiked, climbed, and rested in the forest.
8. We saw incredible plants birds and insects.
   We saw incredible plants, birds, and insects.
9. On the ground were fire ants harvester ants and army ants. On the ground were fire ants, harvester ants, and army ants.
10. The ants looked dangerous but they left us alone.
    The ants looked dangerous, but they left us alone.

Conventions 447

Reader's and Writer's Notebook, p. 447

Writing Workshop

Use pp. WP•1–WP•10 for this week's writing instruction.

Wrap Up Week 4 Review!

✔ **Content Knowledge** *What rules help to improve your school?*

✔ **Literary Elements** *Summarize the plot of* Two Bad Ants.

✔ **Prefixes and Suffixes *un-, dis-, -ful*** *How can learning common prefixes and suffixes help you learn new words?*

Preview DAY 5

Tell students that tomorrow they will review *Atlantis.*

Review Week 5

Content Knowledge
Review Oral Vocabulary

Text-Based Comprehension
Review Generalize

Selection Vocabulary
Review Homographs

Fluency
Expression

Phonics/Word Analysis
Review Related Words

Spelling
Review Related Words

Conventions
Review Quotations and Parentheses

Writing
Quick Write for Fluency

Materials

- Student Edition
- Retelling Cards
- Reader's and Writer's Notebook

Common Core State Standards

Speaking/Listening 1. Engage effectively in a range of collaborative discussions (one-on-one, in groups, and teacher-led) with diverse partners on grade 3 topics and texts, building on others' ideas and expressing their own clearly. **Language 4.** Determine or clarify the meaning of unknown and multiple-meaning words and phrases based on grade 3 reading and content, choosing flexibly from a range of strategies. **Language 6.** Acquire and use accurately grade-appropriate conversational, general academic, and domain-specific words and phrases, including those that signal spatial and temporal relationships (e.g., *After dinner that night we went looking for them*).

Content Knowledge

Keeping Your Freedom

REVISIT THE CONCEPT Today students will explore how the question for this unit of study connects to *Atlantis: The Legend of a Lost City.* Remind students of the Question of the Week, *What is the best way to keep your freedom?*

Build Oral Language

DISCUSS FREEDOM Remind students of the question for this unit of study, *What does freedom mean?* Use the prompts and the concept map from Week 5 to discuss how freedom is something people must work to keep.

- What can you do to keep your freedom when it is threatened?
- How do rules and laws about equality help people keep their freedom?
- How can too much freedom or not enough freedom lead to violence?

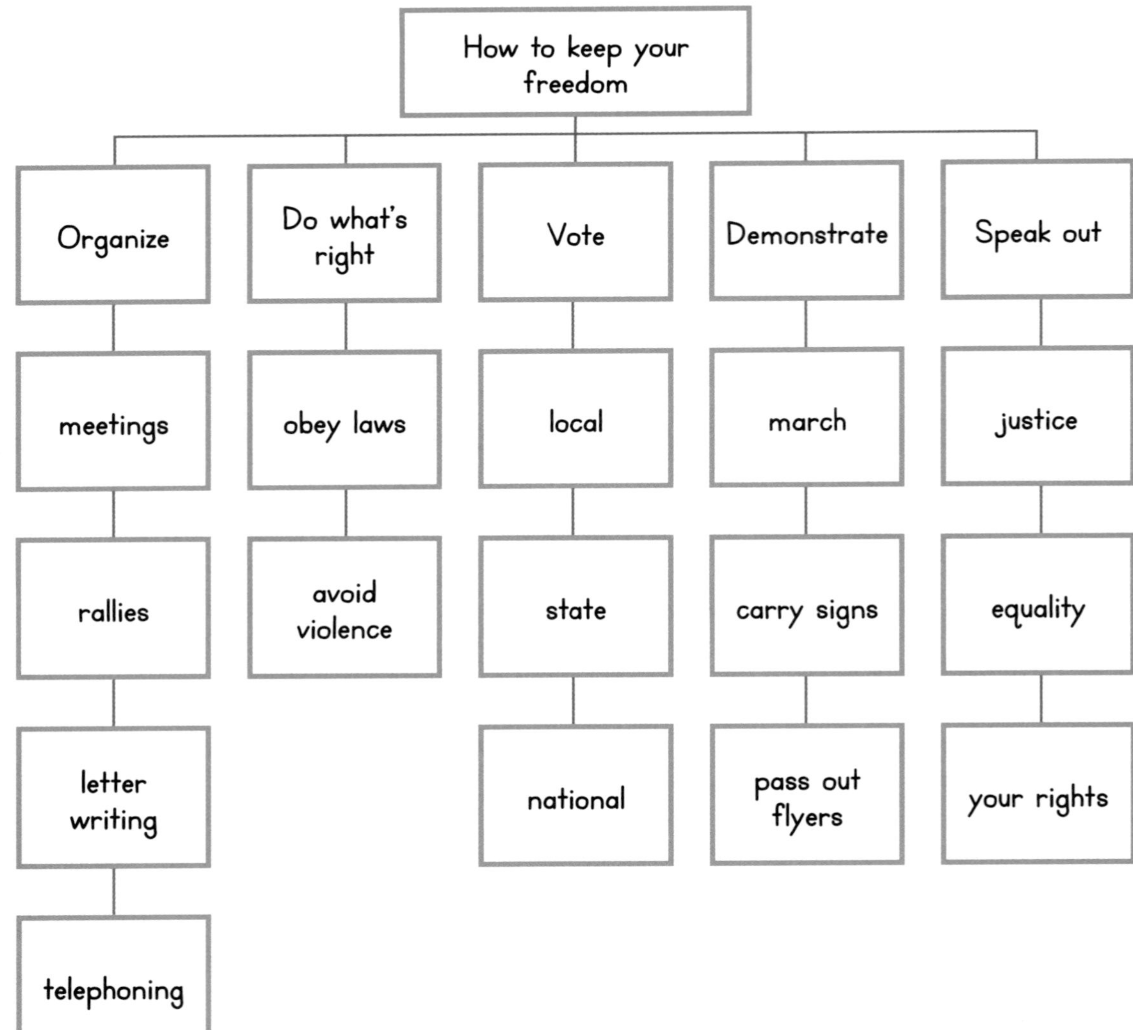

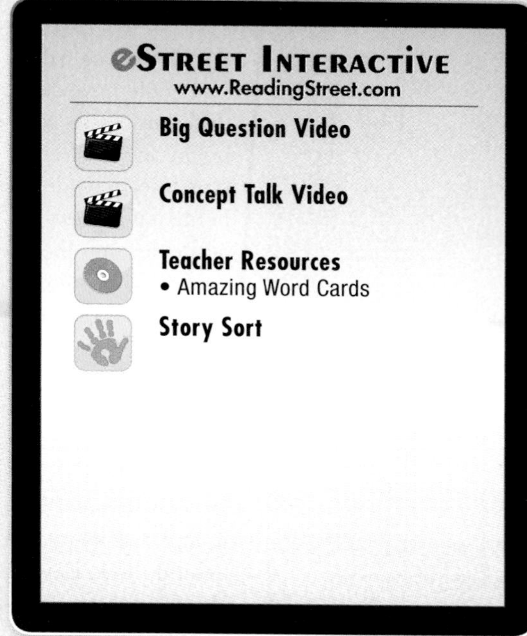

Build Oral Vocabulary

REVIEW AMAZING WORDS Display the Amazing Words for *Atlantis: The Legend of a Lost City.* Remind students that the words are related to the week's concept.

Amazing Words — Robust Vocabulary Routine

1. **Review** Ask students for definitions of the words, starting at the top of the list. Listen for accurate definitions. Prompt students to connect the words to the unit concept of Freedom whenever possible.
2. **Demonstrate** Have students use two or more Amazing Words in the same sentence. Guide the discussion by providing an example that shows the meaning of each word. People *demonstrate* to obtain *justice* for all races. Follow this pattern to the end of the list, covering as many of the nine words as possible.
3. **Apply** Assign the words in random order and have students come up with more new sentences for them. To show that you are becoming more comfortable using these Amazing Words, think up more new sentences for them.

Routines Flip Chart

AMAZING WORDS AT WORK Have students use the Retelling Cards/Story Sort for *Atlantis: The Legend of a Lost City* to talk about the Amazing Words.

CONNECT TO READING Tell students that today they will be rereading passages from *Atlantis: The Legend of a Lost City* and reading "The Story of Echo." As they read, ask students to think about how freedom can be lost or saved.

Amazing Words

witty	mourn
equality	blight
justice	wept
perish	violence
demonstrate	

ELL

Build Background Use ELL Poster 30 to review the Week 5 lesson concept and to practice oral language. Point out and read a question: *What is the best way to keep your freedom?*

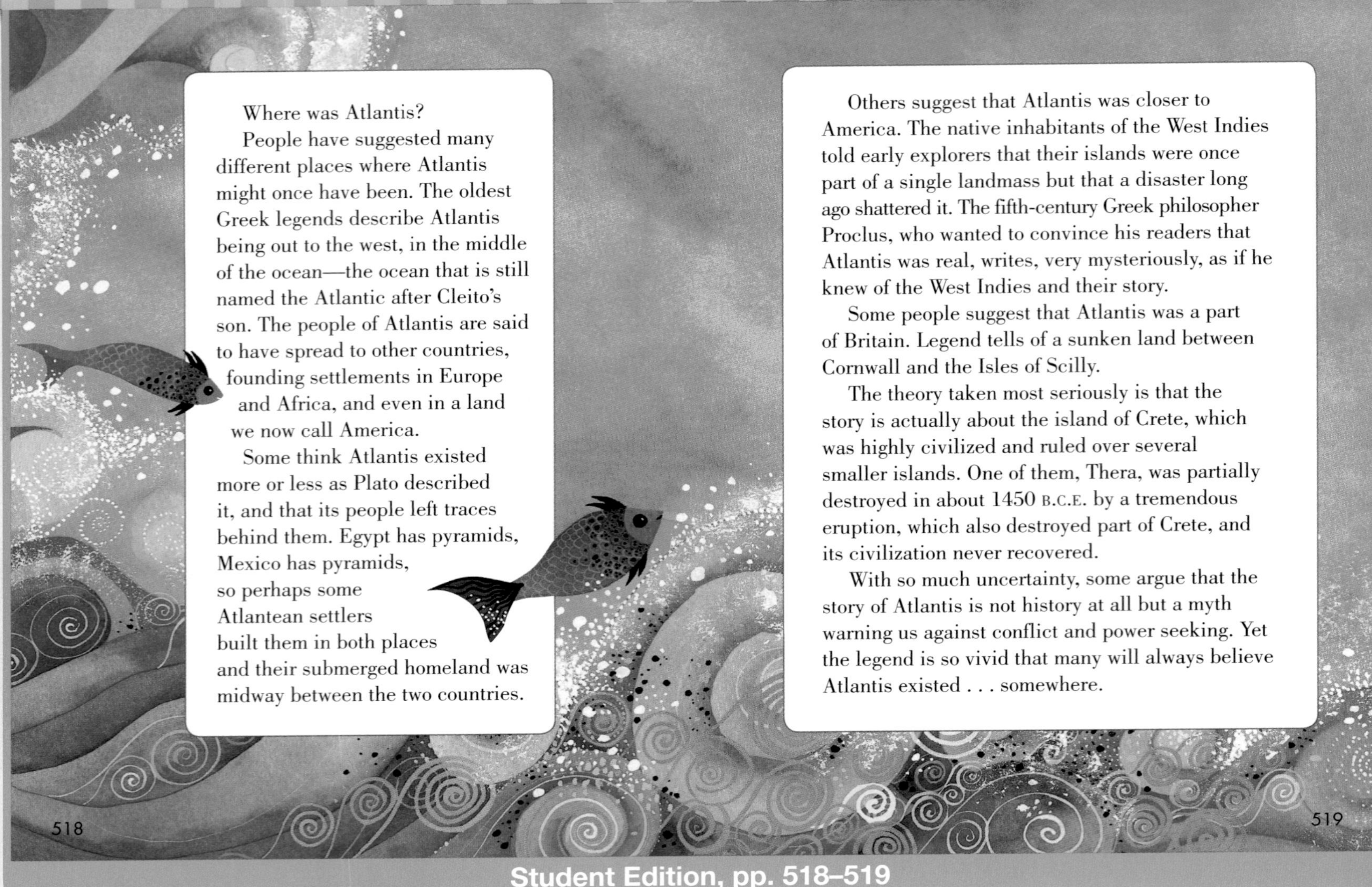

Where was Atlantis?
People have suggested many different places where Atlantis might once have been. The oldest Greek legends describe Atlantis being out to the west, in the middle of the ocean—the ocean that is still named the Atlantic after Cleito's son. The people of Atlantis are said to have spread to other countries, founding settlements in Europe and Africa, and even in a land we now call America.
Some think Atlantis existed more or less as Plato described it, and that its people left traces behind them. Egypt has pyramids, Mexico has pyramids, so perhaps some Atlantean settlers built them in both places and their submerged homeland was midway between the two countries.
Others suggest that Atlantis was closer to America. The native inhabitants of the West Indies told early explorers that their islands were once part of a single landmass but that a disaster long ago shattered it. The fifth-century Greek philosopher Proclus, who wanted to convince his readers that Atlantis was real, writes, very mysteriously, as if he knew of the West Indies and their story.
Some people suggest that Atlantis was a part of Britain. Legend tells of a sunken land between Cornwall and the Isles of Scilly.
The theory taken most seriously is that the story is actually about the island of Crete, which was highly civilized and ruled over several smaller islands. One of them, Thera, was partially destroyed in about 1450 B.C.E. by a tremendous eruption, which also destroyed part of Crete, and its civilization never recovered.
With so much uncertainty, some argue that the story of Atlantis is not history at all but a myth warning us against conflict and power seeking. Yet the legend is so vivid that many will always believe Atlantis existed . . . somewhere.
518
519

Student Edition, pp. 518–519

Common Core State Standards

Literature 1. Ask and answer questions to demonstrate understanding of a text, referring explicitly to the text as the basis for the answers. **Language 2.** Demonstrate command of the conventions of standard English capitalization, punctuation, and spelling when writing.

Access Text

REVIEW GENERALIZE Review the definition of *generalize* on p. 498. Remind students that when they generalize, they tell how some things are mostly or all alike. Tell students that key words, such as *always, never,* and *most,* often signal a generalization.

GUIDE PRACTICE Point out the clue word *some* in the last paragraph on p. 519. Have students restate the generalization in this sentence. Ask them to explain whether or not the generalization is reasonable.

ON THEIR OWN Have students look back at pp. 518–519 of *Atlantis: The Legend of a Lost City* and find another generalization that is signaled by a clue word.

Close Reading

ANALYSIS Reread the first sentence of paragraph 2 on p. 519. Is this a reasonable generalization? Why or why not? It is a reasonable generalization because it includes the word *some,* which allows for other opinions about the location of Atlantis.

INFERENCE What natural occurrences could explain the destruction of Atlantis? an earthquake, a tsunami, a hurricane, or a volcanic eruption

SYNTHESIS According to the author, the story of Atlantis is a warning against conflict and power seeking. What does this mean? Atlantis was destroyed and lost forever because people acted badly and selfishly. People today should keep the story of Atlantis in mind and work together rather than risk losing everything.

Access for All

SI Strategic Intervention

Have students work in pairs to write generalizations about several events in the story. Suggest that they use clue words that signal generalizations.

A Advanced

Have students work in pairs to outline the plot of *Atlantis.* Then have pairs exchange outlines and provide feedback.

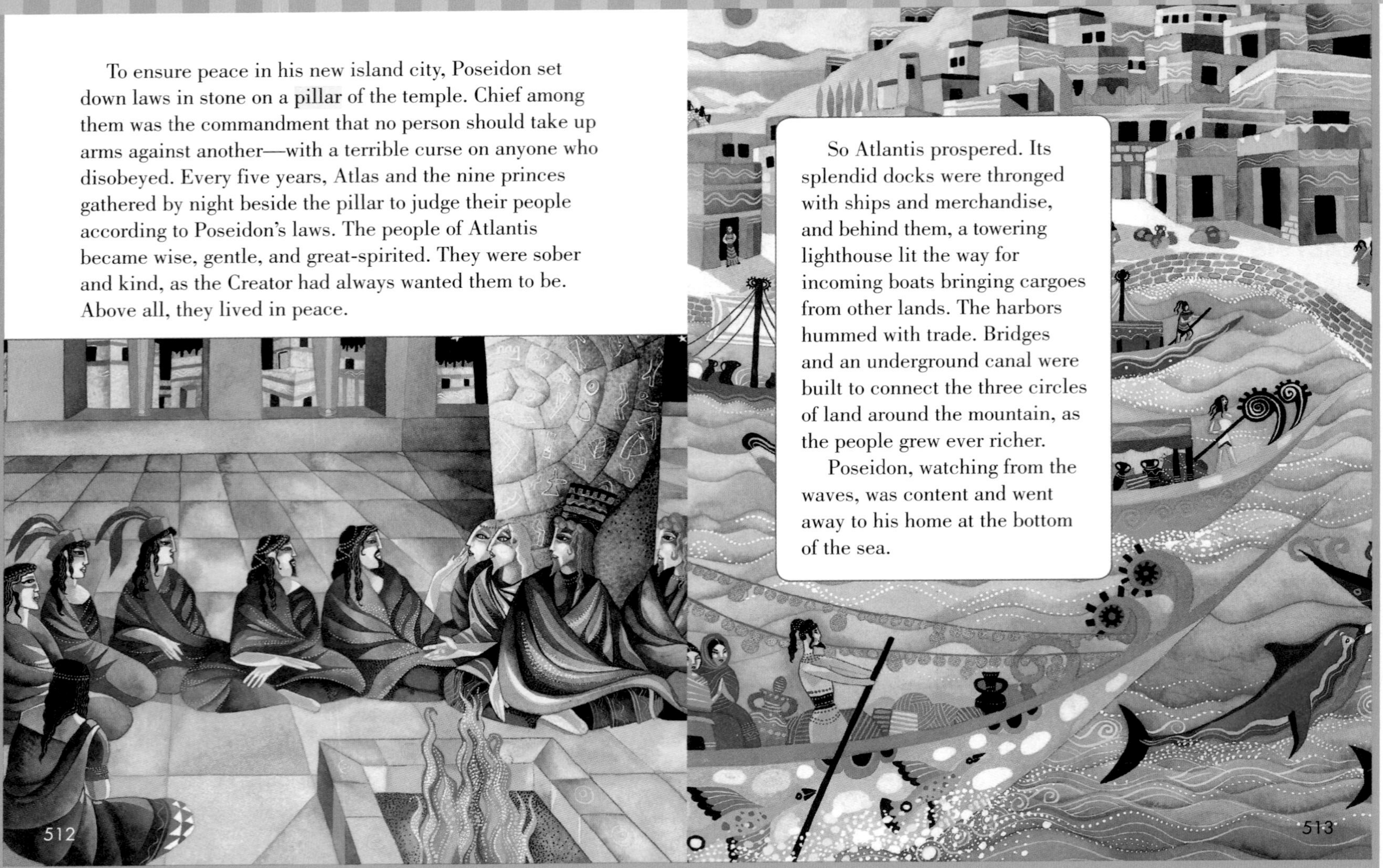

To ensure peace in his new island city, Poseidon set down laws in stone on a pillar of the temple. Chief among them was the commandment that no person should take up arms against another—with a terrible curse on anyone who disobeyed. Every five years, Atlas and the nine princes gathered by night beside the pillar to judge their people according to Poseidon's laws. The people of Atlantis became wise, gentle, and great-spirited. They were sober and kind, as the Creator had always wanted them to be. Above all, they lived in peace.

So Atlantis prospered. Its splendid docks were thronged with ships and merchandise, and behind them, a towering lighthouse lit the way for incoming boats bringing cargoes from other lands. The harbors hummed with trade. Bridges and an underground canal were built to connect the three circles of land around the mountain, as the people grew ever richer.

Poseidon, watching from the waves, was content and went away to his home at the bottom of the sea.

512 513

Student Edition, pp. 512–513

Common Core State Standards

Literature 1. Ask and answer questions to demonstrate understanding of a text, referring explicitly to the text as the basis for the answers. **Foundational Skills 4.c** Use context to confirm or self-correct word recognition and understanding, rereading as necessary. **Language 4.a.** Use sentence-level context as a clue to the meaning of a word or phrase.

Access Text

REVIEW HOMOGRAPHS Review the definition of a homograph on p. 500. Remind students that homographs are words that are spelled the same but have different meanings and sometimes different pronunciations.

GUIDE PRACTICE Point out the word *content* in the last paragraph on p. 513. Explain to students that *content* is a homograph; it has two different pronunciations and meanings. Use each pronunciation of the word in a sentence that defines it. Ask a volunteer to define each usage of the word. Then have students use context clues to determine which meaning and pronunciation of *content* is used in this sentence on p. 513.

ON THEIR OWN Use *Let's Practice It!* p. 430 on the *Teacher Resources DVD-ROM* for additional practice with vocabulary.

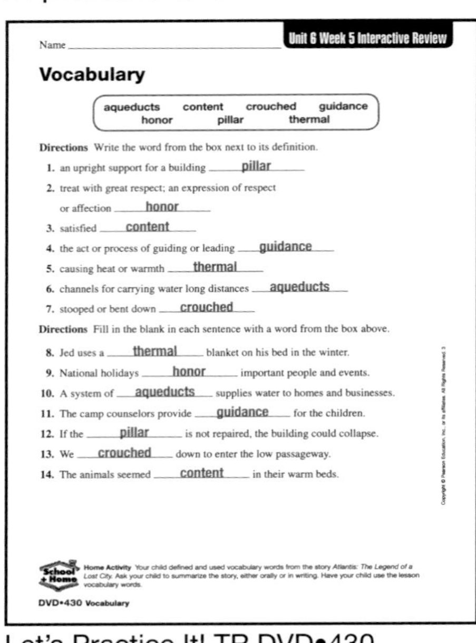

Name ____________ Unit 6 Week 5 Interactive Review

Vocabulary

aqueducts content crouched guidance honor pillar thermal

Directions Write the word from the box next to its definition.

1. an upright support for a building __pillar__
2. treat with great respect; an expression of respect or affection __honor__
3. satisfied __content__
4. the act or process of guiding or leading __guidance__
5. causing heat or warmth __thermal__
6. channels for carrying water long distances __aqueducts__
7. stooped or bent down __crouched__

Directions Fill in the blank in each sentence with a word from the box above.

8. Jed uses a __thermal__ blanket on his bed in the winter.
9. National holidays __honor__ important people and events.
10. A system of __aqueducts__ supplies water to homes and businesses.
11. The camp counselors provide __guidance__ for the children.
12. If the __pillar__ is not repaired, the building could collapse.
13. We __crouched__ down to enter the low passageway.
14. The animals seemed __content__ in their warm beds.

School + Home **Home Activity** Your child defined and used vocabulary words from the story *Atlantis: The Legend of a Lost City.* Ask your child to summarize the story, either orally or in writing. Have your child use the lesson vocabulary words.

DVD•430 Vocabulary

Copyright © Pearson Education, Inc., or its affiliates. All Rights Reserved. 3

Let's Practice It! TR DVD•430

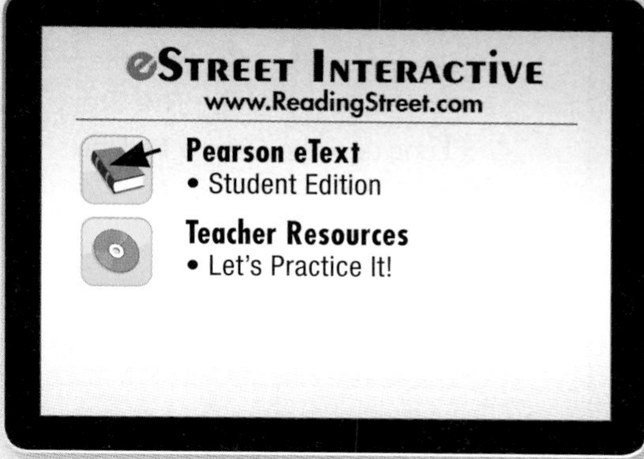

Close Reading

DEVELOP LANGUAGE What is the homograph in this sentence: *The wind was so strong that one of the sails tore in half?* What sentence could you make using the other meaning of the homograph? wind; Sentences should use *wind* as a verb with a long *i,* meaning "to wrap around an object" or "to turn in a series of circular motions."

EVALUATION Which sentence on p. 512 is a generalization about the people of Atlantis? Is it a reasonable generalization? Explain. *The people of Atlantis became wise, gentle, and great-spirited.* Yes, it is reasonable because the rest of the paragraph lists details that support this statement.

SYNTHESIS To ensure peace, Poseidon laid down laws that he expected the citizens of Atlantis to obey. Explain how those laws affected the people of Atlantis. The laws allowed the people of Atlantis to live in peace and to judge each other fairly. As a result, they became wise, gentle, great-spirited, sober, and kind.

SYNTHESIS • TEXT EVIDENCE Based on details on pp. 512–513, explain how following Poseidon's laws helped the people of Atlantis prosper and enjoy freedom. By following the laws, the people of Atlantis had more time to do things that they enjoyed. The laws allowed people to live in peace, so they were free to enjoy their lives and work hard.

Access for All

SI Strategic Intervention
On the board, write two sentences that use the different pronunciations and meanings of the homographs *tear* and *bow.* Have students take turns reading the sentences and explaining the meaning of each homograph.

A Advanced
Have students work in pairs to write two sentences using the different pronunciations and meanings of the homographs *wound, dove,* and *does.* Then have pairs exchange sentences and read them aloud.

Name ____________ **Unit 6 Week 5 Interactive Review**

Read the story. **Answer** the questions.

The Story of Echo

Long ago, the Greeks told the story of a girl named Echo. She was very beautiful, and when she smiled, it was as if a ray of sunshine had shot through the sky.

Echo had something that everyone loved—her voice. It sounded like liquid music, especially when she sang. She was an excellent storyteller, and her stories amused the gods and goddesses for hours. But the more Echo talked, the more she fell in love with the sound of her own voice.

Zeus, king of the gods, had Echo entertain his wife, Hera, so that he could steal away. At first, Hera was charmed by Echo's lovely voice. But when she found out that Zeus had told Echo to distract her, she was very angry.

"You have fooled me in the past, little Echo, but no longer," said Hera. "I shall teach you a lesson you'll never forget!"

With that, Hera took Echo's voice away. Echo could not speak unless someone else spoke first. Even then, Echo could only repeat what the other person said.

Echo regretted tricking Hera, but she could do nothing about it. Day after day she wandered, lonely and sad.

One day in the woods, she came upon a handsome young man gazing into his reflection in a pool. With all her heart, Echo wanted to speak to him, but she had to wait until he spoke first. He, too, was unhappy, because he was in love with only himself.

The young man heard Echo's footsteps. "Who's there?" he demanded.

Name ____________ **Unit 6 Week 5 Interactive Review**

"Who's there?" Echo repeated his words.

The young man tried again. "What is your name?" he asked.

"What is your name?" Echo replied.

Finally Echo could stand it no longer. She ran to the man and tried to touch him, but he pushed her away.

Echo was so sad that she stopped eating altogether. Her body faded away until only her voice remained. To this day, you can hear Echo's voice in some places, but only when you speak first.

1. Underline a generalization that tells about Echo's voice. On the lines below, write a detail that supports the generalization.

   Possible response: It sounded like liquid music.

2. Reread the fifth paragraph. It tells how Hera changed Echo's life forever. Write two ways that Echo's life was changed.

   Hera took Echo's voice away. Echo was forbidden to speak, except to repeat what another person said.

3. Underline the sentence that is the best generalization about the characters in "The Story of Echo."

   All the characters are magical creatures.

   All the characters are either gods or people.

   All the characters have beautiful singing voices.

   All the characters get into trouble.

Home Activity Your child read a myth and found generalizations about the characters and the events. Say a generalization about your child's favorite things; for example, *Chris loves most adventure stories.* Have your child give examples that support the generalization.

Let's Practice It! TR DVD•431–432

Common Core State Standards

Literature 1. Ask and answer questions to demonstrate understanding of a text, referring explicitly to the text as the basis for the answers. **Foundational Skills 4.b.** Read on-level prose and poetry orally with accuracy, appropriate rate, and expression on successive readings. **Foundational Skills 4.c** Use context to confirm or self-correct word recognition and understanding, rereading as necessary. **Language 4.a.** Use sentence-level context as a clue to the meaning of a word or phrase.

Access Text

Have students read "The Story of Echo" and respond to the questions.

REVIEW GENERALIZE Tell students that Greek stories are about great heroes, gods and goddesses, and amazing creatures. Write the sentences below on the board. Ask students to choose the sentence that is the best generalization about Greek stories.

Greek stories are boring.
All Greek stories are about gods and people.
Greek stories have all kinds of characters.
Greek stories tell about people who get into trouble.

Review with students that a generalization is a kind of conclusion about something, and that it is made after thinking about a number of examples or facts and what they have in common.

REVIEW INFERRING Use ideas from the story and what you know about echoes to make an inference about why the Greeks told this story. The Greeks sometimes told stories to explain natural phenomena that they did not understand.

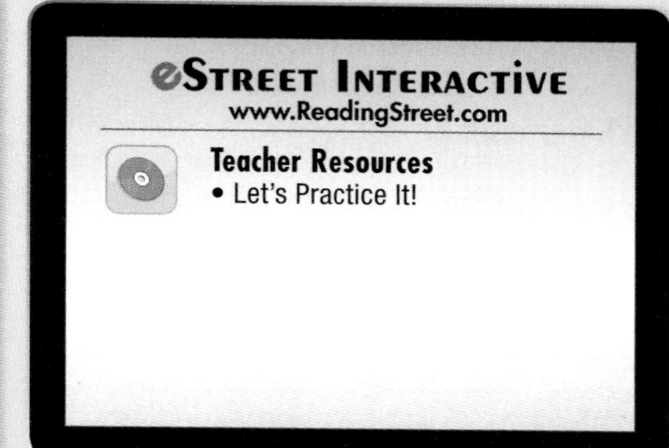

REVIEW HOMOGRAPHS What is the homograph in this sentence? *Echo could not stand the strange conversation.* stand Write a sentence that uses a different meaning of the homograph. Answers will vary, but sentences should use *stand* to mean something other than "to put up with."

Review with students that homographs are two or more words with the same spelling but different meanings and sometimes different pronunciations. Remind them to use context clues to figure out which meaning is being used.

REVIEW GENERALIZE Underline a generalization that tells about Echo's story-telling abilities. Write a detail that supports the generalization. *She was an excellent storyteller.* Her stories amused the gods and goddesses for hours and hours.

Reread for Fluency

MODEL FLUENT READING Have students listen as you read aloud paragraph 2 of "The Story of Echo" on p. 431, using appropriate expression. Explain that you will adjust your voice to stress important words and phrases.

Routine Oral Rereading

1. **Read** Have students read "The Story of Echo" orally.
2. **Reread** To achieve optimal fluency, students should reread the text three or four times.
3. **Corrective Feedback** Have students read aloud without you. Provide feedback about their expression and encourage them to adjust their voice level to stress important words and phrases. Listen for use of appropriate expression.

Routines Flip Chart

Common Core State Standards

Language 2. Demonstrate command of the conventions of standard English capitalization, punctuation, and spelling when writing. **Language 2.c.** Use commas and quotation marks in dialogue. **Language 2.f.** Use spelling patterns and generalizations (e.g., word families, position-based spellings, syllable patterns, ending rules, meaningful word parts) in writing words. **Also Foundational Skills 3., Language 4.c.**

Name ____________ **Unit 6 Week 5 Interactive Review**

Related Words

Directions Circle the word in ( ) that best matches each definition.

1. parents, sisters, and cousins (relate, relatives)
2. to say something again (repeat, repetition)
3. a tool on which you can write or do research (compute, computer)
4. answered a question (responded, response)
5. to make something out of nothing (create, creature)
6. one who plays roles on stage or film (active, actor)
7. one who makes music with the voice (singer, song)
8. to explain what a word means (define, definition)
9. hard to understand (puzzle, puzzling)
10. weapons (arms, army)

Directions Read each pair of related words. Underline the parts that are the same. Use one of the words in a sentence.

Sentences will vary. Sample sentences are given.

11. friendship, friendly
A friendly person is always pleasant to everyone.
12. capture, captive
The soldiers wanted to capture the enemy flag.
13. door, indoors
We painted our front door bright blue last week.
14. scare, scary
I yelled "Boo!" to scare the bully as he went by.
15. natural, nature
I only use natural ingredients when I cook.

School + Home **Home Activity** Your child defined and used related words. Have your child identify the parts in these word pairs that are the same signal, sign; nature, natural. Then have your child use each in a sentence.

Related Words DVD•429

Let's Practice It! TR DVD•429

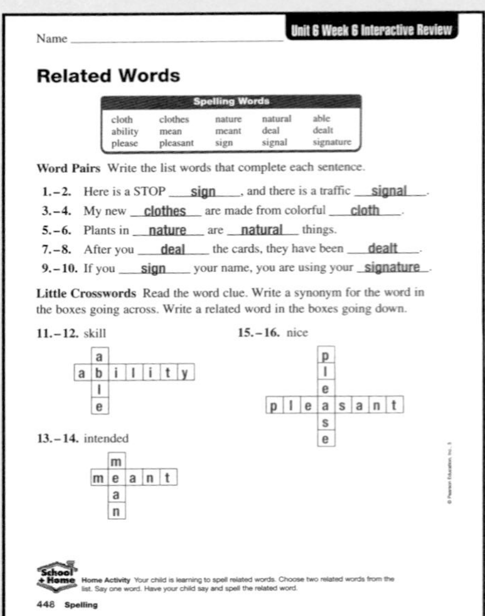

Name ____________ **Unit 6 Week 6 Interactive Review**

Related Words

Spelling Words				
cloth	clothes	nature	natural	able
ability	mean	meant	deal	dealt
please	pleasant	sign	signal	signature

Word Pairs Write the list words that complete each sentence.

1.–2. Here is a STOP sign, and there is a traffic signal.
3.–4. My new clothes are made from colorful cloth.
5.–6. Plants in nature are natural things.
7.–8. After you deal the cards, they have been dealt.
9.–10. If you sign your name, you are using your signature.

Little Crosswords Read the word clue. Write a synonym for the word in the boxes going across. Write a related word in the boxes going down.

11.–12. skill
a b i l i t y
a b l e

13.–14. intended
m e a n t
m e a n

15.–16. nice
p l e a s a n t
p l e a s e

School + Home **Home Activity** Your child is learning to spell related words. Choose two related words from the list. Say one word. Have your child say and spell the related word.

448 **Spelling**

Reader's and Writer's Notebook, p. 448

Word Analysis

REVIEW RELATED WORDS Review how to use related words to figure out word meanings and spellings of unfamiliar words, using *Sound-Spelling Card* 143.

Use *Let's Practice It!* p. 429 on the *Teacher Resources DVD-ROM.*

READ WORDS IN ISOLATION Point out that students know how to read these words. Have students read the words together. Allow several seconds previewing time for the first reading.

READ WORDS IN CONTEXT Point out that there are many words in the sentences that students already know. Have students read the sentences together.

Corrective feedback

If... students have difficulty reading related words,
then... guide them in using the word parts strategy. Have students read all the words repeatedly until they can read the words fluently. Then have students read each sentence repeatedly until they can read the sentences fluently.

Spelling

REVIEW RELATED WORDS Write *sign, signal,* and *signature.* Point out that these are related words. Related words share common letters. Remind students that they have learned how to spell related words.

SPELLING STRATEGY Review related words by having students follow the spelling strategy for spelling these words.

Step 1: Sometimes saying the related word can make spelling easier. For example, the *g* is silent in *sign,* but it is said in *signature.*

Step 2: If you're not sure how to spell a word, say a related word to help you first. For example, think of and say *clean* when you want to spell *cleanse.*

ON THEIR OWN Use p. 448 of the *Reader's and Writer's Notebook* for additional practice with spelling related words.

Conventions

REVIEW QUOTATIONS AND PARENTHESES Review the proper use of **quotation marks** and **parentheses** with students.

GUIDE PRACTICE Write the following sentences, omitting quotation marks and parentheses. Have students correctly punctuate the sentences.

1. **Mom asked, "Would you like a cookie?"**
2. **We collected canned goods (green beans, yams, and carrots) for the food drive.**

ON THEIR OWN For additional practice use the *Reader's and Writer's Notebook,* p. 449.

Routine Quick Write for Fluency — Team Talk

1. **Talk** Have pairs discuss what freedoms were gained and lost for the characters in *Atlantis* and "The Monster in the Maze."
2. **Write** Each student writes a short dialogue between Poseidon and Cleito or Theseus and Ariadne, using quotation marks and parentheses.
3. **Share** Partners act out each other's dialogues and check for the correct use of quotation marks and parentheses.

Routines Flip Chart

eStreet Interactive
www.ReadingStreet.com

Teacher Resources
- Reader's and Writer's Notebook
- Let's Practice It!

Interactive Sound-Spelling Cards

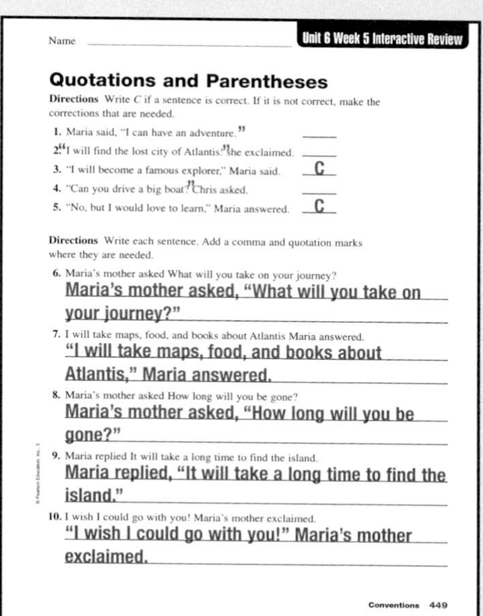

Name ______ Unit 6 Week 5 Interactive Review

Quotations and Parentheses

Directions Write *C* if a sentence is correct. If it is not correct, make the corrections that are needed.

1. Maria said, "I can have an adventure." ____
2. "I will find the lost city of Atlantis!" she exclaimed. ____
3. "I will become a famous explorer," Maria said. C
4. "Can you drive a big boat?" Chris asked. ____
5. "No, but I would love to learn," Maria answered. C

Directions Write each sentence. Add a comma and quotation marks where they are needed.

6. Maria's mother asked What will you take on your journey?
   Maria's mother asked, "What will you take on your journey?"
7. I will take maps, food, and books about Atlantis Maria answered.
   "I will take maps, food, and books about Atlantis," Maria answered.
8. Maria's mother asked How long will you be gone?
   Maria's mother asked, "How long will you be gone?"
9. Maria replied It will take a long time to find the island.
   Maria replied, "It will take a long time to find the island."
10. I wish I could go with you! Maria's mother exclaimed.
    "I wish I could go with you!" Maria's mother exclaimed.

Conventions 449

Reader's and Writer's Notebook, p. 449

Writing Workshop

Use pp. WP•1–WP•10 for this week's writing instruction.

Wrap Up Week 5 Review!

- ✓ **Content Knowledge** *What freedoms do you most enjoy?*
- ✓ **Generalize** *What generalizations can you make about the people of Atlantis based on this week's main selection?*
- ✓ **Homographs** *How can you use context clues to figure out the meaning of homographs?*

Wrap Up Your Unit!

Discuss Content Knowledge Gained Through Reading

What does freedom mean?

WEEK 1

Why do we have symbols that represent freedom?

Students have learned that symbols

- remind us of our history
- remind us of our unity
- stand for freedom

WEEK 2

What does it mean to grant freedom?

Students have learned that freedom

- can be granted to animals
- means pursuing interests
- can be granted through laws

WEEK 3

Why is freedom of expression important?

Students have learned that freedom of expression

- allows us to express ideas or feelings
- can spread a message

What kinds of freedom do you experience in your life every day?

- I experience the freedom to go to school and learn new things.
- I experience the freedom to travel around my town, my state, and the country.

Discuss with students the selections they have explored surrounding the idea of freedom. Throughout discussions, students should support their comments and ideas with evidence from the texts.

How do the different selections you read demonstrate freedom?

- *The Story of the Statue of Liberty:* The Statue of Liberty is a symbol of American freedom.
- *Happy Birthday Mr. Kang:* Mr. Kang sets his bird free because he realizes the importance of freedom.
- *Talking Walls: Art for the People:* The murals that the artists paint reflect their freedom of expression.
- *Two Bad Ants:* The ants learn that rules help keep us safe and protect freedoms.
- *Atlantis: The Legend of a Lost City:* The people of Atlantis lose everything when they disobey laws.

WEEK 4

Why are rules and laws important to freedom?

Students have learned that rules and laws

- keep order
- keep us safe
- remind us to do the right thing

WEEK 5

What is the best way to keep your freedom?

Students have learned that keeping freedom means

- defending it
- working together
- having necessary laws

Talk about freedom.

Think about what you have learned about freedom. How has your idea of freedom changed? (Responses will vary.)

Team Talk Have students work in pairs to talk about the Amazing Ideas related to freedom that they discussed each week. Then have students use these ideas to help demonstrate their understanding of the question, *What does freedom mean?*

Amazing Words

You've learned 296 words this year!

You've learned 049 words this unit to use as you talk about freedom.

Assessment Checkpoints for the Week

Unit Assessment

Use Unit 6 *Benchmark Tests* to check:

- ✔ **Passage Comprehension**
- ✔ **Phonics**
- ✔ **Vocabulary Skills**
- ✔ **Writing Conventions**
- ✔ **Writing**
- ✔ **Fluency**

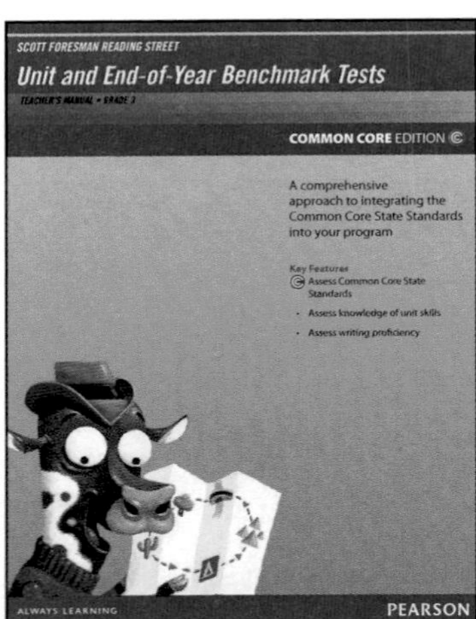

Benchmark Tests

Managing Assessment

Use *Assessment Handbook* for:

- ✔ **Weekly Assessment Blackline Masters for Monitoring Progress**
- ✔ **Observation Checklists**
- ✔ **Record-Keeping Forms**
- ✔ **Portfolio Assessment**

Assessment Handbook

Research Report

Writing Prompt

Write about a monument or statue in the United States that stands for freedom. Use sources such as books, interviews, online searches, and surveys.

Purpose Give information about a monument or statue.

Audience classmates, other students outside of class

INTRODUCE GENRE AND PROMPT In this writing process lesson, you will study a research report and use this genre to write a response to the prompt. In a research report, a writer gathers and organizes facts and details from several sources.

INTRODUCE KEY FEATURES

Key Features of a Research Report

- presents complete, accurate information based on research
- organizes information into paragraphs with topic sentences
- establishes a central idea
- supports the central idea with facts, details, and explanations
- ends with a concluding statement

Academic Vocabulary

In a **research report,** a writer gathers and organizes facts from several sources and writes a composition using these facts.

Introduce Genre Write the word *research* on the board. Underline the word *search* in *research*. Explain that when people research, they search in books, magazines, and other sources for facts about a topic. Discuss with students the key features of a research report.

Common Core State Standards

Writing 5. With guidance and support from peers and adults, develop and strengthen writing as needed by planning, revising, and editing. **Writing 7.** Conduct short research projects that build knowledge about a topic. **Writing 8.** Recall information from experiences or gather information from print and digital sources; take brief notes on sources and sort evidence into provided categories.

Plan and Prewrite

Mini-Lesson Reading Like a Writer

- **Examine Model Text** Let's look at an example of a student's research report on a U.S. monument to freedom. This is the kind of research report you will write. Display and read aloud "The Lincoln Memorial" on Writing Transparency WP36. Ask students to identify key features of a research report in the student model.

- **Evaluate Model Text** Display and read aloud "Traits of a Good Research Report" on Writing Transparency WP37. Discuss each trait as it is shown in the model. For Focus/Ideas, ask students to identify the topic of the research report. Remind them that writing is focused when it stays on topic. For Organization, have them identify the central idea in each paragraph and the essay's concluding statement. Proceed in the same way with the remaining traits, defining them when necessary and asking students to identify evidence of traits in the model.

The Lincoln Memorial

The Lincoln Memorial in Washington, D.C., is one of our country's great monuments. It stands for freedom because it honors Abraham Lincoln. Lincoln, the United States President during the Civil War, helped bring freedom to all Americans.

The Lincoln Memorial is built of white marble. It is rectangular and has 36 columns. It looks like an ancient Greek building. The 36 columns stand for the 36 states in the United States when Lincoln was president.

Inside the Lincoln Memorial are three rooms. A statue of Lincoln sitting in a chair is in the center room. It is 19 feet tall! The other rooms display paintings and two of Lincoln's most famous speeches. They are the Gettysburg Address and the Second Inaugural Address.

The Lincoln Memorial was dedicated in 1922. It has the Potomac River on one side. The Washington Monument can be seen on the other side. The Lincoln Memorial is beautiful. It overlooks Washington and honors a great President. For all these reasons, the Lincoln Memorial is one of Americans' favorite monuments.

Unit 6 Research Report • PLAN and PREWRITE Writing Process 36

Writing Transparency WP36, TR DVD

Traits of a Good Research Report

Focus/Ideas	Report focuses on a monument to freedom in the United States.
Organization	Report has several good paragraphs with topic sentences and a strong conclusion.
Voice	Writer shows thoughtfulness, originality, and thoroughness of research.
Word Choice	Writer uses vivid and precise words (*rectangular, ancient Greek*).
Sentences	Writer uses sentences of different kinds and includes simple, compound, and complex sentences.
Conventions	Writer has good control of spelling, grammar, capitalization, and usage.

Unit 6 Research Report • PLAN and PREWRITE Writing Process 37

Writing Transparency WP37, TR DVD

GENERATE IDEAS FOR WRITING The writing prompt tells you the general topic of your research report: a monument or statue in the United States that stands for freedom. Now you need to think of a specific topic: the actual monument or statue you will research and write about. First, make a list of as many appropriate topics as you can.

USE RANGE OF STRATEGIES Encourage students to try a range of strategies for generating ideas, including these:

- ✔ With other students, brainstorm monuments that stand for freedom, such as the Washington Monument, the Lincoln Memorial, and the Liberty Bell.
- ✔ Visit the library to investigate monuments in Washington, D.C., using both books and online searches.
- ✔ Sort through memories of statues and monuments they have visited by looking through their own journals and photo albums.

NARROW TOPIC Once you have a list of topics, you need to narrow your choices to one topic. Have students look more closely at each of their topics and think about why it is or is not the most suitable topic for the assignment.

Students can also narrow broad topics *(monuments)* by using online search engines and keywords *(Washington, D.C., monuments)*. They can also determine whether a book has information on their topic by skimming the Table of Contents at the front of the book. Remind students to take accurate notes and record their sources during their search.

The Washington Monument is the tallest building in Washington, D.C.	**Author:** Smith, John **Title:** Monuments of the Potomac **Publisher/Year:** Bridge Press, 2008 **Pages:** 24–26

Corrective feedback

If... students have trouble narrowing their topic *(U.S. monuments to freedom)*,
then... help them write a controlling question that limits their focus. *(What makes the Jefferson Memorial unique?)*

AVOID PLAGIARISM Plagiarism is using someone else's words or ideas without giving the person credit. Remind students that when they take notes, they should put quotation marks around any exact phrases or sentences they use as well as acknowledge others' ideas and wording that is close to the original. Paraphrasing, or using one's own words, will help them avoid plagiarism.

Write Guy *by Jeff Anderson*

Use Mentor Texts

Ask students to look back at the unit selection *The Story of the Statue of Liberty*. Tell them that to write the article, the author searched for, gathered, and organized information about the Statue of Liberty. Point out that searching for information about a topic is called *research*. Tell students that they will research the monuments or statues they choose before they write their reports.

Access for All

SI Strategic Intervention

For an alternative writing prompt, use the following: Find an encyclopedia article about a monument. Write three simple facts about the monument in your own words. Write a topic sentence that states the central idea of your facts. Add supporting sentences.

A Advanced

For an alternative writing prompt, use the following: Write a research report about a monument that does not honor a President, such as the Vietnam Veterans Memorial or the U.S. Marine Corps War Memorial. Explain why this memorial is especially important to a particular group of people.

Common Core State Standards

Writing 2.b. Develop the topic with facts, definitions, and details. **Writing 8.** Recall information from experiences or gather information from print and digital sources; take brief notes on sources and sort evidence into provided categories.

Plan and Prewrite

Mini-Lesson Planning a First Draft

- **Use a KWL Chart** Display Writing Transparency WP38 and read it aloud to students.

  Think Aloud **MODEL** This student has used the KWL chart to categorize his ideas. He wrote simple facts and details about The Washington Monument, under *K*. Under *W*, he posed good questions that need specific answers. After researching, the student has written the answers and explanations under *L*. The controlling question he wrote will help him establish his central idea and focus his research.

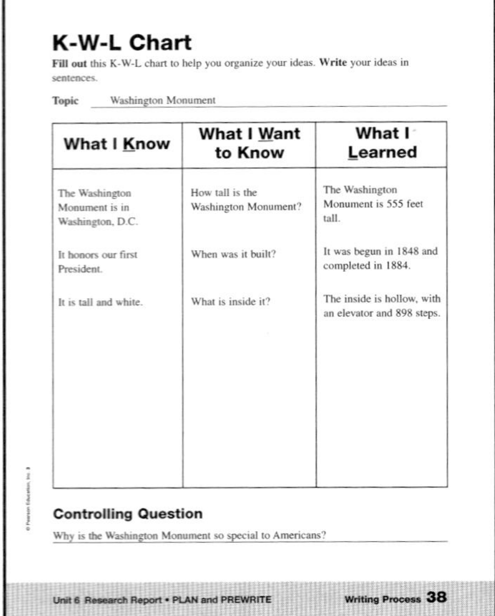

K-W-L Chart

Fill out this K-W-L chart to help you organize your ideas. **Write** your ideas in sentences.

Topic: Washington Monument

What I Know	What I Want to Know	What I Learned
The Washington Monument is in Washington, D.C.	How tall is the Washington Monument?	The Washington Monument is 555 feet tall.
It honors our first President.	When was it built?	It was begun in 1848 and completed in 1884.
It is tall and white.	What is inside it?	The inside is hollow, with an elevator and 898 steps.

Controlling Question

Why is the Washington Monument so special to Americans?

Unit 6 Research Report • PLAN and PREWRITE Writing Process 38

Writing Transparency WP38, TR DVD

- Have students use *Reader's and Writer's Notebook,* p. 450 to help them narrow their topic and begin researching. Before you begin writing, put your ideas in the *K*, *W*, and *L* categories. The question you decide to answer about your topic will establish your central idea.

Name ______ Writing Process Unit 6

KWL Chart

Directions Fill out this KWL chart to help you organize your ideas.

Topic ______

What I Know	What I Want to Know	What I Learned
Answers should include details about each element of the research report.		

Controlling Question ______

450 Unit 6 Writing Process

Reader's and Writer's Notebook, p. 450

Draft

DISPLAY RUBRIC Display Scoring Rubric WP6 from the *Teacher Resources DVD-ROM.* Review with students the criteria for each trait under each score. Explain that students need to keep these criteria in mind as they develop drafts of their research reports. Remind them that this is the rubric that will be used to evaluate their reports when they are finished.

Scoring Rubric Research Report

	4	3	2	1
Focus/Ideas	Well-focused report with one clear topic	Generally focused report with clear topic	Report lacking focus; unclear topic	Report with no focus or clear topic
Organization	Paragraphs with strong topic and detail sentences	Most paragraphs have topic and detail sentences	Few paragraphs with topic and detail sentences	Not organized in paragraphs; no topic sentences
Voice	Interested, informed voice	Voice somewhat interested, informed	Vaguely interested voice	Uninterested or uninformed voice
Word Choice	Evidence of paraphrasing	Some evidence of paraphrasing	Paraphrasing attempted	No paraphrasing
Sentences	Varied, well-constructed simple, complex, and compound sentences	Well-constructed sentences; some variety	Some unclear sentences; little variety	Fragments and run-ons; no variety
Conventions	Few, if any, errors	Some minor errors	Errors that detract from writing	Serious errors that prevent understanding

PREPARE TO DRAFT Have students review the KWL charts they worked on earlier. Ask them to make sure that their charts are complete. If they are not, have students finish them now. You will be using your KWL chart as well as your notes as you write the draft of your research report. Don't worry if your draft doesn't sound exactly the way you want your report to sound. You will have a chance to revise your draft later.

Corrective feedback

If... students do not understand the connection between the Scoring Rubric and their research reports,
then... have them help you use the Scoring Rubric to evaluate and score one or more traits of the model research report on Writing Transparency WP36.

Access for All

Strategic Intervention

Interview students about the topic they have chosen for their report. Take notes on their remarks. Circle ideas that could serve as topic sentences.

Plan a First Draft As students gather information for their research report, guide them toward books, magazines, or Web sites that provide comprehension support through features such as detailed photographs or illustrations, labeled diagrams, strong picture/text correspondence, and text in the home language.

Common Core State Standards

Writing 2.a. Introduce a topic and group related information together; include illustrations when useful to aiding comprehension. **Writing 2.c.** Use linking words and phrases (e.g., *also, another, and, more, but*) to connect ideas within categories of information. **Writing 5.** With guidance and support from peers and adults, develop and strengthen writing as needed by planning, revising, and editing. **Language 1.h.** Use coordinating and subordinating conjunctions. **Language 1.i.** Produce simple, compound, and complex sentences.

Research Report — WRITING — UNIT 6

Name ______

Topic and Detail Sentences

A topic sentence tells the main idea of a paragraph. Detail sentences give supporting facts, descriptions, and examples about the main idea.

Directions Decide how you will organize your paragraphs. Then write a topic sentence and supporting details for each paragraph.

Paragraph 1
Topic Sentence Answers should be topic
Detail Sentences sentences and supporting details on the research topic.

Paragraph 2
Topic Sentence ______
Detail Sentences ______

Paragraph 3
Topic Sentence ______
Detail Sentences ______

Paragraph 4
Topic Sentence ______
Detail Sentences ______

Unit 6 Writing Process 451

Reader's and Writer's Notebook, p. 451

Draft

Mini-Lesson Writing Trait: Organization

■ **Topic and Detail Sentences** Display Writing Transparency WP39. Remind students that a topic sentence states the main, or central, idea of a paragraph, and detail sentences support, or tell about, the main idea with simple facts, details, or explanations.

Think Aloud **MODEL** After I read the first set of details, or supporting sentences, I ask myself: *What is their central idea? Which of the three topic sentences states that central idea?* The third topic sentence goes with these supporting sentences. I would place it as the first sentence in the paragraph.

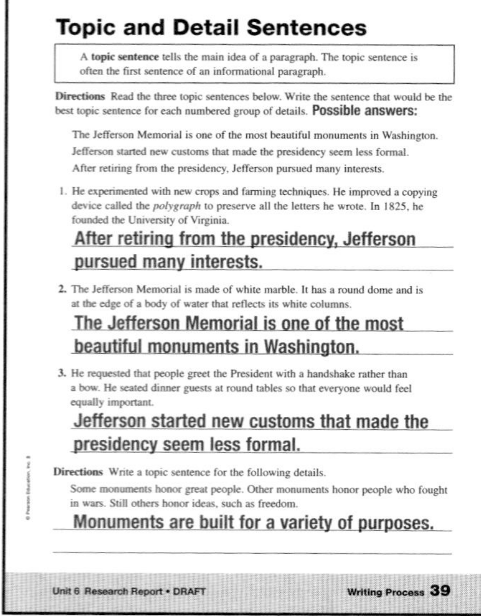

Topic and Detail Sentences

A **topic sentence** tells the main idea of a paragraph. The topic sentence is often the first sentence of an informational paragraph.

Directions Read the three topic sentences below. Write the sentence that would be the best topic sentence for each numbered group of details. **Possible answers:**

The Jefferson Memorial is one of the most beautiful monuments in Washington.
Jefferson started new customs that made the presidency seem less formal.
After retiring from the presidency, Jefferson pursued many interests.

1. He experimented with new crops and farming techniques. He improved a copying device called the *polygraph* to preserve all the letters he wrote. In 1825, he founded the University of Virginia.
After retiring from the presidency, Jefferson pursued many interests.
2. The Jefferson Memorial is made of white marble. It has a round dome and is at the edge of a body of water that reflects its white columns.
The Jefferson Memorial is one of the most beautiful monuments in Washington.
3. He requested that people greet the President with a handshake rather than a bow. He seated dinner guests at round tables so that everyone would feel equally important.
Jefferson started new customs that made the presidency seem less formal.

Directions Write a topic sentence for the following details.
Some monuments honor great people. Other monuments honor people who fought in wars. Still others honor ideas, such as freedom.
Monuments are built for a variety of purposes.

Unit 6 Research Report • DRAFT — Writing Process 39

Writing Transparency WP39, TR DVD

■ Have students use *Reader's and Writer's Notebook,* p. 451 to organize topic and detail sentences in paragraphs for their research report.

Drafting Tips

✔ To avoid plagiarism, write notes in your own words. Also, paraphrase any information you use from books or Web sites.

✔ Your first paragraph should tell readers the central idea of your report, but it should also be interesting so that they want to keep reading.

✔ For your concluding statement, consider using a quotation, a final interesting example, a question, or a suggestion written as a command.

DEVELOP DRAFT Remind students that the focus of drafting is to get their ideas down in an organized way. Display or copy the Drafting Tips for students. Direct students to use what they learned about topic and detail sentences as they write their drafts.

Revise

Mini-Lesson Writer's Craft: Combining Sentences

- One way to revise writing is to combine sentences. A good writer uses simple sentences, compound sentences, and complex sentences. Combining some short simple sentences into compound or complex sentences can better organize and connect your ideas. It can also help your sentences sound smoother. Discuss these sentences with students:

Choppy The Washington Monument is well-known. Most Americans recognize it.

Improved The Washington Monument is well-known, and most Americans recognize it.

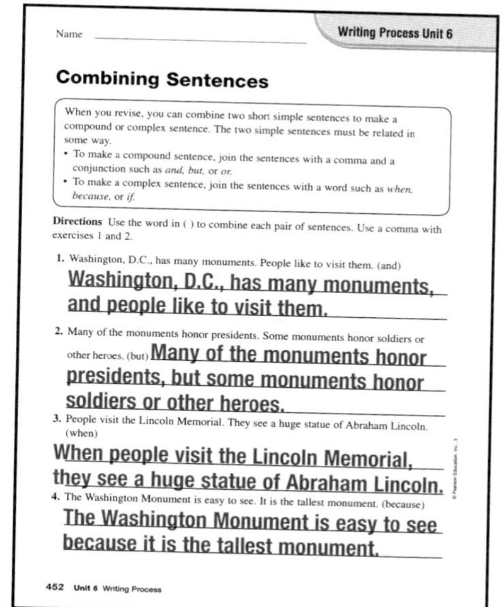

Name ______________ Writing Process Unit 6

Combining Sentences

When you revise, you can combine two short simple sentences to make a compound or complex sentence. The two simple sentences must be related in some way.
- To make a compound sentence, join the sentences with a comma and a conjunction such as *and, but,* or *or.*
- To make a complex sentence, join the sentences with a word such as *when, because,* or *if.*

Directions Use the word in ( ) to combine each pair of sentences. Use a comma with exercises 1 and 2.

1. Washington, D.C., has many monuments. People like to visit them. (and) Washington, D.C., has many monuments, and people like to visit them.
2. Many of the monuments honor presidents. Some monuments honor soldiers or other heroes. (but) Many of the monuments honor presidents, but some monuments honor soldiers or other heroes.
3. People visit the Lincoln Memorial. They see a huge statue of Abraham Lincoln. (when) When people visit the Lincoln Memorial, they see a huge statue of Abraham Lincoln.
4. The Washington Monument is easy to see. It is the tallest monument. (because) The Washington Monument is easy to see because it is the tallest monument.

452 Unit 6 Writing Process

Reader's and Writer's Notebook, p. 452

- Have students practice combining sentences on *Reader's and Writer's Notebook,* p. 452.

REVISE MODEL Display Writing Transparency WP40 and use it to model revising. Point out the revision marks, which students should use when they revise their work. This is part of a research report about the Washington Monument. After changing the informal word *neat* to the more formal word *unique,* the writer combined two simple sentences with a comma and the conjunction *and* to make a compound sentence. This makes those sentences better organized and smoother-sounding.

Ask students to point out and explain other revisions the writer made. (The writer fixed a run-on sentence by making it into two sentences. He added facts to the last sentence to make it a stronger supporting sentence.)

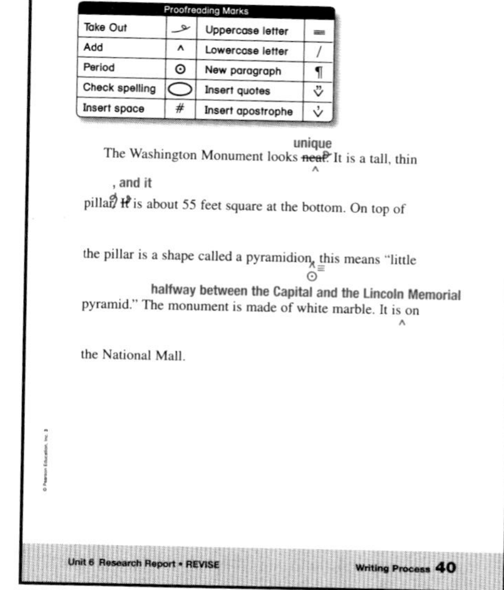

Proofreading Marks			
Take Out	↩	Uppercase letter	≡
Add	^	Lowercase letter	/
Period	⊙	New paragraph	¶
Check spelling	◯	Insert quotes	﹀
Insert space	#	Insert apostrophe	﹀

The Washington Monument looks ~~neat~~ unique. It is a tall, thin pillar, and it ~~It~~ is about 55 feet square at the bottom. On top of the pillar is a shape called a pyramidion. This means "little pyramid." The monument is made of white marble. It is on halfway between the Capital and the Lincoln Memorial the National Mall.

Unit 6 Research Report • REVISE Writing Process 40

Writing Transparency WP40, TR DVD

Access for All

A Advanced

As students revise their work, have them consider ways to improve it.
- Use a mixture of simple, compound, and complex sentences for variety.
- Include at least one quotation from an expert.
- Make sure each paragraph has a topic sentence and supporting sentences.

Support Revising If students include home-language words in their drafts, help them find replacement words in English. Resources can include conversations with you; other home-language speakers; bilingual dictionaries, if available; and online translation sources.

Common Core State Standards

Writing 5. With guidance and support from peers and adults, develop and strengthen writing as needed by planning, revising, and editing. **Writing 6.** With guidance and support from adults, use technology to produce and publish writing (using keyboarding skills) as well as to interact and collaborate with others. **Language 2.** Demonstrate command of the conventions of standard English capitalization, punctuation, and spelling when writing. **Language 2.f.** Use spelling patterns and generalizations (e.g., word families, position-based spellings, syllable patterns, ending rules, meaningful word parts) in writing words.

Revise

REVISE DRAFT Earlier we wrote drafts of research reports about a U.S. monument or statue that stands for freedom. Now we will revise our drafts. When we revise, we try to make our writing clearer and more organized.

PEER CONFERENCING • PEER REVISION Write the Revising Checklist on the board and review the questions with students. Have pairs exchange drafts and follow the directions for peer and teacher conferencing on *Reader's and Writer's Notebook* p. 453. Remind students that their revision suggestions might include where and why some simple sentences could be combined to make compound or complex sentences.

Have students revise their research reports referring to their partner's suggestions and your comments as well as the Revising Checklist and the list of key features of a research report (p. WP•1).

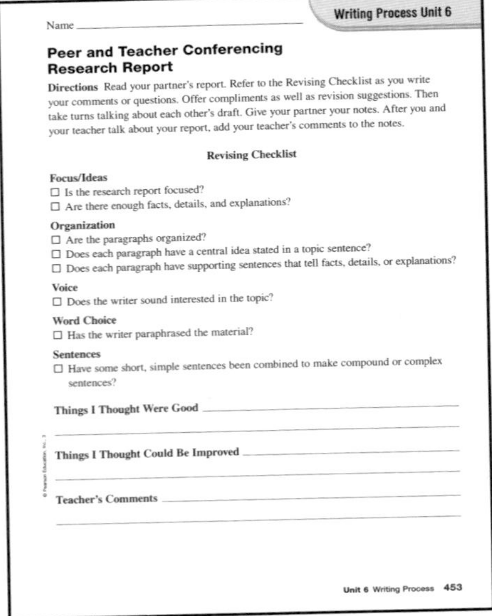

Name ______ Writing Process Unit 6

Peer and Teacher Conferencing
Research Report

Directions Read your partner's report. Refer to the Revising Checklist as you write your comments or questions. Offer compliments as well as revision suggestions. Then take turns talking about each other's draft. Give your partner your notes. After you and your teacher talk about your report, add your teacher's comments to the notes.

Revising Checklist

Focus/Ideas
- ☐ Is the research report focused?
- ☐ Are there enough facts, details, and explanations?

Organization
- ☐ Are the paragraphs organized?
- ☐ Does each paragraph have a central idea stated in a topic sentence?
- ☐ Does each paragraph have supporting sentences that tell facts, details, or explanations?

Voice
- ☐ Does the writer sound interested in the topic?

Word Choice
- ☐ Has the writer paraphrased the material?

Sentences
- ☐ Have some short, simple sentences been combined to make compound or complex sentences?

Things I Thought Were Good ______

Things I Thought Could Be Improved ______

Teacher's Comments ______

Unit 6 Writing Process 453

Reader's and Writer's Notebook, p. 453

Revising Checklist

Focus/Ideas

- ✔ Is the research report focused on one monument or statue?
- ✔ Are there enough simple facts, details, and explanations?

Organization

- ✔ Does each paragraph have a central idea stated in a topic sentence?
- ✔ Does each paragraph have supporting sentences that tell facts, details, or explanations?
- ✔ Does the report end with a concluding statement?

Voice

- ✔ Does the writer sound interested in the topic?

Word Choice

- ✔ Has the writer paraphrased the material?

Sentences

- ✔ Have some short simple sentences been combined to make compound sentences?

Edit

Mini-Lesson Editing Strategy: Line by Line

- Suggest that students use this editing strategy as they check their work: Place an index card under each line and read the line, checking spelling, capitalization, punctuation, and grammar.

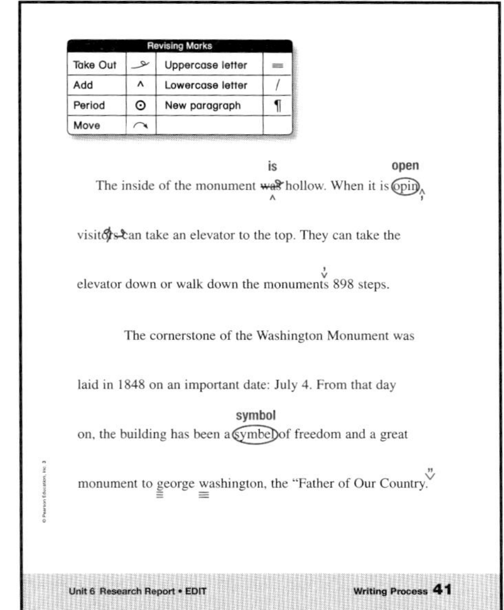

Revising Marks			
Take Out	⌐	Uppercase letter	≡
Add	^	Lowercase letter	/
Period	⊙	New paragraph	¶
Move	↷		

The inside of the monument ~~was~~ is hollow. When it is (opin) open, visitors can take an elevator to the top. They can take the elevator down or walk down the monument's 898 steps.

The cornerstone of the Washington Monument was laid in 1848 on an important date: July 4. From that day on, the building has been a (symbel) symbol of freedom and a great monument to george washington, the "Father of Our Country."

© Pearson Education, Inc. 3

Unit 6 Research Report • EDIT Writing Process 41

Writing Transparency WP41, TR DVD

- Display Writing Transparency WP41 and use it to model the editing process. Point out the proofreading marks, which students should use when they edit. When I check the first line, I see that the verb in the first sentence is not the right tense. The writer has changed it to *is*. I also see that he fixed a misspelled word and added a comma after the clause in the second sentence.

- Ask students to point out and explain other edits the writer made. (In the third line, the writer added an apostrophe to make the singular possessive *monument's*. In the sixth line, he circled and corrected a misspelled word. In the seventh line, he capitalized both words in a proper noun and added closing quotation marks.)

  You can create your own rubric using items from the rubric on p. WP•5 and your own additions or changes and have students use it to edit their own drafts. Have them check their drafts for spelling, grammar, and mechanics. Tell them to use proofreading marks to mark any needed corrections.

Technology Tips

Students who write their research reports on computers should keep these tips in mind as they edit:

- ✔ Do not rely on search engines for getting consistent, accurate information. Access information from encyclopedias, dictionaries, and other reference sources online.
- ✔ For reports that are longer than one page, use the header or footer feature to put page numbers and other identifying information.

Write Guy *by Jeff Anderson*

Express-Lane Edits

In the editing process, students can easily get bogged down by everything that needs to be fixed. Editing one aspect at a time helps students focus their efforts and concentrate on one task. Suggest that they read once looking for spelling errors, a second time looking for punctuation and capitalization errors, and a third time looking for grammar errors.

Support Editing Invite students to read their drafts aloud to you. Observe whether they note any spelling or grammatical errors by stumbling or self-correcting. Return to those errors and discuss how to correct them. Use the appropriate lessons in the *ELL Handbook* to explicitly teach the English conventions.

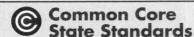

Common Core State Standards

Writing 6. With guidance and support from adults, use technology to produce and publish writing (using keyboarding skills) as well as to interact and collaborate with others.

5 Publish and Present

OPTIONS FOR PRESENTING Have students incorporate peer suggestions and their own revisions and proofreading edits into their research report to write or use a computer to create a final draft. Offer them two options for presenting their work:

Share their research reports in small groups.	Illustrate their reports and post them on a bulletin board.

Mini-Lesson Evaluating Writing

- Display and read aloud Writing Transparency WP42. Model how to evaluate a research report using the Scoring Rubric on p. WP•5.

MODEL I would give this report a 4. It is focused on the Washington Monument. Each paragraph has a topic sentence that tells the central idea and supporting sentences that tell facts, details, and explanations. The writer shows interest and enthusiasm in the topic. He paraphrased material to avoid plagiarism and used simple, compound, and complex sentences. Grammar, mechanics, and spelling are excellent.

The Washington Monument

What is the tallest building in Washington, D.C.? No, it is not a giant office building. It is the Washington Monument. This 555-foot-tall building was completed in 1884 to honor America's first President.

The Washington Monument looks unique. It is a tall, thin pillar, and it is about 55 feet square at the bottom. On top of the pillar is a shape called a pyramidion. This means "little pyramid." The monument is made of white marble. It is halfway between the Capitol and the Lincoln Memorial on the National Mall.

The inside of the monument is hollow. When it is open, visitors can take an elevator to the top. They can take the elevator down or walk down the monument's 898 steps.

The cornerstone of the Washington Monument was laid in 1848 on an important date: July 4. From that day on, the building has been a symbol of freedom and a great monument to George Washington, the "Father of Our Country."

Unit 6 Research Report • PUBLISH and PRESENT Writing Process 42

Writing Transparency WP42, TR DVD

- Have students use the Scoring Rubric to evaluate their research reports. Encourage them to use the evaluation process to help them identify areas for improvement in their future writing.

Looking for Teacher Resources and other important information?

Go online to 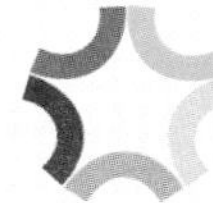 Pearson SuccessNet

eSTREET INTERACTIVE
www.ReadingStreet.com

In the *First Stop* on Reading Street, you will find the following information.

- Research into Practice on Reading Street
- Guide to Reading Street
- Assessment on Reading Street
- Customize Writing on Reading Street
- Small Group Instruction on Reading Street
- ELL on Reading Street
- Customize Literacy on Reading Street
- 21st Century Skills on Reading Street
- Teacher Resources for Grade 3
- Index

LET'S LEARN Amazing Words

Oral Vocabulary for The Story of the Statue of Liberty

Oral Vocabulary Routine

DAY 1	tribute	1 **Introduce** A *tribute* is something done to show thanks or respect. 2 **Demonstrate** The statue is a *tribute* to the soldiers who died in the war. 3 **Apply** Have students name someone or something that they think deserves a *tribute.* 4 **Display the Word** Run your hand under the word parts *trib-ute* as you read the word. Students can decode this word.
	enlighten	1 **Introduce** To *enlighten* means "to give knowledge or wisdom to." 2 **Demonstrate** The boy asked the older man to *enlighten* him about the past. 3 **Apply** Discuss the idiom "to see the light" and help students make the connection to the word *enlighten.* 4 **Display the Word** Identify the spelling of the long *i* sound in the syllable *light.* Students can decode this word.
	contribution	1 **Introduce** A *contribution* is money, help, or advice that is given as a gift. 2 **Demonstrate** Nate's *contribution* to Earth Day was helping to plant trees in the local park. 3 **Apply** Discuss different kinds of *contributions* that people make every day. 4 **Display the Word** Identify the base word *tribute,* the prefix *con-,* and the suffix *-ion.*
DAY 2	competition	1 **Introduce** A *competition* is a contest. 2 **Demonstrate** Tom entered his science project in a statewide *competition.* 3 **Apply** Have students describe a *competition* they've heard of, seen, or been involved in. 4 **Display the Word** Run your hand under the word parts *com-pe-ti-tion* as you read the word.
DAY 3	disgrace	1 **Introduce** A *disgrace* is a shame or a loss of honor or respect. 2 **Demonstrate** It is a *disgrace* to treat other people rudely. 3 **Apply** Discuss situations or conditions that students feel are a *disgrace.* 4 **Display the Word** Identify the long-vowel sound in the word part *grace.* Students can decode the word.
DAY 4	fund	1 **Introduce** A *fund* is a sum of money set aside for a special purpose. 2 **Demonstrate** The school has a *fund* of $4,000 to buy new books. 3 **Apply** Have students think of things at school for which they could raise *funds.* 4 **Display the Word** Students can decode the word *fund.*

Oral Vocabulary for Happy Birthday Mr. Kang

Oral Vocabulary Routine

DAY 1

release

1. **Introduce** To *release* means "to let someone or something go; to set it free."
2. **Demonstrate** Prisoners were *released* after the war. Callie *released* the dog from its kennel and let it run around the yard.
3. **Apply** Work with students to make a list of synonyms for *release.*
4. **Display the Word** Run your hand under the word parts *re-lease* as you read the word.

loyal

1. **Introduce** To be *loyal* is to show lasting affection and support for someone or something.
2. **Demonstrate** Maggie and Andy had been *loyal* friends for years. The soldiers served their country *loyally.*
3. **Apply** Have students discuss how they can show *loyalty* to a friend.
4. **Display the Word** Run your hand under the word parts *loy-al* as you read the word.

deserve

1. **Introduce** *Deserve* means "to be worthy of something" or "to have a right to something."
2. **Demonstrate** The students *deserve* praise for their hard work. The dancers *deserved* applause for their wonderful performance.
3. **Apply** Have students discuss how they might show thanks to someone who *deserves* it.
4. **Display the Word** Run your hand under the word parts *de-serve* as you read the word.

DAY 2

affectionate

1. **Introduce** *Affectionate* means "loving or showing tenderness."
2. **Demonstrate** My dad is *affectionate* toward his mother.
3. **Apply** Ask students to tell with whom they are *affectionate.*
4. **Display the Word** Run your hand under the word parts *af-fec-tion-ate* as you read the word.

DAY 3

nag

1. **Introduce** *Nag* means "to annoy someone by complaining about something that needs to be done."
2. **Demonstrate** I will clean up my room if you won't *nag* me about it any longer!
3. **Apply** Have students come up with additional sentences that use the word *nag.* Point out that an old, worn-out horse is also call a *nag.*
4. **Display the Word** Students can decode the word *nag.*

DAY 4

wandering

1. **Introduce** *Wandering* is moving from place to place without any real purpose.
2. **Demonstrate** We spent the rainy afternoon *wandering* through the museum. Jan likes to *wander* through the woods.
3. **Apply** Have students describe times when they like to *wander.*
4. **Display the Word** Identify the ending *-ing* in *wandering.* Students can decode this word.

Oral Vocabulary for Talking Walls: Art for People

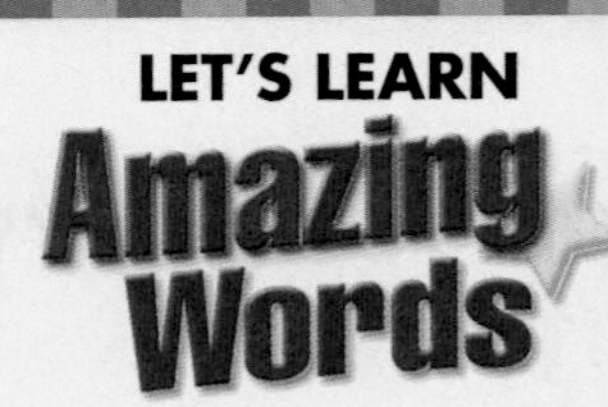

Oral Vocabulary Routine

DAY 1	expressive	1 **Introduce** Something that is *expressive* is full of meaning or feeling. 2 **Demonstrate** Bill's *expressive* voice was perfect for reading the Gettysburg Address at the school assembly. 3 **Apply** Have students read or recite something using an *expressive* voice. 4 **Display the Word** Run your hand under the word parts *ex-pres-sive* as you read the word. Identify the suffix *-ive.*
	emotion	1 **Introduce** An *emotion* is a strong feeling of any kind. Joy, grief, fear, hate, love, anger, and excitement are *emotions.* 2 **Demonstrate** Eric couldn't hide his *emotions* when he walked into the surprise birthday party. 3 **Apply** Discuss with students how people show various *emotions* such as joy, fear, anger, and excitement. 4 **Display the Word** Run your hand under the word parts *e-mo-tion* as you read the word.
	artistic	1 **Introduce** Someone who is *artistic* shows talent in music, dance, painting, writing, or the other arts. 2 **Demonstrate** Steve has many *artistic* skills and can draw, paint, and write. 3 **Apply** Have students talk about what they think it means to be *artistic.* 4 **Display the Word** Run your hand under the word parts *ar-tis-tic* as you read the word.
DAY 2	lecture	1 **Introduce** A *lecture* is a talk on a certain subject given to an audience. 2 **Demonstrate** Dr. Haines gave a *lecture* to the historical society on the history of our area. 3 **Apply** Ask students to name a topic that would be interesting for a *lecture.* 4 **Display the Word** Identify the vowel sound in the first syllable.
DAY 3	pause	1 **Introduce** To *pause* means "to stop somewhere for a short time." 2 **Demonstrate** Paul *paused* for a moment to look in the store window. 3 **Apply** Have students list synonyms for *pause.* 4 **Display the Word** Students can decode the word *pause.*
DAY 4	lyrics	1 **Introduce** Lyrics are the words of a song. 2 **Demonstrate** Tammy memorized the *lyrics* of her favorite song. Vic is going to write new *lyrics* for an old song. 3 **Apply** Have students name songs for which they know the *lyrics.* 4 **Display the Word** Run your hand under the word parts *lyr-ics* as you read the word.

Oral Vocabulary for Two Bad Ants

Oral Vocabulary Routine

DAY 1

consequence

1. **Introduce** A *consequence* is a result of something.
2. **Demonstrate** The *consequence* of Ned's fall was a broken leg. If you break the rules, you'll have to face the *consequences.*
3. **Apply** Point out to students that a *consequence* is typically a negative result. Have them discuss *consequences* they might have encountered.
4. **Display the Word** Run your hand under the three syllables *con-se-quence* as you read the word.

obey

1. **Introduce** To *obey* is to do what you are told or to follow the law.
2. **Demonstrate** The drivers will *obey* the traffic signal. Good citizens *obey* the law.
3. **Apply** Have students name synonyms and antonyms of *obey.*
4. **Display the Word** Identify the long *o* vowel sound in the first syllable of *obey.*

permission

1. **Introduce** *Permission* is allowing someone to do something.
2. **Demonstrate** My mom gave me *permission* to stay over at Margaret's house. We don't have *permission* to cross the busy street.
3. **Apply** Have students discuss things they need *permission* to do.
4. **Display the Word** Run your hand under the word parts *per-mis-sion* as you read the word.

DAY 2

fascinate

1. **Introduce** *Fascinate* means to interest greatly or to charm.
2. **Demonstrate** Charlie is *fascinated* by the colors and designs of African art. Sasha was *fascinated* by the story of how her great-great grandmother came to America.
3. **Apply** Discuss with students things that they think are *fascinating.*
4. **Display the Word** Run your hand under the word parts *fas-ci-nate* as you read the word.

DAY 3

encounter

1. **Introduce** To *encounter* is to meet something or someone, sometimes unexpectedly, or to deal with something.
2. **Demonstrate** Do you think we will *encounter* any wild animals on our hike? We did not expect to *encounter* any problems on our trip.
3. **Apply** Have students tell about a time when they *encountered* a friend in an unexpected place.
4. **Display the Word** Point out the diphthong /ou/ spelled *ou* in *encounter.*

DAY 4

eerie

1. **Introduce** *Eerie* means that something is strange or scary.
2. **Demonstrate** We heard an *eerie* moaning sound coming from the abandoned house. Tanya played *eerie* music at the Halloween party.
3. **Apply** Have students discuss things they think are *eerie.*
4. **Display the Word** Run your hand under the word parts *eer-ie* as you read the word.

Oral Vocabulary for **Atlantis**

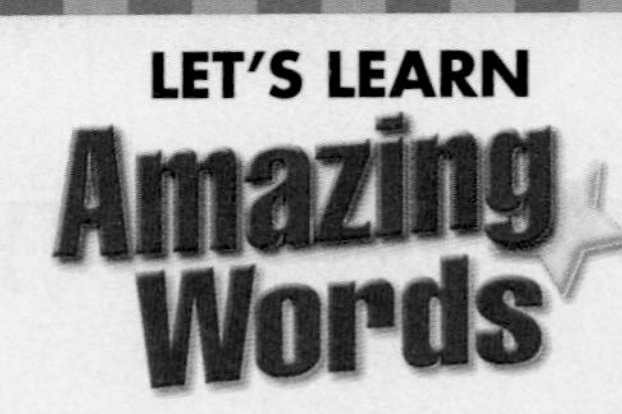

Oral Vocabulary Routine

DAY 1

equality

1. **Introduce** *Equality* means being equal, especially having equal rights and responsibilities.
2. **Demonstrate** In many countries, people have *equality* under the law.
3. **Apply** Have students give an example of *equality* that is guaranteed by our laws.
4. **Display the Word** Identify long *e* spelled *y* at the end of the word.

justice

1. **Introduce** *Justice* has to do with being fair and right.
2. **Demonstrate** Sarah never doubted the *justice* of her cause. Laws provide equal *justice* for everyone.
3. **Apply** Have students discuss ways in which laws guarantee *justice* and how individuals can treat each other with *justice.*
4. **Display the Word** Run your hand under the two word parts *jus-tice* as you read the word.

DAY 2

perish

1. **Introduce** To *perish* means "to die" or "to be destroyed."
2. **Demonstrate** Without water, the crops will *perish.* If they cannot escape, forest animals will perish in a forest fire.
3. **Apply** Ask students to tell what they can do to keep a houseplant from *perishing.*
4. **Display the Word** Run your hand under the word parts *per-ish* as you say the word.

mourn

1. **Introduce** *Mourn* means "to feel very sad and show sorrow about something."
2. **Demonstrate** The family *mourned* the loss of their pet dog.
3. **Apply** Have students talk about situations in which people might *mourn* something.
4. **Display the Word** Students can decode the word *mourn.*

DAY 3

wept

1. **Introduce** *Wept* is the past tense of *weep* and means "to cry."
2. **Demonstrate** Anne admits that she has *wept* at sad movies. Carrie *wept* with joy when she won the award.
3. **Apply** Have students discuss why someone might have *wept.* Point out that it doesn't always have to be a sad occasion.
4. **Display the Word** Point out the final blend /p//t/. Students can decode this word.

Teacher's Edition

Text

KWL Strategy: The KWL Interactive Reading Strategy was developed and is used by permission of Donna Ogle, National-Louis University, Skokie, Illinois, co-author of *Reading Today and Tomorrow,* Holt, Rinehart & Winston Publishers, 1988. (See also the *Reading Teacher,* February 1986, pp. 564–570.)

Photographs

Cover (B) ©Mark Kostich/Getty Images, (Bkgd) ©Chlaus Lotscher/Getty Images

Every effort has been made to secure permission and provide appropriate credit for photographic material. The publisher deeply regrets any omission and pledges to correct errors called to its attention in subsequent editions.

Unless otherwise acknowledged, all photographs are the property of Pearson Education, Inc.

Student Edition

Student Edition, page 552

Student Edition, page 553

Student Edition, page 554

Student Edition, page 555

TEACHER NOTES

TEACHER NOTES

TEACHER NOTES

Looking for Teacher Resources and other important information?

Go online to  Pearson SuccessNet

eSTREET INTERACTIVE
www.ReadingStreet.com

In the *First Stop* on Reading Street, you will find the following information.

- Research into Practice on Reading Street
- Guide to Reading Street
- Assessment on Reading Street
- Customize Writing on Reading Street
- Small Group Instruction on Reading Street
- ELL on Reading Street
- Customize Literacy on Reading Street
- 21st Century Skills on Reading Street
- Teacher Resources for Grade 3
- Index

Looking for Teacher Resources and other important information?

Go online to  Pearson SuccessNet

eSTREET INTERACTIVE
www.ReadingStreet.com

In the *First Stop* on Reading Street, you will find the following information.

- Research into Practice on Reading Street
- Guide to Reading Street
- Assessment on Reading Street
- Customize Writing on Reading Street
- Small Group Instruction on Reading Street
- ELL on Reading Street
- Customize Literacy on Reading Street
- 21st Century Skills on Reading Street
- Teacher Resources for Grade 3
- Index